THE OXFORD HANDBOOK OF

EARLY MODERN WOMEN'S WRITING IN ENGLISH, 1540–1700

THE OXFORD HANDBOOK OF

EARLY MODERN WOMEN'S WRITING IN ENGLISH, 1540–1700

Edited by
ELIZABETH SCOTT-BAUMANN,
DANIELLE CLARKE, *and* SARAH C. E. ROSS

OXFORD
UNIVERSITY PRESS

OXFORD
UNIVERSITY PRESS

Great Clarendon Street, Oxford, OX2 6DP,
United Kingdom

Oxford University Press is a department of the University of Oxford.
It furthers the University's objective of excellence in research, scholarship,
and education by publishing worldwide. Oxford is a registered trade mark of
Oxford University Press in the UK and in certain other countries

First Edition published in 2022
Impression: 2

Published in the United States of America by Oxford University Press
198 Madison Avenue, New York, NY 10016, United States of America

British Library Cataloguing in Publication Data
Data available

Library of Congress Control Number: 2022940747

ISBN 978–0–19–886063–1

DOI: 10.1093/oxfordhb/9780198860631.001.0001

Printed and bound in the UK by
TJ Books Limited

For Elizabeth Clarke

Acknowledgements

We have many people to thank for their support for this book, but first and foremost we would like to pay tribute to the enthusiasm, determination, and resilience of our contributors who never wavered in their commitment to the project despite the very real challenges posed by Covid-19. The project has for the most part been completed over two years of lockdowns and travel restrictions, and the scholars represented in this volume have been a community of conversation and a mainstay of hope through global networks realised only electronically. We would also like to thank here the librarians and archivists who worked so hard to enable access to collections and texts and the wider community of early modern scholars who assisted with locating articles and primary texts, often from their personal archives.

We have been privileged to work with Emma Rayner, Victoria Coldham-Fussell, Emer McHugh, and Harriet Hughes, each of whom brought their insight and vision to the project. We are grateful to them for all of their careful work on these chapters and for their support for the Handbook's aims and principles—it is a better piece of scholarship because of their input.

We would like to thank Kate Chedgzoy, Jane Grogan, and Sarah McKibben for their incisive and perceptive comments on Chapter 1, and wish to acknowledge the generosity of Jaime Goodrich and Paula McQuade, and the contributors to the double special issue of *Criticism*, 'Beyond Canonicity: The Future(s) of Early Modern Women's Writing' (2021) for allowing us to read these provocative and challenging essays in advance of publication. These framed and guided our thinking in profound ways.

At Oxford University Press, we wish to thank Jacqueline Baker for her initial interest in this idea, and Eleanor Collins, Aimee Wright, Karen Raith, and Emma Collison for guiding us from commissioning to submission. We would also like to thank Marilyn Inglis, Dawn Preston, and Kayalvizli Ganesan for their copy-editing and production work. And thank you to Francis Young for the index.

Funding for editorial assistance and indexing is gratefully acknowledged from the College of Arts and Humanities at University College Dublin, the English Department at King's College London, and the Faculty of Humanities and Social Sciences at Te Herenga Waka—Victoria University of Wellington.

We are very grateful to the following institutions for allowing us to reproduce images: Victoria and Albert Museum London; The New York Public Library; Folger Shakespeare Library; Royal Collection Trust; Koninklijke Bibliotheek; Rijksmuseum; Bodleian Library, University of Oxford; National Records of Scotland; Lakeland Art Trust—Abbott Hall Gallery and Museum.

To say that the editing of this book presented some domestic challenges would be an understatement: between us we have children ranging from those on the cusp of adulthood to those born during this book's production, and we think that we understood many of the women represented in this volume better, as we attempted to produce intellectual work in sometimes fraught and crowded domestic spaces. We would like to thank our families: Róisín, Asher, and Annie (Danielle); Benjie, Edward, Will, and Phoebe Way and Mike and Alison Scott-Baumann (Lizzie); and Andru, Milly, and Henry Isac (Sarah).

Contents

PART II FORMS AND ORIGINS

PART III PLACES

List of Illustrations

List of Abbreviations

EEBO	Early English Books Online
ODNB	Oxford Dictionary of National Biography
OED	Oxford English Dictionary (online)
PLRE	Private Libraries in Renaissance England
PMLA	Publications of the Modern Language Association of America
RECIRC	The Reception and Circulation of Early Modern Women's Writing 1550–1700
STC	Short Title Catalogue

List of Contributors

Nadine Akkerman is Professor in early modern English Literature at Leiden University. She is author of the critically acclaimed *Invisible Agents: Women and Espionage in Seventeenth-Century Britain* (OUP), and of *The Correspondence of Elizabeth Stuart, Queen of Bohemia* (OUP), the third and final volume of which will be published in 2023. Her latest book is a biography, *Elizabeth Stuart, Queen of Hearts* (OUP, 2021). She has also published extensively on women's history, diplomacy, and masques, and curated several exhibitions, including the popular 'Courtly Rivals' at the Haags Historisch Museum. In 2017 she was elected to The Young Academy of the Royal Netherlands Academy of Arts and Sciences, and received a Special Recognition Award from the World Cultural Council. Most recently, in April 2019, she received an Ammodo Science Award for fundamental research in the humanities, while a Visiting Fellow at All Souls' College, Oxford.

Bernadette Andrea is Professor of Literary and Cultural Studies in the Department of English at the University of California, Santa Barbara. She is the author of *The Lives of Girls and Women from the Islamic World in Early Modern British Literature and Culture* (University of Toronto Press, 2017) and *Women and Islam in Early Modern English Literature* (Cambridge University Press, 2007). She edited and introduced *English Women Staging Islam, 1696–1707* (University of Toronto, Centre for Reformation and Renaissance Studies, 2012) for the series 'The Other Voice in Early Modern Europe'. Her co-edited collections include *Travel and Travail: Early Modern Women, English Drama, and the Wider World*, with Patricia Akhimie (University of Nebraska Press, 2019), and *Early Modern England and Islamic Worlds*, with Linda McJannet (Palgrave Macmillan, 2011). She currently serves as a co-editor, with Julie Campbell and Allyson Poska, of *Early Modern Women: An Interdisciplinary Journal*, and is the President of the Shakespeare Society of America.

Jake Arthur is a DPhil candidate and Clarendon Scholar at Oxford University. He has recently completed his thesis examining early modern women's work in translation and paraphrase. Titled '"The stuffe not ours": the work of derivation in women's writing, 1560–c.1664', the thesis seeks to reclaim the expressive and intellectual possibilities of 'derivative' works. In collaboration with Sarah C. E. Ross, he is co-editor of the poetry section of *The Palgrave Encyclopedia of Early Modern Women's Writing*. He also has work published in *The Seventeenth Century* and *Early Modern Women: An Interdisciplinary Journal*, and a chapter in *Early Modern Women and Complaint: Gender, Form, and Politics*.

Peter Auger is Lecturer in Early Modern Literature at the University of Birmingham. His first monograph, *Du Bartas' Legacy in England and Scotland*, was published in 2019. He continues to work on Franco-British literary relations, and has written articles and book chapters on topics including transnational and comparative literature, literary reception, translation and imitation practices, the history of reading, manuscript studies, epic and religious poetry, language learning, and cultural diplomacy. With Sheldon Brammall, he is editing a volume of essays about multilingual practices in early modern Europe.

Liza Blake is an Associate Professor of English at the University of Toronto, working at the intersection of literature, science, and philosophy in early modernity, with additional interests in women writers, textual bibliography, and scholarly editing. She has articles published and forthcoming in the journals *postmedieval*, *Studies in English Literature*, *English Literary Renaissance*, *Journal for Early Modern Cultural Studies*, and *Criticism*, as well as several book chapters. She has edited (with Jacques Lezra) the collection *Lucretius and Modernity*, and is the editor of a forthcoming special issue of the journal *Studies in Medieval and Renaissance Teaching*, entitled 'Teaching Women Writers Today'. Blake is at work on two in-progress book projects: a monograph called *Early Modern Literary Physics*, and a multimodal monograph entitled *Choose Your Own Poems and Fancies: An Interactive Digital Edition and Study of Margaret Cavendish's Atom Poems* (under contract with Electric Press http://electric.press/books/cavendish.html). She has also produced two full scholarly editions: *Margaret Cavendish's Poems and Fancies: A Digital Critical Edition* (http://library2.utm.utoronto.ca/poemsandfancies/), and, with Kathryn Vomero Santos, *Arthur Golding's A Morall Fabletalke and Other Renaissance Fable Translations*. She has also edited poems by Hester Pulter for *The Pulter Project* (http://pulterproject.northwestern.edu/).

V.M. Braganza is a PhD candidate at Harvard University who works on early modern women's writing and book ownership, and their intersections with premodern critical race theory, genre studies, Milton, and Shakespeare. Her work has appeared in *Studies in Philology*, *Shakespeare*, *English Literary Renaissance*, the Early Modern Female Book Ownership Blog, and the born-digital *Palgrave Encyclopedia of Early Modern Women's Writing*. Her public-facing writing has appeared in the *LA Review of Books* and *Smithsonian Magazine*. She is the lead curator for an exhibit on how British and American women authors crafted their identities through books ('500 Years of Women Authors, Authorising Themselves') for Harvard's rare books and manuscripts repository, the Houghton Library; and she has also guest-curated an exhibit for the Library of Congress in the past. Her dissertation and first book project, currently in progress, explores the pervasive influence of codes and ciphers on the early modern literary imagination.

Victoria E. Burke is Associate Professor of English at the University of Ottawa. She has published numerous articles on early modern women's manuscript writing, many on the topic of miscellanies, in journals including *English Manuscript Studies 1100–1700*, *Literature Compass*, and *Women's Writing*, and in essay collections including *Manuscript*

Miscellanies in Early Modern England (Ashgate) and *The History of British Women's Writing, 1610–1690* (Palgrave Macmillan). She has edited the manuscript poetry of Julia Palmer and Marie Burghope, and selections from Hester Pulter's poetry for *The Pulter Project: Poet in the Making* (http://pulterproject.northwestern.edu), where she is also a member of the advisory board. She was the inaugural winner of the Margaret P. Hannay Short-Term Fellowship co-sponsored by the Society for the Study of Early Modern Women and Gender and by the Folger Shakespeare Library in 2017. Her most recent article is on Hester Pulter's rethinking of the metaphysical astronomy poem (*Journal for Early Modern Cultural Studies*), and she has forthcoming articles on the roles played by Madame de Sablé and Aphra Behn in the development of the maxim genre in France and England, and on Pulter's poetic emblems. She is the section editor for 'Manuscript' for *The Palgrave Encyclopedia of Early Modern Women's Writing in English.* She is editing *Seneca Unmasqued* for Cambridge University Press's complete works of Aphra Behn, and she is completing a monograph on women's methods of compilation in their devotional writing, tentatively entitled, *Compiling and Creating: Devotional Manuscript Writing by Seventeenth-Century Women.*

Hero Chalmers is a Fellow, College Lecturer and Director of Studies in English at Fitzwilliam College, Cambridge. She is the author of *Royalist Women Writers, 1650–1689* (Oxford: Clarendon Press, 2004) and co-editor, with Julie Sanders and Sophie Tomlinson, of *Three Seventeenth-Century Plays on Women and Performance* (Manchester: Manchester University Press, 2006), for which she edited Margaret Cavendish's *The Convent of Pleasure.* She has published a variety of articles and chapters on Mary Carleton, Margaret Cavendish, and on Fletcher and Shakespeare's *Henry VIII.* Recent publications include, '"But not laughing": Horsemanship and the Idea of the Cavalier in the Writings of William Cavendish, First Duke of Newcastle', *The Seventeenth Century*, 32 (2017), Issue 4: *New Modelled Cavaliers*; 'Romance and the Problem of the Passions in Lucy Hutchinson's *Order and Disorder* and Hester Pulter's *The Unfortunate Florinda*', in *Timely Voices: Romance Writing in English Literature*, edited by Goran Stanivukovic (Montreal: McGill-Queens University Press, 2017); 'The Cavendishes and their Poetry', in *A Companion to the Cavendishes*, edited by Lisa Hopkins and Tom Rutter (Kalamazoo: ARC Humanities Press, 2020). She is currently working on a monograph examining the complex relationships between poetics and political allegiance in writings by women of apparently opposed affiliations in the Civil War and Restoration.

Danielle Clarke is Professor of English Renaissance Language and Literature at University College Dublin. She has published widely on women's writing, gender, and poetry. Recent articles include work on the reception of Teresa de Ávila, on complaint, and on recipe books. She has just completed an edition of the recipe books from Birr Castle, Co. Offaly, Ireland (Irish Manuscripts Commission) and is currently working on a book called *Becoming Human: Women's Writing, Time, Nature and Devotion 1550–1700.* She is a section editor (Theories) for *The Palgrave Encyclopedia of Early Modern Women's Writing in English.*

Marie-Louise Coolahan is Professor of English at the University of Galway. She is the author of *Women, Writing, and Language in Early Modern Ireland* (Oxford University Press, 2010) and co-editor of *Katherine Philips: Form, Reception, and Literary Contexts* (Routledge, 2018). She has written articles and essays about all forms of women's writing, miscellany culture, early modern identity, the literary culture of early modern Ireland, and textual transmission. Most recently, she has edited a special issue of the *Journal of Medieval and Early Modern Studies*: 'The Cultural Dynamics of Reception'. She is Principal Investigator of the ERC-funded project, *RECIRC: The Reception and Circulation of Early Modern Women's Writing, 1550–1700* (https://recirc.nuigalway.ie/).

Line Cottegnies is Professor of Early Modern English Literature at Sorbonne Université. Her research interests include early modern drama and poetry, translation history and cultural exchanges between France and England. She has published extensively on seventeenth-century literature, from William Shakespeare and Walter Raleigh to Margaret Cavendish, Aphra Behn, and Mary Astell. She is the author of a monograph on the politics and poetics of wonder in Caroline poetry, *L'Éclipse du regard* (Droz, 1997), and has edited or co-edited several collections of essays and journal issues, including *Authorial Conquests: Essays on Genre in the Writings of Margaret Cavendish* (Associate University Presses, 2003), with Nancy Weitz, *Women and Curiosity in Early Modern England and France* (Brill, 2016), with Sandrine Parageau, and, more recently, *Henry V: A Critical Guide* (Bloomsbury, 2018), with Karen Britland. She has edited fifteen plays for the bilingual Gallimard Complete Works of Shakespeare (2002–2015) and 2 *Henry IV* for *The Norton Shakespeare* 3 (2016). She has published *Robert Garnier in Elizabethan England,* with Marie-Alice Belle (MHRA, 2017). She is currently working on an edition of three of Aphra Behn's translations from the French (*La Montre,* 1686, *Agnes de Castro* and *A Discovery of New Worlds,* 1688) for the Cambridge Complete Works (general editors, Elaine Hobby, Claire Bowditch, and Gillian Wright).

Lara Dodds is Professor of English at Mississippi State University and the author of *The Literary Invention of Margaret Cavendish.* Her research areas include Margaret Cavendish, early modern women's writing, John Milton, and adaptation studies, and she has published in each of these fields. Recent essays include 'Envy, Emulation, and the Problem of Romance in Mary Wroth's *Urania*' (*ELR* 2018) and 'Virtual or Immediate Touch: Queer Adaptation of *Paradise Lost* in Fantasy and Science Fiction', which appeared in *Queer Milton*, edited by David Orvis (Palgrave MacMillan, 2018). She is currently a member of the advisory board and a contributing editor of *The Pulter Project: A Poet in the Making,* an innovative online edition of Hester Pulter's poetry. With Michelle M. Dowd, she is the author of 'A Feminist Case for a Return to Form' (*Early Modern Women* 2018), an essay that examines the field of early modern women's writing from a methodological perspective.

Michelle M. Dowd is Hudson Strode Professor of English and Director of the Hudson Strode Program in Renaissance Studies at the University of Alabama. She is the author of *Women's Work in Early Modern English Literature and Culture* (Palgrave, 2009), which won the Sara A. Whaley Book Award from the National Women's Studies Association, and of *The Dynamics of Inheritance on the Shakespearean Stage* (Cambridge, 2015). She has co-edited *Genre and Women's Life Writing in Early Modern England* with Julie A. Eckerle (2007); *Working Subjects in Early Modern English Drama* with Natasha Korda (2011); *Early Modern Women on the Fall: An Anthology* with Thomas Festa (2012); *Historical Affects and the Early Modern Theater* with Ronda Arab and Adam Zucker (2015); and, most recently, *Feminist Formalism and Early Modern Women's Writing: Readings, Conversations, Pedagogies* with Lara Dodds (2022). She has also published numerous articles on early modern drama and women's writing in such journals as *Modern Philology, Modern Language Quarterly, Shakespeare Studies, Early Modern Women: An Interdisciplinary Journal, Renaissance Drama,* and *English Literary Renaissance.* She is the editor of a new book series, *Strode Studies in Early Modern Literature and Culture,* published by the University of Alabama Press.

Julie A. Eckerle is a professor of English and Gender, Women, and Sexuality Studies at the University of Minnesota Morris. She is the author of *Romancing the Self in Early Modern Englishwomen's Life Writing* (2013) and the co-editor of *Women's Life Writing & Early Modern Ireland* (2019, with Naomi McAreavey) and *Genre and Women's Life Writing in Early Modern England* (2007, with Michelle M. Dowd). She is currently completing an edition of seventeenth-century Englishwoman Dorothy Calthorpe's two unpublished manuscripts, and she continues to write and publish on early modern life writing, especially by women and in or about Ireland.

Lotte Fikkers is a postdoctoral researcher on the ERC-funded project FEATHERS at Leiden University, led by Nadine Akkerman. She works at the intersection of law and literature in the early modern period and has published on women's position in the English courts of law, the records of the Court of Wards and Liveries, and the representation of wardship on the seventeenth-century stage. She is currently working on a monograph on women's self-fashioning in legal records.

Julia Flanders is a Professor of the Practice in the Department of English and the Director of the Digital Scholarship Group in the Northeastern University Library. She also directs the *Women Writers Project* and serves as editor in chief of *Digital Humanities Quarterly*, an open-access, peer-reviewed online journal of digital humanities. Her work in digital humanities began at the *Women Writers Project* and the Brown University Scholarly Technology Group in the early 1990s and continued with contributions to the development of digital humanities organisations such as the Text Encoding Initiative and the Alliance of Digital Humanities Organisations. She has served as chair of the TEI Consortium and as President of the Association for Computers and the Humanities, and has served on the steering committee of the Alliance of Digital Humanities Organisations. At the *Women Writers Project* she has led a comprehensive curriculum of workshops and tutorials on topics in scholarly text encoding, XML technologies, and digital humanities research methods, and has taught a wide range of workshops on text encoding; she has also served as a consultant and advisor on numerous digital humanities projects. Her research interests focus on data modelling, textual scholarship, and humanities data curation. She is the co-editor, with Neil Fraistat, of the *Cambridge Companion to Textual Scholarship* (Cambridge University Press, 2013), and the co-editor, with Fotis Jannidis, of *The Shape of Data in Digital Humanities* (Routledge, 2019). She holds undergraduate degrees from Harvard University and Cambridge University, and a doctorate in English Literature from Brown University.

Jaime Goodrich is an Associate Professor of English at Wayne State University. She has published numerous articles and book chapters on the lives and writings of early modern Catholic women, especially Benedictine and Franciscan nuns. Her first monograph analyses early modern Englishwomen's devotional translations (*Faithful Translators: Authorship, Gender, and Religion in Early Modern England*, Northwestern University Press, 2014), and her second monograph examines Benedictine nuns' writings in order to consider the philosophical implications of religious community (*Writing Habits: Historicism, Philosophy, and English Benedictine Convents, 1600–1800*, University of Alabama Press, 2021). She is currently preparing scholarly editions of works produced in Benedictine and Franciscan convents for Englishwomen on the Continent.

Carrie Griffin is Lecturer in English at the University of Limerick. She is the author of *Instructional Writing in English, 1350–1650: Materiality and Meaning* (Routledge 2019) and *The Middle English Wise Book of Philosophy and Astronomy: A Parallel-Text Edition* (Winter 2013). She has also co-edited several essay collections, including *Spaces for Reading in Late Medieval England* (Palgrave, 2016) and *Text, Transmission and Transformation in the European Middle Ages* (Brepols, 2018). She is an executive member of the *Centre for Early Modern Studies, Limerick* and on the steering committee of the *Irish Renaissance Seminar*. Her current projects include work on fragments in the Bolton Collection, University of Limerick, and work on medical writing in late medieval Ireland.

Meghan E. Hall earned her PhD in English from the University of Pennsylvania in 2020. Her research concerns representations of travel, empire, and the discourses of race in seventeenth-century women's writing. Her dissertation, titled 'Out of Compass: English Women's Writing and the Cultures of Travel, 1604–1680', challenges current scholarly frameworks for evaluating the experiences of traveling women in the early modern period as either exceptional, transgressive, or liberatory, looking to literary and auto-biographical writings by Elizabeth Cary, Mary Wroth, Margaret Cavendish, and Quaker itinerants, such as Alice Curwen, to illuminate the complex and uneven relationships between travel, women's labour, and social power. Hall's work has greatly benefitted from the support of the scholarly community fostered by the Folger Shakespeare Library's 2017–2018 colloquium, 'Gender, Race, and Early Modern Studies.'

Brenda M. Hosington, Professor of Translation Studies (now retired) at the Université de Montréal, is at present Research Fellow at the University of Warwick and Senior Research Fellow at University College London. She has published widely on medieval and Renaissance translation. She co-edited *Renaissance Cultural Crossroads. Translation,*

Print and Culture in Britain, 1473–1640 (Brill, 2013) and *Thresholds of Translation. Paratexts, Print, and Cultural Exchange in Early Modern Britain (1473–1660)* (Palgrave, 2018). Her guest-edited special issues of journals are *Translation and Print Culture in Early Modern Europe* (*Renaissance Studies*, 2015) and *Issues in Translation Then and Now: Renaissance Theories and Translation Studies Today* (*Renaessanceforum*, 2018). Two co-edited special issues to be published in 2019 are *Transformative Translations: Textual, Material, and Cultural Encounters in Early Modern England (Renaissance and Reformation) and 'Transformissions': Linguistic, Material and Cultural Transfer in England and France (c. 1470–1660)* (*Canadian Review of Comparative Literature*). Finally, she is the creator and principal editor of *Renaisssance Cultural Crossroads: An Online Catalogue of Translations in Britain 1473–1640* and co-creator and co-editor of the online *Cultural Crosscurrents Catalogue of Translations in Stuart and Commonwealth Britain 1641–1660*. In the field of neo-Latin studies, she has published on translation history and on women writers and translators. Her co-edited book, *Elizabeth Jane Weston Complete Writings* (2000), won the Josephine Roberts award from the Society for the Study of Early Modern Women. Brenda Hosington has been the recipient of various research grants from the Social Sciences and Humanities Research Council of Canada, the Leverhulme Trust, the British Academy, the British Council, and the Bibliographical Society, and she has held the William Ringler, Jrn. and Mayers Fellowship at the Huntington Library. Finally, she has served as: President, International Association for Neo-Latin Studies; President, Canadian Society for Renaissance Studies; Assistant General Secretary, Fédération internationale des langues et littératures modernes; Member, Advisory Board of the Neo-Latin Society; Member, editorial boards of *Moreana* and *Florilegium*.

Kevin Killeen is Professor of English Literature at the University of York. He is the author of the forthcoming *The Unknowable in Early Modern Thought: Natural Philosophy and the Poetics of the Ineffable* (Stanford University Press, 2023); *The Political Bible in Early Modern England* (Cambridge University Press, 2017), and *Biblical Scholarship, Science and Politics in Early Modern England: Thomas Browne and the Thorny Place of Knowledge* (Ashgate, 2009). He is the editor, together with Helen Smith and Rachel Willie, of *The Oxford Handbook of the Bible in Early Modern England, c. 1530–1700* (Oxford University Press, 2015), with Liz Oakley-Brown, of 'Scrutinizing Surfaces in Early Modern Thought', a Special Issue of *The Journal of the Northern Renaissance* (2017) and with Peter Forshaw, of *Biblical Exegesis and the Emergence of Science in the Early Modern Era* (Palgrave, 2007). He has edited *Thomas Browne: 21st Century Oxford Authors* (Oxford University Press, 2014), and is currently editing with Jessica Wolfe and Harriet Phillips, Browne's *Pseudodoxia Epidemica*, in two volumes for the *Oxford Works of Sir Thomas Browne*.

Leah Knight is Professor (Early Modern Non-Dramatic Literature) in the Department of English Language and Literature at Brock University (Canada). She is the author of two monographs, *Of Books and Botany in Early Modern England: Sixteenth-Century Plants and Print Culture* (2009) and *Reading Green in Early Modern England* (2014), on the intersections between the green world and textual culture in the sixteenth and seventeenth centuries; both were awarded the British Society for Literature and Science book prize. Her current research, funded by the Social Sciences and Humanities Research Council of Canada, contributes to the history of reading and early modern women's cultural studies. This work led her to co-edit, with Micheline White and Elizabeth Sauer, *Women's Bookscapes in Early Modern Britain: Reading, Ownership, Circulation* (2018). With Wendy Wall, she co-directs the ongoing *The Pulter Project: Poet in the Making* (launched 2018), an international collaborative effort to represent the long-neglected verse of Hester Pulter (1605–1678). The website associated with this project was selected in 2019 as the best project in digital scholarship, new media, or art on women and gender by the Society for the Study of Early Modern Women and Gender and awarded the 2020 Modern Language Association prize for Collaborative, Bibliographical, or Archival Scholarship. She is currently developing a website, *Fragments of a Renaissance Reader: Text Lives of Early Modern Women*, which will represent the reading experiences of Anne Clifford and contemporary female readers.

Laura L. Knoppers is George N. Shuster Professor of English Literature at the University of Notre Dame. Her research focuses on the intersections of literature, politics, religion, and visual culture in seventeenth-century England, especially the works of John Milton and of early women writers. Knoppers is the author of *Historicizing Milton: Spectacle, Power, and Poetry in Restoration England* (University of Georgia Press, 1994); *Constructing Cromwell: Ceremony, Portrait, and Print, 1645–1661* (Cambridge University Press, 2000); and *Politicizing Domesticity from Henrietta Maria to Milton's Eve* (Cambridge University Press, 2011). She has edited or co-edited five essay collections, including *The Cambridge Companion to Early Modern Women's Writing* (2009) and *The Oxford Handbook of Literature and the English Revolution* (2012). Knoppers is currently writing a book on luxury, cultural politics, and the court of Charles II and editing the seventeenth-century volume in the *Oxford History of Poetry in English.*

Katherine R. Larson is Professor of English at the University of Toronto and Vice-Dean Teaching, Learning, and Undergraduate Programs at the University of Toronto Scarborough. Her research and teaching centre on sixteenth- and seventeenth-century English literature and culture, with particular interests in early modern women's writing, gender and language, rhetoric and embodiment, and music (especially opera and song). Her first monograph, *Early Modern Women in Conversation* (Palgrave, 2011; paperback 2015), considers how gender shaped conversational interaction in England between 1590 and 1660. She has also co-edited two essay collections, *Re-Reading Mary Wroth* (Palgrave, 2015) and *Gender and Song in Early Modern England* (Ashgate, 2014; repr. Routledge, 2016). Her most recent book, *The Matter of Song in Early Modern England: Texts in and of the Air* (Oxford University Press, 2019), situates song as a multidimensional form that demands to be considered in embodied, gendered, and performance-based terms; it also features a companion recording. She is currently collaborating on the development of *Early Modern Songscapes* (songscapes.org), an intermedia project that aims more fully to animate song's least tangible, yet essential facets: its generic fluidity; its ability to register multiple meanings and permeate boundaries in unexpected ways; and its rootedness in the air. Katherine's work has been supported by the Social Sciences and Humanities Research Council of Canada, the Connaught Foundation, the Folger Shakespeare Library, the Bodleian Library, the Renaissance Society of America, and the Jackman Humanities Institute. A Member of the Royal Society of Canada's College of New Scholars, Artists, and Scientists, she is also the recipient of a number of awards, including the 2008 John Charles Polanyi Prize for Literature and a Rhodes Scholarship.

James Loxley is Professor of Early Modern Literature at the University of Edinburgh. He has published extensively on many aspects of seventeenth-century poetry, drama, and politics, including his first monograph, *Royalism and Poetry in the English Civil Wars*, which explored the ways in which the polemicisation of culture in the 1630s and 1640s shaped the practice of poetry within both established and improvised institutional frameworks. He has further pursued some of these questions in work on Katherine Philips, Andrew Marvell, Thomas Hobbes, and John Milton. He has also written extensively on Ben Jonson and the dynamics of Jacobean literary and theatrical culture, including—with Anna Groundwater and Julie Sanders—an edition of a hitherto unknown eyewitness account of Jonson's walk from London to Edinburgh in the summer of 1618. His other publications include a study of the theory of performativity from Austin to Butler and a co-authored exploration, with Mark Robson, of the claims of the performative in the context of early modern drama. He has also led a number of digital humanities projects, focusing in particular on digital literary mapping, and co-curated an exhibition on Shakespeare in Scottish collections at the National Library of Scotland in 2011–2012. His current research and knowledge exchange work includes an edition of Dekker's *The Shoemakers' Holiday* for Arden Early Modern Drama, digital literary projects with the Edinburgh International Book Festival and Edinburgh City of Literature Trust, and a monograph on Ben Jonson and the experience of work.

Christina Luckyj is Professor of English and McCulloch Chair at Dalhousie University in Halifax, Nova Scotia, where she specialises in early modern literature. She is the author of *Liberty and The Politics of the Female Voice in Early Stuart England* (Cambridge University Press, 2022) and *'A Moving Rhetoricke': Gender and Silence in Early Modern England* (Manchester University Press, 2002), and editor of *The White Devil* (New Mermaids, 2008) and *The Duchess of Malfi: A Critical Guide* (Arden, 2011). She co-edited (with Niamh J. O'Leary) *The Politics of Female Alliance in Early Modern England* (University of Nebraska Press, 2017), which won the Society for the Study of Early Modern Women Award for Best Collaborative Project published in 2017. Author of a range of essays on early modern drama and on women writers, including two essays on Rachel Speght in *English Literary Renaissance*, she also published '"A Woman's Logicke": Puritan Women Writers and the Rejection of Education', in *The Routledge Companion to Women, Sex and Gender in the Early British Colonial World* (2019). Her new Introduction to *Othello* for the New Cambridge Shakespeare appeared in 2017, and she is section editor (Jacobean period) for *The Palgrave Encyclopedia of Early Modern Women's Writing in English*. She is currently editing *The Winter's Tale* for Cambridge

Shakespeare Editions, and (with Danielle Clarke and Victoria E. Burke) the works of Anne Southwell for *The Other Voice in Early Modern Europe*.

Paula McQuade is Professor of English at DePaul University in Chicago and the author of multiple articles on early modern women's writing, including, most recently, 'How Christiana Learned Her Catechism: Catechisms, Family Religion, and Lay Literacy in Seventeenth-Century England' (2018). Her monograph, *Catechisms and Women's Writing in Seventeenth-Century England* (Cambridge: Cambridge University Press, 2017) is a study of early modern women's literary use of catechising. Drawing upon the methodology of local history, McQuade examines original works composed by women—both in manuscript and print, as well as women's copying and redacting of catechisms—and the construction of these materials from other sources. By studying female catechists, McQuade shows how early modern women used the power and authority granted to them as mothers to teach religious doctrine, to demonstrate their linguistic skills, to engage sympathetically with Catholic devotionals texts, and to comment on matters of contemporary religious and political import—activities that many scholars have considered the sole prerogative of clergymen. Paula McQuade received her PhD from the University of Chicago in 1998. The recipient of a 1996 Charlotte Newcombe Fellowship, McQuade is the author of multiple articles on early modern women and gender. Her article on the female catechist Dorothy Burch was selected as the best article published in 2010 by the Society for the Study of Early Modern Women Writers. She is also the recipient of an Excellence in Teaching Award from DePaul University.

Dianne Mitchell is Assistant Professor of English at the University of Colorado, Boulder. Her work explores the compelling intersections of materiality and form through the study of Renaissance English lyrics. Mitchell's articles have appeared in *Modern Philology*, *English Literary Renaissance*, the *Journal for Early Modern Cultural Studies*, and *Studies in Philology*. Her essays can also be found in *Shakespeare/Text* (Arden, ed. Claire Bourne, 2021) and *Feminist Formalism and Early Modern Women's Writing: Readings, Conversations, Pedagogies* (Nebraska, eds Lara Dodds and Michelle Dowd, 2022). Mitchell is working on her first book, *Paper Intimacies*, which contends that the material lives of handwritten poems afford unexpected models of intimate contact.

Erin Murphy is Associate Professor in the Department of English and the Women's, Gender, and Sexuality Studies Program at Boston University. She has published *Familial Forms: Politics and Genealogy in Seventeenth-Century English Literature* (University of Delaware Press, 2011), and authored articles on John Milton, Lucy Hutchinson, and Mary Astell. She co-edited *Milton Now: Alternative Approaches and Contexts* (Palgrave, 2014) with Catharine Gray, as well as a special issue of *Criticism* on the work of Eve Kosofsky Sedgwick with James Keith Vincent. She is currently working on two book projects, *Wartimes: Seventeenth-Century Women's Writing and its Afterlives* and *Rude Reading: Gender, Race, Sexuality, and the Work of John Milton*. As part of Northeastern University's NEH-supported 'Intertextual Networks' project, she is currently developing a digital exhibit on biblical marginalia in Lucy Hutchinson's *Order and Disorder* with

Chelsea Clark. The exhibit will be published online in 'Women Writers in Context' as part of the Women Writers Project. With Sarah Wall-Randall, she co-leads the interdisciplinary seminar on Women and Culture in the Early Modern World at Harvard's Mahindra Humanities Center.

Michelle O'Callaghan is Professor of Early Modern Literature in the Department of English Literature at the University of Reading. She is the author of *The 'shepheards nation': Jacobean Spenserians and Early Stuart Political Culture* (Oxford, 2000), *The English Wits: Literature and Sociability in Early Modern England* (Cambridge, 2007), *Thomas Middleton* (Edinburgh, 2009), *Crafting Poetry Anthologies in Renaissance England: Early Modern Cultures of Recreation* (Cambridge, 2020), and co-editor of *Verse Miscellanies Online*, with Alice Eardley. She has published various articles, including '"My printer must, haue somwhat to his share": Isabella Whitney, Richard Jones, and Crafting Books', *Women's Writing*, 26 (2019), '"Good Ladies be working": Singing at Work in Tudor Woman's Song', *Huntington Library Quarterly*, 82 (2019), '"An uncivill scurrilous letter": "womanish brabbles" and the Letter of Affront', in *Cultures of Correspondence in Early Modern Britain, 1550–1640*, edited by James Daybell and Andrew Gordon (University of Pennsylvania Press, 2016), and 'The "great Queen of Lightninge flashes": The Transmission of Female-Voiced Burlesque Poetry in the Early Seventeenth Century', in *Material Cultures of Early Modern Women's Writing*, edited by Rosalind Smith and Patricia Pender (Palgrave Macmillan, 2015).

Michele Osherow is Associate Professor of English and affiliate faculty of Judaic Studies at the University of Maryland, Baltimore County. She is the author of *Biblical Women's Voices in Early Modern England* (Ashgate, 2009) along with numerous articles and essays on Early Modern Literature, Shakespeare, and the Early Modern Bible. Her current research project, 'Keeping the Girls in Stitches: Embroidering Biblical Narrative in the Seventeenth Century' continues her work on gendered negotiations and the Bible by exploring domestic needlework of the seventeenth century as a form of women's biblical commentary. In addition, she has served for several academic terms as Interim Executive Director of the Shakespeare Association of America. Osherow is Resident Dramaturg for the Folger Theatre, part of the public programming division of the Folger Shakespeare Library in Washington, DC, where she has contributed to more than forty professional productions of Shakespeare and other classics. At UMBC, she has collaborated with faculty in the departments of Theatre, Visual Arts, the Imaging Research Center, Gender and Women's Studies, and Mathematics. The play 'The Mathematics of Being Human' co-written with mathematician and novelist Manil Suri and based on their collaborative teaching experiences, has been performed is various locations in the US and abroad, including the Museum of Mathematics in New York.

Patricia Pender is an Associate Professor of English and Writing at the University of Newcastle, Australia. She is the author of *Early Modern Women's Writing and the Rhetoric of Modesty* (2012), the editor of *Gender, Authorship and Early Modern Women's Collaboration* (2017), and the co-editor, with Rosalind Smith, of *Material Cultures* *of Early Modern Women's Writing* (2014). She has recently been appointed one of the General Editors of the large-scale digital *Palgrave Encyclopedia of Early Modern Women's Writing in English.*

Patricia Phillippy is Professor of Material and Cultural Memories and Director of the Centre for Arts, Memory, and Communities at Coventry University. Her scholarship engages early modern literature and culture from a comparative and transdisciplinary point of view, with a focus on manuscripts, monuments, and memorial writings and productions. Recent publications include *Painting Women: Cosmetics, Canvases and Early Modern Culture* (Johns Hopkins, 2006), and *Shaping Remembrance from Shakespeare to Milton* (Cambridge, 2018). She is the editor of *An English Sappho: The Writings of Elizabeth Cooke Hoby Russell* (CRRS/ITER, 2011) and *A History of Early Modern Women's Writing* (Cambridge, 2018). Her research in progress studies premodern climate change, understood as anthropogenic and racialized, exploring how the changed global ecology emerging from English and European mercantile and colonial expansion is registered in memorial creations and parochial settings by women in seventeenth-century England and colonial New England.

Sarah Prescott is Professor of English, Principal and Dean of the College of Arts and Humanities at University College Dublin and a member of the Learned Society of Wales. She specialises in seventeenth- and eighteenth-century British and Irish women's writing and pre-1800 Welsh writing in English and has published many articles and chapters in her subject field. She is the author of *Women, Authorship, and Literary Culture, 1690–1740* (2003), *Women and Poetry, 1660≠1750* (co-ed. 2003), *Eighteenth-Century Writing from Wales: Bards and Britons* (2008), and *Writing Wales from the Renaissance to Romanticism* (co-ed. 2012). She has just completed a co-written volume for the forthcoming *Oxford Literary History of Wales*, volume 3 'Welsh Writing in English, 1536–1914' (with Professor Jane Aaron). Professor Prescott is the Principal Investigator for the Leverhulme-funded project 'Women's Poetry from Ireland, Scotland, and Wales: 1400–1800', a joint project between University College Dublin, Aberystwyth University, the University of Edinburgh, the University of Glasgow, and the National University of Ireland, Galway. A multilinguistic anthology and accompanying comparative critical study will be forthcoming from Cambridge University Press.

Anna Reynolds is a Lecturer in English at the University of St Andrews. Prior to this she was an Associate Lecturer at the University of York, where she received her PhD in 2018. She works at the intersection of material practices and imaginative thought in early modern England, focusing in particular on the physical biography of paper and the metaphorical life of books, loose sheets, and textual fragments. She has published an article on early modern encounters with binding waste in *The Journal of the Northern Renaissance* (2017) and is currently completing her first monograph, *Privy Tokens: Waste Paper in Early Modern England*, as well as co-editing the collection *The Paper Trade in Early Modern Europe: Practices, Materials, Networks* (Brill, 2021). With Adam Smyth

(University of Oxford) and Megan Heffernan (DePaul University) she is designing an open-access, online database of early modern printed waste paper.

Jennifer Richards is Joseph Cowen Chair of English Literature at Newcastle University, UK, and the Director of the Newcastle University Humanities Research Institute. She is the author of articles in *Renaissance Quarterly*, *Huntington Library Quarterly*, *Criticism*, *Journal of the History of Ideas*, *Bulletin of the History of Medicine*, and *Past and Present*, and of *Rhetoric and Courtliness in Early Modern Literature* (Cambridge University Press, 2003), *Rhetoric: The New Critical Idiom* (Routledge, 2007), *Voices and Books in the English Renaissance: A New History of Reading* (Oxford University Press, 2019; winner of the biennial ESSE Book Prize 2020; highly commended, SHARP DeLong Book History Prize). She is a general editor of *A New Critical Edition of Thomas Nashe* (forthcoming, Oxford University Press), and the lead on The Thomas Nashe Project (AHRC-funded) and the digital project, *Animating Texts at Newcastle University*. With Virginia Cox (NYU), she is co-editing *Rhetoric in the Renaissance 1380–1640, Volume III*, in *The Cambridge History of Rhetoric*, gen. eds: Rita Copeland and Peter Mack (Cambridge University Press, forthcoming).

Sarah C. E. Ross is Associate Professor of English at Te Herenga Waka–Victoria University of Wellington, Aotearoa New Zealand. She has published widely on early modern women's poetry, religious and political writing, and manuscript and print culture, and she is the author of *Women, Poetry, and Politics in Seventeenth-Century Britain* (2015) and editor of *Katherine Austen's Book M: Additional Manuscript 4454* (2011). She has co-edited *Editing Early Modern Women* (2016, with Paul Salzman) and *Early Modern Women's Complaint: Gender, Form, and Politics* (2020, with Rosalind Smith), and her teaching anthology with Elizabeth Scott-Baumann, *Women Poets of the English Civil War* (2017), won the Society for the Study of Early Modern Women and Gender's prize for Best Teaching Edition in 2018. She is currently completing a project on early modern women's complaint, and is a section editor for *The Palgrave Encyclopedia of Early Modern Women's Writing in English*.

Paul Salzman FAHA is Emeritus Professor at La Trobe University (Australia). He has published widely on early modern women's writing, and on the history and theory of editing, including *Reading Early Modern Women's Writing* (Oxford University Press, 2006). Recent publications include *Editors Construct the Renaissance Canon 1825–1915* (Palgrave Macmillan, 2018) and, co-edited with Sarah C. E. Ross, *Editing Early Modern Women* (Cambridge University Press, 2016). He has edited four World's Classics volumes of early modern writing, and online editions of Mary Wroth's poetry and of her play *Love's Victory*. He is currently working on a book for the Cambridge Elements Shakespeare and Text Series titled *Shakespeare Reproduced: Early Facsimiles and the History of Shakespeare Editing*.

Julie Sanders is Professor of English Literature and Drama and Deputy Vice-Chancellor and Provost at Newcastle University. She has published widely on early modern literature, not least on women's writing, including essays on Margaret Cavendish and the Tixall Sisters, and articles on Jacobean and Caroline drama in *English Literary Renaissance, Modern Language Review, Shakespeare Survey* and *Theatre Journal*. Her monographs include *The Cultural Geography of Early Modern Drama, 1620–1650* published by Cambridge University Press in 2011 and winner of the British Academy Rose Mary Crawshay prize in 2012 and she co-authored *Ben Jonson's Walk to Scotland* with James Loxley and Anna Groundwater (Cambridge University Press, 2015). She has edited several plays by Jonson and others including *The New Inn* for the *Cambridge Complete Works of Ben Jonson* and she co-edited *Three Seventeenth-Century Plays on Women and Performance* with Hero Chalmers and Sophie Tomlinson for the Revels Drama series (Manchester University Press, 2011). Her current research project is on the social life of things in early modern London and she is also co-editor of a commissioning series on 'Early Modern Literary Geographies' with Garrett A. Sullivan Jr for Oxford University Press.

Elizabeth Scott-Baumann is Reader in Early Modern Literature at King's College London and her monograph *Forms of Engagement: Women, Poetry, and Culture 1640–1680* came out in 2013. She has co-edited essay collections including *The Intellectual Culture of Puritan Women, 1558–1680* (with Johanna Harris, 2010); *The Work of Form: Poetics and Materiality in Early Modern Culture* (with Ben Burton, 2014); *Shakespeare's Sonnets: The State of Play* (with Hannah Crawforth and Clare Whitehead, 2017) and two collections of poems, *On Shakespeare's Sonnets: A Poets' Celebration* (with Hannah Crawforth, 2016) and *Women Poets of the English Civil War* (with Sarah C. E. Ross, 2017, winner of the 'Best Teaching Edition' prize of the Society for the Study of Early Modern Women and Gender). She is also a contributing editor for *The Pulter Project* http://pulterproject.northwestern.edu/. Her articles appear in *The Seventeenth Century, English Literary History, Women's Writing*, and *Huntington Library Quarterly*. She has held fellowships at Yale University's Beinecke Library, Chawton House Library, and Massey University, New Zealand.

Helen Smith is Professor of Renaissance Literature and Head of the Department of English and Related Literature at the University of York. She has published widely on materiality, books and the book trades, and on early modern women's work and writing. Helen is author of *Grossly Material Things: Women and Book Production in Early Modern England* (2012, winner of the Roland H. Bainton Prize for Literature and the SHARP DeLong Book History Prize). She has co-edited *Renaissance Paratexts* (with Louise Wilson, 2011), *The Oxford Handbook of the Bible in Early Modern England* (with Kevin Killeen and Rachel Willie, 2015, winner of the Roland H. Bainton Reference Prize), and *Conversions: Gender and Religious Change in Early Modern Europe* (with Simon Ditchfield, 2017). Helen was CI on the AHRC-funded project, 'Conversion Narratives in Early Modern Europe', and PI on the AHRC Network 'Imagining Jerusalem, c.1099 to the Present Day'. Her current book project explores early modern ideas about matter, and the material ways in which those ideas were reproduced and explored. With J. T. Welsch, Helen is founding co-director of Thin Ice Press, a letterpress studio based at the University of York.

Rosalind Smith is Professor of English at the Australian National University and works on gender, form, politics, and history in early modern women's writing. She is the author of *Sonnets and the English Woman Writer, 1560–1621: The Politics of Absence* (2005) as well as multiple book chapters and journal articles including publications in *English Literary Renaissance, Textual Practice, Women's Writing* and the *Journal of Medieval and Early Modern Studies*. She co-edited the collections *Material Cultures of Early Modern Women's Writing* (2014), *Early Modern Women and Complaint: Gender, Form, Politics* (2020), and a special issue of *Parergon* on *Early Modern Women and the Apparatus of Authorship* (2012), and is the general editor (with Patricia Pender) of *The Palgrave Encyclopedia of Early Modern Women's Writing*. Her current research project is an Australian Research Council Future Fellowship on early modern women's marginalia, partnering with the University of Oxford and the Folger Shakespeare Library. She also leads a research project collaborating with State Library Victoria on the Emmerson collection, Australia's first early modern archive of scale, that seeks to understand and contextualise this recent bequest of over 5000 early modern books as well as provide digital pathways for scholarly and public engagement with the collection.

Daniel Starza Smith is Senior Lecturer in Early Modern English Literature (1500–1700) at King's College London, having previously held roles at University College London, the University of Reading, and Lincoln College, Oxford, where he was British Academy Postdoctoral Fellow. His books include *John Donne and the Conway Papers* (Oxford University Press, 2014) and, edited with Joshua Eckhardt, *Manuscript Miscellanies in Early Modern England* (Ashgate, 2014). He is General Editor of the Oxford edition of the letters of John Donne, and, with Jana Dambrogio, is co-director of the Unlocking History research group, researching letterlocking.

Jane Stevenson was educated at Newnham College, Cambridge. She then became Drapers' Research Fellow at Pembroke College. She was appointed to a lectureship in History at Sheffield University, and in 1995, became an Interdisciplinary Research Fellow in the Faculty of Arts at the University of Warwick. In 2000, she joined the University of Aberdeen, where she was Regius Professor of Humanity. She is now Senior Research Fellow at Campion Hall, University of Oxford. Her principal academic publications are *The 'Laterculus Malalianus' and the School of Archbishop Theodore* (1995), *Early Modern Women Poets*, with Peter Davidson (2001), and *Women Latin Poets: Language, Gender and Authority from Antiquity to the Eighteenth Century* (2005), and *Baroque Between the Wars* (2018). Additionally, she has published a biography of the painter Edward Burra, and six novels.

Mihoko Suzuki is Professor of English and Cooper Fellow in the Humanities, Emerita at the University of Miami. She has written extensively on early modern women's political writings, in *Subordinate Subjects: Gender, the Political Nation, and Literary Form in England* (2003) and in *Antigone's Example: Early Modern Women's Political Writing in Times of Civil War, from Christine de Pizan to Helen Maria Williams* (2022) and numerous essays, including, 'Political Writing across Borders', in Patricia Phillippy (ed.), *A*

History of Early Modern Women's Writing (2018); and 'Women's Political Writing: Civil War Memoirs', in Amanda Capern (ed.), *Routledge History of Women in Early Modern Europe* (2019). She is the editor of *The History of British Women's Writing*, vol. 3, 1610–1690 (2011); and the co-editor of *Debating Gender in Early Modern England, 1500–1700* (2002); *The Rule of Women in Early Modern Europe* (2009); *Women's Political Writings, 1610–1725* (4 vols, 2007); and *Early Modern Women: An Interdisciplinary Journal* (2011–2018). Her current projects include women's manuscript writings as political discourse in early modern England and women as authors of epic in early modern Europe.

Martine van Elk is a Professor of English at California State University, Long Beach. She has published extensively on early modern drama, Shakespeare, vagrancy, and early modern women writers. Early on in her career, she worked primarily on English drama with a concentration on Shakespeare and vagrancy. Her essays appeared in journals such as *Studies in English Literature* and *Shakespeare Quarterly*, while she also co-edited a collection of essays entitled *Tudor Drama Before Shakespeare*, which came out with Palgrave in 2004. Other publications include an edition of *Gammer Gurton's Needle* for the *Broadview Anthology of Medieval Drama* (2013) and a chapter on Terence's influence on early modern English drama for the *Blackwell Companion to Terence* (2013). Recently her interests have shifted decisively to writings by early modern women and in particular to developing comparative and cross-cultural approaches to their work. In 2017, her book *Early Modern Women's Writing: Domesticity, Privacy, and the Public Sphere in England and the Dutch Republic* was published by Palgrave. Essays on English and Dutch women and emblems, women's poetry, English and Dutch actresses and on two Dutch female playwrights have come out in edited collections and journals such as *Early Modern Women* and *Early Modern Low Countries*. She has published on book history in Bloomsbury's *Women's Labour and the History of the Book in Early Modern England* (2020), edited by Valerie Wayne, and on Dutch female glass engravers in *Renaissance Quarterly* (2020). Current projects include work as a section editor for the new *Palgrave Encyclopedia of Early Modern Women's Writing in English* as well as a book-length comparative study of women on and behind the stage in England, the Dutch Republic, and France. Finally, she maintains two blogs, one entitled *Early Modern Women: Texts, Lives, Objects*, and the other *Early Modern Female Book Ownership*.

Leah Veronese is undertaking her AHRC-funded DPhil in the rhetoric of early modern petition at Balliol College, Oxford. She has worked as a research intern at Lambeth Palace Library and as a research assistant for the *Variorum Edition of the Poetry of John Donne* and Gateway to Early Modern Manuscripts projects.

Sebastiaan Verweij is Senior Lecturer in Late Medieval and Early Modern English Literature at the Department of English, University of Bristol. He holds a PhD from the University of Glasgow, and previously worked at Cambridge and at Oxford. His research interests are in late medieval and early modern Scottish and English literature (especially poetry) and the history of the book. He is interested in the intersections between the book as material text and more literary questions. He also has an interest in the Digital Humanities; in editorial theory and practice; and in the manuscript and print histories, and the poems and prose texts, of John Donne. His first book, *The Literary Culture of Early Modern Scotland: Manuscript Production and Transmission, 1560–1625* (Oxford University Press 2016), won the Saltire Society's 'Scottish Research Book of the Year 2016' award. He has otherwise widely published on Scottish and English literature and history. He is currently at work, with Professor Peter McCullough, on the Textual Companion volume in *The Oxford Edition of the Sermons of John Donne*. With Noah Millstone he recently completed the AHRC-funded project 'Manuscript Pamphleteering in Early Stuart England'.

Wendy Wall is Avalon Professor for the Humanities and the Charles Deering McCormick Professor of Teaching Excellence at Northwestern University. A specialist in Renaissance literature and culture, she is author of *The Imprint of Gender: Authorship and Publication in the English Renaissance* (Cornell University Press, 1993), *Staging Domesticity: Household Work and English Identity in Early Modern Drama* (Cambridge University Press, 2002), and *Recipes for Thought: Knowledge and Taste in the Early Modern English Kitchen* (University of Pennsylvania Press, 2015). With Leah Knight, she co-created and is general editor for *The Pulter Project: Poet in the Making* (2018), an open-access, collaborative, digital edition of the poems of seventeenth-century writer Hester Pulter. This site pioneers a new mode of editing by making available multiple 'authorised' and contrasting versions of poems, created collaboratively by a team of international scholars. Professor Wall has published on topics as wide-ranging as Renaissance poetry, cookbooks, domesticity, editorial theory, gender, national identity, the history of authorship, women's writing, theatrical practice, and Jell-O. Her public humanities work includes partnerships with the Chicago Shakespeare Theater, the Newberry Library, the Northwestern Prison Education Program, the Shakespeare Slam, and the Chicago Humanities Festival. She is a past president and trustee for the Shakespeare Association of America and served as co-editor for *Renaissance Drama* for seven years.

Helen Wilcox is Professor Emerita of Early Modern English Literature at Bangor University, Wales, having previously taught at universities in the Netherlands and England. Early in her career she was a co-editor of the pioneering anthology of seventeenth-century women's autobiographical writing, *Her Own Life* (Routledge, 1989), and editor of *Women and Literature in Britain, 1500–1700* (Cambridge, 1996). Among her extensive list of articles and essays are more than forty that partly or wholly concern early modern women's writing, particularly devotional lyrics and life-writing, and/or discuss feminist critical approaches to the editing and interpretation of early modern texts. She has given research lectures throughout Europe, as well as in North America, South Africa, China, Japan, Australia, and New Zealand. She is the editor of the acclaimed *English Poems of George Herbert* (Cambridge, 2007), and has been elected a fellow of the Royal Society of Literature, the English Association, the Royal Society of Arts and the Learned Society of Wales. Among her more recent publications are *1611: Authority, Gender and the Word in Early Modern England* (Blackwell, 2014) and two co-edited works, *The Oxford Handbook of Early Modern English Literature and Religion* (Oxford, 2017) and *All's Well That Ends Well* (Arden, 2019). She is the editor of *Oroonoko* in the forthcoming *Works of Aphra Behn* (Cambridge, 2023). Her further critical interests include the relationship of literature with other art forms, particularly music and the visual arts, and the role that literary reading can (and ought to) play in our contemporary communities.

Susan Wiseman teaches English literature at Birkbeck College, University of London. Her publications include: *Writing Metamorphosis in Renaissance England, 1550–1700* (Cambridge University Press, 2014); *Conspiracy and Virtue: Women, Writing, and Politics in Seventeenth Century England* (Oxford University Press, 2006); *Politics and Drama in the English Civil War* (Cambridge University Press, 1998); and *Aphra Behn* (Writers and Their Work Series: Northcote House, 1996; second edition expanded and revised, published 2007).

Ramona Wray is Professor in Renaissance Literature at Queen's University, Belfast. She is the editor of the Arden Early Modern Drama edition of Elizabeth Cary's *The Tragedy of Mariam* (2012), the author of *Women Writers in the Seventeenth Century* (2004), and the co-author of *Great Shakespeareans: Welles, Kurosawa, Kozintsev, Zeffirelli* (2013). She is the co-editor of *The Edinburgh Companion to Shakespeare and the Arts* (2011), *Screening Shakespeare in the Twenty-First Century* (2006), *Reconceiving the Renaissance: A Critical Reader* (2005), *Shakespeare, Film, Fin de Siècle* (2000), and *Shakespeare and Ireland: History, Politics, Culture* (1997). Her articles on Shakespeare appropriation and early modern women's writing have appeared in *Early Theatre*, *Shakespeare Bulletin*, *Shakespeare Survey*, *Shakespeare Quarterly*, *Memory Studies*, and *Women's Writing*.

CHAPTER 1

WHAT IS EARLY MODERN WOMEN'S WRITING?

DANIELLE CLARKE, SARAH C. E. ROSS, AND ELIZABETH SCOTT-BAUMANN

If academic book series, editions, scholarly journals, professional organisations, panels at major conferences, and funded projects are anything to go by, then early modern women's writing is clearly now a fully fledged field.[1] The idea of early modern women's writing as a 'field' has gained additional heft with a double issue of *Criticism* (2021), edited by Jaime Goodrich and Paula McQuade, devoted to exploring future directions for scholarship on early modern writing by women.[2] Other key recent publications also speak to, and engage critically with, the idea of early modern women's writing as a distinct body of material, albeit with contested borders, and an uncertainly defined interior.[3] The idea of a 'field' speaks eloquently to an accumulated body of scholarship with shared assumptions, and to an idea—however contested—that women who write

[1] See the two volumes of the *Collected Works of Lucy Hutchinson*, eds David Norbook, Elizabeth Clarke et al. (Oxford 2012; 2018); Leah Knight and Wendy Wall (eds), *The Pulter Project: Poet in the Making* (2018). Northwestern University. http://pulterproject.northwestern.edu; Liza Blake (ed.), *Margaret Cavendish's Poems and Fancies: A Digital Critical Edition* (2019). University of Toronto. http://library2.utm.utoronto.ca/poemsandfancies/; an eight-volume edition of the works of Aphra Behn is forthcoming from Cambridge University Press, edited by Elaine Hobby, Gillian Wright, Mel Evans, and Alan Hogarth, see https://www.aphrabehn.online/ (accessed 6 May 2021).

[2] See Diane Purkiss, 'Rooms of All Our Own: A History of Ignoring Early Women Writers', *Times Literary Supplement* (15 February 2019), 10–11; Jaime Goodrich and Paula McQuade (eds), 'Special Issue: 'The Future(s) of Early Modern Women Writers', *Criticism*, 63.1–2 (2021); Laura Knoppers (ed.) *The Cambridge Companion to Early Modern Women's Writing* (Cambridge, 2009); Patricia Phillippy (ed.) *A History of Early Modern Women's Writing* (Cambridge, 2018); Patricia Pender and Rosalind Smith (gen. eds), *The Palgrave Encyclopedia of Early Modern Women's Writing* (Palgrave, forthcoming).

[3] See, for one recent example, Kimberly Anne Coles and Eve Keller (eds), *The Routledge Companion to Women, Sex, and Gender in the Early British Colonial World* (London, 2018) and an important, much earlier precedent Margo Hendricks and Patricia Parker (eds), *Women, 'Race', and Writing in the Early Modern Period* (New York, 1994).

in the early modern period share something structurally and culturally significant. The idea of this shared basis in a structural inequality based specifically on gender speaks, too, to the structural inequalities of preservation, circulation, and transmission, absent presences which indelibly mark our objects of enquiry. These inequalities, however, are not one-dimensional; rather, they are complicated by, and implicated in, other dimensions of social, cultural, and economic life in the early modern period. The exploration of these questions is crucial to future scholarship.

This 'fieldness' of early modern women's writing—a framing to which this Handbook contributes—is something to celebrate, as it gestures towards some degree of parity with longer established areas of study. Potentially, however, it risks courting limitation or suggesting monoculture. The metaphor of a field is territorial: it implies ownership, and the creation of boundaries between itself and other things. It may be productive, but at the cost of importing resources from elsewhere, rather than existing symbiotically with them. By the same token, the metaphor suggests a space that might accommodate multiple organisms, connected in complex ways in space and in time. Two key and necessarily unresolved questions for us throughout the planning and execution of this Handbook have been where to draw the boundary to our subject (or indeed whether to), and how to reconcile the particular and specific demands of studying texts by women from 1540 to 1700 with their complex and wide-ranging connections to a thrilling array of other things happening at the time: food, science, religion, medicine, travel, agriculture, furniture, building, painting, language, mathematics, clothing, books, to start only a partial list. Women's writing is bound up in complex ways with questions of circulation, transmission, and access to resources—both in their own moment and across the history of the academic study of their work. Yet openness to other areas and disciplines is also a cornerstone of the study of early modern women's writing, connecting to multiple histories (religious, material, intellectual, social) and plural modes (manuscript, print, oral) and, from its beginnings, asking key questions about periodisation, epistemic shifts, and ideas of teleology.

This Handbook developed from two perceptions: on the one hand, the 'fieldness' of early modern women's writing, and, on the other, accelerated change, a need for more systematic approaches at scale in order to draw larger conclusions from the hugely important scholarship on which our field rests. This volume aims to integrate the disciplinary challenges raised by early modern women's writing more fully into critical work on the Renaissance. In particular, it seeks, through a range of approaches, to ask larger questions about women's writing and its relationship(s) to texts and culture more generally. It questions the category of 'women's' writing, by examining how far gender and constructions of gender inflect authorship, reception, and style, and how the field can integrate provisional and partial identifications into understanding of early modern women's discourses. The chapters interrogate the degree to which women's writings and their innovations, often born out of constraints of various kinds, in fact spearhead a number of key developments in thought and writing over the course of the sixteenth and seventeenth centuries. These might include the valorisation of the vernacular, the development of demotic literary forms, the move away from rhetorically driven literary production, altered notions of privacy, and ultimately the development of a range of vernacular, domestic forms. The emphasis throughout is on innovation as a response to specific cultural, ideological, and sometimes very local conditions. The cumulative effect of the chapters is, we hope, to alter the critical emphasis from uniqueness and exceptionalism to a focus on commonality and embeddedness, while exploring the unique conditions—including material, social, cultural, religious—that structure the production of early modern women's writing.

ORIGINS

It is impossible to survey the field of early modern women's writing now without some sense of its origins and history. Virginia Woolf's *A Room of One's Own* (1929) and her invention of a talented and tragic sister to William Shakespeare has been a defining narrative for feminist scholarship on women writers of the past, bequeathing a framework of occlusion and loss, exclusion and defiance, and a desire to recover matrilineal literary traditions. Writing of the Elizabethan period, Woolf wondered 'why no woman wrote a word of that extraordinary literature when every other man, it seemed, was capable of song or sonnet', and she laid the blame squarely on social and material conditions that precluded women's access to the space or independent income that enabled the penning of texts in genres central to the literary canon: a sonnet, a 'fiction', or a play.[4] Germaine Greer echoed these terms of exclusion and genre hierarchies in her groundbreaking edition of seventeenth-century women's verse, *Kissing the Rod* (1989), declaring Renaissance poetry the domain of 'classically educated males' and envisioning the women poets she anthologised as '*guerilleras*', 'storming the highest bastion' of elite literary production.[5] The absence of women from conventional early modern literary histories, conceived of as male authors publishing in print, provoked the energies of en masse feminist textual recovery in the 1980s and 1990s. Crucial work included the *Women Writers Project* and the *Perdita* project's archaeological excavation of women in early modern manuscript culture. The recovery of 'lost' women writers continues to drive the editing of women's texts across a wide range of print and digital media. Expanding the canon of early modern women writers over recent decades has taken at least two predominant forms, in practice and in theory. On the one hand, feminist scholars valorising the literary qualities of early modern women's writings have fought to insert women into the existing literary canon, fighting for space in the *Norton Anthology of English Literature* and comparable volumes. On the other, extensive work in early modern women's writing and adjacent areas of enquiry has focused on expanding the definitions of the canon itself, emphasising the particularities of the genres and forms in

[4] Virginia Woolf, *A Room of One's Own* (London, 2004; 1928), 48.

[5] Germaine Greer, Susan Hastings, Jeslyn Medoff, and Melinda Sansone (eds), *Kissing the Rod: An Anthology of Seventeenth-Century Women's Verse* (New York, 1988), 1.

which women wrote, and arguing the need for different modes of presentation and anthologisation to bring these materials to new generations of students and scholars.

Even before Woolf, early modern women's writing had never been entirely lost. Compiling his *Memoirs of Several Ladies of Great Britain, Who Have Been Celebrated for their Writings, or Skill in the Learned Languages, Arts and Sciences* in 1752, George Ballard documented over sixty women, including queens Catherine of Aragon, Katherine Parr, and Elizabeth I, the Cooke sisters, and the calligrapher and miniaturist Esther Inglis. He also noted women for whom the trail had begun to run cold, sketching the traces of a diverse range of early modern women poets, letter-writers, and scholars, including Anne, Lady Southwell, Aemilia Lanyer, Lady Ranelagh, and Anna Maria van Schurman.[6] Ballard's *Memoirs* is only one of many volumes before Woolf to highlight the writings of early modern women. George Colman and Bonnell Thornton published an anthology of *Poems by Eminent Ladies* in 1755, with revised editions in 1773 and 1785. Alexander Dyce's *Specimens of British Poetesses* (1825) included eighty-nine women poets, and its 'positive reception' among writers like Leigh Hunt and William Wordsworth attests to its readership and reach.[7] Frederic Rowton published another anthology, *The Female Poets of Great Britain*, in 1848, largely following Dyce's selection. Woolf's fiction of Elizabethan women writers' absence from the literary record, then, is fertile and enduring, but it is a 'creative fact' rather than a true one, even in her own time.[8] Its dominance says much about literary tastes rooted in the eighteenth and nineteenth centuries, and about how these shaped what remained visible and what fell from view.[9] There is, as Paul Salzman has described, as 'a history of forgetting' about the 'rich and diverse' reception histories of early modern women writers, and of work on them, including that of women scholars.[10] To set against this, there is a long sense of the field in which early modern women writers have been celebrated and memorialised according to the 'the pressures and exigencies' of any given time, as Paul Salzman and Marie-Louise Coolahan describe in their chapters in this volume.[11] Considering these longer histories foregrounds the ways in which the visibility or otherwise of early modern

6 George Ballard, *Memoirs of Several Ladies of Great Britain* (London, 1752), vii.

7 Paul Salzman, *Editors Construct the Renaissance Canon, 1825–1915* (Cham, 2018), 8; and see Margaret J. M. Ezell, *Writing Women's Literary History* (Baltimore, MD, 1993), Chapter 4.

8 Paul Salzman points out that Virginia Woolf was 'in a number of instances, exposed more directly' to early modern women's writing than *A Room of One's Own* suggests (*Reading Early Modern Women's Writing* (Oxford, 2006), 34–5.

9 See Margaret J. M. Ezell, 'Invisibility Optics: Aphra Behn, Esther Inglis and the Fortunes of Women's Works', in Phillippy, *History*, 27–45; Jennifer Summit, *Lost Property: The Woman Writer and English Literary History, 1380–1589* (Chicago, IL, 2000).

10 Salzman, *Reading Early Modern Women's Writing*, 219–20. Recent studies in book history, and in histories of reading and reception, have recuperated, for example, the work of Louise Guiney on Aphra Behn and Katherine Philips in the early twentieth century.

11 Salzman, Chapter 42, 'Editing Early Modern Women's Writing: Tradition and Innovation': Coolahan, Chapter 43, 'Reception, Reputation, and Afterlives', p. 645. See also Marie-Louise Coolahan, 'Loss and Longevity: Rhetorics and Tactics of Early Modern Women's Writing', *Criticism*, 63.1–2 (2021), 23–32.

women's writing, and the writing of women's literary histories, reveals much about literary aesthetics and taste, reputation and reception, and concepts of canonicity across multiple centuries—including our own.

While feminist teleologies have, then, tended to overwrite a longer and more recursive history of work on early modern women writers, there is little question that the contours of the field as it is today came into view with the second-wave feminist moment of the 1980s along with much of its conceptual and research infrastructure. Joan Kelly-Gadol asked 'Did Women Have A Renaissance?' in 1976, questioning the extent to which conventional critical schemas, including that of periodisation, applied to early modern women.[12] Margaret Ferguson provided one particularly trenchant answer in her much-quoted formulation, 'If women did not have a Renaissance, they certainly had a Reformation', and Michelle Dowd engages further with the question of periodisation in Chapter 49 of this volume.[13] Religious writings exemplify the pressure that the recuperation and reconsideration of women's texts, in conjunction with the historicism of the 1980s and 1990s, placed on literary and cultural histories of the 'Renaissance' and early modernism. Religious writing by women, often of a kind not readily recognisable as 'literary' (prayers, sermon notes, catechisms, and mothers' advice, for example), came to be understood as prolific, probably enabling, potentially oppositional, and certainly emergent out of richly verbal and material socio-historical contexts.[14] More broadly, historicist and materialist studies radically expanded the scope of enquiry and the variety of texts contained within it, providing granularity to the historicisation of early modern women's lives and textual production. Bringing the insights of feminist historicism to bear on women's writing in *Writing Women's Literary History* (1993), Margaret Ezell brilliantly articulated vital questions about 'our critical assumptions concerning gender and authorship, gender and genre' and 'the very terms we use to describe, categorize, and analyze early women's lives and texts'.[15] Ezell's analysis influentially articulated the ways in which the confluence of second-wave feminism and historicism shifted the terms of the discussion and expanded categories of text, authorship, and publication themselves in early modern women's writing, and in early modern and literary historical studies more broadly. These expansions and points of pressure on conventional categorisations are a signal contribution of early modern women's writing to early modern studies as a whole, and continue to define work in the field and in the multiple cognate areas of research with which it intersects.

Work on early modern women, gender, and textuality now challenges and exceeds the limitations of the category 'early modern women's writing', as the scope of this

[12] Joan Kelly, 'Did Women Have a Renaissance?' in *Women, History, and Theory: The Essays of Joan Kelly* (Chicago, IL, 1984), 19.

[13] Margaret W. Ferguson, 'Moderation and Its Discontents: Recent Work on Renaissance Women', *Feminist Studies*, 20, no. 2 (1994), 352.

[14] See, for example, Margaret Hannay's *Silent but for the Word*, and Elaine Beilin's *Redeeming Eve*, among others. Margaret J. M. Ezell's *The Patriarch's Wife: Literary Evidence and the History of the Family* (1987) and Elaine Hobby's *Virtue of Necessity: English Women's Writing, 1649–1740* (1988).

[15] Ezell, *Writing Women's Literary History*, 5.

Handbook reflects. Since the dominance of historicism in the 1980s and 1990s, several critical turns have intersected with, challenged, or been driven by feminist early modernism. Categories of text and authorship have expanded further into the material cultures of marginalia, paper, etchings, embroidery, histories of reading and book collecting, and even more radically into capacious notions of authorship and agency, including collaborative authorship, patronage, performance, and song.[16] All of these expansions are represented in the chapters of this volume. A (re)turn to formalism is revealing the intricacy of women writers' engagement with canonical early modern poetry and prose, recalibrating the historicist expansion of genre and authorship, and exploring the critical narratives of literary exclusion exemplified in Greer's image of women poets as '*guerilleras*'.[17] As Alice Eardley has argued, women's writing was often 'perceived as a practical interaction with the social environment rather than a literary achievement'.[18] At the same time, recent interrogations of voice and signature as markers of women's authorship are destabilising categories of voice, authorship, and writing. In Chapter 2 of this volume, Rosalind Smith identifies a 'paradox at the heart of our theorisation of the field of early modern women's writing', as a field that takes its initial impetus from a 'stable connection between texts and a single, embodied, historical woman' and engages and embraces anonymous, pseudonymous, collaborative, and communal paradigms of textual and authorial performance and performativity. Such tensions lie at the centre of the designation, 'early modern women's writing', and arguably always have done. Analytics asserting the indeterminacy of 'women' (for example, in the influential work of Denise Riley) are in constant friction with cultural feminism's important insistence on patriarchal social determinants of early modern girls' and women's experience.[19]

Approaches to women writers have expanded and diversified considerably in the last decade, certainly with regard to sexuality, authorship, and the household. And this pluralisation continues apace, with very recent work addressing not only the urgent imperatives of race and gender identity, but also attending to the structural conditions

[16] See, for example, Patricia Pender and Rosalind Smith (eds), *Material Cultures of Early Modern Women's Writing* (Basingstoke, 2014); Susan Frye, *Pens and Needles: Women's Textualities in Early Modern England* (Philadelphia, PA, 2010); Patricia Pender (ed.), *Gender, Authorship, and Early Modern Women's Collaboration* (Basingstoke, 2017); Julie Crawford, *Mediatrix: Women, Politics and Literary Production in Early Modern England* (Oxford, 2014); Katherine R. Larson, *The Matter of Song in Early Modern England: Texts in and of the Air* (Oxford, 2019); Scott A. Trudell, *Unwritten Poetry: Song, Performance, and Media in Early Modern England* (Oxford, 2019); Amanda Eubanks Winkler, *Music, Dance, and Drama in Early Modern English Schools* (Cambridge, 2020).

[17] See, for example, Elizabeth Scott-Baumann, *Forms of Engagement: Women, Poetry, and Culture 1640–1680* (Oxford, 2013); the essays in Leah Knight and Wendy Wall (eds), 'Special Issue: The Poetry of Hester Pulter: Revolution and Remediation', *Journal for Early Modern Cultural Studies*, 20.2 (2020); and Lara Dodds and Michelle M. Dowd (eds), *Feminist Formalism and Early Modern Women's Writing: Readings, Conversations, Pedagogies* (Lincoln, NE, 2022).

[18] Alice Eardley, 'Recreating the Canon: Women Writers and Anthologies of Early Modern Verse', *Women's Writing*, 14.2 (2007), 270–89, 273.

[19] Denise Riley, *'Am I That Name?' Feminism and the Category of 'Woman' in History* (Minneapolis, MN, 1988).

which shape and frame these expressions. This is nowhere more apparent than in the area of food studies, where recent work attends simultaneously to specific recipe books, scientific knowledge, relationships to global foodways. and the complex inscriptions of identity shaped by these factors.[20] That knowledge and existing scholarship requires constant revision as new materials and authors continue to be found is both a strength and a weakness of the field. This is conceptually distinct from some longer established areas of early modern studies where the key documents and texts are well known and available in authoritative editions, but available for the iterative criticism that marks forward momentum, the 'ongoing critical colloquy' that frames the developing canon of early modern writing.[21] There is a difference between adding new texts to a body of known evidence, and reinterpreting often familiar evidence with different priorities in mind (Before Shakespeare, #ShakeRace). Re-reading known (established, edited) literary texts through new critical frameworks (queer, ace, trans) is distinct from continuing to fundamentally alter the parameters of the known evidence.[22] Bernadette Andrea draws attention to the implications of this difference in her chapter in this volume, pointing out that there has been a tendency for early modern women's writing to sideline premodern critical race studies, while premodern critical race scholars have for the most part focused their analyses on male-authored literary texts. She issues a trenchant challenge to both fields in her call 'to refute the sidelining of premodern critical race studies within early modern women's studies *and* to urge scholars of premodern critical race studies to integrate into their analyses (and not simply to mention) historical women's cultural productions'.[23] The potential to position newly discovered texts within radical, questioning, and challenging critical paradigms (including editorial and textual paradigms) is one that the field is yet to realise fully.[24]

Work in queer and trans studies also requires a continued rethinking of the author figure, gendered identities, and a range of linear and teleological narratives. Queer theoretical approaches offer huge potential for thinking more expansively about gender and gendered bodies in the early modern period, as the work of Melissa Sanchez, Penelope Anderson, and others has begun to show. Julie Crawford's recent article on Milton's *Paradise Lost* and Hutchinson's *Order and Disorder* suggests that women in particular had powerful motivations for wanting to think beyond a dyadic model for gender ontologically linked to biology.[25] Established models for chronology, similarly, have often presupposed sequential unfolding through time, rather than recursive stops and starts, or connections across time and space—ironic perhaps in a period so committed to

[20] For example, see Gitanjali G. Shahani, *Tasting Difference: Food, Race, and Cultural Encounters in Early Modern Literature* (Ithaca, NY, 2020).

[21] Wendell V. Harris, 'Canonicity', *PMLA* , 106.1 (1991), 110–21, 111.

[22] See Phillippy, *History*, 11.

[23] This volume, Chapter 47, 'Early Modern Women, Race, and Writing Revisited' 703–16.

[24] See Melissa Sanchez and Ania Loomba (eds), *Rethinking Feminism in Early Modern Studies: Gender, Race, and Sexuality* (London, 2016).

[25] Julie Crawford, 'Transubstantial Bodies in *Paradise Lost* and *Order and Disorder*', *Journal for Early Modern Cultural Studies*, 19.4 (2019), 75–93.

typological rather than linear reading, and a field so marked by repeated rediscovery. With a multiplicity of editions of women writers now available in a multiplicity of forms, the potential to read early modern women's writing differently is clear, and intimated in the pages of this volume. It is a vibrant, plural, and increasingly theorised field of investigation, with the added dimension that there are still genuinely new things to discover and each new discovery has the potential to redraw or at least reposition the boundaries of the field.

DIRECTIONS

This Handbook is neither a history nor a survey, rather it is a kind of prospectus for future directions and explorations: it aims to look forward. Each chapter is anchored in the analysis of primary evidence and many authors also provide theoretical overviews or pose new questions and dimensions for consideration. This combination of bringing new or lesser-known material to light, and its capacity to suggest new conceptual frameworks or the need to modify accepted interpretations is a crucial dynamic in the field as a whole, even as this requires constant revision and renewal. These directions are not only critical (for a useful snapshot of current debates, see the articles gathered for the fiftieth anniversary issue of *English Literary Renaissance*), but professional. As editors, we have tried to cast our net wider than established voices in line with the principle that work focused on early modern women and gender now challenges and exceeds the restrictions of the category 'early modern women's writing' and is central to much historical and critical work that falls outside the traditionally defined male canon. We have commissioned scholars who work on materials that include, but are not confined to, writings by women and our contributors represent every stage of the profession from emerita to current doctoral students. We have attempted to be geographically inclusive as well—though the heavy Anglophone emphasis both of the field and of scholarly publishing has led to limitations here. Our focus is on work in English, but this volume attempts to place such work in the framework of writing in other languages (Latin, Greek, Spanish, French, Dutch). The need to think multilingually and transnationally is an urgent imperative for the future, particularly as new work turns a long overdue lens on the global, on race, on the loss and erasure of difference, questions that are necessarily only partially addressed if we omit work in languages other than English. A radical decentring is needed in order to understand the early modern period more fully. We have tried to present women writers as part of complex transnational and translingual networks, while reflecting their relatively limited opportunities for language learning—navigating cultural, linguistic, and racial difference was a key part of many women's lives, experiences that need to be more central to our understanding of the period.

Our approach in this Handbook is driven in part by an increasing need to draw larger conclusions from the hugely important scholarship that has become the foundation of our field or at least to suggest ways in which this might be done. Much work in the field depends heavily on the use of case studies (often focused on a specific writer, context, or time span), even where a larger thesis is in play.[26] Focusing on particular authors or texts as exemplifying larger trends and ideas is a justifiable intellectual response to examining wide-ranging examples often united by little other than the gender expression of 'authors', yet this leads to a certain asymmetry whereby individual women are inserted into historical narratives that do not necessarily map to their lived experience. As a consequence, larger patterns over longer time spans are often harder to discern. Such larger patterns and considerations might include questions of canonicity, periodisation, whether it is possible to identify a narrative of early modern women's writing within the dates identified in this volume, questions of access to mainstream culture, and, what it might mean to write without expectation of circulation, or how to approach the question of belatedness/derivation. Many of these questions are intrinsic to the study of women and gender, but increasingly work on women writers is also engaged with concerns shared by premodern studies more broadly: affect and embodiment, sexualities, race, capital and trade, the global, all of which construct and inflect gendered experience in complex ways and in turn are impacted by gendered agency. Just as the 1980s, 1990s, and 2000s were marked by continual reinvention and remaking (for example, multiple editions of key texts, mostly pedagogically oriented) and occlusion/loss, our hope is that the field will continue to be defined by reinvention and process as much as by the apparent fixity of research and reference tools as these develop. As work on—in particular—race, sexuality, materiality, and textuality calls into question the traditional categories of literary/critical analysis, there is transformative potential for thinking about how women's writing is engaged with such questions. The relative lack of work at scale has perhaps led to a tendency to underplay or overlook innovation by women writers (as opposed to literary firsts in forms inaugurated by men), namely the ways in which constraints on their circumstances drove invention and the creation of playfully hybrid forms. What does it mean, for example, that one of the earliest collections of generically diverse poetic materials is gathered together under a woman's signature, that of Isabella Whitney? Or that women are centrally involved in the development and evolution of narrative prose forms such as autobiography, letters, romance, and fiction, that come to dominate the mainstream of literary culture in the late seventeenth and early eighteenth centuries?

There is an urgency about our current context, a pressing need to communicate our work beyond and outside the academy, and an imperative to understand the tangled and troubled roots of our varied political situations.[27] The current generation of scholars has not yoked their research imprint exclusively to the field of early modern women's writing—as Erin McCarthy's analysis in the recent special issue of *Criticism* shows, the

[26] Examples include Gillian Wright, *Producing Women's Poetry, 1600–1730: Text and Paratext, Manuscript and Print* (Cambridge, 2013); Erica Longfellow, *Women and Religious Writing in Early Modern England* (Cambridge, 2004); and Christina Luckyj, *Liberty and the Politics of the Female Voice in Early Stuart England* (Cambridge, 2022).

[27] Coolahan, 'Loss and Longevity'.

marker of esteem around which everything in early modern studies is centrifugally placed is Shakespeare (or possibly Milton).[28] Increasingly, the positioning of work on early modern women shares more rather than less with male authors who fall outside the top ten. Meanwhile, more mainstream work that engages with women writers is often aligned with disciplinary fields other than English.[29] It is unsurprising given the intense pressure being placed on the premodern in the Anglophone world as a consequence of the shrinkage of the humanities that many newer scholars who work on women's writing do so in the context of other (usually) male authors. Most scholars of early modern women's writing, however historicist, are members of English departments and this aligns women's writing—sometimes problematically—with evaluative and formalist questions.[30] The field is now more attentive to how these categories are formed and promulgated, with the consequence of a theoretically sensitive and welcome attention to form in women's writing.[31] There remains much work to be done here, however.

Incrementally, scholars have added writers, interpretations, critical materials, editions, websites (early modern women's writing was, from the start, interested in the potential of digital media—and has maintained this focus) to what was and could be known. Much of this early work was grounded in old-fashioned historicism (which often seemed a more amenable framework than new formalism) crossbred with second-wave feminism, grounded in empirical work. It is easy, from the vantage point of the challenges facing premodern scholarship in 2022, to forget that many scholars who worked on this material did so without the benefit of any specific critical infrastructure and did so at significant cost to their own career trajectories and scholarly reputations.[32] To bring women writers into the classroom and onto the conference platform at that time represented a radical challenge to critical and canonical orthodoxies. These initial foundations proved determining of future directions—with a number of significant occlusions and blind spots which remain under-addressed and underdeveloped.

One of the key legacies of the study of early modern women's writing is a wholesale turn to the archive in literary study and a consequent (but not uncontested) turn away from literature as a category defined by aesthetic evaluations.[33] An understanding that the terms in which archives are classified, framed, and represented are critical to the

[28] Erin A. McCarthy, 'Is there Room for Judith Shakepeare and her Brother, Too?', *Criticism*, 63.1–2 (2021), 33–44.

[29] See for example, Alec Ryrie, *Being Protestant in Reformation Britain* (Oxford, 2013); Adam Smyth, *Autobiography in Early Modern England* (Cambridge, 2012); and Peter Auger, *Du Bartas' Legacy in England and Scotland* (Oxford, 2019).

[30] See Jaime Goodrich and Paula McQuade, 'Beyond Canonicity: The Future(s) of Early Modern Women Writers', *Criticism*, 63.1–2 (2021), 1–22.

[31] See, for example Lara Dodds and Michelle M. Dowd. 'Happy Accidents: Critical Belatedness, Feminist Formalism, and Early Modern Women's Writing', *Criticism*, 62.2 (2020), 169–93.

[32] See Purkiss, 'Rooms All of our Own', and Joyce MacDonald's response in 'How Race Might Help Us Find "Lost" Women's Writing', *Criticism*, 63.1–2 (2021), 45–53; see also Steven W. May, 'The Renaissance Women's Canon, Past, Present, and Future', *Criticism*, 63.1–2 (2021), 131–40.

[33] For a counter to this trend, see Catherine Bates, 'Recent Studies in the Renaissance' [annual omnibus review], *SEL: Studies in English Literature, 1500–1900*, 59.1 (2019), 203–41.

ways in which critics approach *all* marginalised subjects is crucial to the future (and of course, not all marginalised subjects are marginalised in the same way, or even only in one way), as Julia Flanders' chapter in this volume so lucidly explores. The multiple tools and directions used to locate traces of early modern women can potentially be applied to finding other 'missing' or 'lost' subjects.[34] And the iterative nature of these losses, erasures, and omissions is a question requiring our careful attention. Or, to put this differently, the 'subject' will be understood to be partial, contradictory, fragmentary, and produced by multiple formations outside and beyond the self. Attention to the discursive construction of different identities also permits a reconsideration of key categories—sex and gender may be discontinuous (and indeed sex, as much work in queer studies demonstrates, is itself a construction). The physical body to which historicist criticism implicitly refers is itself not a stable entity (as the maiden, wife, widow formulation for female identity acknowledges) but is 'contingent in its terms', changing through age, sexuality, death, and reproduction in addition to physical labour, skin colour, and social status.[35] The study of early modern women has too often been the unacknowledged study of whiteness, but the tools and methodologies developed in the field (traditional and digital) remain useful as ways of locating and reading subjects who have been rendered marginal to what the 'Renaissance' traditionally represents and continues to represent. The recognition that Renaissance women, for all that their status was legally and ideologically inferior, were heavily implicated in other types of oppressions and subjugations has, though, been shockingly slow to arrive—despite three decades of scholarship on early modern race, much of it specifically addressing female subjects. Questions of female agency are complex in a context where women cannot own property or spend money on their own behalf, yet can participate in processes of racialisation and centring whiteness culturally and socially. It is not only scholars of women's writing who have failed to acknowledge, let alone engage with or analyse what Kim Coles calls 'ugly history'—swathes of the Renaissance canon is taught and analysed as if all forms of violence (racial, economic, sexual) can be aestheticised away, as if ornament conceals violence, rather than itself being an act of violence, as Patricia Parker, Kim F. Hall, and others amply demonstrate.[36] There is more work on Mary Wroth and race than on Philip Sidney and race, despite the recurrent use of similar racialised tropes and genres in both writers. So while criticism of early modern women's writing must address questions of race, and the role that texts written by women play in racialisation and the centring of whiteness, its own relative marginality risks sequestering this most important of ethical imperatives. Early modern women's writing, as Erin McCarthy's analysis suggests, remains stubbornly marginal where it matters: publications and hiring.[37] In this, as in

[34] See MacDonald, 'How Race Might Help Us', and Melissa E. Sanchez, 'What Were Women Writers?', *Criticism*, 63.1–2 (2021), 63–74.

[35] Kimberly Anne Coles and Eve Keller, 'Introduction', in Coles and Keller (eds), *The Routledge Companion to Women, Sex, and Gender in the Early British Colonial World* (London, 2018), 19.

[36] Kimberly Anne Coles, '"Undisciplined": Early Modern Women's Writing and the Urgency of Scholarly Activism', *Criticism*, 63.1–2 (2021), 55–62, 55.

[37] McCarthy, 'Is there Room'.

so much else, early modern women's writing needs to continue its alignment with the priorities of Renaissance studies more broadly, and to make sure that its unique voice (both its texts and those who write about them) is heard. Continued revision of the theoretical models that frame the feminisms practised in the field is urgent, necessary work. After over forty years of professional scholarly work, scholars are now closer to a fuller sense of the dimensions of the evidence and this provides a strong basis from which to move forward. Open to debate, however, is *how* this is to be done: we hope that this Handbook demonstrates the deeply plural nature of contemporary work on women writers, engaging theoretical positions from queer theory, premodern critical race studies through to digital, archipelagic, and network based approaches.

READING THIS HANDBOOK

Reflecting the multiplicity of approaches to work on early modern women writers, and crucial intersections with diverse fields of scholarship, the chapters in this Handbook are arranged neither by author nor by chronology. Instead, it is composed of six parts, each focused on a broadly conceived aspect of early modern women's writing: Voice and Knowledge; Forms and Origins; Places; Translingual and Transnational; Networks; and Tools and Methodologies. Each cluster of chapters spans multiple authors, a range of genres of writing and often a wide chronology—our date parameters are set according the to earliest and latest writers discussed. While the index and keywords allow readers to locate chapters on particular writers or texts, we hope that this structure will reconfigure the narrative around early women's writing, through exploring ideas that were crucial to writers in the early modern period, and those that have been foundational to modern thinking about this field.

Part I. VOICE AND KNOWLEDGE

This Handbook aims to put pressure on the idea of women's voices and women's texts, while still articulating their conceptual importance. Chapters here ask how best to read female-voiced texts that are anonymous or whose attribution to women is contested, and how to interrogate our own assumptions and methods. While the humanist schoolroom has been identified as the central technology of the Renaissance, girls and women were external to the classroom and its formal modes of learning. Chapters in this section ask how girls and women learned the rhetorical techniques, modes, and stances that define humanist learning, and their distinctive investments in cultures of religion, textiles, science, and practical knowledge.

Identifying and understanding women's 'voice' remains complex. The first two chapters in this section reveal the complexities of voice, both the production of women's voice through education and the precarious relationship of voice to authorship in the texts we study. In Chapter 2, Rosalind Smith explores the ideological and material implications of authorship debates in relation to women's writing. She focuses on the still vigorously debated case of Anne Locke, often said to be the author of the first printed sonnet sequence in English, but whose authorship of this sequence remains debated. Despite the knowing tentativeness of her title, 'How Lady Jane Grey *May* Have Used Her Education', in Chapter 3, Jennifer Richards presents a radical re-evaluation of the ways in which women use others' words in motivated ways, exploring Grey as a case study of the multiple forms of agency involved in the production of women's voices and texts. In Chapter 4, Jane Stevenson traces the use of Latin and Greek by women in diplomacy, translation, private correspondence, and conversation, identifying both confessional difference and chronological change, from the erudition of the sixteenth-century Bacon sisters to the Restoration writings of Mary Mollineux and Lucy Hutchinson.

Subsequent chapters turn to women's knowledge in terms of textile production, practical texts, book ownership, and philosophy. Michele Osherow, in Chapter 5, uses the exemplary figure of the biblical Queen Esther to challenge and expand definitions of women's texts and textiles, and the relationship between these two forms of agency and articulation. In Chapter 6, Carrie Griffin demonstrates the role of texts of instruction—conduct books, midwifery, medicine, and recipes—in the formation of gendered identity. Helen Smith shows how women including Anne Conway and Margaret Cavendish used letters for philosophical exchange, developing a 'manifesto for a supple epistolary methodology' (Chapter 7). Finally in this section, Leah Knight investigates the impact of new technologies and methodologies on our understanding of the relationships between women and their books, especially in revealing 'how particular women experienced reading and participated in book culture not in isolation but as members of social networks' (Chapter 8).

Part II. FORMS AND ORIGINS

Women's relationship with literary forms and genres intersects with current questions about form in recent scholarship on early modern writing as a whole; it also represents a rather different history of critical approaches to gender. The burgeoning of 'women's writing' as a scholarly field in the 1980s and 1990s was broadly synchronous with historicism and its investment in a capacious sense of 'the text', but a swing towards formal analysis (one rooted in political and theoretical questions) is changing the focus and dimensions of the field. The particularities of women's education and rhetorical training addressed in Part I inflected the forms in which they wrote: ode, sonnet, romance, biblical paraphrase, satiric prose, and diverse more popular (and often populist) forms. This section engages both in the foundations and more recent debates around women and form, investigating women's innovations and deviations from conventional, canonical frameworks. Chapters explore the dazzling generic diversity of women writers in the early modern period, considering how certain genres were feminised, and also how certain dominant and highly valued forms of writing were pioneered by women. The chapters here represent different responses to major questions such as whether we can—or, crucially, should—expect women to be using the same literary forms as men in the period. Moreover, this part demonstrates the ways in which the study of early modern women's writing often uses formal analysis alongside a rich variety of historical and theoretical approaches such as queer theory, manuscript study, and political theory.

Christina Luckyj's chapter locates texts from the *querelle des femmes* in the context of the Overbury scandal, showing how 'the woman's voice is deployed to counsel, inform or castigate misogynists or male rulers' (Chapter 9). In Chapter 10, Katherine R. Larson shows how the woman singer was a textual agent, active in multiple locations and producing various kinds of song from psalms to ballads. In Ramona Wray's impassioned and deeply reasoned account, the canon of Renaissance drama has been woefully obstinate to the increasing numbers of known plays by women and their crucial importance in the development of early modern drama (Chapter 11). Wray demonstrates the multiple factors involved, from the dates used by anthologies, the value judgement implicit in the labels ('private', 'domestic', 'household', and 'closet') commonly used to define (and exclude) women-authored texts, to the intersection of gender and race. In '"Sing and let the song be new": Early Modern Women's Devotional Lyrics' (Chapter 12), Helen Wilcox shows that the common trope of the inadequacy of language to write of (and to and for) God is also the motivating force of women's devotional lyric, from Mary Sidney, to Elizabeth Major, An Collins to Mary Mollineux. In 'Lyric Backwardness' (Chapter 13), Dianne Mitchell acknowledges critical prejudices about women's writing (that it is belated, archaic, retrograde). She instead uses queer theory to frame the poetry of Mary Wroth, Anne Southwell, and Hester Pulter, identifying an innovative backwardness in women's poetry in three spheres: emotion, form, and materiality. Turning to prose in Chapter 14, Kevin Killeen argues that Anna Trapnel pioneered an experimental spiritual poetic style, crafted specifically to be turbulent: 'the proper, necessary response to a deeply unstable spiritual-political ontology, in a world whose fragility had been repeatedly exposed, by civil war, regicide, and the fast-moving events of the Republic and Protectorate'. Victoria Burke, in Chapter 15, captures the wide range of poetic, scientific, and religious practices of compilation and argues that in religious compilation, we can 'see a space where women such as Katherine Clarke and Anne Waller were encouraged to participate in this mode of organising, shaping, and responding to texts, sometimes turning constraints into creation'. Julie A. Eckerle's chapter on life-writing (Chapter 16) makes two distinct interventions: that we should see women's 'textual labour as a form of stewardship' and that we should 'broaden our analytical lens to the entire British Atlantic Archipelago', a strand that will be pursued further in Part III. In Chapter 17, Lara Dodds traces associations of women with negative stereotypes of fiction from Woolf to the present, showing that 'the feminisation of fiction has its origins in misogyny, but became a resource, both rhetorical and social, for readers and writers'. V. M. Braganza argues in Chapter 18 that women writers fundamentally changed the relationship between romance and race, transforming it 'from a genre about the discovery of identity to one which foregrounds identity's instability and loss', especially racialised identity.

Part III. PLACES

Part III examines how women imagined and theorised identity as embedded in locations and communities, from village to court. Recent work in this area draws on cultural geography, local history, and anthropology, and sheds light on the archival records of, for instance, performances in aristocratic households and regional patronage circles. Chapters explore the local and regional, urban and rural, and familial and dynastic, as well as the complex economics, religious, national, and racial implications of these. As we see from Paula McQuade's 'A Place-Based Approach to Early Modern Women's Writing' (Chapter 19), there are long-standing connections between women scholars and the study of place, especially 'the local, peripheral, and everyday'. McQuade shows how a place-based approach to a seventeenth-century catechism by Dorothy Burch functions as a powerful defence of her parish community's beliefs, 'emulating ministerial authority'. In Chapter 20, Michelle O'Callaghan focuses on the urban setting of London, showing that the writings of Isabella Whitney and Jane Anger bring 'into focus the part played by non-elite urban cultures in shaping the literary landscape and other locales for humanist practice outside of the more conventional domains of the all-male schoolroom, the court, and elite households'. O'Callaghan identifies the impact of migration and poverty, as well as of education and commercialisation. Financial pressures are at play in Lotte Fikkers' analysis of women in the law courts (Chapter 21). With examples including Anne Halkett and Katherine Austen, Fikkers shows how women moved beyond the literary and social convention of the loud, litigious widow. Finally alongside chapters in this volume by Eckerle, Larson, Blake, Griffin, and others, Wendy Wall explores in Chapter 22 the multiple roles adopted by women in relation to knowledge production and, in this case those revealed by recipe books: 'cook, herbalist, researcher, information organizer, and editor'.

Julie Sanders investigates in Chapter 23 the role of terminology in canon-formation, an issue that emerges in several chapters in this Handbook. Like Ramona Wray in Part II, Sanders challenges the labels of 'household' and 'closet' drama, conceptualising these works as 'site-specific' drama. She explores ways in which women dramatists tailored their works to the 'production houses' in and for which they wrote, from Mary Wroth's Penshurst to Rachel Fane's Apethorpe. Turning to the courtly context of masque production in Chapter 24, Laura L. Knoppers explores the many ways in which women used masque culture in their writings: Aemilia Lanyer strategically; Mary Sidney Herbert innovatively; Margaret Cavendish nostalgically; Mary Wroth subversively. Combining places of dramatic performance and imagined locations, Meghan E. Hall interrogates in Chapter 25 moralised attributes of stillness and mobility in Elizabeth Cary's *Tragedy of Mariam*, asserting that early modern women were supposed to be 'chaste, silent, obedient, and most importantly, still'. Building on critical work on race, space, travel, and power, Hall argues that the respective fates of the play's female protagonists—'Mariam enclosed in a tomb; Salome free to travel but thoroughly vilified—offer Cary's readers a bleak view of the limits of women's autonomy in a globalising world'. Looking at relationships between women's writing in Wales, Scotland, Ireland, and England, Sarah Prescott argues in Chapter 26 for an 'Archipelagic Feminism', an approach which reveals the limitations of 'always comparing and contrasting to English paradigms'. An archipelagic perspective places conventional poetic genre categorisations in a new light, from the sonnets of the Scottish poet Elizabeth Melville to the bardic keens of the Irish poet Caitlín Dubh.

Part IV. TRANSLINGUAL AND TRANSNATIONAL

Building on the previous part with its focus on the local, regional, and archipelagic, this cluster of chapters looks further afield to the transnational and translingual connections of early modern women's writing in English, and the diverse and fertile Anglophone literary cultures beyond England. Recent research on women's translations has opened up new avenues of scholarship on the ways in which English women's writing interacts with its European peers and influences, also connecting to earlier chapters in this Handbook by Stevenson on Latin and Greek, and Akkerman on women spies. This section explores women's geographical and translingual allegiances, via translation, travel, migration, and exile. Taking account of devolutionary and global approaches to the field, it ranges from work on English women's international networks, to the transfer of texts and objects by women across borders both national and linguistic and the distinctive literary influences of European on Anglophone writing by women.

In Chapter 27, '"Mistresses of tongues": Early Modern Englishwomen, Multilingual Practice, and Translingual Communication', Brenda Hosington showcases the under-appreciated scale and diversity of women translators. Diverse in their class, education, genre, and source texts, women translators were also 'remarkably visible' in this period, mostly named rather than anonymous. In a brilliant rereading of Margaret Tyler's *The Mirrour of Princely Deedes and Knighthood*, Jake Arthur challenges in Chapter 28 previous modes of reading early modern women's translations, and makes a compelling case for Tyler's creative Englishing of her Spanish source's concerns, including adding the vocabulary of law and contract. In so doing, he places Tyler within cultures of Renaissance translation and of legal discourses that challenge women's exclusion from paradigms of humanist thought and writing. Line Cottegnies' chapter demonstrates how a wide range of English women writers, from Wroth to Mary Astell, engaged with French texts and styles (often represented as 'fashions'), especially the broader movement of *préciosité* (Chapter 29).

Transnational and translingual explorations of early modern women's writing reveal diverse and fertile Anglophone literary cultures beyond England. Peter Auger, for example, considers Anne Bradstreet in Chapter 30 as both a transatlantic poet and a transatlantic commodity at the two very different moments of her works' publication: 1650 and 1678. Martine Van Elk's chapter (31) on women and the Dutch Republic explores women's engagement of 'public femininity', through a threefold focus on intellectuals, publishers, and writers, giving a broad sense of women as authorial and cultural agents through the seventeenth century. In Chapter 32, 'Political Theory Across Borders', Mihoko Suzuki demonstrates women's ambition and effectiveness as political theorists by focusing on the influence of Christine de Pizan, Niccolò Machiavelli, and Jean Bodin on Elizabeth Cary, Margaret Cavendish, and Anne Clifford.

Part V. NETWORKS

Women were central to literary communities and networks, contributing to the theory as well as the practice of patronage, kinship, and friendship in early modern Britain. Women often engaged with the cultures of those institutions from which they were formally excluded (universities, Inns of Court, learned societies), through kinship and affective connections, while the engagements of barely literate women with 'writing' can be traced through song, prayer, tapestry, and precarious archival traces.

In Chapter 33, Jaime Goodrich examines the writings of Lucy Knatchbull, a Catholic woman who left England to join the English Benedictine cloister in Brussels, to investigate the continental networks enabled by religious communities. These, she argues, demonstrate that 'cloistered authorship was a networked phenomenon'. In Chapter 34, 'Gifts that Matter', Patricia Pender explores the New Year's gift that Princess Elizabeth presented to Henry VIII in 1545, an embroidered manuscript translation of Katherine Parr's *Prayers or Meditations*. Pender teases out multiple interactions created by this exchange, including Parr's facilitation of Elizabeth's place at court and Elizabeth's own strategic networking. Sebastiaan Verweij then reveals in Chapter 35 how Scottish women's texts were embedded in their wider contexts and communities, challenging ideas of lyrical inwardness (the focus of so much work on women's devotional writing), and exploring Melville's possible use of her uncle's extensive library. In Chapter 36, Daniel Starza Smith and Leah Veronese reveal a little known archive of correspondence by a late-sixteenth century woman, Elizabeth Bourne. Spanning issues of domestic violence and epistolary style, their chapter also explores the critical implications of studying writing by women that has never had any public reception. Extending this attention to letters, Nadine Akkerman's Chapter 37, 'Women's Letters and Cryptological Coteries', shows how women including Elizabeth I and Aphra Behn employed code in their epistolary communications 'both to form and maintain sometimes fragile social networks and to communicate across enemy lines'. In Chapter 38, 'Non-Elite Networks and Women', Susan Wiseman explores the rewards and pitfalls of network theory in understanding relationships (both textual and lived) between non-elite women, from settler and Native American women in New England to household servants at a Derbyshire estate. Moving to writers of the English Civil War period, Hero Chalmers demonstrates in Chapter 39 how Lucy Hutchinson carefully repositions royalist imagery to set up her husband as an exemplar of the kinds of moral and spiritual qualities that characterise true kingship as represented in the Scriptures. In Chapter 40, James Loxley uses the concept of topopoetics to delicately unpick the complex meanings of retirement and privacy in the poetry of Katherine Philips, Lucy Hutchinson, and Hester Pulter. Turning to print itself as a form of network in Chapter 41, Liza Blake demonstrates the many ways in which women challenged the boundaries of print and manuscript. Margaret Cavendish and Isabella Whitney both worked with many 'print collaborators': Cavendish to create unusual printed presentation copies of her works and Whitney to maximise profit.

Part VI. TOOLS AND METHODOLOGIES

This final section explores the ways in which early modern women's writing has been at the forefront of many methodological developments in the field of early modern studies more broadly, from studies of reading and reception, to editorial theory and the use of digital media. It has also had a more complex, sometimes vexed, relationship with other critical approaches such as queer theory and premodern critical race studies. The chapters in this section illuminate these differences and suggest ways forward. There is much more to do.

The first three chapters here work in tandem to explore the overlapping fields of editing, reception studies, and digital scholarship. In Chapter 42, Paul Salzman explores early modern transmission itself as a form of editing, tracing a far longer history of 'editing', and of early modern women's writing as a 'field', than is often recognised, from the sixteenth century to the present. Marie-Louise Coolahan also advocates in Chapter 43 for a '*longue durée* perspective' on early modern women's writing, explicating reception studies as a way of thinking afresh about literary histories and their construction. Partly by defining reception broadly as 'a record of engagement with a female author and/or her work', the *RECIRC* project (*Reception and Circulation of Early Modern Women's Writing, 1550–1700*) led by Coolahan has been able to trace evidence of thousands of previously undocumented cases of engagement. Julia Flanders, in Chapter 44, both celebrates the role of digital tools in retrieving and making available women's writing, and shows how digital methodologies can work to reinscribe 'heuristics of classification and differentiation' which may reinscribe structures of exclusion. Investigating the 'material turn' in early modern studies in Chapter 45, Anna Reynolds' analysis of women's practical knowledge of writing materials, including paper, leads into a revelatory reading of Mary Wroth's *Urania* (complementing Michele Osherow's discussion of women's embroidery in Part II). In Chapter 46, Patricia Phillippy draws together the rich recent scholarship on memory, matter, and women's writing, to show how memory can be understood as a 'gendered competency', focusing on Anne Clifford's writings as 'emporia of objects, artifacts, creations, and commodities'. Bernadette Andrea's 'Early Modern Women, Race, and Writing Revisited' (Chapter 47) points to the powerful intellectual genealogy of Margo Hendricks, Kim F. Hall, and Joyce Green MacDonald and also explores Hendricks' romance writing (as Elysabeth Grace) as using the 'mode of speculative realism in order to remain true to ethnic literature's utopian allegiance to social justice'. Andrea shows how race and gender studies have each been 'sidelin[ed]' in different ways and argues that scholars of premodern critical race studies need to integrate analysis of women, and urging scholars of early modern women to place race studies at the centre of their work. In Chapter 48, Erin Murphy's crucial account of the tensions between feminist and queer scholarship in the last three decades, as well as the risk of queer feminism's universalisation and hence racial exclusions, leads into a deft reading of Aemilia Lanyer's *Salve Deus Rex Judaeorum* which shows how biblical typology can be interpreted through a queer feminist understanding of temporality.

In Chapter 49, Michelle Dowd challenges the 'logic of exceptionalism that still governs how women's writing is often framed within early modern studies as a whole', arguing that we should instead demonstrate all the ways in which women's writing 'encourages us to change the rules that we have learned'. As we enter a phase of urgent and much-needed reflection around the intersections of feminism, race, and sexuality, this chapter shows that the early modern period (in Dowd's words) 'needs women' and also that early modern women's writing needs the many approaches with which it has long been in dialogue (feminism, manuscript and book history, reception studies) and also those with which its relationship is just starting (queer theory, trans studies, premodern critical race studies). With its history of disciplinary eclecticism, theoretical sophistication, and historical depth, the scholarly field of early modern women's writing is ready for the next phase of both timely and 'untimely innovation' (Dowd). This Handbook is one step along that path.

PART I

VOICE AND KNOWLEDGE

CHAPTER 2

AUTHORSHIP, ATTRIBUTION, AND VOICE IN EARLY MODERN WOMEN'S WRITING

ROSALIND SMITH

There is a paradox at the heart of our theorisation of the field of early modern women's writing, and it concerns authorship. We know that early modern subjects approached authorship very differently to now, privileging rhetorical display grounded in imitation, addition, and collaboration over originality, copyright, and ownership, and that these structures changed over the sixteenth and seventeenth centuries according to different modes and technologies of textual dissemination. Understanding this, however, has not altered the ways in which we have conceptualised the field of early modern women's writing, which still carries the legacy of its early theoretical underpinnings, predicated on the stable connection between texts and a single, embodied, historical woman subject as original author. This model has produced rich scholarship, changing the way in which we understand women's contributions to the textual, religious, political, and recreational cultures of early modern societies and making necessary incursions into the male-authored canon of Renaissance literature. However, it is also a model under revision—recently and gradually broken open and reassembled. The material turn has changed the range of authorial and extra-authorial roles through which women contributed as textual agents, reinforced by scholarship on the intersection of print, scribal, and oral cultures and increasingly complex understandings of how women's roles, identities, and names shifted throughout their lifetimes.[1] New understandings of the rhetorical habitus

[1] See Helen Smith, *'Grossly Material Things': Women and Book Production in Early Modern England* (Oxford, 2012); Julie Crawford, *Mediatrix: Women, Politics, and Literary Production in Early Modern England* (Oxford, 2014); Patricia Pender and Rosalind Smith (eds), *Material Cultures of Early Modern Women's Writing* (Basingstoke, 2014); Leah Knight, Micheline White, and Elizabeth Sauer (eds),

of early modern subjects in relation to the humanist schoolroom are producing revised evaluations of women's access to rhetorical forms and modes, and digital projects have highlighted the complexities of authorship and reception that attend our definitions of women's writing.[2] The result is that how we understand ideas of authorship, attribution, and voice in early modern women's writing is being recast after decades of relative stasis. These revisions attend to the differences between how texts were produced or 'authored' and how texts were received, both in the forms of contemporary ascriptions—evidence of authorship written in documents—and longer, dispersed histories of attribution. They also extend to how texts were circulated and reproduced through processes of imitation including prosopopoeia, song, and other kinds of performance (see this volume, Chapter 3, Jennifer Richards, 'How Lady Jane Grey May Have Used Her Education', and Chapter 43, Marie-Louise Coolahan, 'Reception, Reputation, and Afterlives').[3] This chapter directly addresses the question of how authorship has been, is, and might be conceived in early modern women's writing. It tests its hypotheses through a sixteenth-century case study concerning one of the most innovative, but problematic, writers from this period: Anne Locke. Finally, the chapter offers at its close a new, expanded approach to authorship as a way of negotiating this potentially generative aspect of early modern women's writing.

Exactly what constituted early modern authorship has been the topic of sustained critical debate. Enlightenment models of the individual author producing fixed and stable texts that circulated under their signature have gradually been dismantled, making way (in theory at least) for writing practices that were collaborative, polyphonic, or choral and based on cultures of imitation and exchange. This remains highly contested critical territory: ranging from the position that for all early modern texts, even those that present as unified and stable, 'collaboration is the paradigmatic mode of textual production', to proponents of computational stylistics who argue that they can detect the early modern subject's compulsion 'to create a distinctive identity in language'.[4] Despite these

Women's Bookscapes in Early Modern Britain: Reading, Ownership, Circulation (Ann Arbor, MI, 2018); Valerie Wayne (ed.), *Women's Labour and the History of the Book in Early Modern England* (London, 2020); Katherine R. Larson, *The Matter of Song in Early Modern England: Texts in and of he Air* (Oxford, 2019) and Jennifer Richards, *Voices and Books in the English Renaissance: A New History of Reading* (Oxford, 2019).

[2] Lynn Enterline, *Shakespeare's Schoolroom: Rhetoric, Discipline, Emotion* (Philadelphia, PA, 2012) and '"Past the Help of Law": Epyllia and the Female Complaint', in Sarah C. E. Ross and Rosalind Smith (eds), *Early Modern Women's Complaint: Gender, Form and Politics* (Cham: Palgrave Macmillan, 2020), 315–27. For an overview of the ways in which digital projects intersect with authorship, see Marcy L. North, 'Ambiguities of Female Authorship and the Accessible Archive', in Kimberly Anne Coles and Eve Keller (eds), *The Routledge Companion of Women, Sex and Gender in the British Colonial World* (London and New York, 2019), 73–87.

[3] I am drawing here on the crucial distinctions between ascription and authorship made by Marie-Louise Coolahan and Erin A. McCarthy in their essay 'From Manuscripts to Metadata: Understanding and Structuring Female-Attributed Complaints', in Ross and Smith (eds), *Early Modern Women's Complaint*, 269–90, 272.

[4] The quotation for the first view is taken from Gordon McMullan, '"Our Whole Life is Like a Play": Collaboration and the Problem of Editing', *Textus*, 9 (1996), 437–60, 454; the second, from Hugh Craig,

polarised positions, it is clear that early modern authorship can no longer be viewed exclusively through the paradigms of either individuation or collaboration, and that possibilities for individual authorship coexisted with a range of other authorial options that included, but were not limited to, imitation, translation, transcription, annotation, emendation, co-writing, exchange, performance, and patronage as well as the myriad practices associated with the labour of textual production, oral, scribal, and print.[5] Valerie Wayne's recent collection of essays illuminates how authorship can be material and embodied as well as part of the imaginative habitus of the early modern subject, building upon Helen Smith's arguments that the co-labour of book production in the period held 'a potent originary power'.[6] In these new, expanded approaches to authorship, ideas of ownership and accountability are seen to operate across a spectrum, from unambiguous claims to authorship in print and manuscript to the anonymous circulation of texts for others to imitate, copy, or repackage. In 1624, when Esther Inglis pastes a pen and ink self-portrait with her name on the verso of the title page of one of her calligraphic manuscripts, she makes a claim to authorship.[7] Yet at the same time, she is not the only author of the text, but its scribal copyist, producing a calligraphic manuscript of the French verses in the 1601 print text *Octonaires sur la Vanité et Inconstance du Monde* side by side with an English translation and enclosed in an embroidered binding.[8] Her authorship practice encompasses multiple roles, many of them collaborative and speculative, but her claims to authorship also signal individuation and singular ownership. Her text is one example of how different models of authorship and textual production coexisted in the period and were not seen to be mutually exclusive, or even contradictory, by early modern subjects.

APPROACHES TO EARLY MODERN WOMEN'S AUTHORSHIP

Inglis' flexible approach to authorship, ownership, and textual production has not always been the way in which early modern authorship (and women's authorship in particular) has been understood. Early modern women as authors were first recovered

'Style, Statistics, and New Models of Authorship', *Early Modern Literary Studies*, 15.1 (2009), 41 paras, para. 41, accessed 12 June 2021.

5 See the essays collected in Patricia Pender (ed.), *Gender, Authorship and Early Modern Women's Collaboration* (Basingstoke, 2017).

6 Wayne, *Women's Labour*, 11–19; Smith, '*Grossly Material Things*', 52.

7 Washington, DC, Folger Shakespeare Library, MS v.a.91, fol. 4.

8 See Georgianna Ziegler, '"More than Feminine Boldness": The Gift Books of Esther Inglis', in Mary E. Burke et al. (eds), *Women, Writing and the Reproduction of Culture in Tudor and Stuart Britain* (Syracuse, NY, 2000), 19–37; Susan Frye, 'Materializing Authorship in Esther Inglis' Books', *Journal of Medieval and Early Modern Studies*, 32 (2002), 469–91.

in histories of the seventeenth and eighteenth centuries, where 'lost' women writers were 'found' in the service of political, religious, and social reimaginings of the past.[9] An interest in encyclopaedic reference works gave rise to collections such as Thomas Heywood's nine-volume history of women, *Gynaikeion*, first published in 1624 and reissued in 1657, which refers to a handful of sixteenth-century early modern women writers, and Edward Phillips' 1675 *Theatrum Poetarum*, which includes brief references to thirteen English women writers.[10] In the mid-eighteenth century, George Ballard's *Memoirs of Several Ladies of Great Britain* provided entries on sixty-one early modern women described on the title page as 'celebrated for their writings or skill in the learned languages', although as Margaret J. M. Ezell points out, the women he selected largely conformed to a 'controlling design' of inclusion according to their existing fame, relationship to accomplished men, and Christian virtue.[11] This didactic construction of the early modern woman as author reproduced eighteenth-century models of ideal femininity—'modest, middle-class, well-read, pious and charitable'—and shaped understandings of women's writing as different from that of their male counterparts, demonstrating that the separation model that we often attribute to early feminism and gynocriticism is, in fact, deeply embedded in histories of transmission of women's writing.[12] A preference for early modern women writers who conformed to a restricted range of models of femininity persisted through the nineteenth century. For example, Alexander Dyce's *Specimens of British Poetesses* includes twenty-five poets from the sixteenth and seventeenth centuries and often reprints examples of their poetry for the first time, as do his many imitators.[13] Ezell has argued persuasively that the range of early modern women's types of authorship became increasingly constrained during the nineteenth century and shaped their later portrayal. But as Paul Salzman has shown more recently, there were exceptions to this rule to be found in sources such as the *Dictionary of National Biography* and early twentieth-century editions of writers such as Aphra Behn; indeed he suggests that those who disappeared from view were 'perhaps not proportionately more numerous than male writers who dropped off the literary map'.[14] Further, women were recognised as authors in these early histories in surprisingly diverse ways:

[9] For accounts of recovery and loss, see Margaret J. M. Ezell, *Writing Women's Literary History* (Baltimore, MD, 1993); Jennifer Summit, *Lost Property, The Woman Writer and English Literary History, 1380–1589* (Chicago, IL, 2000); Paul Salzman, *Reading Early Modern Women's Writing* (Oxford, 2006); Marie-Louise Coolahan, 'Reception, Reputation, and Early Modern Women's Missing Texts', *Critical Quarterly*, 55.4 (2013), 3–14, and Marie-Louise Coolahan (ed.), 'Special Issue: The Cultural Dynamics of Reception', *Journal of Medieval and Early Modern Studies*, 50.1 (2020).

[10] Thomas Heywood, *Gynaikeion: or Nine Bookes of Various History Concerning Women* (London, 1624); Thomas Heywood, *The Generall Historie of Women* (London, 1657); Edward Philips, *Theatrum Poetarum, or A Compleat Collection of the Poets* (London, 1675).

[11] George Ballard, *Memoirs of Several Ladies of Great Britain* (London, 1752); Ezell, *Writing*, 84–5.

[12] Ezell, *Writing*, 88.

[13] Alexander Dyce (ed.), *Specimens of British Poetesses* (London, 1825). His imitators include George Bethune, *The British Female Poets* (London, 1848) and Thomas Percy, *Reliques of English Poetry of the Latter Part of the Sixteenth Century* (London, 1765).

[14] Salzman, *Reading*, 34–5.

as women of learning within familial, religious, and social networks, as participants in print and scribal cultures, and as occupying authorial roles that included translation and imitation—Lady Mary Wroth is described by Phillips as 'an Emulatress perhaps of Philip Sidney's *Arcadia*'—alongside examples of originary and singular authorship.[15]

From the mid-twentieth century, early modern women's writing has been investigated at larger scale by feminist scholars seeking to revise understandings of Renaissance authorship as exclusively male. These recoveries expanded ideas of literary authorship, following Rosalie Colie in acknowledging that the early modern period was characterised by 'inclusionism: uncanonical forms, mixed kinds and *nova reperta*', and that women writers often wrote 'outside the genres which are traditionally studied as literature': prayers, essays, confessions, diaries, letters, dedications, and prefaces.[16] An expanded definition of authorial roles has underpinned scholarship on early modern women's writing from the 1970s, even if the gynocritical imperatives of this scholarship, which sought to establish a separate canon of early modern women's writing characterised by an inherent difference from male-authored texts, often erased other complexities of authorship. Gynocritical analyses tended to privilege pious, 'private', and familial writing, and elided complexities surrounding attribution in favour of stable writing subjects.[17] A contested attribution might be noted, but not explored, as more and more women writers and works were added to the field and collected in anthologies.[18] Nevertheless, the male-authored canon remained the norm against which women's authorship was measured, as critics sought to understand women's experience of authorship through their participation in print cultures, assuming that authorship and publication were coterminous and women's authorial strategies were tied to their restricted position in the culture. In scholarship of the 1990s, in particular, entry into print was seen as difficult, transgressive, and exceptional—with the effect that at the same time as a range of early modern women's authorship was being uncovered, it was also seen to be circumscribed, especially if measured against late modern models of authorship, originality, and ownership.[19] As Ezell commented in 1999: 'we have had

15 Phillips, *Theatrum Poetarum*, x.

16 Rosalie Colie, *The Resources of Kind: Genre Theory in the Renaissance* (Los Angeles, CA, 1973), 76; and Betty Travitsky (ed.), *The Paradise of Women: Writing by Englishwomen of the Renaissance* (New York, 1982; repr. 1989), 13.

17 For an incisive analysis of how scholarship has tended to privilege 'works with authors', see Marcy L. North, *The Anonymous Renaissance: Cultures of Discretion in Tudor-Stuart England* (Chicago, IL, 2003), 11–12.

18 Early anthologies include Ann Stanford, *The Women Poets in English: An Anthology* (New York, 1972); Travitsky, *Paradise*; Angeline Goreau, *The Whole Duty of a Woman: Female Writers in Seventeenth-Century England* (New York, 1985); Germaine Greer et al. (eds), *Kissing the Rod: An Anthology of 17th-Century Women's Verse* (New York, 1988).

19 See, for example, the complex analyses of women and print culture in Wendy Wall, *The Imprint of Gender: Authorship and Publication in the English Renaissance* (Ithaca, NY, 1993), followed by Barbara Smith and Ursula Appelt (eds), *Write or Be Written: Early Modern Women Poets and Cultural Constraints* (Aldershot, 2001). Wendy Wall has recently reflected on the impact of the *Imprint of Gender* upon constructions of the author in early modern women's writing: Wendy Wall, 'Female Authorship', in Catherine Bates (ed.), *A Companion to Renaissance Poetry* (Oxford, 2018), 128–40.

to come up with some quite extraordinary methods to erase—or rather to mask—the differences between past and present and ... we are positively flummoxed by the writer who had no desire to see his or her work in print or to play our games of authorship.'[20]

Insisting that we pay attention to texts' material circulation in the period and develop a fuller, historicised understanding of authorship, Ezell's own work has been instrumental in changing where we look for early modern women's authorship and how we understand its forms, practices, and place in literary history. Foregrounding scribal and social authorship practices, her work has led the past two decades of scholarship on women's participation in manuscript culture, which has shown the richness and diversity of this once overlooked form of authorship.[21] This work has uncovered a wealth of new authors, texts, and authorial practices, including collation, compilation, copying, and annotation—practices for which authorial ascription is frequently absent, contested, speculative, or fictional.[22] Concurrent revisions of the authorial apparatus in print have further pushed the boundaries of what might be considered authorship to include activities such as patronage and editing as well as, more recently, the labours that make up the material production of the book, from collecting the rags to make the paper, through to its printing and publishing.[23] The material turn in early modern studies has been critical in these expanded conceptualisations of book authorship, reminding us how many processes and potential agents go into the making of a text, whether graffiti, embroidery, a manuscript poem, or a print folio, and how extended that process of making can be, as subsequent readers and writers annotate, write over, tear out, cut up, or in myriad ways, reuse a text.[24] As Matt Cohen reminds us, publication is both an extended 'event' and 'choral', the work of many hands and, as Jennifer Richards rightly

[20] Ezell, *Writing*, 19.

[21] See, for example, George L. Justice and Nathan Tinker (eds), *Women's Writing and the Circulation of Ideas: Manuscript Publication in England, 1550–1800* (Cambridge, 2002); Margaret J. M. Ezell, *Social Authorship and the Advent of Print* (Baltimore, MD, 2003); Jonathon Gibson and Victoria E. Burke (eds), *Early Modern Women's Manuscript Writing: Selected Papers from the Trinity/Trent Colloquium* (Aldershot, 2004); Gillian Wright, *Producing Women's Poetry: Text and Paratext, Manuscript and Print* (Cambridge, 2013); and the pioneering *Perdita* project led by Elizabeth Clarke, which amassed information about early modern women's manuscript cultures in a digital archive. See Elizabeth Clarke et al. (eds), *Perdita*, University of Warwick http://web.warwick.ac.uk/english/perdita/html, accessed 12 June 2021, and *Perdita Manuscripts, 1500–1700*, Adam Matthew Digital, https://www.amdigital.co.uk/primary%E2%80%93sources/index.php?option=com_content&view=featured&Itemid=101, accessed 12 June 2021.

[22] Smith, '*Grossly Material Things*'; the essays in Pender and Smith (eds), *Material Cultures*; Pender (ed.), *Gender and Collaboration*; Knight, White, and Sauer (eds), *Women's Bookscapes*.

[23] For example, Heidi Craig, 'English rag-women and early modern paper production', in Wayne (ed), *Women's Labour*, 29–46; and see this volume, Chapter 45, Anna Reynolds, 'Material Texts: Women's Paperwork In Early Modern England And Mary Wroth's *Urania*'.

[24] Seminal work on expanded ideas of the texts that might be included in an expanded canon of women's work include Juliet Fleming, *Graffiti and the Writing Arts of Early Modern England* (London, 2001) and Susan Frye, *Pens and Needles: Women's Textualities in Early Modern England* (Philadelphia, PA, 2010). For textual use and abuse, see Adam Smyth, *Material Texts in Early Modern England* (Cambridge, 2018).

notes, many voices.[25] Recent scholarship on voice, song, and performance emphasises just how extended the publication event of a text might be, encompassing performances where a singer or speaker materially embodies a text in order to make it their own in that moment of inhabitation (see this volume, Chapter 10, Katherine Larson, 'The Songscapes of Early Modern Women'). For Richards, 'voicing and understanding were ... understood to work in partnership': the physical feeling of 'words in the mouth' was integral to their 'digestion' by the reader.[26] This process extends to song, where, as Scott Trudell argues, women's performances 'helped foster a dynamic, collaborative mode of production in which it was difficult to ignore a performer's power to reshape meaning'.[27] Examples of single historical women writers who attach their signature to print texts form only one kind of authorial practice within the dynamic and various world of print, scribal, material, vocal, and oral textual cultures with which women are now understood to have engaged. Even those examples of print texts are now seen as the work of multiple originary practices, many of which might be considered authorial.

At the same time as authorship as a role has been expanded and detached from a single, stable point of origin, the ways in which gender intersects with the author function has also come under pressure. What does it mean when the adjective 'woman' is attached to author? What 'extraordinary methods' have we come up with to fix that connection in ways that reflect our own ideological, cultural, and political pressures rather than the complex and messy world of early modern textual cultures? A history of critique surrounding the stability of the term 'woman' can be traced across the last two decades of scholarship, complicating straightforward relationships between authorial gender and the text, emphasising gendered signature as the marker of whether a text was read as by a woman, and arguing that texts of uncertain attribution are either admissible to an expanded canon of early modern women's writing or valuable as objects of study in their own right.[28] These problems also attend the early modern male-authored canon, and have come under similar scrutiny, especially in editing projects where the case for texts which cannot be attached securely to an author have increasingly been considered as part of that author's works on the basis of circulation and reception, as, for example, in the case of Michael Rudick's historical edition of the poems of Sir Walter

25 Matt Cohen, *The Networked Wilderness: Communicating in Early New England* (Minneapolis, MN, 2010), 12–25; Richards, *Voices and Books*, 201–2.

26 Richards, *Voices and Books*, 68–75.

27 Scott A. Trudell, 'Performing Women in English Books of Ayres', in Leslie C. Dunn and Katherine R. Larson (eds), *Gender and Song in Early Modern England* (Farnham, 2014), 15–30, 29.

28 See Danielle Clarke, 'Nostalgia, Anachronism, and the Editing of Early Modern Women's Texts', *Text*, 15 (2003), 187–209, and Danielle Clarke, introduction to Clarke and Elizabeth Clarke (eds), *'This Double Voice': Gendered Writing in Early Modern England* (Basingstoke, 2001), 1–15; Rosalind Smith, *Sonnets and the English Woman Writer, 1560–1621: The Politics of Absence* (Basingstoke, 2005), 1–12; and 'Reading Mary Stuart's Casket Sonnets: Reception, Authorship, and Early Modern Women's Writing,' *Parergon*, 29.2 (2012), 149–76; Kimberly Anne Coles, *Religion, Reform and Women's Writing in Early Modern England* (Cambridge, 2008), 8–11.

Raleigh.[29] However, while an expanded definition of authorship has gained widespread acceptance in the field of early modern women's writing, an expanded definition of 'women's authorship' has been less enthusiastically received. At a deep and often unspoken level, it conflicts with the project of recovery of early modern women's writing that initiated the field and continues to perform ideological work in representing the past in ways that include diverse voices and experiences. This includes those of historical women whose gender was a key determinant in how they were produced and regulated as political subjects, albeit alongside other factors such as race, ethnicity, geography, and rank. Women writers are now included in major anthologies—although selectively and in small numbers—and new texts and authors continue to be uncovered in ways that make it impossible to ask the question, as once was routine, if women wrote at all in the Renaissance. Yet these canonical incursions are small, contingent, and potentially reversible. The costs of dismantling or complicating secure attributions to women writers and blurring the edges of the field are high if they threaten the legitimacy and theoretical underpinnings of decades of work in establishing the critical field itself. Changing models of authorship carry both gains and losses for the study of early modern women writers, particularly where the precondition of entry into certain cultural forms, most notably the anthology, is still often predicated on the existence of single, identifiable, historical authors. Nonetheless, although the majority of work in the field of early modern women's writing remains focused on texts with stable attributions, recent anthologies, editions, essays, and digital projects are beginning to challenge assumptions about the relationship of embodied woman writer, signature, and text.

As Marcy North has recently argued, increased access to digital resources provided by platforms such as Early English Books Online (EEBO), individual libraries, and comprehensive bibliographies and indices mean that scholars can newly investigate for themselves questions of attribution, ascription, and authenticity.[30] This is not to say that the digital environment, and its attendant epistemologies, have been wholly positive for scholarship on women writers; as Jacqueline Wernimont and Julia Flanders have shown, digital forms—particularly large additive databases—have the potential to bury and obscure early modern women's writing in new ways (see this volume, Chapter 44, Julia Flanders, '"A Telescope for the Mind": Digital Modelling and Analysis of Early Modern Women's Writing').[31] This field is evolving, however, and the increasing number of digital resources now available means we are less reliant on the inclusion of texts in

[29] Michael Rudick, *The Poems of Sir Walter Ralegh: A Historical Edition* (Tempe, AZ, 2000). See also the case made for 'social editing' in Christopher Burlinson and Ruth Connolly (eds), 'Editing Stuart Poetry', *Studies in English Literature* 52.1 (2012), 1–12. For recent scholarship on editing early modern women writers, see the introduction and essays in Sarah C. E. Ross and Paul Salzman (eds), *Editing Early Modern Women* (Cambridge, 2016).

[30] North, *Ambiguities*, 82.

[31] Jacqueline Wernimont, 'Whence Feminism? Assessing Feminist Interventions in Digital Literary Archives', *Digital Humanities Quarterly*, 7.1 (2013), www.digitalhumanities.org/dhq/vol/7/1/000156/000156.html, accessed 12 June 2021; Jacqueline Wernimont and Julia Flanders, 'Feminism in the Age of the Digital Archive', *Tulsa Studies in Women's Literature*, 29.3 (2010), 425–35.

anthologies and editions, and the expert opinion of editors, in admitting or excluding texts of complex attribution. The affordances of scale and space in digital resources mean that texts of uncertain attribution can be, and are, included in databases alongside those of stable attribution, with diverse authorship roles and degrees of stability now able to be assigned, delineated in detailed taxonomies, and searched.[32] In the case of Esther Inglis' copy of the *Octonaires*, for example, her scribal authorship is known but her agency in other authorial practices—making its embroidered binding or translating the text—is less certain.[33] Such complexities cannot be elided or avoided in creating a searchable database, as each category must be given a value, foregrounding the intricacy and indeterminacy of authorial identity and status both within texts and across a corpus. The capaciousness of the digital allows for fine gradation at scale in ways that we have not encountered before, foregrounding crucial research questions for our field and providing a generative instance where quantitative and qualitative methods might inform one another, contrary to the sometimes antagonistic ways in which they have been positioned in recent scholarship.

At the same time as the complexities of authorship, ascription, and attribution are being newly mapped and theorised through the creation of digital resources, a step change is occurring in our conception of authorship and *auctoritas* itself. Lynn Enterline's work on the institutions of education in Tudor England is particularly important here in its emphasis on the ways in which humanism operated through the creation of a rhetorical habitus for the early modern subject, schooled in patterns of thought where the student was invited to inhabit the speaking position and voice of another through the figure of prosopopoiea.[34] This training, coupled with the popularity of Ovid's *Heroides*, meant that the imitation of women's voices became an integral part of fiction-making within the educational institutions of the schoolroom and Inns of Court, and such 'habits of alterity' extended beyond their borders to wider literary cultures.[35] Earlier criticism has suggested that such prosopopoeiae were disincentives to women's authorship, with Josephine A. Roberts noting that the popularity of mimed female discourse 'may well have been a contributing factor in discouraging sixteenth-century Englishwomen from writing their own lyric poetry'.[36] Enterline's work, alongside that of Gavin Alexander and Jennifer Richards, suggests the opposite: that the widespread rhetorical and cultural practice of occupying other subjectivities—male and female—as sites

[32] See Coolahan and McCarthy, 'From Manuscript to Metadata', as well as Jake Arthur and Rosalind Smith, 'Women's Complaint, 1530–1680: Taxonomy, Voice, and the Index in the Digital Age', in Ross and Smith (eds), *Early Modern Women's Complaint*, 269–90 and 291–312.

[33] In discussing Folger MS V.a.665, Georgianna Ziegler comments that it is 'possible that Inglis embroidered the binding herself' and notes that she was praised by a contemporary, Robert Rollock, for her skill with the pen as well as the needle. See Georgianna Ziegler, 'A Recently Discovered Esther Inglis Manuscript', *The Library*, 19.4 (2018), 490–9, 493.

[34] Enterline, *Shakespeare's Schoolroom*, 19–21, 79–85.

[35] Enterline, *Shakespeare's Schoolroom*, 7.

[36] Josephine A. Roberts, 'The Phallacies of Authorship', in Susan Dwyer Amussen and Adele F. Seeff (eds), *Attending to Early Modern Women* (Newark, 1998), 38–57, 49.

of affective imagination was fundamental to the act of authorship itself, underwriting the creation of character, the communication of emotion, and the shaping of authorial identities, historical and imagined.[37] This work has ramifications for how we understand ascription, attribution, and signature, especially when attached to female-voiced works in certain genres such as complaint—as provisional, fictional, and shaped by rhetorical imperatives rather than claims of textual ownership. It casts a new aspect, for example, on Spenser's prosopopoeia of Mary Sidney's voice in 'The Doleful Lay of Clorinda', where he inhabits her subject position as chief mourner following her brother's death through the orthodox practice of imagining the kind of poem she might write and perform: 'In sort as she it sung, I will rehearse'.[38] But it cuts the other way as well, with women newly imagined as capable of taking up fictional subject positions across gender boundaries; in multiple authorial roles; and in print, scribal, and oral forms. These new investigations of what the female voice meant in early modern cultures of reading, writing, and identity formation have reshaped our understanding of the rhetorical possibilities attached to practices of authorship, attribution, and ascription in the period.

Finally, very recent work in identity studies in the early modern period is breaking down how we understand and conceptualise the early modern woman author in other ways: insisting on new formulations surrounding race and ethnicity, gender and sexuality, status and power, community and habitus, which overturn previous models of the woman author that have circulated in different articulations since the seventeenth century.[39] These intersectional analyses reveal how limited our imaginations have been in reconstructing the early modern woman as author. In some ways, the canonical incursions of the last fifty years of scholarship have relied upon a series of restricted models of both women and writer that have masked how complex, diverse, and provisional authorship was in the early modern period. This leads me to ask how compelling any 'hard-won legitimacy' can be if it is built on anachronistic constructions?[40] How much do we want to hold on to these models as a field? How certain are we that women authors did not embrace authorial ambiguity strategically, as a form of rhetorical performance, or simply as an accepted model of experimentation that was only at times, and contingently, attached to a historical woman writer of their own name? To what extent

[37] See Richards, *Voices and Books*, especially her arguments about women's education, 114–18; and Alexander, 'Prosopopoeia'.

[38] Edmund Spenser, in William A. Oram, et al. (eds), *The Yale Edition of the Shorter Poems of Edmund Spenser* (New Haven, CT, 1989), 577. For an earlier version of this argument complicating the attribution, see Danielle Clarke, '"In sort as she it sung": Spenser's "Doleful Lay" and the Construction of Female Authorship', *Criticism*, 42.4 (2000), 451–68.

[39] See for example, Jaime Goodrich, 'Reconsidering the Woman Writer: The Identity Politics of Anne Cooke Bacon', in Patricia Phillippy (ed.), *A History of Early Modern Women's Writing* (Cambridge, 2018); Bernadette Andrea, *Women and Islam in Early Modern English Literature* (Cambridge, 2007); Ania Loomba and Melissa E. Sanchez (eds), *Rethinking Feminism in Early Modern Studies: Gender, Race, Sexuality* (London and New York, 2016).

[40] This phrase is used by Patricia Pender and Alexandra Day, 'Introduction: Gender, Authorship, and Early Modern Women's Collaboration', in Patricia Pender (ed.), *Gender, Authorship and Early Modern Women's Collaboration* (Basingstoke, 2017), 1–19, 1.

did women engage with the rhetorical structures underpinning humanist education and fiction-making? Did women create prosopopoeiae of their own authorial characters—as Gavin Alexander suggests was part of authorial practice—that built upon, engaged with, or resisted other prosopopoeiae circulating under their signatures?[41] How did such 'authentic' and 'fictional' identities interact for readers and performers as well as writers? To think through these questions, I am going to turn to an attribution debate attached to the publications of Anne Locke, an important early writer in canonical accounts of the Tudor lyric.

ANNE LOCKE AND THE FIRST ENGLISH SONNET SEQUENCE

On 15 January 1560, a translation of Jean Calvin's four *Sermons of John Calvin Upon the Songe that Ezechias Made* was entered in the Stationers' Register. It was published by John Day in London shortly afterwards, presumably before the new calendar year began on 25 March, as the British Library copy contains the inscription 'Liber Henrici Lock ex dono Annae vxoris suae. 1559' (A book of Henry Locke by gift of Anne his wife. 1559).[42] The sermons are preceded by a dedicatory epistle to Katherine Brandon, Duchess of Suffolk, subscribed with the initials A. L.; by correlating the initials with the marginal inscription, the dedicatory epistle and translation have been attributed to Anne Locke. Locke was born into a London-based Protestant merchant family, married Henry Locke from the same milieu, and became part of the community of Protestant exiles in Geneva from May 1557. Her copy text for the translation of Calvin's sermons was volume three of Denis Raguenier's manuscript record of Calvin's 'ordinary weekday sermons' and her translation in 1560 was their first publication (Lock, lxix). Locke later went on to translate Jean Taffin's *Of the Markes of the Children of God* in 1590, dedicated to the Countess of Warwick, and circulated under her signature as Anne Prowse (her second married name); she was praised by John Field as a 'scholler in [God's] schoole' and by Richard Carew for her 'rare learning'.[43] Locke's status as translator is not contested, but the same consensus does not attach to the poetry that follows both of these prose texts, especially the meditation appended to Calvin's sermons, 'A Meditation of a Penitent Sinner: Written in a Maner of a Paraphrase upon the 51. Psalme of David'. Comprising five prefatory sonnets 'expressing the passioned mind of the penitent sinner' followed

[41] Alexander, 'Prosopopoeia', 105.

[42] Susan M. Felch, (ed.), *The Collected Works of Anne Vaughan Lock* (Tempe, AZ, 1999), lxix–lxx. All further references cite this edition as 'Lock'. In her introduction, Felch makes a persuasive argument that two subsequent editions, now lost, were printed by John Day in 1569 and 1574.

[43] Discussed in Micheline White, 'Women Writers and Literary-Religious Circles in the Elizabethan West Country: Anne Dowriche, Anne Lock Prowse, Anne Lock Moyle, Ursula Fulford, and Elizabeth Rous', *Modern Philology*, 103.2 (2005), 187–214.

by twenty-one sonnets paraphrasing Psalm 51, this is the first known sonnet sequence in English, scribal or print. It is published on a separate octavo gathering to the translation, which ends on sig. G7v with G8 left blank. The gathering of eight leaves containing the meditation, numbered only A.ii on the second leaf and Aa.3 on the third, were added after the translation, as indicated by its preface identifying the meditation as delivered by a 'frend' and incorporated into the volume 'for that it well agreeth with the same argument':

> I have added this meditation folowyng unto the ende of this boke, not as a parcell of maister Calvines worke, but for that it well agreeth with the same argument, and was delivered me by my frend with whom I knew I might be so bolde to use and publishe it as pleased me. (Locke, 62)

This is not an unproblematic case for attribution to Anne Locke, and nor has it been considered as such in the now considerable scholarship on the meditation. The ways in which this sequence has been attributed exposes some of the difficulties of assigning authorship in early modern women's writing as well as the gains and losses of such different approaches.

Drawing on surviving correspondence from John Knox to Anne Locke, early twentieth-century scholars made a tentative attribution of the meditation to John Knox: 'perhaps Knox's work'; 'possibly written by Knox himself'.[44] Given that Knox produced very little poetry in his substantial corpus, and that poetry was metrically uneven, inflected by Scots dialect, and comparatively unsophisticated, the attribution to Knox has never been seriously considered. From the mid-1980s, most critics have taken one or more of the following three approaches. They attribute the meditation to Locke and ignore the preface; read the preface as the work of the printer John Day, in which case 'the frend' who delivered the manuscript could conceivably be Anne Locke; or they view the preface as an example of Locke's participation in rhetorical traditions of modesty, in which case its narrative of delivery by a friend should not be read literally, but as the adoption of a feigned stance instantly recognisable to an early modern reader.[45] These approaches can be indexed to the period in which they were written. Early gynocritical accounts tended to ignore the preface and make the attribution; later analyses emphasising Locke's difficulty as a woman in circulating original work in print, or composing a psalm paraphrase deviating from Scripture, cluster in criticism when such views were orthodox in the 1990s and in the first decade of the twenty-first century;

[44] Patrick Collinson, 'The Role of Women in the English Reformation Illustrated by the Life and Friendships of Anne Locke', *Studies in Church History*, 2 (1965), 258–72, 265; W. Stanford Reid, *Trumpeter of God: A Biography of John Knox* (New York, 1974), 141.

[45] For the first view, see, for example, Michael R. G. Spiller, *The Development of the Sonnet* (New York and London, 1992), 93; for the second, see Margaret P. Hannay, '"UnLock My Lipps": The Miserere mei Deus of Anne Vaughan Lock and Mary Sidney Herbert', in Jean M. Brink (ed.), *Privileging Gender in Early Modern England* (Kirkesville, MO, 1993), 21–2; and for the third see Patricia Pender, *Early Modern Women's Writing and the Rhetoric of Modesty* (Basingstoke, 2012), 17–18.

interest in modesty rhetoric aligns with the more recent formalist and material turns in literary criticism. Dissenting views have always existed, however. Susan Felch's sceptical stance towards Locke's use of modesty tropes and thematic links between the separate sections of the text, which she views as 'common currency among nonconformist writers', has been matched by Micheline White's view that 'the evidence is still inconclusive' and my own arguments against dismissing the disclaimer in favour of keeping the uncertainty of the attribution alive.[46] More recent work on Locke has focused on her collaborative authorship and the social networks within which she circulated.[47]

Steven May has recently suggested a new candidate for authorship of the sonnets in Thomas Norton, reading the disclaimer literally and searching for a candidate for the 'frend' who might have delivered the meditation to the as yet undetermined 'I' of the preface.[48] He makes a case on the grounds of the possible friendship between Norton and Locke. They lived in proximate neighbourhoods in London; they were both acquainted with Calvin and held similar religious views, and in 1576, sixteen years after the publication of the *Sermons*, a T. N.—possibly Norton—contributed a verse memorialising Locke's second husband, Edward Dering.[49] If this circumstantial evidence is not overwhelmingly convincing, the evidence provided by Norton's poetic career is more plausible: he composes a Surreyan sonnet in *Tottel's Miscellany*, the same rhyme scheme used in the *Meditation*, and he translates two poems in Calvin's *Institutiones* as well as contributing thirty-four poems to the *Whole Booke of Psalmes*, including a version of Psalm 51 in couplets.[50] As Kimberley Coles points out, Norton had access to Locke's 1560 translation of Calvin's sermons and the appended meditation to draw upon before the publication of the 1562 *Whole Booke of Psalmes*, and there are parallels between the language of the two texts.[51] For May, the crowning argument comes through his search using EEBO for nine unusual words and meanings located both in the *Meditation* and in Norton's substantial corpus, that May contends are not to be found in Locke's very slight corpus (comprised mainly of translations) and only occasionally in the work of other contemporary poets.[52] As digital humanities methodologies go, this is not a very robust one: the disparity in size between the corpora of Norton and Locke biases

[46] Lock, liv; Micheline White, 'Dismantling Catholic Primers and Reforming Private Prayer: Anne Lock, Hezekiah's Song, and Psalm 51', in Alec Ryrie and Jessica Martin (eds), *Private and Domestic Devotion in Early Modern Britain* (Farnham, 2012), 94; Smith, *Sonnets*, 30–2.

[47] White, 'Women Writers'; and 'The Perils and Possibilities of the Book Education: Anne Lock, John Knox, John Calvin, Queen Elizabeth, and the Duchess of Suffolk', *Parergon*, 29.3 (2012), 9–27.

[48] Steven W. May, 'Anne Lock and Thomas Norton's Meditation of a Penitent Sinner', *Modern Philology*, 114.4 (2017), 793–819.

[49] May, 'Anne Lock', 808–9.

[50] May, 'Anne Lock', 809–12.

[51] Coles, *Religion*, 136–41. May also notes the verbal parallels but does not consider the circulation of the 1560 print text. Instead he asks: 'Could she have given Norton a copy of her Meditation before its publication in 1560 which then influenced his translation of this penitential Psalm for the metrical Psalter?'. He finds this hypothesis 'rather implausible in itself, given the lack of any evidence that Lock was a poet by 1560' (May, 812).

[52] May, 'Anne Lock', 813–18.

the search from the outset and the sample of nine words is both statistically insignificant and selected through a loosely defined and evidenced category of 'rarity' based on basic searches of EEBO that do not include alternative spellings.[53] Compared to computational stylistics methods developed over the last fifty years to provide evidence for authorship, and which focus on small, common function words, large corpora, and statistically defensible comparisons, May's methods of counting are idiosyncratic at best.[54] Nonetheless, for May this constitutes 'Norton's distinctive verbal "fingerprint"', allowing him to 'be recognized at last as the creator of these moving devotional sonnets'.[55] Despite its triumphal cast, his essay ends rather anxiously noting that Norton's abilities as a rhetorical innovator were formally constrained by 'lengthy set speeches' in *Gorboduc* and the 'longline technical forms of mid-century' in his psalm translations; it is only in the 1560 *Meditation* that his poetic skills are 'unconstrained' and can achieve full expression to constitute 'the high point of Norton's career as a poet'.[56] One senses that even May does not fully believe the case he has made for Norton as the author of the *Meditations*; he seems unable to fully reconcile the disparity between Norton's known work and the rhetorical sophistication and innovation of the 1560 sequence.

CONCLUSION

May's article is of interest less for the case that it makes for Norton's authorship of the *Meditation* than for the challenges it poses to approaches to authorship in early modern women's writing. The question of whether it is sufficient to make attributions to women writers by default, or on the grounds of probability, without fully exploring cases for alternative authors, is an important one that the field has been reluctant to address. For the *Meditation*, candidates other than Norton might be suggested, such as the Scots psalmist William Kethe, who was also part of the Genevan exile community, or William Stewart, who published a sonnet to celebrate the metrical psalms in the Scottish prayer book of 1565 and contributed twenty of its psalm translations. But as May's article also demonstrates, such identifications are not always definitive. Rather than single, stable attributions to historical writers, what most sixteenth-century texts show, in fact, is how complex and diverse authorship was in the early modern period. Within the covers of the British Library copy of *The Sermons* are multiple kinds of writing of differing degrees of originality, including marginalia, dedicatory prose, prose translation, religious sonnets,

[53] For a forensic examination of May's criterion of rarity and his narrow search methods, see Jake Arthur, 'Anne Lock or Thomas Norton? A Response to the Re-attribution of the First Sonnet Sequence in English', *Early Modern Women: An Interdisciplinary Journal*, 16.2 (2022), 213-36.

[54] For an introduction to computational linguistics and authorship, see Hugh Craig and Brett Greatley-Hirsch, *Style, Computers, and Early Modern Drama: Beyond Authorship* (Cambridge, 2017).

[55] May, 'Anne Lock', 818–19.

[56] May, 'Anne Lock', 818–19.

and psalm paraphrase, and these correspond to diverse authorial roles including annotator, patron, author, translator, and editor. All of these author functions are assigned to different subjects within the text itself, some fully identified (Catherine Brandon, John Calvin, Henry Locke), some partially identified (A. L.), and some obscured ('I', 'my frend'). Rather than the work of a single individual, the book is 'authored' by many hands and many agents, extending beyond the book's covers to the circulation, transcription, and performance of its metrical psalm paraphrases in manuscript Scottish songbooks.[57] Viewed using this model of expanded authorship, *The Sermons* also demonstrates the provisionality of such authorial roles: largely anonymous except to coterie circles, the question of who wrote, translated, or contributed to this text looms far larger for late modern readers than it did for their early modern counterparts. For the majority of early modern readers, Anne Locke was not understood to be the author of any of its parts—all the print sections of the text itself use strategies of anonymity as its overarching approach to authorship. What use, then, is our continued investment in making the attribution to Locke except to perform what Danielle Clarke refers to as a 'nostalgic desire for stable texts' that is deeply anachronistic, and to artificially boost claims for women's authorship of a significant poetic work?[58] I would like to suggest that such an approach does our field no favours. We are better served by attending carefully to how authorship is framed in a text, in each of its constituent parts, acknowledging the complexity and range of authorial positions that women could, and did, adopt. These included the construction of an authorial self as part of prosopopoeic practices, alongside equally important and widely practised strategies of anonymous and semi-anonymous circulation.

Such an approach will result in losses: neither the *Meditation* nor a text such as Mary Sidney's 'Doleful Lay of Clorinda' could be claimed for a canon of early modern women's writing based on single authorship if this were our model. Yet in the last two decades, the scale of texts and authors that have been recovered has increased significantly, by opening up restricted models of authorship in print to cultures of manuscript and performance, and by broadening our models of textual agency. This corpus will only continue to grow, as scholars continue to find new sites of women's writing, whether in overlooked genres and modes, from neglected groups of writers, or in entire fields of practice such as marginalia. Such recent work does not constitute the rediscovery of the same 'lost' women writers, nor the reattribution of the same texts, but broader expansions, often methodologically and technologically driven, and conducted in conversation with the broader field of early modern studies. This chapter opened with a paradox, a methodological problem that once enabled and drove scholarship in our field but has more recently complicated its progress. Yet authorship also has the possibility

[57] Susan Felch has shown that the second song of the third section of the St Andrews Psalter 'is the polyphonic setting of Anne Lock's first psalm sonnet'. Susan Felch, 'The Public Life of Anne Vaughan Lock: Her Reception in England and Scotland', in Julie D. Campbell et al. (eds), *Early Modern Women and Transnational Communities of Letters* (Farnham, 2009; repr. 2016), 137–58, 141–2.

[58] Clarke, 'Nostalgia', 188.

to be a generative site of new knowledge about women and their texts, if approached in ways that attend to the specificity and diversity of its use by women writers, in the constituent parts of their texts and in shaping their reputations, across a spectrum of positions from anonymity to overt claims of authorial ownership.

FURTHER READING

Alexander, Gavin. 'Prosopopoeia: the speaking figure', in Sylvia Adamson, Gavin Alexander, and Katrin Ettenhuber (eds), *Renaissance Figures of Speech*. Cambridge, 2007, 95–112.

Coolahan, Marie-Louise (ed.). 'The Cultural Dynamics of Reception', Special Issue of *Journal of Medieval and Early Modern Studies*, 50.1 (2020).

Enterline. Lynn. '"Past the Help of Law": Epyllia and the Female Complaint', in Sarah C. E. Ross and Rosalind Smith (eds), *Early Modern Women's Complaint: Gender, Form, and Politics*. Cham: Palgrave Macmillan, 2020, 315–27.

Larson, Katherine. *Texts in and of the Air: The Matter of Song in Early Modern England*. Oxford, 2019.

North, Marcy L. *The Anonymous Renaissance: Cultures of Discretion in Tudor-Stuart England*. Chicago, IL, 2003.

Richards, Jennifer. *Voices and Books in the English Renaissance: A New History of Reading*. Oxford, 2019.

CHAPTER 3

HOW LADY JANE GREY MAY HAVE USED HER EDUCATION

JENNIFER RICHARDS

I want to begin by explaining why I have chosen to give this chapter such a tentative title, drawing attention to how Lady Jane Grey might have used her education, not how she actually used it, and to acknowledge the difficulties and frustrations of trying to locate the agency of historical women. Lady Jane Grey (1537–1554) is an especially difficult person to attribute agency to, as her confession on the scaffold suggests: 'I am condempned to dye ... only for that I consented to the thing which I was inforced unto'.[1] She had an eventful but short life, over which she had little control. On 21 May 1553 she was married, probably against her will, to Guildford Dudley. A few months later, on 10 July 1553, she was crowned Queen of England thanks to the machinations of her ambitious father, Henry Grey, and her new father-in-law, John Dudley, Duke of Northumberland, and the dying Edward VI's '*Devise*' for the succession, which named Jane and her male heirs his successors, dispossessing his sisters, Mary and Elizabeth. Nine days later she was deposed by the woman she had supplanted, Mary I. She was found guilty of treason, but pardoned, yet she was executed on 12 February 1554 after her father was implicated in Thomas Wyatt's rebellion (1554), in which she had played no part.[2] She became a Protestant martyr whose life and words were appropriated well into the eighteenth century.[3]

Lady Jane Grey did leave behind writings in her own name, a sign, surely, of some authorial agency. This chapter will focus on the collection of four short texts, supposedly written in the Tower of London while she was awaiting execution, and printed posthumously in 1554 by the clandestine Protestant printer John Day. The texts are: 'An Epistle',

[1] Lady Jane Grey, *An Epistle of the Ladye Jane a Righte Vertuous Woman, To a Learned Man of Late Falne From the Truth of Gods Most Holy Word, for Fear of the Worlde* ([London?], [1554?]), sig. B7v.

[2] Alison Plowden, 'Grey, Lady Jane', *ODNB*; Dale Hoak, 'Edward VI', *ODNB*.

[3] Edith Snook, 'Jane Grey, "Manful" Combat, and the Female Reader in Early Modern England', *Renaissance and Reformation/Renaissance et Réforme*, 32 (2009), 47–81.

written to 'a learned man of late falne from the truth of Gods most holy word', who has been identified as John Harding, chaplain to the Duke of Suffolk, by John Foxe; 'A Certayne Communycation' in the form of a catechism, supposedly a record of a dialogue between Grey and Mary I's chaplain, the Abbott of Westminster, John Feckenham, 'Word for Word, her own hand being put therto' (*Epistle*, sig. B2v); a letter to her sister Katherine, titled 'An Exhortation', which was supposedly written by Grey in the 'ende' of her Bible, 'the New testament in Greke' (*Epistle*, sig. B6r); and, finally, 'The Lady Janes wordes upon the Scaffold' (*Epistle*, sig. B7v). The style of these texts is described by Edith Snook as 'unusually direct and confrontational'.[4] Others have described her tone as 'acerbic' and 'arrogant'.[5] It is not hard to see why. 'What kind of girl', asks Louise Horton, would call their addressee a '"defourmed impe of the divel"' and '"the stincking & filthy kenell of Sathan"'?[6] And what kind of teenager, I also wonder, would 'openlye' tell the chaplain sent to prepare her to die that unless he repents, they will never meet again since he is in 'an evyl case', adding that God 'hath geven you his great gift of utteraunce, if it please him to open the eyes of your hart to his truth' (*Epistle*, sig. B5v). However, doubt is now cast over Grey's authorship of these texts, which were, after all, printed posthumously, first by Day, then in a second edition in the same year by the Scoloker press. There are many variants between the two editions, although both printers implied they 'set from copy which was or was taken from Jane's own autograph'.[7]

That Grey wrote *something* is not in doubt, but what exactly is less clear since her manuscripts have not survived; nor do we understand the history of their transmission. It has long been assumed that Day's 1554 edition is 'a faithful reproduction' of Grey's manuscripts, which were supposedly passed to John Foxe by the Swiss reformer Heinrich Bullinger, who obtained them from John Banks, a printer and friend to a tutor in the Grey household.[8] John Foxe added new material to the Grey canon in *Acts and Monuments* in 1563 and 1570, also printed by Day. In 1563, he added a prayer supposedly penned by Grey.[9] In 1570, he added verses she had supposedly written with a pin on

[4] Snook, 'Jane Grey', 48.

[5] Megan L. Hickerson, *Making Women Martyrs in Tudor England* (Basingstoke, 2005), 165.

[6] Louise Horton, 'The Clerics and the Learned Lady: Intertextuality in the Religious Writings of Lady Jane Grey', in Patricia Pender (ed.), *Gender, Authorship, and Early Modern Women's Collaboration* (London, 2017), 149–74, 156, citing Grey, *Epistle*, sig. A2r.

[7] The second edition is titled *Here in this Booke ye Haue a Godly Epistle made by a Faithful Christian. A comunication betwene Fecknam and the Lady Jane Dudley. A letter that she wrote to her syster Lady Katherin. The ende of the Ladye Jane upon the scaffolde. Ye shal have also herein a godly prayer made by maister John Knokes* (London, [1554?]). On key differences see Eric Ives, *Lady Jane Grey: A Tudor Mystery* (Chichester, 2011), 21–3; e.g., the version of Grey's speech on the scaffold in this edition 'take[s] the story beyond Jane's speech and describe[s] the actual execution'.

[8] Horton, 'The Clerics and the Learned Lady', 151; John N. King, *Foxe's Book of Martyrs and Early Print Culture* (Cambridge, 2006), 26. On the challenges of knowing what Grey authored see also Ives, *Lady Jane Grey*, 17–23.

[9] John Foxe, *Actes and Monuments of these Latter and Perillous Dayes Touching Matters of the Church* (London, 1563).

the walls of the prison—a standard trope of prison writing[10]—as well as a letter to her father, written in her prayer book, alongside amended versions of the original scaffold speech and of the 'ostensibly verbatim account' of her meeting with Feckenham.[11] Horton suspects the involvement of Protestant clerics, along with Day, in the creation of Grey's canon, to build her identity as a Protestant martyr. She discovers echoes of words and sentences from the works of contemporary male reformers who were also printed by Day—Thomas Becon, John Bale, Miles Coverdale—as well as Erasmus and 'other reformers'.[12] Grey's 'Epistle' to Harding, Horton observes, is a patchwork of quotations from Coverdale's Bible, 'shaped to reflect [her] circumstances', while the likely source for Grey's 'Communycation', supposedly written in 'her own hand' four days before her execution, is a text written thirty years previously, 'one of Erasmus' well known colloquies, *Abbatis et Eruditae* or, in English, *The Abbot and the Learned Lady*'.[13] There are doubts, then, about the stability of Grey's writings. It is hard 'to imagine [her] alone, in a room of her own, within the Tower urgently writing for posterity'.[14] Even if we did recognise Grey as an author, Horton concludes, we still need to allow that 'many of the underlying phrases belong to male clerics, who themselves were producers of biblically influenced works', and that 'the printed books that contain her writing', including Foxe's *Acts and Monuments*, 'act as a collaborative interface in which clerics and [Grey] coincide'.[15]

This chapter approaches the problem of Lady Jane Grey's authorship and agency in a slightly different way, while accepting the argument that these texts are best understood as collaborations. It acknowledges the difficulties just recounted, but it also recognises that Grey received a humanist education, which would have equipped her to write directly and confidently, and that the tissue of quotations we find in her work is typical, rather than remarkable, in the writing of this period. I will also argue that they serve a specific purpose in relation to the 1554 pamphlet of prison writings, which creates a powerful speaking part for Lady Jane Grey and her future readers. To make my case, I will shift attention away from the question of authorship to the cultural act of attribution, arguing that even if the words we read were not spoken or written entirely by Grey, their attribution to her is meaningful because it creates a different script for future readers (of either gender), that is unusually direct, confrontational, and female (see also this volume, Chapter 2, Rosalind Smith, 'Authorship, Attribution, and Voice'). Such an emphasis means focusing less on the contribution her prison writings made to the construction of her identity as a Protestant martyr, and more on the active role that the

[10] On graffiti on prison walls and windows see Ruth Ahnert, *The Rise of Prison Writing in the Sixteenth Century* (Cambridge, 2013), 32–42; see also Juliet Fleming, *Graffiti and the Writing Arts of Early Modern England* (London, 2001), 56.

[11] John Foxe, *Actes and Monuments of these Latter and Perillous Dayes Touching Matters of the Church* (London, 1570). See Ruth Ahnert, 'Writing in the Tower of London during the Reformation, ca. 1530–1558', *Huntington Library Quarterly*, 72 (2009), 168–92, 182.

[12] Horton, 'The Clerics and the Learned Lady', 156.

[13] Horton, 'The Clerics and the Learned Lady', 155, 159.

[14] Horton, 'The Clerics and the Learned Lady', 165.

[15] Horton, 'The Clerics and the Learned Lady', 165–6.

reading of her 1554 book can play in reinforcing an argument of the Reformation, that our knowledge of God should come from Scripture, not Church tradition.[16] This focus does not intend to sideline the role of Foxe and others in the construction of Grey's authorial identity, and Protestant historical legacy. Rather, I propose that so influential (and huge) a tome as Foxe's *Actes and Monuments* should not overshadow Grey's little book, which discreetly makes its own case for the role of women as teachers of scriptural wisdom. For this is the argument of this chapter, and I will explore how that case is successfully made by Grey in my conclusion.

There is a context for this argument, which I set out in an earlier study in 2019.[17] It begins, for me, with Erasmus' argument in *Moriae Encomium* (1511) that a nuanced reading aloud of the Bible reveals its meaning more readily than does the commentary of erudite divines, and his decision to place that argument in the mouth of a literate speaker without a formal university education, a seemingly foolish woman. When Folly speaks the same verses from the Bible over which the divines labour, their literal meaning is made clear.[18] Folly is a fictional character, of course, and the point she is making is an abstract one: Erasmus is not defending the right of women to speak through and use the Bible. But this argument would be made by the reformer John Bale in relation to a historical woman, Anne Askew, who was burned as a heretic in 1546. In another textual collaboration, Bale defended the right of this modestly educated woman to speak to obstinate male Catholic clerics through Scripture.[19] It is the same imperative that gives Grey's slim octavo coherence and purpose. The difference is that Jane Grey was not modestly but exceptionally well-educated; although, as I will argue, it is the humble vernacular Bible, not classical literary writing, that gives her a voice.

LADY JANE GREY'S EDUCATION

First, though, I need to say something about Grey's education since this will help to explain how the Bible gives her a voice. Education in the Renaissance was segregated. Boys learned 'Latin, grammar, logic, and mathematics' so they could 'become members of the social and political world'.[20] They also, crucially, studied rhetoric, which helped them

[16] Grey, *Epistle*, B4v: 'I ground my faith upon gods word, & not upon the church'.

[17] Jennifer Richards, *Voices and Books in the English Renaissance: A New History of Reading* (Oxford, 2019).

[18] Richards, *Voices and Books*, 122.

[19] Richards, *Voices and Books*, 198. Anne Askew, *The First Examinacyon of Anne Askewe, Latelye Martyred in Smythfelde, by the Romysh Popes Upholders, with the Elucydacyon of Johan Bale* (Wesel, 1546); *The Lattre Examinacyon of Anne Askewe, Latelye Martyred in Smythfelde, by the Wycked Synagoge of Antichrist, with the Elucydacyon of Johan Bale* (Wesel, 1547).

[20] Kathryn M. Moncrief and Kathryn R. McPherson, '"Shall I teach you to know?": Intersections of Pedagogy, Performance, and Gender', in K. M. Moncrief and K. R. McPherson (eds), *Performing Pedagogy in Early Modern England: Gender, Instruction, and Performance* (Farnham and Burlington, VT, 2011), 1–17, 2. See also James Daybell, *Women Letter-Writers in Tudor England* (Oxford, 2006), 11–12.

to write and perform Latin (and English) orations persuasively. Women, in contrast, 'remained at home to receive both domestic and religious training', and, depending on their social status, they might have studied singing, dancing, lute-playing, needlework, and learned French.[21] This is a well-established narrative and a fair assessment of the restricted educational opportunities even for many elite women. But some of them, especially those on whom the dynastic ambitions of their families rested, often did receive a humanist education, although this was not equal to that of their male peers. This is the message of Aysha Pollnitz's excellent *Princely Education* (2015), which contrasts the education of the young prince Edward with that of his female relations, all of whom were future Scottish and English queens. Many of Edward VI's juvenile writings survive, showing how his skill in argument developed as he progressed from the writing of familiar epistles, to the tasks set out in Aphthonius' *Progymnasmata*, including the *chreia*, an exposition of a saying or example.[22]

We have far less evidence for Edward VI's female relations. What we do know is that their education started later, and that it 'commanded fewer resources'.[23] This is certainly the case with Mary, Queen of Scots (1542–1587), whose study of Latin started late, in the autumn of 1554. Although she performed a deliberative oration just a year later in 1555, before 'King Henri, the queen, and all the court', it is likely that 'some staging was involved'.[24] Indeed, Mary struggled when it came to live performance. Pollnitz tells the painful story of a meeting between Mary and John Knox in 1561. In the words of the English ambassador to Scotland, Thomas Randolph: 'Mary got few words in before the reformer "knocked so hashelye upon her harte that he made her weepe"'.[25] To be sure, 'many sixteenth-century monarchs would have found themselves confounded by a subject as arrogant as Knox, regardless of their sex or education', Pollnitz points out. Nonetheless, Mary, Queen of Scots struggled to reason extempore in public when faced with less daunting opponents.[26] Even the formidably capable Elizabeth I (1533–1603) did not have the same level of tutoring lavished on her brother. It is unlikely she started to study Latin before the middle of 1544, and while we can see Edward 'climbing the ladder of the *Progymnasmata* swiftly', her juvenile writings reveal that she 'stuck to writing familial letters' and translating 'prayers and devotional texts'.[27]

These limitations would have been true also of Grey's education, even though she was far more advanced as a multilingual humanist, certainly than Mary, Queen of Scots.[28]

[21] Moncrief and McPherson, '"Shall I teach you to know?"', 2; see also Norma McMullen, 'The Education of English Gentlewomen 1540–1640', *History of Education*, 6 (1977), 87–101, 95.

[22] On Edward VI's exercises (*chreia* and the declarative deliberation), see Aysha Pollnitz, *Princely Education in Early Modern Britain* (Cambridge, 2015), 154–6. On Edward VI and for an introduction to Aphthonius' *Progymnasmata*, 'a graded sequence of fourteen exercises in composition', see Peter Mack, *Elizabethan Rhetoric: Theory and Practice* (Cambridge, 2002), 26–31.

[23] Pollnitz, *Princely Education*, 201.

[24] Pollnitz, *Princely Education*, 213.

[25] Pollnitz, *Princely Education*, 215. British Library, Cotton MS Caligula B X, fol. 160r.

[26] Pollnitz, *Princely Education*, 216.

[27] Pollnitz, *Princely Education*, 242–3.

[28] Pollnitz, *Princely Education*, 219.

Grey was competent in several languages: Greek, Hebrew, Chaldaic, Arabic, French, and Italian. Michelangelo Florio, the author of the first history of Jane Grey (1607), claims to have taught her Italian and Latin, and he dedicated his *Regole de la lingua thoscana* to her.[29] We know she was a fluent reader of ancient Greek because Roger Ascham tells us so in *The Scholemaster* (1570). When visiting Bradgate Park in 1550, he discovered the thirteen-year-old Grey 'in her Chamber'—a semi-private space, not a schoolroom—'readinge *Phaedon Platonis* in Greeke, and that with as moch delite, as som gentleman wold read a merie tale in *Bocase* [Boccaccio]'. For Ascham, Grey exemplifies the good effects of a gentle (male) schoolmaster, who is able to instil a love of learning. When asked why she was not outside hunting in the grounds with her family, she supposedly responded: 'I wisse, all their sporte in the Parke is but a shadoe to that pleasure, that I find in *Plato*'. Grey tells Ascham she prefers her schoolmaster's company to that of her 'sharpe and severe Parentes', who threaten her 'with pinches, nippes, and bobbes, and other waies'.[30] Her gentle schoolmaster was John Aylmer (1520/21–1594), whose studies at Cambridge University had been subsidised by Henry Grey. Aylmer would become the Bishop of London lampooned for his conservative tendencies by Puritan Martin Marprelate, who renamed him 'mar-elme',[31] but in the late 1540s he was 'a yong man singularly well learned both in the latine and greke tonge', and a committed reformer. Under his guidance, Grey wrote letters in Latin to Bullinger between 1551 and 1553, three of which survive. They reveal her ability to write Latin fluently, her desire to study Hebrew, and her characterisation of her relationship with Bullinger as that of a student indebted to a wise master, comparing herself to, among others, the mother of the Roman Emperor Alexander Severus, who was taught Christian doctrine by Origen.[32]

As her cameo in *The Scholemaster* suggests—and as Ascham would have us believe—Grey was educated in pious contemplation, not rhetorical debate. Indeed, Plato's *Phaedo* is an interesting choice for Ascham to choose to spotlight. It is evidence of her proficiency in ancient Greek, the language that Erasmus studied midlife so he could translate the Bible into Latin, but it is also used here as evidence of her (Christian) modesty: *Phaedo* is a philosophical dialogue on the immortality of the soul. Even the way she is discovered reading this work is revealing. We might compare the vignette of Jane's reading alone in her chamber with the homosociality Ascham commends when he recalls reading aloud with his student and bedfellow, John Whitney: 'I read unto him

[29] Carla Rossi, *Italus ore, Anglus pectore: studi su John Florio*, vol. I (London, 2018), 67–8. See also Michelangelo Florio, *Historia de la vita e de la morte de l'illustriss. Signora Giovanna Graia* (Middelburg, 1607).

[30] Roger Ascham, *The Scholemaster* (London, 1570), sigs. E3v–E4r.

[31] Martin Marprelate (pseud.), *Oh read over D. John Bridges, for it is worthy worke: Or an epitome of the fyrste booke, of that right worshipfull volume, written against the puritanes, in the defence of the noble cleargie, by as worshipfull a prieste, John Bridges, presbyter, priest or elder, doctor of Divillitie, and Deane of Sarum* [The Epistle] (East Molesey, 1588), 20–1. See Brett Usher, 'Aylmer, John', *ODNB*, citing Thomas Becon, *The Jewel of Joye* (London, 1550), sig. D2v.

[32] Nicholas Harris Nicolas, *The Literary Remains of Lady Jane Grey: With a Memoir of Her Life* (London, 1825), 1–21.

Tullie de Amicitia, which he did everie day twise translate, out of Latin into English, and out of English into Latin agayne' (*Scholemaster*, sig. K4v).

Yet Grey, like other elite women, did not only benefit from the oversight of male schoolmasters. In 1547, the ten-year-old Jane was made a ward of Thomas Seymour, who had married Katherine Parr, Henry VIII's widow, on the promise that Seymour would engineer a marriage with Edward VI; she stayed in this household for eighteen months, until the death of Parr in 1548.[33] Her closeness to Parr is clear: Grey was the chief mourner at her funeral, and the prayer book now known as 'Lady Jane Grey's Prayer Book' which Grey took to the scaffold, was originally Parr's. It was likely gifted to her by Parr on her deathbed, when she 'lay dying of puerperal fever after giving birth to her only child, a daughter, Mary'.[34] The connection with Parr is significant. Parr created an alternative humanist schoolroom in which the vernacular Bible was a key reading text.[35] In the absence of anything like the resources we have to tell the story of Edward VI's education—and the obvious fact we cannot hear Parr and her circle reading Scripture aloud—I am obliged to imagine a different scenario based on what we know about shared Bible reading involving women: that it took place out loud, that it was accompanied by discussion and exposition, and that, certainly later in the century, it was an extension of auditing in church.[36]

A circle of this kind would help to explain Parr's involvement in the translation of one of the most important books of the English Reformation after the Bible itself: Erasmus' *Paraphrases in Novum Testamentum*, a work that would come to be seen as '"required reading" for every English church'.[37] Parr rewarded the printers; she employed its editor and one of its translators, Nicholas Udall; she persuaded the Princess Mary to translate the paraphrase of the Gospel of John, and she may herself have translated the paraphrase of the Gospel of Matthew.[38] The aim of this work, Udall explains, is to make the

33 Plowden, 'Grey, Lady Jane'.

34 British Library, Harley MS 2342. The prayer book originally belonged to Katherine Parr. See Janel Mueller, 'Prospecting for Common Ground in Devotion: Queen Katherine Parr's Personal Prayer Book', in Micheline White (ed.), *English Women, Religion, and Textual Production, 1500–1625* (Burlington, VT, 2011), 127–46, 127.

35 Elizabeth Mazzola, 'Schooling Shrews and Grooming Queens in the Tudor Classroom', *Critical Survey*, 22 (2010), 1–25, 15–18.

36 See Lady Margaret Hoby, in Joanna Moody (ed.), *The Private Life of an Elizabethan Lady: The Diary of Lady Margaret Hoby 1599–1605* (Stroud, 1998).

37 Desiderius Erasmus, in Nicholas Udall (trans. and ed.), *The First Tome or Volume of the Paraphrase of Erasmus Upon the Newe Testament* (London, 1548). On Parr see Patricia Pender, 'Dispensing Quails, Mincemeat, Leaven: Katherine Parr's Patronage of the *Paraphrases* of Erasmus', in Patricia Pender and Rosalind Smith (eds), *Material Cultures of Early Modern Women's Writing* (Basingstoke, 2014), 36–54. On the translation see John N. King, *English Reformation Literature: The Tudor Origins of the Protestant Tradition* (Princeton, NJ, 1982). 'According to [Nicholas] Udall', King writes, 'paraphrase embodies [Thomas] Cranmer's program of Bible reading as a means of lay education': '"a plain settyng forth of a texte or sentence open, clere, plain, and familiar, whiche otherwyse should perchaunce seem bare, unfruictefull, hard straunge, rough, obscure, and derke to be understanded of any that wer […] unlearned"', 130–1, citing Erasmus, in Udall (trans. and ed.), *Paraphrase*, sig. B7r.

38 Pender, 'Katherine Parr's Patronage', 40.

gospels 'open, clere, plain, & familiar' so they are understood by everyone, including any who are 'unlearned or but meanly entred' (*Paraphrase*, sig. A1r). I admit that the kind of reading I am imagining would not have offered a formal education that could rival that of Edward VI, and yet it shares some elements *if* we understand that the art of rhetoric simply describes effects that work in everyday persuasive practice. Recognising this creates a space for female voices. Girls in early modern England who were denied access to the all-male schoolroom were still able to observe and study these effects by auditing in church, and by reading and conversing at home. Girls did not practise the formal exercises outlined in *Progymnasmata*, whether *chreia* or, of more relevance here, *ethopoeia*, 'a certaine Oracion made by voice, and lamentable imitacion, upon the state of any one',[39] and its sub-genres, *eidolopoeia*, when we speak in the voice of a dead person; *prosopopoeia* (impersonation) when the character we speak through is entirely invented; and *ethopoeia* (again), when we create a character for a known person.[40] But they would have read and heard examples; sometimes they performed them out loud; sometimes they wrote them.[41] Indeed, *ethopoeia*, or *prosopopoeia* as we know this exercise now, is both a formal exercise and something that happens anyway 'when readers perform the voices that writers have created'.[42] Our examples of *ethopoeia* are usually drawn from the all-male schoolroom, and here I give two examples that show how women's voices and emotions were constructed (and why we might want to find alternatives created by or attributed to living women). But I also want to argue that reading the voices of the Bible is *ethopoeia*, and so too is reading the *Paraphrases*, which brings tone and emotion to an often plain and cryptic text, putting God's word in the mouths and ears of ordinary men and women.

ETHOPOEIA: THE VOICE OF LADY JANE GREY

I pause over one type of *ethopoeia*—animating the voices of Scripture—because it gives us a different, often 'male', speaking part for women to the ones with which we are already familiar from the male grammar schoolroom, which have provided a dominant model for female-inflected speech, especially in drama, and whose models were usually classical rather than biblical. Though they were not usually physically present, the voices of women were heard—squeaked, if you listen to Shakespeare's Cleopatra—by young schoolboys, and their emotions impersonated or, depending on your point of

[39] Richard Rainolde, *A Booke Called the Foundacion of Rhetorike* (London, 1563), sigs. N1r–N2r; Aphthonius, *Progymnasmata* (London, 1572), sigs. Y8v–2A7v.

[40] Ibid. See also George A. Kennedy, *Progymnasmata: Greek Textbooks of Prose Composition and Rhetoric* (Atlanta, 2003), 115.

[41] For a recent study of female-authored complaint, see Sarah C. E. Ross and Rosalind Smith (eds), *Early Modern Women's Complaint: Gender, Form, and Politics* (Cham: Palgrave Macmillan, 2020).

[42] See Gavin Alexander, 'Prosopopoeia: The Speaking Figure', in Sylvia Adamson, Gavin Alexander, and Katrin Ettenhuber (eds), *Renaissance Figures of Speech* (Cambridge, 2007), 97–112, 109.

view, given imaginative expression.[43] Female voices mattered a great deal in the male schoolroom because their impersonation enabled boys to express extraordinary loss and suffering beyond their experience: 'O me miseram! … O me infelicem!', laments Hecuba, the vanquished Queen of Troy, 'if only I had never married, nor born so many children for such great misfortune'.[44]

Undoubtedly, this schoolroom exercise has given us some remarkable female characters who speak to the experience of women confronted with terrifying violence on their person. Take Shakespeare's *Rape of Lucrece* for example. Raped by Tarquin, and struggling to understand the violence committed against her, Lucrece looks upon a tapestry depicting the scene of the destruction of Troy, including the grief of Hecuba, and she uses this moment both to berate the artist who has given Hecuba 'so much grief and not a tongue' because he has chosen to anatomise 'beauty's wreck' instead, and to right this wrong.[45] 'Poor instrument', she declares, referring to Hecuba's tongue, before she promises to do what Hecuba cannot: 'I'll tune thy woes with my lamenting tongue' (1465).

The Rape of Lucrece is a product of Shakespeare's grammar-school education, and Lucrece does what any schoolboy would do when asked to give expression to grief: she turns to the past and it is Hecuba she chooses to speak through. She uses her tongue to identify with the victims of Greek brutality thereby to express her own grief: 'She lends them words, and she their looks doth borrow'.[46] In so doing, she temporarily overcomes the difficulties of her own situation both as a woman traumatised by her experience, and as a female speaker, whose eloquence is 'modest', and audibly defined, as Huw Griffiths suggests, by the figure of impossibility, *adynaton*: the impossibility of expressing her feelings in words.[47] Indeed, Lucrece's speech is marked by failure from the beginning: first, the failure to dissuade Tarquin, then the failure to find words to express her pain. Confronting Tarquin at the start: 'She puts the period often from his place, / And midst the sentence so her accent breaks, / That twice she doth begin ere once she speaks' (565–567). That is, we are to imagine her initial attempt to speak as halting and hesitant. Later, traumatised, she cannot find the words to describe what has happened since, like Hecuba, 'more is felt than one hath power to tell' (1288).

[43] William Shakespeare, *The Tragedy of Antony and Cleopatra*, in Stanley Wells et al. (eds), *The Oxford Shakespeare: The Complete Works*, 2nd edn (Oxford, 2005), 5.2.216.

[44] Reinhard Lorich, *Aphthonii progymnasmata* (Cambridge, 1631), 271–2: 'Utinam nunquam viro nupsissem, nec in magnam calamitatem tot liberos peperissem'.

[45] Shakespeare, 'The Rape of Lucrece', in Wells et al. (eds), *The Oxford Shakespeare*, 1463, 1451.

[46] Lynn Enterline, *Shakespeare's Schoolroom: Rhetoric, Discipline, Emotion* (Philadelphia, PA, 2012), 126.

[47] Huw Griffiths, 'Letter-Writing Lucrece: Shakespeare in the 1590s', in Jennifer Richards and Alison Thorne (eds), *Rhetoric, Women and Politics in Early Modern England* (London, 2007), 93. For a nuanced defence of female silence see Christina Luckyj, *'A Moving Rhetoricke': Gender and Silence in Early Modern England* (Manchester, 2002), esp. 164–74, which contrasts male reanimations and appropriations of mute Philomela with the resistance offered by female authors.

This tradition of schoolroom *ethopoeia* gives us one script for the voice of Grey: Drayton's impersonation of her voice in *Englands Heroicall Epistles* (1597). In this case Grey's script is an imagined semi-public performance: a letter to her husband, written while they were imprisoned in the Tower of London, awaiting execution. Drayton was sympathetic to the education of women. He likely served as tutor to one of the female dedicatees of his *Epistles*, Elizabeth Tanfield, who grew up to become the first woman to publish a play in print, Elizabeth Cary.[48] But despite this, and his willingness to represent women as eloquent interlocutors, they struggle to perform.[49] Drayton may exonerate Lady Jane Grey of treason, but he does so by taking away her agency in three rather important ways. Firstly, he (rightly) makes clear in his preface that the fault lies not with Grey and her husband, but with their 'ambitious Fathers', who attempted 'to bring the Crowne unto theyr Children, and to dispossesse the Princesse Mary, eldest daughter of King Henry the eyght, heire to King Edward her Brother'.[50] Secondly, he gives Grey a prophetic voice, using her as the vehicle to predict the triumph of the Reformation, as the reign of Catholic Mary is superseded by that of Elizabeth I who 'Roote[s] out the dregs Idolatry hath sowne' (*Heroicall Epistles*, sig. L1v). Thirdly, he gives Grey a tragic voice much like that of Shakespeare's Lucrece: halting, uncertain, overwhelmed.

Drayton's epistle is striking, I suggest, not so much because of what Lady Jane Grey says so much as how she says it, certainly initially. At the start, we find her in the Tower, visited by her 'Keeper', who arrives with a message—a greeting—from her husband. When she tries to return this, however, she is immediately overwhelmed with grief, and speech fails her: 'Grief stops my words,' she writes. Then, at the very point at which she is finally able to speak, that is, when 'through [her] lips [her] hart thrusts forth', the 'amaz'd' keeper hastes away. Grey's words are not carried out of the cell, then, but 'Drive[n] backe'. They go nowhere, and they reach no one because they are 'drownd' out by the 'dolefull sound' of the prison door closing. When this sound is 'some-what hush'd', her words do sound but to no effect: 'the eccho doth record, / And twice or thrice reiterats my word' (*Heroicall Epistles*, sigs. K6v–K7r). Danielle Clarke has helpfully identified a tradition that represents female speech as 'self-cancelling', inspired by the example of Ovid's Echo, 'the nymph punished by Juno for her protection of Jove through talk', who provides a model for imitation in the schoolroom. Drayton offers a literal example of a woman's speech as echo.[51] Grey's struggle does not end here, though. Words are replaced with sighs, but even these barely escape because she is overwhelmed with emotion: 'Thus strive my sighes, with teares ere they begin, / And breaking out, againe sighes drive them in' (sig. K7r). And spoken words become sighs, while written words become blotches on a page damp with tears. This is another example of *adynaton*: Grey communicates the

[48] On this possibility see Bernard H. Newdigate, *Michael Drayton and His Circle* (Oxford, 1941), 77.

[49] Alison Thorne, '"Large Complaints in Little Papers": Negotiating Ovidian Genealogies of Complaint in Drayton's *Englands Heroicall Epistles*', *Renaissance Studies*, 22 (2008), 368–84.

[50] Michael Drayton, *Englands Heroicall Epistles* (London, 1597), sig. K6v. See also sigs. L1v–L2r.

[51] Danielle Clarke, 'Speaking Women: Rhetoric and the Construction of Female Talk', in Richards and Thorne (eds), *Rhetoric, Women and Politics*, 70–88, 77.

impossibility of communicating. We might contrast Grey's linguistic struggle with the ease with which her husband speaks in his answer letter, where he finds words to express his grief, and the grace—and directness—with which he does so: 'Swan-like I sing'; 'For if I speake, and would complaine my wrong, / Straightwayes thy name doth come into my tongue' (sigs. L2v–L3r).

We might also recall the example of Mary, Queen of Scots, who was left tongue-tied and weeping when John Knox debated with her. Yet, the historical Lady Jane Grey is very different from the Queen of Scots, while the writing attributed to her in 1554 bears no relation whatsoever to the voice created by Drayton. In 1554, she speaks boldly, not haltingly, and she is sharp and direct rather than grief-stricken, secure in her knowledge of Scripture. She is rather more like the reformist preachers with whom she is associated in Foxe's *Actes and Monuments* than Drayton's tragic lady: Bishops Cranmer, Ridley, and Latimer as well as John Rogers and John Bradford. Grey has not created an original literary voice, to be sure. As noted above, her epistle to the recusant John Harding is a collocation of sentences quoted or paraphrased from Coverdale's Bible. But that is the point. Grey writes—*and* speaks (since epistles are oral writings)—through Christ to her addressees. It is clear from the start of this epistle why she does this. 'Wherfore hast thou taken upon the[e], the testament of the lord in thi mouth?', she asks Harding, only to yield 'thi body to the fire, and blodi handes of cruel tirauntes' (*Epistle*, sig. A2v). In short, he has capitulated to the Catholic regime of Mary I. In this epistle Grey reminds Harding of what he already knows since he used to be 'a publicke professour of [God's] name' (sig. A3r). She asks questions, presuming on his knowledge of Scripture: 'What saith the prophet Barucke [Baruch], wher he reciteth the epistel of Jeremi, written to the captive Jewes?'. Or she jogs his memory: 'These, & such lyke words, speaketh Jeremy unto them, wherby he provoth them but vain thinges, and no gods' (sig. A4r–v). Scripture, Grey repeatedly reminds Harding, is alive with voices speaking, reciting, saying the word of God. Indeed, Scripture incites us to *hear* and also to *repeat* the words of God and his prophets: 'Heare what Esay saith: Feare not the cursse of men, be not afraid of theyr blasphemies & revylynges . . . I am the Lord thy God . . . I shal put my word in thy mouth' (sigs. A7v–A8r). This is why she speaks Scripture to him. 'Doest thou not remember the saying of David a notable king', she asks:

> which teacheth thee a myserable wretche, in hys. ciiii. Psalme, wher he sayth: When thou takest away thy spirite (O Lorde) from men, they dye, and ar turned againe to their dust, but when thou lettest thy breath go fourth, they shalbe made, & thou shalt renew the face of the earth?[52]

[52] Grey, *Epistle*, sig. A5v. See Coverdale's translation of Psalm 103 [104]: 'thou shalt take awaye their sprete, and they shall dye, and returne agayne into theyr dust./ Sende out thy sprete, and they shalbe created, and thou shalt renue the face of the erthe' ('auferes spiritum eorum, & deficient, et in pulverem suum revertentur / Smitte spiritum tuum, et creabuntur: et renovabis faciem terre'), in Miles Coverdale (trans.), *The Psalter or Boke of Psalmes Both in Latyn and Englyshe* (London, 1540), sig. M1r.

Grey here recalls the two different meanings of breath ('spirit'): on the one hand, the breath of life, which God can take away; on the other, the breath we use to express our love for God. 'I wyll synge unto the Lorde in my lyfe', this psalm concludes in Coverdale's translation, bringing these two meanings together, especially when they are said or sung aloud: 'I wyll prayse my God, aslonge as I have my beynge' (*Psalter or Boke of Psalmes*, sig. M1r).

Grey speaks with even more directness in the catechism that follows: 'A Certayne Communycation'. John Feckenham, Abbott of Westminster, is the catechist, and Grey is his catechumen or student. His lesson, though, does not go according to plan. He starts well enough with a simple question: 'What thing is required in a Christian?' (*Epistle*, sig. B2v). But Grey's firm responses to this and other questions make clear she is an unwilling student. On the contrary, she communicates her reformed beliefs clearly, asserting that 'faith (as S. Paule saith) *only* justifieth' (emphasis mine) and that the bread and wine of the Communion are merely bread and wine, not the transubstantiated body of Christ (sig. B2v). As she explains to Feckenham: 'I receyve the benefites that cam bi breaking of his bodi, & bi the sheddyng of his bloud on the crosse for mi sins' (sig. B3v). With such clear-sighted responses, and with Grey's recourse to Scripture, the identity of master and scholar begin to blur. 'By what scripture find you that?', she asks early on, to which Feckenham shiftily replies: 'well, we will talke therof hereafter' (sig. B3r). By mid-point, the reversal is complete: 'But I pray you answer me to thys one question', asks Jane, now rather insistently, 'wher was Christ when he sayd: Take, eate, this is my body?' (sig. B4r–v).

To be sure, these words may not be solely Grey's given that her work was printed posthumously. As noted earlier, Horton hears echoes of her reformist male contemporaries, as well as of Erasmus. But I hope I have given enough of a context to explain why we should not take agency away from Grey: she had the kind of education and reading experience that would have enabled her to speak and write and *teach* through Scripture. Recognising the likelihood that these are collaborative writings, and the difficulty of defining how much of the text is Grey's, does, though, prompt a new question: why was it so important that this powerful voice should belong to her? The same question is appropriate for Anne Askew, a woman of the middling sort whose words were edited by Bale. The answer I gave in *Voices and Books* stands here too: she represents the right of a woman—and, arguably, of all Christians—to speak and embody Scripture.[53] But we can add further to this answer, noting the creation of an educational context in the early English Reformation in the mid-century in which women's voices could be heard, and carry weight. Different books of the Bible were translated into English in the 1520s and 1530s, while the first complete English Bible, the 'Coverdale Bible', was printed in 1535, followed by the Taverner Bible in 1539, bringing the Word of God to ordinary men and women.[54] In the following decade, Katherine Parr's *Prayers and Meditations*

[53] Richards, *Voices and Books*, 198.

[54] For discussion of the Bibles available in the first half of the sixteenth century, and the Bible Askew likely read in Lincoln Cathedral, see John N. King, 'How Anne Askew Read the Bible', *Reformation*, 25 (2020), 47–68.

(1545), written for her household servants, was printed; this was shortly followed by Askew's writings (1546 and 1547), then Parr's *The Lamentation of a Synner* (1547).[55] A year later, in 1548, *The First Tome or Volume of the Paraphrase of Erasmus* was printed, thanks to Parr's patronage, while Thomas Chaloner's translation of Erasmus' *Moriae Encomium*, in which Scripture is delivered (and explained) in the voice of a literate woman, was printed in 1549, the same year as *The Book of Common Prayer*, the liturgy for the Reformed Church read in English to ordinary men, women, and children. Grey's writings, printed at the start of the Marian regime, belong to this earlier moment in the English Reformation when the voices of women carried the promise of more to come.

FURTHER READING

Brayman Hackel, Heidi. *Reading Material in Early Modern England: Print, Gender and Literacy*. Cambridge, 2005.

Horton, Louise. 'The Clerics and the Learned Lady: Intertextuality in the Religious Writings of Lady Jane Grey'. In Patricia Pender (ed.), *Gender, Authorship, and Early Modern Women's Collaboration*. London, 2017, 149–74.

Molekamp, Femke. *Women and the Bible in Early Modern England: Religious Reading and Writing*. Oxford, 2013.

Moncrief, Kathryn M. and Kathryn R. McPherson (eds). *Performing Pedagogy in Early Modern England: Gender, Instruction, and Performance*. Farnham and Burlington, VT, 2011.

Pender, Patricia. 'Dispensing Quails, Mincemeat, Leaven: Katherine Parr's Patronage of the *Paraphrases* of Erasmus'. In Patricia Pender and Rosalind Smith (eds), *Material Cultures of Early Modern Women's Writing*. Basingstoke, 2014, 36–54.

Pollnitz, Aysha. *Princely Education in Early Modern Britain*. Cambridge, 2015.

Snook, Edith. 'Jane Grey, "Manful" Combat, and the Female Reader in Early Modern England', *Renaissance and Reformation / Renaissance et Réforme*, 32.1 (2009), 47–81.

White, Micheline. 'Katherine Parr, Henry VIII, and Royal Literary Collaboration'. In Patricia Pender (ed.), *Gender, Authorship, and Early Modern Women's Collaboration*. London, 2017, 23–46.

[55] On the importance of this educational context see Mazzola, 'Schooling Shrews'. On Parr's significant religious writing see especially Micheline White, 'The Psalms, War, and Royal Iconography: Katherine Parr's *Psalms or Prayers* (1544) and Henry VIII as David', *Renaissance Studies*, 29 (2015), 554–75 and 'Katherine Parr, Henry VIII, and Royal Literary Collaboration', in Pender (ed.), *Gender, Authorship*, 23–46.

CHAPTER 4

LATIN AND GREEK

JANE STEVENSON

PERHAPS the most interesting thing about early modern Englishwomen's use of Latin and Greek is how much it changes over time. The idea that these languages, once their primary purpose had become the definition of the identity of a male cultural elite, should also be studied by women has fluctuated remarkably over the centuries (as, of course, has the use of Latin more generally).[1] There were, for example, highly sophisticated and literary women active in the twelfth century, most of whom were nuns or noblewomen, such as Adela of Blois, Countess of Champagne.[2] For twelfth-century noblewomen such as Adela, Latin studies were linked with training in public speaking and the exercise of authority.

However, a variety of factors, probably including the rise of the universities (for men only), increasingly elaborate administrative structures which made it less necessary for women aristocrats to deputise for their husbands, and an increasing availability of vernacular literature, meant that thirteenth- to fifteenth-century women were almost entirely excluded from the study of classical languages. Of course, women who read romances such as William Caxton's *Recuyell of the Historyes of Troye* (presented to Margaret of York) or John Lydgate's *Troy Book* might well be familiar with stories, themes, tropes, and characters originating in the classical tradition.

[1] Edmund Leach, *Culture and Nature, or La Femme Sauvage* [*The Stevenson Lecture*] (London, 1968), 7. On the varying fortunes of Latin, see Françoise Waquet, in John Howe (trans.), *Latin, or the Empire of a Sign from the Sixteenth to Twentieth Centuries* (London and New York, 2001).

[2] Gerald A. Bond, *The Loving Subject: Desire, Eloquence and Power in Romanesque France* (Philadelphia, PA, 1995), 129–57.

THE RISE OF HUMANISM

The idea that women should study Latin and Greek was revived, like much else, in fifteenth-century Italy. Once more, there were women who had a public, political role. For example, Bianca Maria Visconti, only daughter of the Duke of Milan, was humanistically educated. She married the condottiere Francesco Sforza in 1441, aged sixteen, when her talents for both diplomacy and administration were already evident.[3] They were very much joint rulers, as, in the next generation, were Battista Sforza (her niece by marriage) and Battista's husband, Federico da Montefeltro of Urbino.

This new Renaissance ideal of the learned princess seems to have reached England early in the sixteenth century. Due to the essentially transnational nature of the Latin language, new ideas about elite women's education could easily spread from country to country. Its arrival in England is due perhaps to the influence of Catherine of Aragon, who had been taught by the leading humanists Antonio and Alessandro Geraldini. As an adult, she was recognised as a skilful diplomat versed in languages and knowledgeable in affairs of state. In the hiatus between the end of her marriage to Prince Arthur and her marriage to his younger brother Henry, her father King Ferdinand gave her formal credentials as a diplomat, in parallel with the Spanish ambassador. She was provided with a cipher and learned both to decipher Ferdinand's letters, and, eventually, to encipher her replies (see this volume, Chapter 37, Nadine Akkerman, 'Women's Letters and Cryptological Coteries').[4] She was also made governor of the realm and captain-general during Henry's absence on campaign in France between 30 June and 21 October 1513, and she took it for granted that her daughter Mary should receive a humanist education. She commissioned a Spanish humanist, Juan Luis Vives, to write *De Institutione Feminae Christianae*, a treatise on the education of girls, for her daughter, and it is perhaps indicative of this cultural change that Queen Catherine's sister-in-law, the other Mary Tudor, began learning Latin as an adult in the 1520s.

Similarly, in the French and Hapsburg courts of the early sixteenth century, some royal ladies acted both as regents and as diplomats, and were educated to perform these functions. Anne de Beaujeu, who herself acted as regent for her brother Charles VIII, educated a whole group of girls including Marguerite of Hungary, Louise of Savoy, and her own daughter, Suzanne de Bourbon. She based their education on the Church Fathers and Plato, who was studied together with Boethius' commentaries.[5] The peace treaty between François I and Emperor Charles V signed in Cambrai on 3 August 1529

[3] Daniela Pizzagalli, *Tra due dinastie. Bianca Maria Visconti e il ducato di Milano* (Milan, 1988). See Margaret L. King and Alfred Rabil (trans.), *Her Immaculate Hand* (Asheville, NC, 1997), 39–41, 44–6, for Latin orations in praise of Bianca Maria by Costanza Varana and Ippolita Sforza (Bianca Maria's own daughter).

[4] G. A. Bergenroth (ed.), *Calendar of State Papers, Spain* (London, 1862), 405, 412, 413, 426.

[5] Eliane Viennot and T. Clavier (eds), *Anne de France: Enseignements à sa fille, suivis de l'Histoire du siège de Brest* (Saint-Etiennee, 2007).

was brokered by Louise of Savoy, mother of François I, and Margaret of Austria, aunt of Charles V, and was consequently known as 'La Paix des Dames'.

Later in the century, Catherine de Clermont, Duchesse de Retz, was among the intellectual leaders of the court of Henri III.[6] A poem addressed to her by Marie de Romieu of Viviers stresses that 'Greek is familiar to you, and Latin and the Italian language are ordinary'.[7] When a group of Eastern European notables came to Paris in 1573 to offer the crown of Poland to Henri III, it was the Duchesse who played the extremely responsible role of official interpreter and she also gave a Latin oration. Thus, through the sixteenth century, a full humanist education continued to be a useful asset for a female aristocrat who wanted to play a part in the public life of a court. In England, apart from Elizabeth herself, whose extensive education was much publicised, the most conspicuous woman intellectual was Mildred Cecil, née Cooke, wife of Lord Burghley, seconded by her sister Anne, who had married Sir Nicholas Bacon.

The idea that women who had been educated like men might assume roles normally assigned to men, or act as adjuncts to men, continued to develop. Johann Sturm, Strasbourg theologian and humanist, wrote to Francis Walsingham in 1577:

> In my sleep I wished that the Lord Treasurer [Lord Burghley] was in Denmark with his wife, or someone else of the same rank, whose wife could speak Latin; and that this person should bring from our Queen presents to the King of Denmark's wife, and messages to himself, as good neighbours should.[8]

Sturm thus argues that there was a special role for women in the diplomatic process, advancing policy through a parallel mission to the female members of the court.[9] Women did sometimes go abroad. Lady Burghley's third sister Elizabeth, who was also fluent in Latin and Greek, had accompanied her husband Thomas Hoby when he was sent to Paris as ambassador, and perhaps intended to play some part in public life at the court of Charles IX, interacting with women such as the king's sister Marguerite de Valois, an acknowledged scholar and literary patroness.[10] In the event, the embassy was cut short by Thomas Hoby's death after only four months so we cannot know how her role would have developed.

To sum up, sixteenth-century women's principal reason for studying Latin was to take part in public life. The capacity to speak Latin fluently and correctly was more important than an ability to write it, in England as elsewhere. Europe-wide, there is a very great deal more evidence for women speaking Latin than writing in it, a complete reversal of

[6] Frances Yates, *The French Academies of the Sixteenth Century* (London, 1947), 105.

[7] 'le grec t'est familier ... le latin t'est commun et la langue italique'; Marie de Romieu, *Les Premiers oeuvres poetiques de M. Damoiselle Marie de Romieu, Vivaroise* (Paris, 1581), 11.

[8] Gemma Allen, *The Cooke Sisters: Education, Piety and Politics in Early Modern England* (Manchester, 2013), 134.

[9] Allen, 134–5.

[10] C. J. Blaisdell, 'Marguerite de Navarre and Her Circle (1492–1549)', in Jean R. Brink (ed.), *Female Scholars: A Tradition of Learned Women before 1800* (Montréal, 1980), 36–53.

the pattern of Latin language use today.[11] A few women translated from Latin or Greek, or wrote Latin verse, but no Englishwoman was a philologist, editor, or grammarian, or wrote an original work in Latin prose. Their use of Latin was therefore quite different from that of a university-trained scholar.

GREEK

Very few Englishwomen studied Greek. While Latin served a variety of useful purposes, women only studied Greek as an aid to the serious study of Christian writers or of medicine. Lady Jane Fitzalan (1536–1576) translated Isocrates' 'Evagoras' from Greek to Latin and translated Euripides' *Iphigeneia* into English. These were New Year's gifts to her father. In the Euripides, she claims to translate from the Greek but evidently also made use of Erasmus' Latin translation, since her text includes a translation of Erasmus' Latin *argumentum*.[12] She is unusual in confining her attention to classical authors: the other early modern Englishwomen who studied Greek read or translated Christian writers. (For women's translations, see this volume, Chapter 27, Brenda Hosington, '"Mistresses of Tongues"'.) Lady Anne Conway, associated with the Cambridge Platonists, is a seventeenth-century exception to this generalisation.[13]

Probably the most famous women humanists in England were the daughters of Sir Thomas More. Margaret More's understanding of Greek was sophisticated enough for her to be able to emend a corrupt passage in the Greek writer Cyprian of Alexandria.[14] She attempted to engage Roger Ascham as a tutor for her own children and, though she was not successful, her daughter Mary Roper, later Clarke, also studied Greek.[15] John Harpsfield asserted that Roper was:

> well experted in the latine and greeke tonges; she hath very hansomely and learnedly translated out of the greeke into the englishe all the ecclesiasticall storye of Eusebius, with Socrates, Theodoretus, Sozomenus and Euagrius, albeit of modestie she suppresseth it, and keepeth it from the print.[16]

[11] Jane Stevenson, 'Women's Education', in Philip Ford, Jan Bloemendal, and Charles Fantazzi (eds), *Brill's Encyclopaedia of the Neo-Latin World*. (Leiden and Boston, 2014), 87–99, 94.

[12] For the text, see Diane Purkiss (ed.), *Three Tragedies by Renaissance Women* (London, 1998).

[13] See Marjorie Hope Nicolson and Sarah Hutton (eds), *The Conway Letters: The Correspondence of Anne, Viscountess Conway, Henry More, and Their Friends 1642–1684* (Oxford, 1992).

[14] Thomas Stapleton, in E. E. Reynolds (trans.), *The Life and Illustrious Martyrdom of Sir Thomas More* (London, 1967), 104 and n.

[15] Maria Dowling, *Humanism in the Age of Henry VIII* (London, 1986), 222.

[16] James McConica, *English Humanists and Reformation Politics under Henry VIII and Edward VI* (Oxford, 1968), 266.

However, she presented a manuscript volume to the future Queen Mary Tudor, with her Latin version of the first book of Eusebius' *Ecclesiastical History* and an English version of the first five books.[17] Thus, for both mother and daughter, the study of Greek was a gateway to Byzantine theologians, not classical philosophers.

Mildred Cecil's study of Greek was well known. Giles Lawrence, of Christ Church, Oxford, was her Greek tutor in her youth and claimed that she 'egalled if not overmatched' contemporary male Grecians.[18] Like the Catholic Mores, the Protestant Mildred Cecil's primary purpose in learning Greek was the study of theology. Her manuscript translation of a sermon on Deuteronomy 15.9 by St Basil the Great survives as British Library, MS Royal 17.B.xviii. It was made for Lady Somerset, who was her patron in the early years of her marriage and, like herself, a convinced Protestant. Her sister Anne, wife of Nicholas Bacon, also studied Greek theologians with attention.[19]

A short dedicatory poem in Greek, written by Cecil, survives in a presentation manuscript of the *Giardino cosmografico coltivato* by the Italian Protestant doctor Bartholo Sylva of Turin, made for Elizabeth I by a circle of Protestant activists.[20] She and Bathsua Makin are the only Renaissance Englishwomen known to the author of this chapter actually to have composed a short original text in ancient Greek.

The most practical reason for studying Greek was studying medicine, since Galen, who wrote in Greek, remained a primary medical authority. One early sixteenth-century woman who is known to have done so was the daughter of the immensely learned John Aylmer. In an encomium on her son, John Squire, we are told that:

> Dr Ailmer, tutor of Lady Jane Grey, who later became bishop of London, took one Adam Squire as his chaplain, Doctor of divinity and afterwards master of Balliol college. This Bishop [Aylmer] would say, that if the Hebrew bible were lost, he could supplie it, with the help of his two chapplains Dr Squier, and Dr Duport, both being exact linguists, well seene in that originall text. At last Dr Squire marryed Mris Judith, daughter to Bishop Ailmer, a rare scholler of that sex, furnished with the Greeke and Latine tongue and withall a very good physicion, not an empiricke, but grounded in theory, as well as expert in the practise, being able to deale with Galen as he wrot in his owne language.[21]

Judith Aylmer, Mildred Cecil, Mary Clarke, and Lady Lumley all flourished in the mid-sixteenth century. In subsequent generations, evidence for Englishwomen's study of Greek is scant. According to Thomas Heywood, a woman of the next generation, Theophila Berkeley (b. 1596), is said to have known Greek, but there is no evidence that she did anything with this knowledge:

17 London, British Library, MS Harley 1860.

18 Retha M. Warnicke, *Women of the English Renaissance and Reformation* (Westport, CT, 1987), 105.

19 Allen, 31–3.

20 Cambridge, Cambridge University Library MS Ii.5.37.

21 Los Angeles, William Andrews Clarke Memorial Library, MS L6815 M3 C734, fol. 181.

> The severall tongues in which you so excell
> Greek, Roman, French, Castillian, and with those,
> Tuscan, Teutonic, in all which you pose
> The forreigne linguist.[22]

She is one of a variety of Englishwomen who are said to have studied classical languages, but who have left no evidence of why they made the effort.

SEVENTEENTH CENTURY

Although Latinate women are a highly visible aspect of English court life up to the end of the sixteenth century, this is not true of the seventeenth. Amanda Shepherd has commented:

> humanist ideas about female education resulted in a flurry of exceptionally well-educated women, some of whom participated at least to a limited degree in public life. Nevertheless, this apparent revolution in education had no lasting impact. By the middle of the seventeenth century, there are no comparable examples of female educational excellence. Even the notorious Margaret Cavendish, Duchess of Newcastle, lacked any formal education.[23]

This is, in fact, a misunderstanding of the situation, brought about, in part, by the high visibility of the poorly educated Duchess of Newcastle, and by the assumption that if any women studied Latin and Greek, they would be at court and in public, as had been true in the sixteenth century. But the important contextualising fact is that in the sixteenth century, Latin was the spoken language of international diplomacy, and it was therefore necessary for women rulers and the ambitious to be able to speak it. But in the seventeenth century, French had taken over as the international *lingua franca*, a movement which began, naturally, at the French court. The deputation who offered the Polish throne to Henri III were astonished by how few people in the French court had adequate conversational Latin. In Stuart England, or seventeenth-century France, that would not have seemed surprising at all.

James I had no love for learned women; therefore, learning was not an avenue of advancement for a woman at his court. Notoriously, 'When a learned maid was presented to King James for an English rarity, because she could speake and rite pure Latine, Greeke and Hebrew, the King ask'd "But can shee spin?"'. This was almost certainly Bathsua Rainolds, who later married a courtier.[24] Though James' wife Anne of

[22] Thomas Heywood, *The Exemplary Lifes and Remarkable Acts of Nine the Most Worthy Women of the World* (London, 1640). Dedication.

[23] Amanda Shepherd, *Gender and Authority in Sixteenth-Century England* (Keele, 1994), 129.

[24] *The Commonplace Book of John Collet 1633*, in William J. Thoms (ed.) *Anecdotes and Traditions Illustrative of Early English History and Literature* (London, 1839), 125.

Denmark could both write and read Latin, she had no occasion to do so in public. The next queen of England, Henrietta Maria, the youngest child of Marie de Medici, was not classically educated. She brought a marked French influence to the English court, so, for those ambitious to play a part in court life, French was the most relevant language. Many seventeenth-century Englishwomen studied French, and read classical literature in English or French translation (see this volume, Chapter 31, Line Cottegnies, 'French Connections: English Women's Writing and *Préciosité*'). Similarly, in the court of James II, the Italians who came to England with his queen, Mary of Modena, brought translations of Greek and Latin poems with them, and encouraged English women to translate romances from French and Italian vernacular sources.[25] However, though humanist education had ceased to be the qualification for court life that it had been in the sixteenth century, Latin learning for women continued in quite different cultural contexts.

RECUSANTS

Sir Thomas More was not precisely a recusant: the Recusancy Acts were framed under Elizabeth in 1558, as an attempt to coerce Catholics into attending Anglican services. Recusant Catholicism as it developed was, just as much as Protestantism, a religion of books. With access to priestly instruction limited or non-existent, recusants turned to works such as Robert Southwell's *Short Rule of a Good Life* or Robert Person's *Christian Directory* for their religious instruction: these were printed in large numbers both by clandestine Catholic presses in England and by English Catholic presses in Belgium and Northern France.

Though it was possible to send Catholic boys to St Omer's, and some girls intended for a life in the world were educated in Continental convents, smuggling children abroad was extremely difficult. Additionally, parents had to reckon with not seeing them again for six years or more, a sacrifice not everyone was prepared to make. A number of devout Catholic families therefore educated their children at home. Since any girl who decided to become a nun needed to learn Latin, if she did not know it already, recusant women had a particular reason to study the language in childhood. For example, in the manor house of Braddocks, between Thaxted and Saffron Walden (Essex), Thomas and Jane Wiseman educated all eight of their children in Latin in the 1580s: 'the daughters as well as the sons were brought up to learning of the Latin tongue and Mr Wiseman, every Friday, would make an exhortation in Latin thereby to exercise them in that language as also to give them good instruction'.[26] The four daughters all became nuns: two were

[25] Carola Oman, *Mary of Modena* (London, 1962), 35–50.

[26] C. S. Durrant, *A Link between Flemish Mystics and English Martyrs* (London, 1925), 422.

Bridgettines in Portugal, and two were Augustinian canonesses in Louvain. The Louvain chronicle reports of one of them:

> In this year [1633] upon the 8th day of July died most blessedly our worthy Mother Prioress [Mary Wiseman]. She had her Latin tongue perfect, and hath left us many homilies and sermons of the holy fathers translated into English, which she did with great facility, whilst some small respite of health permitted her.[27]

Richard Woodcoke complains of the Catholics that 'every child and audacious woman amongst them presuming to speak Fathers and Doctors as if their idolatrous priests and familiars did speake in them', which suggests that significant numbers of Catholic women were serious readers—some, perhaps, in translation (see this volume, Chapter 33, Jaime Goodrich, 'Networked Authorship'). Tobie Matthew, for example, translated Augustine's *Confessions*, and Thomas Stapleton translated Bede's *Ecclesiastical History*, for recusant readers.[28]

Elizabeth Grymeston, who died in 1603, was another Latin-literate recusant. Her book *Miscellanea, Meditations, Memoratives* was a counselling tract for her son Bernye.[29] Though she was certainly far more interested in Christian than in classical texts, nonetheless, musing on fortune in the fourteenth of her 'Miscellanea', the examples which come to her mind are Troy, Hecuba, Alexander the Great, Caesar, and Xerxes. Quoting in Latin (apparently from memory, since her citations are not entirely accurate) from standard works on fortune, possibly via a handbook, she draws on Seneca's *Troades*, Ovid's *Epistolae ex Ponto* IV, Manilius' *Astronomica* IV.60, and Juvenal's X.185. She sometimes moves between English and Latin in the same sentence, writing, for instance, 'I must confine my selfe to the limits of an epistle, *Quae non debet implere sinistram manum*' ('which ought not to fill the left hand'), quoting Seneca. Similarly, the Catholic controversialist Jane Owen certainly read the Latin Bible, because she quotes it freely: 'Gods sacred Word assureth you, that you may buy Heauen with Good Workes: *Venite possidete paratum vobis regnum; Esurivi enim, et dedistis manducare*, &c. Matth. 25.'; 'It may be said of you, as was said of Cornelius the Centurion, Act. 10 *Elleemosinae vestrae commmoratae sunt in conspectu Dei*'.[30]

[27] Adam Hamilton (ed.), *The Chronicle of the English Augustine Canonesses Regular of the Lateran at St Monica's in Louvain, 1625–1644*, 2 vols (Edinburgh, 1906), vol. 2, 104.

[28] Richard Woodcoke, *Godly and Learned Answer to a Lewd and Unlearned Pamphlet* (London, 1608), sig. A3.

[29] Elizabeth Grymeston, *Miscellanea, Meditations, Memoratives* (London, 1604); repr. St Omer, 1620 and Antwerp, 1565, respectively.

[30] Jane Owen, *Antidote against Purgatory. Or Discourse, Wherein is Shewed that Good-workes, and Almes-deeds, Performed in the Name of Christ, are a Chiefe Meanes for the Preuenting, or Migatating the Torments of Purgatory* (St Omer, 1634), sig. *6.

WOMEN, LATIN, AND WORK

By the sixteenth century, a classical education was potentially a passport to employment. If a potential woman ruler needed to be fully competent in speaking and reading Latin, the job of teaching her might go to a distinguished humanist, or, in a significant number of cases, it might go to a learned maiden. Thus the Italian Olimpia Morata, the daughter of a professional grammarian, was invited to court by Renée, Duchess of Ferrara, in a role somewhere between tutor and companion to her daughter Anna, who was five years younger.[31] The practicality of entrusting the education of princesses to well-trained humanist women seems to have struck a number of European courts at about this time. Similarly, Luisa Sigea was tutor to the Infanta Doña Maria of Portugal (1521–1577), daughter of King Manoel by his third wife, Eleanor of Austria.[32] She taught her to some purpose: Paul Allut quotes a Latin letter written by Maria to her mother Eleanor after the latter had made a second marriage to François I of France, which is both fluent and elegant.[33] Furthermore, the Infanta Maria sought to create a correspondence with her cousin Mary Tudor in 1546; her letter speaks of 'having heard of the fame of her virtuous learning'.[34] A long Latin poem to the Infanta, quoted by Nicolás Antonio, describes her as another Zenobia or Eudocia, both of whom were famously learned.[35] Anna Utenhovia, niece and pupil of the distinguished Belgian humanist Karel Utenhove, was invited by Princess Eleanor of Prussia to come and teach French to her daughters in 1591. For reasons which are not stated, she refused to do so; Utenhove's letter of apology for this survives, as does a letter to his friend Galien Wier, asking him to smooth matters over.[36] There are plenty of other examples.

Because women such as Morata and Sigea were written up in the catalogues of learned and virtuous ladies which are a notable feature of Renaissance culture, the association between women's Latin learning and court service was a matter of record. It therefore occurred to a number of seventeenth-century women to try their luck in this respect. Two of them were English: Bathsua Makin and Rachel Jevon.

[31] Renée, Duchess of Ferrara was the daughter of Anne de Bretagne and Louis XII, sister of Queen Claude. She was brought up with her cousin Marguerite d'Angoulême, later the Queen of Navarre, and known as one of the most learned women in France. She was very concerned with her children's education; see Holt N. Parker (trans.), *Olimpia Morata: The Complete Writings of an Italian Heretic* (Chicago, IL, 2003), 10.

[32] António Moro and Sánchez Coello, 'A princesa esquecida: D. Maria de Portugal (1521–1578)', in Annemarie Jordan (ed.), *Retrato de corte em Portugal: O Legado de António Moro (1552–1572)* (Lisbon, 1994), 63–72.

[33] Paul Allut, *Aloysia Sygea et Nicolas Chorier* (Lyon, 1862). 11.

[34] David Loades, *Mary Tudor* (Oxford, 1997), 132. Another Latin letter from the Infanta to Eusebius of Coimbra is mentioned by Nicolás Antonio, *Biblioteca Hispana*, 4 vols (Madrid, 1783–1788), vol. 2, 346.

[35] Antonio, *Biblioteca Hispana*, 346.

[36] München, Bayerische Statsbibliothek, MS Latin 10369, fols. 161, 169.

Bathsua Rainolds, later Makin, published a collection of polyglot verse, *Musa Virginea*, in 1616, when she was sixteen. She was the daughter of a schoolmaster in Ipswich, and *Musa Virginea* is patently a bid for royal patronage: it contains fifteen poems in Latin, Greek, and French. Seven of these are encomia, and the addressees include James VI, Frederick V, the Count Palatine, who married James' daughter Elizabeth in 1613, Queen Anna of Denmark, and Prince Charles. The British Library copy is the one given to King James and the Cambridge copy is the one given to Prince Charles; both are personalised for their recipients with manuscript additions. Rainolds had obviously missed the boat as far as the education of Princess Elizabeth was concerned, since the princess was married and out of England by 1616, but her work may nonetheless have borne fruit. She was asked to educate Elizabeth, youngest daughter of Charles I, in 1640, when the child was five.[37] On the outbreak of the English Civil War in 1642, Princess Elizabeth and her brother Henry, Duke of Gloucester, were placed under the care of Parliament, who assigned their guardianships to several noblemen in succession. In 1643, the seven-year-old Elizabeth broke her leg and, in that same year, she and Prince Henry were moved to Chelsea where she was again tutored by Bathsua Makin, though only until 1644, when she was nine.

However, through the rest of her life, Makin did everything she could to make capital of her three years as a royal tutor:

> the princess Elizabeth, daughter to king Charles the first, to whom Mrs Makin was tutress, at nine Years old could write, read, and in some measure understand Latin, Greek, Hebrew, French and Italian. Had she lived, what a Miracle she would have been of her sex! ... A School is lately erected for Gentlewomen, at Tottenham-High-Cross, where Mris Makin is Governess, who was sometimes Tutoress to the Princess Elizabeth, daughter of King Charles the First.[38]

William Marshall made an engraving of Makin in the 1640s; circling her image are the words 'BATHSUA MAKIN PRINCIP. ELIZAB. LATINIS, GRAECIS & HEBRAEIS'; that is, 'Bathsua Makin, [tutor] of princess Elizabeth in Latin, Greek and Hebrew'.

Makin's *Essay to Revive the Antient Education of Gentlewomen* makes the argument for the utility of woman's learning directly: 'Here is a sure Portion ... How many born to good Fortunes, when their Wealth hath been wasted, have supported themselves and Families too by their Wisdom?' Dr William Denton, erstwhile physician to Charles I, wrote from his impoverished exile in France, to Lady Mary Verney, about his daughter Anne:

> My highest ambition of all is to have her so much Latin as to understand a Latin testament which is enough to understand a Drs bill and to write one and then I could (if God bless me with life and health) leave her a portion without money ... I would

[37] Frances Teague, *Bathsua Makin: Woman of Learning* (Lewisburg, PA, 1998), 38.

[38] Bathsua Makin, *An Essay to Revive the Antient Education of Gentlewomen* (London, 1675), 10, 42.

> faine have her of as many trades as I could to get her living by, for I am in no great likelihood to provide her a portion.[39]

What he means is that with an adequate command of Latin, Anne Denton could find work as a pharmacist.

A somewhat later example of the would-be royal tutor is the figure of Rachel Jevon. She was educated at home by her father, and, on the restoration of Charles II, presented the king with a poem of fulsome flattery in parallel versions, Latin and English. This was followed up by two petitions for a court position after the king's marriage. It is far from certain that by the 1660s Charles II would have seen the slightest point in educating a daughter in this fashion, but, even if he had, the continued infertility of Catherine of Braganza meant that no such opportunity arose.[40]

Women did not become university professors but they certainly worked as teachers, both as private tutors and in schools. Another example is Anne Norman, daughter of Thomas Norman of Botolph Street, Bishopsgate. She married Roger Ley, Curate of St Leonard's Church, Shoreditch, in Middlesex in 1622. They kept a school in Shoreditch to eke out their income, where she taught Greek and Latin.[41]

EDUCATION FOR ITS OWN SAKE

Some women were educated simply because their fathers thought them educable. According to the testimony of her cousin, Mary Mollineux (1651–1696) was one such. Her parents were Catholic, and

> being of a large natural Capacity, quick, witty, and studiously inclined, her Father brought her up to more Learning, than is commonly bestowed upon our Sex; in which she became so good a Proficient, that she well understood the Latin Tongue, fluently discoursed in it; and made a considerable Progress in Greek also.[42]

She used her Latin to converse privately with her husband when other people were present and wrote verse both in Latin and English (*Fruits*, sig. B3r–v). The better-known Lucy Hutchinson, similarly, was instructed in Latin because her father, Sir Allen Apsley, recognised her precocity. She could read English by the time she was four, so by the

[39] Miriam Slater, *Family Life in the Seventeenth Century: The Verneys of Claydon House* (London, 1984), 135.

[40] Joseph Crowley, 'Rachel Jevon, *Exultationis Carmen* (1660)', in Helen Ostovick and Elizabeth Sauer (eds), *Reading Early Modern Women: An Anthology of Texts in Manuscript and Print 1550–1700* (New York and London, 2004), 393–4.

[41] William Andrews Clarke Memorial Library, MS L6815 M3 C734, fol. 181.

[42] Mary Mollineux, *Fruits of Retirement: or, Miscellaneous Poems, Moral and Divine: Being Some Contemplations, Letters, &c. Written on Variety of Subjects and Occasions*, 5th edn (London, 1761), sig. A4.

time she was seven he was having her taught Latin by the chaplain to the Tower of London where they lived.[43] She kept up her Latin in later life, since, as is well known, she translated Lucretius when she was a young mother, and, in widowhood, a difficult work by a contemporary theologian, John Owen.[44] As in the previous century, some women who read Latin translated, of whom Hutchinson is the most important. Additionally, others wrote verse: Rachel Jevon was the most ambitious of them. And a few, such as Bathsua Makin and Dorothea Moore, could write a Latin letter and were thus able to participate directly in international exchanges of ideas (see this volume, Chapter 20, Martine van Elk, 'Early Modern Dutch and English Women Across Borders'.) However, not one seventeenth-century Englishwoman actually wrote a book in Latin on any subject. Though Anne Conway's *Principles of the Most Ancient and Modern Philosophy* was published in Latin in Amsterdam, this was a translation by François van Helmont.[45]

One of the ways life changed for Englishwomen in the seventeenth century is that, increasingly, the libraries of educated men contained translations of classical texts as well as, or instead of, the originals. The sixteenth century, and still more, the seventeenth, saw a significant democratisation of the classical tradition. After the Reformation, a concatenation of social changes greatly increased the proportion of literates in the population, and in the later sixteenth and seventeenth centuries the book trade expanded enormously. The proportion of Latin-literate gentry also increased due to the expansion of the universities. Many of the men who attended Oxford and Cambridge colleges came away with a taste formed by years of intensive education in Latin, but did not go on to lead lives that kept their Latin fluent. Many of them therefore preferred to do their leisure reading in English, and bought books that were thus potentially accessible to their wives and daughters. A girl who became an avid reader by devouring romances, a familiar pattern in the seventeenth century, might also take to browsing in her father's library, and take down North's Plutarch or Sandys' Ovid: in some families, she might even be encouraged to do so. A sorrowing John Evelyn reported of his daughter Mary, who died at nineteen in 1665, that she had educated herself in his study, reading 'aboundance of History, and all the best poets, even to Terence, Plautus, Homer, Virgil, Horace, Ovide'.[46]

While Mary Evelyn clearly read in translation, such reading could also be a stepping-stone to more serious study. By the age of eleven, the future Lady Mary Wortley Montagu was hiding from her governess and working in her father's library with a Latin dictionary and grammar from ten till two and from four till eight.[47] In later life, Lady

[43] Lucy Hutchinson, 'The Life of Mrs Lucy Hutchinson, Written by Herself', in Julius Hutchinson (ed.), *Memoirs of the Life of Colonel Hutchinson, Governor of Nottingham Castle and Town* (London, 1806), 1–18, 16.

[44] See Lucy Hutchinson, in Reid Barbour and David Norbrook (eds), *Translation of Lucretius* (Oxford, 2012) and Lucy Hutchinson, in Jane Stevenson (ed.), *Of Theologie* (Oxford, 2018). The latter is Hutchinson's translation of John Owen's *Theologoumena Pantodapa*.

[45] Anne Conway, in François van Helmont (trans.), *Opuscula philosophica: quibus continentur Principia philosophiæ antiquissimæ & recentissimæ* (Amsterdam, 1690).

[46] Margaret Ezell, *The Patriarch's Wife: Literary Evidence and the History of the Family* (Chapel Hill, NC, and London, 1987), 13.

[47] Robert Halsband, *The Life of Lady Mary Wortley Montagu* (Oxford, 1956), 5–7.

Mary advised her daughter on her granddaughter's education: 'she should learn to read the Classics in the original, but should not be allowed to "think herself learned, when she can read Latin or even Greek"'.[48] As Lady Mary evidently understood, the ability to read for pleasure and information is not the same as the intensive philological and grammatical study undertaken by contemporary male classicists in the universities. But while formal education was still out of reach for women, the increasing number of domestic libraries in which self-education was possible wrought a slow and subtle change in women's personal opportunities.

Mary Oxlie was most probably either the daughter of the master of the Morpeth grammar school or married to one of his three sons, all of whom were educated at Christ's College, Cambridge. Her commendatory poem to William Drummond of Hawthornden was prefixed to the posthumous edition of his works edited by Edward Phillips and printed in London. She writes:

> I Never rested on the Muses bed
> Nor dipt my Quill in the Thessalian Fountaine,
> My Rustick Muse was rudely fostered,
> And flies too low to reach the double mountaine.[49]

Maybe so, but she still knew who the Muses were, that they lived on the double-headed mountain Parnassus, and that the fountain of Hippocrene was the source of poetic inspiration.[50] As this suggests, increasing numbers of seventeenth-century women could access classical knowledge, whether or not they knew Latin and Greek.

FURTHER READING

Allen, Gemma. *The Cooke Sisters: Education, Piety and Politics in Early Modern England.* Manchester, 2013.

Ezell, Margaret. *The Patriarch's Wife: Literary Evidence and the History of the Family.* Chapel Hill, NC and London, 1987.

Pal, Carol. *The Republic of Women: Rethinking the Republic of Letters in the Seventeenth-Century.* Cambridge, 2012.

Stevenson, Jane, 'Women's Education'. In Philip Ford, Jan Bloemendal, and Charles Fantazzi (eds), *Brill's Encyclopaedia of the Neo-Latin World.* Leiden and Boston, 2014, 87–99.

Teague, Frances, *Bathsua Makin: Woman of Learning.* Lewisburg, PA, 1998.

[48] Lady Mary Wortley Montagu, in James Dallaway (ed.), *The Works of... Lady Mary Wortley Montagu, Including Her Correspondence, Poems and Essays*, 5 vols (London, 1803), vol. 4, 180–3.

[49] William Drummond, in Edward Phillips (ed.), *Poems by That Most Famous Wit, William Drummond of Hawthornden* (London, 1656), sig. A4r-v.

[50] Though she has got slightly confused between two mountains associated with the Muses: the double-headed mountain Parnassus is in Thessaly but Hippocrene is on Mount Helicon, in Boeotia.

CHAPTER 5

'AT MY PETITION'

Embroidering Esther

MICHELE OSHEROW

THE Hebrew Bible's Queen Esther was the most popular biblical heroine featured in seventeenth-century domestic needlework.[1] These pictures, stitched by women whose names we seldom know, lay plain the craft, wisdom, risk, and courage that characterise Esther's performance in her narrative. Though Esther is not a biblical prophetess, she nonetheless demonstrates the ability to pronounce the right word in a given situation.[2] Language is key to her several victories. The women working this narrative perhaps recognised the clash between Esther's linguistic successes and the silence imposed upon women in the early modern English world. The biblical narrative repeatedly underscores the significance of Esther's discourse: 'the *decree of Esther* confirmed these matters... and it was *written in the booke*'.[3] Esther's heroism shows itself in words written and spoken, in texts circulated and chronicled. Her success is marked by an invitation to 'write ... in the Kings name' (Esther 8.8). Within the stitched boundaries of needlework pictures, Esther's linguistic authority is recognised similarly, demonstrating an interplay between word and image, text and textile. Women's needlework embroiders Esther's narrative, offering a reading of Scripture beyond the printed page. This chapter considers the commentary inscribed by needle in an embroidered Esther from the textile collection of the Victoria and Albert Museum. Though I focus on a single embroidered work, its richness and complexity are characteristic of this medium at this

[1] Ruth Geuter, 'Reconstructing the Context of Seventeenth-Century English Figurative Embroideries', in Moira Donald and Linda Hurcombe (eds), *Gender and Material Culture in Historical Perspective* (London, 2001), 97–111, 98.

[2] In his 1657 commentary, John Trapp considers Esther 'no less active in her generation' than prophetesses Miriam and Deborah though he does not link Esther's activity specifically to speech. See John Trapp, *A Commentary or Exposition Upon the Books of Ezra, Nehemiah, Ester, Job and Psalms* (London, 1657), 191.

[3] The Holy Bible, King James Version (1611) 400th Anniversary Edition (Peabody, MA, 2010). Esther 9.32, emphases mine. All citations of the Bible and Apocrypha reference this KJV edition.

time. The piece, marked with the initials 'M. I.' and the year 1665,[4] is a brand of biblical exegesis inked in silks on satin by a woman who engaged fiercely and perceptively with the 'sincere milke of the word'.[5]

DOMESTIC EMBROIDERY

Embroidered scenes were at their height of popularity in England in the latter half of the seventeenth century.[6] Such images were everywhere: stitched into cushions, bed valances, or other furnishings, and commonly used to cover books, cabinets, and mirrors, or they were framed as pictures for display. M. I.'s piece was likely intended for framing, stitched as it is on white satin, a popular choice for needlework pictures.[7] As is the case with the majority of women who produced these pieces, we know nothing about M. I., though the materials she used were fine, suggesting she was of the middling or upper class. But women of all ranks used their needles. During the seventeenth century, according to Carol Humphrey, 'most of the population would have considered female needle skills more important than literacy' for women.[8] Needlework was considered a show of virtue and piety, perhaps owing to the stitching woman's posture which required her to sit with head bowed.[9] Girls began sewing samplers as young as age six and continued developing their skills with increasingly complex patterns and stitches. By the age of fourteen a girl was expected to be an 'accomplished needlewoman'.[10] Conduct books for women endorse needlework as a path to feminine virtue, a benefit promoted by John Taylor in his verse preface to *The Needles Excellency*: 'Thus hoping that these workes may have this guide / To serve for ornament, and not for pride: / To cherish vertue, banish idlenesse, / For these ends, may this booke have good successe'.[11]

Domestic embroidery regularly featured female figures who served as exemplary models for girls and women crafting these pieces. Their examples, writes Ruth Geuter, were used to 'instill in them such specifically female virtues as modesty, humility, and

[4] The practice of initialing and dating embroidered works became more common over the course of the seventeenth century. The majority of dated pieces, though representing only a percentage of extant work, were made in the decade in which M. I. produced this picture. See Ruth Geuter, 'Embroidered Biblical Narratives and Their Social Context', in Andrew Morrall and Melinda Watt (eds), *English Embroidery from the Metropolitan Museum of Art, 1580–1700* (New Haven, CT, 2009), 57–77, 72. A curiosity regarding M. I.'s signature is its appearance in ink, perhaps a marker for stitches left unfinished.

[5] KJV, To the Reader, n.pg.

[6] Geuter, 'Social Context', 57.

[7] Liz Arthur, *Embroidery 1600–1700 at the Burrell Collection* (Glasgow, 1995), 68.

[8] Carol Humphrey, *Sampled Lives: Samplers from the Fitzwilliam Museum* (Cambridge, 2017), 13.

[9] Arthur, *Embroidery*, 36.

[10] Arthur, *Embroidery*, 59.

[11] John Taylor, *The Needles Excellency: A New Booke Wherin Are Divers Admirable Workes Wrought with the Needle* (London, 1631), n.pg.

obedience, and above all chastity'.[12] These exemplars 'provided women with a chance to portray alternative selves' which, suggests Susan Frye, may account for the popularity of Old Testament heroines in these embroidered works.[13] According to Geuter, 43 percent of extant needlework produced in England in the seventeenth century featured biblical themes and subjects.[14] But for all the duty implied by this choice, biblical embroidery of the period offers more than a show of piety. Approaching needlework as a kind of women's text enables us to recognise how women's embroidered representations of the Bible function as biblical commentary in its own right. Women's stitched narratives and characters communicate meaning.

TEXTILES AS TEXTS

For the last decade, scholars have been increasingly attentive to the ways early modern women's textiles function as women's texts. In *Pens and Needles: Women's Textualities in Early Modern England*, Susan Frye impressively outlines the many intersections between these tools and suggests that attending to products of both 'presents an alternative way to read'.[15] Frye encourages attention to women's 'multiple textualities' that span the verbal and the visual: 'for many early modern English women, writing, visual design, and needlework were not considered mutually exclusive activities; rather, they were related ways to create texts'.[16] Frye points to the potential of stitched texts as a means to access the lives of women otherwise lost, 'their existence registered only by the needlework that they left behind and by their choice of narratives'.[17] The rhetoricity of needlework has been taken up by feminist rhetorical scholars who remind us that embroidery and other stitched samplers and pictures were 'made to be seen' and are thus a means to shape female identity.[18] Maureen Daly Goggin and Beth Fowkes Tobin demonstrate across several rich collections the 'dynamic relationship of women, gender, culture, politics, and needle arts'.[19] Scholars turning towards material culture acknowledge the needle as a potent rhetorical tool that offered women opportunities for reflection and

[12] Geuter, 'Social Context', 57.

[13] Susan Frye, *Pens and Needles: Women's Textualities in Early Modern England* (Philadelphia, PA, 2010), 145.

[14] Geuter, 'Social Context', 57.

[15] Frye, *Pens*, xvi.

[16] Frye, *Pens*, 3.

[17] Frye, *Pens*, xv.

[18] Aimee E. Newell, 'Tattered to Pieces: Amy Fiske's Sampler and the Changing Roles of Women in Antebellum New England', in Maureen Daly Goggin and Beth Fowkes Tobin (eds), *Women and the Material Culture of Needlework and Textiles, 1750–1950* (Burlington, VT, 2009), 51–68, 55.

[19] Maureen Daly Goggin, 'Introduction: Threading Women', in Maureen Daly Goggin and Beth Fowkes Tobin (eds), *Women and the Material Culture of Needlework and Textiles, 1750–1950* (Burlington, VT, 2009), 1–12, 2.

transformation. Needlework constitutes a rhetoric of display that enables its audience to imagine possibilities for action.[20]

Approaching seventeenth-century biblical embroidery through this lens enables us to see how these pieces serve as an alternative site of discourse for women and, moreover, how they function as epistemic spaces.[21] Early modern women knew their Bibles and that knowledge shows itself in their renderings which frequently resist or contradict dominant interpretations.[22] Even women working prepared canvases (on which a scene was printed or drawn) adapted, altered, or embellished pieces as they saw fit. Embroidered pictures were not bound to scriptural accuracy, enabling women to explore situations and relationships within and among narratives. Recognisable characters are placed unexpectedly in scenes, and several episodes may be worked into a single stitched piece. What emerges in these pieces is a stunning complexity of material very much in keeping with the textual intricacies of the Bible itself.

ENCOUNTERING ESTHER

The woman who stitched the Esther examined here showcases Esther's wisdom and moxie[23] as well as a sophisticated understanding of narrative events and structure. Told in a brief ten chapters, Esther's story is a kind of Cinderella tale in which a Jewish orphan living in exile becomes Queen of Persia and miraculously saves her people when they are threatened with genocide. The narrative describes her as 'faire and beautiful' (Esther 2.7), but her cleverness and courage are more extraordinary. Esther's progress from concubine to queen happens quickly. The bulk of her narrative attends to Haman the Agagite's campaign against the Jews, Esther's efforts to subvert him, and the establishment of Esther's Uncle Mordecai in King Ahasuerus' court. The narrative concludes with a celebration of the Jews' victory over their enemies, and announces the origin of the Festival of Purim, the observance of which 'Jewes do, even to this day'.[24]

[20] Heather Pristash, Inez Schaechterle, and Sue Carter Wood, 'The Needle as the Pen: Intentionality, Needlework and the Production of Alternate Discourses of Power' in Maureen Daly Goggin and Beth Fowkes Tobin (eds), *Women and the Material Culture of Needlework and Textiles, 1750–1950* (Burlington, VT, 2009), 15–27, 15.

[21] Maureen Daly Goggin, 'Stitching a Life in 'Pen of Steele and Silken Inke': Elizabeth Parker's circa 1830 Sampler,' in Maureen Daly Goggin and Beth Fowkes Tobin (eds), *Women and the Material Culture of Needlework and Textiles, 1750–1950* (Burlington, VT, 2009), 31–50, 35.

[22] Women's engagement with the Bible and other 'godly books' has been noted by numerous scholars of early modern women's texts and history. Patricia Crawford refers to the 'systematic reading' of the Bible by Protestant women; see *Women and Religion in England 1500–1720* (New York, 1993), 79. Elaine Hobby refers to women's 'extravagant' use of Scripture in seventeenth-century vindications; see *The Virtue of Necessity: English Women's Writing 1649–88* (Ann Arbor, MI, 1988), 45.

[23] 'Courage, audacity, spirit; energy, vigour; enterprise; skill, shrewdness' ('moxie', n.OED, accessed 8 December 2020.

[24] *The Geneva Bible: A Facsimile of the 1560 Edition* (Madison, WI, 1969), 222 gl.

The story's moral in early modern Christian terms is its demonstration of 'the great mercies of God . . . who . . . when all hope of worldely helpe faileth . . . he sendeth comfort and deliverance' (Geneva Bible, 218). Esther's narrative was hardly confined to stitched pictures. She is one of nine of the most worthy women of the world as judged by Thomas Heywood.[25] Her narrative is the subject of poetic, dramatic, and visual retellings. Esther's book was one in which early modern readers were well versed, which accounts for the extraordinary number of early modern texts in which her name appears. Esther is referenced as freely in religious tracts as she is in a justification for the use of cosmetics.[26] She became an allegorical figure for the Protestant church, observes Michelle Ephraim, in need of deliverance from Catholic oppression.[27] Her character served any group resisting oppression or positioning itself as intercessor. If Esther represented Protestant causes, so too did she represent Catholic interests. Her name was evoked by both Royalists and Parliamentarians; her ethos was prominent throughout the Civil War, lending scriptural authority to political, religious, or other claims. As Alison Thorne astutely observes, early modern engagement with the Book of Esther 'was shaped by a distinctive set of ideological, political, and religious conventions and priorities'.[28]

M. I.'s embroidered canvas presents Esther's story though a selection of six scenes (see Figure 5.1). The most familiar of these appears at the centre, and features Esther's bold approach to King Ahasuerus in chapter 5. Esther's Jewish identity has been kept secret at court, but Mordecai alerts her to the danger facing her people and encourages her intervention: 'who knoweth whether thou art come to the kingdome for such a time as this?' (Esther 4.13–14). Esther agrees, and makes clear her risk: 'Whosoever . . . shall come unto the King into the inner court, who is not called, there is one lawe of his to put him to death, except such to whom the King shall hold out the golden sceptre' (4.11). This unbidden approach is the go-to moment for representations of Esther, and this scene is the most elaborately stitched of those M. I. selected for her canvas.[29] It is rendered largely in stumpwork, a style of raised, three-dimensional embroidery

[25] Thomas Heywood, *The Exemplary Lives and Memorable Acts of Nine The Most Worthy Women of the World: Three Jewes, Three Gentiles, Three Christians* (London, 1640), title page.

[26] Hannah Woolley references Esther to justify women's use of cosmetics, 'sweet perfumes', and 'whatsoever was then in fashion'. See Hannah Woolley, *The Gentlewomans Companion; or, A Guide to the Female Sex* (London, 1673), 242.

[27] Michelle Ephraim, *Reading the Jewish Woman on the Elizabethan Stage* (Burlington, VT, 2008), 33.

[28] Alison Thorne, 'The Politics of Female Supplication in the Book of Esther', in Victoria Brownlee and Laura Gallagher (eds), *Biblical Women in Early Modern Literary Culture 1550–1700* (Manchester, 2016), 95–110, 101.

[29] There is no way of knowing if M. I. herself prepared this canvas, if the pattern was printed, or drawn by another hand. Compositional aids or pattern books were likely used for details such as the fountain, flowers, and creatures. As I have argued elsewhere, use of patterns or prepared canvas does not negate the needleworker's agency. Embroiderers routinely amended or adjusted cartooned images. To date, I have found no stitched Esther that duplicates this piece to any significant degree. I attribute the choices made on this canvas to the embroiderer whose initials appear at centre. See Michele Osherow, 'Brooding on Bathsheba: Working the Davidic Narrative in Seventeenth-Century Embroidery', Durham Early Modern Conference, Durham University, 23 July 2019.

FIGURE 5.1 *Esther and Ahasuerus* (1665), Museum no. T.125–1937 © Victoria and Albert Museum London.

featuring a variety of materials including silk and metal threads, padding, wooden pieces, beading, mica, and more. M. I.'s king and queen have faces sculpted in silk satin, and each figure is embellished with finely embroidered robes, seed pearls, lace, and other flourishes. They are outfitted in mid-seventeenth-century fashion; both heads are covered in thick curls and their accessories include jewellery, hair ornaments, garters, hose, and ribbons.

Though M. I. chooses a familiar moment around which to construct Esther's story, her depiction distinguishes itself from popular representations, and distances itself from the source on which other artists relied. Paintings by Tintoretto (1546), Rubens (1620), and Artemisia Gentileschi (1628–1630) feature Esther's approach to Ahasuerus' court and depict her fainting into the arms of the women who accompany her. Esther's daring, then, is obscured by a show of feminine weakness. Her fainting is not a detail found in the biblical text, rather, it appears in the Apocrypha's 'Additions to the Book of Esther'.[30] In the apocryphal account of Esther's approach, Ahasuerus 'looked very

[30] The Septuagint's Book of Esther contains six extended passages (107 verses) not found in the Hebrew text. Jerome, recognising that these additions had no Hebrew counterpart, doubted their authenticity. He shifted the passages to the book's close in his Latin Bible. Protestants declared the

fiercely upon her: and the Queene fell downe and was pale, and fainted' (Additions to Esther 15.7). Other representations of the scene, such as in paintings by Paolo Veronese (1556), Antonio Negretti (1574), and Hans Jordaens (1630), show Esther kneeling before Ahasuerus' throne, on her knees before male authority. M. I.'s depiction contains no such deferential or weak-kneed display. She favours Esther as she appears in the Bible's pages, her own source of triumph. The Apocrypha's additions, dedicated largely to the manufacture of Esther's modesty, weakness, and faith indicate just how removed Esther is from any show of these in the canonical narrative.

The choice to present Esther in a subjective pose is in keeping with sixteenth- and seventeenth-century commentary. Routinely, Esther is held up as a model of obedience. Thomas Adams commends Esther for the obedience shown to her uncle and encourages parishioners to follow her example in their duty towards God.[31] Joseph Hall has Esther announce her obedience outright, and Heywood presents Esther as the remedy to the 'evill' of a disobedient wife and the crisis of Empire that comes from unruly women.[32] In his *Monument of Matrons* (1582), Thomas Bentley praises Esther for duty and humility, noting that she '[t]hough ... a royal queene, yet was obedient unto ... her poore kinsman ... and did in everything after his counsel and advise'.[33] Bentley's text precedes M. I.'s needlework by several generations; nonetheless, an insistence on Esther's humility and obedience continued throughout the seventeenth century. In his epic retelling of Esther's narrative, Francis Quarles asserts a '[wife's] obedience never's out of season, / So long as either Husband lasts, or Reason'.[34] John Trapp, who published his commentary on the Book of Esther within a decade of the year marked on M. I.'s needlework, applies the words 'obey', 'obedience', or 'obedient' to the narrative nearly two dozen times. Trapp locates Esther's virtue in obedience and commends her, too, for 'ruling her tongue that unruly member'.[35]

But M. I.'s embroidered Esther lifts the character beyond a show of duty and positions her as one to whom obedience is due. This queen is confident in her majesty and very much the king's equal. The tent that covers Ahasuerus finds a complement in the canopy held above Esther; the couple wear identical crowns. Esther's retinue exceeds

passages uncanonical and placed them in the Apocrypha. The Greek verses spiritualise Esther's narrative, introducing divine agency and prophecy. The additions reference God over fifty times, in contrast to the Hebrew text which contains no reference to God whatsoever. The Apocrypha sections in both the Geneva and King James Bibles indicate that the Additions to Esther are not based upon Hebrew text.

31 Thomas Adams, *A Commentary or, Exposition Upon the Divine Second Epistle Generall* (London, 1633), 116.

32 Joseph Hall, *Contemplations Upon the Principall Passages of the Holy Storie*, 8 vols, (London, 1626), *VIII*, 503; Heywood, *Exemplary Lives*, 49.

33 Bentley refers to Esther 4.13–14. He does not acknowledge that though Mordecai prompts Esther to action, the devices by which Haman will be defeated are left entirely to her. Thomas Bentley, *The Monument of Matrons, The Seventh Lampe of Virginitie* (London, 1582), 149.

34 Francis Quarles, *Hadassa or The History of Queene Ester with Meditations Thereupon, Diuine and Morall* (London, 1621), Meditation 3, n.pg.

35 Trapp, *Commentary*, 118.

Ahasuerus' so that even the fauna and flora endorse her. A lion on the far right brings up Esther's entourage, signalling the ferocity she has in store for her enemies. Flowers embroidered on Esther's gown replicate in miniature the flora stitched across the canvas so that Esther emerges as Shushan's natural queen. M. I. presents her heroine standing tall in a moment of victory with Ahasuerus' sceptre extended towards her. His gesture shows she 'obtained favour in his sight'; her response is to 'touch the top' (Esther 5.2). Esther's touch is a sign of 'reverence and subjection' according to Arthur Jackson's 1646 *Annotations*; Trapp reads it as a form of wifely submission.[36] But in M. I.'s rendering, any submissiveness on Esther's part is more assumed than shown. In the narrative, the queen merely touches the rod, but the embroidered picture locks her hand there, signalling a hand-off of authority and the contributions to governance Esther will make by her book's end.[37] M. I.'s rendering anticipates Esther's influence over the king, and over political and religious leadership. She replaces the popular display of Esther's frailty with a show of ability and ambition.

WHAT IS THY PETITION?

A remarkable detail of the embroidered picture is the text M. I. stitched at its centre. A tiny scroll, or speech ribbon, unfurls from Esther's hand reading 'At my petition'. The words are hers, lifted from chapter 7 where she pleads for the lives of Jews: 'let my life be given me at my petition, and my people at my request' (Esther 7.3). Esther's petitions are central to her narrative, and she will make several of these. She notably preserves the Jewish people, of course, but her various petitions also enable her to contribute to policy, to influence secular and religious law, to empower the weak, to promote moral leaders, to punish the guilty, and to secure royal endorsement of her voice. Esther's popularity during the English Civil Wars was certainly linked to her skilful petitioning as a path towards change and justice. Her history demonstrates, as Richard Heyrick reminds his parishioners, that even the 'poorest subject may have liberty to prefer his Petition'.[38]

References to Esther appear in early modern petitions made by both men and women. But the popularity of her figure in needlework and, consequently, in domestic spaces, suggests that her history bolstered women's political engagement and authorised women to go beyond the private sphere. Esther is among exemplars whose

[36] Arthur Jackson, *Annotations Upon the Remaining Historicall Part of the Old Testament* (Cambridge, 1646), 801; and Trapp, *Commentary*, 147.

[37] The caterpillar stitched beneath the sceptre underscores the moment as one of transformation. See George Ferguson, *Signs & Symbols in Christian Art* (London, 1961), 13.

[38] Richard Heyrick, *Queen Esthers Resolves: or, A Princely Pattern of Heaven-Born Resolution, for All The Lovers of God and Their Country* (London, 1646), 5.

'actions and words carried vast political significance'.[39] The Civil War periods saw a marked increase in women's petitions and Esther is figuratively recruited among these women's ranks. In 'The most humble Petition of the Gentlewomen, Tradesmens-wives, and many others of the Femall Sex', Esther's history is used to justify the women's approach to Parliament:

> Neither are wee left without example in Scripture, for when the State of the Church, in the time of King *Abasuerus* was by the bloudy enemies thereof sought to bee utterly destroyed, wee find that *Ester* the Queene and her Maids fasted and prayed, and that *Ester* petitioned to the King ... On which grounds wee are imboldned to present our humble Petition unto this Honourable Assembly.[40]

Petitioning women were wise, too, to the use of Esther's narrative beyond its heroine. Haman is a ready stand-in for corrupt authority as shown by 'divers afflicted Women-Petitioners to the Parliament on the behalf of Mr. John Lilburn': 'Your Honours may please to consider whether the late unjust and illegal Act against Mr. *Lilburne* was not obtained by such an enemy as proud *Haman* was, having no more cause for so doing, then *Haman* had ... (though a favourite, as *Haman* was)'.[41] Esther, with whom the petitioners identify, appears in stark contrast to the crooked politico: 'Your Honours may please to call to minde ... Esther that righteous woman being encouraged by the justness of the Cause (as we at this time are)' (*Afflicted*, n.pg.).

Esther's speech had applications beyond Parliament's doors. Margret Fell justifies women's speaking by directing audiences to 'see what glorious expression Queen *Hester* used to comfort the People of God'.[42] She is featured in the *querelle des femmes* as an example of a woman who 'wrought mervailes ... to the ... perpetuall memorie of the feminine sexe'.[43] Among those marvels is a voice that demands to be heard and that thoroughly silences enemies. Esther's success in this could not have been lost on Ester Sowernam, who adopted this pseudonym to speak out against Joseph Swetnam's misogynist attacks (see this volume, Chapter 9, Christina Luckyj, 'The *Querelle des Femmes*'). She petitions her readers, 'Let mee speake freely, for I will speake nothing but truly, neither shall my words exceede my proofe'.[44]

[39] Frye, *Pens*, 145.

[40] *A True Copy of the Petition of The Gentlewomen, and Tradesmens-Wives in and about the City of London* (London, 1642), 5.

[41] *Unto Every Individual Member of Parliament the Humble Representation of Divers Afflicted Women-Petitioners to the Parliament, on the Behalf of Mr. John Lilburn* (London, 1653), n.pg.

[42] Margaret Fell, *Womens Speaking Justified, Proved and Allowed of by the Scriptures* (London, 1667), 16–17.

[43] Alexandre de Pontaymeri, *A Womans Woorth, Defended Against All the Men in the World*, attrib. Anthony Gibson (London, 1599), 7.

[44] Ester Sowernam, *Ester hath Hang'd Haman* (London, 1617), 35.

VALUED SPEECH

M. I.'s insertion of the 'At my petition' text at the centre of her needlework establishes Esther's speech as essential to her heroism and reminds her audience that a woman's speech warrants royal attention. The choice to stitch these words inside the events of Esther chapter 5 underscores the value assigned Esther's language within her narrative. With Ahasuerus' extended sceptre comes a petition of his own: 'What wilt thou, Queene Esther? and what is thy request? *It shall bee even given thee to the halfe of the kingdome*' (Esther 5.3, emphasis mine). The king sets Esther's entreaty at a high rate and the familiar reader knows this. The Book of Esther opens with an appraisal of Ahasuerus' wealth in which 180 days are required to show his riches (Esther 1.4). Though Ahasuerus has no knowledge of what Esther will request, he nevertheless assigns a value to her speech. Spotlighting Esther's petition in the context of this scene indicates the value of all Esther proposes in the narrative and expands the scope of those demands. The words 'At my petition' function as kind of caption for the central image. The proximity of the text to the hand Esther places on the sceptre implies that this petitioner aims at nothing short of her husband's authority. M. I.'s pairing of text and image notably shifts the dynamics of this scene. Esther, in need of a pardon for her free approach to the king, instead makes a bid for his power.[45]

That this queen might successfully yield that power and serve a turn as king is a suggestion made and remade on M. I.'s canvas. The scene at bottom right presents events from Esther chapter 6, an after-hours episode in which 'could not the King sleepe, and hee commaunded to bring the booke of Records of the chronicles; and they were read before the king' (v.1). M. I. stages the scene with precision: we find a bed, a reclining figure sporting a crown, and an oversized book. Oddly, this king is unlike the Ahasuerus elsewhere on the canvas. His figure lacks the facial hair he is given in each of M. I.'s other displays. Magnification of the textile reveals no identifiable pinpricks in the satin face; no amber-coloured remnants peek out from face or neck. The absence of facial hair makes this figure's gender presentation ambiguous, resembling the Esther on this canvas as much, perhaps more, than it does Ahasuerus. Whether the face was simply left unfinished, or whether the needleworker winks at us by tucking the heroine into Ahasuerus' bed, the image offers an Esther-like figure matched with an impressive text.

M. I. promotes a woman's engagement with text as a narrative subject—a fitting move given that this book *is* Esther's, one of only two biblical books named for a woman. The surprise of finding Esther where we expect Ahasuerus in this scene also exposes the difference between the characters' textual experiences: Ahasuerus has texts read to

[45] That Esther requires a pardon for her unsolicited approach is recognised consistently in biblical commentary and retellings. See William Ainsworth, *Medulla Bibliorum, The Marrow of the Bible, or, A Logico-Theological Analysis of Every Several Book of the Holy Scripture* (London, 1652), 83; and Hall, *Contemplations*, 505.

him (Esther 6.1); Esther writes her own (9.29). Esther's contribution to texts written and spoken shows itself most when she petitions Ahasuerus for a written decree 'to reverse the letters devised by Haman ... which hee wrote to destroy the Jewes' (Esther 8.5). It is in response to this request that the king empowers her to 'Write ye ... for the Jewes, as it liketh you, in the Kings name'.[46] The narrative's repeated attention to language, writing, and decrees affirms to excess the power of the word. And increasingly, these words are Esther's. Her petition will result in nearly two dozen references to writing, writers, and written commandments.[47] Esther emerges as an essential begetter of texts; it is she, says the biblical narrator, who 'wrote with all authoritie' (Esther 9.29). Esther's appropriation of her husband's authority is implied by the king's obsessive attention to her requests. He asks her some form of 'what is thy petition' more than half a dozen times,[48] a behaviour that leads Trapp to criticise him for being 'only ... clay and wax' in Esther's hands.[49]

CRAFTING INVENTION

M. I.'s visual substitution of Ahasuerus with Esther is in keeping with narrative themes, and provides evidence of the needleworker's sophisticated reading. The Book of Esther contains no shortage of substitutions: Esther substitutes for Vashti (Ahasuerus' former queen), Mordecai for Haman, both Esther and Mordecai for the king, and so on. M. I. plays with substitutions on her canvas. The clearest example is the depiction of Mordecai and the king shown top right of centre. We see Mordecai being honoured on the king's horse as described in Esther 6 (the rider heading right); his appearance mirrors the king's (shown heading left), with the exception of the crown Ahasuerus wears. The rendering visually drives the theme of substitution while foreshadowing Persia's good fortune: the land is in need of capable leadership and Mordecai will fill that gap.[50] The substitution of Mordecai for Haman, which happens quite literally when Mordecai takes Haman's post and property (Esther 8.2), is anticipated across M. I.'s canvas. The

[46] The text underscores the significance of the written word by noting that 'the writing which is written in the Kings name ... may no man reverse'. See Esther 8.8.

[47] See Esther 8.5, 8–10, 13–14. Esther's discursive authority extends in chapter 8 to Mordecai who works with the royal scribes to issue the decree 'unto every province according to the writing thereof, and unto every people after their language'. See Esther 8.9.

[48] See Esther 5.3,6; 7.2; 9.12.

[49] Trapp, *Commentary*, 185.

[50] Susan Frye sees the two men on horseback both representing Mordecai in his precession 'around the entire kingdom', but I hold that the choice to show only one figure wearing a crown is a significant indication of difference. I note a prioritising of theme over narrative here because events depicted do not strictly follow biblical text. Haman is not shown leading Mordecai through Shushan (Esther 6.11). Instead, both of M. I.'s riders are led by a clean-shaven officer, perhaps Harbonah. The visual juxtaposition of king and Mordecai also emphasises how thoroughly Mordecai is honoured through this likeness, an observation that fuels Haman's rancour towards the Jews. For Frye's reading of this scene, see *Pens*, 147–8.

two men are given similar facial features, clothing, colouring, length of hair and beard. These and other choices in M. I.'s rendering riff on stylistic distinctions in the written work, demonstrating a correspondence between the handiwork of pens and needles, and manifesting in textile form the intricacies of textual invention.

Any eye attentive to pattern would delight in The Book of Esther. Its narrative relies on literary symmetry to reinforce the book's themes, and its highly stylised language draws attention to linguistic patterns in a way most biblical narratives do not. A symmetrical pattern making use of Esther chapter 6 as a pivotal scene frames the whole of the book. Key events prior to chapter 6 correspond to the events that follow: Esther, a Jew, identifies as gentile in chapter 2, and gentiles identify as Jews in chapter 8; an anti-Jewish edict is approved in chapter 3, a pro-Jewish edict in chapter 8; and the list goes on.[51] These correspondences translate to irony in Jackson's reading: 'that day which [Haman] designed as the onely lucky day for the massacre of the Jews proved quite contrary, a happy day to them, and fatall to their enemies'.[52] The narrative's series of inversions result in an overall chiastic structure. Indeed, Esther's story is chock-full of crossings—from poverty to riches, weakness to strength, danger to safety, fear to exaltation—all reinforcing the book's theme of the reversal of fortune.[53] M. I.'s embroidered picture conspicuously attends to those reversals. At upper right are two representations of Mordecai. One shows him at the king's gate in 'sackcloth and ashes' (Esther 4.2), a sharp contrast to the Mordecai on horseback in 'royall apparell' (6.8). The juxtaposition of these images realise the description of Mordecai who 'waxed greater and greater' (9.4). Haman's inverted course is illustrated on the opposite side of the canvas. His execution appears in the upper left corner. Directly beneath this is the centre stumpwork scene where Haman stands at Ahasuerus' right hand. The spear Haman holds directs our eyes up towards his gallows to his grim, well-deserved fate.

The chiastic structure of the written text works in conjunction with a pervasive doubling and parallelism that affects both plot and poetry. The excessive linguistic patterning of the biblical Hebrew is not lost in English translation.[54] The language gushes with verbal dyads of all sorts, ranging from pairs of linked noun and/or verb phrases ('nobles and princes,' 'slew and destroyed'), doubled-pair phrasing ('law and judgement,' 'sackcloth and ashes'), inclusion ('both to great and small'), and duplications ('what is thy petition and what is thy request?').[55] The text showcases a variety of repetition poetics including repeated root sequences, ideas, and expressions ('for the writing

[51] Generally, occurrences before the pivotal chapter are considered neutral or negative events, whereas the analogous events following Esther 6 are uniformly positive. See Jon D. Levenson, *The Old Testament Library: Esther, A Commentary* (Louisville, KY, 1997), 8.

[52] Jackson, *Annotations*, 807.

[53] The reversal of fortune is announced outright in the narrative's conclusion, which celebrates the shift 'from sorrow to joy, and from mourning into a good day' (Esther 9.22).

[54] The cumulative effect of this linguistic play leads biblical scholar Althalya Brenner to liken the book to 'a hall of mirrors'. See Athalya Brenner, 'Looking at Esther Through the Looking Glass', in Athalya Brenner (ed.), *A Feminist Companion to the Bible: Esther, Judith and Susanna* (Sheffield, 1995), 71–80, 71.

[55] There are many, many examples; those provided appear in Esther 1.3, 9.6, 1.13, 4.3, 1.20, 5.6.

which is written', 'the king was very wroth, and his anger burned', 'If I perish, I perish').[56] M. I. expertly extends the narrative doubling to her visual display. Each of the scenes presented in the needlework is among those that repeat, or 'double', in the biblical text. The episode at centre depicts Esther's initial visit to the inner court, and potentially represents her second approach described in Esther chapter 8. The gallows scene (top left) depicts Haman's execution, and those same gallows will host Haman's sons (9.13).[57] Esther's banquet table (bottom left), is set in chapter 5 and again in 7. Even the mysterious body between the sheets (bottom right) points to Esther's not-so-chaste entry to Ahasuerus' court. She was among the virgins who nightly 'came … unto the king … out of the house of women' (Esther 2.13). M. I. marks Esther's own change of fortune: she appeared in Ahasuerus' bed first as courtesan, and later as queen.

CUNNING STITCHES

M. I. supplements the parallels within Esther's narrative with astute biblical associations beyond it, confirming not only the depth of her biblical knowledge but also her choice to publish the connections she makes in the discursive space of her canvas. We see this in the representation of the crucial banquet scene (bottom left) in which Esther reveals her Jewish identity, petitions the king for the lives of Jews, and exposes Haman's plans for genocide (Esther 7.4). M. I. has Esther gesturing towards Haman as though at his ruin even now: 'The adversary and enemie, is this wicked Haman' (7.6). Esther's raised hand is unusually large, disproportionate to the rest of her body, and is outlined in red. The choice to display Esther's *left* hand is a detail as smart as it is telling—an unsubtle reminder of Esther's Benjaminite heritage (Esther 2.5). Among Israel's twelve tribes, the Benjaminites are most linked to cunning, trickery, and worse practices. Their history features deft use of the left hand.[58] John Mayer tactfully notes that Benjaminites used 'their left hands as their right' to indicate double-dealing.[59] To mark Esther as a Benjaminite is to highlight her skill for cunning and deception. Esther's keeping her identity a secret, her dramatic delay in petitioning the king, the repeated banquet

56 Again, examples abound. Those quoted are found in Esther 8.8, 1.12, 4.16.

57 The wasp, a symbol of death, hovers near the gallows appropriately marking either event. The wasp's association with death is linked to St Paul's 'O death where is thy sting' (I Corinthians 15.55). See Hope B. Werness, *The Encyclopedia of Animal Symbolism in World Art* (New York, 2006), 427.

58 See Judges 19, 20, and 21, specifically the episodes of the Levite's concubine, the rape of 400 virgins at Jabesh-Gilead, and the abduction of the daughters of Shiloh. Eleven of Israel's tribes find the Benjaminites' actions so abhorrent that they 'turned againe upon the children of Benjamin and smote them with the edge of the sword' (Judges 20.48). For reference to a Benjaminite's deft left hand, see Ehud's slaying of the Moabite king in Judges 3. The narrative details Ehud's use of his left hand to access a knife hidden on his right thigh (v.21). Use of a non-weapon hand enables the deception.

59 John Mayer, *Many Commentaries in One: Upon Joshuah, Judges, Ruth, 1 and 2 of Samuel, 1 and 2 of Kings, 1 and 2 of Chronicles, Ezra, Nehemiah, Esther* (London, 1647), 172.

invitations that make Haman's fall more devastating all smack of Benjaminite strategy.[60] Marking Esther as a Benjaminite distances her, too, from the obedience so often ascribed to her. Saul, Israel's first king and a Benjaminite, lost his throne for disobeying God.[61] Benjaminites move in and out of God's favour, but even their goodly actions feature a degree of craft and artifice.[62]

There is a certain virtue in documenting feminine cunning by way of the needle: 'cunning' was the signature term used to describe skilfully wrought things.[63] M. I.'s embroidered banquet cleverly hints at Esther's cunning beyond what appears in her book. M. I. sews Esther into a tight bodice in this scene, cleavage shaped by the same red running stitch used to outline the heroine's left hand. This sexualised representation affects an understanding of the events that follow, and which lead to Haman's end. In the narrative, Ahasuerus briefly leaves Esther's banquet after Haman's plans are exposed; the king then returns to find the villain 'fallen upon the bed whereon Esther was' (Esther 7.8). Haman's pleas to Esther for mercy are mistaken by Ahasuerus for an ill-timed sexual advance. Haman's sentencing is swift (7.8). M. I.'s choice to outfit Esther for seduction implies Esther's manipulation of these events. She prompts her husband's misreading by effecting his arousal.[64]

M. I. underscores Esther's potential for danger through another striking and unexpected parallel. The most carefully wrought figure in the banquet scene is Harbonah, Ahasuerus' chamberlain, rendered in stumpwork (to the right of Haman). The choice to feature this character is unusual. He is mentioned in only a single verse where he proposes a method of execution appropriate for Haman: 'Behold ... the gallowes, fiftie cubites high, which Haman had made for Mordecai ... standeth in the house of Haman' (7.9). M. I. fashions Harbonah's brand of retributive justice as an intention fit for a queen. A quick glance at the needlework reveals unmistakable similarities between the stumpwork figures of chamberlain and queen (as she appears at centre). Harbonah's features are effeminate: his face mirrors Esther's, his hair is curled and the same colour

[60] The narrative emphasises Haman's ego throughout. Adele Berlin argues that Esther's invitations are designed to 'disarm Haman and make him think he was the center of attention'. See Adele Berlin, *The JPS Bible Commentary: Esther* (Philadelphia, PA, 2001), 54.

[61] King Saul was essentially the poster-child for disobedience in early modern religious texts and commentary: 'God had set up Saul to reign over Israel, so for his ... Disobedience the same God that exalted him deposed him'. See John Strype, *David and Saul a Sermon Preached on the Day of National Thanksgiving* (London, 1696), 3–4.

[62] Henry Ainsworth characterises Benjaminites as 'wolves' but writes: 'Neither need it be thought any dishonour to Benjamin'. Ainsworth's reference likely comes from Jacob's blessing in Genesis 49.27. See Henry Ainsworth, *Annotations Upon the Five Bookes of Moses* (London, 1627), 169. In Renaissance art, the wolf is a marker of cunning and menace, including sexual menace. See Werness, *Animal Symbolism*, 437.

[63] The preface to *The Needles Excellency* assures the reader that 'this Booke, some cunning workes doth teach'. See Taylor, *Needles*, n.pg.

[64] Alison Thorne rightly notes the suggestive language used by Esther to manipulate the king's desire by beginning her petition '[i]f I have found favour in thy sight, O King' (Esther 7.3). Thorne, 'Supplication', 98.

as hers. Unlike key male figures on the canvas, Harbonah has no facial hair. Only he and Esther are adorned with blue feathers. The symmetry that unlocks meaning in the written text is used to pointed effect in M. I.'s stitched translation. Her association of Harbonah and Esther underscores the heroine's taste for vengeance and, moreover, frames the queen as a kind of executioner. M. I. extends Harbonah's role on her canvas, stitching him in miniature as the hangman working Haman's gallows.

Esther's militant inclinations, or, at the least, her interest in punishment, is not subtle. The decree she issues permits Jews to defend themselves on the day Haman assigned for their slaughter (Esther 8.12). Ahasuerus reports those casualties to his queen: 'The Jewes have slaine and destroied five hundred men in Shushan the palace, & the ten sonnes of Haman; what have they done in the rest of the kings provinces? ... now what is thy petition?' (Esther 9.12).[65] Esther responds by demanding more: 'Let it bee granted to the Jewes ... to doe tomorrow also, according unto this dayes decree' (9.13). M. I.'s association of Esther with Harbonah highlights the queen's interest in her enemies' destruction. The upshot of Esther's final petition is the Jews' slaying of 'their foes seventy and five thousand' (9.16). No other biblical heroine is responsible for deaths of this magnitude.[66] '[W]as not this a most bloudy minde in *Ester*,' asks Mayer, 'to desire that ... killing and slaying?'[67]

WORKING ESTHER

As any reader of the Bible knows, the biblical narrator seldom exposes the working of heroes' minds, but Esther's mind is less a subject of this canvas than is the embroiderer's own. M. I. celebrates the biblical heroine without compromising Esther's strength, and without denying her those behaviours that counter early modern feminine ideals. Those complications include not only her public speech, but also her sexual history, cunning, practiced deception, and a suspected 'bloudy minde'. If, as Frye suggests, embroidering heroines enabled needleworkers 'to portray alternative selves' it is hard to think that the self M. I. explores through Esther aims at humility or obedience.

M. I.'s choice to set Esther's narrative not in the land of Shushan but in one more like that outside her door invites us to look more broadly at what she displays in this picture, and to note how the piece shifts from Esther's narrative to the needleworker's own. Embroidering biblical or mythical figures in contemporary dress was not uncommon

65 Ahasuerus' query regarding the provinces suggests his ignorance of the extent of the day's violence. Such displays contribute to Berlin's description of him as 'a caricature of a ... bumbling monarch'. See Berlin, *JPS Commentary*, xx.

66 The violent end of this narrative is not addressed often or in great depth in early modern commentary. Jackson regards Esther's petition as 'aiming at Gods glory'; Trapp distances Esther's person from the proposal, insisting it was 'not out of private and personal spleen to any'. See Jackson, *Annotations*, 808; Trapp, *Commentary*, 185.

67 Mayer, *Commentaries*, 71.

in the period, but those are not the only familiarising markers on M. I.'s canvas. The men in her retelling resemble Stuarts: the faces, hair length, and beards on Haman and Mordecai are strikingly like those of Charles I; Ahasuerus is reminiscent of Charles II (though the biblical king is bearded). This attention to royal figures, in a piece completed in 1665, commemorates the Restoration. The nod towards both Stuart kings in a single work announces a general support of the monarchy. Symbols of both Charles I and II—the caterpillar for the father, butterfly for the son—are stitched throughout the canvas, and float beneath the primary scene.[68] The caterpillar seems intent on occupying the space where the sceptre meets Esther's hand. This Stuart symbol may also be a referent of the inserted text, as though the heroine's petitions advanced a royal cause.

M. I. asserts her political allegiance on the back of a narrative in which a woman's allegiance makes all the difference. Esther preserves her people and strengthens the governance of her king. By implication, so might the woman who imagines herself an Esther.[69] Using Esther's story to advantage, the needleworker illustrates the terms of that allegiance: at her approach the king will extend his sceptre, and with it an invitation to speak. This is the moment around which M. I. embroiders her narrative, preserving a space for a woman's speech and memorialising the petition stitched in her hand.

FURTHER READING

Arthur, Liz. *Embroidery 1600–1700 at the Burrell Collection*. Glasgow, 1995.

Frye, Susan. *Pens and Needles: Women's Textualities in Early Modern England*. Philadelphia, PA, 2010.

Geuter, Ruth. 'Reconstructing the Context of Seventeenth-Century English Figurative Embroideries', in Moira Donald and Linda Hurcombe (eds), *Gender and Material Culture in Historical Perspective*. London, 2001, 97–111.

Goggin, Maureen Daly and Beth Fowkes Tobin (eds). *Women and the Material Culture of Needlework and Textiles, 1750–1950*. Burlington, VT, 2009.

Parker, Rozika. *The Subversive Stitch: Embroidery and the Making of the Feminine (1984)*. London and New York, 2010.

Taylor, John. *The Needles Excellency: A New Booke Wherin Are Divers Admirable Workes Wrought with the Needle*. London, 1631.

[68] In addition to the caterpillar and butterfly, popular Royalist symbols included oak leaves and acorns in reference to Charles II's refuge in Boscobel Wood, 1651. See Arthur, *Embroidery*, 88.

[69] Sarah C. E. Ross explores an identification with Esther in the texts of Royalist poet Hester Pulter. Ross describes Pulter's 'deeply emblematic self-styling' as Esther and examines that styling in relation to Quarles' representation of the heroine in his *Hadassa* poem. See Sarah C. E. Ross, *Women, Poetry, and Politics in Seventeenth-Century Britain* (Oxford, 2015), 139–69.

CHAPTER 6

PRACTICAL TEXTS

Women, Instruction, and the Household

CARRIE GRIFFIN

EARLY modern practical texts range across a wide variety of topics and the term 'practical' can be applied to any text that is didactic or instructional, directing the reader on how to perform tasks, how to behave, and how to, for instance, cook, make, and cure. Among the first books produced in print in England were 'how-to manuals and handbooks, covering many types of skills and knowledge from cookery and measuring time to animal care and calculating interest', and practical works remained popular, seemingly within all levels of society, in the period to 1700 (see this volume, Chapter 22, Wendy Wall, 'The World of Recipes').[1] However, these works often resist neat categorisation given the frequent overlap between, say, conduct and cooking (discussed further on), but also because they respond to investigation that is motivated by a range of interests, among them political, literary, and social.[2] Though women are frequently evoked as readers and patrons of printed practical texts, most often the authors are male. However, at times female authors made their mark in this masculinised sphere, self-consciously stepping into a particular space and adopting a strong voice like their counterparts in the world of literature. Crucially, practical texts in print intended for women scaffolded female creativity and book production in domestic contexts, as well as the sharing of knowledge and advice, and household books are often key locations from which we can glean actual evidence of use or at least interest in print culture among women. In this context, women were active participants in a textual culture that witnessed a crossover of forms. From the late Tudor period onwards the textual space associated with manuscript was increasingly feminised as women compiled their own receipt/recipe books, continuing with traditional methods of manuscript production even as they preserved tried and tested receipts and formulae, folding that textual work

[1] Natasha Glaisyer, 'Popular Didactic Literature', in Joad Raymond (ed.), *The Oxford History of Popular Print Culture, Volume I: Cheap Print in Britain and Ireland to 1660* (Oxford, 2011), 510–19, 510.

[2] Glaisyer, 510–11.

into the work of the home. These women were, in the words of Heather Wolfe, actors in a 'climate in which handwritten documents were produced in Renaissance England' that was 'not unlike a symbiotic and osmotic sphere, with information flowing from speech to manuscript to print and back again in a continuous cross-fertilizing circle'.[3] Women seem to have been important agents in this circle since, as noted by Mary E. Fissell, there was a surge in interest in printed receipt books during the Interregnum. According to Fissell, this increased interest was prompted by the popular publication of the *A Choice Manual of Rare and Select Secrets in Physick and Chyrurgery* in 1653, attributed to Elizabeth, Countess of Kent, an example of yet another way in which the flow between manuscript and print can be conceptualised.[4]

PRACTICALITY AND MORALITY: GOUGE AND MARKHAM

As noted earlier, much printed practical writing for women was male-authored, and it absorbed the flavour of contemporary moral and epistemological writings about women. It normally firmly located the woman in the domestic sphere, and was heavily influenced by ideological positions on the public conduct of women. It was concerned, therefore, with her contribution to society, specifically her role in the health and well-being of the nation. Even the most straightforwardly practical of texts were infused with the philosophy that women—in particular, married women—should perform virtue in all aspects of their existence and in relation to the household, thereby providing applied instruction blended with the correct measure of behavioural and moral guidance. That blend of practical and moral instruction is a hallmark of several practical texts, including William Gouge's *Of Domesticall Duties* (1611), one of many published across the early modern period to comment on role of the wife in the maintenance of an orderly household (and on the role of the husband in ensuring correct wifely behaviour), predicated on the principle that the private lives of women are a matter for public debate and scrutiny. Correct behaviour for women was a complex matter, both publicly debated and privately managed: in Gouge's words, the 'outward reverence' of a woman

[3] Heather Wolfe, 'Manuscripts in Early Modern England', in Donna B. Hamilton (ed.), *A Concise Companion to English Renaissance Literature* (Malden, MA, 2006), 114–35, 115.

[4] Mary E. Fissell, 'Women in Healing Spaces', in Laura L. Knoppers (ed.), *The Cambridge Companion to Early Modern Women's Writing* (Cambridge, 2009), 153–64, 157. See also Jayne Elisabeth Archer, 'Women and Chymistry in Early Modern England: The Manuscript Receipt Book (c. 1616) of Sarah Wigges', in Kathleen P. Long (ed.), *Gender and Scientific Discourse in Early Modern Culture* (London, 2010), 191–216, for comments on the sophistication of the recipes in this publication. I return to the compilation of household books below.

towards her husband was a 'manifestation of her inward due respect of him'.[5] Whether privately in the home or expounded upon in the public space of the printed page the female self—the private self—was managed and instructed, supported by a textual tradition that favoured imperative language and that lacked ambiguity and nuance. And although practical writing in print from this period often transgressed the 'borderlines between literary and non-literary writing', the concentration of precise instruction alongside broader expressions of appropriateness around behaviour strongly suggests that the management of women was envisaged practically, and in line with cultures of instruction for both genders.[6] Indeed the question-and-answer format favoured by Gouge locates his treatise heavily in the medieval didactic tradition, but we might also say that his prescriptions for the ideal wife mimic the textual quality of a recipe (or receipt), recommending (among others) specific measures of sobriety, mildness, meekness, 'reverend speech', courtesy, and obedience. The instructions for 'wive-like mildness' are especially formulaic, consisting of a specific balance of ingredients (and noting the 'thicke cloudes overspreading the heavens in a Summers day' when these are not present); moreover it follows that we discover in Gouge firm ideas around the expected outward presentation of a wife, who should order her 'countenance' and manifest a 'pleasingness' before her husband.[7]

Gouge's tract is underpinned by specific discourses around female behaviour—as we might expect, he frequently cites particular verses from the Bible—but his treatise can also be read as a practical work that sets down 'rules governing the orderly household'. And although it offers guidance not just on female duties but on those of servants, children, parents, and indeed husbands, it may have been criticised for its strong stance on women since Gouge defends himself in the preface, rejecting any suggestion that he is a 'hater of women'.[8] He was not alone among male authors to articulate connections between domestic order and personal conduct. Similar expressions of the relationship between female public and private selves, and correct female behaviour, are discernible in otherwise practical writing. Such sentiments are strongly present, for instance, in Gervase Markham's *The English Housewife* (1615), in which the practical instruction of women involves not just consideration of the moral duties of women in the home but the blurred lines between public and private.[9] In a manual focused on household tasks

[5] William Gouge, *Of Domesticall Duties* (1622), extracted in Suzanne Trill, Kate Chedgzoy, and Melanie Osborne (eds), *'Lay By Your Needles Ladies, Take the Pen': Writing Women in England, 1500–1700* (London, 1997), 112–18, 113.

[6] Irma Taavitsainen and Päivi Pahta, 'Authority and Instruction in Two Sixteenth-Century Medical Dialogues', in Matti Peikola, Janne Skaffari, and Sanna-Kaisa Tanskanen (eds), *Instructional Writing in English: Studies in Honour of Risto Hiltunen* (Amsterdam, 2009), 105–24, 108, in which the authors focus on the literary frame of William Bullein's *The Feuer Pestilence* (1564).

[7] Trill et al. (eds), *'Lay By Your Needles'*, 114.

[8] Trill et al. (eds), *'Lay By Your Needles'*, 112.

[9] Gervase Markham, *The English Housewife*. Markham's compilation was first published in London in 1615 as book two of his *Countrey Contentments*, but it enjoyed considerable success as a distinct edition throughout the 1600s; see Carrie Griffin, *Instructional Writing in English, 1350–1650: Materiality and Meaning* (London, 2019), 168. See also Archer, 'Women and Chymistry', who observes that texts like

such as home-brewing, distilling, and cooking and baking, Markham also constructs a private domestic sphere that is a place of public concern and, like his fellow polemicists, extends the reach of the instruction to promote correct behaviour in women. As noted by Wendy Wall, the tract 'links the virtues of womanhood to tasks important for the "generall good of this kindgome"', also strongly stating that such virtues are requirements 'for the woman to be "compleat" both inwardly and outwardly'.[10]

Markham's 1623 edition presents an ideal 'compleat' woman in the person of Frances, the Countess Dowager of Exeter, to whom he writes a dedicatory epistle and who is intended as a model for the anticipated female reader; this idealised persona cultivated in the opening pages is present to the extent that Markham is heavily invested in the 'ideal of an orderly hierarchical society led by an aristocracy that was noble in action as well as in birth'.[11] That sense of order is crucial for Markham throughout his tract: his housewife must be organised and of good mind when approaching certain tasks around health and medicine, or working with herbs, or cookery and distilling: physically and psychologically ready to devote herself to her role. And Markham's domestic goddess, like Gouge's, should suppress any emotion or feelings of rage, translating her innate inward virtue into an outward calm and serenity, and should always prefer modesty over coyness in her attire, which should be 'comely and strong, made as well to preserve the health, as adorne the person, altogether without toyish fashions ... and as farre from the vanity of new and fantastique fashions, as neere to the comely imitations of modest Matrons' (sig. B2r–v). The orderly conduct, both practical and behavioural, expected of the woman in the domestic context is directly modelled by Markham in his layout, the 'organisational tidiness' of which is one of the ways in which it can be distinguished from other handbooks of the kind and from the same period.[12] Nonetheless, Markham's female reader, cultivated particularly in the second edition of 1623 and in subsequent versions, is afforded a measure of respect by him. Although we again encounter here the familiar mingling of practical and moral instruction, the author inserts what might be regarded as a direct evocation of the authority of the housewife, especially in specific spaces of the home wherein she is an officer or 'marshall' (sig. R4r–v), terms of course instantly and exclusively associated with male roles in domestic cultures of service; such specific terms applied in a certain context perhaps shore up rather than challenge the heavily demarcated and prescribed role of the housewife in the home and in society but may also be designed to satisfy the concerns of a patron or an eager reading public.

Markham's presumed that women needed a 'range of intellectual and practical skills that were intimately linked to a set of moral, specifically Christian and "feminine" qualities' (198).

[10] Wendy Wall, 'Reading the Home: The Case of *The English Housewife*', in Helen Smith and Louise Wilson (eds), *Renaissance Paratexts* (Cambridge, 2011), 165–84, 165; title page, 1615 edition. See also Griffin, *Instructional Writing*, 168.

[11] Michael R. Best (ed.), *The English Housewife* (Montreal, 1986; repr. 1994, 1998), xi.

[12] Best, *English Housewife*, xix.

OBSTETRICS AND GYNAECOLOGY, AND THE FEMALE INSTRUCTOR

I have so far discussed practical texts that were male-authored, intended to be read by men and sometimes by women, or by men to women, and as Lynette Hunter has observed, 'most household or behaviour books, while for and about women's lives, assumed that women would get their knowledge by way of the men in their lives—or at least that they were the correct channel'.[13] Of course that paradigm was acceptable as long as the woman in public discourse was imagined to be a 'weak creature not endued with like strength and constancy of mind', and the very firm notion persisted that women's acquisition of learning should be a private matter, to be managed in the home.[14] However, practical instruction increasingly became a more public, visible enterprise, a fact perhaps reflected in the common exhortations in print about private responsibility around consumption and regulation.

That public–private tension that characterised much practical writing is perhaps best evidenced in the fields of obstetrics and gynaecology. In certain contexts women publicly entered into the male-dominated world of print, and did so often in the context of practical writing around female health, cultivating thereby 'female textual communities'.[15] Such communities, perhaps particularly adhering to matters of health, would have been associated with knowledge that was principally transmitted orally before the advent of print. Since the late medieval period, texts relating to obstetrics and gynaecology demonstrate the gendering of women's healthcare and mediate the private matter of pregnancy and childbirth, thereby pushing back at the dominance of men in medical practices and discourses.[16] Indeed the texts in circulation for and by women are not academic, and midwives and women practitioners were considered to have been 'less learned in physiological theories and therefore less capable in practice'.[17]

Early modern women were perhaps influenced by, or aware of, the widely circulated *Trotula* texts (medieval midwifery tracts, so-called for their purported author, Trota of Salerno) and traditions of the medieval period that frequently encouraged women to take control of their own healthcare and literacy. Midwives and women writers of the early modern period placed a similar emphasis on the need for education and support among women with respect to healthcare. Early *Trotula* texts in English articulated a

[13] Lynette Hunter, 'Books for Daily Life: Household, Husbandry, Behaviour', in J. Barnard and D. F. McKenzie (eds), *The Cambridge History of the Book in Britain, vol. IV: 1557–1695* (Cambridge, 2002), 514–32, 524.

[14] *Homily on Marriage* (1652), quoted in Trill et al., *'Lay By Your Needles'*, 3.

[15] Jennifer Wynne Hellwarth, *The Reproductive Unconscious in Medieval and Early Modern England* (London, 2002), 15.

[16] For which see Monica H. Green, *Making Women's Medicine Masculine: The Rise of Male Authority in Pre-Modern Gynaecology* (Oxford, 2008), 182–4.

[17] Hellwarth, *The Reproductive Unconscious*, 11.

tension between private concerns and a sense of communal responsibility to other women, often directly appealing to female readers who are 'lettyrde' to read the text 'to other unlettyrd and help hem and conceyle [*advise*] hem [*them*] in here maladyes withowytn scheuynge here desyre to man', but also attempting to safeguard against the male reader who might read it for 'dyspyte' or 'sclaundure' of women.[18] Statements of community and solidarity are a feature of similar texts in print, and early modern readers of Jane Sharp's *The Midwives Book* (1671) would have found similar sentiments, here addressed primarily to her 'sisters' in professional midwifery while simultaneously cultivating a wider public.[19] Sharp's intended readers are first and foremost fellow midwives, distinguished by the author from those who practise without adequate knowledge of anatomy and related disciplines. Sharp's authority is twofold, derived from experience and a bookish knowledge resting on her consultation of different versions of midwifery texts across several vernaculars and, in an interesting extension of the situation in the later Middle Ages, she is concerned to valorise book-learning even in the face of the growing professionalisation and masculinisation of medicine.[20] Sharp's condemnation of 'unskilful Midwives' is balanced by an impassioned defence of the practical and speculative knowledge of the female practitioner. Positioning the midwife as key to the responsible transmission and application of knowledge, Sharp carefully moderates her admiration for the formal education received by male practitioners ('I cannot deny the honour due to able *Physicians* and *Cyrurgions*') with the equally valid knowledge possessed by women, which she describes as 'the natural propriety of women to be much seeing into that Art [of midwifery]'. Sharp acknowledges, however, that 'though nature be not alone sufficient to the perfection of it, yet farther knowledge may be gain'd by a long a diligent practice, and communicated to others of our own sex' (sig. B2r).

Although her main concern is to distinguish her experience and service from that of her male counterparts, Sharp's words of warning around the dangers of unskilled medical practitioners echo those found in other popular medical treatises in circulation at the time, notably *The Birth of Mankind* by Eucharius Rösslin (1540), a midwifery manual that similarly warns against hasty and rash midwives, remaining in print in the revised and extended version of 1545 for more than one hundred years.[21] Rösslin's text, prepared for English readers by Richard Jonas and Thomas Raynalde, warns men against misuse

[18] *The Knowing of Woman's Kind in Childing*: translator's prologue, quoted in Jocelyn Wogan-Browne, Nicholas Watson, Andrew Taylor, and Ruth Evans (eds), *The Idea of the Vernacular: An Anthology of Middle English Literary Theory, 1280–1520* (Exeter, 1999), 158.

[19] Jane Sharp, *The Midwives Book. Or the Whole Art of Midwifery Discovered. Directing Childbearing Women How to Behave Themselves in their Conception, Breeding, Bearing, and Nursing* (London, 1671). For extracts see Kate Aughterson (ed.), *Renaissance Women: A Sourcebook*. (London, 1995).

[20] Green, *Making Women's Medicine*, xiii.

[21] The 1540 edition is dedicated to Katherine Howard, the fifth wife of Henry VIII. The text, according to Hobby was the 'first published text in English that sought to explain to the general reader where babies came from and how to look after them in their infancy'. See Hobby, '"Dreams and plain dotage": The Value of *The Birth of Mankind*', *Essays and Studies: Literature and Science*, 61 (2008), 35–52, 35.

of its information, perhaps thereby implying that the expected audience is male though, as noted by Elaine Hobby, Raynalde's re-editing of the work introduces a new subtitle—'The Women's Book'—and directly addresses a female reader in certain sections.[22] Sharp seems to want to clearly define a place for her work—the first in print to have been written by a female midwife—in this long tradition of male-authored print. She is a public advocate for the education of women and their midwives but is as cautious as her male counterparts about the more negative implications of publication. Once again we find here a strong statement of duty around the sharing of knowledge, combined with an overt warning about the evils of unregulated reading that is often replicated in medical works from this period.[23] Sharp's Courteous Reader' should practise:

> modesty ... as I have endeavoured to do in the writing of it, considering that such an Art as this cannot be set forth, but that young men and maids will have must just cause to blush sometimes, and be ashamed of their own follies, as I wish they may, if they shall chance to read it, that they may not convert that into evil that is really intended for a general good. (Sig. B3r)

There are no such conditions attached to the only extant almanac written by a woman in this period. Almanacs were a common source of practical knowledge, often incorporating a combination of calendar material, predictions, cures, and receipts and, though they were accessed by many members of a household, they were nearly always compiled by men.[24] Like Sharp, Sarah Jinner directly addresses the issue of the marginalisation of women's expertise and problems in a healthcare landscape by the male-dominated professions.[25] However, her 1659 almanac marshals the problem of modesty in order to directly discuss the reluctance of women to seek help for gynaecological matters, and in so doing shows little of the respect that Sharp affords to male physicians. Ostensibly the work gives little indication that it is intended for female readers save for an engraving of a woman on the title page, opening with the usual staples of printed almanacs of this period, including a Zodiac Man (a diagram indicating body parts ruled and influenced by signs of the zodiac) and a calendar. Unlike Sharp, Jinner's epistle dedicatory, prefacing a section on prognostications, recipes, and remedies, expresses the ineffectiveness of some physicians in quite assertive tones. Though she claims to avoid offensive language, her chief purpose is to present her cures as 'helps to Nature', suitable

[22] Hobby, '"Dreams"', 37, 41.

[23] The lengthy prefaces to John Hall's 1565 edition of Lanfranc of Milan's surgical text contain similar advice and warnings; see Griffin, *Instructional Writing*, 1–32.

[24] See further Bernard Capp, *Astrology and the Popular Press: English Almanacs, 1500–1800*. London: 1979; repr. 2008.

[25] According to Kristine Kowalchuk (ed.), *Preserving on Paper: Seventeenth Century Englishwomen's Receipt Books* (Toronto, 2017), the seventeenth century saw a 'profusion of male-authored manuscript and printed texts dealing with food and medicine at both the household and professional level, and these texts were mixed in their acceptance of women's authority' (20–1). Sarah Jinner, An Almanack and Prognostication for the Year of our Lord 1659 (London, 1659).

for those who for the sake of modesty are 'shie of acquainting Physicians'. The author is roundly dismissive both of modesty and incompetence:

> Onely they will carry their water to a Physician, and tell him they have a pain in the bottom of their bellies; and the Physician is such a Dunce, he cannot discern the true cause of the Distemper; so the party suffers. (sig. B1r)

Jinner does not exclusively address women at first in this short epistle, instead evoking the 'natural comfort of man and woman', but as she begins to recommend texts that are useful for healthcare, female procreation and modesty and virtue in such matters become her focus, as does the matter of access to knowledge for women.[26]

Early in the epistle, Jinner discusses the fact that her promulgation of women's secrets (medical advice) may have been offensive to some readers, as noted earlier. This, her first almanac, perhaps drew some criticism: 'this year', she writes, 'I here present thee with some other of the like nature, avoiding such Language, as may, perhaps, be offensive to some, whose tender Ears cannot away with the hearing of what, without scruples they will do' (sig. B1r). The criticism, according to Weber, may have come in the form of a mock-almanac by one Sarah Ginnor, a response to the opening up of women's matters and the robust defence of women's writing alongside 'a critique of a society that excluded women from serious intellectual endeavour'.[27] Importantly, Jinner aligns herself, in her evocation of Levinus Lemnius and A. Massarius, with a 'learned and written tradition of medicine, not a folk-herbalist or oral body of knowledge as one might expect judging from the popular nature of the almanac'.[28] The openness characterising Jinner's approach in her early almanacs is replaced in later editions by a more clandestine approach to 'abortifacient and emmenagogic [menstrual-inducing] drugs, such as pennyroyal and mugwort', particularly in the 1660 edition, though, like many male writers of the time she 'never mentions these drugs in connection with aborting a live foetus'.[29]

The receipts gathered by Jinner are neutrally worded around the delicate issue of menstruation: there are several of the same type, variously comprising formulas for syrups and electuaries, but also including receipts to ease conception, pills to expel a dead child, and potions to help with excessive bleeding in childbirth. In the same way that Jinner is indebted, according to Weber, to Massarius' *The Woman Counsellour* (1657) for several of these texts, we can easily imagine this kind of receipt being transcribed into the household books that women compiled, shared, and consulted certainly with more

[26] Specifically Levinus Leminus' *The Secret Miracles of Nature* (1658) and A. Massarius' *The Woman Counsellour* (1657), both of which were published by John Streater, Jinner's own publisher. Several of the female cures listed in Jinner are drawn from the latter; see Alan S. Weber (ed.), *Almanacs: Printed Writings, 1641–1700: Series II, Part One, Volume 6: The Early Modern Englishwoman: A Facsimile Library of Essential Works & Printed Writings* (London, 2002), n.p.

[27] See Weber, *Almanacs*, n.p., where the mock-almanac is reprinted in facsimile.

[28] Weber, *Almanacs*, n.p.

[29] Weber, *Almanacs*, n.p.

regularity from the late 1500s. These rich repositories incorporate material of all kinds relating to domestic work and food but also healthcare and the fabrication of materials and stuff needed in busy households, and many examples of these books have been now curated and made available to scholars via the database *Perdita Manuscripts 1500–1700*, by the Folger Shakespeare Library, and the Wellcome Library among others. However, it is worth noting that many more such volumes are held in institutions and libraries globally, often miscatalogued or hidden, bound with other materials.[30] As scholars like Elaine Leong have shown, the feminised early modern domestic space was an active 'site of knowledge production', and its books (like the Fairfax recipe book that is the subject of her study) demonstrate that householders produced homemade medicines, cures, and other substances, like ink.[31] Household books often provide evidence that early modern women were not only active consumers of printed works but that they were heavily invested in textual transmission and exchange and in the production of new books and repositories of knowledge, some intensely personal and particular to a family or group of women. Moreover, like their sisters who carved out a place in the male-dominated landscape of printed books, they were also interested in the education of women in their family or employ.

DOMESTIC BOOK PRODUCTION AND PRACTICAL TEXTS

The textual culture of the manuscript was mobilised by women in incredibly resourceful ways, perhaps because of its accessibility and flexibility. One useful example that demonstrates just how actively women engaged with print culture is the household book of Dorothy Lewkenore which is preserved as part of the composite and complex manuscript Bodleian Library Ashmole 1477, and is dated by Dorothy's hand to 1576.[32] The two sections of this manuscript that can be linked to Dorothy show evidence that the compiler accessed printed books but also availed of communities of knowledge exchange when compiling her book. There are sections copied from William Clever's *The Flowre*

[30] See *Perdita Manuscripts, 1500–1700*, Adam Matthew Digital, https://www.amdigital.co.uk/primary-sources/perdita-manuscripts-1500-1700, accessed 30 June 2020; Szilvia Szmuk-Tanenbaum and Stephen Schmidt (eds), *Manuscript Cookbook Survey*, https://www.manuscriptcookbookssurvey.org/, accessed 30 June 2020; and 'Wellcome Library | Recipe books', The Wellcome Library, https://wellcomelibrary.org/collections/digital-collections/recipe-books/, accessed 30 June 2020.

[31] Elaine Leong, 'Collecting Knowledge for the Family: Recipes, Gender and Practical Knowledge in the Early Modern English Household', *Centarus*, 55 (2013), 82.

[32] See further Griffin, *Instructional Writing*, 144 ff., and Catherine Field, '"Many hands hands": Writing the Self in Early Modern Recipe Books', in Michelle M. Dowd and Julie Eckerle (eds), *Genre and Women's Life Writing in Early Modern England* (Aldershot, 2007), 49–64, 52–3. For the catalogue description of BL, MS Ashmole 1477 see https://medieval.bodleian.ox.ac.uk/catalog/manuscript_275, accessed 30 June 2020.

of Phisicke (1590) and Thomas Lupton's *A Thousand Notable Things, of Sundry Sortes* (1579), both popular works in print, the latter of which was written in plain English 'to better profit a great sorte, then to feede the fancies of a few'.[33] Moreover, statements of efficacy relating to receipts are testament to the transmission of texts in the community are also common, like that attached to the medicine 'for ye plague, used at Redding w[ith] great good successe [. . .] July 1 1603'.[34]

It is important to note that, although some women were engaged in the production of printed practical texts in this period, the 'archive suggests that *more* women than men were involved in the compilation of manuscript recipe books, just as it is true that *more* men than women were involved in the creation of printed agricultural, husbandry, and household texts, as well as professional cookbooks and medical books'.[35] The recognition of household books as a significant part of the landscape of early modern women's writing has come to the fore as part of a broader conceptualisation of what might be included in such a category, requiring a welcome readjustment of what might be said to be rather a narrow view on authorship.[36] Receipt books can seem predominantly practical, but they may also contribute to an understanding of the public–private divide, functioning as repositories of knowledge that may have been shared or communally formed, acknowledging networks and practices of exchange, and at the same time being intensely personal compilations that can be examined as 'forms of the selves who created them'.[37] Because the lives of middling status women (those most likely to have produced such books) were closely tied up with the 'performance of domestic work, scholars have suggested that writing about household issues might constitute a form of life-writing' that reflected 'interior thoughts and feelings, attitudes and outlooks in a range of written forms'.[38] And as Catherine Richardson further suggests, the ways in which these books 'mix culinary with medical recipes links them to the conception of household activity which came across so strongly from women's diaries'.[39] We can see evidence of some of this desire to personalise in, for instance, the receipt book of Constance Hall (1672) which has a fine decorative title page with calligraphic flourishes, giving prominence to her name and the ownership of the book.[40]

Household books that preserve medical, culinary, and household material are significant in many respects, bearing witness to female networks, and demonstrating that the

[33] For further examples see Archer, 'Women and Chymistry', 205, which cites several printed sources for the receipts copied by Sarah Wigges into her book.

[34] Griffin, *Instructional Writing*, 145.

[35] Kowalchuk, *Preserving on Paper*, 21.

[36] Kowalchuk, *Preserving on Paper*, 4.

[37] Richardson, Catherine. 'Household Writing', in Caroline Bicks and Jennifer Summit (eds), *The History of British Women's Writing, 1500–1610* (London, 2010), 89–107, 98.

[38] Richardson, 'Household Writing', 98, citing Margaret J. M. Ezell, 'Domestic Papers: Manuscript Culture and Early Modern Women's Life Writing', in Dowd and Eckerle (eds), 33–48, 44.

[39] Richardson, 'Household Writing', 99.

[40] Washington, DC, Folger Shakespeare Library, MS V.a.20, f. 1^r; see Kowalchuk, *Preserving on Paper*, 159–243.

traditionally male-dominated practices of manuscript production had been adopted and adapted by women by the latter half of the sixteenth century. Their construction of authority, though perhaps not directly comparable with women's writing in print, is nonetheless evidence of an 'increasing desire to textualise knowledge'.[41] In household books, 'experience met with the written word' affording the practices of women 'a parity with previously printed male example'.[42] The feminised spaces of the household become in the physicality of the receipt book firmly connected to textual production, and the book is a space in which women's voices and identities are symbolically and practically aligned with not just the work of the home but also, importantly, with the traditionally male spheres of instruction, textual production, and education. Effectively, then, women fashioned their own textual authority in and through these books. Evidence of the profound relation with textuality can often be found preserved in the books themselves, such as the recipes for ink-making that are carefully copied into several receipt books. One such is the receipt book that is attributed to Mary Granville, the daughter of Sir Martin Westcomb, and her daughter Anne Granville D'Ewes (Washington, DC, Folger Shakespeare Library, MS V.a.430).[43] A large paper book that begins with 'remedies rather than recipes, which is somewhat rare … amongst receipt books', the manuscript contains three recipes for making ink that are heavily linked to the women's male relatives and acquaintances.[44] One, attributed to Mary's brother John Westcomb, appears to have been copied into the household book in his hand, and is especially detailed, giving instruction on how to make 'double Incke kalled In ffrench ancre Luisante' and calling for all of the regular ingredients for home-made ink at this time, such as vitriol, gum Arabic, and oak galls; the attribution and date of January 1671 are recorded in Mary's hand.[45] A second recipe in English is attributed to Mr William Fens, and the attribution records that it had been given to Mary in Malaga in 1646, while yet another, this time in Spanish, was had from Juan Baqueriso in Cadiz.[46] The attribution of recipes, as we have seen, is not at all unusual, but the direct link here between the male relatives and acquaintances (and in one case an act of copying undertaken by one such relative) highlight the recipes as sites of familial exchange that directly rests on literacy

[41] Richardson, 'Household Writing', 99.

[42] Richardson, 'Household Writing', 99, and quoting Field, '"Many hands hands"', 54.

[43] See also Kowalchuk, *Preserving on Paper*, 61ff., for an edition of the recipes in the volume and an introduction to the book's textual history. According to Kowalchuk the volume measures 21x16.5 cm, with a vellum binding that has metal catches. The volume can be dated *c* 1640–1750. Sir Martin Westcomb was the English consul in Cadiz.

[44] Kowalchuk, *Preserving on Paper*, 61.

[45] Kowalchuk, *Preserving on Paper*, 105. On recipes for ink and book-arts from this period see Griffin 73–109.

[46] Kowalchuk, *Preserving on Paper*, 104–5, 151; see also Helen Smith, 'Women and the Materials of Writing,' in Patricia Pender and Rosalind Smith (eds), *Material Cultures of Early Modern Women's Writing* (London, 2014), 16–35. On this and other instances of the preservation of recipes particularly from this region see Madeline Bassnett, 'A Language Not One's Own: Translational Exchange in Seventeenth-Century Englishwomen's Iberian Recipes', *Journal for Early Modern Cultural Studies*, 19.1 (2019), 1–27.

and literate practice. Similar recipes, many of which were transmitted from the medieval period, are extant in early modern household books; for instance, the receipt book of Sarah Wigges preserves recipes for ink, as does that compiled by Elizabeth Bourne.[47] Account and household books from this period also show evidence that paper and the ingredients for ink were often part of the purchases organised by women in this period. The world of literacy was not closed off to women, but rather was a large part of the work of the household, work that involved 'the production of everything contained in the equivalent of a bathroom cabinet, kitchen cupboards, and the contents of your desk'.[48] Such recipes had been in circulation since the later medieval period and seem to have been transferred to women with more frequency in the early modern period, eliciting interest from women like, for instance, Elizabeth Elstob.[49]

The persistence of practical texts relating to writing and ink-making should not surprise us. It is perhaps self-evident that women involved in textual production would need the materials and skills to make this happen: the ability to cut and maintain quills; the preparation of paper; the fabrication of ink; and the application of wax for letters.[50] As the Granville volume shows, recipes for ink in circulation in this period were often not complex, and paper was more widely available to purchase. However, this tangible interest in literacy may well point to household books as important sites for practical instruction for women who otherwise may not have access to education, and certainly not to contexts in which 'their learning might have had a practical application'.[51] The practical function of receipt books may well have extended beyond the preservation of useful knowledge to the realm of literacy and education. Kowalchuk argues that consideration of receipt books greatly alters our understanding of literacy rates among early modern Englishwomen, challenging Cressy's estimate of a low literacy rate of ten per cent until the late seventeenth century. Coupled with Clarke's assertion that women 'readers and writers could, and did, adopt and adapt the mainstream habits of literacy current in their world' it may offer fresh perspectives on political and social implications of gathering practical texts together in this way.[52] And indeed some household books show direct evidence of education in action: Mary Fothergill's book, dated 1692, is copied in several hands, with signs that an unpractised hand copied the ends of some recipes (for instance

[47] London, Royal College of Physicians, MS 65; see Archer, 'Women and Chymistry', 191; James Daybell, *Women Letter-Writers in Tudor England* (Oxford, 2006), 53. Daybell notes an ink receipt in the Dering Family Remembrance Book, Folger V.b.296. There are two recipes for ink in Glasgow University Library, Ferguson MS 15, a receipt book from *c* 1700. I am currently preparing a study of ink recipes and evidence for paper and pen use in household books.

[48] Hunter, 'Books for Daily Life', 514.

[49] The antiquarian Elstob copied Glasgow University Library, MS Hunter 330 from a printed text on how to make coloured and gilded letters 'as are to be seen frequently in old manuscripts' in 1710.

[50] James Daybell and Andrew Gordon, 'The Early Modern Letter Opener', in *Cultures of Correspondence in Early Modern Britain* (Philadelphia, PA, 1999), 1–26, 6.

[51] Danielle Clarke, *The Politics of Early Modern Women's Writing* (London, 2001), 23.

[52] Kowalchuk, *Preserving on Paper*, 29; Clarke, *Politics*, 23, who cites David Cressy, *Literacy and the Social Order* (Cambridge, 1980), 42–61.

at fol. 56v).[53] Ink recipes and related shorter, practical texts might be usefully reimagined as 'embedded discourses' that can offer insights into some of the ways in which practical writings were marshalled in more political ways.[54] Women were also able to access such material in printed form, and manuals designed to appeal to a female readership very often blended household recipes with everyday medical remedies and recipes for ink.[55] In many ways this collocation makes sense, since the recipe format was familiar to women, the text-type often favouring the 'take and make' formula. And scholars, among them Helen Smith and Wendy Wall, have noted the symbolic and imaginative synergies between the work expected by the housewife and the material processes behind writing and other aspects of manuscript production.[56]

The kinds of reading and literary activity that were deemed appropriate for women seem to have been less restrictive when it came to practical matters, though the instructional literature that was produced for the printing presses and chiefly by male authors was often framed by moralistic statements on the correct behaviour of a woman, publicly and privately. The ideal woman in the home is, paradoxically, both a public and private figure, and the practical books produced by women themselves in the home have the quality of both private and public documents. They are unique and personal, often evidencing careful penmanship and visible and dramatic statements of ownership and authorship, but they also anticipate other readers and at times record changes in ownership between women. And perhaps they are also governed by this sense of duty that often characterises practical writing from this period: the duty of the housewife to collect, compose, and distribute recipes, in particular those for healthcare and of the greatest benefit to others. Household books, I suggest, even in their most basic forms, perform that public–private split that seems to have been at the heart of a great many practical texts concerning women from this period but it is also possible to say that their sense of responsibility was first and foremost to other women.

FURTHER READING

Burke, Victoria E. and Jonathan Gibson (eds). *Women and Early Modern Manuscript Culture.* Aldershot, 2004.

Clarke, Danielle. 'Dorothy Parsons of Birr: Writing, Networks, Identity, 1640–1670'. *The Seventeenth Century* 37.1 (2022), 23–45.

53 Edinburgh, National Library of Scotland, MS W10231.

54 Susan Leonardi, 'Recipes for Reading: Pasta Salad, Lobster a la Riseholme, Key Lime Pie', *PMLA*, 104.3 (1989), 340, quoted in Kowalchuk, *Preserving on Paper*, 5.

55 For example John Partridge's *The Widdow's Treasure* (1595) contains an ink recipe at sig. B5v, while *The Book of Secrets* (1596), compiled by William Phillips, has several. See Daybell, *The Material Letter in Early Modern England: Manuscript Letters and the Culture and Practices of Letter-Writing 1512–1635* (Basingstoke, 2012), 38–9.

56 Smith, 'Women and the Materials of Writing'; Wendy Wall, 'Household "Writing": or the Joys of Carving', in Rebecca Ann Bach and Gwynne Kennedy (eds), *Feminisms and Early Modern Texts: Essays for Phyllis Rackin* (Cranbury, NJ, 2010), 25–42.

Di Meo, Michelle and Sara Pennell (eds). *Reading and Writing Recipe Books, 1500–1700*. Manchester, 2013.

Kowalchuk, Kristine (ed.). *Preserving on Paper: Seventeenth-Century Englishwomen's Recipe Books*. Toronto, 2018.

Leong, Elaine. *Recipes and Everyday Knowledge: Medicine, Science and the Household in Early Modern England*. Chicago, IL, 2018.

Wall, Wendy. *Recipes for Thought: Knowledge and Taste in the Early Modern Kitchen*. Philadelphia, PA, 2016.

CHAPTER 7

CULTURES OF CORRESPONDENCE

Women and Natural Philosophy

HELEN SMITH

'MADAM', writes Margaret Cavendish, near the beginning of her *Philosophical Letters* (1664):

> You have been pleased to send me the Works of four Famous and Learned Authors, to wit, of two most Famous Philosophers of our Age, *Des Cartes*, and *Hobbs*, and of that Learned Philosopher and Divine Dr. *More*, as also of that Famous Physician and Chymist *Van Helmont*. Which Works you have sent me not onely to peruse, but also to give my judgment of them, and to send you word by the usual way of our Correspondence, which is by Letters, how far, and wherein I do dissent from these Famous Authors, their Opinions in *Natural Philosophy*.[1]

Cavendish's clarification that she and her friend habitually correspond through letters might seem self-evident to the modern reader. In the seventeenth century, though, 'correspondence' frequently meant simply intercourse or communication: it could be as much an in person encounter as an epistolary activity.[2] The term also had particular meanings in natural philosophy: it described how objects or materials mirrored one another, articulating relationships of agreement or similarity.[3] Scientific inquiry

[1] Margaret Cavendish, *Philosophical Letters, or, Modest Reflections Upon Some Opinions in Natural Philosophy* (London, 1664), sig. B1r. 'Natural philosophy' is also the phrase now preferred by historians of premodern science, reflecting the early modern period's interest in the thought of ancient Greece and Rome and capturing the oscillations between hypothesis and practical experiment that characterised scientific inquiry at a moment when 'science' retained a capacious sense of knowledge, study, or learning.

[2] *Oxford English Dictionary* (*OED*), 'Correspondence', *n.* def. 5.

[3] *OED*, 'Correspondence', *n.* defs 1a, 2a.

was 'analogical ... its insights and expression had the structure of a rhetorical figure'; philosophers hunted parallels throughout and beyond the observable universe.[4]

This chapter explores the importance of correspondence in both senses to women's natural philosophy. Epistolary exchange offered an arena in which a small number of women negotiated their desire for scientific learning, finding a space to articulate ideas or pursue clarification. More than that, I propose, and especially for Cavendish, letters were a philosophical method in their own right. After outlining early modern Englishwomen's varied engagements with natural philosophy, this chapter explores several important epistolary exchanges, and demonstrates how Anne Conway and Margaret Cavendish engaged with questions of correspondence and antithesis, as well as the rhetorical uses of similitude, as they grappled with questions about the nature of the soul and the operations of matter. The chapter closes with Cavendish's reinvention of the letter form in her *Philosophical Letters*, arguing that this witty, peculiar book, exemplary of Cavendish's creative and mobile thought, is a manifesto for a supple epistolary methodology.

'DR MORE AND MY GALLY POTS': WOMEN AS NATURAL PHILOSOPHERS

Cavendish is one of the seventeenth century's best-known woman philosophers; recent scholarship has embraced her inventive prose and verse, tracing how formal and philosophical concerns combine to create distinctive modes of thought and expression.[5] She was known as a philosopher in her own day: in her anonymously published defence of women's education, Bathsua Makin declared: 'The present Dutchess of *New-Castle*, by her own Genius, rather than any timely Instruction, over-tops many grave Gown-Men'.[6] Makin's text builds on a tradition of catalogues of learned women, which used classical and biblical exemplars to defend female learning. In a short chapter designed to prove that 'Some Women have understood the *Mathematicks*', Makin moves between ancient and contemporary models, the latter including the Dutch painter, engraver, poet, and scholar, Anna Maria von Schurman and the influential Veronese humanist 'Isola Navarula' (Isotta Nogarola). Makin recollects that 'A Lady of late, I have forgot her name, is so well skilled in the Mathematicks, that she hath printed divers Tables' (sig. B4r),

[4] Claire Preston, *The Poetics of Scientific Investigation in Seventeenth-Century England* (Oxford, 2015), 5.

[5] See especially, Liza Blake, 'After Life in Margaret Cavendish's Vitalist Posthumanism', *Criticism*, 62.3 (2020), 433–56; Lisa T. Sarasohn, *The Natural Philosophy of Margaret Cavendish: Reason and Fancy During the Scientific Revolution* (Baltimore, MD, 2010); Jay Stevenson, 'The Mechanist-Vitalist Soul of Margaret Cavendish', *Studies in English Literature, 1500–1900*, 36.3 (1996), 527–43.

[6] Bathsua Makin, *An Essay to Revive the Antient Education of Gentlewomen* (London, 1673), sig. B1v.

probably a reference to the Silesian astronomer Maria Cunitz, who published a version of Johannes Kepler's *Rudolphine Tables* under the title *Urania propitia* (1650).[7]

As these examples suggest, women's natural philosophy took numerous forms. After the death of Elizabeth Stuart, Queen of Bohemia and Electress Palatine, a servant described the loss of her 'beautiful cabinets, full of rarities, books, and papers', suggestive of extensive collections.[8] Lucy Hutchinson, whose biblical poem *Order and Disorder* powerfully combines theology and natural philosophy, translated Lucretius' controversial *De rerum natura* as a young mother. Mary Evelyn, wife of the diarist and writer John Evelyn, learned mathematics in Paris. Her surviving papers include a series of manuscript sundials, and she designed the frontispiece to her husband's 1656 translation of Lucretius.[9] Women's interest in practical mathematics is further attested in the frontispiece to *The Catholique Planispaer, which Mr Blagrave Calleth the Mathematical Jewel,* which features a sullen-looking woman with a book (presumably Blagrave's *Jewel*), a pair of compasses, and a dial on the table before her.[10] In their poems, Anne Bradstreet, Hester Pulter, and Anne Southwell explore the intersecting grounds of natural philosophy and devotion.[11]

Some women had access to laboratories and equipment: John Aubrey described Mary Sidney Herbert as 'a great Chymist, and spent yearly a great deale in that study', and noted that she employed Adrian Gilbert, Sir Walter Raleigh's half-brother, as 'her Laborator in the house'.[12] Cavendish and her husband shared an impressive collection

[7] Warm thanks to Grace Murray for this suggestion.

[8] William Curtius' letter to Charles Louis of 21 March (presumably Old Style) 1662, Munich, Bayerisches Hauptstaatsarchiv, Geheimes Hausarchiv, Korrespondenzakten 1031, no folio, item, or page number, trans. and cited by Nadine Akkerman, 'Introduction', *The Correspondence of Elizabeth Stuart, Queen of Bohemia*, 3 vols, i: *1603–1631* (Oxford, 2015), 1. On Elizabeth's use of ciphers, see Chapter 37, Nadine Akkerman, 'Women's Ciphers'.

[9] London, British Library, Add MS 15950, fols. 178–88. See Frances Harris, 'Living in the Neighbourhood of Science: Mary Evelyn, Margaret Cavendish and the Greshamites', in Lynette Hunter and Sarah Hutton (eds), *Women, Science and Medicine, 1500–1700: Mothers and Sisters of the Royal Society* (Stroud, 1997), 198–217.

[10] For more on dialling, including this image, see Boris Jardine, 'The Book as Instrument: Craft and Technique in Early Modern Practical Mathematics', *Learning by the Book: Manuals and Handbooks in the History of Science, BIHS Themes*, 5 (2020), 111–29.

[11] On Bradstreet, see Patricia Phillippy, 'Anne Bradstreet's Family Plots: Puritanism, Humanism, Posthumanism', *Criticism*, 62.1 (2020), 29–68; on Pulter, see Cassandra Gorman, 'The Imperfect Circle: Hester Pulter's Alchemical Forms', in Subha Mukherji and Elizabeth Swann (eds), *The Poetics of Scientia in Early Modern England* (London, forthcoming) and Leah Knight and Wendy Wall (eds), 'Special Issue: The Poetry of Hester Pulter: Revolution and Remediation', *Journal for Early Modern Cultural Studies*, 20.2 (2020); on Southwell, see Kevin Killeen, 'Coles from thine altar Tipp'd theyr tongues with cunning': The Decalogue Poetry of Anne Southwell', in Sophie Read (ed.), *Literature and the Bible* (London, 2019).

[12] John Aubrey, in Kate Bennett (ed.), *Brief Lives with an Apparatus for the Lives of our English Mathematical Writers* (Oxford, 2015), 251. Elsewhere, Aubrey reports that Gilbert 'was an excellent Chymist, and a great favourite of Mary Countess of Pembroke, with whom he lived and was her Operator ... Some curious Ladies of our country, have rare Reciepts of his' (242). See Margaret P. Hannay, '"How I these Studies Prize": The Countess of Pembroke and Elizabethan Science', in Lynette Hunter and Sarah Hutton (eds), *Women, Science and Medicine, 1500–1700* (Thrupp, 1997), 108–21.

of microscopes and telescopes, with one described specifically as 'my Lady's multiplying glass'.[13] In a letter to John Locke, Damaris Masham, author of the anonymously published *A Discourse Concerning the Love of God* (1696) and *Occasional Thoughts in Reference to a Vertuous or Christian Life* (1705), painted an entertaining scene of the realities of attempting philosophical pursuits in her closet, while secluded on a country estate. 'I can but think', she tells Locke:

> how you would smile to see Cowley and my Surfeit Waters Jumbled together; with Dr More and my Gally Potts of Mithridate and Dioscordium; My Receits and Account Books with Antoninus his Meditations, and Des Cartes Principles; with my Globes, and my Spining Wheel.[14]

Domestic medicines jostle with play texts; philosophical writings with pill and ointment pots; directions to make foodstuffs and medicines with records of household finance and stoic advice on withdrawing from worldly things. The medley is designedly playful, lamenting Masham's inability to focus on the life of the mind, while flaunting her wit and learning. Putting Descartes' *Principles of Philosophy* alongside globes and spinning wheels, for instance, makes reference not only to his book's concern for the physical principles governing the movement of objects, but to the printer's device of the publisher Joan Blaeu, an armillary sphere, which featured prominently on Descartes' title page.

In a section of his popular *The Jewell House of Art and Nature* (1594) which offers 'Divers Chimicall Conclusions Concerning the Art of Distillation', Hugh Plat promises to proceed to 'such matters as I am assured that everie Gentlewoman that delighteth in Chimical practises wil be wiling to learne'.[15] A late seventeenth-century manuscript offers evidence of one such woman, Sarah Horsington, who compiled *Arcana, or, Mysteries in ye Theory of Physiology and Chymistry: Being Authentick Rules, for Preparing Spagyricall* [alchemical] *Medicaments, for my own Observation and Satisfaction* from the papers of her husband, a doctor, as well as the writings of Robert Boyle and others.[16] The manuscript receipt book of Sarah Wigges, compiled between 1616 and *c* 1670 brings together medical and culinary receipts with illustrations of a stillroom, instructions for making the Philosopher's Stone, and accounts of how to counterfeit precious stones.[17] Lynette Hunter has noted the extent to which the well-stocked kitchen and

[13] Emma Wilkins, 'Margaret Cavendish and the Royal Society', *Notes and Records of the Royal Society of London*, 68.3 (2014), 245–60.

[14] Damaris Masham to John Locke, 14 November 1685, in Jacqueline Broad, *Women Philosophers of Seventeenth-Century England: Selected Correspondence* (Oxford, 2019), 163.

[15] Hugh Plat, *Divers Chimicall Conclusions* (separate dated title page, pagination, and register), sig. C2v, in *The Jewell House of Art and Nature* (London, 1594).

[16] Los Angeles, William Andrews Clark Memorial Library, MS 2009.015.

[17] London, Royal College of Physicians, MS 654. For a detailed account of the book, see Jayne Elisabeth Archer, 'Women and Chymistry in Early Modern England: The Manuscript Receipt Book (c.

stillhouse contained the necessary equipment for experimental philosophy and argues that men frequently made use of this space in ways that relied upon and encouraged collaborations with women (see this volume, Chapter 22, Wendy Wall, 'The World of Recipes'). In particular, Hunter posits that Katherine Jones, Lady Ranelagh, worked closely with Boyle, her brother, as well as other male philosophers, and that Boyle drew upon Ranelagh's kitchen observations in his published writings.[18] One of Ranelagh's two surviving recipe books contains detailed chemical recipes, and closes with a guide to 'our' chemical symbols, suggesting a collaboration based in the sharing of experiential knowledge and written codes.[19]

Even without overt claims to physiological and chemical knowledge, women engaged extensively with the phenomena that fascinated empiricist philosophers, responding to the properties and behaviours of ingredients, and possessing an intimate knowledge of natural processes. Wendy Wall has argued for 'a rich and previously unacknowledged literate and brainy domestic culture' centred around the kitchen, while Elaine Leong explores in detail the 'household science' or 'quotidian home-based investigations of the natural world' manifested in the textual flurry she describes as the 'recipe fever' of the seventeenth century.[20] In a suggestive reading of Aphra Behn, Edith Snook charts how Indigenous knowledge, specifically of the Americas, 'functioned for the English in the early modern period as a kind of vernacular science', and argues 'that women, as users of this knowledge, are part of a culture that in recipes both forgets this history of sources and remembers Indigenous practices and technologies'.[21] These interventions encourage us to take more seriously than Masham the inclusion of receipt books and domestic medicines among the materials of learning.

EPISTOLARY PHILOSOPHY

Letters were crucial philosophical tools. As Henry Oldenburg put it in a letter to Stanislaw Lubienietzki:

1616) of Sarah Wigges', in Kathleen P. Long (ed.), *Gender and Scientific Discourse in Early Modern Culture* (Farnham, 2010), 191–216.

[18] Lynette Hunter, 'Sisters of the Royal Society: The Circle of Katherine Jones, Lady Ranelagh', in Hunter and Hutton (eds), *Women, Science and Medicine*, 178–97, esp. 182–4.

[19] London, British Library, Sloane MS 1367.

[20] Wendy Wall, Recipes for Thought: Knowledge and Taste in the Early Modern English Kitchen (Philadelphia, PA, 2016), 1. Elaine Leong, *Recipes and Everyday Knowledge: Medicine, Science, and the Household in Early Modern England* (Chicago, IL, 2018), 4, 2.

[21] Edith Snook, 'English Women's Writing and Indigenous Medical Knowledge in the Early Modern Atlantic World', in Patricia Phillippy (ed.), *A History of Early Modern Women's Writing* (Cambridge, 2018), 382–97, 384.

> The elements of human knowledge ... are scattered and dispersed throughout the globe. I think there is no better way of assembling them than by constantly bringing together the zealous and the inventive in regular correspondence.[22]

Letters were 'the conduit through which news was relayed, orders were conveyed, plans were laid, and trade was transacted'.[23] They made the writer present to and with the reader, creating, in Erasmus' formulation, a 'mutual conversation between absent friends'.[24] Cavendish encapsulates this popular sentiment at the beginning of *CCXI Sociable Letters*, published in the same year as the *Philosophical Letters*:

> I am never better pleased, than when I am reading your Letters, and when I am writing Letters to you; for my mind and thoughts are all that while in your Company: the truth is, my mind and thoughts live alwayes with you, although my person is at distance from you.[25]

The effect of intimate presence was achieved not only through words designed to capture (or appear to capture) the writer's inmost thoughts and feelings, but also through the letter's shape and size: a sheet or few sheets of paper, tightly folded for secure carrying and to deter unwelcome readers. The art of letterlocking exemplifies how letters helped create the boundary between 'private' and 'public', keeping the promise of confidentiality in constant tension with the possibility of interception or circulation to unanticipated audiences.[26] Letters were also an important genre of print publication: numerous manuals instructed would-be correspondents on effective epistolary techniques, while classical, humanist, and biblical letters—especially Paul's Epistles—circulated on bookstalls alongside printed books of letters offering up news (including about Cavendish's husband, William), secrets, military strategy, and scandal.

A number of women engaged in extended correspondence on natural philosophical topics, using letters to develop and maintain social bonds at the same time as they expanded their understandings and contributed to the processes of philosophical knowledge-making. Extant correspondence provides evidence for 'a more intensely collaborative and gender-inclusive history [of science] than some previous narratives

[22] Henry Oldenburg to Stanislaw Lubienietzki, 23 July 1666, in A. Rupert Hall and Marie Boas Hall (eds), *The Correspondence of Henry Oldenburg*, 9 vols (Madison, 1965–1973), 3, 192, cited in Claire Preston, 'Utopian Intelligences: Scientific Correspondence and Christian Virtuousos', in Anne Dunan-Page and Clotilde Prunier (eds), *Debating the Faith: Religion and Letter Writing in Great Britain, 1550–1800* (Dordrecht, 2012), 139–58.

[23] Alan Stewart, *Shakespeare's Letters* (Oxford, 2008), 5.

[24] Erasmus, *De conscribendis epistolis*, in J. K. Sowards (ed.) and Charles Fantazzi (trans.), *Collected Works of Erasmus: Literary and Educational Writings*, 86 vols, xxv (Toronto, 1985), 20.

[25] Margaret Cavendish, *CCXI Sociable Letters Written by the Thrice Noble, Illustrious, and Excellent Princess, the Lady Marchioness of Newcastle* (London, 1664), sig. A1v.

[26] See the essays collected in James Daybell and Andrew Gordon (eds), *Cultures of Correspondence in Early Modern Britain* (Philadelphia, PA, 2016). On letterlocking, see http://letterlocking.org, accessed 17 June 2021.

have suggested', albeit one that remains focused on elites.[27] More generally, as Nadine Akkerman argues in this volume, extant letters witness women's ability to negotiate and make use of rhetorical, generic, and social conventions, and to foster and give shape to family and friendship networks (see this volume, Chapter 37, 'Women's Letters').

Cavendish's description of her philosophical epistles, with which I opened this chapter, reflects the realities of letter-writing in early modern England. Letters were often accompanied by gifts: in this case, four books representing the most on-trend developments in seventeenth-century thought. Ranging from René Descartes' meditations on the nature of matter and sensation to Thomas Hobbes' concern for the motion of physical phenomena, Henry More's rationalist theology to Jan Baptist van Helmont's investigations into spontaneous generation and the properties of gases, these volumes suggest the scope of scientific inquiry in mid-seventeenth-century England. They highlight natural philosophy's internationalism, and the importance of translation in disseminating continental thought to readers who were not fluent in modern European languages or in Latin, the international language of scholarship. Cavendish was one of those readers: she comments that 'The Authors whose opinions I mention, I have read, as I found them printed, in my native Language, except Des Cartes, who being in Latine, I had some few places translated to me out of his works' (sig. b2r).

Though the gift Cavendish describes is a fiction, it is a plausible one: several women received books from their correspondents.[28] In a sprightly letter to Locke, Masham asked:

> Is it possible that you should be Angry with your Governess, and that for no other Cause but not reading your Books. I must Confess indeed that beleeveing at present I should have no use of the Art of Navigation, the first look into it Discouraged me from proceeding farther, But if you are of an other Mind, and think it is as usefull to me, as some here do Architecture, and Trigonometri, I shall set about the understanding of them all, as fast as I can.[29]

The books Masham cannot bear to read are not texts authored by Locke, but volumes he has sent to advance her quest for autodidactic opportunities. The range of reading recommended to Masham—navigation, architecture, trigonometry—outlines the variety of practical and theoretical philosophy women might (or, in Masham's case, might not) tackle. In another letter, again thanking Locke for a book and excusing her delay in reading it, Masham, like Cavendish, laments her lack of language skills: 'For any other Books I leave it to you to do as you Please ... since I perceive that which I should be most desireous to see is not writt in a Language which I understand'.[30]

[27] Broad, *Women Philosophers*, 1.

[28] Cavendish sent presentation copies of her books to Walter Charleton, Thomas Hobbes, and Henry More, among others.

[29] Damaris Cudworth to John Locke, *c* 14 August 1682, in Broad, *Women Philosophers*, 142.

[30] Cudworth to Locke, 8 October 1684, in Broad, *Women Philosophers*, 150.

Elizabeth Stuart's daughter, Elisabeth, Princess Palatine of Bohemia, engaged in extensive correspondence with Descartes, quizzing him on physics, the passions, the nature of virtue, and the relationship between the substances of mind and body.[31] As Akkerman points out, Elisabeth did not adopt a subservient position in this relationship (see this volume, Chapter 37, 'Women's Letters'). It was at her request that Descartes wrote a short treatise defining the passions, to which she responded in a letter of 25 April 1646, and which he published in 1649 as *The Passions of the Soul*. Elisabeth also wrote to John Pell to discuss Descartes' philosophy, and engaged in a brief exchange with Nicholas Malebranche. In her letters to Descartes, Elisabeth critiques what she sees as Kenelm Digby's misreadings of his French contemporary and requests books by Hogelande and Regius. She tells Descartes about phenomena she has witnessed, with an emphasis on diseases and cures. In August 1648, for instance, Elisabeth recounted a walk in an oak wood during which she and her party 'were overcome in an instant by a sort of redness over the whole body, except for the face'. Dismissing the superstition of those who suspected witchcraft, Elisabeth reports peasant knowledge about the cause of the illness and notes the futility of the remedies attempted by the group. 'I give you this account', she concludes, 'because I presume that in it you can find something to confirm some of your doctrines'.[32] Elisabeth poses the group's mysterious affliction as a puzzle for further reflection, but hints that she has already recognised something in Descartes' writings which her observations will reinforce.

Early in their epistolary friendship, Elisabeth depicts her doubts about Descartes' theories as social beings: 'I entertain these sentiments only as friends which I do not expect to keep, assuring myself that you will explicate the nature of an immaterial substance and the manner of its actions'.[33] This striking conceit suggests Elisabeth's willingness to entertain a variety of ideas, and be persuaded of her errors, at the same time as it emphasises the sociability of the epistolary form. She closes the letter with a warm statement of affection towards her correspondent: 'I will never have stronger or more constant designs than that of being all my life, Your very affectionate friend, at your service, Elisabeth' (70). With a keen sense of social bonds, Elisabeth presents her correspondence with Descartes as wholly sympathetic. She asks him to continue correcting Seneca:

> not because your manner of reasoning is most extraordinary, but because it is the most natural that I have encountered and seems to teach me nothing new, but instead allows me to draw from my mind pieces of knowledge I have not before been aware of.[34]

[31] See also Lisa Shapiro, 'Princess Elizabeth [*sic*] and Descartes: The Union of Mind and Body and the Practice of Philosophy', *British Journal for the History of Philosophy*, 7.3 (1999), 503–20. Descartes also engaged in correspondence with Christina, Queen of Sweden (1626–1689), a monarch who aimed to establish Stockholm as a seat of philosophical excellence to rival ancient Athens.

[32] Elisabeth to Descartes, 23 August 1648, in Princess Elisabeth of Bohemia and René Descartes, in Lisa Shapiro (ed. and trans.), *The Correspondence Between Princess Elisabeth of Bohemia and René Descartes*, (Chicago, IL, 2007), 174.

[33] Elisabeth to Descartes, 10 June 1643, in *Correspondence*, 68.

[34] Elisabeth to Descartes, 16 August 1645, in *Correspondence*, 100.

The pair's correspondence on paper draws out the correspondence of their minds, allowing Elisabeth to experience classical learning as something she has always known. Masham discloses a similar, if more playful, sense of 'correspondence' with Locke, commenting, when he had been stuck in Oxford as she felt herself to be marooned in Cambridge: 'You cannot easielie immagine what a Tenderness the Parellel betweene our twoo Conditions was begining to have begot in me for you'.[35] In these examples, natural philosophical correspondence allows absent friends to indulge in and reinforce the sociable fantasy of unfettered access to one another's thoughts.

Ranelagh too engaged in correspondence with several philosophers, including Boyle and Samuel Hartlib. Like Elisabeth, she is frequently concerned with bodily infirmity and medicine. Among Hartlib's surviving papers is a short, scribal copy of 'Extracts out of My Lady Ranalaughs letter from Lismore', featuring three recipes. 'One of these enclosed receipts', Ranelagh notes, 'I have experienced for sharpe hot humors, *the* other was given me by Sir Kenelme Digby, with most Extraordinary Commendation from his owne experience against festers & inflammation'. 'The other', she concludes, 'is a probable one against that kind of fire, that possibly may bee his inflammation'.[36] Ranelagh's speculation about 'his inflammation' make it clear that these medicines—included as a separate paper or papers within the letter—were intended to contribute to the cure of a specific individual; the fact they were extracted suggests their circulation and use. Ranelagh's interest in alchemy, the precursor of modern chemistry, is apparent from a long letter to Hartlib recounting what she had been able to discover about an alchemist named Butler. While Ranelagh is most interested in the social specifics surrounding Butler's attempts to make gold in Paris, her account is striking for its acknowledgement of extra-European scientific expertise. Her informant, she relates, learned from some 'Slaves *that* had binn taken in Barbary' that, in his boyhood, Butler had been sold 'to the Basha of Tunis, who [was?] a great Philosopher, & tooke this Buttler to make his fier & blow his bellows'.[37] This letter forms part of a pattern whereby Ranelagh reports interesting tales to Hartlib, urging him to further investigation.

A sustained epistolary relationship between Anne (Finch) Conway and the Platonist Henry More, from the 1650s onwards, was brokered by Conway's brother, John Finch. In a letter to Conway, John also asked Anne to 'remember me to your library keeper Mrs Sarah', a testament to Conway's extensive book collection.[38] More too sent books with his

[35] Damaris Cudworth to John Locke, 10 June 1682, in Broad, *Women Philosophers*, 138.

[36] Sheffield, The University Library, Extract & Recipes in Scribal Hands, 11 September 1658, Hartlib Papers, MS 61, 66/8, 1A.

[37] New Haven, CT, Beinecke Rare books Library, Yale University, The James Marshall and Marie-Louise Osborn Collection, Lady Ranelagh to Hartlib, 5 April 1659, Document 38, 1A–B. On women and Indigenous philosophy, see Snook, 'English Women's Writing'; Jennifer Park's forthcoming *Thinking Racecraft through Recipes*; and Gitanjali Shahani, *Tasting Difference: Food, Race, and Cultural Encounters in Early Modern Literature* (Ithaca, NY, 2020).

[38] John Finch to Anne Conway, 10–20 Nov 1651, in Marjorie Hope Nicolson and Sarah Hutton (eds), *The Conway Letters: The Correspondence of Anne, Countess Conway, Henry More, and their*

letters: in his first extant letter to Conway, he referred to 'that Booke I have sent you [his *The Third Lash of Alazonomastix* (1651)], together with this third part of Des Cartes'.[39] Even among illness and house moves, Conway found time to ask More 'if you can procure us a copy of the second volume of Des Cartes letters'.[40] In January 1652 or 1653, More sent two copies of his latest book for Conway's husband and Mr Clifton, promising 'I differ [defer] your own till I come to Cambridge that I may send it more handsomely bound when I shall send Mrs Clifton one also'.[41] Elaborate gift copies are reserved for the women rather than their husbands, functioning within relationships that combined compliment with shared philosophical concerns. In letters which reinforce the tight connections between theology and natural philosophy across the seventeenth century, Conway reveals her interest in the relationship between soul and body. She presses More to elaborate his concept of 'vital congruity', a theory of harmonious correspondence between body and soul.[42] Elsewhere, More urged Conway towards a sympathetic mode of thought. Responding to a theological query about a biblical passage, he suggested: 'you will finde little difficulty of discovering the right sense of it, if you do but consyder, that the whole context is a perpetuall Metaphor, or Similitude'.[43] The comparison of one thing to another, along with the recognition of their correspondence, or likeness, was central to More's and Conway's shared biblical hermeneutics, as well as their theories of the tight connection between body and soul.[44] Through correspondence, Conway and More foregrounded their friendship, creating an epistolary intimacy that exemplified their shared philosophical understanding.

'THE FOUNDATION OF ALL SYMPATHY': CORRESPONDENCE AND ANTIPATHY

In *Principles of the Most Ancient and Modern Philosophy* (1690, first translated into English in 1692), Conway invites her readers to see sympathy as a material phenomenon: it is 'a thing of very great moment' that all creatures are connected:

Friends 1642–1684, rev. edn (Oxford, 1992), 57. On Conway's circles, see Sarah Hutton, 'Ancient Wisdom and Modern Philosophy: Anne Conway, F. M. van Helmont, and the Seventeenth-Century Dutch Interchange of Ideas', *Quaestiones Infinitae*, 4 (1994), 1–16.

[39] Henry More to Anne Finch, 12 Feb 1650, in *Conway Letters*, 51.

[40] Conway to More, 12 September 1661, in *Conway Letters*, 191.

[41] More to Conway, 6 January 1652 or 1653, in *Conway Letters*, 69.

[42] For More's use of allegory to explore the theory of vital congruity, see Cassandra Gorman, 'Allegorical Analogies: Henry More's Poetical Cosmology', *Studies in Philology*, 114.1 (2017), 148–70.

[43] More to Conway, 28 Nov 1652, in *Conway Letters*, 68. Conway and More are discussing Isaiah 5.24.

[44] For more on Conway's views on identity and the 'sameness of soul', see Emily Thomas, 'Anne Conway on the Identity of Creatures over Time', in Emily Thomas (ed.), *Early Modern Women on Metaphysics* (Cambridge, 2018), 131–49.

> by means of Subtiler Parts interceding or coming in between, which are the Emanations of one Creature into another, by which also they act one upon another at the greatest distance; and this is the Foundation of all Sympathy and Antipathy which happens in Creatures.[45]

All living things, for Conway, are linked by the finest of material connections, a 'Unity' that is still more pronounced within a single body, the parts of which, even when divided:

> send certain subtile Particles one to another, and to the Body from whence they came, and the Body sends the like unto them ... by means whereof the Parts and Members so apparently separated, still retain a certain real Unity and Sympathy. (sig. I2v)

Conway offers two startling illustrations of this phenomenon: one in which a man received a prosthetic nose made of another's flesh, which corrupted and dropped off when the donor died, and another in which a man whose leg had been amputated experienced urgent pains when his distant limb was cut. Her crowning example of material correspondence, though, is the unity of friendship:

> For if two Men intirely love one another, they are by this love so united, that no distance of place can divide or separate them; for they are present (one with another) in Spirit; so that there passeth a continual Efflux, or Emanation of Spirits, from the one to the other, whereby they are bound together, and united as with Chains. (sig. I3r)

There is a striking parallel between Conway's use of letters to reduce physical distance and her philosophical invocation of an emotional connection that quite literally transcends separation. Correspondence, in the form of continual material interchange, is central to her vital monism, part of a philosophy with constant, insistent communication at its core.

In contrast to Conway, Cavendish is frequently sceptical about the utility of correspondence for natural philosophical thought. Grappling with Hobbes' views on imagination, she argues that words are a product of sensation and reason rather than vice versa, and that 'Thoughts are not like *Water upon a plain Table, which is drawn and guided by the finger this or that way*'. Thoughts are created of rational matter, she explains, whose parts move in different directions, since 'though there is great affinity and sympathy between parts, yet there is also great difference and antipathy betwixt them' (sig. I2r). Cavendish disagrees with the specifics of Hobbes' analogy, demonstrating a characteristic distrust of metaphor as a mode of philosophical reasoning, and emphasising the importance of disagreement to the motions of matter and the mind.

[45] Anne Conway, *The Principles of the Most Ancient and Modern Philosophy* (London, 1692), sig. C7r.

On numerous occasions, however, Cavendish relies on correspondence both as a physical explanation and as a rhetorical mode. In section 2, letter 10, she dwells on the necessity of sympathy and antipathy: 'some of [Nature's] Parts are pleased and delighted with other parts, but some of her parts are afraid or have an aversion to other parts; and hence is like and dislike, or sympathy and antipathy, hate and love' (sig. T1r). 'Oftentimes', she argues, five letters later, 'the rational corporeal motions may so agree with the sensitive, as there may be no opposition or crossing at all, but a sympathetical mutual agreement betwixt them' (sigs. Zz1v–Zz2r). In this letter, dealing explicitly with physical principles of concord and agreement, Cavendish draws on the rhetorical resources of metaphor and analogy to a striking degree. As the Epicurean philosopher Walter Charleton put it in a commendatory letter to Cavendish, 'they who read your Books with design to be informed in points of Philosophy, find themselves at the same time introduced also in Rhetorique'.[46] Cavendish compares the changeability of thought to writing, observing that: 'Man writes oftentimes false, and seldom so exact, but he is forced to mend his hand, and correct his opinions, and sometimes quite to alter them, according as the figures continue or are dissolved and altered by change of motion' (sig. Zz2r). The shifting opinions and blotted writing Cavendish describes blur together in the space of the sentence, reinforcing the correspondence at the heart of her philosophy, in which things, whatever their diversity, are joined in their capacity for motion.

This is not the only point at which Cavendish asks readers to consider writing and books as analogous. In her second letter, Cavendish clarifies the concept of 'Infinite matter' introduced in her *Philosophical Opinions*. Suggesting there are different types and degrees of infinity, she identifies that which is infinite in 'bulk and quantity' with 'the Onely matter': the constitutive substance of all things (sig. B1v). Drawing on an influential trope, derived from Aristotle and Lucretius, that compares the swirl of atoms to the formation and reformation of the alphabet, Cavendish argues that other types of infinity, including of quality and time, 'are contained in the Onely Matter as many Letters are contained in one Word, many Words in one Line, many Lines in one Book' (sig. B2v).[47] Cavendish's words reorient the reader's relationship to the letters, words, lines, and pages before them. Drawing attention to writing as material and the analogical power of the parts of writing, she positions her philosophy as correspondent with the infinite variety of the world.

Elsewhere, Cavendish reflects on the ability of one object to cause movement in another and the question of whether something physical passes between them. She argues her case—that these movements are not material—by recalling her reader to the scene of writing:

[46] *Letters and Poems in Honour of the Incomparable Princess, Margaret, Dutchess of Newcastle* (London, 1676), sig. Bb1r.

[47] For an extended discussion of this trope in Lucretius and its influence on early modern thought, see Gerard Passanante, *The Lucretian Renaissance: Philology and the Afterlife of Tradition* (Chicago, IL, 2011), 85–6.

> if you say, that these tranferrable [*sic*] motions are material, then every action whereby the hand moves to the making or moving of some other body, would lessen the number of the motions in the hand, and weaken it, so that in the writing of one letter, the hand would not be able to write a second letter, at least not a third. (sig. X1v)

Possessing its own distinctive mobility, this passage encourages the reader to picture Cavendish pen in hand, and, concurrently, to imagine a very different conclusion to the volume they are reading: a counterfactual, considerably more slender book where Cavendish's force has been exhausted in the act of writing, and her letters trail into silence.[48] Questions of correspondence are at the heart of Cavendish's epistolary enterprise: she tests the limits of physical sympathy and of analogy in supple, similising prose.

MARGARET CAVENDISH'S EPISTOLARY METHOD

As noted at the beginning of this chapter, Cavendish embraced and transformed the affordances of the letter as a form of scientific method. Positioning *Philosophical Letters* as a development of her *Philosophical and Physical Opinions*, Cavendish argues that:

> to find out a Truth, at least a Probability in Natural Philosophy by a new and different way from other Writers, and to make this way more known, easie and intelligible, I was in a manner forced to write this Book. (sig. a1v)

Where the other letters discussed in this chapter share the hallmarks of epistolary exchange—they are handwritten, identify their addressee, and suggest meaningful dialogue between participants—Cavendish's are distinctively designed for print. The supposed recipient of her 162 *Philosophical Letters* remains unnamed and is generally agreed to be a convenient fiction: a patient, malleable reader for Cavendish's designedly erratic opinions, notably more receptive than the male contemporaries with whom Cavendish engaged in sometimes tense correspondence. By creating an epistolary fiction in which her correspondent has actively sought her views, Cavendish places herself in the position of philosopher rather than student, embracing the freedom created by not addressing her natural philosopher targets directly.

This triangulation is most evident in the seventh letter of section 2, in which Cavendish engages in circumlocutory argument with Henry More. Cavendish quotes More directly on the question of self-moving matter:

[48] For more on the materiality of Cavendish's writing, see Helen Smith, 'Women and the Materials of Writing', in Patricia J. Pender and Rosalind Smith (eds), *Material Cultures of Early Modern Women's Writing: Production, Transmission, Reception* (London, 2014), 14–35.

> Suppose, says he, Matter could move it self, would meer Matter with self-motion amount to that admirable wise contrivance of things which we see in the World?— All the evasion I can imagine, our adversaries may use here, will be this: That Matter is capable of sense, and the finest and most subtil of the most refined sense; and consequently of Imagination too, yea happily of Reason and Understanding. (sig. Qq1v)

These lines are extracted, more or less verbatim, from More's *The Immortality of the Soul* (1659, sigs. G2v–G3r). Cavendish reworks them into an argument, selectively quoting More, and inserting her own defence:

> I answer, it is very probable, that not onely all the Matter in the World or Universe hath Sense, but also Reason; and that the sensitive part of matter is the builder, and the rational the designer; ... But, says your Author, Let us see, if all their heads laid together can contrive the anatomical Fabrick of any Creature that liveth? I answer, all parts of Nature are not bound to have heads or tayls; but if they have, surely they are wiser then many a man's. I demand, says he ... I answer ... Again, says he ...

Rewriting More's published work as a debate, Cavendish takes control of all elements of the natural philosophical epistolary duologue, voicing the authoritative male philosopher while giving herself space to respond, and to shape the outcome of the dispute. Her riposte includes a ribald dig at the male sex, suggesting that the self-moving matter of animal heads or tails is notably more rational than men's corresponding members. The one role she does not take on is that of enquirer, a position securely filled by the fantasy of a female correspondent.

Cavendish uses her addressee to entertain and answer doubts and questions. In letter 25, she opens briskly: 'MADAM, I Perceive you are not fully satisfied with my former Letter concerning Eccho, and a figure presented in a Looking-glass' (sig. Y1v). Creating a quizzical reader, Cavendish gives herself grounds to elaborate the ideas she expressed earlier in the volume, creating, and as quickly closing, a space for different views. Elsewhere, Cavendish imagines doubts not as 'real' interventions but as prospective objections: 'But you will say, Motion may be granted, but not Life, Sense, and Reason. I answer, I would fain know the reason why not; for I am confident that no man can in truth affirm the contrary' (sigs. Iiii2r–v). Though Cavendish quickly dispatches readerly quibbles in this example, she repeatedly uses the form of the letter as a tool to entertain and allow for doubt as an ethical and philosophical approach. It is as important, in Cavendish's natural philosophy, to be able to not know certain things, as to be able to identify the movements and properties of others. In a searing reaction to More, Cavendish closes one letter with the reflection:

> that Man, though counted the best of Creatures, is not made with such infinite Excellence, as to pierce into the least secrets of God; Wherefore I am in a maze when I hear of such men, which pretend to know so much, as if they had plundered the Celestial Cabinet of the Omnipotent God ... But I, *Madam*, confess my Ignorance, as having

> neither divine Inspirations, nor extraordinary Visions, nor any divine or humane learning, but what Nature has been pleased to bestow upon me: Yet in all this Ignorance, I know that I am, and ought to be,
> MADAM,
> Your humble and faithful Servant. (sig. Nnn2r)

Cavendish insists upon her lack of certainty as ethically and theologically apt, even as she uses the conventions of letter writing and the formality of address to assert herself as a point of certainty among the whirl of philosophical opinions.

Over and over, Cavendish uses the formal close of a letter to inscribe herself within the relational bonds of polite society, articulate her disagreement with male philosophical opinion, and assert her singularity as both thinker and instance of natural matter. Disputing More's views on the vacuum, for instance, Cavendish concludes:

> if Vacuum be not created, and shall not be annihilated, but is Uncreated, Immaterial, Immoveable, Infinite, and Eternal, it is a God; but if it be created, God being not a Creator of Nothing, nor an annihilator of Nothing, but of Something, he cannot be a Creator of Vacuum; for Vacuum is a pure Nothing. But leaving Nothing to those that can make something of it, I will add no more, but rest,
> MADAM,
> Your faithful Friend and Servant. (sigs. Zzzzz1r–v)

Delightfully dismissive in tone and effect, Cavendish reduces urgent inquiry into the nature of the vacuum and the possibility of creation *ex nihilo* to the busy fictions of idle brains, desperate to build something from nothing. This philosophical buzz stands in striking contrast to her secure presence, manifested in the closing refrain, 'Your faithful Friend and Servant'.

These elegant endings are more than witty ways to finish letters. In settling on the epistle to set out her philosophical views, Cavendish finds a form that makes space for her variety of thought and opinion. This is characteristic of Cavendish's embrace of an open-mindedness so insistent as to verge on the chaotic: in her *Observations upon Experimental Philosophy* (1666), Cavendish presents a quite extraordinary 'war' between 'the latter and former thoughts and conceptions of my mind', which can only be resolved by offering the jarring totality of her ideas and positions to the 'judicious and impartial reader'.[49] As we have seen, letters established natural philosophy as socially situated, forcing a balance between the robust exchange of views and the polite maintenance of bonds in the face of distance. They occupy a shifting ground between private exchange and public commentary and build in modes of delay and interruption: the writers I have discussed in this chapter frequently note in their correspondence that letters have been long awaited or gone astray. And they insist, as Cavendish does throughout her writings, on development and change as appropriate philosophical responses, making hay from the provisionality and open-endedness of correspondence as a mode of collaborative or contestatory exchange. The bulk of the letters I have cited demonstrate women's skilled

[49] Margaret Cavendish, *Observations upon Experimental Philosophy* (London, 1666), sig. c2r.

negotiation of the letter form to fulfil and advance the dual projects of philosophy and friendship; Cavendish goes further, exploiting the fiction of epistolary friendship to forge a philosophical method that relies on doubt, self-interrogation, sceptical reading, and a willingness to pattern out changes in conception and opinion. It is only fitting to give Cavendish the last word, as she so carefully gives it to herself. The closing lines of letter 15 set a term to philosophical speculation on the nature of infinity, using the conventions of the letter to insist upon Cavendish's emotional and material constancy amid the infinite transformations of words and the world:

> But though Infinite is without end, yet my discourse of it shall be but short and end here, though not my affection, which shall last and continue with the life of
> MADAM,
> Your Faithful Friend and Humble Servant. (sig. O2r)

FURTHER READING

Clarke, Desmond M. and Catherine Wilson (eds). *The Oxford Handbook of Philosophy in Early Modern Europe*. Oxford, 2011.

Daybell, James and Andrew Gordon (eds). *Cultures of Correspondence in Early Modern Britain*. Philadelphia, PA, 2016.

Hunter, Lynette and Sarah Hutton (eds). *Women, Science and Medicine, 1500–1700: Mothers and Sisters of the Royal Society*. Stroud, 1997.

Leong, Elaine. *Recipes and Everyday Knowledge: Medicine Science, and the Household in Early Modern England*. Chicago, IL, 2018.

Long, Kathleen P. (ed.). *Gender and Scientific Discourse in Early Modern Culture*. Farnham, 2010.

Preston, Claire. *The Poetics of Scientific Investigation in Seventeenth-Century England*. Oxford, 2015.

Thomas, Emily (ed.). *Early Modern Women on Metaphysics*. Cambridge, 2018.

Wall, Wendy. *Recipes for Thought: Knowledge and Taste in the Early Modern English Kitchen*. Philadelphia, PA, 2016.

CHAPTER 8

LIBRARIES NOT ONLY THEIR OWN

Networking Women's Books and Reading in Early Modern England

LEAH KNIGHT

As early as the Great Depression of the 1930s, scholars knew that 'the great ladies of the English Renaissance were frequently learned'.[1] The aim even then was to broaden the understanding of the books and reading of early modern women to rest on more than the examples of the few titled figures about whom most evidence seemed to survive. This evidentiary bias was logical, since high-ranking families more often possessed the continuous property ownership that permits the archiving of household papers and the intergenerational ownership of books and libraries. It was in part for this reason that, in 1931, when Louis B. Wright sought the reading materials of the 'average woman of the period', he relied for the most part not on primary sources but on descriptive, prescriptive, and proscriptive remarks in early modern printed books. On this basis, he concluded that women's reading, especially of pious and practical books, found reasonably broad cultural support—at least from his sources, who had various stakes in cultivating a larger audience (whether as educators, evangelists, or simply authors with books to sell).[2] An increase in the number of vernacular printed books throughout the sixteenth century, as well as the emergent Protestant emphasis on personal Bible reading (which often involved women teaching that skill to children), boosted female literacy among the middling sorts. Paradoxically, though, both ecclesiastical schisms and the increased prevalence of print (with so much of it touching on religious sensitivities)

[1] Louis B. Wright, 'The Reading of Renaissance English Women', *Studies in Philology*, 28.4 (1931), 671–89, 671.

[2] Wright, 'Reading', 671–4. For statistical analysis of women's literacy in the period, see Eleanor Hubbard, 'Reading, Writing, and Initialing: Female Literacy in Early Modern London', *Journal of British Studies*, 54.3 (2015), 553–77.

fomented a moral panic about the dangers of women reading for pleasure or without supervision—especially imaginative literature, and still more especially the much-maligned genre of romance, although plays and non-devotional poetry were also suspect.[3] Nearly a century of studies subsequent to Wright's suggests that his understanding was right enough, despite being reached largely through the commentary of early modern men, including writers of fiction and satire, to whose partial and problematic proofs Wright turned only because direct records of 'the learning of bourgeois women' were apparently so 'scanty'.[4]

Historians of reading still often seek in vain for such records; even as previously unnoticed association copies (books whose ownership is known), library inventories, and annotations attract scholarly attention, evidence for women's reading still proves more elusive than that for men.[5] The best-stocked case studies of early modern female book ownership, moreover, remain those of the 'great ladies' about whom we already know a good deal.[6] As recently as the turn of this century, David McKitterick echoed Wright in stating categorically that 'we know extraordinarily little about exactly which books belonged to women in the sixteenth and seventeenth centuries'; he lamented the lack of a single monograph on the subject.[7] Subsequently, monographs like Heidi Brayman Hackel's *Reading Material in Early Modern England* established the critical

[3] On women reading romance, see Julie A. Eckerle, *Romancing the Self in Early Modern Englishwomen's Life Writing* (Farnham, 2013), 25–54; on play reading, see Marta Straznicky, 'Reading Through the Body', in Marta Straznicky (ed.), *The Book of the Play: Playwrights, Stationers, and Readers in Early Modern England* (Amherst, MA, 2006) 59–79, and Kitamura Sae, 'Shakespeare of One's Own: Female Users of Playbooks from the Seventeenth to the Mid-Eighteenth Century', *Palgrave Communications*, 3 (2017), doi: 10.1057/palcomms.2017.21. On verse, see Sasha Roberts, *Reading Shakespeare's Poems in Early Modern England* (Houndmills, 2003), 20–61.

[4] Wright, 'Reading', 675.

[5] The proportion of female and male book owners and users may be roughly measured by their populations in current indices. In the 2018 update of David Pearson's *English Book Owners in the Seventeenth Century: A Work in Progress Listing*, only 3 per cent of inventories listed are women's. *Private Libraries in Renaissance England* sees over 15 per cent of its contents related to women. The figures behind these percentages are from Joseph Black, 'Manuscript and Women's Booklists', in Patricia Pender and Rosalind Smith (eds), *Palgrave Encyclopedia of Early Modern Women's Writing in English* (forthcoming). About 13 per cent of the owners, compilers, and scribes are female in *RECIRC: The Reception and Circulation of Early Modern Women's Writing, 1545–1700*, Marie-Louise Coolahan (principal director), recirc.nuigalway.ie, accessed 2 February 2021.

[6] Recent studies of the books and reading of high-ranking (gentle or noble) women include Elizabeth Zeman Kolkovich, 'Reader, Maker, Mentor: The Countess of Huntingdon and Her Networks', in Valerie Wayne (ed.), *Women's Labour and the History of the Book in Early Modern England* (New York, 2020), 225–42; Lori Humphrey Newcomb, 'Frances Wolfreston's Annotations as Labours of Love', Wayne (ed.), *Women's Labour*, 243–66; Micheline White, 'Katherine Parr's Marginalia: Putting the Wisdom of Chrysostom and Solomon into Practice', in Leah Knight, Micheline White, and Elizabeth Sauer (eds), *Women's Bookscapes in Early Modern Britain* (Ann Arbor, MI, 2018), 21–42; Leah Knight, 'Reading Proof: Or, Problems and Possibilities in the Text Life of Anne Clifford', in Knight, White, and Sauer (eds), *Women's Bookscapes* 253–73; and Elaine Leong, '"Herbals she peruseth": Reading Medicine in Early Modern England', *Renaissance Studies*, 28.4 (2014), 556–78.

[7] David McKitterick, 'Women and Their Books in Seventeenth-Century England: The Case of Elizabeth Puckering', *The Library*, 1.4 (2000), 359–80, 363.

role of gender in the period's readerly culture, and Edith Snook's *Women, Reading, and the Cultural Politics of Early Modern England* flipped Wright's technique to produce evidence of women's reading from within their own writing, while other monographs focused on a particular genre as read by women.[8] McKitterick might also take heart from essays in *Reading Women*, or in *Women's Bookscapes in Early Modern Britain*, or in 'Marking Books: Owners, Readers, Collectors, Annotators', part of *Women's Labour and the History of the Book in Early Modern England*.[9] Many more studies of individual readers reside in journal articles and unindexed in chapters of biographies or other studies with a broader remit than women's books and reading; like early modern primary sources, current secondary sources in this interdisciplinary field are hard to locate comprehensively.[10] Inventories of books owned by named women are also increasingly featured in the ongoing publication of *Private Libraries in Renaissance England* (*PLRE*), which allows filtering by gender (by selecting, in its online extension, 'woman' among the 'Owner's Identifier' categories).[11] The same is true of such valuable resources as the *UK Reading Experience Database*, the *British Armorial Bindings* database, and the gender-related data cloud of the 'Legacy Libraries' project in *LibraryThing*, which assembles several dozen records of sixteenth- and seventeenth-century women's books, mainly drawing from New England probate inventories, most of which feature only a few, often unidentified books and otherwise unknown owners.[12]

[8] Heidi Brayman Hackel, *Reading Material in Early Modern England: Print, Gender, and Literacy* (Cambridge, 2005); Edith Snook, *Women, Reading, and the Cultural Politics of Early Modern England* (Burlington, VT, 2005). On women's devotional reading, see Femke Molekamp, *Women and the Bible in Early Modern England: Religious Reading and Writing* (Oxford, 2013); and on romance, see Helen Hackett, *Women and Romance Fiction in the English Renaissance* (Cambridge, 2000).

[9] Heidi Brayman Hackel and Catherine E. Kelly (eds), *Reading Women: Literacy, Authorship, and Culture in the Atlantic World, 1500–1800* (Philadelphia, PA, 2008); Knight, White, and Sauer (eds), *Women's Bookscapes*; Wayne (ed.), *Women's Labour*. See also Snook, 'Recent Studies in Early Modern Reading', *English Literary Renaissance*, 43.2 (2013), 343–78, especially sections on 'Female Literacy', 357–8, and 'Gentlewoman Readers', 369, and several dozen sources on women readers and gendered reading practices throughout other sections.

[10] Among recent articles, see Nicole LaBouff, 'An Unlikely Christian Humanist: How Bess of Hardwick (ca. 1527–1608) Answered "the Woman Question"', *Sixteenth Century Journal*, 4.7 (2016): 847–82. See also Victoria Brownlee, *Biblical Readings and Literary Writings in Early Modern England, 1558–1625* (Oxford, 2018), 143–67, and Lara M. Crowley, *Manuscript Matters: Reading John Donne's Poetry and Prose in Early Modern England* (Oxford, 2018), 173–210. In some studies, one or more chapters might elucidate female experience with books, as with Kate Narveson's *Bible Readers and Lay Writers in Early Modern England: Gender and Self-Definition in an Emergent Writing Culture* (Farnham, 2012), which balances attention between two men and two women (Anne Venn and Grace Mildmay).

[11] By the 2020 printing of the tenth volume in the series, *PLRE* featured twenty-one lists associated with women; its online extension raises the total to fifty-seven at time of writing (8 December 2020). See also R. J. Fehrenbach and Joseph L. Black, 'General Introduction', in Fehrenbach and Black (eds), *Private Libraries in Renaissance England: A Collection and Catalogue of Tudor and Early Stuart Book-Lists*, x (Tempe, AZ, 2017), xxiii. See Black, 'Manuscript', for a summary of relevant materials in *PLRE* and its online extension, plre.folger.edu.

[12] The *UK Reading Experience Database*, an open-access project which records the experiences of actual (not fictional) readers, allows searches by gender; selecting 'female' and limiting results to the sixteenth and seventeenth centuries yields over 500 reading experiences by women; isolating readers

Resources like these suggest how well the field has been served by relatively new and interactive media, as well as by the open-ended assemblage and open-access distribution of data sets (see this volume, Chapter 44, Julia Flanders, '"A Telescope for the Mind"'). Relevant data include not just textual records but high-resolution images of the type required to identify ownership inscriptions, armorial bindings, and the hands of previously unidentified annotators (for which reverse-image search technologies and digital tools such as retroReveal offer ways forward).[13] With the value of image-sharing in mind, the collaboratively produced blog *Early Modern Female Book Ownership* has joined forces with more conventional scholarly publications in order to document—in separately authored, sequentially dated, and lavishly illustrated essays—scattered individual volumes featuring female signatures. Crowd-sourcing of additional materials is encouraged by the blog's intersection with Twitter, where contributors and readers alike have popularized the tag '#herbook' as a way to flag related finds. Similarly, David Pearson has transformed his online PDF listing of 'English Book Owners in the Seventeenth Century' (first published in 2008 and periodically updated) into *Book Owners Online*, a database presented as a deliberately incomplete resource receptive to further contributions. In addition, the database form (unlike its static predecessor) enables searches by the category 'women,' rather than requiring users to scan the list for female forenames or automate searches for feminine pronouns.[14] Likewise, the database associated with *RECIRC: The Reception and Circulation of Early Modern Women's Writing, 1545–1700*, which amasses records of engagement by men and women with books by female authors, lets researchers hone in on thirty-three women who engaged with such books as owners, scribes, and compilers; results may be exported as graphs or spreadsheets.[15] Recent trends in the genres and forms taken by studies in the field—both

who were owners of the books read yields slightly fewer than 200 results, with most associated with only a few well-known figures (such as Margaret Hoby and Anne Clifford). *British Armorial Bindings* filters by owner, century, and gender, which yields armorial stamps of thirty-five female book owners for the period pertinent to this volume; the full-colour reproduction of the stamps should facilitate further identifications as association copies arrive on the market or arise in previously uncatalogued library holdings. For this search, see *British Armorial Bindings* [by John Morris and Philip Oldfield], University of Toronto, armorial.library.utoronto.ca/stamp-owners-by-centuries?field_gender_value=F&items_per_page=100, accessed 2 February 2021. To find women's books and libraries in 'Legacy Libraries', use the 'Data Clouds' feature and select 'female' from the cloud called 'gender': 'Legacy Libraries: Female', librarything.com/legacylibraries/list/1249151596&sort = date&fieldFromCloud = 5&fieldFromCloud_name = female, accessed 2 February 2021.

13 On retroReveal, see retroreveal.org, accessed 2 February 2021; on its value in the field, see Heather Wolfe, 'Uncancelling the Cancelled: Recovering Obliterated Owners of Old Books', *The Collation: Research and Exploration at the Folger* (3 April 2019), collation.folger.edu/2019/04/uncancelling-the-cancelled, accessed 2 February 2021.

14 Pearson, *English Book Owners*, https://bibsocamer.org/BibSite/Pearson/Pearson.pdf, accessed 2 February 2021. David Pearson, *Book Owners Online*, n.d., University College London Centre for Editing Lives and Letters, https://bookowners.online/Main_Page, accessed 2 February 2021.

15 The relevant *RECIRC* database search is found at recirc.nuigalway.ie/explore#people, accessed 2 February 2021. The requisite search strategy is complex enough to deserve description: in the 'People' section of the database, select 'Person' in the first search field, and 'Is Owner/Compiler/Scribe' in the second; then click 'Add', which locates *all* owners, compilers, and scribes of women's reading, for a total

relatively conventional book chapters, journal articles, and essay collections, but also open-ended series of booklists, blog entries, tweets, databases, filters, clouds, graphs, and spreadsheets, including hybrids between print and digital media—suggest that McKitterick, in wishing for a monolithic monograph, may have sought the wrong medium for a message rapidly being written ever larger: that women's book ownership and access to books in early modernity was much more widespread, and remains better documented, than was once imagined. The body of evidence in the field is rapidly evolving and expanding along with approaches to its discovery and representation.

CHALLENGES AND OPPORTUNITIES

The challenge remains to extrapolate beyond individual case studies without letting the methodological pendulum swing into excessive generalisation or meaningless accounting. Georgianna Ziegler addressed that challenge by identifying patterns in the book ownership of an astonishing 840 women, tracked through provenance data collected by the Folger Shakespeare Library in its open-access Hamnet catalogue and extracted through the painfully analogue process of searching for common female forenames in the 'Copy Notes' field.[16] Joseph Black has similarly parsed the *PLRE* booklists in order to make cautious comparative claims about such matters as the relative popularity of particular titles and genres with male and female owners—the latter proving twice as likely as men to own works of imaginative literature, for instance.[17] Such comparisons between books owned and read by women and by men suggest the value of resources that, rather than isolating women's books in a library of their own, instead sets them on equal footing with their male counterparts, as is the case with both the Folger's catalogue and *PLRE*'s booklists. The ideal next step for a project like Ziegler's would be to emulate the *PLRE*'s publication of its data (through its collaboration with the Folger), by converting the spreadsheets in which she collected data on female book-owners into an open-access format, as Liza Blake has done in 'Locating Margaret Cavendish's Books', which tracks, in sortable charts and zoomable maps, copies of all books written (not owned) by Cavendish.[18] Given the value of cumulative data sets in

of 264; to limit these to women, add more search terms: select 'Sex' in the first box, then 'Equals', then 'Female', then 'Add'; this time, thirty-three female book users appear after the green 'Search' button is clicked. Selecting an individual's name shows which book or books she engaged with, while drilling deeper sometimes leads to parallel panes presenting transcriptions and images.

[16] Georgianna Ziegler, 'Patterns in Women's Book Ownership, 1500–1700', in Wayne (ed.), *Women's Labour*, 207–24.

[17] See Black, 'Manuscript'; see also the related analysis in Black, 'Women's Libraries in the *Private Libraries in Renaissance England* Project', in Knight, White, and Sauer (eds), *Women's Bookscapes*, 214–31.

[18] Liza Blake, 'Locating Margaret Cavendish's Books: Database, Map, and Analysis' (2018), *The Digital Cavendish Project* (14 November 2018, updated 6 December 2019), in Shawn Moore and Jacob Tootalian (directors), *Digital Cavendish*, digitalcavendish.org/original-research/locating-margaret-cavendish, accessed 2 February 2021.

this area of study, combined with the velocity at which new information is accruing and the ease of publishing spreadsheets and databases, the institutional creation and sustenance of authoritative repositories remains a pressing need. Meta-analyses, drawing together from related projects such data as can be cleanly layered, offer another method through which advances might be made. So much would usefully conjoin the 'contextually complete' booklists of *PLRE* with the 'stray provenances' (individual association copies, say, or reading notes in a woman's correspondence) deliberately excluded from that project's parameters but tracked elsewhere.[19]

These shifts in representation of information dovetail with a related intellectual reframing of the field, which has led scholars to foreground how particular women experienced reading and participated in book culture *not* in isolation, or necessarily as owners, but as members of social networks and sharing communities. The creative deployment of network analysis tools therefore also has a role in the next generation of studies of early modern women's books and reading. Many of the readerly networks with which we are most familiar were familial, as with the Cooke sisters, Elizabeth Isham's birth family, the libraries associated with Anne Bradstreet's relations, and the jointly claimed collection of books inscribed with the names of Isabella and Thomas Hervey.[20] In the past, regarding bookish women primarily as products of their families (especially their fathers and husbands) has been a potentially reductive framework (see this volume, Chapter 4, Jane Stevenson, 'Latin and Greek'). Anne Clifford's most recent biographer, for instance, diverts to her father and first husband the 'original ownership' of several books depicted in her famous portrait, *The Great Picture*, even though Clifford stands alone before what seems clearly intended to signify her personal possessions.[21] Richard T. Spence conjectures, for instance, that the copy of Ortelius' *Theatrum Orbis Terrarum* in the painting was either a gift from Clifford's father or 'a memorial to him', a claim based solely on the paper-thin warrant that 'maps were Earl George's province, as an expert navigator and oceanic privateer'—which ignores the fact that maps were

[19] On *PLRE*'s favouring of 'records that are contextually complete in themselves' and the project's exclusion of 'stray provenances, however many might be discovered for a single owner', see Black, 'Women's Libraries', 221.

[20] See Gemma Allen, *The Cooke Sisters: Education, Piety and Politics in Early Modern England* (Manchester, 2013), 18–55; Edith Snook, 'Elizabeth Isham's 'own Bookes': Property, Propriety, and the Self as Library', in Knight, White, and Sauer (eds), *Women's Bookscapes*, 77–93; Elizabeth Sauer, 'Book Passages and the Reconstruction of the Bradstreets' New England Library', in Knight, White, and Sauer (eds), *Women's Bookscapes*, 59–77; Emma Smith, 'Marital Marginalia: The Seventeenth-Century Library of Thomas and Isabella Hervey', in Katherine Acheson (ed.), *Early Modern English Marginalia* (Routledge, 2018), 155–72.

[21] *The Great Picture* (attributed to Jan van Belcamp, 1646, and housed at Abbot Hall, Kendal, UK), artsandculture.google.com/asset/the-great-picture/ugHL4_ozVj1f3g, accessed 2 February 2021; and see this volume, Chapter 46, Patricia Phillippy, 'Memory and Matter', Fig. 46.1). For a description of the books portrayed, see Leah Knight, 'Anne Clifford', in R. J. Fehrenbach (ed.), *Private Libraries in Renaissance England: A Collection and Catalogue of Tudor and Early Stuart Book-Lists, ix* (Tempe, AZ, 2017), 347–63. For speculation on the 'original ownership' of the books portrayed, see Richard T. Spence, *Lady Anne Clifford, Countess of Pembroke, Dorset and Montgomery (1590–1676)* (Sutton, 1997), 191ff.

equally his daughter's province, both when lobbying for properties divested from her by his will and when commissioning maps of her extensive holdings.[22] Given such unwarranted undermining of one early modern women's book ownership, it is easier to understand why evidence for it was so long imagined to be lacking—even for 'great ladies' like Clifford, whose *Great Picture* works tirelessly to ensure that such evidence should stare us in the face.

Newer studies imbricating women's books in their families of origin or of marriage, in contrast, are better evidenced and less biased towards patriarchal presumptions. Such is the case with Michael Edwards' teasingly titled article, 'The Lost Library of Anne Conway', on the recently discovered remains of a collection which still, alas, remains all but lost, with that 'all but' encompassing just four books at Jesus College, Cambridge, found by Edwards to feature the philosopher Conway's signature, along with two more volumes bearing her uncle's signature. Edwards frames his findings with an eye to patterns of intellectual exchange within her family, including her husband, father-in-law, and brother, as well as that uncle; his account thus intercalates Conway's reading into a largely masculine intellectual network, but without displacing her centrality or erasing her readerly agency—unlike the librarian who, as Edwards wryly notes, crossed out her signature (thus aiding the disappearance of her books from intellectual history) while leaving her uncle's signature untouched.[23]

Julie Crawford undertakes related work by detecting Margaret Cavendish's hypothetically crossed-out signature on a 1719 sales inventory of her family's library.[24] The library auctioned as that of her husband and stepson was housed at Welbeck Abbey, where Cavendish also resided; it is logical to treat her, therefore, as co-owner of these books in all but name, as well as an active reader of them, which Crawford substantiates by locating allusions to the library's titles in Cavendish's writings. Caroline Bowden has argued similarly, in her treatment of the library of Mildred Cecil, that the books marked by her name or binding formed only a small part of the familial book collections to which she had access, both by birth into the household of a learned father, Anthony Cooke, and by marriage to William Cecil, Lord Burghley. More generally, she argues that 'educated aristocratic women would have had access to the book collections in their homes and many would have had little need to act on their own initiative, to buy and inscribe their own books'.[25] Something similar may be argued about Elizabeth Gray,

[22] At the age of 86, Clifford was still commissioning new maps of parts of her properties: in January 1676 alone, she paid John Webster for copying maps on three occasions; see Clifford, in Jessica L. Malay (ed.), *Anne Clifford's Autobiographical Writing, 1590–1676* (Manchester, 2018), 232, 234, 238.

[23] Michael Edwards, 'The Lost Library of Anne Conway', *The Seventeenth Century* (2019), 1–29, 19. On cancelled signatures, see Wolfe, 'Uncancelling'; on the role of such cancellation in obliterating another significant female reader's book ownership, see Sarah Lindenbaum, 'Written in the Margent: Frances Wolfreston Revealed', *The Collation: Research and Exploration at the Folger* (2018), https://collation.folger.edu/2018/06/frances-wolfreston-revealed/, accessed 2 February 2021.

[24] Julie Crawford, 'Margaret Cavendish's Books', in Knight, White, and Sauer (eds), *Women's Bookscapes*, 94–116.

[25] Caroline Bowden, 'The Library of Mildred Cooke Cecil, Lady Burghley', *The Library*, 6.1 (2005), 3–29, 7, 10–11.

Countess of Kent, whose 179 known books were catalogued after her death only in order to distinguish them from her partner John Selden's several-thousand-strong library in their shared home—yet surely the books bequeathed to the Bodleian as his, though not her property in a conventional sense, were at least accessible to her, as Tara Lyons argues.[26] The point about shared access may be extended to non-aristocratic women, who often shared close quarters with the books we tend to identify as owned by the men in their lives. We might therefore reconsider which parent wrote out a list of 'The books which my daughter Elizabeth hath read unto me at nights till she read ym all out'. All studies to date presume that the list's author, and thus the books' listener, was Thomas Browne, and many of the titles listed appear in a library catalogue identified (much as in Cavendish's case) as the property of Elizabeth Browne's father and brother; however, nothing precludes her mother, Dorothy Browne, from being Elizabeth's audience instead or as well.[27] One sense of the verb 'to own' emergent in the early seventeenth century was 'to call (a person or thing) one's own; to acknowledge as belonging to oneself, esp. in respect of kinship or authorship; to acknowledge as an acquaintance; to recognize as familiar' (*OED*, 3b). How many books in early modern women's lives, in their very households, did they recognise as familiar, and acknowledge as acquaintances, and thus call their own in a sense that we have since lost?

NETWORKS OF ACCESS: BEYOND POSSESSIVE INDIVIDUALISM

To think more flexibly and inclusively about the matter of ownership within the bookish environs of early modern women like Conway, the Cavendishes, Cecil, Gray, and the Brownes is to think beyond the narrowness and possible anachronism of a form of possessive individualism, or individual possessivism, that attributes household property to a sole proprietor—usually male, given the asymmetrical property laws and practices of early modern England.[28] The tendency and its tendentiousness may be analogous to the excessive ascription of texts to single authors, a characteristic of a later intellectual property regime at odds with an earlier culture of commonplacing, in which both

[26] Tara L. Lyons, 'Lady Elizabeth Grey', in Fehrenbach (ed.), *Private Libraries*, 324–61.

[27] For the book list, see 'Elizabeth Lyttelton's Commonplace Book' (UL MS Add. 8460), *Scriptorium: Medieval and Early Modern Manuscripts Online*, Cambridge Digital Library, University of Cambridge, https://cudl.lib.cam.ac.uk/view/MS-ADD-08640/1. See Victoria E. Burke, 'Contexts for Women's Manuscript Miscellanies: The Case of Elizabeth Lyttelton and Sir Thomas Browne', *The Yearbook of English Studies*, 33 (2003), 316–28; and Rebecca Bullard, '"A Bright Coelestiall Mind": A New Set of Writings by Lady Dorothy Browne (1621–1685)', *Huntington Library Quarterly*, 73.1 (2010), 99–122.

[28] Amy Louise Erickson notes that 'legal restrictions placed on English women at this time were exceptionally severe even by the standards of other early modern European countries'. See Erickson, *Women and Property in Early Modern England* (Abingdon, 1993,repr. 2005), 3.

writerly and readerly ownership of a text was often more distributed than siloed. Books, perhaps especially in early modernity, should instead be considered not solely in relation to registered owners but with a view to the concentric and intersecting spheres of access they have travelled through over time. Emma Smith has recently proposed something similar: 'contrary to its popular associations of permanence and fixity, any library is always in motion across numerous axes [...] the very portability of books makes transferability, dissemination, and movement the element in which print operates'—neither more nor less than manuscript.[29] One nostrum in the historiography of reading reminds us that a book owned is not necessarily a book read, but a book known for a particular owner is also not likely a book read only, predominantly, or most interestingly by that owner.[30] If it is utterly uncontroversial that women writers benefit from rooms of their own, it is equally true that women readers benefited, then as now, from libraries *not* their own, or those not only or officially so, just as they did from books they made their own through such historically specific practices as the memory arts and extraction into miscellanies and commonplace books. Such modes of access to texts, though sometimes harder to study, matter at least as much as individually attributed ownership of whole volumes.

Not all networks in which scholars might locate female readers, moreover, were familial; nor do they all imbricate women in the text lives of the men who were generally better positioned to purchase, possess, and pass on large libraries. Women religious, for instance, might not have owned books in a traditional sense, but their communal life among the same shared and often intergenerational sets of books, and codified institutional protocols for engaging with them, offer rich evidence of differently networked text lives (see this volume, Chapter 33, Jaime Goodrich, 'Networked Authorship').[31] Religion could also be the impetus for other arrangements in which women played crucial roles as readers and book owners, as in the recusant networks that enabled the surreptitious

[29] Smith, 'Marital Marginalia', 168.

[30] On this formula, see, *inter alia*, Jason Scott-Warren, 'News, Sociability, and Bookbuying in Early Modern England: The Letters of Sir Thomas Cornwallis', *The Library*, 1.4 (2000), 381–402, 382, and Stephen Colclough, *Consuming Texts: Readers and Reading Communities, 1695–1870* (Houndmills, 2007), 2.

[31] Jaime Goodrich, 'Common Libraries: Book Circulation in English Benedictine Convents, 1600–1700', in Knight, White, and Sauer (eds), *Women's Bookscapes*, 153–70; Caroline Bowden, 'English Reading Communities in Exile: Introducing Cloistered Nuns to Their Books', in Knight, White, and Sauer (eds), *Women's Bookscapes*, 171–92, as well as Bowden, 'Building Libraries in Exile: The English Convents and their Book Collections in the Seventeenth Century', *British Catholic History*, 32.3 (2015), 343–82, her '"A Distribution of Tyme": Reading and Writing Practices in the English Convents in Exile', *Tulsa Studies in Women's Literature*, 31.1/2 (2012), 99–116, and her 'Books and Reading at Syon Abbey, Lisbon in the Seventeenth Century', in E. A. Jones and Alexandra Walsham (eds), *Syon Abbey and its Books: Religious Communities and Communication in Late Medieval and Early Modern England* (Woodbridge, 2010), 177–202. See also Nicky Hallett, 'Philip Sidney in the Cloister: The Reading Habits of English Nuns in Seventeenth-Century Antwerp', *Journal for Early Modern Cultural Studies*, 12.3 (2012), 87–115.

distribution of smuggled Catholic books.[32] In the secular realm, too, literature could provide the glue for informal communities of writers and readers, male and female, sharing readerly experiences beyond the nuclear family. Karen Britland, for instance, has recently punctured excessively literal interpretations of Hester Pulter's literary claims to isolation by establishing her Hertfordshire estate's proximity—'within walking distance'—to an active literary community centred on the Stanleys, a 'youthful family with profoundly literary connections'.[33] As Britland observes: 'Pulter's original prose romance chimes with [poet, translator, and literary patron Thomas] Stanley's fascination for European romances, while her poetry reflects her royalist neighbours' interests in astronomy, astrology, philosophy and Epicurean/Lucretian atomism'.[34] Britland considers how the Stanley network's presence in Pulter's environs might reverse claims about the influence of a canonical writer like Andrew Marvell on Pulter's verse by leading us to consider, instead, the possibility that her poems influenced his work, as well as that of Abraham Cowley and others, through the tracery of their social matrix.

Even Anne Clifford—so often perceived to be depressively solitary in her youth, and isolated in her northern fiefdom in her maturity—may valuably be reimagined as a hub surrounded by the spokes of friends, employees, and relations who constituted a communal textual life. To characterise Clifford's reading is also to remember that of many others: her governess Ann Taylor, associated by proximity with a neat stack of books in *The Great Picture*; her tutor Samuel Daniel, similarly associated with another stack; Clifford's first husband, Richard Sackville, who 'sat and read by' her when they were not at odds; Robert Domville, a curate who read to her, not Scripture, as one might expect, but 'a great part of the History of the Netherlands'; Christopher Marsh and George Rivers, who spent a couple of weeks reading her Montaigne's *Essays*; her niece, Mary or Moll Neville, who read her *The Faerie Queene* and *Arcadia*; Richard Rand, a clergyman who read the Bible with her until her husband put a stop to it; Katherine or Kate Burton, the gentlewoman servant who took up the role of reading Clifford the Bible, along with a book of preparation for the sacrament; the apparently indefatigable Walter or Wat Conniston, the gentleman servant who read her all of St Augustine's *City of God* in under a month, as well as, at other times, King James' book *A Meditation upon the Lord's Prayer*, Thomas Sorocold's *Supplication of Saints* (a gift from her husband), *Leicester's Commonwealth*, and Josephus' *Antiquities of the Jews*; her 'cousin Mary' who read her Ovid's *Metamorphoses*, as well as Edmund Bunny's Protestant adaptation of Robert Parsons' book of devotion; Sir Francis Slingsby, who read her father's accounts of their shared sea voyages; Elizabeth Gray and John Selden (mentioned earlier), from whom she borrowed an influential copy of Chaucer; Mr Grasty, the parson who read

[32] For a study of a female-dominated example of a recusant network, see Elizabeth Patton, 'Women, Books, and the Lay Apostolate: A Catholic Literary Network in Late Sixteenth-Century England', in Knight, White, and Sauer (eds), *Women's Bookscapes*, 117–34.

[33] Karen Britland, 'Conspiring with "Friends": Hester Pulter's Poetry and the Stanley Family at Cumberlow Green', *Review of English Studies*, 69.292 (2018), 832–54, 835.

[34] Britland, 'Conspiring with "Friends"', 840–1.

Bible chapters in her chamber every Wednesday and Sunday in her last months of life, as well as the Book of Common Prayer's exhortation for receiving the sacrament; the domestic servants in the north, to whom she regularly presented books of devotion; and the same servants, male and female, who copied out and pinned around her chamber the passages Clifford called to mind as a basis for their conversations.[35] Clifford's well-known library remains critical in part because it is, so manifestly, not only her own: it is instead a crossroads for many kinds of evidence (written and painted, material and circumstantial) and the great variety of readers (male and female, elite and otherwise) who formed a reading community around her.[36]

CONCLUSION

When discovering, documenting, or developing analyses of the bookcases of individual readers, in coordinating meta-analyses of book-ownership patterns and networks, and by contextualising individual women in their bookish environments, this century's scholars are opening up extensive evidence of early modern female books and reading in ways enabled by digitally enriched, open-access bibliographic data and a flexible array of lenses and forms for seeing and shaping it. Thanks to new, nuanced, and networked approaches, we know more not only about the reading materials and practices of named individuals, but also how such figures and their reading experiences intersected with other, often more ordinary (and thus representative) women and men, whether neighbours, friends, relations, or employees. Creative and bold searches for connections among disparate readers, joined by books across space and time—what we might call transverse case studies—offer a happy medium between projects that burrow into a single individual and the distant-reading analyses of aggregated data which sometimes, perhaps necessarily, sacrifice any sense of the personal impact of books and reading. The knock-on effects of book ownership and reading experiences, as phenomena not only of individuals but of interpretive communities, present the next arena for studies of the role of books and reading in the lives of early modern women. This focus should lead to the salutary redirection of some scholarly attention away from records of formal ownership of individual volumes—still disproportionately sparse for women, and inevitably skewed towards an elite minority—and towards the relations that saw texts travel through circuits of influence not explicitly legible in linear book lists. Beyond collecting

[35] Taylor and Daniel are portrayed near the top of the left wing of *The Great Picture*. On Sackville, Domville, Marsh, Rivers, Neville, Rand, Burton, Conniston, Mary, Slingsby, and Grasty, and servants' books, see Malay (ed.), *Autobiographical Writing*, 42–4, 50, 53, 56, 59, 66, 76, 78, 79, 93, 94, 88, 227ff., and 231; on Elizabeth Gray, London, see British Library, MS Harley 7001, fol. 212r; on servants pinning quotations, see Edward Rainbowe, *A Sermon Preached at the Funeral of the Right Honorable Anne, Countess of Pembroke, Dorset, and Montgomery* (London, 1677), 40.

[36] See Jessica Malay, 'Reassessing Anne Clifford's Books: The Discovery of a New Manuscript Inventory', *Papers of the Bibliographical Society of America*, 115.1 (2021), 1–41.

names from ownership inscriptions and titles from inventories, we need richly rounded accounts of female readers networked through families, communities, and generations. In re-envisioning a bookish early modern version of the sharing economy, we can learn more from the data that is increasingly at our fingertips about the reading materials and habits that shaped women writers in early modern England.

FURTHER READING

Black, Joseph. 'Manuscript and Women's Booklists', in Patricia Pender and Rosalind Smith (eds), *Palgrave Encyclopedia of Early Modern Women's Writing in English*. London, forthcoming.

Brayman Hackel, Heidi. *Reading Material in Early Modern England: Print, Gender, and Literacy*. Cambridge, 2005.

McKitterick, David. 'Women and Their Books in Seventeenth-Century England: The Case of Elizabeth Puckering'. *The Library*, 1.4 (2000), 359–80.

Snook, Edith. *Women, Reading, and the Cultural Politics of Early Modern England*. Burlington, VT, 2005.

Ziegler, Georgianna. 'Patterns in Women's Book Ownership, 1500–1700', in Valerie Wayne (ed.), *Women's Labour and the History of the Book in Early Modern England*. New York, 2020, 207–24.

PART II

FORMS AND ORIGINS

CHAPTER 9

THE *QUERELLE DES FEMMES*, THE OVERBURY SCANDAL, AND THE POLITICS OF THE SWETNAM CONTROVERSY IN EARLY MODERN ENGLAND

CHRISTINA LUCKYJ

In his 1616 commonplace book *The Rich Cabinet*, Thomas Gainsford includes wildly divergent descriptions of 'Woman' in the chapter he devotes to her. On the one hand, she is a 'purgatory on earth' for 'if she be honest, she will be imperious, if faire, she wil be venerious: if foule, she is loathsome: if a wanton, full of fraude or treason: if proud, costly above thy ability: if witty, impudent to shame thee'. On the other:

> Woman is endued with the same vertues as man: for there hath beene as valiant, wise, godly, magnanimous, pollitick, judicious, great spirited, and learned women as men: yea, our histories are filled with the glorious actions and famous conquests of wo[men] as well as Emperours, or other persons of honour, elloquence, learning, and judgement.[1]

Gainsford's work encapsulates the dizzying oppositions of the *querelle des femmes*, a debate about the nature of women rooted in both classical and medieval tradition that permeated virtually every genre in early modern England. Juxtaposing attacks with defences of women, Gainsford provides commonplaces that can be mobilised for either perspective—woman herself simply serving as the pretext for 'intellectual

[1] T. G., *The Rich Cabinet; Furnished with Varietie of Excellent Discriptions, Exquisite Charracters, Witty Discourses, and Delightfull Histories* (London, 1616), fol. 163v–164r.

calisthenics', as Linda Woodbridge calls them.[2] Yet while some writers certainly tapped into the debate as a form of rhetorical self-display, others found in it a useful resource for trenchant political critique. In this chapter, I suggest that at moments of particular historical pressure the *querelle des femmes* could be deployed across multiple genres to call male monarchs to account. Around the time of Gainsford's publication, for example, the so-called 'Swetnam controversy' of 1615–1617 generated a spate of male-authored misogynist attacks as well as female-voiced defences of women. Usually read simply as contributions to the gender debate, these texts exploit the gendered discourses surrounding contemporary court scandal to offer thinly veiled criticism of the monarch, building on a tradition of female authors and voices speaking truth to power.

THE *QUERELLE*, POLITICAL CRITIQUE, AND THE FEMALE VOICE

The Swetnam pamphlets build on a history of debates about women in which female voices became engines of covert political critique and advice. An important influence on the sixteenth-century English *querelle*,[3] Christine de Pizan's *Livre de la cite des dames* (1405)—translated over a century later as the *Boke of the Cyte of Ladyes* (1521)—downplays de Pizan's authorship to exploit her female voice as narrator. Downcast upon reading a misogynist author, 'Christine' has a vision of three Ladies (Reason, 'Ryghtwysnesse', and Justice) who offer her a catalogue of female worthies as well as a defence of female 'prudence' as a foundation for good civil 'governaunce'.[4] Translator Bryan Anslay, attached to the household of Henry VIII's first queen, Catherine of Aragon, probably designed the text as support for her daughter the young Princess Mary's claim to the succession, though it had an extended life in English royal circles as support for female rulers.[5] In 1521, when relations between the royal couple had soured after the birth of King Henry VIII's illegitimate son, the *Boke* could have been read as celebrating both Catherine, who in 1513 rode out and faced down the Scots as a 'warrior queen like the ones praised in the *Cite des dames*', and her five-year-old legitimate daughter Mary, who deserved to be educated as a prince.[6] Yet, as Jennifer Summit argues, the *Boke* was

[2] Linda Woodbridge, *Women and the English Renaissance: Literature and the Nature of Womankind, 1540–1620* (Urbana, 1984), 17.

[3] Stephanie Downes, 'Fashioning Christine de Pizan in Tudor Defenses of Women', *Parergon*, 23 (2006), 71–92.

[4] De Pizan, in [Bryan Anslay (trans.)], *Here Begynneth the Boke of the Cyte of Ladyes* (London, 1521), sigs. Cc 2r–3r; Do3r–v.

[5] Anslay remained in the household of the new queen, Anne Boleyn, whose alleged lover William Brereton possessed a copy, and tapestries depicting its scenes came into the possession of Queen Elizabeth; see Hope Johnston, 'How *Le livre de la Cite des Dames* First Came to be Printed in England', in Liliane Dulac et al. (eds), *Desireuse de plus avant enquerre* (Paris, 2008), 385–96, 395–6.

[6] Johnston, 387–9.

pitched by printer Henry Pepwell at upwardly mobile gentlemen who might well have seen its women as models for themselves as 'counselors who could wield power not directly but through their influence on those inhabiting official positions of power'.[7]

Moved by the same cause more than a decade later, Thomas Elyot made one of the *Boke*'s worthy women—the learned and warlike Queen Zenobia—the central character of his *Defence of Good Women* (1540). Probably composed around 1532, the *Defence* served as propaganda again in favour of Catherine, whom Henry was then threatening to divorce (thereby making Mary illegitimate). Though Elyot's treatise initially takes the form of a dialogue between the misogynist Caninius and the 'gentyll' humanist Candidus, the latter's argument for Zenobia's 'nobylitye vertue and courage' is clinched by the appearance of the renowned woman who speaks for herself to demonstrate the 'courage, constance, and reason' of all women.[8] Advocating strategic submission to her husband, Zenobia aims 'to give him wise counsaile, [rather] than to appere dissobedient or sturdy' (sig. E2r). After his death, she becomes regent and puts her education in moral philosophy to use, offering views based on 'good reason' to her nobles and counsellors (sig. E3r–v). As a result, Zenobia not only defends her own realm but conquers others, 'by renowne of juste and politike governaunce' (sig. E5r). Elyot himself 'complied with royal policy and even participated in Henry's government', but secretly joined a conspiracy 'prepared to welcome on English shores the forces of Charles V, depose Henry, and place Catherine on the throne as regent for Mary'.[9] By giving Zenobia her own eloquent voice in the *Defence*, Elyot recreates in her an image of the learned queen whom Henry himself recognised as 'a proud stubborn woman of very high courage' capable of bringing him down.[10] Elyot may also have seen in the good wife and counsellor Zenobia an image of himself—a loyal subject whose duty to his governor remains subordinate to his conscience and his reason.

The political nature of the *querelle* was most explicit in the clash between the Scot John Knox's attack on Queen Mary's rule in his *First Blast of the Trumpet Against the Monstrous Regiment of Women* (1558) and John Aylmer's defence of Queen Elizabeth in his *Harborowe for Faithful and Trewe Subjectes* (1559). Excusing Knox as a 'Straunger' who extends Queen Mary's atrocities to all women, Aylmer defends Elizabeth's rule by turning woman's 'weakness' into evidence that she can be, like David or Judith, empowered by God to punish tyranny. Excavating Aristotle's *Economics* for its model

[7] Jennifer Summit, *Lost Property; the Woman Writer and English Literary History, 1380–1589* (Chicago, IL, 2000), 103.

[8] Thomas Elyot, *The Defence of Good Women* (London, 1540), sigs. A3r, D7r, D7v.

[9] Constance Jordan, 'Feminism and the Humanists: The Case of Sir Thomas Elyot's *Defence of Good Women*', in Margaret W. Ferguson, Maureen Quilligan and Nancy Vickers (eds), *Rewriting the Renaissance: The Discourse of Sexual Difference in Early Modern Europe* (Chicago, 1986), 242–58, 246. Similarly, David Clapham's 1542 translation of Heinrich Cornelius Agrippa's 1509 *Treatise of the Nobilitie and Excellencye of Woman Kinde* was 'almost certainly' read as support for 'the two young princesses whose succession to the throne was in jeopardy, in part because they were female'—though because Clapham was a friend of Genevan exile John Bale, his translation likely championed the claim of the young Protestant Princess Elizabeth; Constance Jordan, *Renaissance Feminism: Literary Texts and Political Models* (Ithaca, NY, 1990), 122.

[10] Jordan, 'Feminism', 257.

of 'an equall authoritie betwixte the wife and the husbande', Aylmer claims that 'the Philosopher leaveth a kind of rule to the woman, whiche is hers so muche by nature, as the husbande pullinge it from her, entreth into a kinde of tirannie and violateth the moste naturall and best ordre'.[11] In his suggestion that women embody ideals of rule by counsel, Aylmer builds on Heinrich Cornelius Agrippa's denunciation of 'the great tyranny of men' in favour of the 'councelle' of women.[12] These sixteenth-century treatises not only defend women rulers but associate them with a style of leadership open to consultation with parliament and people, implicitly critiquing autocratic male rulers.

Aylmer's *Harborowe* also uses prosopopoeia—the rhetorical figure that ventriloquises an imagined, absent, or dead person or entity[13]—to imagine England herself as a mother calling to her subjects. 'Obey your mistres and mine which God hath made lady over vs, bothe by nature and lawe', cries the country. 'You can not be my children, if you be not her subjectes: I wyll none of you, if you will none of hir' (sig. R2r). The authoritative female voice was a key element in the repertoire of the defence: Elyot imagines Zenobia delivering her own speeches, and Agrippa's more Christian defence finds authority for the female voice in scripture: 'By ye voyce of the lorde [Abraham] was commanded thus: *What so euer Sara saythe to the here her voice*', he writes (sig. E2r). In each case, the woman's voice is deployed to counsel, inform, or castigate misogynists or male rulers. William Thomas, who represents his own 1551 defence as the extension of a gentlewoman's rebuttal of misogyny, hints at the reforming impulses built into defences of women in his dedication of *The vanitie of the worlde* (1549) to Lady Anne Herbert:

> because I have founde so muche negligence in man, that almost he deserveth not to be warned any more of his folie: therefore did I determine to dedicate my boke unto a woman, to prove whether it maie take any roote in theim: to the entent that men ashamed, thorough the vertuouse examples of women, maie be provoked therby to refourme theim selfes, which no kinde of admonicion can persuade theim to dooe.[14]

The potential didacticism of defences of women can be fully understood only in the context of their particular historical moment, however. As Constance Jordan argues, they

11 John Aylmer, *An Harborowe for Faithful and Trewe Subjectes* (London, 1559), sigs. B1v, I3v.

12 Heinrich Cornelius Agrippa, in David Clapham (trans.), *A Treatise of the Nobilitie and Excellencye of Woman Kinde* (London, 1542), sigs. F7v–F8r. Though Woodbridge 'cannot believe that it was meant to be taken seriously' (*Women*, 40), Diane S. Wood maintains that this work 'is consistent with Agrippa's other declamations and, like them, presents serious theological arguments of a persuasive nature'; 'In Praise of Women's Superiority: Heinrich Cornelius Agrippa's *De nobilitate*', in Barbara K. Gold, Paul Allen Miller, and Charles Platter (eds), *Sex and Gender in Medieval and Renaissance Texts: The Latin Tradition* (Albany, NY, 1997), 189–206, 190.

13 'Proso-poia is a fayning of any person, when in our speech we represent the person of anie, and make it speake as though he were there present'; Abraham Fraunce, *The Arcadian Rhetorike* (London, 1588), sig. G2v.

14 William Thomas, *The Vanitie of this Worlde* (London, 1549), sig. A2v. Thomas defends women in his *An Argument Wherin the Apparaile of Women is Both Reproved and Defended* (London, 1551).

tend to be 'occasional, each defence motivated in some measure by a need to address a specific audience at a particular moment in history'.[15]

THE *QUERELLE* AND THE OVERBURY SCANDAL

The early seventeenth-century 'Swetnam controversy' is situated at just such a particular historical moment. Swetnam's misogynist *Araignment of Lewd, Idle, Froward and Unconstant Women* appeared in 1615, the year when the notorious 'Overbury scandal' broke, and the three responses to Swetnam printed in 1617 followed closely upon the highly public 1616 murder trials of Robert Carr, Earl of Somerset, his wife Frances Howard, and their alleged accomplices. The scandal itself illuminates the politics of gender at court.[16] In 1606, Frances Howard, daughter to the Earl of Suffolk, wed Robert Devereux, third Earl of Essex, in a marriage designed to unite the pro-Spanish, crypto-Catholic Howard faction with the Protestant Sidney/Essex faction. The marriage was a miserable failure, and in 1613 Howard sued for divorce. By this time she had fallen in love with the king's powerful favourite Robert Carr, who began to implement James I's pro-Spanish policies, brokering the unpopular match of Prince Charles to the Spanish Infanta.[17] After successfully procuring an annulment of her marriage on the grounds of non-consummation, Howard married Carr in December 1613 in a lavish celebration bankrolled by the king. When Carr's friend Thomas Overbury objected to the match, he was imprisoned in the Tower where he apparently died of natural causes. In 1615, however, the Essex faction released evidence to suggest that Overbury had in fact been poisoned by Carr, Howard, and their accomplices, including the widow Anne Turner.[18] Carr and Howard were arrested and imprisoned while their alleged accomplices were tried and executed. In January 1616, the pair were indicted and, in May 1616, brought to trial. The 'greatest scandal of the Jacobean age' had a devastating impact on the reputation of James I and his court: David Lindley observes that the explosive nexus of sex and violence 'confirmed in the minds of auditors what they already believed of the court, that it was an immoral and villainous place. This posed something of a problem for the prosecutors, in that the mud could so easily stick to the King himself'.[19] Because two of the accused were women, the initial outpouring of responses to the scandal was deeply misogynistic, the scapegoating of women functioning as metonymy for a court

[15] Jordan, 'Feminism', 247.

[16] For a full account see Alastair Bellany, *The Politics of Court Scandal: News Culture and the Overbury Affair, 1603–1666* (Cambridge, 2002), and David Lindley, *The Trials of Frances Howard: Fact and Fiction at the Court of King James* (London, 1993).

[17] Bellany, *Politics*, 57.

[18] Bellany, *Politics*, 68, 202.

[19] Lindley, *Trials*, 1, 162.

culture that was often perceived as 'intrinsically effeminate'.[20] Howard in particular was widely excoriated as a sexually insatiable 'witch, a poysoner, and a whore'—a 'monster of excess'.[21]

The scandal re-energised the *querelle des femmes*. Despite Barnaby Rich's disingenuous claim to writing '*harmelese lynes, that never did conspire, / In any sort, to slaunder or detect*', his *Excellency of Good Women* (1613) builds on Howard's notorious divorce suit to launch a searing attack on 'a wicked woman wel knowne to be infamed'.[22] And, when Joseph Swetnam's pamphlet *The Araignment of Lewd, Idle, Froward and Unconstant Women* appeared two years later, the association of the Overbury murder with stereotypes of female lust, adultery, and witchcraft was at its height. While Howard herself is never mentioned, the reader would doubtless recognise her in passages like these: 'her brest will be the harbourer of an envious heart, and her heart the storehouse of poysoned hatred, her head will devise villany, and her hands are ready to practise that which her heart desireth'.[23] As a 'hotter' sort of Protestant whose *Araignment* encoded criticism of James' pro-Spanish policies as well as his corrupt and 'effeminate' court, Swetnam exploits James' own identification of himself with the anointed King David to remind the reader of the latter's adulterous love for Bathsheba: 'And was not *David* the best beloved of God, and a mighty Prince?' he writes. 'Yet for the love of women he purchased the displeasure of his God' (10).[24] For Swetnam, king, court, and nation are corrupted by the effeminising passions manifest in the Overbury affair. As Alastair Bellany observes, 'the crime of poisoning ... helped connect Overbury's murder—and by implication the royal court—to such frightening transgressions as demonic witchcraft, popery, and the political corruption of courts under wicked rulers'.[25] As an 'intertextual *bricolage* of considerable subversive power', Swetnam's 'carnivalesque' pamphlet targets the strumpet to indict the court that apparently licensed her sins.[26]

In his *Asylum Veneris, or A Sanctuary for Ladies* (1616), Daniel Tuvil includes what Woodbridge terms a 'confusion' of misogynistic and pro-woman discourses that in fact provide alternate forms of critique.[27] An Essexian 'patriot' who contributed a poem to the seventh edition of *Sir Thomas Overburie his Wife*,[28] Tuvil initially indicts women

[20] Lindley, *Trials*, 61.

[21] Bodleian MS Malone 23, fol. 6r; cited by Lindley, *Trials*, 178, 177.

[22] Barnaby Rich, *Excellency of Good Women* (London, 1613), 33, 10.

[23] Joseph Swetnam, *The Araignment of Lewd, Idle, Froward and Unconstant Women* (London, 1615), 15.

[24] See Christina Luckyj, '*A Mouzell for Melastomus* in Context: Rereading the Swetnam-Speght Debate', *English Literary Renaissance*, 40 (Winter 2010), 113–31, and David Underdown, who suggests Swetnam's work 'was inspired by the Overbury affair'; *A Freeborn People: Politics and the Nation in Seventeenth-Century England* (Oxford, 1996), 64.

[25] Bellany, *Politics*, 148.

[26] Diane Purkiss, 'Material Girls: The Seventeenth-Century Woman Debate', in Clare Brant and Diane Purkiss (eds), *Women, Texts and Histories 1575–1760* (London, 1992), 69–101, 73.

[27] Woodbridge, *Women*, 105.

[28] Daniel Tuvil, 'On Sir Thomas Overbury's Poem The Wife', in Donald Beecher (ed.), *Characters* (Ottawa, 2003), 173. Michelle O'Callaghan defines 'patriots' as 'hispanophobes' and 'defenders of traditional liberties [who] oppose corruption at court'; '*The Shepheards Nation*': *Jacobean Spenserians and Early Stuart Political Culture, 1612–1625* (Oxford, 2000), 18.

who '*doe not feare by poyson to remove / A worthy Husband, for a worthlesse Love*', neatly conflating the Earl of Essex with Overbury as Howard's victims.[29] In his first seven chapters, Tuvil rehearses misogynist arguments much like Swetnam's, drawing anti-feminist material from jest books and commonplaces to mount the same kind of anti-court critique. The last three chapters, however, on women's learning and knowledge, wisdom and discretion, and valour and courage respectively, are entirely different in tone. Obliquely alluding to the Overbury affair, Tuvil redirects blame from such women to the *men* responsible for their falls, suggesting that overweening male authority is responsible for female transgression. 'Let him consider likewise if his owne Lordlynesse bee not a maine efficient of her lewdnesse', he writes (147). That he intends this in a political sense is made clear by what follows: 'The deedes of men in authority, are alwaies Patrons for those of lower ranke. A subject usually eies nothing but the example of his Superiour' (151). But he goes well beyond this to suggest that women, 'endued with such learning, wisdome, courage, and other the like abilities, which Men, overwhelmed with self-conceit presumptuously entitle Masculine', have shown that they can rule more effectively than men (86). His examples include Queen Isabella of Spain, who—like Elyot's Queen Zenobia—defends and enlarges her kingdom while choosing good counsellors, practising 'the chiefest Art that belongeth unto Soueraignetie' (103). Deploying female rulers to implicitly critique James' failures, Tuvil includes both a lengthy paean to Elizabeth I's 'prudence in governing' and 'religion in performing' (105) and a tribute to Queen Anne's 'wisdome and discretion' (107). He then daringly invokes Helena, Queen of Cyprus, 'who perceiving that hir husbands weakenesse was a blot whereon the greatest part of his nobility continually plaied ... tooke the governement into hir owne hands, to the release of the Land, and the reliefe of all hir subjects' (108–9). Here Tuvil may be drawing less on an actual female ruler than on the 'political marriage metaphor' as support for parliament in curbing the monarch's excesses.[30] As Melissa Sanchez observes: 'marriage offered a model of a voluntary and reciprocal relation in which the sovereign would secure legitimacy by submitting to law and counsel'.[31] 'I am the Husband, and all the whole Isle is my lawfull Wife', James proclaimed in his first speech to parliament,[32] and Tuvil extends the logic of James' own analogy in posing the question: 'shall hee, that is blinde in his understanding disdaine to be directed by her, who by the ordinance of God, and the rules of sacred Wedlocke, is alotted him a fellow-helper in all his businesses?' (97). Two years earlier, the king had dissolved the so-called 'Parliament of love' for its attempts to offer him advice and impose on his prerogative.[33]

[29] D[aniel] T[uvil], *Asylum veneris, or a Sanctuary for Ladies* (London, 1616), sig. A6r.

[30] See Christina Luckyj, 'Reading Overbury's *Wife*: Politics and Marriage in 1616', in Hannah Crawforth and Sarah Lewis (eds), *Family Politics in Early Modern Literature* (London, 2017), 39–56.

[31] Melissa E. Sanchez, *Erotic Subjects: The Sexuality of Politics in Early Modern English Literature* (Oxford, 2011), 13.

[32] 'Speech to Parliament', in Charles H. McIlwain (ed.), *Political Works of James I* (New York, 1965), 272.

[33] David Colclough, *Freedom of Speech in Early Stuart England* (Cambridge, 2005), 159–68.

Championing the role of woman as counsellor who corrects her husband/ruler's defects, Tuvil uses the defence to offer and endorse political counsel.

The shift from attack to defence in Tuvil's pamphlet may also map a shift in attitudes to the women at the centre of the scandal. By early 1616, Howard and Turner, the disorderly women on whom Swetnam's political critique relied, were heralded as models of Christian virtue even as Carr obstinately refused to confess and the king refused to have him executed. Accused at her trial of being 'a whore, a bawd, a sorcerer, a witch, a papist, a felon and a murderer', Turner gave such a compelling display of 'deepe sighes, teares, confessions, ejaculations of the soul' at the scaffold while leading the audience in prayer and preaching reform, that she was heralded as a latter-day Mary Magdalen who 'now enjoyes the presence of hirs and our Redeemer'.[34] During her own well-attended trial in May 1616, Howard quietly begged for mercy, showing herself so 'touched with remorse and sense of her fault' that even her chief prosecutor Sir Francis Bacon argued that she should be treated with 'compassion' in view of 'her youth, her person, her sex, her noble family; yea, her provocations'.[35] Eyewitness Edward Palavicino recorded his impression of Howard as 'truly noble, fashioned to act a tragedy with so much sweetness, grace and good form, as if all the graces had heaped their whole powers to render her that day the most beloved, the most commiserate spectacle'.[36] Her penitence, combined with the public execution of male accomplices, had the effect of directing most of the remaining rage at Carr—and beyond him at the king, the man who fostered this serpent in his bosom. The 'amazing volte-face' in perceptions of the women in the Overbury affair between 1615 and 1617 provides essential context for the pamphlets of the Swetnam controversy.[37] No longer viewed as malicious agents but as scapegoated victims of a court rife with masculine corruption, women and their voices could be deployed to redirect blame at the king and his disgraced and unrepentant base-born favourite.

THE OVERBURY SCANDAL, WOMEN WRITERS, AND POLITICAL CRITIQUE

Perhaps finding in Howard's demeanour a nobility (of character and of blood) they shared, women who left impressions of her include Lady Anne Clifford, who records in her diary that Howard was 'much pitied by all beholders' and Lady Anne Southwell, whose 'Epitaph upon the Countess of Sommersett' heralds Howard as 'Natures admired

[34] BL MS Cotton Titus B.vii, fol. 476; cited by Lindley, *Trials*, 179.

[35] T. B. Howell (ed.), *Complete Collection of State Trials* (London, 1816) 2, 957; cited by Lindley, *Trials*, 150; James Spedding (ed.), *The Letters and Life of Francis Bacon* (London, 1869), 5. 297, cited by Lindley, *Trials*, 178.

[36] PRO SP 14/87/34 (Palavicino to Carleton: 29 May 1616), cited by Bellany, *Politics*, 242.

[37] Lindley, *Trials*, 178.

Juell' and 'a Princly dame / the Fenix of Great Hawardes name'.[38] And, in her 1621 *Urania*, Lady Mary Wroth includes a thinly veiled fictional account of the Overbury affair in a tale that begins with a group of 'cruel' women whipping a king—an act that elicits the misogynistic comment that 'women inraged they say are Devils'.[39] The perspective soon shifts, however, when one of the women recounts a hasty marriage in which she lived a wife, 'and yet a maid' while her 'affection was tied and wedded to this king ... of ungratefulnes and cruelty' (564). After her lover / king (aka Carr) divulges the affair to another man (aka Overbury), he 'defamd and forsook' her. 'To tel ... and forsake me to?' she cries, as she tries to scratch him, before asking 'pardon' and retreating to her castle (565). By suppressing Howard's involvement in Overbury's murder, representing her as Carr's victim and fashioning her perspective of events, Wroth participates in Howard's defence.[40] For all these women—staunch Protestants normally opposed to women like Howard and Turner 'suspected of Catholic leanings'[41]—the politics of class and gender trump the politics of religion, though Turner's reported renunciation of Catholicism at her death would doubtless have gratified them.[42]

The first woman to participate publicly in the defence of women after the Carr–Howard trials in May 1616 was twenty-year-old Rachel Speght, whose *Mouzell for Melastomus* was entered five months later into the Stationer's Register. And it is to just such 'Ladies Honou*rable or Worshipfull ... loving their just reputation*' that Speght appeals, looking well beyond Swetnam to give 'content unto the wronged' by denouncing 'the scandals and defamations of the malevolent'.[43] Refuting the 'vulgar ignorant [who] might have beleeved his Diabolicall infamies to be infallible truths' (3), she derides not only Swetnam but also an emergent news culture that disseminated scores of manuscript libels related to the scandal. 'Heere lyes hee that once was poore / Then rich, then great, then lov'd an whore. / Hee woed, then wedd: and in conclusion / His love and whore, was his confusion', reads a pithy and representative one.[44] For Speght, Swetnam represents what Richard Niccols calls the 'ignoble vulgar cruell, mad in minde':

38 Anne Clifford, 'The Diary of Lady Anne Clifford', in Randall Martin (ed.), *Women Writers in Renaissance England* (New York, 2010), 253; Anne Southwell, 'An Epitaph upon the Countess of Sommersett', in Jean Klene (ed.), *The Southwell-Sibthorpe Commonplace Book* (Tempe, 1997), 35.

39 Lady Mary Wroth, in Josephine A. Roberts (ed), *The First Part of The Countess of Montgomery's Urania* (Binghamton, 1995), 563.

40 Wroth, in Roberts (ed.), 563.29, 789.

41 Lindley, *Trials*, 165.

42 'And (now) to make her penitence, more cleare, / That *Image*-worship, that her breast once bare / A heart *Devote*-to; shee in death denide, / And *Rome*, and Romes fowle *Heresie* defide'; Thomas Brewer, *Mistres Turners Repentance* (London, 1615), n.p.

43 Rachel Speght, *A Mouzell for Melastomus*, in Barbara Kiefer Lewalski (ed.) *The Polemics and Poems of Rachel Speght* (Oxford, 1996), 3, 5, 3.

44 [Anon.], 'Heere lyes hee that once was poore', in Alastair Bellany and Andrew McRae (eds), *Early Stuart Libels: An Edition of Poetry from Manuscript Sources*, Early Modern Literary Studies Text Series I (2005), http://www.earlystuartlibels.net/htdocs/overbury_murder_section/H6.html, accessed 28 November 2020.

> The muddie spawne of euery fruitlesse braine,
> Daub'd out in ignominious lines, did staine
> Papers in each mans hand, with rayling rimes
> Gainst the foule Actors of these wel-knowne crimes.[45]

In her response to 'unjust imputations', Speght finds authority in 'the winde of Gods truth' and 'the Word of Gods Spirit' (3–4). 'If the feare of God reside in [women's] hearts, maugre all adversaries, they are highly esteemed and accounted of in the eies of their gracious Redeemer', she asserts (4), perhaps recalling Turner's 'Coelestiall comfort' in her final moments.[46] Speght's excoriation of slanders that circulate 'without any answere at all' (3) may even be offered to defend women such as Howard, forced by codes of feminine modesty to remain 'silent during her hearing'.[47] And, in a neat inversion of the 'link between women and poison' in the Overbury affair,[48] Speght accuses her 'pestiferous enemy' of providing a 'deadly poyson for women', and shooting 'poysoned shafts' (3, 4). Though Speght never refers explicitly to the Overbury affair, she taps into the backlash against its misogynist scapegoating of women.

In the main part of her *Mouzell*—which takes the form of a marriage sermon—Speght eschews the misogyny that fuels Swetnam's political critique by echoing defences like Elyot's and Tuvil's that represent the female voice as a model of resistance to monarchical abuse through moderation and counsel. Many scholars have observed that 'representations of love and marriage offer documents of political ideas',[49] and Speght's 'domestic' treatise also taps into the politicised discourse in which the king declared himself husband/ruler to his wife/subject the nation. 'Yet was shee not produced from *Adams* foote, to be his too low inferiour', writes Speght, 'nor from his head to be his superiour, but from his side, neare his heart to be his equall' (18). Such commonplaces of puritan doctrine with their implicit support for people and parliament undergird her more daring moments of monarchical critique: 'he who was the soveraigne of all creatures visible, should have yeelded greatest obedience to God' (15), she writes (of Adam in Genesis); 'a King doth not trample his Crowne under his feete, but highly esteemes of it' (22), she insists (of the wife in Proverbs). Though the man is '*the Womans Head*', he must not 'domineere' (23); as his 'collaterall companion', the woman must 'give good councell unto her husband, the which hee must not despise' (19). Offering just such 'good councell' to authoritarian 'Lords and Rulers' who 'stand a tip-toe' (24), Speght's female voice becomes an instrument of political critique.

Because Speght founds her critique largely on Scripture, however, she has been described as 'hobbled by her faith', restricted to parroting 'patriarchal' discourses.[50] For this reason she has usually been excluded from the more boisterous company of

45 Richard Niccols, *Sir Thomas Overburies Vision* (London, 1616), 3.

46 Brewer, n.p.

47 Lindley, *Trials*, 184.

48 Lindley, *Trials*, 166.

49 Kevin Sharpe, *Politics and Ideas in Early Stuart England* (London, 1989), 60. For an extended version of this argument see Luckyj, '*A Mouzell for Melastomus*'.

50 Woodbridge, *Women*, 90; Purkiss, 'Material Girls', 94.

the female-voiced defences that followed hers the same year: Ester Sowernam's *Ester Hath Hang'd Haman* and Constantia Munda's *Worming of a Mad Dogge*.[51] But this underestimates the ludic quality of *Certaine Quaeres to the Bayter of Women*, the brief text appended to the *Mouzell* which anticipates both Munda and Sowernam. Having demonstrated in the *Mouzell* that she is capable of writing a 'literate Responsarie, Speght justifies the irregular shape of her *Quaeres* because 'a crooked pot-lid well enough fits a wrie-neckt pot' and Swetnam's 'promiscuous mingle-mangle' invites an 'immethodical' answer in kind (31). In *Quaeres* she responds to Swetnam's individual arguments, correcting his readings of Scripture and his flawed and contradictory logic. But she also plays exuberantly with language, exposing his '*wonder-foole*' grammatical errors '*Asse*' they are found in his book (35). And she devises a mock arraignment for Swetnam, deciding by syllogism that the '*Bayter of women* hath blasphemed God, *Ergo*, he ought to die the death' (38). The unruly play evident in the *Quaeres* unsettles the prevailing idea that Speght is 'sober and sophisticated' and maintains a consistently 'pious tone'.[52] But it also interrogates Diane Purkiss' argument that the voice of the 'unruly woman' she finds in Sowernam's and Munda's texts would inevitably have been received as 'a theatrical performance of femininity which indicates a joke at women's expense'.[53] For if—as Speght later claims—*Mouzell* was read by some contemporaries as the work of her father, a puritan clergyman writing under her signature (45), such playfulness did not compromise the religious authority of a supposed 'transvestite' female author or the seriousness of 'her' text. This evidence should inform our reading of the pseudonymous female-voiced attacks on Swetnam that followed Speght's.

THE SWETNAM CONTROVERSY, THE FEMALE VOICE, AND POLITICAL CRITIQUE

Once hailed as women writers because of their 'passionate conviction' in representing woman's cause,[54] Sowernam and Munda are now more often identified as disorderly transvestite figures whose pseudonymous texts—unlike Speght's supposedly more decorous pamphlet—advertise 'not proper names, but improper stories'.[55] Yet if Sowernam appears to slight 'the slenderness of [Speght's] answer' in the opening epistle to *Ester*

[51] Purkiss, 'Material Girls', 85.

[52] Joad Raymond, *Pamphlets and Pamphleteering in Early Modern Britain* (Cambridge, 2003), 286; Woodbridge, *Women*, 88.

[53] Purkiss, 'Material Girls', 84–5.

[54] See 'Part 1: Contexts', in Katherine Usher Henderson and Barbara F. McManus (eds), *Half Humankind: Contexts and Texts of the Controversy about Women in England, 1540–1640* (Urbana, IL 1985), 3–133, 21.

[55] Purkiss, 'Material Girls', 84.

Hath Hang'd Haman, she nonetheless shares serious political allegiances with 'the Maide in her *Muzzell*' whose arguments she later imitates.[56] Along with Speght's publisher Thomas Archer, Sowernam's publisher Nicholas Bourne was later engaged in printing ultra-Protestant news books or corantos that James attempted to suppress,[57] activities for which 'Archer had been imprisoned in summer 1621, and ... Bourne frequently ran afoul of the authorities'.[58] Sowernam's title, with its allusion to the virtuous Queen Esther who successfully denounces the king's wicked favourite to have him hanged and 'preserve her people' (12), would doubtless have brought to mind Robert Carr, King James' favourite, who in 1617 was also sentenced to hang. Declaring herself on her title page as 'neither Maide, Wife nor Widdowe, yet really all, and therefore experienced to defend all', Sowernam may even be figuring herself as champion for Howard, identified in contemporary libels as 'a mayd a wife a widow and a whore'.[59] To mount her defence, Sowernam builds on Speght's fleeting mock-trial of Swetnam by arraigning *olde fornicators* who, like those in Scripture accusing the woman taken in adultery (John 8.7), 'throw the first stone' but must now face a *fowle reckoning against themselves* (sig. A4v).[60] Her formal arraignment of Swetnam indicts 'under his person, the arraignment *of all idle, franticke, froward, and lewd men*' (27) who corrupt women only to blame them for corruption. Indeed, in her dedication to the apprentices of London—a group often 'caught up in various forms of civil disorder'—Sowernam launches a more pointed barb.[61] If a man *rayle at women, who in his owne experienced tryall had made many bad, he shall shew himselfe a decompounded K.* she declares, adding darkly *I doe not meane Knight* (sig. A4v). As a common abbreviation for King, 'K.' glances at James himself, the 'decompounded' monarch whose behaviour risks squandering his claim to unite his subjects.

In the rest of the pamphlet, Sowernam's 'patriot' allegiances are on full display: in her snubbing of the King James Bible to invoke 'the [Geneva] Bible printed 1595' (7), in her anti-court critique of sumptuously attired men who 'gallant it at the Court one day, & brave it in the Country the next day' (38), and in her celebration of the rule of women, especially Queen Elizabeth, 'a patterne for the best men to imitate' (21).[62] Identifying

56 Ester Sowernam, *Ester Hath Hang'd Haman* (London, 1617), A2v, 6.

57 S. A. Baron, 'Bourne, Nicholas', *Oxford Dictionary of National Biography* [online edn], (3 January 2008), Oxford University Press, https://doi-org.helicon.vuw.ac.nz/10.1093/ref:odnb/68205, accessed 13 July 2020.

58 Chris R. Kyle, *Theater of State: Parliament and Political Culture in Early Stuart England* (Stanford, CA, 2012), 85.

59 Bodleian MS Rawlinson D 1048, fol. 64; cited by Lindley, *Trials*, 178.

60 On the charge of adultery as a key component in the case against Howard, see Lindley, *Trials*, 167–70.

61 Purkiss, 'Material Girls', 87.

62 Although Purkiss, 'Material Girls', reads Sowernam as 'the voice of the unruly woman' (86), she observes her 'political critique' in the praise of Elizabeth, suggesting that 'the praise may reflect upon the perceived dissolution of moral and sexual boundaries at the court of James I' (85). See also Mihoko Suzuki, 'Elizabeth, Gender, and the Political Imaginary of Seventeenth-Century England', in Cristina Malcolmson and Mihoko Suzuki (eds), *Debating Gender in Early Modern England 1500–1700* (New York, 2002), 232–3.

herself with Experience—a Judge who will 'curbe in the prodigall' (28)—Sowernam excoriates 'prodigall spend-thrifts' (44) in an unsubtle allusion to a court characterised by 'wild riot, excess, and devastation of time and temperance'.[63] Even as she vindicates Eve as assaulted by 'a serpent of the Masculine gender' and a 'mischievous Politician' (7),[64] she echoes biblical discourses circulating around the Overbury scandal, as in this ventriloquised lament by 'Mistris Turner': 'With *Eue* I might haue liv'd in Paradice, / But that a Serpent did my Soule intice'.[65] Throughout, Sowernam argues that men should accuse not women but themselves, for 'who is guiltie of his lascivious disease but himselfe?' (37). Her view had special significance in 1617, when the men who scapegoated women in the Overbury affair were exposed as sources of their corruption. One contemporary libel mockingly asks Robert Carr, 'hath fortune kyste thee, & now doth she byte' only to answer, 'O noe I wronge her twas not shee that threwe / thee on thy necke or was thy ruins cause / but lustfull leacher twas thy self that drewe / thy selfe into confutions Jawes'.[66] Similarly, Sowernam lambasts male treatment of women, complaining: 'It is a shame he hath hardned her tender sides, and gentle heart with his boistrous & Northren blasts' (43–4). Here, she may be following the lead of Michael Drayton, who according to Michelle O'Callaghan insinuated in his 1606 *Poemes* that 'James is the "cold northern breath" … blasting the English pastoral landscape'.[67] Adopting the figure of *parrhesia* ('candour') to 'speake freely' (35), Sowernam taps into the same rhetoric of '*libertie*' (16) used by parliamentarians to counsel the king and critique the failures of his 'government (43)'.[68]

Unlike Speght's or Sowernam's, Munda's pamphlet has been identified as a 'railing' text which, because 'more vehement, physical, insulting, aggressive and sharply satirical than in any previous defence',[69] clearly violates 'early modern codes of femininity as meekness, modesty, domesticity, and submissiveness'.[70] Many scholars therefore claim that her work is probably male-authored and 'heavily coded as misogynist impersonation'.[71] Yet, like Sowernam, Munda signals her serious political critique in the paratexts

[63] 'Letter from Sir John Harington to Mr. Secretary Barlow, 1606', in Robert Ashton (ed.), *James I by His Contemporaries* (London, 1969), 244.

[64] It is worth noting the double meaning of 'politician' as both 'schemer' and 'statesman' (*OED* 1a and 2a).

[65] *The Just Downefall of Ambition Adultery and Murder* (London, 1615), sig. D1r.

[66] [Anon.], 'Why how now Robine? discontented quite', in Bellany and McRae (eds), *Early Stuart Libels*, http://www.earlystuartlibels.net/htdocs/overbury_murder_section/H12.html, accessed 28 November 2020.

[67] O'Callaghan, '*The Shepheards Nation*', 13. *Michael Drayton, Poemes. Lyrick and Pastorall* (London, 1606), sig. F1r.

[68] See Colclough, *Freedom of Speech*, 160.

[69] Gwynne Kennedy, *Just Anger: Representing Women's Anger in Early Modern England* (Carbondale, IL, 2000), 43.

[70] Maria Prendergast, *Railing, Reviling and Invective in English Literary Culture 1588–1617: The Anti-Poetics of Theater and Print* (London, 2016), 182–83.

[71] Elizabeth Clarke, 'Anne Southwell and the Pamphlet Debate: The Politics of Gender, Class, and Manuscript', in Malcolmson and Suzuki (eds), *Debating Gender*, 37–53, 48.

of *The Worming*. Identifying herself as '*dux femina facti*' on the title page, she alludes via Virgil's Dido to Elizabeth whose Armada victory was commemorated with a coin bearing the same motto.[72] And while the pseudonym 'Constantia' reinforces the association with Elizabeth, whose motto was '*semper eadem*' (always the same), constancy as defined by Flemish humanist Justus Lipsius was a politically charged notion, a 'symbolic form of resistence to the consolidation of monarchical power and an assertion of the immanent power ... of the nobility'.[73] In the dedication to her mother 'Prudentia', Munda suggests that constancy is born of prudence, another virtue prized by Lipsius as 'most necessarie for a Prince', who requires 'good advise and counsell'.[74] That Munda herself intends to give such advice is clear from her resolve to write to *stop the curs wide throat / Until the haltar came* (sig. A1v). 'Cur' may or may not be a pun on 'Carr' ('Ker' in the original Scottish), but, at a time when most believed (rightly) that the king would commute Carr's death sentence, Munda excoriates her opponent '*As a malefactor* [who] *changeth place / From Newgate unto Tiburne, whose good hope / Is but to change his shackels for a rope*' (sig. A1v). 'Sith Car & Carter then soe well agree / Let none them part till they at Tyburne bee', reads a contemporary libel on Carr.[75] '[*T*]*hough the eyes / Of judgement wink, his soule still guilty cries*', Munda claims in an indictment that glances beyond Swetnam to apply to the king's failure to execute justice on his favourite (19).

Much like Speght—whose 'modest and powerfull' defence is fully acknowledged (15)—Munda stigmatises Swetnam's pamphlet as an appeal to the 'itching eares of silly swaines, and rude / Truth-not-discerning rusticke multitude' (sig. A2r). Unlike Speght, however, Munda mounts a strident defence of class as much as gender. Heavily larded with Italian, Greek, and Latin quotations, *The Worming* illustrates the elite education that elevates Munda above the 'mercenary Pasquils' of her opponent (sig. B1r). If Swetnam threatens 'the dissolution of class and wealth boundaries', observing '*Jone* is as good as my Lady' (9), Munda objects to his slandering equally 'the nobly-descended Ladies, as the obscure base vermine' (9), so that no woman 'of what parentage or royall descent and lineage soever, how well soever nurtured and qualified, shall scape [his] convicious violence' (13).[76] Munda may share contemporary concerns that prosecution of a Lady of noble blood threatened the power and prestige of aristocratic families, potentially diminishing their advisory role as a caution on the monarch's power.[77] But Munda's attack on Swetnam as a 'base phreneticall brain-sicke babler' whose 'insolent

[72] Constantia Munda, *The Worming of a Mad Dogge: or, A Soppe for Cerberus the Jaylor of Hell* (London, 1617); William Camden, *Remaines of a Greater Worke, Concerning Britaine* (London, 1605), 174.

[73] Julie Crawford, *Mediatrix: Women, Politics, and Literary Production in Early Modern England* (Oxford, 2014), 40, 46.

[74] Justus Lipsius, in William Jones (trans.), *Six Bookes of Politickes or Civill Doctrine* (London, 1594), 41, 40.

[75] [Anon.], 'From Car a Carter surely tooke his name', in Bellany and McRae (eds), *Early Stuart Libels*, http://www.earlystuartlibels.net/htdocs/overbury_murder_section/H13.html, accessed 28 November 2020.

[76] Purkiss, 'Material Girls', 76.

[77] See Lindley, *Trials*, 173–5.

invective madnesse' must be punished (1–2, 6) also recalls libels directed at the base-born Robert Carr, the 'upstart and alien favorite'.[78] '[W]hat new strange maddness did possese thy mynde / what Franticke humor haunted thee, what fitte?' asks one such satirical lampoon of Carr, continuing, 'how worthie for it arte thou to be ract / and pecemayle in some fearefull Engine torne'.[79] The punishments Munda envisages for Swetnam are equally corporeal. 'Our pens shall throttle you or like *Archilochus* with our tart Iambikes make you *Lopez* his godson' (16), she writes in a phrase that could apply equally well to Carr, who was associated not only with the 'tarts' that allegedly poisoned Overbury, but also with entanglement in Spanish interests for which Dr Lopez, Queen Elizabeth's physician and alleged poisoner, was executed in 1594. Like Sowernam's, Munda's energetic attack on Swetnam gestures beyond him to the 'execrable designes and inexcusable impudence' of men of the court (26). Concluding by borrowing a long passage from John Cooke's searing response to John Webster's Character of 'An Excellent Actor' (34–5), Munda's pamphlet aligns itself with Cooke's political views, expressed in his Character 'Of an Apparatour' in the Overbury collection, a posthumous tribute to the victim.[80] The sergeant in an ecclesiastical court, an apparatour, writes Cooke, is 'a chick of the egg, Abuse, hatcht by the warmth of authority'.[81]

In her warning to Swetnam, whom she hears 'groule against the Author with another head like the triple dog of hell' (16), Munda pays tribute to Speght as an 'Author'—that is, not only as writer, but also as 'creator' and 'authority' (*OED* 4, 5).[82] If, as Speght observes, authorship of the *Mouzell* subjected her to the 'Censure ... inevitable to a publique act' (45), in this 'publique' act she put herself at risk to serve 'the best interests of the community or nation' ('public' *OED* 7). Adopting the female voice that Speght uses so effectively, both Munda and Sowernam imitate her in building on the same anti-misogynist, anti-court critique that grew out of the Overbury scandal. Whether Munda or Sowernam were men or women, they chose to encode their similarly reformist politics in the female voices of 'Ester' and 'Constantia'.[83] Far from signalling 'feminine unruliness' or political

[78] Lindley, *Trials*, 161.

[79] [Anon.], 'Why how now Robine? discontented quite', in Bellany and McRae (eds), *Early Stuart Libels*.

[80] The work by Cooke (identified only as a 'Gentleman' by Munda) was originally published in John Stephens, *Satyrical Essayes, Characters and Others* (London, 1615), sig. B1r–v. See Deirdre Boleyn, 'Because Women are not Women, Rather Might be a Fit Subject of an Ingenious Strategist', *Prose Studies*, 32 (2010), 38–55, 50.

[81] John Cooke, 'An Apparatour', in Beecher (ed.), *Characters*, 235. Cooke claims authorship of this Character of the Overbury collection in Stephens, *Satyrical Essayes*, sig. A8r.

[82] Munda uses 'Author' in the latter sense elsewhere: 'What sin is wrought by ill example, soone / The displeased Author wisheth it undone', 19.

[83] Clarke, 'Anne Southwell and the Pamphlet Debate', fleetingly proposes Anne Southwell as Munda (37), while Donald W. Foster proposes Frances Prannell, Countess of Hertford, as Sowernam; 'Stuart [*née* Howard; *married name* Prannell], Frances, duchess of Lennox and Richmond [*other married name* Frances Seymour, countess of Hertford]', *Oxford Dictionary of National Biography* [online edn] (3 January 2008), Oxford University Press, https://doi-org.helicon.vuw.ac.nz/10.1093/ref:odnb/70952, accessed 21 July 2020.

disorder, Sowernam and Munda—like Speght—tap into models of conciliar opposition to monarchical absolutism and corruption that had long been associated with both female authors and female voices in the *querelle des femmes.*[84]

FURTHER READING

Bellany, Alastair. *The Politics of Court Scandal: News Culture and the Overbury Affair, 1603–1666*. Cambridge, 2002.

Fine, Emily. 'Polemical Conversation and Biblical Hermeneutics in the Jacobean Gender Pamphlet War', in Kristen Abbott Bennett (ed), *Conversational Exchanges in Early Modern England*. Cambridge, 2015, 132–61.

Jordan, Constance. *Renaissance Feminism: Literary Texts and Political Models*. Ithaca, NY, 1990.

Lindley, David. *The Trials of Frances Howard: Fact and Fiction at the Court of King James*. London, 1993.

Prendergast, Maria. *Railing, Reviling and Invective in English Literary Culture 1588–1617: The Anti-Poetics of Theater and Print*. London, 2016.

Purkiss, Diane. 'Material Girls: The Seventeenth-Century Woman Debate', in Clare Brant and Diane Purkiss (eds), *Women Texts and Histories 1575–1760*. London, 1992, 69–101.

Wayne, Valerie. 'The Dearth of the Author: Anonymity's Allies and *Swetnam the Woman-hater*', in Susan Frye and Karen Robertson (eds), *Maids and Mistresses, Cousins and Queens: Women's Alliances in Early Modern England*. Oxford, 1999, 221–40.

Woodbridge, Linda. *Women and the English Renaissance: Literature and the Nature of Womankind, 1540–1620*. Urbana, IL, 1984.

84 Purkiss, 'Material Girls', 84.

CHAPTER 10

THE SONGSCAPES OF EARLY MODERN WOMEN

KATHERINE R. LARSON

As the field of early modern women's writing has flourished, scholars have become adept at confronting and destabilising moralistic claims about women's silence. Yet even with growing attention to the scope, formal and stylistic innovation, and transnational impact of women's literary contributions, the acoustic and musical dimensions of those writings tend to be muted in critical and pedagogical contexts, resulting in a misleading and dissonant stereo effect. Despite the emergence of sound studies alongside the field of early modern women's writing, critical amplification of women's voices and attention to the complex vocality of women's texts too often collide with disembodied assumptions about their textual production and circulation. This is particularly true when considering women's contributions to early modern song culture as writers and as singers.

This chapter considers how the wide-ranging evidence for women's song performance in sixteenth- and seventeenth-century England opens up new ways of thinking about women's textual production. My approach to women's song performance begins from two premises: first, that song demands to be read in performance-based terms; and second, that singing constitutes an interpretive and creative practice that was integral to early modern women's cultural agency. In recognising that literary production in the period was closely intertwined with musical circulation, my argument enters into dialogue with recent work by Michelle O'Callaghan, Julie Crawford, and others that demonstrates how women's contributions as readers, patrons, editors, and creative practitioners radically expand the parameters of what we understand by women's 'writing' and 'authorship'.[1]

[1] See Michelle O'Callaghan, *Crafting Poetry Anthologies in Renaissance England: Early Modern Cultures of Recreation* (Cambridge, 2020); Julie Crawford, *Mediatrix: Women, Politics, and Literary Production in Early Modern England* (Oxford, 2018); Valerie Wayne (ed.), *Women's Labour and the History of the Book* (London, 2020); Patricia Pender (ed.), *Gender, Authorship, and Early Modern Women's Collaboration* (Basingstoke, 2017).

I begin by charting the musical genres with which women engaged as singers and the varied social settings in which they sang. Surviving cultural and literary documents provide vivid insight into the breadth of women's singing practices. They also underscore the complex networks of artistic transmission to which women contributed. These processes destabilise any singular claim to musical authorship and expose the permeability of textual boundaries. They enrich the historiography of women's performance in early modern England. And they demonstrate the creative role of the performer in bringing a song to life, as well as in mediating its rhetorical impact on auditors. In the second part of the chapter I turn to the recently launched *Early Modern Songscapes* platform (songscapes.org), to unpack these issues in more detail. The performance-based analysis enabled by *Early Modern Songscapes* illustrates the multidimensionality of song and its tendency to confound generic, architectural, physiological, and sociocultural boundaries. The beta iteration of the platform focuses on Henry Lawes, a composer and musical educator whose output reflects the cross-pollination between poetic and lyric circulation in the period and who was a strong and public advocate for 'Musicians of both Sexes'.[2] The textual and performance examples from his *Ayres and Dialogues* (1653) that are featured on the site provide insight into how women's voices are embodied and inhabited through song. They also foreground the interplay between the performance of individual songs and the representation of gendered experience.

SINGING WOMEN IN EARLY MODERN ENGLAND

Women's singing voices formed a vital and vibrant part of the early modern English songscape and animated many vocal genres. Women were accustomed to singing psalms in congregational settings and within the home. Margaret Hoby, for instance, refers in her diary to the importance of psalm-singing as a part of her household devotional practice.[3] The acoustic effects of Hoby's solo practice would have been very different from the nasal and ponderous singing associated with congregations of the period.[4] In both contexts, however, women were encouraged to situate their voices within the 'I' of the psalms, whose communicative efficacy was understood to be intensified through song.[5] In a prefatory section to his 1621 *Whole Booke of Psalms*, Thomas Ravenscroft advocates the 'singing of Psalmes' because it 'uniteth the Creature to his Creator' and

[2] Henry Lawes, *The Second Book of Ayres, and Dialogues* (London, 1655), sig. av.

[3] Lady Margaret Hoby, *The Diary of Lady Margaret Hoby 1599–1605*, in Joanna Moody (ed.), *The Private Life of an Elizabethan Lady* (Phoenix Mill, 1998), 42, 158.

[4] Christopher Marsh, *Music and Society in Early Modern England* (Cambridge, 2010), 419–34.

[5] Micheline White, 'Protestant Women's Writing and Congregational Psalm Singing: from the Song of the Exiled 'Handmaid' (1555) to the Countess of Pembroke's *Psalmes* (1599)', *Sidney Journal*, 23 (2005), 61–82.

advertises the affective relief—and the communicative value—promised by particular psalms.[6] Extant manuscript settings of Mary Sidney Herbert's Psalm 51 and 130, now preserved at the British Library, illustrate how the penitential psalms might have been incorporated into the musical and spiritual practice of a talented amateur singer.[7] They also exemplify the critical implications of considering from a musical perspective texts that have attracted attention for their stylistic virtuosity.[8]

We know too that women sang and sold ballads. While ballads were of course used for gendered didactic and moralistic purposes, the genre offered women a spectrum of expressive possibilities.[9] Complicating already porous lines between private and public, ballads served as a tool for political commentary in early modern Europe and a form of journalism that aimed to provoke audience response.[10] Ballad-singing was a labour-oriented and commercial enterprise as well, and women were among the sellers and criers who advertised their wares in song on street corners and in marketplaces.[11] As such, ballads offer important insight into the musical practices of non-elite and working women.[12] Like the psalms, however, ballads moved fluidly across class boundaries and social spaces, borne through the air on the musical breath and pasted on the walls of homes and taverns. The genre was equally embraced by the status-conscious Margaret

[6] Thomas Ravenscroft, *The Whole Booke of Psalmes* (London, 1621), n.p.

[7] London, British Library, Add. MS 15117, fols. 4v–5v. See Linda Austern, '"For Musicke Is the Handmaid of the Lord": Women, Psalms, and Domestic Music-Making in Early Modern England', in Linda Phyllis Austern, Kari Boyd McBride, and David. L. Orvis (eds), *Psalms in the Early Modern World* (Farnham, 2011), 77–114. Performances of these settings can be heard on the online companion recording to Katherine R. Larson, *The Matter of Song in Early Modern England: Texts in and of the The Air* (Oxford, 2019), performed by Larson and lutenist Lucas Harris. The recording is open access: OUP Companion Website: 'Larson: The Matter of Song in Early Modern England', https://global.oup.com/booksites/content/9780198843788/, accessed 12 March 2021.

[8] Larson, *Matter of Song*, 48–63.

[9] See Bruce R. Smith, 'Female Impersonation in Early Modern Ballads', in Pamela Allen Brown and Peter Parolin (eds), *Women Players in England 1500–1660: Beyond the All-Male Stage* (London, 2008), 281–304; Sandra Clark, 'The Broadside Ballad and the Woman's Voice', in Cristina Malcolmson and Mihoko Suzuki (eds), *Debating Gender in Early Modern England, 1500–1700* (Basingstoke, 2002), 103–20; and Sarah F. Williams, *Damnable Practises: Witches, Dangerous Women, and Music in Seventeenth-Century English Broadside Ballads* (Farnham, 2015). On the affective work of ballad tunes and texts, see Patricia Fumerton and Anita Guerrini (eds), *Ballads and Broadsides in Britain, 1500–1800* (Farnham, 2010).

[10] Angela McShane, '*The Gazet in Metre; or the Rhiming Newsmonger*: The English Broadside Ballad as Intelligencer', in Joop W. Koopmans (ed.), *News and Politics in Early Modern Europe (1500–1800)* (Leuven, 2005), 131–52; Una McIlvenna, 'When the News Was Sung: Ballads as News Media in Early Modern Europe', *Media History*, 22 (2016), 1–17.

[11] See Angela McShane, 'Political Street Songs and Singers in Seventeenth-Century England', in Luca Degl'Innocenti and Massimo Rospocher (eds), 'Street Singers in Renaissance Europe', special issue of *Renaissance Studies*, 33 (2018), 94–118; and Natasha Korda, 'Gender at Work in the Cries of London', in Mary Ellen Lamb and Karen Bamford (eds), *Oral Traditions and Gender in Early Modern Literary Texts* (Aldershot, 2008), 117–35.

[12] Michelle O'Callaghan, '"Good Ladies Be Working": Singing at Work in Tudor Woman's Song', in Jennifer Richards and Richard Wistreich (eds), *Voicing Text 1500–1700*, special issue, *Huntington Library Quarterly*, 82, (2019), 107–26.

Cavendish, Duchess of Newcastle, who identified her own singing and writing with the 'natural' and impactful declamation she associated with ballads.[13] Ballads could be powerful agents of gendered control, working to silence women perceived to be disorderly, dramatising executions, and voicing women's dying laments. But the intertextual resonances activated by the interweaving of text and tune and the interpretive potential afforded by performance speak to the ballad's musical and performative capacity to resist those boundaries.[14]

Extant print and manuscript sources attest to the centrality of singing in women's education and to women's vocal skill as amateur solo performers. Elizabeth Davenant's songbook, dating from the 1620s and now held at Christ Church College Library in Oxford, provides an excellent example of these pedagogical settings.[15] The virtuosic ornamentation preserved in the songbook testifies to Davenant's skill as a singer as well as to the interplay between musical notation, memory, and the body in bringing those notes off the page.[16] As Scott Trudell has shown, women were avid consumers of the lute songbooks that were popularised in the late sixteenth century, which enabled performers to experiment with a range of gendered personae.[17] Women also wrote songs, exemplified by the settings by Lady Mary Dering included in Lawes' *Second Book of Ayres and Dialogues* (1655) and the possible collaboration of Mary Wroth and Alfonso Ferrabosco on the surviving setting of 'Was I to Blame' from the second part of *The Countess of Montgomery's Urania* (1621).[18]

Talented female singers would have made appearances in indoor and outdoor entertainments, including household drama and masques. The surviving score of

[13] Larson, *Matter of Song*, 96–109, and James Fitzmaurice, '"When an Old Ballad Is Plainly Sung": Musical Lyrics in the Plays of Margaret and William Cavendish', in Mary Ellen Lamb and Karen Bamford (eds), *Oral Traditions and Gender in Early Modern Literary Texts* (Aldershot, 2008), 153–68.

[14] See Christopher Marsh, 'The Sound of Print in Early Modern England: The Broadside Ballad as Song', in Julia Crick and Alexandra Walsham (eds), *The Uses of Script and Print, 1300–1700* (Cambridge, 2004), 171–90; Marsh, *Music and Society*, 288–327; and Sarah F. Williams, 'Witches, Lamenting Women, and Cautionary Tales: Tracing 'The Ladies Fall' in Early Modern English Broadside Balladry and Popular Song', in Leslie C. Dunn and Katherine R. Larson (eds), *Gender and Song in Early Modern England* (Farnham, 2014), 31–46. The *English Broadside Ballad Archive*, directed by Patricia Fumerton, enables visitors to explore the musical, visual, and textual facets of ballads: see https://ebba.english.ucsb.edu, accessed 12 March 2021.

[15] Oxford, Christ Church Library, MS Mus. 87. The manuscript may also have been used by another seventeenth-century woman. The inscription 'Kath: Law: May the 6th [?] 1663 / began my Exercises' appears on the side of the first page.

[16] Examples from Davenant's songbook can be heard on *Mistress Elizabeth Davenant, Her Songs*, performed by soprano Rebecca Ockenden and lutenist Sofie Van Den Eyde. On memory in musical circulation, see Rebecca Herissone, *Musical Creativity in Restoration England* (Cambridge, 2013), 315–91.

[17] Scott A. Trudell, 'Performing Women in English Books of Ayres', in Leslie C. Dunn and Katherine R. Larson (eds), *Gender and Song in Early Modern England* (Farnham, 2014), 15–30.

[18] For Mary Dering's settings, see Lawes, *Second Book of Ayres and Dialogues*, 24–5. On Ferrabosco's setting of 'Was I to Blame' and Wroth's possible involvement in the compositional process, see Gavin Alexander, 'The Musical Sidneys', *John Donne Journal*, 25 (2006), 95–102. Dering's setting of 'In vain fair *Chloris*' and 'Was I to Blame' can be heard on the companion recording to *The Matter of Song* (Tracks 9 and 12).

'Sweet Echo', the Lady's song from John Milton's *A Masque Presented at Ludlow Castle* (1634), testifies to the significance of this piece as a showcase opportunity for the fifteen-year-old Alice Egerton, who was studying music with Henry Lawes.[19] Little evidence survives of the performance history of women's theatrical writings, but textual traces gesture towards the possibility of musical elements. Jane Cavendish and Elizabeth Brackley's Civil War entertainment *A Pastorall* (*c* 1645), for example, includes explicit details about vocal genres as well as stage directions that suggest the spacing of domestic music-making.[20] Performances need not have been lavish to incorporate music, but the resources of some early modern estates were impressive. Nonsuch, for instance, where Lady Jane Lumley resided when she translated *Iphigenia at Aulis* (*c* 1554), had one of the best music libraries and instrument collections in the country. If Lumley wished to stage her translation with musical elements she would have had ample materials on which to draw.[21] Representations of female singers on the commercial stage, meanwhile, refracted popular ideas about gender and music and Continental models of women's performances through the bodies of transvestite actors, complicating historiographical narratives of women's involvement in the English theatre.[22]

THE DRASTIC NATURE OF SONG

In all of these instances, animation of early modern women's musical activities and of song as a prevalent mode of creative expression necessitates a recognition that song was a protean and capricious thing. Once voiced, songs lived in the air, overheard across hedges and walls, permeating architectural and physiological boundaries in unexpected ways, and, for early moderns, carrying significant power to affect the minds of hearers.[23]

[19] The piece appears in London, British Library, MS Add. 53723, 37v.

[20] Oxford, Bodleian Library, MS Rawl. poet. 16, 60–1.

[21] Charles W. Warren, 'Music at Nonesuch', *The Musical Quarterly*, 54.1 (1968), 47–57; John Milsom, 'The Nonsuch Music Library', in Chris Banks, Arthur Searle, and Malcolm Turner (eds), *Sundry Sorts of Music Books: Essays on the British Library Collections* (London, 1993), 146–82. On the entertainments that might have informed *Iphigenia*, see Marta Straznicky, *Privacy, Playreading, and Women's Closet Drama* (Cambridge, 2004), 41–2; Alison Findlay, *Playing Spaces in Early Women's Drama* (Cambridge, 2006), 75–9; and Marion Wynne-Davies, 'The Good Lady Lumley's Desire: *Iphigeneia* and the Nonsuch Banqueting House', in Rina Walthaus and Marguérite Corporaal (eds), *Heroines of the Golden Stage: Women and Drama in Spain and England 1500–1700* (Kassel, 2008), 111–28. On the translation's musical possibilities, see Larson, *Matter of Song*, 153–8.

[22] Brown and Parolin, *Women Players in England*; Natasha Korda, *Labors Lost: Women's Work and the Early Modern English Stage* (Philadelphia, PA, 2011); Clare McManus and Lucy Munro (eds), 'Special Issue: Renaissance Women's Performance and the Dramatic Canon', *Shakespeare Bulletin*, 33 (2015), esp. McManus' article "Sing It Like Poor Barbary': *Othello* and Early Modern Women's Performance', 99–120.

[23] See Linda Phyllis Austern, Candace Bailey, and Amanda Eubanks Winkler (eds), *Beyond Boundaries: Rethinking Music Circulation in Early Modern England* (Bloomington, IL 2017); Penelope Gouk, 'Raising Spirits and Restoring Souls: Early Modern Medical Explanations for Music's Effects', in Veit Erlmann (ed.), *Hearing Cultures: Essays on Sound, Listening, and Modernity* (Oxford, 2004), 87–105, and 'Some English Theories of Hearing in the Seventeenth Century: Before and After Descartes',

The product of the body and the breath, song resists capture on the page. Where musical notation does survive, it constitutes a mnemonic shorthand—what Bruce Smith refers to as a 'somatic' trace—that reminds a performer what to do with their body.[24] The virtuosic ornamentation preserved in songbooks like Davenant's constitutes an especially good example of this. To perform them well, ornaments must be internalised within the body and the vocal apparatus through careful practice. In performance, they rely on elements of creative improvisation. Their survival in extant scores is ultimately a testament to the role of aural memory in musical transmission and to the creative input of musicians to what was ultimately a collaborative compositional process.[25]

Musicologist Carolyn Abbate has influentially distinguished between 'gnostic' readings of music represented by academic, text-based analysis, and the 'drastic' experience of music in performance.[26] For Abbate, the deep emotion, imperfection, and sheer 'wildness' of the drastic are impossible to capture analytically. The drastic facets of song as a performance medium, however, demand to be factored into readings of early modern texts. Appreciation of the drastic activates the embodied musicality that was central to early modern literary culture and creates the conditions for a more elastic understanding of early modern form, authorship, and textual transmission.[27] Such an approach proves especially productive when considering early modern women's writing, a field which is itself predicated on complex renderings of voice and vocality and which has been instrumental in complicating established categories of gender, form, and authorial and editorial practice. Part of this work entails expanding the notion of what constitutes 'text', a shift reflected in critical recognition that women's 'writing' encompassed embroidery, herbals, gardening, visual art, as well as oral contributions like trial testimonies. Song needs to be included among these feminist 'counterarchives'.[28] So too does song performance, which reflects the complex networks of creative production and reception to which early modern women contributed, destabilises singular claims to authorship and 'voice', and reframes assumptions about formal and generic boundaries.

What does it mean to search for drastic traces of song and of singing bodies in extant texts of early modern women? Part of this work entails a creative leap. The sound of early

in Charles Burnett, Michael Fend, and Penelope Gouk (eds), *The Second Sense: Studies in Hearing and Musical Judgment from Antiquity to the Seventeenth Century* (London, 1991), 95–113; Smith, *Acoustic World*, 101–6; and Larson, *Matter of Song*, 64–109.

24 Smith, *Acoustic World*, 112.

25 See Herissone, *Musical Creativity*, 360–2, 379–81; and Richard Wistreich, 'Vocal Performance in the Seventeenth Century', in Colin Lawson and Robin Stowell (eds), *The Cambridge History of Musical Performance* (Cambridge, 2012), 408–10.

26 Carolyn Abbate, 'Music—Drastic or Gnostic?' *Critical Inquiry*, 30 (2004), 505–36.

27 Jennifer Richards has argued in related terms for the aurality of reading. See *Voices and Books in the English Renaissance: A New History of Reading* (Oxford, 2019).

28 Natasha Korda, 'Shakespeare's Laundry: Feminist Futures in the Archives', in Ania Loomba and Melissa E. Sanchez (eds), *Rethinking Feminism in Early Modern Studies: Gender, Race, and Sexuality* (London, 2016), 96. See also Patricia Pender and Rosalind Smith (eds), *Material Cultures of Early Modern Women's Writing* (Basingstoke, 2014).

modern song as it was experienced in the sixteenth and seventeenth centuries is lost to us. Even the most sophisticated historical performance practices can never recover those musical soundscapes—many of which were never notated in the first place. This is not to discount the insights that can be gleaned from historical performance practices and from 'scholartistic' collaborations, exemplified by recent performance as research initiatives in early modern studies.[29] But tracing the embodied dimensions of any historical genre necessitates a willingness to confront absence, volatility, and silence.

Where notation does survive, contemporary interpretations remain distanced from the embodied reality of the early modern women who would have voiced those songs and from the cultural resonances that would have been activated by their singing bodies. Both men and women had to grapple with the implications of choosing a particular instrument or musical genre, the affective resonances associated with dissonance and particular modes, and the risks of music-making when practised beyond moderate bounds.[30] These tensions were especially fraught for women, for whom educational expectations concerning decorous musical activities coexisted with the sexualisation of the interplay between body and instrument. Literary and visual depictions of women's music-making capitalise on this dynamic, as do representations of unsupervised music lessons.[31] When singing, of course, the open-mouthed, resonating body becomes one's instrument, taking such concerns to their extreme. Wildness indeed.

The methodological and critical implications for the study of early modern women's writing of considering song in 'drastic' terms are significant. Take, for instance, the work of Mary Wroth. Wroth was herself a talented musician, and she devotes considerable attention to music and to women's musical expression throughout her works. In the context of her manuscript miscellany, now held at the Folger Shakespeare Library, and the published version of *Pamphilia to Amphilanthus* (1621), reading lyrics with the generic marker of 'song' as signalling the possibility—or perhaps a memory—of musical performance, attunes us to the dynamic movement of Wroth's lyrics.[32]

[29] See, for example, 'Performing the Queen's Men: Exploring Theatre History through Performance' http://thequeensmen.ca, accessed 12 March 2021; 'Performance as Research in Early English Theatre Studies: *The Three Ladies of London in Context*', http://threeladiesoflondon.mcmaster.ca, accessed 12 March 2021; and Amanda Eubanks Winkler and Richard Schoch (eds), 'Performing Restoration Shakespeare', https://www.qub.ac.uk/schools/ael/Research/ResearchinArts/ResearchImpact/PerformingRestorationShakespeare/, accessed 12 March 2021.

[30] Linda Austern's work on music and gender in early modern England has been particularly influential. In addition to her many articles, see *Both from the Ears and from the Mind: Thinking about Music in Early Modern England* (Chicago, IL, 2020). See also Dunn and Larson, *Gender and Music*, and Larson, *Matter of Song*, 64–96.

[31] See Linda Phyllis Austern, 'Portrait of the Artist as (Female) Musician', in Thomasin K. LaMay (ed.), *Musical Voices of Early Modern Women: Many-Headed Melodies* (Aldershot, 2005), 15–59; Richard Leppert, *The Sight of Sound: Music, Representation, and the History of the Body* (Berkeley, CA, 1993); Rochelle Smith, 'Admirable Musicians: Women's Songs in *Othello* and *The Maid's Tragedy*', *Comparative Drama*, 28 (1994), 311–23; Marsh, *Music and Society*, 198–203; Katie Nelson, 'Love in the Music Room: Thomas Whythorne and the Private Affairs of Tudor Music Teachers', *Early Music*, 40 (2012), 15–26.

[32] Washington, Folger Shakespeare Library, MS. V.a.104. See Larson, *Matter of Song*, 114–38.

Lyrics from the Folger miscellany pop up in *Urania* in scenes explicitly associated with musical performance, and Wroth's avatar Pamphilia was herself a talented singer. In her groundbreaking biography of Wroth, Margaret Hannay imagines Wroth and her family gathering to read and perform selections from the *Urania*, domestic events that may well have included musical performance.[33] The empty spaces left for lyrics in the Penshurst manuscript of *Love's Victory* (*c* 1619) similarly testify to song's tendency to float free of textual boundaries and across varied contexts of circulation and performance.[34] Recent productions of Mary Wroth's *Love's Victory* led by Alison Findlay and director Martin Hodgson and staged at Penshurst Place, meanwhile, have demonstrated the play's musicality, rendering many of the interspersed lyrics as song.[35]

When I was working on *The Matter of Song in Early Modern England* and its companion recording, the experience of voicing songs like 'Was I to Blame' (Track 12), from the second part of *Urania*, or 'My Father Faine Would Have Me Take a Man That Hath a Beard' (Track 1), a darkly comic air from Robert Jones' 1610 collection, *The Muses Garden of Delights*, which was dedicated to Wroth, deepened my own understanding of Pamphilia, who is depicted as a singer throughout *Urania* and frequently turns to song to voice her experience, and of Wroth's broader critiques of faithlessness and of forced marriage. This is not to suggest that my perspective as a feminist academic and classically trained soprano singing in a twenty-first-century recording studio with all the related benefits of editing technology is consistent with Wroth's, or with early modern women more generally. Like song itself, the notion of a woman's 'voice'—and indeed that of gendered 'embodiment'—are hardly stable concepts, either in the early modern English context or in feminist studies.[36] But it shifts the nature of a reader's encounter with a text like *Urania* or *Love's Victory* to experience (or even to imagine) their many songs as sung. In addition to illuminating the aural and musical textures that contributed to the development of these texts, listening for song demonstrates the affective and communicative significance of the genre for Wroth's female protagonists.

[33] Margaret Hannay, *Mary Sidney, Lady Wroth* (Farnham, 2010), 182–3.

[34] See. Marta Straznicky, 'Lady Mary Wroth's Patchwork Play: The Huntington Manuscript of *Love's Victory*', *Sidney Journal*, 34, no. 2 (2016): 81–91. See also Larson, *Matter of Song*, 167–78.

[35] Lady Mary Wroth, *Love's Victory*, dir. Martin Hodgson, perf. Shakespeare's Globe, Penshurst Place, Kent, 8 June 2014. Alison Findlay discusses the production in '*Love's Victory* in Production at Penshurst', *Sidney Journal*, 31 (2016): 107–21. Hodgson directed the first professional performance of *Love's Victory* in the Baron's Hall at Penshurst on 16 September 2018. The performance was filmed as a part of the 'Dramatizing Penshurst' Festival on Mary Wroth, coordinated by Alison Findlay.

[36] The scholarship in this area is significant, but key interventions on gendered and embodied vocality within early modern literary and feminist studies include Danielle Clarke and Elizabeth Clarke (eds), '*This Double Voice*': *Gendered Writing in Early Modern England* (Basingstoke, 2000); Gina Bloom, *Voice in Motion: Staging Gender, Shaping Sound* (Philadelphia, PA, 2007); and Valerie Traub (ed.), *The Oxford Handbook of Shakespeare and Embodiment: Gender, Sexuality, Race* (Oxford, 2016).

EARLY MODERN SONGSCAPES AND THE 'AYRE' IN PERFORMANCE

Entering into the experience of song from a performance-based perspective invites readers to attend more closely to the musical matter of literary texts and to women's wide-ranging engagement with song culture in sixteenth- and seventeenth-century England. And yet, like early modern vocal treatises, traditional forms of scholarly circulation, notably the essay and the monograph, risk being at odds with the multidimensionality and drastic wildness of song as performance practice, even when accompanied by recordings. *Early Modern Songscapes* is an intermedia project codeveloped by Scott Trudell, Sarah Williams, and myself that aims more fully to animate song's least tangible, yet essential facets: its generic fluidity; its ability to register multiple meanings and permeate boundaries in unexpected ways, and its rootedness in the air.[37] The term intermedia—rather than multimedia—highlights the non-static relationships and synergies among media forms and reminds us that early modern songs are preserved in multiple forms and moved across varied textual and acoustic environments.[38] An intermedia approach also registers song's textual and authorial complexity as a multidimensional genre encompassing lyric, musical setting, and performance.

The project focuses on 'ayres', songs that emphasise the clear communication of text and that typically included instrumental accompaniment. Popularised in the late sixteenth century with the printed lute song collections of John Dowland and Thomas Campion, the air later developed into the declamatory vocal style associated with Henry Lawes, reflecting the speech-like rhythms of verse. Lawes was a composer and a musical collaborator committed to communicating the 'sense' of language through musical setting.[39] Milton famously commemorated the composer in a 1646 sonnet that celebrated his unprecedented skill in creating music that 'tun'st [the] happiest lines in Hymn, or Story' and for 'First [teaching] our English Music how to span / Words with just note and accent'.[40] These are features that Lawes himself highlights as musical aims in his *Second Book of Ayres, and Dialogues* (1655): 'the way of *Composition* I chiefly profess . . . is to shape *Notes* to the *Words* and *Sense*' (sig. av).

[37] The project is a collaboration between the Digital Scholarship Unit at the University of Toronto Scarborough and the Maryland Institute for Technology in the Humanities at the University of Maryland.

[38] Daniel Fischlin (ed.), introduction to *OuterSpeares: Shakespeare, Intermedia, and the Limits of Adaptation* (Toronto, 2014), 3–4. On the significance of intermediality for understandings of song, see Scott Trudell, *Unwritten Poetry: Song, Performance, and Media in Early Modern England* (Oxford, 2019); and Patricia Fumerton, *The Broadside Ballad: Moving Media, Tactical Publics* (Philadelphia, PA, 2020).

[39] Ian Spink, *Henry Lawes: Cavalier Songwriter* (Oxford, 2000); and *English Song: Dowland to Purcell* (London, 1974), 75–99.

[40] *John Milton: Complete Poems and Major Prose*, ed. Merritt Y. Hughes (New York, 1957), 144.

Lawes' airs exemplify the rich interplay between lyric composition, musical setting, and song performance in early modern England. They also provide insight into women's contributions as performers to early modern song culture, not least because Lawes was a strong and public advocate for female musicians. He dedicated his first book of airs to Alice Egerton, by then Countess of Carbury, and her sister Mary, both of whom, he declares in the dedicatory epistle, 'excell'd most Ladies, especially in *Vocall Musick*'.[41] His second book of airs was dedicated to Lady Mary Dering and prepared 'for the ease of Musicians of both Sexes' (sig. av); his inclusion of Dering's song settings in the collection attests to Lawes' admiration for her as a performer and a composer.[42] Dering joined Alice Egerton and her sister, as well as Margaret Cavendish and Lady Elizabeth Brackley, as guests at the musical gatherings Lawes hosted during the Interregnum, which featured the poetry of Royalists like Katherine Philips and the performances of talented female singers like Mary Knight.

The beta version of *Early Modern Songscapes*, which was launched in February 2019, includes Text Encoding Initiative (TEI) and Music Encoding Initiative (MEI) editions of the songs included in Lawes' *Ayres and Dialogues* (1653), as well as their manuscript variants. Visitors to the site experience airs as protean documents whose variants provide insight into the mapping of song across time and space. One of the benefits of a digital humanities approach is that it facilitates non-linear exploration. As such, *Early Modern Songscapes* shares features with recent digital editions of early modern women's writing that resist the notion of a single static text and facilitate comparison of multiple versions. Paul Salzman's electronic edition of Mary Wroth's poetry and *The Pulter Project*, codirected by Wendy Wall and Leah Knight, are both excellent examples.[43] Another priority of *Early Modern Songscapes* is to illuminate song in performance. The site features recordings (both live and studio produced) of Lawes' airs interpreted by mezzo-soprano Rebecca Claborn, tenor Lawrence Wiliford, and lutenist Lucas Harris.

The selection of Lawes' airs included on *Early Modern Songscapes* provide a valuable case study for considering women's engagement with early modern song culture and for thinking through questions of gendered vocality, particularly in musical contexts. An early modern singer browsing Lawes' *Ayres and Dialogues* would have been able to select from an array of settings, including lyrics by Robert Herrick, William Herbert, Thomas Carew, and Richard Lovelace, and to experiment with many different kinds of personae. While men and women performed songs representing differently gendered experiences, Lawes' collection makes space for women's song performance by including a number of songs addressed to singing women. Others are voiced from women's perspectives.

[41] Henry Lawes, *Ayres and Dialogues* (London, 1653), sig. a2r.

[42] The volume also includes dedicatory poems by Katherine Philips and Mary Knight, as well as a setting of Philips' 'Come my Lucatia', which can be heard on the companion recording to *The Matter of Song* (Track 8).

[43] Paul Salzman (ed.), *Mary Wroth's Poetry: An Electronic Edition*, La Trobe University, 2012, http://wroth.latrobe.edu.au, accessed 12 March 2021, and Wendy Wall and Leah Knight (eds), *The Pulter Project: Poet in the Making*, http://pulterproject.northwestern.edu, accessed 12 March 2021.

A particularly virtuosic example of the latter is the first piece in the collection, 'Theseus, O Theseus', a setting of a text by William Cartwright that dramatises Ariadne's lament following the desertion of Theseus (1–7). The *Songscapes* edition of this piece reflects the musical and textual variants preserved in three extant versions: Lawes' autograph manuscript, now held in the British Library, the published 1653 version, and the text preserved in the 1651 collection of William Cartwright's *Comedies, Tragi-Comedies with Other Poems*. Visitors to the site can hover over the score and see the different variants highlighted and pop open as hyperlinks, experiencing the multiplicity registered by this one song. The site also includes two full performances by mezzo-soprano Rebecca Claborn in studio and live settings, along with Rebecca's interpretation of one of the variant sections.

'Theseus, O Theseus' is essentially a series of miniature operatic scenes, and a demanding sing. We approached the studio recording by breaking the lament into sections. On a practical level, this helped Rebecca to pace herself vocally. Working section by section also opened up fascinating conversations about Ariadne's emotional and narrative trajectory. For an early modern performer, this piece would have provided significant affective scope. In her current work on women's song and the complaint, Sarah C. E. Ross has underscored the importance of thinking in terms of lyric taxonomies that illustrate the points of connection between the complaint genre and various modes of expression, including musical.[44] 'Theseus, O Theseus' (which fittingly is subtitled 'Ariadne deserted by Theseus Sittinge upon a Rock in the Island Naxos thus Complaines') exemplifies Ross' observation.

Working with Rebecca on the recording process and in preparation for the recital that took place at the 2019 *Early Modern Songscapes* conference also provided insight into the process by which a singer—regardless of historical context—gradually moves a piece like this into the voice. Not surprisingly for a Lawes setting, textual nuance was crucial. 'Theseus, O Theseus' exemplifies Lawes' declamatory style, and the rehearsals and studio sessions with Rebecca underscored the importance of textual communication in helping to offset some of the technical challenges of the setting. Comments throughout the production process about finessing breath support or pitch were often resolved by reminders about the propulsive energy of consonants, moments of alliteration, and the narrative arc of individual phrases. Such emphasis on diction was crucial to early modern vocal practice as well. As Giulio Caccini puts it in *Le nuove musiche* (1602), which set the tone for discussions of solo vocal performance on the Continent and in England well into the seventeenth century, music that 'prevent[s] any clear understanding of the words, shatters both their form and content'.[45] The breath was understood to be crucial to that communicative efficacy.

[44] Sarah C. E. Ross, 'Woe is She: "Female Complaint" and Women's Songbooks in Early Modern England', *Female Experience in Early Modern England Symposium* plenary address, University of Auckland, New Zealand, 6 November 2020.

[45] Giulio Caccini, in H. Wiley Hitchcock (ed.), *Le nuove musiche* (Madison, WI, 1970), 44.

Another example speaks to the interpretive implications of inhabiting and voicing songs from differently gendered perspectives. As we were working with Rebecca and Lawrence, we solicited their preferences for repertoire choice. Sometimes their selections reflected consistent gendering with the text's persona, sometimes not; in a number of cases the 'I' of the text is ambiguous. This flexibility is also reflective of early modern performance practice. With this in mind, we played with the effect of having two different singers voice the same song. 'Come, my Lucasta heer's the Grove (Love and Loyalty)', a setting of a poem by Charles Lucas (Margaret Cavendish's brother) (25), depicts an amatory encounter in a sheltered grove. When performed by Lawrence, the song comes across as a classic 'carpe diem' piece, accentuating the seduction and temptation intrinsic to the scene from a heterosexual perspective, while also hinting at the potential threat of that scenario for the beloved Lucasta. The apparent comfort signalled by the phrase 'No dangers in this Arbour ly' becomes much less reassuring when it collides with the explicit potential of violence in stanza two: 'None but Foes commit a Rape' (25). Is the singer, the audience is left to wonder, a friend or a foe?

When sung by Rebecca, in contrast, the song opens up into a constellation of potential interpretations. One could imagine it as voiced by Lucasta herself, recounting an amorous encounter that is recalled either with joy or with bitter acknowledgement of deception given the possibility of violence at play in the text. As we were preparing the piece for performance, we also discussed the song's homoerotic resonances when voiced by a woman singer. Listening to Rebecca perform the piece evoked Katherine Philips' friendship poetry, which Lawes also set to music. In this context, the first lines of stanza two convey a contrast between the possibility of male deception and violence and the protective, feminised space carved out by the singer and her addressee, Lucasta:

> Here we'l discourse, and think, and smile,
> Let guilty men seek how to scape;
> He cannot love that can beguile,
> And none but Foes commit a Rape. (25)

Like the notion of embodiment itself, these personae are by no means fixed. It would be just as possible for a female singer to imagine herself inhabiting the role of a male seducer, or for a male singer to experiment with a woman's perspective, however effeminising that might have been deemed in the early modern context. Alternatively, could that lyric perspective be rendered as entirely ambiguous? And if so, what might that look like? How, moreover, would this song have resonated for hearers in different kinds of spaces and for different audiences? We situated Lawrence's and Rebecca's performances of 'Come My Lucasta' back-to-back in recital, foregrounding the scope and malleability of the gendered perspectives at play in this piece, as well as in the collection as a whole. The performance powerfully illustrated how the experience of hearing a song voiced by different singers changes the affective encounter with that work.

Song constitutes a central—and too often silenced—example of women's rhetorical contributions in the sixteenth and seventeenth centuries. The traces of women's musical interests and their singing voices are preserved in many extant texts, including manuscript collections, pedagogical documents, and lyrics that circulated under the generic marker of 'song', even in the absence of musical notation. As a generic category that itself refuses to adhere to clear boundaries and is reflective of the capricious movement of air, song helps to deepen the textures of our understanding of early modern women's writing, whose innovations demand to be considered in relation to more flexible taxonomies of form and genre. From a methodological perspective, meanwhile, performance-based approaches to extant song texts underscore the fundamental musicality of literary production and circulation in the period and illuminates the extent of women's engagement with song culture. In a contemporary context, these 'drastic' elements of early modern women's songscapes are perhaps best approximated in intermedia frameworks like the *Early Modern Songscapes* site, and of course in live performance. But the drastic can, I think, also change the typically gnostic nature of scholarly encounters with extant women's texts. Tuning our ears as readers and as writers to the musical dimensions of women's writing holds the potential to transform not only our understanding of early modern literary culture and the nature of women's 'writing', but also the form and circulation of contemporary scholarship.

FURTHER READING

Austern, Linda Phyllis. *Both from the Ears and Mind: Thinking About Music in Early Modern England.* Chicago, IL, 2020.

Austern, Linda Phyllis, Candace Bailey, and Amanda Eubanks Winkler (eds). *Beyond Boundaries: Rethinking Music Circulation in Early Modern England.* Bloomington, IL, 2017.

Dunn, Leslie C. and Katherine R. Larson (eds). *Gender and Song in Early Modern England.* Farnham, 2014.

Fumerton, Patricia and Anita Guerrini (eds), with the assistance of Kris McAbee. *Ballads and Broadsides in Britain, 1500–1800.* Farnham, 2010.

Herissone, Rebecca. *Musical Creativity in Restoration England.* Cambridge, 2013.

LaMay, Thomasin (ed.). *Musical Voices of Early Modern Women: Many-Headed Melodies.* Aldershot, 2005.

Larson, Katherine R. *The Matter of Song in Early Modern England: Texts in and of the Air.* Oxford, 2019.

Marsh, Christopher. *Music and Society in Early Modern England.* Cambridge, 2010.

CHAPTER 11

RECEIVING EARLY MODERN WOMEN'S DRAMA

RAMONA WRAY

DRAMA is arguably the literary genre most readily associated with the early modern period. Certainly, it is the genre that has attracted the greatest wealth of critical commentary. This should be welcome news for scholars of early modern women writers since drama was a genre in which early modern women excelled. Accomplishment occurs throughout the period—for instance, Jane Lumley's *Iphigeneia at Aulis* (*c* 1554) is the earliest English translation of Euripides, Mary Sidney's *The Tragedie of Antonie* (1592/5) is the first English Cleopatra drama, and Elizabeth Cary's *The Tragedy of Mariam* (1613) is the only early modern play to open with a woman speaking *sola* and to dramatise gendered discourses of race. Such landmarks are not defined by gender; rather, they are important cultural developments which underline the fact that dramatic work by women is lively, original, interventionist, and innovative.

From the early 1980s onwards, feminist critics brought women playwrights to light, and follow-up work has played a key role in establishing the historical and contextual energies informing women's drama. There is now substantial scholarship on the subject, and almost all of the plays produced by women in this period have been edited, some on several occasions. Marion Wynne-Davies' important overview highlights the multiple ways in which plays by women have been reproduced so as to accentuate their accessibility and artistry.[1] But—and it is a big 'but'—this scholarship has not really impacted on the field of early modern studies as a whole. In a wide-ranging review, Diane Purkiss argues that 'women's writings' can still be viewed 'as hermetically sealed off, not relevant, not of immediate concern', and this is certainly the case for drama.[2] The canon of early modern drama remains overwhelmingly male, and, outside of studies of women's

[1] Marion Wynne-Davies, 'Editing Early Modern Women's Dramatic Writing', in Sarah C. E. Ross and Paul Salzman (eds), *Editing Early Modern Women* (Cambridge, 2016), 156–75.

[2] Diane Purkiss, 'Rooms of All Our Own: A History of Ignoring Early Women Writers', *Times Literary Supplement* (15 February 2019), 10.

writing, women dramatists are by and large bypassed. Mainstream work in Renaissance drama tends to omit or downplay women's examples, and, in general, performance criticism and theatre history pivot around male-authored plays. Part of this is to do with the continuing authority of Shakespeare, of course, yet, even when we bring non-Shakespearean drama into discussion, women do not feature consistently. A recent instance is Jeremy Lopez's *Constructing the Canon of Early Modern Drama* (2014) in which women are conspicuous by their absence. In a study centred on the 'broad expansion of the range of early modern dramatic texts available for scholarship, pedagogy, and appreciation', one might expect, as one finds in Wynne-Davies' essay, reflection on the effort both to recover and then publish women's dramatic creations.[3] However, women playwrights, and the accompanying richness of critical writing, are unspoken; it is as if they do not exist. The problem is replicated in anthologies. The latest edition of *The Routledge Anthology of Early Modern Drama* (2020) runs to 1,138 extra-large pages. It claims to demonstrate 'the astonishing range of styles and forms ... that characterised early modern English drama' and to 'achieve the goal of broad historical representation'.[4] It includes no women dramatists. *De facto*, this means that—through silence and omission—early modern drama is constituted as a wholly male-authored preserve. In some ways, we appear to have travelled backwards. In comparison, the less voluminous 2003 incarnation of the Routledge anthology includes both a woman dramatist and engagement with how women playwrights are explored in the critical record. The contrast with the situation in 2020 suggests a trend towards *less* awareness of women in drama rather than more.

The exclusion matters. If women do not appear in a standard anthology, then they will not to be taught, and this impacts directly on the women students who increasingly take humanities programmes. And, in the specific case of drama, the stakes are higher again: what is taught affects what we get to see on stage. As Pascale Aebischer and Kathryn Prince recognise in relation to non-Shakespearean drama, 'there is a connection between the academic labour of ... scholars ... amateur productions of early modern drama ... in higher education settings [and] fully realised productions at fringe and mainstream theatres'.[5] Staging plays by early modern women is to be responsive to the possibilities inherent in dramatising intersections between gender, class, and race. As Kim Hall notes, and as early modern drama by women demonstrates, 'race, as much as class, [is] a crucial category used by women writers to differentiate between female characters'.[6] This chapter asks questions about early modern women's drama and its relationship to dominant culture both in the early modern past and in the academic and

[3] Jeremy Lopez, *Constructing the Canon of Early Modern Drama* (Cambridge, 2014), 18.

[4] Jeremy Lopez, 'General Introduction', in Jeremy Lopez (ed.), *The Routledge Anthology of Early Modern Drama* (Abingdon and New York, 2020), 1–3, 1.

[5] Pascale Aebischer and Kathryn Prince, 'Introduction', in Pascale Aebischer and Kathryn Prince (eds), *Performing Early Modern Drama Today* (Cambridge, 2012), 1–16, 12.

[6] Kim F. Hall, *Things of Darkness: Economies of Race and Gender in Early Modern England* (Ithaca, NY, 1995), 182.

theatrical here-and-now. Why do women dramatists remain largely peripheral to discussion of drama as a genre? Why are women's plays—in a majority of cases—explored only by female scholars and inside 'female' traditions? Why do plays by women so rarely form part of the contemporary theatrical repertory? What are the costs of ignoring women's dramatic representations of intersectional identity? Why do the insights of feminist critics working on drama tend to be left out of more general or mainstream praxis? Although scholarship on early modern women's drama has proliferated, this scholarship has not and is not being heard. By attending to the multiple ways in which women dramatists converse with early modern writing and culture, this chapter hopes to encourage a new dialogue in the present.

REPUTATION, STAGE, LABOUR

The 2020 Routledge *Anthology* does not provide a rationale for leaving out women dramatists. Indeed, women dramatists are not mentioned at all, either as a grouping or as individuals. Presumably, there was a decision to exclude; the alternative, that representation of women's drama was not considered, doesn't bear thinking about. Yet, without a rationale, we can only speculate about the reasons. Can the decision be related to dates? The anthology offers 'a representative sample of drama written and performed in England between the 1560s and the 1630s'.[7] While perhaps not the most expansive construction of 'the early modern', these dates would nevertheless have allowed the editor to include Mary Sidney's *The Tragedie of Antonie*, which retells the story of Antony and Cleopatra by foregrounding female characters and discovering Cleopatra in a heroic light. It could also include: Elizabeth Cary's *The Tragedy of Mariam*, which recreates a Jerusalem setting to elaborate the beautiful but ill-fated Mariam, 'Queen of Jewry'; and Mary Wroth's *Love's Victory* (1614–1619), a comic celebration of female virtue and heterosexual passion. If the dates had been extended just a few more years either side, the anthology might have accommodated Jane Lumley's *Iphigeneia at Aulis*, the dramatic account of a woman sacrificed to political conflict, and Jane Cavendish and Elizabeth Brackley's *The Concealed Fancies* (1643–1645), a lively civil war drama featuring besieged yet proactive young women who attempt to determine their own marital choices. If the anthology had stretched to include an incomplete play text, drama by Elizabeth I might have featured (a translation of a scene from Seneca's *Hercules Oetaeus* which begins with the chorus of the Aetolian women) or dramatic fragments (*c* 1627) by Rachel Fane (one of which dramatises a widowed duchess assuming the responsibilities of a householder).[8] With greater generosity still, the anthology might have pointed to the fact that

[7] Lopez, 'General Introduction', 1.

[8] See Alison Findlay, *Playing Spaces in Early Women's Drama* (Cambridge, 2006), 40–2.

these are only the extant texts. We do know, for instance, that several plays by women are now lost, including a drama by Elizabeth Cary set in Syracuse, Sicily.[9]

But if the dates reveal the potential for women-authored choices, they also implicitly close things down by signalling a particular kind of drama, a kind of drama that women did not write, did not necessarily want to write, and could not write. Michelle M. Dowd highlights periodicity and the ways in which it often works to exclude women, and, in a similar fashion, the dates in the 2020 Routledge *Anthology* prioritise plays written for the commercial theatre (see this volume, Chapter 49, Michelle M. Dowd, 'Untimely Developments'). While women wrote drama throughout the early modern period, they did not write for the commercial theatre/public stage until the early 1660s. As Marta Straznicky notes:

> the public sphere of a commercial theatre is not unambiguously available for the presentation of a woman writer's plays . . . the secular, public nature of commercial theatre [is seen not least in the] . . . anti-theatrical and moral writings [to be] . . . fundamentally incompatible with the conception of female virtue as domestic.[10]

Instead, women wrote drama for domestic audiences and for family and friends. However, this does not mean that the drama women produced was radically different to that produced by men, not least because, as many critics have noted, distinctions made between plays that were composed with reference to a public and paying audience, and plays that were created for the benefit of an immediate family and its circle, are not as hard and fast as we might think. In fact, recent work has demonstrated that the lines separating public and private drama, and domestic and commercial drama, are often blurred. To begin with, as one appraisal has established, a 'play that is not intended for commercial performance can nevertheless cross between private play reading and the public sphere through the medium of print'.[11] The fact, then, that two dramas by women were published in the period—Mary Sidney's *The Tragedie of Antonie* and Elizabeth Cary's *The Tragedy of Mariam*—means that these plays could have captured a sizeable reading public. Moreover, the circulation of manuscripts was not restricted only to the family milieu. Its elaborate—and multiple—prologues and epilogues suggest that Jane Cavendish and Elizabeth Brackley's *The Concealed Fancies* may have moved beyond the immediate family. Similarly, dedicatory details, as A. C. Dunstan and W. W. Greg observe, confirm that *The Tragedy of Mariam* 'must have circulated in manuscript among Lady Cary's friends'.[12] And, while we can assume he was probably not a 'friend', it is clear that Thomas Middleton was both aware of Cary's drama and imitated

9 'To Diana's Earthly Deputess', in Ramona Wray (ed.), *The Tragedy of Mariam* (London, 2012), 14. All further citations are included parenthetically in the text.

10 Marta Straznicky, 'Private Drama', in Laura Lunger Knoppers (ed.), *The Cambridge Companion to Early Modern Women's Writing* (Cambridge, 2009), 247–59, 258, 247.

11 Marta Straznicky, *Privacy, Playreading, and Women's Closet Drama, 1550–1700* (Cambridge, 2004), 1.

12 A. C. Dunstan and W. W. Greg (eds), *The Tragedy of Mariam* (Oxford, 1914), ix.

it (in *The Second Maiden's Tragedy*, 1611). As R. V. Holdsworth suggests, the only way that Middleton could have come 'to know an unpublished play which is unlikely to have received a professional London production' is if 'he read it in manuscript'.[13] Of course, *The Tragedy of Mariam* is an example of a play which circulated in both print and manuscript, supporting the idea that plays could have overlapping incarnations and multiple chances for visibility. To put the point in another way, as does Karen Raber:

> the blend of 'amateur' genre and print publication these women achieve implicitly interrogates the assumption that a choice must be made between amateur literary courtiership and professional authorship, between the coterie and the marketplace.[14]

In its material form, we can conclude, women's drama was not limited in terms of its consumption, readership, and reception.

The idea that drama could only be considered drama if enacted on the commercial stage was not one that would have been understood in early modern England. We know that early modern women were acknowledged as dramatists by their contemporaries. As S. P. Cerasano and Marion Wynne-Davies note in their seminal collection: 'Early modern women dramatist[s] ... were perfectly well known in their own period and were the subject of numerous panegyric commentaries'.[15] Recent studies have highlighted the extent to which Elizabeth Cary achieved fame in her own time as both translator and dramatist. John Davies honoured Cary's achievements in dramatic 'Art' and 'Language' in a 1612 treatise.[16] Similarly, the printer of the 1633 edition of the dramatic works of John Marston singled out Cary in his prefatory dedication: '*your Honour is well acquainted with the Muses*', he writes, a formulation that suggests her place in the contemporary theatrical world.[17] Other dramatists were no less eulogised. Thus, Samuel Daniel, in a 1594 poem, likens Mary Sidney's *The Tragedie of Antonie* to a 'star of wonder' that inspires him 'To sing of state, and tragic notes to frame', while Ben Jonson, via allusions to Cupid and Venus in a 1640 sonnet, demonstrates profound appreciation of Mary Wroth's *Love's Victory*.[18] These and related encomiums both testify to the recognition of women dramatists and confirm their association with seventeenth-century theatrical culture.

The acknowledgement of a gendered contribution accords with work highlighting women's wider participation in dramatic production and public theatre. Elizabeth Schafer devotes a recent special issue to 'women theatre makers', while Clare McManus and Lucy Munro, in a further special issue, explore 'women's multiple roles within

[13] R. V. Holdsworth, 'Middleton and *Mariam*', *Notes and Queries*, 33 (1986), 379–80, 380.

[14] Karen Raber, *Dramatic Difference: Gender, Class, and Genre in the Early Modern Closet Drama* (Newark, 2001), 23.

[15] S. P. Cerasano and Marion Wynne-Davies, 'Introduction', in S. P. Cerasano and Marion Wynne-Davies (eds), *Readings in Renaissance Women's Drama* (London, 1998), 1–5, 1.

[16] John Davies, *The Muses Sacrifice* (London, 1612), sig. *3v.

[17] John Marston, *The Workes* (London, 1633), sig. A4r.

[18] Samuel Daniel, 'Samuel Daniel to Mary Sidney' and Ben Jonson, 'Jonson and Wroth', in Cerasano and Wynne-Davies (eds), *Readings*, 11, 15.

theatrical culture'.[19] Their language choices are revealing, pointing up both a desire for inclusivity and a material reality in which women not only performed on stage but also patronised, produced, and published the drama of others. Women's roles as sponsors or patrons of drama is an urgent field of enquiry, and in the interstices of dramatic dedications we may extrapolate both a bid for female patronage and gratitude for support received.[20] Exemplary are Samuel Daniel's prefatory verses to his *Cleopatra* (1594) which, as well as identifying *The Tragedie of Antonie* as a source of inspiration, suggest that he was commissioned by Mary Sidney to write a sequel.[21] A concomitant practice occurs in masques such as Robert White's *Cupid's Banishment* (1617), performed by the 'young Gentlewomen of the Ladies Hall in Deptford' for Queen Anna of Denmark, and Walter Montagu's *The Shepherd's Paradise* (1633), in which Queen Henrietta Maria had a speaking part.[22] The presence of a monarch, either in the audience or on stage, and the fact that both masques were infused with tropes familiar from related royal panegyrics, have led Alison Findlay, Stephanie Hodgson-Wright, and Gweno Williams, in the ground-breaking volume *Women and Dramatic Production 1550–1700* (2000), to argue for Anne and Henrietta Maria themselves as 'creators', precisely because of the regularity with which they 'commissioned and performed' court entertainment.[23] The analysis of relationships suggests that, if we are open with our understanding of 'early modern women's drama', an increasing number of examples is generated.

The masque form, of course, enabled and legitimated early modern women barred from acting on the commercial stage. Thanks to the work of Barbara Ravelhofer, we now have a much more informed sense of how women, performing in masques, were able to dance, sing, improvise, and command attention via intricate costumes, virtuoso insets, and displays of physical dexterity.[24] Her scholarship has generated a lively discussion of female performance across a variety of social expressions and in a range of cultural modes. Ravelhofer's work has been extended into new findings, with James Stokes showing that, 'with the exception of professional English troupes ... women participated as performers ... at every level of society during the medieval and early modern periods', taking active roles in street festivities, guild shows, itinerant musical

[19] Elizabeth Schafer, 'Introduction', *Early Theatre*, 17 (2014), 125–32, 125; Clare McManus and Lucy Munro, 'Renaissance Women's Performance and the Dramatic Canon', *Shakespeare Bulletin*, 33 (2015), 1–7, 2.

[20] David M. Bergeron, 'Women as Patrons of English Renaissance Drama', in Cerasano and Wynne-Davies (eds), *Readings*, 69–80, 71–2.

[21] Samuel Daniel, 'Samuel Daniel to Mary Sidney', in Cerasano and Wynne-Davies (eds), *Readings*, 11–12.

[22] Robert White, *Cupid's Banishment*, in S. P. Cerasano and Marion Wynne-Davies (eds), *Renaissance Drama by Women* (London and New York, 1996), 83.

[23] Alison Findlay, Stephanie Hodgson-Wright, and Gweno Williams, *Women and Dramatic Production 1500–1700* (Harlow, 2000), 7–8.

[24] Barbara Ravelhofer, *The Early Stuart Masque: Dance, Costume, and Music* (Oxford, 2006), 107–20.

demonstrations, and all manner of popular entertainments (dancing, exhibitions of 'monsters', and fortune-telling).[25] Accompanying Stokes' explorations are levelling implications and broadening effects. Early modern women's drama was restricted neither by social status nor by site of activity, the extraordinary richness of kinds of performance operating to sensitise us to women who purposefully engaged in playing actions across of range of institutional and informal, licensed and unlicensed, settings. Alison Findlay, Stephanie Hodgson-Wright, and Gweno Williams maintain that 'political or religious demonstrations' and testimonies staged in 'public spaces' emphasised the inherently theatrical modes in which some women were able to express themselves, going so far as to suggest that such practices and pursuits made manifest a seventeenth-century form of 'alternative' theatre.[26] The thesis that early modern women took advantage of all manner of performance acts and spaces has been fruitfully developed by others, not least in relation to martyrs, prophets, women speaking in church, and women writing from prison.

In a related development, Natasha Korda has gone backstage (if not under-stage) to uncover a rich array of labour performed by women in the theatres, complementing, in so doing, existing knowledge about women as audience members and shareholders. Spotlighting female-stamped ephemera such as 'dress pins, hooks ... lace, fringe and beads' found in excavations of the Rose and Globe playhouses, Korda argues for the prioritising of women's work in the early modern theatre and for contributions that, by extension, expose the 'paradigm of "all male" theatre' as a 'myth'.[27] Such archival recoveries reveal an expanse of occupations and classes, and, as with discussion that amplifies conceptions of theatre, the significances are multiple. By recognising a spectrum of female involvement, we can progress from theorising about women as 'singular' or 'exceptional' authors to thinking through alliances between, and networks shared among, women as playwrights, performers, patrons, and employees, all providers of 'labour'. There is also the potential for reflecting on the ways in which the work women produced (the products of their labour) appeared on stage as a material manifestation of the intersectional gendered work of theatrical institutions.

In this connection, it is relevant to discuss the extent to which drama authored by men and women participate in similar debates and traverse comparable thematic territories. Women dramatists in the period embrace the cultural questions and political projections also entertained in the work of their male counterparts. The relationship might be a proximate one: for example, Samuel Daniel's closet drama, *Cleopatra*, and Mary Sidney's *The Tragedie of Antonie* are intimately allied in their ventilating of anxieties about foreign invasion and domination.[28] Or the relationship might be more

[25] James Stokes, 'The Ongoing Exploration of Women and Performance in Early Modern England', *Shakespeare Bulletin*, 33 (2015), 9–31, 9.

[26] Findlay, Hodgson-Wright, and Williams, *Women*, 6.

[27] Natasha Korda, 'Insubstantial Pageants: Women's Work and the (Im)material Culture of the Early Modern Stage', *Shakespeare*, 7 (2011), 413–31, 413, 414.

[28] Margaret P. Hannay, *Philip's Phoenix: Mary Sidney, Countess of Pembroke* (Oxford, 1990), 127, 128.

attenuated and suggestive. Jane Lumley's *Iphigeneia at Aulis*, in its coded engagement with religion and politics, lends comparison with male-translated versions of Seneca in the 1550s and 1560s distinguished by their interventions in discussion about 'tyranny, power abuse, and resistance'.[29] Simon Barker and Hilary Hinds describe *The Tragedy of Mariam* as 'central to the debates that characterise contemporary critical interest in Renaissance drama as a whole', pointing to the play's thematic congruity with Thomas Heywood's *A Woman Killed with Kindness* (1603), Ben Jonson's *Epicoene* (1609), and Thomas Middleton and Thomas Dekker's *The Roaring Girl* (1611), and an intensity of characterisation that recalls the protagonists of Shakespeare's *King Lear* (1603–1606) and *Richard III* (1591).[30] Other areas of overlap include Marlowe's major plays, as suggested in parallels in phrasing and a preoccupation with social status, as well as Shakespearean tragedies, *Othello* (1601–1602), *Hamlet* (1599–1601), and *Antony and Cleopatra* (1606–1607), as suggested in costuming decisions, racial dynamics, and a concern with reputation.[31] Critics have now established that women dramatists were working within well-rooted traditions of adaptation and reinvention: Jane Lumley repurposes Euripides in her translation, Mary Sidney reworks Robert Garnier's Roman plays, and Mary Wroth reanimates masque and pastoral conventions (see this volume, Chapter 24, Laura L. Knoppers, 'Changing Places'). For her part, Cary's appropriative practice and use of Old Testament history tie her closely to playwrights such as Philip Massinger, whose *The Duke of Milan* (1623) similarly relies on Thomas Lodge's translation of Josephus' Herod and Mariam narrative. Similar Continental instances, such as plays by Hans Sachs and Alexandre Hardy, are suggestive here, and the parallels that emerge point to the potential of exploring further what Robert Henke has described elsewhere as 'a common European theatrical language'.[32] Receiving early modern women's drama in terms of its wider pressures, practices, and contexts allows us to dismantle some recent understandings and approaches. Early modern women's drama fails to be contained within the public/private dichotomy; rather, it needs to be judged in terms of continuing interactions with the politics and priorities of theatre in all of its forms, including the commercial stage.

[29] Linda Woodbridge, 'Resistance Theory Meets Drama: Tudor Seneca', *Renaissance Drama*, 38 (2010), 115–39, 115.

[30] Simon Barker and Hilary Hinds, 'Elizabeth Cary, *The Tragedy of Mariam*', in Simon Barker and Hilary Hinds (eds), *The Routledge Anthology of Renaissance Drama* (Abingdon, 2003), 191–3.

[31] See Elizabeth Gruber, 'Insurgent Flesh: Epistemology and Violence in *Othello* and *Mariam*', and Maureen Quilligan, 'Staging Gender: William Shakespeare and Elizabeth Cary', in Karen Raber (ed.), *Ashgate Critical Essays on Women Writers in England, 1550–1700: Elizabeth Cary* (Farnham, 2009), 477–94, 527–51.

[32] Robert Henke and Eric Nicholson, 'Introduction', in Robert Henke and Eric Nicholson (eds), *Transnational Exchange in Early Modern Theatre* (Aldershot, 2008), 1–22, 2.

CLASSIFICATION, PERFORMANCE, HISTORY

In contradistinction to playwrighting produced for the public stage, women's drama has been unhelpfully labelled 'private', 'domestic', 'household', and 'closet'. Each one of these terms contains a value judgement—what is valuable and valued is that which is commercial and public. These judgements are, of course, unfavourably inflected in terms of gender and not dissimilar to some arguments made in relation to female-authored drama, novels, or television today: pejorative assumptions are made about domestic subject matters and about the quality of drama that is read rather than performed. We know this, yet the tenacity of these classifications persists. In feminist criticism now, the tendency is for the terms to be deployed and disavowed at one and the same time. Hence, Laura Lunger Knoppers' important collection, *The Cambridge Companion to Early Modern Women's Writing* (2009), divides drama into 'private' and 'public' categories, with the distinction between the two essentially a matter of dates.[33] Simultaneously, in her excellent chapter in the collection, Marta Straznicky is frank and upfront about the 'conceptual and rhetorical limitations' of 'public' and 'private' and keen to query the distinctions they exacerbate.[34] As critics, we recognise the damage the terms do, but we still struggle to shake them off entirely.

Of all the labels attached to early modern women's drama arguably the most damaging has been, in the words of Elizabeth Schafer, 'the anachronistic and inappropriate nineteenth-century term "closet drama"' (see this volume, Chapter 23, Julie Sanders, 'Daughters of the House').[35] Inside a discipline which defines itself in terms of the Shakespearean and the non-Shakespearean (with 'masque studies' occupying subsections of these two groupings), a play designated 'closet drama', no matter how significant in other ways, is often seen as failing to fit into the 'early modern drama' canon. 'Closet drama' suggests that many outputs by women were never performed but were—at the most—designed to be read aloud in some sort of family or domestic gathering; some commentators have gone further, seeing the plays as not only unperformed but also unperformable.[36]

Perhaps the most important riposte to the exclusion of women dramatists, therefore, has been to refuse the judgement that brands drama by women as theatrically unviable. This argument—first developed by Alison Findlay, Stephanie Hodgson-Wright, and Gweno Williams—holds that we cannot deduce from the absence of evidence for a

[33] Laura Lunger Knoppers (ed.), *The Cambridge Companion to Early Modern Women's Writing* (Cambridge, 2009), vi.

[34] Straznicky, 'Private Drama', in Knoppers (ed.), *Companion*, 247.

[35] Schafer, 'Introduction', 125.

[36] Marta Straznicky, 'Closet Drama', in Arthur F. Kinney (ed.), *A Companion to Renaissance Drama* (Oxford, 2002), 416–30, 416.

play's performance in the early modern period a lack of theatrical responsiveness or ambition on a woman dramatist's part. As they observe:

> in composing a play, a woman made an active and informed choice of genre. Her script was written with a theatrical arena in mind, whether or not evidence of a production has survived … It is mistaken to assume that plays for which we have no production history are unperformable and not even intended for performance.[37]

Subsequent work further corroborates these claims by identifying specific performance signals in early modern women's drama. For example, Marta Straznicky points out that Jane Lumley's *Iphigeneia at Aulis* strips out much 'rhetorical dilation', reduces 'indirect speech' and 'descriptions of offstage events', and maintains a steady narrative pace: the conclusion is unmistakably that Euripides' play was translated with 'an eye to performance'.[38] Marion Wynne-Davies has gone further, holding that other elements of *Iphigeneia at Aulis*, including 'prose' that suits 'spoken dialogue', the implied movement of the 'cast', and the 'use of the St Paul's Boys by Lumley's father', suggest 'an envisaged performance'.[39] Translation, as critics have richly demonstrated, does not preclude a cognisance of performance opportunity.

Undoubtedly, the fullest discussion around the performativity of early modern women's drama has been conducted with reference to *The Tragedy of Mariam*. All recent editors of the play direct attention to the duelling scene between Constabarus and Silleus which famously includes one of the most frequently used stage directions of the period, 'They fight' (stage direction at 2.4.92). The first to flag up the performativity of *The Tragedy of Mariam* was Jonas Barish who, in 1993, noted the play's 'sense of action hastening forward, of event erupting into event … an effect alien to closet drama but familiar on the stage'.[40] Elizabeth Schafer has taken these remarks to the next level, maintaining that 'the play was very definitely written' with a view to 'performance': she points out, for example, the 'long entrances, typical of the public playhouse' and the presence on stage of Herod's attendants (they serve little purpose in a read-only iteration).[41] Details of costumes and props are also suggestive. In act four, Mariam, much to the annoyance of her tyrannical husband, elects to dress herself not in Herod's favoured fashion of 'fair habit' (5.1.142) but, rather, in black, which she, like Hamlet, claims refracts her mood. Props include standard theatrical objects like a flower ('Much like this flower which today excels', states Salome; 3.1.21) and a cup ('A drink procuring love', explains the Butler; 4.4.1). The gestural and kinetic energy embedded in the lines is self-evident.

[37] Findlay, Hodgson-Wright, and Williams, *Women*, 3.

[38] Straznicky, 'Private Drama', 249.

[39] Wynne-Davies, 'Editing', 172.

[40] Jonas Barish, 'Language for the Study; Language for the Stage', in A. L. Magnusson and C. E. McGee (eds), *The Elizabethan Theatre XII* (Toronto, 1993), 19–43, 38.

[41] Elizabeth Schafer, 'An Early Modern Feminist', *Times Higher Education* (6 June 2013), https://www.timeshighereducation.com/features/an-early-modern-feminist/2004327.article?nopaging=1, accessed 20 December 2020.

Most recently, exciting work by Jennifer Richards on 'the sound of print' enjoins us to attend to the text of *Mariam* 'as a script for female oral readers ... with breath marks that provide pauses and patterns, stops and starts ... in rhetorically punctuated sentences'.[42] Her brilliant reading of the opening lines of the play opens up the possibility that punctuation may have functioned as signals to verbal performance, as spaces within which to read aloud and imitate the character's own psychic processes. The radical potential of recovering the voice as it appears on the printed page is captured in Richards' question, 'how would it feel ... to physically voice Salome's bold promise to divorce Constabarus in a culture in which women had no legal escape from marriage?'[43] Even without more self-evident staging clues, the punctuational organisation of words and lines points to individual or group modes of spoken delivery with far-reaching implications for rhetoric and self-expression.

If convincing arguments have been made that early modern women's drama contains staging clues and was written in terms of projected performance, the issue then becomes not the texts themselves but the lack of a conventional performance history. After all, it is only at the point where the individual play is staged that hypotheses about performability can be fully tested. A growing consensus suggests that some plays by women were performed in early modern venues beyond the commercial stage. For example, Mary Sidney's *The Tragedie of Antonie* may have received performances at several of the Pembroke properties, including Ivychurch, Ramsbury, and Wilton, with individual architectural environs dictating and shaping the play's unique theatrical flavour.[44] Both the 'Shakespeare and his Sisters' and the 'Early Modern Women Research Network' projects are detailing how Mary Wroth's *Love's Victory* exists in two manuscript versions, with the latter (Huntington) manuscript suggesting a text performed at Surrenden Dering, Pluckley, Kent: tell-tale signs include the removal of pages, evidence that individual parts were cut up to give to the performers and the stitching together of the whole.[45] In the same way that archaeological work can revise assumptions about women and theatre, so too can manuscript examination, and exploration of provenance and ownership, bring to light staging possibilities if not staging histories.

Because critics are generally habituated to thinking that early modern drama by women is not performable, a record of their stage history rarely troubles theatrical accounts. In this regard, Elizabeth Schafer's appendix to her *Early Theatre* special issue, 'Modern Performances of Plays by Early Modern Women', breaks new ground by constructing a performance history for the first time. Space cannot do justice to the detail, but the listing shows that there have been multiple performances of Elizabeth

[42] Jennifer Richards, *Voices and Books in the English Renaissance: A New History of Reading* (Oxford, 2019), 119.

[43] Richards, *Voices and Books*, 286.

[44] Findlay, *Playing Spaces*, 24, 29.

[45] Paul Salzman, 'Lady Mary Wroth: *Love's Victory*', Early Modern Women Research Network (2017–2020), Centre for 21st Century Humanities, https://c21ch.newcastle.edu.au/emwrn/, accessed 20 December 2020; Alison Findlay, 'The Manuscripts of *Love's Victory*', Shakespeare and His Sisters, wp.lancs.ac.uk/shakespeare-and-his-sisters, accessed 20 December 2020.

Cary's *The Tragedy of Mariam*, Jane Cavendish and Elizabeth Brackley's *The Concealed Fancies*, Mary Sidney's *The Tragedie of Antonie*, Jane Lumley's *Iphigeneia at Aulis*, and Mary Wroth's *Love's Victory*.[46] Distinctively, Schafer's listing includes, as well as fully-fledged productions, excerpts and staged readings. A staged reading of Mary Wroth's *Love's Victory* as part of the 'READ Not Dead' education project at Penshurst Place, Kent, in 2014, for example, pointed up the comedic complexities of the play's characterisation and the ways in which the windows of the Great Hall framed its absorption in the natural world.[47] The conditions of the event are suggestive of the ways in which women's drama—when it does make its way to a stage—is often performed not by established companies but by amateur and local groups.

The lack of an established company repertoire for early modern women's drama is undoubtedly a factor in the historical occlusion of their work, yet, as a recent polemic points out, this can also be a plus: 'by operating on the margins of theatre practice, these productions can ignore commercial pressures and ... take more risks, be less conventional'.[48] Part of the break with the conventional is the opening up of explicitly gendered perspectives. Discussing why she chose to stage *The Tragedy of Mariam* as a rehearsed reading in a London pub, for example, director Rebecca McCutcheon cited 'the numerous extended and complex female roles ... the unprecedented ... focus on female experience and ... voices'.[49] *The Tragedy of Mariam* also provides roles for raced actors, allowing for an embodiment of Kim Hall's argument that 'the language of beauty and favour ... troped through the dark/light binary works primarily to define females'.[50] Like Shakespeare's Desdemona, Mariam is described in terms of lightness and whiteness—typical is Herod's lament, 'If [Mariam] had been like an Egyptian, black, / And not so fair, she had been longer lived' (5.1.239–40). In this formulation and others, women are ranked according to the way in which they are racially distinguished. In contrast to the fair/pale Mariam, the play's anti-heroine, Salome, as Dympna Callaghan observes, 'is conspicuously dark and morally tarnished'.[51] The hierarchy of colour is registered in Herod's sense that Salome, when placed alongside Mariam, appears 'a sunburnt blackamoor' (4.7.106). In showing how racial identifiers dictate an aesthetic competition between women, the play is one of the earliest examinations of the ways in which beauty is always racially constructed (see this volume, Chapter 25, Meghan E. Hall, 'Race and Geographies of Escape'). For the dramaturge, the staging possibilities are legion—all the

[46] Schafer, 'Introduction', 129–32.

[47] Naomi J. Miller, 'Playing with Margaret Cavendish and Mary Wroth', *Early Modern Women*, 10 (2016), 95–110, 96, 106; Marta Straznicky and Sara Mueller (eds), *Women's Household Drama: 'Loves Victorie', 'A Pastorall', and 'The concealed Fansyes'* (Tempe, AZ, 2018), 45.

[48] Schafer, 'Introduction', 128.

[49] Rebecca McCutcheon, 'A Performance Studies Approach to *The Tragedy of Mariam*', *Early Theatre*, 17 (2014), 187–201, 189.

[50] Hall, *Things of Darkness*, 206.

[51] Dympna Callaghan, 'Re-reading Elizabeth Cary's *The Tragedie of Mariam, Faire Queene of Jewry*', in Margo Hendricks and Patricia Parker (eds), *Women, 'Race', and Writing in the Early Modern Period* (London and New York, 1994), 163–77, 175.

more significant when we bear in mind that, as Joyce Green MacDonald argues, male-authored Renaissance drama is usually marked by 'female racial disappearances'.[52] In a context in which early modern women's drama is under-represented, performances have the capacity to be ideologically transformative in the present.

The existence of a performance history—the fact that drama by early modern women is actually being staged—approves the inherent theatricality of their creations. But, crucially, we need not only to document the performances but also to dedicate ourselves to their analysis and assessment. In short, we need academic work on actual performance that is taken seriously. Hence, while reviews of early modern drama by women are still few and far between, it is a positive development that critics have begun the task of producing scholarship on early modern women's drama in its performance manifestations. This new work challenges the consensus by drawing attention to—and providing in-depth appreciation of—issues such as casting, costume, lighting, set, and movement that have been somewhat bypassed in studies of early modern women's drama thus far. Typical is Alison Findlay's discussion of a 2013 production of Jane Lumley's *Iphigeneia at Aulis* by the Rose Company: her subtle and finessed reflections on the 'eclectic mix of modern dress' and centenary setting (the outbreak of the First World War) point up how, in performance, the play 'continues to function as a palimpsest that revivifies the past in order to disturb the present'.[53] My own discussion of the 2013 Lazarus Company production of *The Tragedy of Mariam* in the small box space of the Tristan Bates Theatre notes the production's retention of many of the play's racialised references and the 'colour conscious' casting decisions—three women of colour play Mariam, Salome, and Doris respectively—making visible the link between competition among women and racialised constructions of beauty.[54] The hordes of red roses that adorned the stage in this production keep discourses of beauty at the forefront and highlight as emancipatory Salome's understanding that beauty is both socially constructed and transient ('Beauty is a blast', Salome states, 'like this flower ... it will not last'; 3.1.20–2). For the Lazarus *Mariam*, racial inequities translate eloquently into staging aesthetics.

We are only at the beginning of assembling a production history scholarship. Even so, we cannot now doubt that early modern women's drama constitutes an actable entity or that it invites and enables a spectrum of performance options, from site-specific to London fringe. Early modern drama by women is excitingly compatible with different kinds of theatrical space, both traditional and experimental, and plays takes on varying domestic and political complexions according to cuts and adjustments in emphasis. Crucial here is Marion Wynne-Davies' sense that:

52 Joyce Green MacDonald, *Women and Race in Early Modern Texts* (Oxford, 2002), 9. On the paucity of '"racialised and gendered" representations on the contemporary Shakespearean stage', see Delia Jarrett-Macauley, 'Introduction', in Delia Jarrett-Macauley (ed.), *Shakespeare, Race and Performance: The Diverse Bard* (London and New York, 2017), 1–19, 11.

53 Alison Findlay, 'Reproducing *Iphigenia at Aulis*', *Early Theatre*, 17 (2014), 133–48, 134, 146.

54 Ramona Wray, 'Performing *The Tragedy of Mariam* and Constructing Stage History', *Early Theatre*, 17 (2014), 149–66.

> what matters in ... performance is not scholarly ... pigeonholing but the fluidity of interpretation ... achieved through ... speech, movement, costume, set, light—that enable a director to edit a play so that it focuses on issues that are relevant to a present-day audience.[55]

As this brief summary of performance history has implied, we are moving to a place where strategies of staging more familiar from, say, Shakespeare's plays in the theatre are starting to be visited on early modern women dramatists. Such creativity—and an accompanying scholarship of performance—has the potential to give women dramatists the afterlives denied by the most recent Routledge *Anthology* while fundamentally altering our sense of each dramatist's achievement.

As we move into the third decade of the twenty-first century, a wealth of scholarship on early modern women's drama presents itself, and we stand to reap its dividends. Yet questions about how deeply the resulting knowledge has been internalised remain open. What is required is a commonality of purpose and a parity of treatment so that early modern drama by women is properly integrated, in both curricular and performance terms. How, then, should critics working today on women's drama go forward? We need to continue to make our case. To emphasise intersectionality. To insist on performability. To flag up translation as a creative act. To remake our terms and to abandon the ones—like private, domestic, household, and closet—that are no longer serving us. We need to insist on the capaciousness of the field, to stress fluid definitions, and to demand that early modern drama by women moves inside less straitjacketed interpretive terrains. This is our work and we are ready to do it. More than this: the argument of this chapter has been that we are doing it already. Generally speaking—and there are some notable and important exceptions—the scholarly and performative labour around women's drama has been and is being undertaken by women. It is hard not to think that this might be a factor in the continuation of critical neglect. We need to keep doing our work, but, crucially, we also need to be heard. Unless the work that has been conducted on women's drama is listened to, engaged with, and properly taken into account in the broader assessments and constructions of early modern studies, progress will falter. The exploration of early modern women's drama is a vital and flourishing endeavour, but its ongoing success depends not only on articulation but also on reception.

FURTHER READING

Aebischer, Pascale and Kathryn Prince. 'Introduction', in Pascale Aebischer and Kathryn Prince (eds), *Performing Early Modern Drama Today*. Cambridge, 2012, 1–16.

Cerasano, S. P. and Marion Wynne-Davies. 'Introduction', in S. P. Cerasano and Marion Wynne-Davies (eds), *Readings in Renaissance Women's Drama*. London, 1998, 1–5.

55 Wynne-Davies, 'Editing', 174–5.

Findlay, Alison, Stephanie Hodgson-Wright, and Gweno Williams. *Women and Dramatic Production 1500–1700*. Harlow, 2000.

Knoppers, Laura Lunger (ed.). *The Cambridge Companion to Early Modern Women's Writing*. Cambridge, 2009.

Raber, Karen. *Dramatic Difference: Gender, Class, and Genre in the Early Modern Closet Drama*. Newark, 2001.

Schafer, Elizabeth. 'Introduction'. *Early Theatre*, 17 (2014), 125–32.

Straznicky, Marta. *Privacy, Playreading, and Women's Closet Drama, 1550–1700*. Cambridge, 2004.

Wynne-Davies, Marion. 'Editing Early Modern Women's Dramatic Writing', in Sarah C. E. Ross and Paul Salzman (eds), *Editing Early Modern Women*. Cambridge, 2016, 156–75.

CHAPTER 12

'SING AND LET THE SONG BE NEW'

Early Modern Women's Devotional Lyrics

HELEN WILCOX

'DEVINE POESYE': THE NATURE OF DEVOTIONAL LYRICS

In 1627, Lady Anne Southwell wrote to her friend, Lady Ridgway, articulating a passionate and eloquent defence of the 'banquett of soules, devine Poesye'.[1,2] Troubled by the realisation that her correspondent is a 'sworne enemye to Poetrie', Southwell begins with broad claims on its behalf: poems are 'the Herald of all Ideas' and the 'true vocall Harmonie' of the world, encompassing and holding together all other arts in the way that a 'silke thredd' strings together a 'chayne of pearle' (sig. 3r). Southwell does not shrink from Plato's awkward charge that 'Poesye is a fiction, & fiction is a lye' (sig. 3r), asserting the higher truth of the poetic imagination: poetry offers a 'patterne' for living and shows, defiantly, that 'Imagination goes before Realitye' (sig. 3r). Aware that some scandalous secular poems may have cast a cloud over the clear light of such exemplary poetry, Southwell asserts that the fault lies in the subject, not the art itself. She concludes her defence with a splendid account of the highest, untainted form of poetry, religious verse:

[1] With thanks to the editors for their generous support, and Marije van Lankveld for invaluable assistance.

[2] Washington, DC, Folger Library, MS V.b.198, fol. 3v. See Jean C. Cavanagh, 'Lady Southwell's Defense of Poetry', *English Literary Renaissance*, 14.3 (1984), insert bound between 284–5; and Jean Klene (ed.), *The Southwell-Sibthorpe Commonplace Book: Folger V.b.198* (Tempe, AZ, 1997).

> will you behold Poesye in perfect beautye: Then see the kingly Prophett, that sweete singer of Israell, explicating the glory of our god, his power in creating; his mercye in redeeming, his wisedome in preserving making these three, as it were the Coma, Colon, & Period to every stanza. (Sig. 3v)

Citing the Psalms of the 'kingly Prophett', David, as the ultimate instance of poetry's 'perfect beautye', Southwell here ingeniously outlines the material of religious poetry in specifically textual terms, likening its key elements to the three main punctuation marks—'Coma, Colon, & Period'—of a written verse. Having thus neatly expressed her sense of the underpinning and framing of a poem by its sacred subject, Southwell can only exclaim in conclusion: 'O never enough to bee admired, devine Poesye' (sig. 3v).

Southwell's letter is a remarkable piece of literary criticism, and sets the relationship between women, religion, and poetry firmly centre stage. As a religious poet herself, Southwell writes with the authority of experience, and as a correspondent she radically establishes a dialogue between two women about God and the nature of poetry. Far too often, modern literary critics have assumed that the impact of religion on early modern women was a negative one—and with good reason, of course. The constraints of biblical precedent, from Eve to St Paul as well as in subsequent interpretation by the Church Fathers, would appear to keep women firmly in their place as the weaker sex, subject to the patriarchal dominance of God, church leaders, and husbands.[3] However, it is important *not* to underestimate the agency that the Christian faith could offer to early modern women, both in their lives and for their writing. As Aemilia Lanyer showed in the spirited 'Eves Apologie' section of *Salve Deus Rex Judaeorum* (1611), the secondary position allotted to women could make possible the consequent claim that Adam should be deemed far more responsible for the fall than Eve.[4] As Anna Trapnel knew, an acceptance of women's weakness could make the female body and voice a readier channel for the prophecies of God.[5] In other words, as Kimberly Anne Coles has written: 'women appropriated the terms of religion for their own use; in fact, in the struggle against oppression, the terms of religion, properly negotiated, were among the most effective tools that women could employ'.[6] When it came to poetry, writing verse on sacred subject matter was regarded as the most appropriate and acceptable choice for a woman author. Lady Mary Wroth discovered this to her cost, facing harsh criticism for writing 'lascivious tales and amorous toys' in contrast to the positive example of her 'virtuous and learned aunt', Mary Sidney, Countess of Pembroke, whose verse

[3] See Genesis 2–3, and 1 Timothy 2.9–15, among many other passages.

[4] Aemilia Lanyer, in Susanne Woods (ed.), *The Poems of Aemilia Lanyer: Salve Deus Rex Judaeorum* (New York, 1993), 84–7.

[5] 'The Lord will give [me] words ... I will be nothing', asserts *Anna Trapnel's Report and Plea*, in Elspeth Graham et al. (eds), *Her Own Life: Autobiographical Writings by Seventeenth-Century Englishwomen* (London, 1989), 78.

[6] Kimberly Anne Coles, *Religion, Reform, and Women's Writing in Early Modern England* (Cambridge, 2008), 7.

translations of the Psalms were widely admired.[7] Indeed, it could be said that the devotional lyric became a vitally important creative outlet for women of the early modern period. As I hope to show, a remarkable number of sixteenth- and seventeenth-century women found textual expression in metrical biblical paraphrases, devotional love lyrics, religious complaints, introspective poetic questioning, and versified dialogues with God and with their own souls. Spiritual experience enabled them to find a poetic voice, giving rise to notable literary inventiveness and rhetorical skill as they expressed their devotion—in all its complexity—in verse.

Before looking more closely at the work of some of the poets involved, it is helpful to consider two fundamental questions. First, what exactly is meant by 'devotional' when the adjective is applied to poetry? Anne Southwell has offered us a useful starting point: in describing the Psalms as a means of 'explicating the glory of god'—glory shown in his 'power in creating; his mercye in redeeming, his wisedome in preserving'—she highlights several key aspects of devotional verse. The writer is likely to be addressing God and contemplating the greatness of creation, the gift of divine forgiveness, or the providence at work in the world. This range of topics is close to those featured in the 'Prayer of General Thanksgiving' from the *Book of Common Prayer*, in which God is thanked for 'our creation, preservation, and all the blessings of this life, but above all for [his] inestimable love in the redemption of the world by our Lord Jesus Christ'.[8] These parallels indicate not only some of the focal subjects and moods of devotional poetry, but also its frequent closeness to prayer: both are fundamentally modes of conversation. Poetry that is devotional in nature is less likely to debate points of theology or doctrinal controversy (features of the ampler genre known as 'religious poetry') than to give voice to a dialogue, often with God—Father, Son, or Holy Spirit—sometimes with a saint or, most commonly, with or between different aspects of the speaker's self, such as body and soul. In its range of genres, then, devotional poetry can take the form of (or overlap with) many Renaissance poetic forms, including complaints, dialogues, elegies, and love sonnets. A devotional poem frequently originates as a meditation on a biblical text or scene, or in response to an unusual or providential occasion in the life of the speaker; it can apply religious knowledge to the practical and personal challenges of sin, loss, joy, doubt, and faith, often testing the boundaries of what can be expressed and believed. Such poetry may therefore also be defined as much by its devotional *purpose* and usage as by its specifically poetic features or spiritual concerns. David Manning has argued that early modern 'devotional discourse' was 'more than a category of literature': it was 'invariably not just about God, or directed at God, but something which gained

[7] The comment was made by Lord Denny; see Josephine A. Roberts (ed.), *The Poems of Lady Mary Wroth* (Baton Rouge, LA, 1993), 34.

[8] *The Book of Common Prayer* (1662), though these words appear to have been based on a prayer attributed to Elizabeth I. See Brian Cummings (ed.), *The Book of Common Prayer: The Texts of 1549, 1559, and 1662* (Oxford, 2011), 268, 762.

its meaning through the grace of God and in the presence of God'.[9] A devotional lyric straddles the worlds of language and belief, testing the limits of both in creative and prayerful practice.

If 'devotional' is a thought-provoking literary category, so too is 'lyric'. At its basic level, it forms part of the ancient generic categorisation, predicated upon the distinction between short verse forms and longer epic or narrative poems.[10] In this chapter, the religious poetry of Aemilia Lanyer (narrative) and Lucy Hutchinson (epic) will therefore not be a primary focus of the discussion. However, to take a less reductive approach to an understanding of lyric, we may turn once more to Anne Southwell, who provides us with a helpful point of departure by asserting the profound relationship between poetry and music. Southwell's sense of poetry as the world's 'true vocall Harmonie' assumes the musical principle of concord that gives shape to this verbal art form. When praising the Psalms of David, Southwell adds: 'who would not say, the musicall spheares did yeeld a cadencye to his songe' (sig. 3v). Through this rhetorical question, Southwell asserts that the Psalms, those foundational devotional lyric poems, are songs whose sounds echo the music of the spheres, the idealised unheard music of the creation. The closure of a poem, the final line that seals its meaning, functions like a 'cadencye' or cadence, the last chords of a harmony.[11] When we apply the term 'lyric' to an early modern poem, therefore, the primary implication is a form of verse either constructed with its own in-built sense of melodic and harmonic structure, or written in anticipation of a musical setting. Thus the most easily identifiable lyrics will be the many poems simply entitled 'Song' or taking the form of an air, madrigal, ballad, or hymn—or even a sonnet, which in the original Italian means 'little song'. However, as this period was also a great age of artful solo singing accompanied by lute or viols, the lyric poem further developed complex and subtle stanza forms to match the rhythmic shape of the music, real or implied, that might accompany it; this is evident in the verse of poet-musicians such as Thomas Wyatt, Thomas Campion, George Herbert and—as we shall see—Mary Sidney. The early modern lyric is thus, by implication, a performative poetic mode and, as a consequence, assumes the social context of a speaker/singer and an addressee/listener. This has significant consequences for its function and contents, and suggests that a lyric is likely to be an implied dialogue expressive of an individual perspective and taking on a particular voice exploring its relationship with another person, the world, God, or the self. As Constance M. Furey has rightly observed, in the early modern period 'what we

[9] David Manning, 'What was devotional writing? Revisiting the community at Little Gidding, 1626–33', in Elizabeth Clarke and Robert W. Daniel (eds), *People and Piety: Protestant Devotional Identities in Early Modern England* (Manchester, 2012), 25–42, 28.

[10] For useful general discussions of lyric as a genre, see David Lindley, *Lyric* (London, 1985), Scott Brewster, *Lyric* (London, 2009) and Marion Thain (ed.), *The Lyric Poem: Formations and Transformations* (Cambridge, 2013).

[11] Compare George Herbert's poem 'Virtue'—'My musick shows ye have your closes', in Helen Wilcox (ed.), *The English Poems of George Herbert* (Cambridge, 2007), 316.

now describe as self-exploration was a relational dynamic'.[12] In the case of devotional lyrics, this relational approach has some fascinating implications: how far is the speaker to be identified with the author, what is the proper role of rhetorical artifice in the relationship with one's maker, and to what extent is the poet constructing an unreliable perspective on the conversation, in order for it to be corrected and redeemed in the course of the poem?

As we explore these questions in relation to early modern women's devotional lyrics, the interaction of tradition and innovation—the familiar and the new—will become increasingly evident. The quotation in the title of this chapter, 'Sing and let the song be new', is the first line of Mary Sidney's verse translation of Psalm 96; the subsequent line identifies the subject and recipient of that song, 'him that never endeth'.[13] Sidney's opening phrase encapsulates the lyric impulse in her command to 'sing' a devotional 'song' to and about God, a creative act which echoes and continues the biblical tradition of poetic praise. On the other hand, in the same breath she declares that the song must be 'new', freshly reinvented, and rewritten to suit changing contexts and perspectives. All the women whose poetry is celebrated in this chapter were looking both backwards and forwards in their devotional poems: backwards to the established biblical models and preceding poetic or ecclesiastical traditions, but forwards in their realigning of the devotional lyric to suit the expression of female spiritual experiences.[14] In the following two sections, the emphasis in the first will be on preceding sources and traditions for the women's poems of devotion, while the second will be more concerned with the newer aspects of the female devotional voice emerging in their lyrics.

'MY JOY AND ALL MY TREASURE': PRECEDENTS FOR POETIC DEVOTION

Any poet writing about God faces a double dilemma: the knowledge that human language can never be sufficient to match the divine subject, and (paradoxically) the anxiety that anything that can be uttered on the matter has been said before, and probably better. The first of these dilemmas is irresolvable, resulting from the inevitable gap between creature and creator; the sense of inadequacy recurs as a concern and a challenge—indeed, even as a compelling dynamic—in almost every devotional lyric. The second dilemma can be tempered, if not overcome, by turning for inspiration to preceding models of devotional expression. In the Christian tradition, the greatest of

[12] Constance M. Furey, *Poetic Relations: Intimacy and Faith in the English Reformation* (Chicago, IL, 2017), 3.

[13] Mary Sidney, *The Psalms of David*, in Hannibal Hamlin, Michael G. Brennan, Margaret P. Hannay, and Noel J. Kinnamon (eds), *The Sidney Psalter: The Psalms of Sir Philip and Mary Sidney* (Oxford, 2009), 184.

[14] See this volume, Chapter 13, Dianne Mitchell, 'Lyric Backwardness'.

these is the Bible itself, the very text whose language might also mitigate the first dilemma by providing divine words to enable the praise of God who 'in the beginning was the Word'.[15] As Gertrude More wrote in her poem 'To Saint Augustine', God is 'My joy and all my treasure'—both the blissful subject of her verse and the source or treasury of her inspiration.[16] For early modern writers of devotional lyrics, there were two overarching biblical models of poetic engagement with God, both from the Hebrew Bible though interpreted as prefiguring the love of Christ for humanity: the Psalms and the Song of Songs. It is therefore not surprising that the influence of these passionate and richly metaphorical biblical books underpins a great many women's devotional lyrics from the early modern period.[17] What is notable, however, is that female poets not only identified with the 'sweete singer' of the Psalms (to use Southwell's term for David) and the speaker–addressee of the Song of Songs, but also transformed these roles into their own lyric personae and voices, frequently with a particularly gendered slant.

Anne Locke was a sixteenth-century pioneer: the first poet—male or female—to write and publish a sonnet sequence in English, and the first significant female devotional lyricist of the two centuries under discussion here (on the authorship debate, see this volume, Chapter 2, Rosalind Smith, 'Authorship, Attribution, and Voice in Early Modern Women's Writing'). Her sonnets, entitled *A Meditation of a Penitent Sinner*, take their inspiration from Psalm 51, each poem being a paraphrase of a verse of this popular penitential psalm.[18] It is noteworthy that Locke chose to use the sonnet not for secular purposes, as Wyatt and Surrey had done with their occasional sonnets before her, but to rewrite a biblical text and inflect it with her own intense vision. Here, immediately, is an instance of devotional lyrics looking back to familiar sources of inspiration—biblical and literary—while also making something entirely new, both spiritually and poetically, out of it. In spite of this boldness—or perhaps precisely because of it—Locke published her poems anonymously as an appendix to her translation of sermons by Calvin.[19] The material context of the poems, printed along with the work of a great Protestant reformer, alerts us to the vital role of reformed theology in the rise of the devotional lyric: both place special emphasis on the individual's interaction with God. In Locke's sonnets,

[15] John 1.1, *The Bible: Authorized King James Version*, eds Robert Carroll and Stephen Prickett (Oxford, 1997). All subsequent references will be to this edition.

[16] Gertrude More, 'To Saint Augustine', in Robert S. Miola (ed.), *Early Modern Catholicism: An Anthology of Primary Sources* (Oxford, 2007), 252.

[17] For further discussion, see Margaret P. Hannay, '"So may I with the Psalmisty truly say": Early Modern Englishwomen's Psalm discourse', in Barbara Smith and Ursula Appelts (eds), *Write or Be Written: Early Modern Women Poets and Cultural Constraints* (Aldershot, 2001), 105–34, and Elizabeth Clarke, *Politics, Religion and the Song of Songs in the Seventeenth Century* (Basingstoke, 2011).

[18] Preceded by a preface consisting of five sonnets, the sequence consists of twenty-one; in two cases, the first and fourth verses of the Psalm, Locke uses two sonnets (numbers 1–2 and 5–6) to paraphrase one verse. All Locke's sonnets take the form of three quatrains and a couplet, later known as the Shakespearian variety of this lyric sub-genre.

[19] *Sermons of John Calvin, upon the songe that Ezechias made after he had been sicke* (London: 1560). The pages of the sonnet sequence, *A Meditation*, announced with a separate title page after the sermons, are unnumbered.

unlike many other such poems, this relationship is not so much a friendship or loving partnership with God as a hierarchical structure within which the speaker's position is utterly penitent. The insistence and invention of Locke's rhetoric of abjection may be perceived, ironically, to amplify and personalise the argument of abasement. This is all too clear in the rhetorically powerful nineteenth sonnet, which employs a sustained metaphor of starvation: she dreads that the suffering of her 'dyeng hart' may be like that of a 'fainting corps' with a 'starved appetite', to whom food, when it finally comes, is 'offred all in vaine'. Lines 9–10, marking the volta in this anguished yet accomplished sonnet, confirm that the speaker is drawing a parallel with her fear of rejection from God's grace: 'My pining soule for famine of thy grace / So feares alas the faintnesse of my faithe'. Locke's whole sequence effectively conveys an overwhelming impression of what it feels like, physically and spiritually, to suffer from a 'famine' of God's grace. The sonnets are formally accomplished and make effective use of repetition and wordplay, even punning on her own name in Sonnet 11 when pleading with God to 'loke' upon her. Together the poems plead cumulatively, relentlessly, for a glimpse of God's 'face of mercie and swete relefe' (Sonnet 13).

Writing a generation after Locke (whose poems were published in 1560), Mary Sidney also drew upon the Psalms as the inspiration for her devotional lyrics (circulating in manuscript from about 1595). However, whereas Locke's sonnet sequence is a series of meditative paraphrases elaborating upon a single psalm, Sidney's achievement was to translate all 150 psalms, building on, revising, and completing her late brother Philip's unfinished project and crafting the Psalms as lyrics. The metrical and structural ingenuity of Mary Sidney's *Book of Psalms* is such that she barely repeats any stanza forms in more than 170 poems.[20] Its formal invention is perhaps the most striking feature of this remarkable collection of devotional lyrics, giving rise to Hallett Smith's famous description of it as a 'School of English Versification'.[21] However, the technical prowess shown by Sidney should not be allowed critically to overshadow its emotional range and spectrum of devotional moods. As Aemilia Lanyer wrote in 1611, Sidney was admired for 'Her love, her zeale, her faith, and pietie' shown in the psalm translations, but this devotional impact is only made possible by the formal and rhetorical skills that supply its poetic music.[22] One example must suffice here—and to highlight the contrast of moods that are possible within devotional poetry even when inspired by a shared source (Sidney is here translating the same text as Locke paraphrased), this is the opening stanza of Sidney's translation of Psalm 51:

> O Lord, whose grace no limits comprehend;
>   Sweet Lord, whose mercies stand from measure free;

[20] The statistics are those of the Oxford editors; see Sidney, *Psalms*, xxiii.

[21] Hallett Smith, 'English Metrical Psalms in the Sixteenth Century and their Literary Significance', *Huntington Library Quarterly*, 9 (1946), 269.

[22] Lanyer, *Poems*, 29.

To me that grace, to me that mercy send,
    And wipe, O Lord, my sins from sinful me.
    Oh, cleanse, oh, wash, my foul iniquity;
        Cleanse still my spots, still wash away my stainings,
        Till stains and spots in me leave no remainings. (97)

Despite the familiar desire here to be washed from 'foul iniquity', and the (witty) longing for God to take the 'sin' out of 'sinful', the lyrical optimism of this translation shines through Sidney's stanza in contrast to the mortal dread enclosed in Locke's sonnets. In spite of their shared penitential context, the starting point in Sidney's version is limitless grace, the very gift that Locke's speaker fears she has been denied. Sidney's lyric form underlines the hope implicit in this stanza: in a verse 'measure', it is crucial that divine mercies are said to be unlimited, 'from measure free', a belief mirrored in the verse structure as the last word, 'free', is itself set free on the pause at the end of the second line. Similarly, the choice of a so-called 'feminine' rhyme for the closing couplet allows the stanza to lilt to its conclusion, 'stainings' being cheerfully displaced to 'leave no remainings'. The lyric control and beauty of the poem, with its inventive seven-line stanza enabling flexibility of expression in the melody of its metre and the harmony of its rhyme, perfectly matches the devotional focus on what Sidney succinctly describes in the fifth stanza as God's 'breathing grace' (98).

Both Locke and Sidney wrote from a Protestant perspective in the later sixteenth century; Gertrude More, by contrast, was a Catholic nun whose poetry dates from the early seventeenth century. Interestingly, however, she shared with Locke the experience of living and writing abroad, though for reasons that were politically and doctrinally very different: Locke was in Geneva with the Calvinist exiles of the mid-sixteenth century, whereas More was a recusant in the English Benedictine convent in Cambrai (see Jaime Goodrich's chapter in this volume). Despite their theological differences, More understood, as did Locke and Sidney, that devotional poetry was communal as well as singular, and could draw on shared spiritual resources. More was steeped in the rhetoric and liturgical traditions of the old faith, and inspired by the inheritance of Catholic devotion and martyrdom: as the editor of her works wrote (when publishing them posthumously in 1658), Dame Gertrude was the 'pious fspring [sic] of that noble and Glorious Martyr Sir Thomas More, Chancellor of England'.[23] This reassuring sense of precedents, particularly the inspiring lives and writings of the saints, was not only important to her Catholic readers but also infuses her lyrics. In a poem addressed to St Augustine, 'whose heart did burn / And flame with love divine', she implores that writer of 'truly sweet' words to 'Remember me, most sinful wretch'.[24] The focus on Augustine's heart, and not his theology, is revealing: for More, it is the love-filled sweetness of the saint's words that offers hope and comfort. Like so many writers of devotional verse, More perceives her

[23] Dom Augustine Baker, in Dom Augustine Baker (ed.), *The Spiritual Exercises of the Most Vertuous and Religious D. Gertrude More* (Paris, 1658), n.p. (after 104). More was the great-great-granddaughter of Thomas More.

[24] Miola, *Catholicism*, 252.

own poetic efforts as an 'oblation' or offering to God, humbly returning a gift to him and, in doing so, attempting to 'stir up my poor frozen soul / By love itself to raise' (254). Her poems are infused with the language of one who is 'sick with love': in 'A Short Oblation', the speaker borrows a standard trope of secular romance (elevating and cross-dressing it at the same time) by threatening to engrave 'on every tree / The name and praise of him she loves' (254). Elsewhere, in 'Cantum Cygnaeum', she longs to 'enjoy my God, my all', and in eternity to be united with him 'by a knot of love' (251). In this language of the mystical union of the soul with God, More is clearly drawing on another precedent, the Song of Songs; the inspiration of biblical examples was by no means limited to the Protestant poets, central though the Scriptures were to their reformed faith. More's devotional lyrics are shot through with the yearning expressed in the Song of Songs, where the speakers are 'sick' with love and seek fulfilment as expressed in the reciprocal phrase, 'my beloved is mine, and I am his'.[25] In her poem 'If we would die unto ourselves', More employs this scripturally sanctioned language of desire as she sums up her deepest spiritual craving:

> No gifts, or grace, or comforts here,
> How great so e'er they be
> Can satiate my longing soul,
> While I possess not thee. (253)

The intensity of such verse is a reminder of the liberating force that a devotional experience could signify for early modern women—and how the focus of devotional lyrics permitted the written outpouring of female desire in a way that would have been almost unthinkable in a secular setting.

'O REND THE VAIL THROUGHOUT': SINGING A NEW SONG

While Gertrude More was writing lyrics of religious ecstasy in her Continental convent, an unidentified woman was growing up in England who, two decades after More's death, would publish her own collection of devotional poems in the tradition of the Song of Songs. However, this anonymous volume, entitled *Eliza's Babes* (1652), was on the cusp of something new, drawing on the inspiration of preceding examples but, in doing so, creating a radically fresh devotional voice.[26] Whereas More's work seems to be the culmination of a long tradition of mystical writing that includes Julian of Norwich as well

[25] The Song of Songs, 2.5, 2.16. The relationship described is generally interpreted as the mystical marriage between Christ and the church.

[26] *Eliza's Babes: Or the Virgins Offering* (London, 1652). All page references are to this original edition. See also L. E. Semler (ed.), *Eliza's Babes (1652): A Critical Edition* (Madison, NJ, 2001).

as earlier male writers, the poems that are the 'babes' of the unknown 'Eliza' adopt the tropes from the Song of Songs but set them firmly in her contemporary society. These ballad-like verses not only address God as the speaker's lover, but also speak directly to her 'sisters', her readers, challenging them unflinchingly to reassess their worldly lives in her spiritual terms.[27] And if they demur, she briskly tells them that she has no time for their 'odd words':

> All you that goodness doe disdaine,
> Go; read not here:
> And if you do; I tell you plaine,
> I doe not care.
> For why? above your reach my soule is place'st,
> And your odd words shall not my minde distaste. (1)

This is a new voice, merging the spiritual and the social with a down-to-earth and quarrelsome immediacy. Despite this, there is no doubting the devotional nature of her poems, focused as they are on a celestial relationship: as she declares in 'The Rapture', 'I'le arise, and to Heaven goe,—I will not tarry here below' (10), and the reason for this trajectory, given in 'My Robes', is that Christ is 'my Spouse, and my lov'd Lord' (21). The Song of Songs remains the source of her confident verse, but the immediate contexts are social and familial. When the speaker finds that she must marry an earthly husband, she complains to Christ in 'The Gift' that her heart is not available since she has pledged it to him already: 'To thee I onely gave my heart, / Wouldst thou my Lord from that gift part?' (42). Though she later gratefully admits that Christ gave her a husband who possessed 'sweet discretion' (44), it is always Christ of whom she boasts as her 'Lover' (24–5). There is a genuine joy in this relationship, enhanced by a sense of female emancipation, as expressed towards the end of 'The Gift':

> It was my glory I was free,
> And subject here to none but thee,
> And still that glory I shall hold
> If thou my Spirit dost enfold. (43)

In the pen of 'Eliza', devotional lyrics may be those 'babes' that proceed from the 'heavenly dew of grace' (54)—as she claims when answering back 'To a Lady that Bragged of her Children'—but the real energy of her verse appears to derive from a combination of her passion for Christ with a much more worldly sense of feminine freedom and defiance. Where her rival simply has children, Eliza has her poems; where this 'Lady' has a mere earthly husband, Eliza has God.

By the mid-seventeenth century, women's devotional verse seems to achieve a new confidence, in that it still draws richly upon the essential precedents of the Bible and

[27] In one case, this includes rebuking a female friend for her 'naked breasts' (*Eliza's Babes*, 56).

church traditions, but it mingles temporal and spiritual worlds more comfortably together. An Collins' printed collection of *Divine Songs and Meditacions* (1653) includes mainly autobiographically inclined devotional lyrics which create, as she puts it, 'the image of her mind', and her many songs speak of the blessings of God's 'sacred presence'.[28] However, the volume also features 'A Song composed in time of the Civill Warr', lamenting the impact of the 1640s conflict on 'Lady Verity', and looking forward to the 'auspicious dayes' when the 'godly' prevail over the wicked and 'Truth will spread and high appeare' (61, 63). Politics and prayer are never far apart in the devotional lyrics of this period, from whichever side of the divide they emerge. Jane Cavendish, also writing during the English Revolution, tends to merge the presence of her earthly father, the Duke of Newcastle, with the heavenly father to whom she addresses her poems. In 'On the 30th of June, to God' (1643), Cavendish offers God the Father her 'soules devotion' and declares her thanks 'To thee great God who gave thy bounty large / Saveing my Father from the Enemies charge', after Newcastle led the Royalist army to victory in the battle at Adwalton Moor.[29] However, towards the end of the poem, when Cavendish promises to 'keepe this thy victoryes day', the border between the two fathers grows blurred, and precisely whose victory is being celebrated becomes nicely ambiguous. Indeed, Cavendish writes vividly of the perplexing tensions between heaven and earth, faith and despair, and can find herself in two minds as the eternal realm and the transitory but pressing world of everyday temptations collide:

> I have now received thy Sacrament, soe fynd
> The difference 'twixt my soule, and bodies mind
> My soule that hath spoke guilty yet 'tis sav'd
> And yet my bodies mind that still doth rave
> And as I'm clearely wash'd from all my sinn
> Yet doe my mind still harsh dispare suck in. (94)

Here the dialogue of devotional poetry becomes a crowded conversation, as the speaker is joined not only by the addressee of the poem, God, but also by the voice of her own soul and the 'ravings' of her wilful body.

The devotional lyrics written by women in the mid-seventeenth century are significantly greater in number and variety than in the previous century, spanning a range of denominations, poetic modes, moods, and concerns. This may be assigned to several causes, including the gradual increase in women's access to education, the opening up of print culture during the 1640s and 1650s, the enhanced role of women in new branches of the reformed religion such as Baptists and Quakers, and a stronger sense of the place of the humble individual, male or female, in the chorus of devotional voices. This new

[28] An Collins, in Sidney Gottlieb (ed.), *An Collins: Divine Songs and Meditacions* (Tempe, AZ, 1996), 9, 47.

[29] Jane Cavendish, in Jill Seal Millman and Gillian Wright (eds), *Early Modern Women's Manuscript Poetry* (Manchester, 2005), 93.

self-awareness, which might be thought of as 'rending the Vail' (to borrow the phrase of Mary Mollineux cited at the start of this section) may be exemplified poetically in the writings of Elizabeth Major.[30] The few poems published in her devotional volume, *Honey on the Rod* (1656), combine humility with self-expression, ingenious and accomplished formal structures. Delighting in acrostics and anagrams, she uses three devices in one poem, entitled 'The Authors Prayer': words from the text of her simple prayer form the opening of each line; an acrostic of her own name is embedded as the opening letters of the last word of each line, and the whole poem, despite the complexity of being framed in this way, is a perfect sonnet. Finding a unique poetic form to embody herself and encompass her devotion, Major breaks new ground.[31] Mary Carey, on the other hand, who was also writing in the 1650s, did seem able to let go of herself, as well as to accept, sorrowfully, the loss of a baby; her elegies on the deaths of her children acknowledge her fate with almost distressingly complete submission to God. Yet here too we may discern a new boldness, a bargaining with God, even in the depths of despair. In 'Upon the Sight of my abortive Birth', Carey works her way painfully through maternal grief to reach a moment of outspoken questioning of God's purpose: 'I only now desire of my sweet God, / The Reason why he took in hand his Rod?'[32] Crucially, the experience recounted in this intense and powerful poem, and Carey's challenge to God, are both profoundly female: after making her supplications to God, she prays, 'Let not my heart, (as doth my Womb) miscarry' (57). The insecurity of the devotional voice is potentially identified with the weakness of a female body, the miscarrying womb, thus giving the heart and mind greater freedom to engage in debate with God.

The newness of early modern women's devotional poetry, then, takes many forms: the boldness of biblical appropriation, the merging of secular and sacred, the range of poetic invention, and the intensifying of gendered perspectives on faith and experience. I would suggest two further aspects of 'letting the song be new': poetic ambition, and the expression of new aspects of belief. The poems of Julia Palmer, written between 1671 and 1673, signify an enormous undertaking: two 'Centuries' of devotional lyrics make up a body of original verse even larger than that of Mary Sidney's psalms. Palmer would have regarded her writing as a means of accounting for herself before God, akin to the writing of diaries, journals, and conversion narratives so fundamental to the development of Protestant spirituality. Each lyric painstakingly observes an aspect of faith or an experience of the soul, as a sample of their titles reveals: 'Christ a perfect pattern, & compleat saviour'; 'The souls complaint from a sence of its inntabilyty, and unconstancy, in this imperfect state', or, perhaps most representatively, 'The soull reaching out after what it

[30] Mary Mollineux, *Fruits of Retirement* (London, 1702), 147.

[31] See Elizabeth Major, *Honey on the Rod* (London, 1656), 191. Mary Sidney uses acrostic devices in her psalm translation—there is nothing missing from her formal armoury—but her poems take *David's* prayer as their starting point, rather than, in Major's case, her own.

[32] Oxford, Bodleian Library, Rawlinson MS D.1308, fol. 114r–117v, cited from Rachel Adcock, Sara Read, and Anna Ziomek (eds), *Flesh and Spirit: An Anthology of Seventeenth-Century Women's Writing* (Manchester, 2014), 55.

most desires'.[33] Gone are the otherwise untitled 'Songs' of the late sixteenth and earlier seventeenth century, with their complex lyric stanza forms; each of Palmer's poems carefully announces a specific focus or purpose, many are dated as in a spiritual diary, and all are written in what might be called the Presbyterian plain style. Though her poems represent the journal of an individual soul, and remained in manuscript until this century, in fact their clarity of manner is akin to that of the congregational hymn. The female devotional lyric has evolved with the religious and sociopolitical developments of the era and taken on an accessible simplicity. However, the understated power of Palmer's verse can surprise and arrest the reader, as in the opening stanza of 'Admirings of Christ & longings to be with him':

> Oh my redeemer dear
> How excelent thou art
> Oh that thou wouldest, now draw neer,
> To iradiate every part. (10)

Amidst the vocabulary of adoration, the verb 'iradiate' bursts like the very illumination for which the speaker pleads—all the more effectively because of the unpretentiousness of the surrounding language. Palmer's lyrics strive to achieve what she wonderfully describes as a 'holy familiarity' with God in her poem 'On praer': by the 'art' of her prayerful and apparently artless lyrics, she hopes to 'wind' her way into the heart of her saviour (51).

The intimate tone of Palmer's 'Centuries' is a salutary reminder that the devotional lyric remains, at its core, love poetry—and with all the potential for the shifting of moods, from praise and joy to anger, sorrow, and despair, that is so integral to human relationships. Yet still this genre retains its capacity to say something fresh and new, especially in the hands of the women who took to it and moulded it in the early modern period. At the very end of the seventeenth century, Mary Mollineux, a Lancashire Quaker, wrote a series of devotional poems published posthumously as *Fruits of Retirement: or Miscellaneous Poems, Moral and Divine* (1702), a volume whose subtitle hints at the move away from intimate devotion towards the more 'moral' public voice heard in religious poems of the eighteenth century. Mollineux's lyric, 'Retirement' is a devotional rather than doctrinal or moralising verse, and still draws strongly upon the inspiration of the Song of Songs. Despite the pre-Augustan ideal of 'Retirement' hinted at in the book's title, Mollineux's poem plays on the double meaning of its own title: the speaker desires the soothing retirement of 'A Solitary Place to ease my Mind', but the poem actually originates in a sense that God has 'withdrawn' or retired from her reach, leaving her oppressed by her own '*Wounds*' and '*Stains*'.[34] In the absence of God, the speaker adopts an all too familiar posture of abjection, though here with an added

[33] Los Angeles, Clark Library, MS P1745 M1 P744 1671–1673, cited from Julia Palmer, in Victoria Burke and Elizabeth Clarke (eds), *The 'Centuries' of Julia Palmer* (Nottingham, 2001), 41, 143, 77.

[34] Mollineux, *Fruits*, 146.

gendered inflection: 'Lord, cast thine Eye upon a Worm, whose State / Is even like a Widow desolate!' (147) This feminised speaker desires to see the '*Resplendent Beams*' of her Lord, the 'Great Spring of Light'—imagery given a new urgency in the context of the central focus on light in Quaker belief. The speaker is desperate to show and put to the test her 'Zeal', 'Fervour', and 'Sincerity' (147), a new vocabulary of sentiment and enthusiasm that marks the turning of the era. When she urges her 'Lord' to 'rend the Vail throughout' (147), this ostensible reference to the tearing of the veil of the temple on the first Good Friday becomes a metaphor for removing the obstacles that would separate her from God's love. It also resounds as an image for all that the lyrics of early modern women instigated in the language and experience of devotion.

'CAST US NOT AWAIE': A LEGACY OF LYRICS

These lyric voices are simply a sample of the work of the numerous female devotional poets who found a significant mode of poetic self-expression through their religious experience in the sixteenth and seventeenth centuries. We have seen how their writing was retrospective, drawing extensively on textual precedents such as the Bible, church liturgy, and earlier poets, both male and—in the later generations—female.[35] Yet in almost all cases they were also looking firmly forwards, writing verse that was pioneering in form, in focus, and in the perspective from which they viewed their spiritual and material worlds. Indeed, the legacy of their poetry is vital and varied. Although the quoted examples have all been in English, we should not forget that early modern women from Great Britain also wrote devotional lyrics in Latin, Greek, French, Scottish Gaelic, and Welsh (see this volume, Chapter 26, Sarah Prescott, 'Archipelagic Feminism').[36] The poets span not only the denominational range from Roman Catholic to Quaker, but also the full political spectrum, particularly in the turbulent years of the mid-seventeenth century. The immediate settings of their writings were also immensely varied, from Gertrude More's French convent to Jane Cavendish's besieged Welbeck Abbey, and the differences of social rank are indicated by the grandeur of Wilton House, in which Mary Sidney translated the Psalms, in contrast to the lowliness of a Presbyterian preacher's household in Westminster, where Julia Palmer wrote her lyrics. The starting-point of

[35] For example: Locke is sure to have known the work of earlier sonneteers; Mary Sidney is likely to have been aware of Locke's paraphrases; Lanyer and others drew on the model of Mary Sidney's *Psalms*; Collins, 'Eliza', and Palmer were clearly influenced by George Herbert, while Herbert himself was inspired by Mary Sidney.

[36] Poets using vernacular languages other than English include Catrin Ferch Gruffydd ap Hywel o Llanddeniolen, Esther Inglis, Katherine Killigrew, Elizabeth Melville, Lilias Skene, and Jane Vaughan. See also Jane Stevenson and Peter Davidson (eds), *Early Modern Women Poets: An Anthology* (Oxford, 2001).

devotional verse was often spiritual anxiety or biblical comfort, though they were also occasioned by personal or domestic events such as the prospect of marriage in the case of 'Eliza' and the devastating loss of Mary Carey's children. Had space permitted here, we could also have seen religious lyrics triggered by the unhappy seclusion of Hester Pulter in a country grange, Christmas celebrations in the household of Anna Ley, and Frances Cooke's miraculous escape from a shipwreck.[37] There is very little that is dull or even predictable in this deceptively straightforward genre.

Many questions remain to be pondered by modern readers of this remarkable body of what Anne Southwell called 'Devine Poesye'. It is important to consider, for example, how these poems reached us, whether through early modern printing, either contemporary or posthumous (Major and More, for example), through circulation and as a presentation manuscript (Sidney), or through the recent rediscovery of preserved family manuscripts (Pulter and Palmer). Were the works published anonymously (Locke), pseudonymously ('Eliza'), or with full acknowledgement of the female author (Mollineux)? Some lyrics emerged by less direct routes, such as musical settings (Sidney) or, in the case of the poems of Elizabeth Tyrwhit, their inclusion in Thomas Bentley's 1582 compendium volume, *The Monument of Matrones*, a fascinating early modern source of texts by women as well as ideas about them. Tyrwhit's 'Hymne of the daie of judgment' includes the phrase 'cast us not awaie', addressed by Tyrwhit to Christ but used in the title of this section to remind us not to cast away or overlook the poetic legacy discussed here.[38] In valuing the work of these women devotional poets—and continuing to seek out further examples of it—we need to keep a number of issues in mind. Where we see (to borrow Mary Sidney's phrase again) the 'song' being sung 'new' and developments emerging in the genre across a period of a century and a half, to what extent are these phenomena specific to women writers, or to the devotional lyric, as opposed to being inherent in the patterns of literary or religious history? While we might perceive the transition from the sonnet to the hymn, for instance, as part of a wider stylistic shift, it is crucial to note that women writers (Locke in one case and Palmer in the other) were in fact in the forefront of both these formal innovations rather than following trends set by others. Several of the poets under discussion also actively participated in the aesthetic debate on the place of artistry in the poetic expression of devotion, a controversial subject for the early modern church as well as among writers: while An Collins declared that 'want of skill' as a poet was less 'blameworthy' than 'want of good will', Julia Palmer put her trust in the 'holy art' of her prayerful words.[39] Above all, whether they are (paradoxically) expressing unadorned penitence in a perfectly

[37] See Hester Pulter, in Alice Eardley (ed.), *Hester Pulter: Poems, emblems and the unfortunate Florinda* (Toronto, 2014); Anna Ley, in Millman and Wright (eds), *Manuscript Poetry*, 77–86; Frances Cooke, *Mris. Cookes meditations* (London, 1650). For the poems of Hester Pulter see also this volume, Chapter 8, Leah Knight, 'Libraries Not Their Own' and this volume, Chapter 13, Dianne Mitchell, 'Lyric Backwardness'.

[38] Elizabeth Tyrwhit, 'Hymne of the daie of judgment', in Thomas Bentley (ed.), *The Monument of Matrones* (London, 1582), 131.

[39] Collins, *Divine Songs*, 9; Palmer, *'Centuries'*, 51.

formed sonnet or unfolding complex spiritual ideas in disarmingly familiar language, the contradictions and challenges of devotional lyrics are magnificently on display in the poetry of these early modern women. Their exploration of devotional experience in lyrical verse was no doubt largely intended for the sake of God and their own souls, and perhaps for the comfort and enlightenment of their contemporaries, but it is now rightly recognised as an enrichment of the literary canon and a delight to readers in our own day.

FURTHER READING

Clarke, Elizabeth. *Politics, Religion and the Song of Songs in the Seventeenth Century.* Basingstoke, 2011.

Coles, Kimberly Anne. *Religion, Reform, and Women's Writing in Early Modern England* Cambridge, 2008.

Longfellow, Erica. *Women and Religious Writing in Early Modern England.* Cambridge, 2004.

Molekamp, Femke. *Women and the Bible in Early Modern England: Religious Reading and Writing.* Oxford, 2013.

Smith, Barbara and Ursula Appelts (eds). *Write or Be Written: Early Modern Women Poets and Cultural Constraints.* Aldershot, 2001.

CHAPTER 13

LYRIC BACKWARDNESS

DIANNE MITCHELL

In an imagined conversation between two of Hester Pulter's daughters, the younger sister gives voice to a startling concept: a future that is indistinguishable from what has come before.

> And if what's future prove like what is past,
> I'll patient be; I can but die at last.
>
> (Hester Pulter, 'A Dialogue Between Two Sisters, Virgins Bewailing Their Solitary Life', 51–2)[1]

Likely composed during the last years of the English Civil Wars or the early Interregnum, the poem's vision of continuity seems curiously out of joint with the fast-changing political landscape of mid-seventeenth-century England. Yet, by situating her daughters within a *literal* landscape, Pulter invokes alternate models of temporality more suited to an isolated female life. In the 'Dialogue', the fading primroses and pruned cypress tree on which Anne and Penelope Pulter gaze become symbols of the speakers' diminishing hope for a life outside 'sad obscurity' (45). For these sisters, futurity signals not progress but more of the same.

This chapter contends that there is something backward about the forms of early modern women's poetry. For many, the adjective 'backward' will summon terms like 'retrograde' or 'archaic', invoking the seeming belatedness of Mary Wroth's choice of the sonnet form or the 'quaint' spellings, reproduced in conservative editions, that cause poets like Anne Southwell to feel hopelessly 'embedded in … [their] own original period'.[2] But as the increasing accessibility of female-authored lyrics has compelled

[1] In Leah Knight and Wendy Wall (eds), *The Pulter Project: Poet in the Making* (2018), Northwestern University, http://pulterproject.northwestern.edu, accessed 13 November 2020. All quotations are from the Elemental Editions.

[2] Leah Marcus, 'Editing Queen Elizabeth I', in Sarah C. E. Ross and Paul Salzman (eds), *Editing Early Modern Women's Writing* (Cambridge, 2016), 139–55, 143. For example, Christopher Warley assesses Mary Wroth's gendered reversal of subjectivity as 'just a particularly obvious and clunky version' of a

increased attention to their formal effects, women poets have proven alert to both tradition and trend.[3] Paradoxically, it is their very innovations that can cause friction. As Liza Blake has argued, the historic centrality to literary studies of exemplary male lyricists like John Donne has generated a particular set of interpretive tools, not all of which are effective for close-reading a poem like Pulter's 'Dialogue'.[4] Those of us cued, for instance, to elide the dialogic form with disagreement might miss how Pulter transforms it into a source of mutual consolation. Drawn from conventions of feminine complaint poetry, the daughters' exchange seems less invested in persuasion than in a kind of consciousness-raising.

By referring to poetry by early modern women as backward, then, I signal and celebrate its divergence from lyric 'norms' calcified by a scholarly tradition that has historically excluded women's writing. But I also want to ask how formalist criticism might better heed the perverse trajectories pursued by these lyrics. Pulter's invocation of a future that merely repeats the past is just one moment in the female poetic canon that resists a logic of progress or forward motion. Fortunately, methods not traditionally seen as formalism's allies—queer theory and the history of material texts—offer compelling models for recuperating the formally recalcitrant. This chapter draws on these critical strands to argue for backwardness as a meaningful condition of early modern women's lyric. Extending our understanding of form to accommodate effects of textual materiality, temporal delay, or authorial affect, we realise how often women's poems work against long-held ideals of linearity and progress, demanding a richer set of assumptions.

This chapter traces three related kinds of formal 'backwardness' across a trio of authors working partly or entirely in manuscript—sometimes seen as a 'backward-looking' medium—during the first half of the seventeenth century. The first section considers the 'negative, shameful, and difficult' feelings Heather Love influentially terms 'feeling backward'.[5] Exploring Wroth's and Pulter's reluctance to 'move on', it argues that these poets elide forward momentum with injury, preferring alternative emotional trajectories. Next, it considers the temporal backwardness of Pulter's and Southwell's lyrics. If these poets betray strange intimacies with the past, I suggest, it is because their

'move' practised since Petrarch himself; see 'Un-canonizing Lady Mary Wroth?', in *Arcade: Literature, the Humanities, & the World* (2010), Stanford University, https://arcade.stanford.edu/blogs/un-canonizing-lady-mary-wroth, accessed 16 November 2020. Warley cites the claim that Wroth's poetry is 'boring—conventional and repetitious'; see Elizabeth Hanson, 'Boredom and Whoredom: Reading Renaissance Women's Sonnet Sequences', *The Yale Journal of Criticism*, 10 (1997), 165–91, 166.

[3] Elizabeth Scott-Baumann, *Forms of Engagement: Women, Poetry, and Culture 1640–1680* (Oxford, 2013). By accessibility, I refer both to the increased availability of digital surrogates and to the availability of modern-spelling print and digital editions of women writers.

[4] Liza Blake, 'Reading Poems (and Fancies): An Introduction to Margaret Cavendish's *Poems and Fancies*', in Liza Blake (ed.), *Margaret Cavendish's Poems and Fancies: A Digital Critical Edition* (2019), University of Toronto, http://library2.utm.utoronto.ca/poemsandfancies/introduction-to-cavendishs-poems-and-fancies/, accessed 16 November 2020.

[5] Heather Love, *Feeling Backward: Loss and the Politics of Queer History* (Cambridge, MA, 2007), 127.

practices of composition and compilation generate radically unlinear models of time. Finally, the chapter asks how the materiality of Southwell's and Wroth's extant poetic manuscripts can incite literal modes of backward reading. Where will these poets take us if we follow rather than resist their backward turns?

FEELING BACKWARD

Renaissance sonnets are full of bad feelings. Despair, shame, losses repeated so often they begin to feel desired—all are built-in components of what we might think of as the ultimate lyric technology of self-harm.[6] Yet, even among the masochistic English sonnets of the 1590s and early 1600s, Mary Wroth's collection known as *Pamphilia to Amphilanthus* has felt to readers unusual in its negative affects. Constant to an ideal of love that causes psychic and even physical pain (the sonnets memorably begin with Venus shoving a burning heart inside the cavity of its speaker's breast), Wroth's persona seems incapable of sustaining joy or hope for more than a few lines. When combined with Wroth's authorial preference for syntactical and emotional indirection, the effect has been described as one of 'retreat' into a place so dark it is inscrutable.[7]

What is the payoff for reading poems that afford neither clarity nor psychological resolution?[8] According to a recent editor of Wroth's manuscript lyrics, Wroth's interpretive challenges are designed to occlude evidence of an incestuous love affair so explosive that its traces had to be censored out of the 1621 printed version of the sonnets.[9] Yet, buying into the biographical premise of this argument—that Wroth's lyrics are 'dramatic' and 'suspenseful' because they disguise a rich, if thwarted, erotic life—comes at the cost of the very shadowed effects that shape Wroth's poetic forms.[10] Read instead as a virtuosically crafted script for feminine survival, these lyrics stand out precisely for their refusals: of comfort, of recovery, of progress in any sense.

[6] Melissa Sanchez, '"In My Selfe the Smart I Try": Female Promiscuity in *Astrophil and Stella*', *English Literary History*, 80 (2013), 1–27. On the 'estranging' potential of sonnets' negative affects, see Jyotsna G. Singh, '"Th'expense of spirit in a waste of shame": Mapping the "Emotional Regime" of Shakespeare's Sonnets', in Michael Schoenfeldt (ed.), *A Companion to Shakespeare's Sonnets* (Oxford, 2007), 277–89, 288.

[7] Nona Fienberg, 'Mary Wroth and the Invention of Female Poetic Subjectivity', in Naomi J. Miller and Gary Waller (eds), *Reading Mary Wroth: Representing Alternatives in Early Modern England* (Knoxville, TN, 1991), 175–90, 176.

[8] On Wroth's 'intentional opacity', see Paul Salzman, 'Not Understanding Mary Wroth's Poetry', *Parergon*, 29 (2012), 133–48, 135.

[9] Ilona Bell, '"Joy's Sports": The Unexpurgated Text of Mary Wroth's *Pamphilia to Amphilanthus*', *Modern Philology*, 111 (2013), 231–52.

[10] Bell, '"Joy's Sports"', 231.

Wroth's eighth sonnet exemplifies the poet's disconcerting willingness (in Bronwyn Wallace's evocative phrase) to 'cohabit with loss' rather mastering it:[11]

> Led by the powre of griefe, to waylings brought
>   by faulce consiete of change fall'ne on my part,
>   I seeke for some smale ease by lines, which bought
>   increaseth paine; griefe is nott cur'd by art:
>
> Ah! how unkindness moves within the hart
>   which still is true, and free from changing thought
>   What unknowne woe itt breeds; what endles smart
>   with ceasles teares which causelessly ar brought.
>
> Itt makes mee now to shunn all shining light,
>   and seeke for blackest clouds mee light to give,
>   which to all others, only darknes drive,
>   they on me shine, for sunn disdaines my sight
>
> Yett though I darke do live I triumph may
> Unkindness, nor this wrong shall love allay. (Sonnet 8, 1–14; *Pamphilia*)[12]

As Love observes, 'it is hard to know what to do with texts that resist our advances'.[13] Wroth's persona's 'ceasles teares' (8) and preference for shunning (9) rather than embracing undermine the feminist fantasy that premodern women writers are reaching towards us with the same desire for intimate contact that we bring to them. Like the queer modernist writings Love explores—texts whose 'passivity, escapism, self-hatred, withdrawal, bitterness, defeatism, and loneliness' mark their authors' sense of being painfully out of joint with their own times—Sonnet 8 demands of its readers not the possibility of repair but a willingness to feel as 'backward' as its speaker.[14] Yet, in experiencing with Wroth's speaker a near-permanent state of crisis, we learn something important: that moving forward, far from being desirable, is a trap.

From the first words of Sonnet 8, 'Led by the powre of grief' (1), Wroth associates momentum with injury. Her speaker is 'brought' to 'waylings'—an emotional state couched as an undesirable destination—by something or someone she calls 'faulce consiete of change' (2). Desiring what she terms 'some smale ease by lines' (3), Wroth's poetic persona finds to her dismay that writing only 'increaseth paine' (4). This is an incredible claim. Rather than enabling mental catharsis, the constituent materials of

[11] Bronwyn Wallace, 'Intimate Exegesis: Reading and Feeling in Early Modern Devotional Literature' (PhD Diss., University of Pennsylvania, 2015), 107. Wallace is referring to Amelia Lanyer's lyrics, but her chapters on Lanyer and Anne Locke trace and model a feminist hermeneutics of bad feeling.

[12] Ilona Bell and Steven May (eds), *Pamphilia to Amphilanthus in Manuscript and Print* (Toronto, 2017). I have expanded Wroth's abbreviations (preserved in Bell and May's edition) for ease of reading.

[13] Love, *Feeling Backward*, 8.

[14] Love, *Feeling Backward*, 4.

lyric are reduced here to 'lines', a false trajectory the poet nonetheless feels compelled, punishingly, to follow. But if Sonnet 8 exposes the lie that 'griefe' can be 'cur'd by art' (4), it also encodes its own practices of resistance to what Wallace calls 'the propulsive force of form'.[15] In the context of the 'driv[ing]' motion Wroth's speaker associates with 'others' (11), her repetition of the rhyme ending 'brought' (1, 8) becomes a subtle act of rebellion, privileging reiteration over novelty even at the risk of repeating past injuries. Indeed, a cancellation in the manuscript suggests that this poem has actually become more reiterative over time: line 8 originally read 'ceaseles teares which causelessly *ai wrought*' (emphasis mine). This 'lost' version shows us a poet actively choosing the 'darke' (13) over the unwelcome force of 'shining light' (9). For in the face of the bleak future promised by the movement of 'unkindness' within the heart (5), Wroth's persona doubles down on her commitment to 'shady, murky modes of undoing, un-becoming, and violating'.[16] To those who would demand a more seemly emotional plasticity, Wroth merely reverses the valuations aligned with lyric imagery of despair. Black clouds are recoded as a light source; the words 'shine' and 'sunn' (12) collapse into the verb 'shunn' (9), a motion distinct from being 'led' by grief (1). 'Triumph' (13), for Wroth's speaker, is thus bound up with a form of negative persistence. To read this as no triumph at all is to reject her very terms of survival.

The backward feelings Wroth's sonnets invoke and provoke resonate within the emergent canon of early modern women's lyric. This is not to say that only female poets favour positions of loss and isolation. Nor should woman authored lyrics be seen as bleakly monochromatic. Yet, one cannot help but be struck by the frequency with which elegy, complaint, or spiritual introspection jump the boundaries of genre within the corpus of women's poetry to take on the status of overarching moods or dispositions. We do a disservice to these authors if we fail to acknowledge that the 'triumph' of early modern women's increasing prominence in scholarship and teaching is bound up with the requirement to close read almost unendurable scenes of hurt.

One compelling body of work for readers willing to take on the risks of feeling backward are the lyrics of Hester Pulter. Entering our purview belatedly, Pulter's collection missed the politicised, often affirming, wave of early feminist recovery efforts. Consequently, her readers have not shied away from the melancholia and suicidal urges that permeate Pulter's lines.[17] The evocatively titled 'Universal Dissolution, Made When I Was with Child, of my 15th Child, my Son, John, I Being, Everyone Thought, in a Consumption, 1648' is representative of Pulter's fatalistic collection in its effortless shuttling between an embrace of embodied personal loss and a more 'Universal' acknowledgement of mankind's fragility. The poem opens:

15 Wallace, 'Intimate Exegesis', 85.

16 Jack (Judith) Halberstam, *The Queer Art of Failure* (Durham, NC, 2011), 4.

17 See, for instance, Alice Eardley, '"Saturn (whose aspects soe sads my soule)": Lady Hester Pulter's Feminine Melancholic Genius', in Michael Denbo (ed.), *New Ways of Looking at Old Texts, IV: Papers of the Renaissance English Text Society, 2002–2006* (Tempe, AZ, 2008), 239–54.

My soul, why art thou sad at the decay
Of this frail frame, this feeble house of clay?
What can be expected from the humble birth
Of this frail fabric, but to fall to earth? ('Universal Dissolution', 1–4)

Notable here is Pulter's repetition of 'frail', first deployed to indicate the particular condition of her exhausted maternal body, then used to gesture to the grossly corporeal nature of humankind. These opening couplets play virtuosically, in short, with scale. Pulter's reiterative use of the device of the rhetorical question suggests that unsparing self-scrutiny shares its work with the pursuits—frequently coded masculine—of philosophical meditation or religious speculation.

Pulter's elision thus offers a provocation. What if we were to treat the intellectual and spiritual life of the early modern period as intimately bound up with the lyric forms of women's sadness? What if, no less than the break with Rome or the founding of the Royal Society, the feminised conditions of chronic illness, child- or friend-loss, marital unhappiness, physical and emotional isolation, and political helplessness—all experiences evoked by Pulter, Wroth, and her contemporaries—informed the developments that make our period the early *modern*? What if, finally, the sense of forward motion we call 'progress' cannot be separated from the backward feelings that suffuse the female-authored elegy, epitaph, or complaint? Without losing sight of these questions, I would like to turn now to another deviant trajectory: temporal backwardness. More particularly, I will ask how women's backward looks generate alternative ways of navigating and residing in time.

LOOKING BACKWARD

In his comprehensive *Theory of the Lyric*, Jonathan Culler proposes as one of lyric's defining features its capacity to usher in a kind of 'lyric present', a period he terms 'the special "now"' of lyric utterance.[18] The idea that one of lyric's superpowers is to pause or slow time is compelling. Yet, it falters when confronted with poems such as 'Universal Dissolution, Made When I Was with Child, of my 15th Child, my Son, John, I Being, Everyone Thought, in a Consumption, 1648', one of Pulter's many verses whose retrospective glance effectively scatters the lyric present into several distinct moments. How should we understand such poems, predicated not on an ability to stop time, but on the need to continually renegotiate a relationship with the past?

Pulter's title situates composition at a moment in time that is not the poet's own. The fact that Pulter can name and sex the child she was creating as she 'Made' the poem suggests that this is a retrospective title, added when Pulter was compiling her lyrics

[18] Jonathan Culler, *Theory of the Lyric* (Cambridge, MA, 2015), 226.

for transcription into the manuscript that is her writings' sole witness.[19] The messy realities of manuscript 'publication'—the preferred medium for many (though not all) early modern women—thus complicate still further the ideal of a lyric present, with its fantasy that lyric utterance and lyric materiality inevitably overlap. When Pulter refers to herself, for instance, as 'Being, Everyone Thought, in a Consumption', she retroactively applies a particular state of embodiment to her poem, suggesting that her work is recognisably shaped by the wasting disease she endured. Yet, the poem's odd material expansion—four lines have been added in the margin, likely closer to the period of the poem's transcription than to its original composition—work against the image of 'Consumption' which the title evokes. Pulter's puzzling qualification 'Everyone Thought' simultaneously calls into question the very experience implied to have prompted the poem's melancholy reflections.

Pulter's ambivalence towards temporal linearity emerges especially acutely in her elegies. Precisely because elegies often bewail lives curtailed 'before their time', poems such as Pulter's moving elegy for her daughter Jane could be read as laments as much for a normative temporal progression as for an individual. Consequently, such lyrics might seem to shore up rather than disrupt the social and biopolitical 'lockstep' of generational progression to which a queer understanding of time is opposed.[20] Yet, one cannot help but wonder if the expectations of generational continuity that define 'straight time' really obtain for Pulter, who was predeceased by thirteen of her fifteen children. Indeed, the sheer volume of extant Renaissance child elegies suggests that these losses were part of the 'fabric' (to use Pulter's term) of familial temporalities.

For Pulter, elegy thus offers the ideal medium in which to question time's perceived relation to emotion. 'Upon the Death of My Dear and Lovely Daughter Jane Pulter' marks the second anniversary of the passing of Pulter's twenty-year-old child. Yet, it simultaneously rejects the commonplace that grief can be bounded within limits calculable by one's temporal distance from an occasion of loss. As Elizabeth Zeman Kolkovich shows, Pulter's near-identical couplets 'Yet still my heart is overwhelmed with grief / And tears (alas) gives sorrow no relief' (13–14) and 'Yet still my heart is overwhelmed with grief, / And time, nor tears, will give my woes relief' (21–2) talk back to a long tradition of injunctions to temper maternal despair. What Pulter's temporally charged and five-times repeated phrase 'twice hath' (as in 'Twice hath the Earth thrown Chloris' mantle by' (7)) stubbornly insists, then, is not that life goes on, but precisely that it does not.[21] Instead, the cyclical rotations of the earth, migrations of birds, and movements of heavenly bodies Pulter codes as natural only emphasise the poet's dislocation in time. When she confesses, 'My heart to heaven with her bright spirit flies / Whilst she (ah me!) closed up her lovely eyes' (55–6), Pulter's mixing of present and past tense ('flies', 'closed')

[19] Leeds, Brotherton Collection, MS Lt q 32.

[20] Eve Kosofsky Sedgwick, *Touching Feeling: Affect, Pedagogy, Performativity* (Durham, NC, 2003), 147. See also Carla Freccero, 'Queer Times', *South Atlantic Quarterly*, 106 (2007), 485–94, 489.

[21] Elizabeth Zeman Kolkovich, 'In Defense of Indulgence: Hester Pulter's Maternal Elegies', *Journal for Early Modern Cultural Studies*, 20.2 (2020), 43–70.

gives the impression of being temporally fractured by Jane's death. Reflecting on Jane's corpse prompts a reciprocal response in her own body, repeated as often as she thinks on Jane: 'my sad heart, for her still pining, dies' (26).

In Pulter's elegies, inscribing 'a past that does not understand itself as a past' becomes a powerful (and often politicised) act of rewitnessing.[22] Yet, Anne Southwell's epitaph on her friend Cicely, Lady Ridgeway suggests that absence from—or unawareness of—a scene of past loss can equally provoke a temporal crisis in verse. Crucially, Southwell's lyric responds both to Ridgeway's death and to Southwell's own earlier poem for Ridgeway. In 'An Elegie written by the Lady A. S. to the Countesse of London Derrye supposyenge hir to be dead by hir long silence', Southwell had playfully attempted to resume contact with an uncommunicative correspondent, unaware that Ridgeway really was deceased at the time of writing. Southwell's subsequent epitaph recasts this period of ignorance as one of subconscious knowledge. Her lyric thus attempts an unusual compensatory gesture: the creation of a sense of retrospective dismay.

Southwell's epitaph opens with a self-rebuke:

> Now let my pen bee choakt with gall,
> since I have writt propheticall
> I wondred, that the world did looke,
> of late, like an unbayted hooke
> Or as a well, whose springe was dead
> I knew not, that her soule was fledd. ('An Epitaph', 1–6)[23]

While female-authored mourning poems often express a desire for release through weeping or inarticulate cries, Southwell's lyric describes instead a wish for blockage: 'let my pen bee choakt with gall' (1).[24] The word 'gall' refers to bile or bitterness, but it reminds us that oak galls were a common ingredient in ink recipes. Might a gall-choked pen have produced the 'blotted lines' (13) Southwell self-consciously describes in her earlier 'Elegie'? Southwell's inditement of her own (in hindsight) 'propheticall' (2) verse recalls Wroth's contention that the material act of generating 'lines' only 'increaseth pain' (Sonnet 8, 4). For both poets, the labour of composition becomes a source of harm, one that demands mitigating strategies.

Southwell's approach is to revisit the period she twice terms 'of late' (4, 9). Precisely because its referent is so vague, 'of late' becomes a temporal arena ripe for reinscription.

[22] Penelope Anderson and Whitney Sperrazza, 'Feminist Queer Temporalities in Aemilia Lanyer and Lucy Hutchinson', in Merry E. Wiesner-Hanks (ed.), *Gendered Temporalities in the Early Modern World* (Amsterdam, 2018), 159–84, 165. On the politics of Pulter's elegies, see Sarah C. E. Ross, *Women, Poetry and Politics in Seventeenth-Century Britain* (Oxford, 2015), 135–78.

[23] Jane Stevenson and Peter Davidson (eds), *Early Modern Women Poets: An Anthology* (Oxford, 2001). In Southwell's manuscript, Washington, DC, Folger MS V.b. 198, fol. 21r, the epitaph is erroneously titled 'An Epitaph, uppon Cassandra Mac Willms wife to Sr Thomas Ridgway Earle of London Derry by ye Lady A. S.'.

[24] See, for instance, the 'piercing groans' and 'gasping numbers' of Katherine Philips' 'Orinda Upon Little Hector Philips', in Ross and Scott-Baumann (eds), *Women Poets of the English Civil War* (Manchester, 2018), 198.

Writing in the wake of this blurry expanse, the poet depicts it as a time of such disjointedness that it made her 'wonder' (3), a verb that combines the act of marvelling with a more negative state of doubt. Southwell's uneasy image of a world 'like an unbayted hooke' (3) invokes a sensation of dread and thwartedness.[25] Yet, even as her subsequent metaphor of a well without a source doubles this feeling of dysfunction, the syntactical ambiguity of the phrase '*as* a well' (5, emphasis mine) suspends the possibility that Southwell, the 'I' of the following line, is also eliding *herself* with the defunct water source. The poet thus becomes her own object of wonderment, caught up in the temporal flux the epitaph unfolds as well as in the queer landscape evoked by a line structure that equates Ridgeway's departed 'soule' (6) with Southwell's longed-for 'springe' (5).[26]

It is hard to know whether to read the suicidal desire with which Southwell concludes her epitaph for Ridgeway—'I'le prayse noe more, hir blest condicion, / But follow hir, with expedition' (15–16)—as an effect of the poet's grief or a response to her uncanny sensation of belated temporal reckoning. Southwell's poem is framed by two words that suggest immediacy: 'Now' and 'expedition'. Yet, these words' injunctions to face both the present moment and an unknown future ('I'le . . . follow hir') bookend a lyric that is very much about Southwell's uncomfortable relation with the recent past. In this Southwell may be aligned with her younger contemporary Pulter, whose breathless anticipations of the afterlife are bound up with the profoundly recursive experience of her own and others' mortality. Turning the time of lyric into jarringly 'non-linear, repetitive . . . constellations of desire', both poets suggest that a lyric present—and a lyric future—are possible only by dwelling in and remediating the past.[27]

TURNING BACKWARD

What to do, then, with a poem like 'The Revolution'? In this startling lyric, Pulter imagines an alternate existence as a fiery comet hurtling through the atmosphere at the world's end. Explicitly welcoming this state, she writes:

> Nor back again I would not turn
> Though I a thousand worlds might burn;
> It would too long my joys adjourn. ('The Revolution', 52–4)

Pulter's fantasy of exultant, destructive futurity might seem to work against the backward trajectories I have located in early modern women's lyrics. Yet, her poem's meteoric

[25] Marie-Louise Coolahan argues that this phrase refers to the failure of Southwell's mock-elegy; see *Women, Writing, and Language in Early Modern Ireland* (Oxford, 2010), 191.

[26] For a queer reading of the 'propheticall' elegy, see Kate Lilley, 'Fruits of Sodom: The Critical Erotics of Early Modern Women's Writing', *Parergon*, 29 (2012), 181–2.

[27] Anderson and Sperrazza, 'Feminist Queer Temporalities', 179.

resistance to the backward turn is only possible, I propose, because Pulter has exchanged one kind of matter for another: bodies for blazing motes of dust. We who read female-authored verse, on the other hand, are forced to reckon with an unrepentantly earth-bound set of materials: collections that are often handwritten, ad hoc, collaboratively produced, and/or cryptically arranged.

Danielle Clarke describes the impulse to straighten out this wayward lyric matter as 'a nostalgic desire for stable texts'—one that derives in large part from the fantasies of coherence produced by centuries of intensively edited male-authored early modern verse.[28] Rather than giving into this desire, however, I want to consider what it would mean to take seriously the false starts and quite literal backward turns required of us by women's lyric manuscripts. As Anna Reynolds' chapter in this volume reminds us, form and matter are inevitably entangled. Might it be possible to look at these texts and see not incoherence, but rather a different kind of order?

The material composition of Southwell's poetic manuscript (Folger Shakespeare Library MS V.b.198) has proven particularly recalcitrant to readers. A hybrid object compiled by numerous household hands, its fusion of notebook and tipped-in leaves generates some odd effects. For instance, a few leaves of Southwell's poetry were inserted backwards (likely by Southwell's husband after her death), meaning that in order to read a poem or part of a poem 'correctly', one must start on the verso (back) of the page and then turn the page to the right.[29] Household inventories and decades-old financial records jostle with poems by Southwell and several contemporaries, all copied out by a range of scribes. While the recurring presence of Southwell's hand implies some sense of authorial control, her textual interventions scarcely stabilise or finalise her lyrics. Indeed, one might even say that these alterations impede our ability to read in an expected way, demanding that we pause or even reverse normal progression.

A memorable example of this material disorientation occurs in Southwell's sixteen-page Decalogue poem 'Thou shalt keepe holy the saboth daye'. Trained to value lyrics as 'well-wrought urns', readers may already be flummoxed by the poem's engorgement of one of the snappy Christian Ten Commandments.[30] Compounding this perplexity is the presence of a paper slip inscribed with six lines and glued like a flap over one of the poem's stanzas (fol. 41r). Prevented from progressing 'normally' down the page, the reader must decide how to understand the relationship between the lyric stanza written underneath the slip and the stanza on the slip itself. Which of the two stanzas should go first? And how might the Decalogue poem's problem of stanzaic flux converse with the backward-tipped-in leaves, the linear logic of whose contents seems to have been a low priority even for its early audience?

[28] Danielle Clarke, 'Nostalgia, Anachronism, and the Editing of Early Modern Women's Texts', *Text*, 15 (2003), 187–209, 188.

[29] Jonathan Gibson, 'Synchrony and Process: Editing Manuscript Miscellanies', *SEL Studies in English Literature 1500–1900*, 52 (2012), 85–100, 88–9.

[30] On feminised formal choices as provocations to New Critical modes of reading, see Elizabeth Scott-Baumann, 'Hester Pulter's Well-Wrought Urns: Early Modern Women, Sonnets, and the New Criticism', *Journal for Early Modern Cultural Studies*, 20.2 (2020), 118–43.

If answers elude us, we may need to ask different questions. For instance: how might the material disruption of structural coherence actually generate its own hermeneutic? Might it afford greater readerly agency ('choose your own stanza')? A sense of interpretive dislocation suitable to the fraught exegetic histories of Southwell's biblical matter? Precisely because it resists familiar reading practices, Southwell's manuscript (helpfully digitised by the Folger Shakespeare Library) affords students of early modern lyric the chance to develop formalisms unfreighted by expectations about how poems 'ought' to proceed. Rather than closing in on an ideal version of Southwell's texts, more inventive critical models might instead account for the way Southwell's poems expand and contract or abruptly turn back on themselves.

This work takes on an urgency even when we encounter more familiar poetic forms like Wroth's sonnets. Trained by editions of male sonneteers to expect certain formal conventions, including a sense of 'narrative continuity and the progression of discrete poetic units', scholars have understandably brought to Wroth's autograph manuscript of sonnets and songs (Folger Shakespeare Library MS V.a.104) a wish for *sequence*.[31] Yet, if Wroth's text is less haphazard than Southwell's collaborative notebook, it still 'resists, or at least considerably vexes, the concepts of fixity and unity'.[32] Features that might consolidate logical development—catchwords, poem numbers, the so-called 'closural' symbol known as the 'fermesse'—are deployed inconsistently or recursively, thwarting efforts to turn individual poems into a story of Pamphilia's emotional development. Organisational logics emerge only to fade on the next leaf.

The enigmatic appearance of Pamphilia's 'signature' is a case in point. Inscribed in two different places in Wroth's manuscript, this name is said to afford a sense of an ending, leading to the identification of three distinct narrative groupings at work within the larger collection.[33] But the question of why readers should grant the name 'Pamphilia' any such unifying force, given the resistances to formal momentum and psychological coherence that attend Wroth's speaker, remains largely unexamined. It might be more productive to acknowledge that Wroth's collection, like her individual sonnets, is marked by a tendency to 'turn and counterturn', re-opening wounds we thought were closed.[34] On folio 54 verso, the signature 'Pamphilia' concludes an untitled sonnet instructing the speaker's 'now hapy' muse to lay her self 'to rest' (13) and shake off the hurt of desire. But on 55 recto, Pamphilia returns to the very position of abjection from which we thought she had just emerged: 'Unquiet griefe search farder,

[31] Rebecca L. Fall, 'Pamphilia Unbound: Digital Re-Visions of Mary Wroth's Folger Manuscript, V.a.104', in Katherine R. Larson and Naomi J. Miller (eds), *Re-Reading Mary Wroth* (New York, 2015), 193–207, 194.

[32] Fall, 'Pamphilia Unbound', 197.

[33] See, for instance, Ilona Bell, 'The Circulation of Writings by Lady Mary Wroth', in Margaret P. Hannay, Mary Ellen Lamb, and Michael G. Brennan (eds), *The Ashgate Research Companion to the Sidneys, 1500–1700*, Vol. 2: *Literature* (Burlington, VT, 2015), 77–87, 79.

[34] Clare R. Kinney, 'Turn and Counterturn: Reappraising Mary Wroth's Poetic Labyrinths', in Katherine R. Larson and Naomi J. Miller (eds), *Re-Reading Mary Wroth* (New York, 2015), 85–102, 85.

in my hart' ('Sonett', 1). What seems final is, in this collection, always open, sometimes painfully so.

This sense of endless reworking is reinforced by a marginal note Wroth inscribed in a personal copy of her printed *Urania* (1621), to which *Pamphilia to Amphilanthus* forms a coda. Wroth's handwritten interventions to this copy, now at the University of Pennsylvania Library, largely correct stationers' errors. But next to the opening stanza of Sonnet 19:

> Come darkest Night, becomming sorrow best,
> Light leave thy light, fit for a lightsome soule:
> Darknesse doth truely sute with me opprest,
> Whom absence power doth from mirth controule

we find a phrase that is not a correction: 'For absence'.[35] Like the figure of Night herself, who appears throughout the collection as Pamphilia's intimate companion, the inscription 'For absence' seems to speak to this sonnet's availability to Wroth during a familiar experience of isolation or abandonment. For Wroth's modern students, it suggests reading practices attuned to the cyclical nature of experience. Wroth's 'obsessive repetitions' might prompt us to read affect as a set of recurring forms.[36] Rather than looking for resonances among neighbouring sonnets, we might trace Wroth's reuse of verbal patterns (for example, the confluence of the rhyme words 'night', 'delight', and 'spite') across the manuscript as a whole, discovering thematic concerns such as Wroth's perplexing and racialised investment in 'becomming' dark.[37]

Such practices would offer a powerful alternative to 'sequence'. With its compulsive quest for development and coherence, the sequence is an ideal whose qualities can feel inimical to the material realities of writing—perhaps existing—as a woman in early modern England. By refusing this narrow definition of order in favour of something more like an 'assembly of fragmented parts', the manuscripts of Wroth and Southwell signal form's capacity to invite contingency, playfulness, and a range of creative agencies.[38] Admittedly, it is disorienting to find ourselves at the frontiers of such a form. Yet, if we allow ourselves to be guided by the affordances of pasted-in slips or a preference for cycle and reversal, we might find less a map than a reminder that it is always possible, even advisable, to take an unexpected turn.

[35] *The Countesse of Mountgomeries Urania*, Philadelphia, Kislak Center for Special Collections—Rare Book Collection, Folio PR2399.W7 C68 1621, fol. Bbbbv.

[36] Heather Dubrow, '"And Thus Leave off": Reevaluating Mary Wroth's Folger Manuscript, V.a.104', *Tulsa Studies in Women's Literature*, 22 (2003), 273–91, 281–2.

[37] Kim F. Hall, *Things of Darkness: Economies of Race and Gender in Early Modern England* (Ithaca, NY, 1995), 105–7.

[38] Whitney Sperrazza, 'Knowing Mary Wroth's Pamphilia', *Journal for Early Modern Cultural Studies*, 19 (2019), 1–35, 20.

CONCLUSION: CRITICAL BACKWARDNESS

This chapter has modelled what it might look like to pursue unfamiliar lyric trajectories. Exploring or inhabiting conditions of emotional abjection, temporal dislocation, and material perplexity, it has argued that our encounters with early modern women's poetic forms must account for effects we do not yet have names for. While this chapter has made visible Southwell's, Wroth's, and Pulter's strategic use of certain familiar tropes and devices (repetition, metaphor), it has also shown that these choices are but a small part of what we must mean when we talk about form. How can our interpretive language accommodate accidents of material compilation or lyrics' bifurcated temporalities? What would it mean to delineate the forms of feeling?

If pondering such questions means embracing lyric backwardness, then being backward can be no bad thing. Yet, this chapter's celebration of poetic divergences—swerves so forceful they threaten to topple the conventions of literary history—has exposed, too, less salutary forms of critical backwardness. In particular, this chapter's use of 'women' or 'female-authored text' may feel regressive, its apparent premises (that 'woman' is a unified category, that texts are 'authored' by individuals) overly simplistic. Indeed, my emphasis on material conditions partly outside of writers' control would seem to undermine the assertion that what I have called 'backwardness' is a peculiarly feminised condition in the history of poetics. Does formal backwardness attend only certain more legible (socially exalted, *white*) forms of femininity? Or is backwardness collaboratively produced, uncoupled from a single gendered body? Might backwardness be contagious, infecting lyrics to, about, voiced by, or copied alongside those of women?

The greatest risk of backwardness is, of course, collision. Yet, the costs of a lyric formalism without women would seem to far outweigh such a risk.[39] A poetics gendered female exposes women's conditions of living and working as forces that shape form, in the most expansive sense of the word. Following where these backward forms take us, we cannot help but defy Pulter: literary history will not, must not, prove like what is past.

FURTHER READING

Clarke, Danielle and Marie-Louise Coolahan. 'Gender, Reception, and Form: Early Modern Women and the Making of Verse', in Ben Burton and Elizabeth Scott-Baumann (eds), *The Work of Form: Poetics and Materiality in Early Modern Culture*. Oxford, 2014, 144–61.

Dodds, Lara and Michelle M. Dowd. 'Happy Accidents: Critical Belatedness, Feminist Formalism, and Early Modern Women's Writing', *Criticism*, 62 (2020), 169–93.

39 Lara Dodds and Michelle Dowd, 'The Case for a Feminist Return to Form', *Early Modern Women: An Interdisciplinary Journal*, 13 (2018), 82–91, 86.

Dodds, Lara and Michelle M. Dowd (eds). *Feminist Formalism and Early Modern Women's Writing: Readings, Conversations, Pedagogies*. Lincoln, 2022.

Lilley, Kate. 'Fruits of Sodom: The Critical Erotics of Early Modern Women's Writing', *Parergon*, 29 (2012), 175–92.

Ross, Sarah C. E. *Women, Poetry and Politics in Seventeenth-Century Britain*. Oxford, 2015.

Sanchez, Melissa E. *Queer Faith: Reading Promiscuity and Race in the Secular Love Tradition*. New York, 2019.

Scott-Baumann, Elizabeth. *Forms of Engagement: Women, Poetry, and Culture 1640–1680*. Oxford, 2013.

CHAPTER 14

'PEOPLE OF A DEEPER SPEECH'

Anna Trapnel, Enthusiasm, and the Aesthetics of Incoherence

KEVIN KILLEEN

AFTER twelve days of hard prophecy and public spectacle like no other, Anna Trapnel, exhausted and exhilarated, described the breaking of language, how it ceases to mean, how even the Bible can empty itself, becoming a mere bloated corpse of Scripture. Cromwell or the addled Council of State can speak still, but it is only 'dead men, dead things' speaking. Gideon-Cromwell's words infect him, even as he speaks them: 'Does not he confound himself in his own language?'.[1] Trapnel's prophecy, in the winter of 1654, was remarkable for many reasons. Begun in the precincts of Westminster, attracting large crowds, it was an event of vehement prophetic impropriety and another cacophonous fortnight in the country's political–spiritual perma-crisis ('This is the saddest day that ever poor England had' (67)). Taken down in shorthand, as near a record of prophecy as we are likely to find, it is also a text that is exuberant about its own plunging into the unspeakable.

Trapnel's *The Cry of a Stone* (1654) is perhaps the most notable piece of women's prophetic writing in the era, in its length, its dramatic scope, and ferocity. Hers is a style that is at once exegetically precise and politically tempestuous, in its class-conscious hermeneutic that lambasts the obfuscation of 'university learning', which wilfully obscures the otherwise limpid Scriptures. Speaking of her eschatological times as themselves corrosive of meaning, Trapnel understood herself to be living in an era not only of political fracture and fragmentation, but also of a more thoroughgoing crisis of language: 'many are infected, their language is infected, it was sweet before, but now it is confused, it had

[1] Anna Trapnel, *The Cry of a Stone* ([London?], 1654), 67–8. All quotations from this edition. See also Anna Trapnel, ed. Hilary Hinds, *The Cry of a Stone* (New York, 2001).

an harmony, but now it hath no relish' (37). Scripture, chopped and minced by the uncompromising civil war prophet, needed to pulse dangerously close to incoherence—there was nothing to be clear about—before it might become suddenly interpretable, in a dazzle of political revelation.

This chapter argues that prophetic language in the era wholly embraced and crafted its turbulent style as the proper, necessary response to a deeply unstable spiritual-political ontology, in a world whose fragility had been repeatedly exposed, by civil war, regicide, and the fast-moving events of the Republic and Protectorate. It makes the case that Trapnel, and women prophets of the revolution more generally, understood themselves to be working within a scriptural poetic that could properly be termed experimental, in the literary sense, that they were consciously aiming to disrupt the parameters of language and coherence, and that the nature of this cracked language underlay their appeal and their authority, such as it was. The flamboyant guise and unruly rhetoric of the prophet was adopted by plenty of men as well in the era, but it was a mode most fully and brilliantly adopted by women, with some 300 of such visionaries being known, as Phyllis Mack notes.[2] Closely connected with this was the fact that prophecy involved outlandish performance—bodily and unbodied, unearthly and gutsy. The Word was a wind through the prophet, body and soul: 'thy Spirit takes the Scripture all along, and sets the soul a swimming therein' (67). The soul immersed and drowning in the near-incomprehensible Word is a characteristic state for prophetic women writers, channelling or channelled by the divine. This was a speech that was barely voluntary and there was little a prophet could do about it when it seized them, whether Trapnel in Whitehall, Hosea 'whoring' in Samaria, or Isaiah naked in Judah. All respond to an ontological instability with answerable style, delirium, and fabulous theatrics.

To argue thus for Trapnel, however, demands that we square apparently incompatible positions: first, that her performance is generically astute, exegetically subtle in its weaving of the biblical and the political, as well as alert to and guileful in response to patriarchal, as much as political, context; then, second, that she is genuine in her religiously infused stupor, that the biblical spirit's rending her body, her language, and her soul is how she and how the times construe reality, construe incoherence. To suppose that Trapnel is not wholly, rigorously, certain that the divine was bellowing through her body is to undermine her seriousness, and her terms of reference. We cannot secularise. If these positions seem initially irreconcilable—that it might be a ruse and resolutely cannot be a ruse, that she can be both conscious of her literary-exegetical manoeuvres and genuinely betranced—they converge in the early modern understanding of prophecy. The prophet is gripped and powerless, but also a fearless voice of political truth, which speaks outside the ordinary temporal fabric, such that the scriptural past is manifested in the eschatological and political present.

[2] Phyllis Mack, *Visionary Women: Ecstatic Prophecy in Seventeenth-Century England* (Berkeley, CA, 1994), 1.

Prophetic writing, since it first came to serious scholarly attention in the work of Hilary Hinds, Phyllis Mack, and others, has not been neglected, but its alienating biblical idiom has remained at least slightly baffling, and for many unappealing, in its temporal tangles of the thickly biblical-apocalyptic and the immediately political. Hilary Hinds, in *God's Englishwomen*, comments on writings which are audacious, in political–religious as well as literary terms, which are rhetorically sophisticated and playful, and which frequently brought down mockery, poverty, and imprisonment upon the early modern prophets.[3] Though a great deal has changed since Hinds' 1996 work in terms of the canon of women writers, it remains the case that women prophets are often a hard sell compared with what Teresa Feroli calls women writing in the 'Tory cause', an aristocratic poetry of friendship, education, and politics of privilege. The prophetic mode with its apocalyptic fireworks is not, however, intrinsically radical—Lady Eleanor Davies, a fervent royalist, is similarly turbulent, to quite different ends.[4] The abrasive, biblical medium of this style of thought is not to modern taste. Phyllis Mack's work made the case that prophecy has almost invariably been secularised, if not pathologised, as emotional excess and catharsis, as psychological instability, not *thinking* as such, but being soaked in theology. 'Did the female prophet have a mind?' she asks rhetorically, in response to these women's abrogation of authorship as such, their adopting a role as merely and vehemently the vessel for God's political wrath.[5] Susan Wiseman writes of the unlocatable nature of the prophetic female voice channelling an irredeemably male God-voice, and the predicament of feminist responses to this ventriloquising role.[6] Even reading prophecy as a sublimated radical politics in which women appropriate a traditionally male discursive and social space (though in some ways this is clearly the case) cannot escape the crude effects of a secularisation that tries to make it more palatable.

Trapnel is more readily accessible than many early modern female prophets, thanks to Hilary Hinds' excellent edition of *The Cry of a Stone* (2001) and, subsequently, the quasi-martyrological and autobiographical *Report and Plea* (2016), telling of her travels, trials, and arrest following her public prophecy in Whitehall against Cromwell. Some impressive scholarly writing on Trapnel has done a good deal to contextualise and make sense of her, including, for example, work on the pathology and performativity of the fasting female body, the dynamics of the prophetic and gender, and the larger cultural–political

[3] Hilary Hinds, *God's Englishwomen: Seventeenth-Century Radical Sectarian Writing and Feminist Criticism* (Manchester, 1996).

[4] Teresa Feroli, *Political Speaking Justified: Women Prophets and the English Revolution* (Newark, 2006), 29.

[5] Mack, *Visionary Women*, 119.

[6] Susan Wiseman, 'Unsilent Instruments and the Devil's Cushions: Authority in Seventeenth-Century Women's Prophetic Discourse', in Isobel Armstrong (ed.), *New Feminist Discourses* (London, 1992), 176–96. See also Diane Purkiss, 'Producing the Voice, Consuming the Body: Women Prophets of the Seventeenth Century', in Isobel Grundy and Susan Wiseman (eds), *Women, Writing, History 1640–1740* (London, 1992); Alexis Butzner, '"Taken Weak in My Outward Man": The Paradox of the Pathologized Female Prophet', *Early Modern Women*, 13 (2018), 30–57; Kate Chedgzoy, 'Female Prophecy in the Seventeenth Century: The Case of Anna Trapnel', in William Zunder and Suzanne Trill (eds), *Writing and the English Renaissance* (London, 1996) 238–54.

context.[7] With a few exceptions, however, it is also the case that criticism on Trapnel's prophecy has gone quiet in recent years.

TRAPNEL IN WHITEHALL

Trapnel wrote in a number of genres, from the prison narrative of *Report and Plea* (1654), to the autobiographical confessional experience in *A Legacy for Saints* (1654). She produced a printed collection of poem-hymns, *A Voice for the King of Saints and Nations* (1657), many of which are reproduced in the vast single printed copy of a titleless work in the Bodleian.[8] A brief report, *Strange and Wonderful Newes from White-Hall* (1654), describes the same events that occupy her major and most famous prophetic experience, which appeared as *The Cry of a Stone* (1654). The latter is unique, however, as a record of a prophetic event, narrated 'live', as opposed to a report of visions, or a conversion experience. The events were fraught and dramatic, but have been described in many of the critical works cited, so I will be brief on the background, wanting rather to describe the generic and exegetical character of prophecy.

Trapnel's trance and ecstasy began at Whitehall in January 1654, following the arrest of a fellow Fifth Monarchist, Vavasor Powell and in the context of a widespread disillusionment of the radical godly at Cromwell's de facto monarchical assumption of power as Lord Protector, after the dissolution of the uncompromising Barebones Parliament. Her prophesying in song and in prose continued for eleven or twelve days, and became a public spectacle, with a large and political crowd, including members of the Council of State, ejected Members of Parliament, and prominent London ministers, as well as the spy and pamphleteer, Marchamont Needham, who reported with some disdain back to Cromwell.[9] *The Cry of a Stone* emerged, incomplete, from what an exhausted 'Relator' could take down of Trapnel's words, once it became clear that this was an ongoing marvel. '[O]f the four first days no account can be given', he explains, 'there being none that noted down what was spoken' (2). At times, the crowd was too great, at times her voice too weak, or the relator not sufficiently indefatigable, but the text accrued, from

[7] Key points of reference in the political sphere include Catie Gill, '"All the Monarchies of this World Are Going down the Hill": The anti-monarchism of Anna Trapnel's *The Cry of a Stone* (1654)', *Prose Studies*, 29 (2007), 19–35; Katharine Gillespie, *Domesticity and Dissent in the Seventeenth Century: English Women Writers and the Public Sphere* (Cambridge, 2004) 62–114; James Holstun, *Ehud's Dagger: Class Struggle in the English Revolution* (London, 2000), 257–304; Erica Longfellow, *Women and Religious Writing in Early Modern England* (Cambridge, 2009), 149–79; David Loewenstein, *Representing Revolution in Milton and his Contemporaries: Religion, Politics, and Polemics in Radical Puritanism* (Cambridge, 2001), 92–124; Marcus Nevitt, '"Blessed, Self-Denying, Lambe-Like"? The Fifth Monarchist Women', *Critical Survey*, 11 (1999), 83–97.

[8] Anna Trapnel, [Poetical addresses or discourses delivered to a gathering of 'Companions' in 1657 and 1658] (1659), Arch. A c.16

[9] Calendar of State Papers, Needham to Protector, 7 February 1654

ad-libbed hymns and a scriptural hopscotch of prose, both apocalyptic and contemporary in their scope. What post note-taking revision and reconstruction took place, and the extent to which Trapnel might have overseen or been involved in readying the transcription for publication, remains elusive. Occasionally the relator clarifies to whom Trapnel is referring, bracketing his comments in the text, with the implication that the words are otherwise hers.[10]

The preliminaries to the prophecy itself are quite extensive, including an autobiographical account, which may pre- or post-date it. That this is separate from the actual prophecy matters; it is a different kind of narration, more carefully crafted. It attests, after a fashion, to Trapnel's good character and social propriety, but is far from meek. It includes details of her spiritual battles, her fasting into hallucinatory vision states, her being buffeted by a suicide-inducing Satan, her prophetic induction in her mother's dying words, and her series of wild visions and prognostications of war, from the late 1640s and 1650s. She sees a vision of a bull, whose 'Countenance was perfectly like unto *Oliver Cromwels*' who runs furiously at her, 'neer with his horn to my breast' and thence at the saints in his violent rage 'scratching them with his horn, and driving them into several houses, he ran still along, till at length there was a great silence, and suddenly there broke forth in the Earth great fury coming from the Clouds' (13). This is fervent and spectacular, but it is not live prophecy as such, rather a remembrance of visions past. The prophecy within *The Cry of a Stone*, by contrast, has no real visionary element. It is less hallucination than hermeneutics.

Prophecy is an awkward, if not an embarrassing, category for the modern historian or literary historian. Even when hedged with the proper caveats—that it is less soothsaying and prognostication than interpretation and appropriation of a biblical form, that its ventriloquising the fury of the divine provided a conduit for political speech—even when it is understood as holy delirium brought on by excessive fasting, or a ruse to wriggle out of clearly real class and gender constraints, or an expression of separatist religiosity, it remains hard to credit and, what is worse, repetitive. In verse, the accusation goes, it is doggerel and in prose it is a tissue of biblical rags. Whatever we make of it, it is hard to make literature of it, and while scholars are less likely these days to voice criticism in any haughty fashion, it is nevertheless the case that Trapnel, and prophecy more broadly, fails to make it regularly onto literature curricula.[11] Despite this, it is a genre. Could we say that, in the 1650s, it was an experimental genre? That it was a little avant garde? That Anna Trapnel was a radicalised Virginia Woolf, a H.D. for her times? If this is preposterous (where's the chaise longue?), it remains the case that this writing was formally shocking (in the literary sense). Radical writers, Fifth Monarchist women in particular, established what were essentially new literary-scriptural forms as the

[10] Ramona Wray, 'What Say You to [This] Book? [. . .] Is It Yours?': Oral and Collaborative Narrative Trajectories in the Mediated Writings of Anna Trapnel', *Women's Writing*, 16 (2009), 408–24.

[11] See, for example, Champlin Burrage, 'Anna Trapnel's prophecies', *The English Historical Review*, 26 (1911), 526–35 (527) on her 'rambling rhymes'. She receives short shrift in B. S. Capp's *The Fifth Monarchy Men* (London, 1972), 102.

vehicle for their theological-apocalyptic ideas.[12] For all its potential anachronism, there is something both appealing and off-kilter in understanding prophesy as, for example, an *écriture feminine* in that its riot of eschatological thought is so consciously disruptive, wild, and ranting—an *écriture prophétique* at least.[13]

RANTING WITH TRAPNEL

Trapnel has a capacious knowledge of the Bible and her prose is an intricate weave of quotations bearing on the present calamities, a temporal knot of ancient Israel, the contemporary, and the eschatological. But she rejects with some vehemence the specious chicanery of the learned and their distortions of Scripture: 'what disputing, what reasoning ... vaine conceits, vaine speculations, and high notions' (38). This disdain for 'university learning' runs deep in the text, and across radical prose of the era. Indeed, as per Christopher Hill, it is almost the defining watermark of radicalism. Even very learned radicals, of whom there are many, voice this disdain for university chop-logic.[14] It not necessarily the case that writing which styles itself as enthusiastic, from Ranter to Quaker and Baptist literature, is in any sense primitive, or less adept at producing the tumble of precise biblical reference characteristic of the era. For Trapnel, something other than mere density of learning is at play in the high-flown vapidity of the learned: 'they say these waters are very clear and sweet that come from men, but at length they make the Soule very muddy' (35). This oozy capacity to taint even the Scriptures, turning it to thick sludge rather than sweet water ('many are infected, their language is infected') is a product of blighted times and self-interested sophistry. One can say complex things that mean nothing at all. Such are universities. Nor is this garble new. Citing Isaiah 33.19, where the Assyrians issue their commands in a wilfully obscure tongue, Trapnel warns the learned ('all you Disputants, Monarchs, Scribes, and Rabbies of the world'), with their tricksy impenetrable language, that their day is done, that they cannot oppose the spirit of prophecy:

> because thine are of a stammering speech, and of stuttering tongue, but thou hast promised that the time shall come that there shall not be a people of a deeper speech then thy people, and they shall not be of a stammering tongue. (37–8)

12 See Susan Wiseman, *Conspiracy and Virtue: Women, Writing, and Politics in Seventeenth-Century England* (Oxford, 2006), 176.

13 Christine Berg and Philippa Berry, '"Spiritual Whoredom": An Essay on Female Prophets in the Seventeenth Century', in Francis Barker et al. (eds), *1642: Literature and Power in the Seventeenth Century* (Colchester, 1981), 37–54; Hinds, *God's Englishwomen*, 125; Paul Salzman, *Reading Early Modern Women's Writing* (Oxford, 2008), 109–34.

14 Christopher Hill, *The English Bible and the Seventeenth-Century Revolution* (London, 1993), 380.

There are two kinds of deeper speech here, the obfuscatory—whether that of the Assyrian, of university churchmen, or, latterly, of Cromwell—and the promised new prophetic fog, a deeper deep, 'a people of a deeper speech' whose prophetic language passes through incoherence—the stammering speech and stuttering tongue associated with reluctant biblical prophets—Moses, Isaiah, Jonah, and Jeremiah—into its preternatural clarity, where all the 'Scriptures cohere. But that time has not yet come'.

Trapnel's prophecy is dazzlingly atonal. It is generically amorphous, breaking into hymns, threats, self-exculpatory digressions, exhortation, and jeremiad; it is a complex tapestry of palimpsestic times and rhetorical modes. It is breathtakingly rude, aggressive, and threatening. And it revels in its wild state and its unpredictable sea changes. If we wanted to characterise its style, we might think in terms of an aesthetics of incoherence. For both biblical and early modern political prophets, the fragmented form of the text, its rapid shifts, and broken logic are a correlate to deranged times. It expresses a madness of what is beyond expression. It hurls itself at the impenetrable, insisting on its access to the mysterious: 'go into the Marrow, what matters it for the bone' (38). The bone is not internal enough. While Trapnel has some aphoristic gems of this kind (albeit they may be common property), the rhetorical effect of her prophecy is only experienced in the more extended zigzag of her prose:

> Oh, But who is he or she that admires the Lord Jesus through all, in all, and above all; He is all in nothing-Creatures, the Creature is nothing, but thou hast said, thou dost great things through nothing: Oh, that thine were taken with Truth for Truths sake, that they would seek into the bottome, and goe into the golden Mine, and not onely gather up the shavings thereof, let them not take up the sparks but the fire it selfe. That a poor Creature should subsist without sustenance, what a gazing is there at this poor thing, while you forget the glory that is in it, go into the Marrow, what matters it for the bone, let them have the Spirits, it is no matter for any thing else. (38)

Trapnel rants. Trapnel is also keen to disassociate herself from Ranting, but notes too how, at points, she had been intrigued and tempted by its resources—albeit that was Satan tempting her in the midst of her periodic spiritual buffeting, prior to the Whitehall events, when: 'he [Satan] endeavoured to bring me into those Familistical ranting Tenents, that I had almost spent my lungs in pleading against' (10). No doubt Trapnel understood Ranters at least in part through the lens of heresiography, such as Edwards' *Gangraena*, or she may of course have known those underground groups or the pamphlets that have come to be grouped as Ranter texts. There does not seem to have been any formal association between Ranters and the Fifth Monarchist visionaries of a quite different bent, but there was very possibly a rhetorical association, in their shared rejection of the dry diet of university language, their shared sense of the wild 'whisperings of the spirit' (50), what Nigel Smith calls the radical 'culture of Illumination'.[15] Clement Hawes speaks of Enthusiasm as a mode of speech that managed

[15] Nigel Smith, *Perfection Proclaimed: Language and Literature in English Radical Religion, 1640–1660* (Oxford, 1989), 16–18.

to encompass both a mystic annihilation of self and a sense of manic omnipotence, enunciation bordering on the sublime, a language at once purgative and apophatic in its conscious irrationality, as well as being resolutely class-conscious.[16] If not ranting, Trapnel is certainly enthusing. Her sense of the prophetic is not incidentally incoherent, but is so at the level of structure—the text's rapid-fire shifts of genre—as well as at the level of the sentence, its local rhetoric.

Sometimes, it is true, a Renaissance sentence (and a text more broadly) has an intricate rhetorical structure, architectural in its balanced clauses and curlicues. But at other times, with no less design, it is a swarm of bees. The desired effect of the sentence is one of calculated disorientation, all its parts akimbo, working according to a mysterious pattern.[17] The early modern sermon, for example, while it may have its formal rhetorical staging—exordium, peroration, and so on—can seem in any individual sentence mad as a box of frogs, hopping between scriptural example and its typological valence. This scriptural steeplechase is in some respects a thoroughly domesticated form of writing in a culture that routinely collated texts and commonplaced its ideas. However, in the case of the era's most radical syntactical thinkers, whether a Thomas Nashe, the prophets, or the Ranters, the polyphonic motion of the thought and the fate of the sentence was often precariously balanced between sense and nonsense. That, in the case of Trapnel, this is by design rather than accident we know from how often she comments on the practice.

Trapnel produces meta-prophetic commentary on her own state of bodily and scriptural incoherence, reporting on her audience's rationalistic and quasi-medical diagnosis: 'They say these are convulsion fits and Sickness, and diseases that make thy handmaid to be in weakness' (29). This, she suggests, both is and is not the case—it matters that the prophet is a woman, and a starving one at that, in a state of hallucinatory fasting and self-mortification. But the holy anorexia, and its paroxysms, are not the real issue. Trapnel has one and one only explanation of what is happening: 'But oh they know not the pouring forth of thy Spirit, for that makes the body to crumble, and weakens nature' (29). She is, so to speak, beside herself, outside her own control, beset by the spirit, possessed of an enthusiasm that has seized her rationality, the divine throb of dissatisfaction coursing through her: 'thy Servant is made a voyce, a sound, it is a voyce within a voyce, anothers voyce, even thy voyce through her' (42). This is a convulsion poetics, in its pauselessness, its surge beyond the powers of the Relator to take down, as the Word torrents through her, and as extempore verse flows into expository prose, here political, there exegetical, a hodgepodge at the edge of coherence. This godly ventriloquism demands that the listener—the august audience cramming into her room—and the reader not only follow the logic, but accept the disorientation, the illogic. The spirit veers drunkenly, and not only does the individual sentence swarm with its garble of scriptural

[16] Clement Hawes, *Mania and Literary Style: The Rhetoric of Enthusiasm from the Ranters to Christopher Smart* (Cambridge, 1996), 2, 10.

[17] Thanks to Jenny Richards for this thought, in a passing discussion of Thomas Nashe and Thomas Browne on a traffic-swarming Euston Road.

quotations, but the form of the prophecy across its eleven or so days is likewise turbulent, reeling in the unbidden spasms of prophetic woe.

CHARACTER OF THE PROPHECY

The Cry of a Stone twists and turns in its fast-paced shifts of idiom, subject matter, and addressee. It includes numerous songs to the soldiers, sergeants, and merchants of the city; it involves extensive typological reformulating of Israelite kingship as English Protectorship, quotidian one moment, eschatological the next, but all continually voicing the anguish of the betrayed saints and God, frustrated by the lukewarm English. Again and again she turns to the rank treatment of the poor, the hypocrisy of those ostensibly saintly ex-soldiers who betray the revolution by pandering to the wolfish aristocrats, to whom Cromwell has sold out. Though much of the detail must be passed over here, it is worth unfolding a couple of instances of her political style. Over its week of transcription, the politics of Cromwell's apostasy is often to the fore, and the infamy of Trapnel's text was grounded on its bracingly non-deferent political critique, and its fearlessness, her pulling no punches. But its reputation was very much a product of its prophetic performance and what was for its contemporaries the worrying (or heartening) possibility that it was genuine, that it was really God's manifestation, because it is clear that many of its auditors and subsequently its readers believed it, or did not disbelieve it. The fact that Trapnel was arrested and accused subsequently only added to its plausibility. But it was plausible (or it was not) insofar as its auditors credited its prophetic character. And this was wholly bound up with its tone and style, its habits of discontinuity, and enthusiastic propulsion. This is where it most evidently generates its 'literary' quality or quirks, a punk poetics that produced its particular hallmarks within its discursive, prophetic parameters, a channelling of scriptural reality to oust worldly self-interest.

A prominent motif of this style, alongside and intertwined with its more evidently political comments, was its exposure and lamenting of the pernicious malleability of sacred language, wrought to unholy purposes. Indeed, the millennial cast of *Cry of a Stone* is frequently couched as a battle around pure and corrupt language. Trapnel speaks of how Cromwell, formerly capable of godly speech, is now able to utter only a 'confounded' bastard language: 'And how has thy Servant disputed, declared, remonstrated and appeared in the field against Antichrist, and how is his language now confounded?' (42). This was New Babel. He, Cromwell, might try to speak, and might indeed be wholly eloquent, but his words were empty and spiritless. This is a recurrent idea for Trapnel, that one must inhabit the scriptural, and body forth an inner meaning of its words. The very same language could be vital, alive, and shimmering with truth, or it could be corpse-like, rotten, and spiritless.

At the point when the 'relator' begins to record things, on the fifth day, Trapnel's prayer-song interweaves the captivity of the Israelites in jeering Babylon with

Christological escapology, 'Oh but what fastness, what locks, what bolts that could keep in a Jesus', and she sings of his escape from the prison-grave, transposing as she goes to the present: 'Thou knowest who are the Babylonians that are now about thine'. The 'thine' here are the undauntable, endlessly imprisonable speakers of truth to Cromwell, in constant yearning 'to understand more of the mystery, and of the entrals of scripture' (17). The biblical improvisation on the entrails of Scripture continues, but 'because of the press of people in the chamber', the relator misses the full riff, returning only when Trapnel shifts genre into song, when she readies her listeners for the coming reckoning, in a political taxonomy of those colluding with and corrupting the government.

In a series of anaphoric anathemas, she invokes the reprobate lackeys of the regime, whose crimes will be recorded, one by one: 'Come write down how those sparkling ones . . .', 'Oh write that those great Counsellors . . .', 'Oh write also that Colonels / And Captains they shall down ...' (19).[18] The list will be long: 'you shal have great Rols of writ / Concerning Babylons fall', and it will conclude at the top table of political malice:

> Write how that Protectors shall go, And into graves there lye:
> Let pens make known what is said, that, They shall expire and die. (19–20)

What most grieves Trapnel, perhaps, is the lower classes falling into line as the 'sergeants' and enforcers of the Protectorate:

> Poor Serjeants that were honest men
> Oh how are you fallen,
> Oh how are you now taken with
> The vanity of men? (20)

Such singing with intermittent prayer continues 'four or five hours together', the exhausted relator reports, and what we have is the mere snippet, albeit full throttle calumny, quite sufficient to have her arrested, after the fact. The recorder notes on a number of occasions the fact of her continual singing and the political nature of the hymns. As verse, it needs to be understood as psalmic, in a culture attuned to slow rousing Davidic psalmody, a sung form whose dynamics and rhythms differ from poetry. It is certainly the case that we misread Trapnel's verse if we imagine it as lyric or read it as balladry. Its alternating with and its interaction with the prose-prophecy produces, on the one hand, a quality of the liturgical, and, on the other, a continual wrong-footing, an unpredictable element to the prophecy, as it veers from prose exegesis to verse.

[18] *The Cry of a Stone* appears in two editions in 1654, designated in Hinds' edition via the Cambridge University Library copy (CUL) and the British Library version (BL). See the textual note, and collation of editions, in *God's Englishwomen*, xlix–l. The EEBO copy is the British Library version. The differences are in typesetting and layout, most notably the introduction of stanzaic form in the British Library (presumably the latter) copy, which Hinds suggests serves to 'emphasise the "poetic" nature of Trapnel's spontaneous prophesying' (xlix).

If on some days the subject was a more loosely defined backsliding of the godly nation, on others the relator finds Trapnel in vehemently political mood. In quick-shuffle typology, she takes up Cromwell's favourite Old Testament identity and mantle as Gideon, who in Judges refused to accept the proffered crown of Israel:

> If he were not (speaking of the Lord *Cromwell*) backsliden, he would be ashamed of his great pomp and revenue, whiles the poore are ready to starve, and art thou providing great Palaces? Oh this was not *Gideon* of old, oh why dost thou come to rear up the pillars, the stones which are laid aside? tell him, Lord, thou art come down to have a controversie with him ... (50)

Over the course of several pages, ostensibly still in trance and laid out on her bed, Trapnel produces an intricate mesh of biblical–political thought, the calamity of kingship in Samuel and Deuteronomy, the wretched national betrayals, and the promised retribution 'When thou, Lord, pluckest him from thence' (54). Cromwell's malign turn has dragged soldiers, sergeants, and advisers in its wake: 'O poore Souldiers, take heed that you never draw your sword against the Saints; do not smite with your tongue, as they did against *Jeremiah!*' (56). At times, this can seem to be policy as much as prophecy, the nitty-gritty of government and allegiance, albeit policy with an eschatological tinge, infused with dark warnings, richly amplified with biblical examples of neglectful rulers and their fall. In tempo, in its analytic mode, in its taut political typologies, this is consummately political, in the biblical manner of the time. It is also a quite phenomenal act of scriptural collation, and we might wonder if she knows the Bible by heart? We see such compilations in Fast Sermons, for instance, but the presumption is that these are the work of careful commonplacing, rather than improvisation. This latter part of the prophecy is quite different from the borderline apophasis of the earlier days, when she dealt with the involutions of the spirit, the channelled voice, the deeper speech plumbing the unutterable. Towards the end, by contrast, Trapnel seems awake, alert, astute, rather than in stupor, transported in vision, and the relator is keen to note the very public nature of the prophecy, 'the press and noise of people in the chamber' (56).

The electrifying finale brings together many of her concerns with the apostasy of those who surrender their integrity to Cromwell, but she also returns to the issue of language: language that is dead, and that which is infused with the elusive spirit. In a remarkable statement of the somatic Word, she warns the reprobate soldiers, 'Oh when the hand-writing is come up in their veins, will not their knees smite together?' (62). The very blood that pulses through the veins carries the handwritten liquid Word that both constitutes them—this is the scriptural stuff of life—and condemns them. A stark justice is to come and Trapnel exemplifies this fate, noting Ananias and Sapphira in Acts 5, 'who did lie against the Holy Ghost' in withholding their money from the common pot, breaking the communist property rules of the early church, for which they were struck dead on the spot (Acts 5:3–5). Trapnel prophesies that not only is a wholesale and revolutionary change imminent, but that when it comes, it will be accomplished with such summary justice. No longer will the Word allow itself to be manipulated: 'Wilt not thou come forth and confound their language?' (62). This usurpation of spiritual authority by 'feeble, poore, low creatures', this spiritual world turned upside down is the great threat of Trapnel's prophecy. She is positively enacting the change by which the words of the 'wise' are shown to be empty, when God comes to 'confound their language', to reduce them to Babel-like babble. It is, at once, a gendered challenge to the patriarchal morass of Cromwellian rule, and those who would pathologise her prophetic state, and, at the same time, it is an impassioned defence of unlearning, swimming in Scripture, and the benefits of being an idiot:

> thy servant was one that was simple, an Ideot, and did not study in such things as these, and must thy servant now float upon the mighty and broad waters? [meaning of the Spirit] thou saidst indeed that thy servant should declare in *Gath* and publish in *Askelon:* They will say the spirit of madness and distraction is upon her, and that it is immodesty; but thou knowest Lord, that it is thy Spirit; ... let them know that it is so too, by the language of it, by the Rule through which it comes; how is the written Word carried forth in it! thy Spirit takes the Scripture all along, and sets the soul a swimming therein; oh, those things that are concealed are made manifest, when thy Spirit comes forth; oh that they might know what is the true fountain, and what is pudled water. (67)

Such a passage, at the culmination of Trapnel's prophetic trance, embodies the drama of a revolution that is at once social and spiritual. This is the moment when madness reveals itself to be sanity. This is the world turned upside down because language rids itself of fear. When Trapnel is instructed to 'declare in Gath and publish in Askelon', she is being asked to do what David demanded *not* be done, at the death of Jonathan, 'lest the daughters of the Philistines rejoice, lest the daughters of the uncircumcised triumph' (2 Samuel 1.20). This is the moment when language is to be 'tried', in the sense of separating out the true from the false, the ore from the dross. Cromwell's downfall will be his descent into incomprehensibility when, in the coming eschaton, the spiritless, barren language of the kingly is revealed as shallow 'pudled water', and the madness, the cacophony of ranting prophecy comes to be sane and full, holy idiocy and boundless flow.

CONCLUSION

Denys Turner, in *The Darkness of God*, his impressive history of medieval mysticism, writes of a 'theological tradition which consciously *organised* a strategy of disarrangement as a way of life'.[19] The prophetic writings of mid-seventeenth-century enthusiasm have something of this about them, organising disarray. Trapnel's *The Cry of a Stone* is disarranged, is awry and elliptical, because that is how the spirit blows. But this is not

[19] Denys Turner, *The Darkness of God: Negativity in Christian Mysticism* (Cambridge, 1995), 8.

to suggest a wholesale lack of control, or that, as an oral text, it is not crafted. Trapnel can write a martyrology and can life-write her tale of Satan and Free-Grace, when she so chooses. *The Cry of a Stone*, however, speaks of disorder at the root of things, in language, in the State coming apart at its seams, and Time collapsing in on itself, and its form—literary, prophetic, typological, deranged—is a part of that. Poor Cromwell cannot even speak—his spiritless words have become mere gibber. Such is the spiritual nature of language. Such is the decay of England on its knife-edge, with its pampered and self-indulgent Council of State, behaving like courtiers and kings: 'you Councel, you think you have done well in this, but surely the passing-Bell shall ring for you', she warns, but to little effect, till revenge is wrought and kingdom come: 'this is the saddest day that ever poor *England* had' (67). *The Cry of a Stone* is a text, a performance, as political as it comes, in which a lower-class woman commands centre stage in a twelve-day Whitehall drama, and demonstrates a mesmerising command of that most crucial political language of early modernity, the biblical past patterned onto and folded into the eschatological. If it remains alien to us in its scriptural obsessions, it is also clear that Trapnel, in both literary and in political terms, mattered and dazzled in her brief interregnum spectacle.

FURTHER READING

Hawes, Clement. *Mania and Literary Style: The Rhetoric of Enthusiasm from the Ranters to Christopher Smart*. Cambridge, 1996.

Hinds, Hilary. *God's Englishwomen: Seventeenth-Century Radical Sectarian Writing and Feminist Criticism*. Manchester, 1996.

Holstun, James. *Ehud's Dagger: Class Struggle in the English Revolution*. London, 2000.

Mack, Phyllis. *Visionary Women: Ecstatic Prophecy in Seventeenth-Century England*. Berkeley, CA, 1994.

Wiseman, Susan. *Conspiracy and Virtue: Women, Writing, and Politics in Seventeenth-Century England*. Oxford, 2006.

CHAPTER 15

COMMONPLACING, MAKING MISCELLANIES, AND INTERPRETING LITERATURE

VICTORIA E. BURKE

TYPICALLY considered private, idiosyncratic collections of verse and prose, early modern manuscript miscellanies are difficult to categorise. Commonplace books—compilations of thematically organised quotations often arranged under topic headings—are easier to define but challenging to study since in their purest forms they were compiled by schoolboys in Latin. Commonplacing and making miscellanies in their strictest senses were different activities (the former arguably concerned with collecting and organising pithy, sententious extracts and the latter with copying longer poems and prose passages, potentially for a more literary motive), and yet both get at the heart of how many early modern people responded to and created discourse. Research into these related genres has demonstrated that the modes of compilation evidenced by surviving manuscripts and printed volumes tapped into wide-reaching practices of reading and writing that ultimately helped determine how educated early modern people interacted with their world. Women were among the readers and writers who engaged with these processes of compilation, sometimes offering a unique insight into the written record of the past, because differences of focus are apparent in some female-authored collections. This chapter explores the extant manuscript record for women's participation in compilation as a form of writing, the settings that were amenable to female engagement, and some of the varied ways that writers in manuscript, including Sarah Cowper, Katherine Clarke, and Anne Waller, and print, including Isabella Whitney, used this technique to interpret their reading. This mode of thinking and compilation was not marginal in the early modern period; John Milton kept commonplace books, and Margaret Cavendish, who professed herself to be unencumbered by formal learning, was in conversation with this mode of interpreting literature, even if ultimately to reject it.

MANUSCRIPT COMMONPLACERS AND MISCELLANY MAKERS

Angus Vine has recently noted 'the simultaneous ubiquity of commonplace thinking and relative rarity of commonplace practice (at least in its strictest humanist form)',[1] with reference to the lament of Simonds D'Ewes:

> I spent a great part of this month [July, 1620] amongst other private studies in framing several scholastic heads, as physics, ethics, politics, economics, and the like, and inserting them into two great commonplace books I had newly caused to be bound up in folio; but this cost and labour, by my sudden departure from the University, was in a manner lost, those paper books remaining still by me with little or nothing inserted into them.[2]

While D'Ewes indicates the gap that could occur between prescription and practice, commonplacing was the most expected of Renaissance activities in that it followed humanist practices of turning to past writers in order to imitate them and to generate one's own writing. Passages were gathered and then framed under headings, encouraging 'a method of reading that shaded into invention, a creative use of text that was self-perpetuating and potentially inexhaustive'.[3] Women do not appear to have compiled commonplace books at the most scholarly end of the spectrum, but if a working definition is a book in which extracts were collected for reference under topic headings, then some manuscript collections do fit that standard. I have shown elsewhere that six extant manuscript collections (by Ann Bowyer, Katherine Butler, Sarah Cowper, Anne Ley, Anne Southwell, and Jane Truesdale) could apply, and there are no doubt others.[4] Each of these, in at least some of its pages, gives evidence of a compiler organising their reading thematically. The extracts were sometimes shaped as if they came from authoritative classical sources, though in English translation (as in the case of Truesdale and in one example from Bowyer), but more often the passages were extracted from popular printed vernacular texts (such as those by Michael Drayton and Chaucer, plus *The Mirror for Magistrates* in Bowyer's case, and Joseph Hall's works in Ley's case).[5] Adam

[1] Angus Vine, *Miscellaneous Order: Manuscript Culture and the Early Modern Organization of Knowledge* (Oxford, 2019), 31.

[2] William T. Costello, *The Scholastic Curriculum at Early Seventeenth-Century Cambridge* (Cambridge, MA, 1958), 32.

[3] Abigail Shinn and Angus Vine, 'Introduction: Theorizing Copiousness', *Renaissance Studies*, 28 (2014), 167–82, 177–8. For the terminology of gathering and framing, see Mary Thomas Crane, *Framing Authority: Sayings, Self, and Society in Sixteenth-Century England* (Princeton, NJ, 1993).

[4] Victoria E. Burke, 'Recent Studies in Commonplace Books', *English Literary Renaissance*, 43 (2013), 153–77.

[5] Victoria E. Burke, 'Ann Bowyer's Commonplace Book (Bodleian Library Ashmole MS 51): Reading and Writing Among the "Middling Sort"', *Early Modern Literary Studies*, 6 (2001), paragraph 9, Sheffield

Smyth's suggested criteria for detecting commonplace book culture open up possibilities for seeing this mode of categorising knowledge and literary expression in many sites, and broaden the evidence for women's participation in these activities. Smyth puts forward sixteen characteristics to account for compilers' eclectic practices, arguing that scholars have focused too narrowly on prescriptions.[6]

The range of possible motivations in compiling manuscripts of this type was no doubt broad, but Peter Beal's influential formulation of commonplace books as the 'useful' and miscellanies as the 'pleasurable' ends of the spectrum offers a starting point.[7] The term 'miscellanies' is much more capacious than 'commonplace books', though the labels are sometimes used interchangeably, since in their broadest sense miscellanies can include verse and prose of various types and by different writers compiled with or without any order. While it is not always easy to determine a role a woman might have played in making a miscellany, Erin McCarthy has provided some fascinating statistics about extant verse miscellany manuscripts. McCarthy discovered sixty-nine verse miscellany manuscripts (which contain verse by multiple authors, sometimes with other types of writing included), or about thirty per cent of the surviving total, that she could link with 'female agents'. She defines the latter as 'owners and inscribers, compilers, and "author scribes" who copied their own compositions alongside those of other authors', roles that often overlap.[8] Her research on nineteen of these manuscripts, which contain one or more poems by John Donne, demonstrates that women readers tended to choose the same poems that readers in general did. It is not always possible to claim a difference in miscellanies linked with female reception from those assumed to have a male reception, a fact which is complicated by the number of anonymous collections, and of manuscripts associated with multiple compilers and users.

While research in this field tends to proceed on a case-by-case basis, the RECIRC project at the National University of Ireland, Galway, will allow for more quantitative assessments such as McCarthy's about women's miscellanies.[9] Many important studies

Hallam University, http://purl.oclc.org/emls/06-3/burkbowy.htm, accessed 23 November 2020. Bowyer included a couplet from Timothe Kendall's *Flowers of Epigrammes* (London, 1577) which he attributed to 'Adrastus, out of Euripides', but which Bowyer simply attributes to Euripides. It should be noted that there is evidence in Anne Ley's manuscript that she knew Latin.

6 Adam Smyth, 'Commonplace Book Culture: A List of Sixteen Traits', in Anne Lawrence-Mathers and Phillipa Hardman (eds), *Women and Writing, c.1340–c.1650: The Domestication of Print Culture* (Woodbridge, 2010), 90–110.

7 Peter Beal, 'Notions in Garrison: The Seventeenth-Century Commonplace Book', in W. Speed Hill (ed.), *New Ways of Looking at Old Texts: Papers of the Renaissance English Text Society, 1985–1991* (Binghamton, NY, 1993), 131–47, 143.

8 Erin A. McCarthy, 'Reading Women Reading Donne in Manuscript and Printed Miscellanies: A Quantitative Approach', *The Review of English Studies* new series, 69 (2018), 661–85, 664–5.

9 *RECIRC: The Reception and Circulation of Early Modern Women's Writing, 1550–1700*, directed by Marie-Louise Coolahan, https://recirc.nuigalway.ie/, accessed 23 November 2020. See also Victoria E. Burke, 'Women's Verse Miscellany Manuscripts in the Perdita Project: Examples and Generalizations', in Michael Denbo (ed.), *New Ways of Looking at Old Texts, IV: Papers of the Renaissance English Text Society, 2002–2006* (Tempe, AZ, 2008), 141–54. For a discussion of which female authors were read and in what forms, see this volume, Chapter 43, Marie-Louise Coolahan, 'Reception, Reputation, and Afterlives'.

have been published in recent years, but overviews of the practices of commonplacing and making miscellanies sometimes bypass women's participation (such as in Vine's book), making it all the more pressing to assert women's engagement.[10] While the conventional settings of poetic miscellany compilation were the male-dominated spaces of the universities, Inns of Court, and even the tavern, other locations fostered female participation, including the family, the court, and specific religious networks. Geographically, London and university towns have been considered centres of literary activity, but the provinces were also sites of literary production and exchange. Readers consulted printed books and manuscript sources of different types (loose sheets, small booklets, or codices),[11] depending on a range of factors such as access to various networks of transmission. The most famous sixteenth-century example of a miscellany with a large female presence is the Devonshire Manuscript,[12] formerly appreciated primarily as a source of poetry by Sir Thomas Wyatt, but now also seen as an important collection associated with three women at Henry VIII's court. Elizabeth Heale has described the multiple hands involved in writing lines in praise of and in critique of women, which sometimes altered words from their sources to either defend or blame their target.[13]

One key issue these manuscripts raise is that of interpretation: how were compilers interpreting the writing they read, and how do scholars today interpret those choices? It is perhaps unsurprising that academics are drawn to compilers who seem to be engaging creatively with the literature they inscribe in their manuscripts, as in the case of the Devonshire Manuscript and of a manuscript owned by a Margaret Bellasis.[14] Lara Crowley takes seriously the question of what role this early modern woman might have played: compiler, reviser, scribe, owner, or reader? She suggests that though only the last is certain, other roles are possible, and demonstrates that revisions to all eight of the poems by John Donne included in the manuscript serve to regularise metre, soften bitterness, and enhance love and optimism.[15] In the case of some of the changes to the female-voiced lyric 'Break of Day', the revisions are arguably aesthetic improvements.

[10] Mary Hobbs, *Early Seventeenth-Century Verse Miscellany Manuscripts* (Aldershot, 1992); Harold Love, *Scribal Publication in Seventeenth-Century England* (Oxford, 1993); Arthur F. Marotti, *Manuscript, Print, and the English Renaissance Lyric* (Ithaca, NY, 1995); H. R. Woudhuysen, *Sir Philip Sidney and the Circulation of Manuscripts, 1558–1640* (Oxford, 1996); Richard Beadle and Colin Burrow (eds), *Manuscript Miscellanies c.1450–1700*, special issue of *English Manuscript Studies, 1100–1700*, 16 (2011); Joshua Eckhardt and Daniel Starza Smith (eds), *Manuscript Miscellanies in Early Modern England* (Farnham, 2014); Vine, *Miscellaneous Order*.

[11] Steven W. May and Arthur F. Marotti, 'Manuscript Culture: Circulation and Transmission', in Catherine Bates (ed.), *A Companion to Renaissance Poetry* (Oxford, 2018), 78–102, 79–80.

[12] London, British Library, MS Add. 17492.

[13] Elizabeth Heale, '"Desiring Women Writing": Female Voices and Courtly "Balets" in some Early Tudor Manuscript Albums', in Victoria E. Burke and Jonathan Gibson (eds), *Early Modern Women's Manuscript Writing: Selected Papers from the Trinity/Trent Colloquium* (Aldershot, 2004), 9–31, 19–21.

[14] London, British Library, MS Add. 10309.

[15] Lara M. Crowley, *Manuscript Matters: Reading John Donne's Poetry and Prose in Early Modern England* (Oxford, 2018), 173–210.

This compiler preserved Donne's wit but offered an interpretation in their transcription of his verse, in a manuscript which contained many erotic poems. Laura Estill has demonstrated that the three dramatic extracts in the manuscript, from plays by Middleton and Jonson, each comment on gender, but notes that their meaning is uncertain, due to the miscellany's juxtaposition of different voices and views.[16] The compilers of this volume made choices about what to include, how to position their extracts, and how to alter their source texts for their own reasons, most of which we cannot decode.

One of Sarah Cowper's extant manuscripts began life as a commonplace book in 1673, with passages transcribed beside and under alphabetically arranged topics, to which she later returned and added more poems and prose.[17] Harold Love argues that the commonplace book was Cowper's adaptation of parts of the so-called 'Buckingham Commonplace Book', which she probably obtained from her friend Martin Clifford, but it is intriguing to see what she chose to include from her sources, whether mediated by Clifford or not.[18] As Robert D. Hume and Harold Love note, Cowper included nine passages from Shakespeare's *Hamlet*.[19] Her choice of extracts and her placement of them in thematic categories sometimes surprise. In the category 'obserue' comes Hamlet's insight, 'That one may smile, and smile, and be a Villain' (198, no. 9).[20] In 'Poetry' appear three couplets whose lineation has been preserved (unlike in other passages which are transcribed as prose). The rhyming couplet spoken by Claudius at the end of Act 3, Scene 3 ('My words fly up my thoughts remain below / Words without thoughts neuer to heauen go', 97–8) is followed by two passages from Act 1, Scene 2: Hamlet's lines that close the scene, 'Foul deeds will rise / Though all the earth orewhelm them to mens eies' (255–6) and Gertrude's earlier comment, 'All that liue must die / passing through Nature to Eternity' (72–3) (260, nos 3, 4, and 5). Even with the slant rhyme of the last couplet, these evidently stood out to Cowper as superior poetry. A condensed version of 'To Be or not to be' (3.1.58–90) appears beside the theme 'Question' (269, no. 3); perhaps even in the later seventeenth century the question as framed by Shakespeare was recognised as a highlight of the play (though neither of the two manicules on this page of seven passages

16 Laura Estill, '"All the Adulteries of Art": The Dramatic Excerpts of Margaret Bellasys' BL MS. Add. 10309', in Michael Denbo (ed.), *New Ways of Looking at Old Texts, V: Papers of the Renaissance English Text Society, 2007–2010* (Tempe, AZ, 2014), 235–45.

17 Hertford, Hertfordshire Archives, Penshanger MS D/EP F37. A digitised copy of this manuscript is available in facsimile from *Perdita Manuscripts, 1500–1700*, an Adam Matthew database available by subscription (https://www.amdigital.co.uk/primary-sources/perdita-manuscripts-1500-1700, accessed 23 November 2020).

18 Harold Love, 'How Personal is a Personal Miscellany? Sarah Cowper, Martin Clifford, and the "Buckingham Commonplace Book"', in R. C. Alston (ed.), *Order and Connexion: Studies in Bibliography and Book History* (Cambridge, 1997), 111–26.

19 Robert D. Hume and Harold Love (eds), *Plays, Poems, and Miscellaneous Writings Associated with George Villiers, Second Duke of Buckingham*, vol. 2 (Oxford, 2007), 154. For Cowper's reading of Katherine Philips, see Victoria E. Burke, 'The Couplet and the Poem: Late Seventeenth-Century Women Reading Katherine Philips', *Women's Writing*, 24 (2017), 280–97.

20 William Shakespeare, *Hamlet*, in Stanley Wells et al. (eds). *The Oxford Shakespeare: The Complete Works* (Second Edition) (Oxford, 2005), 1.5.109.

points to this speech). Finally, in the section 'Precept', come some expected quotations (lines from Polonius' sententious advice to Laertes, such as 'To thy own self be true', 1.3.78), and some passages which are less expected, but which also fit (227, nos 4, 5, and 6). The first quotation of this cluster is taken from Hamlet's haranguing words to his mother in Act 3, Scene 4 to confess her sin, repent what is past, avoid what is to come, assume a virtue that she may not have, and refrain, so that the next abstinence will be easier. By changing the play's 'Refrain tonight' (3.4.152) to 'refrain but once', Cowper has turned a specific instruction to a widely applicable moral. Similarly, at the end of Polonius' lines of advice, Cowper has seamlessly added lines spoken earlier by Laertes (1.3.25–7). His warning to Ophelia that she should weigh Hamlet's words against his actions have been altered by Cowper to 'it fitts your wisedome so farr to beleive as *men* do give their saying deed' (emphasis mine). This no longer concerns Ophelia in relation to Hamlet (who 'in his peculiar sect and force / May give his saying deed') but is instead advice to everyone, and perhaps given the original context is meant to urge women to be wary of men's words. Here is a snapshot of one female compiler's treatment of one text among hundreds of pages of extracts. In these passages, Cowper demonstrates a fondness for extractible wisdom and for flowers of expression, a feature of many miscellanies and commonplace books. Documents such as Cowper's can offer historians of reading precise examples of choices people made, thus hinting at what they found interesting or pleasurable or, in the case of the adaptations of Donne in the Bellasis manuscript, in need of improvement.

PRACTICAL DIVINITY AND COMMONPLACING

Readers compiled rhyming couplets, entire poems, and passages from plays. They also used these techniques on genres we cannot as easily deem to be literary. Men and women turned to devotional texts and created documents that witnessed their religious lives, collecting, reordering, and reshaping writing that we might consider practical divinity, and that we should consider as writing worth studying in itself. Scholarly techniques were not systematically taught to women, but, as Kate Narveson has noted of Grace Mildmay, humanist modes of organising and responding to one's reading were adapted by less educated compilers. Narveson argues that in her manuscripts Mildmay is echoing the scholarly humanist *mise en page*, by using 'extensive marginal citations, tie-letters to the text, and running heads'.[21] Narveson sees both commonplacing and collation (comparing passages of Scripture with each other) as a gateway that 'provided

[21] Kate Narveson, 'Authority, Scripture, and Typography in Lady Grace Mildmay's Manuscript Meditations', in Micheline White (ed.), *English Women, Religion, and Textual Production, 1500–1625* (Farnham, 2011), 167–84, 170.

a mode of rhetorical invention, helped Bible readers develop an effective style, and allowed a sense of authority' which ultimately 'allowed lay people to write moving devotions in their own words'.[22] Mildmay created lengthy devotional meditations using scripture as her primary source, 'editing, interlacing, and reassembling Biblical texts to sometimes vivid effect'.[23] Reading, selecting, organising, compiling, sometimes adding one's own words—they were all forms of interpretation, if not of 'literature' then of the crucial Protestant text, the Bible. It was the most authoritative text, especially to early modern women whose sanctioned writings tended to be devotional in nature.

Scriptural commonplacing involves collecting and organising passages which relate to particular themes or topics, using the Bible as the primary text. Nicholas Byfield and Isaac Ambrose are two among many writers who advised readers on how to collect biblical passages under headings, and both stressed that there was room for individual choice in not only which passages to choose, but in formulating the headings themselves.[24] Indeed, surviving scriptural commonplace books compiled by lay people, including women, can sometimes indicate different perspectives. In his description of Katherine Clarke's life and her death in 1675, her husband Samuel describes the pious manuscripts that Katherine compiled during her lifetime. He mentions a collection to which he has given the marginal notation: 'Promises to strengthen her Faith', which comprises twenty biblical verses. He summarises this manuscript as 'These Texts of Scripture having been as so many Cordials unto her in Times of Temptation, it is hoped that they may prove so to others, and therefore for their sakes they are here set down'.[25] Another book also contains scriptural extracts, described by Samuel as gathered for the purpose of ministering 'great Comfort against Satans Temptations' (154 [162]). The cluster of verses that follow stress our temptations and God's mercy in spite of them. Another section contains 'Promises made to Gods People in the most dangerous Times. What confidence we should have in God' (163). While each verse could be said to fit the theme of trusting to God in dangerous times, the passages she has found in the Psalms seem especially apt (such as, 'When the Wicked even mine Enemies, and my Foes came upon me to eat up my Flesh, they stumbled and fell', Psalm 27.2). After many psalm passages, Katherine Clarke evidently decided that five verses from the Pauline epistles also fit, including one approving as righteous that God metes tribulation on those who trouble you (2 Thessalonians 1.6). Within an overarching theme, Katherine Clarke

[22] Kate Narveson, *Bible Readers and Lay Writers in Early Modern England: Gender and Self-Definition in an Emergent Writing Culture* (Farnham, 2012), 62. In this section, Narveson demonstrates how Elizabeth Hastings and Elizabeth Egerton gained a kind of 'alternative rhetorical education' from reading the Bible.

[23] Alec Ryrie, *Being Protestant in Reformation Britain* (Oxford, 2013), 305.

[24] Nicholas Byfield, *Directions for the Private Reading of the Scriptures* (London, 1618), sigs. A5r–A12r; Isaac Ambrose, *Prima, Media, & Ultima, the First, Middle, and Last Things in Three Treatises* (London, 1659), 477–88. Unlike the two examples I discuss here by Katherine Clarke and Anne Waller, Byfield and Ambrose recommend just citing the biblical book, chapter, and verse and not transcribing the passages.

[25] Samuel Clarke, *The Lives of Sundry Eminent Persons in this Later Age in Two Parts: I. Of Divines, II. Of Nobility and Gentry of Both Sexes*, part two (London, 1683), 157–8.

marries passages that exalt in the punishment of the wicked with those that comfort God's people. It is not always obvious why certain verses are chosen instead of others, but arguably a patchwork rather than a narrative unfolds; the places in Scripture where Katherine Clarke has chosen to pause show her own process of making meaning.[26] Evidently losing steam, Samuel explains that he transcribed the above promises made to God's people but that he now will list only the heads, 'to prevent tediousness'. Twenty-six headings follow (with several subheadings), many of which have the word 'Promises' or 'Comforts' in the title (164).[27] The impression that Samuel's account of his wife's manuscript writing gives us is of a compiler who read the Bible with an attentive eye to the topics of comfort, hope, and salvation, mining Scripture for messages of consolation and hoping to strengthen her faith.

When looking at manuscripts created by compilers whose motivations are opaque, various interpretive lenses present themselves. If we look for gender commentary are we twisting the evidence to fit a feminist interest that may be only tangentially there? If we want evidence of aesthetic engagement and a literary sensibility in order to prove a compiler's agency, are we in danger of applying literary criteria to non-literary material? Methodologically, the process of reconstructing someone's reading practices through tracing their sources can get us closer to their historical milieu and their reading material, but their desires might not line up with a scholar's desires to make each choice in a patchwork significant and worthy of study.

Another writer, Anne Waller, also used commonplacing techniques in two of her manuscripts.[28] The Folger manuscript is a mixture of Scripture collation and commonplacing, sermon notes, records of autobiographical events, and commentary on current political upheaveals from the late 1640s to the early 1660s. Many pages are arranged into two columns, often with further horizontal divisions within those columns. Waller often uses the terminology of commonplacing in her headings: numerous biblical passages are listed as 'places', 'promises', or 'helps'. On page two, for example, the six headings are: 'prays' [i.e., presumably 'praise'], 'prayer', 'fayth', 'remarkable', 'Commands', and 'who are blesd'; under these headings are listed many passages, primarily from the Psalms. What makes a passage 'remarkable' to Waller is up for debate, and this is a term she uses at several points in the two manuscripts. Her second manuscript, now at the British Library, was compiled in two main phases, and contains sermons compiled between 1641 and 1642 and more heterogeneous material entered in the late 1640s, including quotations from Scripture and sermons, plus a statement of faith. Her practices of note-taking, gathering, summarising, and ordering, all show a reader fully engaged with her religious life, and one sometimes attuned to matters we

[26] For a discussion of the 'patchwork logic' of manuscript miscellanies, see Piers Brown, 'Donne, Rhapsody, and Textual Order', in Joshua Eckhardt and Daniel Starza Smith (eds), *Manuscript Miscellanies in Early Modern England* (Farnham, 2014), 39–55, 55.

[27] The word 'Promises' appears in twelve headings and 'Comforts' (or 'Comfort') in seven.

[28] Washington, DC, Folger Shakespeare Library, MS V.b.376 and London, British Library, MS Harley 6028.

might consider aesthetic or formal. A striking image might have been one cause to label a passage as 'remarkable'. In the Folger manuscript, she has one heading on page 68 which reads 'remarkable pasadges', although there is only one entry. This is, 'it may fall out that a Mans religious dutys be the stage upon which all a Mans lusts doe eminently act,—as the pharises who did all to be seen of Men'.[29] It does seem a remarkable and noteworthy idea that the performing of religious duties could be a stage for a man's lusts rather than for his piety. In the British Library manuscript there are other passages labelled 'remarkable' and exactly why the compiler found them to be so is unclear. But one section headed 'plases of sripture speasially observable' (fol. 106r) contains a cluster of passages from the Song of Songs which do seem especially interesting in their natural imagery, their eroticism, and in their use of a sometimes female speaking voice desiring a male beloved. These are followed by more 'plases of sripture speasially remarkable' (fol. 106v), which include more lines from the Song of Songs, and a passage from the Psalms which begins, 'Kiss the sonne lest he be angry' (2.12), and then 'speasiall remarkable pasadges in the profesy of esay' (i.e., Isaiah; fols. 107v–108v). One can guess that the striking imagery and the eroticism of some of the Song of Songs and Psalm verses, plus the often bloody and bizarre nature of some of Isaiah's prophecies, would qualify as noteworthy. These passages are remarkable and observable for what they suggest about the suffering of God's chosen people, and for the yearning and sensuality that religious expression can encompass.

Perhaps in the cases of Katherine Clarke and Anne Waller, commonplacing and making compilations was less about interpreting literature than about interpreting their own lives. Men and women used methods of commonplacing to many different ends, but women's collections of miscellaneous materials can have distinct profiles, and are worth examining for what they can teach us about their compilers' sense of cultural capital and of their literary and religious lives. Sometimes organised by topic or by writer, or apparently not organised at all, these volumes are above all records of textual interpretation. Scholars on the lookout for flashes of creativity, agency, and surprising imagery risk misconstruing the texts before them, and yet an openness to uncertainty in how we should be interpreting these documents might allow us to get closer to understanding their audiences and functions. Compilation was widely understood to be a form of writing in the early modern period and so all documents of this type are worth studying, though asking undergraduates to stop reading Shakespeare in favour of commonplace books and miscellanies is an unlikely proposition. What we could do in addition to reading literary texts like Shakespeare's poetry and plays is to investigate how readers like Sarah Cowper read them, in order to study canonical literature through a historical lens. If we include less literary texts—such as the Bible, sermons, and other religious material of the kind Katherine Clarke and Anne Waller read—we might be able

[29] In my transcriptions from both manuscripts I have silently expanded abbreviations. This passage comes from a section of Anthony Burgess, *Spiritual Refining* (London, 1652), 16, a tract from which she quotes elsewhere.

to construct a picture of what motivated our ancestors to interact with many of the most popular examples of the printed word, the steady sellers of their day.[30]

PRINT WRITERS USING (AND NOT USING) COMMONPLACE TECHNIQUES

It may be a little artificial to distinguish clearly between mere readers and compilers, on the one hand, and writers of original works, on the other. As many scholars such as Peter Stallybrass have reminded us, invention was based on using the inventory of the past, and our modern notions of originality are not appropriate.[31] But it is reasonable to note that some women chose to seek an audience, in print and/or in manuscript, and could thus be considered writers in a more straightforward way. What did the techniques of commonplacing and miscellany compilation offer to a writer putting their work out into the world? Ben Jonson and John Milton are among many erudite writers who made use of these methods. Jonson's *Timber: Or, Discoveries* was printed posthumously, but it contains extracts from classical and contemporary writers organised with marginal glosses into topics.[32] Milton kept a multilingual commonplace book which contains passages from ninety-five authors written under topics arranged into three indexes (moral, economic, and political). Thomas Fulton has argued that Milton used it to collect ideas rather than aphorisms, which then found expression in his printed tracts.[33]

The value judgement implicit in the claim that Milton collected ideas rather than aphorisms is one with which many scholars would agree. Our preference for incisive thought rather than proverbial truisms makes it difficult to study the first half of Isabella Whitney's *A Sweet Nosegay* (1573), a versification of 110 prose aphorisms. Mary Ellen Lamb has argued that the 883 commonplaces in Whitney's source, Hugh Plat's *Floures of Philosophie*, are 'entirely unexceptional' and that critics have been puzzled over their appeal to Whitney.[34] But Whitney evidently valued both her source material and her transformation of it, surrounding her 110 quatrains with a number of items that draw attention to her labour in gathering and framing these flowers. This commentary on her

[30] For a discussion of Protestant bestsellers and steady sellers, see Ian Green, *Print and Protestantism in Early Modern England* (Oxford, 2000).

[31] Peter Stallybrass, 'Against Thinking', *Publications of the Modern Language Association*, 122 (2007), 1580–7, 1584.

[32] Ben Jonson, *Timber: Or, Discoveries; Made upon Men and Matter: As They Have Flow'd out of His Daily Readings; or Had Their Refluxe to His Peculiar Notion of the Times*, in *The Workes of Benjamin Jonson* (London, 1641).

[33] Thomas Fulton, *Historical Milton: Manuscript, Print, and Political Culture in Revolutionary England* (Amherst, MA, 2010), 38–81.

[34] Mary Ellen Lamb, 'Isabella Whitney and Reading Humanism', in Leah Knight, Micheline White, and Elizabeth Sauer (eds), *Women's Bookscapes in Early Modern Britain: Reading, Ownership, Circulation* (Ann Arbor, MI, 2018), 43–58, 48.

efforts figures in the items that preface the posy (her dedicatory epistle and her poetic address to the reader, as well as the commendatory poem by 'T. B.') and the two poems that follow it (a short receipt to make a conserve with a fleur-de-lis and a farewell to the reader). Elizabeth Sauer reminds us of the humanist labour involved in products that we would consider to be derivative: Whitney carries on Plat's own work of 'reading, selection, imitation, versification, and assembly' from his pseudo-Senecan sources and employs the arts of 'mimesis, adaptation, [and] translation' in her ordering of Plat's garden.[35] But even more than simply participating in a respectable and creative scholarly activity, Whitney uses the authorial metaphor of 'gathering' in a gendered manner, according to Whitney Trettien.[36] In *A Sweet Nosegay*, Isabella Whitney plays on the long tradition of describing textual extracts as flowers and cuttings from her main source text, but Trettien argues that Whitney adds a pun on 'slips' as embroidered squares, something women produced, to evoke both floral and textual slips, and 'to carve out a space for her own composition'.[37] Trettien's interpretation—which links reading, writing, picking flowers, and sewing—reminds us that compilation practices can have a distinctly gendered angle. The second half of Whitney's volume, comprising poems of complaint often addressed to family members, and the funny and biting mock-will to London that excoriates the city's indifference to the poor, has appealed most to today's readers. One way to integrate the aphorisms with the more original poetry is to find thematic parallels, as Lamb persuasively does in Whitney's treatment of friendship, the dangers of slander, and economic vulnerability, and in her self-presentation as a virtuous, sensible person.[38] Whitney selects, paraphrases, versifies, and integrates her own readings of a source text she deems authoritative, obliging today's readers to consider how she interpreted Plat's garden even though they are more eager to interpret the verse epistles and the mock-will.

Margaret Cavendish, Duchess of Newcastle would appear to be the last person to discuss in relation to commonplaces and stores of proverbial wisdom since she makes a point of proclaiming her singularity, originality, and lack of reading. She states her desire to be 'Margaret the First' in the preface to *The Blazing World* (1666) and she claims the primacy of a self-generated fancy, or imaginative inspiration, in her poetic and scientific writing.[39] At various points Cavendish disavows scholarly learning, such as in

[35] Elizabeth Sauer, 'Anthologizing Practices, Women's Literary History, and the Case of Isabella Whitney', in Arthur F. Marotti (ed.), *New Ways of Looking at Old Texts, VI: Papers of the Renaissance English Text Society, 2011–2016* (Tempe, AZ, 2019), 103–16, 110–11.

[36] Whitney Trettien, 'Isabella Whitney's Slips: Textile Labour, Gendered Authorship, and the Early Modern Miscellany', in *The Renaissance Collage: Toward a New History of Reading*, special issue of *Journal of Medieval and Early Modern Studies*, 45 (2015), 505–21.

[37] Trettien, 'Isabella Whitney's Slips', 516.

[38] Lamb, 'Isabella Whitney and Reading Humanism', 51–6. Dana E. Lawrence also discusses thematic links across Whitney's volume in 'Isabella Whitney's "Slips": Poetry, Collaboration, and Coterie', in Patricia Phillippy (ed.), *A History of Early Modern Women's Writing* (Cambridge, 2018), 119–36, 127–30.

[39] Sylvia Bowerbank and Sara Mendelson (eds), *Paper Bodies: A Margaret Cavendish Reader* (Peterborough, ON, 2000), 153.

her epistle 'To Natural Philosophers'. She writes that she 'never read nor heard of any English book to instruct [her]' and that her lack of knowledge of 'mother tongues' [Latin and Greek, presumably] 'in which learning is propagated, makes [her] ignorant of the opinions and discourses in former times'.[40] She also eschews the principle of imitation, a Renaissance literary strategy which could be aided by collecting passages from other writers. The soul of the character called the Duchess of Newcastle in *The Blazing World* explains that:

> her ambition being such, that she would not be like others in any thing if it were possible; I endeavour, said she, to be as singular as I can; for it argues but a mean Nature to imitate others; and though I do not love to be imitated if I can possibly avoid it; yet rather then imitate others, I should choose to be imitated by others.[41]

This desire for exceptionalism would seem to leave little room for responding to tradition. Cavendish's conception of the mind in several of her poems in her collection *Poems and Fancies* (1653) is a good indication of how she views the role of fancy or invention. In the first half of 'Similizing the Mind', she depicts the mind as a merchant, searching for opinions in the ocean of the brain; he then lays goods (that have been brought by imagination's ships) in the warehouse of remembrance. In this account of thinking, opinions are to be found in the brain, not in reading authorities' words, and the goods that are to be stored in memory have been brought by imagination, not by learning. Though this is one of many poems in which Cavendish contemplates how cognition might work (for example, another poem in the collection is titled 'The Fairies in the Brain May Be the Causes of Many Thoughts'), it is a good barometer of her inventive approach to tradition. Elizabeth Spiller and Lara Dodds are two critics who have investigated Cavendish as a reader, and they have shown that her various poses of unlearned amateur and self-generator of ideas do not give credit to the extent to which she read and responded to contemporary debates and to classical learning.[42] Dodds, for example, demonstrates how Cavendish refuses to read Plutarch's *Lives* in a way that would allow her to extract morals for use, and prefers instead to offer her own sceptical analysis.[43] Cavendish rejects humanist processes of reading and so her lack of interest in commonplacing is a logical part of her self-presentation.

Ann Moss argues that by the late seventeenth century, new methods of scientific enquiry and new modes of taste which countered the abundance and contradiction of the

[40] In Liza Blake (ed.), *Margaret Cavendish's Poems and Fancies: A Digital Critical Edition* (2019), University of Toronto, http://library2.utm.utoronto.ca/poemsandfancies/2019/05/04/to-natural-philosophers/, accessed 25 November 2020.

[41] Bowerbank and Mendelson, *Paper Bodies*, 245.

[42] Elizabeth Spiller, *Science, Reading, and Renaissance Literature: The Art of Making Knowledge, 1580–1670* (Cambridge, 2004), 137–77; Lara Dodds, *The Literary Invention of Margaret Cavendish* (Pittsburgh, PA, 2013).

[43] Dodds, *Literary Invention*, 23–56.

commonplace book led to the form's decline.[44] But less scholarly versions of the practice of commonplacing, and of compiling extracts from one's reading into miscellanies, persisted. Whether compiled by women or men, these documents are distinguished by their variety. This variety is found in their contents, in the social circumstances of their compilers, in the individual choices of placement of items and of layout: each document negotiates these choices differently. In the sphere of religion we see a space where women such as Katherine Clarke and Anne Waller were encouraged to participate in this mode of organising, shaping, and responding to texts, sometimes turning constraints into creation. Women's compilations, whether literary, devotional, educational, or all or none of these categories, can offer windows into how readers interpreted their worlds.

FURTHER READING

Burke, Victoria E. 'Recent Studies in Commonplace Books', *English Literary Renaissance*, 43 (2013), 153–77.

Eckhardt, Joshua and Daniel Starza Smith (eds). *Manuscript Miscellanies in Early Modern England*. Farnham, 2014.

McCarthy, Erin A. 'Reading Women Reading Donne in Manuscript and Printed Miscellanies: A Quantitative Approach', *The Review of English Studies*, 69 (2018), 661–85.

Narveson, Kate. *Bible Readers and Lay Writers in Early Modern England: Gender and Self-Definition in an Emergent Writing Culture*. Farnham, 2012.

Smyth, Adam. 'Commonplace Book Culture: A List of Sixteen Traits', in Anne Lawrence-Mathers and Phillipa Hardman (eds), *Women and Writing, c.1340–c.1650: The Domestication of Print Culture*. Woodbridge, 2010, 90–110.

[44] Ann Moss, *Printed Common-Place Books and the Structuring of Renaissance Thought* (Oxford, 1996), 255–81.

CHAPTER 16

WOMEN'S LIFE WRITING AND THE LABOUR OF TEXTUAL STEWARDSHIP

JULIE A. ECKERLE

As studies of both life writing and early modern Englishwomen's writing have proliferated in recent decades, they have often intersected, yielding an enriched understanding of sixteenth- and seventeenth-century women's engagement in life writing, as well as a revised perspective on auto/biographical writing more generally.[1] Most significantly, analysis of life writing by early modern women—in combination with a broader feminist critique—has forced us to completely rethink the terminology applied to life-writing texts and the generic requirements of some life-writing forms, especially 'autobiography'.[2] Until quite recently, this relatively modern term and its definition as a 'unified, retrospective first-person narrative [that] uniquely totalizes its subject as both author and hero' determined how scholars approached most life writing.[3] Yet

[1] I use the phrase 'auto/biographical writing' as a synonym for 'life writing', both of which encompass autobiographical *and* biographical forms.

[2] See, for example, Shari Benstock, *The Private Self: Theory and Practice of Women's Autobiographical Writings* (Chapel Hill, NC, 1988), who wrote that 'The very requirements of the genre are put into question by the limits of gender', 20.

[3] Michael Mascuch, *Origins of the Individualist Self: Autobiography and Self-Identity in England, 1592–1791* (Stanford, CA, 1996), 23. Even in a 2009 publication, *The Cambridge Companion to Early Modern Women's Writing*, the essay devoted to life writing is titled 'Autobiography', though the essay itself addresses diaries, memoirs, conversation narratives, and more. See Ramona Wray, 'Autobiography', in Laura Lunger Knoppers (ed.), *The Cambridge Companion to Early Modern Women's Writing* (Cambridge, 2009), 194–207. The dates most often noted for the first recorded use of the term 'autobiography' are 1797 in David Booy, 'General Introduction', in David Booy (ed.), *Personal Disclosures: An Anthology of Self-Writings from the Seventeenth Century* (Aldershot, 2002), 3; and 1809 in Felicity A. Nussbaum, *The Autobiographical Subject: Gender and Ideology in Eighteenth-Century England* (Baltimore, MD, 1989), 1. See also Linda Anderson, *Autobiography* (London, 2001), 7; and Mascuch, *Origins of the Individualist Self*, 19.

'autobiography' so understood precludes the kind of self-writing that women, especially in earlier periods, tended to produce; it fails to account for most forms of life writing beyond the most cohesive birth-to-late-adulthood narratives; and generally assumes authorship by a male public figure. Consequently, once the scholarly lens was freed from the limitations of this approach, a rich corpus of highly varied texts by writers from a range of social contexts became visible, and illuminating analyses of just what early modern life writing meant for its practitioners have followed at a fast and furious pace.

Life writing neither conveys a factual record of the historical past nor provides 'easy access to a "true self"'.[4] Yet reassessing the past through a female-narrated perspective inevitably yields an altered, differently nuanced historical picture. For example, analysis of early modern women's life writing composed in or about Ireland often conveys a very different impression of Ireland than that provided by the more traditional (male) political and colonial angle at the same time that it forces us to reexamine notions of gendered, religious, political, and national identity in this highly complicated context.[5] As several of the essays in the recent collection *Women's Life Writing and Early Modern Ireland* demonstrate, '"Ireland" and "Irishness" are floating signifiers for women, with the potential to mean different things at different times and for different purposes'.[6] This critical reminder that the scholarly approach to the early modern period was for too long patriarchal in nature also points to the Anglocentric bias that has thus far determined much of our work on early modern women's writing in English.[7]

That said, all life writing by early modern women used auto/biographical expression to engage in, process, manage, and sometimes intervene in a variety of life circumstances, both local and global. Put simply, life writing offered its female practitioners a practical means of agency, as well as, in many cases, a more personal and intellectual means of understanding and managing identity, an aspect of life writing that I call textual stewardship. In this chapter, I first provide an overview of the most common characteristics of early modern women's life writing as we now understand it, incorporating throughout specific textual examples that highlight women's innovation, flexibility, and creativity. I next illustrate how our understanding of early modern women's life writing becomes richer and more accurate if we think of their textual labour as a form of stewardship and

4 Wray, 'Autobiography', 195.

5 For a useful overview of women's early writing in Ireland, much of it 'life writing,' see Marie-Louise Coolahan, 'Writing Before 1700', in Heather Ingman and Clíona Ó Gallchóir (eds), *A History of Modern Irish Women's Literature* (Cambridge, 2018), 18–36.

6 Julie A. Eckerle and Naomi McAreavey, 'Introduction', in Julie A. Eckerle and Naomi McAreavey (eds), *Women's Life Writing and Early Modern Ireland* (Lincoln, 2019), 1–21, 10.

7 See Chapter 26, Sarah Prescott, 'Archipelagic Feminism'. In addition to Coolahan, 'Writing Before 1700', see Kate Chedgzoy, 'The Cultural Geographies of Early Modern Women's Writing: Journeys across Spaces and Times', *Literature Compass*, 3/4 (2006), 884–95, who claimed that 'the study of early modern women's writing might benefit from being situated in relation to more expansive, detailed and complex cultural geographies of the period', 884. This approach has become increasingly popular in recent years, with variations like 'multi-centred', 'Three Kingdoms', 'Four Nations', and 'New British History'. See also work on Scotland, such as David George Mullan's important anthology *Women's Life Writing in Early Modern Scotland: Writing the Evangelical Self, c. 1670–c. 1730* (Aldershot, 2003), and on Wales.

if—as I have just suggested—we broaden our analytical lens to the entire British Atlantic Archipelago (see this volume, Chapter 26, Sarah Prescott, 'Archipelagic Feminism').[8]

EARLY MODERN WOMEN'S LIFE WRITING: AN OVERVIEW

As a result of critical work since the late twentieth century, several aspects of early modern women's life writing have become clear. First, early modern women made use of *multiple* life-writing forms, many of which are only now coming to be understood as life writing. In addition to familiar, canonical genres like diary, memoir, and autobiographical prose narrative, women also produced prophetic discourse, conversion narratives, spiritual testimony, lives (often of fathers and husbands), travel narratives, memorandum books, meditations, genealogical records, prison narratives, chronicles, mothers' legacies, and autobiography-inflected fiction like the *roman à clef*.[9] They also left auto/biographical fragments in the margins of recipe books, in letters, in prefaces to literary texts, and even via the words engraved on monuments.[10] Auto/biographical

[8] An important intervention in the study of early modern women is to recognise and reframe their contributions to and participation in rhetorical and textual developments as 'labour'. Valerie Wayne (ed.), *Women's Labour and the History of the Book in Early Modern England* (New York, 2020), is an excellent example.

[9] In the early modern period, 'memoir' denoted both autobiographical and biographical accounts. See Helen M. Buss, *Repossessing the World: Reading Memoirs by Contemporary Women* (Waterloo, 2002), esp. 1–26, for an overview of the history and development of the memoir form. Wray's 'Autobiography' describes the memoir as 'a text which ... offer[s] a denser and more retrospective rehearsal of the life story', 198, than the early modern diary. The term 'biography' came into use in the seventeenth century, but 'life' was far more common; the term 'history' could also apply to a textual 'life'. For meditations as life writing, see Raymond A. Anselment, 'Introduction', in Anselment (ed.), *The Occasional Meditations of Mary Rich, Countess of Warwick* (Tempe, AZ, 2009), 1–36.

[10] For recipes, see Chapter 22, Wendy Wall, 'The World of Recipes' and Catherine Field, '"Many hands hands": Writing the Self in Early Modern Women's Recipe Books', in Julie A. Eckerle and Michelle M. Dowd (eds), *Genre and Women's Life Writing in Early Modern England* (Aldershot, 2007), 49–63. The epistolary genre is a topic unto itself, though certainly a sub-genre of life writing as well. See James Daybell, 'Recent Studies in Seventeenth-Century Letters', *English Literary Renaissance*, 36 (2006), 135–70, and *Early Modern Women's Letter Writing, 1450–1700* (New York, 2001) and, in this *Handbook*, Chapter 7, Helen Smith, 'Cultures of Correspondence: Women and Natural Philosophy'; Chapter 36, Daniel Starza Smith and Leah Veronese, 'Desire, Dreams, Disguise: The Letters of Elizabeth Bourne' and Chapter 37, Nadine Akkerman, 'Women's Letters and Cryptological Coteries'. For prefaces, see Julie A. Eckerle, 'Prefacing Texts, Authorizing Authors, and Constructing Selves: The Preface as Autobiographical Space', in Dowd and Eckerle (eds), *Genre and Women's Life Writing*, 97–113. Both literal monuments and texts memorialize via life writing. It is no coincidence, for example, that Lucy Hutchinson describes her biography of her late husband, *The Life of John Hutchinson of Owthorpe*, as a 'monument' (17) to him, in N. H. Keeble (ed.), *Memoirs of the Life of Colonel Hutchinson with a Fragment of Autobiography* (London, 1995), or that Arnold Boate refers to his *The Character of a Trulie Vertuous and Pious Woman* (Paris, 1651) as a means of providing his deceased wife, Margaret, with 'a farre statelier monument' (A3).

tales were incorporated into law cases and depositions and can be extrapolated from book inscriptions and wills.[11] In short, early modern women's life writing was highly varied and much more common than we have hitherto thought.

Second, early modern women were extraordinarily flexible and creative in their auto/biographical writing, often combining aspects of multiple life-writing forms in a single text.[12] Indeed, it is fair to say that variety and generic complexity are the defining features of this remarkable corpus, in part because the various forms of life writing with which early modern women engaged were themselves much more flexible than later codification allowed for and in part because female life writers applied flexibility, ingenuity, creativity, unique personal goals, and an often fluid sense of self to their self-constructions. Although there are often many formulaic aspects of their texts, generally speaking, women tended to produce hybrid texts that defy both expectation and categorisation. Precisely how or how much female life writers innovated depended on a number of factors, such as the writer's purpose, skill, degree and type of literacies, and material and geographical environment. Yet they consistently made use of a variety of elements from different genres and subgenres for the creation of unique life-writing texts. In many cases, furthermore, generic blending entailed a more, rather than less, rigorous approach to genre, and evidence suggests that early modern women were often keenly aware of formal requirements and expectations. For example, as Michelle M. Dowd has demonstrated of mothers' legacy author Elizabeth Richardson (1576/77–1651), Richardson strategically blended elements of different forms in *A Ladies Legacie to her Daughters* (1645) and deliberately undermined specific generic expectations in the construction of the text best suited to her purpose, allegiances, and individual context. In this way, '[g]eneric hybridity ... becomes a ... useful ... literary tool', one consistently manipulated by early modern women.[13]

Third, these women used form to construct and represent particular versions of self, sometimes multiple selves across different forms. Women's generic choices thus reveal

[11] For law cases, see Chapter 21, Lotte Fikkers, 'The Self-Portrayal of Widows'. For depositions, see the extensive, now-digitized 1641 Depositions (http://1641.tcd.ie, accessed 30 June 2021), which collected the testimony of both male and female settlers (i.e., New English Protestants) after the 1641 rising in Ireland and contains a wealth of auto/biographical information, although obviously mediated in complex ways. As Coolahan explains in 'Writing Before 1700', 'The act of deposing encouraged self-representation and the terms of the commission supplied a narrative structure', 23. Furthermore, on some occasions, as 'in the case of Lady Elizabeth Dowdall, the act of deposing prompted the composition of a separate first-person account ... that is unshackled from the pro-forma constraints of a deposition', 24.

[12] As early as 1996, Elspeth Graham argued that the key commonality in early modern women's life writing was its 'exploration and exploitation of a variety of forms, rather than adherence to a recognized format for articulating the self'. Although not speaking of women's writing in particular, Adam Smyth notes that 'generic unfixity and experimentation' are not only common in early modern auto/biographical writing but actually 'a *condition* of autobiographical writing'. See Graham, 'Women's Writing and the Self', in Helen Wilcox (ed.), *Women and Literature in Britain 1500–1700* (Cambridge, 1996), 123; and Smyth, 'Introduction', in Adam Smyth (ed.), *A History of English Autobiography* (Cambridge, 2016), 6, 7 (emphasis added).

[13] Michelle M. Dowd, 'Structures of Piety in Elizabeth Richardson's *Legacie*', in Dowd and Eckerle, *Genre and Women's Life Writing*, 116.

the complex ways they thought about personal identity, as well as the various literacies and texts that they drew on in order to record written versions of self or selves. Whatever the genre or narrative formula, the relationship between form and self, or language and selfhood, proves to be mutually constitutive, such that women chose (and often manipulated) particular forms based on the self they intended to present in a particular text.[14] Such is the case with Mary Rich, Countess of Warwick (1624/5–1678), whose autobiography and multivolume diary, as a number of scholars have observed, convey drastically different versions of her marriage and spouse.[15] In her autobiography, Charles Rich (*c* 1623–1673) is the appealing and idealised suitor of romance, and Rich is the woman who defies father and family to marry him. However, in her diaries, Charles is a constant source of conflict and consternation, and Rich is a martyred wife who relies on devotions and prayers to 'bringe my minde into frame'.[16] Although both texts impose a spiritual lens on Rich's past and present, '[t]he disparity between these two versions of Rich's life illuminates the shifting ground between competing constructions of "truth", between narrative convention and autobiographical insertion, and between generic trajectory and personal life journey'.[17] In other words, genre determines self.

Fourth, as is true of all auto/biographical texts, early modern women's life writing is intensely and thoroughly rhetorical, driven by authorial purpose, intended audience, and the unique confluence of time, place, geographical context, and personal identity as perceived at that moment. As rhetorical documents, then, life-writing texts contain evidence of women's rhetorical and narrative skill and technique, as well as the writers' pressing concerns, efforts at legacy building, and self-justification. But the texts are always fundamentally unstable, since the textual representations therein vary according to the rhetorical context at the moment of writing and sometimes beyond that moment, as women not infrequently revised or even rewrote their texts as circumstances changed. This was the case, for example, with Alice Thornton (1626/27–1706/7), who rewrote her first autobiographical narrative by expanding it into a much longer three-part version, thus resulting in four different manuscript texts.[18] Similarly, Elizabeth Freke (1641/42–1714) produced two versions of her *Remembrances*, the latter of which 'both retells and revises the earlier version, adding and deleting material to

[14] The mutually constitutive relationship between form and self is a key idea in all the essays in Dowd and Eckerle (eds), *Genre and Women's Life Writing*. See also Booy, 'General Introduction', 6.

[15] See, for example, Julie A. Eckerle, *Romancing the Self in Early Modern Englishwomen's Life Writing* (Aldershot, 2013), 148–58, and Ramona Wray, '[Re]Constructing the Past: The Diametric Lives of Mary Rich,' in Hank Dragstra, Sheila Ottway, and Helen Wilcox (eds), *Betraying our Selves: Forms of Self-Representation in Early Modern English Texts* (London, 2000), 148–65. Rich's autobiography was published posthumously as *Some Specialities in the Life of M. Warwicke*, in T. C. Croker (ed.), *The Autobiography of Mary Countess of Warwick* (London, 1848), 1–38. Her life-writing corpus also includes spiritual meditations.

[16] Mary Rich, London, British Library, Additional MS 27351, vol. 1, fol. 140v.

[17] Wray, 'Autobiography', 199.

[18] For the textual history of Thornton's complex corpus, see Raymond A. Anselment, 'Seventeenth-Century Manuscript Sources of Alice Thornton's Life', *SEL: Studies in English Literature 1500–1900*, 45.1 (2005), 135–55.

gain a tighter chronological continuity'.[19] Significantly, revisions like Thornton's and Freke's are not purely editorial, reminding us that a textual self is far from fixed and that a woman's agency in penning her self could also be enacted by changing that self when and how she deemed fit.

Fifth, early modern women's life writing was rarely published in print, yet it *was* published and often circulated in manuscript. Thornton, for example, shared her first version of her narrative among friends not long after her daughter's controversial marriage in an effort to defend her choices in relation to the match.[20] Female-authored biographical texts, such as *The Life of William Cavendish Duke of Newcastle* (1667) by Margaret Cavendish (1623–1673), were more likely to see print.[21] But looking only to print obscures the sheer quantity and variety of early modern women's life writing. Archival research has been essential to the study of this corpus and in fact continues to reward, having in recent years yielded the fascinating epistolary account of Mrs. Briver (fl. 1641), wife of the local mayor during the 1641 rebellion at Waterford in Ireland; the biographical romance (or *roman à clef*) *A Short History of the Life and Death of Sr Ceasor Dappefer* by Dorothy Calthorpe (1648–1693); and the memorandum book of Elizabeth Boyle, Countess of Cork and Burlington (1613–1690).[22] Increasingly, both print and digital editions are making these manuscripts more accessible, ideally in ways that fully and accurately reveal their authors' unique editorial and artistic decisions, but manuscript archives continue to be essential to ongoing research.[23]

19 Raymond A. Anselment, 'Introduction', in Raymond A. Anselment (ed.), *The Remembrances of Elizabeth Freke, 1671–1714* (Cambridge, 2001), 20.

20 Anselment, 'Seventeenth-Century Manuscript Sources', 136. At issue were the daughter's age (fourteen), potential fraud, and the possibility that Thornton herself was interested in the groom. For more on the impetus for Thornton's energetic and insistent life writing, see Anselment, 'Seventeenth-Century Manuscript Sources,' and '"My first Booke of my Life": The Apology of a Seventeenth-Century Gentry Woman', *Prose Studies*, 24 (2001), 1–14.

21 Margaret Cavendish, in C. H. Firth (ed.), *The Life of William Cavendish Duke of Newcastle* (London, 1886).

22 For analysis and a transcription of Briver's narrative, see Naomi McAreavey, 'An Epistolary Account of the Irish Rising of 1641 by the Wife of the Mayor of Waterford [with text]', *English Literary Renaissance*, 42.1 (2012), 90–118, and '"This is that I may remember what passings that happened in Waterford": Inscribing the 1641 Rising in the Letters of the Wife of the Mayor of Waterford', *Early Modern Women: An Interdisciplinary Journal* 5 (2010), 77–109. Calthorpe's two extant manuscripts, one of which includes the romance, will be published with The Other Voices in Early Modern Europe Toronto series as *News from the Midell Regions and Calthorpe's Chapel*, Eckerle (ed.) (Toronto, forthcoming). See also Eckerle, *Romancing the Self*, 163–74. Boyle's manuscript memorandum book, which Ann-Maria Walsh is editing for the Irish Manuscripts Commission, is 'Elizabeth Lady Burlington Memorandum Book', Chatsworth, Cork MSS, Miscellaneous Box 5.

23 Some editions, such as Rich's *Memoir of Lady Warwick: Also Her Diary* (London, 1847), were published in the nineteenth century, but most of these are highly problematic due to their editors' tendency to excerpt, selection criteria, and over-zealous correction, among other concerns. In contrast, Heather Wolfe's 2001 edition of *Elizabeth Cary Lady Falkland: Life and Letters* (Cambridge and Tempe) is exemplary for the way it captures the textual complexities of its manuscript sources.

LIFE WRITING AS TEXTUAL STEWARDSHIP

Taken together, these basic points about early modern women's life writing underscore just how rich, complex, and varied this body of material is. Female life writers came from many political and spiritual persuasions, they produced both spiritual and secular texts, and their motives were as diverse as their individual experiences. Quite often women wrote out of self-concern, in order to justify an act, defend behaviour, or counter rumour. But they also composed life writing out of concern for others—as was often the case when writing a life of a maligned relative or simply a very beloved one—and most often women wrote out of a combination of motives, sometimes for self and others at the same time. Regardless of the individual whose life is constructed, however, women's life writing was often an act of stewardship: creating, solidifying, protecting, and/or maintaining an individual's reputation via text. Through careful stewardship of the details that comprise a life, a woman could do her part towards assuring that her preferred version of that life persisted into posterity.

Calthorpe's authorial choices throughout her corpus offer a case in point. For example, her fictional representation of her uncle John Reynolds (1625–1657) in *A Short History* notably elides both his Parliamentarian affiliation (a problematic detail in a post-Restoration text) and a scandal that had tainted his heroic reputation near the end of his life; consequently, as *A Short History*'s Hilarious Vare, he remains 'the bravest man and the greatest warrior in that age'.[24] Since *A Short History* represents Calthorpe's family in the guise of fiction, she is able to project not just an idealized image of individuals like Reynolds but also of the Calthorpe family as a whole and even herself. Significantly, Calthorpe makes stewardship an explicit theme of her work, as in *A Short History* she traces the development of Caesor and Jewlious Dappefer (who represent her father and grandfather) into ideal stewards of the Calthorpe name and property.[25] This point is not-so-subtly reinforced in the fictional surname Calthorpe assigns them, as 'dapifer' is literally a term for 'one who brings meat to table; hence, the official title of the steward of a king's or nobleman's household' (*OED*). Significantly, as I have noted elsewhere, Calthorpe's earliest recorded ancestors actually held the position of dapifer in their local religious community; her use of this name, then, demonstrates not only her thorough knowledge of her family's history but also, most significantly, the thoughtfulness with which she constructed her most immediate male ancestors' textual reincarnation

[24] Calthorpe, *Short History*, fol. 54r. All references to Calthorpe's manuscripts are to my forthcoming edition, *News from the Midell Regions and Calthorpe's Chapel*. Reynolds' excellent reputation as a Parliamentarian army officer and member of the Cromwell inner circle had been tainted by his 'friendly but noncommittal interview with James, duke of York' not long before his death at sea (*ODNB*).

[25] Caesar and Jewlious represent Calthorpe's paternal grandfather, Sir Henry Calthorpe (1586–1637), and her father, Sir James Calthorpe (1626–1659), respectively.

in her writing.[26] Indeed, in a move that brings together the spiritual and the familial, Calthorpe introduces these characters and their prodigal-son like story only after her 'A Discription of the Garden of Edden', a prose narrative in which Adam apologises to his descendants for so carelessly losing their inheritance. Although both Caesor and Jewlious also behave somewhat carelessly in their youth, they eventually heed the lesson of Adam's story and mature into their ideal roles over time. As the narrator says of Jewlious in a kind of afterword, he had 'provided for us all out of his own industerry without being be holding to his famely'.[27] This, she further suggests, is the logical and right conclusion of an individual's story: *A Short History* can end because there is 'no reason to unreauell any furder [unravel any further]'.[28] But of course the story *does* continue in the form of descendants (the 'us' of Calthorpe's comment). Indeed, although she does not write herself into *A Short History* as a character, she *does* take care to embody in her life the kind of Calthorpe stewardship represented in her text. Most significantly, she demonstrates fiscal responsibility with a bequest for the founding of an almshouse, and she explicitly defends the family name with her *Short History*. She is, in other words, the logical product of a line of exemplary Christian stewards.

Whether performing the work of an ideal widow by seeing her husband's remains into print, as Jane Bonnell (*c* 1670–1745) did for James (1653–1699), Accountant-General of Ireland; Calthorpe implying her own Christian stewardship as the logical descendant of her idealised forefathers; or someone like Lady Ann Fanshawe (1625–1680) producing her own memoir via a text that was 'ostensibly written as a biography of her husband', Sir Richard Fanshawe (1608–1666), women's biographical writing is always some form of self-writing as well.[29] As Ramona Wray puts it, 'the biographical project in the period was inextricably intertwined with the autobiographical, and ... for women, the particular and local distinctions between autobiographical and biographical representations are simply not sustainable'.[30] Approaching female life writers as stewards of their own and others' lives thus usefully underscores the agency they were able to wield in the act of authoring auto/biographical texts. In the kinds of examples I have provided, written when the biographical subjects are already deceased, the female writers or curators clearly manage the way the world will remember the 'heavenly remains' of their loved ones.[31] In this way, while certainly not equivalent in most cases to a man's agency within a patriarchal culture, life writing offered early modern women a kind of power that—depending on the woman's circumstances and class—varied widely

[26] The most thorough treatment of Calthorpe's life, family, and texts is available in the introduction to my forthcoming edition, *News from the Midell Regions and Calthorpe's Chapel.*

[27] *Short History*, fols. 61v–62r.

[28] *Short History*, fol. 61v.

[29] Coolahan, 'Writing Before 1700', 28. Bonnell did not write her husband's life herself but was nonetheless the key driver behind its ultimate publication, in 1703, as William Hamilton's *The Exemplary Life and Character of James Bonnell.*

[30] Wray, 'Autobiography', 200.

[31] Bonnell used this phrase in a 1701 letter to William King. Dublin, Trinity College Dublin, MS 1995–2008/752.

in purpose, degree, and efficacy. Sometimes, for example, deploying agency in the act of life writing might mean simply assuring that an author appears to meet her culture's standards for an exemplary woman: appropriately modest, dutiful, and obedient. Many life-writing genres, especially lives and spiritual testimonies, were in fact based on the idea of providing in print exemplary models of pious living. But it behooves us to read carefully, with a full awareness of rhetorical context, to see where other motives and actions might be at work.

Even at the level of grammar, syntax, and style, there is often much to be learned. For example, early modern women's diaries are frequently sparse and, as Wray notes, often contain repetitive, formulaic phrases. Yet, as her brief analysis of Rich's diary-writing demonstrates, '[a]ttention to linguistic habits, syntactical arrangements and recurring motifs ... offers heightened awareness of this particular writing subject's domestic conditions'.[32] The extensive corpus of Anne Clifford, Countess of Pembroke (1590–1676) perhaps best illustrates the rewards of carefully attending to life writing that—from a twenty-first-century perspective—appears unengaging at first glance. Motivated primarily 'by a secular desire to establish a record of [her] life and achievements', Clifford produced numerous texts, including both daily and annual diaries, an autobiographical sketch, and other forms of self- and familial accounting.[33] The diaries in particular contain numerous repeated phrases (like Rich's) and seem obsessed with tracing Clifford's movements not only from one property to another but also from one room to another within a property. Thanks to the work of scholars like Megan Matchinske, we can now see how Clifford's repetitive placement of herself within certain locations and properties was, among other things, a means of claiming her right to the inheritance out of which she believed she had been cheated (and that she ultimately regained after years of legal battles).[34] For Clifford, writing herself into diaries, auto/biographical narratives, and genealogical records meant writing herself into the legal and familial histories of buildings and properties, as well as the actual physical spaces.

And yet, as the result of archival research and a widened geographic lens that have highlighted different aspects of familiar texts and writers and introduced altogether new women and manuscripts, Clifford no longer appears entirely unique in her approach to the textual stewardship of family name, property, and self. On the contrary, she now appears as one of many life writers in a complex, multifamily network with deeply engrained life-writing habits. Clifford herself was neither Irish nor terribly concerned about Ireland in her life writing beyond brief notes of fact.[35] Yet her case is illustrative

[32] Wray, 'Autobiography', 198.

[33] Wray, 'Autobiography', 196. Only recently has Clifford's entire auto/biographical corpus been gathered into one edition: Jessica L. Malay (ed.), *Anne Clifford's Autobiographical Writing, 1590–1676* (Manchester, 2018).

[34] See esp. Megan Matchinske, 'Serial Identity: History, Gender, and Form in the Diary Writing of Lady Anne Clifford', in Dowd and Eckerle (eds), *Genre and Women's Life Writing*, 65–8. See also this volume, Chapter 46, Patricia Phillippy, 'Memory and Matter: Lady Anne Clifford's 'Life of Mee''.

[35] For example, she notes in her *Great Books of Record* that her father, George Clifford, 'was in the northe parte of Ireland' when his eldest son died, having landed there when 'himselfe and his shippe was cast in by tempest about twelve or fowrteen dayes before'. See Anne Clifford, in Jessica L. Malay

because *even it*—when probed more deeply—reveals how interconnected women's lives of the early modern period were and how privileging 'English' voices has left us with only a partial picture of early modern women's life writing.[36]

Clifford's brief Irish references are most useful in this regard when she turns to Elizabeth Boyle, Clifford's second cousin and—as noted earlier—the writer of a memorandum book. Elizabeth had married Richard Boyle (1612–1698), brother of Rich and son of First Earl of Cork Richard Boyle (1566–1643), and thus joined a powerful New English (or settler) family. Clifford's meticulous recording of the physical movements of all her relatives means that Elizabeth, too, is tracked. For example, in Clifford's 1652 memoir, she writes, 'it was about the 8th day of September did my cousin, the Countess of Cork, with her six children go from Bristol over sea into Ireland to Lismore and Cork and those places in Munster to her husband Richard' (127).[37] In Clifford's 1656 memoir, she notes movement in the opposite direction: 'And about Midsummer this year, did my cousin Elizabeth Clifford of Cork come from her husband Earl of Cork out of Ireland with their two sons and their daughter Elizabeth for a while into England' (141). In this way, Ireland gradually becomes part of Clifford's habitual marking of time and space, primarily as the place to which Elizabeth goes upon her marriage and the place from which she comes on visits to England.

But this attention to Elizabeth's comings and goings was more than casual familial interest, for Elizabeth was not just any cousin to Clifford: she was the sole surviving child and heir of Henry Clifford, the Fifth Earl of Cumberland and the man to whom Clifford's inheritance had ultimately passed as a result of her father's decision to will what should have been hers to his brother Francis, Henry's father. Given Clifford's decades-long struggle to reclaim what she believed was rightfully hers, 'she did not'—as Barbara K. Lewalski usefully noted in an early, ground-breaking essay—'define herself or her place in society through [her] marriages, titles, and roles, but referred to herself on every possible occasion and in every possible document as "sole Daughter and Heir to my illustrious Father" '.[38] Therefore, the existence of a rival heiress—however tenuous that rival's claim might be—was no small matter, and it is no surprise that, in her Great Books, she used identical language to highlight Elizabeth's identity as '*sole daughter and heire* to her parents'.[39] As 'sole daughter and heir', each woman occupies a notable

(ed.), *Anne Clifford's Great Books of Record* (Manchester, 2015), 708. And she includes in her April 1616 diary the news that her 'cousin Sir Oliver St John was made Lord Deputy of Ireland', 31. All references to Clifford's life writing, with the exception of the Great Books, are to Malay (ed.), *Anne Clifford's Autobiographical Writing* and will be cited parenthetically in the text.

36 I am grateful to Jessica L. Malay for the opportunity to present an early version of this material at the 'Anne Clifford: Engagements in Culture' Symposium in July 2018.

37 Elizabeth Boyle was then 2nd Countess of Cork.

38 Barbara K. Lewalski, 'Re-Writing Patriarchy and Patronage: Margaret Clifford, Anne Clifford, and Aemilia Lanyer', *The Yearbook of English Studies*, 21 (1991), 87–106, 90.

39 Clifford, *Anne Clifford's Great Books* (715, emphasis added). Clifford's Great Books include her genealogical work on the Clifford family, a life of her mother, and an autobiographical narrative called 'Life of Mee'.

position in a system that tended not to respect women's right to property. Perhaps their similar positions would even have inspired Clifford's empathy for her cousin if not for the niggling worry that—as Jessica L. Malay notes in her edition of Clifford's auto/biographical writing—'Anne feared that ... Elizabet[h] would attempt to thwart the stipulation of her as heir after the male heirs of her uncle Francis Clifford' (110n68).[40] As if this rivalry were not enough to grant Elizabeth significance in Anne's life, their relationship became even more intertwined over time: Clifford became godmother to Boyle's daughter Elizabeth ('Betty') in 1642, and this goddaughter married Clifford's grandson Nicholas Tufton in 1664.

Thus we have two aristocratic life-writing women whose complex relationship meant that each was not only acutely aware of the other's movements—physical, legal, and otherwise—but also often gave space to the other in her auto/biographical texts. Several aspects of their shared life-writing practice are worth noting. First, they both seemed to privilege familial life writing. Boyle's memorandum book, which she maintained from 1659 through October 1689, not long before her death, traces her own family history, starting with her marriage in 1634, and generally 'focused on tracking the Boyles' movements at the apex of Irish and English society'.[41] Therefore, although she is credited with only one non-epistolary autobiographical text—as opposed to Clifford's *many*—there are striking similarities between the two women's life-writing method. Second, both women developed their life-writing habits in part because of familial influence. Clifford learned the art of epistolary negotiation and the value of collecting and maintaining documentary evidence from her mother, Margaret Clifford, though she took the practice much further by producing not simply a 'collection of documents' but—to use Malay's words—'an epic narrative of dynastic power and honour, through which she interwove her own identity'.[42] Across the Irish Sea, Boyle showed a similar reverence for official documents, always noting when they were revised and where they were stored. Upon her marriage, Boyle had become a member of an extraordinary life-writing family with deeply engrained life-writing habits. The First Earl himself wrote both a diary and an autobiographical account. As Ann-Maria Walsh notes, it was he who began '[t]he practice of keeping records and preserving the family's papers', since, 'as a New English Protestant planter, [he] recognized the importance of using textual and other (non-textual) media to legitimize and consolidate his status as a landowner and as a member of the ruling elite in

[40] For instance, on 28 February 1649, Clifford wrote to her agent and friend Christopher Marsh with concerns about a property in London, asserting, 'My Lady of Cork will cozen me of it, if she can'. Quoted in George Charles Williamson, *Lady Anne Clifford* (1922), 210.

[41] Ann-Maria Walsh, 'The Boyle Women and Familial Life Writing', in Eckerle and McAreavey (eds), *Women's Life Writing*, 79–98, 86. I am indebted to Walsh's work on the Boyle women, who have long been overlooked among early modern Anglophone women writers and whose collective extant writings include 'letters, a diary, an autobiography, a memorandum book, account books, medical receipt books, prose treatises, and pious meditations'. See Walsh, 'The Boyle Women', 79; as well as Walsh, *The Daughters of the First Earl of Cork: Writing Family, Faith, Politics and Place* (Dublin, 2020).

[42] Jessica L. Malay, 'Introduction', in Jessica L. Malay (ed.), *Anne Clifford's Great Books*, 7, 12.

Ireland'. These practices, as well as the 'intense focus on fashioning and maintaining an "English" identity, ... conditioned the upbringing of the natal Boyle women and shaped the cultural understanding of those other women who subsequently married into the family'.[43] In other words, the Boyle family was thoroughly committed to life writing; even its women wrote letters, engaged in intellectual debate, recorded significant life moments, created personal narrative, attended to history via textual accounting, and used epistolary networks to manage estates and legal battles. And third, some of the key life events that Boyle and Clifford recorded were the same.

Consequently, reading their life writing together enables us to see how two aristocratic women approached the same subject, such as Skipton Castle. This North Yorkshire property, a particular point of contention between the cousins, was part of the Clifford hereditary estates that should have passed to Clifford and thus played a critical role in her self-justifying family history. Among the many titles she claims for herself, for instance, is 'Lady of the Honour of Skipton in Craven' (95). In various autobiographical texts, she relates numerous events that happened or—significantly—*should* have happened at Skipton, including her older brother's death there seven weeks before she was born (96); her own birth there on 30 January 1590 (95); her christening at the parish church the next month; her first meeting with her father when he joined his family at Skipton in March of that year (96); his funeral at Skipton church (85–6); her and her mother's inability to visit in October 1607, when 'the doors thereof [were] shut against us by my uncle of Cumberland's officers in an uncivil and disdainful manner' (101); and—perhaps most poignantly—her inability to bury her mother there. Her 29 May 1616 diary entry notes Clifford's extraordinary grief 'when I considered her body should be carried away, and not be interred at Skipton' (37). Yet Boyle also writes Skipton into her family's story and also suffers when she or a family member is kept from the property. Indeed, Skipton appears in the very first entry of Boyle's memorandum book: 'I was marryed in ye Chappell at Skipton Castle July ... ye 3^{d} 1634'.[44] A rehearsal of her children's births includes the detail that 'My daughter Katherine was born at Skipton Castle on Tuesday ... ye 10 of oct: 1637'.[45] It was also the site of Boyle's grandfather Francis Clifford's death in 1641, Boyle's own birth—23 years after Clifford—in 1613, her sister Francis' death, and her father's burial. Since her father's death led to Clifford's triumph in the matter of the inheritance, it is the same moment that leaves Boyle disenfranchised, barred—in legal terms at least—from a key place in her life and her father's final resting place.

In other words, the threads that bound Clifford and Boyle to one another and Clifford to Ireland are both familial and textual, encoded into the women's attempts to record their lives, their selves, and their very complex relationship. Furthermore, by shifting our lens on Clifford just slightly to include Ireland, she changes from the

43 Walsh, 'The Boyle Women', 79.

44 Elizabeth Boyle, 'Elizabeth Lady Burlington Memorandum Book', 1v. I am grateful to Ann-Maria Walsh for sharing her transcription of this manuscript with me. All references are to her transcription.

45 Boyle, 'Elizabeth Lady Burlington Memorandum Book', 2r.

entirely singular woman she is typically treated as to one of a network of aristocratic, life-writing women—a participant in a cultural and familial milieu in which life writing was a common practice, even among women and especially in connection with the kinds of antiquarian, legal, and estate management interests that frequently drove her own self and familial accounting.[46] To recognise this is not to alter or diminish Clifford's powerful and exemplary role within both her immediate and extended family but, on the contrary, to better contextualise and thus understand it.

In the end, Clifford and Boyle are simply two among many early modern life-writing women who used narrative, generic form, and personal ingenuity to textually construct their selves and—in the process—enact stewardship of those selves. Like all life writers, they found in life writing a particularly malleable and often effective means of agency, however mediated. Indeed, such malleability was—for female life writers—not only useful but also essential, since—as women—their agency was inhibited or explicitly denied because of patriarchal norms and laws. Thus they put personal narrative to the service of fighting legal battles, idealised male relatives to help create a particular authorial or personal ethos, and changed their own stories based on genre and the associated audience. In all cases, they acted as stewards of lives, properties, reputations, and personal stories by using the tools of pen, paper, and genre. Furthermore, although women were long understood as writing in sanctioned genres—perhaps the mothers' legacy or spiritual meditations—we now know that no genre or combination of genres was off limits. As we open our eyes to more of this writing, including texts from the entire British Atlantic Archipelago and those not written in English (an acknowledged weakness of my own work here), such findings are likely to be reinforced. After all, constructing one's self on the page often entails moving out of the margins, and managing identity perforce means reconciling or justifying those aspects of the self that are most marginalised or misunderstood. The further we move our scholarly lens from Anglophone aristocratic women, in other words, the more we will learn about the ways in which early modern women's textual labour worked to create, project, and safeguard the self and how their texts bear the evidence of complex, active, and fluid identities.

FURTHER READING

Anderson, Linda. *Autobiography*. London, 2001.

Coolahan, Marie-Louise. 'Writing Before 1700', in Heather Ingman and Clíona Ó Gallchóir (eds), *A History of Modern Irish Women's Literature*. Cambridge, 2018, 18–36.

Graham, Elspeth, Hilary Hinds, Elaine Hobby, and Helen Wilcox. 'Introduction', in Elspeth Graham, Hilary Hinds, Elaine Hobby, and Helen Wilcox (eds), *Her Own Life: Autobiographical Writings by Seventeenth-Century Englishwomen*. Routledge, 1989, 1–27.

[46] Networks have become an increasingly common and useful means for approaching early modern women. Note, for example, how Part V of this volume is devoted to 'Networks and Communities'.

Mullan, David George (ed.). *Women's Life Writing in Early Modern Scotland: Writing the Evangelical Self, c. 1670–1730*. Aldershot, 2003.

Smith, Sidonie and Julia Watson (eds). *Women, Autobiography, Theory: A Reader*. Madison, WI, 1998.

Smyth, Adam. 'Introduction', in Adam Smyth (ed.), *A History of English Autobiography*. Cambridge, 2016, 1–10.

CHAPTER 17

WOMEN AND FICTION

LARA DODDS

VIRGINIA Woolf invented her influential and notorious thought experiment—or fiction—of Judith Shakespeare as part of a larger investigation of the question of 'women and fiction'. She begins her essay by acknowledging an apparent disparity: 'But, you may say, we asked you to speak about women and fiction—what, has that got to do with a room of one's own?'. Woolf's wide-ranging exploration of the relationship between women's literary creativity and the social and economic circumstances of their lives comes about because of the complexity of her original topic, 'women and fiction', which may mean 'women and what they are like, or it might mean women and the fiction that they write; or it might mean women and the fiction that is written about them, or it might mean somehow all three are inextricably mixed together'.[1] The topic is equally complex for the contemporary scholar, and this chapter returns to Woolf's essay in order to ask how early modern women engaged with and shaped the development of fiction. Women played active roles as patrons, translators, readers, and, increasingly from the mid-seventeenth century onwards, as authors and theorists of fiction (see this volume, Chapter 28, Jake Arthur, '"The Surplusage": Margaret Tyler and the Englishing of Spanish Chivalric Romance'). At the same time, women were the subject of fictional writing and also central to debates about its moral and aesthetic qualities. Though the majority of authors, and likely readers, of early modern fiction were men, critical discourse had and has a tendency to feminise the form. Thomas Overbury's oft-cited character, or fictional portrait, of a chambermaid who likes to read romance is both notorious and exemplary: 'She reads *Greenes* works over and over, but is so carried away with the *Myrrour of Knighthood*, she is many times resolved to run out of her selfe, and become a Ladie Errant'.[2] Overbury's portrait casts the reading of fiction as simultaneously a source of delusion and a threat to social order. The maid becomes an object of satire because she mistakes fiction for reality, but in doing so she imagines possibilities

[1] Virginia Woolf, *A Room of One's Own* (New York, 1989), 1.

[2] Thomas Overbury, *New and Choise Characters* (London, 1615), sig. J4v.

for her life outside her current lived reality. Overbury's portrait joins a long line of critical commentary that places women and fiction at the centre of debates about the nature of representation and the moral value of reading. Whether in Vives' warning in *The Instruction of a Christian Woman* (1529) that women must avoid fiction as they would 'serpentes or snakes' or in contemporary references to women's fiction as chick lit, the association between women and fiction can too often be used to discredit both.[3]

This chapter explores how early modern women writers engage with this complex landscape of women and fiction. Women participated in fiction as translators, patrons, writers, and readers, and they took on each of these roles in a discursive context that persistently gendered fiction. Against a background of detraction and satire, women nevertheless played essential roles in the development of early modern fiction and, as readers and writers, they developed flexible and innovative theories about the power of fiction to reflect and shape the conditions of women's lives.

WOMEN READERS AND THE FEMINISATION OF FICTION

In the twenty-first century literary landscape, fiction is a general term for narrative works in prose, of which the novel is the most prominent. Studies of fiction have traditionally been preoccupied with the origins or 'rise' of the novel, and definitions of fictionality likewise centre on the novel. This critical history has shaped studies of premodern fiction, creating a tendency, as Paul Salzman observes, to 'look *back* at the earlier period in order to understand the developmental model'.[4] In Catherine Gallagher's influential argument, the novel 'discovered' fiction, a claim she supports by citing, in part, changes in the use of the word 'fiction' over the course of the seventeenth century.[5] Whereas 'fiction' was once used to refer to the 'feigning' of imaginary incidents, sometimes for the purposes of deception, it took on its now-dominant sense as a distinct literary form in the later seventeenth century and after.[6] Certainly there is no single word in the early modern period to describe prose narratives of this type; writers may use fiction, romance, tale, story, or even poesy to describe works that twenty-first-century readers

[3] Juan Louis Vives, *A very frutefull and pleasant boke called the instruction of a Christen woman* (London, 1529), sig. F2r. See also Jennifer Lee Carrell, 'A Pack of Lies in a Looking Glass: Lady Mary Wroth's *Urania* and the Magic Mirror of Romance', *SEL: Studies in English Literature 1500–1900*, 34 (1994), 79–107, 81. For examples of gendered detraction extending from the seventeenth century to the twentieth, see Joanna Russ, *How to Suppress Women's Writing* (Austin, TX, 2018).

[4] Paul Salzman, 'Theories of Prose Fiction in England: 1558–1700', in Glyn P. Norton (ed.), *The Cambridge History of Literary Criticism* (Cambridge, 1989), 295.

[5] Catherine Gallagher, 'The Rise of Fictionality', in Franco Moretti (ed.), *The Novel* (Princeton, NJ, 2006), 336–63, 337.

[6] 'fiction, n.' *OED*, 3a. and 4a.

would likely call fiction. This semantic variety is matched by a proliferation of fictional genres and subgenres, as demonstrated by Salzman's comprehensive survey of prose fiction of the period. Renaissance fiction, he concludes, 'was pre-eminently a series of mixed forms', as authors creatively reworked earlier traditions and created new ones.[7] Given this context, I have found Julie Orlemanksi's 'minimalist conception' of fiction to be a more fruitful approach than the search for precursors of novelistic fictionality in premodern literature. Orlemanski productively defines fiction as:

> a semantic mode of unearnest reference that depends on the recognition by some interpretive community of a representation's distinction from one or another idiom of actuality—from history, philosophy, factuality, religious doctrine, a sacrament's performative efficacy, or everyday speech.[8]

This approach acknowledges that fiction is not absolute and unchanging, but instead exists in varying relation to other discourses. Caroline Levine's appropriation of the concept of affordances, which are defined as the 'potential uses or actions latent in materials and designs', from design theory offers further purchase on early modern women's engagement with fiction. As we shall see, many early modern women writers and theorists of fiction are quite sensitive to the changing status of fiction across different contexts. Writers use the opposition to discourses of actuality such as history or philosophy both to gain authority and in order to intervene in these discourses through their fiction. Levine argues that the concept of affordances is useful for thinking about literary form because it allows critics to attend to 'both the specificity and the generality of forms—both the particular constraints and possibilities that different forms afford, and the fact that those patterns and arrangements carry their affordances with them as they move across time and space'.[9] For the writers considered in this chapter, the discourse of 'women and fiction' defines the affordances of fiction in complex ways, offering constraints and possibilities that shape their fictional, and in some cases nonfictional, works.

Overbury's portrait of the reading chambermaid creates the impression that women were a primary audience for fiction, but research by Helen Hackett and others demonstrates that passages such as these are not descriptive, but instead have an ideological and rhetorical purpose. Hackett's review of the evidence of women's fiction reading suggests that the idea of a large group of female readers of fiction in the later sixteenth or earlier seventeenth centuries, promulgated by early scholars such as Louis B. Wright, is 'exaggerated.' By the mid-seventeenth century, however, women readers of fiction were likely both more numerous and also a 'fairly unremarkable' phenomenon.[10]

[7] Paul Salzman, *Engish Prose Fiction: 1588–1700* (Oxford, 1985), 348.

[8] Julie Orlemanski, 'Who Has Fiction? Modernity, Fictionality, and the Middle Ages', *New Literary History*, 50 (2019), 145–70, 147.

[9] Caroline Levine, *Forms: Whole, Rhythm, Hierarchy, Network* (Princeton, NJ, 2015), 6.

[10] Helen Hackett, *Women and Romance Fiction in the English Renaissance* (Cambridge, 2000), 9.

Nevertheless, the association of fiction with women readers became, as Lori Humphrey Newcomb argues, a 'powerful literary convention'.[11] This convention can be observed in a scholar like Wright, who attributed increased interest in romance fiction to women readers who 'never subscribed to realism'; consequently 'love stories with happy endings found favour with the Elizabethans even as with feminine readers today'.[12] As Newcomb explains, 'educated men pretended to consign romance to women, displacing ambivalence about a genre long on appeal but short on cultural sanction'.[13] Critics and authors can distance themselves from aesthetic and moral qualities of fiction that are deemed negative by feminising them.

Fiction, and especially romance fiction, was frequently framed through concepts of leisure, privacy, frivolity, and illicit sexuality that were themselves feminised. These concepts come together in a memorable way in John Lyly's prefatory letter to all 'Ladies and Gentlewomen' in *Euphues and his England* (1580):

> It resteth Ladies, that you take the paines to reade it, but at such times as you spend in playing with your little Dogges, and yet will I not pinch you of that pastime, for I am content that your Dogges lye in your laps, so Euphues may be in your hands, that when you shall be wearie in reading of the one, you may be ready to sport with the other: or handle him as you doe your junkets, that when you can eate no more, you tye some in your napkin for children, for if you bee filled with the first part, put the seconde in your pocket for your wayting maydes: Euphues had rather lye shut in a Ladies casket, then open in a Schollers studie.[14]

This passage likens fiction to pets, sweets, and the secret contents of a woman's 'casket'. These comparisons trivialise fiction, while simultaneously sensationalising it. But Lyly's preface also implicitly invites gentlewomen to share their reading with children and servants. While reading across class boundaries can be a source of satire, as in Overbury's portrait of the chambermaid, it is also a reminder of the potential of fiction to expand access to reading and the pleasures it provides. Released from the scholar's study, fiction prompted new modes of reading that were 'extensive, relaxed, and empathetic' in contrast to the purposeful reading of humanism.[15]

[11] Lori Humphrey Newcomb, 'Gendering Prose Romance in Renaissance England', in Corinne Saunders (ed.), *A Companion to Romance: From Classical to Contemporary* (Malden: Blackwell, 2004), 121–39, 121.

[12] Louis B. Wright, *Middle-Class Culture in Elizabethan England* (Chapel Hill, NC, 1935), 110. See also Louis B. Wright, 'The Reading of Renaissance English Women', *Studies in Philology*, 28 (1931), 671–89.

[13] Newcomb, 'Gendering Prose Romance', 121.

[14] John Lyly, *Euphues and His England* (London, 1580), sig. ¶1v.

[15] Newcomb, 'Gendering Prose Romance', 123. For humanist reading practices, see Lisa Jardine and Anthony Grafton, '"Studied for Action": How Gabriel Harvey Read his Livy', *Past and Present*, 129 (1990), 30–78.

As with all topics in the history of reading, it is difficult to say with certainty how many women read fiction or precisely how they interpreted what they read.[16] Over the course of the seventeenth century, however, references to reading fiction proliferate in women's letters, autobiographies, and other forms of life writing. These references demonstrate both a knowing awareness of the cultural expectation of 'women and fiction' and evidence of creative engagement with the transformative possibilities of fiction. For instance, Margaret Cavendish's epistolary fiction *Sociable Letters* (1664) takes women's reading as one of its primary subjects, but in doing so reproduces the rhetorical convention that women read fiction naively. In a critique of the unjust limitation of women's education, Cavendish complains that women resort to fiction in the absence of other alternatives:

> the chief study of our Sex is Romances, wherein reading, they fall in love with the feign'd Heroes and Carpet-Knights, with whom their Thoughts secretly commit Adultery, and in their Conversation and manner, or forms or phrases of Speech, they imitate the Romancy-Ladies. (Letter 21)[17]

Sociable Letters repeatedly warns against mistaking the illusions of fiction for reality. By contrast, in Dorothy Osborne's letters to Sir William Temple, shared reading of fiction advances the couple's courtship and provides a framework for literary expression as Osborne rewrites her experience through the tropes of romance.[18]

Women's reflections on reading fiction often display a tension between an extensive knowledge and clear enjoyment of fiction's conventions and an ironic distance that can be attributed to the negative associations of 'women and fiction'. Lucy Hutchinson's biography of her husband, *The Memoirs of Colonel John Hutchinson*, illustrates this tension well in its account of the courtship and marriage of Lucy and John. Hutchinson shapes the courtship narrative with romance tropes, including an enchanted house that is 'so fatal for love that never any young disengaged person went thither who returned again free'.[19] The conventions of romance fictionality serve Hutchinson in the opening pages of the biography as a means to establish the characters of Lucy and John. These conventions cast John as a romance hero, while simultaneously establishing Lucy's desirability and preserving her modesty. The same conventions serve Hutchinson in a different way, however, when she dismisses them at the conclusion of the courtship

[16] Heidi Brayman Hackel, *Reading Material in Early Modern England* (Cambridge, 2005); Sasha Roberts, 'Engendering the Female Reader: Women's Recreational Reading of Shakespeare in Early Modern England', in Heidi Brayman Hackel and Catherine E. Kelly (eds), *Reading Women: Literacy, Authorship, and Culture in the Atlantic World 1500–1800* (Philadelphia, PA, 2007), 36–54. For a case study of Margaret Cavendish's reading, see Lara Dodds, 'Reading and Writing in Sociable Letters; Or, How Margaret Cavendish Read Her Plutarch', *English Literary Renaissance*, 41 (2011), 189–218.

[17] Margaret Cavendish, in James Fitzmaurice (ed.), *Sociable Letters* (Ontario, 2004), 68.

[18] Hackett, *Women and Romance Fiction*, 190. Dodds, 'Reading and Writing', 199–200.

[19] Lucy Hutchinson, in N. H. Keeble (ed.), *Memoirs of the Life of Colonel Hutchinson* (London, 1995), 45.

episode: 'I shall pass by all the little amorous relations which, if I would take the pains to relate, would make a true history of more handsome management of love than the best romances describe'.[20]

As Orlemanski argues, fiction is recognised in contradistinction to variously defined discourses of actuality. Hutchinson highlights that distinction here—a distinction between 'true history' and the 'best romances'—at a crucial point in the narrative. Fiction functions to highlight the legitimacy of Hutchinson's biographical narrative—affirming the *truth* of the relationship between John and Lucy—and it also aligns with a shift in the narrative from personal and local events to the narration of the historical antecedents of the Civil War and her husband's participation in this event of national significance. The opposition between 'romance' and 'history' works straightforwardly to assert the 'truth' of the courtship narrative and Hutchinson's reliability as a narrator. But this rhetorical strategy also functions to highlight the broader aim of the work, which is to vindicate John Hutchinson's role in history. The opposition between fiction and history draws a line under the narrative's concern with John Hutchinson's private life—and his association with women—in order to signal his fulfilment of public roles and responsibilities. Hutchinson's multivalent use of 'women and fiction' suggests that women readers approached this discourse flexibly and creatively. The feminisation of fiction has its origins in misogyny, but became a resource, both rhetorical and social, for readers and writers.

TRANSLATORS, PATRONS, AND EDITORS; OR WOMEN'S HIDDEN CONTRIBUTIONS TO EARLY MODERN BRITISH FICTION

The outsized presence of women in the discourse of fiction, what I have called 'women and fiction', has sometimes obscured the important roles played by historical women in the development of early modern fiction. Consider Margaret Tyler's translation of the first book of *Espejo de principes y cavalleros* by Diego Ortúñez de Calahorra as *The Mirrour of Princely Deedes and Knighthood* (1578). Tyler's translation of this text was the first of a Spanish chivalric romance into English, and it 'set a vogue which lasted almost until the end of the seventeenth century'.[21] Beyond this, however, as Joyce Boro argues in her excellent edition of the translation, Tyler was responsible for 'modernizing and anglicizing the romance, adapting it to the cultural and aesthetic sensibilities of her

[20] Hutchinson, in Keeble (ed.), *Memoirs*, 51.

[21] Tina Krontiris, 'Breaking Barriers of Genre and Gender: Margaret Tyler's Translation of "The Mirrour of Knighthood"', *English Literary Renaissance*, 18 (1988), 19–39, 20.

era'.[22] As Jake Arthur demonstrates elsewhere in this volume, Tyler's modernisations introduced a vocabulary of law and contract that is at odds with the chivalric world of romance.[23] While the work's many sequels were translated by other writers, it was Tyler's translation that provided the foundation for both the continuing popularity of the chivalric romance in Britain and the eventual parodic responses to it. Almost four decades after the publication of Tyler's translation, Overbury's portrait identifies *The Mirrour of Princely Deedes and Knighthood* as a favourite of his fictional chambermaid, which testifies to both its staying power and broad reach.

As Woolf observed, 'women and fiction' includes both the stories—whether acknowledged as fiction or not—that men write about and for women as well as the stories that women write in response. Tyler anticipates this insight in the letter to readers that prefaces her translation:

> But to return, whatsoever the truth is—whether that women may not at all discourse in learning for men lay in their claim to be sole possessioners of knowledge, or whether they may in some manner that is by limitation or appointment in some kind of learning—my persuasion hath been thus: that it is all one for a woman to pen a story as for a man to address his story to a woman. (50)

Tyler acknowledges but rejects the presumption that knowledge is a male prerogative: if men are to 'address' stories to women for their reading and edification, then women can be expected to write stories in response. Tyler creates an equivalence—'it is all one'—between the reading and writing of fiction and suggests that the writing of fiction is a natural consequence of reading it. Further, Tyler's preface explores the interaction between gender and the affordances of fiction. Tyler anticipates that one of the objections to her writing will be the decorum (or lack thereof) of writing about war as a woman. She rejects the premise that her work's subject matter is 'more manlike then becommeth my sexe' and reminds readers that it is fiction: 'I trust every man holds not the plough which would the ground were tilled, and it is no sin to talk of Robin Hood though you never shot in his bow' (49). Sidney's *Defense of Poetry*, the most well-known theoretical account of fiction in the period, emphasises mimesis and emulation as central to the function of fiction: poets are able 'not only to make a Cyrus, which had been but a particular excellency, as nature might have done, but to bestow a Cyrus upon the world to make many Cyruses, if they will learn aright why and how that maker made him'.[24] Tyler's understanding of fiction acknowledges the importance of emulation, but extends beyond it to stress the possibilities of invention and imagination, especially for women writers and readers who may not otherwise aspire to be Cyruses.

22 Margaret Tyler, in Joyce Boro (ed.), *Mirror of Princely Deeds and Knighthood* (London, 2014), 1.

23 See this volume, Chapter 28, Jake Arthur, '"The Surplusage": Margaret Tyler and the Englishing of Spanish Chivalric Romance'.

24 Philip Sidney, 'The Defense of Poesy', in Stephen Greenblatt et al. (eds), *The Norton Anthology of English Literature: The Sixteenth Century [and] the Early Seventeenth Century*, 10th edn (New York, 2018), 546.

Renewed attention to women's participation in the development of fiction in the early modern period has the potential to expand ideas of authorship and transform literary history. This potential is best illustrated by Sir Philip Sidney's pastoral romance, *The Countesse of Pembroke's Arcadia*, which was named for and dedicated to his sister. This framing privileges women's literary judgement and positions the Countess as the patron and ideal reader of the work. As the dedicatee of the *Arcadia*, Mary Sidney Herbert is the paradigmatic example of what Julie Crawford calls the 'mediatrix', a 'politically and culturally powerful' woman who is 'at once a patron to be honored and a force to be reckoned with, a maker of texts and a maker of careers'.[25] The 1593 folio edition of *Arcadia* was overseen by the Countess and, in contrast to the first edition, is 'augmented and ended' with versions of the final two books of the romance. It has been traditional to describe the Countess' involvement in the *Arcadia* as that of an editor or curator, but Sarah Wall-Randell's recent research demonstrates that she should equally be described as the text's 'co-author'.[26] Further, the centrality of Philip Sidney's works to English literary history and the very idea of the author are largely due to Mary Sidney Herbert's efforts to preserve Philip Sidney's legacy. Patricia Pender describes these efforts as a poignant irony: Sidney Herbert's success was to create a 'poetic mythology whose enduring influence would eventually obscure her own decisive role in its development'.[27] An address to the reader in the 1593 edition of *The Arcadia* identifies the Countess as the agent who took 'in hand' the imperfections of the previous edition, correcting, editing, and completing the revisions left unfinished at Philip Sidney's death. As Wall-Randell demonstrates, the full legacy of women in early modern fiction has rarely been acknowledged, even though, as the paratexts to the 1593 edition explain, one of the most highly regarded fictional works of the early modern period is 'by more then one interest *The Countesse of Pembrokes Arcadia:* done, as it was, for her: as it is, by her'.[28]

WOMEN WRITERS AND THE AFFORDANCES OF FICTION

Though apparently unknown to Woolf, Lady Mary Wroth's 1621 romance *The Countess of Montgomery's Urania* suggests how capacious and productive the rubric of women

[25] Julie Crawford, *Mediatrix: Women, Politics, and Literary Production in Early Modern England* (Oxford, 2014), 2.

[26] Sarah Wall-Randell, '"All by her directing": The Countess of Pembroke and her *Arcadia*', in Valerie Wayne (ed.), *Women's Labour and the History of the Book in Early Modern England* (London, 2020), 163–85, 177.

[27] Patricia Pender, 'The Ghost and the Machine in the Sidney Family Corpus', *SEL Studies in English Literature 1500–1900*, 51 (2011), 65.

[28] Sir Philip Sidney, *The Countesse of Pembrokes Arcadia* (London, 1593), sig. ¶4v.; Wall-Randell, 'All by her directing', 163–75.

and fiction can be. *Urania* is a massive and innovative fictional text, written by a woman, dedicated to a woman, and about women. Further, *Urania* is notable for its numerous episodes that depict women as storytellers, as poets, and as readers and writers of fiction. The emphasis on metafictional and metapoetic reflection is highlighted in the text's very first episode, in which Urania questions Perissus' storytelling and offers an alternative interpretation of the events he relates, in spite of his verdict that, because she is a woman, her judgement is 'not much to be marked'.[29] Urania listens attentively to Perissus recount the self-nominated 'saddest story' about his adulterous love for Limena and her husband's retaliatory abuse. But though Urania sympathises with Perissus and recognises his worth, she does not agree with his interpretation of events. Picking up immediately on a missing plot detail—the lack of confirmed evidence of Limena's death—Urania counters his despair with an alternative plan of action. As Naomi Miller argues, 'Wroth alters generic conventions in order to re-present the relation between gender, genre, and culture from a woman's perspective', and this initial episode is a good illustration of this alteration.[30] Urania's interpretive autonomy in this scene implicitly valorises women's reading of fiction and also prepares readers for the multiple, interlocking, and sometimes competing narratives that will follow.

Wroth's innovations in romance offer a productive vantage point on the affordances of fiction. One of the most remarked upon aspects of the fiction of *Urania* is its complex relationship to the life of its author. Often described as a *roman á clef*, *Urania* is a work that troubles the distinction between fiction and actuality by highlighting parallels between fictional characters and historical figures. Though the parallels between the romance's central characters, Pamphilia and Amphilanthus, and the experiences of Wroth and her lover William Herbert, are clear, Wroth's use of this convention is far from straightforward. As Josephine Roberts explains, 'Wroth created a highly complex fiction that provides for the intermittent shadowing of actual lives and events, often under multiple figures' and featuring 'competing and often conflicting representations of the same person'.[31] Orlemanski's focus on medieval fiction highlights the strategy of 'referential dappling', which describes works that display a mixture of different levels of fictionality in their narratives, and I have found this a useful concept for describing Wroth's narrative strategies.[32] Wroth's narrative does not simply translate biography into fiction, nor distinguish fiction from biography; instead she juxtaposes episodes with varying levels of referentiality in order to show characters and readers the transformative potential of fiction. As Jennifer Lee Carrell describes it, 'the author and her characters

[29] Mary Wroth, in Josephine A. Roberts (ed.), *The First Part of the Countess of Montgomery's Urania* (Tempe, AZ, 1995; repr. 2005), 4.

[30] Naomi J. Miller, '"Not much to be marked": Narrative of the Woman's Part in Lady Mary Wroth's Urania', *SEL: Studies in English Literature 1500–1900*, 29 (1989), 121–37, 126. Crucially, as Miller further argues, Urania's perspective is featured, but does not become representative of a singular or unitary female identity in the romance. Instead, multiple female perspectives and voices are explored through her friendship with Pamphilia and others (130).

[31] Wroth, in Roberts (ed.), *The First Part of the Countess of Montgomery's Urania*, lxx.

[32] Orlemanski, 'Who Has Fiction?', 161.

participate in an endless creation of stories within stories; all these storytellers, especially Wroth, stand outside their fictions, looking in at *and being changed by* distorted reflections of themselves'.[33] Referential dappling is common throughout *Urania*, but can be illustrated effectively by the story of Lindamira, which is recounted by Pamphilia as a 'tale, feigning to be written in a French story' (499). Lindamira is a woman in service to the Queen and secretly in love with a man also loved by her mistress. A jealous rumour results in her exile from the court, but her constancy is rewarded when she is visited by her beloved and finally reveals her love. The pair enjoy a brief moment of happiness, but, like so many of the heroines of *Urania*, Lindamira is abandoned. The fictionality of this episode is complex. Lindamira is a fictional character discovered by Pamphilia in a book. Feeling affinity with Lindamira's story, Pamphilia turns fiction into lyric in a sonnet sequence called 'Lindamira's complaint'. Dorolina, who listens to Pamphilia's storytelling, believes the story is 'something more exactly related than a fiction', which posits Lindamira as a fictional character invented by Pamphilia as a way to covertly express her experiences and passions (501). Pamphilia, of course, is also a fictional character, a protagonist of *Urania*, believed by many readers to shadow the experiences and emotions of that work's author, Lady Mary Wroth. These multiple layers of fictionality suggest the two-fold affordances of women and fiction. On the one hand, fiction is a veil; it allows women to share beliefs and experiences at a distance, in a discrete and decorous form. On the other, Lindamira is not Pamphilia and Pamphilia is not Wroth; fiction is gain (and loss) that occurs in the imaginative transformation of one into the other.

The most prolific writer of fiction among the women writers of the next generation is Margaret Cavendish. In addition to authoring fiction in several different subgenres, including romance, fantasy or proto-science fiction, and epistolary fiction, Cavendish's numerous and extensive paratexts offer one of the most thorough theoretical considerations of the political and aesthetic possibilities of fiction in seventeenth-century British literature. As we have seen, the danger of 'women and fiction' is that it can be reduced to a caricature or burden. Cavendish falls prey to this burden when she recalls Wroth's fictional masterpiece through the framework of male detraction, opening *Poems and Fancies* (1653) with a reference to Sir Edward Denny's libellous poem. She claims that it is likely that men 'will say to me, as to the lady that wrote the romance: Work lady, work, let writing books alone, / For surely wiser women ne'er wrote one'.[34] As Liza Blake observes elsewhere in this volume, Cavendish misquotes or misremembers this couplet.[35] She overcompensates for the possibility of detraction with a hyperbolic repetition of the most negative associations of 'women and fiction'. Cavendish's desire

[33] Carrell, 'A Pack of Lies', 80.

[34] Margaret Cavendish, 'To All Noble and Worthy Ladies', in Liza Blake (ed.), *Margaret Cavendish's Poems and Fancies: A Digital Critical Edition* (2019), University of Toronto, http://library2.utm.utoronto.ca/poemsandfancies/, accessed 30 November 2020. Cavendish also cites this passage in the dedicatory epistle to William Cavendish that prefaces *Sociable Letters*; Cavendish, in Fitzmaurice (ed.), *Sociable Letters*, 38.

[35] See Chapter 41, Liza Blake, 'Early Modern Women in Print and Margaret Cavendish, Woman in Print'.

to write socially useful works, as well as her desire to deflect criticism, makes the danger of fiction, or more specifically romance, a refrain throughout her work. In the preface to *Natures Pictures* (1656; 1671), she acknowledges that some of her stories are 'Romancical', but hopes that no one will mistake her for a fan (or a writer) of romance, 'for I never read a Romancy Book throughout in all my life'.[36] Cavendish goes so far as to assert that if her own works 'should create Amorous thoughts in idle brains, I would make blots instead of letters' and 'never suffer them to be printed' (sig. c2v). Cavendish maintains that her tales will, by contrast, 'rather quench Passion, than enflame it' and 'beget chast Thoughts, nourish the love of Vertue, kindle humane Pitty, warme Charity, increase Civillity, strengthen fainting patience, encourage noble Industry, crown Merit, and instruct Life; and recreate Time' (sig. c2v). The distinction Cavendish draws between her own writing and the romances she claims not to have read is an excellent illustration of Margaret Doody's definition of romance as the term used 'in literary studies to allude to forms conveying literary pleasure the critic thinks readers would be better off without'.[37] Cavendish worries that to call her writing romance would interfere with the social and political values she intends to promote with her fiction, and this tension is never resolved. Cavendish wrote *Natures Pictures* in exile, and her writing often reflects the disjunctions between what is, what should be, and what might be. A desire to promote social order jostles with the representation of alternative lives for women in Cavendish's fiction, perhaps most intensely in the science fictional and utopian *The Blazing World*, which finds space for both female self-actualisation and ideal government only in an explicitly fantastic setting.

This tension is illustrated as well in 'Assaulted and Pursued Chastity', a story published in *Natures Pictures* that begins with the assertion of a moral and didactic purpose: to 'show young women the danger of travelling without their parents, husbands or particular friends to guard them'.[38] From this opening, readers might expect the story that follows to be a grim tale of female suffering and punishment for transgression of patriarchal order. But though this story centres upon chastity, a traditional feminine virtue, it severs this virtue from obedience and places it under a woman's own control.[39] The central dilemma faced by the protagonist is that of determinism and free will: is her fate determined by the ill fortune that besets her—war, exile, shipwreck, and sex trafficking to start—or can she change it? The narrative makes it very clear that virtue does not guarantee safety. 'Heaven doth not always protect the persons of virtuous souls from rude violences', but instead lends a 'human help' (48). The protagonist quickly learns

[36] Margaret Cavendish, *Natures Picture* (London, 1656), sig. c2r. The *OED* records Cavendish's usage of 'romancical' as the first in print. See 'romancical, adj.' *OED*. For further exploration of the different terms used by seventeenth-century writers to describe what we would call *fiction*, *romance*, and the *novel*, see James Grantham Turner, '"Romance" and the Novel in Restoration England', *The Review of English Studies*, 63 (2011), 58–85.

[37] Margaret Doody, *The True Story of the Novel* (Newark, NJ, 1997), 15.

[38] Margaret Cavendish, in Kate Lilley (ed.), *The Blazing World and Other Writings* (London, 1994), 47.

[39] See Kathryn Schwarz, 'Chastity, Militant and Married: Cavendish's Romance, Milton's Masque', *PMLA*, 118 (2003), 270–85.

that she will have to furnish the help she needs on her own. In the beginning of the story she is tricked into entering a brothel and threatened with rape by the Prince. Recognising that 'the gods would not hear her, if she lazily called for help and watched for miracles neglecting natural means' (50), she acquires a gun and, when the Prince will not listen to reason, she shoots him. With this action, the protagonist—called Miseria at this point in the story—disrupts the opposition between honourable death and dishonourable life that characterises most early modern rape narratives. By breaking this powerful fiction of women, Miseria eventually escapes the brothel and the Prince and launches herself into a series of adventures that allow her to explore different identities and different modes of gendered experience. These possibilities are signified by the different names she takes on over the course of the story. In the long middle part of the narrative, the protagonist—now Travellia—joins with a kind fatherly figure, dresses as a young man, and explores new and strange worlds. As Travellia, she becomes an imperialist, gains the love of a queen, and leads armies to victory.[40] Meanwhile, however, a letter she left behind when she escaped the Prince dubs her Affectionata, a name that prepares for the ending of the story, which sees her married to the Prince, her would-be rapist. As in many of Cavendish's dramatic works, this conclusion threatens to foreclose the multiple possibilities explored by the narrative in favour of slotting the heroine into the heteronormative expectations of married life. The Queen, thwarted in her love for Travellia, is likewise *deus ex machina*-ed into marriage with a man she rejected, and her lament about the capriciousness of Fortune captures well the limitations of Cavendish's fiction: 'Must all your works consist in contradiction? / Or do we nothing enjoy but Fiction?' (102).

Cavendish is not the author of a dedicated treatise on fiction; instead, her extensive comments on literary theory are found scattered throughout her works, in letters and prefaces to her literary and scientific works as well as in several short essays collected in *The Worlds Olio* (1655; 1671) and the essay-like letters of *Sociable Letters* (1664). There has not yet been a comprehensive study of Cavendish's contributions to literary theory, though her writings on the topic demonstrate knowledge of the work of previous theorists as well as a characteristic preoccupation with form and the social and epistemological functions of literature.[41] Cavendish does not use *fiction* as a stand alone generic category, but instead as a quality displayed by different types of writing to a lesser or greater degree.[42] In *The Worlds Olio*, her thinking on fiction is developed through

[40] Travellia's adventures include a sojourn in a fantasy country inhabited by people of purple and orange complexions. Here she escapes captivity to become an imperialist figure who transforms the inhabitants into 'a civilized people' (75). For further discussion of this episode see Sujata Iyengar, 'Royalist, Romancist, Racialist: Rank, Gender, and Race in the Science and Fiction of Margaret Cavendish,' *English Literary History*, 69 (2002).

[41] Lara Dodds, 'Form, Formalism, and Literary Studies: The Case of Margaret Cavendish,' in Brandie R. Siegfried and Pamela S. Hammons (eds), *World-Making Renaissance Women: Rethinking Early Modern Women's Place in Literature and Culture* (Cambridge, 2022), 136–50.

[42] In Cavendish's critical vocabulary, the term that is most similar to modern *fiction* is romance or romancy. For instance: 'Romancy is an adulterate Issue, begot betwixt History and Poetry; for Romancy is as it were poetical fancies; put into a Historical stile; but they are rather tales then fancies; for tales are

a discussion of poesy, which includes but is not limited to works in verse.[43] In an essay called 'The Difference between Poesy and History', she defines each through a sequence of oppositions: 'History draws the minde to look back, Poesy to look right forth'; 'Poesy is simulising, History is repetition'; 'Poesy goeth upon his own ground but History goeth upon the ground of others' and, of course, 'Poetry is most fiction, and History should be truth' (7). Each of these oppositions offers a rich starting point for exploring the aesthetic and epistemological potential of poesy, but most important for our purposes is the opposition between fiction and truth. Fiction's most important quality is that it is something made up, a meaning that resonates with the etymology of the word, which comes from *fingere*, 'to fashion or form'. This understanding of fiction informs Cavendish's writing throughout her career. In *Poems and Fancies* (1653), she explains that she wrote about atomic theory in verse because:

> I thought *Errours* might better passe there, then in *Prose*; since *Poets* write most *Fiction*, and *Fiction* is not given for *Truth*, but *Pastime*; and I feare my *Atomes* will be as small *Pastime*, as themselves: for nothing can be lesse then an *Atome*. ('To Natural Philosophers', sig. C2v)

Cavendish makes a familiar move here, deflecting criticism by relegating her scientific verse to the realm of fiction, implying that it is false or made up. Yet this strategic defence hides within it another claim about the affordances of fiction that turns on the figure of the atom. Atoms are small, but:

> My desire that they should please the readers is as big as the world they make; and my fears are of the same bulk. Yet my hopes fall to a single atom again, and so shall I remain an unsettled atom, or a confused heap, till I hear my censure. If I be praised, it fixes them, but if I am condemned, I shall be annihilated to nothing. But my ambition is such, that I would either be a world, or nothing. ('To Natural Philosophers', sig. C2v)

Atoms are small, trivial, not to be marked; atoms are everything, the stuff of the world, the sign of a poet's ambition. The poems that follow describe how atoms make up the world and establish poetry—and fiction—as a space for philosophical speculation and world-building, a promise spectacularly fulfilled by Cavendish's best-known work, *The Blazing World* (1666), which invites all of its readers to follow the example of its author, and 'if they cannot endure to be subjects, they may create worlds of their own, and govern themselves as they please' (225).

number of impossibilities: put into a methodical discourse, and though they are taken from grounds of truth, yet they are heightned to that degree, as they become meer falshoods; where poetry is an Imitatour of nature to create new, not a falsefying of the old: and History gives a just account, not inlarging the reckning. History, if it be simuliseing, and distinguishing, it is pure poetry, if it be a lie made from truth it is Romancy'; Margaret Cavendish, *The Worlds Olio* (London, 1655), 9.

[43] Margaret Cavendish, *The Worlds Olio* (London: 1655), 8–9.

CONCLUSION

The discourse of 'women and fiction' is a flexible rubric through which to explore women's engagement with literary culture in the early modern period. To Woolf's original list of topics—the fiction women wrote, the fiction written about women, and what women are like—we can add several additional areas of inquiry. The concept of 'women and fiction' encompasses as well the rhetorical conventions that feminised fiction and shaped its reception, the reading strategies that women and others brought to fictional works, women's often unacknowledged contributions to the development of fiction, as well as the particular affordances that fiction provided to women writers who engaged with the form. Women writers cast fiction as other to different idioms of actuality, such as lived experience, history or biography, and philosophy, as a means to both gain the authority of those discourses of actuality and also to innovate within them. In *The Blazing World*, the original distinction between the romancical, the philosophical, and the fantastic opens space for experimentation within both philosophy and fiction. The episode in which the Empress and the Duchess create fictional worlds from different philosophical systems demonstrates how philosophy can engage with fiction and vice versa, providing the foundation for what will eventually become speculative fiction. The boundary between fiction and history—whether defined as the history of an individual life or of a nation—is engaged in different ways by Hutchinson and Wroth. For Hutchinson, the skilful manipulation of the opposition between fiction and history underlies the writing of a biography that transcends the authority that might be given a wife in order to encompass the most tumultuous events of the seventeenth century. Wroth, on the other hand, exploits the resources of fictionality to their limit through strategies of referential dappling also used by Cavendish for the setting and characters of *The Blazing World*. Encompassing both rhetorical conventions of detraction and creative transformation, women and fiction offers a critical framework from which to explore women's contributions to literary history.

FURTHER READING

Aït-Touati, Frédérique. *Fictions of the Cosmos: Science and Literature in the Seventeenth Century*, trans. Susan Emanuel. Chicago, IL, 2011.

Gallagher, Catherine. 'The Rise of Fictionality', in Franco Moretti (ed.), *The Novel: Volume I*. Princeton, NJ, 2006, 336–63.

Glomski, Jacqueline and Isabelle Moreau (eds). *Seventeenth-Century Fiction: Text and Transmission*. Oxford, 2016.

Hackett, Helen. *Women and Romance Fiction in the English Renaissance*. Cambridge, 2000.

Mentz, Steve. *Romance for Sale in Early Modern England*. New York, 2006.

Newcomb, Lori Humphrey. 'Prose Fiction', in Laura Lunger Knoppers (ed.), *The Cambridge Companion to Early Modern Women's Writing*. Cambridge, 2009, 272–86.

Orlemanski, Julie. 'Who Has Fiction? Modernity, Fictionality, and the Middle Ages'. *New Literary History*, 50.2 (2019), 145–70.

Salzman, Paul. *English Prose Fiction: 1588–1700*. Oxford, 1985.

CHAPTER 18

ROMANCE AND RACE

V. M. BRAGANZA

FICTIONS that link romance and race in seventeenth-century English literature flow largely from the pens and imaginations of women.[1] This is no coincidence. Female writers during this period employ these categories to explore their own identities and, in doing so, end up reshaping the intersection between them. This development is the continuation of a long-standing correspondence between romance and race. Romance's dynamic form coheres, according to Frederic Jameson, around a racialised binary of 'good' and 'evil' that the texts addressed in this chapter problematise:

> In the shrinking world of today, indeed, with its gradual leveling of class and national and racial differences, it is becoming increasingly clear that the concept of evil is at one with the category of Otherness itself: evil characterizes whatever is radically different from me, whatever by virtue of precisely that difference seems to constitute a very real and urgent threat to my existence. So from earliest times, the stranger from another tribe, the 'barbarian' who speaks an incomprehensible language and follows 'outlandish' customs ...[2]

Jameson's trans-periodising view misses a key turn in seventeenth-century prose romance: with the entry of women writers into what had previously been considered a masculine genre, the Other becomes the Author. Christine Lee offers one account of this shift by tracking romance as an evolving semantic and conceptual category which, until the end of the sixteenth century, 'centered on the deeds of illustrious men', but, by the early seventeenth century, had begun to acquire connotations of effeminacy and the erotic.[3] This perceivedly feminine turn from wars to *amours*, the noticeable (and

[1] This chapter is in loving memory of Cecilia and Blaise Castelino.

[2] Frederic Jameson, 'Magical Narratives: Romance as Genre', *New Literary History*, 7.1 (1975), 135–63, 140.

[3] Christine S. Lee, 'The Meanings of Romance: Rethinking Early Modern Fiction', *Modern Philology*, 112.2 (2014), 287–311, 291.

contemporarily noticed) increase in women writing romances, and the conceptualisation of romance as a genre at once dangerous and peculiarly suited to the female reader, collectively reoriented its investment in identity.[4]

In women's hands, romance transforms. It is not only the fact of women's authorship that changes romance, but that their interventions regarding race transform it from a genre about the discovery of identity to one which foregrounds identity's instability and loss. Romance protagonists characteristically possess a hidden noble identity which the narrative to must after a long delay created by dilatory storylines.[5] Although 'a recognizable social identity and a role' finally materialise for the protagonist, the fact of their transformation implies the antecedent absence of social identity in which the narrative dallies.[6] On one hand, romance 'posits its progress on the ultimate triumph of the stranger and the youth, the "Fair Unknown" who earns both a name and a place'.[7] On the other, this progress is premised upon a prior condition of alienness which the text does not relegate to a position of otherness, but develops as a fully realised subjectivity throughout most of its course. In this way, romance has always contained the possibility that the Other, far from being 'radically different from me', is vividly imaginable as the self.

Consequently, romance itself has an ambiguous identity. It is not shaped by a binary opposition between self and other, but by their unlikely proximity and transmutability. Women writers capitalise on this metamorphic potential to attempt to offset the gendered otherness of the female subject. They do so, as Kim F. Hall suggests, by centralising the woman's subject position relative to the alternative peripheral reference point of racialised identities.[8] This reorientation transforms romance from a genre of identification to one in which identity itself, particularly those of non-white persons, is the casualty. The mutual transformations of romance and race by women make genre an epistemological category which shapes black and brown subjects into emblems of self-loss in various ways and makes stable identity a fiction.

[4] On the dangers of women reading romance, see Juan Luis Vives, in Foster Watson (ed.), *Vives and the Renascence Education of Women* (London, 1912), 59–62.

[5] See Patricia Parker, *Inescapable Romance: Studies in the Poetics of a Mode* (Princeton, NJ, 1979), 8.

[6] Nandini Das, *Renaissance Romance: The Transformation of English Prose Fiction, 1570–1620* (London, 2011), 14.

[7] Das, *Renaissance Romance*, 5–6.

[8] Kim F. Hall, '"I Rather Would Wish to Be a Black-Moor": Beauty, Race, and Rank in Lady Mary Wroth's *Urania*', in Margo Hendricks and Patricia Parker (eds), *Women, 'Race', and Writing in the Early Modern Period* (New York, 1994), 178–94. This essay is later expanded into Hall's *Things of Darkness: Economies of Race and Gender in Early Modern England* (Ithaca, NY, 1995), 178. Both volumes are foundational to further work on the intersections of race and gender in Renaissance texts.

MARY WROTH AND MARGARET CAVENDISH: 'WHO THUS TO BLACKNESS RUN'

Lady Mary Wroth's *Countess of Montgomery's Urania* (1621) is well-known for its autobiographical mode of identity-seeking, as Lara Dodds establishes (this volume, Chapter 17, 'Women and Fiction'). But its resolution, like that of Wroth and her lover, William Herbert, Third Earl of Pembroke, is infinitely deferred by an incomplete text. The anticipated union of their fictional counterparts, the lovers Pamphilia and Amphilanthus—the expected endpoint of romance—is ultimately denied us because the Second Part of the *Urania* is unfinished. Blackness, a symbol both of undesirability and unfulfilled erotic promise, facilitates this open-endedness. In the First Part of the *Urania*, Pamphilia couches her desire to be desired only by Amphilanthus in terms of racial alternatives. She says that she 'rather would wish to be a Black-moore, or anything more dreadfull, then allure affection to me, if not from [Amphilanthus]; thus would I be to merit [his] loved favour, the other to shew my selfe purer, then either purest White or Black'.[9] Hall complicates the routine aesthetic troping of black skin as undesirable in early modern texts by noting that 'this assumption almost never turns out as anticipated, and men end up in the arms of black women in these texts', perhaps revealing both a desire of difference and a fear of it.[10]

But, if blackness 'highlights the lack of subject position offered by the language of beauty', the typical trajectory of romance suggests that powerlessness and ill fortune will eventually give way to status and union.[11] Pamphilia's unrewarded constancy is typical of the protracted suffering of the romance protagonist which is, usually, eventually resolved. Further, she metaphorically racialises her identity to convey this passive suffering. In terms of the intersection between narrative structure and racialisation, Wroth owes a particular debt to Heliodorus' *Æthiopica*(ca. 3–4th cen. CE), in which race similarly contributes to the proliferating narratives of romance as well as being a hidden facet of the protagonist's identity. The *Æthiopian History* was translated from Greek into English several times during the sixteenth and seventeenth centuries, beginning with Thomas Underdown's 1569 translation.[12] Heliodorus' tale of an

[9] Mary Wroth, in Josephine A. Roberts (ed.), *The First Part of the Countess of Montgomery's Urania* (Binghamton, NY, 1995), 465.

[10] Hall, *Things of Darkness*, 205.

[11] Hall, *Things of Darkness*, 205.

[12] See Heliodorus, in William L'Isle (trans.), *The Faire Æthiopian*, (London, 1631); see also Heliodorus, in Thomas Underdown (trans.), *An Æthiopian Historie* (London, 1659). Underdown's translation came to be well-known and was republished in five subsequent editions in 1577, 1587, 1605, 1606, and 1622. Wroth would certainly have been familiar with Heliodorus. Although no record of her own personal library survives, records show that the *Æthiopica* was to be found in at least one (probably Italian) edition in the library at Penshurst; see Gilbert Spencer, in Germaine Warkentin, Joseph L. Black, and William R. Bowen (eds), *The Library of the Sidneys of Penshurst Place Circa 1665* (Toronto, 2013), 188.

abandoned, white-skinned Ethiopian princess's journey back to her kingdom owes its peregrinations to the fact that the protagonist's racial identity is belied by her colour. The heroine, Charikleia, and her beloved, Theagenes, frequently despair of their tragic fortunes throughout a seemingly endless narrative in which their superlative—and emphatically white—noble beauty makes them objects of unsolicited desire and envy. They are also repeatedly (and, in Charikleia's case, incorrectly) identified as Greeks, both for their whiteness and the language they speak. From bands of 'blacke coloured, & euell favoured' Egyptian bandits, to Arsake, the wife of the Persian satrap (or governor) and a 'Lover of Greekes, & al handsomnesse', their antagonists are figured as racialised foils to their Greekness.[13] Consequently, the ultimate recovery of Charikleia's sovereignty is also implicitly an act of aesthetic and cultural colonisation from within Ethiopia—a recontainment of blackness within whiteness for which Charikleia serves as an emblem.

Heliodoran resonances emerge several times in this chapter. Pamphilia, like Charikleia, asserts an inner blackness. Wroth's formulation, however, harnesses the racial and aesthetic peripherality of blackness as a metaphor for erotic alienation. In its 1621 printed version, Wroth's romance was accompanied by a sequence of songs and sonnets, 'Pamphilia to Amphilanthus'.[14] In one of these sonnets, blackness recurs as the driving conceit which conveys the isolated inwardness of Pamphilia's identity as lover:

Like to the Indians, scorched with the sun,
The sun which they do as their God adore,
So am I used by love, for ever more
I worship him, less favours have I won,
Better are they who thus to blackness run,
And so can only whiteness' want deplore
Than I who pale and white am with grief's store,
nor can have hope, but to see hopes undone;
Besides their sacrifice received in sight
of their chose saint: mine hid as worthless rite;
Grant me to see where I my offerings give,
Then let me wear the mark of Cupid's might
In heart as they in skin of Phoebus' light,
Not ceasing offerings to love while I live.[15]

The poem shores up Pamphilia's aesthetic association of blackness or brownness with ill favour with an Ovidian allusion to Phaëthon, who disastrously crashed Phoebus'

[13] Underdown, *An Æthiopian Historie*, 2, 95.

[14] For a more detailed discussion of the relationship of the sonnet sequence to the *Urania*, see Josephine Roberts (ed.), 'The Nature of the Poetry', in *The Poems of Lady Mary Wroth* (Baton Rouge, LA, 1983). See also Paul Salzman, 'Lady Mary Wroth's Poetry', in *The Ashgate Companion to the Sidneys, 1500–1700*, vol. 2 (Farnham, 2017).

[15] Mary Wroth, 'Like to the Indians (PA Transcription)', in Paul Salzman (ed.), *Mary Wroth's Poetry: An Electronic Edition*, http://wroth.latrobe.edu.au/row-075.html, accessed 10 September 2020.

sun-chariot, burning the inhabitants of Ethiopia black in the process. Wroth, however, argues punningly that not to be favoured by one's beloved, or by love itself, is a worse fate than being ill-favoured because one is black. Pamphilia's blackness is an emblem both of devotion and of Cupid's ill use. The sonnet develops the themes Pamphilia introduces in the 'Black-moore' passage of the *Urania*.

For Pamphilia (and Wroth), blackness is symptomatic of finding oneself othered. But this metaphor is also perversely vindicating. To be black is purportedly to be ill-favoured (aesthetically *and* romantically), but it also becomes a sign of an ardent worshipper, evidence that erotic favour is deserved. Pamphilia's blackness is not only symptomatic of melancholy, but of unjust alienation.[16] The bitterness of rejection generates the turn in the sonnet's second quatrain which separates the elision of other and self out again—this time, with the Indians, not the white subject, in the enviable position. As a result, blackness is double-edged. Requital is figured as basking in the rays of one's idol and growing sunburned; at the same time, to be rejected is to be burned by love. Unlike Ben Jonson's *Masque of Blackness*, in which Wroth herself performed at court in 1605, and which ends with the whitewashing of the black daughters of Niger, blackness is the inevitable conclusion of Pamphilia's plight.

The fact that blackness here is a metaphor for an emotional state which is constitutive of Pamphilia's identity, rather than a marker of her race, differentiates her from Charikleia. The troping of blackness lends it power as a figure of female Petrarchan subjectivity. However, it consequently lacks the indelibility associated with blackness as racial identity and therefore fails to produce the desired outcome. The meanings of whiteness and blackness widen over the course of the sonnet to include this unattainability. While the Indians inevitably grow 'with Phoebus' amorous pinches black', in Shakespeare's apt formulation, Pamphilia remains sickly pale with unrequited love. In her pallor, she puts on the inner blackness of the final tercet. This last turn transforms blackness's aesthetic association with ill favour into a symbol of Amphilanthus' lack of favour and the fantasy of basking in the favour she craves. Blackness in the *Urania* evokes a topos of impossibility which we actually expect romance to reverse. At the same time, it defies our, and perhaps Wroth's, generic expectations that love will find a way. The incomplete romance appears ultimately to defer to an anticipated biographical fulfilment. The unfinished Second Part of the *Urania* introduces the character Fair Design, a figure both for Wroth's son by Herbert and a cryptic monogram which adorns two of her surviving books.[17] The implied invitation to Herbert to 'decipher' the design and supply a real-world ending to the fiction by acknowledging his children by Wroth goes unanswered. Wroth's quest for identity is never completed.

[16] For a discussion of Pamphilia's blackness as melancholy, see Elizabeth Spiller, *Reading and the History of Race in the Renaissance* (Cambridge, 2011), 153–201.

[17] V. M. Braganza, '"Many Ciphers, Although But One For Meaning": Lady Mary Wroth's Many-Sided Monogram', *English Literary Renaissance*, 52.1 (2022), 124-152.

CAVENDISH'S IMAGINED EMPIRE

Over thirty years later, Margaret Cavendish invokes the final lines of Edward Denny's polemical 'hermaphrodite' poem attacking Wroth and the *Urania* twice in her own published works. She perversely paraphrases Denny in her prefaces to *Poems and Fancies* (1654) and *Sociable Letters* (1664), predicting that men 'will say to me, as to the lady that wrote the romance: Work lady, work, let writing books alone, | For surely wiser women ne'er wrote one.'[18] Cavendish's search for literary and epistemological authority draws inspiration from Wroth's bravura act of female authorship. Although she speciously claims in the preface to *Natures Pictures* (1656) that she has never read a romance, she evidently delights in considering herself a thoroughly unwise woman by Denny's standard, for she writes many. In fact, she innovates vigorously in the genre by building upon it a vision of imperial female identity.

Romance is no stranger to imperial themes. However, Cavendish renegotiates the terms of these themes in *The Blazing World* (1666) according to the gender and racial politics of colonialism and natural philosophy. In this endeavour, she casts herself as '*Margaret* the *First*' in direct parallel to real-world male sovereigns.[19] Her imaginative empire offsets the loss of social rank and title that the Royalist Cavendish and her husband, William, Duke of Newcastle, suffered during the Interregnum when they were exiled to Antwerp. It also creates for Cavendish an epistemological sovereignty as a woman weaponising the derogatory allegation of 'fancy' usually levelled at romance.[20] The hegemony which animates Cavendish's romance is not over land, but over knowledge and ideas. *The Blazing World* has a tripartite generic identity, 'the first part whereof is *romancical*, the second philosophical, and the third is merely *fancy*.'[21] A resonance between the world-making involved in fanciful romance and the knowledge-making of natural philosophy drives this threefold structure. In *The Worlds Olio* (1655), Cavendish suggests that poetic invention has the potential to create unified and universal knowledge. Unlike competing natural philosophers who advance discordant theories, poets:

> are quick of invention, easie to conceive, ready in executing, and flies [*sic*] over all The world, yet not so swiftly, but They take a strickt notice of all things, and knowes perfectly The laws, and wayes which inables Them to judge more uprightly, and

[18] Margaret Cavendish, 'To All Noble and Worthy Ladies,' in Liza Blake (ed.), *Margaret Cavendish's Poems and Fancies: A Digital Critical Edition* (May 2019), accessed 20 August 2020. See also Margaret Cavendish, in James Fitzmaurice (ed.), 'To His Excellency the Lord Marquis of Newcastle,' in *Sociable Letters* (New York, 2004), 38.

[19] Margaret Cavendish, *The Blazing World*, in Kate Lilley (ed.), *The Blazing World and Other Writings* (New York, 2004), 124.

[20] Lee, "The Meanings of Romance," 306.

[21] Cavendish, *The Blazing World*, 124.

> having an universal knowledg, joyned to his natural wit, makes him The best general judge.[22]

Poets are wide-ranging close observers, but their judgement is also the product of invention. By this account, knowledge is made more than it is uncovered by experimentation—a suggestion which resonates with Cavendish's extensive critiques of mechanical philosophy. The result is that knowledge-making and world-making become mates in empire. This imperialist vision uses social hierarchy as the basis for the romance protagonist's identity and race as the basis for hierarchy. Within this hierarchy, racialised characters themselves are evacuated of any independent identity.

The Blazing World begins conventionally with its female protagonist, a figure for Cavendish, taking to the sea to flee the rapacious advances of a lusty merchant. However, romance itself soon undergoes a sea change as she crosses over into a different world, where she encounters beings of varied half-animal shapes who take her for a goddess, crown her Empress, and perform scientific investigations in her name. The Blazing Worldians are, as Sujata Iyengar observes, 'racially diverse in two different senses: they have skins of varying colors, and they belong to diverse species'.[23] Moreover, the text organises social hierarchy and functional differentiation according to these physical forms. Members of the 'imperial race', including the Empress herself, consume a youth-giving gum which gives them advantages of physical strength and form (155–6). The 'ordinary sort of men' are 'of several complexions; not white, black, tawny, olive or ash-coloured; but some appeared of an azure, some of a deep, some of a grass green, some of a scarlet, some of an orange-colour, etc'.[24] The 'rest of the inhabitants' are members of various humanoid species—'bear-men', 'worm-men', 'fish- or mear-men', 'bird-men', 'fly-men', etc.—although their physical appearances are never described beyond this litany of hybrid names (133–4).

The imperial hierarchy of knowledge production which licenses '*Margaret* the *First*' to pass judgement on the animal-men's scientific findings is a representation of the epistemological and authorial power which allows Margaret Cavendish to fashion these same characters as fictionalisations of her ideas about race. As the animal-men present their scientific discoveries to the Empress on topics ranging from the cosmos to the natural world, she acts not as a consumer of knowledge, but a controller of methods and scrutiniser of conclusions. Displeased with the bear-men's competing theories of the stars, for example, she threatens to break their telescopes, which she calls 'mere deluders' (142). This repudiation of the limitations of experimental science places knowledge at the level of speculations controlled by Cavendish herself. Race-making occurs within

[22] Margaret Cavendish, *The Worlds Olio*, in Shawn Moore, Jacob Tootalian, and Liza Blake (eds), *Digital Cavendish: A Scholarly Collaborative*, http://digitalcavendish.org/complete-works/worlds-olio-1655/, accessed 20 August 2020.

[23] Sujata Iyengar, 'Royalist, Romancist, Racialist: Rank, Gender, and Race in the Science Fiction of Margaret Cavendish', *English Literary History*, 69.3 (2002), 649–72, 650.

[24] Cavendish, *The Blazing World*, 133.

the parameters of this agency. In the second edition of *Observations On Experimental Philosophy* (1668), Cavendish adds a claim in a substantial passage absent from the first edition (1666) that '*black Moors* ... seem a kind or race of men different from the white', and further asserts that black people are of an entirely 'different species'.[25] She also rejects the theory that blackness is created by the absence of light in the pores of substances like charcoal, and its corollary that 'a black Moor would have larger pores than a man of a white complexion'. This is also a repudiation of Robert Hooke, who argued in his *Micrographia* (1665) that the 'pores' he observed in charcoal appeared black because 'from each ... no light was reflected'.[26] Cavendish's jab at his theory resurfaces in *The Blazing World* in nearly the same terms as in *Observations*, only to be similarly rejected by the Empress when the bear-men—all that remains of the hapless Hooke in her fiction—present her with a piece of charcoal.

This deliberate conversation between natural philosophy and romance makes romance a venue for exploring race's social consequences. For Cavendish, racial hierarchy is about hegemony over knowledge production. Romance's basis in invention permits her to assume this hegemony and rewrite race in polygenetic terms while rearranging its differences into an imagined society. Within this social order, the animal-men have neither autonomous identity nor interiority (a choice aimed simultaneously at empirical scientists and colonised subjects), but are defined only by the functions of scientific inquiry they serve for the Empress. This vision of racialised categories as functionally subordinate non-identities renegotiates romance in terms of colonial dominance. Cavendish's romance is centred on European identity formation. The irony of this focus, of course, is that, in the Blazing World, it is the Empress herself who is the foreigner of another race, the stranger on strange shores. Nonetheless, epistemological hegemony displaces the prolonged geographic wandering of a traditional romance. This reinvention demonstrates that colonial social structures depend on the ability to control knowledge and social identity.

HESTER PULTER AND APHRA BEHN: DARK SHADOWS, FAIR PICTURES

The last two texts in this chapter feature racialized subjects. The first, Hester Pulter's *The Unfortunate Florinda* (*c* 1661), constructs a world which blurs the line between self and other. The framing narrative of this unfinished two-part romance is the rape of the obstinately chaste maiden, Florinda, by the Spanish king, Roderigo, and the subsequent retributive Moorish invasion of Spain. Pulter draws this part of the narrative and many

[25] Margaret Cavendish, in Eileen O'Neill (ed.), *Observations Upon Experimental Philosophy* (Cambridge, 2001), 115.

[26] Robert Hooke, *Micrographia* (London, 1665), 100–1.

passages almost verbatim from a contemporary historical source, *The Life and Death of Mahoment, The Conquest of Spain, Together with the Rysing and Ruine of the Sarazen* (1637), a text spuriously attributed to Walter Raleigh, and may have been drawn to the story by William Rowley's dramatic adaptation, *All's Lost By Lust* (1633).[27] However, the First Part of the text centres upon a romance subplot invented by Pulter, which follows the trials and tribulations of a mixed-race couple: the African Moorish woman, Fidelia, and her beloved Amandus, the King of Naples and France.

Perhaps because the romance is incomplete, the Fidelia/Amandus subplot is more substantial than digressive. It reads as a wholesale takeover of the unfinished story, reorienting the narrative's themes with a force all its own. Pulter also rewrites the racial politics of Heliodorus' *Æthiopica*. From the moment that Fidelia, former companion to Roderigo's wife, the Moorish princess Zabra, washes up on Spanish shores, a certain gravity pulls the romance into orbit around the focal point of her narrative, in comparison to which even the main narrative of Florinda's rape becomes temporarily peripheral. This magnetism is aesthetic. The topos of the hero/heroine's beacon-like noble beauty is a familiar one in romance. Generically, it is unsurprising that Fidelia, the 'beautiful stranger' whose entrance earns the wonder of Roderigo's court, successfully intercepts the narrative.[28] However, Pulter deploys the exceptional beauty topos with the difference that Fidelia, resolving the tension in the opening line of the 'Song of Songs', is both black *and* comely.

It seems overwhelmingly likely that Pulter models Fidelia and her narrative trajectory on Heliodorus' Charikleia. Both characters are culturally Europeanised African heroines. Like Charikleia, Fidelia is subject to protracted misadventures as her beauty makes her a perpetual object of desire and persecution. Both women bemoan the cruelty of their fortunes repeatedly in explicitly tragic terms, and Fidelia even '[repines] at nature for burdening her with such an alluring beauty' (335). Beauty also functions as a disaster magnet for the white male beloveds in both texts. Heliodorus' Theagenes is captured and nearly gifted to the Persian king as a royal servant because of his extraordinary beauty. Likewise, Pulter's Amandus enters the story as a captive sent to Fidelia's father because he is 'judged a present for none but a prince' (294). Both women's 'propensity to read events through the medium of the tragic mode ... [is offset] against a providential narrative trajectory that the heroine fails to recognise'.[29] Additionally, the fact that Fidelia is a woman of colour reads as an engagement with the tension, always deferred in the *Æthiopica*, between a European ideal of whiteness and a beautiful African heroine.

Pulter uses these romance paradigms in turning towards a centralised black subject. She undoes the aesthetics of romance and race in which blackness is 'other', but does

[27] Peter C. Herman, 'Lady Hester Pulter's *The Unfortunate Florinda*: Race, Religion, and the Politics of Rape', *Renaissance Quarterly*, 63.4 (2010), 1206–46, 1216.

[28] Hester Pulter, 'The Unfortunate Florinda', in Alice Eardley (ed.), *Poems, Emblems, and The Unfortunate Florinda* (Toronto, 2014), 285.

[29] Goran Stanivukovic, *Timely Voices: Romance Writing in English Literature* (Montreal, 2017), 309.

so incompletely. Elsewhere in her manuscript, Pulter deploys the indelibility topos, using the well-known emblem of 'washing the Ethiop white' in her Royalist poem, 'The Complaint of Thames' (1647) to excoriate London itself for betraying Charles I.[30] Interestingly, her descriptions of Fidelia avoid specifying the colour of her skin. At first, she is 'a young lady in a Moorish habit', her ethnicity marked only sartorially, while her brother, Ithocles, is 'a Barbarian, whose person and deportment demonstrated his extraction to be noble' (285). While the text apparently finds the combination of Ithocles' North African identity and noble features unremarkable, it fails to provide a similar description of Fidelia. Instead, what Peter C. Herman calls Pulter's tendency to '[refer] to her African ladies as fair as much as she refers to the European Florinda as fair' bolsters her defence of women by capitalising on the associations of fairness with virtue and beauty, even as it tacitly ignores the word's literal reference to whiteness.[31] Additionally, as Herman points out, Pulter's African women are pagans rather than Muslims. Thus Fidelia, like the Greek-speaking Charikleia, is culturally Europeanised.

Pulter's assimilationist tack downplays Fidelia's racial difference and effaces her colour. When the text does mention Fidelia's blackness, it is a fleeting shadow. Initially, the unnamed African king who desires Fidelia mistakes her for one of the statues in her father's house and asks him 'whether the tenth statue were Diana, or Venus, for, he said, it were too lovely to be Minerva, and why all the rest were white, and the cheeks of one of them were blushing according (as one says) to the English barbarism' (306). The king's question replaces the expected colour contrast between white and black skin with a material one between white marble and pink paint. At the same time, it reverses the more usual application of 'barbarism' to non-European cultures by placing the word in the mouth of an African king as a commentary on the English practice of painting statues. While this moment conceals the colour of Fidelia's skin, it promotes whiteness by suggesting that white marble is most appropriate to pagan iconography.

However, the text later reveals that Fidelia is not white. Ironically, she is initially mistaken for a painted work of art and multiple men subsequently fall in love with her painted portrait, which Amandus carries. Amicla later fights Amandus for possession of the portrait, which the latter claims is an image of the Virgin Mary. Amicla asks 'the reason that this picture (though it be incomparably lovely) hath so dark a shadow and that I ever saw of the immaculate virgin are infinitely fair' (342). His gesture to Christian iconography echoes the African king's reference to classical statuary and re-establishes the traditional symbolism of 'fair' as linking whiteness to virtue. Moreover, the description of the portrait's blackness as a 'shadow' minimises Fidelia's darkness, hinting that it is almost insubstantial. Amandus' reply that 'our Lady of Loretta is much blacker (even as black as an Ethiopian) but what the reason is I know not' augments this effect, gesturing to a primarily white iconography of the Virgin Mary. Amandus' reference to

[30] She writes that it is 'more impossible [i.e., to expunge Parliament's guilt] than 'tis to change | The skins of Negroes that in Afric range' (ll. 19–20). See Pulter, *Poems, Emblems, and the Unfortunate Florinda*, 59–60.

[31] Herman, 'Lady Hester Pulter's *The Unfortunate Florinda*', 1223.

the much darker statue of the Virgin Mary—which still stands in the Basilica della Santa Casa in Loreto, Italy—attempts to lighten Fidelia's brown skin by contrast.

Pulter's incorporation of a black, beautiful, and virtuous protagonist into romance shifts the conventions of the genre, but a white over black hierarchy lingers over the text's aesthetics. Aphra Behn's *Oroonoko* (1688) also confronts this hierarchy. This time, romance itself comes undone. Unlike the previous texts in this chapter, *Oroonoko* does not foreground a search for white female identity. Behn's narrator is a white woman, but she is unnamed and nearly invisible until she takes an active role in manipulating the hero into perpetual slavery. In one sense, she is the fulfilment of a fantasy of the assimilation of the female author: she is at once unmarked and confident in the power of her authorial voice to 'make [Oroonoko's] name to survive to all ages'.[32] Interestingly, the last word which flows from the white female author's pen is the name of Oroonoko's wife, 'Imoinda', a black woman and perhaps the most voiceless character in the romance. If white women have, by this point, gained an authorial voice despite their gender, black women are silenced by colour and gender.[33]

The narrator's gender takes a back seat to themes of race and identity. Oroonoko begins his narrative already in possession of the noble identity which constitutes most romance protagonists' hard-won endpoint. Like Fidelia, blackness and beauty are in tension in Oroonoko, whose:

> Face was not of that brown, rusty Black which most of that Nation are, but a perfect Ebony, or polish'd Jett. His Eyes were the most awful that wou'd be seen, and very piercing; the White of 'em being like Snow, as were his Teeth. His Nose was rising and *Roman*, instead of *African* and flat. His mouth, the finest shap'd that cou'd be seen; far from those great turn'd Lips, which are so natural to the rest of the *Negroes*.[34]

This description uses lustre and proportion as an apology for colour. Its distinctions between 'rusty' and 'polish'd' black draw on classical Ovidian juxtapositions between *ater*, *niger*, *albus*, and *candidus*, terms which distinguish between dull and lustrous varieties of black and white.[35] Behn's implicitly classical vocabulary evokes, and perhaps responds to, Cavendish's repudiation of the absence of light in blackness. Still, her description of Oroonoko blazonically latches onto any whiteness at all that can be found in his countenance, even if it is his teeth or the whites of his eyes. Behn's is a much more elaborate apology for blackness than that which Pulter offers. Nobility still inheres, according to romance, in European features, even when romance turns to a black subject.

[32] Aphra Behn, in Joanna Lipking (ed.), *Oroonoko* (New York, 1997), 65.

[33] Thomas Southerne's dramatic adaptation of *Oroonoko* (1668) dilates upon this juxtaposition, but turns Imoinda into a white woman.

[34] Behn, *Oroonoko*, 13.

[35] See C. Arius Abellan, '"Albus-Candidus, Ater-Niger, and Ruber-Rutilus" in Ovid's *Metamorphoses*: A Structural Research', *Latomus*, 43.1 (1984), 111–17.

This black subject is a product of a colonising European imagination on an authorial and a narrative level. The failure of the European imagination to transcend the very aesthetic hierarchy it establishes threatens the essence of identity politics in romance. It presents the possibility that, although there *is* an art to find the noble mind's construction in the face, it may be disregarded by society. A post-regicide England nearing the height of the British slave trade fittingly asks of romance what nobility is worth in a world capable of indifference to it. The reply is the breakdown of identity, an awakening to new horrors where neither status nor human dignity are protected—and where this nightmare is the natural sequel to the writings of Wroth, Cavendish, Pulter, and many others. Oroonoko begins at the traditional romance protagonist's endpoint only to follow an inverted trajectory of identity loss via enslavement. Behn's female narrator becomes visible as an agent of this downward spiral. While the slave owner Trefry feeds Oroonoko with false promises of eventual freedom, the narrator '[gives] him all the Satisfaction I possibly cou'd' by feeding him tales of heroism, 'the Lives of the Romans, and great men, which charm'd him to my Company' (41). Emily Griffiths Jones points out that, 'While the friends' enjoyment of romance and of each other seems sincere, their superficially radical community is a contrived tool of the enslaving establishment'.[36]

Herein, the accusations of idle fancy and danger levelled at romance return in an ominous form, as do the associations of romance and fancy with women.[37] The narrator's tales have an effeminising effect on Oroonoko, who 'lik'd the Company of us Women much above the Men' (41). Romance's feminine connotations become agents of racially motivated social death and physical slaughter. In an ironised reference to Lucan's *Pharsalia*, Oroonoko takes the epic name of Caesar because 'he wanted no part of the Personal Courage of that Caesar, and acted things as memorable'; but, in stark contrast to Cavendish's protagonist, the name of Caesar relegates him to the status of a slave (36–7). Tales of martial deeds lull him into a false belief that his identity will eventually be restored via his manumission—a deferral truly without end.

CONCLUSION

Fiction, within and beyond romance, will always be about identity. Criticism presents a concomitant opportunity to examine these representations of identities and investigate the ways in which texts blur the declared lines between self and other. These investigations should extend to questioning existing critical judgements of centrality and peripherality. Nearly fifty years after Jameson, we face a world in which the 'leveling of racial differences' or inequalities is no longer a given, in which we find our own

[36] Emily Griffiths Jones, *Right Romance: Heroic Subjectivity and Elect Community in Seventeenth-Century England* (University Park, 2020), 187–225.

[37] Lee, 'The Meanings of Romance', 306.

protracted journey towards racial equality in the West violently deferred. Under these circumstances, scholarship must insist upon aiding the resolution, not prolonging the deferrals. Half a century after studies of early modern women writers were first made possible by a generation of pathbreaking work, Renaissance criticism is still in the process of incorporating conversations about these women into the mainstream of a historically male-dominated canon.[38] This volume is a stepping stone in that vital work, which must be performed as ubiquitously and ardently as critics everywhere take up Shakespeare, if scholarship is to be historically representative. Further, the work of important intersections between women's texts and other 'othered' identities, particularly racialised ones, is largely yet to be performed. In an essay whose provocations to intersectionality resonate today, Laura Brown argues that:

> *Oroonoko* can serve as a theoretical test case for the necessary connection of race and gender, a model for the mutual interaction of the positions of the oppressed in the literary discourse of its own age, and a mirror for modern criticism in which one political reading can reflect another.[39]

Not only must the field take the analysis of categories like gender in new and intersectional directions, it must also reject the positioning of these categories as niche or optional by contrast to the study of canonical male writers. To accept this positioning is to take Renaissance judgements of otherness on the bases of race and gender as representing historical fact and dictating selective critical prominence—rather than attending holistically who was really writing and being read at the time and the ideas which made up the intellectual fabric. Only by recognising race and women writers as central, for they are, can we perceive the past accurately and write a better future.

FURTHER READING

Habib, Imtiaz. *Black Lives in the English Archives, 1500–1667*. Farnham, 2008.

Hackett, Helen. *Women and Romance Fiction in the English Renaissance*. Cambridge, 2000.

Hall, Kim F. *Things of Darkness: Economies of Race and Gender in Early Modern England*. Ithaca, NY, 1995.

Hendricks, Margo and Patricia Parker (eds). *Women, 'Race', and Writing in the Early Modern Period*. New York, 1994.

[38] Most recently on this subject, see Lara Dodds and Michelle M. Dowd, 'Happy Accidents: Critical Belatedness, Feminist Formalism, and Early Modern Women's Writing', *Criticism*, 62.2 (2020), 169–93.

[39] Laura Brown, *Ends of Empire: Women and Ideology in Early Eighteenth-Century English Literature* (Ithaca, NY, 1993), 27. The pathbreaking work on this intersection which the field must build on moving forwards is Margo Hendricks and Patricia Parker's edited collection *Women, 'Race,' and Writing in the Early Modern Period* (New York, 1994).

Jones, Emily Griffiths. *Right Romance: Heroic Subjectivity and Elect Community in Seventeenth-Century England*. University Park, 2020.
Loomba, Ania. *Gender, Race, Renaissance Drama*. Manchester, 1989.
MacDonald, Joyce Green. *Women and Race in Early Modern Texts*. Cambridge, 2004.
Thompson, Ayanna (ed.). *The Cambridge Companion to Shakespeare and Race*. Cambridge, 2021.
Traub, Valerie (ed.). *The Oxford Handbook of Shakespeare and Embodiment*. Oxford, 2016.

PART III

PLACES

CHAPTER 19

A PLACE-BASED APPROACH TO EARLY MODERN WOMEN'S WRITING

PAULA MCQUADE

NEARLY ten years ago, while researching a book on early modern women's writing, I encountered a seventeenth-century catechism written by a woman named Dorothy Burch. *Early English Books Online* (EEBO) made it easy to download a copy of Burch's catechism, which was available in print only at the British Library and the Huntington, to my desktop in Chicago. Figuring out what to do with Burch's catechism was much more difficult. The study of early modern women's writing at that time focused largely upon either aristocratic women who wrote in recognisably literary genres or religious radicals whose works subverted the established religious and political order. Burch was neither. As far as I could tell, she was an ordinary wife and mother who dedicated her text, *A Catechism of the Several Heads of the Christian Religion* (1646) to her children, whose good, she writes in the preface, 'I must and will desire as my own'.[1] It was the only work Burch ever published. Together with the baptismal records of her children, it provides the only certain textual evidence of her existence.

As I puzzled over Burch's text, I became increasingly intrigued by the catechism's title page announcing that it had been written by 'Dorothy Burch, living at Strood in Kent'. Why did the title page deliberately associate the catechism and its author with a specific village? This question emerged in part from my long-standing interest in local history, a branch of history that 'deals with the social, economic, and cultural development of particular localities, often using local records and resources'.[2] What would

[1] I would like to thank Danielle Clarke, Sarah C. E. Ross, Elizabeth Scott-Baumann, and Joshua Scodel for providing helpful comments on an earlier draft of this chapter. Dorothy Burch, *A Catechism of the Several Heads of the Christian Religion*, in Paula McQuade (ed.), *Catechisms Written for Mothers, Schoolmistresses and Children, 1575–1750* (Aldershot, 2008).

[2] 'Local History' (*OED n.* (b)).

happen, I wondered, if I shifted my attention from Burch's identity as a woman writer to the community in which she wrote? The article that I eventually published on Burch relied upon local history to uncover why Burch determined to write and publish her catechism. Drawing upon the traditional sources of local history—churchwardens' accounts, taxation records, and town histories—it traced the catechism's origin to a dispute within her local parish. Many of these sources originally existed only in manuscript, but thanks to the efforts of late nineteenth- and early twentieth-century-local historians, they were now readily available to me in printed form. My analysis suggested that Burch adapted a genre associated with mothers and children in order to witness her scriptural knowledge and Protestant orthodoxy, as well as that of her fellow church members. In response to the claim of a newly arrived Laudian minister that the members of St Nicholas were a 'poore, ignorant and simple people', Burch countered that they were 'a knowing people, and precious in the sight of God' (sig. A3v). She intended her catechism's publication, I concluded, to defend lay Scripture reading, a controversial issue during the Civil War.[3]

My personal interest in local history had developed in part because I believed that it offered a valuable way of thinking about the past, one which acknowledged the importance of the lives of otherwise unremarkable women and men. I also found its eclecticism appealing: local historians, often working collectively, were able to use a variety of sources and methodologies, including oral histories, material culture, and field work, in their efforts to understand the past. Local history is a field, observes the pioneering agricultural historian Joan Thirsk, which encourages 'heterodoxy and experimentation'.[4] But I also knew that most academics dismissed local history as insufficiently rigorous, a hobby for enthusiastic but untrained amateurs, so I was careful to maintain a strict division between it and my professional publications. My experience writing about Burch and her catechism, however, made me realise that local history could provide a way for scholars to better understand the origin, composition, and importance of early modern women's writing, especially the textual productions of non-elite women who lived in smaller villages and towns. Since the sixteenth century, local historians have documented the geography, socio-economic structure, and religious history of their communities. These compilations include a variety of documents useful to the modern researcher, including maps, genealogical tables, drawings of ecclesiastical buildings and manor houses, and descriptions of the landscape, soil, and economy. These are monumental works, often the culmination of a lifetime of labour. They also offer an alternative way of considering the past. Unlike professional academic histories that focus upon 'great men' and their involvement in events of national

[3] Paula McQuade, '"A Knowing People": Early Modern Motherhood, Female Authorship, and Working-Class Community in Dorothy Burch's *A Catechism of the Several Heads of the Christian Religion* (1646)', *Prose Studies*, 32 (2010), 167–86.

[4] Joan Thirsk, 'Women Local and Family Historians', in David Hey (ed.), *The Oxford Companion to Family and Local History* (Oxford, 2008), 100–10, 108.

and international significance, local histories attest to the dignity of non-elite people living in villages and small towns and foreground how these women and men helped to create the religious and civic institutions which shape community life. Local histories acknowledge human beings' relation to the natural world, frequently emphasising how a region's economy develops in response to the landscape. Often, they are written by a group of women and men who, working together, willingly devote large amounts of time and intellectual energy to contemplating the history of a particular place. It is an 'amateur' approach to history, but in 'the original good sense' of the word, an endeavour which emerges from affection for a place and 'gives a great deal of pleasure to a great deal of people'.[5] I came to believe that local history offers an alternative model for inquiry into the textual productions of early modern women writers, one which insists upon the value of an emotional attachment to one's subject and the significance of community. Its emphasis upon collaboration helps recapture the sense of community that local histories seek to describe.

This chapter seeks to explore in more detail the usefulness of local history for the study of early modern women's writing, especially for the writings of women like Burch who may have possessed considerable power and authority within local communities but played no role in national, let alone international, events. It has two parts. In the first part, I draw upon my interest in local history, as well as work by literary scholars Kate Chedgzoy, Diane Purkiss, and Micheline White, to develop what I will term a 'place-based approach', to early modern women's writing.[6] Elaborating and expanding upon the work of local historians from the seventeenth century to the present, a place-based approach considers how geography and landscape shaped both the development of a community and, as importantly, a women's position within that community. Socio-economic structure is an additional consideration: what were the various occupations and working conditions of community members? Finally, it pays attention to the centrality of religion and the parish church to community life. In the second part, I use Dorothy Burch's catechism as a case study demonstrating the usefulness of a place-based approach to early modern women's writing. After analysing the geography of Strood and its impact upon the village's socio-economic structure, I turn to a series of public debates between Presbyterian ministers and religious enthusiasts at Rochester Cathedral in 1655. These debates reveal that St Nicholas parish was closely connected to Presbyterian churches in Rochester. I suggest that we might best understand Burch's catechism as participating in a more widespread effort by the Presbyterian clergy of Strood and Rochester to defend their doctrinal beliefs against sectarianism. By adopting a

[5] W. G. Hoskins, *Local History in England* (London, 1984), 4–5.

[6] Kate Chedgzoy, *Women's Writing in the British Atlantic World: Memory, Place and History, 1550–1700* (Cambridge, 2007); Diane Purkiss, 'Anna Trapnel's Literary Geography', in Johanna Harris and Elizabeth Scott-Baumann (eds), *The Intellectual Culture of Puritan Women, 1558–1680* (Basingstoke, 2010), 162–75; Micheline White, 'Women Writers and Literary-Religious Circles in the Elizabethan West Country', *Modern Philology*, 103 (2005), 187–214.

place-based approach, we are better able to understand the extent to which Burch's decision to compose and publish a catechism emulates—and to some extent, appropriates—ministerial authority.

A place-based approach to women's writing invites contemporary scholars to connect their work to a tradition of women researchers, whose exclusion from the professional study of history has enabled them to develop distinctive ways of thinking about the past. Women have been active local historians since the seventeenth century, energetically writing about the people, landscape, economies, and religious histories of their communities. Celia Fiennes (1687–1702) crossed England on horseback, describing the people, customs, and industries she encountered. The diarist Sarah Cowper (1644–1720) composed a manuscript local history that addresses the landscape, destroyed monastic houses, and trades of the counties of England. The manuscript local history of Elizabeth Freke (1641–1714) considers the relationship between landscape and human settlement.[7] In the nineteenth century, essayist Harriet Martineau (1802–1876) addressed 'the landscape, archeological remains … settlement history, local industries, household economies and local lifestyles' of England's Lake District in a chapter for a published local history. The *Victoria County History* (1899), a monumental work of local history, has been described as 'a history for gentleman, largely researched by ladies'.[8] Recently, many female local historians have migrated online, creating easily accessible repositories of photographs, wills, oral histories, and local industries within their communities.[9] In the twentieth century, a number of professional women historians, including Jacqueline Eales, Margaret Spufford (1935–2014), and Joan Thirsk (1922–2013), incorporated some characteristics of local history into their work.[10] Thirsk relates women's long-standing interest in local history and methodological creativity to their historical exclusion from academia: 'Long exempt from professionalizing influences', observes Thirsk, women's 'experimental flair was not curbed'.[11] By adopting a place-based approach, scholars of early modern women's writing can emulate the heterodoxy and enthusiasm of female local historians. We can come to understand our work as participating within a tradition of women researchers who have also insisted upon the importance of the local, peripheral, and everyday.

[7] Christopher Morris (ed.), *The Illustrated Journeys of Celia Fiennes, 1685–1712* (London, 1982); Sarah Cowper, Hertfordshire Archives and Local Studies, D/EP F36; Elizabeth Freke, British Library, Add. MS 45720. Thirsk attests to women's long-standing engagement with local history when she observes that Fiennes' work was edited for publication by a kinswoman, Emily Griffiths, in 1888; 'Women Local and Family Historians', 101.

[8] Thirsk, 'Women Local and Family Historians', 103, 105.

[9] See, for example, the website created by the Ewas Lacy Study Group, http://www.ewyaslacy.org.uk.

[10] Jacqueline Eales, *Puritans and Roundheads: The Harleys of Brampton Bryan* (Cambridge, 1990); Margaret Spufford, *Contrasting Communities: English Villagers in the Sixteenth and Seventeenth Centuries* (Cambridge, 1979); Joan Thirsk, *Alternative Agriculture: A History* (Oxford, 1997).

[11] Thirsk, 'Women Local and Family Historians', 108.

A SENSE OF PLACE

Taking its cue from the types of documentary material contained within local histories, a place-based approach begins by exploring the geography of a region, considering how it might have impacted the economic and social development of a community. What is the soil quality? Is the land flat and thus suitable for tillage? Or hilly and thus better for sheep? Is the earth rich in natural minerals such as iron? Early modern local historian and diarist Sarah Cowper, for example, observes of Derbyshire that it is 'rich in iron, lead, and coals' (D/EP F36). A place-based approach also considers topography and landscape, perhaps drawing upon early modern local histories which contain county maps indicating forested areas and fields. It also recognises the importance of rivers in a region's development, since they provided residents with fresh water and food and were an important (and under-recognised) mode of transporting people and goods, as well as books and ideas, in early modern England. Elizabeth Freke uses the course of the River Tamar to structure her narrative, observing at one point that it runs 'high into Salt Esse, a pretty market town' (British Library, Add. MS 45720). William Dugdale does likewise in his *Antiquities of Warwickshire* (1656). Rivers were also engines of economic growth, as William Somner observes his *Antiquities of Canterbury* (1640) when he writes that the River Stour powered the King's mill, as well as five other mills, and thus contributed to the growth of Canterbury.[12]

By studying the county maps included in many early modern local histories, a place-based approach considers how roads and river ways might have connected women who lived in small villages with other communities. Roman roads continued to be heavily used in the early modern period. For example, Watling Street (today's A2) linked London with the Channel ports; Fosse Way connected Lincoln to Exeter. Dugdale includes a map which demonstrates where Fosse and Watling intersect in Warwickshire.[13] Women writers who lived in villages adjacent to these roadways could easily travel to London, where they could participate in its print and political culture. At the same time, we should remember that Roman roads also connected smaller and mid-sized communities: a woman who lived in a small village might not need to travel all the way to London if she could shop in a larger nearby town. Even apparently isolated villages were often connected by serviceable roads to other small communities. Writing of Morebath, a 'small and remote' village in Devon, Eamon Duffy observes that it was not far from Bampton, a market town of about 600 people. The townspeople of Morebath could (and did) access its 'community of gentry, merchants, tradesmen, artisans [and] lawyers'.[14]

[12] William Dugdale, *The Antiquities of Warwickshire Illustrated* (London, 1656), sig. B3r; William Somner, *The Antiquities of Canterbury* (London, 1640), 37.

[13] Dugdale, *The Antiquities of Warwickshire*, 2.

[14] Eamon Duffy, *The Voices of Morebath: Reformation and Rebellion in an English Village* (New Haven, CT, 2001), 5.

A place-based approach can draw upon the wills, genealogical charts, and church memorials contained within local histories to determine a woman writer's socio-economic position within her community. Churchwardens' accounts, frequently transcribed and published by nineteenth-century local historians, can also be consulted, especially if they include assessments made upon all members of a parish based on their wealth. If a woman (or her husband) is included in this group, it is fairly easy to determine her economic position relative to the other members of her community: what marks a person as wealthy in a small village would not necessarily do the same in London. At the same time, wealth does not absolutely correlate with status: a long-standing community member who has fallen into penury might be accorded more respect than a newcomer with greater assets. Household account books can provide a researcher who adopts a place-based approach not only with income and expenditures, but also insight into the local community. The *Household Account Book of Sarah Fell* (1673–1678), for example, includes payments to the local Society of Friends, as well as insight into local trades and occupations. Surviving wills and probate inventories detail a person's wealth at the end of their life; they can also demonstrate a woman writer's legal acumen. The Protestant conformist writer Katherine Thomas, for example, lived in a small village on the Welsh border. She composed a manuscript miscellany which reveals her engagement with Catholic devotional texts, as well as England's ecclesiastical history.[15] A local history group has made her will, which she composed after her husband died intestate, as well as an inventory of her household goods and pictures of her house, including tiles imprinted with the date 1609, accessible online.[16] Finally, churchwardens' accounts and wills can provide a rough approximation of male literacy rates within a community. Female literacy rates will of course be much lower.[17]

Sixteenth- and seventeenth-century local histories frequently include detailed drawings of the exterior and interior of local churches, as well as descriptions of notable people and events associated with the church. Recognising that the parish church was frequently a focal point for community life, a place-based approach can use parish records to provide a rough estimate of church membership. Attentive reading of these records can reveal alliances within a community, as well as schisms.[18] It might also examine monuments and memorials to community members within the parish church. A place-based approach should also consider the minister of a parish. If he published his sermons, they can provide a good indication of the type of piety practised within the parish. Published ministerial catechisms can illuminate the relationship between a minister and his parishioners. For example, when the Welsh minister Vavasor Powell

[15] Sarah Fell, in Norman Penney (ed.), *The Household Account Book of Sarah Fell of Swarthmoor Hall* (Cambridge, 1920); Katherine Thomas, National Library of Wales, MS 4340A.

[16] *The History of Ewas Lacey* (updated 2020), Ewas Lacey Study Group, http://www.ewyaslacy.org.uk/ , accessed 11 December 2020.

[17] David Cressy, *Literacy and the Social Order* (Cambridge, 1980), 145.

[18] Duffy, *Voices of Morebath*, 61. See also Alan Stewart, 'The Familial Lives of Martha Moulsworth and Constance Lucy', in *The Oxford History of Life Writing*, vol. 2 (Oxford, 2018), 183–98.

published a catechism in 1646, he dedicated it 'to my dear Christian friends of Dartford in Kent, whose hopeful and forward children I taught herein, for whom chiefly I intended it'.[19] Urban parishes, in a large city like London or even in a mid-sized city like Rochester, are slightly different, since urbanites were not as closely associated with a particular parish. But, as Diane Purkiss has shown in her discussion of the urbanite Anna Trapnel, we can learn a great deal about an early modern woman's religiosity by tracking her voluntary association with particular parishes.[20] A place-based approach, then, adapts the local historian's interest in geography, socio-economic structure, and religion to consider how the writings of early modern women were shaped by their communities and parishes.

RELIGIOUS RADICALISM IN STROOD

Let us return to Dorothy Burch, 'living at Strood in Kent'. How might a place-based approach improve our understanding of her decision to compose and publish a catechism? Turning our attention to Strood's geography, we see that Strood was near excellent transportation networks that connected its residents both to London and the Continent. The village is located on the River Medway, which the eighteenth-century local historian Edward Hasted describes as a 'spacious river, of great width and force of water'. Hasted relates that it divided Strood from Rochester, as it passed through Rochester Bridge, and by the 'towns of Strood, Rochester, and Chatham' and at Chatham [there are] large and extensive docks, buildings, and other accommodations for the use of the royal navy'. Eventually, it flows into the North Sea.[21] Unsurprisingly, Strood's riverfront location shaped its economy: its inhabitants consisted largely of sailors, fishermen, and oyster dredgers. It also helped make Strood a trading centre. Hasted remarks that ships would unload cargo, 'on the east to the river Medway and Rochester bridge'.[22] From there, the merchandise could be sent throughout the country. *The Churchwardens' Accounts of St. Nicholas, Strood* reveal a surprising number of international visitors; presumably, they arrived from the North Sea via the River Medway.[23]

[19] Vavasor Powell, *Scripture's Concord* (London, 1646), 1. On ministerial catechisms, see Ian Green, *The Christian's ABC: Catechisms and Catechizing in England, 1550–1700* (Oxford, 1996), 93–170.

[20] Purkiss, 'Anna Trapnel's Literary Geography'. See this volume, Chapter 14, Kevin Killeen, '"People of a Deeper Speech": Anna Trapnel, Enthusiasm, and the Aesthetics of Incoherence'.

[21] Edward Hasted, 'Parishes: Strood', in *The History and Topographical Survey of the County of Kent: Volume 3* (Canterbury, 1797), 546–60, *British History Online*, https://www.british-history.ac.uk/survey-kent/vol3, accessed 10 December 2020.

[22] Edward Hasted, 'General history: Rivers', in *The History and Topographical Survey of the County of Kent: Volume 1*, (Canterbury, 1797), 272–93. *British History Online*, http://www.british-history.ac.uk/survey-kent/vol1/pp272–293, accessed 31 January, 2021.

[23] Henry Plomer (ed.), *The Churchwardens' Accounts of St. Nicholas, Strood* (Kent, 1927), 183–4.

Although small, Strood was not isolated. A map included in John Phillipot's account of Kent, *Villare Cantianum* (1659), reveals that it was only one and a half miles from Rochester, a mid-sized city with a population of approximately 2,000 people.[24] Hasted observes that historically part of Strood was within 'the bounds of the corporation of the city of Rochester'.[25] Dorothy Burch could easily enter Rochester simply by crossing Rochester Bridge. At the same time, she could easily journey to other towns in the area, including Chatham and Maidstone, via the River Medway.[26] As significantly, she would have been able to access good roadways: Watling Street (which residents called 'High Street') ran along Strood's southern edge and multiple contemporary sources suggest that residents of Strood frequently travelled it to London.[27] Watling Street also connected Strood's residents with other similarly sized villages along its route. This includes Dartford, a prosperous market town, where Vavasor Powell was minister from 1639 to 1645. Powell may have preached at St Nicholas in 1639.[28] There is some evidence, admittedly incomplete, suggesting that Watling's route from Rochester to London may have contributed to the spread of religious radicalism in the region.[29]

A place-based approach next considers the socio-economic position of Dorothy Burch. Analysis of *The Churchwardens' Accounts for St. Nicholas* can provide a good estimate of her financial position: an assessment inventory of uncollected taxes in 1645 places Burch and her husband Peter in the upper middle of St Nicholas' parishioners who were unwilling or unable to pay the tax. They were not as rich as some members of their church community, but they were certainly wealthier than many.[30] This provides some context for her claim in her catechism that she writes on behalf of her fellow congregants at St Nicholas, whom she acknowledges as poor and variously literate, observing that 'the Lord hath promised to teach his people, though not all like' (sig. A3v). *The Churchwardens' Accounts* also illuminates the social position of Dorothy Burch. In 1639, Dorothy's husband Peter was selected to serve as churchwarden. Typically, men

[24] John Phillipot, *The Parishes, Burroughs, Villages, and Other Respective Mannors Included in the County of Kent* (London, 1659), 401.

[25] Hasted, 'Strood'.

[26] Hasted, 'General History: Rivers'; Hasted, 'Strood'.

[27] *Churchwardens' Accounts of St. Nicholas*, 182–6. In the *Serpent's Subtility* (London, 1656), Walter Rosewell relates that he sent a message to the lodging of Richard Coppin one evening but Coppin 'was gone to London and came not home till Saturday night' (4).

[28] In 1639, Powell was an itinerant preacher; a 'Mr. Powell' preached at St Nicholas Parish in 1639. That is also the year in which Peter Burch was churchwarden; *Churchwardens' Accounts of St. Nicholas*, 182–6. Powell published a catechism with Mathew Simmons in 1646, in the same year and with the same publisher as Dorothy Burch. Although Powell was subsequently considered a religious radical, Steven Roberts observes that Powell was 'willing to present himself as an orthodox' Presbyterian as late as 1646. See Stephen K. Roberts, 'Vavasor Powell', *ODNB*.

[29] Vavasor Powell was minister from 1642 to 1646 at Deptford, a community bisected by Watling Street. Watling Street connected Deptford with both London and Strood. Diane Purkiss observes that Blackheath, which occurs in Anna Trapnel's prophetic vision as 'Hermon Hill', was 'traversed by Watling Street, carrying stagecoaches en route to the Channel ports', 170.

[30] McQuade, *Catechisms and Women's Writing* (Cambridge, 2017), 159, n. 25, provides an extended discussion of taxation rates at St Nicholas parish.

who were chosen to serve in this position were well respected within their community. Peter Burch's tenure as churchwarden also provides some insight into the nature of his piety—and likely that of his wife. It includes a number of activities, such as an increase in the number of visiting ministers, which were typically associated with the 'hotter' sort of Protestants.[31] Finally, a place-based approach might draw upon *The Churchwardens' Accounts* to understand the degree of literacy in the parish. By comparing the number of men who were able to sign the accounts with those who signed with an 'X' (or, in one case, a carefully drawn anchor!) we learn that Strood had higher literacy rates than many similarly sized communities.[32] These higher rates may result from its proximity to Rochester and London, since residents of urban areas generally enjoyed a higher degree of literacy. But, more significantly, we find evidence that Peter Burch enjoyed greater fluency; his written account is so vivid, so full of detail, that Henry Plomer, the nineteenth-century editor of *The Churchwardens' Accounts,* independently characterises it as 'very interesting'.[33] Dorothy Burch appears to have shared her husband's high degree of literacy, as well as his religiosity. For example, to the question, 'What is true Repentance?' Burch responds with some eloquence: 'this is a mightie worke of God upon his people, when he opens their understandings, and so lets them see their sins, which was a cause that Christ did suffer for them that bitter death upon the Crosse, which causeth them to mourne as one that mourneth for his first-borne, Zachary 12.10' (sig. B2r).

A place-based approach is perhaps most revealing when it considers the religious culture of Strood. Elsewhere, I have explored the immediate local religious context for Dorothy Burch's decision to write and publish a catechism in 1646. Here, I would like to turn our attention forward nine years to consider the role of St Nicholas Church in a series of disputations concerning religious radicalism in 1655 that I believe shed retrospective light upon Burch and the religious community of St Nicholas in Strood. In the autumn of 1655, the Ranter Richard Coppin began to preach weekly at Rochester Cathedral. He may have decided to preach in Rochester because Joseph Solomon, a Parliamentary soldier turned Ranter, had lectured there during the preceding four or five years with considerable success. Walter Rosewell, minister at Chatham, observes of Solomon that 'his language was smooth and taking, especially with carnal auditors that delight more in play-books than in the Book of God' (*Serpent's Subtilty*, 1). Coppin advocated such heretical doctrines as universal salvation, Christ's sinfulness, and the non-resurrection of the body. One of his clerical opponents described Coppin as preaching that 'Christ the redeemer was a sinner in respect of his human nature, that all of mankind was the body of Christ to be redeemed and to be saved by him, [and] many more pestilent errors' (*Serpent's Subtilty*, 13). Underpinning all of these doctrines was Coppin's allegorical interpretation of Scripture. In response to a divine who accused him 'of abusing the scripture', Coppin insisted that 'the scriptures are an allegory and a great

[31] *Churchwardens' Accounts of St. Nicholas*, 182.

[32] For a more extensive analysis of literacy rates in Strood, see McQuade, *Catechisms and Women's Writing*, 159, n. 27.

[33] *Churchwardens' Accounts of St. Nicholas*, xxviii.

mysterie ... there is a spiritual meaning to be understood in it all along'.[34] A charismatic orator, Coppin converted many of his listeners. As one of his clerical opponents put it, Coppin 'by good words and fair speeches [did] deceive the hearts of the simple'.[35]

Conformist ministers in Rochester were understandably alarmed by Coppin's success. Worried that their congregations might adopt Coppin's heretical views, four ministers 'resolved to establish on a scripture foundation some of those precious truths which Coppin (by perverting scripture) had determined to undermine' (*Serpent's Subtilty*, 7). In December 1655, they debated Coppin on four successive Sundays, before a packed congregation which was made up of both community members and Parliamentary soldiers. Daniel French, vicar of St Nicholas in Strood, was the second minister to debate Coppin. The debate, which took place on 9 December, covered such topics as the possibility of redemption from hell and Christ's role in the final judgement. Coppin's allegorical interpretation of Scripture clearly perturbed French, who accused Coppin of 'turning scripture every way you list ... like a nose of wax' (*A Blow*, 27). But French's friends gloated that he had forced Coppin to 'betray many of his damnable errors concerning heaven, the ascension of Christ into heaven and his second coming to judgment' (*Serpent's Subtilty*, 6).

The debates attest to the strong religious and pastoral connections between Strood and Rochester. French played a prominent role in the disputations. The other ministers see him as a ministerial 'brother' whom they can call upon to refute sectarian error. A published account of the debate remarks approvingly upon his willingness to leave 'his own congregation' to assist his fellow ministers (*A Blow*, 15). Coppin dismissively lumped all four ministers together as a 'Presbyterian sect' (*A Blow*, 78). Nor is there any discernible difference between the theology espoused by French and that articulated by the other ministers. They saw themselves as members of the same theological tradition: an orthodox Calvinism, whose doctrine was supported by a strong 'scripture foundation'. They affirmed the importance of ministerial preaching and catechising as a way to inoculate the laity so that 'all sorts (even children) might be antidoted' against sectarian error (*Serpent's Subtilty*, 13).

At the same time, the debates reveal a strong undercurrent of religious radicalism in Strood. It thus supports Jacqueline Eales' conclusion that Kent was a county which, during the revolutionary period, was filled 'with so many sects and schisms'.[36] In his response to Coppin, Walter Rosewell reminds his congregation that he has been their minister for nine years and that 'while I have been with you, grievous wolves have come upon you and amongst yourselves have risen upon men speaking perverse things to

[34] Richard Coppin, *A Blow at the Serpent* (London, 1655), 21. Christopher Hill, *The World Turned Upside Down* (London, 1972), 217–23, discusses Solomon and Coppin. See also Nigel Smith, 'Coppin, Richard', *ODNB*.

[35] Edward Garland, *An Answer to a Printed Book* (London, 1657), sig. B1.

[36] Jacqueline Eales, 'So Many Sects and Schisms: Religious Diversity in Revolutionary Kent, 1640–1660', in Christopher Durston and Judith Maltby (eds), *Religion in Revolutionary Kent* (Manchester, 2006), 226–49.

draw disciples after them' (*Serpent's Subtilty*, 1). Throughout the debates, the ministers lament that they were overly tolerant of Solomon's radical preaching. With the benefit of hindsight, they now recognise that Solomon advocated nearly the same doctrinal beliefs as Coppin, but less boldly: 'he [Solomon] desperately undermined the whole mystery of godliness and sowed the seeds of ranting familism, yet managed his devilish designs so slyly and cunningly that it was not easy for an ordinary hearer to discover them' (*Serpent's Subtilty*, 1). Coppin and Solomon were probably brought to Rochester by labourers within the community: Rosewell observes that Coppin was 'brought down from London' by 'Hils the searcher, [and] Robert Cosins, John Phinehas, Carpenters'. These same men, Rosewell points out, had also been 'principall sauters and followers of Salomon' (*Serpent's Subtilty*, 1).

These debates, which Eales describes as 'the most high profile disputation to take place in Kent in the revolutionary period', represent a concerted effort by Presbyterian orthodoxy in and around Rochester to defend their congregations from sectarianism.[37] Daniel French played a significant role in these debates because St Nicholas Parish was closely associated with other Presbyterian churches in Rochester. Moreover, at the same time, Presbyterian ministers in London were battling religious radicals in print. It is not implausible that the two responses were connected, especially given the excellent transportation routes connecting the two regions. We know that ministers in Strood and Rochester were aware of London-based religious initiatives: in 1626, St Nicholas Church participated in a collection spearheaded by William Gouge and other ministers in London for Calvinist churches in the Palatinate. Viewed in this context, the 1655 disputations in Rochester seem to have been part of a larger effort by Presbyterian clergy throughout the country to defend their religion.

Having analysed Strood's location, Burch's socio-economic position, and the religious ecosystem in Strood and Rochester, we are able to ask: what might these debates reveal concerning Burch's decision to compose and publish a catechism nine years earlier? First, they suggest that Dorothy Burch saw herself as a defender of Calvinist orthodoxy in Strood—just as Daniel French would nine years later. Burch relates as much, explaining that she wrote the catechism, 'asking herself questions and answering of them' in order to demonstrate her doctrinal knowledge—and that of her community—to a newly arrived 'minister of the Parish where I live' who follows a 'way' 'descended from Rome' (sig. A2r). To be sure, they battled different enemies: Burch sought to defend her beliefs against those of High Church clergymen, while French and his fellow ministers disputed doctrines associated with radical sectarianism. But Burch and the ministers would have agreed that both positions shared a common error: an overly spiritualised or allegorical interpretation of Scripture. Near the end of his account, Rosewell himself explicitly connects Roman Catholicism and Coppin's beliefs; in each case, he suggests, the doctrinal errors result from an incorrect interpretation of Scripture (*Serpent's Subtilty*, 16). This helps make sense of both Burch's and the ministers' insistence upon their

[37] Eales, 'So Many Sects and Schisms', 241.

scriptural literacy. They believed that it was because they understood Scripture correctly, grounding their doctrine in 'the plainest historical and doctrinal passages of the Old and New Testament', that they could defend Calvinist doctrine against sectarians (*Serpent's Subtilty*, 1).

A place-based approach also enables us to better understand the shifting status of Presbyterianism in revolutionary England, by considering Burch's 1646 catechism alongside the ministerial debates of 1655. Under Archbishop Laud, Calvinist conformist churches had become religious outsiders, whose reliance upon biblical principles set them apart from the Church of England. But by the 1650s, the ground had shifted: Presbyterians were now forced to defend their doctrines against an increasing variety of radically sectarian beliefs. No longer outsiders, they had come to represent the religious mainstream. As Eales observes, there were 'intense struggles between conformists and their opponents before the war broke out' but 'as the war progressed, the Presbyterian clergy became established, even conservative figures'.[38] A place-based approach amplifies our appreciation for Burch's composition by allowing us to see her catechism as participating in a larger, minister-led effort to defend Calvinist doctrine.

A place-based approach to Burch's catechism also usefully complicates our understanding of the relationship between doctrinal orthodoxy and early modern women writers. As I suggested at the beginning of this chapter, most scholarship on early modern women's religious writing focuses upon religious radicals, women who opposed the prevailing religious orthodoxy. Their voices are undeniably bold, brilliant, and compelling. Mary Cary claims the ability to interpret God's will as revealed in Scripture while denying any prophetic experience; Anna Trapnel prophesies from her bedchamber, enacting a form of early modern performance art.[39] Presbyterian ministers in London devoted considerable rhetorical energy to attacking the claims of these women.[40] Burch, in contrast, adapts a form associated with everyday maternal experience and uses it to defend orthodox doctrine. She explains that she published her catechism largely because she hoped 'that it may do good to my children, whose good I must and will desire as my own: if any gaine any good or profit by it, I desire God may have all the honour and praise thereof, and so I rest, thy friend in Christ, Dorothy Burch' (sig. A3r). Her catechism's publication has attracted neither public notice nor scholarly attention. A place-based approach to Burch's text reveals its unexpected significance: it encourages us to see Burch's catechism as participating within a tradition of published defences of Calvinist doctrine in and around Rochester—and perhaps even in London. When we do so, we can see that by publishing a catechism defending the beliefs of her

[38] Eales, 'So Many Sects and Schisms', 234.

[39] On Cary, see Erica Longfellow, *Women and Religious Writing* (Cambridge, 2004), 154, and David Loewenstein, 'Scriptural Exegesis, Female Prophecy, and Radical Politics in Mary Cary', *SEL Studies in English Literature*, 46 (2006), 133–53. On Trapnel, see Katharine Gillespie, *Domesticity and Dissent in Seventeenth-Century England* (Cambridge, 2004) and Hilary Hinds, *Anna Trapnel's Report and Plea* (Tempe, AZ, 2016).

[40] For an orthodox response to Cary, see anon, *The Account Audited* (London, 1649). McQuade discusses this response in *Catechisms and Women's Writing*, 174–8.

parish community, Burch emulates ministerial authority. Otherwise unremarkable, Burch positioned herself, through the publication of her catechism, as the primary defender of Protestant doctrine and belief in Strood. A place-based approach allows us to see that although the form and content of Burch's catechism was ordinary and orthodox, her decision to act as the spokesperson for her parish community was extraordinary and radical.

CONCLUSION

A place-based approach, then, offers an alternative way of considering the textual productions of early modern women. Because it studies the geography, economy, and religious development of particular places, it encourages researchers to explore the local contexts of early modern women's writing. Such an approach is especially valuable when considering the writings of non-aristocratic women residing in smaller communities, such as Dorothy Burch, but it can also be used to study neighbourhoods and networks within cities or even counties.[41] By adopting a place-based approach, we can better appreciate how Burch's catechism intersects with broader religious and political debates concerning lay Scripture reading and Calvinist doctrine.

I would like to conclude by suggesting that a place-based approach also reveals the extent to which the contemporary study of early modern women's writing continues to be shaped by nineteenth-century disciplinary structures. With the professionalisation of history in the nineteenth century, academic historians increasingly dismissed works of local history as antiquarian follies, formless collections which were chockablock full of idle curiosities, fawning genealogies, and useless etchings of ecclesiastical furnishings. By 1849, E. A. Freeman, father-in-law of the English archaeologist and linguist Arthur Evans, could unselfconsciously sneer that 'the first phase of ecclesiology was simple antiquarianism'.[42] The academic perception of local history was not helped by the field's association with women. By the nineteenth century, the female antiquary, a hapless spinster who spent her time searching for relics and curios, was a popular subject for literary satire.[43] Rather than accept these designations, we might see the nineteenth-century professional historian's desire to distinguish between their own work and that of the unpaid (often female) local historian as a policing of boundaries, through which academic historians sought to reinforce their own prestige and interests. By exploring local histories from the seventeenth century to the present, we learn that, unlike professionals who focus largely upon 'great' men and national politics, local historians recognise the

[41] See especially, Purkiss, 'Anna Trapnel's Literary Geography' and White, 'Women Writers and Literary-Religious Circles'.

[42] 'Antiquarianism' (*OED*).

[43] Anon, 'The Female Antiquary', in *The Lady's Magazine, or Mirror of the Belle-Lettres, Fine Arts, Music, Drama, and Fashions* (London, 1830).

dignity of non-elite men and women and foreground their importance in creating and maintaining community life. They thus provide an admirable model for contemporary scholars of early modern women's writing who similarly seek to value the local and the everyday.

FURTHER READING

Goodrich, Jaime. 'The Antiquarian and the Abbess: Gender, Genre, and the Reception of Early Modern Historical Writing', *Journal of Medieval & Early Modern Studies*, 50, 1 January 2020, 95–113.

Gough, Richard. In David Hey (ed.), *The History of Myddle*. New York, 1986.

Hey, David. *The Oxford Companion to Local and Family History*. Oxford, 2008.

Hoskins, W. G. *Local History in England*, 3rd ed. London, 1984.

Thirsk, Joan. 'The History Women', in Mary O'Dowd and Sabine Wichert (eds), *Chattel, Servant or Citizen: Women's Status in Church and State*. Belfast, 1995, 1–11.

Woolf, Daniel. 'A Feminine Past? Gender, Genre, and Historical Knowledge in England, 1500–1800', *American Historical Review*, 102, 1997, 645–79.

CHAPTER 20

LONDON AND THE BOOK TRADE

Isabella Whitney, Jane Anger, and the 'Maydens of London'

MICHELLE O'CALLAGHAN

PRINTED books were a urban phenomenon. When Isabella Whitney famously sends her readers to St Paul's churchyard to buy books from 'my Printer', Richard Jones, her familiarity with the book trade and her own engagement with its economic, transactional practices makes up the matter of her poem:[1]

To all the Bookebinders by Paulles
  because I lyke their Arte:
They e[ver]y weeke shal mony have,
  when they from Bookes departe.
Amongst them all, my Printer must,
  have somwhat to his share:
I wyll my Friends there Bookes to bye
  of him, with other ware.[2]

Bookbinders are also drawn into the ambit of this description, resulting in a fleshed out scene of book production that maps the experience of those sixteenth-century readers who bought *A Sweet Nosgay* from Jones' bookstall and had it bound in one of the nearby

[1] On Whitney and Jones, see Kirk Melnikoff, 'Isabella Whitney Amongst the Stalls of Richard Jones', in Valerie Wayne (ed.), *Women's Labour and the History of the Book in Early Modern England* (London, 2020), 145–61; and Michelle O'Callaghan, '"My Printer Must, Haue Somwhat to his Share": Isabella Whitney, Richard Jones, and Crafting Books', *Women's Writing*, 26 (2019), 15–34.

[2] Isabella Whitney, 'Wyll and Testament', in Danielle Clarke (ed.), *Isabella Whitney, Mary Sidney and Aemilia Lanyer: Renaissance Women Poets* (London, 2000), 24–5. All references to Whitney's poems are taken from this edition.

shops within the precinct of St Paul's. The passage of the book from production to consumption is woven by Whitney into the lived texture of the early modern city.

Once neglected, Whitney is now regarded as one of the most significant authors of the London literary imaginary.[3] Whitney fashioned herself as a print author, who addressed not only her own sex, but a wider urban non-elite readership, often new to book buying, and who provided a ready market for the type of recreational vernacular literature sold on Jones' stalls. His own ballad before Whitney's *The Copy of a Letter* opens with the cry of the bookseller before his shop, 'What lack you Maister mine?', and ends with a sales pitch:

> Therfore, bye this same Booke,
> of him that heere doth dwell:
> And you (I know) wyll say you haue
> bestowed your mony well.[4] (Sig. A1v)

The bookseller's appeal to potential buyers speaks to the tangible experiential urban world of the London book trade. Book shops and their wares were open to those passing by, physically, visually, and audibly. Title pages of books hung on posts outside stalls and were advertised through the type of sales pitch set out by Jones. His ballad describes a scenario in which his text is performed to passersby much like ballads sung by ballad sellers to encourage sales. Here, the bookseller's cry is also that of other traders who sold an array of goods on the London streets and it acts to incorporate the work of this woman author into the transactional and acoustic worlds of early modern London.

Whitney is distinct among other early modern women writers—and many contemporary male writers—in terms of how firmly she embeds her authorial identity within the book trade and weaves it into the social fabric of early modern London.[5] The personas fashioned in *The Copy of a Letter* and *A Sweet Nosgay* and in the various signatures she adopts are themselves an urban phenomenon that tells of the social and economic provisionality characterising the lives of those who worked in London, from the lower orders to the middling sort. While *Copy of a Letter* is marketed as the work of 'a Yonge Gentilwoman', the authorial identities deployed in *A Sweet Nosgay* are more multivalent and unsettled. Alongside the gentlewoman author is the former maidservant who addresses an advice poem 'to two of her yonger Sisters servinge in London' and bemoans her own loss of service to 'a virtuous Ladye' in her verse epistle to her brother, and the 'Auctor' who places herself among the dispossessed urban poor of early modern London. The literary communities fashioned through her works are not those

[3] See Andrew Gordon's *Writing Early Modern London: Memory, Text and Community* (Basingstoke, 2013), 84–109; Whitney is notably absent from Lawrence Manley's *Literature and Culture in Early Modern London* (Cambridge, 1995).

[4] *The Copy of a Letter* (London, *c* 1567), sig. A1v.

[5] See Laurie Ellinghausen, *Labor and Writing in Early Modern England, 1567–1667* (Aldershot, 2008), 8–35.

of elite women authors and readers but are instead instructively socially diverse in ways that ask us to recalibrate our models of early modern cultural production, especially in relation to women. The way Whitney embraces the identity of a working woman allows us to consider how women's participation in book production involved different types of labour, as writers, as readers, and as makers and sellers of books and ballads; work that engaged women from a range of social classes, from the urban poor to the aristocracy.[6]

Whitney is not only a distinctive, but also a seemingly singular figure in the history of early modern women's writing. Even if we consider the ephemerality and anonymity of cheap print, the non-elite woman author certainly was not a widespread phenomenon (see this volume, Chapter 38, Susan Wiseman, 'Non-Elite Networks and Women'). Nonetheless, other texts attributed to variants of this urban author function were available on the London bookstalls alongside those of Whitney. The same year Jones published Whitney's *The Copy of a Letter*, Thomas Hacket put out *A Letter Sent by the Maydens of London, to the Virtuous Matrones & Mistresses* (1567). Much like Jones, Hacket was a 'speculator in the burgeoning market for printed texts'.[7] This pamphlet, a response to Edward Hake's now lost satire, *A Mery Metynge of Maydes in London*, is written in defence of London maidservants and speaks in their interests.[8] Another pamphlet presented under a non-elite female signature, *Jane Anger Her Protection for Women* (1589), would appear on Jones' stall later in the sixteenth century (see this volume, Chapter 9, Christina Luckyj, 'The *Querelle des Femmes*'). Anger's pamphlet, like that of the London maidservants, responds to books that have newly come into her hands from the London bookstalls, specifically the now lost pamphlet, 'His Surfeyt in love. with a farewel to the folies of his own phantasie', and evokes a wider cityscape in which the woman question is being hotly debated. These lost pamphlets are reminders of the ephemerality of this type of literature, printed cheaply and quickly, often in response to other recently published works. For Rosa Salzburg, writing of Renaissance Venice, these forms of cheap print, like the ballad and small pamphlet, 'offer a uniquely privileged way into the transient, quotidian, as well as the extraordinary, life of the city that is challenging to access by other means'.[9] Of all the ballads printed in the sixteenth century, estimated at around 4,000, only 260 survive, including duplicate copies.[10] Only one copy survives of Whitney's *The Copy of a Letter* and *A Sweet Nosgay*, which is itself a fragment, missing the first few leaves, and of *A Letter Sent by the Maydens of London* and *Jane Anger Her Protection for Women*. *The Copy of a Letter* and *A Letter Sent by the*

[6] See Helen Smith, *'Grossly Material Things': Women and Book Production in Early Modern England* (Oxford, 2012) and the essays in Wayne (ed.), *Women's Labour*.

[7] Kirk Melnikoff, 'Thomas Hacket and the Ventures of an Elizabethan Publisher', *The Library*, 10 (2009), 257–71, 257.

[8] R. J. Fehrenbach, '*A Letter Sent by the Maydens of London* (1567)', *English Literary Renaissance*, 14 (1984), 285–304, 285–6.

[9] Rosa Salzburg, *Ephemeral City: Cheap Print and Urban Culture in Renaissance Venice* (Manchester, 2014), 3–4.

[10] Carole Rose Livingston, *British Broadside Ballads of the Sixteenth Century: A Catalogue of the Extant Sheets and an Essay* (New York, 1991), 32.

Maydens of London are small octavo pamphlets, printed on two sheets. *A Sweet Nosgay* and *Jane Anger* are more substantial productions—the former is an octavo volume made up of five sheets, and the latter a quarto of four sheets. There is also something more to all these works that is belied by the concept of ephemerality. While ephemerality helpfully conceptualises the flow of printed material around the early modern city, it also diverts attention away from the literary ambitions of many of these texts. Instead, what is needed is a more expansive modelling of non-elite literature that can account for its responsiveness to more conventional 'Renaissance' concerns.

These texts are part of the wider 'democratisation' of humanism that operated through the printing press and bookshops of London and its artisanal and mercantile communities.[11] To these communities, we can add London servants and apprentices who were 'extraordinarily literate'.[12] Whitney digested George Turberville's just published translation, *The Heroycall Epistles of the Learned Poet Publius Ovidius Naso* (1567), in her *Copy of a Letter* for these urban readerships. She then turned her attention in *A Sweet Nosgay* to Hugh Plat's *The Floures of Philosophy* (1572), also new, repurposing his commonplace book into a more accessible form.[13] A similar process of acculturation is at work in *A Letter Sent by the Maydens of London* and *Jane Anger Her Protection for Women*, which take the humanist mode of the *querelle des femmes* to the streets of London. Whitney digests humanist books, out of the reach of many non-elite readers, partly through cost, partly because of content, into more accessible forms by translating their matter into idioms more familiar from cheap print. Also sold from Jones' shop alongside *The Copy of a Letter* was *A Handefull of Pleasant Delites*, an anthology of ballads on the topic of love and courtship, similarly marketed to readers browsing the stalls of St Paul's churchyard: 'Here may you have such pretie thinges, / as women much desire' (sig. A1v). The language of love animating these ballads, as we shall see in the case of 'Faine would I have a pretie thing', is not courtly or Petrarchan, but more prosaic, often dealing with the business of courtship and contracting marriages.[14]

When humanism is translated into the idioms of cheap print, the boundaries between learned and unlearned cultures become instructively blurred, bringing into focus the part played by non-elite urban cultures in shaping the literary landscape and other locales for humanist practice outside the more conventional domains of the all-male schoolroom, the court, and elite households. Whitney in *A Sweet Nosgay* puts forward a seemingly paradoxical non-elite, unlearned, yet thoroughly humanist author function. In the verse epistle, 'The Auctor to the Reader', this woman author takes advantage of

[11] Mary Ellen Lamb, 'Isabella Whitney and Reading Humanism', in Leah Knight, Micheline White, and Elizabeth Sauer (eds), *Women's Bookscapes in Early Modern Britain: Reading, Ownership, and Circulation* (Ann Arbor, MI, 2018), 43–58, 44; Angus Vine, *Miscellaneous Order: Manuscript Culture and the Early Modern Organization of Knowledge* (Oxford, 2019), 126–33.

[12] David Cressy, *Literacy and the Social Order: Reading and Writing in Tudor and Stuart England* (Cambridge, 2006), 129.

[13] Vine, *Miscellaneous Order*, 170; Lamb, 'Isabella Whitney', 58–61.

[14] On these ballads see Michelle O'Callaghan, *Crafting Poetry Anthologies in Renaissance England: Early Modern Cultures of Recreation* (Cambridge, 2020), 82–8.

'leasure good, (though learning lackt) some study to apply: / To reade such Bookes, whereby I thought my selfe to edify' (3–4). By 'learning lackt', Whitney does not mean that this woman author is illiterate or unread; rather 'learning' refers to instruction within formal education institutions, such as the grammar schools and universities, which indeed were largely closed to women. Instead, this non-elite author is self-taught and her schoolroom is the bookshops of early modern London, especially those of her printer, Jones.[15]

Whitney instructs fellow women readers in edifying humanist reading practices that are attuned to the scope of action designated to them within gender relations. In 'The Admonition', the author presents herself to fellow 'yong Gentilwomen: And to al other Maids being in Love' as a critical reader of Ovid, dismissing his 'Arte of Love' (*Copy of a Letter*, 21) for teaching men tricks to deceive women, 'To wet their hand and touch their eies: / so oft as teares they lacke' (23–4). Instead, she asks young women to look to other classical female exemplars, citing Scilla, Oenone, Phillis, and Hero, and to learn from their stories of male perfidy. Whitney's mode of imitation is pragmatic and prosaic, selecting apt figures that can serve as examples for determining actions. Hence, the 'unconstant lover' is advised by the speaker to 'Example take by many a one / whose falsehood now is playne' (31–2), and she proceeds to list Aeneas, Theseus, Jason, and Paris, before offering faithful Troilus as an alternative exemplar. Classical texts are excerpted, turned into matter that is to be 'studied for action'; a prosaic 'goal-directed reading' that differs markedly from our conventional sense of this humanist enterprise, in which these practices belong to male professional domains and pursue civic goals to do with holding public office.[16] Here, the scope of action is the everyday matter of courtship, including those cases of broken promises that came before the Elizabethan church courts.[17] The speaker opens with an accusation that, while familiar from the vocative openings of *The Heroides*, is located in the here and now of early modern London:

As close as you your weding kept
  yet now the trueth I here:
Which you (yer now) might me have told
  What need you nay to swere? (1–4)

[15] See also Melnikoff on Jones' bookshop as Whitney's library, 'Isabella Whitney', 145–6. On auto-didacticism, see this volume, Chapter 3, Jennifer Richards, 'How Lady Jane Grey May Have Used Her Education' and on non-elite learning, see this volume, Chapter 39, Susan Wiseman, 'Non-Elite Networks and Women'.

[16] Lisa Jardine and Anthony Grafton, '"Studied for Action": How Gabriel Harvey Read His Livy', *Past & Present*, 129 (1990), 30–78. On an elite woman's goal-directed reading habits, see also Julie Crawford, 'How Margaret Hoby Read her De Mornay', *Mediatrix: Women, Politics, and Literary Production in Early Modern England* (Oxford, 2014), 86–120.

[17] Martin Ingram, *Church Courts, Sex and Marriage in England, 1570–1640* (Cambridge, 1990), 131–3.

When Jones advertises that the 'matter' of *Copy of a Letter* 'is true as many know' (sig. A1v), he is alluding both to the familiarity of the story and its applicability to its readership, how this text might be 'studied for action' as well as read for leisure.

Through these reading practices, Whitney is turning classical exemplars to everyday proverbial uses. At the heart of 'The Admonition' is the popular proverb, 'try before you trust', which acts as the heading under which classical examples are gathered. Whereas Scilla trusted 'to much / before that she dyd trye' (41–2), 'Hero did trie Leanders truth, / Before that she did trust' (73–4) concluding 'alwayes trie before ye trust, / so shall you better speede' (87–8). Proverbs are mobile and highly portable, straddling humanism and the realms of cheap print. These were common cultural codes that punctuated ballads and moralising poetry and were part of the shared cultural matter of urban life. Humanist collections of proverbs, such as Erasmus' *Proverbs or Adages* (1552) and the many proverbs gathered in John Heywood's *Woorkes* (1562), were a staple of early print trade. Proverbs were used in the schoolroom to train students in rhetorical composition. Whitney is following humanist educational practice when she uses proverbs as 'proofs' to comprehend and impose a moralising reading on classical texts. Categorised as the common idiom of the people, these common sayings were conceptualised as 'speech acts' and could be deployed to signify the oral, spoken, and lived properties of texts.[18] In John Heywood's 'A Dialogue Containing the Number of the Effectual Proverbs in the English Tongue', an older man advises a younger acquaintance on choosing a wife. The stories he tells are set in the houses of the middling sort, where they eat, drink, and converse. The second chapter begins:

> Friend, (quoth I), welcome! And with right good will,
> I will, as I can, your will herein fulfil.
> And two things I see in you, that show you wise.
> First, in wedding, ere ye wed to ask advice.[19]

This plain-speaking vocative style is shared with Whitney's *Copy of a Letter*, and it works to actualise ancient, proverbial lore in the present moment, demonstrating how these common sayings can be acted upon through everyday social exchanges.

A Sweet Nosgay is an overtly urban collection. The author fashioned across the collection identifies herself as a writer in and of the city. The dedication to George Mainwaring, a family friend from Chester, is signed 'From Abchurch Lane, the 20. of October, 1573. / By your welwillyng Countrywoman Is. W.' and tells an early modern story of migration from the country to the city for employment. Abchurch Lane was in Candlewick Street ward, bounded by Eastcheap, which housed the butchers' market, one of the first stops in 'Wyll and Testament'—'First for their foode, I Butchers lea[v]e' (34), and near to the Thames, where 'you shal have Brewers store' (36). An urban life is

[18] Manley, *Literature and Culture*, 411–13.

[19] John Heywood, *A Dialogue*, Chapter II, in John S. Farmer (ed.), *The Proverbs, Epigrams, and Miscellanies* (London, 1906), 5.

narrativised as it is lived and practised on the streets.[20] The author takes the air to refresh herself, weary from reading, and 'walked out: but sodenly a friend of mind mee met: / And sayd, yf you regard your health: out of this Lane you get' (15–16); the author returns home and reads Hugh Plat's *Floures of Philosophy*, but, since 'businesse bad mee hye' (33), returns to the streets, taking with her 'A slip' from this nosegay 'to smell unto, which might be my defence' (36) on the 'stynking streetes, or lothsome Lanes which els might mee infect' (37). The narrative, in which author ventures out onto the streets of London at a time of sickness, presumably plague, with the book-as-nosegay pressed against her nostrils to ward off infection, materialises the florilegium idiom of the healthful, prophylactic effects of the proverbs and adages gathered in printed commonplace books like Plat's and, by derivation, Whitney's *Sweet Nosegay*.

'Wyll and Testament' in *A Sweet Nosgay* completes the path of travel through the London streets begun at the start of the collection. In the closing complaint in the 'Certain familier Epistles', 'Is. W. beyng wery of writyng, sendeth this for Answere', the author, beset by misfortune, explains that 'For now I wyll my writting cleane forsake / till of my griefes, my stomack I discharg' (10–11). The following headnote to 'Wyll and Testament', takes this a step further:

> The Aucthour (though loth to leave the Citie) upon her friendes procurement, is constrained to departe: wherefore (she fayneth as she would die) and maketh her WYLL and Testament, as foloweth: With large Legacies of such Goods and riches which she most aboundantly hath left behind her: and therof maketh London sole executor to se her Legacies performed.

Whitney is experimenting with literary forms, from the mock testament to her signature style of the female-voiced complaint, which she uses to personify London; except this faithless lover's 'great cruelnes' is to do with the economics of city living, rather than love, since London fails to extend credit 'to boord me for a yeare' ('Wyll and Testament', 22) and 'with Apparell me releve / except thou payed weare' (23–4). Whitney is describing the nature of early modern economy: because there were few coins in circulation, buying and selling relied on credit, which the author has been refused; instead, if she wants goods she must pay.[21]

'Wyll and Testament' gives a contemporary inflection to a medieval complaint tradition that held the city to account for its lack of charity and, by association, its failure to maintain its citizens, especially the poor. Whitney's ballad shares its peripatetic structure and perspective on the bustling city streets with other London complaints,

[20] See Jean Howard, 'Textualizing an Urban Life: The Case of Isabella Whitney', in Ronald Bedford, Lloyd Davis, and Philippa Kelly (eds), *Early Modern Autobiography: Theories, Genres, Practices* (Ann Arbor, MI, 2006), 217–33.

[21] Craig Muldrew, *The Economy of Obligation: The Culture of Credit* (London, 1998), 4; for a detailed analysis of the mock testament and a credit economy in relation to *A Sweet Nosgay*, see Jill Ingram, *Idioms of Self-Interest: Credit, Identity, and Property in English Renaissance Literature* (New York, 2006), 73–90.

including John Lydgate's early fifteenth-century ballad, 'London Lickpenny', which is voiced by a countryman who travels to London to present his complaint about the city's lack of charity to the poor:

> To Westminster-ward I forthwith went,
> To a man of law to make complaint.
> I said, 'For Mary's love, that holy saint,
> Pity the poor that would proceed'.
> But for lack of money I could not speed.[22]

This last line provides the refrain and, like the author of 'Wyll and Testament', the countryman is forced to leave London because he cannot thrive and suffers economic hardship. The forms of spatiality set in motion by these departing and migrant figures provide the groundwork for counter narratives of the city. In these complaints, the city is represented as it is experienced by the urban poor on the streets. Since the city is experienced from below, the body of the speaker is subject to the deprivations of the poorest inhabitants, hence the identification of the 'Aucthor' of 'Wyll and Testament' with the inmates of prisons and the urban poor. Whitney takes over the medieval 'Auctor' of complaint not in order to claim a commanding view of the city, but rather to take up the paradoxical position of an inhabitant who is also an outsider, on the point of departure, and so can clearly see both London's bounty and inequities.[23] This view from the streets and on the margins comes with its own tactical satiric privileges.

The soundscape of 'London Lickpenny', with its cries of costermongers and other street sellers, was part of the cultural memory of London. John Stow's *Survey of London* used Lydgate's ballad to describe the goods and activity marking out certain streets in West Cheap:

> In westcheape (saith the song) he was called on to buy fine lawne, Paris thread, cotton Umple, and other linnen clothes and such like ... In Cornehill to buy olde apparel, and houshold stuffe, where he was forced to buy his owne hoode, which hee had lost in Westminster hall: in Candlewright street Drapers profered him cheap cloth, in Eastcheape the cookes cryed hotte ribbes of beefe rosted, pyes well baked, and other victuailes: there was clattering of pots, harpe, pipe, and sawtry, yea by cocke, nay by cocke, for other greater oathes were spared: some sang of Jenken and Julian &c. all which melodie liked well the passenger, but he wanted money to abide by it, and therefore gat him into Gravesend barge and home into Kent.[24]

[22] John Lydgate, 'London Lickpenny', in Lawrence Manley (ed.), *London in the Age of Shakespeare: An Anthology* (University Park, 1986), 3–7.

[23] For an alternative Ovidian reading of this phenomenon, see Lindsay Ann Reid, 'The Brief Ovidian Career of Isabella Whitney: From Heroidean to Tristian Complaint', in Sarah C. E. Ross and Rosalind Smith (eds), *Early Modern Women's Complaint: Gender, Form, and Politics* (Cham; Palgrave Macmillan, 2020), 89–113.

[24] John Stow, *A Survay of London*, (London, 1598), 171.

It is striking that a complaint about lack is remembered as a song of a city full of stuff, of clothes, goods, food, smells, and sounds. This very material accumulation of things, places, and people makes the city tangible as a dynamic lived space. 'Wyll and Testament' similarly fashions a rhetoric of the city based on this principle of street-based urban mercantile *copia*, in which 'fayre streats there bee, / and people goodly store' (29–30). An accumulative structure characterises other London ballads, including the very popular, 'Faine would I have a pretie thing / to give unto my Ladie', which circulated widely and was printed by Jones in *A Handefull of Pleasant Delites*. To find 'a pretie thing' the speaker goes shopping, 'I walke the towne, and tread the streete, / in every corner seeking' an action that takes him by mercers, silk wives, down Cheap Street, and past engravers.[25] Like 'Wyll and Testament', the mode of writing the city is peripatetic and embodied, a 'pedestrian speech act' creating an urban topography made up of shops that act synecdochically for the whole city.[26] Whitney's topography is more multifarious. The rhetoric of walking in 'Wyll and Testament' sets in motion a series of narrative turns and counterturns, which construct paths between places that carry satiric meaning. The narrator moves from places of sustenance, trade, and commerce, to the margins of the city and its prisons, finally disposing of herself as she departs not only London, but 'out of this vale so vile' (274), repudiating worldly vanity. This is the well-trodden path of the complaint. As Danielle Clarke first noted, this woman author's rhetorical command over place, as she scripts the city through the modes of complaint, balances material dispossession with poetic self-possession.[27]

The woman author Whitney puts into circulation in poems gathered in the 'Certain familier Epistles' and 'Wyll and Testament' is economically distressed, luckless, a 'poore Kinsewoman', and 'unfortunate' (*Sweet Nosgay*, 13, 16). Although she is enfolded within kinship networks and exchanges verse letters with friends, familial relations are also compromised and attenuated. Her brother, G. W., who 'must be chiefest staffe that I shal stay on heare' ('To her Brother. G. W.', 8) does not reply to her letters, and she also has no news of her brother B. W.—'none can tell, if you be well, nor where you doo sojourne' ('To her Brother. B. W.', 2). The author of 'Wyll and Testament' declares herself 'so weake / that none mee credit dare' (189–90), hence even imprisonment for debt in Ludgate is not available to her. Her poverty is so extreme that in death, as Andrew Gordon points out, 'she is unable to dispose of herself', requesting only a 'shrowding Sheete' (266), and refusing all other ceremonies 'for cost' (270); instead 'in oblivion bury mee / and never more mee name' (267–8).[28] Acts of dispossession are, of course, a feature of the mock testament and take on a jesting tone within its frame through their very extremity. Even so, the local detail of London's credit economy provided by Whitney grounds the

25 'Faine would I have', in Clement Robinson (ed.), *A Handefull of Pleasant Delites* (London, 1584), sig. D5v; O'Callaghan, *Crafting Poetry Anthologies*, 92–4.

26 On 'pedestrian speech acts' and a 'rhetoric of walking', see Michel de Certeau, in Steven Rendall (trans.), *The Practice of Everyday Life* (Berkeley, CA, 1984), 97–100.

27 Danielle Clarke, *The Politics of Early Modern Women's Writing* (Harlow, 2001), 212–13.

28 Gordon, *Writing Early Modern London*, 106.

genre within a lived city. 'Wyll and Testament' gives voice to the experience of being a Londoner in the Elizabethan period, when many had migrated to the city, and so were without kin, and haphazard communication systems meant it was difficult to hear news or to maintain ties with relatives. As Patricia Fumerton concludes, 'there is a sense in which displacement, transience, and instability were inherent or native to early modern London.'[29]

In Whitney's advice poem, 'A Modest Meane for Maides in Order Prescribed, by Is. W. to Two of Her Yonger Sisters Servinge in London', a domestic civic modelling of a working woman's moderate, temperate self goes hand-in-hand with the risk attendant upon women's work within gentry households and outside kinship networks.[30] According to the order prescribed by Whitney, a well-governed household is not simply achieved through masters and mistresses but relies on the self-governance and labours of domestic servants. The ability of maidservants to maintain this domestic and godly order is constantly hedged round by dangers, from unspecified others in the household who are vectors of corruption and especially from ungoverned words and behaviour. The sisters will be especially vulnerable when their sister 'shal further from you dwell' (1), which necessitates this advice poem. Maidservants are instructed to 'listen to no lyes: / Nor credit every fayned tale, that many wyll devise', with proof provided through the proverb: 'For words are but winde, yet words may hurt you so' (17–19). Whitney's defence of maidservants is shared with *A Letter sent by the Maydens of London, to the virtuous Matrones & Mistresses* (1567). This pamphlet accuses 'those fonde and malicious Dialogues of *The Mery meting of Maydens in London*' of so maligning maidservants that their mistresses will set 'about immediately to abridge us of our lawful libertie'.[31] This defence does not operate in jesting fashion to confirm by rhetorical sleight of hand the licentiousness attributed to maidservants in Hake's pamphlet, but instead procedurally addresses his accusations to claim for these young working women a type of domestic civic subjectivity in which they are necessary to the functioning of the household as a microcosm of the commonwealth. Using a body–household analogy, only cooperation between mistress and maidservant can ensure the healthy functioning of the household, for as 'we alone doe stande you in, as diverse membres of the body altogether do stande the body in' (294). The right to a holiday is defended through the concept of healthful recreation being necessary in a working life: maidservants 'being with honeste exercises and pastimes refreshed, may the better fal to their labor again' (295). Liberty is therefore not a synonym for licentiousness but employed in a civic humanist sense of the liberty of the citizen, the freeman, as opposed to the slave, to argue for certain rights attendant upon service. In a similar move to Whitney's later 'Order Prescribed' for maidservants, the civic humanist idiom attributed to these maidservants of London promotes a

[29] Patricia Fumerton, *Unsettled: The Culture of Mobility and the Working Poor in Early Modern England* (Chicago, IL, 2006), 12–13.

[30] See also Lamb, 'Isabella Whitney', 52–3.

[31] Fehrenbach, '*A Letter*', 294.

feminised model of citizenship that establishes the female domestic servant as necessary to the healthy working of the household and, by association, the commonwealth.

Much of the discussion of this pamphlet has focused on the question of authorship.[32] We can usefully view this pamphlet as an example of prosopopoeia, without disenfranchising these maidservants, if we understand this rhetorical strategy in terms of fashioning a female subject position that is then available to be inhabited and performed by others. The pamphlet draws attention to the question of authorship specifically in relation to fashioning a collective identity for the maidservants of London. Hake's pamphlet had seemingly cited six maidservants by name, each embodying different vices. *A Letter* takes over these names on its title page—'Answering the / Mery Meeting by us / Rose, Jane, Rachell, / Sara, Philumias, and / Dorothie—but points out that 'when he recited six of us by name, ... under those sixe names [are] above sixe thousand of us' (297). Here, the generic status of these 'named' authors is acknowledged and turned into a figure for a wider collective of London maids in whose interests this pamphlet speaks. By this means, maidservants are voiced and identified as a distinct subclass within the London citizenry. This 'collective' points out Hake's lack of knowledge of the everyday working lives of maidservants. Rather than 'overmuche libertie', maidservants only have one holiday in the week, on Sunday, when the 'forenoone' is either spent at church or finishing 'necessarie businesse at home', meaning there is very little time 'after noone' to 'stray abroade', given that 'they ring the first peale to Eve[n]songe before that we have washed up halfe our dishes' (295–6). This defence of maidservants is grounded in the reality of women's working lives within the household. Alongside Whitney's texts, it contributes to a body of urban literature fashioning female working subjectivities and readerships.

A Letter Sent by the Maydens of London is a version of the *querelle des femmes*. The way it mobilises the defence of women formula in the interests of maidservants illustrates the flexibility of this genre. Another *querelle* pamphlet, *Jane Anger her Protection for Women*, shares many features with both *A Letter* and Whitney's 'Admonition' in her *A Copy of a Letter*—it also shares its printer, Jones, with Whitney. When placed alongside Whitney's work, it suggests a broader interest in fashioning a space for the woman author in print. The *querelle des femmes* is a highly formalised humanist genre, with its origins in a scholastic exercise of *pro et contra* debate, hence its close affiliation with the all-male institutions of the universities and Inns of Court.[33] That said, the *querelle* is also an exemplary case of the 'democratisation' of humanism through the printing press, which brings these domains into conversation with other environs. Many *querelle* texts fabricate pamphlet wars, responding to or predicting other entries in the battle of the sexes. This publishing strategy locates these pamphlets among the London printing houses and bookshops and gives the genre an urban complexion. The defence of women pamphlets devoted considerable energy to fashioning female author functions

[32] Fehrenbach, '*A Letter*', 286–8.
[33] Clarke, *Politics*, 50.

and readers. *A Letter Sent by the Maydens of London* interpellates an urban audience of fellow maidservants and their mistresses. *Jane Anger Her Protection for Women* distinguishes between two female readerships along the lines of social class. The first, 'the Gentlewomen of England', are learned women conversant with the humanist formula of this genre: 'Gentlewomen, though it is to be feared that your settled wits will advisedly condemn that which my choleric vein hath rashly set down ... yet ... I hope you will rather show yourselves defendents of the defender's title than complainants of the plaintiff's wrong' (31). The second, general woman reader is more well versed in the idiom of cheap print as it circulates through London:

> Fie on the falsehood of men, whose minds go oft a-madding and whose tongues cannot so soon be wagging, but straight they fall a-tattling! ... O Paul's steeple and Charing Cross! A halter hold all such persons. Let the streams of the channels in London streets run so swiftly as they may be able alone to carry them from that sanctuary. (32)

Characterised as slander, 'male' entries in the *querelle des femmes* are figured through a scatological rhetoric of the city as the sewage that flows through the London streets.

The different registers, tropes, and other rhetorical formulae employed across these epistles to signify different classes of women authors and readers points to the diversification of the early modern print marketplace. An array of female reader and author functions were fashioned and circulated across the social spectrum, from elite to non-elite, through different print genres. Whitney provided a precedent for the woman author at home in the London book trade. 'The Lamentacion of a Gentilwoman', which closes the anthology *A Gorgious Gallery of Gallant Inventions* (1578), is now thought to be the work of Whitney, partly because it was published by her printer, Jones.[34] Also part of the reason why this gentlewoman author sounds like Whitney is that she too frames her authorship through the bookstalls of St Paul's churchyard, setting up a rival poet whose ballad 'hanges at Pawles as every man goes by' (41). The gentlewoman of 'The Lamentacion' may take us to a particular author—Isabella Whitney—but she also designates a type of woman author who is identified with certain genres—the complaint, the admonition, and the *querelle des femmes*—that, in turn, take on a distinctive orientation in response to an urban environment.

FURTHER READING

Clarke, Danielle. *The Politics of Early Modern Women's Writing*. Harlow, 2001.
Ellinghausen, Laurie. *Labor and Writing in Early Modern England, 1567–1667*. Aldershot, 2008.

[34] Randall Martin, 'Isabella Whitney's "Lamentation upon the death of William Gruffith"', *Early Modern Literary Studies*, 3 (1997), 2.1–15.

Gordon, Andrew. *Writing Early Modern London: Memory, Text and Community.* Basingstoke, 2013.

Howard, Jean. 'Textualizing an Urban Life: The Case of Isabella Whitney', in Ronald Bedford, Lloyd Davis, and Philippa Kelly (eds), *Early Modern Autobiography: Theories, Genres, Practices.* Ann Arbor, MI, 2006, 217–33.

Ingram, Jill. *Idioms of Self-Interest: Credit, Identity and Property in English Renaissance Literature.* New York, 2006.

Lamb, Mary Ellen. 'Isabella Whitney and Reading Humanism', in Leah Knight, Micheline White, and Elizabeth Sauer (eds), *Women's Bookscapes in Early Modern Britain: Reading, Ownership, and Circulation.* Ann Arbor, MI, 2018, 43–58.

Melnikoff, Kirk. 'Isabella Whitney Amongst the Stalls of Richard Jones', in Valerie Wayne (ed.), *Women's Labour and the History of the Book in Early Modern England.* London, 2020, 145–61.

Smith, Helen. *'Grossly Material Things': Women and Book Production in Early Modern England.* Oxford, 2012.

CHAPTER 21

THE SELF-PORTRAYAL OF WIDOWS IN THE EARLY MODERN ENGLISH COURTS OF LAW

LOTTE FIKKERS

ACCORDING to T. E. in his *The Lawes Resolution of Womens Rights* (1632), early modern English women were understood to be 'either married or to bee married'.[1] Indeed, women's legal status was attached to their marital status: women were thus identified as maid, wife, or widow. Under the common law, married women were classified as *femes covert*, because the legal principle of *coverture* considered their legal identities subsumed, or covered, by their husbands upon their marriage. As a result, they were unable to enter into contracts, start suits, or own property without their husband's approval. Maids and widows were labelled as *femes sole* and were not restricted by the rules of *coverture*. The tripartite framework of maid, wife, and widow was thus tied to women's legal identity.

This rigid three-part model has, however, been challenged by various historians and literary scholars alike. Amy Froide, for example, has suggested that a two-part model does more justice to early modern perceptions of women's legal status. She proposes that we should distinguish never-married women (single women) from ever-married women (married women and widows), because of the different roles and positions these groups of women occupied in early modern English society.[2] Although single women and widows were both considered *femes sole*, Froide argues that their shared legal status

[1] T. E., *The Lawes Resolution of Womens Rights* (London, 1632), 6.

[2] Amy M. Froide, *Never Married: Singlewomen in Early Modern England* (Oxford, 2005), 16. See also Amy M. Froide, 'Marital Status as a Category of Difference: Singlewomen and Widows in Early Modern England', in Judith M. Bennett and Amy M. Froide (eds), *Singlewomen in the European Past, 1250–1800* (Philadelphia, PA, 1998), 236–69.

was only theoretical: while the appropriate role of a never-married woman was that of household dependent, wives could assist their husbands, and widows were capable of running their own households.[3] More recently, Rebecca Mason has argued that neither two-part nor three-part structures do justice to women's actual legal positions. She suggests that we should look at how women effectively used the law, rather than at what legal handbooks prescribed. The variety of women's legal identities as noted down by clerks in Scottish burgh and commissary courts reveals that those women could occupy different positions at the same time, such as wife *and* daughter. A woman's legal position was thus not only dependent on marital status, but also on other intersecting factors including the presence of siblings or any existing property rights.[4] Indeed, the legal archives contain many records featuring women who do not neatly fit the strict tripartite characterisation of maid, wife, or widow. According to Subha Mukherji, this situation is mirrored on the early modern stage, as 'Renaissance drama is full of men and women with an uncertain and indeterminate marital status'.[5] One example is *Measure for Measure*'s Mariana, who is 'neither maid, widow, nor wife' after Angelo refuses to recognise her as his wife (Shakespeare, 5.1.176–7).[6] The tripartite division thus does not do justice to the diversity of women's legal identities—neither in real life nor on the early modern stage.

Particular attention has been paid to demonstrate that this is true for married women. According to Tim Stretton, for instance:

> the idea that married couples became one flesh before God and one person at law provided a handy shorthand for lawyers and commentators, especially in the area of property, but it does not capture, not does it explain, the full complexity of married women's status in day-to-day life.[7]

Mason, too, has convincingly demonstrated that married women, in particular, could alternate between personas depending on the case at hand: married female litigants could choose to appear as daughters in one suit, but emphasise that they were married women in the next.[8] Rather than having one fixed, stable legal identity, then, married women could and did invoke different versions of the self in different legal contexts.

Shaping their legal identities to match a particular context was not a strategy reserved to wives, however. This chapter shows that widows, too, could draw on an array of

[3] Froide, *Never Married*, 17.

[4] Rebecca Mason, 'Women, Marital Status, and Law: The Marital Spectrum in Seventeenth-Century Glasgow', *Journal of British Studies*, 58 (2019), 787–804, 795.

[5] Subha Mukherji, *Law and Representation in Early Modern Drama* (Cambridge, 2006), 17.

[6] William Shakespeare, *Measure for Measure*, in John Jowett, William Montgomery, Gary Taylor, and Stanley Wells (eds), *The Oxford Shakespeare: The Complete Works* (Oxford, 2005).

[7] Tim Stretton, 'The Legal Identity of Married Women', in Andreas Bauer and Karl H. L. Welker (eds), *Europa und Seine Regionen: 2000 Jahre Rechtsgeschichte* (Cologne, Weimar, and Vienna, 2007), 309–21, 312.

[8] Mason, 'Women, Marital Status, and Law', 803.

different labels when representing themselves in the courts of law. Indeed, it was particularly important for relicts (widows) to pay attention to their self-representations, as there were various stereotypes of what Stretton refers to as the 'bad widow' in existence against which they had to defend themselves.[9] At the same time, as this chapter aims to demonstrate, litigating widows could draw on literary models to help shape their legal persona as the 'good widow' in the court room. The 'biblical widow' and the 'eternal wife' were potent templates of self-representation, rooted in literary texts, and employed by women in their life-writing to counter negative stereotypes about widowhood. After discussing these stereotypes, this chapter analyses Lady Anne Halkett's and Katherine Austen's identification with the 'biblical widow' and the 'eternal wife' in their life-writing. By reading autobiographies, diaries, and meditations alongside legal records, it will then show that these literary models were not only used in literary texts, but also applied by litigants in a legal context. Working with records from the Court of Requests, this chapter ultimately argues that negative stereotypes both necessitated and allowed relicts to draw on literary models in the court room to escape the strict three-part legal framework of maid, wife, and widow.

THE LITERARY WIDOW: STEREOTYPES AND MODELS

The position of widows was a hotly debated issue in early modern England.[10] According to Barbara J. Todd, early modern English society required that 'the household should be headed by a man'; where a woman headed the household, this contradicted the patriarchal ideal.[11] Yet Eleanor Hubbard has calculated that roughly eighty per cent of London's relicts lived independently.[12] This large number of widows performing the role of head of the household would certainly have led to anxiety amongst those in favour of patriarchal norms. As a result, widows were the subject of scrutiny: those who remained single were feared and those considering remarriage could be seen as hypocritical or

[9] Tim Stretton, 'Widows at Law in Tudor and Stuart England', in Sandra Cavallo and Lyndan Warner (eds), *Widowhood in Medieval and Early Modern Europe* (Abingdon, 2014), 193–208, 205.

[10] Renu Juneja, 'The Widow as Paradox and Paradigm in Middleton's Plays', *The Journal of General Education*, 34 (1982), 3–19, 4–5. See also Vivien Brodsky, 'Widows in Late Elizabethan London: Remarriage, Economic Opportunity and Family Orientations', in Lloyd Bonfield, Richard M. Smith, and Keith Wrightson (eds), *The World We Have Gained: Histories of Population and Social Structure* (Oxford, 1986), 122–54; Elizabeth Foyster, 'Marrying the Experienced Widow in Early Modern England: The Male Perspective', in Sandra Cavallo and Lyndan Warner (eds), *Widowhood in Medieval and Early Modern Europe* (Harlow, 1999), 108–24.

[11] Barbara J. Todd, 'The Remarrying Widow: A Stereotype Reconsidered', in Mary Prior (ed.), *Women in English Society 1500–1800* (London and New York, 1985), 54–92, 55.

[12] Eleanor Hubbard, *City Women: Money, Sex and the Social Order in Early Modern London* (Oxford, 2012), 261–2.

intimidating, given their financial independence and sexual experience.[13] As both remarriage and staying single could be sources of apprehension, relicts had to walk a fine line.

This made the position of widows ripe material for early modern dramatists. On the one hand, widows could be portrayed as societal misfits for staying single. An example is mother Sawyer in Rowley, Dekker, and Ford's *The Witch of Edmonton* (1621), who is the stereotypical perennial relict heading her own household: she is feared by her community, accused of witchcraft, and ostracised by society. Indeed, the stereotypical witch was thought to be a widowed, elderly, post-menopausal woman.[14] At the same time, dramatists frequently used the trope of the rapidly remarrying widow. Such widows were often exposed as hypocritical. The widowed Eudora in George Chapman's *The Widow's Tears* (*c* 1605), for instance, vows to remain 'a fort of chastity' by refusing to remarry.[15] The play demonstrates 'how short-lived widows' tears are', when only a few lines later in the same scene Eudora does choose to remarry (1.1.141–2). Playwrights thus had two potent stereotypes they could draw on when depicting women who had lost their husband: the widowed witch and the hypocritical widow seeking a quick remarriage.

A third stereotype regarding the relict which playwrights could use was that of the loud and litigious widow.[16] She was frequently found on the early modern stage: litigating stage-widows include Thomas Middleton's Valeria in *The Widow* (*c* 1615), John Webster's Leonora in *The Devils Law-Case* (*c* 1617), and John Fletcher and Philip Massinger's Jacintha in *The Spanish Curate* (1622). A particularly loud and litigious widow is depicted by William Wycherley in *The Plain Dealer* (1676). The list of characters preceding the play already identifies widow Blackacre as a 'petulant, litigious widow, always in law', and other characters describe her as a 'litigious she-pettifogger', 'as vexatious as her father was, the great attorney … and as implacable an adversary as a wife suing for alimony'. Moreover, 'she has no pleasure, but in vexing others'.[17] The litigious widow, too, was thus a frequently used trope on the early modern stage.

[13] Ulrike Tancke, *'Bethinke Thy Selfe' in Early Modern England: Writing Women's Identities* (Leiden, 2010), 146.

[14] James Sharpe, *Instruments of Darkness: Witchcraft in Early Modern England* (Philadelphia, PA, 1996), 176; Lyndal Roper, *Oedipus & the Devil: Witchcraft, Sexuality and Religion in Early Modern Europe* (London and New York, 1994), 211.

[15] George Chapman, in Akihiro Yamada (ed.), *The Widow's Tears* (London, 1975), 1.1.125.

[16] A fourth stereotype, which will not be discussed in detail here, is that of the older, rich widow, hunted by suitors for her money. Amy Louise Erickson has demonstrated that this stereotype was not rooted in reality: widowers remarried more often than widows, and wealthy widows remarried less often than less well-off widows; *Women and Property in Early Modern England* (London and New York, 1993), 196. For more on the representation of the widow hunt on the early modern stage, see Ira Clark, 'The Widow Hunt on the Tudor-Stuart Stage', *SEL: Studies in English Literature 1500–1900*, 41 (2001), 399–416 and Renu Juneja, 'Widowhood and Sexuality in Chapman's "The Widow's Tears"', *Philological Quarterly*, 67 (1988), 157–75.

[17] William Wycherley, *The Plain Dealer*, in Peter Dixon (ed.), *The Country Wife and Other Plays* (Oxford, 1996), 283–399 (289), 1.1.391–410.

The stereotypical litigious widow was based on her real-life historical counterpart. This stereotype must have been so persistent, or so feared, that it caused Juan Luis Vives to insist in his conduct book that relicts should avoid entering into legal proceedings, because doing so would harm their reputation of modesty.[18] Sure enough, immediately upon the death of their husband, women often found themselves thrust into the legal arena. Widows could be appointed as executrix or administratrix of their late husband's affairs, roles in which they would have to settle affairs with creditors and debtors—often in court. Even if they were not officially appointed to oversee their late husband's estate, widows could find themselves in court to deal with the legal and financial consequences of widowhood. As 'up to 45% of all women could expect to be widowed at some time in their lives', as Amy Louise Erickson has calculated, a large proportion of relicts was thus bound to engage with the law.[19] This experience, peculiar to widows, led to the stereotype of the litigious widow.

As a result, any widowed woman writing for a (perceived) audience would have to deal with these stereotypes regarding widowhood. Stretton has demonstrated that litigating widows and their legal counsel attempted to 'distance themselves from these damaging stereotypes of the "bad" widow'.[20] However, because widows could anticipate invocations of litigiousness or deviation from the accepted patriarchal norms, they were also able to prepare a carefully constructed persona to counter any such allegations: 'the "good" widow'.[21] This holds true not only for litigating widows, but for all relicts who attempted to create a written portrait of the self. A widow's self-portrayal thus had to be, and could be, carefully navigated—both in and outside the courts of law. This could be done by making use of literary models. Two models were particularly potent and will be discussed here: the biblical widow and the eternal wife. In each case, the model allowed widows to ameliorate the anxieties regarding a relict's renewed status as *feme sole*, as becomes clear by looking at the life-writing of Lady Anne Halkett and Katherine Austen.

Lady Anne Halkett, née Murray, (1622–1699) was a prolific life-writer: she produced her autobiographical 'True accountt' (1677–1678) and twenty-one manuscript volumes full of 'Meditations' (1658–1699).[22] In one of her meditations ('vpon my deplorable beeing a Widow'), she reflects on her status as a widowed woman.[23] She introduces the 'biblical widow' as a model for her own behaviour. This biblical widow is what:

[18] Juan Luis Vives, in Richard Hyrde (trans.), *A Very Frutful and Pleasant Boke Called the Instruction of a Christen Woman* (London, 1547), sigs. 137r–138v.

[19] Erickson, *Women and Property*, 154.

[20] Stretton, 'Widows at Law', 205.

[21] Stretton, 'Widows at Law', 205.

[22] The autobiographical 'True accountt' is held at the British Library, Add. MS. 32376; the extant volumes of the 'Meditations' are held at The National Library of Scotland, MS. 6490–502.

[23] Suzanne Trill (ed.), *Lady Anne Halkett: Selected Self-Writings* (Aldershot, 2007), 34. All references to the 'Meditations' are taken from this edition.

> St Paul Calls a Widow Indeed (Oh to bee such a one)[,] desolate (wch I understand to bee alone & retired)[,] trusting in God[,] & Continuing in Suplications & Prayers Night & day. [B]lamelese, well reported of for Good workes[,] brought up chilldren[,] Lodged strangers[,] washed the Saints feet[,] releeved the afflicted[,] diligently followed every good worke[. T]his Lord I desire to doe. (37)[24]

Halkett thus strives to live a God-fearing life, dedicating her time to prayer and doing good deeds. This is the kind of widow few people could object to: rather than unsettling patriarchal norms by boldly heading a household, this type of widow served society by leading a charitable life.

The biblical widow not only does good deeds, however; she also requires God's provision as she lives in relative poverty as a result of giving away all her money and material property to those in need. In Psalm 68, God is described as the 'Father of the fatherless and protector of widows' (5).[25] Halkett is well aware of this and specifically seeks out God's protection: 'For thou hast promised to establish the border of the widow <*and*> to Execute the Iudgementt of the fatherlese'. This protection, for Halkett, is shaped in the form of financial prosperity, as she desires God 'to multiply what is yet left[. T]hat the Credittors may bee Sattisfied *and* wee may Liue vpon the rest' (35). The biblical widow is thus the giver of charity as well as the potential receiver of it.

The model is also a useful shield against unwanted suitors. In the same section of her 'Meditations', Halkett considers remarriage. A new husband would offer financial security and allow Halkett to be 'inabled to pay my depts *and* bee more usefull to the poore'. While such relief from financial worries would be welcome, Halkett asks God to provide 'strength to resist this Temptation' of remarriage. She ultimately decides against accepting her suitor's 'Riches' and instead chooses to 'place more true Contentt in my quiett retirementt' (49). The model of the biblical widow thus offered the widow an acceptable way of styling herself in order to mediate patriarchal anxieties.

Halkett was in particular need of such careful and strategic styling, given her eventful and rather scandalous past.[26] The 'True accountt' details her romantic involvement with the Royalist spy Joseph Bampfield. This relationship left Halkett vulnerable to gossip, as her lover was, unbeknown to Halkett at the time, already married to someone else. Much of her autobiography is therefore an attempt at vindicating her own life.[27]

[24] In her paraphrasing of 1 Timothy 5.5–10, Halkett conveniently leaves out 5.9, where Paul preaches against the giving of charity to a widow under the age of sixty. She wrote this passage in 1670, when she was 48 years old.

[25] *The Bible, English Standard Version*, 2016, https://www.bible.com/bible/59/PSA.68.5-6.ESV.

[26] For the rhetorical strategies Halkett employs in her autobiographical work, see Judith Kearns, 'Fashioning Innocence: Rhetorical Construction of Character in the Memoirs of Anne, Lady Halkett', *Texas Studies in Literature and Language*, 46 (2004), 340–62.

[27] Nadine Akkerman, *Invisible Agents: Women and Espionage in Seventeenth-Century Britain* (Oxford, 2018), 182–203; Sheila Ottway, 'They Only Lived Twice: Public and Private Selfhood in the Autobiographies of Anne, Lady Halkett and Colonel Joseph Bampfield', in Henk Dragstra, Sheila Ottway, and Helen Wilcox (eds), *Betraying Our Selves: Forms of Self-Representation in Early Modern English Texts* (Basingstoke, 2000), 136–47.

For this reason, perhaps, Halkett sought to align herself with the biblical widow in her 'Mediations', which she uses, according to Suzanne Trill, 'to (re)construct herself in accordance with the rather more solemn, biblical example of "a Widow Indeed"'.[28] Regardless of whether she was the embodiment of the biblical widow, Halkett certainly had good reasons to portray herself as one.

Relicts could also choose to model their self-portrayal on the type of the eternal wife. The clergyman William Gouge thought that for many spouses 'their love of a former husband or wife departed is so fast fixed in their heart, as they can never againe so intirely loue any other. They who are so minded are not fit to be joined with another yoke-fellow after they are loosed from one'.[29] Such spouses could choose to remain eternally married to their partners, becoming, in the case of women, perpetual wives. Widows aspiring to such a status could turn to Homer's *Odyssey* for an example. In this epic, Penelope, wife of Odysseus, becomes a symbol of marital fidelity by refusing all her suitors during her husband's twenty-year absence. She even devises several tricks to keep the suitors at bay. Katherine Austen (1628–1683), diarist and poet, is one such widow who turned to Penelope's example.[30] In her diary *Book M*, Austen writes that she does not want to remarry, out of 'perticular esteeme to my D*eare* Friend'.[31] Consequently, she describes herself to a suitor as 'like pennelope, alwayes employed' (148). The suitor for her hand in marriage recognised Austen's literary allusion to Penelope: 'I ses he her lovers could not abide her for it' (148).[32] Austen's comparison to Penelope is, however, not merely a sign of her fidelity to her husband, but also, according to Sarah C. E. Ross, driven 'by a desire to preserve his patrimony for her eldest son'.[33] Like the biblical widow, then, the model of the eternal wife could be strategically adopted to create a certain image of the self, even if there were ulterior motives.

While Austen portrays herself consistently as an eternal wife,[34] Anne Halkett uses this model in her 'Meditations' but deviates from it in her autobiography. In her 'Meditations', Halkett styles herself as a perpetual wife and is resolved to 'ever ... Live like

[28] Suzanne Trill, 'Introduction', in Suzanne Trill (ed.), *Lady Anne Halkett: Selected Self-Writings* (Aldershot, 2007), xvii–xlii (xviii).

[29] William Gouge, *Of Domesticall Duties* (London, 1622), 226.

[30] She also adopted the persona of the biblical widow, as is argued in Raymond A. Anselment, 'Katherine Austen and the Widow's Might', *Journal for Early Modern Cultural Studies*, 5 (2005), 5–25, 7.

[31] Katherine Austen, in Sarah C. E. Ross (ed.), *Katherine Austen's Book M: British Library, Additional Manuscript 4454* (Tempe, AZ, 2011), 116. All quotations from *Book M* are taken from this edition.

[32] For a more thorough analysis of the simile between Austen and Penelope, see Pamela S. Hammons, 'Introduction', in Pamela S. Hammons (ed.), *Book M: A London Widow's Life Writings* (Toronto, 2013), 19–20.

[33] Sarah C. E. Ross, '"Like Penelope, Always Employed": Reading, Life-Writing, and the Early Modern Female Self in Katherine Austen's *Book M*', *Literature Compass*, 9 (2012), 306–16, 313.

[34] She is less consistent in adopting the model of the 'biblical widow': according to Pamela Hammons, Austen represents herself 'both as a helpless, persecuted widow and as a prophet with divine gifts' ('Widow, Prophet, and Poet: Lyrical Self-Figurations in Katherine Austen's "Book M" (1664)', in Barbara Smith and Ursula Appelt (eds), *Write or Be Written: Early Modern Women Poets and Cultural Constraints* (Aldershot, 2001), 3–27, 4).

[her late husband's] Widow' (38). And so she did: Halkett remained a widow for twenty-nine years after her husband's death, rebuking at least one suitor. Throughout most of her autobiography, on the other hand, Halkett makes a point of styling herself as a single woman. This autobiography was written in *c* 1677/8, when she had, in fact, already been widowed for some years (Sir James Halkett died in 1670). Rather than presenting her work under her husband's name, however, the 'True accountt' bears Anne's maiden name, Murray. Although the choice for Murray over Halkett may have been an editorial one, the fact that the autobiography focuses on Halkett's life as a single woman gives reason to believe that 'Murray' may have been a strategic choice made by Anne herself. The reason behind the self-representation as a single woman may, yet again, be found in Halkett's tumultuous past. It is possible that Halkett did not want to tarnish her late husband's name with her past disreputable behaviour and therefore distanced herself from him by styling herself as a single lady, while in her widowhood. If so, Halkett presented herself in line with the task at hand, and offered a different version of her life and herself in each different case. For Susan Wiseman, this means that Halkett's life is captured by 'a complicated web of texts, available to different readers at different moments'.[35] Suzanne Trill, too, argues that attention needs to be paid to 'the plurality of Halkett's "lives"' as captured in her various texts.[36] This does not hold true only for Halkett: all early modern widows could, and did, present themselves and the relationship to their late husbands according to their text's purpose and its intended audience.

THE LEGAL PERSONA OF THE WIDOWED LITIGANT

The literary models were not reserved to the writers of literary texts only. They served litigating widows particularly well, too, when these women tried to move beyond the restrictive tripartite model in a bid to strengthen their case. Certainly, some women simply and straightforwardly describe themselves, or let themselves be described by their legal counsel, as widows or relicts. Often, however, they offer more detailed self-portrayals that move beyond the label of 'widow'. But where widowed life-writers were capable of switching personas within their texts, and across their texts, litigating widows had to offer a singular version of the self to meet the demands of the legal case at hand. The two models, biblical widow and eternal wife, could help them in doing so.

[35] Susan Wiseman, '"The Most Considerable of My Troubles": Anne Halkett and the Writing of Civil War Conspiracy', in Jo Wallwork and Paul Salzman (eds), *Women Writing, 1550–1750* (Bundoora, Vic, 2001), 25–45, 29.

[36] Suzanne Trill, 'Beyond Romance? Re-Reading the "Lives" of Anne, Lady Halkett (1621/2?–1699)', *Literature Compass*, 6 (2009), 446–59, 454.

The model of the biblical widow gave widowed women the opportunity to counter the stereotype of the litigious widow and cast themselves in the role of helpless creature wholly dependent on the Court. This was particularly the case before the Court of Requests, as has been demonstrated extensively in Stretton's seminal study of women's participation in this Court.[37] The Court of Requests was a London-based equity court, which, according to the lawyer Thomas Ridley (b. before 1548–1629), was established to handle 'poore miserable persons causes, as Widowes and Orphans, and other distressed people, whose cases wholly rely on pietie and conscience'.[38] Placing themselves in a dependent role was something women did before this Court anyway, regardless of their marital status: maids, wives, and widows alike tended to make clear that they desperately needed legal relief. Such demands for help are so frequent that they become formulaic; almost all pleadings contain opening phrases such as: 'yo*ur* said orato*r* is w*ith*owt all remedy yf yo*ur* greate Favor be not to her extended in this behalfe'.[39] Widows, however, modified such formulaic phrases at the beginning of their pleadings to further emphasise their helplessness. Johane Coppe, for example, suggests in her bill of complaint that 'she havinge nothinge ells to releve or comforte her w*ith*all beinge a woman of the age of threeschore yeares and above to her utter undowinge *and* overthrowe if some spedy remidie be not by your ma*jestie* herin p*ro*vided'.[40] The Court here is cast as the widow's only saviour. If the Bible named God as protector of widows and orphans, here the Court of Requests is placed in the same position. Rather than portraying themselves as litigious, then, these women cast themselves as completely helpless and at the mercy of the Court.

Weakness and dependency thus become two key rhetorical elements in a biblical widow's self-representation in the Court of Requests, not just at the beginning of pleadings, but throughout them. Elizabeth Bedell, for example, refers to herself as 'being both aged and verye Impotent'.[41] Maryan Smythe, too, mentions her age as a form of weakness, 'she beinge lxxx yeres of age and not hable to helpe her self', 'she beinge also an Anncyent p*ar*isshioner', 'a sillye woman of lxxx yeres of age', and 'a verye Aged woman of lxxx yeres of ages *and* cannot travell'.[42] Alice Cowper describes her dependency on the Court by stating she was 'w*ith*out any frande'.[43] Poor health, old age, and the lack of support network were thus all forms of weakness and dependency that widows could use to align themselves with the biblical widow.

The same holds true for lack of money. Styling oneself as a 'pore widowe' is so common in legal pleadings that the phrase becomes an empty formulation. Widows thus modified it to their specific circumstances. Margerie Themilthorpe, for instance,

[37] Tim Stretton, *Women Waging Law in Elizabeth England* (Cambridge, 2005).

[38] Thomas Ridley, *A View of the Civile and Ecclesiasticall Law* (London, 1607), 229.

[39] London, The National Archives, Req 2/138/62, *Bygge v Pycke* (1577).

[40] London, The National Archives, Req 2/141/18, *Coppe v Smith* (1596).

[41] London, The National Archives, Req 2/50/27, *Bownest v Bedell*, answer of Elizabeth Bedell (1600).

[42] London, The National Archives, Req 2/48/25, *Huntington v Smythe*, answer of Maryan Smythe (1591).

[43] London, The National Archives, Req 2/140/36, *Clerke v Cowper*, answer of Alice (1594).

refers to herself as 'very poore and overchardged *with* manie children'[44] and Anne Davie claims that '*your* highenes sayd poore subiect hathe many poore fatherless children, whereof sundrye of them bene of fewe yeres and verie chargdable to *your* highnes poore subiect to bringe upp'.[45] Agnes Bridges' children required extra care: she describes herself as 'a verye olde woman and not able to gett her lyvinge, having twoe sonnes thone blynde and thother lame'.[46] Other widows had to take care of other family members alongside their own children: Margaret Carter has to 'maynteyne her selfe and her pore mother and two children'[47] and Elizabeth Thomas has 'her poore Children and fammlye' to think about.[48] To back up the claim of being a 'poor widow', then, women would share details about those whose mouths they needed to feed.

The weakness of a widow was not just absolute, it was also relative to their powerful legal opponents. Johan Fowles, for instance, describes herself as 'a very power and nedy widow and the seid John Sencler [her legal opponent] A worshipfull esquier'.[49] Margaret Pralyng describes herself similarly: she 'beinge Wyddowe verie simple and ignorant leste altogether frendles and Fatherles and the defende*n*tes verie coninge craftie and subtill people'.[50] This juxtaposition serves to make the widow appear even more helpless, as well as question the morality of the legal opponent, who is described as somebody with power and skills that are employed to destroy a poor, dependent relict.

That women chose to model their self-representation on the biblical widow does not mean that they were, in fact, poor or weak at all.[51] Anne Hooton, for example, presents herself as poor when she may not have been. She describes herself as 'lefte a verye poore ignoraunt weake and unbefrended woman charged *with* young Children' after the death of her husband, but according to her legal opponent she is actually 'a woman of great wealth and abillytie'.[52] It is difficult to establish who is right in this case, but because Hooton was capable of settling her late husband's debt with apparent ease, it seems likely that her claims of poverty are, at the very least, exaggerated. As such, the archetype of the biblical widow could be used by all widows, whether poor or not.

The model of the biblical widow thus contained three main elements: a petition to an authority figure, a self-deprecating portrayal of the widow, and a comparison to a powerful legal opponent. This made the biblical widow the perfect model to counter the persistent stereotype of the litigating widow. Rather than wanting to go to court, biblical

[44] London, The National Archives, Req 2/44/59, *Themilthorpe v Ecerton*, bill of Margerie Themilthorpe (1600).

[45] London, The National Archives, Req 2/43/51, *Davie v Davie*, bill of Anne Davie (1588).

[46] London, The National Archives, Req 2/56/87, *Bridges v Shynner and Obey*, bill of Agnes Bridges (1578).

[47] London, The National Archives, Req 2/188/6, *Carter v Hogge and Rowland Bates*, bill of Margaret Carter (1595).

[48] London, The National Archives, Req 2/41/99, *Thomas v Finche*, bill of Elizabeth Thomas (1575).

[49] London, The National Archives, Req 2/44/51, *Fowles v Sencler* (1559).

[50] London, The National Archives, Req 2/42/76, *Pralyn and Pralyng v Lloyd* (1594).

[51] Tim Stretton has already demonstrated this, see Stretton, 'Widows at Law', 206–7; Stretton, *Women Waging Law*, 185–7.

[52] London, The National Archives, Req 2/50/26, *Williams v Hooton and Hooton* (1598).

widows were forced to do so for their survival, and rather than evoking irritation, the biblical widow invites pity. This model could help widows not only to try and win their case, but also to present themselves in a certain way to the outside world—a way which could deviate from reality. As such, the choice to model oneself on the biblical widow in the courts of law is a deliberate form of self-fashioning.

The model of the eternal wife, too, could be a potent template for self-fashioning. Where Katherine Austen explicitly invoked the comparison to Penelope, however, no litigating widow chose to portray herself so openly as eternal wife. Instead, widows aimed to associate themselves with their late husbands and, as such, portrayed themselves in more subtle ways as the perpetual wife.

Customary law, the law practised in manors and boroughs, could require widows to remain single and chaste after the death of their husband in order to continue to enjoy the legal rights they had held while still married.[53] There was therefore a strong incentive for women to associate themselves with their late husband. We see this in the case of Alice Bowdon, who finds herself at law over a property in Northam, Devon. According to Bowdon:

> there is a custome whiche (From the tyme whereof there is no memorie of manne to the contrarye[)] hathe ben that the wiefe of euerye suche Ten*a*nte seased of any the customarye landes and tenementes of the said mann*or* shall haue her widower estate whiche is so longe as she lyuethe sole and unmaryed allthoo she be not named in the coppie.[54]

Here, Bowdon argues that Northam maintains a custom that relicts are entitled to succeed their husbands as tenants, as long as they live 'sole and unmaryed'.[55] Even if the widow is not mentioned in the copyhold, living chaste and single allows her to enjoy such privileges. As such, legal rights are attached to her status as a widowed *feme sole* and her compliance with this role.

However, in these types of cases, widows refrain from explicitly labelling themselves as a *feme sole*. Although they *act* like *femes sole* by starting legal proceedings and heading their own household, they opt for terminology such as 'relict', 'widow', or 'then Wife' in their self-descriptions. Alice Tilcocke, for example, refers to herself as 'wydowe the late Wief and Relict of William Tylcocke' and 'then Wife and nowe his relict and wydowe' in her pleading.[56] This decision to act like a *feme sole*, but describe themselves in relation

[53] Such local cases could be tried before the Court of Requests, which could serve as a court of appeal for local suits or at first instance (for example, if parties feared the bias the of local court).

[54] London, The National Archives, Req 2/42/49, *Bowdon v Beaple* (1566).

[55] Such stipulations are numerous in the court records. We find them, for example, in the following cases: London, The National Archives, Req 2/42/49, *Bowdon v Beaple* (1566); Req 2/210/118, *Grove v Gould and Peverell* (1571); Req 2/35/50, *Grove v Thynne* (1573); Req 2/41/36, *Tilcocke and Tilcocke v Iuxton* (1579); Req 2/168/19, *Allambrigge v Allambrigge* (1586); Req 2/56/34, *Soppe v Weekes* (1594); Req 2/187/49, *Cosynes v Morgan and Brodribbe* (1560).

[56] London, The National Archives, Req 2/41/36, *Tilcocke and Tilcocke v Iuxton* (1579).

to their late husband suggests that widows (and their legal counsel) had a solid understanding of what the case at hand required: the affiliation to their late husband was what gave these widows their legal rights, while their ongoing claims to these rights rested on the condition of remaining single. While they did not explicitly invoke the trope of the eternal wife, then, the more subtle strategy these litigating widows employed was closely related to it.

This styling as implicit eternal wife is tied to very specific legal circumstances. As a result, there are only a few cases in which widows would want to present themselves as such. No legal situation required relicts to explicitly express their love and devotion to their late husbands. For that reason, we do not meet Penelope in the legal archive. This shows us that the legal action a widow was involved in determined, in large part, how she portrayed herself. Another reason litigating widows did not opt for the label of eternal wife was perhaps that the trope of the biblical widow was simply more powerful: she was in more need of protection and charity than the eternal wife.

Women were thus capable of fashioning themselves beyond the tripartite model of maid, wife, and widow, both in and outside the courts of law. The literary models of the biblical widow and eternal wife offered widows the opportunity to escape negative connotations attached to the label of 'widow', including the challenges she posed to early modern patriarchy and the idea that all widows were loud and litigious. The most potent of the two models was certainly that of the biblical wife. This countered the stereotype of the loud and litigious widow and invoked pity rather than anxiety. Moreover, it could be used as a framework by all women who had lost their husbands. This made it a powerful model for all widows seeking to create a written self-portrait. The template of the eternal wife, on the other hand, served little purpose in the courts of law, and was for that reason a less attractive model. At the same time, we do see it used by widows in their life-writing, which suggests that widows made conscious decisions about their self-portrayal—in and outside the court room. The type of text, its purpose, and its perceived audience are important factors when it comes to making such decisions. Where life-writing offered widows much flexibility to style themselves, relicts involved in legal suits were hampered by the nature of their law suit and the brevity required in legal pleadings. In all situations, however, widows had to carefully consider which version of the self would serve them best in the case at hand, and the models of the eternal wife and biblical widow helped them to do so.

FURTHER READING

Anselment, Raymond A. 'Katherine Austen and the Widow's Might', *Journal for Early Modern Cultural Studies*, 5 (2005), 5–25.

Flannigan, Laura. 'Litigants in the English "Court of Poor Men's Causes," or Court of Requests, 1515–1525', *Law and History Review*, 38 (2020), 303–37.

Kearns, Judith. 'Fashioning Innocence: Rhetorical Construction of Character in the Memoirs of Anne, Lady Halkett', *Texas Studies in Literature and Language*, 46 (2004), 340–62.

Mason, Rebecca. 'Women, Marital Status, and Law: The Marital Spectrum in Seventeenth-Century Glasgow', *Journal of British Studies*, 58 (2019), 787–804.

Mukherji, Subha. *Law and Representation in Early Modern Drama*. Cambridge, 2006.

Shepard, Alexandra. *Accounting for Oneself: Worth, Status, and the Social Order in Early Modern England*. Oxford, 2015.

Stretton, Tim. 'Widows at Law in Tudor and Stuart England', in Sandra Cavallo and Lyndan Warner (eds), *Widowhood in Medieval and Early Modern Europe*. Abingdon, 2014, 193–208.

Trill, Suzanne. 'Beyond Romance? Re-Reading the "Lives" of Anne, Lady Halkett (1621/2?–1699)', *Literature Compass*, 6 (2009), 446–59.

CHAPTER 22

THE WORLD OF RECIPES

Intellectual Culture in and around the Seventeenth-Century Household

WENDY WALL

EARLY modern recipe ('receipt') books are not, as modern people might expect, synonymous with cookery books; instead they freely intermixed information about creating edibles (such as lemon creams, roast lamb, spinach fritters, or stewed eels) with advice on how to make herbal and chemical medicines, cosmetics, inks, dyes, letters, home decorations, pain relievers, cordials, wines, perfumes, pesticides, and even artistic food spectacles. Because Galenism, a dominant physiology of the day, saw disease as an imbalance of bodily humours, the housewife's management of the household diet was at the core of healthcare. In a world in which culinary and medical knowledge were inextricable, recipes enable us to understand women's role in a literate domestic culture, one in which they were called to mobilise a range of knowledges through daily acts in the kitchen.

Until recently, recipes had not been imagined to be promising sources for scholarship, largely because they were technical, formulaic, and prescriptive. As recent online blogs, transcribathons, recreated kitchen tutorials, and scholarly journals attest, recipes have become the subject of lively discussion and debate. With digitisation, searchable platforms, and transcriptions making early modern recipes newly accessible, they have been adopted as indispensable tools for refining our understanding of early modern science, medicine, food, labour, women's history, material book studies, social networks, and women's writing.[1]

[1] A partial list of important recipe scholarship includes: the *Early Modern Recipes Online Collective (EMROC)*, Hypotheses (2012), https://emroc.hypotheses.org/, accessed 5 December 2020; Michelle DiMeo and Sara Pennell (eds), *Reading and Writing Recipe Books 1550–1800* (Manchester, 2013); Elaine Leong et al. (eds), *The Recipes Project*, Hypotheses, https://recipes.hypotheses.org/,

Over the course of the seventeenth century, printed recipes emerged as a site for debating social status, national identity, and gender roles. This began in 1573 when John Partridge presented something novel to Western Europe: his recipe book, *The Treasurie of Commodious Conceits, & Hidden Secrets and May Be Called, the Huswives Closet, of Healthfull Prouision*, was pointedly marketed to women and non-nobles. England then emerged as the most active site of cookery publication in Europe (until the 1650s) and the only country marketing recipe books specifically for women. The male-authored recipe books that flooded the market included cheap pocket-sized collections such as Hugh Plat's bestselling *Delightes for Ladies* (1602), which offered the fashionable medical and culinary secrets of an international elite. By contrast, Gervase Markham's equally popular estate manual *The English Housewife* (1615) defined domestic labour in terms of English national character, Protestant ethics, and utilitarianism. England's robust print market for recipe books in the seventeenth century attracted consumers to join a global commerce system that stretched from the Spice Islands to Caribbean sugar plantations.

In the 1650s, book publishers began to market English recipe books as the collections of individual (often female) practitioners, including those of Elizabeth Grey (Countess of Kent) and Aletheia Talbot (Countess of Arundel). Some publications aired fierce politically partisan debates: readers could show Royalist sympathy by buying recipes attributed to the exiled Queen Henrietta Maria or join in mocking the inelegant recipes of Oliver Cromwell's wife Elizabeth.[2] But times were changing: alongside volumes privileging aristocratic knowledge, a new genre emerged that placed the kitchen front and centre as an *entrepreneurial* site of practice. Two groups battled for control over a market-saturated cuisine: female housekeepers (such as Hannah Woolley) who placed cooking in the domain of domestic management, and male chefs (such as Robert May) who saw cooking as a professional male skill far from the drudgery of housework. Woolley set the terms for eighteenth-century female recipe writers, including Sarah Harrison, Eliza Haywood, Elizabeth Moxon, Elizabeth Raffald, and Eliza Smith. Recipe

accessed 5 December 2020; Sara Pennell, 'Perfecting Practice? Women, Manuscript Recipes and Knowledge in Early Modern England', in Victoria Burke and Jonathan Gibson (eds), *Early Modern Women's Manuscript Writing: Selected Papers from the Trinity/Trent Colloquium* (Burlington, VT, 2004), 237–58; Wendy Wall, *Recipes for Thought: Knowledge and Taste in the Early Modern English Kitchen* (Philadelphia, PA, 2015); Elaine Leong, *Recipes and Everyday Knowledge: Medicine, Science, and the Household in Early Modern England* (Chicago, IL, 2018); Elizabeth Spiller (ed.), *Seventeenth-Century English Recipe Books: Cooking, Physic and Chirurgery in the Works of Elizabeth Grey and Aletheia Talbot* (Burlington, VT, 2008); David Goldstein, *Eating and Ethics in Shakespeare's England* (Cambridge, 2013); Sandra Sherman, *Invention of the Modern Cookbook* (Santa Barbara, CA, 2010); and Kristine Kowalchuk, *Preserving on Paper: Seventeenth-Century Englishwomen's Receipt Books* (Toronto, 2017).

[2] See Laura Knoppers, *Politicizing Domesticity from Henrietta Maria to Milton's Eve* (Cambridge, 2011); and Jayne Archer, 'The Queens' Arcanum: Authority and Authorship in *The Queens Closet Opened* (1655)', *Renaissance Journal*, 1 (2002), 14–25.

publication throughout the seventeenth century thus made visible a robust cultural dispute about who should manage bodies (through healthcare and diet) and what that management signified in terms of ideologies of class, nationality, and gender.

Male-authored recipe texts invited women to read and participate in these debates. But did women actually use these books? Scholars have sought to answer this question by examining women's annotations in printed recipe books and bringing to light hundreds of *handwritten* recipe collections.[3] 'Jane Staveley Her Recept Book', 'Grace Blome Her Booke': ownership marks such as these suggest that noblewomen, affluent gentry, yeomen's wives, merchants' wives, and other anonymous contributors not only actively consumed printed books but also compiled, annotated, and exchanged recipes—sometimes in expensively bound folio texts (see Figure 22.1) and sometimes in ragged working notebooks which were heavily annotated and marked with corrections.

Yet even signed collections do not directly evidence authorship or a single individual's knowledge, because collections routinely expanded as they travelled to family and friends or were handed down through generations in a family. On the day of her daughter's wedding, Mary Granville, for instance, modestly regifted her recipes to her daughter, and signed the flyleaf: 'Mrs Anne Granville's Book which I hope she will make a better use of then her mother'.[4] As recipes circulated, new owners annotated recipes and added new sections. Recipes were thus fashioned within a collaborative circuit of exchange and inheritance. Recipe writers also *textually* gathered people by attributing individual recipes to 'donors', citing either people they knew (for example, neighbours, cousins, or local healers) or their aspirational social networks (including famous authors, doctors, or social superiors). In citing the Countess of Warwick's way to make almond butter or Dr Willis' kidney stone drink, a writer might fantasise that one was in the recipe company of the rich and famous. When Sarah Longe, reputedly a tradesman's wife, tells how to make the caraway biscuits that King James and his wife 'have eaten with much liking', she implies that she not only has the resources to make expensive desserts but also is 'in-the-know' about the latest elite fashions.[5] Crowding a recipe collection with names could serve as a communication strategy, a tool for social mobility, and/or a display of cultural capital.

It is tricky to establish the identities of recipe compilers. Who was the 'Mary Bent' who loved oyster pies and legs of pork camouflaged as Westphalia hams? Who referred to herself in the royal 'we' ('you may put alittel pepper in if you please', she writes of preserved cucumbers, 'but we do not')?[6] Even without pinpointing the exact provenance of recipe collections, we appreciate that they offer crucial evidence about their

[3] I have consulted manuscript recipe collections at the Wellcome Library for the History of Medicine, the British Library, the Folger Shakespeare Library, the University of Iowa Library, the New York Public Library, and the University of Pennsylvania Library.

[4] Washington, DC, Folger Shakespeare Library, MS V.a.430., flyleaf. Granville's married name was Dewes. On this collection, see Wall, *Recipes for Thought*, 192–5.

[5] Washington, DC, Folger Shakespeare Library, MS V.a.425, fol. 20.

[6] London, Wellcome Library, MS 1127, fol. 2.

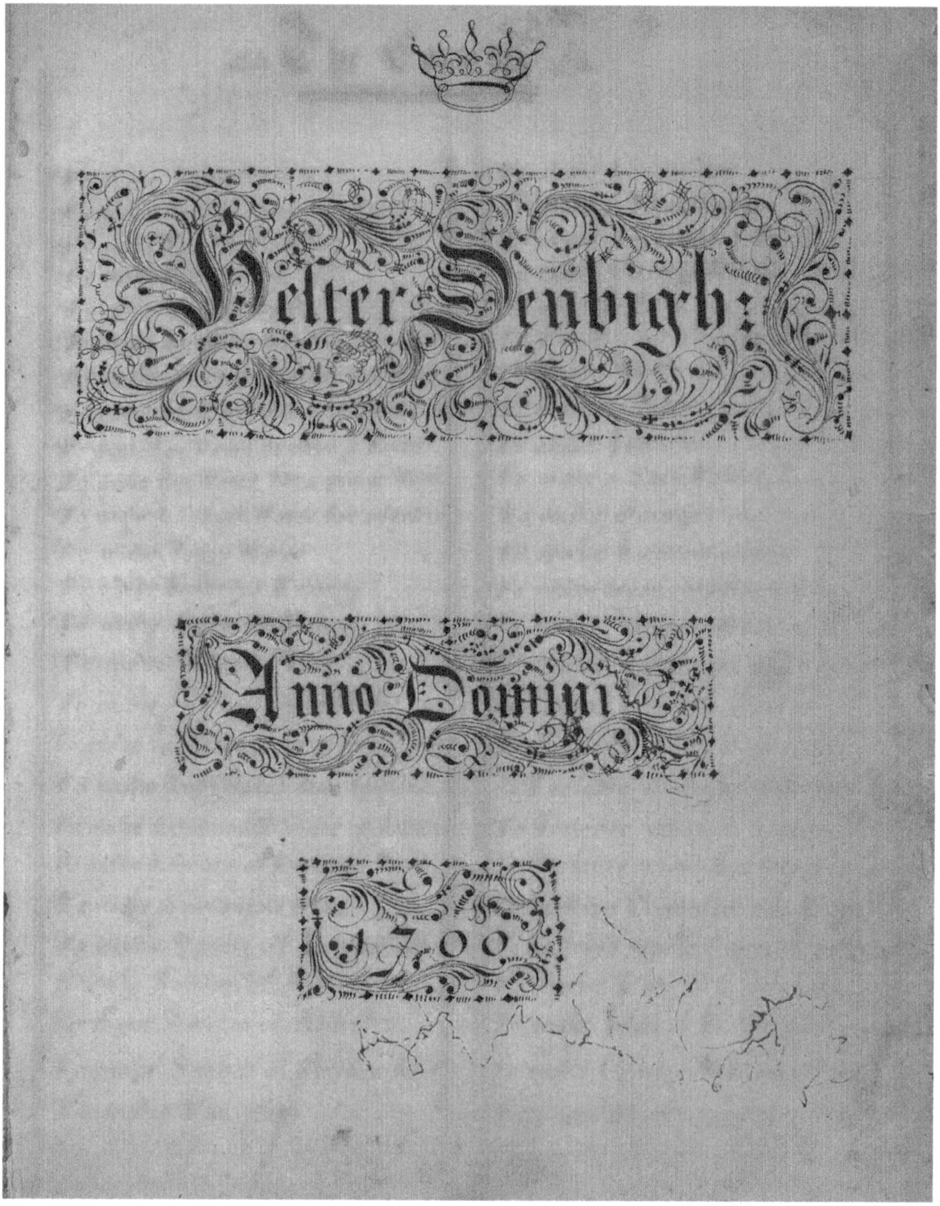

FIGURE 22.1 Hesrer (Hester) Denbigh, Cookery and Medical Receipts. Whitney Cookery Collection, Manuscripts and Archives Division, The New York Public Library, Astor, Lenox and Tilden Foundations, MssCol 3318, 1700, vol. 11, fol. 1.

functions: on blank pages amidst stained recipes, writers recorded family births, love letters, accounting sums, penmanship practice, biblical verses, and prayers. These texts were part of a manuscript culture that is becoming crucial for correcting the misperception that women had only a limited participation in early modern intellectual life.[7] Now a rich literature has emerged showing how recipes are indispensable sources for understanding global foodways; hospitality; women's relationship to the environment, including animal studies, gardening, botany, and ecofeminism; women's relationship to mortality, violence, and time; national and racial identities; religious identities; and authorship studies.[8] Recipes clearly have more than a documentary function for revealing the complexity and capaciousness of the pre-industrial *domus*; they are not just *windows* onto lived experiences, but also textual forms of writing themselves. They thus widen our conceptions of what constituted knowledge production in the seventeenth century and who was able to participate in its various manifestations.

THE HOME LAB AND MEDICAL SCHOOL: THE CASE OF ELIZABETH OKEOVER'S RECIPES

Scholars such as Elaine Leong and Rebecca Laroche have demonstrated how important recipes are for understanding early modern women's medical reading practices and assessing their role in healthcare (as neighbourhood authorities, authors, apothecaries, gardeners, herb gatherers, midwives, and local healers).[9] In a world in which physicians

[7] Margaret Ezell, *The Patriarch's Wife: Literary Evidence and the History of the Family* (Chapel Hill, NC, 1987), 36–61.

[8] On global foodways, see Robert Appelbaum, *Aguecheek's Beef, Belch's Hiccup, and Other Gastronomic Interjections* (Chicago, IL, 2006) and Ken Albala, *The Banquet: Dining in the Great Courts of Late Renaissance Europe* (Champaign, IL, 2007). On hospitality, see David Goldstein, *Eating and Ethics*, esp. 1–26; 139–70. On women's relationship to the environment, including animal studies, gardening, botany, and ecofeminism, see three essays in Jennifer Munroe and Rebecca Laroche (eds), *Ecofeminist Approaches to Early Modernity* (New York, 2011): Amy Tigner, 'Preserving Nature in Hannah Woolley's *The Queen-Like Closet; or Rich Cabinet*', 129–49; Michelle DiMeo and Rebecca Laroche, 'On Elizabeth Isham's "Oil of Swallows": Animal Slaughter and Early Modern Women's Medical Recipes', 87–104; and David Goldstein, 'Woolley's Mouse: Early Modern Recipe Books and the Uses of Nature', 105–27. On women's relationship to mortality, violence, and time, see Wendy Wall, *Staging Domesticity: Household Work and English Identity in Early Modern Drama* (Cambridge, 2002); 192–201; Wall, *Recipes for Thought*, 167–208; and Anita Guerrini, 'The Ghastly Kitchen', *History of Science*, 54 (2016), 71–97. On food as it relates to national and racial identities, see Kim F. Hall, 'Culinary Spaces, Colonial spaces: The Gendering of Sugar in the Seventeenth Century', in Valerie Traub, Lindsay Kaplan, and Dympna Callaghan (eds), *Feminist Readings of Early Modern Culture: Emerging Subjects* (Cambridge, 1996), 168–90; Wall, *Recipes for Thought*, 44–58; Gitanjali Shahani, *Tasting Difference: Food, Race, and Cultural Encounters in Early Modern Literature* (Ithaca, NY, 2020); Wall, *Staging Domesticity*, 1–42. On cookery books and religious identities, see Lauren F. Winner, 'The Foote Sisters' Compleat Housewife: Cookery Texts as a Source in Lived Religion', in DiMeo and Pennell (eds), *Reading and Writing Recipe Books*, 135–55. And on how cookbooks relate to authorship studies, see Michelle DiMeo, 'Authorship and Medical Networks: Reading Attributions in Early Modern Manuscript Recipes', DiMeo and Pennell (eds), *Reading and Writing Recipes Books*, 25–46.

[9] Rebecca Laroche, *Medical Authority and Englishwomen's Herbal Texts, 1550–1650* (Farnham, 2009); Leong, *Recipes and Everyday Knowledge*; Elaine Leong, 'Making Medicines in the Early Modern

were expensive and rare, non-formally trained practitioners did not just treat coughs and colds but also devised regimens of purgatives (including vomits and bloodletting); treated epilepsy, plagues, and heart disease; and undertook minor surgery. Women were called upon to use their extensive knowledge of plants' 'virtues' (physical healing properties). One case in point is a collection of recipes attributed to Elizabeth Okeover but which bears signs of multiple writers. This handwritten collection consists of over 250 recipes for ointments for sores; gynaecological and bladder treatments; remedies for kidney stones; and a few food recipes (including for cheesecake, collared beef, and preserved currants). Begun by an unknown female member of the Okeover family in Derbyshire, this collection was continued by Elizabeth Okeover, who amended formulas, cross-referenced information, provided an index, and cited relatives, friends, elite women, printed guides, and doctors as her sources.

In her recipes, Okeover not only presents herself as a medical practitioner, but also as a curious researcher who sifts received information. 'This is the salve I allwais make', she writes while customising her mother's 'ointment of flowers' by adjusting the ingredients and measurements.[10] Okeover offers advice about how to understand weights for cherries, choose the best sugar candy for cock water (medicinal, spiced chicken soup), and economise when stewing rabbits. Beside a remedy for scrofula (called the 'kings evill'), she observes that a key ingredient, 'green flag', resembles the 'sword flagg and growes in the water', the root of which, she notes, 'may be knowne in being of a red or flesh couler' (20). In addition to displaying botanical knowledge, Okeover seeks to create a user-friendly book by directing readers to *categories* of remedies scattered throughout the collection and correcting *errata*. 'Resits in this book', she writes, were erroneously 'writ twice over' (65). Okeover thus left abundant traces of her activities as a cook, herbalist, researcher, information organiser, and editor.

Okeover's collection modelled for users the importance of testing received information. For example, one balsam remedy (written before Okeover owned the book) concludes with testimony to a sensational, if gruesome, success: 'I: pr: this cured a head that was burned to the very skull' (88). The 'I' that 'pr.' or 'proved' (tried or authorised) the remedy insisted that validity be established by trial, advice that Okeover took to heart after inheriting the collection: she assiduously tested family recipes, added new and variant curatives, and backtracked through her own contributions to update methods and elaborate instructions. She was so enthusiastic about a 'blast salve' made up of cream, marigolds, chamomile, and hyssop (a palliative ointment for 'blasted' or infected sores) that she not only glossed it as 'Most Exelen', but also marked it with a note: 'this I make Eliz: Okeover now Eliz. Adderley' (229). This inscription identifies

Household', *Bulletin of the History of Medicine*, 82 (2008), 145–68. See also Linda Pollock, *With Faith and Physic: The Life of a Tudor Gentlewoman, Lady Grace Mildmay 1552–1620* (London, 1993). On women and early modern medicine in general, see Margaret Pelling, *Medical Conflicts in Early Modern London: Patronage, Physicians, and Irregular Practitioners, 1550–1640* (Oxford, 2003) and Lucinda McCray, *Sufferers and Healers: The Experience of Illness in Seventeenth-Century England* (London, 1987).

10 London, Wellcome Library, MS 3712, fol. 219.

who she is—both the recipes' compiler (who has linked two families by marrying) and someone whose act of *making* validates her knowledge. Okeover thus held up for the reader's scrutiny her own grounds of expertise and the relationship of text to practice. In characterising recipe writing as more than an ancillary legitimising of what was already known, Okeover validated the empirical process that the Royal Society was elsewhere shaping as a model of evidentiary standards.

Recipe collections such as Okeover's have enabled scholars to form a revisionary history of science: books of secrets (the progenitors of recipes) help to redefine Aristotelian conceptions of *praxis* and scholastic notions of experience; and the craft practices of artisans, gardeners, tradesmen, and mechanical artists' labours are now understood as a popular basis for experimental science.[11] Sara Pennell laid the groundwork for understanding the epistemological implications of recipe studies by theorising the ways in which the recipe format shaped knowledge in the period.[12] Rather than simply storing previously substantiated knowledge (about the natural world, medicine, chemistry, and food), recipes were grammatically structured, edited, and circulated in ways that enabled them to prove 'truth'—whether they concerned the most effective means for preserving raspberries or the right temperature for evaporating liquids. Acting as a script that demanded that readers *do* something in the world ('take', 'make', or 'grind'), recipes called for active, embodied completion; the knowledge they offered was contingent on the next user's materialisation of a recommended formula. The fact that recipes kept the circuit of 'reproving' information alive was crucial in the climate of seventeenth-century England, where empirical and deductive methods were hotly debated. In Okeover's domestic experimental culture, *making* extended from the transformations conjured up in the kitchen to the formats by which knowledge was authorised.

PRESERVING MATERIALS AND MEMORIES: THE CASE OF HOPESTILL BRETT'S RECIPES

When Hopestill Brett recorded a recipe for conserved barberries, she was not doing anything unusual.[13] In a world without mass-produced canning or refrigeration, it was imperative to delay the expiration date of produce from the garden or market. Conserves

[11] See William Eamon, *Science and the Secrets of Nature: Books of Secrets in Medieval and Early Modern Culture* (Princeton, NJ, 1994); Deborah Harkness, *The Jewel House: Elizabethan London and the Scientific Revolution* (New Haven, CT, 2007); Pamela Smith, *The Body of the Artisan: Art and Experience in the Scientific Revolution* (Chicago, IL, 2004); and Lynette Hunter and Sarah Hutton (eds), *Women, Science, and Medicine 1500–1700: Mothers and Sisters of the Royal Society* (Stroud, 1997).

[12] Pennell, 'Perfecting Practice?'.

[13] Philadelphia, PA, Esther Aresty Collection, Kislak Center for Special Collections, University of Pennsylvania Library, MS codex 626.

and preserves were, for this reason, the most popular subjects of seventeenth-century recipe collections. Numerous recipes for preserving fruits (gooseberries, currants, raspberries) and flowers (roses, violets) concluded with a reassuring mantra: 'this will keep' or 'keep as long as you please'. Preserves were additionally popular because they could signify status (as expensive desserts displayed at social events) as well as frugality (a virtue lauded in post-reformation conduct literature). The promise of 'keeping' in recipes extended beyond technical functionality to encompass abstract forms of preservation and remembrance.

Almost half of the 176 recipes in Hugh Plat's popular published recipe book, *Delightes for Ladies,* fall within the section entitled 'The Art of Preserving', which included the making of candies, jams, marzipans, jellies, and durable pastes. In an unusual poetic preface, Plat hyperbolically presents making conserves and confectionery as an art practice through which humans can triumphantly master time:

> When chrystall frosts hath nipt the tender grape,
> And cleane consum'd the fruits of euery vine,
> Yet here behold the clusters fresh and faire,
> Fed from the branch, or hanging on the line.[14]

Secured from nature's devouring destruction, the grape seems reincarnated for the reader or diner to 'behold', both in the recipe book itself and in the tasty preserves it describes. Plat's grandiose claims make sense when read through the lens of contemporary medical theory, where foods were seen as drugs used to ward off disease and death. In fact, the word 'preservation' appears frequently in recipes in reference to medical care, such as when Granville offers a recipe for a precious water that promised to 'preserveth the body from putrifying' (Granville, 39). As Plat's preface suggests, recipes fused multilayered notions of preservation. Using the family recipe book required the compiler to move seamlessly between the 'keeping' of perishable goods and collective memories. 'As a form through which celebrated figures or the dead might be memorialised and re-encountered every time one read or made a dish or medicine', write Sara Pennell and Michelle DiMeo, 'recipe collections exert a powerful associative and even psychic force'.[15] When consulting a family collection, a woman might visualise her dead grandmother making currants or her aunt concocting sugar cakes—memories etched in the idiom of food.

Let us return to Brett, whose 1678 recipe collection not only commemorates the past but also introduces family members' implicit debates about food preferences and tasks. A recipe telling how to pickle oysters according to 'my sister Higginbothams way' (fol. 4v) is followed by 'My cosen Betty's waye' (fol 5r); 'My sister Knowles' way to whit[en] Cloath]' (fol. 134v) rests face to face with 'my oune way' (fol. 135r). 'My owne

[14] Hugh Plat, *Delightes for Ladies* (London, 1602), sig. A3r.

[15] Michelle DiMeo and Sara Pennell, 'Introduction', in DiMeo and Pennell (eds), *Reading and Writing Recipe Books*, 14.

mothers way for hogspudding' (fol. 47r) is followed by 'My hogspudding' (fol. 60r).[16] The book stages Sister Higgins and Cousin Betty debating methods for pickling oysters; Brett improves her mother's hogspudding by adding sack. Family members emerge as a chorus of characters animating the experiences of eating and reading, forming what David Goldstein sees as a convening (or gathering together) of community guided by an ethic of commensality: 'The dishes are yoked to those who donated them as if at a kind of communal table—a table called into being by the fact of the book'.[17]

Brett also followed the well-worn custom of using blank leaves in her compilation as an all-purpose storage site for memorandum. Beside recipes for wild duck sauce, preserved berries, Goody Barber's rolls, Madam West's diet drink, and puddings in guts, Brett scribbled lists of household goods and recorded the deaths of friends. On the book's final leaves, she lists her family members' favourite Bible verses: 'A Time to be born and a time to die' (her mother; fol. 141v); 'Then shall the dust return to the earth as it wase: and the spirit shall return unto god who gave it' (her father; fol. 142r); 'I am not as the Cloude is consumed: and vanised a way: Soe hee that goeth down to the grave shall com ye no more' (her own selection; fol. 141v). Drawing out common biblical themes about the vanity of life and necessity of death, this diary record adds charged meanings to a recipe collection handed down in time; for these meditations are proximate to the mundane work of preserving harvest from the garden and preserving bodies from decay. Recipe collections, which shared with Bibles the function of recording family births and deaths, served as a technology of memory safeguarding against inevitable loss as well as a source of practical advice.[18]

TRANSLATION STUDIES IN THE KITCHEN: THE CASE OF SARAH HUGHES' RECIPES

Recipes are helpful in mapping international foodways, such as the routes by which spices were introduced into England through Roman invasion, the Crusades to the Middle East, or colonisation of the 'new world'. Several early modern women's collections commented on the border-crossings of recipes. Ann Fanshawe, for example, not only marked the voyage of a novel hot chocolate drink into England, but also registered anthropological curiosity about its origins. In addition to noting that

[16] University of Pennsylvania Library, MS codex 626. On Brett, see Janet Theophano, *Eat My Words: Reading Women's Lives Through the Cookbooks They Wrote* (New York, 2002), 15–24.

[17] Goldstein, *Eating and Ethics*, 145.

[18] For recipe collections that record family histories, see Frances Springatt (Ashford), London, Wellcome Library, MS 4683; Grace Randolph (Blome).

she procured the recipe in Madrid (presumably while her husband was English ambassador to Spain), she includes a drawing of a Native American chocolate pot, typical in 'the Indies'.[19] Fanshawe's collection was not unusual in welcoming foreign dishes and methods from Spain, North Africa, or France, without xenophobic commentary. In doing so, recipe compilers largely ignored the advice of Gervase Markham, whose *English Housewife* warned readers they should use only native and home-grown ingredients (though he did not follow his own advice).[20] Although Markham's idea that diet was a fundamental signifier of national identity was confirmed in numerous stage representations, husbandry manuals, travel writings, and dietaries, it seemed to have little sway in the praxis of the recipe world, which was pointedly more cosmopolitan.

Recipe writing afforded a female compiler named Sarah Hughes with the opportunity not only to learn Spanish but also to contemplate ways that grammars, words, and materials could (and could not) be translated across cultures. Hughes' bilingual collection opens with ninety-five Portuguese recipes in Spanish (*Libro de Recetas de Portugal para hacer Peuetes y Pastillas y adrecar Guantes perfumados*), followed by her own collected recipes in English, a translation of the Spanish recipes, and abundant marginal commentary making clear that cooking was a site of cultural and linguistic diversity.[21] The volume includes its own English glossary of Spanish terms and idiomatic expressions (fol. 2r) as well as a list of words that stymied the translator.[22] In addition to marking the flow of international foodways, this collection attends to the fissures that arise when goods and information cross linguistic borders; it marks the boundaries of what had to remain alien and untranslatable.

When readers consulted recipes on cookery and medical care in Hughes' collection, they were ushered into a sustained examination of what we now call translation studies. The translator/compiler comments on the labour of converting the Spanish 'third person' ('tomar' or 'one takes') into the English second-person imperative voice 'more usuall and familiar in our idiom' ('take'; fol. 81v). 'It is to bee noted that, the spanish coppy is very ill pointed' [punctuated], the translator observes, 'it hath Divers false orthographies' (fol. 81v). As the reader looked for recipes to make perfumes or cure a toothache, she could not avoid thinking about grammar and syntax. She was told that underlined words signalled that 'the Spanish translated in every particle verbatim' are

[19] Fanshawe's recipe 'To dresse Chocolatte' is marked 'Madrid, 10 Aug. 1665'; London, Wellcome Library, MS 7113, fol. 332. For other collections marking the family's Iberian travels, see Glyd in BL Add MS 45196; and Granville, Folger Shakespeare Library, MS V.a.430. For astute discussions of bilingual recipe books, see Madeline Bassnett, 'A Language Not One's Own: Translational Exchange in Seventeenth-Century Englishwomen's Iberian Recipes', *Journal for Early Modern Cultural Studies*, 19 (2019), 1–27; and Amy L. Tigner, 'Trans-border Kitchens: Iberian Recipes in Seventeenth-Century English Manuscripts', *History of Retailing and Consumption*, 5 (2019), 51–70.

[20] Gervase Markham, *The English Housewife* (London, 1623), 3–4.

[21] Bassnett, 'A Language Not One's Own', [3], notes that the attribution is a compilation of the 'Mrs. Hughes' mentioned in the second section and 'Lady Sarah' from the third. The sections are in different, and yet unknown, hands.

[22] London, Wellcome Library, MS 363, fol. 81v.

'found harsh in English & not bee ... altogether intelligible' (fol. 81v). She learned that the Spanish word 'coale' was not a black rock, as an English reader might think, but a fruit (fol. 83r). And she was invited to experience the frustration of simply suspending certain knowledge: coming to the phrase '*en camo de Rosas*', the translator frankly confessed, 'but whether bee meant ... Rosewater or no; I know not' (fol. 82v). A recipe for marzipan tablets 'that my Lady' created for flatulence prompted complete exasperation 'Lady?': 'lord knowes who', the translator exclaims (fol. 96v). In Hughes' collection, kitchen work is a contact zone airing the estranging nature of knowledge systems.

THE CELEBRITY RECIPE WRITER: THE CASE OF HANNAH WOOLLEY

Hannah Woolley emerged in the 1660s as the first female professional domestic writer and the most popular author of recipe books. She embodied a rags-to-riches narrative that allowed readers to see domestic expertise as a path for upward social mobility. Orphaned as a child, she apprenticed as a servant and married Benjamin Woolley, the master of a boarding school, where she served as nurse and manager. After being widowed, she used her professional stints as a housekeeper and cooking teacher to launch a successful career as a published recipe book writer; her frequently reprinted texts included *The Ladies Directory in Choice Experiments* (1662); *The Cook's Guide* (1664); *The Queen-Like Closet; or, Rich Cabinet* (1670, see Figure 22.2); and *A Supplement to the Queen-Like Closet* (1674). By 1670, Woolley was an established figure, so popular that publishers sought to capitalise on her name and to consolidate a cult of personality around her. Three additional books were attributed to her, some of which recirculated material from her works—*The Gentlewomans Companion; or, A Guide to the Female Sex* (1673; a text Woolley disavowed); *The Accomplisht Ladys Delight in Preserving, Physick, Beautifying and Cookery* (1675); and *The Compleat Servant Maid, or the Young Maidens Tutor* (1677). As Margaret Ezell has argued, Woolley's celebrity was enhanced by publishers who marketed assembled information under Woolley's brand, consolidating the authority of the recipe author through the strategic use of portraits and prefaces.[23] Woolley's texts dramatically expanded recipe topics to include manners, parenting advice, decorating, arithmetic, money handling, wax working, and moral behaviour. She insistently classified penmanship and letter writing as a vital part of housework, offering sample letters that concretely addressed the gritty problems of impoverishment, violence, and family loss.

In *A Supplement to the Queen Like Closet*, Woolley explicitly based her medical authority on her own experience: 'I have been *Physician* and *Chirugian* in my own House

[23] Margaret Ezell, 'Cooking the Books; or, The Three Faces of Hannah Woolley', in DiMeo and Pennell (eds), *Reading and Writing Recipe Books*, 159–78.

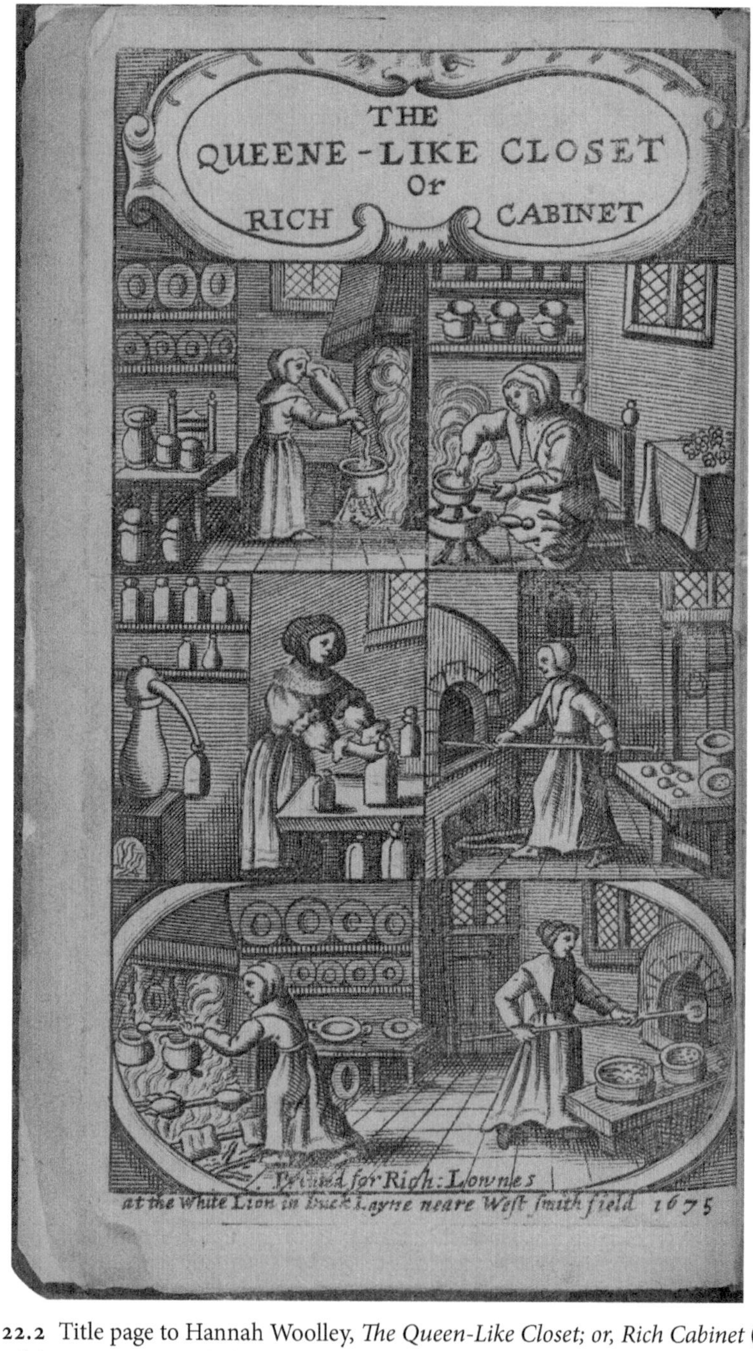

FIGURE 22.2 Title page to Hannah Woolley, *The Queen-Like Closet; or, Rich Cabinet* (London, 1675). Used by permission of the Folger Shakespeare Library under a Creative Commons Attribution-ShareAlike 4.0 International License.

to many', she wrote, 'and also to many of my Neighbors, eight or ten miles round'.[24] She insisted that food preparation was not the purview of elite male chefs, whose books she found overly technical, but instead was requisite knowledge of a lady, housewife, or servant. Woolley explained that her domestic advice was necessary precisely because of the social upheaval of the English Civil War: 'I find many Gentlewomen forced to serve whose Parents and Friends have been impoverished by the great Calamities, *viz.* the Late Wars, Plague, and Fire, and to see what mean Places they are forced to be in, because they want Accomplishments for better'.[25] Her advice books defined requisite skills for all levels of domestic service: from lowly servants to nursemaids, from housekeepers to ladies. She unabashedly instructed readers on how to improve their resumés so as to take advantage of job opportunities. Woolley was thus an important figure in reshaping recipes as part of an English domesticity validating not just the well-run home but also the service relations and marketplace underpinning that institution. Recipes could enable a female career, in the home and in the print marketplace.

DELICIOUS LITERACY: THE CASE OF LETTICE PUDSEY'S RECIPES

Recipe writing allowed early modern women to participate not only in the circulation of domestic knowledge but also in sites for literacy formation and demonstration. Witness this ownership mark: 'Lettice Pudsey, her Booke of recipts, these following are written with my owne hand' (see Figure 22.3). Pudsey introduced her recipes by boasting of her ability to form letters as well as puddings, pies, and wafers. While she does not claim to have invented the individual recipes (which are freely borrowed from others), she does claim the physical book object, the skill of its making, and her literate status (her 'owne' hand).

Amongst Pudsey's recipes for how to make rabbit fricassees, eye ointments, puddings, laxatives, fake venison, kidney stone cures, fritters, perfumes, antidepressants, and vegetarian stews, Pudsey includes a gooseberry cake recipe that concludes: 'Doe somwhat on them: ether letters or what you please'.[26] Pudsey's offhand comment indicates that alphabets were among the classic designs used in confectionery. In numerous recipes for sweets (called banqueting dishes) readers were invited to concoct elaborate enterprises of almond paste, some moulded as architectural designs (e.g., castles) or animals (e.g., rabbits, birds, deer). 'Print them as you please', many recipes conclude, as if the kitchen were a domestic print shop equipped to stamp tarts with family crests, abstract shapes, flowers, and/or religious signifiers. In *Treasurie of Commodious Conceites*, to take one

[24] Hannah Woolley, *A Supplement to the Queen Like Closet* (London, 1674), sig. A2v.

[25] Hannah Woolley, *The Queen-like Closet* (London, 1670), 378–9).

[26] Washington, DC, Folger Shakespeare Library, MS V.a.450, fol. 20v.

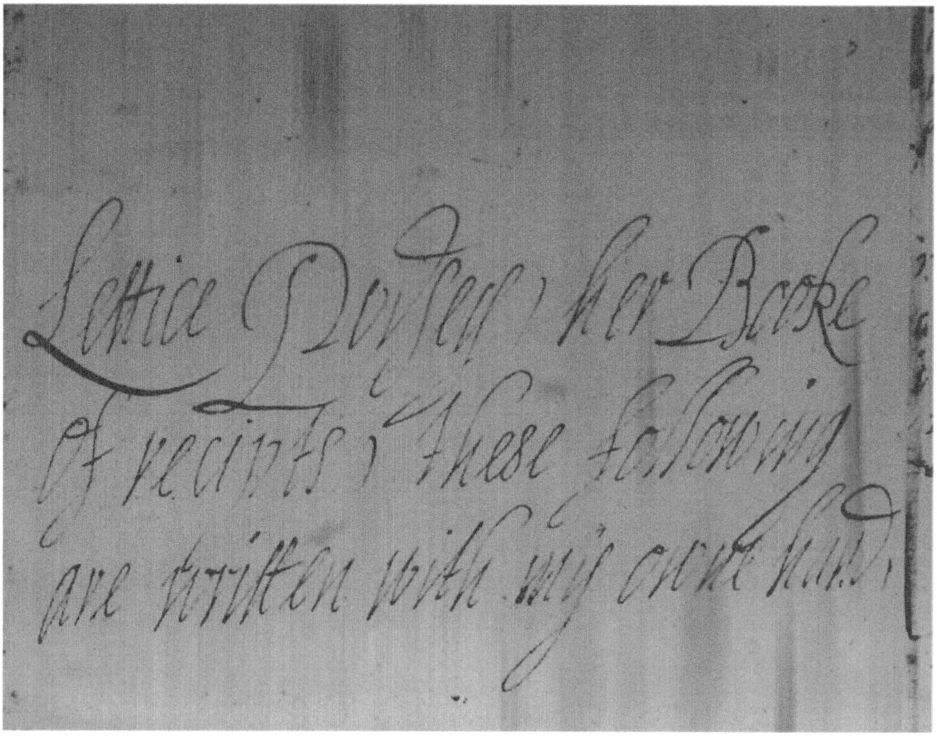

FIGURE 22.3 *Lettice Pudsey Her Booke of Receipts*, *c* 1675, Folger Shakespeare Library, MS V.a.450, fol. F7v. Used by permission of the Folger Shakespeare Library under a Creative Commons Attribution-ShareAlike 4.0 International License.

fascinating example, Partridge casually recommends that the user emblazon a dessert with 'the name of Jesus, or any other thing whatsoever'.[27]

Published recipe writers such as Plat and John Murrell revelled in kitchenwork as a site of fantasy and artistry, urging readers to craft sophisticated foods which demonstrated a cultured wit. Plat directed readers to shape marzipan into 'letters, knots, Arms, Escocheons, beasts, birds, & other fancies' (sig. B9v) or to trick diners with dessert conceits that *seem* to be savoury roasted meats (sig. B4r). Murrell not only detailed techniques for creating edible designs and alphabets, but also asked readers to show off knowledge of specific fonts by fashioning 'faire capitall Romane letters'.[28] Renaissance literary theorist George Puttenham saw edible 'posies' (short emblematic sayings or poems) as a customary feature of dinner party culture; they might be 'printed or put upon their banketting dishes of suger plate, or of march paines, & such other dainty meates as by the curtesie & custome every gest might carry from a common feast

[27] John Partridge, *The Treasurie of Commodious Conceites* (London, 1573), sig. B5v.

[28] John Murrell, *A Daily Exercise For Ladies and Gentlewomen* (London, 1617), sig. F9v.

home with him'.[29] Pudsey's attention to writing underscores a tactile kitchen literacy that extended from tasty sweets to her own handwritten recipes.

CONCLUSION

Some early modern writers warned that a woman's submissive place was in the home, where housework might suppress female inventiveness and ensure a spiritual focus. 'Domesticke charge doth best that sex befit', Thomas Overbury advised, 'Contiguous businesse; so to fixe the mind, / That leisure space for fancies not admit'.[30] Yet, the recipe archive makes us wonder whether such writers actually knew much about what was going on amid the pots and pans of the early modern household. The acts of making in the household hardly 'fixed' or suppressed social, creative, or intellectual energies in ways that necessarily absorbed workers into a narrowly conceived ideological role. Indeed, as we have seen, recipes documented and encouraged resourceful invention and the active curation of information. Existing in the transformation of nature into art—shapeless *materia* into cultural product, the raw into the cooked—recipe writing invited scrutiny of the weighty issues that acts of domestic *poesis* (or making) entailed: what it meant to shape the material world of which humans were a part; how epistemological confirmation took place in the circulations of texts as well as management of goods; how the lines between 'nature' and 'art' could blur; and how humans managed temporality and mortality through language and other signifying systems. It was all in a day's work.[31]

FURTHER READING

Bassnett, Madeline. 'A Language Not One's Own: Translational Exchange in Seventeenth-Century Englishwomen's Iberian Recipes', *Journal for Early Modern Cultural Studies*, 19 (2019), 1–27.

DiMeo, Michelle and Sara Pennell (eds). *Reading and Writing Recipe Books 1550–1800*. Manchester, 2013.

Early Modern Recipes Online Collective (EMROC). *Hypotheses* (2012). https://emroc.hypotheses.org/. Accessed 5 December 2020.

[29] George Puttenham, *The Arte of English Poesie*, eds Frank Whigham and Wayne A. Rebhorn (Ithaca, NY, 2007), 146–7.

[30] Thomas Overbury, *His Wife with Additions of New Characters* (1614), repr. in Edward F. Rimbaul (ed.), *The Miscellaneous Works in Prose and Verse of Sir Thomas Overbury* (London, 1890), 41.

[31] We have yet to understand fully how female literary writers (such as Hester Pulter, Katherine Philips, and Margaret Cavendish) mobilised domestic expertise to adapt and query received genres and belief systems, but see Samantha Snively, '"The Quintessence of Wit"': Domestic Labor, Science, and Margaret Cavendish's Kitchen Fancies', *Newberry Essays in Medieval and Early Modern Studies* 9 (2015), 21–8.

Hall, Kim F. 'Culinary Spaces, Colonial spaces: The Gendering of Sugar in the Seventeenth Century', in Valerie Traub, Lindsay Kaplan, and Dympna Callaghan (eds), *Feminist Readings of Early Modern Culture: Emerging Subjects*. Cambridge, 1996, 168–90.

Leong, Elaine. *Recipes and Everyday Knowledge: Medicine, Science, and the Household in Early Modern England*. Chicago, IL, 2018.

Pennell, Sara. 'Perfecting Practice? Women, Manuscript Recipes and Knowledge in Early Modern England', in Victoria Burke and Jonathan Gibson (eds), *Early Modern Women's Manuscript Writing: Selected Papers from the Trinity/Trent Colloquium*. Burlington, VT, 2004, 237–58.

Wall, Wendy. *Recipes for Thought: Knowledge and Taste in the Early Modern English Kitchen*. Philadelphia, PA, 2015.

CHAPTER 23

DAUGHTERS OF THE HOUSE

Women, Theatre, and Place in the Seventeenth Century

JULIE SANDERS

PLACE and place studies have been important proving grounds for interdisciplinary scholarship and not least for the cultural–geographical turn in early modern literary studies. In this chapter I will explore the place-based work of a number of seventeenth-century women playwrights, arguing for the site-specificity of their output. Political geographer John Agnew identified three fundamental aspects to place theory: location, locale, and sense of place.[1] All of these have resonance for dramatic work created by the women under discussion here, and each of these categories mobilise important reflections around family, neighbourhood, material culture, lived experience, and site. The heartland of these works is, I will argue, the household estate.

PRODUCING HOUSES

In September 2018, an audience gathered at Penshurst Place in Kent, the ancestral home of the Sidney family, to witness a production of a *c* 1620 play by a female member of that literary circle, Lady Mary Sidney Wroth's *Love's Victory*. The production took place in the Baron's Hall and used the gallery space therein to enable the framing Venus and Cupid scenes. It built from earlier experiments with partial stagings and staged readings, and asked spectators to think about a production in the here and now as a simultaneous, albeit partial, point of entry into the ways the play might have been performed in Wroth's own time.[2] That intellectual and experiential oscillation is familiar to those who deploy

[1] John Agnew, *Place and Politics* (Boston, MA, 1987).

[2] The project entitled 'Dramatizing Penshurst: *Love's Victory* and the Sidneys' which enabled the production was led by Alison Findlay. Her practice-based research has been fundamental in reclaiming

practice-based research to explore the sometimes difficult-to-reach aspects of theatre history. In previous decades those difficulties were compounded by limited scholarship and limiting assumptions about early modern women's writing, but understanding is increasingly gaining energy and substance from performance studies as well as earlier archival retrievals by 1990s feminist scholarship. In addition to Wroth's play, examples will be offered from Lady Rachel Fane's 1620s family masques and entertainments written and performed at the family home in Apethorpe Hall, Northamptonshire, and the quasi-dramatic texts created by the Cavendish sisters, Lady Jane Cavendish and Lady Elizabeth Brackley, during their period of house imprisonment at the family estate in Welbeck, Nottinghamshire during the 1640s English Civil War.

Margaret Hannay and Alison Findlay, among others, have speculated as to exactly which location *Love's Victory* might have been performed in and written for.[3] Both explore possible linked occasions such as family weddings at a range of locales, but Findlay settles on Penshurst as the most likely, identified so closely as the play's interpretative layers are with the Sidney family story.[4] Wroth actively references her uncle's romantic relationships as well as her own in a series of veiled allusions, and Findlay rightly notes how offensive some of this would have been if staged on her husband's estates.[5] Coded references are frequently the lifeblood of this form of household drama. Family members and local people—neighbours or estate employees and their children—appear to have taken part in readings and performances. Rachel Fane's cast list, appended to her Maytime masque from *c* 1627, identifies family relations as performers but also names three other children, including five-year-old Richard Burton, who were 'probably family dependents or servants'.[6] How this very human aspect of the works interacted with the significant local meanings of spatial settings will be the focus of the following section. Documentary evidence like this points, as Paul Salzman has indicated, to the likelihood or possibility that plays like *Love's Victory* were also 'written for semi-private

Love's Victory for consideration as a dramatic work; see, for example, *Playing Spaces in Early Modern Women's Drama* (Cambridge, 2006), 83–94. Findlay was also the driving force behind the 2016 staged reading at Penshurst in collaboration with the Shakespeare's Globe 'Read not Dead' series.

[3] Margaret Hannay, *Mary Sidney, Lady Wroth* (Farnham, 2010), pp. 219–20; Findlay, *Playing Spaces*, 90.

[4] Findlay, *Playing Spaces*, 90. Cf. Martin Butler, 'Private and Occasional Drama', in A. R. Braunmuller and Michael Hattaway (eds), *The Cambridge Companion to English Renaissance Drama* (Cambridge, 1990), 131–63.

[5] Findlay, *Playing Spaces*, 89. On the layered referencing of the family story, see the introduction to Marion Wynne-Davies and S. P. Cerasano's edition of the play in their *Renaissance Drama by Women: Texts and Documents* (London, 1996), 94. All quotations from *Love's Victory* will be from this edition.

[6] Findlay, *Playing Spaces*, 41. She observes that a 'Dick Burton' was clearly part of Rachel's household after her marriage; Todd Gray (ed.), *Devon Household Accounts Part II: Henry 5th Earl of Bath and Rachel, Countess of Bath, Tavistock and London 1637–1655* (Exeter, 1996), 176, 178, 206, 239. Marion O'Connor has identified this complete masque, which is collated along with a series of other dramatic and verse fragments in a handbound silk volume labelled by a later hand as Fane's 'Dramatic Pastimes for Children', as a Maytime occasional drama due to its internal references and dating; 'Rachel Fane's May Masque at Apethorpe, 1627', *English Literary Renaissance*, 36 (2006), 90–113, 94–5. Fane's notebooks and juvenilia are housed in the Kent Archives in Maidstone, Sackville MSS KAO U269.

performance, with those in the know able to appreciate the allusions'.[7] Household texts could well have had afterlives beyond an initial reading or 'occasional' performance, circulated in manuscript as they were and therefore available for interpretation in different locales. This was certainly a Sidney family tradition and *Love's Victory* survives in two variants which connect to other producing households in the region. One manuscript was in the possession of Sir Edward Dering, who is known to have performed non-professional staged readings of plays at his Surrenden estate in Kent just twenty-five miles from Penshurst.[8] The line between amateur and professional performance is porous in the context of early seventeenth-century household theatre, and the tendency to categorise women's experimentations as 'amateur' has undoubtedly had a detrimental effect, delimiting an appreciation of their contribution to wider patterns of professional and commercial performance.[9] At the very least, the situating of writers like Wroth, Fane, and the Cavendishes in a circle of manuscript circulation indicates networks of affinity and textual exchange which provided the formative context for elite women's writing.[10] But it also pulls these texts away from the literary margins and allows for their direct influence on (as well as influence by) professional writers such as Ben Jonson and John Milton who interacted throughout their literary careers with these significant families and their regional 'producing houses'.

Whatever the actual or imagined location that shaped these women's literary productions, we are, in Lindsay Yakimyshyn's terms, dealing with dramatic and semi-dramatic works that were 'written and performed for the household, by household members, and in household spaces', and in this respect they are intensely informed by the physical and social aspects of those places, these 'producing houses' as I am labelling them here.[11] Part of what creates the enabling atmosphere for women in these producing houses to write and perform is certainly family associations with literature, and the attendant communities so essential to female literary agency in this period. In Wroth's

[7] Paul Salzman, '*Love's Victory*, Pastoral, Gender, and *As You Like It*', in Paul Salzman and Marion Wynne-Davies (eds), *Mary Wroth and Shakespeare* (London, 2014), 125–36, 127.

[8] The Dering-owned manuscript is Huntington MS HM600. For a detailed discussion of his household theatre, see the case study in my 'Making the Land Known: *Henry IV, Parts 1 and 2* and the Literature of Perambulation', in Claire Jowitt and David McInnis (eds), *Travel and Drama in Early Modern England* (Cambridge, 2018), 72–91, 84–7. See also Paul Salzman and Marion Wynne-Davies, 'Introduction', in Salzman and Wynne-Davies (eds), *Wroth and Shakespeare*, 1–5, 2, and Hannay, *Mary Sidney*, 220.

[9] For a wider discussion of the history and politics of scholarship on early modern women's writing, see this volume, Chapter 11, Ramona Wray, 'Receiving Early Modern Women's Drama'.

[10] Julie Crawford, *Mediatrix: Women, Politics and Literary Production in Early Modern England* (Oxford, 2014), 6. Michelle O'Callaghan's chapter in this volume on Isabella Whitney makes the case for her as a 'seemingly singular figure in the history of early modern's women writing' with her crafting of urban settings and personae (see this volume, Chapter 20, O'Callaghan, 'London and the Book Trade'); nevertheless there are intriguing links to be drawn between the focus on everyday lived experience that O'Callaghan traces in Whitney's poetry and the influence of estate life on the works of the elite women writers I am exploring here.

[11] Lindsay J. Yakimyshyn, 'Security and Instability: Mary Wroth, the Cavendish Sisters, and Early Stuart Household Plays', PhD Diss., University of Alberta, 2014, 18.

case, her uncle was a renowned poet and prose writer as a well as a courtier of note and she actively signals his influence in her mirroring choices of form, from her sonnet sequence *Pamphilia to Amphilanthus* which echoes Sir Philip Sidney's *Astrophil and Stella* to her pastoral prose romance *The Countess of Montgomery's Urania* (published 1621, and for which a 1620–1630 composed manuscript continuation is extant) which links to his *Countess of Pembroke's Arcadia.* Sidney's text explicitly honoured his sister, Wroth's aunt, Mary Sidney Herbert, Countess of Pembroke, who translated French tragedy. It is also of note that Wroth's father Robert was both a patron of music and the arts more generally and a practising poet.

Literary families inevitably meant literary collecting as a household activity and in this way the privileged households of the Sidneys, Fanes, and Cavendishes were enablers of female production through their provision of access to libraries, education, and regular exposure to intellectual networks and debate. Apethorpe Hall, Fane's family home, certainly had a Jonson 1616 Folio in its collection at some point in the seventeenth century, along with plays by Beaumont and Fletcher.[12] Jane Cavendish's poetry and letters clearly situate her in an active dialogue with household visitors, several of them notable literary figures whose work her father both collected and commissioned.[13] For Jane Cavendish and her sister Elizabeth, the family estates in Nottinghamshire were also a site of theatrical performance with two of Ben Jonson's specially written masques staged at Welbeck Abbey and Bolsover Castle in 1633 and 1634 respectively.[14] In the sisters' *The Concealed Fansyes* and *A Pastorall* we can see the influence of these events, whether this is the authors' direct memory of being in the audience or having heard about it from family members.[15]

A Pastorall includes, alongside a developed understanding of stage directions and use of properties, two anti-masques. This is a structure directly attributable to Jonson's development of the masque form and evident in his Midlands entertainments for the Cavendish family, but in particular derived from those works he created in collaboration with Queen Anna of Denmark at the Jacobean court. That we are working with a series of overlapping literary circles and communities of practice here, in which Jonson is often a recurring feature, is underscored by the fact that Rachel Fane's 'May Masque' includes an anti-masque of estate workers that has been interpreted through the frame

[12] O'Connor, 'Rachel Fane's May Masque', 93.

[13] Alexandra G. Bennett (ed.), *The Collected Works of Jane Cavendish* (London, 2018), 'Introduction', 2. All quotations from Cavendish will be from this edition, which uses the Bodleian Library manuscript, Oxford, Rawlinson MS Poet 16 as its copy text.

[14] Bennett says of *The King's Entertainment at Welbeck* and *Love's Welcome at Bolsover*: 'Though there is no evidence to guarantee that Jane would have seen the original productions of either ... she certainly could have read the texts for manuscript copies were kept in her father's library. Jonson's site-specific stagecraft, along with the plays of several of his contemporaries, would eventually influence her own dramatic writings'; *Collected Works*, 4.

[15] Both these co-authored dramatic writings by the Cavendish sisters are contained in Oxford, Bodleian Library, Rawlinson MS Poet 16.

of Jonsonian influence.[16] Furthermore, Mary Wroth had herself performed, dancing silently as was the norm for female courtiers at this early point in the masque's evolution, in *The Masque of Blackness* (1605). Masquing terminology and understanding permeates Wroth's texts, as Penny McCarthy has noted: in *Urania*, Lindamira, who has fallen from the queen's favour in a storyline that has parallels with Wroth's life story, is described at one point in these terms: 'remaining like one in a gay Masque, the night passed, they are in their old clothes, againe, and no appearance of what was'.[17] It is a vivid evocation of the ephemeral spectacle of courtly masquing, let alone of the precarious life of a Jacobean courtier.

For the Cavendish sisters, their inheritance of wider masquing traditions and form was further inflected by Elizabeth's marriage to John Egerton, Viscount Brackley and future second Earl of Bridgewater, in 1641. In 1634, Brackley had, along with his brother, his fifteen-year-old sister Lady Alice Egerton, and their music tutor Henry Lawes, performed in John Milton's *A Masque Presented at Ludlow Castle*. That Alice performed an extensive speaking part as the 'Lady' means that again we can register family precedents for the theatrical, and specifically female, agency evident in the work of the women writers being examined here.[18] Alice's younger brothers also had direct experience of court masques which they could bring to bear on the Ludlow production, having performed as pages in Thomas Carew's 1632 *Coelum Britannicum*. The Egerton household was another active collector of printed plays; the Earl's wife Lady Frances Stanley notably purchasing texts by Jonson among others.[19] Writing with performance scholar Susan Bennett, I have previously made the case that the Ludlow masque, usually studied as part of the singular authorial career of John Milton, is better viewed as a complex site-specific coproduction between Milton, Lawes, and the Egerton family. By adopting this approach, we begin to view this masque less as a stand-alone in a male author's canon than as part of the wider overlapping histories of family and household productions I am mapping here. Site-specific performance is, I would argue, a less limiting term than 'closet drama' which seems governed by an assumption of women's spatial (and by extension psychosocial) restrictions to the home-space. Site-specific performance situates the household-based dramatic work of early modern women in a far broader literary context of place-based writing.

Pioneering work by Jennifer Richards on cultures of voice in this period has redrawn our understanding of the significance of performative reading. There were many contexts for reading aloud in early modern England—from churches to universities, colleges, schools, theatres, ordinaries, and barbers. Many of these we might construct

[16] On the estate worker anti-masque in the 'May Masque' and the significance of the use of specific props, see O'Connor, 'Rachel Fane's May Masque', 101.

[17] Penny McCarthy, 'Autumn 1604: Documentation and Literary Coincidence' in Salzman and Wynne-Davies (eds), *Wroth and Shakespeare*, 37–46, 40.

[18] See Susan Bennett and Julie Sanders, 'Rehearsing Across Space and Place: Rethinking *A Masque Presented at Ludlow Castle*', in Anna Birch and Joanne Tompkins (eds), *Performing Site-Specific Theatre: Politics, Place, Practice* (London, 2012), 37–53.

[19] See Bennett and Sanders, 'Rehearsing Across Space and Place', 38.

as distinctly masculine spaces but the practices learned in the early modern schoolroom also found purchase in middling to large households and we need therefore to factor this in as part of the productive learning space of young women as well as men.[20] Alice Egerton's acting and musical learning alongside her brothers is again a salient reference point and clearly helped to shape the literary content and dramatic form of the Ludlow *Masque*. Richards' research invites us, then, to reimagine the dramatic text not only as material artefact but as an immersive experience and 'social event'.[21] Even if quasi-dramatic writings by women were not granted a theatrical performance, she stresses that we should not regard the reading experience simply as precursor to 'full' performance but understand it on a continuum with their lived experiences of commercial drama in the London playhouses and wider masquing cultures.[22] Through their active reading cultures and spatial practices, the regional power bases of families such as the Cavendishes, Sidney-Wroths, Fanes, Derings, and Egerton-Brackleys, let alone the Newdigates and Stanleys, helped to foster women who were part of a dynamic national, as well as regional, exchange of ideas, words, and practice.[23]

What comes into view is a place-based and place-shaped, as well as place-making, understanding of influence and exchange, one in which women are active participants rather than passive bystanders. These influential families and their household 'bases of operation' are significant when unpacking the literary productions of these women but not solely as examples of daughters benefiting from patriarchal support.[24] The everyday lived experience and practice of these sites was a crucial foundry for the writings of these women. These households were complex sites and, as Crawford stresses, 'by no means simply mutually supportive or hermetically sealed cultural encounters'.[25] The remainder of this chapter will focus, therefore, on the tensions as well as possibilities created by the material site in which these women produced their work.

[20] Jennifer Richards, *Voices and Books in the English Renaissance* (Oxford, 2019). Discussing 'the vocality of reading' (29), Richards observes that 'at the most basic level ... learning to read and perform in elite households was a family affair involving both male and female members' (116).

[21] Richards, *Voices and Books*, 14.

[22] I argue for this continuum elsewhere; see Julie Sanders, *The Cultural Geography of Early Modern Drama, 1620–1650* (Cambridge, 2011). Salzman, '*Love's Victory*' (132) observes that 'Wroth provides space for women on her stage, reflecting the way that performance extends beyond the professional theatre to allow for women's presence in various venues, from the court masque to private, or perhaps we should say, less public productions'.

[23] See Julie Sanders, 'Geographies of Performance in the Early Modern Midlands', in Susan Bennett and Mary Polito (eds), *Performing Environments: Site-Specificity in Medieval and Early Modern English Drama* (London, 2014), 119–37, 121. On the Newdigates, see M. J. Kidnie, 'Near Neighbours: Another Early Seventeenth-Century Manuscript of *The Humorous Magistrate*', *Renaissance Quarterly*, 52 (1999), 402–39.

[24] Crawford, *Mediatrix*, 15.

[25] Crawford, *Mediatrix*, 7.

SITE-SPECIFIC PRODUCTIONS

Theatrical writing is best considered as a social event, imagined or embodied in some way as or by acts of assembly. For early modern elite women their most regular site of assembly was the household; by extension, 'Even in the absence of any concrete evidence for a performance, it is logical to suppose that the scripts of figures such as Mary Sidney Herbert, Elizabeth Cary, Jane Cavendish, and Elizabeth Brackley were informed by the spatial practices of their family estates'.[26] Houses and the estates in which they nested were, as Susan Bennett and Mary Polito have argued, 'replete with different registers of legibility based on the ways an individual or a group interacted with (or had access to) that specific place.'[27] The dramatic writings of Wroth, Fane, and the Cavendish sisters all benefit therefore from the application of methodologies derived from more contemporary studies of site-specific performance. My case is that viewing these women's creative impulses through the lens of site-specific performance frees them from the implicit value judgements of previous categories of their work as closet or coterie drama. It releases agency and a very present sense of coproduction and mutual influence.[28]

Gay McAuley has argued that place is more than simply a venue in which to host a theatrical performance; rather, it:

> is involved in complex ways in the genesis of the work and even in its subject matter. The performance may be inspired by the place, or it may be a means of exploring and experiencing that place. In some cases the place is the pretext for the performance, which functions to celebrate or attempt to transform it; in others the performance may exploit the place for its own purposes and in still others it may play at the interface of the experience of the real and fictional.[29]

At different moments in the texts under review here McAuley's suppositions play themselves out. In thinking about *Love's Victory* and its association with Penshurst, and the wider symbolic and cultural capital of the Sidneys, we can see how Wroth was influenced by the literary precedents and romantic histories of her family. We see in her pastoral drama the interface between real and fictional that McAuley delineates. But there is something more quotidian and material in the relationship of this play to place which also speaks to McAuley's account of the ways in which site-specific theatre is inspired by and a pretext for exploring actual sites.

[26] Findlay, *Playing Spaces*, 17.

[27] Susan Bennett and Mary Polito, 'Thinking Site: An Introduction', in Bennett and Polito (eds), *Performing Environments*, 1–13, 6.

[28] See Bennett and Sanders, 'Rehearsing Across Space and Place', 50, for an extended version of this argument that the 'turn to site-specificity' enables a more active understanding of early modern household and estate-based theatre as hybrid, peripatetic, and coproduced.

[29] Gay McAuley, 'Place in the Performance Experience', *Modern Drama*, 46 (2003), 598–613 (599). See also Bennett and Polito, 'Thinking Site', 7.

The archival record of Rachel Fane is a helpful point of entry to analysing how daily household operations helped to shape both the content and casting of her family entertainments, let alone the active cognitive associations audience members would bring to any performance. There are multiple internal references in her entertainments to practical aspects of household management—from preserving fruits to the making of bread and sugar loaves to needlework—and the 'May Masque' deploys a number of farm tools such as mattocks, spades, and ladders as props that would have been readily available on the Apethorpe estate:[30]

> Enter . . . A sheperd in a gray cote and dog in won
> hand & sheep hooke in ye other; a man fooling
> him wt a tabier & pipe, in a red wascote a gray
> payre of breches, won fooled him we {x} matucks
> & spades & companye bearing a maypole
> wit outhers fooling wt laders & outher toles.[31]

Marion O'Connor notes how these 'appurtenances' are 'put straight to work as pastoral signifiers'.[32] These allusions to kitchen and farm work and other spatially prescribed activities map intimately onto the spatial locations that were either the actual venue for, or proximate to, the performance space of the Great Hall at Apethorpe. The Hall 'was close to the housekeeper's room, the still-room and the store-room, [and consequently Fane's] scenes of women's work take on the power to transform the everyday'.[33] Here are both the everyday and transformative aspects that McAuley cites as being central to place-specific theatre. In the same way that the casting of household servants and family members mobilises spectatorial associations with the working life and operations of the household, so this referencing of household and estate work mobilises the active production of meaning central to site-specific performance. Use of family-owned clothes and properties enabled reimaginings of the everyday that would further charge the space in which these dramas were embodied through shared readings or performance. As Bennett and Polito note, what women's household theatre does is draw attention to the inherent theatricality of a normal residential property, 'a set of coordinates in which all kinds of social performances happen'.[34]

[30] O'Connor, 'Rachel Fane's May Masque', 103, notes that the dramatic fragment that precedes the May masque in the notebook talks of domestic matters such as 'petticoat-sewing and apple preserving'; see also Findlay, *Playing Spaces*, 42.

[31] Rachel Fane, 'May Masque', Kent Archive Office, Sackville MSS KAO U269, sig. 2r, col a (transcription from O'Connor, 'Rachel Fane's May Masque', 106).

[32] O'Connor, 'Rachel Fane's May Masque', 102.

[33] O'Connor, 'Rachel Fane's May Masque', 43.

[34] Bennet and Polito, 'Thinking Site', 6.

In Fane's family entertainments, as in the quasi-dramatic writings of the Cavendish sisters which we will unpack in more detail in the next section, we witness directly the household functioning as performance venue, and therefore oscillating between site of play and of work. This is heightened by the use of actual rooms for the performance but also by the suggestion that audience members transport their minds to other nearby spaces, interior and exterior. In Wroth's *Love's Victory*, a self-conscious pastoral as we have already established, this associational spatial technique extends to the estate gardens and cultivated walks as well as the nearby River Medway which flowed through the Penshurst estate. In *Love's Victory* we hear of 'Meadows, paths, grass, flowers, / Walks, birds, brook ...' (1.2.17–18). In this moment, Philisses overtly maps his surroundings, conjuring perhaps for an indoors performance a very real sense of the cartography of the landed estate just outside. This is a veritable dramatic survey, bringing the outside in for spectators familiar with that real landscape, at the same time as mourning through traditional pastoral tropes Philisses' (presumed) unrequited love for Musella. Throughout Wroth's play, Petrarchan discourse is both utterly literary and idealistic and yet physically tied to the material landscapes in which the action is presumed to take place.[35]

As well as meadows, woodlands, and brooks, gardens, walks, parterres, arbours, and groves, are specifically relevant sites to *Love's Victory* and its settings, especially if we are imagining a Penshurst estate performance in the 1610s. This imagery once again functions metaphorically and mythologically and is familiar from other works in Wroth's canon such as *Pamphilia to Amphilanthus*, where labyrinths, mazes, and knot gardens inform the spatial awareness of the corona of sonnets. But these allusions also have direct links to the estates in which Wroth lived and worked. Additionally, these allusions in *Loves Victory* would have had Penshurst-specific resonance in a site-specific performance, many of them female inflected. Another presiding female influence at Penshurst was Wroth's mother, Barbara Gamage Sidney, Countess of Leicester.[36] She is directly mentioned in Jonson's 1611 poem-paean to the estate 'To Penshurst' ('Thy copse named of Gamage', l.19) and Findlay notes the ways in which Wroth's play draws attention to her bower and the long shady walk of trees which extant contemporary surveys indicate were important parts of the estate.[37] This makes sense of the play's emphasis on spaces of shady retreat at various act beginnings and Findlay suggests that many of the deictic references to 'This place' (1.1.78) imply the possibility of an al fresco performance.[38] In Act 1, Scene 3, for example, it is in the available shade that the women decide to share their various stories of love and to perform the female singing game:

[35] On links to family history, see Wynne Davies and Cerasano, *Renaissance Drama by Women*, 94, and Salzman, '*Love's Victory*', *passim*.

[36] Crawford, *Mediatrix*, 17.

[37] Findlay, *Playing Spaces*, 90. All references to Ben Jonson's poems and drama in this chapter are from *The Cambridge Works of Ben Jonson*, gen eds David Bevington, Martin Butler, and Ian Donaldson, 7 vols (Cambridge, 2012).

[38] Findlay, *Playing Spaces*, 92.

DALINA: The sun grows hot, 'twere best we did retire.
LISSIUS: There's good shade. (1.3.1–2)

Even if this was not an actual promenade performance—although similar kinds of hybrid indoor/outdoor performances have been posited for both the *Masque Presented at Ludlow* and *Love's Welcome at Bolsover*[39]—it is apt that these feminocentric estate spaces would be brought to mind at these specific junctures in any performance. Light and shade references can of course also be understood through a distinctly Petrarchan lens. Philisses' response to the women's instructions to find good shade is to claim in a self-dramatising aside that there is no shade possible for him: 'But here's a burning fire' (1.3.2). What intrigues me, however, is that the women characters are invariably associated with more realistic references and in turn with the very real passing of time that is being evoked. It is they who are rooted in place, a point that the final section of this chapter will argue is no literary coincidence. The women's scenes are intricately engaged with the passing of time, both in terms of marking the literal passing of the hours as registered by the peak of midday heat followed by failing light and via the idea of leisure time and practised recreation. In Act 2, Scene 1, Dalina suggests 'Let's play / At something while we yet have pleasing day' (1–2). We perhaps register here the potential for a staged reading or full production to connect in a very tangible way with the shared light of performance and the shifts in natural light that might occur. This could have been further heightened if there was an indoor/outdoor blend to the performance, but it is also possible to see the light-filled spaces such as the Hall at Penshurst or the Long Gallery at Apethorpe as receptive venues for this kind of wordplay.

Reflecting on stagings of *Love's Victory* at Penshurst, Findlay notes the ways in which the script invokes Penshurst as a geographical location in order to promote the Sidney family's wider reputation and their values of good estate management and neighbourliness that Jonson also espoused in 'To Penshurst'.[40] In the same way that Rachel Fane's use of props derived from real-life estate management, this play's discourse of shepherds and flocks of sheep is intrinsic to the pastoral mode but the lexicon of farming, as with the light/shade references, also introduces some highly practical resonances. This slippage from pastoral to everyday and back again situates the work of these women engaged in place-based writing in a wider context of influence and contribution than a specifically 'female' version of either pastoral or household drama. The interface of pastoral and georgic modes is not uncommon in pastoral drama. Shakespeare's *As You Like It* is a fine working example, with its carefully staged dialogues between Corin the shepherd and Touchstone the jester bringing courtly and practical values into debate with each other in the process. Nevertheless, an awareness of the Wroth-Sidney family locales from Penshurst to Wilton—which were sites of practical estates husbandry and sheep farming—suggests that the interplay of the literary and actual of the kind we

[39] See Sanders, *Cultural Geography*, 75–84, 104–7.
[40] Alison Findlay, '*Love's Victory* in Production at Penshurst', *Sidney Journal*, 34 (2016), 107–22.

are identifying in the work of the women in focus in this chapter might be especially pertinent to the experience of this kind of household theatre.[41] The remainder of this chapter focuses on a more detailed consideration of practical estate management and its presence in the writings of the Cavendish sisters, as well as of Wroth and Fane. This was an everyday fact of these women writers' lives and fed directly into their literary experimentations with both the pastoral form and place-based writing.

Tim Cresswell observes that 'places are constructed by people doing things'.[42] The dramatic writings of Wroth, Fane, and the Cavendish sisters, whether read aloud or partially or fully staged, 'constituted a route for transforming place into space' but they are also about 'people doing things' in both a heightened literary sense and a practical everyday context. Their dramatic work manifests itself via an active understanding of the practice of place.[43] Underpinning these efforts, we identify a strategic but also risky claiming of household and estate space by these literary women.

PRODUCTIVE ESTATES

Wroth's *Love's Victory* can best be understood, then, not only through intertextual relationships with the work of Jonson and her famous Sidney family relations, but also as a site-specific work imbued with the spatial practices that informed family life on the Kent estate. Julie Crawford's work has been instrumental in highlighting the empowering but also unstable positions for elite women as part of these powerful dynasties and the architectural entities they occupied. It was often not these educated 'daughters of the house' who inherited the estates they had cared for and contributed to over sustained periods of time, but more often their brothers and cousins. Many daughters ceded control of any rights to family lands and properties to their husbands upon marriage, and wives in turn often lost status when they became widows or, conversely, inherited the crushing responsibility of family debts incurred by male partners. Legal battles for control of estates characterise the life narratives of significant Jacobean women such as Lady Anne Clifford, Lady Christian Bruce Cavendish, Countess of Devonshire, and indeed Wroth herself.

Wroth was forced to sue to Queen Anna of Denmark to grant her the freedom to improve the estate at Loughton Hall after Sir Robert Wroth's death in the wake of the considerable debts he bequeathed her. She would eventually hold the estate in her own name, but it was a fight. It is a story we see repeated several times in the archive.[44]

[41] Wilton House, for example, was 'an estate dominated by sheep farming'; Findlay, *Playing Spaces*, 81.

[42] Tim Cresswell, *Place: A Short Introduction* (Oxford, 2004), 37; cited in Bennett and Polito, 'Thinking Site', 9.

[43] Findlay, *Playing Spaces*, 3.

[44] See, for example, the story of debt and lawsuits bequeathed to her by her husband, recounted in Christian Bruce Cavendish, Countess of Devonshire's letters to William Cavendish, Earl of Newcastle,

Writers such as Jonson were alert to this fact: his 1616 play *The Devil is an Ass*, written at the time when Wroth and Fane among others were embarking on their literary and theatrical endeavours, has at its heart a woman disinvested of her lands by marital law.[45] That Jonson could fashion commercial drama from this material suggests that this was a common enough situation to be recognisable to audiences but also that his personal exposure to the lived reality of women such as Clifford and Wroth (Jonson dedicated his 1610 play *The Alchemist* to Wroth, and Clifford was known to him through her performances in several of his masques) had a profound impact upon him.

Women who found themselves enabled by being educated on wealthy regional estates were also genuinely engaged with the daily practices of estate management.[46] Lady Margaret Hoby's Yorkshire diaries depict her in a variety of sociospatial encounters on the family estates, for example receiving corn in the granary and visiting fields where the hay was being brought in as well as collecting rents and paying wages.[47] Crawford is keen to stress that these women were equally bound up with the national political issues of the day—'Women's governance of great estates . . . was not only a matter of money and ground-level husbandry', she says—but I remain interested in how that 'ground level husbandry' makes itself felt in their estate-based writing.[48]

In reading the specific example of *Love's Victory*, we need to read beyond pastoral tropes and ludic play in the world of shepherds and shepherdesses and see this as a play informed by the real work of caring for a flock. If we accept the active spectatorship of site-specific performance argued for earlier, then we are perhaps less inclined to view this material simply as generic convention but rather as important detail pertaining to lived experience that is to be relied on as part of any audience response. The comic character of Rustic is key to making this case. Lissius speaks in conventional pastoral discourse: 'For we should women love but as our sheep, / Who being kind and gentle give us ease' (2.1.67–8); but it is Rustic's pragmatic responses that offer up a more practical understanding of estate operations, where sheep are part of the national economy of the wool trade. His analogies are throughout rooted in this aspect of estate production ('whiter than lamb's wool' (1.3.57)), undercutting the Petrarchan metaphors of the other lovers, while bringing the outside in in terms of a great hall performance by conjuring up the working fields and pastures just outside: 'Thy eyes do play / Like goats with hay' (1.3.61–2). Comic when placed in juxtaposition with the lover-protagonists though this

University of Nottingham Library, Portland Papers Pw1. See also Victor Slater, Cavendish (née Bruce), Christian [Christiana], Countess of Devonshire, *ODNB*.

45 Helen Ostovich, 'Hell for Lovers: Shades of Adultery in *The Devil is an Ass*', in Julie Sanders with Kate Chedgzoy and Susan Wiseman (eds), *Refashioning Ben Jonson: Gender, Politics and the Jonsonian Canon* (London, 1998), 155–82.

46 In a related chapter in this volume, Anna Reynolds emphasises the knowledge of the practicalities of the domestic environment that informed the thinking of elite, middling, and lower status women (and by extension their touchpoints with literary creation in its intellectual and material forms). See this volume, Chapter 45, Anna Reynolds, 'Material Texts'.

47 Crawford, *Mediatrix*, 20.

48 Crawford, *Mediatrix*, 17.

material is, there is something else here that interweaves the play with practical place-based understanding.

In Act 4, Scene 1, Rustic enters just as Philisses and Musella declare love for each other to say he has been 'Marking [Tending] some cattle and asleep I fell' (146); Musella playfully echoes his language of tending for the estate flocks and herds (and the hard labour involved there is signified by his exhaustion) to describe her romantic encounter: 'And I was seeking of a long-lost lamb, / Which now I found, ev'n as along you came' (4.1.147–8). Alongside the elevated pastoral, what I am suggesting is equally worth noting here are these drumbeat references to the working nature of the estate on which the play is set (and in performance perhaps being actively staged). Rustic's world is a practical one, more influenced by the georgic tradition, where coats need mending and where loss of property is a serious thing:

> What call you love? I've been to trouble moved,
> As when my best cloak hath by chance been torn,
> I have lived wishing till it mended were.
> And but so lovers do; nor could forebear
> To cry if I my bag or bottle lost,
> As lovers do who by their loves are crossed. (2.1.86–91)

For the same reasons, he can scarcely bear the lovers' games of wit which are the product of copious leisure time:

> Truly, I cannot riddle, I was not taught
> These tricks of wit; my thoughts ne'er higher wrought
> Than how to mark a beast, or drive a cow
> To feed, or else with art to hold a plough
> Which if I knew, you surely soon would find
> A matter more of worth than these odd things. (4.1.391–6)

Rustic's expertise is not simply dismissed in these comic interjections and comparisons. As with Corin's ripostes to Touchstone in *As You Like It*, there is implicit recognition of the value of local place-based knowledge. Without the skill to drive a cow to feed present in their community of practice, the privileged existence of the Sidney-Wroths would soon face economic hardship and challenge. Rachel Fane's equally active references to the objects and practices of women's household work in her family entertainments has already been registered. The rural anti-masque that commences her May Masque makes direct allusion through its pastoral character types of shepherds and shepherdesses to family members' roles in the management of their Northamptonshire estate.[49] Another pastoral drama (co)authored on a significant household estate is *A Pastorall*, created by Jane Cavendish and Elizabeth Brackley when they were running the Welbeck Abbey

[49] Findlay, *Playing Spaces*, 100. The household actively employed shepherds in 1627.

estate for their father, William Cavendish. In the 1640s, William was either embroiled in military affairs or exiled to mainland Europe. The text of the sisters' household drama actively makes meaning from household practices, incorporating the agricultural and dairying routines that must have determined their responsibilities and coping rituals at the time. Again, we see the choice of pastoral by place-based women writers having its roots both in literary tradition and highly localised practice.

The absent patriarch who looms over *A Pastorall* was himself a great patron of plays and masques (not least the aforementioned Jonsonian creations staged on the family properties in the 1630s) and a playwright in his own right. But his influence can also be felt in this more practical domain. The language of tenant farming informed the negative republican political discourse which attached to William Cavendish at this time. Alexandra Bennett has demonstrated how he was directly criticised for driving poor labourers off their tenant farms—'their Sheepe, Oxen, and other Cattell, being driven away, and sold before their face'—and also how the troops he led on the Civil War battlefields were described as 'Newcastle lambs'.[50] What might seem standard pastoral tropes of lambing and the tending of sheep and cattle in the sisters' semi-dramatic work accrete very localised and at times politicised meanings as a result. As also seen in Wroth's oeuvre, female-authored household dramatic writing invites us to be very active readers of cues and coded references.

The two Jonsonian-influenced anti-masques of *A Pastorall* are of particular interest in any place-based reading. As already noted, Jane Cavendish and Elizabeth Brackley's use of the anti-masque form is indebted to their exposure to wider masquing conventions, but it is important to see how these are, certainly in the case of *A Pastorall*, very much remade through the sisters' direct experiences on the family's Nottinghamshire estates. In a manner akin to Jonson's deliberately discordant anti-masques with their communities of 'outsiders' from traveller gypsy communities to witches to labouring artisans, Cavendish and Brackley incorporate decidedly non-elite and potentially subversive voices into their work.[51] The first anti-masque ushers in a group of witches who are in their activities not only a palpable threat to livestock on the farm, to 'Kine & sheepe' but also to its food security (82). The witches' malign interventions have set local families at war with each other. In the second anti-masque, we also receive a dialect-strewn thick description of gossiping local neighbours involved in a local illicit economy of foodstuffs being smuggled in baskets out of households. Once again these are scenes that deliberately juxtapose the pastoral mode with comic realism. This is a highly place-based version of witches' *maleficium*—the harm they can do is to farmsteads, injuring livestock, disrupting processes in the dairy, and therefore the essential food supply chain of cheese, milk, and butter. And this is the direct subject of the neighbours' discourse in the second anti-masque: 'But these Witches, out upon them they can cunier [conjure] our Kine & sheepe from us' (82). The song that follows elaborates on this theme:

50 Bennett, *Collected Works*, 16.

51 On non-elite women's writing, see this volume, Chapter 20, Michelle O'Callaghan, 'London and the Book Trade' and this volume, Chapter 38, Susan Wiseman, 'Non-Elite Networks and Women'.

Naunt Henn, Gossip Pratt, Goodman Hay, and Goodman Rye—even the nomenclature is grounded in the livestock and growing regimes of the estate—account for their very real losses:

> HE: I have lost my melch Cow
> PR: And I have lost my Sow.
> RY: And for my Corne I cannot keepe,
> HA: Nether can I my pritty sheepe.
> HE: And I have lost fowre dozen of Eggs
> PR: My Pigs are gone, & all their Heads. (83)

The reference to, and anxiety about, empty purses at the end of the song is palpable:

> RY: Since that wee haue noe plenty
> HA: And our Purses, they are empty. (83)

Writ large in these moments of the sisters' pastoral are the brutal realities of siege and lockdown. These charged aspects of place-based works by women sit in tension with the pastoral idyll which is the framework through which their household theatre tends to be viewed. The one does not cancel out the other, but the productive tension registered in the Cavendish sisters' creation has deep kinship to the version of *Loves Victory* I have been advancing in its hybridity and blending of the pragmatic, political, and literary.

Our ways of reading women's writing are themselves steeped in a form of gender politics as well as exclusionary and inclusionary approaches to place-based writing. Categories and epistemologies of the amateur are used to render some of this work 'secondary' or peripheral to the mainstream. New ways of accounting for women's work in this period enable a different point of entry to the production of theatre by 'daughters of the house': 'the labors they practiced, enabled and oversaw—... estates ... relied on the unseen and often highly exploited labour of others—were rarely separable into ready categories'.[52] Literature and theatre, like dairy goods and wool, are local household products.

FURTHER READING

Bennett, Susan and Mary Polito (eds). *Performing Environments: Site-Specificity in Medieval and Early Modern English Drama*. London, 2014.

Birch, Anna and Joanne Tompkins (eds). *Performing Site-Specific Theatre: Politics, Place, Practice*. London, 2012.

Cerasano, S. P. and Marion Wynne Davies (eds). *Renaissance Drama by Women: Texts and Documents*. New York, 1996.

[52] Crawford, *Mediatrix*, 24.

Crawford, Julie. *Mediatrix: Women, Politics and Literary Production in Early Modern England.* Oxford, 2014.
Findlay, Alison. *Playing Spaces in Early Modern Women's Drama.* Cambridge, 2006.
Richards, Jennifer. *Voices and Books in the English Renaissance: A New History of Reading.* Oxford, 2019.
Sanders, Julie. *The Cultural Geography of Early Modern Drama, 1620–1650.* Cambridge, 2011.
Wroth, Mary. *Love's Victory.* Alison Findlay, Philip Sidney, and Michael G. Brennan (eds). Manchester, 2021.
Wynne-Davies, Marion. '"My Seeled Chamber and Dark Parlour Room": The English Country House and Renaissance Women Dramatists', in S. P. Cerasano and Marion Wynne-Davies (eds), *Readings in Renaissance Women's Drama.* London, 1998, 60–8.

CHAPTER 24

CHANGING PLACES

Relocating the Court Masque in Early Modern Women's Writing

LAURA L. KNOPPERS

Gerrit van Honthorst's masque-like 1628 painting, *Apollo and Diana*, depicts Charles I as Apollo, god of art and learning, and Queen Henrietta Maria as the virgin goddess Diana, seated on a cloud as they welcome the allegorised figures of the Seven Liberal Arts (see Figure 24.1).[1] The royal couple's costumes and starlight crowns (a half-moon for Henrietta Maria and a sun for Charles I), as well as their elevated cloud-like seat, evoke the spectacle, light, and splendour of a Stuart court masque.[2]

Yet, arguably, two focal points vie for the viewer's attention in Honthorst's *Apollo and Diana*. While the king and queen appear illuminated in the upper-left corner, Honthorst places George Villiers, Duke of Buckingham and likely commissioner of the painting, in the centre of the composition, along with the personated Seven Liberal Arts who follow in his train. Buckingham, a favourite of King Charles as he had been of King James, dresses as the classical god Mercury, a role he had earlier taken in court masques. Overhead, two winged cherubs are poised to give Buckingham a laurel crown. Envy and Hate seem banished not by monarchical virtues but by Buckingham's own entrance. In moving the court masque into an elaborate, seemingly complimentary painting, Buckingham places himself centre stage.

The dynamic interaction, even tension, in Honthorst's painting offers an important perspective on four early modern women who, I will argue, likewise relocate the place and language of court masques into their writing. This chapter will consider women

[1] My description of Honthorst, *Apollo and Diana*, is drawn from J. Richard Judson and Rudolf Ekkart, *Gerrit van Honthorst, 1592–1656* (Doornspijk, 1999), 107–8, plates 45, 45a.

[2] On the masque, see Stephen Orgel, *The Illusion of Power: Political Theatre in the English Renaissance* (Berkeley, CA, 1975); Stephen Orgel and Roy Strong, *Inigo Jones: The Theatre of the Stuart Court*, 2 vols (Berkeley, CA, 1973); and David Bevington and Peter Holbrook (eds), *The Politics of the Stuart Court Masque* (Cambridge, 1998).

FIGURE 24.1 Gerrit van Honthorst, *Apollo and Diana* (1628). Royal Collection Trust © Her Majesty Queen Elizabeth II, 2020/Bridgeman Images.

within elite courtly networks, from Mary Sidney Herbert, Countess of Pembroke (closely aligned with Queen Elizabeth I and Queen Anna of Denmark) and Sidney's niece, Lady Mary Wroth (participant in court masques under Queen Anna), to Aemilia Lanyer (of more humble origins, but appealing to Queen Anna and court women for patronage), to Margaret Cavendish, Duchess of Newcastle (maid of honour to Queen Henrietta Maria in Oxford and Paris and part of elite aristocracy after her 1645 marriage to William Cavendish, then-Marquis of Newcastle).

In recreating the place of the court, these women draw on the masque as a vital performance space for elite girls and women under the influence of Anna of Denmark and Henrietta Maria of France. Scholars have shown how, by sponsoring and staging all-female masques and pastoral entertainments, both queens promoted their own authority, aligning themselves with Continental courts and furthering their religious, cultural, and political agendas. Female masque performance also gave visibility and agency to women within the court, enabling their own expressivity and feminine creation of meaning through dance, costume, music, and (in a few cases) speech. Female bodies on the masque stage were both structured by, and a potential threat to, court conventions and gendered hierarchies.[3]

[3] See the groundbreaking work of Clare McManus, *Women on the Renaissance Stage: Anna of Denmark and Female Masquing in the Stuart Court, 1590–1619* (Manchester, 2002); Clare McManus (ed.),

The queen's court was not only a material place but also a symbolic locale that facilitated elite women's cultural agency, performativity, and self-representation more broadly.[4] Most pertinent to my interests, the place of the masque manifests itself in surprising literary genres: Sidney's psalm translation; Lanyer's devotional poetry; Wroth's pastoral prose fiction; and Cavendish's utopia. Exegetically and poetically innovative in her masque-like depictions of the heavenly court, Mary Sidney evokes a sense of place for devotional purposes. In *Salve Deus Rex Judaeorum*, Aemilia Lanyer strategically places her would-patrons as recipients of a divine entertainment. By purposefully misplacing masques in her *Countess of Montgomery's Urania* (1621), Mary Wroth underscores the failure to uphold courtly virtues. Margaret Cavendish's nostalgic and utopian relocation of the masque transforms centre and periphery, displaying aristocratic virtues.

Strikingly, all of these court-connected and (except for Lanyer) aristocratic women write largely from places outside the court, and their writing establishes new or transformed connections. Residing at the primary Pembroke estate at Wilton, Sidney constructs a heavenly court as model for the earthly one. Living in financial straits in London, Lanyer makes the court masque a new locale in which social relations are reconstituted and transformed. While she was largely removed from court after the death of her husband in 1614, Wroth's misplaced masques continue to engage courtly codes as a means of self-fashioning and social critique. Cavendish, exiled with her husband on the Continent or, after 1660, retired into the countryside, stages a display of aristocratic loyalty that not only displaces but implicitly critiques an ungrateful monarch. If, in Honthorst's masque-like painting, the figure of Buckingham threatens to overshadow the monarchs whom he ostensibly serves and flatters, we will see that by changing the place of the court masque, these women even more radically and boldly reconfigure their own places in and beyond the world of the court.[5]

MARY SIDNEY: PLACES IN A HEAVENLY COURT

While the court connections of Mary Sidney have long been noted, that relation has often been characterised in oppositional terms. Scholars have focused on how Sidney

Women and Culture at the Courts of the Stuart Queens (New York, 2003); and Karen Britland, *Drama at the Courts of Queen Henrietta Maria* (Cambridge, 2006).

[4] See especially Clare McManus, 'Introduction: The Queen's Court', in McManus (ed.), *Women and Culture*, 1–17.

[5] I draw on the three meanings of place (locale, sense of place, and location) articulated in John A. Agnew, *Place and Politics: The Geographical Mediation of State and Society* (Winchester, MA, 1987). See also Tim Cresswell, 'Place; Part I', in John A. Agnew and James S. Duncan (eds), *The Wiley-Blackwell Companion to Human Geography* (Oxford, 2011), 235–44.

promotes the international Protestantism of the Dudley–Sidney alliance through implicit admonition of Queen Elizabeth and through stress on court envy and backbiting in her translations of the Psalms.[6] Yet, the countess's connections at court were deep and long lasting, and I would argue that Sidney uses the language of the court and the court masque more centrally and constructively than has been recognised. Depicting places in a heavenly court, Sidney engenders a new devotional subjectivity in herself and in her readers.

The Sidney faction was powerful in the Elizabethan court, with the countess's uncle, the Earl of Leicester, as the queen's favourite and sometime suitor. Sidney's mother was a close intimate of Elizabeth I before her disfigurement from smallpox (the result of nursing Elizabeth herself with the disease). Elizabeth wrote a warm invitation for Mary to join her court after the death of Mary's sister, Ambrosia, who had been herself a lady-in-waiting. It is well known that Mary spent two years in Elizabeth's court before marrying the powerful William Herbert, Earl of Pembroke, some thirty years her senior. Later, she would write a fulsome letter to Queen Elizabeth asking for a place in court for her son William.[7]

Under Queen Anna and King James, the widowed Sidney was less frequently at court, but her family members remained highly visible. Sidney's two sons, William and Philip, were much favoured by James, and frequently participated in court masques. William's marriage to Mary Talbot was celebrated lavishly at court, including with a masque, and James honoured Philip in turn by making him the Earl of Montgomery. Sidney's two daughters-in-law, Mary Talbot and Susan de Vere, danced in the queen's *Masque of Blackness*; De Vere became a great favourite of the queen, and participated in five of the eight masques for which records are extant. Robert Sidney, Mary's brother and father of Lady Mary Wroth, served as Queen Anna's Lord Chamberlain, and Wroth herself danced in the queen's *Masque of Blackness* and sat with the royal spectators for *Masque of Beauty*.[8]

The Sidney Psalter, for which Mary completed the translations (Psalms 45–150) begun by her brother Philip (Psalms 1–44), was not published until the nineteenth century, but it circulated widely in manuscript. For this audience, and for an envisioned royal audience, Sidney uses language of the court and of the courtly masque far more often than in earlier psalms translations.[9] A comparison of the vocabulary of the Book of Common

[6] See, for example, Margaret P. Hannay, '"Doo What Men May Sing": Mary Sidney and the Tradition of Admonitory Dedication', in Margaret P. Hannay (ed.), *Silent but for the Word: Tudor Women as Patrons, Translators, and Writers of Religious Works* (Kent, OH, 1985), 149–165 and Margaret P. Hannay, '"Princes You as Men Must Dy": Genevan Advice to Monarchs in the *Psalmes* of Mary Sidney', *English Literary Renaissance*, 19 (1989), 22–41.

[7] On Sidney's biography, see Margaret P. Hannay, *Philip's Phoenix: Mary Sidney, Countess of Pembroke* (Oxford, 1990).

[8] See Hannay, *Philip's Phoenix* and Leeds Barroll, *Anna of Denmark, Queen of England: A Cultural Biography* (Philadelphia, PA, 2001), ch. 4.

[9] Sidney writes two dedicatory poems to Queen Elizabeth, anticipating the queen's visit to Wilton House in 1599. See Michael G. Brennan, 'The Queen's Proposed Visit to Wilton House in 1599 and

Prayer Psalter, the Geneva Bible, and the Bèze-Marot French *Psaumes* shows much more usage of the words 'court', 'royal', 'king', 'queen', 'grace', 'present' (royal gifts), and 'seat' (throne). Language unique (or unique in its courtly sense) to the Sidney Psalter includes 'attend' or 'attending', 'traine', 'state', 'entertaine', 'honor', 'viands', 'check-role', 'suit', and 'propp' (stage property for a masque such as a throne).[10]

Envisioning particular court places in her royal psalms and psalms of divine praise, Sidney not only articulates her elite class identity but forges common ground with Queen Elizabeth and with a scribal audience. While other translations allegorise the celebration of Solomon's marriage to an Egyptian princess in Psalm 45 as representing the marriage of Christ and the Church, Sidney evokes courtly spaces. In her praise of the king, Sidney adds language of 'honor', 'triumph', and of a courtly train ('thie breathing odors all thie traine excel'; 32; *Psalmes* 39). She describes the king's women as 'Daughters of kings among thie courtlie band' (33), compared to the Geneva's 'thy honorable wives', and the Psalter's 'honorable women'. Sidney counsels the new queen to 'with awe ... entertaine' her husband, while receiving suitors herself: 'richest nations moe / with humble sute thie Roiall grace to gaine, / to thee shall doe such homage as they owe' (44, 46–8), in contrast to 'make thir supplication' (Psalter) and 'do homage' (Geneva).

Even more striking, the stanza describing the new queen and her women evokes resplendent court costume and the politics of place:

> This Queen that can a king hir father call,
>   doth only shee in upper garment shine?
> Naie, under clothes, and what shee weareth all,
>   golde is the stuffe the fasshion arte divine,
>   brought to the king in robe imbrodred fine,
>   hir maides of honor shall on hir attend:
>   with such, to whome more favoure shall assigne
>   in neerer place their happie daies to spend. (45.49–56; *Psalmes* 39–40)

Sidney adds the courtly terms 'attend' and 'maides of honor' (the first usage in the *OED*), rather than 'virgins' (Psalter and Geneva). She inserts the telling detail that the most favoured ladies are assigned a 'neerer place' to the queen, resonating with her own time—as well as the variable success of her daughters-in-law—at court.

Sidney also consistently figures God himself in courtly and even masque-like terms, riding on the clouds driving his enemies before him, attended by followers or a courtly train. In her Psalm 97, God comes to reign in a triumph of spectacle and power:

the "Sidney Psalms"', in Margaret P. Hannay (ed.), *Mary Sidney, Countess of Pembroke* (Surrey, 2009), 175–201.

[10] Mary Sidney Herbert, *Psalmes*, in Margaret P. Hannay, Noel J. Kinnamon, and Michael G. Brennan (eds), *The Collected Works of Mary Sidney Herbert, Countess of Pembroke*, 2 vols (Oxford, 1998), vol. 2.

Cloudes him round on all sides,
and pitchy darknesse hides.
  Justice and judgment stand
  as propps on either hand,
whereon his throne abides. (5–9; *Psalmes* 146)

Her Psalm 135 replaces the generic verb 'stand' of the Geneva and the Psalter with a picture of courtly servants 'whose attendance in [God's] howse is shown, / and in the courtes before his howse we see' (3–4; *Psalmes* 228).

Sidney depicts herself as attending upon God, like a maid-of-honour waiting on a monarch. Her Psalm 73 reads 'but as I was, yet did I still attend, / still follow thee' (67–8; *Psalmes* 94). In Psalm 86, she describes herself as one 'who in thy service have attended / and of thy handmaid am descended' (39–40; *Psalmes* 126). In Psalm 138, Sidney envisions a courtly space within which she—like the angels—serves a divine monarch: 'Ev'n before kings by thee as gods commended, / and Angells all, by whom thou are attended, / in harty tunes I will thy honor tell' (1–3; *Psalmes* 233). Sidney uniquely imagines that the 'pallace where thy holines doth dwell, / shall be the place, where falling downe before thee, / with reverence meete, I prostrate will adore thee' (4–6). Sidney's *Psalmes* activate a courtly space that correlates with her Dedicatory poems to Queen Elizabeth. In 'Even Now that Care', Sidney imagines the Psalter itself as a royal gift, from King David to Elizabeth: 'A King should onely to a Queene bee sent / Gods loved choise unto his chosen love' (53–4; *Collected Works* 1.103). Translating the Psalms is Sidney's 'handmaids task', encouraged by the queen's regard, 'that light / which lively lightsome Court, and Kingdome cheeres' (90, 91–2; *Collected Works* 1.104). Relocating the masque into her Psalms translation for devotional purposes, Sidney stands as a devout handmaid before her earthly queen, and before her heavenly Lord.

AEMILIA LANYER: PLACING PATRONS

In her *Salve Deus Rex Judaeorum* (1611), Aemilia Lanyer praises Margaret Russell, Countess of Cumberland, that 'Thou from the Court to the Countrie art retir'd, / Leaving the world, before the world leaves thee'.[11] Yet despite this seeming rejection, the tropes and figures of the court masque pervade Lanyer's work, from the language of attendance and entertainment, to noblewomen figured as classical goddesses, to the allegorised virtues of Christ himself. While gender and, to a lesser extent, religion have dominated critical conversation about Lanyer, I want to suggest that class and courtly codes also crucially shape her space of female performance and patronage.

[11] Aemilia Lanyer, *Salve Deus Rex Judaeorum*, in Susanne Woods (ed.), *The Poems of Aemilia Lanyer* (Oxford, 1993), 58 (lines 161–2). References to Lanyer's poems will be from this edition.

Although she came from humble origins, Lanyer herself had earlier experience of the court. As a young woman, she became the mistress of Henry Cary, Lord Hunsdon, powerful Lord Chamberlain to Elizabeth I; when, after several years, Lanyer became pregnant with Hunsdon's child, she was married off to another court musician, Alfonso Lanyer. She seems to have spent time in the household of Susan Bertie, Dowager Countess of Kent, and she was unusually well educated for a woman not of the upper class. Lanyer's husband apparently squandered her dowry, and, by 1611, when she published her *Salve Deus Rex Judaeorum*, Lanyer was in financial straits.[12]

Lanyer situates Queen Anna and a number of aristocratic women as honoured masque participants and recipients. In 'To the Queenes Most Excellent Majestie', Lanyer links Queen Anna with the classical goddess Pallas Athena (whom she had personated in Samuel Daniel's 1604 masque, *Vision of the Twelve Goddesses*), as well as with Juno and Venus. Lanyer depicts Anna sitting in state as the 'Muses doe attend upon your Throne' (19; *Poems* 4). Artists, sylvan gods, and satyrs likewise pay homage to the queen, whom even 'shining Cynthia with her nymphs attend' (23). Like a monarch to whom a masque is presented, Anna will be the 'welcomest guest' at the 'feast' Eve herself will present; in turn, Anna looks down, resplendent: 'From your bright spheare of greatnes where you sit, / Reflecting light to all those glorious stars / That wait upon your Throane' (25–7).

Lanyer offers laudatory addresses in masque-like terms to eleven other women, for a total of twelve; significantly, the same distinctive number as the female dancers in Anna's masques (e.g., *Twelve Goddesses*).[13] She depicts other dedicatees and hoped-for patrons as likewise seated, honoured, and entertained by classical gods. In a dream vision, Lanyer imagines Mary Sidney, Countess of Pembroke, seated in Honour's chair, and surrounded by virgins who 'with due reverence [her] / Did entertaine, according to that state / Which did belong unto her Excellence' (30–2; *Poems* 23). In a masque-like spectacle, the goddess Bellona descends in a chariot drawn by four dragons and likewise honours Sidney.

In turn, Lanyer guides her dedicatees themselves to wait or attend upon the main masque, featuring God himself both as the victorious deity of the Psalms and the grieving and suffering Christ, defined by allegorised virtues. *Salve Deus* proper opens with Queen Elizabeth ('Cynthia') having ascended to heaven, 'Where Saints and Angells do attend her Throne, / And she gives glorie unto God alone' (7–8; *Poems* 51). The Passion of Christ itself features allegorised virtues and an antimasque of evil. Lanyer depicts Mary, Christ's 'woefull Mother', as 'wayting on her Sonne' (1009; *Poems* 94); the 'beauty of heaven and earth' being in the grave, the '*Maries* doe with pretious balmes attend' the tomb (1287; *Poems* 106). But Christ himself triumphs over Death to become 'that Bridegroome that appeares so faire' (1305; *Poems* 107).

Lanyer situates Margaret Russell, Countess of Cumberland, as prime recipient of the masque of Christ's Passion: 'On your Deserts my Muses doe attend: / You are the Articke

[12] Woods, 'Introduction', in Aemilia Lanyer, *Poems of Aemilia Lanyer*.

[13] On this point, see Karen Britland, 'Women in the Royal Courts', in Laura L. Knoppers (ed.), *Cambridge Companion to Early Modern Women's Writing* (Cambridge, 2009), 132.

Starre that guides my hand, / All what I am, I rest at your command' (1838–1840; *Poems* 129). It is little surprise, then, that when we get to 'The Description of Cooke-ham', all of nature receives the Countess: the 'Walkes put on their summer Liveries' (21; *Poems* 131), while birds in 'chirping notes . . . / . . . entertaine' and 'oft come to attend' her (29–30, 47; *Poems* 131–2). A masque-like scene honours Cumberland as she sits, monarch-like, by a stately oak:

> Where beeing seated, you might plainely see,
> Hills, vales, and woods, as if on bended knee
> They had appeard, your honour to salute,
> Or to preferre some strange unlook'd for sute. (67–70; *Poems* 133)

By relocating the court masque into her meditative work, Lanyer builds common ground with her noble and aristocratic dedicatees—in particular, Margaret Russell and her daughter Anne Clifford, who fondly remembered her own participation in masques under Queen Elizabeth.[14] In doing so, Lanyer also asserts her own creative and authorial power by placing all these women in positions that she has determined for them. In depicting the feast of Christ the Bridegroom, Lanyer imagines a new locale 'Where he that is the greatest may be least' (16; *Poems* 41) and where 'God makes both even, the Cottage with the Throne' (19; *Poems* 42). Placing would-be patrons as recipients of a transformative divine masque, Lanyer also changes and transforms her own humble place.

MARY WROTH: MISPLACING MASQUES

Mary Wroth, as we noted earlier, herself participated in court masques early in Queen Anna's reign and was closely aligned with the court, especially through family connections. These included her father as Queen Anna's Lord Chamberlain and her cousins William Herbert, Earl of Pembroke (with whom she had a romantic liaison that produced two illegitimate children) and Philip Herbert, Earl of Montgomery, as well as Philip's wife, Susan de Vere, the Countess of Montgomery to whom she dedicates *Urania*.[15] By the time the widowed Wroth was writing the two parts of her long prose romance, *The Countess of Montgomery's Urania*, she was away from the court, although

[14] Jessica L. Malay argues that Lanyer may be primarily appealing to Anne Clifford, given the greater opportunities for herself and her musician husband in Clifford's household, 'Positioning Patronage: Lanyer's *Salve Deus Rex Judaeorum* and the Countess of Cumberland in Time and Place', *The Seventeenth Century*, 28 (2013), 251–74.

[15] On Wroth's participation in masques, see Josephine A. Roberts, 'Introduction', in Lady Mary Wroth, *The First Part of The Countess of Montgomery's Urania* (Binghamton, NY, 1995), xxxi; and footnote 16.

she continued to be involved in court activities.[16] Noting Wroth's use of masques and their language, scholars have explored how she appropriates Queen Anna's oppositional voice, writes her own aristocratic identity, and gestures through the actions of Pamphilia and Amphilanthus (shadowing herself and Pembroke) in masque-like enchantments towards a potential happy ending for her lived experience.[17] I want to look, in contrast, at unhappy endings, at masques run amok. Through purposefully misplacing masques—showing how their laudatory aims are misdirected, mistaken, or feigned—Wroth both participates in and critiques courtly culture, underscoring the failure to uphold courtly virtues.[18]

In the first 'marriage masque' that we encounter in part one of *Urania* (published 1621), Leandrus relates a tragic story of star-crossed love. Landing on the island of Cephalonia, Leandrus comes upon the celebration of the marriage of the daughter of the Lord of Cephalonia and the son of Lord of Zante ('a fine and spritefull youth', 41). A celebratory masquer lauds the honour and joy of the newly married couple, after which 'twenty Gentlemen presenting souldiers' perform a dance and the company moves to a rich banquet. But at the moment when the bride should be taken away from the banquet to bed, she instead heads for the hills. The uneasy celebrants and the perplexed groom wait to see if the bride will nonetheless turn up in bed; when that does not happen, general disorder ensues. Suspicion first falls on the masquers, but they clear themselves and join (as does Leandrus) the hunt for the bride. Eventually, Leandrus and his companion find the bride, hidden in a vineyard, kissing and embracing her true lover.

The masquers' praise of honour and joy turns out to have been woefully misdirected. The Lord of Cephalonia has forced the marriage, virtually imprisoning his daughter, who loves another, until the wedding day. The bridegroom is killed by Leandrus' companion and, in turn, one of the bridegroom's servants stabs and kills the unarmed lover. The bride avows constancy to her dead lover and commits herself to a nunnery but, two days later, 'she fell ill, not sicke in body, but dead in heart', and she soon joins her lover in death (44). The masque ideals of honour and love pertain not to the forced marriage but to the faithful lovers, with whom Leandrus sympathises.

Things also go awry in a second masque-like entertainment recounted by Dolorindus. Having fallen in love with the beautiful Selinea, Dolorindus is given a noble welcome

[16] Margaret P. Hannay, 'Sleuthing in the Archives', in Katherine R. Larson and Naomi J. Miller (eds), *Re-reading Mary Wroth* (New York, 2015), 19–36, dispels the long-held assumption that Wroth was ostracised by the court after her affair with her cousin.

[17] See Marion Wynne-Davis, 'The Queen's Masque: Renaissance Women and the Seventeenth-Century Court Masque', in S. P. Cerasano and Marion Wynne-Davies (eds), *Gloriana's Face: Women, Public and Private, in the English Renaissance* (Detroit, MI, 1992), 79–104; Mary Ellen Lamb, 'Topicality in Mary Wroth's *Countess of Montgomery's Urania*: Prose Romance, Masque, and Lyric', in Andrew Hadfield (ed.), *The Oxford Handbook of English Prose, 1500–1640* (Oxford, 2013), 235–50; and Julie D. Campbell, 'Masque Scenery and the Tradition of Immobilization in *The First Part of the Countess of Montgomery's Urania*', *Renaissance Studies*, 22 (2008), 221–39.

[18] On Wroth's biographical 'shadowing', see Roberts, 'Introduction', in Lady Mary Wroth, *The First Part of The Countess of Montgomery's Urania*, lxx–lxxi.

by her unsuspecting husband, Lord Redulus, and stays on as a guest until he has won Selinea's love. Indeed, he remains for years, enjoying 'Maskes, Justs, [and] Huntings' at their house (184). Only when the seemingly unattached Dolorindus spurns the love of a new lady does Lord Redulus begin to suspect the affair. The jealous husband, feigning good 'cheere' but with a 'heart never more foule', then uses an elaborate masque-like show ('neither Masque nor properly any one thing but a mingle of divers sorts') to garner evidence and get revenge. Placing Dolorindus between the two ladies as they view the show, Redulus watches their 'close looks as spiders flyes, with numbers of her webs' (185). He then conceives of a way to throw a 'spitefull jarre' among the three (185), breeding distrust in Selinea who rejects her lover. The heartbroken Dolorindus leaves Selinea and the country, bemoaning his hard fate.

Equally misdirected is a masque aimed at winning Pamphilia in the second part of the *Urania* (which remained unpublished). Rodomandro, King of Tartaria, after having been shipwrecked onto the kingdom of Morea, falls in love with Pamphilia and presents a masque to woo her. Wroth consistently depicts Rodomandro, a figure perhaps showing the influence of the *Masque of Blackness*, as valiant, civil, noble, and brave: he knows the courtly codes.[19] Rodomandro's masque, which includes dancing and elaborate costumes, focuses on honour. Cupid chides the Tartars for abandoning the ladies of Tartaria to gaze on the fair-skinned ladies of Morea. Rebuked in turn by Honour, Cupid reforms and, by the end of the masque, lauds Honour, not desire and whimsy, as the King of true love: 'Butt lett harts and voices singe: / Honor's Cupids just borne Kinge'.[20] But Rodomandro is unaware of the secret love of Pamphilia and Amphilanthus, who have just that morning secretly taken *de presentia* marriage vows. Neither the elegant masque nor Rodomandro's valiant service in military action against the usurping king of Sophy moves Pamphilia: only when Amphilanthus marries another does she consent to give Rodomandro her hand in marriage, while nonetheless withholding her heart.

If Wroth purposefully misplaces masques to contrast true love and honour with forced and unhappy marriages, jealous husbands, and the fickleness of male lovers, the anti-masquers 'in strange habit and farr stranger fashion' who entertain the married Amphilanthus in a later scene at Urania's court (412) seem more suitably placed. Amphilanthus' behaviour has failed to follow courtly ideals, even as he is presented as the consummate courtier. The anti-masquers are defined as having 'such a scarcetie of good Civilitie as little ore non[e] was seene in them' (142), a description that might well apply to Amphilanthus himself.

By depicting masques run amok, the aristocratic Wroth appeals to her coterie audience and writes herself into those circles as an authority not only on keeping courtly codes, but, even more significantly, on their violation. Court masques continue

[19] On Rodomandro, see Helen Hackett, 'Lady Mary Sidney Wroth: *The Countess of Montgomery's Urania*', in Margaret P. Hannay, Mary Ellen Lamb, and Michael G. Brennan (eds), *The Ashgate Research Companion to the Sidneys, 1500–1700, Volume 2: Literature* (Burlington, VT, 2015), 139–40.

[20] Lady Mary Wroth, *Urania*, in Josephine A. Roberts (ed.), *The Second Part of The Countess of Montgomery's Urania*, completed by Suzanne Gossett and Janel Mueller (Binghamton, NY, 1999), 49.

to facilitate Wroth's cultural engagement, creative production, and authorial self-fashioning, long after she has completed her final dance.

MARGARET CAVENDISH: DISPLACING MONARCHS

Margaret Cavendish might seem to be negative about the royal court in her writing. In her brief autobiography, she depicts herself as shy and homesick after joining the court of Queen Henrietta Maria at Oxford in 1642. During their courtship in Paris, Margaret (as lady-in-waiting) and the exiled William Cavendish, defeated royalist general and then-Marquis of Newcastle, faced opposition from the court and the queen to their marriage. Cavendish's late play *The Presence* gently mocks Henrietta Maria's cult of Platonic love in a princess who has fallen in love with a shadow met in a dream; and Cavendish's alter ego, Lady Bashful, is surrounded by ladies-in-waiting who gossip, scheme, and try to obstruct her relationship with Newcastle's figure, Lord Loyalty.

Yet Cavendish, too, draws on courtly forms, including the masque. Familiar with masques from her own court experience and through her husband, who had patronised Ben Jonson, lavishly entertained Charles I and Henrietta Maria, and himself composed masques, Cavendish uses the masque for both nostalgic and utopian purposes. Masques constitute an important and still-understudied aspect of Cavendish's generic experimentation and hybridity, as well as of her authorial and, in particular, aristocratic self-fashioning.[21] Most notably, I will suggest that when Cavendish moves the place and language of the masque into her writing, she replaces the monarch with aristocratic women who not only evince elite class virtues but bear a strong resemblance to herself.

In the eclipse of the monarchical court in England, Cavendish radically interiorises her 'Phantasm's Masque', included in *Poems, and Fancies* (1653): 'The scene is poetry. / The stage the brain whereon it is acted'.[22] While Fancy speaks a Prologue 'to Judgment, as king', Vanity and Honour speak Epilogues to 'Thoughts, which are spectators' (266). The masque itself tells Cavendish's own life story under the allegory of a voyaging ship.

[21] On Cavendish and the masque, Tanya Caroline Wood argues that while 'Phantasm's Masque' shows the failures of monarchy in the civil war, Cavendish redeploys masque elements in *The Blazing World* to reassert absolutism absolutely; 'The Rise and Fall of Absolutism: Margaret Cavendish's Manipulation of Masque Conventions in "The Claspe: *Fantasmes* Masque" and *The Blazing World*', *In-Between: Essays & Studies in Literary Criticism*, 9 (2000), 287–99; Jennifer Low looks at how Cavendish both disclaims and is drawn to the court, in 'Surface and Interiority: Self-Creation in Margaret Cavendish's *The Claspe*', *Philological Quarterly*, 77 (1998), 149–69; and Holly Faith Nelson and Sharon Alker point to masque elements in the spectacular self-memorialisation of the grieving widow, Madam Jantil, in 'Memory, Monuments, and Melancholic Genius in Margaret Cavendish's *Bell in Campo*', *Eighteenth Century Fiction*, 21 (2008), 13–35.

[22] Margaret Cavendish, 'Phantasm's Masque', in Brandie Siegfried (ed.), *Poems and Fancies with The Animal Parliament* (Toronto, 2018), 266–74 (266).

Sailing towards the 'land of riches', with sails of 'high ambition' and 'winds of praise and beauty's flowing tide', the ship is soon beset with 'rebellious clouds' and tossed high on 'sorrow's billows', before finally arriving at 'a haven of great France' (267). There a 'noble lord' (Newcastle) buys the ship, launching it on another voyage of content and love, although it will once again be beset, this time by 'a storm of poverty', 'showers of miseries', and the noise of 'thund'ring creditors' (268).

At the centre of the masque are resplendent figures of the Bride and Groom, shadowing Cavendish and Newcastle. The Bride wears a gem-encrusted crown:

> A crown of jewels on her head was put,
> And every jewel like a planet cut.
> The diamond, carbuncle, and sapphire,
> Ruby, topaz, and emerald was there. (271)

But the light of the Bride's face outshines even the jewels: 'Her face was like the sun, which shined bright; / And all those jewels, from her face took light' (271). Wearing a 'crown of loyalty' (271), the Bridegroom is led by Fortitude and Justice. Triumphing over Envy's opposition, the couple arrives at the Temple where the gods join them in wedlock bands. In the absence of the royal court in England, Cavendish reimagines the masque as aristocratic self-fashioning.

In Cavendish's short prose fiction, 'The Contract', published in 1656 in *Natures Pictures Drawn by Fancies Pencil to the Life*, the court masque serves as a scene of triumph for Cavendish's beautiful, aristocratic, and decidedly uncourtly young heroine.[23] The orphaned heiress Lady Deletia, raised in the country by her Uncle, is so innocent and inexperienced that she asks, 'Pray ... what is a masque?' (9). The Uncle describes an elaborate masque spectacle—'painted scenes to represent the poet's heavens and hells, their gods and devils, and clouds, sun, moon, and stars', actors, music, lords and ladies, and dancing (9). Yet when Lady Deletia arrives at court, her appearance 'like a glorious light' strikes all with amazement, so that 'few looked on the masque for looking on her' (14).

The court masque itself all but forgotten, the only spectacle that matters is that of Lady Deletia—her splendid dress, her beauty, her flawless dancing. The men, especially the Viceroy and the Duke who has earlier spurned her, fix their eyes on only her. Similarly, when the Viceroy gives a second ball, all the men want to dance with Deletia, so that nobody asks the other ladies to dance, incurring their envy and gossip. Ultimately Lady Deletia triumphs over all obstacles, reforming and marrying the wayward Duke. Cavendish uses a disordered court space as a foil for female aristocratic virtue and its power to change and transform.

When, in 1667, Cavendish published her now-best-known work, *The Description of a New World, Called the Blazing World*, Charles II had been restored to the throne. Yet

[23] Margaret Cavendish, 'The Contract', in Kate Lilley (ed.), *The Blazing World & Other Writings* (London, 1994).

Cavendish places her idealised court far from England and constructs its spaces and figures through the masque form that is both nostalgic and utopian. Shrinking the representation of Charles II to a brief cameo, Cavendish reimagines centre and periphery, placing her aristocratic alter-ego Empress at the centre and moving the monarch to the margins. If in Honthorst's masque-like painting with which we began the Duke of Buckingham rivals the royal couple, Cavendish barely allows the king to come onto the stage.

Arguably, then, the very extravagance of the Empress in *Blazing World*, which has been used as evidence of Cavendish's royalist absolutism, linked to various historical queens, conveys a very different message as a depiction of aristocratic loyalty and merit. As in her 'Phantasm's Masque', the opening utopian narrative echoes Cavendish's own biography. After a dangerous sea voyage, the Lady finds herself in the court of the Emperor of the Blazing World, who marries her on the spot. The Lady-turned-Empress dresses in what can be seen as the most extravagant of masque costumes:

> on her head she wore a cap of pearl, and a half-moon of diamonds just before it; on the top of her crown came spreading over a broad carbuncle, cut in the form of the sun; her coat was of pearl, mixed with blue diamonds, and fringed with red ones; her buskins and sandals were of green diamonds.[24]

With a buckler made of multicolored diamonds, cut in an arch that 'showed like a rainbow', and a spear 'made of a white diamond, cut like the tail of a blazing star', the Empress is ready, we are told, 'to assault those that proved her enemies' (133).

But the extravagant bejewelled costuming of the Empress then all but disappears from the text. The various beast scientists and the spirits with whom the Empress converses do not seem to notice her attire. Nor does her new friend and scribe, a second alter ego, the Duchess of Newcastle. Only in the Second Book of *Blazing World* does the costume come into play, when the Empress seeks to help the beleaguered monarch in her own former country, EFSI (transparently England, France, Scotland, and Ireland). The Empress' entertainment-like appearance above the water at night—with a description of her glittering diamonds, rubies, crown, coat, and spear repeated virtually verbatim from Book One—stuns, bewilders, and overwhelms her former countrymen.

Strikingly, the masque-like spectacle aims to evince the Empress' loyalty. She declares that she has come only to aid her king: 'All the return I desire, is but your grateful acknowledgment, and to declare my power, love and loyalty to my native country' (210). Although now 'a great and absolute princess, and empress of a whole world', she was once 'a subject of this kingdom', and she vows to 'destroy all your enemies' and 'make you triumph over all that seek your ruin and destruction' (210). Needless to say, the rebels themselves are doomed; the Empress distracts them with her blazing sight and her

[24] Margaret Cavendish, *The Blazing World*, in Lilley (ed.), *Blazing World*, 133.

imperial robes of diamonds, rubies, and carbuncles, while the real work is done by her fish-men who torch the rebel ships with fire-stones.

While Cavendish extravagantly displays her own loyalty, she also repeatedly characterises her husband as loyal. Her biography of William underscores his unstinting devotion to the king, while in her play, *The Presence*, William's alter-ego is dubbed Lord Loyalty. Back in England after the Restoration, the Cavendishes lived in retirement, repairing their devastated country estates, and were largely unheeded by the king. Newcastle had ruinously lent his wealth to Charles I and Henrietta Maria and had striven to advise Charles II in exile, fervently loyal to Stuart monarchy. But Charles II had neglected to reward and repay his loyal servant.[25] In *Blazing World*, the masque-like Empress (not to mention her advisor, the Duchess of Newcastle, or the author herself as '*Margaret* the *First*', 124) shows how eminently deserving the loyal and aristocratic Cavendishes are, upholding court ideals that the king himself has neglected and spurned.

We have explored how four early modern women writers use the quintessential courtly form of the masque to imagine and inscribe courtly places, innovating with literary genre and form. In changing the place of the court masque, these women change their own place as well. If under Queens Anna and Henrietta Maria, girls and women were given new cultural agency, visibility, and power by their participation in the vital performance spaces of the court masque, these women writers take on even more of the masque parts. Exercising authorial agency and creativity, they sponsor, patronise, write, direct, and perform in their own masques, however interiorised and on the page. Their relocation of the masque into their own writing gives them a place alongside, and in relation to, court culture. And the bold innovation of their written work gives them a place in an emerging literary tradition of women's writing that itself would open symbolic and enabling spaces for girls and women for many years to come.

FURTHER READING

Barroll, Leeds. *Anna of Denmark, Queen of England: A Cultural Biography*. Philadelphia, PA, 2001.

Bevington, David and Peter Holbrook (eds). *The Politics of the Stuart Court Masque*. Cambridge, 1998.

Britland, Karen. *Drama at the Courts of Queen Henrietta Maria*. Cambridge, 2006.

McManus, Clare. *Women on the Renaissance Stage: Anna of Denmark and Female Masquing in the Stuart Court, 1590–1619*. Manchester, 2002.

McManus, Clare (ed.). *Women and Culture at the Courts of the Stuart Queens*. New York, 2003.

[25] For discussion of Newcastle's situation, and the ways in which Cavendish intervenes on his behalf, see Lisa T. Sarasohn, 'Margaret Cavendish, William Newcastle, and Political Marginalization', *English Studies*, 92 (2011), 806–17.

CHAPTER 25

RACE AND GEOGRAPHIES OF ESCAPE IN ELIZABETH CARY'S *THE TRAGEDY OF MARIAM*

MEGHAN E. HALL

THIS chapter argues that foreign geographies and transnational travel play a crucial role in Elizabeth Cary, Viscountess Falkland's 1604 drama, *The Tragedy of Mariam* (printed 1613), and its meditations on power, space, and the limits of (white) feminine virtue. While the play is set entirely within the living quarters of the royal court of pre-Christian Judea and therefore does not depict travel directly, I suggest that our understanding of the play benefits from bringing to bear on the play's depiction of women the rich critical conversations on travel, expansionism, and globality that have thrived in early modern studies for the past three decades. After all, the two main storylines hinge on two women's willingness to leave their native country: the stoic Mariam initially flirts with the emancipatory possibilities of 'ranging' freely, only to disavow her desires and reject an opportunity to immigrate abroad, while her scheming sister-in-law, Salome, pursues a visiting Arabian prince precisely so she can relocate to his kingdom and overthrow his father (1.1.26).[1] Both women use distinctly spatial, sometimes navigational, language to express themselves and their desires, to the effect that it highlights the reciprocal relationship between their domestic lives as royal women and the tense geopolitical landscape that is unfolding between Judea and the surrounding Roman provinces. Faced with heightened scrutiny, Mariam and Salome each cling to opposite sides of a racially inflected binary of the 'fair' and 'virtuous woman' who is chaste, silent, obedient, and most importantly, still; and the 'base' and immoral woman, whose self-interest drives

[1] All quotations for *Mariam* come from Susan P. Cerasano and Marion Wynne-Davies (eds), *Renaissance Drama by Women: Texts and Documents* (New York, 2013). I discuss the resonances of the term 'range' further on.

her to transgress both social and physical boundaries. Their respective fates—Mariam enclosed in a tomb; Salome free to travel but thoroughly vilified—offer Cary's readers a bleak view of the limits of women's autonomy in a globalising world.

This chapter draws together several critical conversations regarding *Mariam*, and within early modern studies in general. One concerns the racial epistemologies Cary upholds in the play's depiction of womanhood. Responding to early feminist readings of *Mariam* that presumed Salome to be the more sympathetic of the two women, Dympna Callaghan's foundational reading of Salome as an example of the early modern trope of the hyper-sexualised, morally tarnished dark woman has engendered a small but rich body of scholarship on the play's presentation of racialised femininity.[2] Salome is othered within the Judean court in response to her mixed parentage: Mariam attacks her sister-in-law's birth, exclaiming 'thou parti-Jew and parti-Edomite, Thou Mongrel, issued from rejected race!' and she colours Salome's schemes as 'black acts' (1.3.235–6, 244–5). Meanwhile, as Callaghan observes, 'faire Mariam' progresses towards a 'dazzling' whiteness over the course of the play, and her stoic, even stubborn, adherence to ideals of feminine virtue and her harsh treatment of Salome locates her within the early modern trope of the pious but vicious white Christian woman.[3]

This chapter also builds on rich critical discussions of space and power in *Mariam*. The play offers an especially lucid portrayal of the ways in which patriarchal authority structures lived environments, consequently restricting the choices of the women who live within them. In *Mariam*, women of all circumstances struggle against barriers to their desires and self-interests: barriers that include legal inequality, controlling husbands, and the intense social stigma they encounter when acting against gendered social norms. Indeed, as Carol Mejia-LaPerle, Lynette McGrath, and Michelle M. Dowd have all suggested, social boundaries have physical lives in *Mariam*, and vice versa: power takes shape through the walls and guarded structures of the Judean court, while physical spaces define and reshape the social lives of the female characters.[4] While this scholarship has thus far limited its discussions of space to the play's domestic and

[2] For scholarship on *Mariam* and race, see Dympna Callaghan, 'Re-reading Elizabeth Cary's *The Tragedy of Mariam*', in Margo Hendricks and Patricia Parker (eds), *Women, 'Race' and Writing in the Early Modern Period* (New York,1994), 173–93.; Kimberly Poitevin, '"Counterfeit Colour": Making up Race in Elizabeth Cary's *The Tragedy of Mariam*', *Tulsa Studies in Women's Literature*, 24.1 (2005), 13–34; Evelyn Gajowski, 'Intersecting Discourses of Race and Gender in Elizabeth Cary's *The Tragedy of Mariam*', *Early Modern Literary Studies*, 27 (2017), 297–314; Suzy Beemer, 'Masks of Blackness, Masks of Whiteness: Coloring the (Sexual) Subject in Jonson, Cary, and Fletcher', *Thamyris*, 4 (1997), 223–4; M. Lindsay Kaplan, 'The Jewish Body in Black and White in Medieval and Early Modern England', *Philological Quarterly*, 92 (2013), 41–65.

[3] Callaghan, 'Re-reading', 174–6.

[4] For discussions of space in *Mariam*, see Carol Mejia-LaPerle, 'Access and Agency in Elizabeth Cary's *The Tragedy of Mariam*: Early Modern Closet Drama and the Spatialization of Power', *Literature Compass*, 3.2 (2006), 80–94; Lynette McGrath, *Subjectivity and Women's Poetry in Early Modern England: Why on the Ridge Should She Desire to Go?* (New York, 2017); Michelle M. Dowd, 'Dramaturgy and the Politics of Space in *The Tragedy of Mariam*', *Renaissance Drama*, 44.1 (2016), 101–22; Miranda Nesler, 'Closeted Authority in *The Tragedy of Mariam*', *SEL: Studies in English Literature 1500–1900*, 52.2 (2012), 363–85; Jennifer L. Heller, 'Space, Violence, and Bodies in Middleton and Cary', *Studies in English*

courtly environments, it does the crucial work of establishing linkages between the spatial language of the play and the play's setting as the characters live in and experience it.

Finally, this chapter draws upon the growing body of scholarship that contemplates the experiences of women who travelled in the early modern period. Patricia Akhimie and Bernadette Andrea's 2019 essay collection, *Travel and Travail: Early Modern Women, English Drama, and the Wider World*, began the crucial work of recovering historical instances of travelling women, and of establishing the historically specific linkages between gender, mobility, and power.[5] Though their work indicates that women did travel—far more often than we have assumed—it also sheds light on a dominant cultural narrative that broadly deemed women who travelled to be promiscuous and untrustworthy. Travel manuals of the period assumed an exclusively male readership, generally ignoring the possibility that women might need their advice and, in a few cases, explicitly forbidding women to travel.[6] For example, Thomas Palmer's 1606 travel manual counts women among those unfit for travel (alongside infants, the mentally ill, and the physically disabled), while Fynes Moryson's 1617 *Itinerary* states that 'women for suspition of chastity are most unfit for [the] course [of travel]'.[7] *Mariam*, as I shall argue, upholds the association between travelling women and promiscuity via the character of Salome, whose plans to travel are entangled with her unrestrained sexual desire.

From a young age, Elizabeth Cary was fascinated by the world beyond England's shores. In her adolescence, Cary completed an English translation of Abraham Ortelius' popular pocket atlas, *L'Epitome du Théâtre du Monde*, which she titled *The Mirror of the Worlde*. As Lesley Peterson, modern editor *of The Mirror*, demonstrates with her meticulous examination of Cary's alterations and penmanship, the *Mirror* translation was a considerable investment of time and labour.[8] She dedicated the manuscript to Sir Henry Lee, her great-uncle and an aristocrat known for the extensive educational travels he undertook in his youth; her dedication explicitly compares his knowledge of geography, garnered through first-hand experience, to her own knowledge, limited because it comes entirely from books.[9]

Literature 1500–1900, 45.2 (2005), 425–41; Katherine O. Acheson, '"Outrage your face": Anti-theatricality and Gender in Early Modern Closet Drama by Women', *Early Modern Literary Studies*, 6.7 (2001), 1–16.

5 See Patricia Akhimie and Bernadette Andrea, 'Introduction: Early Modern Women, English Drama, and the Wider World', in Patricia Akhimie and Bernadette Andrea (eds), *Travel and Travail: Early Modern Women, English Drama, and the Wider World* (Lincoln, NE, 2019), 1–24.

6 Akhimie and Andrea, 'Introduction', 1–2; Patricia Akhimie, 'Gender and Travel Discourse: Richard Lassels' 'The Voyage of the Lady Catherine Whitenhall from Brussells into Italy' (1650)', in Akhimie and Andrea (eds), *Travel and Travail*, 121–38, 124.

7 See Thomas Palmer, *An Essay of the Meanes How to Make our Travails into Forraine Countries, the More Profitable and Honouable*. London, 1606; and Fynes Moryson, *An Itinerary Written by Fynes Moryson*. London, 1617.

8 For detailed descriptions of the *Mirror* manuscript, see Lesley Peterson, 'Introduction: Early Encounters with the World: Elizabeth Tanfield and her Work', in Lesley Peterson (ed.), *The Mirror of the World: A Translation* (Montréal, 2012), 3–21.

9 See Elizabeth Cary, *The Mirror of the Worlde*, in Peterson (ed.), *The Mirror of the World*, 119.

As a favourite of Lee's, Cary no doubt grew up listening to stories of his adventures on the Continent, but she had little hope of travelling in the same way. The only daughter of a self-made barrister and his social-climber wife, Cary was groomed for a financially and politically advantageous marriage.[10] Married by the age of seventeen, Cary lacked the time, financial independence, and social support for travelling educationally, and the humble, nearing disappointed tone that the dedication takes reflects that she regretted her restricted circumstances.

In addition to the *Mirror* manuscript, small details from *The Lady Falkland, her Life*, the biography written by four of her children in 1630, gesture to Cary's sharp interest in the larger world. According to the *Life*, Cary was a voracious reader and self-taught polyglot, fluent in seven languages, including one she learned 'of a Transilvanian' simply through extended conversation.[11] She was also a prolific writer in the early years of her marriage; the writing 'sayd to be the best' was a verse chronicle about the world conqueror, Timur, which she based on Christopher Marlowe's popular 1597 play, *Tamburlaine*.[12] While her early writings were marked by a fascination with the larger world, Cary's view of travel shifted in adulthood, as her marriage to Henry Cary became increasingly strained. Travel, in *Mariam*, functions not solely as an opportunity for self-enrichment, but as an escape from personal and systemic oppression.

Mariam is about the tragic downfall of Queen Mariam of Judea, wife of Herod the Great. It begins just after news reaches the court that Herod, a cruel tyrant whose oppressive nature has made even his most loyal followers miserable, has been executed in Rome for the regicides he committed against Mariam's grandfather and older brother. This news throws the court into chaos, as several characters view the sudden power vacuum as an opportunity to advance politically: political betrothals and marriages are broken, new alliances are forged, and several characters produce competing visions of Judea's political future. The chaos comes to a sudden halt in act three when Herod returns, proving reports of his death to have been false and inflicting severe consequences on the courtiers who had acted opportunistically.

Herod's sister, Salome, is one of the first to take advantage of his apparent death. No longer answerable to her brother, she decides to seek a divorce from her husband, Constabarus. Though she acknowledges that Judean law allows only men to petition for divorce and, furthermore, that she will be judged harshly for remarrying, she nonetheless proclaims 'I'll be the custom-breaker, and begin to show my sex the way to freedom's door' (1.4.319–20). In these lines, Salome uses a familiar navigational metaphor—(sexual) freedom is represented as a threshold, to which Salome must first travel and then cross—to highlight how divorce will entail trespassing both legal and social boundaries. With these lines, Salome previews the strategic 'moves' she will make for

[10] See Lucy Cary et al. *The Lady Falkland, Her Life*, in Heather Wolfe (ed.), *Elizabeth Cary, Lady Falkland: Life and Letters* (Tempe, AZ, 2001), 103–4.

[11] Cary, *The Lady Falkland*, 106.

[12] Cary, *The Lady Falkland*, 106.

the remainder of the play as Herod returns and she must deflect attention away from her indiscretions.

Mariam, on the other hand, refuses to make any plans in the wake of Herod's alleged death. Consumed by the memory of his abuse, she instead struggles with how she should respond appropriately, vascillating in her opening lines between relief, shame, grief, and confusion. 'Oft have I wished that I from him were free ... Oft have I wished his carcass dead to see', she admits bitterly, then swiftly admonishes herself for failing to return 'the tender love that he to Mariam bare' (1.1.16–18; 1.1.32). Completely aware of how Herod has betrayed her, Mariam nonetheless upholds Judea's rigid social demands on a wife's unconditional love and loyalty to her husband, and so she refuses to be moved to action. This ultimately contributes to her tragic end: when Salome frames Mariam for attempted regicide, Mariam refuses to retaliate and is executed.

Thus, both women desire to escape their marriages and, more broadly, the patriarchal legal and social structures that limit their personal freedom, yet only Salome is willing to cross social boundaries to achieve that escape. Throughout the play, Salome is associated with transgressive and uncontrolled movement. Even before she spurns him, Constabarus chastises her 'wavering thoughts', claiming that her mind 'to inconstancy doth run', and that it would be 'as good [to] go hold the wind as [to] make her stay' (1.6.474, 1.3.321, 2.2.318–23). Herod decries Salome's inability to 'be still', Mariam refers to Salome as 'unsteadfast', and even Salome acknowledges her own 'wandering heart' (5.1.157, 1.3.263, 1.4.331). While these comments refer literally to Salome's propensity to stray romantically and to the moves she makes to elevate her political standing, they simultaneously align her figurative mobility with her willingness to cross social and physical boundaries. Salome is often found in places she should not be, meeting secretly with the Arabian prince, Silleus, and appearing over Herod's shoulder to convince him to punish Mariam.

She also actively desires immigration abroad, perhaps more than she desires Silleus himself. Indeed, Salome's desire for Silleus is inextricably linked to her political ambitions. This is reflected in her language. Like most at the Judean court, Salome calls Silleus 'the Arabian', or simply 'Arabia', conflating the prince and his kingdom. Though others call him 'Arabia' as a reference to his ambassadorial function, Salome's use of the metonym tends to frame Silleus as desirable precisely because he commands territory. Describing her desire for him, she exclaims 'Oh blest Arabia, in best climate place, I by the fruit will censure of the tree: 'tis not in vain the happy name thou hast, / if all Arabians like Silleus be' (1.4.269–73). Here, Salome playfully fantasises about the possibility that all Arabian men are as worthy as Silleus via an arboreal generational metaphor. Beneath her sexual desire, however, lies political desire. Her reference to Arabia's 'happy name' identifies Silleus' homeland as Arabia Felix, the southern and largest of three Arabian territories that sat south of Judea. Early modern atlases and geographical texts lauded this region for its abundance of natural resources. For example, George Abbot's 1599 atlas, *A Brief Description of the Whole World*, explained that Arabia Felix earned its name from the 'fruitfulnes of the ground, and convenient standing everie way towarde the sea', and that 'it yeeldeth many things in aboundance, which in other parts of the world are not to be had' (143). Abbot names some of the 'fruits' of Arabia Felix as frankincense, myrrh, fruits, spices, and some 'precious stones' (44). In explorer Nicolas de Nicolay's account of the region, he claims it is 'most pleasant and abundant of things pretious & Aromaticke', such as olives, corn, cinnamon, and timber (56).

In both Abbot's and Nicolay's accounts of Arabia Felix, the region is prized for its natural resources. Thus, Salome's formulation that Arabia deserves the name 'happy' because the fruit (Silleus) reflects positively on the tree (Arabia) evokes the natural resources (the fruitfulness) that Arabia holds for merchants. In fact, Arabia's root, 'arav', was thought by early modern Europeans to be derived from 'arov', meaning 'to exchange' or 'to merchandise', associating the country's name with economic transactions.[13]

Salome's desire for Silleus is likewise coloured with the language of exchange and conquest. 'Tis not for glory I thy love accept, / Judea yields me honors worthy store: / had not affection in my bosom crept, / my native country should my life deplore' (1.5.357–64). Here, Salome coyly insists that her love for Silleus is untainted by greed or ambition, yet she does so through specialised language that betrays her ulterior motives. The 'glory' to which she claims indifference refers quite plainly to the concept of *grandezza* in Florentine political theory. Translated into English as 'glory', *grandezza* referred to a polity's drive towards territorial expansion. Therefore, given the nature of Salome and Silleus' arrangement, her statement that 'tis not for glory I thy love accept' reads as a coy acknowledgement of the land she expects to receive as a result of their union.

Additionally, Salome's claim to an abundance (a 'store') of honour conceals her dissatisfaction with life at the Judean court. We know that Herod's tyranny extended to his sister. When he returns in the third act, she angrily exclaims that Herod 'will give her foot no room to walk at large', predicting that Herod will prevent her from moving abroad (3.1.71). Salome also endures vicious attacks from Mariam, Constabarus, and others: though her kinship with Herod has secured her a place at court, Salome is positioned as something of an outsider, marked as a 'mongrel' because of her mixed parentage. She has little honour and also little power, even over herself. Thus, her desire for territorial sovereignty is linked to a desire for self-sovereignty.

Silleus, too, participates in Salome's fantasy of conquest, apostrophising Arabia to 'prepare [its] earth with green' in preparation for Salome's arrival. 'Her foot is destined to depress thy brow. / Thou shalt faire *Salome* command as much / as if the royal ornament were thine' (1.3.348–52). Though elsewhere Silleus makes it clear that he intends to quietly overthow his father, Obodas, whose weakness has primed the Arabian people to support a new king, the lines which begin this passage, describing Salome's foot pressing into the brow of an anthropomorphised territory, suggest a more forceful, dominating relationship between Salome and Arabia. Arabia does not merely represent a land to be

[13] *OED*, 'Arab, n. 1'.

travelled to, a land to be inhabited, or a dynasty to marry into, but a land to be conquered. If we compare Silleus' promise of Arabia to one of Salome's earlier lines, 'Lives Salome to get so base a style, as foot to the proud Mariam?', we see that Silleus' promise of territorial sovereignty compensates for her own degraded position in the court at Judea (1.3.261–2).

While Salome's mobility is characterised as fickle or unpredictable, it is worth noting that her scheming is far from directionless. Rather, Salome works strategically to obtain a better political position at court and her scheming mirrors the political machinations of the men around her. Herod's marriage to Mariam, for instance, is motivated not merely by possessive lust but by a desire for the throne. Constabarus, too, has chased political power: in a heated argument, Salome reminds her husband of the personal debt he owes her for saving him from execution after he attempted to wrest control of Idumea, an outpost of Judea, away from Herod. His marriage to Salome was also a political move, as the marriage granted him a modicum of protection from Herod's erratic violence. Analogously, Salome's affections have 'wandered' up the political ladder: from her first husband, Josephus, Herod's uncle, to the social climber, Constabarus, and finally to a man who can deliver to her the throne, Silleus. Salome is certainly not unaware of the different standards of behaviour that women, especially of her rank, experience. But she makes the conscious decision to disregard it and spends the play navigating the complex social world that sees her autonomy as improper.

If Salome's portion of *Mariam*'s plot is preoccupied with emigrating abroad, Mariam's portion seems, at first, to be preoccupied with stillness. Indeed, Mariam insists on the stillness of her affections, and her refusal to dissemble is matched by her refusal to leave Herod, either through scheming or through legal means. I would argue, however, that Mariam has a far more complex set of feelings about mobility and travel than is at first apparent. Her views on travel are characterised by a conflicted set of desires, an acute awareness and fear of the social stigma connected to women's mobility, and a negotiation of this stigma through the mechanisms of race.

In the opening lines of the play, Mariam carefully negotiates with herself the social cost of movement through a series of pained contradictions. 'Blame me not', she exclaims, 'for *Herod's* jealousy / had power even constancy it self to change: / For he by barring me from liberty, / to shun my ranging, taught me first to range. / But yet too chaste a scholar was my heart, / to learn to love another then my Lord' (1.1.23–8). Here, Mariam admits that she was driven to inconstancy, but immediately claims that she could never be inconstant. She desired to 'range', but was too 'chaste' to ever consider ranging. Another contradictory passage follows. 'Why now me thinks the love I bare him then, / when virgin freedom left me unrestrained, / doth to my heart begin to creep again' (1.1.71–3). 'Virgin freedom', like her former liberty, is aligned with a life before marriage, and it implicitly gestures towards a subjunctive future where Mariam *could* again be unrestrained, free to range again in the wake of Herod's death. Yet Mariam abandons this desire as soon as she states it, firmly insisting upon her own chastity.

Of course, the freedom to range refers primarily to the sociality Mariam enjoyed in her youth: in limited usage, to 'range' meant to change one's romantic attachments, to be inconstant. However, her romantic attachments have a spatial dimension.[14] When Herod 'barred' her from liberty, he effectively confined her physical movements, restricting the spaces she could occupy and the relationships she could build. Thus, Mariam's desire to be unrestrained is partly a desire for freedom of movement. To emphasise that desire for movement, Cary uses the loaded term 'range', connoting a laterally wider and spatially dispersed area of movement than many of its synonyms, such as 'wander' or 'ramble', both of which were also used to describe inconstant behaviour. Ranging was travelling, roaming, prospecting; in early modern nautical texts, to range was to explore coastlines in uncharted territories. Etymologically linked to the verbs 'rank' and 'arrange', ranging captured geographic mobility and social mobility through its implicit emphasis on categorisation and charting.[15] Thus, the geographical resonances of Mariam's speech suggest that while she refers directly to marital arrangements and her life at the Judean court, she indirectly invokes a desire for physical movement.

Yet, such desires seem wholly inappropriate to Mariam, who is keenly aware that in the social world of the play, women who show autonomy through their movements are considered suspicious. The social stigma attached to mobile women shapes Mariam's relationship to the larger world, leading her to bury her desires for spatial freedom in insistences of her own constancy and refuse opportunities that promise greater personal freedom and political power. Early in the play, Mariam's mother Alexandra laments, 'Where if thy portraiture had only gone, / his life from *Herod, Anthony* had taken: / he would have loved thee, and thee alone, / and left the brown *Egyptian* clean forsaken / and *Cleopatra* then to seek had been, / so firm a lover of her wayned face' (1.2.187–92). If only Anthony had seen Mariam first, then she and not Cleopatra would have been Antony's love, and the power of Rome would have been in Mariam's hands. Cleopatra's 'wayned face', a phrase which is rarely glossed but might equally refer to a loss of beauty or to a decline in her political power, contrasts with the portraiture of Mariam's face, which is mobilised as a proxy for her availability on the marriage market. Mariam replies to her mother unequivocally, 'Not to be empress of aspiring *Rome*, / would *Mariam* like to *Cleopatra* live: / with purest body will I press my Tomb, / and wish no favors *Anthony* could give' (1.2.199–202). Comparing her pure (as in chaste, obedient, and implicitly white) body to Cleopatra's brown one, Mariam activates a set of associations with dark-skinned women, and Cleopatra more specifically, that vilifies both their mobility and their desire for power.

The association Mariam makes between Cleopatra, emotional mobility, and physical mobility was not new to texts of the period. A common story about Egyptian society was that their gender roles were inverted, with women attending market and working in trade and men staying at home, an idea that originated in the writings of fifth-century historian Herodotus.[16] In this inversion, men stay and women go, their spatial

[14] *OED*, 'Range, v. 4'.

[15] *OED*, 'Range, v. 1a'.

[16] Ania Loomba, 'Introduction', in Ania Loomba (ed.), *Antony and Cleopatra: Authoritative Text, Sources, Analogues, and Contexts* (New York, 2011), 266.

reach widened by their association with trade: the prominence of Egyptian ports in the Mediterranean trade provided women access to the commodities and people of the larger world. The association between Egyptians and mobility is even more pronounced if you consider the slippage between 'Egyptians' and 'gypsies' in early modern discourse. Gypsies, a term applied to a nebulous category of emigrants and vagabonds in sixteenth-century England as well as to the actual Romanies who had settled in England, were considered a social ill because of their alleged propensity to lie, cheat, and steal, which certainly informs Mariam's derision of 'false Cleopatra'. Yet, their mobility also seems to have been a problem. Over the course of the sixteenth century, laws against vagrancy increasingly included gypsies among the common perpetrators. Henry VIII's *Egyptians Act of 1530* describes the gypsies as 'outlandish people, calling themselves Egyptians, using no craft nor feat of merchandise, *who have come into this realm, and gone from shire to shire, and place to place*, in great company'.[17] The threat of these Egyptians' mobility—and their sheer numbers—is subtended in the *Act* by the implication that they serve no productive function in England: they allegedly make nothing and trade nothing, and so by implication they add no economic value to the country.

In English representations of Cleopatra, who is certainly aligned with Egyptian women and gypsies but who is also a sovereign, her emotional mobility (her fickleness and her quickness to anger) is coupled with her desire for power. At the end of Cary's play, Mariam again names Cleopatra as an example of greedy and inconstant women: 'The wanton queen that never loved for love, / False Cleopatra, wholly set on gain, / With all her sleights did prove, yet vainly prove, / For her the love of Herod to obtain' (5.8.136–9). Cleopatra's falseness—her willingness to employ cunning in drawing the affections of a king—is integrally tied to her desire to increase her power and, implicitly, her territorial sovereignty, and it serves, in turn, as a foil to Mariam's presumed stillness.

Given the web of racial and gendered affiliations that attend to Cleopatra's representations in early modern literature, Mariam's rejection of territorial sovereignty is clearer. To seduce Caesar in a bid for power would not only be a transgression of her cherished ideals of chastity, but it would be a transgression of the racial line she works to police throughout the play. For Mariam, to desire and seek out political power and to embrace what Lynette McGrath has called a 'nomadic subjectivity', is to align herself with the play's dark women.[18]

In fact, Mariam clings so tightly to her ideals of 'fair honesty' that she can scarcely recognise herself as a sovereign. One could argue that Mariam's tragedy is that she is persistently unwilling or incapable of understanding her marriage to Herod as a political relationship that matters to the future of Judea and to the geopolitics of the Mediterranean under the Roman Empire. She may die a good woman, but she hardly dies a good queen. When Alexandra describes Mariam's marriage in terms of transactions, recounting the

[17] Henry VIII, King of England, 'An Act Concerning Outlandish People, Calling themselves Egyptians', in Danby Pickering (ed.), *The Statutes at Large, From the First Year of K. Richard III to the 31st Year K. Henry VIII, Inclusive* (London, 1763), 205.

[18] McGrath, *Subjectivity and Women's Poetry*, 171.

gifts she sent and her strategic circulation of Mariam's picture among world leaders, Mariam can only responds to her in terms of love and morality, lamenting that Herod did love her, despite his violence, and insisting that she owed him her love. Alexandra busies herself with planning for the political future of Judea, over which Mariam now has great power; Mariam is wholly consumed with questions of her duty as a wife and her propriety as a woman.

Consider her response to Herod's counsellor, Sohemus, who advises that for the sake of her children—the heirs to the Judean throne—she should hide her enmity towards Herod:

> Oh what a shelter is mine innocence, to shield me from the pangs of inward grief: against all mishaps it is my fair defense, and to my sorrows yields a large relief. To be commandress of the triple earth, and sit in safety from a fall secure: to have all nations celebrate my birth, I would not that my spirit were impure. (3.3.171–6)

Here, Mariam repeats her disparagement of Cleopatra and prioritises the safety of her conscience over her physical safety. Katherine Eisaman Maus and David Bevington gloss the phrase 'triple earth' as referring 'probably [to] Rome, Egypt, and Jerusalem', the holy geography.[19] Marion Wynne-Davies, on the other hand, traces it to classical mythology, arguing that the 'triple earth' comprises the heavens, the seas, and the underworld.[20] The phrase also bears similarity to the opening lines of Shakespeare's *Antony and Cleopatra* (1608), in which Antony is described as the '(triple Pillar of the world) transform'd', the 'triple Pillar' (1.1.11) referring to the triumvarite, the political association between Antony, Octavius, and Lepidus that made up the Roman Empire. Finally, the phrase brings to mind the tripartite medieval T-O maps, which included Asia, Europe, and Africa circumscribed in a circle. Though these had been supplanted by Ptolemaic maps in the sixteenth century, they would still have been familiar to those well-read in cartography in the early seventeenth century, as Cary surely was. Regardless of the scope evoked in the phrase 'triple-earth'—geographical or cosmological, three distinct regions or three continents)—the position of power that Mariam rejects is rooted in territorial sovereignty. Adding that 'all nations [would] celebrate her birth' underlines this, referring to the material or symbolic tribute individual countries would pay to their imperial sovereigns.

Her conflicted feelings towards territorial sovereignty are tested when, in a moment that parallels Salome and Silleus' plot, Herod offers to conquer Arabia for Mariam to rule. Sensing her unhappiness upon his return, he offers, 'If thou think *Judaea's* narrow bound, / too strict a limit for thy great command: / thou shalt be Empress of *Arabia* crowned, / For thou shalt rule, and I will win the Land' (4.101–4). Mariam answers, '*I* neither have of power nor riches want, / *I* have enough, nor do I wish for more: / your offers

19 David Bevington et al. (eds), *English Renaissance Drama: An Anthology* (New York, 2002), 28.

20 Susan P. Cerasano and Marion Wynne-Davies (eds), *Renaissance Drama by Women: Texts and Documents* (New York, 2013), 211.

to my heart no ease can grant, / except they could my brothers life restore' (4.1.109–12). Mariam's rejection of Herod's offer mirrors Salome's response to Silleus' offer, though with a more earnest tone. While Salome coquettishly claims not to seek glory, Mariam's outright rejection of 'power and riches' accompanies a solemn reference to her brother's murder. Her refusal of this offer becomes clearer a few lines down, when she states bluntly, 'I cannot frame disguise, nor never taught / my face a look dissenting from my thought' (4.1.144–5). Refusing to dissemble, like refusing power and riches, is again a rejection of the safe and beneficial position in order to maintain an ideal of moral purity.

Salome's and Mariam's respective gazes beyond the borders of Judea signal their awareness of the possibilities that travel holds for gaining territorial sovereignty and, perhaps more importantly, for gaining the self-sovereignty not available to them under Herod's patriarchal tyranny. In *Mariam*, the power to subvert the bonds of political marriage and escape oppressive governance lies in outward movement, in the fugitive migration of the female subject to areas beyond their reach. This anticipates Cary's decision to encourage her daughters' emigrations to learned convents in France three decades after the play was written.

Despite parallels in their desires, Salome's and Mariam's respective fates could not be more different. While Salome is chastised by Herod for her part in Mariam's downfall, she presumably lives. Successfully uncoupled from Constabarus (he is executed for a political matter), she presumably is free to travel to Arabia with Silleus, where she will depose his father and assume rulership. Her horizon is significantly spatially broadened. Mariam, on the other hand, is executed offstage, her final resting place a 'vault or some den enclose'd' (5.1.251). Mariam's final words are not directly depicted, but rather, Herod's agent, Nuntio, recalls her final pleas of innocence: Mariam loses the space to speak to power herself. Mariam's tragedy, it seems, lies in her refusal to be moved across physical and conceptual boundaries, even to save her own life.

Rather than locate Cary's sympathies with either Mariam or Salome, I argue that the two women serve as counterpoints in Cary's meditation on the affordances and consequences of using travel as an escape. Though at the play's end, Salome presumably leaves to become Arabia's queen, she is remembered as a duplicitous woman who would stop at nothing to gain power. Mariam, on the other hand, stays within the boundaries of feminine propriety and is remembered as a virtuous woman, but is ultimately put to death.

FURTHER READING

Akhimie, Patricia and Bernadette Andrea. 'Introduction: Early Modern Women, English Drama, and the Wider World', in Patricia Akhimie and Bernadette Andrea (eds), *Travel and Travail: Early Modern Women, English Drama, and the Wider World*. Lincoln, NE, 2019, 1–24.

Callaghan, Dympna. 'Re-reading Elizabeth Cary's *The Tragedy of Mariam*', in Margo Hendricks and Patricia Parker (eds), *Women, 'Race' and Writing in the Early Modern Period*. New York, 1994, 173–93.

Harris, Jonathan Gil. 'Mobility', in Ania Loomba (ed.), *A Cultural History of Western Empires in the Renaissance (1450–1650)*. London, 2018, 127–46.

Mejia-LaPerle, Carol. 'Access and Agency in Elizabeth Cary's *The Tragedy of Mariam*: Early Modern Closet Drama and the Spatialization of Power', *Literature Compass*, 3.2 (2006), 80–94.

Peterson, Lesley. 'Introduction: Early Encounters with the World: Elizabeth Tanfield and her Work', in Lesley Peterson (ed.), *The Mirror of the World: A Translation*. Montréal, 2012, 3–21.

CHAPTER 26

ARCHIPELAGIC FEMINISM

Anglophone Poetry from Ireland, Scotland, and Wales

SARAH PRESCOTT

In its emphasis on reframing and reimagining the relationship of the perceived geographical margins to the metropolitan centre, an archipelagic approach to literary studies has always contained feminist potential. In the most obvious way, it is the devolutionary impulse of archipelagic studies, the focus on the previously peripheral (both spatial and canonical), that speaks to the parallel feminist methodology of literary historical recovery and expansion of the accepted literary canon. As John Kerrigan argues in his influential study, *Archipelagic English*: '[t]o devolve is to shift power in politics or scholarly analysis from a locus that has been disproportionately endowed with influence and documentation to sites that are dispersed and skeletally understood'.[1] This chapter aims to make this connection more explicit and to explore some insights that a methodological intersection between feminist literary history and archipelagic literary study might yield. In particular the chapter will address in what ways feminist recovery work and archipelagic studies can come together to address the double marginalisation of early modern women who produced Anglophone poetry from Scottish, Irish, and Welsh contexts. Through what we might term 'archipelagic feminism' or 'archipelagic feminist recovery', the chapter argues that a devolved attention to the geographically marginal can result not only in reappraisal of that perceived marginality, but also lead to different conclusions as to the status of particular poets, the significance of their poetry, and that of individual poems. In addition, the chapter considers the implications of an archipelagic approach for a reassessment of the 'canon' of women's literary production in the period and the contexts from which it can be read and interpreted. Overall,

[1] John Kerrigan, *Archipelagic English: Literature, History, and Politics 1603–1707* (Oxford, 2008), 80. The term 'archipelagic' stems from a foundational article by J. G. A. Pocock, 'British History: A Plea for a New Subject', *Journal of Modern History*, 47 (1975), 601–21.

the chapter poses the question: 'How can archipelagic literary criticism expand and challenge the parameters of the feminist recovery project'?

In what follows I suggest some different ways we can approach this question both in terms of archival and scholarly recovery and in terms of methodology and textual interpretation. Firstly, and most straightforwardly, archipelagic approaches can work simply to expand the range of women poets under discussion by deliberately problematising an exclusively Anglocentric scholarly focus or, at the very least, consciously acknowledging when the focus is on English examples and English paradigms of authorship and literary production (often hidden under the use of 'British'). Paradigms of English women writers are routinely taken as the norm against which Irish, Scottish, and Welsh writers are judged as marginal. Of course, as Kate Chedzgoy has argued: 'the work of remembering forgotten women is not just a matter of expanding the canon of women's writing, but of reconsidering the criteria—geographical, social and linguistic, as well as aesthetic—we have used to define it'.[2] As Chedzgoy goes on to note, we need 'a rebalancing of the casual anglocentricity of much early modern scholarship'.[3] This 'casual anglocentricity' is more pernicious than just benign neglect as it also affects the theoretical paradigms employed in relation to women's poetic production. For example, Sarah M. Dunnigan discusses the 'double marginalisation' of 'writing by women, and as writing which is Scottish', noting that '[f]ew of the works combining an interpretative or theoretical 'feminist' practice with new archival discoveries or evaluation of early modern women's writing include Scottish material'.[4] The same could be said for Irish and Welsh examples and could stem also from disciplinary differences between 'English Studies', 'Scottish Studies', 'Irish Studies', and 'Celtic Studies', disciplines that are clearly complementary but which often fail to speak to each other sufficiently. As C. R. A. Gibbon points out, 'the recovery of writing by women—now so well advanced in scholarship of English literature—lags behind in Scotland'.[5]

Missing pieces of the archipelagic jigsaw can change the overall picture, not just expand parameters within the same methodological frame. This approach is not about inclusion alone but involves asking different questions and acknowledging diversity. Archipelagic methods force what might seem to be obvious questions, but they are often ones that rarely get asked if we approach national traditions in isolation or collectively under a 'British' umbrella. As Dunnigan has argued, again in relation to the context in Scotland:

[2] Kate Chedgzoy, *Women's Writing in the British Atlantic World: Memory, Place and History, 1550–1700* (Cambridge, 2007), 124.

[3] Chedgzoy, *Women's Writing in the British Atlantic World*, 124.

[4] Sarah M. Dunnigan, 'Introduction', in Sarah M. Dunnigan, C. Marie Harker, and Evelyn S. Newlyn (eds), *Woman and the Feminine in Medieval and Early Modern Scottish Writing* (Basingstoke, 2004), xiv–xxx.

[5] C. R. A. Gibbon, 'The Literary Cultures of the Scottish Reformation', *The Review of English Studies*, 57.288 (2006), 64–82, 68.

> Because of its linguistic and cultural diversity (arguably in comparison to English women's writing of the period), this literature questions notions of homogeneity or uniformity; its very 'marginality' invests it with the power to re-evaluate conventional paradigms of culture.[6]

In the first instance, then, what do we gain from an archipelagic approach in relation to Scottish women poets? The first insight might be that while there are considerably fewer women poets in early modern Scotland when compared to England, there are many more surviving examples of women composing Anglophone poetry in the Scottish context than in Ireland and Wales; a basic fact we miss if the focus is only on a comparison with England. As Chedgzoy notes: 'Scotland demonstrates by far the highest level of literary activity by women of the three countries with texts produced in significant quantities in English, Scots and Gaelic, and a sprinkling in French and Latin too'.[7] Moreover, as Dunnigan reminds us, 'it is the Scottish Gaelic tradition which offers the earliest and richest examples of late medieval women's writing'.[8] Furthermore, as Colm Ó Baoill notes, 'Scotland far exceeds Ireland in the number of Gaelic women well known as poets'.[9]

In contrast to the relative wealth of poetic output by women from the Scottish Gaelic tradition, 'until the post-Reformation period, very little material composed in Lowland Scots survived', and very little reached print.[10] What does survive in manuscript from sixteenth-century Scotland can be seen to emerge from literary circles and coteries of predominantly male poets. As Jane Stevenson outlines:

> [t]hree women's names are associated with the group of poets which grew up around James VI in the last two decades of the sixteenth century, Christian Lindsay, whose surviving poems (if she is not a literary fiction) defend Alexander Montgomerie; Elizabeth Douglas, who wrote two poems in praise of William Fowler's Petrarch translations; and Lady Mary Beaton, also a friend of Fowler's.[11]

Christian Lindsay (fl. 1580/86) 'was part of a circle of court poets active in Scotland in the mid-1580s, known as "the Castalian Band"' in Edinburgh.[12] Her only surviving poem, 'Cristen Lyndesay to Ro. Hudsone', is a plea for support on behalf of Montgomerie and

6 Dunnigan, *Woman and the Feminine*, xvi.

7 Chedgzoy, *Women's Writing in the British Atlantic World*, 97. See also Suzanne Trill, 'Early Modern Women's Writing in the Edinburgh Archives, c. 1550–1740: A Preliminary Checklist', in Dunnigan, Harker, Newlyn (eds), *Woman and the Feminine*, 196–201.

8 Dunnigan, 'Introduction', xxiii.

9 Colm Ó Baoill, '"Neither out nor in": Scottish Gaelic Women Poets, 1650–1750', in Dunnigan, Harker, Newlyn (eds), *Woman and the Feminine*, 136–52, 137.

10 Dunnigan, 'Introduction', xxiii.

11 Jane Stevenson, 'Reading, Writing and Gender in Early Modern Scotland', *The Seventeenth Century*, 27.3 (2012): 335–74, 336.

12 Jane Stevenson and Peter Davidson (eds), *Early Modern Women Poets: An Anthology* (Oxford, 2001), 83.

signals that a woman could be active on behalf of her fellow artists despite the masculine makeup of the group. Similarly, Lady Mary Beaton may have influenced Fowler's 1587 vernacular translation of Petrarch.[13] In addition, the Maitland Quarto manuscript is associated with Mary Maitland, a 'member of a prominent and educated family'.[14] Needless to say, all these women appear to have been both elite and educated as well as supported by their male counterparts.

The seventeenth century witnessed an increase in the prevalence and survival of Scottish women's writing in English and the model of communal literary practices that centre on influential male mentors continues in different contexts. As Stevenson notes: '[i]n the generation after Fowler, women formed part of the cultural nexus around Drummond of Hawthornden (Fowler's nephew) and his brother-in-law Scot of Scotstarvet [Sir John Scot]'.[15] For example, the shadowy and complex figure of Mary Oxlie (fl. 1656) appears to have been the author of a commendatory verse 'To William Drummond of Hawthornden', 'prefixed to the *Poems* of William Drummond' in 1656 and signed 'Mary Oxlie of Morpet (1656)'.[16] As Stevenson and Davidson argue, the poem displays evidence of 'a fair amount of education' in her reference to Drummond's poetry and in the use of classical allusion.[17] Although we know little more about Oxlie apart from her possible authorship of two broadsides, the opening of this poem reflects on her background as a 'Rustick ... rudely fostered' and comments on the 'hoarse encumbrances of houshold care' (l. 9) that hold her back as a female writer due to the lack of 'an untroubled mind' (l. 7). The genre is familiar as a 'poetic *apologia* for female creativity'.[18] It is clear, then, that literary coteries and their attendant manuscript cultures were enabling for women poets in Scotland and indeed the period after 1600 witnessed the emergence of two significant poets with a body of work in print. Elizabeth Melville's *An Godlie Dreame* (1603), 'the first religious text by a Scottish woman to be published', was printed in Edinburgh first in Scots and then in an anglicised version in the same year.[19] Her work has, until recently, been marginal to the mainstream canon of women's writing, but she was also marginalised from the canon of Scottish studies

[13] Sarah M. Dunnigan, 'Scottish Women Writers c. 1560–c. 1650', in Douglas Gifford and Dorothy McMillan (eds), *A History of Scottish Women's Writing* (Edinburgh, 1997), 15–43, 26. Stevenson also argues that '[a] 'Sonnet' in Fowler's MSS, NLS Ms 2065, fol. 6r, composed in the 'Castalian' interlaced rhyme scheme and signed M.L.B., urges that Fowler abandon lyric and take up translation/imitation of Petrarch'. See Stevenson, 'Reading, Writing and Gender', 365, note 6.

[14] Evelyn S. Newlyn, 'A Methodology for Reading Against the Culture: Anonymous, Women Poets, and the Maitland Quarto Manuscript (c. 1586)', in Dunnigan, Harker, Newlyn (eds), *Woman and the Feminine*, 89–103, 92.

[15] Stevenson, 'Reading, Writing and Gender', 336.

[16] Stevenson and Davidson, *Early Modern Women Poets*, 170–1.

[17] Stevenson and Davidson, *Early Modern Women Poets*, 170.

[18] Dunnigan, 'Scottish Women Writers', 26.

[19] Dunnigan, 'Introduction', xiii. See also, Deanna Delmar Evans, 'Holy Terror and Love Devine: The Passionate Voice in Elizabeth Melville's *Ane Godlie* Dreame', in Sarah M. Dunnigan, C. Marie Harker, and Evelyn S. Newlyn (eds), *Woman and the Feminine in Medieval and Early Modern Scottish Writing* (Basingstoke, 2004), 153–61, 160.

due to her Calvinist background.[20] In 1644, the Lowland Borders writer Anna Hume, published a translation of Petrarch, *The Triumphs of Love: Chastity: Death: Translated out of Petrarch*, which 'can justly claim to be the first printed example of women's secular writing in Lowland Scotland'.[21] Despite the prominence of Hume's verse, however, it is still apparent that 'devotional or spiritual writing [...] offers the richest source of vernacular Scottish women's writing.[22]

As in Scotland, the paucity of women in Wales producing poetry in English is offset by the relatively high number of surviving Welsh-language manuscript examples of women's poetry; although, like Scotland again, 'the majority of known women poets before 1800 have only one surviving poem to their name'.[23] A rare exception is Alis ferch Gruffudd ab Ieuan (fl. c 1540–1570), 'a poet whose surviving canon includes about eight strict-metre poems' and who was associated through her family with the broader bardic culture of North Wales.[24] Cathryn A. Charnell-White provides an insightful comparative overview from a Welsh perspective:

> The Welsh female canon before 1800 comprises over 200 individual items by about 80 individuals, mainly from manuscript sources but also, by the eighteenth century, from print sources. This compares with around 200 items by 25 individuals who composed in Scottish Gaelic before 1800, around 100 items by 35 individuals who composed in Scots, and around 40 items by 15 named individuals who composed in Gaelic/Irish before that date.[25]

The findings of this ostensibly quantitative comparison are potentially radical if we follow Charnell-White and look at the non-Anglophone poetic productions of women in early modern Britain and Ireland as a group rather than always comparing and contrasting to English paradigms. The genres used by Welsh women poets are familiar, with an emphasis on elegy, occasional poetry, love poetry, devotional and religious verse

[20] Gibbon notes that 'since the seventeenth century, the Scottish literary canon has been forged in a climate deliberately opposed to the theological ideas—especially the Calvinist ideas—that repeatedly appear at its heart'. See Gibbon, 'The Literary Cultures of the Scottish Reformation', 65. For recent challenges to this climate and an informative overview of the more recent 'cultural turn' in early modern Scottish studies, see Karin Bowie, 'Cultural, British and Global Turns in the History of Early Modern Scotland', *The Scottish Historical Review*, XCII.234 (2013), 38–48. For an excellent example in literary studies of the positive developments noted by Bowie, see Sebastiaan Verweij, *The Literary Culture of Early Modern Scotland: Manuscript Production and Transmission, 1560–1625* (Oxford, 2016).

[21] Sarah M. Dunnigan, 'Daughterly Desires: Representing and Reimagining the Feminine in Anna Hume's *Triumphs*', in Dunnigan, Harker, Newlyn (eds), *Woman and the Feminine*, 120–35, 122.

[22] Dunnigan, 'Introduction', xiii.

[23] Cathryn A. Charnell-White, 'Problems of Authorship and Attribution: The Welsh-Language Women's Canon before 1800', *Women's Writing*, 24.4, (2017), 398–417, 398. For an anthology of Welsh women's poetry, see Charnell-White, *Beirdd Ceridwen: Blodeugerdd Barddas o Ganu Menywod hyd tua 1800* (Swansea, 2005).

[24] Charnell-White, 'Problems of Authorship and Attribution', 398. Another example is Catrin ferch Gruffudd ap Hywel (fl. *c* 1555) of Anglesey.

[25] Charnell-White, 'Problems of Authorship', 400.

as well as 'subliterary genres like the mother's advice poem'. However, overall, the contextual framework is distinct as the 'surviving female canon was shaped by the bardic culture of its time and reflects the vicissitudes of strict metre and free metre during the course of the early modern period'.[26] Most Welsh women participating in poetic culture were not only part of a privileged elite, but also associated with 'a familial bardic circle' that enabled proficiency in strict-metre composition. In fact, 'family bonds were as important as poetic networks to budding amateur poets, both male and female'.[27] Furthermore, rather than thinking about these women as constituting a coherent tradition, 'it is more useful to think of Wales' medieval and early modern women poets in terms of a diversity of independent, localized poetic coteries (both mixed and women only) that occasionally interlinked'.[28]

In contrast to the localised contexts of Welsh women's poetic production, early modern Irish women operated in a national framework that was intrinsically archipelagic. As Marie-Louise Coolahan has argued:

> [t]he literature of early modern Ireland is always a drama of archipelagism; an island co-habited by Gaelic Irish, 'Old' English, 'New' English and Scots settlers can only be a space in which competing identities confronted and shaped each other in a variety of languages. […] Irish literary history—from any linguistic perspective—cannot but be archipelagic, despite its avowedly national paradigm.[29]

For women writing in Gaelic, both in its elite bardic form and, as the seventeenth century progressed, in increasingly non-bardic vernacular production, there are comparisons with Scotland more obviously, but also with Wales. Coolahan draws a connection between the elite Gaelic poetry of Brighid Fitzgerald (*c* 1589–1682) and Scottish contemporaries Aithbhreac inghean Coirceadail (fl. 1470s) and Iseabal Ní Mheic Cailéan (1459–*c* 1493), suggesting that the 'archipelagic context enables us to consider the more complete picture of elite Gaelic women's literary composition and to overcome assumptions about the solitary text'.[30] In the seventeenth century the five keens composed by Caitlín Dubh in the period 1624–1629 are the production of a non-elite woman, but one who, nonetheless, was able to employ bardic tropes for political effect in her work. Furthermore, as both Coolahan and Chedgzoy suggest, Dubh's keen on Donnchadh Ó Briaín, the fourth earl of Thomond, for example, evokes the archipelagic frame of composition: '[i]n these familial poems the local is privileged

[26] Charnell-White, 'Problems of Authorship', 400–1.

[27] Charnell-White, 'Problems of Authorship', 403–4.

[28] Charnell-White, 'Problems of Authorship', 408.

[29] Marie-Louise Coolahan, 'Whither the archipelago? Stops, starts, and hurdles on the four nations front', *Literature Compass*, 15.11 (2018), 1–12, 7.

[30] Coolahan, *Women, Writing, and Language in Early Modern Ireland* (Oxford, 2010), Kindle edn, 1052.

within a complexly archipelagic context, and memory and mourning are deployed to map shifting relations between Thomond, Ireland and English authority'.[31]

Neither Ireland nor Wales produced a discernible body of early modern Anglophone poetry by women, although there are examples of women's writing in other genres (such as petitions and legal pleadings as well as letters and life writing). However, 'the experience of living in Ireland also impacted on the writing of women now established in the canon of women's writing in English—women who migrated from and returned to Britain'.[32] Two prominent examples are the Munster planter Anne Southwell who 'lived in Cork for almost three decades before returning to London about 1630', and Katherine Philips, who spent a year in Dublin between 1662 and 1663.[33] There are no native-born Anglophone poets whose work has survived from Ireland or Wales in the period covered by the present volume. As I have previously noted elsewhere, Katherine Philips is the only woman writing in English out of Wales in the entire seventeenth century. This is just one of the insights concerning the locations of women's literary production that comes to light if due attention is paid to non-metropolitan geographies.

Thus far I have been attempting to illustrate how an inclusive expansion of the canon of women's writing along archipelagic lines can lead to a reassessment of accepted paradigms of women's engagement in poetic cultures. Such an approach has highlighted both the dangers of assuming homogeneity, or clear 'traditions' of women's poetry, as well as shown some of the cross-cutting generic similarities between women in different national and local contexts. However, in addition to increased inclusivity as a result of a widened geographical range, archipelagic feminist approaches can also disrupt methodological and theoretical conventions. As I have argued elsewhere in relation to Katherine Philips, one conceptual framework for reassessing the work of women writers perceived to have been producing poetry on the geographical margins is that of 'archipelagic coterie space'. Following Kerrigan, such an approach is achieved by '[r]eframing the local or localised as an interactive component of a broader archipelagic frame, rather than as a narrowing constraint on female literary production'.[34] In the case of Katherine Philips, a well-known and frequently studied writer primarily recognised for her friendship poetry and her Royalism, such an approach allows for a reassessment of the centrality of Philips' Welsh location for her poetry and her coterie practice. In fact, Philips lived the majority of her writing life in Wales as she moved there in the 1640s on her mother's marriage to Sir Richard Phillips of Picton Castle in Pembrokeshire and then on to Cardigan from 1648 following her marriage to Colonel James Philips in that year. As such, it can be argued that, rather than serving as a form of rural isolation from

[31] Chedgzoy, *Women's Writing in the British Atlantic World*, 84; Coolahan, *Women, Writing, and Language*, Kindle edn, 3971–2. See also Coolahan, 'Caitlín Dubh's Keens: Literary Negotiations in Early Modern Ireland', in Victoria Burke and Jonathan Gibson (eds), *Early Modern Women's Manuscript Writing: Selected Papers from the Trinity/Trent Colloquium* (Aldershot, 2004), 99–102.

[32] Coolahan, *Women, Writing, and Language*, Kindle edn, 1055.

[33] Coolahan, *Women, Writing, and Language*, Kindle edn, 1050.

[34] Sarah Prescott, 'Archipelagic Coterie Space: Katherine Philips and Welsh Women's Writing', *Tulsa Studies in Women's Literature*, 33.2 (2014), 51–76, 52; Kerrigan, *Archipelagic English*.

the metropolitan literary centre leading to a stifling of creativity, Philips' married life in Wales both enabled and also informed her poetry.[35] Such an approach also leads to a re-evaluation of Philips' own body of work and redirects attention not only to the ways in which her poetry is shaped by the archipelagic dimension of her Welsh experience but also to how a significant number of poems in her oeuvre have been critically neglected due to their perceived 'narrow' Welsh or local focus. Thinking about Philips as a 'Welsh' woman writer in an archipelagic frame produces a very different view of her significance, as Coolahan points out:

> the surprise of Prescott's arguments—that Philips reverses expectation of centre/periphery by claiming Wales as a space for literary renewal, that understanding of her Welsh poems facilitates us to consider social connectivity instead of the isolated single author, that she can usefully be constructed as 'an archipelagic bard'—highlights the valuable way in which archipelagic criticism can show us what is hiding in plain sight.[36]

Can the concept of 'archipelagic coterie space' work as a transferable model applicable to other early modern women writers and could it therefore further the recovery project?[37] If we bring together an attention to devolved geographies with a focus on a more fluid and expansive sense of the local what other insights might be possible? One way is to look at Philips alongside two other seventeenth-century Anglophone women poets who also operated in non-metropolitan contexts outside England but who also, although to lesser degrees, produced a discernable body of work: Anne Southwell and Elizabeth Melville. Philips has been read alongside both these writers in different ways and in different contexts. For example, Coolahan juxtaposes Philips and Southwell in terms of their respective experiences in Ireland: Southwell as a Munster planter living near Cork in the early years of the seventeenth century and Philips in terms of her one year spent in Dublin in the period 1662–1663. Coolahan 'examines the literary strategies of two poets [. . .] who used their writing to forge alliances among their peers. Both poets circulated their writing to a network of acquaintances and friends in manuscript, a medium attractive for its facilitation of control over readership'.[38]

In her study of 'Reading, Writing and Gender in Early Modern Scotland', Jane Stevenson acknowledges Elizabeth Melville, Lady Culross (?1570s–after 1630) as Scotland's 'one major published poet' as well as an active participant in manuscript literary culture:

[35] Gillian Wright notes: '[t]he evidence of her own autograph collection, which includes no poems firmly datable before autumn 1649, bears out this association, and suggests that Philips' marriage in August 1648 may have helped make it possible for her writing to flourish'. Wright, *Producing Women's Poetry, 1600–1730: Text and Paratext, Manuscript and Print* (Cambridge, 2013), 119.

[36] Coolahan, 'Whither the archipelago?', 4. See Prescott, 'Archipelagic Coterie Space'.

[37] See this volume, Chapter 16, Julie A. Eckerle, 'Women's Life Writing'.

[38] Coolahan, *Women, Writing, and Language*, Kindle edn, 2376–9.

> Her vision-poem *Ane Godlie Dreame* was printed again and again in Scotland after the first edition in 1603, at least thirteen times down to 1737. Lady Culross also left verse in manuscript: most of what survives is written in the last thirteen leaves of a manuscript volume of sermons by Robert Bruce preached in autumn 1590 and spring 1591, now in New College Library, Edinburgh.[39]

As discussed earlier, other surviving examples of early modern Scottish women writing in English or Scots either in print (Anna Hume) or manuscript are rare, leading Stevenson to pose the question: 'why is there no Scottish Katherine Philips?'[40] Stevenson's question does not take into account the fact that Philips was writing primarily from Wales, but evokes her as an example of the comparative wealth of women poets in England in the seventeenth century. In her discussion of Melville's religious and poetic communities in Scotland, however, Sarah C. E. Ross picks up on Stevenson's 'provocative' question to make the case that 'as Melville's poetry and networks of transmission become increasingly visible, a comparison with Philips has become more productive and more apt'.[41] The comparison is now possible due not only to recognition that Philips herself, far from being isolated in Wales, was both there, and later in Dublin, engaged 'in multiple and overlapping locuses of manuscript culture'. Comparison is also enabled by new insights into Melville's modes of production and engagement in literary and religious coteries and communities that belie the sense of her as a sole or solitary example of Anglophone Scottish women's participation in the literary culture of their day.[42] Central to the reassessment of Philips and Melville, and to a lesser extent Southwell, is the reconfiguration of the local and geographical 'marginal' as part of a more expansive and fluid archipelagic frame based on networks of connectivity and influence. Ross notes that by paying attention to the 'literal' as well as the 'textual' networks of exchange utilised by Melville, it is possible 'to create a cultural cartography that is particular, local, and networked at the same time as it tells us much about comparative national and archipelagic cultures of manuscript production and exchange'.[43] Despite the different national location, this sounds very much like Philips' practice in Wales. Overall, all three of these poets can be said to be enabled, rather than restricted by their 'marginal' locations and localities. Therefore, the sense that these authors are 'isolated' and 'peripheral' is not backed up by their poetic and literary practice across Ireland, Scotland, and Wales. As Ross argues in relation to Elizabeth Melville:

[39] Stevenson, 'Reading, Writing and Gender', 335.

[38] Stevenson, 'Reading, Writing and Gender', 337.

[40] Stevenson, 'Reading, Writing and Gender', 337.

[41] Sarah C. E. Ross, 'Peripatetic Poems: Sites of Production and Routes of Exchange in Elizabeth Melville's Scotland,' *Women's Writing*, 26.1 (2018), 52–70, 54. See also, Sarah C. E. Ross, *Women, Poetry, and Politics in Seventeenth-Century Britain* (Oxford, 2015).

[42] See this volume, Chapter 35, Sebastiaan Verweij, 'Elizabeth Melville'.

[43] Ross, 'Peripatetic Poems', 55.

> Evolving scholarship on Elizabeth Melville continues to enlarge our understanding of a poet whose work makes clear that her religious sonnets and poems in manuscript travelled widely and were very extensively read over several decades in seventeenth-century Scotland—perhaps as widely and extensively as the work of Katherine Philips. Her poems' emergence in new, multiple, and various manuscript contexts is just one indicator that English manuscript culture is in part 'more scrutable' that that of its archipelagic cousins because it has been more scrutinised.[44]

However, archipelagic connections can also work to expose a sense of difference and disruption, revealing sites of tension or even conflict between women's writing rather than reciprocity. Anne Southwell is a fascinating example of a poet who composed her poetry in both Cork and Acton and who, out of the three women highlighted here, was perhaps less expansive in terms of the range of the audience for her manuscript verse.[45] In contrast to Katherine Philips' mutually appreciative experience in Dublin, Southwell's Irish experience is an example of the surfacing of difference as a result of an archipelagic clashing of religious cultures in this instance. For example, Elizabeth Clarke notes Southwell's virulent anti-Catholicism and observes that rather than developing increased religious tolerance, her exposure to Catholicism in Ireland 'seems to have sharpened her disdain for it'.[46] Indeed, in her Decalogue poem on the third commandment Southwell states that, 'Rome holdes not upp more fopperyes then this land' (*Southwell-Sibthorpe Common Place Book*, 131), particularly focusing on Irish funeral traditions as an example of such 'foppery':

> Yf in Hibernia god will haue mee dye,
> I cannott have your capon eaters knell,
> Yet for a pound Ile have a hundred crye,
> & teare theyr hayres like furyes sent from hell.
> (*Southwell-Sibthorpe Common Place Book*, 132)[47]

Coolahan views these lines as 'dramatising the culture clash of coexistence on the island', characterised as a moment that 'articulates dislocation':[48]

> Her self-construction as a poet is overwhelmingly devotional and protestant, and sharply defined by its opposition to the religion of the majority culture surrounding her. The expatriate evaluation of funerary rites, above, is a particularly dramatic moment in the complex figuration of identity in her verse.[49]

44 Ross, 'Peripatetic Poems' 65.

45 As argued by Gillian Wright, *Producing Women's Poetry*, 32.

46 Elizabeth Clarke, 'Anne, Lady Southwell: Coteries and Culture', in Johanna Harris and Elizabeth Scott-Baumann (eds), *The Intellectual Culture of Puritan Women, 1558–1689* (London, 2010), 57–70, 58.

47 Quoted by Clarke 'Anne, Lady Southwell', 58.

48 Coolahan, *Women, Writing, and Language*, Kindle edn, 2387.

49 Coolahan, *Women, Writing, and Language*, Kindle edn, 2414.

Gillian Wright similarly draws attention to the way in which 'Southwell speculates on how the 'poore wretched' Irish, whom 'the Pope doth cozen ... of wealth and wittes', might mourn her death, 'Yf in Hibernia god will have mee dye' (stanza 41.5, 6, 1).'[50]

Exposure to different cultures, therefore, does not always produce reciprocity or appreciation. Attention to an archipelagic frame can also highlight 'dislocation', not only between different cultural traditions but also between contemporaneous and co-located women writers. This can work both ways. As Chedgzoy notes: '[e]arly modern English writings on Ireland are fascinated by practices surrounding death and mourning as a key locus of Irish cultural difference'.[51] However, the keen, or funeral lament, criticised by Southwell by implication, was one of the key genres for women composing in Irish, such as Caitlín Dubh.[52] Indeed, Chedgzoy argues that, in her elegy on the death of Donnchadh Ó Briaín, Dubh turns 'back on the English the quasi-ethnographic gaze they had directed at Irish funerary customs'.[53] Dubh's poems, Chedgzoy argues, confront and complicate such perceptions head on:

> Blending the formal public elegy for a male leader with the more feminine mode of the keen, relocating her feminine lament from Ireland to James' British court, and locating her Gaelic hero within a context which is at once Irish, archipelagic, and European, Caitlín Dubh's poem poses a complex challenge to such perceptions.[54]

Nevertheless, Ireland proved enabling for Southwell to develop her devotional thought and her poetry. 'Rather than languish in Irish isolation among "poor wretched soules"', Coolahan explains, 'she composed religious verse, cultivating social connections among the New English elite through her writings'.[55] For example, her mock-elegy to Cicely Ridgeway (whose husband Sir Thomas was made earl of Londonderry in 1622), 'An Elegie written by the Lady A:S: to the Countess of London Derrye', continues a literary debate about the art of poetry that had begun in an epistolary exchange. She also addressed prominent male figures through her verse often those 'at the front line of the Church of Ireland effort', such as the religious poet Frances Quarles and Bernard Adams, the Bishop of Limerick.[56] As such, like Philips and Melville in their different national contexts, the building of social and the literary networks which make sense of the location in which the poet finds herself are key to the development and circulation of manuscript verse and the self-construction of the poet. Yet, as Wright notes, locality (either in Munster or Acton) as much as any link to a broader readerly community is the feature of Southwell's manuscript practice: 'the social and intellectual influences on Anne

[50] Wright, *Producing Women's Poetry*, 51.

[51] Chedgzoy, *Women's Writing in the British Atlantic World*, 84.

[52] See Danielle Clarke and Sarah McKibben, 'Seventeenth-Century Women's Writing in Ireland', in Ailbhe Darcy and David Wheatley (eds), *A History of Irish Women's Poetry* (Cambridge, 2021), 57–73.

[53] Chedgzoy, *Women's Writing in the British Atlantic World*, 84.

[54] Chedgzoy, *Women's Writing in the British Atlantic World*, 85.

[55] Coolahan, *Women, Writing, and Language*, Kindle edn, 2406.

[56] Coolahan, *Women, Writing, and Language*, Kindle edn, 2515.

Southwell's poetry owe nothing to the coterie networks of the court in London; their sources are at once less privileged, more idiosyncratic and more diverse'.[57]

I would like to conclude by turning to Katherine Philips' brief experience in Dublin in the 1660s and end with a recent reading of her poem 'The Irish Greyhound' as one example of how poetry can engage textually with archipelagic context. Philips spent one year in Restoration Dublin between July 1662 and July 1663 where she wrote and circulated a number of poems to members of the Irish 'Old Protestant' elite, but was most well-known for her English translation of Corneille's *Pompey* (published in Dublin and London in 1663), which was performed at Smock Alley theatre and drew the immediate admiration and support of Roger Boyle, earl of Orrery. However, her ostensible reason for travelling to Dublin was to settle a land investment on behalf of her husband and, as Coolahan explains, because of this she had direct dealings with the institutions and networks that could enable her entrance into Dublin literary society:

> Philips' father had invested £200 as an adventurer in Ireland in 1642: according to the terms of the act, individuals would invest in an army to suppress the 1641 rising in return for land which would be confiscated from Irish rebels. This investment was passed to Philips' husband on their marriage. Conveniently, her friend Edward Dering ('Silvander') was in Dublin as one of seven commissioners appointed to implement the 1662 Bill of Settlement. She had connections to the crown administration and Dublin court; her legal objective involved her in the political wrangling of the new regime.[58]

In addition, Philips had travelled to Dublin from Wales with Anne Owen (Lucasia) who was the second wife of the Anglo-Irish Colonel Marcus Trevor, Viscount Dungannon. She thus arrived in Ireland with a strong base of connections from which to build her literary networks and reputation in Dublin.

The publication circumstances of the poem 'The Irish Greyhound' illustrate very well the success of Philips' acceptance by the Anglophone literary circles primarily focused vice-regal culture of Dublin court. The poem was printed with two further pieces by Philips in *Poems, by Several Persons* (1663), a verse miscellany that also included admiring poems to her by Orrery and Abraham Cowley and which has been described by Peter Beale as 'the very essence of a coterie circulation of verse connected with the Dublin court'.[59] Although 'The Irish Greyhound' is not a typical coterie poem, in that it does not address a particular individual or context, Lee Morrissey has pointed out that the poem 'springs from an inter-island, archipelagic experience', adding that '[a]rriving in Dublin in 1662, Philips was in the right place at the right time to play an

[57] Wright, *Producing Women's Poetry*, 32.

[58] Coolahan, *Women, Writing, and Language*, Kindle edn, 2592–5.

[59] Peter Beal, *In Praise of Scribes: Manuscripts and their Makers in Seventeenth-Century England* (Oxford, 1998), 159. Referenced also by Coolahan, *Women, Writing, and Language*, Kindle edn, 2768; Lee Morrissey, '"Behold this Creature's form and State": Katherine Philips and the Early Ascendancy', *Women's Writing*, 24.3 (2017), 298–312, 299.

important part in the emergence of what came to be known as the Ascendancy. In "The Irish Greyhound", she seized this opportunity'.[60] Morrissey's main point about the poem is that through the animal analogy, Philips is drawing a favourable comparison between Ireland and England that did not replicate the stereotypes of past Anglophone writing on Ireland, but instead was concerned to find 'a new vocabulary for inter-island understanding'.[61] The key dynamic is in the comparison of the English lion to the Irish Greyhound in the poem:

> Behold this Creature's form and State,
> Which Nature therefore did Create,
> That to the World might be exprest,
> What miene there can be in a Beast.
> And that we in this shape might find
> A Lyon of another kind.
> For this Heroick Dog does seem
> In Majesty to Rival him. (ll. 1–8)

The description of the leonine greyhound echoes Philips' use of 'the lion as an image for the English monarchy' elsewhere in her poetry, thus reinforcing this poem's association of the particular breed of dog with broader conceptions of statehood.[62] Such an analogy, argues Morrissey, positively reflects Philips' archipelagic experience of difference. In contrast to Anne Southwell, then, 'it also seems to have made Philips into something of an inter-island advocate for her experience of Ireland, and, thereby, for inter-island relationships', albeit within the elite circles of a pro-monarchy vice-regal court.[63]

Employing an archipelagic framework alongside the feminist imperative to recover the literary history of early modern women poets across Ireland, Scotland, and Wales does not result in easy answers to the questions such an approach poses. What we do not find is the simplicity of homogeneity. In fact, as the geographical range is expanded the contextually specific becomes increasingly significant for understanding both individual and communal poetic practice, as seen clearly in the emerging scholarship on Elizabeth Melville, for example. However, an archipelagic approach can dramatically alter the terms on which we evaluate an individual author's poetry by inviting serious critical attention to be paid to previously under-studied poems that emerge from and respond to the localities in which they were written. As such, a poet conventionally known as an English Royalist poet of female friendship, Katherine Philips, can become an Anglo-Welsh archipelagic bard as well as an Anglo-Irish 'inter-island advocate'.[64] As a result, the range of her 'significant' poems is thus expanded by her authorial redefinition in archipelagic terms. Furthermore, by exploring early modern women poets

60 Morrissey, '"Behold this Creature's form"', 299, 300.
61 Morrissey, '"Behold this Creature's form"', 307.
62 Morrissey, '"Behold this Creature's form"', 302.
63 Morrissey, '"Behold this Creature's form"', 308.
64 Morrissey, '"Behold this Creature's form"', 308.

from Ireland, Scotland, and Wales in an archipelagic frame we become alert as much to productive differences and tensions as well as putative similarities and synergies, as shown by the poetry of Anne Southwell when read alongside that of Caitlín Dubh. Nevertheless, a comparative approach that does not view non-metropolitan sites of poetic production as automatically representative of isolation opens up lines of investigation that can highlight common practices, such as the shared importance of local networks of exchange for women, and also suggest areas of intersection, such as the recurrence of 'non-canonical' poetic genres across different languages and cultures. Overall, the key is not to be prescriptive or dogmatic in the practice of archipelagic feminist inclusivity, but nevertheless to insist that women from Ireland, Scotland, and Wales are not an optional extra but an integral part of the still developing bigger picture of early modern women's poetry in English. It is salutary to note that despite the excellent work achieved by various scholars of early modern women's poetry, the full map of women's poetic production, and our understanding of it, is far from complete or inclusive.

FURTHER READING

Charnell-White, Cathryn A. 'Problems of Authorship and Attribution: The Welsh-Language Women's Canon before 1800', *Women's Writing*, 24.4 (2017), 398–417.

Coolahan, Marie-Louise. 'Whither the archipelago? Stops, starts, and hurdles on the four nations front', *Literature Compass*, 15.11 (2018), 1–12.

Coolahan, Marie-Louise. *Women, Writing, and Language in Early Modern Ireland*. Oxford, 2010.

Dunnigan, Sarah M., C. Marie Harker, and Evelyn S. Newlyn (eds). *Woman and the Feminine in Medieval and Early Modern Scottish Writing*. Basingstoke, 2004, 136–52.

Kerrigan, John. *Archipelagic English: Literature, History, and Politics, 1603–1707*. Cambridge, 2006.

Prescott, Sarah. 'Archipelagic Coterie Space: Katherine Philips and Welsh Women's Writing', *Tulsa Studies in Women's Literature*, 33.2 (2014), 51–76.

Ross, Sarah C. E. 'Peripatetic Poems: Sites of Production and Routes of Exchange in Elizabeth Melville's Scotland', *Women's Writing*, 26.1 (2018), 52–70.

PART IV

TRANSLINGUAL AND TRANSNATIONAL

CHAPTER 27

'MISTRESSES OF TONGUES'

Early Modern Englishwomen, Multilingual Practice, and Translingual Communication

BRENDA M. HOSINGTON

TAKEN from Bathsua Makin's 1673 pamphlet, *An Essay to Revive the Ancient Education of Gentlewomen,* the phrase 'mistresses of tongues' punningly alludes to women's indisputable linguistic abilities but also to the age-old proverbial slur, 'one tongue is enough for a woman'. Actually, Makin continues, 'Women have not been mere talkers (as some frivolous men would make them), but they have known how to use languages when they have had them' (sig. B2r). One way was to put their foreign language learning into multilingual practice through communicating translingually, sometimes orally, as recently discussed in Emilie Murphy's excellent article on language use and proficiency in English convents on the Continent.[1] Often, however, women could demonstrate their linguistic skills through translation. They and their translated texts are the subject of this chapter.

An enormous amount of work has been done over the past two decades in discovering, and especially in reinterpreting, translations penned by early modern Englishwomen. Earlier feminist literary critics viewed translations with a rather jaundiced eye. This was largely because they read them in isolation from other contemporary translations or original compositions, disregarded Renaissance theories and practice of translation and the whole burgeoning field of translation studies from the 1980s on, and were heavily influenced by post-Romantic attitudes that viewed translated works as derivative and secondary. In short, this was to misunderstand the nature of translation, which is interdisciplinary and cannot be divorced from the linguistic and sociocultural developments taking place at a given time and in a given setting. It also underestimated how large and powerful the translation movement was in early modern Europe. As Danielle Clarke

[1] Emilie K. M. Murphy, 'Exile and Linguistic Encounter: Early Modern Convents in the Low Countries and France', *Renaissance Quarterly*, 73 (2020), 132–64.

points out, it was a 'variegated, multiple' and multi-functional activity, accounting in England for a 'significant proportion of both printed and manuscript texts until (and beyond) the Restoration'.[2] Far from being a marginal activity, it was central to the dissemination of knowledge in all fields, thoroughly mainstream, highly respected, and engaged in by people of various stations, classes, and backgrounds, and in a variety of ways. And, most important for our considerations, women translators, through their multilingual practice and translingual communications, were keen participants in that translation movement. Translation studies underwent a sea change in the last decades of the twentieth century, influenced by the writings of Walter Benjamin, who spoke of the ongoing life of a text albeit in a different form, and by Roland Barthes, Michel Foucault, and Jacques Derrida, who dismantled notions of textual and authorial hierarchy and invited readers to focus on the ever-unfolding meanings emanating from the interrelationships between texts. Specialists such as André Lefevere and Susan Bassnet emphasised the intercultural as well as interlingual nature of translating, viewing translated texts as rewritings and recreations in their own right, the result of manipulations dictated by the translator's beliefs, place in time and space, purposes, and goals.[3] Far from being subservient, then, translation was seen as appropriative, mediating texts through the translator's own voice, creative, dialoguing with, not simply echoing, the author, but also manipulative, operating under the constraints of poetics, patronage, and ideology. This changed the former way of evaluating translations in terms of linguistic equivalence based on comparative readings of source and target texts; rather, translation was seen as a form of *écriture*, or to use Lefevere's term, a 'refraction' of the original, not a reflection.[4]

Over the past two decades, translation studies has continued to challenge the old binary paradigms of source/target text and author/translator and advanced the conception of translation as an intercultural as well as interlingual activity.[5] Another very significant innovation has been to adapt material and methods from other areas of scholarly investigation.[6] This interdisciplinarity is suitable for the multifaceted nature of translation, but is also particularly appropriate for early modern studies and, moreover, has far-reaching effects for our appreciation of women translators' contributions in the period.

[2] Danielle Clarke, 'Translation', in Laura Lunger Knoppers (ed.), *The Cambridge Companion to Early Modern Women's Writing* (London, 2009), 167–80, 167. See also Clarke's earlier defence of early modern women's translation in *The Politics of Early Modern Women's Writing* (Harlow, 2001), 13–14.

[3] André Lefevere, *Translation, Rewriting and the Manipulation of Literary Fame* (London/New York, 1992); Susan Bassnet, 'The Translation Turn in Cultural Studies', in S. Bassnet and A. Lefevere (eds), *Constructing Cultures: Essays on Literary Translation* (Clevedon, 1998), 123–40.

[4] André Lefevere, 'Mother Courage's Cucumbers: Text, System and Refraction in a Theory of Literature', *Modern Language Studies*, 12 (1982), 3–20.

[5] Peter Burke, 'Cultures of Translation in Early Modern Europe', in Peter Burke and R. Po-Chia Hsia (eds), *Cultural Translation in Early Modern Europe* (Cambridge: 2007), 7–38.

[6] On this, see Edwin Gentzler, *Perspectives: Studies in Translatology*, 11 (2003), 11–24.

The first part of this chapter presents an overview of thirty-four English women translators working in the years 1500–1660, and the seventy-seven translations they produced, since to date no such broad study has been undertaken. Two monographs have discussed female translators in the period, and both within the context of translation theory, but Deborah Uman's concentrates on only six women, including Aemilia Lanyer, while Jaime Goodrich's deals exclusively with religious translation.[7] My discussion will highlight a salient characteristic of the whole group of translators and corpus of translations but one that has attracted little attention, namely their diverse nature. This will result in me diverging from some received opinions concerning both. I shall then discuss four fields of scholarship that have innovatively merged with studies of early modern translation and early modern women writers to shed light on what it meant for them to translate, and what they accomplished in doing so: the history of print; materiality in book and manuscript studies; the conception of writing as collaboration; and the use of paratexts.

DIVERSITY AND DIVERGENCE

A first general observation concerning the thirty-four translators I have identified is that they do not constitute a homogeneous group and therefore should not be the subject of broad generalisations. To the contrary, they represent great diversity. This is reflected in terms of social class: Tudor royalty (Queen Katherine Parr; Princess Elizabeth; Princess Mary); aristocracy (Lady Margaret Beaufort, Countess of Richmond; Mary Fitzalan, Duchess of Norfolk; Lady Jane Lumley, Baroness; Mary Sidney Herbert, Countess of Pembroke); the courtier class (Lady Anne Bacon [née Cooke]; Mildred Cecil, Lady Burleigh [née Cooke]; Lady Elizabeth Russell [née Cooke]; Lady Bess Carey; Elizabeth Cary, Viscountess Falkland); the gentry (Margaret Roper [née More], Mary Bassett [née Roper, later Clarke], Anna Hume, Anne Jenkinson, Judith Man, Jane Owen, Jane Seager, Agnes Wenman); and the tradesman class (Anne Locke, later Prowse; Dorcas Martin). One is the daughter of a rector (Rachel Jevon); seven are exiled nuns (Barbara Constable, Pudentiana Deacon, Elizabeth Evelinge, Catherine Gascoigne, Catherine Greenbury, Agnes More, Mary Percy); four we know little or nothing about (Margaret Tyler, Susan Du Verger, Elizabeth Arnold, Mrs. C. N.).

It follows that their level of education and linguistic ability also differed widely. Some were taught Greek and Latin by humanist tutors whom they sometimes shared with their brothers; Jevon was taught both languages by her father. Lucy Cary says her mother, Elizabeth, was self-taught in Latin, as well as Spanish and Italian, although this

[7] Deborah Uman, *Women as Translators in Early Modern England* (Newark, 2012); Jaime Goodrich, *Faithful Translators. Authorship, Gender, and Religion in Early Modern England* (Evanston, IL, 2014).

is perhaps questionable.[8] Concerning Latin proficiency, another early misperception needs correcting, namely that very few female-authored translations were made from that language because even fewer women knew it. In fact, sixteen of our translators, or almost half, definitely knew Latin, fifteen of them well enough to translate from or into it. As for their translations, twenty-four, or 32.8 per cent, are made out of or into Greek and Latin. The majority of our women translators will have also studied vernaculars, represented here by French, Italian, Dutch, and Spanish, either through private tutoring, or circumstance (as was the case of some exiled nuns), or even Continental travel and education.[9]

The translators were of varying ages, too, when they penned their translations, thus bringing to their work very different life experiences. Princesses Mary and Elizabeth were prodigies, translating Thomas Aquinas ('Prayor', n.d.), Marguerite de Navarre ('Glasse of the Synneful Soule', 1544), Parr ('Precationes, seu meditationes', 1545), Jean Calvin ('How we Ought to Knowe God', 1545), and a Barnardine Ochino sermon ('Quid Christus sit et quam obrem in mundum venerit', 1547). So, too, was Cary, who translated Ortelius's geographical work ('Mirrour of the Worlde', *c* 1597). All three were between the tender ages of eleven and fourteen. Lumley and Fitzalan were both teenagers when they offered their father their translations from Greek into Latin, Greek into English, and English into Latin. However, the dated translations in our corpus demonstrate that most of the women composed them in their twenties and thirties. Queen Elizabeth was nevertheless still busy at age sixty-five translating Erasmus' Latin version of Plutarch's essay on curiosity, *De curiositate* (1598), and the opening lines of Horace's *De arte poetica* (1598), while Russell published her *Way of Reconciliation* (1605) at age seventy-eight, although she had translated it much earlier.

A second, important observation concerns the frankly impressive diversity of the subjects treated in this corpus, which number no fewer than twenty-one. Again, this diverges from a previous impression that women were restricted to translating religious and domestic works. On the contrary, we find twelve secular subjects, none domestic: pharmacology (Arnold), geography (Cary), history (Princess Elizabeth, Wenman), rhetoric (Lumley, Fitzalan, Elizabeth I), wisdom literature (Fitzalan), philosophy (Jane Seager, Elizabeth I), Petrarchan poetry (Sidney, Carey, Elizabeth I, Hume), French fiction, drama, and verse (Du Verger, Man, Sidney, Mrs. C.N.), Greek and Latin drama (Lumley, Elizabeth I), Spanish romance (Tyler), Restoration poetry (Jevon), and epistolary writing (Elizabeth I). The religious subjects number nine, given here in descending order in terms of numbers of texts: devotional writings (Beaufort, Princess Elizabeth, Basset, Constable, Deacon, Gascoigne, More, Percy), sermons (Princess Elizabeth, Bacon, Locke Prowse, Cecil), theology (Bacon, Cary, Owen, Russell) biblical commentary and paraphrase (Roper, Princess Mary, Jenkinson), the Psalms (Parr,

8 Lucy Cary, 'The Lady Falkland: Her Life', in Barry Weller and Margaret W. Ferguson (eds), *The Tragedy of Mariam the Fair Queen of Jewry, with The Lady Falkland by One of Her Daughters* (Berkeley, CA, 1994), 183–275, 186.

9 See Murphy, 'Exile and Linguistic Encounter', 147–53, for these last two categories.

Locke, Sidney), prayers (Princesses Elizabeth and Mary), hagiography (Evelinge, Greenbury), Church history (Basset), and catechism (Martin).

The religious translations, again notably, account for only forty-one of the seventy-seven works, or 53.2 per cent. Moreover, this is quite directly comparable to the overall percentage of religious translations in England for the years 1473–1640, which is 49 per cent, while the subjects treated in the female-authored translations mirror those found in the male-authored ones.[10] These two facts support Jaime Goodrich's observation concerning similarities between male and female translators' cultural agendas when translating religious texts.[11] Nevertheless, unsurprisingly, women's devotional translations outnumber theological or controversial ones, whereas for men the opposite is true. Bible translating, which dominates male religious output, is notably absent, since women were authorised to translate only the Psalms. A foray into theology and religious controversy would have done nothing to ease a female translator's already delicate entry into print, as indeed Tyler suggests in her address to the reader prefacing her 1578 *Mirrour*, where she distinguishes between writing of 'divinitie', thought more appropriate for a woman than romance, and handling matters of 'controversie', which she eschews for fear of proving incompetent or creating a text that will be 'misconstrued' (sig. A4v) (see also this volume, Chapter 28, Jake Arthur, '"The Surplusage": Margaret Tyler and the Englishing of Spanish Chivalric Romance'). Owen, some forty years later, declares she is writing *An Antidote against Purgatory* (pub. 1634) to advance 'the spiritual good of [her readers'] soules', but immediately adds parenthetically, '(pardon I pray the boldnes of my Sexe heerin)' (sig. 2r). True, Cooke's rather daringly entitled *Fourteene sermons of Barnardine Ochyne, concernyng the predestinacion and eleccion of god*, bearing her initials on the title page, saw print in 1551 but by then the Edwardian Reformation was in full swing, Ochino was well ensconced in England, and her new printer, John Day, was successfully putting out a range of Reformation texts. As for her 1564 translation of John Jewel's *Apologia ecclesiæ anglicanæ*, a theological work of far greater import, it was solicited by the author and received the Archbishop of Canterbury's blessing. On the other hand, her sister, Russell, waited almost half a century before printing *A Way of Reconciliation*, a treatise on the Eucharist, no doubt deeming it too controversial to publish earlier. Cary displayed no such reticence, however, defending her right in 1630 as 'a Catholique, and a Woman' not only to translate the controversial *Reply of the Most Illustrious Cardinall of Perron* but also to print it (sig. A2v).

A final comment on the diversity represented in this corpus pertains to the forms and types of translation found. I have identified five forms: whole works, fragments, selections, composites, and insertions. While the majority of translations render complete works, some are fragments of unfinished translations, poised as if waiting for the translator to return quill in hand. Four are by Queen Elizabeth: lines from the choral ode

10 Percentages and information are based on the latest data in Brenda M. Hosington et al. (eds), *the Renaissance Cultural Crossroads Online Catalogue of Translations in Britain, 1473–1640* (www.dhi.ac.uk/rcc) [accessed 31 May 2021].

11 Goodrich, *Faithful Translators*, 22.

in the pseudo-Senecan *Hercules Oetaeus* (*c* 1589), a passage from Horace's *De arte poetica* (1598), four and a half books of Tacitus' *Annales* (n.d.), and, of questionable attribution, Petrarch's *Trionfo dell'eternità* (n.d.). Another is Jane Lumley's 'Oratio prima Isocrates ad Demonicum'. Other translations are purposely selected portions of a source text. The single chapter of Calvin's *Institution de la religion chrestienne* was a suitable length for the young Princess Elizabeth but, more important, addressed the thorny issue of predestination far more discreetly than the rest of the work, thus lessening the risk of offending her father.[12] Du Verger presented stories she says she 'culled' from Jean-Pierre Camus' collections for her 1639 *Certain Moral Relations* and *Admirable Events*. Throughout her paratexts she positions herself alongside Camus as author, and this power to select strengthened her stance.[13] Two Petrarchan translations are harder to define in terms of form. Bess Carey's *Canzoniere* 146 and 215 (n.d.) are fragments of Petrarch's great sonnet sequence but were probably exercises selected by her tutor.[14] Sidney's *Trionfo della morte* (n.d.) fits neatly into neither the fragment nor selection category, since we do not know whether she translated the remaining *Trionfi*, or intended to, or whether she chose this particular *Trionfo* on account of its theme of death at a time when she was mourning her brother, Philip.[15]

There are only three composite translations, made up of an impressively wide range of texts and authors. The Cambrai Benedictine nun, Barbara Constable, produces all three, using both Latin and French sources: 'Speculum superiorum, composed of diverse collections taken out of the lives & workes of holie persons' (1650), 'A Spirituall Incense composed of divers exercises of prayer' (1657), and a 'Second part . . . Composed of Collections out of the workes & Liues of many H: persons' (1657).[16]

Other translations were inserted seamlessly into a longer original text. Arnold's two passages from Andrés de Laguna's annotations on Dioscorides (Book V, chapters 62 and 69) are placed within Thomas Tuke's 1616 translation of the text, *A Discourse Against Painting and Tincturing of Women*. She gave them an explicit title authorising and describing Laguna and connected them by a linking sentence reinforcing his invective against women. Owen, composing *An Antidote against Purgatory*, took as her 'foundation or groundworke' Cardinal Bellarmino's 1617 *De gemitu colombae siue de bono*

[12] Elizabeth's judicious textual changes and prudent dedicatory epistle to Parr were further self-protecting features. See Brenda M. Hosington, '"How we ought to knowe God": Princess Elizabeth's Presentation of her Calvin Translation to Katherine Parr', in Catherine Batt and René Tixier (eds), *Booldly Bot Meekly. Essays on the Theory and Practice of Translation in the Middle Ages in Honour of Roger Ellis* (Turnhout, 2018), 499–513.

[13] Brenda M. Hosington, 'Fact and Fiction in Susan Du Verger's Translations of Jean-Pierre Camus' *Les Euenemens singuliers, Les Relations morales*, and *Diotrephe. Histoire Valentine*', in Jacqueline Glomski and Isabelle Moreau (eds), *Seventeenth-Century Fiction. Text and Transmission* (Oxford, 2016), 115–29.

[14] Katherine Duncan-Jones, 'Bess Carey's Petrarch: Newly discovered Elizabethan Sonnets', *The Review of English Studies*, 50 (1999), 304–20.

[15] For a discussion of this, see Clarke, *Politics*, 208–13.

[16] Heather Wolfe, 'Dame Barbara Constable. Catholic Antiquarian, Advisor, and Closet Missionary', in Ronald Corthell et al. (eds), *Catholic Culture in Early Modern England* (Notre Dame, IN, 2007), 158–88.

lacrymarum. This devotional and meditative text seems an unlikely edifice on which to build a work proposing practical acts of charity as a means to avoid purgatorial pains, but she succeeds by unifying the work through her choice of title, her paratexts, and certain material features that continue through the whole work.

There are three distinct types of translation represented in this corpus. The great majority are direct; that is, made directly from the original source text. However, fifteen are indirect or mediated; that is, translations made from translations. Indirect translation occurs as a result of a translator's ignorance of the source language, difficulties in obtaining texts, or unequal power relations between languages and cultures. The practice has attracted much interest lately, although not among early modernists. Peter Burke claims briefly that it was frequent and, since it was announced on title pages, must have incurred less disapproval than in later times.[17] This remains to be proved and, in fact, only five titles in our corpus declare that the translations have been made from intermediary sources: Beaufort's *Mirroure of Golde* (1506?), Evelinge's *History of the Angellical Virgin Glorious S. Clare* (1635), Man's *Epitome of Faire Argenis and Polyarchus* (1640), Percy's editions of *An Abridgement of Christian Perfection* (1625 and 1628), and Wenman's *Historyes and Chronicles of the World* (n.d.).

To date, there is no study of indirect translation as it pertains to early modern women translators. Since the *Renaissance Cultural Crossroads Catalogue* identifies only about ten per cent of its 6,540 entries as indirect, whereas in this corpus the percentage doubles to 21.9 per cent, this invites further investigation. Ignorance of the source language, attributable to differences in male and female education and linguistic apprenticeship, is probably the major reason. The majority of the intermediate texts are French, which is also true for male-authored indirect translations in the period (for early modern Englishwomen's use of French, see this volume, Chapter 29, Line Cottegnies, 'French Connections: English Women's Writing and *Préciosité*'). Of the women translators of the Psalms, only Sidney perhaps had a rudimentary knowledge of Hebrew; she used Marot's and de Bèze's French versions, along with the Vulgate, which Parr and Locke also used as their source text. Availability would seem the most likely explanation for Judith Man's translation of Coëffeteau's *Argenis*, since she tells us she found it in a closet, although that was of course a popular topos. Elizabeth's motive for using Erasmus' translation of Plutarch's essay on curiosity is harder to explain but she had already used Latin translations of most of the Greek *sententiae* she translated in 1563, according to Mueller and Scodel, who assert this was a usual habit among early modern non-classical scholars. They nevertheless claim that she was careful to hide the fact. Pride in being a learned woman, greater prestige in translating Greek than Latin, and much earlier praise by Thomas Blundeville on her reading Plutarch in the Greek perhaps explain her reticence.[18]

[17] Burke, 'Cultures of Translation', 27.

[18] Janel Mueller and Joshua Scodel (eds), *Elizabeth I. Translations, 1592–1598* (Chicago, IL, 2009), 373–4, 338.

The third type of translation found in this corpus is self-translation, of which we have but one example: Jevon's two Restoration odes, the Latin *Carmen* and English *Exultationis Carmen*, published in one volume in 1660 to celebrate Charles II's return to England. Self-translation, the creation of a single text in two or more languages by the same author, has also recently attracted attention, since it challenges the binary and hierarchal distinctions between original and translation, languages and cultures, and author and translator, calling into question the whole notion of authority. In Jevon's poem, textual authority is non-existent since we do not know which poem is the original. Linguistic and cultural authority resides in the prestige language, Latin, and its intended readership, an educated elite. Authorial authority is, of course, all Jevon's, which makes the work unusual given her gender. It is also doubly unique in this corpus, since only five other translations are made from texts written by women authors and they are all religious.

INNOVATION AND INTERDISCIPLINARITY

Various disciplines have merged with translation studies to create innovative ways of understanding the translating process. Four, in particular, have been particularly beneficial to studying early modern Englishwomen's translations. The first is print history. Some of the developments in literary criticism and translation studies to which I referred earlier were mirrored in bibliography and print history, changing our understanding of book production, the politics of print, the role of the agents involved, and the ever-shifting, unauthoritative forms of the printed page. The interface thus created between print and translation in early modern England was explored in Anne Coldiron's groundbreaking book, which discusses not translations by women but about them, and in a short piece of my own.[19] More recent research, however, has addressed the subject specifically in terms of women's translations. Helen Smith, for example, has explored various connections between women and the early print trade, including that of translation.[20]

By taking print production into consideration, Micheline White overturned the assertion that in the years 1559–1625 women's religious translations outnumbered original compositions.[21] Princess Elizabeth's 'Glass of the Synneful Soule' and its

[19] A. E. B. Coldiron, *English Printing, Verse Translation, and the Battle of the Sexes, 1476–1557* (Burlington, VT, 2009); Brenda M. Hosington, 'Commerce, Printing, and Patronage', in Gordon Braden, Robert Cummings, and Stuart Gillespie (eds), *The Oxford History of Literary Translation in English. Volume 2, 1550–1660* (Oxford, 2010), 47–57.

[20] Helen Smith, *'Grossly Material Things': Women and Book Production in Early Modern England* (Oxford, 2012).

[21] Micheline White, 'Renaissance Englishwomen and Religious Translations: The Case of Anne Lock's *Of the Markes of the Children of God* (1590)', *English Literary Renaissance*, 29 (1999), 375–400.

metamorphoses at the hands of three different editors, John Bale, James Cancellar, and Thomas Bentley, and three printing presses in 1548, 1567, and 1582, followed a print trajectory that mirrored Elizabeth's progress as she moved from linguistic prodigy seeking to please family members, to young queen establishing herself firmly as the head of the Church of England, then to wise and powerful monarch in mid-reign. The editorial textual and paratextual interventions map these changes; they also bring new light to bear on the translation's varied and underlying layers of meaning, its *skopos* or purpose, and its ongoing value as a propaganda tool.[22] Translations by Beaufort, Roper, Parr, Princesses Mary and Elizabeth, Bacon, and Basset have been considered not as isolated publications, but as part of a whole print context comprising a range of works published 'at the same time, on the same subject, and in similar socio-historical circumstances', and this brings these women into the mainstream of religious activity.[23] Roper's *Precatio dominica* is discussed by Jaime Goodrich in a similar print context, prompting her to consider the question of the translator's private versus public voice, the latter made possible by print.[24] This is a matter of particular pertinence to women translators. Jevon's *Carmen/Exultationis Carmen* was one of over one hundred pamphlets and collections of Restoration poems printed in 1660–1661. As G. M. Maclean says, political poetry was no longer coterie verse distributed in manuscript form, but part of a 'public discourse largely managed by commercially-minded printers'.[25] This sheds a different light on her achievement.

The level and nature of these women's participation in print differed from one translator to another. Beaufort was actively involved in patronising Caxton, de Worde, and Pynson, chose Pynson for her two translations, and probably oversaw their production. Basset helped finance Rastell's *The Workes of Sir Thomas More* and allowed him to include her 'Of the sorowe, werinesse, feare and prayer of Christ before hys taking' in it. The success of the participation also differed from one translator to another, but it is noteworthy that so many of the early Tudor translations went through several editions and reprints, which secured their authors' continuing visibility. Parr's 1544 *Psalmes or Prayers*, published by Thomas Berthelet and part of a programme of Church reform, proved a bestseller, going through twenty-one editions up to 1613.[26] The 'Book of St John', in the 1548 *First Tome or Volume of the Paraphrase of Erasmus upon the Newe Testament*,

[22] Concerning some of these interventions, see Mueller and Scodel (eds), *Elizabeth I. Translations, 1544–1589*, 34–9, and Maureen Quilligan, *Incest and Agency in Elizabeth's England* (Philadelphia, PA, 2005), 51–75.

[23] Brenda M. Hosington. 'Women Translators and the Early Printed Book', in Vincent Gillespie and Susan Powell (eds), *A Companion to the Early Printed Book in Britain 1476–1558* (Woodbridge, 2014), 248–71.

[24] Jaime Goodrich, 'Thomas More and Margaret Roper: A Case for Rethinking Women's Participation in the Early Modern Public Sphere', *Sixteenth Century Journal*, 39 (2008), 1021–40.

[25] G. M. Maclean, 'An Edition of Poems on the Restoration', *Restoration: Studies in English Literary Culture, 1660–1700*, 11 (1987), 117–21.

[26] Kimberly Anne Coles describes the translation as the most enduringly popular devotional text in the period, in *Religion, Reform, and Women's Writing in Early Modern England* (Cambridge, 2008), 47–52.

translated in part by Princess Mary, enjoyed an even wider circulation since the *Paraphrases* became required reading in English churches in 1547, resulting in massive sales in the ensuing five years, and were required again from 1559 to 1583.

Three translators show an understanding of some of the problems that could arise in the printing process. Basset, in her dedicatory epistle to Princess Mary accompanying her two partial translations of Eusebius' *Ecclesiastical History* (1550–1553), complains that the poor quality of the first printed Greek edition has hampered her translating, conjecturing that the base text was either corrupt or 'worne and peryshed' (5r). This complaint was often expressed about early printed editions of Greek texts. Russell explains she has decided to print her *Way of Reconciliation* because she has lent her own copy to a friend and fears it might be printed with errors after her death (sig. A3r). Percy's 1612 *Abridgement of Christian Perfection* was handed over to John Wilson to be printed at the Jesuit St Omer press, but he published it anonymously, although her Epistle bore her initials. In the 1625 edition, the work was assigned to Achille Gagliardi, but without mentioning his collaborator and co-author, Isabella Berinzaga, while the translation and dedicatory epistle were attributed to fellow Jesuit Anthony Hopkins, who added 'An Advertisement to the Reader'; in short, it became an all-male publication. Percy was only rightfully restored as translator with the 1628 edition.

A second field of study pertinent to the history of early modern women translators is that of manuscript culture, which continued well up to and beyond 1660. No longer seen as an inferior mode of literary production but as a site where cultural exchange could take place and compositions be circulated, manuscripts have now assumed much greater importance, particularly with regard to early modern women authors, for some of whom print represented a problematic mode of publication. Despite this, twenty-five of our thirty-four translators published in print, although three also produced manuscript translations: Basset's *Ecclesiastical History*, Sidney's English *Trionfo della morte*, and Princess Mary's 'Prayor of Sainte Thomas of Aquyne'. Sidney, in fact, has been described as a 'liminal figure in the shift from manuscript to print circulation ... in court circles', with the power to decide between which of the two media to choose for her own and Philip's works.[27] For her 1592 *Discourse of Life and Death* and *Antonius*, it was print; her Psalm renditions, however, were widely circulated in manuscript before their appearance in print in 1598.

Five translators offered their manuscript translations as gifts: Fitzalan and Lumley to their father; Princess Elizabeth to her father, stepmother, and brother; Basset to Princess Mary; and Seager to Queen Elizabeth. This did not necessarily imply, however, that they would be entirely private documents. Indeed, Elizabeth tells Parr she hopes none but she will read or see her 'Glasse of the Synneful Soule' before she 'shall rubbe out, polishe, and mende (or els cause to mende)' it.[28] As for Elizabeth's trilingual *Precationes sive meditationes*, Paul Hentzner records having seen it in the Whitehall Palace Library in

[27] Mary Sidney Herbert, in Margaret P. Hannay, Noel J. Kinnamon, and Michael G. Brennan (eds), *Selected Works of Mary Sidney Herbert, Countess of Pembroke* (Tempe, AZ, 2005), 27–32.

[28] Elizabeth I, in Mueller and Scodel (eds), *Elizabeth I. Translations 1544–1589*, 42.

1598, presumably exhibited with her permission.[29] In her Eusebius dedication, Basset fully exploits the topoi of the reluctant, private, and humble translator, yet recounts how the manuscript was circulated twice before being presented, first to friends, then to 'one or twayne very wyse and well learned men' (fol. 4r). Lastly, although Seager makes no allusion to a possible circulation of her 1589 verse translation, 'The Divine Prophecies of the Ten Sibyls', the material craftsmanship involved, learning displayed, positioning of the work within several cultural discourses used in praising the queen and promoting Protestantism, and the perfectly gender-appropriate political gesture of a woman offering a gift to a female sovereign, strongly suggest she was setting her sights on a wider circle of readers.[30]

In the last decade, studies of early modern translation have ventured into yet another new area of investigation, the materiality of printed books and manuscripts. D. F. McKenzie followed his dictum, 'forms effect meaning', by a comment particularly pertinent, if unintentionally so, for translations: 'every reader rewrites [a society's] texts, and if they have any continuing life at all, at some point every printer redesigns them ... different readers [bring] the text to life in different ways'.[31] This redesigning was first examined in the context of early modern English translations by two pioneers in the field, Anne Coldiron and Guyda Armstrong, who investigated how material forms (title pages, *mise en page*, font, visual and discursive paratexts) contributed to transforming foreign texts for a new culture, readership, or ideology.[32] Not a few individual studies have since focused on the material features of women's translations.

One examines the placement of two different translations in one volume, although their source texts had been published separately. This, too, can carry meaning. Marie-Alice Belle and Line Cottegnies argue that Sidney's *Discourse of Life and Death* and *Antonius* can be seen as companion pieces in more than one way.[33] Despite ideological and generic differences, the texts can shed light on each other, while the English reader, confronting them side by side, will respond differently from his or her French counterpart and find new meanings in each. Moreover, by uniting Robert Garnier and Philippe de Mornay, two important French cultural figures, on the pages of her publication, Sidney showed she was *au fait* with current Continental thinking.

[29] Horace Walpole (ed.), *A Journey into England by Paul Hentzner, in the Year 1598* (London, 1758), 30.

[30] See Jessica L. Malay, 'Jane Seager's Sibylline Poems: Maidenly Negotiations Through Elizabethan Gift Exchange', *English Literary Renaissance*, 36 (2006), 173–93, and 'To be a Sibyl. Jane Seager's Sibylline Poems', in Jessica L. Malay (ed.), *Prophecy and Sibylline Imagery in the Renaissance* (New York, 2010), 121–36.

[31] D. F. McKenzie, *Bibliography and the Sociology of Texts* (Cambridge, 1999), 13, 25–6.

[32] A. E. B. Coldiron, *English Printing, Verse Translation and Printers Without Borders. Translation and Textuality in the Renaissance* (Cambridge, 2015); Guyda Armstrong, *The English Boccaccio: A History in Books* (Toronto, 2013) and 'Coding Continental: Information Design in Sixteenth-Century English Vernacular Language Manuals and Translations', *Renaissance Studies*, 29 (2015), 78–102.

[33] Marie-Alice Belle and Line Cottegnies (eds), *Robert Garnier in Elizabethan England. Mary Sidney Herbert's Antonius. Thomas Kyd's Cornelia* (Cambridge, 2017), 22–3.

Visual codes (typography, book design, page design, illustration) also regulate meaning and are connected to the work's function. John Bale's black-letter font for Princess Elizabeth's 'Glasse of the Synnful Soule' evokes a different reader response from the delicately executed italic hand of her manuscript. It brought the text into the mainstream of religious print production since that font was the most commonly used in early sixteenth-century printing, thus increasing its authority and significance. The woodcut on the title page, depicting a young, crowned woman kneeling before Christ and set above a Latin encomium addressing her as the celebrated, learned, and Christian daughter of Henry VIII, reinforces this authority. Translator-authorship, authority, gender, and visibility are similarly embodied in another combination of visual and discursive codes that marks Roper's 1526 *Devout Treatise*. The title page woodcut portrays a studious young woman but also interacts with Richard Hyrde's preface addressing issues of gender and defending women's learning.[34]

The interplay and size of various fonts (black letter, roman, italics) can signal a different focus from that of the original text. On the title page of Judith Man's *Epitome of the History of Faire Argenis and Polyarchus*, Argenis' name is placed first, rather than Polyarchus' as in the French original, and is printed in bold and in capital letters twice the size of those in his name, again in a reversal of the French title. Since the same rearranged title is given in the discursive paratexts, this hints at the translator's feminisation of the work that will ensue.[35]

Page layout and design can, on the contrary, imitate the original work, confirming the translator's familiarity with foreign traditions, or other similar translations, which in the case of women translators and their texts can only contribute to conferring authority. In Hume's 1644 *The Triumphs of Love; Chastity; Death*, explanatory verse 'Arguments', encased in a decorative border at the head of each chapter, are reminiscent of Harington's *Orlando Furioso* or Robert Tofte's *Ariosto's Satyres*, for example, but also of many sixteenth-century Italian works.

Writing and producing the early modern book was of necessity an act of collaboration between the various agents involved (author, editor, proofreader, printer, bookseller). The nature of that collaboration attracted the attention of print historians but also literary critics and theatre historians. Heather Hirschfield, in particular, declared collaboration a particularly important factor for assessing the roles of early modern patrons, translators, and women writers.[36] Nor did its significance escape translation specialists.

[34] The woodcut has been discussed by several critics but see especially A. E. B. Coldiron, 'The Translator's Visibility in Early Printed Portrait-Images and the Ambiguous Example of Margaret More Roper', in Marie-Alice Belle and Brenda M. Hosington (eds), *Thresholds of Translation: Paratexts, Print, and Cultural Exchange in Early Modern Britain* (Cham, 2018), 51–74.

[35] On this material and paratextual feminisation, see Brenda M. Hosington, 'Collaboration, Authorship, and Gender in the Paratexts Accompanying Translations by Susan Du Verger and Judith Man', in Patricia Pender (ed.), *Gender, Authorship, and Early Modern Women's Collaboration* (Basingstoke, 2017), 95–121.

[36] Heather Hirschfield, 'Early Modern Collaboration and Theories of Authorship', *PMLA*, 116 (2001), 609–22.

Christiane Nord's *Skopostheorie* saw translation as an interlingual and intercultural cooperative process, while Françoise Massardier-Kenney argued that concepts of 'collaboration, cooperation, and negotiation, and resistance to binary oppositions in connection with gender-oriented discourse could then be used to characterize feminist translation'.[37] In fact, translation is, in its very essence, collaborative, as Belén Bistué says in *Collaborative Translation and Multi-Version Texts*, for it involves more than one writing subject and more than one interpretative position.[38] It also, of course, involves two texts, languages, and cultures, and two sets of printers and readers.

Several women's translations have been discussed within the context of collaboration. Deborah Uman and Belén Bistué describe Margaret Tyler's *Mirrour* in terms of co-authorship, opening up another dimension to this translation and its famous prefatorial paratexts.[39] Patricia Demers coins the wonderful term 'deferred collaboration' to describe Sidney's reworking of her deceased brother's Psalms, Gemma Allen talks of Bacon's *Apologie or Answere in Defence of the Churche of Englande* being created within a social nexus of agents, and Micheline White writes of Katherine Parr's collaboration with her husband and Thomas Cranmer in producing wartime propaganda through reframing Erasmian prayers calling for peace.[40] Parr also collaborated with Henry, Cranmer, Berthelet the King's Printer, and George Day, her almoner, on her John Fisher translation, the *Psalmes or Prayers*. Alexandra Day has even called for a new theoretical model for discussing Lumley's and Fitzalan's translations and accompanying dedicatory epistles, one 'that can accommodate social, material, and intellectual collaboration as multiple and simultaneous modes of production'.[41]

Collaboration is also a hallmark of the translations made by exiled nuns, supervised, edited, and usually printed and distributed beyond their convent walls by their male superiors. Jaime Goodrich has shown how Evelinge's translations combined with other English Franciscans' translations in order to promote the order's ideals, bolster its powers both within and without the cloister, combat Protestantism, and reach out to

[37] Christiane Nord, *Translation as a Purposeful Activity: Functionalist Approaches Explained* (Manchester, 1997); Françoise Massardier-Kenney, 'Towards a Redefinition of Feminist Translation Practice', *The Translator*, 3 (1997), 55–69.

[38] Belén Bistué, *Collaborative Translation and Multi-Version Texts* (Farnham, 2013), 1.

[39] Deborah Uman and Belén Bistué, 'Translation as Collaborative Authorship: Margaret Tyler's *The Mirrour of Princely Deedes and Knighthood*', *Comparative Literature Studies*, 44 (2007), 298–323.

[40] Patricia Demers, '"Warpe and web" in the Sidney Psalms: The "coupled worke" of the Countess of Pembroke and Sir Philip Sidney', in Marjorie Stone and Judith Thompson (eds), *Literary Couplings: Writing Couples, Collaborators, and the Construction of Authorship* (Madison, WI, 2006), 41–59; Gemma Allen, '"A Briefe and Plaine Declaration": Lady Anne Bacon's 1564 Translation of the *Apologia Ecclesiasticae Anglicanae*', in Anne Lawrence-Mathers and Phillipa Hardman (eds), *Women and Writing, c.1340–1650. The Domestication of Print Culture* (York, 2010), 62–76; Micheline White, 'Katherine Parr, Translation, and the Dissemination of Erasmus' Views on War and Peace', *Renaissance and Reformation/Renaissance et Réforme*, 43 (2020), 67–91. See also Patricia Pender's fine introduction to her *Gender, Authorship, and Early Modern Women's Collaboration*, 1–12.

[41] Alexandra Day, 'Literary Gifts: Performance and Collaboration in the Arundel/Lumley Family Manuscripts', in Patricia Pender (ed.), *Gender, Authorship, and Early Modern Women's Collaboration*, 125–48.

English Catholics.[42] A similar 'collaborative authorship' is how Marie-Louise Coolahan describes the Irish Poor Clares' 'highly politicized religious and linguistic project', for which they commissioned eminent Gaelic scholars.[43] Finally, Helen Smith's section on translation as collaboration in '*Grossly Material Things*' opens with Catherine Greenbury's 1628 *Short Relation of the Life, Vertues, and Miracles of S. Elisabeth*; her authorship was confirmed by Arthur Bellamy, who also saw the work through publication. Translation, Smith asserts, is 'frequently a collaborative venture in which translator and author both worked to discover the full sense of the text'. Men and women alike presented female translators as 'partners' and this partnership took place 'within an extended circuit of exchange, comparison, and mutual correction'.[44]

The fourth area of research to have been co-opted by translation studies and women's writing specialists is the study of paratexts. Gérard Genette's initial taxonomy and description of them as stabilising sites of authorial and editorial control have been found wanting with regard to early printed materials, and he is purposely silent on translation.[45] Yet paratexts accompanying translated works, as well as performing the same functions as for original texts, can 'offer privileged insight into early modern conceptions of the nature and status of translation activities', explaining and justifying the methods used, unveiling any appropriation and manipulation strategies, and giving a voice to the translator.[46] In the field of early modern women's writing, paratexts have proved extremely fruitful for understanding one form of what Sarah C. E. Ross calls 'the apparatus of authorship'; they 'provide the entrée into literary and non-literary texts'.[47]

Like women who compose original works, women translators use discursive paratexts for self-fashioning, authorising their work, and preparing and shaping the reader's response. However, these functions are made more complex in the case of translated texts: visibility is harder to achieve for the translator, textual authority harder to impose, and the 'threshold' into the foreign text has to be adjusted to suit the new readership. This corpus comprises various types of discursive paratexts (dedications, prefaces, addresses to the reader, commendatory verse), which fall into three groups: female-authored paratexts standing alone; male-authored paratexts standing alone; and female- and male-authored paratexts presented side by side. A full study of all these, including a comparison of the female and male meta-discourse employed, would shed new light on how early modern women—and men—perceived female agency in

42 Jaime Goodrich, '"Ensigne-Bearers of Saint Clare": Elizabeth Evelinge's Early Translations and the Restoration of English Franciscanism', in Micheline White (ed.), *English Women, Religion, and Textual Production, 1500–1625* (Farnham, 2011), 83–100.

43 Marie-Louise Coolahan, *Women, Writing, and Language in Early Modern England* (Oxford, 2010), 10.

44 Smith, '*Grossly Material Things*', 32, 40.

45 Gérard Genette, in Jane E. Lewin (trans.), *Paratexts. Thresholds of Interpretation* (Cambridge, 1997). See, amongst other critics, Helen Smith and Louise Wilson (eds), *Renaissance Paratexts* (Cambridge, 2011), 2–9.

46 'Introduction', in Belle and Hosington (eds), *Thresholds of Translation*, 1–23.

47 Sarah C. E. Ross, 'Early Modern Women and the Apparatus of Authorship', *Parergon*, 29 (2012), 1–8.

producing translated texts, both printed and in manuscript, but space will allow only a few observations, limited to the types of paratext written by the women and the subjects addressed.

The great majority are prefatory in nature, but Basset, following humanist translating practices, provides four explicatory marginal glosses in her translation of More's *De trisititia*, while Hume imitates (and often silently translates) the humanist Italian editors of the *Trionfi* by adding 'Annotations' after each chapter to explain points in her translation. Of our seventy-seven translations, forty-one contain dedications; of these, twenty-five, or 61 per cent, are directed to women. Given that Lumley's and Fitzalan's translations account for ten of the sixteen dedicated to men and only two of these male dedicatees are non-family (Tyler's employer and Constable's spiritual advisor), this suggests a rather restricted circle and, with the exception of Tyler, one in which a bid for patronage does not figure prominently, although that is one of the main purposes of the dedicatory epistle.

The circle of female dedicatees is far wider and certainly does include patronage as a motivation, along with the need for protection, either religious, as in the case of the Catholics who invoke Henrietta Maria's help, or secular for some women venturing into print. Kinship plays a far smaller role. Only three dedicatees are relatives: Bacon's mother (*Fouretene Sermons*), Princess Elizabeth's stepmother ('Glasse of the Synneful Soule' and 'How to Knowe God'), and Russell's daughter (*A Way of Reconciliation*). The predominance of female dedicatees suggests that women translators felt safer seeking patronage and protection amongst members of their own gender, that it was perceived as more appropriate, and that their concerns and areas of interest were more likely to harmonise with those of other women.

Prefaces and addresses to the reader provided an important space in which the woman translator could portray herself. The same, of course, held true for male translators but given the social constraints on the early modern woman, the high value put on modesty, and the gendered nature of paratextual rhetoric, her task was more delicate. Yet, contrary to what one might expect, and certainly contrary to what Laurence Venuti claimed concerning seventeenth-century English translators, these women are not invisible.[48] The majority of the titles name the translator, three give her initials, three hint coyly at her identity, which would have been obvious to many, and the majority are signed and contain personal details that merge with authorial claims and justifications. In all, despite earlier assertions about female anonymity, the women translators in our corpus are in fact remarkably visible.

Finally, these female-authored paratexts treat a variety of subjects. Amongst them are comments on the value of translation and nature of the strategies used. The fullest are by Basset in her Eusebius dedication and Cecil in her St Basil one, which both

48 Lawrence Venuti, *The Translator's Invisibility. A History of Translation*, 2nd edn (Abingdon, 2008). A. E. B. Coldiron strongly challenges his view with regard to earlier translations in 'Visibility Now: Historicizing Foreign Presences in Translation', *Translation Studies*, 5 (2012), 189–200, and 'The Translator's Visibility'.

demonstrate they are employing the humanist philological theory of translation. Many of the translators comment on gender issues and notions of femininity, Tyler and Cary the most boldly. Others do so more subtly or implicitly, or employ metaphors such as the wise virgins, who appear in Elizabeth's and Bacon's dedicatory epistles, or the milk of true doctrine and the mother's legacy that Russell speaks of in the dedication of her *Way of Reconciliation* to her daughter. Virtually all, in various ways, serve not simply as a frame for or threshold into these women's translations, but as a setting in which the translators can present themselves authoritatively, yet without breaching codes of decorum, while displaying a remarkable deployment of rhetorical devices.

This study is the first to take into consideration the whole corpus of Englishwomen's translated texts from 1500 to 1660 and thereby to uncover the impressive diversity that they represent. It has built upon the work of many recent scholars who have contributed to situating translation within a culture of female writing, bringing it in, to echo Jaime Goodrich, from the periphery of studies of early modern women writers and early modern literature in general.[49] Print and manuscript circulation broadened these women's visibility and increased the significance of their role in public discussions of a given subject, while authorising and demarginalising them by placing them within a nexus of like-minded—or otherwise—writers and thinkers. Similarly, an assessment of these women's translations through various prisms and a co-opting of resources from various disciplines broaden and render more holistic our view of what these 'mistresses of tongues' achieved.

FURTHER READING

Burke, Peter. 'Cultures of Translation in Early Modern Europe', in Peter Burke and R. Po-Chia Hsia (eds), *Cultural Translation in Early Modern Europe*. Cambridge, 2007, 7–38.

Clarke, Danielle. 'Translation', in Laura Lunger Knoppers (ed.), *The Cambridge Companion to Early Modern Women's Writing*. London, 2009, 167–80.

Goodrich, Jaime. *Faithful Translators. Authorship, Gender, and Religion in Early Modern England*. Evanston, IL, 2014.

Lefevere, André. *Translation, Rewriting, and the Manipulation of Fame*. London/New York, 1992.

Uman, Deborah. *Women as Translators in Early Modern England*. Newark, 2012.

[49] Goodrich, *Faithful Translators*, 188.

CHAPTER 28

'THE SURPLUSAGE'

Margaret Tyler and the Englishing of Spanish Chivalric Romance

JAKE ARTHUR

THE turbulent relationship between early modern Spain and England was characterised by religious difference, military conflict, and oppositional national myth-making. But as Barbara Fuchs has argued, 'early modern taste does not rigidly follow religious or political conviction' and English readers and writers were often 'seduced by [the] Spanish imaginary, language or plots'.[1] According to the *Renaissance Cultural Crossroads* database, Spanish is well represented as a vernacular language of origin for English publications, with 340 printed texts translated from Spanish into English between 1520 and 1641 (its period of data collection), more than Italian (322), German (229), or Dutch (217).[2] These texts are largely Catholic or crypto-Catholic material, treatises on the Americas or on maritime and military subjects, or romances. These categories are not as disparate as they seem. Spain's widely coveted military and naval expertise facilitated its ongoing expansion into the Americas, which in turn captured the European imagination with tales of exotic 'discoveries'. In the New World, reality seemed to collide with romance. Explorers like Álvar Núñez Cabeza de Vaca wrote chronicles styling themselves as Christian heroes surrounded by alien marvels; others took romances with them and were inspired to seek out cities of gold and tribes of Amazonian women.[3] Given Spain's association with adventure and the exotic, it is perhaps no surprise that when Spanish chivalric romances were first translated into English in 1578 they were a sensation, representing a quarter of all Spanish-language texts translated into English in the following three decades.

[1] Barbara Fuchs, *The Poetics of Piracy: Emulating Spain in English Literature* (Philadelphia, PA, 2013), 6.

[2] Brenda Hosington et al., *Renaissance Cultural Crossroads* (2010), The University of Warwick, www.dhi.ac.uk/rcc, accessed 20 December 2020.

[3] See Irving A. Leonard, *Books of the Brave* (Berkeley, CA, 1992).

This vogue for Spanish chivalric romance was initiated by an Englishwoman, Margaret Tyler, and her *The Mirrour of Princely Deedes and Knighthood* (1578), a translation of the first part of Diego Ortúñez de Calahorra's *Espejo de príncipes y cavalleros* (1555). Tyler's *Mirror* is the first secular publication translated into English by a woman and the only publication known to be translated into English from Spanish by a woman in the period.[4] Much of what we know about Tyler we have gleaned from *Mirror*'s dedication and translator's preface. In the dedication, she refers to herself as a former 'servant' in the household of Thomas Howard, Duke of Norfolk, and Duchess Margaret Audley Howard, where she likely took to 'spot translating' romances for entertainment.[5] Returning to what she calls her 'old reading' at a later age, publication offered Tyler income and her printer Thomas East an opportunity to open a new market in romances.[6] Indeed, her translation proved a commercial success. Reprinted in 1580 and 1599, her first part of *Mirror* spawned the publication of eight subsequent volumes (with different translators), as well as inspiring rival offerings, including Anthony Munday's translations of the *Amadís de Gaula* and the various *Palmerín* series.

Much has quite rightly been said about the radical defence of women's writing in Tyler's translator's preface. There she argues that it is 'all one for a woman to pen a story as for a man to address his story to a woman'; for if men dedicate their works to women, then women have the right to read them and, 'if we may read them, why not farther wade in them to the search of a truth?' (*Mirror*, 50). Her intriguing suggestion that translation might be a 'search of a truth'—an involved textual 'wading'—has, however, tempted few critics to turn their attention from her two-page preface to the 358-page romance and fewer still to consider it seriously as a version of, and response to, another text. This oversight is a product of the way earlier scholarship conceived of translation as 'near miss' authorship: a woman's name but a man's text. Mary Ellen Lamb's foundational account of women's translation, which is still regularly cited, contends that translations by Renaissance women are 'different from the translations of Renaissance men in being exceedingly literal', and that women's translations 'deprived them of any original voice'.[7] In Lamb's search for 'authentic' female articulation, the original trumps the imitative and the literary work of translation is overlooked (see also this volume, Chapter 27, Barbara Hosington, '"Mistresses of tongues": Early Modern Englishwomen, Multilingual Practice, and Translingual Communication'). We find a

[4] That is, up to 1640/41, the limit of both the *Renaissance Cultural Crossroads database and A Bibliography of Spanish-English Translations 1500–1640* (2006), King's College London, www.ems.kcl.ac.uk/apps/, accessed 20 December 2020.

[5] Louise Schleiner, 'Margaret Tyler, Translator and Waiting Woman', *English Language Notes*, 29 (1992), 1–8, 4.

[6] Margaret Tyler, in Joyce Boro (ed.), *Mirror of Princely Deeds and Knighthood* (London, 2014), 48. See also Schleiner, 'Margaret Tyler'.

[7] Mary Ellen Lamb, 'The Cooke Sisters: Attitudes toward Learned Women in the Renaissance', in Margaret P. Hanny (ed.), *Silent But for the Word* (Kent, OH, 1985), 107–25, 124–5.

similar argument in Neil Rhodes' 2018 book *Common*. He describes translation as the 'seedbed of Elizabethan literature' but nonetheless describes learned women who translate as 'setting aside the enticements of the imagination in order to produce resources for the commonwealth'; 'as reproducers', Rhodes says, early modern women are suited to translation 'precisely *because* it is reproductive'.[8] The dyad between women and translation that emerges here, in line with John Florio's famous description of translations as 'reputed femalls, delivered at second hand', has proven pernicious for our appreciation of early modern women's translations.[9] By describing translation as mechanical it is deprived of literary interest, and by describing women who translate as similarly mechanical they are deprived of literary agency. The anomaly and interest of women's work at the coalface of the humanist project is effaced by a critical tradition that sees no creativity and no appeal in translation.[10]

Possibilities for creativity or pleasure are obscured by the customary focus on whether a translation is 'accurate'. The way we talk about translation has particular repercussions for early modern women's place in literary history because translations make up a significant proportion of their extant works; but accuracy is a fuzzy term that produces fuzzy criticism. One article describes Margaret Tyler's romance as a 'relatively faithful reproduction' that is 'not strictly word for word', and another critic calls it 'accurate and impressive'.[11] The problem with 'accuracy' is that it implies the meaning of a source text can be measured and then used as a yardstick with which to evaluate the resulting text. Of course, meaning and language elude this kind of quantification. If there is no such thing as a perfect synonym inside a language (if, for instance, you can have a 'stony silence' but never a 'rocky silence'), then the expectation that there could be perfect synonymy *between* languages—and not only between single words but whole texts—seems perverse. But this is exactly what accuracy, and similar terms like 'faithfulness' and 'literalness', imply. Even if we imagine the text alone as the locus of signification, a hypothetical list of semantic attributes would for practical purposes be infinite. Translators must instead

[8] Neil Rhodes, *Common: The Development of Literary Culture in Sixteenth-Century England* (Oxford, 2018), 120–2. For the association between women and translation, see also Danielle Clarke, 'Translation', in Laura Lunger Knoppers (ed.), *The Cambridge Companion to Early Modern Women's Writing* (Cambridge, 2009), 167–80.

[9] John Florio (trans.), *The Essayes or Morall, Politike and Millitarie Discourses of Lord Michaell De Montaigne* (London, 1603), sig. A2r.

[10] More compelling recent scholarship includes: Marie-Alice Belle and Brenda Hosington (eds), *Thresholds of Translation: Paratexts, Print and Cultural Exchange in Early Modern Britain (1473–1660)* (Cham, 2018); Jaime Goodrich, *Faithful Translators: Authorship, Gender, and Religion in Early Modern England* (Evanston, IL, 2013); and Patricia Demers' and Brenda M. Hosington's chapters in Micheline White (ed.), *English Women, Religion, and Textual Production 1500–1625* (Farnham, 2011).

[11] Deborah Uman and Belén Bistué, 'Translation as Collaborative Authorship: Margaret Tyler's *The Mirrour of Princely Deedes and Knighthood*', *Comparative Literature Studies*, 44.3 (2007), 298–323, 299; and Boro, 'Introduction', in Tyler, *Mirror*, 18.

decide which items on their 'list' they believe to be most important and which can be viably combined and preserved in their target language and text. Few English translators of *The Odyssey*, for example, choose to preserve Homer's dactylic hexameters because that meter is so ill-suited to English that it forces difficult concessions in syntax, diction, and length.[12] In short, translation choices are literary choices. The interesting question is not 'how accurate is this translation?' but 'what does this translation attempt—or not attempt—to preserve?' and then 'why?' and 'how?'. In this chapter I hope to model how close, comparative analyses of translations alongside their sources can uncover not potential errors but rather the creative opportunities that inhere in translation. Much like their male counterparts, these are opportunities which early modern women, including Margaret Tyler, took.

ERRANT DEBT COLLECTORS

Joyce Boro's recent edition of *Mirror* begins this comparative work; she finds Tyler's romance a 'hybrid text' that neither wholly removes Catholic and Hispanic content nor leaves it untouched, and rightly suggests that her impulse as a translator is to modernise.[13] I want to demonstrate here that Tyler's most significant interventions respond to the changing social and literary sensibilities of late sixteenth-century England. This is a strategy of many parts, including an emphasis on communicative rather than martial action and an application of forensic rhetoric that infers, or encourages readers to infer, probable arguments that mitigate the romance's narratological and psychological 'gaps'. From the standpoint of adapting a foreign text for an English audience, though, the most striking aspect of Tyler's translation is her insistent use of a lexicon of legal case and contract. These additions leave an unmistakably English mark on this Spanish text and import a mode of social description that threatens to unravel the chivalric world of the romance. The result is a text at odds with itself, as Tyler exposes the ideological clash that would inform seventeenth-century parodies of the chivalric genre in another key moment of Anglo-Spanish exchange: the success of *Don Quixote* and its revisioning in Francis Beaumont's *The Knight of the Burning Pestle*.

Like many of the Spanish romances translated into English in this period, Tyler's *Mirror* is a dynastic chivalric romance. Emperor Trebatio of Hungary is trapped in an enchanted castle for much of the book while his two young sons, the Knight of the Sun and Rosicleer, are scattered across the globe. The reader, enjoying a birds-eye view of

[12] The preface to Emily Wilson's recent translation provides a clear-eyed literary discussion of her translation choices, including her use of iambic pentameter; Emily Wilson (trans.), *The Odyssey* (New York, 2018), 81–91.

[13] Tyler, in Boro (ed.), *Mirror*, 15, 1.

events, awaits realisations and reconciliations that are either tantalisingly delayed or effected only to be undone. These delays and reversals allow for the titular 'princely deedes': opportunities for these 'fair unknowns' to distinguish themselves at jousts, defeat giants, and rescue gentlewomen—that is, opportunities to earn the knightly credentials that their undiscovered noble parentage in fact makes theirs by right. The feudal values of patrilineal virtue and martial distinction that underlie this story and genre are, however, frequently undermined by Tyler's own translation choices. We see this midway through the romance in a battle between the Knight of the Sun (also called Donzel del Febo) and the hideous giant Rajartes:

Mirror	*Espejo*
Again Donzel del Febo repaid him with a plus ultra, the surplusage more than an ordinary interest. And they wounded each other, mangling themselves pitifully (Ch. 21, 104).	De allí él le bolvió la respuesta, y entrambos se golpean con tanta furia que los huessos y las carnes les parescían molerles[14] (1. 171).

Placing *Mirror* alongside its source, we see that Tyler has supplied, along with a newly elevated register, an original conceit. The stroke of a sword is not a 'respuesta' (reply), as in Ortúñez's *Espejo*, but a means by which debt is incurred or repaid.[15] Each blow places the recipient under an obligation to repay and, as here, it is best if the debt is paid with interest—a 'surplusage'. The Knight of the Sun therefore shows his superlative knightly credentials by paying 'more than an ordinary interest', a '*plus ultra*'.

Credit relationships are legal relationships and in sixteenth-century England wayward debtors were increasingly subject to legal actions, either to reclaim the amount of the debt (using the writ of debt) or to claim damages beyond that amount (using action on the case). Litigation quadrupled between 1560 and 1580 at the King's Bench with similarly exponential rates at the Court of Common Pleas, and debt-related cases took up an increasing portion of this growing total, reflecting an expansion of credit as an economic mechanism.[16] The dual meaning of Tyler's word 'surplusage', at once a financial surplus and a supernumerary clause in a law, itself suggests this close relation between economics and law.[17] Craig Muldrew argues that the boom in litigation in

[14] This and subsequent references to the Spanish are from Daniel Eisenberg's edition of the 1555 text (which Tyler also used); Diego Ortúñez de Calahorra, in Daniel Eisenberg (ed.), *Espejo de príncipes y cavalleros* (Madrid, 1975), vol. 1, 171. In my translation of the Spanish: 'From there [the ground], he gave him reply, and between them they hit each other with such fury that they seemed to grind their bones and flesh'. Subsequent English translations in these footnotes are my own.

[15] Elsewhere they are described as 'loan[s]', see Tyler, in Boro (ed.), *Mirror*, 121.

[16] Christopher W. Brooks, *Lawyers, Litigation and English Society Since 1450* (London, 1998), 11, 17 and Craig Muldrew, *The Economy of Obligation* (Basingstoke, 1998), 327.

[17] 'surplusage', *OED*, *n.* 1.a. and 1.b.

England prompted an 'increasing emphasis on the contractual nature of interpersonal economic relationships' and the 'elevat[ion of] the legalism of contract to a privileged social position'.[18] It is this newly elevated status that makes Tyler's debt analogies appropriate, in one sense, as a description of chivalrous deeds.

However, Tyler's persistent addition of a language of debt and contract, entirely absent in Ortúñez's text, has repercussions for the feudal values of *Mirror*'s world and its heroes. We see this when Emperor Trebatio attempts to rescue a gentlewoman from some giants:

Mirror	*Espejo*
without either good-even or good-morrow, he lent the first whom he approached unto such a stroke that the giant would have mortgaged his part in the lady to have made sufficient payment of that blow. For the lifting up his battle axe to receive the blow, the sword cut it into the middest... (Ch. 8, 65).	E no se queriendo detener con ellos en palabras, al primero que llegó tiró un golpe con tanta presteza que no tuvo otro remedio el jayán para librarse dél sino alçar la hacha e recebirlo en ella, la qual cortó la espada... (1. 65).[19]

Again, Tyler opts for a language of debt and repayment. The alternative course of action, not offered in the Spanish, of the giant 'mortgag[ing] his part in the lady', suggests that the giant cannot provide 'sufficient [re]payment' of Trebatio's 'blow' without offering as collateral his investment ('part') in the lady. (To do so would end the fight because the kidnapped lady is exactly what Trebatio seeks to recover.) In this schema, Trebatio's superlative might becomes instead a superlative ability to indebt others to him, turning martial contests into financial coming-to-accounts and chivalric protagonists into errant debt-collectors.

This language extends beyond the battlefield. King Oliverio of Britain is said to have 'advance[d] his private credit and the honour of his country' by exhibiting Rosicleer's feats of arms in his court (Ch. 42, 185). The King's daughter, Princess Olivia, longs to have Rosicleer as a husband but because of his ostensible lack of noble ancestry this is impossible. She complains:

[18] Muldrew, *Economy of Obligation*, 315.

[19] 'And not wanting to stop them for words, as soon as he [Trebatio] reached them he so quickly threw a blow that the giant had no other remedy to escape it but to receive it with his axe, which the sword cut [in half]'.

Mirror

Alas, Rosicleer, my father thinks he hath made a great purchase by thy being here, but I would to God I might be as sure heir to this purchase, as I am otherwise certain to repent thy coming hither! And yet, whatsoever the event be, my love commands in me the contrary. For is it not better . . . [that] by the enjoying of his sight I receive such pleasure than never to have seen him, though I lose the hope of augmenting my state? And truly befall what may, in spite of Fortune's rancour, I will stay myself upon this choice and will not exchange it (Ch. 35, 155).

Espejo

O Rosicler, ¡quánta alegría ha dado al rey mi padre y a todos los cavalleros de su corte tu venida en esta tierra, y quán amarga ha sido para mí, y penosa! Mas ¿qué digo yo, cativa? Quel amoroso fuego en que me abraso me haze desvariar en lo que digo . . . Pues sólo en gozar de su estremada vista recibo tan gran plazer que a haverlo dexado de conoscer, para no poder ser más de lo que antes era, ni esperar de augmentar más mi ser, por pensar que no avía nadie que me meresciesse. Por cierto, venga lo que viniere, y dure mi penar hasta la muerte; que más quiero vivir con tan gloriosa pena . . . que ser libre sin ella[20] (2. 56).

While in the Spanish having Rosicleer in court is a 'great joy' ('quánta alegría') for the King, in Tyler's English it is instead a 'great purchase': a fortuitous exchange of goods by which his reputation is advanced. Olivia also sees Rosicleer as part of a transaction. She wishes to be the 'heir' or recipient of the goods of her father's bargain; that is, to have Rosicleer as a husband. But knowing the marriage to be impossible, she nevertheless prefers to suffer than never to have seen him at all, saying she will 'not exchange it'—or rather, exchange *him*. That Rosicleer can be purchased, inherited, or exchanged recasts his exemplary chivalry as an economic good or service; his effects on Olivia and on Oliverio's reputation are, in Tyler's translation, quantifiable. We see this, too, when Princess Olivia watches Rosicleer fight. In the Spanish, her love for him causes her apprehension ('algún recelo'; 2. 39), but in the English we read that 'the beautiful Princess Olivia could not but be angered at the new knight's jeopardous adventure, as if she had had no small title or claim to his person' (Ch. 33, 149). Rosicleer, though newly arrived in the court at this point, is already a possession and his risking his life in battle is a risk on Olivia's investment.

20 'Oh, Rosicleer, how happy your coming to this land has been for the king my father and for all the knights of his court, and how bitter it has been for me, and sorrowful! But, what say I, captive? The amorous fire that burns in me turns what I say into ravings . . . From the mere enjoyment of your goodly appearance I get such pleasure that, [I wonder that] had I not met him, I would be nothing more than what I was then, wanting nothing to augment myself and thinking there were none that deserved me. Well, come what may, even if my sorrow lasts unto death, I much prefer to live with that glorious sorrow . . . than to be free from it'.

If, as Fuchs argues, Beaumont's *The Knight of the Burning Pestle* imposes on its Cervantine model an 'English commercial subjectivity in contradistinction to the chivalric', then it finds a precedent in the translation of Margaret Tyler.[21] Her changes in diction, often the choice of one alternative over another, acculturates Ortúñez's romance to reflect contemporary English concerns. Indeed, *Mirror* is a striking example of the way that, in England, 'the legalistic language of credit and contractual discourse had permeated all aspects of early modern culture by the late sixteenth century', including the lives and interests of women like Tyler.[22] Applied to a Spanish chivalric romance, this legalese has unpredictable effects, as indeed its satirical descendants suggest. But before I examine these, I first want to examine one of Tyler's longest additions and her most protracted engagement with contemporary legal procedure. For, unlike her more general references to sale and debt, this common law proceeding is unmistakably English.

Rosicleer is participating in a jousting tournament when he looks at Princess Olivia seated in the stands and burns with love. Olivia is then coaxed by Cupid into reciprocating his affection. These particulars appear in both the Spanish and English, but between them Tyler inserts an entire legal proceeding that has no equivalent in her source.[23] Her addition is indicated below in square brackets:

> This was a breathing time for Rosicleer, but yet I am persuaded that it was no playing time although no enemy appeared. For he had a greater conflict within his bones than he professed outwardly, and therefore, his heart, neither fully assured nor yet in danger, gazed upon the beauty of Olivia. Whereby the fire, entering closely by the veins, wasted and consumed his flesh sooner than he felt the flame or could think of remedy. [But better considering that he was within the compass of Love's seigniory, and that his matter was to be tried at the great assize in Love's dominion, he took better advisement to alter it to an action upon the case of covenant against his mistress, the matter arising upon exchange of looks, as you have heard. And for this cause he entertained Sergeant Hope to be his lawyer and feed diverse others to assist him. But Master Despair, an old stager, had won the day of him had not the whole bench, and especially the Chief Justice Desert, stayed upon a demur, which relieved much Rosicleer's courage and made him look more freshly upon Hope to find out better evidence for recovery of his suit. But as Rosicleer thus pled his cause at the bar,] so gentle Cupid attended upon his mistress, faithfully serving

[21] Fuchs, *Poetics of Piracy*, 53.

[22] Muldrew, *Economy of Obligation*, 315.

[23] The Spanish reads: 'Pues en este tiempo el coraçón de Rosicler, no muy consolado ni seguro, la grande hermosura de Olivia contemplava; que encendido en amoroso fuego se du amor, çufría la pena que la falta del remedio le causava, teniéndose del todo por perdido, paresciéndole quel cercano parentesco que con aquella hermosa infanta tenía impedía qualquier remedio que por su parte pudiesse serle dado. Quanto más, que mirando su tan soberana hermosura, merescimiento le parescía a él faltar para osarse publicar por suyo. La qual, en este tiempo, como los mensageros de Cupido la començassen a tentar, mirando con grande atención su tan estremada dispusición y las altas cavallerías que aquel día avía hecho, paresciéndole ansí armado ser el mejor de quantos havía visto, ya tenía abierta la puerta y rendidos todos sus sentidos, para que visto su rostro descubierto ser conforme a su gran bondad, sin ninguna resistencia pudiesse el amor entrar en su libre coraçón, a hazerla subjecta'; Ortúñez, *Espejo*, 2. 25–6.

> him and beating into her head the remembrance of his acts and the beauty of his personage that, the windows of her desire being set wide open, she viewed her fill, wishing yet to see his face, thereby to comfort herself if his visage were answerable to his virtue. (Ch. 32, 145)

The tone is playful, but the case that is fought here reflects real legal procedures and refers to contemporary legal controversy. A few pages earlier, Rosicleer and Olivia have shared a reciprocal 'interchange of looks' which, as in the word 'exchange' in this passage, turns their looks into goods in a transaction. Here, Rosicleer looks at Olivia and burns in love, but his look is not returned. Like the blows of chivalric combat, Rosicleer's look incurs a debt that Olivia is obliged, in his mind, to repay. It is this breach of obligation that is the 'matter' litigated in the courtroom episode. On the advice of his lawyer 'Sergeant Hope', Rosicleer pursues 'an action upon the case of covenant' at the 'great assize in Love's dominion'. Action on the case responded to a civil wrong and the specification of 'covenant' identifies it as a breach of what we would today call contract. Unlike an action of debt, which sought to recover the amount owed, action on the case was often used to seek restitution for damages arising from the non-payment of debt.[24] In other words, to compensate for the damage Rosicleer incurs when he is consumed and burnt by love, he wants more than just a look from Olivia. He wants a 'surplusage'.

However, Rosicleer's case does not go well. We are told that 'Master Despair, an old stager, had won the day of him' entirely but the Chief Justice Desert 'stayed upon a demur', an objection that awaits the 'find[ing] out of better evidence for recovery of his suit'. What is happening here? This case is fanciful because 'looks' are not goods that can be transacted, but if we take it seriously on its own terms, it nonetheless engages aspects of legal debates coming to a head in the common law system of late sixteenth-century England. Rosicleer's attempt to sue action on the case, rather than using than the traditional writ of debt, reflects a point of particular controversy. The issue was 'whether a simple bargain and sale involved an assumpsit, that is, whether when you made a bargain you also implicitly *promised* to uphold your part of it'. If a promise *was* involved, then action of the case could be brought and damages sought, but if not, parties only had recourse to the action of debt.[25] In the 1570s, The King's Bench Court held that a promise was implicit in the transaction itself, enabling litigants to pursue an action on the case if they wished to. The Court of Common Pleas disagreed, arguing that an action on the case could only be brought if there had been a promise to repay *subsequent* to the initial transaction that incurred the debt.[26] If there were only the initial transaction, the Common Pleas contended there were no grounds for bringing an action on the case.

[24] See David Harris Sacks, 'The Promise and the Contract in Early Modern England: Slade's Case in Perspective', in Victoria Kahn and Lorna Hutson (eds), *Rhetoric and Law in Early Modern Europe* (New Haven, CT, 2001), 28–53.

[25] Luke Wilson, 'Ben Jonson and the Law of Contract', in Kahn and Hutson (eds), *Rhetoric and Law*, 143–65, 150.

[26] See David Ibbetson, 'Sixteenth Century Contract Law: Slade's Case in Context', *Oxford Journal of Legal Studies*, 4.3 (1984), 295–317.

This is what happens to Rosicleer's case in *Mirror*. The judge of an assize court could be sympathetic to either the Common Pleas or the King's Bench, and Chief Justice Desert's 'demur' here suggests he favours the Common Pleas.[27] A 'demur' or 'demurrer' is an objection typically used to challenge the sufficiency of a legal action, Chief Justice Desert indicating that Rosicleer's case is not permissible as an action on the case because there is no evidence that Olivia promised to repay, only the fact of their initial 'exchange' of looks. As such, Rosicleer enlists Hope to seek out further evidence, such as a promise from Olivia to repay his love.[28] In the romance, Rosicleer is 'ple[a]d[ing] his cause at the bar', and so is distracted when Olivia finally does return his look, egged on by Cupid. Rosicleer has not won his damages, but the debt has now been repaid.

If Tyler had written Rosicleer's court case thirty years later, it might have had a different result. The impasse between the two courts was resolved in Slade's Case (1596–1602) in favour of action on the case so that the fact of incurring a debt implied in itself a promise to repay, thus combining '[t]he two old concepts of the covenant and the debt-creating bargain'.[29] Rosicleer's gazing upon Olivia, cast as an exchange of goods, would then itself imply a promissory obligation to repay.

'WHO MADE YOU A JUSTICE?'

That Tyler has Rosicleer argue action on the case and then have that action thrown out demonstrates she followed such cases and the contested legal argumentation behind them with close attention. This passage is among the strongest evidence we have that the growing 'law-mindedness' of early modern English society did not leave women's minds, or their pens, untouched.[30] But the detail in this passage would also be exceptional in a male writer, particularly given Luke Wilson's recent warning (using the example of Philip Henslowe's 'law illiteracy') that we are sometimes too eager to read literary texts as 'highly sensitive seismograph[s]' alert to legal developments and nuance.[31] Tyler's addition suggests exactly that degree of sensitivity while also being, in its levity, decidedly literary.

What are we to make of Tyler's choice to insert her interest in English law into her translation of a Spanish chivalric romance? She makes no attempt to retain the

[27] Ibbetson, 'Slade's Case', 301.

[28] That a 'promise of love' might be legally actionable seems less farcical when one considers the potential for hardship when promises of marriages went unfulfilled. Developments in assumpsit led to 'the extension of promissory liability into areas previously outside the scope of law'. See Wilson, 'Ben Jonson', 144. See also John H. Baker, *An Introduction to English Legal History* (Oxford, 2019), 350–85.

[29] Baker, *Introduction*, 369.

[30] This term is from Christopher W. Brooks, *Pettyfoggers and the Vipers of the Commonwealth* (Cambridge, 1986), 9.

[31] Luke Wilson, 'Contract', in Lorna Hutson (ed.) *The Oxford Handbook of English Law and Literature, 1500–1700* (Oxford, 2017), 393–409, 393.

foreignness of the text, for while *Espejo* is not particularly invested in Spain—none of the main cast of *Espejo* are Spanish nor do its events take place in Spain—the hazy exoticism of its various settings is undercut by a turn to the detail of the English courtroom. The effect that this language has on the integrity of Ortúñez's romance is substantial. The insertion of the courtroom scene just before and after Rosicleer defeats a series of foes in one-to-one jousts and combats implies the insufficiency of those typically chivalric deeds to sufficiently recommend him to Princess Olivia's notice. Lorna Hutson has argued that the martial feats which allow the knight of the chivalric romance to 'become visible' to royal patrons such as Olivia are displaced, in the textualised economy of Renaissance England, by feats of mental prowess.[32] That Rosicleer feels no assurance his skills in combat will distinguish him thus feels like an anxiety every bit as contemporary as his attempt to remedy it by suing Olivia in court, though his facility with swords does not necessarily translate to a facility with words.

As this suggests, the penetration of legalistic language into the world of the romance represents an existential threat to the legitimacy of the chivalric knights and the hierarchy that esteems them. This is because, as Muldrew argues, an extension of credit created the need for mechanisms of enforcing credit obligations, resulting in a 'redefin[ition of] both political authority and social relations in extremely legalistic terms' that were premised on 'the necessary equality of justice'.[33] This 'equality of justice' provided an alternative framework through which to measure a person's moral or social value without reference to nobility—namely the law. In the chivalric romance, noble ancestry and knightly virtue are synonymous, but Tyler's translation choices evoke a world in which 'legal power could subvert conventional hierarchy' and all were 'morally equal in their responsibility to honour their bargains'.[34] Only under this alternate model is it conceivable that Princess Olivia might be compelled by her (apparent) social inferior to carry out a contractual obligation.

The clash of these value systems is on full display in the incident where Emperor Trebatio chases down two knights who are attempting to rape a gentlewoman. He remonstrates with them, stating 'let this gentlewoman alone, for it is great villainy to force a woman!'. In a line Tyler adds to the English, one of the knights replies: 'Who made you a justice? Or do you look for an attorney's fee?' (Ch. 49, 221). This comment is a striking encapsulation of the effect Tyler's introduction of legal language has on the chivalric world of *Mirror*. Not only does it import distrust of lawyers and caricatures of their greed from sixteenth-century England, but it introduces a whole alternate system of moral authority: not nobility or God, but the law.[35] We see the same clash of values in Cervantes' *Don Quixote*. At risk of arrest, Quixote protests that 'knights errant are exempt from all jurisdiction ... What knight errant has ever paid tax, duty, queen's patten

[32] Lorna Hutson, *The Usurer's Daughter: Male Friendship and Fictions of Women in Sixteenth-Century England* (London, 1994), 101–3.

[33] Muldrew, *Economy of Obligation*, 327.

[34] Muldrew, *Economy of Obligation*, 316, 318.

[35] Brooks, *Lawyers*, 22.

money, statue money, customs, or toll?'.[36] Cervantes' and Tyler's delinquent knights each ask: what right do you have to judge? And in each text the traditional hierarchy is being questioned. The mere fact of being a knight, or in Trebatio's case the Emperor of Hungary, has no practical bearing on the parties' 'moral equality' before the law—and the law claims sole right of adjudication. That Trebatio subsequently chops the knights into pieces does not resolve the ideological tensions lingering in the air.

By introducing into the chivalric romance a wholly incommensurate set of legal values, Tyler disrupts the genre's nostalgia for a mythical past in which virtue and hierarchical position were perfectly aligned.[37] If romance, a notoriously difficult genre to pin down, can be defined primarily by the way it 'undermines the social ideals of the here and now' by 'express[ing] a powerful longing for what came before', then a modernising impulse would seem to be the one alteration that it cannot accommodate.[38] Yet this is what Tyler attempts here, at once acculturating and modernising her source. While the discordance that results did not seem to affect *Mirror*'s commercial success, it nonetheless helps us to understand the coming decline of chivalric romance. Her translation exemplifies how antithetical the values are that characterise, on the one hand, the emerging early modern social order defined by capital, the law, and the state, and, on the other, the romance order of feudal obligation and patrilineal virtue. These are exactly the tensions that texts like Cervantes' *Don Quixote* and Beaumont's *The Knight of the Burning Pestle* (both of which repeatedly reference the *Mirror* series) would exploit in the seventeenth century as the chivalric knight became an object of satire. In the way she anticipates those parodies, Tyler is shown to be a keen observer of both the law and the changing societal values to which the law responds and occasions.

'MY PART NONE THEREIN BUT THE TRANSLATION'

Examining *Espejo* and *Mirror* together reveals a vexed relationship between source and translated text and provides a vivid example of how small alterations or additions can have cumulatively transformative effects. Critics have taken Tyler at her word when she says that the 'invention, disposition, trimming, and what else in this story is wholly another man's, my part none therein but the translation' (Preface, 49). But translation, by women as well as men, not only invites but necessitates invention, (re-)disposition, and trimming; it is itself an expressive process. If we had a percentage figure of how many of

[36] Miguel de Cervantes Saavedra, in J. M. Cohen (trans.), *The Adventures of Don Quixote* (London, 1950), 410.

[37] For these two senses of 'pastness', see Alex Davis, *Chivalry and Romance in the English Renaissance* (Cambridge, 2003), 190.

[38] This is Fuchs on Northrop Frye; Barbara Fuchs, *Romance* (New York, 2004), 6.

Tyler's sentences have no rough equivalent in the Spanish, we might agree that her text is 'a relatively faithful reproduction'.[39] But I hope this discussion has shown that this kind of quantification is meaningless to translation; there what matters are the expressive gaps left by the necessarily imperfect equivalence between two cultural and linguistic systems. Short additions and a series of changes in diction and emphasis are sufficient to turn the titular 'deedes' from blows and parries on Ortúñez's medieval battlefield to contracts and claims in the early modern courtroom of Tyler's England.

Finally, Tyler's translation shows that a willingness to intervene in foreign texts is not limited to male translators who, we are told in F. O. Matthiessen's foundational account, 'made the foreign classics rich with English associations', discarding 'meticulous imitation' for 'the production of a book that would strike into the minds of their countrymen'.[40] Tyler, too, not only reworks Ortúñez's text with English words but embeds it in English culture, tracking legal, social, and literary developments to create a more modern text that appealed to her readers even as she furnished them with the impossible feats and exotic journeys promised by the chivalric romance and by Spain itself. Appeal it did, but even as *Mirror* triggered a fashion for Spanish chivalric romances, it instantiated the ideological values that decades later would make that tradition such rich material for satire. There is no doubt that Margaret Tyler is a milestone in Anglo-Spanish literary exchange. But that her romance can still challenge our assumptions about early modern women's interests and engagements should spur us to attend with renewed scrutiny to the full range of women's work in translation.

FURTHER READING

Boro, Joyce (ed.). *Mirror of Princely Deeds and Knighthood*. London, 2014.

Braden, Gordon et al. (eds). *The Oxford History of Literary Translation in English: Volume II 1550–1660*. Oxford, 2010.

Cooper, Helen. *The English Romance in Time*. Oxford, 2004.

Fuchs, Barbara. *The Poetics of Piracy: Emulating Spain in English Literature*. Philadelphia, PA, 2013.

Hutson, Lorna (ed.). *The Oxford Handbook of English Law and Literature, 1500–1700*. Oxford, 2017.

Muldrew, Craig. *The Economy of Obligation*. Basingstoke, 1998.

Reynolds, Matthew. *The Poetry of Translation: From Chaucer & Petrarch to Homer & Logue*. Oxford, 2011.

[39] Uman and Bistué, 'Translation', 299.

[40] F. O. Matthiessen, *Translation: An Elizabethan Art* (New York, 1965), 4, 6.

CHAPTER 29

FRENCH CONNECTIONS

English Women's Writing and Préciosité

LINE COTTEGNIES

In early modern England, knowledge of French was widespread among the gentry and the aristocracy, and the language constituted an essential part of the education of women of the upper echelons.[1] Dedicating his 1603 translation of Montaigne to six noble English ladies, John Florio revealed that he had been reading the *Essayes* with his patronesses in private tutorials,[2] adding: 'French hath long time beene termed the language of Ladies'.[3] Peter Erundell, the Huguenot author of *The French Garden: for English Ladyes and Gentlewomen to Walke in. Or, A Sommer Dayes Labour* (London, 1605), called it *Lingua mulierum* (sig. B). Elizabeth I was taught French, also a diplomatic language, and translated Marguerite de Navarre as an exercise. Women of the upper ranks were habitually taught French as a social skill, and French literature was widely read among them. Some extant inventories of women's libraries reveal a significant proportion of French books.[4] Women were also avid readers of translations and some turned their hands to translating from the French.[5] When Mary Sidney Herbert, Countess

[1] Kathleen Lambley, *The Teaching and Cultivation of the French Language in England during Tudor and Stuart Times* (Manchester/London, 1920), 263–73. See also Douglas A. Kibbee, *For to Speke Frenche Trewely. The French Language in England, 1000–1600* (Amsterdam, 1991).

[2] Warren Boutcher, 'Marginal Commentaries: The Cultural Transmission of Montaigne's *Essais* in Shakespeare's England', *Actes des congrès de la Société française Shakespeare*, 21 (2004), 13–28, 22.

[3] *The Essayes, of Moral Politike and Millitarie Discourses of Lo: Michaell de Montaigne* (London, 1603), sig. Rr2.

[4] Lady Bridgewater owned eighteen French books out of 241 items, as well as some translations. See Heidi Brayman Hackel, 'The Countess of Bridgewater's London Library', in Jennifer Andersen and Elizabeth Sauer (eds), *Books and Readers in Early Modern England. Material Studies* (Philadelphia, PA, 2002), 145.

[5] On women and translation, see Tina Krontiris, *Oppositional Voices: Women and Writers and Translators of Literature in the English Renaissance* (London, 1992); Danielle Clarke, 'Translation', in Laura Lunger Knoppers (ed.), *The Cambridge Companion to Early Modern Women's Writing* (Cambridge, 2009), 167–80; and Marie-Alice Belle, 'Locating Early Modern Women's Translations: Critical and Historiographical Issues', *Renaissance and Reformation / Renaissance et Réforme*, 35.4 (2012), 5–23.

of Pembroke, boldly taking over from her brother, looked for models to emulate for a reformation of the English stage, she translated *Antonius* by French dramatist Robert Garnier (1592). She contributed, in her turn, to the militant support of the Protestant cause by translating an essay by Huguenot Philippe du Mornay.

French seems to have been perceived as particularly fashionable at Anna of Denmark's court, which led Edmund Blount to comment scathingly on what he saw as a recent craze in the 1620s: 'that Beautie in Court, which could not Parley Euphueisme, was as little regarded; as shee which now there, speakes not French'.[6] The crowning, in 1625, of Henrietta Maria, sister to Louis XIII, reinforced the importance of French cultural trends among polite circles, and the craze grew for French tutors, musicians, dancing masters, and tailors, while a new interest in French pastoral drama and ballet emerged at court.[7] The interest in French literature gathered momentum during the Commonwealth as a consequence of the exile of many royalists on the Continent and the publication in England of the long French romances of La Calprenède and Scudéry in particular. Although not specifically aimed at women, these romances, whose volumes were published in instalments in quick succession, were particularly successful with a female readership. Interest in French literature continued after the Restoration, when the new court looked towards France as a powerful cultural model to emulate.[8] The popularity of French fiction was such in the Restoration that Mary Astell implored English women to read French philosophy rather than fiction, confirming the supremacy of French among them: 'since the *French Tongue* is understood by most Ladies, methinks they may much better improve it by the study of Philosophy (as I hear the *French Ladies* do) *Des Cartes*, *Malebranche* and others, than by reading idle *Novels* and *Romances*'.[9]

This chapter argues that an engagement with French literature and culture helped early modern English women from the middle and upper echelons transcend the limitations imposed on their gender, and empowered them as readers, patrons, book owners, and social movers, but also translators and authors. As Tina Krontiris has argued, translation often allowed early modern women an oblique and 'soft' point of entry into literature: 'Englishwomen responded in many ways to the obstacles they encountered ... Translation became a popular form of literary expression among women of the period, especially in the acceptable subject of religion'.[10] But women authors also looked towards French literature as sources of inspiration, not just as new material to be tapped, but because it provided them with powerful philogynist models that valorised female agency. Seventeenth-century French society was traversed by a sweeping movement that saw the emergence of the powerful female salon-holder, arbiter of mores and wit (and

[6] 'To the Reader' in John Lyly, *Sixe Court Comedies* (London, 1632), sig. A5v.

[7] See Erin Griffey, *Henrietta Maria: Piety, Politics and Patronage* (Aldershot, 2008) and Barbara Ravelhofer, *The Early Stuart Masque: Dance, Costume, and Music* (Oxford, 2006), e.g., 61–3, 152.

[8] See Gera Stedman, *Cultural Exchanges in Seventeenth-Century France and England* (Farnham, 2013), 63–95.

[9] *A Serious Proposal to the Ladies for the Advancement of their True and Greatest Interest* (London, 1694), 85.

[10] Krontiris, *Oppositional Voices*, 21.

sometimes author) in her own right. This woman-friendly context was conducive to the assertion of published women authors. This chapter touches on the influence on English women of the multifaceted movement subsumed in the concept of *préciosité*, a cultural phenomenon which created a unique stimulation for seventeenth-century French women by allowing them a voice on the social and the literary stages. I argue that a better apprehension of this often misunderstood social and cultural movement, which led to an extensive body of literature, can shed light on English literary phenomena or authors often described in criticism as singular or exceptional. It can help see connections between the alleged craze for 'platonic love' at the court of Henrietta Maria, the fashion for French romances, Margaret Cavendish's fascination with 'heroic women', Katherine Philips' 'Society of Friendship', and the imitation of French pastoral and amorous works by Aphra Behn and Anne Finch in the 1680s. All these can be seen as interconnected creative responses to the consistent, enduring influence of *préciosité* in various guises. By importing French models, English women authors reconfigured and put them to use in different ways, self-fashioning themselves as women authors.

FROM *ASTREA* TO THE FRENCH ROMANCE OF THE 1650S

There is evidence to suggest that French heroic prose romance was immensely popular in England from the 1650s. First, the number of editions indicates that it became economically viable for successful booksellers like Henry Moseley and Henry Herringman to publish translations.[11] Secondly, documents like Dorothy Osborne's correspondence of the mid-century allow one to capture the excitement felt by readers eagerly awaiting instalments of the serialised novels. Osborne reads La Calprenède and Scudéry both (or alternately) in French and English, and complains about the quality of the translations available to English readers.[12] She eagerly discusses specific episodes with her future husband William Temple, and fastidiously reminds him to leave each volume, when he is done, at a certain place for the benefit of the next reader in line, her friend Lady Diana Rich, daughter of the Earl of Holland.[13] This shows a community of readers passionate

[11] See Alice Eardley, 'Marketing Aspiration. Fact, Fiction, and the Publication of French Romance in Mid-Seventeenth-Century England', in Jacqueline Glomski and Isabelle Moreau (eds), *Seventeenth-Century Fiction. Text & Transmission* (Oxford, 2016), 130–42; on the popularity of romance, see Lambley, *The Teaching and Cultivation*, 320–1, and Paul Salzman, *English Prose Fiction 1558–1700: A Critical History* (Oxford, 1985), 177–201.

[12] Osborne, in G. C. Moore Smith (ed.), *The Letters of Dorothy Osborne to William Temple* (Oxford, 1928), 91. Pepys also records buying a French edition of Scudéry's *Ibrahim* for his wife from a London bookseller. Pepys, in Robert Latham and William Matthews (eds), *The Diary of Samuel Pepys: A New and Complete Transcription*, vol. 9, 1668–1669 (London, 1986), 89.

[13] Her favourite romance seems to have been *Le Grand Cyrus* (quoted nine times), but she mentions many others.

about discussing the romances they literally shared as the books circulated among them. The French romances published in translation targeted the upwardly aspiring as well as more elegant readers, both men and women. Each tome was almost immediately translated from French to English. They include: La Calprenède's *Cassandre*, published in two different translations, one by George Digby and the other by Charles Cotterell, in 1652; La Calprenède's *Cleopâtre*, published as *Hymen's Praeludia* between 1652 and 1659; the Scudérys' *Ibrahim* translated by Henry Cogan in 1652 (reissued in 1674); their *Artamène, or the Grand Cyrus*, translated by Francis Gifford and published between 1653 and 1655; and finally Madeleine de Scudéry's *Clelia*, with the first three parts translated by John Davies and parts four and five by George Haver, published between 1655 and 1661 (and reissued in 1678).[14]

Another Englishwoman who avidly read these romances was Katherine Philips, whose friends in the poetic coterie she created in the 1650s and early 1660s were all given romance-inspired pseudonyms, such as Lucasia, Rosania, Poliarchus, or Antenor. Davies dedicated one volume of *Hymen's Praeludia* to her in 1659, which indicates her keen interest in a genre associated with aristocratic values and a female readership.[15] Philips was also close to Cotterell, who had spearheaded the translations of romances with *Cassandra*. As she herself translated several pieces from the French, she was presumably able to read the romances in the original language, however, which is confirmed by the fact that she translated a pastoral song from Scudéry's *Almahide* (1660), a romance which would only be translated in 1677. Philips' interest in romance has often been read as an aspiring poet's desire to align herself with royalist values,[16] but it can be argued that she also found in French romance a literary genre that chimed with her ethical and literary concerns. It is easy to overlook how modern this form might have appeared to a seventeenth-century woman. The French romance offered a synthesis between the Greek romance (in the models of Heliodorus and Longus) and the innovations brought to the genre by Honoré d'Urfé's *L'Astrée*, the first part of which, originally published in 1607, had been translated as *Astrea* in 1620.

L'Astrée, while steeped in the same European pastoral sources as Montemayor's *Diana* or Sidney's *Arcadia*, offered a new concern with the psychology of love and friendship, which it discussed at great length. More fundamentally it feminised the Greek model, focusing on the plight of female heroines. Although it was by no means the only influence on her, Lady Mary Wroth was probably the first English woman author to perceive its potential. Its 1620 translation was dedicated by John Pyper to both Wroth's cousin William Herbert, earl of Montgomery and his wife, her close friend, Susan Herbert,

[14] Parts 1–3 were translated by Richard Loveday (1652, 1654, 1655), Parts 4–7 by John Coles (1656, 1657, 1658), Part 8 by James Webb (1658), and Parts 9–12 by John Davies (1659). Reissued 1663, 1665, 1666, 1668, 1674. It is not known why Moseley published two different translations of *Cassandra* (Digby translated Books 1–3, Cotterell the whole text). See Eardley, 'Marketing Aspiration', 132.

[15] *Hymen's Praeludia, or, Loves Master-Piece Being the Ninth, and Tenth Part* (London, 1659), sig. a.

[16] See Carol Barash, *English Women's Poetry, 1649–1714. Politics, Community, and Linguistic Authority* (Oxford, 1996), 62–6, and Hero Chalmers, *Royalist Women Writers 1650–1689* (Oxford, 2004), 57–72.

countess of Montgomery, the woman to whom she inscribed her own romance, *The Countess of Montgomery's Urania* the following year.[17] Internal evidence, like the focus on heroines and female melancholy, also reveals that Wroth had closely read *Astrea*. More specifically perhaps, an episode close to the end of *Urania* seems to echo, among other references to Sidney and Ovid, the famous episode of the drowning and rescue of Celadon which opens *Astrea*. Close similarities between Galathée's spying of Celadon's 'corpse' in *Astrea*, and Celina's discovery of the dead shepherd in *Urania*, suggest a direct reminiscence.[18] The influence of *L'Astrée* permeated contemporary French literature, and it was also a real, often unacknowledged, presence in England from the 1620s onwards, through the works of Jean-Pierre Camus (translated by Susan Du Verger) or Jacques Du Bosc's *The Accomplish't Woman*, translated in 1639 by Walter Montagu, for instance.[19] Its influence can be traced in the 1630s in the French pastorals that Henrietta Maria staged at court, like Racan's *Les Bergeries*, performed as *Artenice* in 1626,[20] or in Montagu's *The Shepheard's Paradise*, performed in 1633 (published in 1659). It is the Neoplatonism that it contributed to promoting that famously made Howell exclaim against the craze for 'Platonic love', 'love abstracted from all corporeall grosse impressions, and sensuall appetite', which 'sets the wits of the Town on work'.[21]

George de Scudéry's preface to *Ibrahim* acknowledges his debt to *L'Astrée*, praising 'the great and incomparable *Urfé*' as the 'Painter of the soul' who freed romance from the marvellous and the ideal, focusing instead on 'reasonable' verisimilitude: 'every thing in him is naturall, and truly resembling', Scudéry continues.[22] D'Urfé was in turn deeply influenced by François de Sales' devout humanism (a Catholic religious movement that sought to reconcile a secular form of spirituality with life in society), and used the pastoral mode as a vehicle for the latter's ideas. He gave women the upper hand by promoting a form of Neoplatonism that allowed them to be the arbiters of mores, in particular to regulate matters of love and friendship. Later romance writers easily adapted d'Urfé's teaching to the more immediate context of *galanterie*. Translating as 'Civility,

[17] The title itself, with its combination of a patron's name, the Countess of Montgomery, and a heroine's name, Urania, is a homage to Sir Philip Sidney's *The Countess of Pembroke's Arcadia*, and to d'Urfé's *Astrea*.

[18] Mary Wroth, in Jacqueline A. Roberts (ed.), *The First Part of The Countess of Montgomery's Urania* (Binghamton, NY, 2005), 642. See Aurélie Griffin, *La Muse de l'humeur noire. Urania de Lady Mary Wroth: une poétique de la mélancolie* (Paris, 2018), 101–2.

[19] See Alfred Horatio Upham, *The French Influence in English Literature from the Accession of Elizabeth to the Restoration* (New York, NY, 1908), 308–64; Jonathan Mallinson, '*L'Astrée* en Angleterre au XVIIe siècle', *Cahiers de l'Association internationale des études françaises*, 60 (2008), 208; Erica Veevers, *Images of Love and Religion. Queen Henrietta Maria and Court Entertainments* (Cambridge, 1989), 44–7. For a reappraisal, see Karen Britland, *Drama at the Courts of Queen Henrietta Maria* (Cambridge, 2006), 10–14; and Brenda M. Hosington, 'Fact and Fiction in Susan Du Verger's Translations of Jean-Pierre Camus' *Les Euenemens singuliers, Les Relations morales, and Diotrephe. Histoire Valentine*', in Jacqueline Glomski and Isabelle Moreau (eds), *Seventeenth-Century Fiction*, 115–29.

[20] Britland, *Drama*, 35–6.

[21] James Howell, *Epistolae Ho-Elianae. Familiar Letters Domestic & Forren* (London, 1645), 29.

[22] Preface, *Ibrahim. Or The Illustrious Bassa*, trans. Henry Cogan (London, 1652), sig. A4v.

civil Behaviour, genteelness, genteel or courtly way',[23] the concept of *galanterie* refers to the aristocratic ethos shared by 'honnêtes gens' (gentlemen and ladies), an ideal of civilisation and sociability based on courtesy, politeness, the art of conversation, and a particular form of wit. As the expression of an aristocratic coterie society, it flourished best in the contemporary collective miscellanies.[24] In the wake of d'Urfé, and under the conjoined influence of *préciosité*, which attributed to aristocratic women a vital social and intellectual role, *galanterie* and its focus on love became hegemonic in literature. A host of essays, poems, collections of letters, and works of fiction sought to define and regulate love and friendship, particularly from a feminine perspective. Although the term *préciosité* is still contested in French studies, because it was initially coined by critics of the trend in the 1650s, it cannot be denied that mid-seventeenth-century France saw the emergence of an important feminine movement with 'a massive entry of women onto the literary stage and a questioning of their status'.[25] The movement peaked with the debates on love and friendship, and the ideal of feminine heroism in *Clelia* by Madeleine de Scudéry, who had her own salon. It continued in the 1660s as a new generation of women, highly conscious of their specific identity as female arbiters of tastes, literary hostesses, and authors, thrived, even as male voices rose to satirise the trend. La Calprenède's and the Scudérys' romances follow *Astrea* by focusing on heroines and female heroic melancholy; but they tone down d'Urfé's eroticism to adjust to more refined contemporary tastes, in particular by valorising tenderness. Madeleine de Scudéry thus includes the famous emblematic 'Map of Tender' in *Clelia*, which materialises love as an allegorical voyage from 'Inclination' to 'Tender' (or true love).[26] French romance of the 1650s modernised the literary blueprint offered by d'Urfé, treating pastoralism more critically, even satirically, to foreground urban politeness. In formal terms, French romance writers perfected the narrative technique they found in *L'Astrée*, such as the multiplicity of inset narratives, the recurrent use of ekphrasis, the insertion of letters, and formal devices such as citations and collages, emphasising the metaliterary dimension of the genre.[27] New literary genres, in turn, emerged out of these romances, such as collections of 'portraits' (as invented by Scudéry), letters, maxims, and epistolary forms.

[23] Abel Boyer, *Dictionnaire royal françois et anglois* (The Hague, 1702), sig. Ii3.

[24] See Myriam Maître, *Les Précieuses. Naissance des femmes de lettres en France au XVIIe siècle* (Paris, 1999), 427–31; Delphine Denis, *Le Parnasse galant: Institution d'une catégorie littéraire au XVIIe siècle* (Paris, 2001), 146–52.

[25] Philipe Sellier, '"Se tirer du commun des femmes": La constellation précieuse', in *Essais sur l'imaginaire classique* (Paris, 2005), 197–213 (212). Domna C. Stanton, Faith H. Beasley, and Joan DeJean have argued caution about the term *préciosité* which is a contentious construction, but Maître and Sellier have reclaimed the concept as useful to literary history. See Domna C. Stanton, 'The Fiction of *Préciosité* and the Fear of Women', *Yale French Studies*, 62 (1981), 107–34, Faith H. Beasley, *Salons, History, and the Creation of 17th-Century France* (London, 2006), 9–10, Joan DeJean, *Tender Geographies. Women and the Origins of the Novel in France* (New York, NY, 1991), 17–42; Maître, *Les Précieuses*, 15–17.

[26] See Delphine Denis, 'Sçavoir la carte': Voyage au Royaume de Galanterie', *Espaces classiques*, 34 (2002), 179–89.

[27] Anne-Elisabeth Spica, 'Les Scudéry, lecteurs de *L'Astrée*', *Cahiers de l'Association internationale des études françaises*, 56 (2004), 397–416.

In England, French romances paradoxically made *Astrea* fashionable again, and the ubiquitous John Davies even translated it again in the 1650s, dressed to look new: Books 1 and 2 appeared in 1657, and Book 3 in 1658, a joint enterprise of booksellers Moseley, Herringman, and Dring. Davies' contemporaries could thus read *Astrea* as a contemporary romance, an editorial ploy which made the text topical again: Cotton translated several poems from *L'Astrée* as late as in 1689, while Behn used the pseudonyms Astrea and Celadon as code names for herself and William Scott while spying in Antwerp—which led her to use Astrea as her pseudonym as a poet.

KATHERINE PHILIPS AND *PRÉCIOSITÉ*

Katherine Philips has long been labelled an English 'précieuse', although the term is inappropriate in the English context.[28] As a close reader of French literature of the 1640s and 1650s, she was well informed about current trends. Several of her poems come under French titles, although their sources have not all been identified. In a letter, she enthused about the famous *salonnière* and author Madame de La Suze, who 'must needs be an extraordinary woman', after reading some of her poems, probably from collective miscellanies.[29] Philips translated four French poems in a variety of fashionable genres, and wrote two songs after French airs.[30] The first one was drawn from a recent royal ballet, and the second was a court air; both circulated in manuscript and appeared in fashionable miscellanies.[31] Philips' interest in the genre of the song is well known: her friend Henry Lawes set a number of her poems to music, and she wrote original songs for inclusion in her translation of Corneille's *Pompey*.[32] Both Philips and Lawes were attracted to French airs for their aura of fashionable distinction and novelty. It is Philips' foregrounding of tenderness in love and friendship, however, that owes most to *préciosité* and the current debates among the polite circles in Paris. For through her poetry, Philips produces a philosophy of friendship which clearly echoes debates featured in French romances.

Carol Barash and Hero Chalmers have offered convincing readings of royalism and friendship as 'vitally interconnected in Philips' poetry', in the context of the royalist

[28] See Lambley, *The Teaching and Cultivation*, 323.

[29] *Letters from Orinda to Poliarchus* (London, 1705), 16. La Suze's poetry was collected in 1666, but circulated in miscellanies in the 1650s.

[30] 'La Solitude de Saint Amant', 'Tendres desers *out of a French prose*', '*A Pastoral of* Mons. de Scudéry's *in the first volume of Almahide*', and '*Translation* of Thomas a Kempis *into Verse, out of* Mons. Corneille's *lib.3 Cap.2*', in *Poems* (London, 1667), 170–98.

[31] 'Song. To the tune of *Sommes nous pas trop heureux*', and '*Song to the Tune of* Adieu Phillis' (*Poems*, 126, 127). See Line Cottegnies, 'Katherine Philips' French Translations: Between Mediation and Appropriation', *Women's Writing* 23.4 (2016), 445–64.

[32] See Joan Applegate, 'Katherine Philips' "Orinda upon Little Hector": An Unrecorded Musical Setting by Henry Lawes', *English Manuscript Studies, 1100–1700*, 4 (1993), 272–80, 273–5.

culture of civil war and Interregnum England.[33] Through her poetry, they argue, Philips stages her own poetic *salon*, as 'Orinda' celebrates a community that is very much her own creation. The poems are semi-public epistles that could be sent folded in letters but were also read within her circle, and include several philosophical poems on friendship—clearly the soul of her poetical community.[34] Her more passionate poems about female friendship have occasionally been read as homoerotic, and one is reminded that several French *Précieuses*, including Madame de Lafayette, were known for their exclusive friendships.[35] Recent studies have offered to contextualise Philips' poetry by retracing contemporary debates on friendship, which owe a great deal to *préciosité*, although her debt to the latter has only been occasionally mentioned.[36] Philips' poetry is thus closely connected with two English treatises: one by Francis Finch ('Palaemon' in her poetry), published anonymously in 1654 in support of her positions, and Jeremy Taylor's more critical *Discourse of the Nature, Offices and Measures of Friendship, with the Rules of Conducting it* (London, 1657). Friendship is also one of the main subjects of conversation in *Clelia*, which was dedicated to Scudéry's friend Madame de Longueville, and praised, in particular, the superiority of tender over ordinary friendship:

> there is as great difference between a tender friend and an ordinary friend, as between a tender friend and a lover, but better to define tenderness. I think I may call it a certain sensibility of heart, which never soveraignly operates, but in those which have noble souls, vertuous Inclinations, and well weighed spirits, and which makes them when they have friendship, to have it sincerely and ardently, and to feel lively the griefs and joys of those they love as their own.[37]

Fifty years earlier, D'Urfé had promoted a spiritualised form of friendship as the soul's dominant passion between individuals of the opposite sex, who were encouraged to

[33] Chalmers, *Royalist Women Writers*, 58, 59–82; Barash, *English Women's Poetry*, 100. For Kate Lilley, however, Philips' love poetry addressed to women should not be read as political allegory. See Kate Lilley, '"Dear Object": Katherine Philips' Love Elegies and Their Readers', in Paul Salzman and Jo Wallwork (eds), *Women Writing 1550–1750* (La Trobe, 2001), 167.

[34] For autograph poems that were sent folded in letters, see British Library, Add MS 78233, fol. 69–71.

[35] See Harriette Andreadis, 'The Sapphic-Platonics of Katherine Philips, 1632–1664', *Signs: Journal of Women in Culture and Society*, 15.1 (1989), 34–60; Elaine Hobby, 'Katherine Philips: Seventeenth-Century Lesbian Poet', in Elaine Hobby and Chris While (eds), *What Lesbians Do in Books* (London, 1991), 183–204. It is to be wondered, however, whether Philips could have been celebrated as the 'Matchless Orinda', if her poetry was meant to be read as openly homoerotic. See Salzman, *Reading Early Modern Women's Writing* (Oxford, 2006), 194–9. On friendships among *Précieuses*, see Sellier, '"Se tirer du commun des femmes"', 211–12.

[36] For Philips' rapport with *préciosité*, see Kathleen Swaim, 'Matching the "Matchless Orinda" to Her Times', in Kevin L. Cope (ed.), *1650–1850: Ideas, Aesthetics, and Inquiries in the Early Modern Era*, vol. 3 (New York, NY, 1997), 77–108, especially 104–5; and Chalmers, *Royalist Women Writers*, 74–6. On friendship, see Mark Llewellyn, 'Katherine Philips: Friendship, Poetry and Neo-platonic Thought in Seventeenth Century England', *Philological Quarterly*, 81 (2002), 441–68; Chalmers, *Royalist Women Writers*, 56–104; and Harriette Andreadis, 'Re-Configuring Early Modern Friendship: Katherine Philips and Homoerotic Desire', *SEL: Studies in English Literature*, 46.3 (2006), 523–42.

[37] *Clelia* (London, 1678), 22.

'become one spirit in diverse bodies' through 'honnête amitié'.[38] French romances took up this doctrine of 'honest friendship' to promote friendship at the expense of love.[39] Philips' conception of friendship thus seems to echo Scudéry's emphasis on 'Tender Friendship, or Heroick Friendship', with its emphasis on same-sex friendship.[40] One of the principles of Philips' 'Society of Friendship' is the equality between man's and woman's souls—a position for which the Cambridge Platonists, after Descartes, gave a philosophical basis. Although Philips' definition of friendship is not explicitly female-oriented, she concludes from this that women should not be excluded from friendship—it would be 'partial tyranny' ('*A Friend*', *Poems*, 95). Then, like Scudéry, she moves to celebrating female friendship as superior to 'irregular' love because not subjected to desire: ''Tis Love refin'd and purg'd from all its dross' ('*A Friend*', *Poems*, 94). This alarmed Taylor, because friendship is described here as a new form of religion, whose 'sacred Sympathy was lent / Us from the Quire above' ('*To Mrs.* M. A. *at* parting', 74). Philips thus presents friendship as a Neoplatonic conduit to the divine, something like divinity itself: 'A wonder so sublime, it will admit / No rude Spectator to contemplate it' ('*To my* Lucasia', 58); or as the mystical union of two into one, of 'Two Bodies and one Mind' ('The Enquiry', 81):

> Our chang'd and mingled Souls are grown
> To such acquaintance now,
> . . .
> That each is in the Union lost.
>
> ('*To Mrs.* M. A. *at parting*', 74)

This might have featured in Montaigne's or in Donne's writings, but in relation to *male* friendship only.[41] In his essay 'Of Friendship', Montaigne mentions the union of the (male) friends' 'conjoyned' souls.[42] Philips feminises this conception of same-sex friendship and describes it as superior to marriage, which can be tainted by lust: 'But Lust, Design, or some unworthy ends / May mingle there, which are despis'd by Friends' ('Friendship', 79). Probably because this smacked too much of Catholicism, Taylor's rebuttal was firm: 'Marriage is the Queen of friendships', he corrected, made sacred by 'vows and love, by bodies and souls, by interest and custome, by religion and by laws' (Taylor, 53).

[38] Sales, quoted by Frances Harris, *Transformations of Love. The Friendship of John Evelyn and Margaret Godolphin* (Oxford, 2002), 155. This passage draws from my 'Leaves of Fame: Katherine Philips and Robert Herrick's Shared Community', in Tom Cain and Ruth Connolly (eds), *Lords of Wine and Oile: Community and Conviviality in Robert Herrick* (Oxford, 2011), 145–8.

[39] Maître, *Les Précieuses*, 588. As Harris has shown about Evelyn and Godolphin, these ideas could lead to idealised friendships in Restoration England (Harris, *Transformations*, 155).

[40] Madeleine de Scudéry, *Conversations upon Several Subjects* (London, 1683), 57.

[41] For the engagement of Philips' friendship poetry with Donne's love poetry, see Elizabeth Scott-Baumann's *Forms of Engagement: Women, Poetry, and Culture 1640–1680* (Oxford, 2013), 116–25.

[42] *The Essays of Michael, seigneur de Montaigne*, trans. Charles Cotton (London, 1700), 297.

In Philips' poetry, however, friendship is not only a Neoplatonic ideal, and her *Poems* are permeated with melancholy and loss: in the end, Orinda's friendships prove imperfect shadows of the idea of friendship, because they are submitted to change.[43] Incensed at one point by what she calls Rosania's 'betrayal', Orinda accuses her of 'kill[ing] that which gave [her] Immortality' ('*Injuria Amicitiae*', 54). In many respects, the typical friendship poems, in the collection can only be elegiac: they can only offer records of lost moments of union and intimacy.

HEROINES, 'HEROICKESSES', AND *FEMMES DE LETTRES*

In his study of the milieu of the *précieuses*, Sellier offers a psychological-cum-literary portrait of these aristocratic women: a sense of their singularity, a hypertrophied image of the self, and a superior perception of their refinement or *délicatesse*—with, for some like Madame de Rambouillet who wanted to 'debrutalise men', a militant, civilising approach to language and society.[44] This portrait might partly apply to Philips. Contemporary readers commented on the particular smoothness and refinement of her verse, which they saw as a major poetic innovation. Beyond the focus on friendship and its discontents, Philips' *Poems* can also be read as the idealised portrait of a self-crowned poet intent on ensuring her enduring fame.[45] If friendship matters, then, it is as a medium for immortalising Orinda, who remains the focus of her constellation of friends:

> . . . for the way to be
> Secure of fame to all posterity,
> Is to obtain the honour I pursue,
> To tell the World I was subdu'd by you.
>
> ('*To the truly Noble Mrs.* Anne Owen, *on my first Approches*', 33)

Critics have commented extensively on Philips' complex relationship to posterity; and although she might have been ambivalent about print publication it seems clear that Philips was carefully building her public self-image as that of a poet.[46] Like many French *Précieuses*, she fashioned herself as a woman author.

[43] See Penelope Anderson, *Friendship's Shadows. Women's Friendship and the Politics of Betrayal in England, 1640–1705* (Edinburgh, 2012), 69–113.

[44] Sellier, '"Se tirer du commun des femmes"', 205–7, 203.

[45] Paula Loscocco, '"Manly Sweetness": Katherine Philips among the Neoclassicals', *Huntington Library Quarterly*, 56.3 (1993), 259–79, and Chalmers, *Royalist Women Writers*, 98–9.

[46] For Gillian Wright, Philips' self-fashioning is primarily in manuscript (*Producing Women's Poetry, 1600–1730*, Cambridge, 2013, 99–101).

This makes her more akin to her contemporary Margaret Cavendish than might seem to be the case on first sight. Cavendish, more raucously perhaps, and with an apparent disregard for the scandal she caused for flouting the conventions of modesty, declared her ambition for fame in the many preliminary texts with which she framed her works, and her resolute pursuit of 'singularity', as early as 1653.[47] She crowned herself 'Margaret I' in the preface to *The Blazing World* (London, 1666), for instance, and consciously fashioned herself throughout her *œuvre* as a heroic 'authoress', tome after tome.[48] Cavendish had briefly been a maid of honour at the court of Henrietta Maria and lived in exile in Paris in the mid-1640s just before the Fronde (1648–1653, a period of civil and political unrest in France), and, although she allegedly spoke no French, she was exposed to French culture. As she moved to the Netherlands in 1648, she might have crossed paths with Christina of Sweden, who was a celebrity among women intellectuals of her time, greatly admired in the French salons. Cavendish was so fascinated by her that she imitated her in dress and comportment. She was very much influenced by the culture of heroic *femmes fortes* celebrated in romance and poetry on the Continent. The engravings she commissioned from Flemish artist Van Diepenbeeck to illustrate the lavish tomes she published at her own expense show the influence of the baroque iconography Le Moyne had popularised in his often-reprinted *Gallerie des femmes fortes* (Paris, 1647). This book, which was influenced by Bocaccio's *De Mulieribus claris*, extolled a selection of heroic women from the Old and New Testaments, Roman, and more recent history, down to Jeanne d'Arc and Mary Stuart. In a Van Diepenbeeck portrait that she used as frontispiece to *Grounds of Philosophy* (London, 1668), a crowned Cavendish is represented as standing on a pedestal under an arch, framed by a caryatid and an atlantes representing Athena and Apollo. This iconography became central in the imagination of *préciosité* during the period of the Fronde, and led to the fashion for female cabinets decorated with galleries of *femmes fortes* throughout France.[49] Cavendish's works are full of female leaders and martial heroines echoing this tradition, from Lady Victoria in *Bell in Campo* (from *Playes*, London, 1662) to the Empress in *The Blazing World*, both leading their troops to victory. While Cavendish might here have remembered Henrietta Maria leading the troops into Oxford in 1643, she might also be reminiscing about Le Moyne's strikingly illustrated collection of *femmes fortes* which included women warriors like Deborah or Joan of Arc. As Chalmers argues, she might more specifically have had in mind the 1652 translation of Le Moyne's *The Gallery of Heroick Women* by John Paulet, Marquess of Winchester, when she coined the word

[47] Chalmers notes the symbolic importance of 1653 as the date of *Poems, and Fancies*, 'a landmark in the history of Englishwomen's writing' (*Royalist Women Writers*, 1). DeJean also sees 1653 as 'crucial .... in the history of seventeenth-century French feminism', as the year when French salons resumed after the Fronde and Scudéry came into her own (*Tender Geographies*, 51).

[48] Preface, *The Blazing World*, in Kate Lilley (ed.), *The Blazing World and Other Writings* (Harmondsworth, 1992), 124. For 'singularity' and 'authoress', see *Natures Pictures* (London, 1656), 175, 178.

[49] See the 'Cabinet des Femmes fortes' built in the 1640s for Marie de Cossé Brissac, which is now part of the Arsenal Library (Paris).

'heroickesses' in *Bell in Campo* to designate Lady Victoria's women warriors—perhaps as an echo of Paulet's 'Heroesses'.[50]

CODA: APHRA BEHN AND THE SATIRE OF FRENCH *PRÉCIOSITÉ*

While a younger generation of Restoration women authors including Anne Finch continued to look enthusiastically towards France for inspiration, Aphra Behn showed a more complex rapport with the French works she translated and imitated.[51] When Behn turned to translation for a living in the 1680s, French salon culture was in full swing, and dozens of miscellanies had been published gathering the literature collectively produced. Paradoxically enough, although she became the translator of authors identified with *préciosité* in England and thus specialised in genteel literary works, Behn is the only woman author discussed here who is not a gentlewoman, and as a result her attitude towards her sources is ambivalent. This is consistent with her unstable social status as a professional author in the making, and testifies both to her desire to court High Church Stuart sympathisers by absorbing an aristocratic culture that is not her own, and her need, as a commercial author, to cater for the more mixed readership these translations targeted. All the works she translated thus had an aristocratic, fashionable aura that would have appealed to a wide, mixed readership of fashionable city dwellers as well as an aspiring middle class. In quick succession, she published in 1684 an adaptation of Paul Tallemant's *Voyage to the Isle of Love* (originally 1663), an allegorical travel narrative derived from Scudéry's 'Map of Tender'; an imitation of La Rochefoucault's maxims, a work originally redacted for the *Salon* of Madame du Sablé, in 1685; and, in 1686, a translation of *La Montre, or The Lover's Watch* by Balthazar de Bonnecorse, a *précieux* narrative in prosimetron (or prose interspersed with verse), on which Behn freely expanded to produce a work that was twice as long as the original.[52] In 1688 alone, she additionally translated a historical, sentimental novella, *Agnes de Castro*, published anonymously in French that very year,[53] and a translation of Fontenelle's *A Discovery*

[50] Quoted by Chalmers, *Royalist Women Writers*, 41. See also Claire Gheeraert-Graffeuille, 'Margaret Cavendish's *Femmes Fortes*: The Paradoxes of Female Heroism in *Bell in Campo* (1662)', *Revue de la Société d'études anglo-américaines des XVIIe et XVIIIe siècles*, 73 (2016), 243–65.

[51] For Anne Finch's French sources, see Ellen Moody, 'List and Bibliography: All Sources for Finch's Fables, Plays, Lyrics, Satires and Devotional Poetry', http://www.jimandellen.org/masterlist.fables.html (accessed 30/09/2020), and *The Poems of Anne Countess of Winchilsea*, ed. Myra Reynolds (Chicago, IL, 1903).

[52] The Tallemant text was published in *Poems on Several Occasions* (London, 1684); his *Second Voyage* (originally 1667) in *Lycidus* (London, 1688). The translation of La Rochefoucault was published as 'Reflections on Morality, or Seneca Unmasqued', in *Miscellany* (London, 1685).

[53] The novella, by Jean-Baptiste de Brilhac, exploits the craze for Portuguese stories after the success in France of *Lettres portugaises* (1669).

of New Worlds (originally 1686), a major work of scientific vulgarisation in the shape of conversations about astronomy between a philosopher and a marchioness.[54] The Tallemant and Bonnecorse texts had been successful in French, and were reprinted in the numerous editions of the fashionable miscellany ascribed to Madame de la Suze, *Recueil de pièces galantes en prose et en vers*, which Behn used as a basis.[55] In all these translations, except the Fontenelle, Behn treats the French works with similar irony, interlarding the text with personal additions and playful moments of imitation that occasionally alter the tonality of the original. Her treatment of *La Montre* is characteristic of this strategy: in this witty narrative, the beautiful Iris has to leave town, and she sends a watch to her lover, the courtier Damon, together with a strict twenty-four-hour schedule regimenting his activities in her absence. This text is representative of a new fashionable 'object literature' that uses objects such as the compass, almanacs, or maps as allegorical emblems to discuss love. In the wake of Scudéry's compelling 'Map of Tendre', and to cater for the female-oriented culture of salons, the allegory is often apprehended from a female perspective, with a woman narrator playfully lecturing a male lover, as here. Seemingly deaf to the niceties of *galanterie*, however, Behn displaces the wit of the original, and offers a satire of what she perceives as excessive coyness. As a corrective, she introduces poems that are pastiches of pastoral pieces, and tend to exacerbate the erotic titillation that is produced by the woman's ventriloquism of her lover's voice, not to mention the digressions in celebration of the Stuart monarchy.

While Behn's strategy as a translator could be read as betrayal, it can also be interpreted as a form of accommodation and creative adaptation for her English readers, ignorant of the context of *galanterie* and probably, by that time, more receptive to satire and burlesque. Nathaniel Lee's adaptation of Madame de Lafayette's bestselling novel *La Princesse de Clèves* (Paris, 1678) as a licentious farce in 1689 is another example of the plasticity and resilience that some works emblematic of *préciosité* acquired in the English context. In the second half of the seventeenth century, translations of contemporary fiction were in high demand: in 1690 alone, the number of translated works of fiction (31) that were published in London is almost twice that of new works (17).[56] Translated fiction naturally provided a space for experimentation for both male and female authors and opened up possibilities by offering models to imitate.[57] As is obvious from the joint publication of *Agnes de Castro, Oroonoko and The Fair Jilt* as *Three Histories* in 1688, Behn built on her career as a translator when she turned to fiction. Other women also

[54] For a presentation of Behn's translations, see Line Cottegnies, 'Aphra Behn's French Translations', in Janet Todd and Derek Hughes (eds), *The Cambridge Companion to Aphra Behn* (Cambridge, 2004), 221–34. The translation of Fontenelle's *The History of Oracles*, also 1688, is probably not hers, however.

[55] *Recueil de pièces galantes en prose et en vers de Madame la Comtesse de la Suze, et de Monsieur Pelisson* (Paris, 1663). Behn used the 1684 edition.

[56] Leah Orr, *Novel Ventures. Fiction and Print Culture in England, 1690–1730* (Charlottesville, VA, 2017), 184.

[57] Mary Helen McMurran, *The Spread of Novels. Translation and Prose Fiction in the Eighteenth Century* (Princeton, NJ, 2010); Gillian Dow, 'Criss-crossing the Channel', in J. A. Downie (ed.), *The Oxford Handbook of the Eighteenth-Century Novel* (Oxford, 2016), 88–104, 91.

saw French literature as pliant affordances: Catherine Trotter adapted *Agnès de Castro* for the stage; Anne Finch turned to La Fontaine, Madame Deshoulières, and Madame Dacier to fashion her own poetic voice. The extensive and prolific range of strategies adopted by women authors of the period—from literal translation to rejection—illustrate a modern form of *translatio studii* which would soon be reversed when France fully absorbed the English novel. In the early modern period, French literature, as an alternative and fashionable canon, provided endlessly renewable material to be freely tapped, digested, and eventually transformed and rejected.

FURTHER READING

Anderson, Penelope. *Friendship's Shadows: Women's Friendship and the Politics of Betrayal in England, 1640–1705*. Edinburgh, 2012.

Barash, Carol. *English Women's Poetry, 1649–1714: Politics, Community, and Linguistic Authority*. Oxford, 1996.

Britland, Karen. *Drama at the Courts of Queen Henrietta Maria*. Cambridge, 2006.

Chalmers, Hero. *Royalist Women Writers 1650–1689*. Oxford, 2004.

Clarke, Danielle. 'Translation', in Laura Lunger Knoppers (ed.), *The Cambridge Companion to Early Modern Women's Writing*. Cambridge, 2009, 167–80.

Maître, Myriam. *Les Précieuses. Naissance des femmes de lettres en France au XVIIe siècle*. Paris, 1999.

Salzman, Paul. *Reading Early Modern Women's Writing*. Oxford, 2006.

Scott-Baumann, Elizabeth. *Forms of Engagement: Women, Poetry, and Culture 1640–1680*. Oxford, 2013.

CHAPTER 30

OLD ENGLAND AND NEW IN ANNE BRADSTREET'S POETRY

PETER AUGER

THE title page of Anne Bradstreet's *The Tenth Muse Lately Sprung up in America* is dated 1650. It was entered in the Stationers' Register on 1 July that year, and may have already been printed by then: just days later, George Thomason, who was known for obtaining books rapidly after publication, would write 'July 5' on his copy.[1] These dates place the publication of Bradstreet's collection in the same month that Oliver Cromwell had returned from Ireland and was mustering an army to lead into Scotland; this was also the summer of Andrew Marvell's 'Horatian Ode'. Furthermore, the July dating locates the publication of *The Tenth Muse* within an uneasy shift in transatlantic relations that year. In 1650, the newly formed Commonwealth was looking to exert greater control over New England's ports: the second reading of an act to form a council of trade (which would be especially concerned with matters of free trade and free ports) took place in March, and would be read for a final time in August.[2] Katharine Gillespie associates Bradstreet's presentation as a New England poet in the collection with the efforts of her father, Thomas Dudley, to defend the colony's autonomy at this time.[3]

Rather than making a direct intervention in this political debate, though, *The Tenth Muse* marks out the ideological centre ground for closer alliance between reformed Protestants on both sides of the Atlantic. In Edward Holberton's well-informed reading:

> The shape and timing of *The Tenth Muse*, and Nathaniel Ward's involvement in its production, suggests that its publication may have been connected with Ward's

[1] *A Transcript of the Registers of the Worshipful Company of Stationers; from 1640–1708 A.D.*, 3 vols. (London, 1913), 1.346; *Catalogue of the Pamphlets, Books, Newspapers, and Manuscripts [. . . .] Collected by George Thomason, 1640–1661*, vol. 1 (London, 1908), 804.

[2] Robert Brenner, *Merchants and Revolution: Commercial Change, Political Conflict, and London's Overseas Traders, 1550–1653* (London, 2003), 603–4, 606–7.

[3] Katharine Gillespie, *Women Writing the English Republic, 1625–1681* (Cambridge, 2017), 202–3.

> attempts to build links between Massachusetts Congregationalists and Puritans in England (perhaps especially Presbyterians) who were against the radical liberty of conscience favoured by the now-dominant army.[4]

Puritanism had been consolidating its position in England after the Civil War; meanwhile, the Congregational church in New England had formalised its structure through the Cambridge Platform of 1648, which described how it would be governed. By appealing to the values that the two churches and territories shared, the publication of *The Tenth Muse* aligned their religious identities. As Phillip H. Round states: 'To read Bradstreet's text was to bond into a political faction'.[5]

July 1650 is the first time that Bradstreet's works, or indeed those of any poet from New England, appeared in print. The edition presented Bradstreet's poems in a way that was up to date for readers in London. As we have just seen, the dating enables a tightly historicised reading of the print publication's transatlantic dynamics. And yet such precision is only possible because 1650 is the point at which Bradstreet's poetry enters the worlds of English church politics and the London publishing industry. Because seventeenth-century archives are biased towards male actors in metropolitan centres of power, we have many more contextualising dates and details about this initial moment of publication than we do for Bradstreet's life in New England as she composed her poems years earlier.[6]

This matters, especially when considering her poetry's transatlantic relations, because Bradstreet probably had nothing to do with the publication. The critical consensus (which has dissenters, such as Patricia Pender) is that Nathaniel Ward and John Woodbridge brought it to print, and that we should take the prefatory letter of *The Tenth Muse* (anonymous but traditionally attributed to Woodbridge) at its word when it claims that 'I fear the displeasure of no person in the publishing of these Poems but the Author's, without whose knowledge, and contrary to her expectation, I have presumed to bring to public view what she resolved should never in such a manner see the Sun'.[7] Bradstreet's confirmatory displeasure is recorded in the later poem 'The Author to Her Book' that bitterly repeats the phrase 'public view' when complaining that, like a small child, her book 'after birth didst by my side remain / 'Til snatched from thence by friends, less wise than true, / Who thee abroad exposed to public view' ('Author to Her

[4] Edward Holberton, 'Prophecy and Geography in Anne Bradstreet's "Contemplations": A Transatlantic Reading', in Robin Peel and Daniel Maudlin (eds), *Transatlantic Traffic and (Mis) Translations* (Durham, NH, 2013), 157–75, 167.

[5] Phillip H. Round, *By Nature and by Custom Cursed: Transatlantic Civil Discourse and New England Cultural Production, 1620–1660* (Hanover, NH, 1999), 193.

[6] See Kristina Bross, *Future History: Global Fantasies in Seventeenth-Century American and British Writings* (New York, 2017).

[7] Patricia Pender, *Early Modern Women's Writing and the Rhetoric of Modesty* (Basingstoke, 2012), e.g., 150. Anne Bradstreet, in Margaret Olofson Thickstun (ed.), *Poems and Meditations* (Toronto, 2019), 341. Unless a specific seventeenth-century edition is named, all quotations from Bradstreet's poems are from this edition.

Book', 2–4; Bradstreet 265). Bradstreet's most recent editor, Margaret Olofson Thickstun, emphasises that 'there is no evidence that she [Bradstreet] was revising for print publication or that she sought to produce an improved printed volume of her poems'.[8]

If we are to appreciate how Bradstreet responded to her social, cultural, and religious circumstances in colonial America, we must disentangle the poems from their later engagements with transatlantic politics in the two print publications, *The Tenth Muse* and *Several Poems* (1678), in which most of her poems exclusively survive. In other words, we need to separate the poems' reception when they were published in 1650 and 1678 from their moments of authorship in the 1630s and 1640s. This distinction, which numerous scholars have already helped to elucidate, is crucial for women writers like Bradstreet whose gender (as well as her geographical location) restricted her access to the publishers who shaped her poems into a vendible object for new readerships.[9]

This chapter focuses on the narrower issue of how Bradstreet and her first editors presented transatlantic relations in ways that were appropriate for when they were each working. Both at the initial moment of composition and two later seventeenth-century moments of printing, Bradstreet's poems articulate New England's identity in relation to the old country, performing a shared puritan identity that allowed the collection to retain its timeliness. This chapter first reviews why Bradstreet is so interested in the relation between Old and New England in the poems that were subsequently printed in *The Tenth Muse*, then looks closely at how her 'Dialogue between Old England and New' responds to the events of 1642. Next it examines how the publications of 1650 and 1678 repurpose that narrowly transatlantic perspective for new readerships in London and Boston respectively. This culminates in a reading of 'David's Lamentation for Saul and Jonathan' which shows that the more we historicise Bradstreet's poetry to its reception in 1650 (when such historicisation is most possible), the more difficult it becomes to establish how much political relevance the poem contained when composed—and indeed even to be sure whether she wrote it.

We can distinguish these three moments of reception better if we pay close attention to how individual poems are placed in particular time frames. We shall see that Bradstreet and her contemporary editors took an interest in dates for different reasons. Bradstreet supplied dates for many poems, typically for those that address specific events from her familial and devotional life, such as the illness she suffered aged nineteen in 1632 or her mother's death on 27 December 1643. Though her poetry is cherished today for such reflections on her life, these poems are not included in *The Tenth Muse*. The 1650 editors, meanwhile, selectively give dates for the poems that they do print: those printed were probably written between 1638 (the date of the elegy to Philip Sidney, the earliest dated poem in the collection) and 1647 (when Woodbridge returned to England). *Several Poems* contains additional dates, with revealing discrepancies from the earlier edition.

[8] 'Introduction', in Thickstun (ed.), *Poems and Meditations*, 3.

[9] See Gillian Wright, *Producing Women's Poetry, 1600–1730: Text and Paratext, Manuscript and Print* (Cambridge, 2013). Thanks to Prof. Wright for comments on an early draft of this chapter.

Thinking about dates cuts across a dichotomy between private and public poetry to inform our sense of women writers' frames of reference: dates indicate, for example, whether writers are working in common genres like occasional poems (such as Bradstreet's elegies on her parents' deaths) or verse meditations (such as those dated between 8 July 1656 and 30 September 1657 in the Andover manuscript of Bradstreet's work). Above all, dates challenge us to take the fullest account possible of the rich circumstances in which women wrote, and assess how their works might be resituated to advantage for later readerships.

Narrowly Transatlantic

Bradstreet was writing when New England's relations with other English, French, and Dutch colonies were as important as those with England. Carla Gardina Pestana writes that:

> The Atlantic world came to life only after the people residing in these far-flung settlements lost their narrowly transatlantic orientation (looking only to their native land on the other side of the ocean) and began to foster ties to other Atlantic plantations. The creation of that interconnected world was the work of the 1640s.[10]

Bradstreet's poems do demonstrate knowledge of how England's and New England's politics were caught up in wider geographies. *The Four Monarchies*, her longest work, looks back to the Assyrian, Persian, Greek, and Roman empires. 'A Dialogue between Old England and New' refers to Spanish, French, Scottish, and Dutch threats to English sovereignty ('Dialogue', 45–9; Bradstreet 209), and to religious violence in Germany, France, and Ireland (138–45). Yet ultimately even these references look back to Bradstreet's 'native land on the other side of the ocean'. Her 'narrowly transatlantic' perspective validates settler colonialism by making minimal reference to life in New England (aside from the later 'Contemplations', not printed in 1650), and acknowledging neither other Atlantic plantations nor Native American experience.[11] When, decades later, Mary Rowlandson does write about the Algonquian nation in 1682, it is in the context of captivity. She imposes foreign reference points onto the land: even though she had come over to America as a child, she still takes comfort in cattle, paths, and fields that are reassuringly 'English'.[12]

[10] Carla Gardina Pestana, *The English Atlantic in an Age of Revolution, 1640–1661* (Cambridge, MA, 2004), 3.

[11] See Lorenzo Veracini, *Settler Colonialism: A Theoretical Overview* (Basingstoke, 2010), e.g., 77–8.

[12] Mary Rowlandson, *Soveraignty and Goodness of God* (1682), B6r; Myra Jehlen and Michael Warner (eds), *The English Literatures of America, 1500–1800* (London, 1997), xix and 350.

Bradstreet wrote poems in the 1630s and 1640s that strengthened her ties to the old country. This is a central element of her settler poetics (a topic about which much more could be written) that helped make New England a home while keeping open the possibility of return. Although we cannot know how widely Bradstreet's poems may have circulated in manuscript in the 1640s, there must be some truth in Round's claim that 'the bulk of her Ipswich writing seems to have been intended as a kind of dutiful performance, the literary equivalent of keeping up her social status in the community'.[13] From this perspective, Anne Hutchinson's charismatic prophecies in the mid-1630s were an example of how not to acquiesce to the New England church.[14] Margaret Tyndal Winthrop's private correspondence with her husband John (first governor of the Massachusetts Bay Colony) is a more complaisant example of devotional performance, though Bradstreet's poems were probably read by a wider circle of family members and friends.[15] The disparate activities of these relatively wealthy white Protestant women all participated in imposing an Anglocentric world view on the newly christened territory still known today as New England.

Puritanism bound Bradstreet's authorial identity to a wider collective identity in colonial New England.[16] Her poems are appropriate for a female member of a leading family who claimed that she was of the 'self-same blood' (Elegy to Sidney, 28; Bradstreet 220) as Sidney, and who speaks for her community's values while being tied to its sense of propriety. Bradstreet's poetry, in Abram Van Engen's account, displays one puritan quality before all others: fellow-feeling, especially towards puritan co-confessionalists back in England. Puritans used a Calvinist theology of sympathy to assert that they had left England to serve the church, not to break from it: 'This need to assert unity despite a few thousand miles of intervening ocean sent Puritans in search of any language that would overcome and downplay the basic fact that they had physically abandoned England. One language was sympathy'.[17] This perspective helps us understand the rhetorical value of Bradstreet's use of earlier English sources and literary forms.

Bradstreet was evidently reading books that had crossed the ocean such as James Ussher's *Annals of the World*, John Speed's *Historie of Great Britaine*, and Walter Raleigh's *History of the World*. Consulting such books meant that Bradstreet, in Elizabeth Sauer's phrase, 'forged a new transatlantic dynamic'.[18] It is also one aspect of what Catharine

[13] Round, *By Nature*, 164.

[14] Marilyn J. Westerkamp, *Women and Religion in Early America 1600–1850: The Puritan and Evangelical Traditions* (New York, 1999), 39–45.

[15] Joseph Hopkins Twichell (ed.), *Some Old Puritan Love-Letters: John and Margaret Winthrop, 1618–1638* (New York, 1894).

[16] See Christopher Ivic, '"Our British Land": Anne Bradstreet's Atlantic Perspective', in Philip Schwyzer and Simon Mealor (eds), *Archipelagic Identities: Literature and Identity in the Atlantic Archipelago, 1550–1800* (Aldershot, 2004), 195–204.

[17] Abram Van Engen, *Sympathetic Puritans: Calvinist Fellow Feeling in Early New England* (New York, 2015), 5.

[18] Elizabeth Sauer, 'Book Passages and the Reconstruction of the Bradstreets' New England Library', in Leah Knight, Micheline White, and Elizabeth Sauer (eds), *Women's Bookscapes in Early Modern Britain: Reading, Ownership, Circulation* (Ann Arbor, MI, 2018), 59–76, 60.

Gray calls 'a particular brand of Elizabethan nostalgia' in Bradstreet's poetry.[19] We see this in the choice of subjects for her early elegies: Elizabeth I, Sidney, and Guillaume de Saluste, Sieur Du Bartas. The latter, though a French Protestant, was effectively anglicised in the early 1600s through his close association with James VI and I. When Bradstreet is called a 'right *Du Bartas* Girl' (12; Bradstreet 342) in Ward's prefatory verse, it associates the poet with a recent English tradition of Scripture-based verse that was already well-established when Bradstreet was writing. That association points to an editorial preference for historical verse (i.e., the kind of poetry which Du Bartas wrote) over autobiographical works (which he did not).[20] *The Tenth Muse* is dominated by a retelling of world history in *The Four Monarchies*, starting with the Assyrian empire, which began '131 years after the Flood' (Bradstreet 106) and reaching the Roman monarchy, founded in '*Anno Mundi* 3213' (203).

'Dialogue between Old England and New'

In addition to demonstrating a knowledge of English literary culture and world history, Bradstreet reveals her thorough acquaintance with recent political events in 'A Dialogue between Old England and New, concerning their present troubles, Anno 1642', a poem that has attracted substantial critical commentary in recent years. The poem's imagined dialogue between a personified mother and daughter may make it seem idiosyncratic to readers today; however, all of the poem's key features have precedents within and outside her oeuvre that tighten the bonds between New and Old England, and would have made the poem more familiar to its earliest readers than it might feel today. 'Mother England' was a familiar topos that appeared in a dozen other print publications between 1640 and 1650.[21] Bradstreet may have encountered publications from the early 1640s, particularly William Hooke's *New Englands Teares, for Old Englands Feares* (1641), that play up the transatlantic relation. Bradstreet was comfortable imagining parent–child relationships, writing in several places as a mother to her children and as a daughter to Dorothy and Thomas Dudley.[22] 'The Flesh and the Spirit' is another poetic conversation, between sisters, as are the *Quaternions*, probably composed around the same time,

19 Catharine Gray, *Women Writers and Public Debate in 17th-Century Britain* (New York, 2007), 144.

20 Auger, *Du Bartas' Legacy in England and Scotland* (Oxford, 2019), 168–76.

21 From full text search on *Early English Books Online* (August 2020); see also Andrew Hiscock, '"A Dialogue between Old England and New": Anne Bradstreet and her Negotiations with the Old World', in Hiscock (ed.), *Mighty Europe 1400–1700: Writing an Early Modern Continent* (Bern, 2007), 185–220, 194–5.

22 Patricia Pender, 'Disciplining the Imperial Mother: Anne Bradstreet's *A Dialogue Between Old England and New*', in Jo Wallwork and Paul Salzman (eds), *Women Writing 1550–1750* (Bundoora, 2001), 115–31, 123.

which have a precedent in Thomas Dudley's now-unknown poem on 'the four parts of the world' imagined as 'four sisters' (Bradstreet 42). Sauer points to the 'Dialogue upon the Troubles Past' in Josuah Sylvester's *Devine Weekes and Workes* (1605; sigs. 2R3r–5r) as a possible source.[23] This is plausible but would be ironic since—as Bradstreet would not have known—the poem's author is not Du Bartas but the Catholic writer Jean Du Nesme.[24]

Beyond form, Bradstreet is keenly aware of religious politics in her characterisation. The poem's initial readers in manuscript would surely have particularly identified with the perspective of New England, who speaks first. If so, then we can read the poem as dramatising New England's emergence as a knowledgeable and sympathetic interlocutor.[25] Old England begins with a provocative question: 'Art ignorant indeed of these my woes[?]' (9). What follows is a pitch-perfect response that signals New England's, and perforce Bradstreet's, sensitivity to history, religion, and English politics in 1642. In Sauer's words, 'Bradstreet's New England, the daughter colony, succeeds in discerning, historicising, diagnosing, and poeticizing the ills that cripple Old England, and thus she forges alternative connections between Old and New England, past and present'.[26]

New England first recalls the early centuries of English history (28–44), then asks if England's neighbours are the aggressor (45–50). Old England repeats several of these details in her reply, then explains why the land fares so ill at present. These criticisms delineate core puritan convictions: she condemns '[i]dolatry' (91), 'superstitious adoration' (92), lack of respect for the Gospel (94), simony (95), Papism (96), 'Sabbath-breaking', and intemperance (both 105). Old England's next speech refers to various events between 1640 and 1642 (171–83). The poet supports the political position of Robert Devereux, third earl of Essex, a moderate who led the Parliamentarian army, but was open to dialogue with the king: he was '[n]ot false to King nor Country in thy heart' (239). This is the reading in 1650: the later 1678 text reads 'nor to the better part' (sig. N4v), stressing his loyalty to the cause. The 1650 text makes its parliamentary allegiance clear in the final lines: 'Farewell, dear mother. Parliament, prevail, / And in a while you'll tell another tale' (294–5). The 1678 text reads 'Farewell dear Mother, rightest cause prevail' (sig. N5v), acknowledging the Restoration and again placing emphasis on what is right in general. The 1650 text probably was Bradstreet's original that was tweaked to match 'the more moderate and measured tone and the politically conservative position of the 1678 version'.[27]

The conclusion contains a higher density of biblical allusions to assert the scriptural basis for the poet's vision of puritan revival in England. In both versions, New England's final speech rounds out her and the poet's emergence as an authoritative spokesperson

23 Sauer, 'Book Passages', 68.

24 Sergio Capello, 'Jean Du Nesme', in Michel Simonin (ed.), *Dictionnaire des lettres françaises. Le XVIe siècle* (Paris, 2001), 434.

25 See Van Engen, *Sympathetic Puritans*, 130–5.

26 Sauer, 'Book Passages', 71.

27 Sauer, 'Book Passages', 73–4.

for the puritan cause, one whose vision is grounded in biblical knowledge, doctrinal values, and English history and politics. The 'Dialogue' also completed Bradstreet's performance as a knowledgeable and committed puritan as the Civil War in England broke out. For early readers in New England, it would have renewed the colony's sense of mission at such a desperate moment back in the old country.

Late Poems

'A Dialogue' was among those poems that were congenial for turning to fresh purpose in the post-war political circumstances that were outlined at the start of this chapter. *The Tenth Muse*'s contemporary resonance in London in 1650 derives from how it took advantage of Bradstreet's 'narrowly transatlantic' interest in the bilateral relationship between England and its colony. Bradstreet probably knew something of print publications such as Hooke's *New Englands Teares* that addressed the transatlantic connection, and her editors surely also knew of titles published after she had apparently written her poems like Thomas Shepard's *New Englands Lamentation for Old Englands Present Errours* (1645). Christopher D'Addario, writing of how well-connected New England writers were to the London publishing industry, argues that:

> Conspicuously, the New England authors' most vociferous assertion of their Englishness came in the 1640s, when the homeland itself was fighting a war over the identity of the nation. These New England texts, which became something of a genre in the '40s, seem to feel the crisis in English identity just as acutely on the other side of the Atlantic, while also sensing the opportunity to justify and explain their exile as their homeland went through its own transformation.[28]

The doctrinal orthodoxy embedded in the poems for their original 'performance' in the English American settlements now served, in their new publication setting, as testimony for readers back in England that co-religionists across the Atlantic were loyal members of the transnational Protestant church. Women writers in print seemingly had a particular duty to demonstrate such loyalty: Susan Wiseman takes the criticism that Elizabeth Avery's *Scripture-Prophecies Opened* (1647) received when it was first published as evidence that for Bradstreet too (who was related to Avery through marriage) 'aesthetic achievement was, it seems, infinitely more welcome than the refusal of forms and ordinances'.[29] *The Tenth Muse* was a unique publishing venture that reinforced that New England Congregationalism was not innovative, and had retained strong English roots.

[28] Christopher D'Addario, *Exile and Journey in Seventeenth-Century Literature* (Cambridge, 2007), 38.

[29] Susan Wiseman, *Conspiracy and Virtue: Women, Writing, and Politics in Seventeenth-Century England* (Oxford, 2006), 206.

Woodbridge and Ward had to handle carefully these poems that were written several years earlier for readers across the Atlantic. The full title (*The Tenth Muse Lately Sprung up in America*) plays up the Old and New England relation, which is picked up in a prefatory poem whose title notes that Bradstreet is '[a]t Present Residing in the Occidental Parts of the World, in America, alias, Nov-Anglia' (Bradstreet 346). The editors also name 'A Dialogue between Old England and New, concerning the late troubles' on the title page. The final three words are revised from the poem's heading later in the volume, which reads 'their present troubles. Anno 1642'. The new phrase 'concerning the late troubles'—which could easily have been left out—is potentially misleading here as it could well be taken to imply knowledge of more recent events, in particular the king's execution in January 1649. Woodbridge and Ward's phrasing advertises Bradstreet's genuine historical knowledge while avoiding the self-defeating impression that New Englanders were not up to speed with what had happened since 1642.

The editors let most poems seem as though they were composed more recently than they actually were. After the title page's '1650' no further dates are included until 'A Dialogue' on page 180 (sig. N2v). The dedicatory materials emphasise her familial relations to still-active political figures: titles instate her as 'Wife of the Worshipfull Simon Bradstreet Esquire' (sig. A7r) and daughter to 'her most Honoured Father Thomas Dudley Esq' (sig. B1r). Furthermore, that final poem does not include the date which is found in the 1678 edition: 20 March 1642 (sig. A1v). Following on from 'A Dialogue', however, each of the trio of elegies to sixteenth-century figures is dated to that earlier period. We are not left to wonder whether the Sidney elegy was written immediately after he died in 1586, thanks to the subheading 'By A.B. in the yeare, 1638' (sig. N8r) in the 1650 text only. The date is probably Bradstreet's but this phrase (reminding us who wrote it) looks like an editorial addition, as does the date tacked onto the very end of the Elizabeth elegy, '1643' (sig. O6r). Consequently, those elegies are presented as recently written retrospectives contemporary with 'A Dialogue'.

We can contrast these apparent editorial interventions with how *Several Poems* dates these poems and others to boost the impression that the colony was well established by 1678. This posthumous edition prints poems 'by a Gentlewomen in *New England*' (title page) that were already decades old when published in Boston. Dating the elegies was no longer so urgent: while 'A Dialogue' keeps 'Anno 1642' in the title, the Sidney elegy is not dated and, after the poem titled 'In Honour of Du Bartas, 1641', the Elizabeth poem is also undated. 'David's Lamentation' is undated too, but is followed by two poems commemorating her father (deceased 31 July 1653) and her mother Dorothy Dudley (deceased 27 December 1643). *Several Poems* includes further dates that key the collection to Bradstreet's family life in New England, instating these settler lives into New England's history. The preface to her father before *Quaternions* is dated here (sig. A1v), and an apology at the conclusion of *Four Monarchies* refers to the fire in which Bradstreet lost her personal papers (sig. M8r). The final leaves print poems from her papers, including one about her illness in 1632 and several on the deaths of family members: her infant grandchildren Elizabeth (d. August 1665), Anne (d. 20 June 1669), and Simon (d. 16 November 1669); her daughter-in-law Mercy (d. 6 September 1669 according to *Several Poems*, but Thickstun amends to 1670); and finally Anne herself, whose soul 'was taken to its Rest, upon 16th Sept. 1672'.

These dates help the texts argue that the colonisers' presence was long-standing. This was all too timely, seeing that the publication of *Several Poems* was linked to recent colonial violence. After English settlers suppressed various indigenous communities in King Philip's War between 1675 and 1678, colonial administrators such as Simon Bradstreet sought to occupy new land. He came into contact with John Foster, Boston's first printer, in the summer of 1678 to print an advertisement encouraging colonists to settle on former Narragansett land.[30] *Several Poems* probably followed as a result, and was consistent with a perceived need to unite the New England colonies in defence against Native Americans and Dutch colonists. Bradstreet is no longer described as 'lately sprung up', and the dialogue is not mentioned on the title page (quite possibly because its relevance had faded). This second edition is, however, said to have been '[c]orrected by the Author, and enlarged by an Addition of several other Poems found amongst her Papers after her Death' (title page). Like the dates in this edition, these temporal references in 1678 place Bradstreet's poetry at the start of an American canon that is solely English in its language and cultural values.

Inconsistencies in how the elegies in particular are dated in the 1650 and 1678 editions correlate with the different transatlantic circumstances when each was printed. Back in the 1650 edition, the date '1643' for the elegy on Elizabeth I is an instance of what Wright calls the *Tenth Muse*'s 'locally anomalous but strategically adroit' arrangement.[31] It changes the poem's interpretation, binding it to the two preceding it and so directing it to be read in that earlier political context. It cancels an alternative interpretation that would read the Elizabeth elegy in relation to the regicide. Along with one of the book's thickest type ornaments, this date also separates this elegy from the final poem placed under the heading 'Elegies and Epitaphs': 'David's Lamentation'.[32]

A Problem Case

'Davids Lamentation for Saul, and Jonathan, 2 Sam. 1.19' (sig. O6v) is left undated in *The Tenth Muse*, which releases this poem to be read as more recent than the four preceding poems from 1638–1643 that spoke to a historical situation that, by 1650, was firmly in the past. The absence of a date here enables comparisons between the fallen Saul and Charles that are in line with the suggestion made above that Bradstreet's editors presented the volume as being more current than much of it really was. Beginning with Elizabeth Wade White, who argued that the poem is 'an elegy in scriptural disguise',

30 Simon Bradstreet, *An Advertisement* (Boston, MA, 1678); Gillespie, *Women Writing*, 240.

31 Wright, *Producing Women's Poetry*, 83.

32 Thickstun, 'Contextualizing Anne Bradstreet's Literary Remains: Why We Need a New Edition of the Poems', *Early American Literature*, 52 (2017), 389–422, 407.

numerous critics have indeed felt that the poem discreetly alludes to Charles.[33] In Mihoko Suzuki's reading, the poem is unsympathetic to the monarch: it 'functions as a reminder of Charles' role in bringing about his own destruction, and serves to legitimate the parliamentarians as God's anointed'.[34] Wright comments that 'the application of "David's Lamentation" to Charles undoubtedly suggests that Bradstreet—and Woodbridge—wanted to register sorrow at the execution'.[35] There was ample precedent for comparing King Saul with English monarchs, and Hooke's *New England's Sence* had taken a later passage from the same book of the Bible (2 Samuel 10:6–12) as its text.[36] It was certainly expedient for Woodbridge and Ward to include a poem that implied that New Englanders knew about such a key development; otherwise the whole collection might make the colony seem behind the times. When read in the 1650 edition, the versification seems to disclose knowledge of the regicide without speculating about future political scenarios.

What was the relation, then, between this poem's moments of composition and initial publication? Did the author use this poem to introduce topical resonances, or did her editors? Did its first readers even hear those resonances? For centuries, critics have understood that Woodbridge took manuscripts of Bradstreet's poetry to England in 1647. If that is correct, then Bradstreet would have needed to send on a poetic response to the king's death separately for this to be an authorial intervention. This is undoubtedly possible: news of the regicide had reached New England by June 1649 at the very latest, and Bradstreet could have sent a letter across the Atlantic before July the following year, whether or not she meant it for print publication.[37] Bradstreet's latest biographer, Charlotte Gordon, even uses 'David's Lamentation' as evidence that Bradstreet did in fact know about *The Tenth Muse*: she argues that 'Bradstreet was probably involved in the publication decisions surrounding her first book, despite her claims to the contrary'.[38] For Gordon, the poem's moments of authorship and publication are identical.

Another scenario is that Bradstreet had written the poem years before without knowledge of publication or the regicide. Thickstun advocates this approach, noting that 'there is little internal and no extratextual evidence to support' the claim that the poem responds to Charles' execution.[39] It is conceivable that Bradstreet had written the versification years earlier, perhaps along with other now-lost versifications that Woodbridge

[33] Elizabeth Wade White, *Anne Bradstreet: The Tenth Muse* (New York, 1971), 246.

[34] Mihoko Suzuki, 'What's Political in Seventeenth-Century Women's Political Writing?', *Literature Compass*, 6 (2009), 927–41, 935.

[35] Wright, *Producing Women's Poetry*, 96.

[36] Anne Lake Prescott, 'A Year in the Life of King Saul: 1643', in Kevin Killeen, Helen Smith, and Rachel Willie (eds), *Oxford Handbook of the Bible in Early Modern England, c. 1530–1700* (Oxford, 2015), 412–26.

[37] Pestana, *English Atlantic*, 88–9; and David Cressy, *Coming Over: Migration and Communication between England and New England in the Seventeenth Century* (Cambridge, 1987), 253–4.

[38] Elizabeth Ferszt and Ivy Schweitzer, 'A Different, More Complicated Bradstreet: Interview With Charlotte Gordon', *Women's Studies*, 43 (2014), 372–8, 376.

[39] 'Introduction', in Thickstun (ed), *Poems and Meditations*, 23.

took with him. Her editors could simply have included it as a final example of an elegy, one fittingly based on biblical verses which George Wither had described as a 'Patterne for our Funerall Poemes'.[40] In this reading, it is only Bradstreet's modern critics, rather than the poet or her editors, who have tied the poem to its moment of publication in 1650. As the penultimate poem in the collection, it arguably also gives an appropriately scriptural emphasis to the collection's close (as does the final item, 'Of the Vanity of All Worldly Creatures').

Nonetheless, the dates supplied for the preceding elegies do offer some support for critics who fix this poem, like the rest of *The Tenth Muse*, precisely amidst contemporary political developments. Woodbridge certainly could have placed the versification here to hint at the regicide. We could even propose that the poem was not an editor's felicitous discovery among Bradstreet's papers but that someone else wrote it for inclusion here; after all, the only evidence we have that Bradstreet wrote 'David's Lamentation' is its appearance in the 1650 and 1678 editions. The poem does remain in the second edition (which the author is said to have corrected) and Bradstreet's speaker claims in 'The Author to Her Book' that her book has no father (22); a sceptical reader could respond, though, that the 1678 edition looks like it simply took the 1650 edition as an authority. That reader might also posit Ward as a possible author: he composed heroic couplets in *Simple Cobler of Aggawam* (1647) and is known to have condemned Charles' execution. The poem's imitative style is dissimilar from any other work in Bradstreet's known oeuvre and its diction is close to the King James Bible. This makes the poem impossible to attribute securely, which would be consistent with an attempt to pass off someone else's poem as Bradstreet's—but also makes this hypothesis unverifiable.

With reference to poems including 'David's Lamentation', Holberton notes that '[t]his version of Bradstreet makes the New England elite appear more broadly sympathetic amid the opportunities for political realignment that followed the regicide'.[41] We have seen that this 'version of Bradstreet' brings the poet's persona closer to her editors' political stance to the point that we need to ask just how involved her editors might have been in choosing, or even composing, the poem. Readers need to make their own judgement about Bradstreet's denial that she was aware of the *Tenth Muse*'s publication, to listen to 'David's Lamentation' for traces of Bradstreet's voice, and to assess whether its placement in 1650 suggests or not that it was indeed written or included with well-judged allusions to Charles I in mind.

This problem case reveals the risk of historicising women's writing so closely to the moment of its publication that its meaning seems less and less like that of its attributed author. The available evidence for historicised readings can tilt our interpretation away from the author herself and towards her editors. This problem is most acute for women authors whose access to the institutions of print publication was restricted: Bradstreet's gender made it that much easier for her editors to make changes without her apparent

[40] Barbara Kiefer Lewalski, *Protestant Poetics and the Seventeenth-Century Lyric* (Princeton, NJ, 1979), 35.Thank you to Sarah Ross for discussion of this point.

[41] Holberton, 'Prophecy and Geography', 167.

involvement that turned her authorial labour into a print commodity designed for commercial and political ends.

Readers of early modern women's writing need to remember the sometimes substantial distance between what texts meant when they were first written and the new meanings they acquired when they entered print. That is why this chapter has sought to recover Bradstreet's agency as a novel and sympathetic female interlocutor in transatlantic relations in the 1640s while remembering her role in the formation of English settler colonial literature. It has also examined how the editions of 1650 and 1678 superimposed new rhetorical purposes onto her poetry at later points in the colonies' history. All the dates associated with Bradstreet's poems encourage us to consider their coherence and timeliness when they were written. They encourage us to think back to when Bradstreet was actually writing, just as they do for other women writers who dated their works like Anne Southwell, Katherine Austen, and Mary Roper.

The 'narrowly transatlantic' orientation of her poems reminds us that Bradstreet was writing in a specific locale. So were other women writers writing in other languages in the Americas, e.g., Leonor de Ovando, Sor Juana Inés de la Cruz, Marie de l'Incarnation, and the two Hispanophone poets in Peru known to history as Clarinda and Amarilis.[42] Dates mark the way that women writers like Bradstreet were politically engaged, well-informed, and attuned to circumstances. They also expose how susceptible women's writing was to interference as it was repurposed on entering a wider public domain.

FURTHER READING

Bradstreet, Anne. In Margaret Olofson Thickstun (ed.), *Poems and Meditations*. Toronto, 2019.

D'Addario, Christopher. *Exile and Journey in Seventeenth-Century Literature*. Cambridge, 2007.

Engen, Abram Van. *Sympathetic Puritans: Calvinist Fellow Feeling in Early New England*. New York, 2015.

Gillespie, Katharine. *Women Writing the English Republic, 1625–1681*. Cambridge, 2017.

Round, Phillip H. *By Nature and by Custom Cursed: Transatlantic Civil Discourse and New England Cultural Production, 1620–1660*. Hanover, NH, 1999.

Wilcox, Kirstin. 'American Women's Writing in the Colonial Period', in Dale M. Bauer (ed.), *The Cambridge History of American Women's Literature*. Cambridge, 2012, 55–73.

Wright, Gillian. *Producing Women's Poetry, 1600–1730: Text and Paratext, Manuscript and Print*. Cambridge, 2013.

[42] See Kirstin Wilcox, 'American Women's Writing in the Colonial Period', in Dale M. Bauer (ed.), *Cambridge History of American Women's Literature* (Cambridge, 2012), 55–73.

CHAPTER 31

EARLY MODERN DUTCH AND ENGLISH WOMEN ACROSS BORDERS

MARTINE VAN ELK

IN recent years, literary critics and historians have become increasingly attuned to the international aspects of textual production by early modern women. One area that has not been the subject of much study is early modern women's attention to Anglo-Dutch relationships, even though these relationships were close and significant. For individuals in both countries, the other country represented at different times a cultural and economic rival, a religious and political safe haven, and a place of economic opportunity. Dutch reformers of the movement known as the Further Reformation were influenced deeply by English Puritan thought, and English and Dutch Catholics and Protestants of different affiliations felt strong connections with each other.[1] Key political events in the period, from the Dutch Revolt against Spain and the English Civil Wars to the Restoration, the Anglo-Dutch Wars, and the Revolution of 1688, were the subject of lively debates. English royal and Dutch elite families were intertwined, and religious and political communities of refugees and exiles lived on both sides of the Channel.[2] For England and the Dutch Republic, this was a period of political alliance and conflict, economic exchange, and a cultural closeness characterised by Lisa Jardine as 'an extraordinary process of cross-fertilisation'.[3]

1 For an overview, see Cornelis W. Schoneveld, *Intertraffic of the Mind: Studies in Seventeenth-Century Anglo-Dutch Translation with a Checklist of Books Translated from English into Dutch, 1600–1700* (Leiden, 1983).

2 There is a rich body of work on Anglo-Dutch relations, particularly by historians; two interdisciplinary approaches to Dutch representations of the English are Helmer J. Helmers, *The Royalist Republic: Literature, Politics, and Religion in the Anglo-Dutch Public Sphere, 1639–1660* (Cambridge, 2015) and Marjorie Rubright, *Doppelgänger Dilemmas: Anglo-Dutch Relations in Early Modern English Literature and Culture* (Philadelphia, PA, 2014).

3 Lisa Jardine, *Going Dutch: How England Plundered Holland's Glory* (New York, 2008), xv.

Although patriarchal ideology raised obstacles to female participation in public debates, English and Dutch women expressed their opinions on issues that touched both countries. The circulation of their texts not only contributed to the formation of transnational publics and counterpublics focused on Anglo-Dutch relations but also allowed for a variety of representations of public femininity, a phrase I use to designate widely accessible representations of female-gendered agents. As the words 'publics' and 'counterpublics' indicate, I agree with scholars who see Jürgen Habermas' conception of the public sphere—a secular space in which private individuals discuss ideas as equals based on reason—as not yet relevant to the seventeenth century.[4] The plural terms 'publics' and 'counterpublics' suggested by Nancy Fraser highlight the extent to which at this time there was no one dominant public of that type; instead there were overlapping and competing spaces for exchange, especially in print form, that were available to a larger reading public.[5]

Nevertheless, even as political and religious upheaval allowed for the existence of publics and counterpublics, older views of the public realm persisted. Habermas' notion of a premodern 'publicity of representation' or, alternatively, 'representative publicness', is helpful in this respect; it refers to the ways in which the public realm had long been concentrated on the authority of a monarch who embodied the larger collective and through his or her presence created and confirmed community.[6] This older type of public realm marked by representative publicness imagined a public united around the monarch, rather than engaged in debate or fractured by difference. In this context, models of public femininity had a role to play as unifying exemplars of virtue and as evidence of the superiority of elite women. Such models commanded a form of authority on the basis of a visual and embodied, rather than a discursive, female presence. But there was also a push for a different public femininity, one that made space for textual agency and participation in religio-political debates. Expanding on Habermas, Michael McKeon sees the seventeenth century as a period marked by a dialectic between earlier and newer understandings of public and private, which explains why texts by and about women feature conflicting representations of public femininity, some associated with representative publicness and others with more active public and civic participation in matters of national and international politics and religion.[7]

[4] Jürgen Habermas, in Thomas Burger (trans.), *The Structural Transformation of the Public Sphere: An Inquiry into a Category of Bourgeois Society* (Cambridge, MA, 1991), esp. 27. For specific examples of scholarship on early modern women that take this approach, see Susan Wiseman, who sees Habermas' model as not 'applicable' to the period, and Catharine Gray, who uses the terms 'counterpublics' and 'publics' to show that women participated in smaller networks, enabling them to contribute to public debates; Susan Wiseman, *Conspiracy and Virtue: Women, Writing, and Politics in Seventeenth Century England* (Oxford, 2006); Catharine Gray, *Women Writers and Public Debate in Seventeenth-Century Britain* (New York, 2007).

[5] Nancy Fraser, 'Rethinking the Public Sphere: A Contribution to the Critique of Actually Existing Democracy', *Social Text*, 25.26 (1990), 56–80.

[6] Habermas, *Structural Transformation*, 5–14, esp. 7. In this chapter, I use 'publicness' for the nature of the public realm and 'publicity' for a presence in the public realm.

[7] Michael McKeon, *The Secret History of Domesticity: Public, Private, and the Division of Knowledge* (Baltimore, MD, 2005).

In this chapter I look at examples of three types of female contribution to Anglo-Dutch exchange: participation in intellectual networks, book printing and publishing, and the production of poetry about Anglo-Dutch politics. While it would be simplistic to align manuscript with the private and print with the public realm, a woman's name in a printed book as author, contributor, or stationer does not just allow for the circulation of ideas but also creates a representation of public femininity. As David Norbrook puts it, a book can be thought of as 'a public space, a claim to the right to be judged by one's peers and to engage in judgment of them'.[8] In this chapter I explore female interventions in Anglo-Dutch relations not only for their substance but also as discursive public femininities. Writing about matters of transnational concern, I argue, enabled women to imagine their place in, and articulate their relationship to, the public realm of Anglo-Dutch affairs. Due to the political and religious conflicts that pitted royalism against Puritan sectarianism, the women I discuss found in Anglo-Dutch relations a means of clarifying their own allegiances, which allowed them, with varying degrees of success, to redefine public femininity as a matter of transnational identification and public action.

INTELLECTUALS

The Republic of Letters, a precursor to the later public sphere, was potentially open to women, provided they knew Latin. The most famous female participant in this international network was the Dutch woman Anna Maria van Schurman (1607–1678), a polyglot, artist, poet, theologian, and the first woman to attend a Dutch university (albeit behind a screen and in an informal capacity). Her treatise defending female education for women of leisure, *Dissertatio de Ingenii Muliebris ad Doctrinam et Meliores Litteras Aptitudine* ('Dissertation on the Aptitude of the Female Mind for Learning and Letters'; official edition published in 1641), was widely read and translated, bringing her international renown. In addition, she became, as Pieta van Beek and Carol Pal have argued, the centre of a small Republic of Letters made up of highly educated women.[9] More specifically for our purposes, her connections with several English men and women, which included the learned Bathsua Reginald Makin (*c* 1600–*c* 1675), demonstrate an ambition to foster Anglo-Dutch exchange.

By contrast with Van Schurman, who became one of the most public figures of her time, Bathsua Makin never became widely known. Van Schurman herself was deeply

[8] Norbrook is referring specifically to Anna Maria van Schurman's *Opuscula*, discussed later in this chapter; David Norbrook, 'Autonomy and the Republic of Letters: Michèle le Dœuff, Anna Maria van Schurman, and the History of Women Intellectuals', *Australian Journal of French Studies*, 40 (2003), 275–87, esp. 279.

[9] Pieta van Beek, *The First Female University Student: Anna Maria van Schurman (1636)*, trans. Anna Mart Bonthuys and Dineke Ehlers (Utrecht, 2010); Carol Pal, *Republic of Women: Rethinking the Republic of Letters in the Seventeenth Century* (Cambridge, 2012).

conflicted about her own standing, showing the complex publicity associated with female intellectuals. In a study of the reception of Van Schurman in France and England, Anne Larsen observes that the learned woman:

> came under increasing pressure to match her public persona to that of a cultivated woman. The latter's more suitably feminine accomplishments, connected with the rise of salon sociability, focused on domestic skills, dancing, drawing, and music, with the fashionable vernaculars French, Italian, and Spanish.[10]

This absorption of learnedness into the realm of sociability anticipates what Habermas sees as an eighteenth-century development, accompanied by the rise of nation states and the reduction of 'representative publicness' to the royal courts alone.[11] Van Schurman, perennially reluctant about being placed in public view, was torn between her discomfort with being well known and her desire to contribute to theological and political debates. Her career as an intellectual can be read as an attempt to overcome the restrictive conventions of public femininity.

As an elite woman of learning, Van Schurman's connections with England centred mostly, though not exclusively, on royalty. She wrote a poem on the birth of Queen Henrietta Maria's fourth child, and she became a mentor to Princess Elisabeth of Bohemia (1618–1680), daughter of the exiled Elizabeth Stuart, Queen of Bohemia, whose court was in The Hague. She corresponded with Makin, who was herself an educator and governess to Elizabeth Stuart (1635–1650), the daughter of Charles I. But Van Schurman's contacts also included non-royalists, such as Sir Simonds d'Ewes, a Parliamentarian. These and other connections were publicised in *Opuscula Hebræa, Græca, Latina, Gallica, Prosaica et Metrica* ('Minor Work in Hebrew, Greek, Latin, and French, in Prose and Poetry', 1648), a collection of letters, poems, and prose, in a deliberate move to raise her profile as a scholar with international standing. The representation of Van Schurman in this volume contained a strong visual component. The frontispiece (see Figure 31.1), an engraved self-portrait, invites the reader to appreciate Van Schurman's modest and virtuous beauty.[12] Friedrich Spanheim's preface in Latin treats the book itself as a visual display, announcing to the reader, 'the Netherlands show you a young woman who is not only proficient in languages that belong to the domain of scholars, but who is also experienced in almost all disciplines of learning'.[13] Van Schurman thanked Spanheim for his preface in a letter in which

[10] Anne R. Larsen, *Anna Maria van Schurman, 'The Star of Utrecht': The Educational Vision and Reception of a Savante* (London, 2016), 15. Pal, *Republic of Women*, 57, notes a similar duality in scholarship between Van Schurman's position as a 'colleague both to male scholars in the republic of letters and to the intellectual women who would form her female epistolary network' on the one hand and 'the ongoing discourse on female excellence' on the other.

[11] Habermas, *Structural Transformation*, 11.

[12] Katlijne van der Stighelen has convincingly shown the engraving to be a self-portrait; *Anna Maria van Schurman of 'Hoe hooge dat een maeght kan in de konsten stijgen'* (Leuven, 1987), 119–22.

[13] Van Beek, *First Female*, 103.

FIGURE 31.1 Anna Maria van Schurman, *Nobilis. virginis Annae Maria à Schurman Opuscula Hebraea, Graeca, Latina, Gallica. Prosaica et Metrica* (Leiden, 1648), sig. *4v. Koninklijke Bibliotheek, The Hague. Shelfmark KW 188 L 6.

she called it 'une tres-belle statue, que vous avez dedié à mon honneur, et qui ne peut donner aux spectateurs que de tres-avantageuses impressions de mes estudes' ('a very beautiful statue, which you have dedicated to my honour, and which can only give to spectators very favourable impressions of my studies').[14] The use of 'statue' and 'spectateurs' suggests Van Schurman herself was thinking of readers' visual engagement with the book, describing it as a public monumentalisation—a description that matches the elite publicness of representation that Habermas associates with absolutism.

By contrast, the letters and poems that follow the prefatory material construct Van Schurman as an active scholar with a position in multiple transnational publics and networks. Her letters to English contacts solidify this impression, even as they carefully present her political interests in modest terms. Most explicitly, she asks D'Ewes in 1645 to 'communicate unto us (partakers of the same cause) whatsoever shall be atchieved by your Honourable Assemblie either in Peace or Warre'.[15] As Norbrook has noted, she casually expresses her allegiance to Parliament's side in the English Civil War here, claiming a place in an Anglo-Dutch reformed public.[16] By contrast, writing to Makin in Greek in 1640, she asks her Royalist friend more neutrally to let her know 'what the situation is in the church'.[17] In a second letter to Makin, written in 1645, in the midst of the Civil War, Van Schurman calls it 'most admirable that you, despite being kept busy by many domestic obligations, are not seldom found in the company of philosophy and that your Muses have not been silenced in the midst of the tumultuous battle', and she tells her friend to dedicate herself to educating 'the little royal girl, so that you may resurrect the famous Elizabeth for us (under whose holy and just government your island has indeed flourished)'.[18] In spite of her sympathies for Parliamentarians, Van Schurman saw Elizabeth I as a model of Protestant rule and virtuous femininity. While she characterises Makin's tutoring as publicly significant, she also presents a tension between female learning and domesticity as well as war, with learning taking place, as it were, in an alternative space outside public and private, free from distraction. These contradictory gestures show Van Schurman's conflicted relationship to the public realm and the difficulty of articulating a virtuous public femininity that could accommodate open religio-political expression. Late in life, in a radical break with her reputation as a learned woman, Van Schurman decided to become a leader of the sectarian community

[14] Quoted in Pieta van Beek, 'Klein werk: de *Opuscula Hebraea Graeca Latina et Gallica, prosaica et metrica* van Anna Maria van Schurman (1607–1678)', PhD Diss., University of Stellenbosch, 1997, 44. All translations, including this one, are mine unless otherwise noted.

[15] Anna Maria van Schurman, in [Clement Barksdale (trans.)], *The Learned Maid; or, Whether a Maid May Be a Scholar?* (London, 1659) sigs. D5r–v.

[16] David Norbrook, 'Women, the Republic of Letters, and the Public Sphere in the Mid-Seventeenth Century', *Criticism*, 46 (2004), 223–40, esp. 232. Norbrook argues that the examples of Van Schurman and Margaret Cavendish show that public spheres were developing at a different pace in different countries. England, he claims, was less advanced in this regard than France.

[17] Van Beek, *First Female*, 178.

[18] Van Beek, *First Female*, 180.

around Jean de Labadie, a decision she presented as a retreat from the limelight. In fact, it was an attempt to create a new public persona: she published a final work, *Eucleria* ('Choosing the Better Part', 1673), in which she disavowed all former praise in favour of a new public role to which her religion and her theological ideas were primary. Modifying her persona from elite cultivated paragon of virtue to sectarian theologian was successful in terms of supporting small counterpublics, but it inevitably meant a retreat from mainstream public life.

Makin's life and career followed a different trajectory. She too was a prodigy with a remarkable talent for languages, having published poems at the age of sixteen in a collection entitled *Musa Virginea Graeco-Latino-Gallica* ('The Virgin Muse in Greek-Latin-French', 1616). Her connection to the English court came initially via her husband, a minor court official. She was able to work as a tutor to prominent pupils, but she also had children of her own to take care of. Thus, unlike the unmarried Van Schurman, Makin remained relatively unknown. When she published her argument for female education in 1673, the same year the *Eucleria* came out, *An Essay to Revive the Ancient Education of Gentlewomen* did not bear her name and saw her assume a male voice. Makin mentions Van Schurman admiringly more than once and praises the Dutch Republic for its education of women, but she evidently worried that her argument would not be taken seriously if voiced by a woman, even one who had proven her learnedness and educated royalty.[19] Frances Teague has remarked that 'Makin wrote because of financial pressures. Unlike a man of this period, she would not have written to establish her identity as an intellectual'.[20] This observation clarifies the connection between social and marital status on the one hand and openings for publicity as a learned woman on the other. Establishing an identity as a public intellectual was Van Schurman's life's work. Van Schurman favoured Anglo-Dutch exchange, but even for a woman with her recognition and fame, explicit political partisanship and religious sectarianism could not be assimilated into a rhetoric of female virtue and modesty.

STATIONERS

Van Schurman's eventual break with a reputation that was encumbered by conventions of public femininity took the form of her active participation in small religious counterpublics. Non-elite women had long found a place in such smaller networks, and it is there that we encounter a different way in which women could contribute to transnational conversations: as stationers. Feminist book historians have pointed to

[19] Frances Teague (ed.), *Bathsua Makin, Woman of Learning* (Lewisburg, PA, 1998), 117–18, 121, 135.
[20] Frances Teague, 'The Identity of Bathsua Makin', *Biography*, 16 (1993), 1–17, esp. 9.

the importance of female stationers' politics in England, particularly in the late seventeenth and early eighteenth centuries.[21] As Paula McDowell notes of the period from 1678 to 1730:

> women of the widest possible variety of socioeconomic backgrounds in fact played so prominent a role in the production and transmission of political and religio-political ideas through print as to belie simultaneous powerful claims that women had no place in civic life.[22]

This double standard, by which patriarchal ideology created impediments to female expression but the forces of the marketplace ignored gender, shows the complexity of public femininity in this period. The Stationers' Company in England and printers' and booksellers' guilds in the Dutch Republic allowed women to continue running businesses after their husbands (or, less frequently, their fathers) died, so long as they remained unmarried. As a matter of course these stationers produced books, pamphlets, and newspapers that touched on Anglo-Dutch relations, including, for example, publications on the Anglo-Dutch Wars and the accession of William and Mary. This section discusses two female publishers, Mercy Arnold Bruyning (*c* 1618–1698) and Abigail May Swart (*c* 1642–1727), who were members of a community of English separatists in exile in Amsterdam. Despite their non-elite status and gender, they made extensive and lasting contributions to debates on these and other topics related to Anglo-Dutch exchange, and their publications advanced a public femininity that was openly political, sectarian, and transnational.

Related to each other by marriage and born in the Dutch Republic to English parents, Bruyning (active 1673–*c* 1685) and Swart (active 1683–*c* 1711) ran bookshops in Amsterdam for many years after their husbands died. The books and pamphlets they published were related to England, translated from English, and sometimes sold in England. These works were frequently narrowly sectarian but also allowed a wider readership to become acquainted with major voices and events in English politics. Their authors argued against the Church of England, against Jacobites, and in favour of the Revolution of 1688, and this activism did not go unnoticed in England. Paul Hoftijzer writes that the firms of Bruyning and Swart were the subject of several letters to the English government from consul William Carr, who described them in 1681 as 'the printers of all seditious papers', adding 'To these 2 booksellershopps come all the phanaticke English & Dutch merchants & there for a stiver a peace read the newes which afterward is spread upon the Change'.[23] The notion that their works might 'spread' in the

[21] See Paula McDowell, *The Women of Grub Street: Press, Politics, and Gender in the London Literary Marketplace 1678–1730* (Oxford, 1998) and Lisa Maruca, *The Work of Print: Authorship and the English Text Trades, 1660–1760* (Seattle, WA, 2007).

[22] McDowell, *Women of Grub Street*, 6.

[23] Quoted in P. G. Hoftijzer, *Engelse boekverkopers bij de Beurs: De geschiedenis van de Amsterdamse boekhandels Bruyning en Swart, 1637–1724* (Amsterdam, 1987), 140.

larger Dutch marketplace suggests that the English state took these activities seriously as potentially having an impact on Anglo-Dutch relations.

If we think of a book produced by a female stationer as, in Norbrook's words, a 'public space', her presence is marked primarily—and, in most cases, only—on the title page, where her name appears. From this perspective, the title page becomes, as Helen Smith has noted, a key locus of interpretation.[24] Given that authorities fined and prosecuted printers and booksellers for seditious work, the title page was potentially a dangerous place in which to appear in public, through which women showed that they participated, by manufacturing, distributing, and thus endorsing the content of books, in controversial public debates. From a professional perspective, it also helped establish and maintain the reputation of businesses among authors, competitors, and readers. Thus, title pages offer important instances of public representation of women as religio-political agents performing what Lisa Maruca calls 'text work'.[25]

An example of such self-representation is the title page of a sermon by John Tillotson, published by Abigail Swart in 1689.[26] This was shortly after the Revolution of 1688, when the Catholic James II had been ousted and his Protestant daughter Mary II and her Dutch husband William of Orange, the Stadholder (a position similar to prime minister) of the Republic, had assumed the English throne (see Figure 31.2). Tillotson was a moderate Archbishop of Canterbury, not quite the sectarian typically promoted by Swart's firm, but his importance is clarified in political terms by the title page. In a direct translation of the English version of the sermon, the title page states that it was spoken on 10 February 1689, to thank God for making William 'Tot een heerlijk Instrument van de groote Verlossinge van dit Koningrijk van 't Pausdom en de Arbitraire Magt' ('Into a Holy Instrument for the great Deliverance of this Kingdom from the Papacy and the Arbitrary Power'). The juxtaposition of this religio-political statement with Swart's name in the imprint accompanied by the gendered term for bookseller, 'Boekverkoopster', associates her with a position in an international conflict and shows her reaching out to different overlapping publics and counterpublics, from Dutch-reading refugees and immigrants to Dutch readers with an interest in the reception of William as the new joint ruler of England.

Bruyning and Swart specialised in the publication of political and sectarian materials, but they also produced works of wider interest to a Dutch reading public, including two major travel narratives by Englishmen about the Low Countries: Owen's Feltham's *A Brief Character of the Low-Countries* and William Temple's *Observations upon the United Provinces of the Netherlands*. Feltham's book, which had circulated in manuscript from the late 1620s before it was published during the First Anglo-Dutch War in 1652, functioned in England, as Christopher Gabbard notes, as 'an Anglican-royalist response'

[24] Helen Smith, *'Grossly Material Things': Women and Book Production in Early Modern England* (Oxford, 2012), 89.

[25] Maruca, *Work of Print*, 4.

[26] Johan Tillotson, *Predicatie gedaan in de Kapel van Lincolns-Inn, tot London, op den 10. February. 1689* (Amsterdam, 1689).

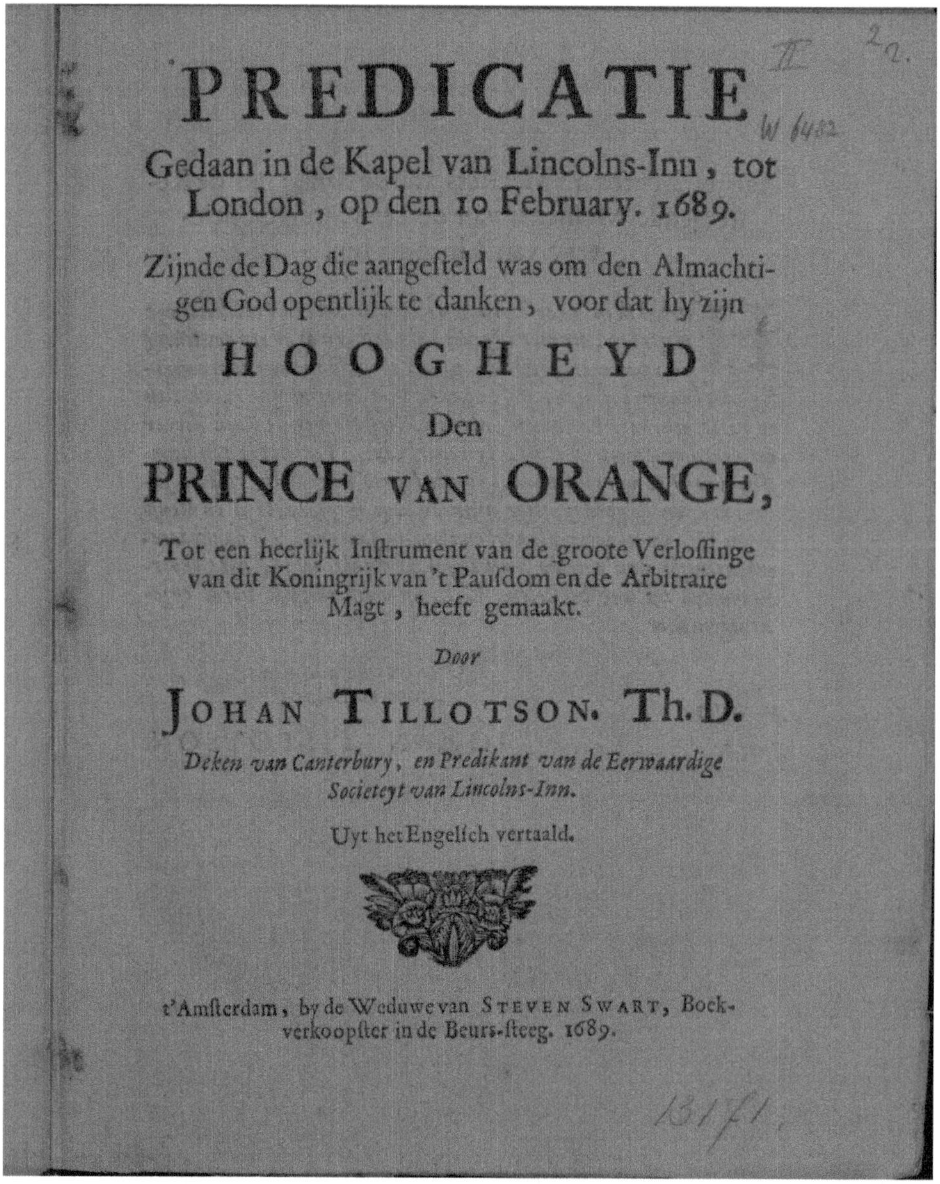

PREDICATIE

Gedaan in de Kapel van Lincolns-Inn, tot London, op den 10 February. 1689.

Zijnde de Dag die aangesteld was om den Almachtigen God opentlijk te danken, voor dat hy zijn

HOOGHEYD

Den

PRINCE VAN ORANGE,

Tot een heerlijk Instrument van de groote Verlossinge van dit Koningrijk van 't Pausdom en de Arbitraire Magt, heeft gemaakt.

Door

JOHAN TILLOTSON. Th.D.

Deken van Canterbury, en Predikant van de Eerwaardige Societeyt van Lincolns-Inn.

Uyt het Engelsch vertaald.

t'Amsterdam, by de Weduwe van STEVEN SWART, Boeck-verkoopster in de Beurs-steeg. 1689.

FIGURE 31.2 Johan Tillotson, *Predicatie gedaan in de Kapel van Lincolns-Inn, tot London, op den 10. February. 1689* (Amsterdam, 1689), title page. Koninklijke Bibliotheek, The Hague. Shelfmark KW Pflt 13171.

to the Republican government of the Low Countries.[27] Steven Swart had published *A Brief Character* for distribution in England, but it was his widow who brought out the first Dutch translation in 1684.[28] Given its satirical presentation of the Dutch, it is a curious choice that is defended in an unsigned prefatory note to the 'Bescheydene Lezer' ('Modest Reader'), by the anonymous translator or possibly Swart herself. The note presents Feltham's anti-Dutch ideas as entertainment and assures the reader that there is a 'Tegen-gift' ('Countergift') at the end of the book in the form of Feltham's equally negative description of the Scottish.

Over a decade before Swart published Feltham's work, Bruyning produced a Dutch translation of Temple's *Observations*, shortly after its appearance in England in 1673. Following the publication of a pirated edition, she put out a second edition of her translation, explicitly presented as 'opnieuws gecorrigeert en verbetert' ('newly corrected and improved').[29] The title page contains a double English-Dutch imprint, including publisher Samuel Gellibrand and printer Anne Maxwell, who were responsible for the English publication. Its attribution and the phrase 'Na de Copye' ('After the Copy') solidify its status as a match with the English edition. Temple's book offers a nuanced look at the Dutch people from a former ambassador, right after 1672, the so-called Year of Disaster, when the Republic was invaded by France, England, and parts of Germany and internal conflicts between supporters of William of Orange and the political elite culminated in the lynching of the political leader Johan de Witt and his brother. While in England Feltham's *Brief Character* contributed to the anti-Dutch climate in 1652 and Temple's *Observations* aroused sympathy during the unpopular Third Anglo-Dutch War, the Dutch translations were brought out in reverse order. This suggests that the latter could encourage a reconciliation with the English, whereas the former came out well after the Anglo-Dutch Wars, when the Dutch were presumably better positioned to be entertained by a satirical depiction of themselves. These publications show that Bruyning and Swart aimed at catering not only to a limited audience of like-minded sectarians and exiles, but also to a larger audience with an interest in Anglo-Dutch relations.

What has been called the 'discussion culture' of the Dutch Republic allowed for relatively open civic and political expression, but, as Helmer Helmers has noted, this culture was in principle off-limits to women.[30] Nevertheless, female stationers could push their ideas and strengthen wider and smaller publics and counterpublics without clear gendered constraints. Thus, they shaped a textual public femininity that contrasted

[27] D. Christopher Gabbard, 'Gender Stereotyping in Early Modern Travel Writing on Holland', *SEL Studies in English Literature, 1500–1900*, 43 (2003), 83–100, esp. 93.

[28] Printed by Swart in *Batavia, or the Hollander Displayed* (Amsterdam, 1675), the translation is entitled *Batavia, of Den ontployden Hollander* (Amsterdam, 1684).

[29] William Temple, *Aenmerckingen over de Vereenigde Nederlandtsche Provintien*, 2nd edn (Amsterdam, 1673). See Hoftijzer, *Engelse boekverkopers*, 86–7.

[30] Helmer J. Helmers, 'Popular Participation and Public Debate', in Helmer J. Helmers and Geert H. Janssen (eds), *The Cambridge Companion to the Dutch Golden Age* (Cambridge, 2018), 124–46, esp. 124, 126.

with the circumscribed public presence of learned women. The paradox of public femininity, as we have seen in the case of Van Schurman, was that greater visibility came with a less flexible public role that could not accommodate strong political or religious affiliation. Van Schurman's acceptance as a prominent intellectual was predicated on her willingness to function as an exemplar of female virtue and modesty. Once she shifted to more vocal religious sectarianism, she was vilified and subsequently appealed only to much smaller groups. Female stationers' presence in the books they produced was associated with a different, purely textual, and potentially more flexible mode of public engagement, especially at times of political upheaval. Although they did not write the works they published, stationers were able to promote their ideas in the marketplace of books, producing a public femininity by virtue of their labour rather than their words or visual presence.

POETS

While elite learned women and working stationers created different representations of public femininity, women writers also articulated their views on Anglo-Dutch relations in order to position themselves in a rapidly changing political environment. Aphra Behn (1640–1689) and Katharina Lescailje (1649–1711) wrote plays for the public theatre, although, unlike Behn, Lescailje did not make her living primarily as an author. She had taken over management of her father's printing and publishing house in Amsterdam after his death in 1679. The female-led firm—Lescailje was in charge along with her sister and later their niece—was the preferred stationer for Amsterdam's only public theatre, the Schouwburg, printing and publishing numerous plays and maintaining close contacts with playwrights and the theatre's board of regents. The public status of Behn and Lescailje was not as constrained or visible as that of the learned women discussed earlier, given their lower social status and the relatively new openness of the theatre to contributions from women playwrights and actresses. Nonetheless, they still relied on patronage and elite contacts as well as a larger audience, potentially limiting their political expression. For both Behn and Lescailje, plays offered the possibility of political and religious commentary in a fictional framework, but the two also composed poems in which they responded more directly to key moments in Anglo-Dutch history, including the Anglo-Dutch Wars, the Revolution of 1688, and the coronation and death of royalty. The public femininity they fashioned in composing these poems points both forwards and backwards, creating openings for female textual agency in adopting public, 'masculine' genres of poetry while relying on traditional views of the public sphere and women's place in it.

Lescailje's political sentiments shifted over the course of her writing career, although most of her poems are attempts to formulate a collective response to a turbulent period in her country's history. Nina Geerdink has explored Lescailje's poetry on William III, which had to navigate between audience support for the Stadholder and her patrons' objections to him. Like other poets', Geerdink writes, Lescailje's support for William became especially pronounced after 1688, when, in spite of her lack of religiosity in other poems, she started introducing religious discourse in her promotion of William's increasingly monarchical status in the Republic.[31] Some of her poems appeared individually in pamphlet form, an indication of Lescailje's ambition to bring them to the attention of a broader readership. Posthumously, however, her descendants created a very different material context for them in the 1731 publication of her collected works, which includes a section on 'Staatsgevallen' ('Matters of State') with twenty-one political poems.[32] The collection includes a frontispiece depicting a monumentalised Lescailje surrounded by muses (see Figure 31.3). While the format of the three volumes is modest—quarto rather than folio—the visual presentation of the poet nonetheless cultivates a public femininity reminiscent of representations that accompanied elite female publication. Someone who read Lescailje's political poems in 1731 would have received a very different impression of the author, in other words, than would the reader who encountered the same poems shortly after the events they describe in pamphlet form.

Generally, Lescailje changes her representation of England depending on the political climate and the events she commemorates, representing the English variously as enemies, brothers, and inferiors. The point throughout is to articulate pride in the Dutch Republic and focus on its leadership. Absolutist and religious rhetoric is used to infuse William's position with a sense of the sacred, most clearly in a poem on the Revolution of 1688, in which England is depicted as in need of a Dutch saviour. William is the '*Oranje Zon*' ('Orange Sun'), the light that 'Trekt alle nevels op van 't kwynende Engeland' ('Draws up all the mists from the withering England'; sig. D2r). Having been sent by God, his invasion is a rescue mission. Lescailje's 1695 elegy on the death of Mary II relies on a similarly absolutist model of representative public femininity, calling for a unified response by England, the Republic, and indeed the entire world.[33] Mary's loss is depicted, with conventional hyperbole, as affecting not just England and the Dutch Republic, but all of Europe. Addressing the English directly, she calls the English court, so secure previously in its power, 'ontbloot' (exposed) since with Mary's death, 'De Kroon is van uw Hoofd gevallen' ('The Crown has fallen off your Head'; sig. A3v). The poem ends with a call on the Dutch Republic to help William, the great warrior leader, mourn, and the speaker promises that Mary's guiding light will lead to peace and victory (sigs. A4r-v). Geerdink notes that the poem is different from other elegies on Mary by women, in its absence of religious rhetoric and confident adoption of male conventions and a gender-neutral voice.[34] The poem also envisions a shared Anglo-Dutch community centred on

[31] Nina Geerdink, 'Cultural Marketing of William III: A Religious Turn in Katharina Lescailje's Political Poetry', *Dutch Crossing*, 34 (2010), 25–41.

[32] Katharina Lescailje, *Tooneel-en mengelpoëzy*, 3 vols (Amsterdam, 1731), vol. 1, sigs. Ar–H2v.

[33] Katharina Lescailje, *Rouwklagt over de dood van de koninginne van Grootbrittanje* (Amsterdam, 1695), sig. A2r.

[34] Nina Geerdink, 'Rouw om een "cieraad grooter vrouwen": Lijkdichten bij de dood van Maria Stuart (1695) door mannen en vrouwen', *Historica*, 32 (2009), 3–5, esp. 4–5.

FIGURE 31.3 Louis Surugue and Nicolaas Verkolje, frontispiece engraving, Katharina Lescailje, *Toneel- en mengelpoezy* (Amsterdam, 1731), volume 1. Rijksmuseum, Amsterdam. Object number RP-P-OB-74.381.

the death of Mary. This absolutist rhetoric precludes representations of debate between individual agents, let alone women, but in becoming its mouthpiece, Lescailje nonetheless assumes an unusual authority to articulate national feeling in response to key moments in Anglo-Dutch history. In contributing to what Geerdink calls 'the cultural marketing' of William III, she took it upon herself to write in a male-dominated genre, and yet in doing so she also perpetuated older forms of public femininity that foreclosed active female civic participation.[35]

Although Lescailje and Behn would seem to be natural opposites in terms of their political and religious views, Behn similarly contributed to formulations of English nationality in response to political turmoil from an absolutist perspective. When her plays and prose featured Dutch characters or settings, Behn frequently resorted to negative stereotypes, and even though individual characters were sometimes more complex, Rebecca Wolsk claims that Behn usually associated the Dutch and Dutchness with negative qualities such as greed, mercantilism, duplicity, and a hypocritical Calvinist morality—concepts that were antithetical to the Cavalier, aristocratic world view Behn espoused.[36] In elegiac poetry on Charles II and praise poetry on James II, Behn used a conventional absolutist style similar to Lescailje's, but 'A Pindaric Poem to the Reverend Doctor Burnet', written in 1689 in response to Gilbert Burnet's request for a poem on the coronation of William III, represents a departure.[37] The poem is not a celebration of the coronation, but an explanation of why she declined to write such a celebration. Thus, Behn turns the conventions of absolutist coronation poetry and the Pindaric around, defending her decision not to speak. Published in pamphlet format, the poem's title page contrasts the names of 'the Reverend Doctor Burnet' and '*Mrs. A. BEHN*' typographically, with the former in bold, black letter and the latter set off in italics. The full title's repeated use of personal pronouns ('On the Honour he did me of Enquiring after me and my MUSE') projects a confident public persona, but there is a slight tension between modesty in acknowledging the 'Honour' implied by the invitation and the emphasis on herself as worthy of such an invitation. This complex female publicity is matched by the ambivalent content of the poem itself.

In a compelling argument, Christopher Loar situates Behn's poem in relation to Habermas' conception of publicness of representation, explaining that by upending the conventions of the coronation poem, Behn redirects the sacredness of the monarch towards 'the individual conscience'.[38] Read this way, the poem becomes an instance of what McKeon has described as key to the development of public and private as opposing categories:

[35] Geerdink, 'Cultural Marketing'.

[36] Wolsk uses the term 'Hollandophobia' coined by Simon Schama for these representations. Rebecca S. Wolsk, 'Muddy Allegiance and Shiny Booty: Aphra Behn's Anglo-Dutch Politics', *Eighteenth-Century Fiction*, 17 (2004), 1–33, 2 and *passim*.

[37] Aphra Behn, *A Pindaric Poem to the Reverend Doctor Burnet, on the Honour He Did Me of Enquiring after Me and My Muse* (London, 1689).

[38] Christopher F. Loar, 'Exclusion and Desecration: Aphra Behn, Liberalism, and the Politics of the Pindaric Ode', *Restoration*, 39 (2015), 125–36, esp. 125.

> a devolutionary movement 'downward,' a progressive detachment of the normatively absolute from its presumed locale in royal absolutism and its experimental relocation in 'the people,' the family, women, the individual, personal identity, and the absolute subject.[39]

This movement of authority inward and downward is what Loar pinpoints in the poem, which presents Behn's refusal to perform the task of endorsing the new Dutch king in melancholy terms of silent watching, 'like the Excluded Prophet', being 'forbid by Fates Decree / To share the Triumph of joyful Victory' (sig. A3v). For this reason, Loar aligns the poem with liberalism.

From the perspective of its gendered qualities, the poem can be seen to make a somewhat different though related argument. Behn starts the poem by comparing her position to that of the male political leader of Rome who is receiving the approbation of the people, but she ends up as another male, Moses, the 'Excluded Prophet', who can only watch matters from afar. She claims she is made 'Useless and Forlorn' (sig. A4r) by the momentousness of William's accession. In the end, she leaves the great work of chronicling 'this Unpresidented Enterprise' to Burnet himself. At the conclusion, Behn finally turns, briefly, from Burnet to William:

> 'Tis you that to Posterity shall give
> This Ages Wonders, and its History.
> And Great *NASSAU* shall in your Annals live
> To all Futurity.
> Your Pen shall more Immortalize his Name,
> Than even his Own Renown'd and Celebrated Fame. (sig. A4v)

The Dutch invasion into England represents, in this poem, both the formation of a new relationship of subject to government, ruled by the 'Pen' rather than the sword, but also, for the female poet, a retreat into silence, enacted in the composition of a Pindaric poem—the most public of political genres—that refuses to fulfil its function as Pindaric. Although in comparing herself to a Roman leader and to Moses she masculinises her position as speaking and non-speaking subject, for Behn the Dutch intervention in English politics heralds a reorganisation of the public sphere in which she, an absolutist without a king she wants to support, will no longer have a place.

As the century drew to a close, the emerging Habermasian bourgeois public sphere limited female participation in religio-political debate, and women were increasingly strongly associated with an ideology of domesticity, a trajectory that is the subject of McKeon's *The Secret History of Domesticity* and has also been noted by book historians. Both McDowell and Maruca describe the mid- to late eighteenth century as a time when women's contributions to public debates as stationers stalled.[40] In the seventeenth

39 McKeon, *Secret History*, xxii.
40 McDowell, *Women of Grub Street*, esp. 9–10, and Maruca, *Work of Print*, 118–19.

century, close relations between England and the Dutch Republic, whether they were a matter of intellectual exchange, religious affiliation, or political and economic conflict, enabled women to gain a voice in transnational debates and thus situate themselves in religio-political terms, presenting themselves as public agents. In doing so, however, they had to work within and against conventions of public femininity and of absolutist publicness of representation, conventions that raised obstacles to controversial modes of expression. Whether they adopted these conventions or rejected them in favour of sectarian or political self-representation, they expressed their views on Anglo-Dutch relationships to fashion their own modes of public femininity and contribute to transnational Dutch and English publics and counterpublics.

FURTHER READING

Elk, Martine van. *Early Modern Women's Writing: Domesticity, Privacy, and the Public Sphere in England and the Dutch Republic*. Cham, 2017.

Gemert, Lia van et al. (eds). *Women's Writing from the Low Countries 1200–1875: A Bilingual Anthology*. Amsterdam, 2010.

Norbrook, David. 'Women, the Republic of Letters, and the Public Sphere in the Mid-Seventeenth Century'. *Criticism*, 46 (2004), 223–40.

Smith, Helen. *'Grossly Material Things': Women and Book Production in Early Modern England*. Oxford, 2012.

Weintraub, Jeff. 'The Theory and Politics of the Public/Private Distinction', in Jeff Weintraub and Krishan Kumar (eds), *Public and Private in Thought and Practice: Perspectives on a Grand Dichotomy*. Chicago, IL, 1997, 1–42.

CHAPTER 32

POLITICAL THEORY ACROSS BORDERS

MIHOKO SUZUKI

In justifying Salic law, which proscribed female rule as well as the transmission of sovereignty through the female line, Jean Bodin, the celebrated French jurist and political philosopher, adduced the 'law of nature which hath given unto men wisdom, strength, courage, and power to command; and taken the same from women'. The 'law of God' further ordains that women should be subject to men and concern themselves with domestic matters. Therefore, it would be an 'absurd and ridiculous thing, for women to busie themselves in mens publicke actions and affaires'.[1] These quotations from Bodin's *Six livres de la république* (1576) are taken from the English translation by Richard Knolles, *The Six Bookes of a Common-weale* (1606). While England decidedly did not follow Salic law—not only did Mary I and Elizabeth I exercise sovereignty in their own right, but Henry V claimed the French crown through Isabella of France—the notion that women should not 'busie themselves' with politics prevailed in England. For example, Richard Brathwait in *The English Gentlewoman* (1631) enjoined his female readership to refrain from engaging in 'discourse of State matters' and 'state political action'.[2]

However, scholarship of the last two decades on early modern women writers has recognised that a substantial number declined to follow such injunctions and concerned themselves with political subjects. At the same time, this scholarship largely assumes that these writers confined their points of reference to the English political context.[3] In addition, their engagements with political theory have yet to be investigated. This chapter discusses three political theorists from 'across [English] borders'—Christine de

[1] Jean Bodin, in Richard Knolles (trans.) and Kenneth Douglas McRae (ed.), *The Six Bookes of a Common-weale* (Cambridge, MA, 1962), 746.

[2] Richard Brathwait, *The English Gentlewoman* (London, 1631), 89–91.

[3] See my 'Political Writing across Borders', in Patricia Philippy (ed.), *A History of Early Modern Women's Writing* (Cambridge, 2018), 364–81, for a discussion of Margaret Cavendish's engagement with the political and cultural context of France, where she lived for four years.

Pizan, Niccolò Machiavelli, and Jean Bodin—whose writings proved to be of importance for Mary Sidney Herbert, Countess of Pembroke; Elizabeth Cary, Viscountess Falkland; Margaret Cavendish, Duchess of Newcastle; and possibly Anne Clifford, Countess of Dorset, Pembroke, and Montgomery.

CHRISTINE DE PIZAN

It is not surprising that Christine de Pizan, several of whose works—*The Book of the Deeds of Arms and of Chivalry* (1404), *The Book of the City of Ladies* (1405), and *The Book of the Body Politic* (1407)—were translated and published in England, would become an influential predecessor for English women who wrote concerning politics. Christine was a respected political thinker of her time, whose renown reached England: Henry IV, for example, sought her services as counsellor. Although Christine declined this invitation from a monarch whom she considered a usurper, she sent a manuscript of her *Epistle of Othea to Hector* (*c* 1400) dedicated to him. Henry VII valued Christine's expertise on military matters, apparently not discounting the authority of a woman on this conventionally masculine subject.[4] William Caxton explains in the epilogue to *Faytes of Armes and of Chevalrie* (1489) that the king commanded him to translate the work, which was ordered to be read by 'euery gentylman born to armes & all manere men of werre'.[5] In 1521, during Henry VIII's reign, translations were published of the *City of Ladies* by Brian Anslay and the *Body Politic* by John Skot.

According to Susan Groag Bell, royal inventories record that Elizabeth I owned tapestries, now lost, illustrating the *City of Ladies*.[6] Such tapestries, displayed in public rooms, would affirm precedents for Elizabeth's rule to those who had access to her court. It would be surprising if Elizabeth, proficient in French as evidenced in her translation of Marguerite de Navarre, would not have been familiar with Christine's political writings in either English or French. Indeed, her sense of responsibility to her subjects as articulated in her speeches to Parliament and her oft-noted effective use of counsellors reflect Christine's views. Mary Sidney, who addressed to Elizabeth 'Even now that care', the dedicatory poem to the translation of the Psalms by her brother Philip and herself, expresses a similar understanding of a monarch's grave responsibilities. Sidney would have been familiar with Christine's promotion of female sovereignty from the tapestries, Anslay's translation, or the French original. *Antonius* (1592), her translation of the

[4] On Christine's English reception, see Jennifer Summit, *Lost Property: The Woman Writer in English History, 1380–1589* (Chicago, IL, 2000), Ch. 2.

[5] Christine de Pizan, in William Caxton (trans.) and A. T. P. Byles (ed.), *Fayttes of Armes and of Chyualrie* (London, 1932), 291.

[6] Susan Groag Bell, *The Lost Tapestries of the City of Ladies: Christine de Pizan's Renaissance Legacy* (Berkeley, CA, 2004).

French playwright Robert Garnier's *Marc Antoine*, represents Cleopatra as a ruler whose passion for Antony leads her to neglect her responsibilities to her subjects.

A generation later, Elizabeth Cary may have been familiar with the 'Cyte of Ladies' tapestries passed on to Henrietta Maria, to whom she dedicated her translation from the French of Cardinal du Perron's *Reply* to James I (1630). Her *History of Edward II*, which she wrote in 1627, remained in manuscript until it was published in 1680, contributing to the political debate during the Exclusion Crisis, in which Parliament sought to prevent James II from succeeding Charles II. Given Cary's interest in political thought and in women as political agents as evidenced in the *History*, she would certainly have known Christine's political writings translated into English; in addition, as in the case of Sidney, Cary's linguistic proficiency would have enabled her to read the French originals of Christine's works.

In the *History*, Cary prominently features the corporate metaphor, which closely follows Christine's version in the *Body Politic*. Christine designates the prince as occupying the head of the political body, but rather than affirm the hierarchical relationship between the head and other parts of the body, she stresses their interdependence and the indispensability of the lower parts of the body: 'a human body cannot go without its feet ... if the republic excluded laborers and artisans, it could not sustain itself'.[7] Like Christine, Cary displays an interest in the commons and the lower orders of the Commonwealth, in squarely laying the blame for the 'sick State' on 'the Head [that] is so diseased', so that 'all the Members suffer by his infirmity'.[8] In emphasising the responsibility of the king to his people, Cary inverts James' claim in *The True Law of Free Monarchies* (1598) that it was the prerogative of the head to sever a diseased limb. In addition, by contrast with James, Cary agrees with Christine in recognising the importance of queens (in the *City of Ladies*) and the commons (in the *Body Politic*) as participants in the polity. Christine thus serves as an antecedent for Cary in her understanding of 'equivalences' between Edward's Queen Isabel and his subjects, an understanding that anticipates Ernesto Laclau and Chantal Mouffe's notion that subaltern groups can articulate new subject positions through an awareness of equivalences with others in relation to the dominant order.[9]

Cristina Malcolmson has suggested that William Cavendish purchased while in France the sumptuous manuscript volume of Christine de Pizan's collected works (British Library, MS Harley 4431), thus making available to Margaret Cavendish the works of her illustrious predecessor.[10] Christine's substantial oeuvre on political subjects

[7] Christine de Pizan, in Kate Langdon Forhan (trans. and ed.), *The Book of the Body Politic* (Cambridge, 1994), 105.

[8] [Elizabeth Cary], *The History of the Life, Reign, and Death of Edward II* (London, 1680), 29, 44.

[9] Ernesto Laclau and Chantal Mouffe, *Hegemony and Socialist Strategy: Toward a Radical Democratic Politics* (London, 1985), 64–5. I have argued for equivalences between male apprentices and women of various classes in *Subordinate Subjects: Gender, the Political Nation, and Literary Form in England, 1588–1688* (Aldershot, 2003).

[10] Cristina Malcolmson, 'Christine de Pizan's *City of Ladies* in Early Modern England', in Cristina Malcolmson and Mihoko Suzuki (eds), *Debating Gender in Early Modern England 1500–1700* (New York, 2002), 15–35.

represents an important example for Cavendish's equally ambitious output of political writing. Moreover, Christine represents for Cavendish a unique female predecessor who explicitly envisioned a future readership for her works.

Mary Sidney, Elizabeth Cary, and Margaret Cavendish follow Christine de Pizan's example in fashioning themselves as political counsellors. Christine called attention to the importance of sound political counsel for the ruler and the qualifications of those who would provide such counsel; her emphasis on the counsellor's speaking truth to those who hold power anticipates Michel Foucault's focus on *parrhesia*, truth-telling, as the *sine qua non* of political counsel and a foundational term for the history of political thought.[11] Christine counselled not only male aristocrats who patronised her but also the queen consort Isabeau of Bavaria to intervene in the civil war between the Armagnacs and the Burgundians to achieve peace. Sidney counselled Elizabeth I concerning her responsibility as a monarch. Cary counselled Henrietta Maria through the negative example of Isabel, another French queen consort. Finally, Cavendish counselled Charles II to refrain from repeating the mistakes made by his father Charles I, whom she implicitly held responsible for his own defeat.[12]

NICCOLÒ MACHIAVELLI

Another political thinker who, perhaps less expectedly than Christine de Pizan, proves to be of importance for early modern women writers is Machiavelli.[13] In *The English Face of Machiavelli*, Felix Raab investigated Machiavelli's influence in early modern England, but his 1964 study does not include mention of any women writers.[14] However, my research has uncovered early modern women writers' sustained engagement, hitherto unrecognised, with Machiavelli, political theorist par excellence. Such engagement, I suggest, indicates the consciousness with which women such as Cary and Cavendish fashioned themselves as political writers.

Early in the *History of Edward II*, Cary explicitly refers to Machiavelli when she criticises Edward's favorite Gaveston for falling short of the standard of what she calls '*Machiavilian* States-men', by displaying 'publick hatred' and failing to 'disguise [his] aims with Vizards, which see and are not seen'. Since '[h]e that will work in State, and thrive, must be reserved', Cary ironically voices her suspicion concerning the accuracy

[11] Michel Foucault, in Frédéric Gros (ed.) and Graham Burchell (trans.), *The Government of the Self and Others: Lectures at the Collège de France 1982–1983* (New York, 2010), 69–71.

[12] For more on these writers as envisioning themselves as political counsellors, see my *Antigone's Example: Early Modern Women's Political Writing in Times of Civil War from Christine de Pizan to Helen Maria Williams* (New York, 2022), Chs 1, 2, 4.

[13] In *Antigone's Example*, I argue that Machiavelli's writings evince his engagement with Christine; his diplomatic missions to France provided him with opportunities to access her work. See Suzuki, *Antigone's Example*, Ch. 1.

[14] Felix Raab, *The English Face of Machiavelli: A Changing Interpretation 1500–1700* (London, 1964).

of her source that claims Gaveston was Italian (26). Raab has shown that Machiavelli's reception during the period 1603–1640 was with very few exceptions hostile, or at best ambivalent.[15] Cary's notable departure from the prevailing negative assessment may be explained partly by her Catholicism, for she does not share her contemporaries' enmity towards Italy, associated with Catholicism. However, it is neither Gaveston, nor even the wily Spencer, who succeeds Gaveston as Edward's favourite, but Isabel, Edward's queen, who exemplifies qualities of Machiavellian statecraft—in accord with the motto Cary had inscribed on her daughter's wedding ring, 'BEE AND SEEME'.[16] In contrast with Gaveston, Isabel 'advances her own affairs by all means possible: She courts her Adversary with all the shews of perfect reconcilement' (90). Although Spencer suspected 'her Cunning', and although he himself was 'as cunning as a Serpent', he 'findes here a female Wit that went beyond him' (90–1). Isabel's shrewdness enables her to prevail over Spencer, 'thus over-reach'd by one weak Woman' (92). Here Isabel not only overcomes her disabling gender but also takes advantage of others' expectations and lulls them into complacency: as one of her adversaries states, 'Alas, what can the Queen a wandring Woman compass, that hath nor Arms, nor Means, nor Men, nor Money' (93). Spencer in fact knows Isabel to be 'a Woman of a strong Brain, and stout Stomach, apt on all occasions to trip up his heels, if once she found him reeling' (86–7). By contrast, Edward mistakenly and fatally believes his monarchical and patriarchal prerogatives to be unassailable: 'The King, a Sovereign, Father, and a Husband, did hope these titles would be yet sufficient to guard his Life, if not preserve his Greatness; but they prov'd all too weak' (126).

Cary devotes the second part of her *History* to the rise of Isabel, concomitant with the decline of Edward: 'Fortune, that triumphs in the Fall of Princes, like a Stepmother, rests not where she frowneth, till she have wholly ruin'd and o'rethrown their Power, that do precede or else oppose her Darlings' (127). This reference to the famous allegory in Chapter 25 of *The Prince* of Fortune as a woman who must be mastered by a prince exhibiting *virtù* exemplifies Cary's use of and departure from Machiavelli, who insistently constructs political agency as masculine—in this example of the sexual mastery of Fortune, as well as in the figuration of Italy as a woman, who will welcome a redeeming prince as her lover. While following Machiavelli's gendering of Fortune, Cary's text departs from his representation of a sexual relationship between the masculine ruler and feminine Fortune by calling Fortune a 'Stepmother' to Edward and by featuring Isabel as Fortune's 'Darling'. In thus designating Isabel as a same-sex favourite of Fortune, Cary suggests a surprising link between Isabel and Edward's favourites Gaveston and Spencer, a link that prepares the way for Cary's severe judgement on Isabel's exercise of power.

Although Machiavelli considers Fortune's favours to be beneficial to a prince, Cary turns against Isabel after Fortune has shifted from favouring Edward to favouring Isabel: she harshly criticises Isabel's 'Tyranny' and her departure from 'her former Vertue

15 Raab, *The English Face*, 90–1.

16 Elizabeth Cary, in Heather Wolfe (ed.), *Elizabeth Cary, Lady Falkland Life and Letters* (Tempe, AZ, 2001), 118.

and Goodness' when she gratuitously insults and exults over Spencer. Cary's criticism of Isabel is not based solely on considerations of *Realpolitik*, as it would be if she were following *The Prince*, but also on ethical considerations: her ostentatious humiliation of Spencer 'savour'd more of a savage, tyrannical disposition, than a judgement fit to comand, or sway the Sword of Justice .... it was at best too great and deep a blemish to suit a Queen, a Woman, and a Victor' (129). The apposition of 'a Woman' and 'a Victor' indicates that the two terms are not in contradiction—as they would be in Machiavelli; at the same time, Cary criticises Isabel for falling short of ethical and political standards, suggesting that the two are not in contradiction, either.

While Machiavelli provides a framework for Cary's political discourse, she departs from his strict gendering of political agency as *virtù* by her focus on Isabel as an *exemplum*. In *The Prince*, where *exempla* of male rulers predominate, Machiavelli briefly discusses in Chapter 20 Caterina Sforza as a negative example of a ruler who mistakenly trusted in a fortress rather than the good will of her own people; their alliance with Cesare Borgia made her vulnerable to his attack. *The Discourses* includes another brief, but memorable, account of the widowed Sforza: the 'Madonna of Forlì' defended the citadel against attackers who had taken her children hostage and defied them by 'expos[ing] her sexual parts to them and said she was still capable of bearing more'.[17] Through this striking gesture, Machiavelli reduces Sforza to the fact of her sex and her reproductive function.

While Cary, unlike Machiavelli in his treatments of Sforza, emphasises Isabel's ability as a ruler, she nevertheless excoriates Isabel's lack of what she calls 'female pity' (72), just as she criticised Edward's ruthlessness when he executed his rebellious subjects. Edward's lapse is not only an ethical error but also a political one: 'So many excellent lives, so ingloriously lost, had been able to have commanded a victorious Army while it had triumpht in some forrain conquest' (73). By showing how both examples of 'Tyranny' bring about political consequences and contribute to the weakening of the ruler, Cary accomplishes a complex and multifaceted gendered critique of and intervention in Machiavellian political thought.

Despite these clear references to *The Prince*, the political thought developed in Cary's *History* owes more to Machiavelli's *Discourses*. For example, Cary criticises Edward for following his private will and not being bound by laws or considerations of the common good, in a manner that recalls Machiavelli's condemnation in the *Discourses* of tyrants, who 'forsaking virtuous deeds, considered that princes have nought else to do but to surpass other men in extravagance, lasciviousness, and every other form of licentiousness' (107). According to Machiavelli, such a state of affairs leads to a revolt of *la moltitudine* (the multitude) and *i potenti* (the powerful); the governments thus formed are legitimate as long as the people 'rule in accordance with the laws' and 'subordinate their own convenience to the common advantage', but they soon degenerate to 'avarice and ambition' (108).

[17] Niccolò Machiavelli, in Bernard Crick (ed.), *Discourses* (Harmondsworth, 1970), 419.

This devolution corresponds closely to the shift in Cary's representation of both Isabel and the people. Cary initially affirms the worth of the commons and the legitimacy of their grievance against Edward: 'The subjects sensible of the disorders of the Kingdom, and seeing into the advantage which promis'd a liberty of Reformation, make choice of such as for their wisdome and integrity deserv'd it' (58). Calling the commons a 'goodly body', Cary affirms their judgement against Spencer: '*Spencer* is, pointblanck charg'd with *Insolency, Injustice, Corruption, Oppression, neglect of the publick and immoderate advancement of his own particular*' (61). Yet she later becomes more critical of them as they become unruly and violent: 'But the actions of this same heady monster Multitude never examine the Justice, or the dependance, but are led by Passion and Opinion; which in fury leaves no Disorder inacted, and no Villainy unattempted' (122). The 'giddy Multitude, who scarcely know the civil grounds of Reason' (129), approves of Isabel's cruel actions towards Spencer, of which Cary is harshly critical, as we have seen. Cary further censures Parliament for committing 'Politick Treason' in deposing Edward:

> It ne're was toucht or exprest by what Law, Divine or Humane, the Subject might Depose, not an Elective King, but one that Lineally and Justly had inherited ... they had just cause to restrain [him] from his Errours, but no ground or colour to deprive him of his Kingdom. (131)

This apparently contradictory judgement of the commons is in keeping with Machiavelli's similar assessment of *la moltitudine*: they can be either benign when bounded by laws and the common good or maleficent if driven by passionate wilfulness and private ends. Interestingly, Machiavelli in the *Discourses* gives Herod's regret for the execution of Mariam as an example of 'reputedly wise princes [who] have put people to death and then wished them alive again' (253)—behaviour often attributed to and blamed on the masses by monarchists. Cary's *Tragedie of Mariam* (1613), indeed, features such a repentant Herod.

Machiavelli and Cary seek to level the monarch and the commons since both can be driven by will and unbounded by law: Cary even speaks of 'Royal Passions' as 'rebellious and masterless, having so unlimited a Power' whereby the monarch's 'Will becomes the Law; his hand the executioner of actions unjust and disorderly' (140). Cary's innovation, however, lies in linking the claims of a female subject in marriage, in this case Isabel, with the claims of the subjects. When Isabel appeals to her brother, the French king, for aid against Edward, she speaks in the name of a 'distressed kingdom', emphasising that ''tis not I alone unjustly suffer' (96). She shifts her allegiance from her husband the king to identify herself as a representative of the English people, who answer her 'intentions not ... to rifle, but reform the Kingdom', by 'com[ing] like Pigeons by whole flocks to her assistance' (118).

Machiavelli was a theorist of political division and civil war and it is entirely appropriate that not only Cary, but also Cavendish found his works useful to think with.[18] In

[18] The relationship between Cavendish and Machiavelli has been noted only obliquely and in passing. For example, Anna Battigelli states, 'I would [not] want to insist that ... Margaret Cavendish was

'Heaven's Library, which is Fames Palace purged from Errors and Vices', included in one of her earliest works, *Natures Pictures* (1656), Jove gives orders to 'purge and cleanse' the library of useless and harmful 'Records'.[19] While among the orators only Thucydides and Demosthenes would be preserved, among the 'Politicks only *Achitophell* and *Machiavell*' escape elimination (389). Cavendish's coupling of Machiavelli with Achitophel indicates that she considered Machiavelli to be a political counsellor whose wise counsel was unjustly impugned.

Cavendish also explicitly refers to Machiavelli in the first two plays included in her second volume of plays, published in 1668. In the *Sociable Companions; Or, the Female Wits* Will Fullwit is found reading '*Plutarch's* Lives, *Thucidides, Machiavel, Commineus, Lucan, Cæsars* Commentaries, and the like' (12, lines 14–16). The discussion concerning the usefulness of history that immediately follows (though presented ironically) reflects Cavendish's knowledge of Machiavelli's notion of exemplary history that informs his oeuvre, including *The Prince*; *The Discourses*, whose Preface discusses the importance of historical knowledge; and *The Florentine Histories*, which begins with the fall of the Roman Empire, the rise and fall of the Goths and the Longobards, and the ascendancy of Venice, Milan, Rome, and Naples.[20] In *The Presence* that follows, the second Gentleman states that '*Seneca* doth express Moral Virtues, and *Machiavillian* Policy better and more properly then Dramatic Poetry; and the Spectators will learn more in one day by reading their Works ... then by seeing forty Plays'; he thus notably associates Machiavelli's 'Policy' with Seneca's 'Moral Virtues', and promotes both as worthy sources of instruction (2, lines 15–19).[21]

In the *Orations* (1662), a privy counsellor paraphrases Machiavelli's well-known question concerning whether a prince should govern through love or fear: 'But when [the people] Fear their Sovereign, they are Obedient; for it is impossible to Work upon their Good Nature, as to make them Obey through Love and Good Will'.[22] However, since Cavendish's practice in the *Orations* is to argue both sides of the question, and

unfamiliar on some level with the political thought of Machiavelli'. See Battigelli, *Margaret Cavendish and the Exiles of the Mind* (Lexington, KY, 1998), 147n.

19 Margaret Cavendish, *Natures Pictures Drawn by Fancies Pencil to the Life* (London, 1656), 358.

20 Ironic, because these were the very texts that Cavendish read and used in writing her works, by contrast to the literal-minded interlocutors who agree that reading history is useless: 'Why such Books, since you are neither *Greek* nor *Roman*? So that those Histories, or Historians of other Nations will not benefit thee'(12, lines 17–19); 'what are their Wars, or Peace to us, unless the same Cause, the same Places, and the same Men, were again in our time?' (13, lines 1–3). We may detect an ironic echo of Machiavelli's critique of those who fail to see the relevance of history: 'as though heaven, the sun, the elements, and men had changed the order of their motions and power, and were different from what they were in ancient times' (*Discourses*, Preface to Book I, 105).

21 In *The Second Part of the Lady Contemplation*, in the *Plays* (1662), Cavendish's heroine significantly affirms the necessity of 'policy': 'for without policy (which is deceit) there can be neither government in peace or war: wherefore it is a vertue in a States-man, or a Commander, to be a dissembler' (222, lines 42–4).

22 Margaret Cavendish, *Orations of Divers Sorts Accommodated to Divers Places* (London, 1662), 116–17.

since she on various occasions has levelled critiques at the monarch, it is by no means certain that she endorses this view. In fact, in another oration, a king, who claims to be 'a Loving Father' to his people, distances himself from a 'Tyrant, that had rather be Fear'd than Loved' by his subjects (130).

In 'Of Queen Elizabeth' in *The Worlds Olio* (1655), though not explicitly naming Machiavelli, Cavendish strikingly describes Elizabeth I's rule referring to his coupling of the lion and the fox and alluding to his recommendation in *The Prince* of the art of dissimulation in order to maintain rule:

> Queen *Elizabeth* reigned long and happy; and though she cloathed her self in a Sheeps skin, yet she had a Lions paw, and a Foxes head; she strokes the Cheeks of her Subjects with Flattery, whilst she picks their Purses; and though she seemed loth, yet she never failed to crush to death those that disturbed her waies.[23]

This rather disquieting portrait of Elizabeth, who was celebrated during the English Civil Wars by the Parliamentarians as a populist queen, is closer to the assessment of modern historians who consider her to have been adept at manipulating Parliament with her masterful rhetorical performance. Despite the general condemnation of such Machiavellian statecraft, Cavendish does not unequivocally condemn the stratagems Elizabeth used in order to maintain her 'long and happy' rule. Her aphoristic account achieves a dialogical effect: the reader is asked *either* to condemn Elizabeth in following the general negative assessment of Machiavelli, *or* to re-evaluate Machiavelli in light of Elizabeth's successful reign. If, as a result, readers are led to acknowledge the soundness of Machiavellian statecraft, they will in fact have accepted a notion of a ruler's *virtù* that is not by any stretch in accordance with Christian virtues.[24]

Cavendish followed Machiavelli in valuing the authority of history. She also agreed with Machiavelli on the importance of deliberative rhetoric and eloquence; she championed the rule of law and the common good against particular interest. In addition, like Machiavelli, she opposed tyranny, and valued mixed government as conducive to the most stable and well-ordered polity. Her *Orations* exemplify the value she placed on political deliberations in which the citizenry participated. Finally, Cavendish even shares Machiavelli's scepticism about religion, which he considers to have been used by political leaders as a tool to manipulate the people, in keeping with her acceptance of Machiavellian *virtù* that contravenes Christian virtues.

Cavendish's oft-noted pursuit of 'Fame' has not, however, been considered as another instance of her transgression of the Christian framework of values. In 'A Dedication to Fortune' in *The Worlds Olio*, Cavendish calls Fortune a 'Powerfull Princess', though she considers her to be an ally rather than an adversary as Machiavelli does:

[23] Margaret Cavendish, *The Worlds Olio* (London, 1655), 126.

[24] Cavendish uses the phrase 'Reason of State'—associated with Machiavelli through the title of Giovanni Botero's attack on Machiavelli, *Della ragion di stato* (1589)—in *Sociable Letters*, Letter 75.

> if Fortune please, with her helping hand, she may place my Book in Fames high Tow'r, where... the whole Volume, like a Cannon Bullet, shall Eccho from Side to Side of Fames large Brasen Walls, and make so loud a Report, that all the World shall hear it. (sig. A)

Together with the invocation of Fortune, her notable use of military imagery to represent 'Fame' calls to mind Machiavelli's *virtù* that brings honour and glory to its possessor—a this-worldly reward whose pursuit would be questionable from a Christian perspective. In fact, Cavendish nowhere mentions providence, which before Machiavelli was equated or closely associated with Fortune. While Cavendish followed Christine de Pizan in imagining a future readership, her affirmation of her own 'Fame' renders her in this instance closer to Machiavelli than to Christine, who posited the afterlife of her works as a means of providing useful counsel to future rulers.

The most important parallel with Machiavelli, perhaps, is Cavendish's oft-noted use of dialogism and contradiction—between contiguous orations, but also between the paratexts and the texts themselves, giving rise to scholarly debate about her position—much as Machiavelli's contradictory promotion of principalities and republics in *The Prince* and *The Discourses* has given rise to disagreement about his political thought. As she herself states in the *Sociable Letters* (1664), 'for my Orations for the most part are Declamations wherein I speak *Pro* and *Con*, and Determine nothing'.[25] According to Maurizio Viroli, Machiavelli 'wrote as an orator'; Viroli considers *The Prince* and *The Discourses* as 'two exemplary texts of political rhetoric', not a contradiction, a 'puzzle' that needs to be deciphered.[26] In discussing political 'turbulence and disorder', Machiavelli, quoting Cicero, also expressed his confidence that 'the people ... are capable of appreciating the truth' (*Discourses*, 119, 120); and that because of 'the people's capacity of judging of things, it is exceedingly rare that, when they hear two orators of equal talents advocate different measures, they do not decide in favour of the best of the two; which proves their ability to discern the truth of what they hear' (*Discourses*, 263). Cavendish may have hoped for similar discernment from her readers.

JEAN BODIN

Although Jean Bodin is largely considered to have been a proponent of absolutism in the history of political thought, he was, in fact, respected as a political thinker by both royalists and Parliamentarians during the English Civil Wars. Among royalists, Robert Filmer published extracts from Knolles' translation of *Six Books* as *The Necessity of the*

[25] Margaret Cavendish, *CCXI Sociable Letters* (London, 1664), sig. C2.

[26] Maurizio Viroli, *Machiavelli* (Oxford, 1998), 3.

Absolute Powers of All Kings: And in Particular of the Kings of England (1648); and among Parliamentarians, Henry Parker and William Prynne referred to Bodin in their works.[27]

In *The Elements of the Law, Natural and Politic* (1640) Hobbes cited Bodin on the indivisibility of sovereignty. Although Cavendish, whose husband William was Hobbes' patron, never explicitly refers to Bodin, I suggest that we can discern her engagement with Bodin in 'The She-Anchoret', included in *Natures Pictures*. In this tale, which Cavendish recommended in particular to her readers in the volume's preface, many men seek out the She-Anchoret for her wisdom. One of the questions concerns the optimal form of the polity among monarchy, aristocracy, and democracy. After weighing the advantages and disadvantages of each, the She-Anchoret concludes that monarchy is the least of all evils, preferring a tyrant to a 'factious Councel' (370). Cavendish thus gives voice to a demystifying pragmatism that endorses the lesser of evils. In this mode of deliberation and in the conclusion she reaches, Cavendish echoes Bodin's Book 6, Chapter 4: 'A Comparison of three lawfull Commonweales, that is, a popular estate, an Aristocraticall, and a royall; and that a royall Monarchie is the best' (700). At the same time, Cavendish slyly counters Bodin's misogyny—for example, in likening democracy to a 'strumpet' (704)—by making her protagonist an anchoret. As I discussed in the beginning of this chapter, Bodin defended Salic law, on the basis of women's unsuitability to engage in 'mens publicke actions and affaires'. Cavendish refutes such an assumption of women's disability by having men seek the opinions of the She-Anchoret on the optimal form of the polity. Cavendish returns to this question in the *Orations*: having different speakers argue in support of each, she declines to make a final assessment and leaves the matter open-ended. In doing so, Cavendish anticipates J. H. M. Salmon's uncertainty concerning the legacy of Bodin: whether he wrote in support of 'absolutism, populism, or constitutionalism'.[28]

In Anne Clifford's case, we have no extant evidence of her having read Bodin, for his is not among the many books represented in the Great Picture; neither is a copy of his work among those that have survived with her distinctive markings and annotations.[29] I will nevertheless suggest that this absence of Bodin does not preclude the possibility of Clifford's engagement with his work, following Pierre Macherey's emphasis on the significance of silence and the unsaid.[30]

[27] Glenn Burgess, 'Bodin in the English Revolution', in Howell A. Lloyd (ed.), *The Reception of Bodin* (Leiden, 2013), 387–407.

[28] J. H. M. Salmon, 'The Legacy of Jean Bodin: Absolutism, Populism, or Constitutionalism?' *History of Political Thought*, 17 (1996), 500–22.

[29] See Leah Knight, 'Lady Anne Clifford', in Joseph L. Black (ed.), *Private Libraries in Renaissance England, ix* (Tempe, AZ, 2017), 348–63; and Ch. 9 in this volume, Knight, 'Libraries Not their Own: Networking Women's Books and Reading in Early Modern England'.

[30] Pierre Macherey, in Geoffrey Wall (trans.), *A Theory of Literary Production* (London, 1978), 85–9. On methodological questions raised by the different kinds of evidence concerning Clifford's reading, see Leah Knight, 'Reading Proof: Or, Problems and Possibilities in the Text Life of Anne Clifford', in Leah Knight, Micheline White, and Elizabeth Sauer (eds), *Women's Bookscapes in Early Modern Britain: Reading, Ownership, Circulation* (Ann Arbor, MI, 2018), 253–73.

Clifford read and marked a number of books on political subjects, such as *The Mirror for Magistrates* (1610), John Selden's *Titles of Honor* (1631), and Anthony Weldon's *The Court and Character of King James* (1651). We can discern the reason why she read these books with special attention. For example, her enthusiastic assent to the depiction of James and his courtiers as corrupt and decadent in the *Court and Character* is in keeping with her anger and resentment over the prominent role James played in attempting to compel her to forfeit her inheritance for a cash settlement; her refusal made it possible for her to inherit the titles and lands forty years later, when her uncle's male line failed.[31]

Selden's *Titles of Honor*, which Clifford read repeatedly, as indicated by the various layers of her distinctive marks, was of interest especially for its presentation of the prerogatives and duties of those who held the baronial title, as suggested in the marked passages concerning the barons' revolt against King John and the signing of the Magna Carta.[32] Selden does not confine his discussion of the 'titles of honor' to England: Clifford marks a passage in which he discusses the Byzantine princess Anna Komnene: 'Lady *Anna Comnena*, daughter to the Emperor *Alexius* ... stiled ... *Queen*, in the title of her *Alexiados*' (27). Komnene's example resonated with Clifford because she also claimed title and sovereignty from her father, whose account of his voyages to the West Indies she commissioned and whose biography she included in the Great Book. Clifford's abiding interest in questions of inheritance can be gleaned in her underlining 'Of feminine Titles, some are immediately Created in Women' and 'others are Transmitted to them from their Ancestors'. However, she leaves unmarked between the two marked passages, 'some are Communicated by their Husbands'—to which she paradoxically calls attention (876) (see Figure 32.1) This conspicuously unmarked passage, I suggest, represents an analogue to Clifford's reading and rejection of Bodin's *Six Books*, which is not included among the books depicted in the Great Picture.[33]

Clifford did state in her 'Knole Diary' that she was reading 'the Turkish History', another book translated by Knolles, *The Generall Historie of the Turkes* (1603).[34] I believe the absence of Knolles' Bodin in the Great Picture is analogous to that of Holinshed and Shakespeare, which she read but found objectionable. Their absence, especially notable

[31] A[nthony] W[eldon], *The Court and Character of King James, and the King of Court Charles* (London, 1651), 124–5, *passim*. Clifford's copy, which she read in June 1669, is held by the Kendal Archive Centre (WDHOTH/1/22).

[32] John Selden, *Titles of Honor* (London, 1631), 209, 213. Clifford's copy, which she read in February–March 1638, is held by the Folger Shakespeare Library (STC 22178, copy 3). See Georgianna Ziegler, 'Lady Anne Clifford Reads John Selden', in Katherine Acheson (ed.), *Early Modern Marginalia*. New York, 2019: 134–54.

[33] Leah Knight characterises Clifford as 'an extremely critical' and a 'resistant' reader from the evidence of her reading three books—all from France—that were considered seditious or were banned; 'Reading Across Borders: The Case of Anne Clifford's "Popish" Books', *Journal of the Canadian Historical Association*, 25.2 (2014), 27–57, 46.

[34] Anne Clifford, in Jessica Malay (ed.), *Anne Clifford's Autobiographical Writing, 1590–1676* (Manchester, 2018), 32.

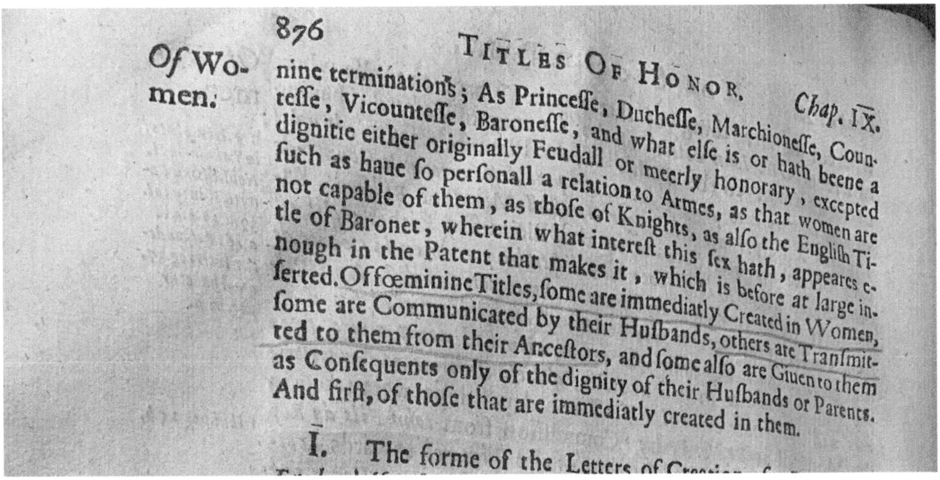

876 TITLES OF HONOR. Chap. IX.

Of Women.

nine terminations; As Princeſſe, Ducheſſe, Marchioneſſe, Counteſſe, Vicounteſſe, Baroneſſe, and what elſe is or hath beene a dignitie either originally Feudall or meerly honorary, excepted ſuch as haue ſo perſonall a relation to Armes, as that women are not capable of them, as thoſe of Knights, as alſo the Engliſh Title of Baronet, wherein what intereſt this ſex hath, appeares enough in the Patent that makes it, which is before at large inſerted. Of fœminine Titles, ſome are immediatly Created in Women, ſome are Communicated by their Huſbands, others are Tranſmitted to them from their Anceſtors, and ſome alſo are Giuen to them as Conſequents only of the dignity of their Huſbands or Parents. And firſt, of thoſe that are immediatly created in them.

I. The forme of the Letters

FIGURE 32.1 John Selden, *Titles of Honor* (1631), 876. STC 22178, copy 3. Photography by Mihoko Suzuki, from the collection of Folger Shakespeare Library.

since the books pictured include many histories as well as Chaucer, Sidney, and Spenser, stems from Clifford's dissatisfaction with their representation of John Clifford. She pointedly contests their account of her ancestor's ruthless killing of the twelve-year-old Edmund, the earl of Rutland; she instead claims, correctly, that Edmund must have been a youth of seventeen when he met his death on the battlefield.[35]

Given Clifford's keen interest in sovereignty over her baronial estates, as indicated in her marks in *Titles of Honor*, it is a strong possibility that she also read Knolles' Bodin; Clifford would have considered Bodin's affirmation of undivided sovereignty not only of 'commonweales' but of baronies as buttressing her own sovereignty in Westmorland. However, Clifford would have strenuously objected to Bodin's affirmation of Salic law, which proscribed female sovereignty and its transmission through the female line. To this end, Bodin argues that a collateral male, however distant, should inherit sovereignty rather than a much closer female. Bodin's prescribed course exactly corresponds to the manner in which Clifford was disinherited by her father, who chose his brother as heir. Although we do not have explicit evidence of Clifford's ownership or reading of Bodin, either in the Great Picture or through an extant copy with her annotations, I suggest that her negative assessment of Bodin can be gleaned from the absence of his volume from the Great Picture—analogous to the similar absence of Hall, Holinshed, and Shakespeare as well as the line she left unmarked in Selden.

[35] Anne Clifford, in Jessica Malay (ed.), *Anne Clifford's Great Books of Record* (Manchester, 2015), 512. A 1684 manuscript inventory of books in Appleby Castle includes Holinshed but neither Bodin nor Shakespeare; the inventory, however, is incomplete, since some of the books depicted in the Great Picture are not listed. See Malay, 'Reassessing Anne Clifford's Books: The Discovery of a New Manuscript Inventory,' *Papers of the Bibliographical Society of America*, 115.1 (2011), 1–41, 21.

CONCLUSION

The women writers I have discussed in this chapter give evidence of their ambition as political thinkers in their engagement with a variety of theorists from beyond the borders of England. Cary, who used the genre of history—an accepted form for political writing, as evidenced in Bacon's *History of Henry VII* (1622)—refers to Machiavelli, but not explicitly to Christine de Pizan, perhaps because she sought to avoid writing from a female subject position; her success in doing so is evidenced in her *History of Edward II* being attributed to her husband when it was published. Nevertheless, her gendered subject position can be gleaned from her revisionary portrayal of Isabel as a Machiavellian ruler. Unlike Cary, Cavendish wrote concerning politics in forms that do not explicitly announce themselves to be political, such as plays and fiction. Nevertheless, she makes multiple references to Machiavelli, and her portrait of Queen Elizabeth, though it does not refer explicitly to Machiavelli, reveals her complex engagement with his political thought as well as with his reception by her contemporaries.

As in the case of Cary using Christine without naming her, Cavendish's oblique use and Anne Clifford's silent rejection of Bodin need to be carefully teased out. In discussing the reception of Bodin during the English Revolution, Glenn Burgess considers writers to have engaged with their predecessors in a variety of ways: for the purposes of this chapter, the most relevant of these are the invocation of a predecessor as an authority or icon, and the use of the earlier work as a source of creative appropriation or adaptation.[36] The women writers examined here engage with prior political thinkers more obliquely than their male counterparts, who tend to invoke them explicitly as an authority or icon. Such engagement is often revisionary and creative, corresponding most closely to Burgess' mode of reception by 'those least likely to be expected'—such as Parliamentary writers' use of Bodin.[37] But even Parliamentarians such as Prynne and Parker named Bodin, while Cavendish pointedly did not, although she was clearly thinking with Bodin. I suggest that women writers often adopt this type of oblique, revisionary, and creative reception and engagement because of their inability as women to claim a direct genealogical descent from male thinkers. However, their exclusion from the polity and the largely patriarchal tradition of political thinkers—with the exception of Christine de Pizan—did not foreclose their active engagement with these thinkers, even from beyond the borders of England. Following the example of Christine de Pizan who characterised herself as '*seulette à part*' (a lone woman on the side)—a phrase that applies also to Cavendish's She-Anchoret—early modern women writers diverged from or questioned the authority of male political theorists who preceded them, intervening critically and creatively in the history of political thought.

[36] Burgess, 'Bodin', 389–91.

[37] Burgess, 'Bodin', 401–2.

FURTHER READING

Bodin, Jean. In Julian H. Franklin (ed.), *On Sovereignty*. Cambridge, 1992.

Falco, Maria J. (ed.). *Feminist Interpretations of Niccolò Machiavelli*. University Park, 2004.

Forhan, Kate Langdon. *The Political Theory of Christine de Pizan*. Aldershot, 2002.

Green, Karen, and Jacqueline Broad. *A History of Women's Political Thought in Europe, 1400–1700*. Cambridge, 2008.

Pizan, Christine de. In Kate Langdon Forhan (trans. and ed.), *The Book of the Body Politic*, Cambridge, 1994.

Pizan, Christine de. In Karen Green, Constant J. Mews, and Janice Pinder (trans. and ed.), *The Book of Peace*. University Park, 2008.

Suzuki, Mihoko. 'Political Writing across Borders', in Patricia Phillippy (ed.), *A History of Early Modern Women's Writing*. Cambridge, 2018, 364–81.

Suzuki, Mihoko. 'Women's Political Writing: Civil War Memoirs', in Amanda Capern (ed.), *Routledge History of Women in Early Modern Europe*. New York, 2019, 287–308.

Suzuki, Mihoko. *Antigone's Example: Women's Political Writing in Times of Civil War from Christine de Pizan to Helen Maria Williams*. New York, 2022.

PART V

NETWORKS AND COMMUNITIES

CHAPTER 33

NETWORKED AUTHORSHIP IN ENGLISH CONVENTS ABROAD

The Writings of Lucy Knatchbull

JAIME GOODRICH

In 1622, Abbess Mary Percy of the English Benedictine convent in Brussels faced a dilemma: her house's controversies over spiritual direction had become known among English Catholics abroad and at home, yet she did not know how the dissidents' complaints had reached the public. In search of answers, Percy inspected the cell belonging to Lucy Knatchbull and reported the surprising results to her superior, the archbishop of Mechelen-Brussels: 'I found in one of the celes of a pri[n]cipal officer divers letters ... in cifers'.[1] As the house's cellarer and depositary (officers in charge of supplies and finances, respectively), Knatchbull had frequent opportunities for contact with the outside world that facilitated the exchange of coded letters. (On ciphers, see this volume, Chapter 37, Nadine Akkerman, 'Women's Letters and Cryptological Coteries'.) Percy suspected that she was corresponding with Toby Matthew (a Jesuit priest who, without Percy's knowledge, was providing Knatchbull with spiritual advice), but the confiscated letters disappeared before Percy could decipher them. Although the case of Knatchbull's encrypted letters is extreme, it illustrates the porousness of enclosure within the convents founded by Englishwomen on the Continent during the seventeenth century. These institutions might appear to have been isolated outposts with little connection to the outside world, but historians and literary scholars have already demonstrated that the Continental cloisters were important hubs for English Catholics. James Kelly has shown that familial and patronage networks in England played major roles in convent recruitment, while Claire Walker has explored how these cloisters

[1] Mechelen, Archdiocesan Archives of Mechelen-Brussels [hereafter AAMB], Engelse Benedictinessen/12.2, Mary Percy to Jacobus Boonen, December 1622.

developed their own patronage systems.[2] Extensive analysis of the political activities of English nuns, especially Benedictines, has revealed their active participation in royalist and Jacobite circles.[3] Letters in particular have offered tantalising evidence of nuns' roles within familial, literary, and textual networks, while also providing material for quantitative network analysis.[4] Extending the critical conversation about cloistered networks, this chapter analyses the interrelationship between Knatchbull's networks and her textual production in order to demonstrate the ways that cloistered authorship was a networked phenomenon.

KNATCHBULL'S LIFE AND WRITINGS

Lucy Knatchbull was one of several charismatic Englishwomen who helped found convents on the Continent specifically for women of their nation during the seventeenth century. Born into the Catholic gentry in 1584 and named Elizabeth by her parents, she left England in 1604 to become a postulant at the English Benedictine cloister in Brussels.[5] The Brussels foundation was then the only English cloister in the Low Countries, but Knatchbull was probably also attracted to this house because of its close ties to Jesuit priests, who heard confessions, provided spiritual guidance, and offered the Spiritual Exercises (a highly popular programme of guided meditations).[6]

[2] James E. Kelly, *English Convents in Catholic Europe, c 1600–1800* (Cambridge, 2020), 21–50; Claire Walker, *Gender and Politics in Early Modern Europe: English Convents in France and the Low Countries* (New York, 2003), 102–29.

[3] Laurence Lux-Sterritt, *English Benedictine Nuns in Exile in the Seventeenth Century: Living Spirituality* (Manchester, 2017), 123–8; Claire Walker, '"When God shall Restore them to their Kingdoms": Nuns, Exiled Stuarts and English Catholic Identity, 1688–1745', in Sarah Apetrei and Hannah Smith (eds), *Religion and Women in Britain, c 1600–1760* (Farnham, 2014), 79–97; Claire Walker, 'Crumbs of News: Early Modern English Nuns and Royalist Intelligence Networks', *Journal of Medieval and Early Modern Studies*, 42 (2012), 635–55; Claire Walker, 'Loyal and Dutiful Subjects: English Nuns and Stuart Politics', in James Daybell (ed.), *Women and Politics in Early Modern England, 1450–1700* (Farnham, 2004), 228–42; Claire Walker, 'Prayer, Patronage, and Political Conspiracy: English Nuns and the Restoration', *The Historical Journal*, 43 (2000), 1–23; Caroline Bowden, 'The Abbess and Mrs. Brown: Lady Mary Knatchbull and Royalist Politics in Flanders in the Late 1650s', *Recusant History*, 24 (1999), 288–308.

[4] Victoria Van Hyning, *Convent Autobiography: Early Modern English Nuns in Exile* (Oxford, 2019), 37–82; Emilie K. M. Murphy, 'Language and Power in an English Convent in Exile, *c* 1621–1631', *The Historical Journal*, 62 (2019), 101–25; Bronagh Ann McShane, 'Visualising the Reception and Circulation of Early Modern Nuns' Letters', *Journal of Historical Network Research*, 2 (2018), 1–25; Jenna Lay, *Beyond the Cloister: Catholic Englishwomen and Early Modern Literary Culture* (Philadelphia, PA, 2016), 120–42; Claire Walker, '"Doe not Supose me a Well Mortifyed Nun Dead to the World": Letter-Writing in Early Modern English Convents', in James Daybell (ed.), *Early Modern Women's Letter Writing* (Basingstoke, 2001), 159–76.

[5] See Caroline Bowden, 'Knatchbull, Elizabeth [name in religion Lucy] (1584–1629), *ODNB*; Toby Matthew, in David Knowles (ed.), *The Life of Lady Lucy Knatchbull* (London, 1931).

[6] On the Jesuits and the Brussels house, see Jaime Goodrich, 'Authority, Gender, and Monastic Piety: Controversies at the English Benedictine Convent in Brussels, 1620–1623', *British Catholic History*, 33

When rumours circulated in early 1609 that Jesuit priests would no longer be allowed to work closely with the Brussels nuns, Knatchbull and several other postulants unsuccessfully attempted to found a new monastery in Louvain. She returned to Brussels shortly thereafter, taking the veil and the name Lucy in December 1609 and making her final vows in 1611. When internal dissension over Jesuit influence at Brussels recurred during the early 1620s, Knatchbull and a few other Brussels nuns established a new cloister in Ghent. After being elected in 1624 as the first abbess at Ghent, Knatchbull served in this capacity until her death in 1629. Under her leadership and with the assistance of English Jesuits, the Ghent cloister flourished and became the pre-eminent English Benedictine convent on the Continent. Abbess Mary Knatchbull, Knatchbull's niece, would later create filiations at Boulogne (1652), Dunkirk (1662), and Ypres (1665), cannily extending her aunt's legacy at a time when the Ghent foundation experienced financial exigency.

Despite her historical importance, few of Knatchbull's writings survive today except for a few texts in common genres of convent writing: financial accounts, letters, and spiritual accounts. As her death notice observes, some of her spiritual works were 'lent and so lost' during her lifetime while 'others through her humility she caused to be burn[ed] before her Death'.[7] In his biography of Knatchbull, Toby Matthew further explains:

> when she grew near her death she called one of her Religious to her ... whom not only she earnestly desired, but expressly also required, to go towards such a Cabinet, and to take out all those Papers which she should find there, and so cast them presently into the fire. All which the other instantly did, with a great deale of exact and humble obedience.[8]

By destroying her own writing, Knatchbull displayed a stringent understanding of humility, an important component of Benedictine piety. For example, the Benedictine Rule states that the eleventh degree of humility requires 'the Religious to refraine her toung from speaking'.[9] Although Knatchbull was apparently content to lend her texts to outsiders, she did not wish her posthumous reputation within the convent to rest on her textual production. Significantly, Knatchbull's obituary omits a third category of works: those written for outsiders, such as letters. The archives of the archdiocese of Mechelen-Brussels contain one set of financial accounts and a handful of letters in Knatchbull's hand, all of which date from her final years at Brussels. Meanwhile, Matthew preserved twenty-three of her spiritual writings in his biography, which was prepared for publication but remained in manuscript: an autobiography, two contemplations, four

(2016), 91–114; and Jaime Goodrich, *Faithful Translators: Authorship, Gender, and Religion in Early Modern England* (Evanston, IL, 2014), 154–7.

7 'Obituary Notices of the Nuns of the English Benedictine Abbey of Ghent in Flanders 1627–1811', *Miscellanea XI* (London, 1917), 11.

8 Matthew, *Life*, 50. All further citations of this work will be parenthetical.

9 *The Rule of the Most Blissed Father Saint Benedict* (Ghent, 1632), 38. On the relationship between Benedictine humility and writing, see Jaime Goodrich, '"Low and plain stile": Poetry and Piety in English Benedictine Convents, 1600–1800', *British Catholic History*, 33 (2019), 599–618.

spiritual accounts, six letters sent to him between 1619 and 1622, and ten spiritual accounts composed between 1624 and 1629 for William Vincent, confessor of the Ghent Benedictines. Our knowledge of Knatchbull as an author has thus been made possible by the preservation of her writings within an external network largely constituted of priests and ecclesiastical officials. Members of this network did much more than simply circulate and safeguard Knatchbull's texts: they mediated her writings through secondary forms of authorship such as translation and editing. Like texts by other early modern women writers, Knatchbull's works thus remain available to us today because male contemporaries deemed them worthy to be read, particularly as exemplary models of female piety.

KNATCHBULL AND HER TRANSLATORS

Knatchbull's letters to Jacobus Boonen, archbishop of Mechelen-Brussels, provide a glimpse into the ways that nuns collaborated with male agents to create and exploit textual networks. As the ground-breaking scholarship of Emilie K. M. Murphy has revealed, monolingualism posed serious problems for English convents on the Continent, which were generally under the jurisdiction of local superiors who had limited or non-existent familiarity with English. Needing to communicate with these superiors both by letter and in person during visitations, English nuns either learned the local language or relied on translators (whether other nuns or male outsiders).[10] The situation was further complicated by the nuns' varying levels of linguistic competence (see this volume, Chapter 27, Brenda Hosington, '"Mistresses of tongues"'). While some women religious read and even translated foreign language texts into English, they did not necessarily feel capable of writing original works in a different tongue and consequently used translators.[11] As Murphy has noted, although reliance on translators created 'a complex collaborative authorial process', the translator's agency was always subordinate to that of the original writer: 'the agency of the female authors was not outweighed by the presence of male translators as the authorial role of the female religious was clearly distinguished'.[12] Indeed, members of the Brussels convent selected translators who sympathised with their perspective and could be trusted to convey their words accurately.[13] While Knatchbull knew some French, she generally wrote to the

[10] See Murphy, 'Language and Power', as well as Emilie K. M. Murphy, 'Exile and Linguistic Encounter: Early Modern English Convents in the Low Countries and France', *Renaissance Quarterly*, 73 (2020), 132–64.

[11] Jaime Goodrich, 'Translating Lady Mary Percy: Authorship and Authority among the Brussels Benedictines', in Caroline Bowden and James E. Kelly (eds), *The English Convents in Exile, 1600–1800: Communities, Culture and Identity* (Farnham, 2013), 114–15.

[12] Murphy, 'Language and Power', 111.

[13] Murphy, 'Language and Power', 120–3; McShane, 'Visualising the Reception', 14–17; Goodrich, 'Translating Lady Mary Percy', 111.

archbishop in English and depended on translators to render her letters into French or Latin. Close analysis of these translations demonstrates the ways that Knatchbull and members of the convent's network successfully collaborated to oust confessor Francis Ward from the Brussels house in 1623.

The earliest extant communication from Knatchbull in the archbishop's papers dates from 1619, when she prepared the house's accounts for inspection in her dual capacity as cellarer and depositary. Gabriel Colford, the father of a Brussels nun and the house's procurator (or financial manager), served then as the convent's primary translator, and he annotated Knatchbull's accounts with French translations.[14] Since this manuscript also includes an undated French list of the house's income in Knatchbull's hand, it seems likely that Knatchbull had some knowledge of the language but did not feel competent to translate most of her accounts, which would have required a considerable vocabulary relating to domestic goods.[15] Colford has also added an English comment of his own, which he translated for the archbishop:

> In this calculation nothing is sett downe for the doctor barbour potticary and his drugges. Nor for soape. Neyther for what is spent by the carpenter mason, Joyner glasier locksmyth etts[etera] yearely for mending making and altering of thinges in the house; nor what is spent in other necessary implements and househould stuffe ... nor alsoe what is spent in ornaments or otherwise for the churche and sacristie. Coales.[16]

This note demonstrates the authorial power Colford wielded in his capacity as intermediary between Knatchbull and the ecclesiastical authorities. By indicating that this document does not provide a complete reckoning of the nuns' expenses, Colford suggests that the archbishop might want to further investigate the house's finances. While Colford does not undermine Knatchbull's authority, he nonetheless possesses a supplemental power of his own in order to influence the way that the archbishop viewed the nuns' financial health.

As a clash over spiritual direction boiled over in 1623, Knatchbull sought out new translators who shared her pro-Jesuit views.[17] A secular confessor named Francis Ward had infringed on the prerogatives of Jesuit priests at the convent, which led Knatchbull, John Daniel (a secular priest), and John Norton, SJ (Knatchbull's brother) to contend that he was seducing a nun named Mary Phillips in order to secure his ouster from the convent.[18] Knatchbull conveyed these explosive allegations in a detailed letter to Boonen dated 16 May 1623, which Daniel then translated into Latin. Comparison of the English and Latin versions reveals that Daniel reworked Knatchbull's text in order to make it

[14] AAMB, Engelse Benedictinessen/12.1, Accounts, 1620–1623. On Colford, see Murphy, 'Language and Power', 108–9, 120–1.

[15] AAMB, Engelse Benedictinessen/12.1, Accounts, 1620–1623.

[16] AAMB, Engelse Benedictinessen/12.1, Accounts, 1620–1623.

[17] AAMB, Engelse Benedictinessen/12.1, Lucy Knatchbull to Jacobus Boonen.

[18] Goodrich, 'Authority, Gender', 102–11.

more rhetorically effective. Knatchbull claimed that Ward used kisses as a special love token: 'to shew his love to her he kissed her before they parted'.[19] Daniel emphasises Ward's intentionality in kissing Phillips by inserting a new clause that mentioned Ward's desire to do so: 'ut amorem nunc suum in illam ostenderet, *voluit ab ea osculum sumere*, quod et sumpsit antequam discederet' (now to show his love towards her, *he wished to take a kiss from her*, which he also took before he left; my emphasis).[20] Similarly, Daniel underscores Phillips' vulnerability to such advances. Knatchbull observes that 'the pore creature ... is so weake, that when she faleth into the ocasion she hath not the strenght to resist the evill it draws her into'. By translating 'weake' with the doublet 'adeo infirma est, et adeo parum sui potens' (she is so weak and so little in control of herself), Daniel reinforces Phillips' spiritual frailty. Finally, Knatchbull concludes with a postscript seeking Ward's removal: 'it is earnestly desired of many that your Lordshipe would dismiss him'. Daniel moves this material into the body of the letter itself, situating it as the final paragraph and conveying Knatchbull's request more pointedly: '*tam meo quam aliarum nomine etiam atque etiam obtestor*, ut Dominum Wardium *quam primum* hinc dignetur amovere' (*both in my name and the name of others I urgently beseech* that it may be thought worthy to remove Master Ward from here *as soon as possible*; my emphasis). Daniel highlights Knatchbull's agency by rendering a passive construction ('it is earnestly desired') as an active verb (*obtestor*; I beseech), referencing Knatchbull's 'name' ('meo ... nomine'; my name), and emphasising her role as a representative of the convent ('aliarum nomine'; in the name of others). He also draws attention to the urgency of the situation by adding the phrase 'quam primum' (as soon as possible). While Knatchbull provided the raw content for the Latin version, Daniel's translation supports her goal of removing Ward in two ways. First, he heightens the dangers posed by Ward in ways that encourage immediate action. Second, he enhances Knatchbull's authority to demonstrate her credibility as a reliable witness and spokesperson for the convent.

Letters sent by Daniel and Norton to Boonen shed further light on Knatchbull's place within a pro-Jesuit network that linked priests with members of the Brussels house. On 31 March 1623, Daniel wrote to Boonen about Ward's problematic behaviour. He had intended to speak to the archbishop in person, 'in nomine sororis Patris Nortoni Dominae Luciae Knatchbull, quae mihi rem totam communicavit nuper' (in the name of the sister of Father Norton, Dame Lucy Knatchbull, who recently communicated the whole matter to me).[21] However, seeing that the archbishop was busy, Daniel instead sent a written summary of Knatchbull's 'urgens ac festinum ... votum quod mihi serio commendaverat, ut significarem quamprimum' (urgent and hasty petition ... which she earnestly entrusted to me so that I should make it known as soon as possible). This communication set the stage for Knatchbull's letter in May by stating that Ward was drawing his face very close to Phillips, 'deosculaturo similis' (like someone about to kiss). Yet from the perspective of networks, what is most remarkable about this letter is

[19] AAMB, Engelse Benedictinessen/12.1, Knatchbull to Boonen, 16 May 1623.
[20] All translations are my own.
[21] AAMB, Engelse Benedictinessen/12.1, John Daniel to Boonen, 31 March 1623.

its treatment of Knatchbull. Daniel first introduces her in terms of biological kinship, as the sister of Norton, a priest well known to the archbishop. He then identifies her as the source of the information contained in the letter while also situating himself in a subordinate role as the bearer of her 'votum' (petition). Making a final intervention that led to Ward's dismissal, Norton himself sent a short missive to Boonen on 21 October 1623 with an urgent message that Ward was preparing to run away with Phillips.[22] Norton concluded by stating that Knatchbull had provided him with this information and was willing to share more with the archbishop in person: 'Domina Lucia ex ore ipsius Mariae Illustrissimae et Reverendissimae Dominationi Vestrae narrabit omnia meque interpretem desiderat' (Dame Lucy will tell Your Most Illustrious and Right Reverend Lordship everything from the lips of Mary herself, and she desires me as an interpreter). Like Daniel, Norton assumes a secondary place as an intermediary and translator for Knatchbull. In both cases, Knatchbull expected Daniel and Norton to convey her messages faithfully, relying on her biological and spiritual network in order to carry out her agenda. The letters of Daniel, Knatchbull, and Norton in turn demonstrate the networked aspects of authorship. While Knatchbull employs male members of her network to transmit and translate her words, they depend on her for knowledge about the cloister. Knatchbull thus functions as an author even in the letters sent by Daniel and Norton, serving as the linchpin in her pro-Jesuit network's larger effort to remove Ward from the convent.

TOBY MATTHEW'S EDITION OF KNATCHBULL'S WORKS

Taking advantage of the authorial agency available to editors, Toby Matthew also mediated Knatchbull's writings in the process of incorporating them into his *Relation of the Holy, and Happy Life, and Death, of the Lady Lucie Knatchbull* (1652).[23] This text offers the most complete record of Knatchbull's textual production since it contains works in a variety of genres, as previously noted. In his capacity as editor, Matthew collected, preserved, and transmitted Knatchbull's writings to present her to English readers as a protosaint. As Matthew himself observes, the contemplative life is so abstract that Knatchbull's own words best convey her interior state: 'I will ... mak[e] use of her own letters and Papers, which I hope will give more satisfaction to others' (122). Yet in deciding to include or exclude certain works, Matthew has constructed the biography's portrait of Knatchbull according to criteria that support his quasi-hagiographic aims.

[22] AAMB, Engelse Benedictinessen/12.1, John Norton to Boonen, 21 October 1623.

[23] On Matthew's interventionist approach, see Marie-Louise Coolahan, 'Nuns' Writing: Translation, Textual Mobility, and Transnational Networks', in Patricia Phillippy (ed.), *A History of Early Modern Women's Writing* (Cambridge, 2018), 257–75.

For example, Matthew comments that he omitted her notes from the Spiritual Exercises: 'they are so very many, and would take up so much room, as would make this discourse too big for that use to which it was principally designed' (140–1). This passage offers the most obvious evidence of the way that Matthew used his intermediary power as an editor in order to fashion a corpus of Knatchbull's works that advanced his agenda as her biographer. While Knatchbull herself provided the source material for this work, Matthew's role as her posthumous editor allowed him the latitude to co-opt her authorship for his own purposes. Matthew's attitude towards Knatchbull's textual production was thus less reciprocal and more assimilative than that of Daniel and Norton. Since Matthew had served as Knatchbull's confessor and commanded her to write an autobiography, his heightened agency fits the model of collaborative authorship typical of confessor-penitent relationships.[24]

Matthew's shaping hand can also be discerned in revisions that he made to Knatchbull's writings. In describing her family background, Matthew observes that while the women in the Knatchbull family were 'eminent and even superexcellent for conceiving, and expressing themselves, and this both by tongue and pen', Knatchbull herself 'might be well enough allowed to win and wear the Prize' in terms of her eloquence (24). Nevertheless, inspection of the manuscript presented by Matthew to the Ghent Benedictines reveals that Matthew himself subtly altered Knatchbull's language at various points. This copy of the manuscript was prepared by a scribe and then revised by Matthew. For example, Matthew anonymises references to specific individuals. In the autobiography, Knatchbull directly petitions 'Mr. Mathew' to pray for her, but Matthew crosses out his own name and substitutes 'Sir'.[25] Likewise, Matthew replaces 'my Sister Digbyes', an allusion to Ghent co-founder Magdalen Digby, with a more euphemistic phrase, 'a great frend of mine'.[26] Often, however, Matthew's alterations are purely stylistic. Matthew carefully revises her account of a vision by crossing out some words and adding in others, represented here in angle brackets: 'It was <but> for a very short ~~space~~ <time>, that I ~~beheld~~ <saw> this Light, <but> yet, it left my soule in much comfort' (*Relation*, fol. 24r). Similarly, Matthew rewrites Knatchbull's description of spiritual aridity: 'It seemed to me, that my soule was now extreame<ly> poore, and beggerly, and that she had ~~availed~~ <improoved> herselfe nothinge, ~~of~~ <by> the time which she had spent in Religion' (*Relation*, fol. 36v). Such substitutions refine Knatchbull's homely language, as when Matthew changes 'extreame' to 'extreamely' or replaces 'of' with 'by'. Likewise, Matthew's introduction of 'but' in the first passage cited produces more sophisticated syntax. Matthew also strives to make Knatchbull's language more direct and precise, changing 'space' to 'time', 'beheld' to 'saw', and 'availed' to 'improoved'. These

[24] Jodi Bilinkoff, for example, comments that life-writing penned collaboratively by confessors and penitents 'reveals as much about male clerics and their agendas as about the women who are their ostensible subjects': *Related Lives: Confessors and Their Female Penitents, 1450–1750* (Ithaca, NY, 2005), 75.

[25] Berkshire, Douai Abbey, Box O IV 1, MS G 13, Toby Matthew, *A Relation of the Holy, and Happy Life, and Death, of the Lady Lucie Knatchbull*, fol. 145v; Matthew, *Life*, 48, n. 1.

[26] Douai Abbey, Matthew, *Relation*, fol. 26v; Matthew, *Life*, 32, n. 1.

minor emendations provide further evidence of the ways that members of Knatchbull's network mediated her writings and left their imprint in the process.

INTERTEXTUALITY IN MATTHEW'S BIOGRAPHY OF KNATCHBULL

Matthew's biography also reveals another network that shaped her textual output: the intertextual system of devotional writings read by Knatchbull. This intertextual web overlaps partially with her social network since Knatchbull alludes to several texts translated into English by Matthew. In one letter to Matthew describing her acts of contrition before receiving the sacrament, Knatchbull mentions petitioning an Italian bandit and convert: 'I thought also upon divers Penitents; and in particular upon Troilo Savelli, whose help amongst the rest, I desired' (135). In 1620, Matthew had published his English translation of Savelli's death, and his preface to this work depicted Savelli as a protosaint: 'it is morally certaine, that the abundant grace of Contrition, and Charity, which God infused into the hart of [Savelli], even by the occasion of his very sins . . . did put him instantly, after his death, into a state so blessed'.[27] It seems likely that Matthew introduced Knatchbull to Savelli since he was serving as her unofficial spiritual advisor at the time. Knatchbull's account of her intercessory prayers to Savelli thus derives directly from her familiarity with Matthew and, probably, his translation. A subtler example occurs in Knatchbull's 1619 autobiography when she describes receiving great comfort in 1609 from a vision of light:

> the eye of my mind . . . [saw] a Light not much bigger than the greatest Star which ordinarily we use to see. . . . I found myself . . . struck with a deep apprehension of the greatness and Majesty of Almighty God; and methought this Light did compass the whole world. (19–20)

In his explication of this moment, Matthew directs the reader to a similar revelation depicted in Book 7, Chapter 10 of Augustine's *Confessions*, where Augustine views:

> the unchangeable light of our Lord. Not this vulgar light, which is subject to the sense of flesh and bloud ... It was greater, and as if it were much, and much more cleare, then the other; and as if it would possesse the whole world by the greatnes thereof.[28]

[27] *A Relation of the Death of the Most Illustrious Lord, Sigr. Troilo Savelli*, trans. Toby Matthew (St Omer, 1620), 23.

[28] Matthew, *Life*, 59; *The Confessions of the Incomparable Doctour S. Augustine*, trans. Toby Matthew (St Omer, 1620), 315.

Much like Knatchbull, Augustine was dumbfounded by this sight: 'I even trembled between love and horror' (316). Matthew knew this text well since he had published an English translation of it in 1620, adding a marginal note calling attention to this passage: 'Ponder wel and wonder at the most elevated discourse of the Saint, in this chapter' (315). Since both the autobiography and this translation were probably composed around 1619, it seems possible that Matthew and Knatchbull discussed her vision in relation to its Augustinian precedent, particularly the divine light's ability to encompass the world. Matthew's guidance thus supplied Knatchbull with textual models that helped shape her understanding of her own spiritual life.

Yet as her biographer, Matthew imposed his own intertextual framework on Knatchbull's life to advance his proto-hagiographical agenda. Knatchbull and Matthew shared a special devotion to St Teresa of Ávila, who is known for both her visions and her writings.[29] Knatchbull's autobiography indicates that her reverence for Teresa dated to at least 1609, when she briefly left the Brussels convent. When her advisors suggested founding a Carmelite house in Louvain, Knatchbull rejected this proposal despite her great esteem for Teresa: 'I had, as I still have, that excellent Saint in high reverence' (31). Knatchbull also records that one of her revelations occurred 'upon the fifth of October, being the Feast of the Blessed Mother Teresa of Jesus' (42). Meanwhile, Matthew's interest in Teresa is best demonstrated by his English translation of her autobiography, *The Flaming Hart or the Life of the Glorious S. Teresa* (1642). Matthew probably undertook his biography of Knatchbull after publishing his translation of Teresa's autobiography, and he consistently presents Knatchbull as an English version of Teresa. After arguing that Knatchbull's visions parallel those of contemporary saints, Matthew portrays the two women as equivalent to one another:

> whosoever will take the pains and pleasure to read St Teresas Life, of the Flaming Heart, will clearly find the truth of that which I am now delivering here. For they are as like one another—I mean not (as I was saying) for Quantity (as it were) and Proportion, but merely for Quality, and Kind—as even two drops of water can be. (124)

Modern scholarship on Matthew's biography has followed his lead by identifying many connections between Knatchbull's writings and Teresa's works.[30] Indeed, David Knowles has claimed that 'practically any page of Dame Lucy's Relations could be paralleled from St Teresa'.[31] Yet as Nicky Hallett has warned in her own edition of Matthew's work, 'It

[29] On Teresa's English reception, see Danielle Clarke, 'Life Writing for the Counter-Reformation: The English Translation and Reception of Teresa de Ávila's Autobiography', *Journal of Medieval and Early Modern Studies*, 50 (2020), 75–94.

[30] Alan Stewart, 'The Revised Lives of Tobie Matthew', in *The Oxford History of Life-Writing*, vol. 3, *Early Modern* (Oxford, 2018), 180; Matthew, *Life*, 44, 46, 49, 128–9, 152; 'The Life of Lady Lucy Knatchbull', in Caroline Bowden (ed.), *English Convents in Exile, 1600–1800*, vol. 3, Nicky Hallett (ed.), *Life Writing I* (London, 2012), 386, n. 5, 387, n. 12; Coolahan, 'Nuns' Writing', 268–9.

[31] Matthew, *Life*, xx.

is difficult to determine ... where the likeness originates, whether Knatchbull or (and) Matthew modelled their Life on a Teresian scheme'.[32] Significantly, while Matthew notes many biographical parallels between Knatchbull and Teresa, he does not identify any allusions to Teresa in Knatchbull's writings, as he had done with Augustine's *Confessions*. Given Matthew's familiarity with Teresa's work as well as his goal of associating the two women, it seems likely that he would have highlighted any obvious intertextual links between Knatchbull and Teresa. Matthew himself is thus primarily responsible for creating the intertextual web that connects his biography of Knatchbull with the works of Teresa.

Indeed, Matthew's emphasis on Teresa has obscured Knatchbull's participation in another intertextual network that was Benedictine in nature. As her autobiography documents, Knatchbull could not agree to become a Carmelite because of her unshakeable zeal for the Benedictine order. Describing the proposed Carmelite foundation as being 'worse to me than all the rest' of difficulties she faced, Knatchbull comments: 'it was not in my power (with all the force that I could use) to draw my affection from the desire of being that [i.e., Benedictine] which now through the grace of God I am' (31). While Matthew showed little interest in Knatchbull's Benedictinism, her writings reveal a familiarity with Benedictine authors. In a contemplation on the Ecce Homo, Knatchbull cites St Bernard of Clairvaux's First Sermon for the Feast of the Epiphany as she recalls how Christ suffered on her behalf: 'For which excess of Love, my heart and Soul doth love and praise his holy name, and with St Bernard humbly at my Saviour's feet say, *Quanto pro me vilior, tanto mihi carior* [the baser he was on my behalf, so much dearer is he to me]' (148).[33] As the Abbot of Clairvaux, Bernard (1090–1153) played a major role in the spread of the Cistercians, a reformed branch of the Benedictines. Knatchbull thus drew inspiration for her own contemplation of Christ's humanity from a highly influential and much revered member of her order, literally joining her voice to his through intertextuality.

Knatchbull also admired Gertrude the Great (b. 1256), who was known for her visions involving Christ's humanity and the sacrament. As the author of Knatchbull's obituary notes: 'She had a most Special devotion to the Great St Gertrude Abbess of Elpidia in Saxony, and to all her works, writing out with her own hand, most, or all, that book of her Insinuations'.[34] Gertrude is often conflated with an abbess at Helfta by the same name, and it seems natural that Knatchbull would have been drawn to works by and about another Benedictine abbess who had mystic revelations. No English version of Gertrude's writings was published in the seventeenth century, but several French editions appeared during Knatchbull's lifetime under the title *Insinuations de la divine piété* (1619, 1620, 1622, 1623). Whether Knatchbull read Gertrude in an English manuscript translation or one of the printed French texts, many of her spiritual accounts (especially those written at Ghent) emphasise sacramental

[32] Nicky Hallett, 'Introduction', in *English Convents in Exile*, 3.xvi.

[33] St Bernard, in Jean Leclercq and Henri Rochais (eds), *Sancti Bernardi Opera*, vol. 4, *Sermones I* (Rome, 1966), 293.

[34] 'Obituary Notices', 7.

revelation.[35] For both Gertrude and Knatchbull, communion results in a closer union with God. As the fourth book of *Insinuations* records:

> le sainct Esprit remassant en soy toutes les perfections du sainct Sacrement, il les versa toutes avec luy mesme dans l'ame de saincte Gertrude & saincte Gertrude se communiant avec la mesme Hostie, Dieu s'unit à ceste ame bien-heureuse d'une union estroicte & inseparable.[36]
>
> (the Holy Spirit gathering in itself all the perfections of the holy sacrament, it poured them all along with itself into the soul of St Gertrude, and St Gertrude taking communion with this same host, God united himself to this blessed soul with a strict and inseparable union)

Similarly, after communion Knatchbull experiences a divine union initiated by God:

> So soon as I had Received, whilst I was adoring, methought our Lord (of whose Presence I had a lively faith) had regard to this poor wretch, and, as it were, fastening my Soule to himself, did unite her to him, even as two things are made one. (150)

Gertrude also experienced God entering into her heart, as when Christ makes this pronouncement to her during Mass: 'estant maintenant chassé du coeur de tous les hommes, je viens me reposer dans le vostre, comme dans mon refuge' [being now chased from every man's heart, I come to rest myself in yours, as in my refuge] (*Insinuations*, 434). Knatchbull likewise finds that God occupies her heart after she receives communion:

> it seemed to me that our Lord did shut himself up into the most innermost part of my heart—in such sort as some person (who for just respects desiring neither to be seen, heard, or known to be in the house, no not so much as to his own Servants) would, for the better concealing himself, make the door fast upon himself in his most retired Chamber or Closet. (164)

While Knatchbull never explicitly refers to Gertrude, the parallels between their mystical visions suggest that the *Insinuations* offered her an important spiritual and textual precedent, one that has been overlooked due to Matthew's focus on Teresa of Ávila.

CONCLUSION

As this chapter has shown, Lucy Knatchbull belonged to a religious network of English priests on the Continent who received and conveyed her works and words to

[35] On Knatchbull and the Sacrament, see Lisa McClain, *Divided Loyalties? Pushing the Boundaries of Gender and Lay Roles in the Catholic Church, 1534–1829* (London, 2018), 214–15.

[36] *Les insinuations de la divine piété* (Paris, 1634), 511.

others. Occupying secondary authorial roles as Knatchbull's editors, translators, and messengers, these men sought to control her reception among two audiences: first, ecclesiastical officials such as the archbishop of Mechelen-Brussels, and second, English Catholics at large. The small corpus of writings that Knatchbull composed for readers outside the convent thus reveals the ways that her social circle functioned as a literary network that facilitated the production, transmission, and preservation of her texts. Viewed from this perspective, Knatchbull's authorship is itself a networked phenomenon. Members of her network circulated her writings even as they shaped her compositions in a variety of ways. Their success in influencing Knatchbull's authorship may be seen in both the eventual ouster of Ward and in the tendency even today for readers to associate Knatchbull with Teresa. Yet Matthew's biography also provides a cautionary example showing why we must recognise the network's participation in constructing Knatchbull's authorship. By emphasising her devotion to Teresa for his own ends, Matthew reveals that the mediation of Knatchbull's works could become a form of appropriation rather than collaboration. Indeed, Matthew's preservation of Knatchbull's spiritual texts exceeded her own intentions to leave her convent with no written trace of her piety. The house's obituary for Knatchbull includes many verbatim citations of works included in Matthew's biography and even directs readers to that text for additional examples of her writing. While Matthew's life of Knatchbull remained unpublished, it nonetheless affected Knatchbull's later reputation among the Ghent Benedictines by bringing works composed for an extramural audience back into the cloister. Ultimately, Knatchbull's circle served as both a conduit and a mediator of her writings inside and outside the convent, offering an intriguing example of the way that cloistered authorship itself could function as an extension of nuns' social networks.

FURTHER READING

Bilinkoff, Jodi. *Related Lives: Confessors and Their Female Penitents, 1450–1750*. Ithaca, NY, 2005.

Coolahan, Marie-Louise. 'Nuns' Writing: Translation, Textual Mobility, and Transnational Networks', in Patricia Phillippy (ed.), *A History of Early Modern Women's Writing*. Cambridge, 2018, 257–75.

Kelly, James E. *English Convents in Catholic Europe, c 1600–1800*. Cambridge, 2020.

Lux-Sterritt, Laurence. *English Benedictine Nuns in Exile in the Seventeenth Century: Living Spirituality*. Manchester, 2017.

Matthew, Toby. In David Knowles (ed.), *The Life of Lady Lucy Knatchbull*. London, 1931.

Stewart, Alan. *The Oxford History of Life-Writing*. Vol. 3. *Early Modern*. Oxford, 2018.

Walker, Claire. *Gender and Politics in Early Modern Europe: English Convents in France and the Low Countries*. New York, 2003.

CHAPTER 34

GIFTS THAT MATTER

Katherine Parr, Princess Elizabeth, and the Prayers or Meditations *(1545)*

PATRICIA PENDER

THE exchange of gifts was a crucial mode of early modern networking—one in which relationships between peers and across power lines were initiated, brokered, celebrated, and cemented.[1] Books—often beautifully designed and decorated books—played an instrumental role in this process, famous examples being the lavishly illuminated copies of *Orlando Furioso* that Sir John Harington gifted to Elizabeth I and her courtiers, and the elaborately embroidered book of Psalms that professional calligrapher and bookmaker Esther Inglis presented to the queen in 1599.[2] For the Tudors, the New Year provided a highly ritualised and very public context for such exchange: gifts given at New Year were designed to be seen rather than secreted; they occupied a central place in the palace for the duration of festivities. This chapter examines the New Year's gift that Princess Elizabeth presented to Henry VIII in 1545: an embroidered manuscript translation of the *Prayers or Meditations*, a text that her stepmother Katherine Parr had published

[1] On gift giving, see Natalie Zemon Davis, *The Gift in Sixteenth-Century France* (Oxford, 2000) and Felicity Heal, *The Power of Gifts: Gift Exchange in Early Modern England* (Oxford, 2014). For recent work on early modern women's networks, see Kate Davison, 'Early Modern Social Networks: Antecedents, Opportunities, and Challenges', *American Historical Review*, 124.2 (2019), 456–82 and Sarah C. E. Ross, 'Coteries, Circles, Networks', in Patricia Phillippy (ed.), *A History of Early Modern Women's Writing* (Cambridge, 2018), 332–47.

I would like to thank the editors of this volume for their patience and perseverance with this chapter, despite the many delays I subjected them to. I am also extremely grateful to Kelly Peihopa, whose contribution to this project, over several drawn-out years, has been invaluable.

[2] See Jason Scott-Warren, *Sir John Harington and the Book as Gift* (Oxford, 2001) and Lisa M. Klein, 'Your Humble Handmaid: Elizabethan Gifts of Needlework', *Renaissance Quarterly*, 50.2 (1997), 459–93. See also Georgianna Ziegler's recently published blog on Esther Ingis, 'Esther Inglis (*c* 1570–1624): Calligrapher, Artist, Embroiderer, Writer', https://estheringliscreativewoman.wordpress.com/, accessed 4 June 2021.

that same year. We can read this gift not only as evidence of Parr's important facilitation of Elizabeth's literary endeavours but also as material, textual, and performative instantiations of Elizabeth's own nascent networking practices.

Less than a year after Katherine Parr published her *Prayers or Meditations* in 1545, her twelve-year-old stepdaughter Elizabeth presented Henry VIII with a manuscript volume of this work translated into Latin, French, and Italian, as her New Year's gift. This chapter examines this gift from three distinct but related perspectives, attending to the familial and literary contexts in which the gift was bestowed, to the embroidered needlework covers with which Elizabeth 'clothed' her manuscript, and to the representation of her own literary labour in the translation's dedication. In doing so it brings together anthropological analysis of the gift-as-gesture, along with material analysis of the book-as-object, and rhetorical analysis of book-as-gift. The gestural, physical, and formal features of this gift, I will argue, illuminate the complex dynamics of allusion and allegiance behind its precocious display of literary and political agency.

LITERARY AND FAMILIAL CONTEXTS

Parr's *Prayers or Meditations* was published by Henry's royal printer Thomas Berthelet in three successive editions of 1545. The first edition appeared on 2 June 1545 under the title *Prayers Stirryng the Mynd unto Heauenlye Medytacions*. A second edition bearing the same date was entitled *Prayers or Meditacions, Wherin the Mynde is Styrred Paciently to Suffre all Afflictions Here*, and a third edition appeared on 5 November 1545 under the long title *Prayers or Medytacions, wherein the Mynd is Stirred, Paciently to Suffer all Afflictions here, to set at Nought the Vayne Prosperitee of this Worlde, and Alwaie to Longe for the Everlastynge Felicitee: Collected out of Holy Woorkes by the most Virtuous and Graciouse Princesse Katherine queen of Englande, Fraunce, and Irelande.*[3] It is this third edition that Parr's most recent editor, Janel Mueller, considers definitive. She and other scholars have argued persuasively that Parr envisaged her text as a private counterpart to the *Exhortation and Litany* that Archbishop Thomas Cranmer had recently

[3] Janel Mueller describes the different states of the three editions in her 'Introduction to *Prayers or Meditations*', in *Katherine Parr: Complete Works and Correspondence* (Chicago, IL, 2011), 369. The first edition appeared on 2 June 1545 under the title *Prayers Stirryng the Mynd unto Heavenlye Medytacions* and reprinted two prayers, one for Henry and one for men entering battle, that had concluded her anonymous publication of *Psalms or Prayers* in 1544. A second edition with the same contents and date was entitled *Prayers or meditacions, wherin the mynde is styrred paciently to suffre all afflictions here.* What Mueller calls the definitive third edition appeared on 5 November 1545 containing the latter of the above prayers and three more, under the long title *Prayers or Medytacions, wherein the mynd is stirred, paciently to suffer all afflictions here, to set at nought the vayne prosperitee of this worlde, and alwaie to longe for for the everlastynge felicitee: Collected out of holy woorkes by the most virtuous and graciouse princesse Katherine queen of Englande, Fraunce, and Irelande.* These are respectively STC 4818; STC 4818.5; STC 4819.

produced at Henry's behest to guide public devotion for the new Church of England. English translations of the Bible had been hitherto prohibited; Cranmer's was the first English translation to receive royal approval, and it is reasonable to assume that Parr too would have needed to obtain the king's permission, as well as the archbishop's approval, for her volume to be printed.[4]

It is significant for our understanding of Elizabeth's translation of the *Prayers or Meditations* that the third iteration of Parr's text unapologetically revealed the queen's authorship of the volume, even if this authorship was presented as compiling or 'collecting'. I have previously argued that the modesty rhetoric of Parr's project—its representation of her own authorial labour in *sermo humilis*, or the humble style—assisted in its reception as dutiful rather than transgressive of the gendered religious discourse to which she aimed to contribute.[5] In a series of recent articles, Micheline White has usefully extended our understanding of Parr's contribution to this period's textual culture by arguing that she is best understood 'as a participant in a collaborative, diglot crown project', in which Henry 'entrusted' to her the translation of an 'important crown-sponsored wartime book'—the *Psalms or Prayers* published anonymously in 1544.[6] White contends not only that Henry and Parr 'must have engaged in serious political discussions' as the materials for this work were 'assembled, translated, and edited' but that in translating the Psalms, Parr was not simply writing *with* Henry, but was engaging in 'a fascinating form of royal ventriloquism' in which she was 'writing *as* Henry'.[7]

It is also significant that, despite the long title indicating that the work was compiled from several holy source works, Parr's *Prayers or Meditations* derives its material almost exclusively from the third book of Thomas à Kempis' fifteenth-century Catholic devotional manual, *De Imitatione Christi* (*c* 1441). When Mueller published her *Complete Works of Katherine Parr* in 2011, she presented the publication of *Prayers or Meditations* under Parr's name as 'the earliest such occurrence for a woman author in England'.[8] The almost inevitable overriding of such claims to chronological priority are made more interesting in this case by the irony that Lady Margaret Beaufort, Henry VIII's

4 Mueller, *Complete Works*, 369–70. See also Kimberly Anne Coles, *Religion, Reform, and Women's Writing in Early Modern England* (Cambridge, 2008).

5 Patricia Pender, '"A worme most abjecte": *Sermo Humilis* as Reformation Strategy in Katherine Parr's *Prayers or* Medytacions', in *Early Modern Women's Writing and the Rhetoric of Modesty* (New York, 2012), 64–91.

6 Micheline White, 'The Psalms, War, and Royal Iconography: Katherine Parr's *Psalms or Prayers* (1544) and Henry VIII as David', *Renaissance Studies*, 29.4 (2015), 554–75, 557.

7 Micheline White, 'Katherine Parr, Henry VIII, and Royal Literary Collaboration', in Patricia Pender (ed.), *Gender, Authorship, and Early Modern Women's Collaboration* (Cham, Switzerland: 2017), 23–46, 30, 33. See also Micheline White, 'Katherine Parr, Translation, and the Dissemination of Erasmus' Views on War and Peace', *Renaissance and Reformation*, 43.2 (2015), 67–91 and 'Katherine Parr and Royal Religious Complaint: Complaining For and About Henry VIII', in Sarah C. E. Ross and Rosalind Smith (eds), *Early Modern Women's Complaint: Gender, Form, and Politics*, (Cham, Switzerland, 2020), 47–65. See also Coles' analysis of 'crown' publication in *Religion, Reform, and Women's Writing*, especially 47–57.

8 Mueller, *Complete Works*, 369–70. Margaret Beaufort, *A Full Devout and Gostely Treatyse of the Imytacion and Folowynge the Blessed Lyfe of Oure Moste Mercyfull Savyoure Criste* (London, 1504).

grandmother, had actually translated the fourth book of Thomas à Kempis' *Imitatio Christi* and published it under her own name almost forty years earlier.

Margaret Beaufort provides an important precedent for Parr's enterprise—and thus for Elizabeth's—in several distinct respects. Henry VIII owed his claim to the English throne partly to his grandmother, whose political machinations helped establish the Tudor line under her son Henry VII. The term 'mediatrix'—highlighted through Julie Crawford's work on influential seventeenth-century powerbrokers such as Lucy Harington, Duchess of Bedford and Mary Sidney Herbert, Countess of Pembroke—was first used, according to the *Oxford English Dictionary*, to describe the combination of literary, social, and political patronage wielded by Margaret Beaufort.[9] Her encouragement of writers, translators, and printers, and her promotion of the education of women through the vernacularisation of scripture, provided a potent and empowering example to subsequent generations of Tudor women, including Catherine of Aragon and Katherine Parr, as well as her great-granddaughters Mary and Elizabeth.

Beaufort's translation of the fourth book of the *Imitatio Christi* in 1504 was published by Richard Pynson alongside translations of the first three books that William Atkinson had undertaken and Pynson had published at Beaufort's behest a year previously.[10] In contrast to Beaufort's translation, which was probably based on the French edition of the *Imitatio* published in Toulouse in 1488, Parr's *Prayers or Meditations* is thought to have been based on an English translation of the third book of the *Imitatio* by a Bridgettine monk of Syon monastery, Richard Whitford, under the title *The Folowynge of Christ* (*c* 1531).[11] While Beaufort focuses on the fourth book, which concerns the Eucharist, Parr concentrates on the third book, and more specifically the final third of that book, from Chapters 16–54.

Early scholars of Parr's work were dismissive of her *Prayers or Meditations*. C. Fenno Hoffman, for instance, opines that 'a line-by-line comparison' of Parr with Whitford reveals that 'the entire *Meditacion* is a piece of schoolboy plagiarism of the *Imitation*'. Similarly, John L. King complains that Parr's 'haphazard selection destroys the methodical character and evocation of inward dialogue which characterise the original'. But while the text was intitially 'tagged as a derivative compilation', subsequent scholarship has reassessed Parr's textual practice and political motivations as carefully designed and deliberately interventionist. For Janel Mueller and the scholars who have followed her lead, Parr's *Prayers or Meditations* 'take shape and substance in a deliberate,

9 Julie Crawford, *Mediatrix: Women, Politics, and Literary Production in Early Modern England* (Oxford, 2014), and *OED*.

10 Beaufort, *A Full Deuout and Gostely Treatyse*.

11 See Patricia Demers, '"God May Open More than Man Maye Vnderstande": Lady Margaret Beaufort's Translation of the De "Imitatione Christi"', *Renaissance and Reformation/Renaissance et Réforme*, 35.4 (2012), 45–61. See also Brenda M. Hosington, '"How We Ovght to Knowe God": Princess Elizabeth's Presentation of Her Calvin Translation to Katherine Parr', *The Medieval Translator/Traduire Au Moyen Age*, 14 (2018), 499–513.

bold, and sustained act of intertextual appropriation that constitutes a genuine claim to authorship'.[12] Mueller sees Parr's translation as explicitly designed to foster 'reformed devotion among the literate laity of the late Henrician church of England by performing a generic reorientation on the masterpiece of late medieval Catholic spirituality'.[13] In this context, Mueller reconceives Parr's *Meditations* 'as a self-certifying gesture, in a literary mode for which she had impeccable precedents, to confirm her rather recently attained membership in the exalted circle of English royalty'.[14] As we will see, Elizabeth finds herself in an uncannily similar situation when she undertakes her own translation of Parr.

TEXTUAL AND TEXTILE CONTEXTS

In order to understand Elizabeth's translation of Parr's *Prayers or Meditations* in its historical and material context, it is necessary to situate her 1545 gift to her father in the company of her other, contemporaneous gifts to the king and queen.[15] Elizabeth's gift to Henry in 1545 was accompanied by a matching gift for Parr, a translation from the French of the first chapter of Calvin's *Institution de la Religion Chrestienne*, entitled *Howe We Ought to Knowe God*.[16] The previous year, in 1544, the then eleven year old Princess Elizabeth presented her stepmother with her translation (from French to English) of Marguerite de Navarre's *Le Mirroir de l'âme pécheresse* (1531) as *The Miroir or glasse of the synnefull soule*, a book also associated with Margaret Beaufort. In 1506 Pynson had published Beaufort's *Mirroure of Golde for the Synfull Soule*, a translation from the French of the *Speculum aureum animae peccatricis* (1480) usually attributed to Jacobus Gruytroede. Like Katherine Parr before her, then, in translating her stepmother's *Prayers or Meditations* Elizabeth was writing herself into an established family genealogy of Tudor women's textual production and translation that traced back to her father's powerful grandmother. Elizabeth Tudor shared a paternal lineage with Margaret Beaufort, and with this translation Elizabeth brokered for an additional source of legitimacy via Katherine Parr—as a royal Tudor woman of demonstrated—and unusually public—learning, letters, and piety.

[12] Hoffman concludes his essay with the judgement that Parr 'has no place among English authors, though the plagiarism of *Prayers or Meditacions* was not a crime to her contemporaries' (367). See C. F. Hoffman, 'Catherine Parr as a Woman of Letters', *The Huntington Library Quarterly*, 23.4 (1960), 349–67.

[13] Janel Mueller, 'Devotion as Difference: Intertextuality in Queen Katherine Parr's "Prayers Or Meditations" (1545)', *The Huntington Library Quarterly*, 53.3 (1990), 171–97, 175.

[14] Mueller, 'Devotion as Difference', 173. See also Janel Mueller, 'Complications of Intertextuality: John Fisher, Katherine Parr and "The Book of the Crucifix"', in Cedric C. Brown and Arthur F. Marotti (eds), *Texts and Cultural Change in Early Modern England* (Basingstoke, 1997), 15–36.

[15] Elizabeth Tudor, *Prayers and Meditations* (1545), London, British Library, Royal MS 7 D X.

[16] Hosington, 'How We Ovght to Knowe God', 499–513.

Gifts to Katherine Parr	Gifts to Henry VIII

FIGURE 34.1 Elizabeth I's gift book designs, 1544–1545.

The table above (see Figure 34.1) provides a sense 'at-a-glance' of the similarity in Elizabeth's gift book designs across the crucial years 1544 and 1545. As these images show, the books are all matching examples of needlework-covered calligraphic manuscripts (see this volume, Chapter 5, Michele Osherow, '"At My Petition": Embroidering Esther').[17] For the purpose of my inquiry, it is useful to look at how the material objects of the books in question present them as pairs—or, more accurately, two pairs (perhaps a quartet)—from which a missing fourth volume, one presented to Henry in 1544, has been persuasively surmised.[18] In the reading that follows, my understanding of the textile rhetoric of these embroideries is deeply indebted to the previous work of Margaret Swain, Lisa Klein, and Susan Frye, who have studied these covers in detail.[19]

[17] Susan Frye, *Pens and Needles: Women's Textualities in Early Modern England* (Philadelphia, PA, 2010), 31–2.

[18] Frye, *Pens and Needles*, 39.

[19] Margaret H. Swain, 'A New Year's Gift from the Princess Elizabeth' N.P. 1 January 1975, 258–66; Klein, 'Your Humble Handmaid'; Susan Frye, *Pens and Needles* and 'Sewing Connections: Elizabeth Tudor, Mary Stuart, Elizabeth Talbot, and Seventeenth-Century Anonymous Needleworkers', in Susan Frye and Karen Robertson (eds), *Maids and Mistresses, Cousins and Queens: Women's Alliances in Early Modern England* (New York, 1999), 165–82. See also Swain, *Figures on Fabric: Embroidery Design Sources and Their Application* (London, 1980), Rozsika Parker, *The Subversive Stitch: Embroidery and the Making of the Feminine* (London, 1984, repr. 1989) and Maureen Quilligan, 'Elizabeth's Embroidery', *Shakespeare Studies*, 28 (2000), 208–14.

Figure 34.2 shows the *The Miroir or Glasse of the Synneful Soule*, which Elizabeth gave to Katherine Parr in 1544 and which now resides in the Bodleian Library. The volume is bound in canvas, embroidered in blue and silver silk, and decorated on the upper and lower covers with an interlace design in silver and gilt thread. In the centre of each cover

FIGURE 34.2 Elizabeth I. 1544. 'Le miroir de l'âme pécheresse' ('The Mirror of the Sinful Soul'). MS. Cherry 36, binding/upper cover. Bodleian Library, University of Oxford.

are the initials 'KP'. Placed diagonally in each corner is a raised embroidered flower, which Swain identifies as heartsease. Klein calls these flowers pansies (also known as 'love-in-idleness'), which she believes Elizabeth intended as a pun on the French word *pensée*, meaning 'thought' or 'idea'.[20] The cover's looping lines 'surround the central initials with lover's knots, forming a cross with six groups of four rings each'. Frye notes that, 'The four rings themselves form a particular kind of knot that appears in many cultures, one that the Vikings called "Frode" or "happiness" '.[21]

Elizabeth's gifts of 1545—*Howe We Ought to Knowe God*, given to Katherine Parr (now held at the National Records of Scotland), and *Prayers and Meditations of Katherine Parr*, given to Henry (now in the British Library) (see Figures 34.3 and 34.4)—show striking similarities in technique and design, and, according to Margaret Swain, share a common origin. Swain notes that:

> All three are worked on canvas in the same stitch, a stitch that is now called plaited Gobelin. The same type of silk and silver thread is used on each. The heartsease [or pansies] in the corners are all worked in the same stitch, a version of detached buttonhole.[22]

The cover of the book given to Henry is red, with a blue and silver monogram; that presented to Katherine is blue (like *The Miroir or Glasse of the Synneful Soul*) with a red and silver monogram. 'The same silks are used on both with the colours reversed'.[23] For both Swain and Frye, these paired manuscripts of 1545 'strongly suggest that in 1544 Elizabeth had also created a matching gift for Henry, in the reverse color scheme of blue on silver', with Frye positing that this was a translation of Erasmus' *Diologus Fidei*.[24] The 1545 volumes, then, 'are identical in design, except that the single "H" at the top and bottom of Henry's book is slightly reshaped to form an "R" for Regina at the top and bottom of Katherine's'.[25]

Looking in particular at Elizabeth's *Prayers and Meditations of Katherine Parr*, given to Henry in 1545, we can see a monogram in the centre worked in 'blue and silver silk, the letters of which can be discerned to spell HENRY KATHERIN, the letter E being reversed, on the left side.[26] Frye suggests that Elizabeth uses the letter 'H' as the cipher's base, while the 'H', 'K', 'P', 'E', and 'R' represent Henry, Katherine, Parr, Elizabeth, Edward, Rex, and Regina.[27] I am intrigued by the idea of the 'E' being reversed, by the idea that Elizabeth is presented as looking back at the other members of her family. And although there is not the time to follow this lead here, we might consider that through

20 Swain, 'A New Year's Gift', 259; Klein, 'Your humble Handmaid', 478.
21 Frye, *Pens and Needles*, 37.
22 Swain, 'A New Year's Gift', 266.
23 Swain, 'A New Year's Gift', 262.
24 Frye, *Pens and Needles*, 39; Swain, 'A New Year's Gift', 265–6.
25 Frye, *Pens and Needles*, 39.
26 Swain, 'A New Year's Gift', 262.
27 Frye, *Pens and Needles*, 35.

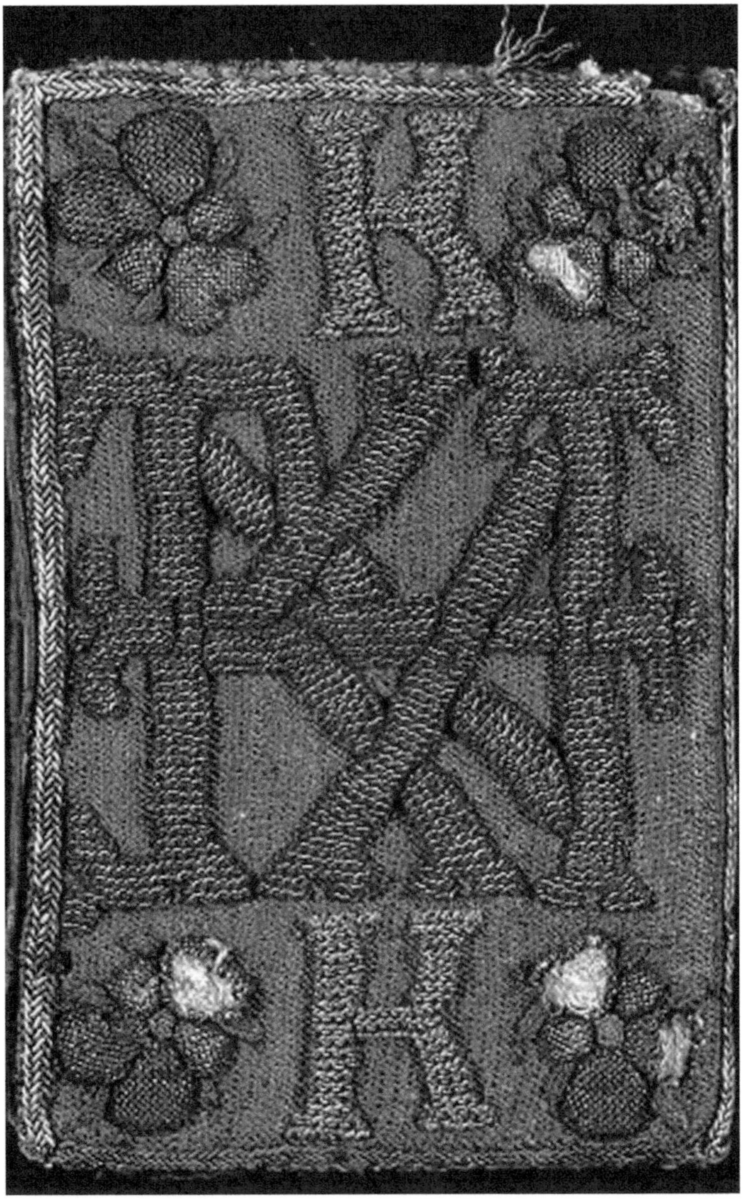

FIGURE 34.3 Elizabeth I. 1545. Religious book written by Princess Elizabeth (later Queen Elizabeth I of England) for her stepmother, Katherine Parr, 1545. RH13/78. National Records of Scotland. Used with permission.

FIGURE 34.4 Elizabeth I. Prayers and meditations (the 'Prayerbook of Princess Elizabeth'). BL Royal MS 7 D. X., embroidered back cover. © British Library Board.

this reversal, Elizabeth could be alluding to what her 'preposterous', or about-faced, inclusion in the new family unit.[28] These letters are moreover connected by '[curious] knots': the places where the letters composing each cipher are stitched to overlap one another. Frye suggests that:

[28] On the preposterous see Patricia Parker, *Shakespeare from the Margins: Language, Culture, Context* (Chicago, IL, 1996).

> Whether sewn in embroidery, penned with ink, or planted in gardens, 'curious knots' are more than interconnected lines. In ciphers, they form the patterns that connect letters to particular meanings, designs that celebrate the tension between separation and joining, [much] like the letters forming Elizabeth's ... ciphers that are individually distinguishable and bound together.[29]

How are we to read these once beautifully bound books as material objects? In the introduction to *Renaissance Clothing and the Materials of Memory*, Ann Rosalind Jones and Peter Stallybrass argue that 'we need to understand the animatedness of clothes, their ability to "pick up" subjects, to mold and shape them both physically and socially, to constitute subjects through their power as material memories'.[30] 'In the livery economy of Renaissance Europe', they argue:

> things took on a life of their own ... one was paid not only in the 'neutral' currency of money but also in material that was richly absorbent of symbolic meaning and in which memories and social relations were literally embodied.[31]

Livery acted 'as the medium through which the social system marked bodies so as to associate them with particular institutions'.[32] In this understanding, 'payment in cloth and clothing was a form of bodily mnemonic, marking the wearer's indebtedness to master or mistress':

> The liveried body ... stitched servants' bodies to their households. Such clothes were 'habits' in the sense that they were persistent material reminders of status and of incorporation.[33]

Jones and Stallybrass go on to suggest that 'laid on tables or hung on the inner walls of their houses', the needlework produced by elite early modern women 'constituted a kind of family livery, one capable of declaring the household's loyalty to one leader or another'.[34] In this context, I want to suggest that we can read Princess Elizabeth's matched sets of needlework gift books to Henry and Katherine precisely as a kind of family livery or uniform: they are 'material mnemonics' that clearly declare her loyalty to her father-leader, but also embody her inclusion in the royal household.[35] They are objects through which she is able to stitch herself into new social and familial relations that instantiate and celebrate her recent reincorporation in the institution of the royal family. In order to appreciate the specificity of these resonances, it is helpful to look at

[29] Frye, *Pens and Needles*, 37.

[30] Ann Rosalind Jones and Peter Stallybrass, *Renaissance Clothing and the Materials of Memory* (Cambridge, 2002), 2.

[31] Jones and Stallybrass, *Renaissance Clothing*, 8.

[32] Jones and Stallybrass, *Renaissance Clothing*, 5.

[33] Jones and Stallybrass, *Renaissance Clothing*, 11.

[34] Jones and Stallybrass, *Renaissance Clothing*, 162.

[35] Jones and Stallybrass, *Renaissance Clothing*, 11.

Elizabeth's immediate historical context. At this point in time, Elizabeth's own position in the family was distinctly tenuous. In 1544, she had apparently offended the king, although details of the incident are unknown. She was banished from his household, and restored only by Katherine Parr's intervention. Elizabeth's legal status was also being negotiated at this time. Declared a bastard before Anne Boleyn's execution in 1536, she was established in the succession by an act of Parliament in 1544, though she was still deemed illegitimate.[36]

Roger Ellis has noted the timeliness of what he calls Elizabeth's 'juvenile translations'.[37] All of the texts she translated in this period were current; most were decidedly topical. Her choice in 1545 to produce a trilingual translation of a work also published that year by the queen registers as an extreme example of such topicality. And it raises interesting (if sometimes unanswerable) questions about the text's production. How did Elizabeth accomplish this ambitious tripartite translation so swiftly? Did Parr encourage or even set her to this Herculean task? Did she start it before Parr published her work in print? Did Elizabeth work from Parr's manuscripts? And if Parr did not set Elizabeth to this task, who did? What were their motivations? Was Elizabeth's willingness to undertake it part of currying Parr's favour and brokering her way back into the royal household?

These questions sound, admittedly, like something from a popular historical novel and many of them may remain unanswered. But I ask them because the fragile extant copy that the British Library has meticulously preserved tells a story of historical success: of a more-or-less completed text; a presentation copy actually presented; a gift given. This should not stop us, however, from asking questions about the hypothetical rough drafts, loose copies, or foul papers that preceded this finished artefact. As scholars we know well that any published outcome is only the tip of the iceberg in terms of the literary labour invested in it. We know *now* that Elizabeth translated Parr's recently published *Prayers or Meditations* in 1545, into three different languages, at the age of twelve. This extraordinary feat has become something of a fait accompli. Of course she did. The fact that her gift was accepted by Henry also assists in a kind of unwitting amnesia, or at least complacency about the *risk* involved in giving such a gift. We need to remember that a gift to the monarch may well be refused, and could sometimes cause grave offence. We know that Elizabeth's position was politically precarious. The fact that she chose to translate a text by one of her several stepmothers was by no means a guarantee of Henry's acceptance; quite possibly the reverse. Katherine was after all called up on charges before the Privy Council not long after the presentation of this gift. And her willingness to debate scripture with the king was precisely the point of her arrest. If we focus solely on the success of Elizabeth's gift, we ignore the risks involved in making, and giving it.

36 Klein, 'Your humble Handmaid', 66.

37 See Roger Ellis, 'The Juvenile Translations of Elizabeth Tudor', *Translation and Literature*, 18.2 (2009), 157–80.

RHETORICAL AND ANTHROPOLOGICAL CONTEXTS

In his influential treatise on precapitalist exchange, Marcel Mauss states that objects in such exchanges can be 'personalised beings that talk and take part in the contract. They state their desire to be given away'. Things-as-gifts, he asserts, are not 'indifferent things'; they have 'a name, a personality, a past'.[38] Mauss emphasises in particular 'the principle of rivalry that prevails in these practices', which he views as agonistic in type.[39] Despite vast temporal and geographic differences, the early modern practice of New Year's gifts to the monarch bears some resemblance to the Indigenous American potlatch and the Oceanic kula rituals on which Mauss' and much subsequent gift theory is based. Gifts of sometimes crippling generosity were bestowed upon Henry and publicly displayed, with the ostensible disinterest of the giver being rewarded, at least theoretically, with the promise of the king's confidence and his future counter-gift.[40] As Mary Douglas notes of Mauss' theory: 'A gift that does nothing to enhance solidarity is a contradiction'.[41]

Both Elizabeth's translation and the rhetoric of her dedication to Henry can be productively read in light of these suggestions. The dedication to Henry is the only letter that has survived from Elizabeth to her father, and it has generally been considered a childish exercise, redolent of uncertainty and humility. Even in Lisa Klein's nuanced analysis of Elizabeth's gifts, this letter smacks of 'the abashed hesitancy of a girl not exactly sure how to address a father who has delegitimised her'. Klein writes: 'Considering Elizabeth's youth, dependency, and insecure status, her gifts exhibit not the coercive display by which wealthy nobles sought to enhance their status, but rather rely upon the giver's modest humility to foster desired, reciprocal relations with her father and stepmother'.[42]

I have argued elsewhere that we should not consider women's modesty tropes to be any more literal than we do men's. Consider the loquacious Othello's faux-apology: 'Rude am I in my speech'.[43] Why should Elizabeth's be any different? Here is some of the extended contractual rhetoric of her dedication to Henry:

> And thus, as your majesty is of such excellence that none or few are to be compared with you in royal and ample marks of honor, and I am bound unto you as lord by law of royal authority, as lord and father by the law of nature, and as greatest lord and

[38] Marcel Mauss, in W. D. Halls (trans.), *The Gift: The Form and Reason for Exchange in Archaic Societies* (Abington, 2008), 8.

[39] Mauss, *The Gift*, 8.

[40] See Maria Hayward, 'Gift Giving at the Court of Henry VIII: The 1539 New Year's Gift Roll in Context', *The Antiquaries Journal*, 85.01 (2005), 126–75.

[41] Mary Douglas, 'Forward', in Marcel Mauss, *The Gift: The Form and Reason for Exchange in Archaic Societies*, trans. W. D. Halls (Abington, 2008), x.

[42] Klein, 'Your humble Handmaid', 61.

[43] See Pender, *Rhetoric of Modesty*.

> matchless and most benevolent father by the divine law, and by all laws and duties I am bound unto your majesty in various and manifold ways, so I gladly asked (which it was my duty to do) by what means I might offer to your greatness the most excellent tribute that my capacity and diligence could discover.[44]

Elizabeth presents herself here not as once or twice, but as quadruply 'bound' to her father-king, in locutions that read not of abashed hesitancy but of meticulous and canny negotiation, conducted through the medium of modesty-legalese. Her repetitive, even excessive, representation of bondage is designed to elicit at base the simple acceptance of her gift, but more penetratingly, an acknowledgement that it is 'the most excellent tribute'—in her own words, 'a most suitable thing', than which '*nothing* ought to be more acceptable to a king' (emphasis mine).[45]

Lest the agonistic strong arm of this rhetoric escape the reader (initially Henry, but also today, ourselves) Elizabeth promises: 'If it is well received, it will incite me earnestly so that ... I will ... respect your majesty more dutifully'.[46] The dynastic recognition Elizabeth bargains for (the counter-gift of kinship status) is nowhere more prominent than in her pledge: 'May I, by this means, be indebted to you not as an imitator of your virtues but indeed as an inheritor of them'.[47] Elizabeth solidifies her status as Henry's daughter, underscoring her newly reinstated position as one of his legal, as well as linguistic, successors.

Claiming kinship and the inheritance of virtues from not only Henry but Parr and Margaret Beaufort, Elizabeth's translation thus celebrates these connections but also writes them anew. She instantiates these connections in both fabric covers and literary content, providing in this process a ready-made version of what anthropologist Annette Weiner calls 'inalienable possessions'—'possessions that are imbued with the intrinsic and ineffable identities of their owners [and] which are not easy to give away'. Ideally, Weiner writes: 'these inalienable possessions are kept by their owners from one generation to the next within the closed context of family, descent group, or dynasty', representing the paradox of keeping-while-giving.[48] Elizabeth's gift would subsequently play this symbolic role across successive English monarchies, from Henry to the present day.

Clothed in a royal family livery then, arguably of her own design and making, Elizabeth's embroidered book gift to Henry in 1545 stitches herself into the family unit in which she has been but recently reincorporated. Jones and Stallybrass argue that:

[44] Elizabeth I, in Leah S. Marcus, Janel Mueller, and Mary Beth Rose (eds), *Elizabeth I: Collected Works* (Chicago, IL, 2002) 9

[45] Marcus, Mueller, and Rose (eds), *Elizabeth I: Collected Works*, 9–10.

[46] Marcus, Mueller, and Rose (eds), *Elizabeth I: Collected Works*, 10.

[47] Marcus, Mueller, and Rose (eds), *Elizabeth I: Collected Works*, 10.

[48] Annette Weiner, *Inalienable Possessions: The Paradox of Keeping-While-Giving* (Berkeley, CA, 1992), 6.

> The end or aim of livery is to mark the body with its debts—debts of love, of solidarity, of servitude, of obedience. Clothes [and in this analysis embroidered book covers] ... like acts of naming, are attempts to stitch together past and future, to constitute genealogy and identity. [As this case shows, they can stitch together] *radically conflicting* pasts and futures, *radically different* genealogies and identities.[49]

Elizabeth's New Year's gift to Henry in 1545 presents an almost literal example of what Jones and Stallybrass call 'Needlework as a record of women's resistance to histories that obliterate them'.[50] In 1545 Elizabeth was still a bastard, but she was a now a bastard in the line of royal succession and she was a member, thanks to Parr's persuasions, of the royal household. Her translation of her stepmother's *Prayers or Meditations* marks this moment in multiple complimentary textualities: translation, dedication, and decoration, demonstrating, in the paradoxical rhetoric of *prestation* and *contre-prestation*, Elizabeth as the true inheritor of Henry's gifts.

FURTHER READING

Coles, Kimberley Anne. *Religion, Reform, and Women's Writing in Early Modern England.* Cambridge, 2008.

Crawford, Julie. *Mediatrix: Women, Politics, and Literary Production in Early Modern England.* Oxford, 2014.

Frye, Susan. *Pens and Needles: Women's Textualities in Early Modern England.* Philadelphia, PA, 2010.

Heal, Felicity. *The Power of Gifts: Gift Exchange in Early Modern England.* Oxford, 2014.

Jones, Ann Rosalind and Peter Stallybrass. *Renaissance Clothing and the Materials of Memory.* Cambridge, 2002.

White, Micheline. 'Katherine Parr, Henry VIII and Royal Literary Collaboration'. In Patricia Pender (ed.), *Gender, Authorship and Early Modern Women's Collaboration.* Cham, 2017, 23–46.

[49] Jones and Stallybrass, *Renaissance Clothing*, 273.

[50] Jones and Stallybrass, *Renaissance Clothing*, 170.

CHAPTER 35

ELIZABETH MELVILLE

Protestant Poetics, Publication, and Propaganda

SEBASTIAAN VERWEIJ

'Introite *per augustam portam. Nam lata est via que ducit ad interitum*' ('Enter in at the straight gate: for it is the wide gate, and broad way that leadeth to destruction').[1] These words, from Matthew 7.13, feature as the motto on the title page of a poem first printed in Edinburgh in 1603, *Ane Godlie Dreame, Compylit in Scottish Meter be M. M. Gentelwoman in Culros, at the requeist of her freindes*.[2] This Calvinist dream vision features a despairing speaker led to a heavenly vision by Christ, which inspires a renewed faith and as a result, upon waking, the dreamer's ecstatic homiletic address to the reader. In this shift from despair to hope, and from inwardness to exhortation, the poem dramatises the speaker's reintegration into a community of the faithful, as it tracks the profound loneliness of a 'sillie saull … tossit to and fro' (21) to the shared experience of 'sillie saulls with paines sa sair opprest' (345).[3] Throughout, *Ane Godlie Dreame* underlines the trope of life as spiritual pilgrimage. The motto found on the title page is reinforced throughout: not only the gate but also, as Christ puts it, 'The way is strait, and thou hes far to go' (148). This way—traversed not only by the dreamer but by every Scottish Presbyterian—is also 'lang' (158), 'wonderous hard' (217, 337), and 'narrow' (466).

The author of this work, 'M. M.' or 'maistres Melville', that is, Elizabeth Melville, Lady Culross (fl. 1599–1631; d. *c* 1640), is often considered a solitary traveller on a long, hard, and narrow way in another sense. Melville was the first Scottish woman whose poetry

[1] I am very grateful to the editors of this volume, as well as to Jamie Reid Baxter, for their generous comments to this chapter which have saved me from some errors.

[2] Elizabeth Melville, *Ane Godlie Dreame, Compylit in Scottish Meter be M. M. Gentelwoman in Culross, at the requeist of her freindes* (Edinburgh, 1603). The translation, slightly modernised, is from the 1560 Geneva Bible.

[3] Citations are from Elizabeth Melville, in Jamie Reid Baxter (ed.), *Poems of Elizabeth Melville, Lady Culross* (Edinburgh, 2010).

reached print, and after the attribution to her of several thousand lines of manuscript verse discovered in 2002, she is now among the most prolific early modern woman writers of the Jacobean age.[4] She is, in the estimation of the foremost Melville scholar and her editor, Jamie Reid Baxter, 'a master'.[5] Melville is, according to Sarah Dunnigan, 'of all known early-modern Scottish women writers […] the most "authoritative" and the most "interpretable"', and in the words of Jane Stevenson, 'Scotland's most important woman poet'.[6] Her singularity has often been stressed, for example by Dunnigan who argues that, despite the fact that Melville's work was 'more readily "assimilable" into existing Scottish literary and spiritual traditions' and exemplary of a 'Protestant poetics', the poetry nonetheless does not belong 'to a recognisable aesthetic or devotional "movement" or "tradition" within early-modern Scottish women's writing' (simply because so little of it has survived, or indeed, was never written).[7]

Melville matched a near unfailing command over the formal demands of her poetry with a tightly controlled vocabulary and subject matter. Almost every Melville poem (sometimes, every line) recalls another because of her continual redeployment of stock figures and phrases, many of which were ultimately quarried from Scripture. Yet underlying this focused poetic output is a wide variety of sources, and as these are being discovered by scholars, it has become possible to place Elizabeth Melville more squarely within the literary cultures of which she was a product, and an exponent (particularly the Scottish 'Protestant poetics' referenced earlier). Rather than signal Melville's singularity, scholars are now more concerned to demonstrate the various ways in which her work negotiates overlapping literary traditions that are first Scottish, second British (or English), and even European. Melville's embeddedness is also being established from further manuscript discoveries. Much of Melville's work was fully enmeshed with her environments: written, circulated, or compiled to provide spiritual solace to friends, often those who found their Calvinist faith beleaguered as the religious climate in Scotland became more hostile to them. As Melville's poetry has resurfaced in various manuscript networks, particularly in her locale at Fife in the east of Scotland, her poems are revealed to have operated also as social texts that do important work within the overlapping circles of friends, family, and spiritual kin groups.

This chapter will explore how we might best conceive of the poetry of Elizabeth Melville and her indebtedness to Scottish and British literary culture. I will draw from

[4] Jamie Reid Baxter, 'Elizabeth Melville, Lady Culross: 3500 New Lines of Verse', in Sarah M. Dunnigan, C. Marie Harker, and Evelyn S. Newlyn (eds), *Woman and the Feminine in Medieval and Early Modern Scotland* (Basingstoke, 2004), 195–200.

[5] Melville, *Poems*, 98; earlier Reid Baxter described Melville's poetic talent in more measured terms: e.g., in comparison with another more 'genuinely gifted poet', James Melville. See Jamie Reid Baxter, 'Elizabeth Melville, Calvinism and the Lyric Voice', in David J. Parkinson (ed.), *James VI and I, Literature and Scotland: Tides of Change, 1567–1625* (Leuven, 2013), 151–72, 153–5.

[6] Sarah M. Dunnigan, 'Sacred Afterlives: Mary, Queen of Scots, Elizabeth Melville and the Politics of Sanctity', *Women's Writing*, 10.3 (2003), 401–24, 414; Jane Stevenson, 'Reading, Writing and Gender in Early Modern Scotland', *The Seventeenth Century*, 27.3 (2012), 335–74, 360.

[7] Dunnigan, 'Sacred Afterlives', 419.

texts in the literary sense, by considering poetic techniques, but also pay attention to their bibliographical nature, the surviving prints and manuscripts that tell of the poetry's social lives within Melville's networks. These books will allow comparison with others like it (for instance several Scottish verse anthologies, but also an English compilation of sermons and verse). Finally, the social lives of Melville's poetry in fact underpin the functions of her verse, as it models not only a profound lyric inwardness (perhaps more readily expected from the poetry of an exceedingly pious woman), but also a commitment to social address through the discourses of practical divinity and homiletics.

POETICS AND INFLUENCES

In the search of sources, influences, and reading practices that shaped Melville's distinct poetic output, *contrafacta* and sacred parodies have proved most revealing. These practices were as well established in Scotland as elsewhere in Europe: secular words or music were turned to devotional use, or Catholic material turned to Protestant gain (or vice versa). In terms of the function of sacred parodies, and in relation to another woman poet (Mary Sidney Herbert, Countess of Pembroke), Beth Wynne Fisken has argued that such adaptations were 'devised as a form of literary religious propaganda, setting up a rival tradition of sacred verse to counter the popularity of love poetry and encourage the individual to worship God with the intensity of romantic love, in fact, to use one as training for the other'.[8] Fisken poses two questions that are important in relation to Melville: first, what poetry or other texts Melville might have read as 'training' (and consequently, where and how she might have accessed such texts), and second, a question that I will return to at the close of this chapter, whether Melville's verse was written as a kind of literary propaganda.

Two *contrafacta* appeared as printed appendices to *Ane Godlie Dreame*. The first, appended from 1603 onwards, is 'Away vaine warld', set to the tune of 'Farewell dear love' (though entitled in the print as 'Sall I let her goe').[9] The original was written and printed in 1600 by English composer Robert Jones, who also parodied his own words in 1609 by reversing his speaker's sex: from his original lovelorn male taking leave of his fickle mistress, to a woman's love complaint. The song was parodied and recopied many times in England and in Scotland.[10] Melville, who must have worked from a printed copy or manuscript intermediary, recast Jones' secular valediction as a godly lyric in which its speaker bids 'Away vaine warld bewitcher of my heart' (1). Where Jones' speakers

[8] Beth Wynne Fisken, '"The Art of Sacred Parody" in Mary Sidney's Psalmes', *Tulsa Studies in Women's Literature*, 8.2 (1989), 223–39, 223.

[9] Melville, *Poems*, 92.

[10] David Greer, 'Five Variations on "Farewell Dear Loue"', in John Caldwell, Edward Olleson, and Susan Wollenberg (eds), *The Well Enchanting Skill: Music, Poetry, and Drama in the Culture of the Renaissance* (Oxford, 1990), 213–29.

wallow in their despair for a full five stanzas, Melville's by stanza 1, line 3, finds solace in God. This allows for a witty reconfiguration of the entire dynamic of the song: from the painful departure of lovers to the welcome opportunity to leave this world and join 'my love' Christ. By virtue of this reorientation many of what seem conventional love words—'mercie', 'slave', 'sweit alluring fo[e]', 'pleasures', 'lusts'—are in Melville's rendition imbued with sacred significance:

> Ten thousand times farewell! Yet stay awhile!
> Sweet, kiss me once; sweet kisses time beguile.
> I have no power to move. (Jones)
>
> A thousand tymes away, ah stay no more,
> Sweete Christ me saif, lest subtill sin devore:
> Without thy helping hand, I have no strenth to stand. (19–21)

Here the lover's sweetness is transferred to Christ and so transformed; whereas the lover simply cannot move, so Melville's speaker can stand, but not alone. A sacred parody never quite cancels out its original but rather enters into a complex dialogue with its secular assumptions, and so Melville's practice reveals her to have been a deep and engaged reader of the secular source.

The textual history of 'Away vaine warld' and its Scottish adaptations is complex, not least because another copy with substantive variants survives in the authoritative manuscript anthology of Alexander Montgomerie's shorter poems, probably compiled by Margaret Ker.[11] Some knotty problems around dating and attribution have never been fully resolved: since Montgomerie died in 1598 he is unlikely to have written the Scots *contrafactum*. Reid Baxter suggested that Ker 'may have seen a manuscript version of Melville's words differing slightly from the 1603 publication, or simply have appropriated and retouched the latter', perhaps 'on Montgomerie's posthumous behalf'.[12]It seems at least equally possible that now lost chains of transmission account for such differences.

What is important here is that two Scottish women engaged with, and perhaps reworked, a poem that would be copied and parodied across the seventeenth century. What sets them apart is that Margaret Ker's copy remained within the comparatively closed confines of a manuscript anthology, whereas Melville's found a wider audience in print. It is difficult to be certain that the route to print demonstrates an author who was more politically or even propagandistically inclined: *Ane Godlie Dreame* was printed '*at the requeist of her freindes*' and there is no evidence of Melville's involvement in the publication process beyond the ambiguous fact and existence of this first printed edition.

[11] Now rejected from his canon, the song was printed in Alexander Montgomerie, in James Cranstoun (ed.), *The Poems of Alexander Montgomerie* (Edinburgh, 1887), 237; cf. Alexander Montgomerie, in David J. Parkinson (ed.), *Alexander Montgomerie: Poems* (Edinburgh, 2000), I, 5–6.

[12] Jamie Reid Baxter, 'The Songs of Lady Culross', in Gordon Munro, Stuart Campbell, Greta-Mary Hair, Margaret Mackay, Elaine Moohan, and Graham Hair (eds), *Notis Musycall: Essays on Music and Scottish Culture in Honour of Kenneth Elliott* (Glasgow, 2005), 143–63, 144–5, 160.

The other printed *contrafactum* was appended to *Ane Godlie Dreame* in later editions, from 1644 onwards, though Melville's authorship seems relatively secure.[13] This poem, 'Come, Sweet Lord', also originated from English song culture, in this case Richard Johnson's 'The Shepheards Joy', which starts 'Come sweet Love, let sorrow cease'. There is once more some evidence that *The Golden Garland* found other Scottish readers, some of them women. This is the verse miscellany compiled by Margaret Robertson of Lude around 1630, which contains a copy of 'Come suet love let sorrow cease' and another song from the *Garland*.[14] Robertson was amongst the most prolific of Scottish readers and copyists of English songbooks: her manuscript contains over sixty lyrics that ultimately derived from as many as seventeen different English printed titles by composers such as William Byrd, Thomas Campion, and John Dowland.[15] Robertson's miscellany also shares some texts with the music and song anthology by another Scottish woman, Margaret Wemyss, who also copied from English sources including Campion and Morley.[16] Such English imports were thus routinely read by Scottish women, and some actively copied this material into their own collections. Yet Elizabeth Melville went a step further than some of her contemporaries, in that her sacred parodies reject, or at least problematise, the values inherent in the secular songs.

These are but two short examples of Melville's reading and poetic practice, chosen because there is also more evidence of their separate circulation in Scotland. Other poems from her canon which cannot be discussed in detail here further reinforce just how deeply embedded Melville was in the literary cultures of her age. This includes another *contrafactum*, of Christopher Marlowe's pastoral wooing song 'Come live with me and be my love' (*Poems*, 7–9). Since its first attributed appearance in *Englands Helicon* (1600), in England it was often copied into manuscript alongside Raleigh's answer poem, and frequently parodied; one Scottish reworking by Alexander Craig was printed in *The Amorose Songes, Sonets, and Elegies* (1606).[17] *Ane Godlie Dreame* stands in the long tradition of Scottish and English late medieval visionary poetry: from Chaucer, to James I, William Dunbar, and David Lyndsay, to the contemporaneous Alexander Montgomerie's *Of the Cherrie and the Slae*. Melville also used the native Scots 'Solsequium' stanza, developed by Montgomerie and often reused by others. Melville's three sonnet sequences (or series, respectively of three, three, and seven poems) have attracted attention as perhaps the most accessible texts for today's readers. These poems explicitly engaged with the Scottish trend for sonneteering in the 1580s and early 1590s at court, but they also showed awareness of English pietistic sonnets, some English secular

13 Reid Baxter, 'Songs', 145–8.

14 National Library of Scotland, Edinburgh, MS 15937.

15 Sebastiaan Verweij, *The Literary Culture of Early Modern Scotland: Manuscript Production and Circulation, 1560–1625* (Oxford, 2016), 221–40.

16 National Library of Scotland, Edinburgh, MS Dep. 314/24.

17 Frederick W. Sternfeld and Mary Joiner Chan, 'Come Live with Me and Be My Love', *Comparative Literature*, 22.2 (1970), 173–87.

sonnets (for instance by Sidney), and further displayed the stylistic features ultimately deriving from European neo-Petrarchism and *amour courtois*.[18]

Other poems have more obscure referents, for instance one of Melville's currently unprinted poems, 'The Winter Nicht', in twenty-one twelve-line stanzas of tail-rhyme, or *rime couée*.[19] Reid Baxter has shown not only this poem's strong similarity to *Ane Godlie Dreame* in terms of subject and stock phrasing, but also that Melville's poem was an explicit response to a poem by the Scottish minister James Anderson, *The Winter Nicht* (*c* 1582).[20] If the source has been clearly established, it is still worth considering what these late Calvinist renditions bring to the long history of tail-rhyme, and especially its Scottish inflections (see this volume, Chapter 13, Dianne Mitchell, 'Lyric Backwardness'). Whereas Middle English poets used it frequently, it was, by Chaucer's time, also ripe for parody (famously in the *Tale of Sir Topas*). Rhiannon Purdie has noted 'the complete absence of tail-rhyme romance in the Scottish corpus', and when it was used by Scots poets, for instance William Dunbar, it served satirical ends.[21] Just as *Ane Godlie Dreame* obliquely builds on English and Scottish dream vision, so Melville's endorsement of tail-rhyme rehabilitates some of the form's potential as it strips away the association with satire and comedy.

The ways in which Melville responded to literary precedent function as indicators of her aesthetic sensibilities, but also underline aspects of the literary cultures that shaped her writing. This begs important questions as to what Melville read, and more broadly, of her cultural education and intellectual milieux. The poet's biography contains some enormous gaps, especially regarding her earlier years. Yet scholars routinely invoke Melville's family environment and strongly Protestant background, including her grandfather Sir John Melville of Raith, and her father, Sir James Melville of Halhill.[22] The latter's career as diplomat and ambassador to France, privy councillor, gentleman of the bedchamber of Queen Anne, but also a memoirist, will at least have made possible a broad and literate education for his children. Though women's educational opportunities were often curtailed, Elizabeth Melville belonged to a family that was well connected, culturally active, and literarily attuned.

It makes sense therefore to consider a resource which has not, to my knowledge, been discussed in relation to the poet or indeed much noticed at all: two surviving library catalogues from Monimail, previously a fine Renaissance palace owned by Cardinal Beaton, and which became in 1592 the home of Sir Robert Melville of Murdocairny, the first Lord Melville (1616) and uncle of the poet (see this volume, Chapter 8, Leah Knight,

[18] Sarah C. E. Ross, 'Elizabeth Melville and the Religious Sonnet Sequence in Scotland and England', in Susan Wiseman (ed.), *Early Modern Women and the Poem* (Manchester, 2013), 42–59.

[19] New College Library, University of Edinburgh, MS Bru. 2, fol. 173v. Subsequent references will be to the 'Bruce manuscript'.

[20] Reid Baxter, 'Songs', 153–9.

[21] Rhiannon Purdie, 'Medieval Romance in Scotland', in Priscilla Bawcutt and Janet Hadley Williams (eds), *A Companion to Medieval Scottish Poetry* (Cambridge, 2006), 165–77, 170.

[22] See further Reid Baxter, 'Calvinism', 152, stressing especially the courtly connections of other family members; cf. Jamie Reid Baxter, 'Elizabeth Melville, Lady Culross: New Light from Fife', *Innes Review*, 68.1 (2017), 38–77, 43–9.

'Libraries Not Their Own'). No family papers from Halhill (the estate of Elizabeth Melville's father) have survived, but she occasionally visited there after her marriage when she had settled at Comrie Wester (near Culross).[23] Monimail was at easy walking distance from Halhill, and both places near to Collessie, site of the Melville Tomb that features the funerary verses also attributed to the poet.

The first book catalogue is undated but likely compiled in the later 1620s. It lists a little over fifty books, stored 'in the Upper Studie off Monymaill'.[24] This is, broadly speaking, a gentleman's library containing a smattering of the classics (Seneca, Tacitus), history, including more current affairs (e.g., a history of the Turks, Holinshed, and reports relating to the House of Orange), Protestant theology, and books on estate management (e.g., horticulture or horsemanship). Works in French include translations of the Psalms and Genesis, as well as chronicles. There are several works of anti-Catholicism, practical divinity, and some literary texts: Sylvester's Du Bartas, James VI's *His Majesties Poeticall Exercises at Vacant Houres* (1591), Overbury's *A Wife* (1614), and what the catalogue lists as 'The anatomie of the World', perhaps Donne's printed poem commemorating Elizabeth Drury (1612). The second catalogue, compiled *c* 1681, is much more exhaustive.[25] It includes around five hundred titles organised under fifteen headings, some of which suggest a more profound, even scholarly, engagement with its subject. Of note in relation to Melville's religiosity are books in the categories of 'Fathers and commentaries on the bible' (*c* 64); 'Bookes of didactick and polemick divinitie' (*c* 84); and 'Bookis of Practicall divinitie' (*c* 48). Virtually all books listed under 'Romances' (*c* 17 titles), the only strictly literary category, date to well after Melville's death, but include the work of her youngest son, 'Sam. Colvilles mock poems'. Since the second catalogue incorporates some titles from the first, it follows that either this Melville library grew exponentially over the middle of the seventeenth century, or the first catalogue was only a partial representation of books already owned by Murdocairny but stored elsewhere.

Some provisos are necessary: Elizabeth Melville's association with Robert Melville of Murdocairny and his library is indirect at best; no physical copies of the books on the lists have (yet) been discovered; we have no evidence the poet ever accessed them; and there are no direct matches between the library catalogues and some of Elizabeth Melville's known sources. We must also remember that the majority of Melville's poetry appears to have been written in the late 1590s through to *c* 1610: anything post-dating these years cannot readily be brought into conversation with the poet's work. However, placing Elizabeth Melville within the bookish culture of her family may ultimately account for some of her wider (and ongoing) education and suggest pathways by which Melville acquired some of her books and formative reading opportunities. The library certainly reflects how book collecting formed part of the family's religious, political, and cultural activities and interests.

[23] Cf. the letter from Elizabeth Melville to John Livingston, 10 December 1631, 'from Helhill' [sic]: W. K. Tweedie (ed.), *Select Biographies* (Edinburgh, 1845), I, 365.

[24] National Archives of Scotland, Edinburgh, GD 26/6/124.

[25] National Archives of Scotland, Edinburgh, GD 26/6/136.

Further research will be needed to support this hypothesis, but consider three poems from the Bruce manuscript: 'Ane exhortatioun for patience with ane prayer for comfort' (fol. 174v), 'Ane lamentatioun for sin with ane consolatioun to the afflicted saull' (fol. 175v), and 'Ane stryfe againes sorrow with ane prayer for comfort, and ane thankisgiving for ane suddane feilling of the samen' (fol. 180r). They follow a similar pattern from complaint and introspection, to answer and comfort. This pattern is also reinforced by two scriptural citations that preface each poem (respectively, Hebrews 12.1–2 and James 5.13; Matthew 5.4 and James 4.10; Psalms 27.14 and Psalms 3.5), which relate the movement from despair to hope, and the promise of God's restitution of his chosen. In the 'exhortatioun' (in twenty-four eight-line stanzas) the speaker addresses their 'woful saull incarcerat / Within this corps of cair' and chides it for 'murning': 'Thy sichis and sobbis do pearce the air / that thou to hevin doth send' (fol. 174v). Most of the poem, before the speaker's 'prayer for comfort' to God, speaks in moral Christian dicta expressed in the imperative: 'Do daylie homage on thy kneyis / vnto thy father deir'; 'Luik on the law if thow wold lear / to lead thy lyfe aricht'. As elsewhere in the corpus the speaker's suffering is aligned with that of Christ:

With patience learne to bear the croce
    from suddane wraith refraine
Tyn not thy hairt for worldlie loss
    lent gudis sall not remaine
If god sall give and tak againe
    Yit blis his holie name
Then pleasure sall cum efter paine
    and honour efter schame. (fol. 175r)

In the second poem, the first thirteen stanzas constitute a 'lamentatioun'. The 'consolatioun' that follows underscores Melville's doctrinal position:

[14]
For thy decrie o lord can not be brokin
no slicht of sin can vanquische thy elect
the word that once out of thy mouth is spokin
sall not returne vntill it tak effect ...

[15]
Yit thy elect can nevir sin to death
becaus thy blud hes stay'd thy fatheris wraith

[16]
Quho sall lay oucht vnto thy chosinis chairge
quhom god doth justifie quho dar condame
thoucht sin abound his grace aboundis more lairge
quhois promis is ay ane and still the same. (fol. 176r)

Expression here of the Covenant of Grace is predicated on what is evident throughout Melville's work: 'its fundamentalist Calvinist theology, complete with predestination, *contemptus mundi* and awareness of Satan's tyrannical persecution of the Elect in this reprobate world'.[26] The speaker finally exhorts to 'Put on the helmet of salvatioun / w[i]t[h] the breistplat of richteousnes', and so armed, finds comfort and joy in the promise of redemption.

These poems are not sacred parodies, yet continue some of the function of Melville's verse at large. I would like to argue that what they particularly seek to achieve may be classified as 'practical divinity': an early modern discourse that was grounded in Scripture, advocating a moral living according to Calvinist principle, in relatively plain style and explicitly didactic. If practical divinity is largely a prose genre, some poetical collections operate in line with its aims. It seems no surprise that some texts of this kind have occasionally been mentioned in relation to Melville, e.g., George Herbert's *The Temple* or John Bunyan's *The Pilgrims Progress*. Bearing in mind the above-mentioned provisos regarding the library at Monimail, it is worth stressing how this family collection invested in what the second catalogue also termed 'practicall divinity'. A few examples focusing on books published within Melville's lifetime must suffice. From the second catalogue, among the foundational authors of the genre is the English puritan William Perkins, whose commentary on the Epistle of Jude and lectures on the first three chapters of Revelations are included (1606, STC 19724; 1604, STC 19731). Works by Scots include Zachary Boyd's *Balme of Gilead* (1629, STC 3445a), three sermons on spiritual sickness predicated on Psalm 107, and Robert Rollock's *A Treatise of Gods Effectual Calling* (1603, STC 21286). Books included in the first catalogue and published within the period when Melville is known to have written poetry include the formative 'Calvines Institutiones in English'. Another is *The Amendment of Life* (1594, STC 23650) by Dutch reformed minister Jean Taffin: this book cataloguing man's sins and duties urges spiritual betterment since, as the title page motto from Matthew observes, 'Amend your liues for the kingdome of heauen is at hand'. Although the exact work is not specified in the list, 'Dubartas translated by Jo. Sylvester' ranks amongst the most important works of Protestant epic in the period (Sylvester published editions from the 1590s onwards), and exceptionally so in Scotland.[27]

It is in some sense perverse to look to establish a reading context for a poet who might argue her entire corpus is predicated on a single text: the word of God. It is also well known that Melville maintained close relationships with a number of Scots divines (e.g., John Livingston, John Welsh, Andrew Melville, Samuel Rutherford), she was known to other Protestant poets (famously to Alexander Hume), and that she offered spiritual comfort to her family and community. It seems reasonable to assume that some of these people furnished Melville with books and ideas, directly and indirectly (e.g., through access to sermons, or by maintaining correspondence).

[26] Reid Baxter, 'Calvinism', 153.

[27] See Peter Auger, *Du Bartas' Legacy in England and Scotland*. Oxford, 2019.

Yet Elizabeth Melville's poetry fits well within the Protestant theology and spiritual practice espoused (in parts of) this family library: it offers new angles on the intellectual culture of the Melvilles and as such, both the library and the poet's potential connections with it, deserve further scrutiny.

PUBLICATION AND PROPAGANDA

Melville's extant corpus divides into three main parts: in print, *Ane Godlie Dreame* (1603 and frequently printed thereafter) and the two appended *contrafacta* lyrics; second, the twenty-nine poems attributed to Melville in 2002 in the Bruce manuscript, appended there to a sermon series on Hebrews XI by the Edinburgh minister Robert Bruce preached in 1590/91; and third, a disparate collection of poems across manuscripts. Completing the corpus is the funerary inscription on the Melville family tomb at Collessie (possibly by Melville), and a collection of thirteen letters (some in autograph) and four addressed to her.[28]

In this section I briefly consider Melville's publication strategies associated with some of these works, and in particular how these supported the social and intellectual work that the poems purport to undertake: that is, to offer spiritual guidance and consolation (in accordance with practical divinity), and perhaps even—in the words of Fisken—a kind of propaganda. In 1605/06 Melville sent a sonnet to John Welsh, a minister with a long track record of challenging the king's ecclesiastical policy and then in prison for disobeying Privy Council orders forbidding a General Assembly.[29] The sole copy of the sonnet survives among the papers of church historian Robert Woodrow.[30] Woodrow's attribution, 'A sonnet sent to Blackness to Mr John Welsh by ye Lady Culross' records the occasion, but judging by his transcription (made over a century later) that indents every other line of the quatrains, Woodrow (or the scribe of his source) missed the acrostic. This suggests the different levels on which the poem operated: readers further removed in time read a conventionally Protestant poem of spiritual consolation (and one entirely in keeping with Melville's oeuvre, with its advice couched in the imperative: e.g., 'w[i]t[h] courage bear ye crosse'; 'wait on his will whoes Blood hath bo[ugh]t ye dear'; 'End out thy faught and suffer for his sake'). However, the recipient (assuming a copy reached Welsh) and perhaps other readers in Melville's immediate circles, read a sonnet that was anchored to the historical moment, tailored to one man's spiritual distress, but also speaking to the spiritual distress shared by co-religionists. Melville's

28 All works are planned for inclusion in Jamie Reid Baxter's forthcoming critical edition. The most comprehensive bibliographical description (no longer complete after new discoveries) is Sarah C. E. Ross, 'Elizabeth Melville: Textual History', *Early Modern Women Research Network* https://c21ch.newcastle.edu.au/emwrn/elizabethmelville, accessed 9 March 2021.

29 Melville, *Poems*, 68.

30 National Library of Scotland, Edinburgh, MS Wod. Qu. XXIX (iv), fols. 10–11.

encouragement was a significant political act with potential consequences, and may have been rendered more safe by its acrostic address that in scribal form could either be highlighted or obscured.

Another manuscript contains a mini-anthology (on a single sheet) of five poems associated with Andrew and James Melville, including two by Elizabeth Melville (one explicitly attributed to her) addressed to Andrew (his association emerges once more from acrostics and anagrams).[31] The sheet was appended to a copy, *c* 1598–1623, of Robert Lindsay of Pitscottie's *History and Chronicles of Scotland*, and is followed by other materials that (owing to their anti-episcopalianism) may be seen to chime with the Presbyterian Melville poems. Similar to the Woodrow collection, the historical tenor of co-texts and compilation impulse suggests that these poems were treated as primary source material or illustration of historical issues. Not all manuscripts containing Melville's verse can be mentioned or discussed here, but some display family relations, for instance a late copy by Elizabeth Bruce Boswell (1673–1734) of Melville's above-mentioned sacred parody of Marlowe. Another is the newly discovered 'East Neuk commonplace book', containing another copy of a poem discussed above, 'Ane lamentatioun for sin with ane consolatioun to the afflicted saull' alongside poetry by James Melville (copied from print), and a host of documents that ties this manuscript firmly to its place of production in Fife.[32]

The importance of such manuscripts cannot be overestimated: they demonstrate that 'Melville strategically, successfully, and extensively exploited manuscript practices to cultivate overlapping poetic coteries and networks'.[33] Reid Baxter's assertion—'that Melville's verse had an existence independent of its author'—based on the East Neuk commonplace book and a further manuscript containing copies from the Bruce collection, finally underlines that the functions of Melville's verse were decidedly plural. To the poet and her direct addressees, these poems united in spirit, and gave voice to their increased suffering at the hands of the establishment. Yet the function of such autograph manuscripts (now lost) can only be inferred from their later copies which in themselves add further cumulative function to the poetry (e.g., commemorative, historical, familial).

A major revisionist study by Reid Baxter (in turn endorsed by Sarah Ross) has finally changed assumptions about the nature of the Bruce manuscript. Its opening sonnet with anagrams in the opening and closing lines ('Sob sille cor') and acrostic partner poem spelling 'ISABELL COR' had been read as referring to the poet and her anguished heart (Latin, *cor*). Yet discovery of an actual Isobell Cor and her anguished life story has turned her into the collection's potential instigator. Thus Reid Baxter has quashed old hypotheses on the manuscript's function and has boldly asserted instead that:

[31] National Library of Scotland, Crawford Collections, Acc. 9769, Personal Papers 84/1/1, 174–5.]

[32] See Reid Baxter, 'New Light'.

[33] Sarah C. E. Ross, 'Peripatetic Poems: Sites of Production and Routes of Exchange in Elizabeth Melville's Scotland', *Women's Writing*, 26.1 (2019), 53–70, 65.

> Isobell Cor commissioned the copying of Bruce's sermons on Hebrews 11 … As Lady Airdrie's [Cor's] personal and spiritual situation grew worse, she sought help from her friend Lady Culross, asking for some of the unpublished 'spiritual exercises in verse' that she knew existed. In response, Melville went back to her own notebooks, and carefully assembled the sequence of poems.[34]

This train of events, if not (yet) provable, accords Cor and Melville central and active roles in the creation of the manuscript, and consequently underscores what is generally becoming clearer in terms of early modern women's sustained engagement with sermons and their manuscripts. The ongoing *Gateway to Early Modern Manuscript Sermons* project (*GEMMS*) has unearthed many such women, who figured commonly as auditors and the subjects of sermons (at funerals, marriages, churchings), and even as patrons (largely an aristocratic prerogative). Women also acted as owners, dedicatees, or givers of sermon compilations, and as scribes, copyists, or sermon notetakers. *GEMMS* to date records about ten named female notetakers, and over twenty manuscript owners including at least one Scottish example, a Margaret Cockburn, owner of a sermon compilation dated to around 1660.[35] More broadly speaking, ownership of such manuscripts must be placed on a continuum with women's devotional practice: in Scotland this has been well documented, e.g., in relation to spiritual autobiography. More particular in terms of book ownership, one Englishwoman, Anne Sadleir (1585–1671/72), author of autobiographical religious mediations and a letter writer, also owned many sermon manuscripts that she ultimately presented to friends and libraries.[36] Another example proves the extraordinary exception to the rule that women were exclusively consumers of sermonic texts: this is Anna Walker, author of a manuscript sermon and several poems and meditations that were transcribed into a presentation manuscript for Queen Anne.[37] As an appeal for patronage this collection functioned differently from the Bruce manuscript, and with additional frisson since its stridently Protestant author addressed a queen who was rumoured to have converted to Catholicism.

Walker is of particular interest in comparison to Elizabeth Melville, whose own homiletic style has long been the subject of attention. Especially the third part of *Ane Godlie Dreame* (229 ff.) functions as sermonic address, or even 'a full-blown verse sermon'.[38]

[34] Reid Baxter, 'New Light', 74.

[35] National Library of Scotland, Edinburgh, Acc. 9270, Pt. 6. See further Jeanne Shami and Anne James, *Gateway to Early Modern Manuscript Sermons* https://gemms.itercommunity.org, accessed 9 March 2021.

[36] Arnold Hunt, 'The Books, Library, and Literary Patronage of Mrs. Anne Sadleir (1585–1670)', in Victoria E. Burke and Jonathan Gibson (eds), *Early Modern Women's Manuscript Writing: Selected Papers from the Trinity/Trent Colloquium* (Aldershot, 2004), 205–36.

[37] Suzanne Trill, 'A Feminist Critic in the Archives: Reading Anna Walker's A Sweete Savor for Woman (c. 1606)', *Women's Writing*, 9.2 (2002), 199–214.

[38] Reid Baxter, 'Calvinism', 168; cf. Deanna Delmar Evans, 'Holy Terror and Love Divine: The Passionate Voice in Elizabeth Melville's Ane Godlie Dreame', in Sarah M. Dunnigan, C. Marie Harker, and Evelyn S. Newlyn (eds), *Woman and the Feminine in Medieval and Early Modern Scottish Writing* (Basingstoke, 2004), 153–61.

> The way to heaven, I sie, is wonderous hard.
> My Dreame declairs that we have far to go:
> Wee mon be stout, for cowards ar debarde,
> Our flesh on force mon suffer paine and wo.
> Thir grivelie gaits and many dangers mo
> Awaits for us, wee can not leive in rest:
> Bot let us learne, sence wee ar wairnit so,
> To cleave to Christ, for he can help us best. (337–44)

At this point the poem once more harks back to the motto on the title page, but also develops the necessity of the 'grivelie gaits' (grievous, arduous, troublesome ways) for spiritual reformation. This type of homiletic discourse, centred on Christ's word and example, and its prescriptive application for good moral living, is also on a continuum with other poems by Melville, as I have suggested above in relation to the poems functioning as practical divinity. (The Melville library at Monimail was also replete with sermons.)

This confluence between *Ane Godlie Dreame* and the Bruce anthology begs further questions about where Melville (and Cor) stand in terms of women's engagement with sermon culture, and of course, how this intersected more broadly with poetry and related forms of art (e.g., godly song). It asks questions, too, of the ways in which women contributed to early modern Protestant poetics, not only as participants in such a culture but also as active proponents of it. Answers to such questions will need to be framed locally, with attention to Scottish Presbyterian practice (and here Reid Baxter's research into the Fife communities once more leads the way), but also include the comparative evidence from other early modern British women (this too is underway, as Melville's work has been compared, for instance, with poetry by Anne Lock, Aemilia Lanyer, Rachel Speght, and Katherine Philips). This chapter has explored some other ways in which Melville's poetry is not only singular, but also embedded in the literary cultures of her age: in reference to other Scottish female compilers, and the bookish culture of the Melville family. This embeddedness is, I demonstrate, also suggested by the combined evidence of *Ane Godlie Dreame* and the lyrical poems from the Bruce manuscript. As Fisken has explained, *contrafacta* and sacred parodies function in part as spiritual propaganda, redirecting amatory impulses to a love for God and Christ. Sarah Ross has read Melville's sonnets alongside English sonnets that were explicitly records of conversion (Henry Constable and William Alabaster), and Jamie Reid Baxter has even suggested that 'the 29 poems in the Robert Bruce MS read like the monuments of a "conversion experience"'.[39] Conversion records are by their nature polemical and exemplary, modelling how other conflicted spirits might follow a similar path. In Melville's lyrics, any outward concerns in terms of the poems' function may seem wholly outweighed by the urgent spiritual distress of their first-person speakers, and that of the single

[39] Ross, 'Religious Sonnet Sequence', 42–3; Jamie Reid Baxter, 'Presbytery, Politics and Poetry: Maister Robert Bruce, John Burel and Elizabeth Melville, Lady Culross', *Records of the Scottish Church History Society*, 33 (2003), 6–27, 21.

addressees of these works (Welsh, Melville, Cor)—all experienced in such anxious privacy. Yet as soon as such poems find wider audiences, like the conversion records, they also model a Calvinist forbearance, and the discourse of spiritual counsel. So in some sense the very propagandistic aspects of Melville's verse, explicitly so the homiletic mode and implicitly so the *contrafacta* and sacred parodies, are supported and made possible by the inwardness of the lyrical poetry: as such, Melville's poetics and the social lives of her poems mutually reinforce each other.

FURTHER READING

Dunnigan, Sarah M., C. Marie Harker, and Evelyn S. Newlyn (eds). *Woman and the Feminine in Medieval and Early Modern Scottish Writing*. Basingstoke, 2004.

Melville, Elizabeth. In Jamie Reid Baxter (ed.), *Poems of Elizabeth Melville, Lady Culross*. Edinburgh, 2010.

Stevenson, Jane. 'Reading, Writing and Gender in Early Modern Scotland', *The Seventeenth Century*, 27.3 (2012), 335–74.

Verweij, Sebastiaan. *The Literary Culture of Early Modern Scotland: Manuscript Production and Circulation, 1560–1625*. Oxford, 2016.

CHAPTER 36

DESIRE, DREAMS, DISGUISE

The Letters of Elizabeth Bourne

DANIEL STARZA SMITH AND LEAH VERONESE

'I taste of fortunes byter spyte more then any body euer dyd', laments Elizabeth Bourne (1549–1599) in one of her letters: 'yf I showld com playne all my grefes to you a whole bybell would not howld them'.[1] Bourne's words reflect many of the concerns and self-presentations encountered in her writing. In the face of untold suffering, she stands defiant against injustice, channelling extreme pain into righteous anger. Her lament—consciously evoking the complaint genre—has an unmistakably literary feel, thanks to the bookish image of an overflowing 'bybell', the striking generic hybridity (would it still be a Bible if it was about her life story?), and her facility with purposefully rhetorical turns of phrase ('fortunes byter spyte'). Bourne undoubtedly experienced appalling life events, but her tendency to portray herself as *uniquely* wronged lends her prose urgency and vivacity. This letter actively interacts with its correspondent, participating in a wider conversation which will collaboratively develop shared imagery and linguistic patterns. Yet even in the midst of her narrative we are told that she is still holding back, that the true depths of her passions remain unknown to us—that they would probably overwhelm us if she were to unleash the full force of her feelings. Joining a tradition of literature in the mode of complaint, Bourne pours out her woes, while insisting on the

[1] London, British Library, Add. MS 23,212, fol. 123r. This MS is a collection of approximately 129 separates found among the Conway Papers and bound in the nineteenth century, rather than a contemporary miscellany. All future references to this MS will be made in the main text, by folio only. The transcriptions are our own; [square brackets] indicate our interpolations and <angle brackets> indicate damaged or illegible text. We are grateful to Caroline Sharp for sharing with us her transcriptions of some of these documents, made during her master's degree at King's College London. Cristina Léon Alfar's and Emily G. Sherwood's edition of Bourne's letters, *Reading Mistress Elizabeth Bourne: Marriage, Separation, and Legal Controversies* (New York, 2021), was published as this chapter went to press.

impossibility of giving them full articulation.[2] In a manoeuvre typical of her authorial self-construction, Bourne insists the reader acknowledge her perspective while simultaneously evading scrutiny. Even while reaching out, her writings frequently express her desire for sanctuary, a principal theme of this essay (see this volume, Chapter 40, James Loxley, 'The Topopoetics Of Retirement'). Deprived of any real physical or psychological safety, in her letters she draws on an astonishing range of rhetorical devices to create spaces of imaginative respite.

Elizabeth was born to Edmund Horne (*c* 1490–1553), a gentleman pensioner of Sarsden, Oxfordshire, and Amy Clarke/Clerke (d. *c* 1581) who, after Edmund's death, married Sir James Mervyn (1529–1611). Elizabeth grew up in considerable privilege; both she and her mother spent time at court, and Elizabeth was clearly educated (her imagery engages with the Bible and contemporary romance).[3] Her life was overturned by her disastrous marriage in 1565 to Anthony Bourne, the son of Sir John Bourne (*c* 1518–1575), Queen Mary's principal secretary of state between 1553 and 1558. Anthony is one of the most well-documented terrorisers of Elizabethan England, 'a pathological cheat, liar, and philanderer, extremely prone to physical violence, and able to raise armed gangs or commission individual thugs to intimidate his enemies'.[4] His crimes against Elizabeth were vicious and unrelenting. Having sworn her 'death and dystruction', Anthony repeatedly beat her, tried to poison her, and threatened to 'blowe upp' the house with gunpowder, with his wife and her children inside.[5] While defrauding his wife of thousands of pounds and spending the money on his affairs, chillingly he even hired a man from France with a burned hand to follow Elizabeth's movements and bribe her servants for information—probably with the intention of murdering her. In the face of active and continuous threats she proved herself forthright, determined, and resourceful, negotiating complex contemporary patronage networks to secure support for her legal case against her husband. It was in this context that Sir John Conway (1535–1603), a former Low Countries soldier, was appointed as her legal guardian. The romance that developed between Elizabeth and Conway can be traced in a series of letters recording both passion and exquisite fantasies.[6]

2 The rehabilitation of Bourne's voice contributes to current critical attempts to challenge the notion that early modern female complaint was usually 'an act of male literary ventriloquy' in the tradition of Ovid's *Heroides*. Furthermore, in her frequent evocation of friendship and patronage (albeit relationships that have failed her), Bourne further confirms that real female-authored complaint tends to situate speakers 'in networks of literary, social, and political exchange', rather than presenting them as utterly abandoned and alone. See Sarah C. E. Ross and Rosalind Smith, 'Beyond Ovid: Early Modern Women's Complaint', in *Early Modern Women's Complaint: Gender, Form, and Politics* (Cham, 2020), 1–26, 2, 11.

3 Charles Angell Bradford, *The Conway Papers (1576–1606)*, 26; unpublished typescript, Folger Shakespeare Library call number DA378.C6 B6. Although he did not employ footnotes, Bradford (1864–1940) was a careful scholar and palaeographer who identified and transcribed a great many relevant documents, and carefully untangled the legal complexities of the Bourne marriage.

4 Daniel Starza Smith, 'Elizabeth Bourne', *Oxford Dictionary of National Biography*, 2021.

5 BL Add. MS 12,507, fol. 204r.

6 Reading Bourne and Conway's relationship very differently, Glynn Parry and Cathryn Enis have argued that Bourne had an unreciprocated 'crush' on Conway, who simply used her to exploit his access

Bourne writes to Conway with unguarded passion about physical and emotional love, a rare quality in surviving women's letters from the period: 'I rejoyse in you more than I am able to expresse ... what creatvre can be mor happyer then I who loves and is loved interchangeable un revokeable' (fol. 123r); 'I never sese to saye I love you and honor you I dye wyth ovt you and lyve and lacke nothing when I haue you' (fol. 145r). Bourne's direct, emotional, and literary rhetoric, and the very personal record of her suffering, mark her out as a unique voice in early modern England, as several recent studies have recognised.[7] Now with an *Oxford Dictionary of National Biography* (*ODNB*) entry and Cristina Léon Alfar's and Emily G. Sherwood's edition of her correspondence recently published, her dramatic life experience and extraordinary writings are increasingly visible to early modern scholars. This chapter is the first critical piece dedicated to a literary reading of her letters.

The corpus of Elizabeth Bourne as poet, eloquent petitioner, and 'one of the most prolific letter-writers of her generation' offers many avenues for future scholars to explore, including the relationship between her letters and the law, her use of dream imagery, and the language of espionage.[8] Bourne astutely utilised networks of kinship and courtiership to advance her legal case and win herself powerful support through eloquent petition. Yet despite all her connections, her writing often emphasises her solitude and abandonment. On occasion this rhetoric could be carefully calculated to evoke sympathy and provoke assistance ('all my ovne kynne haue forsacken me: ther fore yf you euer sayde yo^u wovld frend me nowe is the tyme to showe hit', fol. 127r). Nevertheless, her literary persona insistently returns to isolated spaces: the places where she experienced real entrapment and torment; domestic spaces crushingly devoid of familial love; concealed locations for covert writing ('my stody wheare I doo nothing but wysh for you', fol. 140v); and the charged sites of secret trysts (imagined and, we assume, real). Abandoned, her need for support, kinship, and love drew her to Conway. Their relationship—predicated almost entirely on her perceived *lack* of a wider network—created the conditions of her surviving literary output. It seems most productive, therefore, to concentrate on the ways Bourne imagines and creates space to describe and contemplate her unique life experience. We trace the letters as an erotic space

to her estate; see *Shakespeare Before Shakespeare: Stratford Upon Avon, Warwickshire and the Elizabethan State* (Oxford, 2020), 127. While it is certainly true that the Conways strengthened their estate through marriage with the Bournes, this chapter acknowledges Elizabeth's rhetorical focus on equality and mutuality, which suggests that she at least understood their relationship to be reciprocal.

7 See, e.g., James Daybell, 'Interpreting Letters and Reading Script: Evidence for Female Education and Literacy in Tudor England', *History of Education*, 34 (2005), 695–715; Daniel Starza Smith, *John Donne and the Conway Papers* (Oxford, 2014); Cristina Léon Alfar, *Women and Shakespeare's Cuckoldry Plays: Shifting Narratives of Marital Betrayal* (New York, 2017).

8 James Daybell was the first to draw attention to Bourne's poem 'I hope, what happe? thy happie states retyre'; see Daybell, 'Elizabeth Bourne (fl. 1570s–1580s): A New Elizabethan Woman Poet', *NQ*, 52 (2005), 176–8, 176. For Bourne's use of the petitionary genre, see Leah Veronese and Daniel Starza Smith, 'Elizabeth Bourne', in Patricia Pender and Rosalind Smith (eds), *The Palgrave Encyclopedia of Early Modern Women's Writing* (Cham, forthcoming).

in themselves; how this space was threatened by surveillance; Bourne's and Conway's use of the letters to co-create an imagined sanctuary; and the letters themselves as transformative literary space. The chapter ends by reflecting on a different kind of space, the archive, and its material context as a site for the study of early modern women's writing.

LETTERS AS EROTIC SPACE

As Gary Schneider has usefully argued, 'epistolary contact' in early modern England 'manifested its affective … power not by *being* actual face-to-face contact, but by inscribing rhetorical strategies based on speech, aurality, and bodily presence'.[9] While there are clearly difficulties with dating this correspondence, Bourne and Conway evidently drew on similar language and imagery throughout their surviving letters to one another, envisaging an erotic space in which their material engagements replicate the real physical contact denied them. Conway describes Bourne's missives as embodiments of their sender:

> fo^{r} yor letter ys the Image of yor self and < > thisys most trewe that in the letter of a very ffrynde the harte ys delyghted the eyes plessed, the understandyng cōfo^{r}ted, and all the < > spyrytes rejoysted. (fol. 149r)

Bourne elaborates on the proximity and interaction enabled by their letters, playing with the erotic potential of inscribed bodily presence:

> I … hope that my novne knyght wyll brynge hit so to passe that we at an instante receaue the full of ovr delytes to bothe ovr covmfrtes wyth ovt any respect of psons: this I be leve in this I Joye in this I lyve and hope in yf my bad skryblynges shall ever geve yo^{u} cause to send me the chose of my delytes: nexte to yor ovne presence is the syte of yor leters moste wellcom: there fore I wyll neve sease to please you and delyte you yth < > my playne trewe leters wych never sayth halfe so mch as my hande thinketh … I love you: I well never sease to saye that so [longe] as my hand can wryte hit and < > my tounge can tell hit and you do lyke I should saye so. (fol. 138r)

Like Conway (and following the precepts of early modern epistolary theory) Bourne imagines the letter as the image of her absent correspondent: 'nexte to yor ovne presence is the syte of yor leters moste wellcom'. The repeated emphasis upon her hands and tongue further eroticises the letter as an embodiment of its sender. While Bourne's letters cannot say 'halfe so mch as my hande thinketh', her developing use of 'delyte' is illuminating. 'Delyte' begins as the imagined satisfaction of a future liaison: 'we at an instante receaue

[9] Gary Schneider, *The Culture of Epistolarity: Vernacular Letters and Letter Writing in Early Modern England* (Newark, DE, 2005), 110.

the full of ovr delytes'. She then begins to meld sexual and epistolary contact, as 'delyte' becomes the presence of Conway, either in person or on paper: 'send me the chose of my delytes: nexte to yor ovne presence is the syte of yor leters moste wellcom'. Subsequently seeking to 'delyte you with my playne trewe letters', Bourne transforms physical contact with her letter into contact with her body: 'I well never sease to saye that so [longe] as my hand can wryte hit and < > my tounge can tell hit and you do lyke I should saye so'. The curious sentience of 'my hande thinketh' further entwines the intellectual and sexual. Her thinking hand makes sexual contact an expression of the mind, while blending the script on the page with her own touching hands. Bourne exploits early modern epistolary convention, making her letters a space for the uniquely candid, sophisticatedly constructed expression of her desire, which transcends the restrictions of reality.

In another letter, a recently received letter (or book?) prompts a fantasy about the absent Conway:

> I thanke you much and many tymes for my lytell companyon: but I would thanke you more yf you had brouvght me yor selfe: but oh good god I shall not be so hapye to in Joye so shwete a comforte: howe longe shall I wante hit: when shall I have hit? a lase I dye when I <think?> of the my knight . . . I thinke my < > love wyll scarse keepe in tyll then wyth ovt festryng. (fol. 139r)

The 'lytell companion' familiarly aligns text with person, although her 'festryng' desire makes clear this alternative union is unsatisfying. The increasing ecstasy of the passage, however, creates some kind of textual release, the pulsing rhythms of the sentence—*long*, *want*, *when*, *have*—culminating orgasmically with *die*.

THREATENED SPACE

The frequency of such sexually charged passages throughout the correspondence demonstrates that the letters exchanged between Conway and Bourne offered some room for liaison in absentia. Yet these letters do not represent a safe space: they are rife with imminent threat. Bourne feared, and appeared to be subject to, surveillance at various points in her life. Arranging a clandestine meeting with Conway, Bourne advises:

> yf you com at ten ora leaven of cloke at nyght I can let you in and no body shall knowe hit for thaye be all so faste a slepe as I had mch a do to wake the[m] . . . yf you com on the fryday you may be sure theis no at home. (fol. 138r)

Although the sound sleep of the other people in the house tantalisingly suggests the lovers' freedom to make noise without discovery, it simultaneously evokes listening ears. The sixteenth-century concept of the household as micro-commonwealth authorised both internal and external communities to police behaviour within the home: it was 'permissible for neighbours to spy through windows or cracks in walls to secure proof of sexual misdoings', and for the constable to 'make forcible entry if he had cause to suspect that the crime of adultery or fornication was being committed inside the house'.[10] Whatever the real situation within the household here, Bourne's emphasis on this night-time secrecy lends urgent energy to this letter's proposal.

Bourne and Conway were already subject to public scrutiny and gossip, as Conway's daughter had pointedly remarked:

> mrs elysabeth conwaye tovld me ... my < > mayde covlde tell such tales of you and me asshaull make vs blush and be a shamed. (fol. 143v)

Bourne feared the interception of their letters, and implored Conway, 'I wyshe you to kepe yor letters safe o^r^ burne them fo^r^ you have spyes' (fol. 177r); in another letter, she warned 'wee have enymys nowe to worke our dysguyes' (fol. 138r). Noting that 'I haue other causes wych toucheth me nerer wych I wyll not commit to paper' (fol. 119r), Bourne showed her awareness of the first rule of intelligence: the most cautious writers do not write down anything they would not want in the wrong hands. Detecting enemies on all sides, whether real or imagined, she declared herself 'so care full and so fearefull as I do mystrvst every thing' (fol. 143v). Bourne's response to the risk of interception involved the strikingly sophisticated simultaneous obfuscation of her identity on the one hand, and a coterie-style codified framing of her identity to the right recipient on the other. She used pseudonyms at least twice, signing herself Frances Wesley and Anne Hayes (fols 193 and 199). Two other letters include rhyming fragments which both disguise and underline her role as writer and Conway's as recipient:

> from whens hit camm hit
> hathe no name & whiche
> hit wyll hytt tellethe
> the sam[e]. (fol. 193v)
>
> whyther this gothe hyt hath
> no name from whence
> hyt cometh hytt seythe
> the same. (fol. 199r)

These octosyllabic riddling epigrams operate simultaneously as anti-signatures and signatures, concealing identity while unmistakably identifying the author to its

[10] Amanda Flather, *Gender and Space in Early Modern England* (Woodbridge, 2007), 42. Cf. Catherine Richardson, 'Early Modern Plays and Domestic Space', *Home Cultures*, 2.3 (2005), 269–83, 276; and Lena Cowen Orlin, *Locating Privacy in Early Modern London* (Oxford, 2007), 152–4. For the importance of witnessing adultery in divorce proceedings, especially the role of servants, see also Laura Gowing, *Domestic Dangers: Women, Words, and Sex in Early Modern London* (Oxford, 1996), 188–92.

intended reader. Elsewhere she describes her writing as 'secrete syphers', drawing on the language of intelligence (fol. 193v; see this volume, Chapter 37, Nadine Akkerman, 'Cryptological Coteries'). She even secured some letters with tamper-evident letterlocking techniques—more usually the preserve of professional secretaries (e.g., fols 169–70 and 174–5).

IMAGINING PRIVATE SPACE

Lacking securely private space, in reality or on paper, Bourne and Conway did something remarkable: together they dreamt up a fantasy safe haven. Their collaboratively created imaginative world lies at the heart of our reading of the relationship. In one letter, Conway recalls having read aloud to Bourne from a 'laten hystory', which he offered to translate in full.[11] In the middle of a letter, he takes his reader into a magical clearing in the woods, where he has been led by a colourful bird to a plenteous table of food and drink. Conway strikingly makes no spatial or syntactical attempt to separate the 'translation' from the letter's main text: the letter glides from an image of a zealous lover sweating on horseback to greet his paramour to an encounter within an extraordinary dream vision, as if the dream world has risen up around the questing rider.

> I ame redy ever to < > use my travel . . . putt me to any exercise: throwghe want thereof I growe fatt. I can sweate as hard throwghe the lyghte of the mone in the coole nyght as others can wythe heate of the sonne in the hotte daye. I dyd of late wythe drawe my self from company and all alone I wandered abroode in a wyld wilderness of woodes, when all thyngs was at rest . . . where I was I mett with a byrde of dyvers colors . . . she browght me emydde the wyld wodds to a hwosse where hyt semed there dwelt no body. rest she gave me to comforte my body overwearyed w^{t} travel: most delycatt wyne to dryncke sondrye frutes of the wodd: and most sweete and saverie bread to eate. . . . Good god. I wyshed you there so ofte and so hartely that at length I fell in to Imagination and beleaffe w^{t} my self that I had my wyshe, that you were there, that I did dryncк to and eate to you of every thynge that was there: and that yor Joyes and myne were equall. was hit soo? Or ys hit but a dreame? a dream hit can not be: therefor sens by my wellwyshing and harty prayer you came thither as a gest. tell me who she was, where she ys, and howe she dothe that I meane, and can not name. I longe to knowe, and wyshe she may knowe me better / yf you wyll send me word, when and whyther I shall travel out again to see her . . . I wyll devyse and meanes to brynge my self to her presens . . . lett me receive yor answer to this. (fols 135r–v)

The solitary dreamer 'all alone' in the forest is particularly pertinent in a correspondence so haunted by surveillance. The world of rumour and whisperings is left behind;

11 'This muche I have translated out of the laten hystore I redd to you of late wch you lyked so well: yf the rest plesse you, and that you can rede my ill hand: I wyll translate the whole and send hit you' (fol. 135r).

solitary peace remains 'when all thyngs was at rest'. Contrasting with the limited privacy afforded by Bourne's sleeping household, Conway's forest dwelling is significantly uninhabited—'a hwosse where hyt semed there dwelt no body'—truly a fantasy compared to the two lovers' densely populated domestic reality.[12] As Laura Gowing succinctly puts it: 'The early modern world was not built for privacy'.[13]

The dream vision strikingly reflects the lovers' urgent desire for each other's company. The exclamation 'Good god' and the repeated wish 'so ofte and so hartely' echoes the urgency of Bourne's yearning. Given the segue from Conway's promises of nocturnal athleticism, it does not seem too far a stretch to read the 'most delycatt wyne', 'sondrye frutes of the wodd: and most sweete and saverie bread' as sensuous satisfactions of sexual appetite—especially when the couple eats together.[14] The passage is acutely tuned to the erotic yearning of Bourne and Conway's correspondence. If this were a translation from a romance or another text that could be called a 'Latin history', Conway's choice of passage is highly suggestive.[15] Given the covert nature of their correspondence, it seems just as likely to be an original composition disguised as translation. The strange 'byrde of dyvers colors' is seemingly without a discernible literary source, although birds are frequently used as signifiers in medieval and early modern erotic verse. If we take the text to be Conway's own creation, the final questions seem to invite Bourne both to co-create—'tell me who she was, where she ys, and howe she dothe'—and to cohabit this shared world: 'yf you wyll send me word, when and whyther I shall travel out again to see her'. His promise that 'I wyll devyse and meanes to brynge my self to her presens', is reminiscent of their meetings. Except, in this imagined romance world, they can share the secure space denied them in reality: 'a dream hit can not be: therefor sens by my wellwyshing and harty prayer you came thither as a gest'.

Lena Cowen Orlin describes how 'many extramarital liaisons were conducted in the house's most liminal spaces or, indeed, outside it'.[16] In fact, Conway and Bourne began to conduct their affair even farther afield—in the realm of imagination. And, perhaps most remarkably of all, Bourne accepted the invitation to create a shared fantasy with a generically appropriate dream-vision sequel:

> I chanste of latte to sytt alonne in my mvse and mvsynge fell In to a slepe & dreamyng < > methought ther came amane vnto me whiche sayd vnto me the man that you wotte of ... hathe sent for you & would have you come to such a pllace by

[12] As Lena Cowen Orlin notes, Tudor lives 'appear porous in part because living conditions were so crowded ... there were also powerful social conventions regarding shared bedchambers, communal beds, the personal security to be found in numbers, and the mutual regulation that was so much a feature of early modern culture', *Locating Privacy*, 155.

[13] Gowing, *Domestic Dangers*, 190.

[14] Conway also suggests that 'from heaven I thynke she [the bird] and all the rest came' (fol. 135v), lending the wine and bread a subtly eucharistic feel.

[15] Helen Smith accepts that it is a translation in *'Grossly Material Things: Women and Book Production in Early Modern England* (Oxford, 2012), 67. We have found no Latin text that might be a source for this passage.

[16] Orlin, *Locating Privacy*, 155.

> on of the clocke & sayd to me you mvst make no de lay ... me thought wakyng out of my dreame I had rather have bynne present streayt way then absent but never the les I remembrnge The absence of vs to ys as presence but Rysyng out of my muse I thought to travell to the place & goynge over The felldes at lenthe I came to a howse wher I saw nobody nor I thought nobody dyd In abytt ther ... at last I saw amane whych bad me gooe In to the howse and Sytt downe & rest my sellf over werryd wth travell & beyng very fyrsty & drye ... at Last he gave me a glasse of wynne I dranke & then he gave me frutes to eatt & then he leving me ther alonne went to feach vs som meat & bad yf any body dyd knocke I showld harken what they wer & lett them In att the last I hard on knocke & hearyng nott his voyse I knew nott what he was but he semynge some thyng bould he opned the on dore & came to the other & knocktt & sayd who dwelles heare nobody then I hearyng his voyse knew who he was & opend the dore & he saynge thes wordes ... though my fett have forst to carye my body frome this place ytt my hart wyll not sufer me to torne my head frome you whyche ys the cause that hath mad me this boudly To In trvde my self In to your company this talkyng & drymynge away the tyme satt downe to eatt of that was ther & to drynke of the wynne. (fols 150r–v)[17]

The power of dreams in early modern Europe carried considerable weight, and they were variously interpreted as a means of knowledge and understanding belonging to science, theology, and divination. Scholars including Melanchthon considered them in relation to 'Protestant theories about the nature of the soul, its relationship with the body, and the possibility of continuing divine revelation'.[18] Bourne's own use of the genre, consciously or not, appropriates this cultural authority to present a distinctly gendered vision. Solitude and isolation are an immediate feature of her dream vision. She begins '[sat] alone', and we are twice reminded that the house is unoccupied. In the dialogue with the male entrant, it seems the answer to 'who dwelles heare' is 'nobody'. The quasi-servant figure also withdraws before the man, who we take to be Conway, enters: 'he leving me ther alonne'. Like Conway's promise to 'travel' out again to their dream world, Bourne's dream involves a long physical journey: 'rysyng out of my muse I thought to travell to the place & goynge over The fealdes at lenthe I came to a howse', and a tryst with a set time and location. Once again the lovers share an imagined private

[17] Further suggesting a personal purpose to this text, written in the margin is a note: 'To nobody but to your self wyshyng you as to my owne hartt'.

[18] Ann Marie Plane and Leslie Tuttle, 'Review Essay: Dreams and Dreaming in the Early Modern World', *Renaissance Quarterly*, 67.3 (2014), 917–31, 921. Conway ponders dreams elsewhere in his correspondence. In a long 1576 letter of advice to Anthony Bourne, he implies that his care for the addressee stems in part from a distressing nocturnal vision: 'A dreame I had this night wherin I was troubled wth you so much y^t waking I can not chuse but wryte thus much of good will' (Oxford, Bodleian Libraries, MS Tanner 169, fols 43v–46r (fol. 44v)). In contrast, writing to Elizabeth, evidently during their affair, he relegates faith in dreams beneath the more powerful inspiration of his love for her: 'I see dreames arr butt thynges of fancie, follye, and fallacies, I leav them to fearefulle o^r fonnde myndes to beleav them. hyt is a nother thynge wch moveth Saynctes and subdeweth men, that nowe delyteth me. ask you what it ys? love hyt ys: and of yor selfe; not begonne, conceaved and wrought in me, w^towt cause and consyderation' (BL, Add. MS 23,229, fol. 149r).

space denied to them in reality. Bourne's opening meditation on the relationship between absence and presence, 'absence of us to ys as presence', could summarise their eroticised epistolary contact.

Although Bourne smoothly follows Conway's generic choice, the house in her dream vision, and the activities conducted within it, are poignantly quotidian. Houses, or estates, were the continued site of legal and personal conflict for Bourne. Anthony and Elizabeth did not cohabit during the early years of their marriage, and when they did it was deeply traumatic. Anthony slept with Bourne's own maid, whom she dismissed, only to have him install a sex worker as her new maid.[19] Anthony sold Bourne's own land to finance an affair, and his flight to Calais without the queen's permission almost saw the entire estate confiscated as a penalty.[20] In a letter to her half-sister Lucy in 1584, Bourne expresses the distress of her peripatetic life:

> When I was . . . constrained by necessity to seek the aid of friends to resist the injuries my unkind husband offered me himself, and my children, to the utter overthrow of us all, I first sought my refuge amongst those which by nature were most bound to have yielded me . . . assistance. Being refused . . . I was forced . . . to accept aid amongst strangers . . . I live at Sarisden [i.e., Sarsden], where I mean to secrete myself and my sorrows, until God give me a better estate.[21]

Her weariness of the humiliating search for 'refuge' is palpable. In their dream visions, the house offers refuge for Conway and Bourne respectively 'overwearyed w^{t} travel,' and 'worryd w^{t}h travell', a common symbol for hardship in the allegory of life as journey. Bourne often writes to Conway of him securing peace:

> you put me in comfor you haue devysed a waye < > to ende this trvbellsom lyfe I leade and to bryng e me som quyet in the end of my dayes wych I fere wyll not be many yf I contynewe a prysonor. (fol. 127r)

Elsewhere she expresses a feeling of security with Conway: 'I mst be wyth them as I mst be safe est and most to my lykyng wych wylbe where I am nerest you' (fol. 138r). Dreaming of houses, for Gaston Bachelard, is inextricably tied both to shelter, and the security of the past: 'we see that the imagination builds "walls" of impalpable shadows, comforts itself with the illusion of protection'.[22] Bourne's vision of the lovers 'talkyng & drymynge away the tyme' in an empty room, is an 'illusion of protection', the wish for quietness and safety granted. Furthermore, the man knocking to be let in recalls

19 Bradford, *The Conway Papers*, 54–5.

20 Bradford, *The Conway Papers*, 54.

21 London, The National Archives, SP 12/175 fol. 24r, Elizabeth Bourne to Lucy, Lady Audley (November 1684). Lucy, who became Lady Audley, was the mother of Mervin Touchet, second Earl of Castlehaven. It is hard to know what to make of half-sisters Elizabeth and Lucy spending their lives with two of the cruellest domestic abusers known to us from this period.

22 Gaston Bachelard, *The Poetics of Space* (New York, 2014), 27.

Matthew 7.7: 'seek, and ye shall find: knock, and it shall be opened unto you.'[23] The passage is also reminiscent of Revelation 3.20:

> Behold, I stand at the door, and knock ... If any man hear my voice, and open the door, I will come in unto him, and will sup with him, and he with me.[24]

'Wynne' and 'meat' again lends their meal eucharistic resonance. Their dreamed private space is both quotidian and simultaneously a fantasy of a promised Heaven. For Bachelard, 'through dreams, the various dwelling-places in our lives co-penetrate and retain the treasures of former days.'[25] Notably, Bourne's dream house is more poignant because her domestic past was so troubled. For Bachelard, the dreamed house is imbued with longing for what was; for Bourne it seems to express a longing for a safe marital cohabitation that never was.[26]

TRANSFORMATIVE SPACE

Conway was a soldier for the Protestant cause, rewarded by Queen Elizabeth for his service in Europe. He wrote poetry and devotional works, and was at least a satellite member of the Sidney circle. Now he was quite literally a knight helping his lady, a woman who portrayed herself as besieged by oppressors and in need of a champion. Together they wrote themselves a narrative that could have come straight out of any contemporary romance.[27] Conway may have begun to see their relationship as belonging to the romance tradition, or found in romance the generic conventions required to express his feelings. In this reading of the dream vision, Conway casts himself as a kind of knight errant, led by a magical spirit to a secluded clearing in a wood where he encounters a vision of Bourne, bringing him a temporary transcendence followed by an exquisite yearning. Resituating their affair in the romance world diffuses their adultery, by placing them in the company of such adulterous lovers as Tristan and Isolde and Lancelot and Guinevere, whose love is certainly not without consequence, but is justified by its transcendent passion.[28]

[23] Geneva Bible, Matthew 7. 7.

[24] Geneva Bible, Revelation 3.20.

[25] Bachelard, *The Poetics of Space*, 23–4.

[26] 'Memories of the outside world will never have the same tonality as those of home and, by recalling these memories, we add to our store of dreams; we are never real historians, but always near poets, and our emotion is perhaps nothing but an expression of a poetry that was lost.' See Bachelard, *The Poetics of Space*, 28.

[27] It is even possible Conway and Bourne exchanged romances. Conway 'had drawne a boke ouse' for Bourne's daughter Amy (fol. 143v), and sent Elizabeth one for herself, which she read and responded to directly; fols 143v, 152r. Cf. fols 144r, 135v, and 152r.

[28] Helen Cooper posits that romance adultery offered an opportunity for debate about female sexual conduct, but one which generically must pardon the accused: 'If a work is to remain within the parameters

A language of mutuality, unity, and eternity further recasts and legitimises their affair, echoing the ideals of Protestant marriage. Bourne often revisits the image of the lovers as one body:

> synse ovr loves ar so equall and fynne on to the other that our eyes tell the Joyes of ovr hartes < >, oh howe greate pytye is hit that ovr bodyes should be kept a sonder that do so well deserve on a nother. (fol. 138r)

The married couple as one body is a foundational image both for St Paul and the Book of Common Prayer. Man and wife are one flesh:

> So men are bound to loue their owne wiues, as their owne bodies. Hee that loueth his owne wife loueth him-selfe. For neuer did any man hate his owne flesh, but nourisheth and cherisheth it . . . For this cause shall a man . . . be ioyned vnto his wife, and they two shall be one flesh.[29]

Bourne's use of 'sonder' more specifically recalls the marriage service: 'Those whom God hath ioyned together, let no man put asunder'.[30] Bourne, 'commendyng my selfe to yor < > harte to be noreched and chereched for ever tyll death' (fol. 139r), also picks up on the church's instruction that the husband should 'nourisheth and cherisheth' his wife as his body. The eternal nature of their bond is also enforced by her subscriptions: 'Yors for ever and all'; 'Yor for ever and ever'; 'Yo^{rs} to her laste' (fols 139r, 138r, and 145v). The letter offers Bourne a space where the rhetoric of married union can be achieved, if not its reality.

ARCHIVES ARE NOT SANCTUARIES

Much recent pioneering work on early modern women's writing is in dialogue with a half-century of scholarship on manuscript culture. With the so-called 'archival turn' has come an increasingly sophisticated awareness that archives are not 'neutral and passive vehicles of authoritative or true 'facts', but instead constitute active sites of meaning production which intervene in the construction of individual and cultural identity, and which actively define, control, and legitimise knowledge.[31] These letters were composed

of romance, its final meaning, its *sentence*, must be one of approval: the text constitutes a kind of trial, in which the "sentence" in the forensic sense exonerates the heroine'. See Cooper, *The English Romance in Time: Transforming Motifs from Geoffrey of Monmouth to the Death of Shakespeare* (Oxford, 2004), 270.

[29] *The Booke of Common Praier, and Administration of the Sacramentes, and Other Rites and Ceremonies in the Churche of Englande* (London: Richard Iugge and John Cawode, 1559), sig. Oviiiv.

[30] *The Booke of Common Praier*, sig. Oviv.

[31] Liesbeth Corens, Kate Peters, and Alexandra Walsham, 'Introduction', in Liesbeth Corens, Kate Peters, and Alexandra Walsham (eds), *Archives & Information in the Early Modern World* (London, 2018), 3.

and saved in unambiguously patriarchal circumstances. They describe a relationship between a married man and his female lover, negotiated through male courts and patronage networks. Retained in the archive of the married man who had an affair with Bourne, and who benefited financially by marrying his son to her daughter, they only survive because their male nineteenth-century custodians deigned not to throw them away. Their status as archived texts does not just secure their survival, it conditions our reading experience.

Most of Bourne's letters can be found in the British Library, making access to them relatively straightforward—and Alfar and Sherwood's edition makes them even more accessible. Yet her corpus has required especially patient palaeographical transcription since both she and Conway have difficult hands. Further, our identification of her authorship is partial and often provisional; much of this material plays with anonymity and isolation, and draws attention to its radically insecure contexts of composition. Over the years, willing readers may have been put off by the comment written in a nineteenth-century hand that these are documents 'Of no importance' (fol. 2r). Messy, undated, incohesively ordered, and sometimes fragmentary, these texts pose unique interpretive challenges which often verge on moral quandaries. While writing this chapter, we have frequently asked ourselves to what extent the modern reader (especially a male one)—imposing a conjectured order onto these materials and prying into Bourne's emotional and erotic privacy—continues to invade her space. The abuse, started by her husband, seems potentially perpetuated in the archival process. We are conscious that, as Bourdieu and Passeron have argued, 'every power which manages to impose meanings and to impose them as legitimate by concealing the power relations which are the basis of its force', contributes its own 'specifically symbolic force to those power relations'—the archives not least among them.[32] We found ourselves torn between the desire to protect Bourne's privacy and the knowledge that every new female voice from early modern England enriches our understanding of women's imaginative lives in the period, and found ourselves faced with the opportunity to challenge ostensibly 'legitimate' meaning imposed on the documents by their earlier archivists. Stamped as 'letters of no importance' they symbolically carry 'no importance'; recovered and presented as important, they are empowered against that symbolic violence.

Few spaces for Bourne were truly safe—including, crucially, the archive. Oppressed physically, socially, and legally, Elizabeth Bourne was able to create some kind of escape and find solace in a romantic literary exchange which harnessed the power of language to transcend her situation temporarily. Bourne was not a major figure in Elizabethan England, yet her story conspicuously illustrates the role of the imaginative interior world in female agency. Her story also dramatically demonstrates the major shifts in historiographical assumptions that have taken root only in the last fifty years or so. The provenance of her papers prompts us to consider whether Bourne's letters are as exceptional as

[32] Pierre Bourdieu and Jean-Claude Passeron, in Richard Nice (trans.), *Reproduction in Education, Society and Culture* (London, 1990), 4.

they seem. How common was it for a woman to think like Bourne, and leave traces of those thoughts?

On 27 June 1760, the poet Thomas Gray wrote to William Mason at the British Library. Gray had been asked to transcribe a batch of the Conway Papers, an archive recently bequeathed to the state. Mason had asked what he should do with a pile of Conway Papers he had received from Gray, who replied:

> as I remember they were divided into three parcels, on the least of which I had written the word 'nothing,' or 'of no consequence'. It did not consist of above twenty letters at most; and if you find anything about Mr. Bourne's affairs ... it is certainly so. ... if this is the case, they may as well be burnt; but if there is a good number, and about affairs of State (which you may smell out), then it is one of the other parcels, and I am distressed, and must find some method of getting it up again. I think I had inscribed the two packets that signified anything, one, 'Papers of Queen Elizabeth or earlier,' the other ... 'Papers of King James and Charles the First.' Pray Heaven it is neither of these.[33]

Reading them today, it seems remarkable that these stunningly original, aesthetically beautiful, beguilingly ambiguous, and fantastically informative missives could ever be deemed 'Of no importance'. Yet of course Mason and his contemporaries were sifting Conway family material for State Papers; Elizabeth's letters do not even make it into Gray's summary of the manuscript's contents, which he defines as 'Mr Bourne's affairs'. A clear hierarchy is established between the 'affairs of State' whose loss merits distress, and the un-named woman's 'letters of no importance' which are worthy of a second death in the fire. Countless women's texts must have met similar lamentable fates, permanently erased from the ostensibly 'neutral' archive. If Bourne herself found only partial redress against early modern misogyny, the survival of her papers may at least offer historians and literary scholars an opportunity to overturn the gender and power prejudices of outdated historiographical practices.

FURTHER READING

Alfar, Cristina Léon and Emily G. Sherwood (eds). *Reading Mistress Elizabeth Bourne: Marriage, Separation, and Legal Controversies*. New York, 2021.

Daybell, James. *Women Letter-Writers in Tudor England*. Oxford, 2006.

Gowing, Laura. *Domestic Dangers: Women, Words, and Sex in Early Modern London*. Oxford, 1996.

Orlin, Lena Cowen. *Locating Privacy in Early Modern London*. Oxford, 2007.

Schneider, Gary. *The Culture of Epistolarity: Vernacular Letters and Letter Writing in Early Modern England, 1500–1700*. Newark, DE, 2005.

[33] Thomas Gray, in Duncan C. Tovey (ed.), *The Letters of Thomas Gray*, 3 vols (London, 1900–1912), 2, 149–50.

Veronese, Leah and Daniel Starza Smith. 'Elizabeth Bourne', in Patricia Pender and Rosalind Smith (eds), *The Palgrave Encyclopedia of Early Modern Women's Writing in English*. Cham, forthcoming.

Washington, DC, Folger Shakespeare Library. Bradford, Charles Angell. *The Conway Papers (1576–1606)*. DA378.C6 B6.

CHAPTER 37

WOMEN'S LETTERS AND CRYPTOLOGICAL COTERIES

NADINE AKKERMAN

DECADES of scholarship on early women's epistolary practices has made us reassess overly simplistic assumptions about female literacy and education. Letters are the material witnesses that show how sixteenth- and seventeenth-century women mastered and then manipulated conventions of genre, in the process showing themselves to be able rhetoricians who nurtured kin and wider familial relationships through their correspondence networks. They sought patronage, and acted as political go-betweens for their male kin, but also functioned as diplomats or 'ambassadresses' in their own right, extending their differing forms of influence across Europe, always using letters to first open up and then maintain lines of communication.[1] This chapter examines specific secrecy techniques used by some women letter writers—cryptology, either cryptography or steganography—reminding us that the study of letters can bring unexpected forms of female activity to the surface.

Letters written in cipher or code, that is, those that make use of cryptography, immediately betray that an attempt has been made to obscure their content: their very incomprehensibility broadcasts the fact that the meaning is hidden. By way of contrast, letters using another cryptological technique, steganography, hide their messages in plain sight, through use of invisible inks or analogical wordplay: by not displaying their acts of concealment, they remain deceptively innocuous. This chapter will analyse how early modern women letter writers used both branches of cryptology—cryptography

[1] For an overview of studies of the early 'noughties' see James Daybell, 'Recent Studies in Sixteenth-Century Letters', *English Literary Renaissance*, 35.2 (2005), 331–62; and 'Recent Studies in Seventeenth-Century Letters', *English Literary Renaissance* 36.1 (2006), 135–70, which includes his own foundational work, *Women Letter-Writers in Tudor England* (Oxford, 2006). For recent important work on manuscript letters see Alison Wiggins, *Bess of Hardwick's Letters: Language, Materiality, and Early Modern Epistolary Culture* (Abingdon, 2016); for letters in printed form see Diana G. Barnes, *Epistolary Community in Print, 1580–1664* (Abingdon, 2013). For the role of epistolary correspondence in scientific exchange, see this volume, Chapter 7, Helen Smith, 'Cultures of Correspondence'.

and steganography—to create and maintain their networks, even at times when lines of communication were breaking down. Each technique came with its own challenges: cryptography required painstaking encoding and decoding while steganography demanded the writer display no little creativity and literary skill as they composed their letter. To create a piece of steganography, the writer had to transform a letter into an unrelated, semi-fictional document which nevertheless made sense on its own terms so that it could only be read as factual by the person holding the key. When resorting to steganography, women were in effect compelled to try their hand at fictional discourses. This chapter seeks to highlight cryptology as another layer of 'fiction in the archives', and will cast women letter writers as semi-literary authors, and show how cryptology was a polysemous linguistic technique that women employed both to form and maintain sometimes fragile social networks, and to communicate across enemy lines and borders to ensure that their secret messages remained just that: secret. Finally, it argues that with more knowledge of the mechanics of cryptology, epistolary networks might be mapped that hitherto have remained hidden, and female activity revealed in areas generally considered to be the preserve of men: diplomacy and its darker sister, espionage.

DIPLOMAT, MESSENGER, SOLDIER, SPY, 'RUSTICS, WOMEN, AND CHILDREN'

Ever since the philosophical historian Philippe de Commynes (1447–*c* 1511) suggested that diplomat, messenger, and spy all plied the same trade, it has been a commonplace to refer to an ambassador as an 'honourable spy'.[2] Certainly, both ambassadors and spies were well accustomed to protecting the content of their messages from prying eyes through the use of cipher codes, and the two trades became inextricably entangled at the beginning of the sixteenth century, as organised espionage allowed for the development of more regular diplomatic institutions.[3] Encryption and decryption became an essential part of statecraft, and it was described in manuals such as Giovanni Battista della Porta's *De Furtivis Literarum Notis* (1563).[4] Cryptology became a vital tool of epistolary communication, and the keys needed to lock and unlock the dispatches to and from diplomats and spies alike were closely guarded by those other keepers of secrets, secretaries. Robert Beale (1541–1601), one of Sir Francis Walsingham's right-hand men

[2] Ian Arthurson, 'Espionage and Intelligence from the Wars of the Roses to the Reformation', *Nottingham Medieval Studies*, 35 (1991), 134–54, 134; Maurice Keens-Soper, 'Wicquefort', in G. R. Berridge, Maurice Keens-Soper, and T. G. Otto (eds), *Diplomatic Theory from Machiavelli to Kissinger* (New York, 2001), 88–105, 97.

[3] Arthurson, 'Espionage and Intelligence', 142.

[4] For della Porta, see David Kahn, *The Codebreakers: The Story of Secret Writing* (New York, 1967; repr. 1996), 137–43.

and a pre-eminent clerk of the Privy Council, made this abundantly clear when he wrote of how a secretary needed:

> a speciall Cabinett, whereof he is himselfe to keepe the Keye, for his signetts, Ciphers and secrett Intelligences, distinguishing the boxes or tills rather by letters than by the names of the Countryes or places, keepinge that only unto himselfe, for the names may inflame a desire to come by such thinges.[5]

The secretary needed to keep his secrets to himself even within an organisation, and as a result the National Archives in Kew holds over three hundred cipher keys, from the reign of Elizabeth I to that of Charles II.[6]

Less well known is that while the first half of the seventeenth century still found the overwhelmingly male spheres of rulers, ambassadors, and their intelligencers encrypting communications as a matter of course to protect sensitive political content, the practice had also taken root within elite circles as a second mode of literacy, a way to further distinguish themselves from the masses.[7] In other words, the use of cryptography had quickly stopped being the prerogative of those in diplomatic circles. In his *De Furtivis Literarum Notis*, della Porta bemoaned the spread of cryptography, noting that even the 'pigpen' cipher—a simple substitution system built from a geometric grid and often attributed to the Freemasons or even the Rosicrucians even though it appears to pre-date both movements—was used by ' "rustics, women, and children" '.[8] This observation was one of the things that led della Porta to present more intricate cipher systems to his readers. Della Porta's claim regarding the pigpen cipher seems either to have been an exaggeration or to indicate a local, Italian practice: I have not been able to locate any sixteenth- or seventeenth-century English letters, male or female, that use this simple system. What is true, however, is that before 1642, elite letter writers, female as well as male, mostly employed cryptography for social purposes, that is, to create a sense of intimacy amongst a select circle of correspondents, an intimacy that encompassed a communal sense of privacy. In those elite circles, cryptography did not hide state secrets, but coded messages that were gossipy at best. It is perhaps fitting that the primary use of cipher and code, to keep something secret, has served to obscure the fact that it was also

[5] London, British Library, Robert Beale, 'Instructions for a Principall Secretarie obserued by R: B for Sr Edwarde Wotton', MS Add. 48149, fols. 3v–9v. I cite the printed version: 'A Treatise of the Office of a Councellor and Principall Secretarie to her Ma[jes]tie', in Conyers Read, *Mr. Secretary Walsingham and the Policy of Queen Elizabeth* (Oxford, 1925), 3 vols, i, 428.

[6] The keys are to be found in six bound manuscript volumes: London, The National Archives, 67 vols, SP 106/1–6. While The National Archives might hold the cipher keys they are, unfortunately, held independently of those individuals or messages to which they were originally attached. If you find an enciphered letter, you may just find the key there, though it may take you rather longer than Beale would have thought wise.

[7] Margaret Ferguson, 'The Authorial Ciphers of Aphra Behn', in Steven N. Zwicker (ed.), *The Cambridge Companion to English Literature, 1650–1740* (Cambridge, 1998), 225–49, 227; Edith Snook, *Women, Reading, and the Cultural Politics of Early Modern England* (Aldershot, 2005), 153–4.

[8] Kahn, *The Codebreakers*, 138.

used to delineate and nourish a wide variety of elitist social practices that included early modern women.[9]

A KEY TO HIGH SOCIETY

A cipher code is a way of transforming an original text into one impossible to read without the 'key' with which the original was transformed. To use cipher code, both writer and recipient needed to share such a key. Generally, it took the form of a cipher alphabet and a nomenclator. A cipher alphabet can be constructed in many ways, but the principle is always the same: a letter is replaced with an equivalent, whether this be a number, a letter, or a symbol. For example, the key might progress as follows: a = 8 but also 20; b = 3 but also 4; h = 000 but also 14, etc. The nomenclator will play similar games but with names and particular words: 52 may stand for France; 174 for the Prince of Orange, while the King of England may be referred to as Polyphemus, and so on.[10] The majority of early modern cipher keys are based on such straightforward substitution systems, and are monoalphabetic, that is, each letter corresponds to a fixed equivalent or equivalents (a polyalphabetic cipher uses multiple monoalphabetic ciphers, switching from one to another at pre-designated points or as indicated within the ciphered text itself). Correspondents tended to use the same keys year after year, even if they might easily have replaced these keys more often, especially if they believed they had access to trusted private bearers and protected postal channels. While using a trusted communications channel, letters needed only to be protected from casual glances rather than from concerted attempts to read them. Elizabeth Stuart (1596–1662), sometime Queen of Bohemia, is a case in point, as while she started using ciphers in the 1620s and continued to do so until the 1640s, in all that time she employed only eight different keys, of which only one was polyalphabetic (1.868–76; 2.1055–76).[11] She used individual keys for years on end. One of her keys not only stayed in use for decades, but was treated as a family heirloom: when her son Charles Louis (1617–1680) came of age in December 1635, and thus took over the Palatine government in exile, his mother could not give him the keys to Heidelberg Castle, but she did pass on the cipher key she and her late husband had used since 1622 (see 1.869–72 for 'Key Frederick V').[12] The

[9] This chapter draws heavily upon my chapter 'Enigmatic Cultures of Cryptology', in James Daybell and Andrew Gordon (eds), *Cultures of Correspondence in Early Modern Britain* (Philadelphia, PA, 2016), 69–84, which analyses the social uses of cryptology; as well as on the insights of my full-length study, *Invisible Agents: Women and Espionage in Seventeenth-Century Britain* (Oxford, 2018).

[10] The example is a key used by Sir Balthazar Gerbier between December 1631 and December 1638, which he shared with Elizabeth Stuart, but also with Sir John Coke, and Richard Weston, first earl of Portland: see 'Key 1 Gerbier', in Nadine Akkerman (ed.), *The Correspondence of Elizabeth Stuart, Queen of Bohemia* (Oxford), 2.1057–8. All parenthetical in-text citations refer to my three-volume edition.

[11] See the appendices to the first two volumes of Akkerman (ed.), *The Correspondence of Elizabeth Stuart, Queen of Bohemia* (Oxford, 2011, 2015).

[12] 'Key Frederick V', in Akkerman (ed.), *Correspondence*, 1.869–72.

same tendency is to be found in the correspondence of practically any well-functioning diplomat of the period, however. In 1596, Sir Robert Cecil (1563–1612) received a letter enclosing 'the Alphabet of Mr. Bertons cipher used thes xviii years', while the Dutch ambassador to Sweden, Hugo de Groot aka Grotius (1583–1645), used his keys for at least fifteen years.[13]

The paradox of why early moderns generally employed relatively simple ciphers while they were well-informed regarding cryptography can be explained if we focus on the social aspects of cryptography rather than its potential for espionage and diplomacy. In a social setting, to replace one cipher key with another could potentially sever a 'bond', to use the term of Hannah J. Crawforth, that had taken effort and time to create. Crawforth has explained how in certain circumstances, the significance of cipher is not its effectiveness as a device for secret writing but the fact that it 'creates a bond between writer and recipient that has the appearance of exclusivity'. Cipher, she suggests, was used in 'community-building'.[14] The simple act of letter-writing had been expressed as a route to building a community by Erasmus, but to write in cipher was a way of building communities *within* a community already extant.

This concept of an epistolary 'inner-community' helps to explain the relative simplicity of the cipher keys used by spy and later playwright Aphra Behn (1640–1689), alias Astraea, or royalist agent '160'. Already part of one epistolary community, Behn spent months asking to be granted what was, effectively, access to its inner circle: she begged Secretary of State Henry Bennet (1618–1685), Baron Arlington, to grant her a key of her own. Her constant lobbying met with success, but the key she received was almost childish in its simplicity: a = 2, b = 3, c = 4, d = 5.[15] For Behn, it was receiving the key itself that held most meaning, as it meant that she had been admitted to the next level, so to speak. Its effectiveness as an actual code was largely beside the point, even though this has since been taken as evidence that she was neither well-trained nor well-respected as a spy and ought not be taken seriously. The later dismissal of her spy techniques also betrays a biased attitude towards women's involvement in the dangerous trade of espionage.[16] Cipher alphabets used by male spies or diplomats were not necessarily that much more secure, and were often constructed with a similar uninterrupted sequence of numbers. One of the alphabets of art broker, diplomat, and spy Sir Balthazar Gerbier

[13] For Cecil, see London, The National Archives, P. Proby to Sir Robert Cecil, [12 March 1596], SP 12/256, fol. 186. For Grotius, compare, for instance, letter no. 1966 to no. 4290 of Grotius' correspondence. The seventeen printed volumes of Grotius' *Briefwisseling* (1928–2001) were digitised by the Huygens Institute in 2009: see Grotius, in P. C. Molhuysen, B. L. Meulenbreuk, P. P. Witkam, et al. (eds), *Briefwisseling*, 17 vols, *The Correspondence of Hugo Grotius*, http://www.grotius.huygens.knaw.nl, accessed 3 April 2021.

[14] Hannah J. Crawforth, 'Court Hieroglyphics: The Idea of the Cipher in Ben Jonson's Masques', in Robyn Adams and Rosanna Cox (eds), *Diplomacy and Early Modern Culture* (Basingstoke, 2011), 138–54, 144.

[15] Key reconstructed from London, The National Archives, SP 29/167, fol. 209. The letter is also printed in W. J. Cameron, *New Light on Aphra Behn* (Auckland, 1961), as document no. 2.

[16] Alan Marshall, *Intelligence and Espionage in the Reign of Charles II, 1660–1685* (Cambridge, 1994), 125, 136.

(1592–1663), for instance, demonstrates this clearly: the first letter of the alphabet is out of sequence, 'a' being represented by 36; 37; 38; 39; 40; 41; but from then onwards it is relatively straightforward: for example, 'b' being substituted by 26; 27; 'c' by 29; 30; 31; 'd' by 32; 33; 34.[17] The example of Behn's simple key shows that the social aspects of cryptography remained present even during times of duress such as, in her case, the Second Anglo-Dutch War, when she also used cipher to hide true state secrets. In fact, it might even show that those social aspects were seen as more important than the 'diplomatic' use of ciphering.

Though the efficacy of a cipher code was not of primary importance when it came to delineating its role as a community-building tool for networks of women, that is not to say that it could not be used as a way of asserting one's stature within a relationship. When the philosopher and mathematician René Descartes (1596–1650) sent the Queen of Bohemia's daughter Elisabeth (1618–1680), Princess Palatine, a cipher as part of their long-standing correspondence, the princess was not impressed:

> I examined the code that you sent me and found it very good, but too long to write a whole thought. And if one writes only a bit of a word, one would figure it out by the number of letters. It would be better to make a key of words by alphabet and then to mark a distinction between the numbers that signify letters and those that signify words.[18]

Elisabeth's recommendations on how Descartes might improve his key demonstrate quite clearly that she is in no way the junior partner in their epistolary relationship; by damning the key Descartes introduced to her with faint praise before suggesting an alternative, she gains the upper hand. It is she who will determine the secret language to be used to exchange information by missive (see this volume, Chapter 7, Helen Smith, 'Cultures of Correspondence').

As for Behn, she was not the only individual who had to lobby hard to be granted the honour of communicating in 'secret'. Two years into his eight-year embassy to Constantinople, Sir Thomas Roe (1581–1644) began to beg the Queen of Bohemia for a cipher key. Another two years passed without such a key coming his way (see 1.427–9; 1.490–2).[19] His letter in which he refers to 'a Ciphar w*hi*ch I haue long expected from your Ma.[tie], not p*re*suming to send any of myne', makes it plain that for him to take the initiative—to present a queen with a cipher key—might be taken as insolence.[20] Were Roe to present Elizabeth with a key, it would mean that she would not only have to learn the cipher, which in itself could be rather time consuming, but she would have to submit

[17] 'Key 2 Gerbier' in Akkerman (ed.), *Correspondence*, 2.1058–9.

[18] Elisabeth to Descartes, 10 October 1646, Berlin, in Lisa Shapiro (ed. and trans.). *The Correspondence between Princess Elisabeth of Bohemia and René Descartes* (Chicago, IL, 2007), 147. Their ciphered correspondence is yet to be found.

[19] See Akkerman (ed.), *Correspondence*, 1. letter nos. 301, 340.

[20] Roe to Elizabeth, 25 May 1625, Old Style, Constantinople (Akkerman (ed.), *Correspondence*, 1.536).

herself to his system, which was another thing altogether. It is presumably for this reason that he refrained from taking such a bold step even two years after he had first broached the subject.

What Roe was truly wishing for was the clear sign of favour inherent in a key created (or, at least, chosen) by Elizabeth herself. Edith Snook explains how the cipher key's creator sits 'at the centre of a circle of knowledge', and 'establishes a reading practice in which comprehension of the text depends on being welcomed by the writer into the social relationship that provides access to the code'.[21] In this sense we can see the difference in social standing, and the position within their respective circles, between Elizabeth and Aphra Behn: one was begged to supply a key, while the other begged to received one. By September 1625, Elizabeth had either given Roe permission to send her a key or he finally felt that circumstances necessitated his taking such a step, writing that 'I can safely say nothing of it, but under *the* cyphar, to which *yow* wilbe pleased to bee referred' (1.559).[22] Though she did not create a code herself, by accepting Roe's encoded letters Elizabeth signalled that he was finally considered a member of the inner circle of her most loyal servants.[23]

But Roe received more than simply the confirmation that theirs was now a privileged relationship, as the act of decoding his letters meant that Elizabeth reproduced his very words in her own handwriting—in doing so, Elizabeth becomes Roe's secretary, reversing the hierarchy. Just as a student learns the wisdom of Cicero by copying out his Orations, so Elizabeth would see Roe's words attain extra authority simply by their being inscribed in her royal hand, and Roe, knowing that she always deciphered letters herself, would presumably feel that his words were thereafter effectively endorsed by her. He would also know that Elizabeth would be unable to 'skim-read' any of his letters, as the necessity of deciphering would ensure that the words within would be fully considered by virtue of this process. Cryptography, therefore, did not serve merely to obscure information and protect it from the prying eyes of outsiders, but it also could bind the members of a group together through their shared use of a 'language' particular to them, or, in this case perhaps, a hand. Cryptography served a profound social function: it kept outsiders further away, and bound insiders closer together. As I have argued elsewhere, in many ways, cryptography in epistolary circles mimicked the social act of 'scribal publication', the act which served to bond 'groups of like-minded individuals into a community, sect or political faction, with the exchange of texts in manuscript serving to nourish a shared set of values and to enrich personal allegiances'.[24]

[21] Snook, *Women, Reading*, 155.

[22] Roe to Elizabeth, 9/19 September 1625, Halki. Roe often notes the Julian (Old Style) as well as the Gregorian (New Style) date for Elizabeth's convenience; 9 September and 19 September were in fact the same day, the calendar simply depending on where one found oneself.

[23] For Roe's cipher see Akkerman (ed.), *Correspondence*, 1.873–5.

[24] Harold Love, *Scribal Publication in Seventeenth-Century England* (Oxford, 1993), 177.

A FORBIDDEN ART

The elite circles that employed cryptography rarely felt the need to utilise the more political aspects of the art until 1642, when the civil wars arrived in England. The problem with writing a letter in cipher is, of course, that its deceptive nature is generally broadcast in the numbers or symbols that stare blankly at the reader, whether that is the intended recipient or an eavesdropping interceptor. Queen Henrietta Maria (1609–1669) used cipher as a mark of an epistle's importance, telling her husband not to believe 'the letters which I write by the post, in which there is no cipher [. . .] for they are written for the Parliament'.[25] In 1643, Parliament seemed to have got wise to the trend, and passed a decree forbidding cryptography, declaring that anyone found in possession of a ciphered letter or even cipher key could be prosecuted as a spy and thus ran the risk of a conviction of treason and its accompanying unpleasant end. This decree ensured that from this point, only those in great need of secret communication would use cipher codes. Cryptography was returned to its origins, and was once more a language used only by spies and conspirators, those who peddled information that would damn them if easily read—while being caught with a letter in cipher was extremely risky, being caught with a letter that says in plain text 'we kill all of Parliament tomorrow' left the messenger no wiggle room whatsoever. For the historian, of course, detecting cipher in letters after this date is therefore also a handy way of identifying characters as active in the underbelly of early modern society.

The decree had sounded the death knell of cryptography, however, and by the outbreak of the Second Civil War in 1648 it had all but vanished (it would, as with all such things, be revived some decades later). Those still in need of secrecy had by this time realised that there was another branch of cryptology that offered a way to keep both secrets truly hidden and also themselves as writers and their correspondents as readers protected. Steganography, the art of concealing one message in another, soon replaced cryptography almost completely. Steganography allows the writer to produce a letter that, to anyone lacking the key to its comprehension, seems completely innocuous. Mercantile discourse may be used to communicate military information, for example, as 'receiving an order for two pairs of gloves to be sent to Paris' might translate as 'four regiments of foot soldiers are on their way to Newcastle', an interpretation not immediately open to a surreptitious reader. In using steganographic methods, the need for secrecy and maintaining bonds in communication could still be fulfilled, with correspondents employing invisible inks and coded discourses, but without it being obvious to any interceptor who caught a glance of a letter.

[25] Henrietta Maria to Charles I, [October 1642], The Hague, BL Harley MS 7379, fol. 80b, in Mary Anne Green (trans. and ed.), *Letters of Queen Henrietta Maria, Including her Private Correspondence with Charles I* (London, 1857), 124.

Historiography has mostly been blind to steganography and its fabrications of hidden lies, as steganographic messages are difficult to detect; for instance, as the editor of Elizabeth Stuart's correspondence, I discovered one steganographic message that fooled not only King Charles I (1600–1649) but also a fair few modern scholars. In October 1641, Elizabeth needed to disguise the name of her daughter, Louise Hollandine (1622–1709). Elizabeth wanted to tell a poisonous tale which was so secretive that she begged Roe never to mention it 'to anie bodie liuing for some reasons you shall know when we meet I ~~haue~~ dare not trust it to paper, […] for there by lyes a tale that must not yett be tolde, till you and I meete'.[26] Her mother-in-law had told her that Frederick William (1620–1688), son of the Elector of Brandenburg, had been poisoned by the Count of Schwarzenberch, one of Brandenburg's chief ministers. The count allegedly intended to prevent Frederick William from marrying the Palatine princess Louise Hollandine.[27] Elizabeth thought it would be better to keep Charles I and his ambassador in The Hague, Sir William Boswell (d. 1650), in the dark about this rumour, because she believed their meddling had already harmed the prospects of one of her other daughters, Princess Elisabeth, when, against Elizabeth's advice, Charles had attempted to marry her off to the King of Poland. The resulting negotiations had lasted for seven years and proved fruitless. Elizabeth was thus particularly keen to prevent Charles from causing any more trouble by trying to marry off her other daughters. Elizabeth knew full well that her letters were intercepted and examined by her brother's agents, and if she had simply resorted to her usual cipher alphabet to disguise the name of Louise Hollandine, one of Charles' cryptanalysts could simply have counted the letters to identify her. She wanted a more secure code. She required a singular number from the nomenclator rather than the separate numbers of the cipher alphabet. Louise Hollandine, who had previously seemed of little political importance, did not have her own number in the cipher Elizabeth shared with Roe, however. Elizabeth could not simply add another number to the nomenclator because then Roe would have had no idea what or to whom this new number referred. Her solution was as cryptic as it was cunning, and relied entirely on her personal relationship with Roe.

Elizabeth decided to use the same number for Louise Hollandine as was used for Rupert. To indicate this, she gave Roe a clue, one which only a very few individuals could possibly have fathomed. She gave a description of a private performance of *Medea*, in which 'none but women acted' including Roe's adopted daughter Jane Rupa, her lady-in-waiting, who was 'a graue matron'. She specifically mentioned Louise Hollandine played 'a man and so like Rupert as you then woulde haue ju^s^tlie called her by his name'.[28] This stegotext has always been interpreted literally, as if Louise Hollandine, who is depicted by portraitist Gerard Honthorst as utterly feminine and sensual, in reality would have had either a crude or masculine

[26] Elizabeth to Roe, 10 October 1641, New Style, Rhenen (Akkerman (ed.), *Correspondence*, 2.1004).

[27] See Elizabeth to Roe, 6 January 1642, New Style, The Hague (Akkerman (ed.), *Correspondence*, 2.1020–1).

[28] Elizabeth to Roe, 10 October 1641, New Style, Rhenen (Akkerman (ed.), *Correspondence*, 2.1004).

appearance.[29] In fact, Elizabeth's letter revealed nothing about her daughter's appearance or even her gender-bending theatrical performance; it could even be questioned whether her daughters performed *The Tragedy of Medea* on this occasion, were it not for Sophia's memoirs providing corroborative evidence.[30] The description gave Elizabeth the opportunity to stealthily signal, in a truly steganographic manner, that she would use the same code number for her daughter as they used for her son. From that point on Elizabeth's correspondents indeed referred to Louise Hollandine by Rupert's nomenclator; both names were thereafter encoded with no. 166. Furthermore, the very act of understanding Elizabeth's clue also allowed Roe to confirm his status as a member of her inner circle.

LITERARY INSPIRATIONS

Elizabeth Stuart was an avid reader of prose romances and was particularly well-versed in them, ordering them through her brother's ambassador in France, Sir Isaac Wake:

> I intreat you to doe me the kindness that if there be anie reuerent bookes of Romances newlie come out in print at Paris to send me some espetiallie the second part of *l'Excil de Polexandre* [Martin Le Roy de Gomberville's *Polexandre*] if it be come out, for such studies are verie fitt for this place [her hunting lodge in Rhenen] where we doe nothing but hunt.[31]

She had also indulged in some romance roleplay with her husband, who referred to her as Astraea (the same codename Behn was also later given), while she called him Celadon, the two being protagonists of Honoré d'Urfé's multiple volume prose romance *L'Astrée* (published 1607–1627). They even had Honthorst portray them as such.[32]

Literary names were also put to more serious use in royalist communications during the Wars of the Three Kingdoms. In 1643, for instance, Jane Bingley and her husband swapped letters with their daughter, Susan, who had crossed over to France, using romance conceits. Their correspondence was concerned with the negotiations that Susan's father was engaged in with Lord Wentworth at the royalist stronghold of Oxford, as well as the manner in which parliamentary forces had retaken Arundel Castle. In these letters, Jane was referred to as Fidelia, her husband as Melidora, and Susan as either

29 Jessica Gorst-Williams, *Elizabeth, The Winter Queen* (London, 1977), 150; and Mary Anne Everett Green, *Elizabeth, Electress Palatine and Queen of Bohemia* (London, 1855; rev. 1909), 353. For Honthorst's paintings of Louise Hollandine, see, for instance, Rosalind K. Marshall, *The Winter Queen: The Life of Elizabeth of Bohemia 1596–1662* (Edinburgh, 1998).

30 Sophia of Hanover, 1680, in Sean Ward (ed. and trans.) *Memoirs (1630–1680)* (Toronto, 2013), 41.

31 Elizabeth to Wake, 28 August 1631, Old Style, Rhenen (Akkerman (ed.), *Correspondence*, 1.846).

32 Nadine Akkerman, *Courtly Rivals in The Hague: Elizabeth Stuart (1596–1662) & Amalia von Solms (1602–1675)* (The Hague, 2014), 43–6.

Philitia or Amorella. If these efforts may not have fooled the Black Chamber operative who intercepted at least one of their letters, as this letter was eventually 'decoded', they do seem to have at least delayed the identification of the correspondents. The borrowing of names from romance literature may not have conferred complete anonymity upon an individual, but it might help keep a conspirator from exposure and thus capture for at least a few days or weeks.[33]

Whether or not Elizabeth picked up the habit of hiding identities with the assistance of prose romances from royalists such as Bingley, she would later write about the marital problems of her son Charles Louis in steganographic form, giving those whom it concerned literary codenames. She cast herself in the role of Queen Candace, the famed martial queen Ben Jonson had introduced to the Stuart court in his *Masque of Queens* (1609), thus writing about herself in the third person. Her daughter Sophia (1630–1714), who was resident in Charles Louis' household at the time, she referred to as Madame de Scudéry's Bernice from *Les Femmes Illustres* (1642), while she named her son Charles Louis after Plutarch's Tiribaze, and his estranged wife became the mythological Greek Eurydice.[34] Whatever had influenced this development, Elizabeth had already abandoned cryptography in favour of steganography in the 1640s. In a letter to Sir Charles Cotterell (1615–1701), her master of the household, she included a passage in invisible ink that concerned her daughter Sophia: 'she is an hipocrit to the Root [...] trust her no further than you see cause'.[35] She not only wrote passages in invisible ink, but stopped signing her letters altogether, explaining to the Old Cavalier James Graham, first marquess of Montrose (1612–1650), 'because letters may be taken, I shall not putt all my name to them but this æ cipher'.[36] How this was expected to help when her hand itself was quite easy to identify is another matter, though it may relate to potential evidentiary use further down the line: it would be far easier to claim a cipher as either someone else's or forged than a holograph signature.

GENDERING THE CIPHER

Bingley's prose romance letter was sent up the chain of command by the Black Chamber operative in a bundle marked as 'Letters intercepted from his Ma.^{tys} ministers abroad, 1644/3', accompanied by a note which read: 'Fidelia to Amorella. Note! Some Court

[33] Akkerman, *Invisible Agents*, 168–9.

[34] Barbara Kiefer Lewalski, *Writing Women in Jacobean England* (London, 1993), 46, in particular endnote 6 in which Lewalski speculates on which source texts Elizabeth might have used to pick her codenames. Lewalski erroneously identifies Sophia as Candace.

[35] Elizabeth to Cotterell, 2 December [1650s, no year], private collection (to be published in Akkerman (ed.), *Correspondence*, 3).

[36] Elizabeth to Montrose, 2 September [1649], Old Style, Rhenen, Edinburgh, National Archives Scotland, GD220/3, no. 111 (to be published in Akkerman (ed.), *Correspondence*, 3).

Ladies at Oxford took Names out Some Romancys'.[37] It appears that the parliamentarian intelligencer could not countenance the idea that men such as Jane Bingley's husband, or even John Evelyn (1620–1706) who used the same trick in his correspondence, would ransack such fanciful texts as prose romances to select a code name. This note suggests that this particular cryptological technique, the use of prose romances to furnish codenames, was mistakenly seen as a particularly feminine form of deception.[38] In this sense it joined cryptography, as the employment of cipher keys had previously become associated with women, an idea fully exploited in *The King's Cabinet Opened; or, Certain Packets of Secret Letters & Papers* (1645). This pamphlet presented Charles I's use of cipher as evidence of his emasculation by Henrietta Maria: his French wife was corrupting his power and rhetoric with her feminine ways.[39]

This identification of cryptography with the feminine did have some merit, however, as women had been encrypting and decrypting letters since the sixteenth century, and were increasingly apt to do so.[40] Elizabeth Mazzola even argues that cryptography was an art particularly suited to women, connecting it 'to other early modern writing technologies like needlework, allegory, graffiti, and the masque, activities for which many women had great skill and made enormous investments of time and interests'.[41] Indeed, women might have been particularly skilled at it: if Henry, Lord Howard, is to be believed, King James VI (1566–1625) was taught intricate cipher codes by a woman, Frances, Lady Kildare (d. 1628). James was a man neither 'acquainted nor accustomed to that kind of intelligence', presumably because a king would never (officially) practise any form of deception, unlike a woman (and a Catholic one at that).[42] While cryptography might not have formed part of a king's education, James' mother, Mary Stuart (1542–1587), was taught at the tender age of fifteen to select those passages in the letters she sent to her French mother, Mary of Guise (1515–1560), which were to be enciphered by a secretary.[43] That Mary, Queen of Scots, knew how to wield a cipher code herself would become plain when, out of necessity, she dispensed with any secretarial assistance and enciphered and deciphered her own letters while she languished in prison—a skill shared by another French-born Catholic queen, Henrietta Maria.

While it can of course be questioned whether cryptography truly was a feminine art with so many diplomats practising the same, it is beyond question that women letter

[37] London, The National Archives, Amorella to Fidelia (and not vice versa as the interceptor noted down), 8 Jan. 1643/4, SP 16/506, fol. 8, 236.

[38] Akkerman, *Invisible Agents*, 168–9.

[39] Laura Lunger Knoppers, *Politicizing Domesticity from Henrietta Maria to Milton's Eve* (Cambridge, 2011), 42–67.

[40] For early examples, see James Daybell, 'Secret Letters in Elizabethan England', in James Daybell and Peter Hinds (eds), *Material Readings of Early Modern Culture: Texts and Social Practices, 1580–1730* (Basingstoke, 2010), 47–64, 53–4.

[41] Elizabeth Mazzola, 'The Renaissance Englishwoman in Code: "Blabbs" and Cryptographers at Elizabeth I's Court', *Critical Survey*, 22.3 (2010), 1–20, 10.

[42] Lord Henry Howard to Mr Edward Bruce, 27 August [1602], in David Dalrymple (ed.), *Secret Correspondence of Sir Robert Cecil with James VI, King of Scotland* (Edinburgh, 1766), 209–10.

[43] John Guy, *My Heart Is My Own: The Life of Mary Queen of Scots* (London, 2004), 82.

writers were both drawn to and well suited to steganography, the secret writing method that largely replaced cryptography following its outlawing in 1643. In general, women's letters escaped the interceptor's attention: an italic hand promised nothing but domestic tittle-tattle, surely, and would not be worth the reading. Women realised they could make use of this general assumption that their letters were filled purely with domestic gossip as a potential level of obfuscation. Lucy (1599–1660), Lady Carlisle, for instance, wrote letters to her brother-in-law, with whom she had a difficult relationship at the time, starting in *medias res* with discourses of intimacy: 'my Deerest thinke of me and loue me as the parsone most yours'. She left her letters unsigned, only her seal betraying her authorship, in the hope that an interceptor would have long cast the letter aside as a love letter before reaching the secret, political message relating to the Bishops' Wars.[44]

One network of women, which has invariably been seen to centre around Elizabeth Murray (1626–1698), Lady Dysart, used code names and medical discourse or 'women's complaints' in order to hide both messenger and message from prying eyes. This network was in all likelihood orchestrated by Mrs Catherine Grey (1636–1682), a woman in her own right rather than a simple code name for Dysart as many have assumed, and included Murrough O'Brien (*c* 1614–1674), first earl of Inchiquin, as well as Dysart's sisters Katherine (d. 1670) and Anne Murray (d. 1679), a certain Mrs Hoskinson and, quite possibly, the famed Lady Carlisle herself.[45] The nomenclator used within this circle not only reveals who was important—Lady Anne Murray and Lady Rachel Newport (d. 1661) were amongst those who were accorded their own code name—but also how easy it is for the historian to become confused. Not only was Mrs Grey mistaken for Elizabeth Murray, but Murray herself had two 'spy names': she could be referred to as either Mr or Mrs Legg. Medical discourse was employed alongside the cryptographic nomenclator to prevent any potential interceptor from realising that invisible ink was being used. Grey's invisible ink recipe was expensive—a concoction, therefore, to be used on special occasions only.[46] Each of the correspondents complain of being ill, and at a certain point Inchiquin insists that the time had come to use the 'powder', which they were to apply 'between the Ribbs as belowe'. What Inchiquin meant was that they should write with invisible ink between the lines written in normal ink. It worked. Though the letters were still intercepted, the Black Chamber operatives merely copied out the letters before sending them on, failing to make the invisible ink visible; Lady Dysart's circle thus gave their enemies a pile of letters full of misinformation or literary fabrication, while the

[44] Akkerman, *Invisible Agents*, 91–2.

[45] The fact that Catherine Grey was not a code name was brought to light in Akkerman, *Invisible Agents*, 136–57, and overturned the false assumptions, which were repeated by other scholars ever since, first made by Doreen Cripps, *Elizabeth of the Sealed Knot: A Biography of Elizabeth Murray, Countess of Dysart* (Kineton, 1975), 46–7, 58–9.

[46] For women using 'kitchen chemistry', see Jayne Elisabeth Archer, 'Women and Chymistry in Early Modern England: The Manuscript Receipt Book (ca. 1616) of Sarah Wigges', in Kathleen P. Long (ed.), *Gender and Scientific Discourse in Early Modern Culture* (Farnham, 2010), 191–216, 216. The Inchiquin recipe book is in the National Library of Ireland, NLI 14786, but unfortunately does not include this particular invisible ink recipe. I thank Danielle Clarke for bringing its existence to my attention.

treasonous messages they hid escaped unseen.[47] This technique was, in effect, a sort of double blind—the existence of one form of steganography, invisible ink, was indicated through another form, analogical substitution. In essence, those letter writers who communicated via steganographic discourse were trying their hands at fiction, whether they were reusing tropes and names from prose romances, acting as if lovers instead of bickering in-laws, or pretending that they were sick.

CONCLUSION: TO LOOK WITHOUT SEEING, WRITE WITHOUT READING

The simple fact that instances such as Elizabeth Stuart's conflation of Louise Hollandine with Rupert and the Dysart circle's obtuse indication of invisible ink usage remained unnoticed for nigh on 350 years demonstrates the complexities at work. It is fair to say that we are, at times, responsible for our own failures to read such practices when we encounter them, as modern editorial and archival techniques can work to remove these textural clues, both literally and figuratively. By flattening letters into letterbooks and repairing 'damage', material clues such as letterlocking techniques are literally 'ironed out',[48] while an editor who deciphers a letter and presents it in plain text may enhance legibility, but at the cost of erasing the link to the message's social context which is inherent in the cipher key itself. By destroying these evidentiary signs, we run the risk of making the same mistake as the Black Chamber operative who thought that only women read prose romances, or the operative who failed to read between the lines and caress Inchiquin's letters until they gave up their real secrets. By removing a letter's physical texture, its 'social texture' may become impossible to recover.

Women letter writers created epistolary webs, and during times of duress these webs were maintained by invisible, spidery threads of secrecy. If we study cryptology, we see how wide these networks could reach. The cryptological web can ensnare those who share a cipher or speak the same language. Gerbier, for example, shared a key given to him by Elizabeth Stuart with both Sir John Coke and Richard Weston, first earl of Portland—the very individuals from whom the queen was attempting to protect her messages.[49] This reveals that Gerbier betrayed her, using the sense of security their apparently shared secrecy conferred against her. A fully reconstructed or retrieved cipher

[47] Akkerman, *Invisible Agents*, 152.

[48] See Jana Dambrogio, Amanda Ghassaei, Daniel Starza Smith, et al., 'Unlocking History through Automated Virtual Unfolding of Sealed Documents Imaged by X-Ray Microtomography', *Nature Communications*, 12: 1184 (2021). The article codified the field of letterlocking.

[49] The example is a key used by Sir Balthazar Gerbier between December 1631 and December 1638, which he shared with Elizabeth Stuart, but also with Sir John Coke, and Richard Weston, first earl of Portland: see 'Key 1 Gerbier', in Akkerman (ed.), *Correspondence*, 2. 1057–8.

key also has its own story to tell, as a key is more often than not built up logically and hierarchically: for instance, if the king is 100, the queen is 99, their male heir is 98. With nomenclators running into the hundreds, it can reveal whom the key's maker thought belonged to the same circle, and who was of most importance. Networks can be mapped in a similar way when focusing on steganography. Who in the same circle were 'sick' at the same time, who shared the same discourse? Who pretended to be lovers when they were clearly not anything of the sort? Several invisible ink recipes were published in della Porta's *Magiae Naturalis* (1558), but also noted down in women's recipe books. Who shared their recipes with whom? Spycraft in all its varieties passed from one generation of spies to another, and did the same in female circles. The potential represented by cryptographical techniques to study women's epistolary networks and thus, perhaps, uncover new strands of historical discourse and activity, has yet to be fully exploited.

FURTHER READING

Ahnert, Ruth, Sebastian E. Ahnert, Catherine Nicole Coleman, et al. *The Network Turn: Changing Perspectives in the Humanities*. Cambridge, 2020.

Ahrendt, Rebekah, Nadine Akkerman, Jana Dambrogio, Daniel Starza Smith, and David van der Linden. 'The Letter as Object: Signed, Sealed, and Undelivered', in Howard Hotson and Thomas Wallnig (eds), *Reassembling the Republic of Letters in the Digital Age: Standards, Systems, Scholarship*. Göttingen, 2019, 63–7.

Akkerman, Nadine. *Elizabeth Stuart, Queen of Hearts*. Oxford, 2021.

Akkerman, Nadine. *Invisible Agents: Women and Espionage in Seventeenth-Century Britain*. Oxford, 2018.

Dambrogio, Jana, Amanda Ghassaei, Daniel Starza Smith, et al. 'Unlocking History through Automated Virtual Unfolding of Sealed Documents Imaged by X-Ray Microtomography'. *Nature Communications*, 12.1184 (2021). doi: https://doi.org/10.1038/s41467-021-21326-w.

Marshall, Alan, *'Arcana imperii': A History of Espionage in Early-Modern Britain, 1598–1715*. Manchester, forthcoming.

CHAPTER 38

NON-ELITE WOMEN AND THE NETWORK, 1600–1700

SUSAN WISEMAN

THIS chapter investigates how we can use the idea of the 'network' to think about the relationships of non-elite women. In examining writing by and about women in the swathe of society below gentry status, we can see that there are large differences between such women. They might be village brewers, relatively prosperous townswomen, Native Americans, or busy metropolitan licensed midwives. Not all of these even share frameworks of status. There are also, however, some connections in that many of these women, perhaps most, went into the world with rudimentary or no guidance in reading and writing and that over the long term, scholarship has not focused on them. In taking one term—that of the 'network'—and asking how it can help us to understand more about the writing and thinking lives of such women in the period 1500–1700, the aim is to chart some relatively practical solutions to questions of how we can more accurately and fully recognise individual, smaller groups and, potentially, larger groups of such women as part of a social world, and to investigate what kinds of material might yield results. Because the term 'network' is used extensively in two ways, one literal, small-scale, and informal, and the other using data and combining mathematical and humanistic analysis, this chapter has two sections and seeks to address the relationship between the two with reference to non-elite subjects.

NETWORK PRACTICES AND NON-ELITE WOMEN

Where researchers have significant quantities of textual evidence produced by women, they have generated a substantial amount of material investigating the writings of women who were in specific types of early modern networks. Some work presents itself explicitly as being about networks, but with just a little creativity an investigator can bring into view several other kinds of scholarship that imply or encourage thinking in terms of networks—such as studies of courts, powerful families, the republic of letters, and correspondence. Scholars, including Jane Couchman and Mihoko Suzuki, have tracked the interrelationships of women from the European elites, placing them in relation to intellectual currents; Micheline White and Barbara Harris have tracked the far-reaching influence of women at the Tudor courts; and work exists on philosophical circles of the upper gentry connecting Damaris Masham and John Locke in England, and Elizabeth of Bohemia and René Descartes.[1] The influence of English gentry women in epistolary and literary communities has been established by scholars studying manuscript circles, such as Helen Hackett on the Tixall miscellanies or Gillian Wright on the circle of Katherine Philips.[2] Scholars including James Daybell, Johanna Harris, and Alison Wiggins have explored letters, and the connections fanning out from the aristocracy into the church and radical religion can be explored both through life-writings and funeral sermons, such as those by Anthony Walker for Mary Rich, Countess of Warwick, as suggested by Ramona Wray and others.[3] Such scholarship does not generally use the specific protocols of network analysis, but identifies sets of connections expressed in textual, often epistolary, forms which have both nodes and edges—in this case people and, say, letters—to use network analysis terminology. At times, as Helen Hackett perceptively notes of the scholarship on the Catholic Tixall circle, seeing the spreading and dense connections between gentry families in terms of networks avoids scholarly tendencies to see Catholic and provincial circles in particular as 'inward-looking' and 'provincial'; thinking with networks helps scholars to consider carefully whether the evidence suggests the existence of a coterie, more outward-looking associations or, as often, an inner circle of multiple connections offset by less central nodes.[4] Indeed, thinking about this work on elite and gentry networks—some of women only, most of men and

[1] Leah Knight, Micheline White, and Elizabeth Sauer (eds), *Early Modern Women's Bookscapes: Reading, Ownership, Circulation* (Ann Arbor, MI, 2018); Barbara Harris, 'Women and Politics in Early Tudor England', *The Historical Journal*, 33.2 (1990), 259–81. For Elizabeth of Bohemia and philosophical correspondence start with Lisa Shapiro, 'Elizabeth, Princess of Bohemia', in *The Stanford Encyclopedia of Philosophy* https://plato.stanford.edu/entries/elisabeth-bohemia/ (accessed 22 May 2021); similarly, for Damaris Masham see Sarah Hutton, 'Lady Damaris Masham', https://plato.stanford.edu/entries/lady-masham/ (accessed 22 May 2021).

[2] Helen Hackett, 'Women and Catholic Manuscript Networks in Seventeenth-Century England: New Research on Constance Aston Fowler's Miscellany of Sacred and Secular Verse', *Renaissance Quarterly*, 65.4 (2012), 1094–124; Gillian Wright, *Producing Women's Poetry, 1600–1730* (Cambridge, 2013), and on longitudinal associations see Kate Lilley, 'Katherine Philips, "Philo-Philippa" and the Poetics of Association', in Patricia Pender and Rosalind Smith (eds) *Material Cultures of Early Modern Women's Writing* (Basingstoke, 2014), 118–39.

[3] Carol Pal, *Republic of Women: Rethinking the Republic of Letters in the Seventeenth Century* (Cambridge, 2012); Ramona Wray, [Re]constructing the Past: the Diametric Lives of Mary Rich', in Henk Dragstra, Sheila Ottway, and Helen Wilcox (eds), *Betraying Ourselves* (Basingstoke, 2000), 148–65; Mary Rich, *Memoir of Lady Warwick: Also her Diary* (London, 1847); Anthony Walker, *Eureka, or, The Virtuous Woman Found* (London, 1678).

[4] Hackett, 'Women', 1100.

women—a factor that links them is that they can be thought of as making literary–social shapes or forms. Putting this more strongly, Caroline Levine has argued that 'the network is, like the period and the nation-state, a kind of form', and one that 'invites our attention to patterns of circulation rather than rootedness, zigzagging movements rather than stable foundations'.[5] In grouping together interconnected writers, such work can be said to elucidate the forms of social as well as literary relations in which women—with men—participated in early modern England.

When we turn to the writings of early modern women below the gentry, literary, semi-literary, and literate networks are not as readily visible or represented in extant evidence as those of their more affluent and higher status peers. Clearly, non-elite women had wide-ranging relationships, and we have evidence such as midwives' client lists, letters, and apprentice papers that do evidence these—but the remains are comparatively few. It also seems to be the case at present that more writing by non-elite English men than women is known and locatable, and that this situation may, to some extent, be similar in other parts of Europe. Thus, writing about pan-European chronicling practices and local recording, Judith Pollman finds 'very few' female chroniclers, and writing about families of writers in France, Neil Kenny finds that in families of high commoners, ranked below the elite, families with more than one female writer tend to exist only in the very highest social bands.[6] Many factors make it intuitively very plausible that considerably less material by women from below gentry level might survive than by men. Factors might include that men from non-elite backgrounds, for example, might have their interests joined to those of the elite through family connections (between gentry and, say, the city of London guilds), and might rise through grammar school, business, office, soldiering, or during long days on board ship and even become educated through choral singing; however, women had relatively few paths to mobility open to them. Offices and occupations are at times associated with longer discursive forms and ones with reasons to survive; thus while payments are made to both men and women, more will be made to men. There is also obviously the basic fact that lower down the social echelons fewer women could read and write and it is likely that the papers of poorer families were themselves fewer and more vulnerable to flood, fire, and dispersion.

Besides a brutal economics of illiteracy and vulnerability, it may also be that non-elite women writers are less visible in finding tools, more often marginalised by editors, and unlikely to be cited in significant other projects of investigation because so little of theirs remains or because they are very minor players in an elite game. It seems that we don't have many actual networks of below gentry women—or at least not in the forms with which we are relatively familiar—but it is also the case that to understand whether that is simply a result of relative poverty and attrition, we would need a clearer overall picture of production, transmission, and what survives. In sum, it is clear that in comparison

[5] Caroline Levine, 'From Nation to Network', *Victorian Studies*, 55.4 (2013), 647–66, 667.

[6] Judith Pollmann, 'Archiving the Present and Chronicling the Future in Early Modern Europe', *Past and Present*, Supplement, 11 (2016), 232–52, 237; Neil Kenny, *Born to Write: Literary Families and Social Hierarchy in Early Modern France* (Oxford, 2020), 48–55.

with those of their social superiors, non-elite women's contacts may need additional methods and approaches.

Looking for textual materials by non-elite female writers involves excavating relatively limited circles or following up traces and absences where we can see texts once existed, or finding fragments by authors on the edges of elite networks. However, where materials by non-elite women are available it may be possible to tease out more about the worlds of such writers and readers and about potential textual and other contacts. Keeping in mind the idea of the network can prompt us to ask more questions about evidence, transmission, and methodology. In considering what primary evidence of networks can put non-elite women at the centre of our enquiries, we may need to shift expectations from a large number of texts surviving to different forms of evidence of presence in literate culture. What evidence falls within our remit depends substantially on the object of our study—particularly whether we are looking for women or only for writing; this affects what would constitute evidence of non-elite women's networks and where we would look for them. From the full range of evidence four types are examined here: the non-elite beyond customarily observed borders; family papers; testimony; and—an area in which literal networks are definitely traceable—religion.

First, following Caroline Levine's suggestion that keeping in mind the network invites us to enlarge our thinking beyond customary borders, we are prompted to extend our analysis to cross traditional borders—of nation, of literacy, and of societal organisation. If we consider non-elite women and cultural encounter, for example, we find a range of types of evidence, Here, I select two examples, both from the period of King Philip's or Metacom's war between settlers and Native Americans in late seventeenth-century New England.[7] In the first, John Eliot, whose project was to convert the Native Americans and who, as a consequence, taught them to read, reports in a letter to England on the sufferings of a Native American woman herded into what was virtually a penal colony on Dere Island. Eliot writes:

> Some ungodly & unrulely youth, came upon them where thei were ordered by authority to be, called them forth theire houses, shot at them, killed a child of godly parents wounded his mother & 4 more. The woman lifted up her hands to heaven & saide. Lord thou seest that we have neither done or said any thing against the English th[at] thei th[usdea]le with us.[8]

Evidently, though these may have been her words, this woman's sentiment is reported by Eliot to his patrons as he and they would wish to hear her. She is wholly nameless and—as far as we know—her speech is mentioned only here. Although this subject might be

[7] See Kathryn N. Gray, *John Eliot and the Praying Indians of Massachusetts Bay* (Plymouth, MA, 2013); Matt Cohen, *The Networked Wilderness: Communicating in Early New England* (Minneapolis, MN, 2010), esp. 1–28; see also Hilary E. Wyss, *Writing Indians: Literacy, Christianity and Native Community in Early America* (Amherst, MA, 2000).

[8] John Eliot to Robert Boyle 17 December 1675 in Michael Hunter et al. (eds) *The Correspondence of Robert Boyle*, vol. 4 (London, 2001), 400–1.

considered a node in a network of relations emanating from Eliot, to start from her and to trace her contacts and life via networks seems unlikely to be possible; 'her' networks are likely to have been oral and in textual evidence her presence remains shadowy. A second figure, who was probably not non-elite in her own terms, is discussed by Mary Rowlandson in her account of her capture by Native Americans. This is one of several occasions on which Rowlandson, a hostile witness, imagines the point of view of a woman with power over her:

> By that time I was refresht by the old Squaw, with whom my master was, Wettimores Maid came to call me home, at which I fell a weeping. Then the old Squaw told me, to encourage me, that if I wanted victuals, I should come to her, and that I should ly there in her Wigwam. Then I went with the maid, and quickly came again and lodged there. The Squaw laid a Mat under me, and a good Rugg over me; the first time I had any such kindness showed me. I understood that Wettimore thought, that if she should let me go and serve with the old Squaw, she would be in danger to loose, not only my service, but the redemption pay also.[9]

Such women were often key political players within their own culture, as, for example, warriors.[10] Although themselves not necessarily literate they are mentioned as cultural agents in settler writings and, probably, some of them can be understood as nodes in cultural exchanges that generated textual records. Moreover, as Matt Cohen suggests in his discussion of signifying systems used by Native Americans in the period that settlers brought the codex, once we permit and look for a larger range of signifying practices in a text then, perhaps, we can tease out networks other than, or as well as, those of the settler women.[11] Thinking with and about networks in the context of settler and Native American New England presses us to both discriminate amongst participants and clarify forms of communication that are included in analysis. These examples show that once we introduce the idea of the 'network', it can encompass several forms of contact: writing by women only, writing about women or on their behalf, reported speech, and non-verbal communication.

The family archive is another place where we might expect to find texts by non-elite women. To investigate this we can take the example of the Soresbie archive containing the family papers of a non-elite but relatively prosperous family from Derby and Darley Dale in Derbyshire. When in the seventeenth century Jane Mosley married Edward Soresbie (1665–1729) it seems that two literate families began to mingle their papers. These are typical in their inclusion of accounts, but less typical, perhaps, as Susan Whyman has noted, in their inclusion of records of generations of children,

[9] Mary Rowlandson, in Neal Salisbury (ed.), *The Sovereignty and Goodness of God* (Boston, MA, 1997), 97. Salisbury takes the second Boston edition (1682) as the basis for his edition.

[10] John A. Strong, 'Algonquian Women as Sunksquaws and Caretakers of the Soil: The Documentary Evidence in the Seventeenth-Century Records', in Susan Castillo and Victor M. P. Da Rosa (eds), *Native American Women in Literature and Culture* (Porto, 1997), 193–203.

[11] Cohen, *The Networked* Wilderness,1–28.

male and female, in a long, temporally linear, network. The Soresbie family were not wealthy, nor were they systematic in what they kept, but the archive houses an amazingly used, written in, and rehoused writing book. On the Mosley side we have words from Jane (two vibrant letters asking for special things from the metropolis) and her tedious rejected suitor (two dull but illuminating letters), her recipe book, and writing exercises from her sister.[12] The archive also contains many miscellaneous financial notes and records and stretches on into the eighteenth century. Why the family came to keep all this material is unclear, but it seems that the retention priorities of the archive are: record-keeping in relation to institutions, prompts to memory, and what we think of as 'sentimental' value, apparently naming a relation to objects as memorials and prompts to memory. It seems possible that some records may have acquired perceived value by surviving, and were kept simply because they had already been kept for a length of time.

The Soresbie archive is a collection of fragments shaped by constantly modified individual priorities. It suggests several interlocking networks, such as those between Jane Mosley in Derby and London correspondents and relatives and, from the more rustic country Soresbie side just two letters from a woman who is—at least at that point—a servant. Dorothy Sorsebie writes to 'Cosen Roger', presumably in Darley Dale, in May 1677, and we learn that she has visited him and returned to the household where she is employed as a servant, 'these are to let you know that I gate well to Kneeton [Kniveton?]'. Moreover, she might be able to return sooner than she expected because 'my ladi thinks her jou[r]ni is stayd and if it bee I shall cum the souner but I cnowe not when it will be'.[13] If we start with women, such as the middling Jane Mosley and the serving Dorothy, the archive itself gives us only glimpses of literal networks. However, we can think of this group of texts in terms of networks in several other ways; the idea prompts us to think about the two families spatially (moving around in the middle and south of their Midlands county), diachronically (as spreading and changing over generations) and, if we wanted to trace acts of transmission, although we probably could not trace preservers and inheritors with exactitude, it would be possible to identify both kinds of material (children's writing and music books; accounts) as transmitted between generations. As always, a family archive shows connections outwards and some of these will be between women. Here, we have the materials but we would have to painstakingly reconstruct as far as possible the instances of gifting and inheritance that transmitted them or work with gaps in knowledge. To think in terms of the network and the family archive together, then, prompts reconsideration and reframing of some familiar materials in relation to potentially wider and longer groups.

[12] For a discussion of family reading see Gillian Wright, 'Delight of Good Books: Family, Devotional Practice and Textual Circulation in Sarah Savage's Diaries', *Book History*, 18 (2015), 45–74. See also Susan Whyman, *The Pen and the People* (New Haven, CT, 2009), 83–8.

[13] For example, the Mosley—Soresbie papers, Matlock, Derbyshire Records Office; see, e.g., D331/19/23 Copy Book of Elizabeth Mosely; D331/19/17–18 letters to Jane Mosley from William Chatterton; D331/10/15 Dorothy Soresby to Roger Soresbie.

Testimony is a significant genre for finding out about women and their place in networks, but does not tell us about women writers. It has become a liminal and test case for the positioning of non-elite agency in writing and the generation of texts. The category of testimony—made orally by witnesses to various kinds of courts and written down in set forms—helps us to focus on the issue of how what material is available impacts on what kinds of questions can be productively asked. Do we want to find networks of women writers (in whatever sense) or are we researching texts that tell us about women? Testimony shows very clearly the implications of looking for women versus looking for writers. It is not women's writing, and therefore when we look for a network of women writing it must be excluded. But it does tell us whether women could sign their name not at all (and made a mark), shakily, or with confidence, and therefore gives us some limited sense of a woman's skill at writing. In terms of being primary textual evidence that tells us about women's networks it has much more potential. As Paula Humfrey's work implies, such testimony can be quite long and can disclose much about economic, commercial, household, and other relationships; it shows us women in relation to economic and social equals and superiors and it can tell us about women's economic positions, work networks, and social capital.[14] It also allows us to interpret a situation by starting with a non-elite woman, and by foregrounding her within the narrative. We can consider an example in which the testimony of domestic servants illuminates the networks of the elite and leaves evidence of literacy or lack of it at the same time as allowing us to trace more precisely how relationships between men and women, women and their servants, and the dramas of their households played out in early modern London.[15]

The case of Inchiquin versus Escrick in 1698 is a useful study in what testimony can disclose of non-elite networks of women, specifically that of Martha Pierce, a fifty-three year-old charwoman who, unlike the other servant who testified, only made her mark. Pierce was a poor woman and outside the charmed circle of literacy but, as her editor Paula Humfrey notes, had access to good information.[16] The information the deponents give relates to the attempt of Elizabeth, Dowager Countess of Inchiquin to have her marriage to Charles Howard, Baron of Escrick declared null on the grounds that he was already married—to 'Mrs Hannah Pike', with whom he had two children. As Pierce testifies, she works for the Countess and knows Escrick; she was in the room when Inchiquin asked her minister, Dr Winston Squib, when he had married Mrs Pike and Escrick. She had earlier worked for Escrick and Pike when they lived as man and wife and, upon leaving to work for a Mrs Beckwith, had been recommended to Inchiquin. She had also worked for West, the lawyer acting for Inchiquin, and she knew Hannah Pike's mother (Mrs Edwards) as well as servants on both sides. She had even heard

[14] Paula Humfrey, *The Experience of Domestic Service for Women in Early Modern London* (Abingdon, 2011), 1–38.

[15] See this volume, Chapter 36, Daniel Starza-Smith and Leah Veronese, 'Desire, Dreams, Disguise: The Letters of Elizabeth Bourne'.

[16] See Humfry, *Experience*, 94–9.

Escrick, in the Escrick-Pike household, exclaim that 'he should be damned to all eternity, both body and soul ... for he had married the Lady Inchiquin though his first wife was alive'.[17]

Looking for non-elite women's networks in primary evidence helps us to focus on Martha Pierce as potentially a figure of some cultural reach. She supplied convincing oral evidence that she was appraised of the goings-on throughout the household and neighbourhood. Moreover, she gives a rough sense of the social distance that pertained in direct conversation as opposed to overhearing (she converses with Mrs Pike but does not claim conversation with Inchiquin), and we can see that she had a wide range of acquaintance as well as mobility. The idea of the network, then, is immediately productive in putting her at the centre of our thought and in prompting us to look for connections—as one framework amongst several. Court testimony may take us to literate women, may lead us to texts beyond testimony but definitely is likely to supply us with networks of non-elite women as each subject speaks herself as at the centre of her own actions and world in relation to the testimony. This oral testimony in set forms is both outside consideration in any search for women in networks of writers and, in terms of networks of women, provides the clearest set of named connections so far. Indirect reports of women's ideas, most significantly (in terms of quantity) testimony in court but also reported narratives (such as oral conversion narratives) and embedded within other texts such as family narratives are significant for women whose position gave them no platform or literacy. However, whether we include or exclude them depends on the objectives of particular research, whether those include women, women's texts, both, or a wider field including gender.

Religious networks including non-elite women are, probably, the most readily available networks yielding large numbers of non-elite women. The evidence of these networks is particularly rich from the period of the mid-seventeenth century. From this period and after, we can access print and manuscript texts that are both about non-elite women and by them, but also find cases that complicate that border such as that of Sarah Wight, a young woman in London who ceased to eat and spoke rhapsodically. Her words were recorded by Henry Jessey, a nonconformist minister, who also carefully notes not only those who can vouch for her inedia, such as Wight's mother, Mary; her maid, Hannah Guy; and her mother, but also the men and women who visit and observe—Lady Willoughby and Lady Vermuiden'.[18] Thus, the names that are added to underwrite Wight's honesty are chosen for reasons of status, credibility, and position; they tell us qualitative things about the relations of women in that society and in terms of networks we can map Wight's connectedness to a wide range of men and women. Offered to the reader as evidence that Wight's experience was credited, this material is ripe for analysis of where, and therefore how, rumour and information travelled.

[17] Humfry, *Experience*, 94.

[18] Henry Jessey, *The Exceeding Riches of Grace* (London, 1647), sigs. A1r, B3r, B5r.

A first-person account that is particularly worth considering in relation to the network is a narrative of events from 1674 by the Baptist Agnes Beaumont. The manuscript was originally found valuable because she was 'acquianted [sic] with John Bunyan' (preface to the manuscript) and Bunyan has inscribed her name as a member of a Bedford congregation of Baptists in 1672.[19] In terms of the network, this should be a productive story, being full of events and people. The manuscript describes Beaumont's time of 'great fiery trial Concerning my fathers death'.[20] Events snowball horribly after she travels to a meeting on the back of Bunyan's horse. A local vicar spreads rumours that she and Bunyan were 'nought' together and on her return her father locks her out so that she spends one night in the barn and the next at her brother and sister-in-law's house. When, at last, she gets back in the house, her father makes her promise not to go to meetings; she is sick at heart. Two nights later, as she is sitting up praying, her father suffers a terrible pain in his heart and by the next lunchtime, after a traumatic night of suffering, he is dead. Although with his death the 'fiery trial' might seem to be over, in fact from this point we see Beaumont's faith and conduct tested in relation to a wide range of sacred and secular officeholders and opinion-formers: her local network of authority and information.

Beaumont's second fiery trial is initiated by a local lawyer, Mr Fary (or Farrow) who accuses her of poisoning her father—a crime for which those convicted 'must be burned', as Beaumont reports the lawyer as saying. A doctor is brought and, eventually, she is tried for parricide by a coroner's court. On the way many members of the community, the Baptists, the family, and the neighbourhood are named or cited. Eventually, Beaumont, still steadfast in faith and truth, is cleared. This narrative is slightly unusual in nonconformist writing in that the events take place after her 'awakening', and concentrates on the worldly actions of others through which her faith sustains her. Thinking about this story as a simple network allows us to see it in a semi-spatial schematic in which the sustaining connections—Bunyan, meetings, her religious society—are at the furthest distance from her and she struggles to get to them throughout. Seeing the narrative as a network helps us, perhaps, to see how in her case and in that of many others, the connections she has to others are relations of power, even as, through Bunyan, she is connected to the Baptists. To recast her story as a grid of connections foregrounds the specific precincts or layers of society with which she intersects. At the same time, but significantly, framing the text as a network at least partially effaces the mixed motives that precipitated events and the weave of emotions suggested by the narrative. Thus it would be hard to express the text's hints that Beaumont's father, as well as being furious about her nonconformity, and her connection with its apparent source—Bunyan—at least at moments may have taken some cognisance of the

[19] John Stachniewski with Anita Pacheco, 'Introduction', in *Grace Abounding with Other Spiritual Autobiographies* (Oxford, 1998), xl.

[20] Agnes Beaumont, 'The Narrative of the Persecution of Agnes Beaumont', in Stachniewski with Pacheco (eds), *Grace Abounding*, 193–224, 194.

rumours of her unchastity. Rumour and reputation blend with self-interest when, after his death, the vicar made ruining her reputation his open project—blending her nonconformity with sexual slurs on her and Bunyan. At the local fair, rumours of their liaison 'ran from one End of the fair to the other presently'.[21] Even before the accusation of parricidal poisoning, then, the narrative emphasises that her reputation was in tatters with the world beyond the Baptist community. The narrative shapes the final words of the coroner to Mr Farrow who had accused her as vindication in the secular world when he says: 'You that have defamed this maid after this manner, yow had need make it your business now to repair her reputation Again. You have taken Away her good name from her, and you would have taken Away her life from her if yow could'.[22] In a schematic arrangement, then, which casts the people involved as nodes in a network, people's motivations are not shown. In such an arrangement we can put Beaumont at the centre of connections but it is harder to use the concept of the network to tease out the motivations and significance of the story—the question of reputation; the narrator's assertion that throughout her faith and joy in Christ sustained her (a crucial point); or even, from our own analytical point of view, the huge malice that the slight movement towards the toleration of even a Protestant religious minority could provoke in the everyday lives of Biggleswade folk.

All the Beaumont narrative's nuanced issues can be more readily explored in discursive prose than in a schematic network of nodes but each has virtues. Beaumont's case suggests to us both some of the advantages and disadvantages of formalising network analysis. In reading Beaumont a reader must attend to the shifting weighting of the strands of the story. Religion, chastity, gossip, law, and family all influence events, and the narration presents these woven together so that a reader recognises the nuanced motivations and mixed reactions of the protagonists. This would be hard to show at all in a network abstraction, yet that, as we will see, is likely to both connect onwards and suggest more about the power networks in which she was enmeshed. Beaumont's case seems to have been significant to her in terms of her address to her Baptist fellowship, and within that perhaps has the status of evidence; for Baptists it is a valuable record of God's assistance in persecution; for Baptists and students of Bunyan it is—and perhaps was for many years primarily—notable as a sidelight on Bunyan. For scholars thinking about the family, religious anthropology, and town dynamics it is significant in showing where the borders might lie. The network as a concept does not allow us to follow one line—such as the subtle interaction of Agnes and her father, but thinking with networks does show up these dimensions as layered and overlapping. Beaumont's case suggests what informal thinking with the idea of the network on a small scale can and cannot do.

[21] Beaumont, in Stachniewski (ed.), 'Persecution', 214.

[22] Beaumont, in Stachniewski (ed.), 'Persecution', 221.

NETWORK THEORIES: PROS AND CONS OF ABSTRACTION

The possibilities of abstraction and system are implicit in the idea of the network and this section investigates its potential for the exploration of non-elite women. Given that all abstract theories of the network are designed to illuminate relationships, the focus is on showing what kind of relationships are manifested by three key modes of abstraction: traffic analysis (which can reconstruct a network by identifying its nodes when the content is unavailable); actor network theory (that puts things and people into heterogeneous networks); and social network theory (which traces the density of connections between human members of a network).

The reactions of enthusiasm and scepticism that network theories have encountered have been important in shaping take-up. While at present (2022) it is regarded as specialist within early modern studies, it might in due course become more quotidian. In archaeology, where network theory has been deeply and widely applied for longer than in the field of literary criticism and history, scholars suggest that its reception has followed the 'hype cycle', moving from the 'peak of inflated expectations' and slumping 'disillusionment' to achieve the 'plateau of productivity'.[23] As they note, clearly, network analysis is one tool amongst several. Discussing primarily traffic analysis, whereby the flows of information—not necessarily the information itself, which might be absent—can be mapped, Collar and others illuminate in detail the potential of a theory of the network which allows us to infer connections—*edges*—between nodes where the traces of what actually flowed between them (in our case potentially letters or other materials) are absent. For example, traffic analysis can monitor encrypted messages without their being decoded—perhaps a potentially useful tool for the mapping of networks where the exact content carried by conduits is, or might be, unknown—and therefore abstractly expressed. Collar and her collaborators prioritise starting with the phenomena the project wants to capture. Although they are looking specifically at 'network science', they start from a process equally applicable in informal searches for the networks of non-elite women—'the conceptual process researchers go through, explicitly or implicitly, in deciding whether the phenomena under investigation can be usefully abstracted using network concepts and represented using network data'[24]A similar process of evaluation is underway in early modern studies as scholars respond to each other and reflect on what data sets are available.

One step in the direction of making the methods of network analysis more available is establishing key aims and terms. For Collar and her contributors, a primary virtue

[23] Anna Collar, Fiona Coward, and Barbara J. Mills, 'Networks in Archaeology: Phenomena, Abstraction, Representation', *Journal of Archaeological Method and Theory*, 22.1 (2015), 1–32, 2; see also Albert-László Barabási, *Network Science* (Cambridge, 2016).

[24] Collar et al., 'Networks in Archaeology', 4.

of network analysis is that it can express relationships 'between past (and present) individuals, groups and material culture' even when the content of that relationship is only known in part. A distinguishing feature of evidence that can be helpfully expressed as a network is whether the data can be 'represented as nodes and connections between them', called 'edges'. Thus, a node is a unit (whether a human or, perhaps, a shop) and an edge—a mathematical word for join—is a relationship between nodes. Two measures of the importance of a person or other agent in a network (a node) are 'betweenness' measuring the number of shortest paths that pass through it and eigenvector centrality which measures a node's place in the network by noting its connectedness to all the other nodes in the network.

Collar is writing primarily about traffic analysis, a method that can show that communication did happen even though the literal or material evidence is missing, and there is much to consider in terms of how it might further the study of non-elite women. Thus, where Collar and her collaborators use the example of 'patterns of trade in prehistory' we might place 'patterns of family business writing' or 'patterns of cross-status-relationships upwards and downwards' or, using an example discussed above, we might trace the news of Wight's visions through London starting with the known visitors to her bedside. This might prove a small network indeed—but, beyond literal visitors, it might imply that the news spread to a range of congregations and interest groups. If we have a number of people in a network, but know no more than that they were in contact, it might be helpful to begin a web of connections—a diagram of flows expressed as nodes and edges and, potentially, leading into other networks. Thus, the first question might be what is to be gained from expressing information abstractly—in terms of showing patterns, making small networks diagrammatically comparable, or in showing far-ranging connections and indicating where 'edges' are missing, can illuminate gaps in information. These abstract flows can productively model the individual decisions of cultural agents—people—as well as large shifts, even if they downplay individual human decisions and actions.

Actor network theory has found considerable purchase in literary and historical studies, and is valuable in work that does not want to give humans excessive or special status, but, rather, to equalise relations. Following the work of John Law and Bruno Latour, actor network theory has found productive applications in some branches of early modern studies, having in particular a strong take-up in animal studies where, for example, it allows scholars to map much more fully the reach of animals, alive and dead. Moreover, as Erica Fudge argues, actor network theory is valuable in reshaping the animal's place in the world as the equalisation of agents does away with the constantly troubling relationship between human and non-human animals as agents, in which animals are held in a comparative dynamic with the human.[25] As Rita Felski puts it, one of the features that makes actor network theory so compelling is its reforming and undermining of chains of meaning that—being ideologically saturated—form

[25] Bruno Latour, *Reassembling the Social* (Oxford, 2007); Erica Fudge, 'Renaissance Animal Things', *New Formations*, 76 (2012), 86–100.

naturalised hierarchies, offering instead the compelling 'rhetorical force of the ... quasi-surrealist lists of disparate entities—strawberries, stinkbugs, quarks, corgis, tornadoes, Tin-Tin and Captain Haddock', which, 'through their promiscuous entanglement and equanimous copresence', indicate 'the equal footing of non-human and human actors'.[26] Felski, oddly, is in fact seeking to liberate over-read poems from critical ivory towers and into a greater stream of interpretation, but for those engaged in the study of animals, material culture, or landscape, actor network theory serves more evidently to put them in the frame. The use of actor network theory to research non-elite women of the seventeenth century certainly seems counterintuitive and is unlikely to be a main line of approach; after all, early modern non-elite texts hardly suffer from being excessively interpreted. Given the sheer lack of information about non-elite women subjects, researchers are obviously unlikely to prioritise a theory that invites them to look away from the specificity of these subjects whose connections they want to trace. Nevertheless actor network theory invites us also to keep in mind the constellation of humans with information gleaned from things and places. To consider, for example, that a piece of information that we do have about Dorothy Soresbie (the Soresbie family were entwined with the Mosleys, as discussed earlier in the chapter), the enigmatic word 'Knighton', might apply to a family, a family house, or a place; if a place it might be in Staffordshire, but it might also be Kniveton, which is in Derbyshire. We are already constellating her by things and places and, in the possible event that she is travelling to Kniveton, not Staffordshire, given that even now much of its medieval fieldscape encloses the village (its church has a medieval tower and a font she must have seen) we can, indeed, begin to network her with environments and objects. In doing so, although we are hardly proceeding as invited by actor network theory, we are beginning to see more things (literally) as revealing an early modern world of a non-elite person; if it is indeed Kniveton that Soresbie writes of or means, extraordinarily, we can see contours, monuments, and church furniture that she almost certainly also saw. A step or two away from the main force of actor network theory, we find Matt Cohen writing fusion-fashion to see signification in things—extending the ways of thinking that might be familiar to us with regard to the gift and extending the range of meanings, emotions, and understanding to a whole universe of communication in things, paths, and ways. However, in the study of early modern women, for good or ill, hitherto the emphasis (and self-reflection) has largely been on the terrain of 'recovery' of names, texts, and agency. Accordingly, most take-up of network analysis has not been of actor network theory but, rather, of social network theory.

Social network analysis is amongst the formal network approaches likely to be productive in attempting to trace the connectedness of non-elite women. This takes people as nodes and looks explicitly at connections between them. While a network abstraction can look both simplified and static (expressing relations diagrammatically), such representations can bring to light issues not visible in other systems—such as the impact of previously little-considered figures. As Ruth Ahnert and Sebastian Ahnert argue,

[26] Rita Felski, 'Latour and Literary Studies', *PMLA*, 130.3 (2015), 737–42, 730.

in an essay on their project charting the network of the Tudor State Papers, these social networks can and do tell us new things. Thomas Cromwell has most edges (with a degree—that is a place where two edges meet—of 2,149) and that, contrastingly, 68.1 per cent of nodes (3,937) had only one.[27] Although we might expect Cromwell to be the most contacted figure, as Ahnert and Ahnert remind us, before the 'monumental data cleaning' of the Tudor State Papers we did not even know the total number of correspondents; looking with networks illuminates new routes. However, as they note, network analysis can disclose the writing patterns of overlooked subjects and an example in the Tudor state network is a figure such as John Snowden, the Catholic agent working for the state who sustained relationships with Cecil and a range of Catholics.[28] In this regard, as Evan Bourke puts it, the concept of 'centrality'—here used in the mathematical sense of 'the total number of edges connected to a particular node'—can 'yield surprising results' in showing the infrastructural significance of women within networks previously analysed primarily in terms of male participants.[29] While network analysis can seem to state the obvious—most specifically that people we already know are connected are, indeed, connected—as Ahnert and Ahnert's work indicates, not only the literal counting but also the measuring of centrality and betweenness illuminates things that are not seen in informal analysis. Network theory is clearly productive for looking again at early modern data landscapes—and seeing them afresh.

Working on bringing into view women active within the mid-seventeenth-century network of Samuel Hartlib, Evan Bourke discusses methods that allow correction of the statistical bias inherent in networks where texts by some members have survived whereas others have disappeared. Bourke argues that this can be done by carefully reading and correcting results; by designing the project to incorporate 'mentions' as well as texts, and thereby enabling some suggestion 'of the world beyond the archive' and, finally, by using 'algorithms that reject quantity as a marker of significance and instead highlight infrastructural significance'.[30] Put more simply, as Catherine Medici reminds us, we are likely to come up with different results according to whether we are measuring textual evidence (such as letters as edges joining nodes) or social measurements (whether or not two nodes knew each other). A network model will allow 'triadic closure' in which if we know two people know each other we can assume they must know a third, and, as Ahnert and Ahnert note in predicting involvement in espionage, it is possible to extrapolate subnetworks from repeated patterns of connection.[31]

[27] Ruth Ahnert and Sebastian E. Ahnert, 'Metadata, Surveillance and the Tudor State', *History Workshop Journal*, 87 (2019), 27–51, 27–8.

[28] Ahnert and Ahnert, 38–42.

[29] Evan Bourke, 'Female Involvement, Membership, and Centrality: A Social Network Analysis of the Hartlib Circle', *Literature Compass*, 14.4 (2017), 1–17, 2, 3.

[30] Bourke, 'Female Involvement', 3.

[31] Catherine Medici, 'Using Network Analysis to Understand Early Modern Women', *Early Modern Women*, 13.1 (2018), 153–62. See this volume, Chapter 37, Nadine Akkerman, 'Women's Letters and Cryptological Coteries'.

Social network theory seems like a method that might yield excellent results in networks where women are already named and known but where we do not have extant letters from one to another. It might, for example, enable comparisons of various kinds amongst the roles and centrality of women in distinct nonconformist networks so that the place of women in networks of, say, Quakers, Baptists, and Presbyterians could be compared. Thus, it seems likely that the women who can be captured will have been in some ways acknowledged as central to the social and other form actions of a group. Those, who, like servants, were outside any sense that they were significant are, of course, not likely to be significant in a network in any case and formalisation is unlikely to do a great deal to make them more visible.

NON-ELITE WOMEN AND THE NETWORK: WHAT NEXT?

Thinking about non-elite subjects, particularly non-elite women, in relation to the network has produced several directions that can be pursued—and shown up some obvious problems to be solved next. We can draw practical and conceptual conclusions. In practical terms, if we as researchers want to know more about these women they are going to have to become more traceable. One step any scholar can take is to begin noting the names of non-elite participants in essays and footnotes; these subjects are unlikely to be all of our objects of study, but we can note their names. Record offices and archives are often willing to adapt entries in catalogues; we can ask them to do this to insert names or indicate the contents of boxes. Many small steps can help us to avoid reproducing the status-and-gender-politics of the early modern household, workplace, and religious framework where, as we know, not everyone 'counts' or is counted. These steps and others can work well in informal ways. However, as the discussion of network theory suggests, a crucial step is to generate a data set large enough to be legitimately analysed in the terms offered by mathematically based network analysis. Maybe this in turn offers a question to network theory: how can we trace networks where there will have been connections but there won't have been significant figures to group them around, as in the *Oxford Dictionary of National Biography* or the Hartlib Papers? How can we glean, as well as clean, and make uniform such data so that, eventually, we can ask it questions that it can answer in its own ways—in the language of degree, betweennness, and edge? Ultimately, while network analysis might enable us to map the reach of connection of non-elite women, the most immediate challenge, then, is identifying and generating data that might be analysed.

To return to the question we began with, overall, what do we learn if we put together non-elite women and the idea of the network? First, thinking about these two together invites us to sharpen which understanding of each category we might want to use for a given project. We need to ask whether we are in search of women in a network or a network of women's writing? Do we want to think informally about women and network or are we hoping to locate women using a theorised network? And to put the two in the same frame invites us to look again at largely undisturbed parts of the research field. Thus we have to begin to ask how we can identify non-elite women, how we can track them, and whether we can be in a position to have enough data on them to productively use theorised network methods. It is clear that this can be done but, for example, the National Archive is a huge database of uneven data; there are no doubt many non-elite women in it, but if cleaning the State Papers was a huge job then it is evidently the case that we need to start somewhere else and begin, at least, to more fully document such women. Most significantly, putting together the idea of the network and non-elite women invites us to expand the ways we think about them both and to see them not as isolated fragments but as communicative, often attached both horizontally and to those above themselves, often literate—though potentially not very literate—and leaving traces of existences that, in time and given effort, can be better attached to, and therefore in simple ways reframe more adequately, our wider understanding of literacy, literature, and status.

FURTHER READING

Ahnert, Ruth and Sebastian E. Ahnert. 'Metadata, Surveillance and the Tudor State', *History Workshop Journal*, 87 (2019), 25–51.

Barabási, Albert-László. *Network Science*. Cambridge, 2016.

Bourke, Evan. 'Female Involvement, Membership, and Centrality: A Social Network Analysis of the Hartlib Circle', *Literature Compass*, 14.4 (2017), 1–17.

Fudge, Erica. 'Renaissance Animal Things', *New Formations*, 76 (2012), 86–100.

Levine, Caroline. 'From Nation to Network', *Victorian Studies*, 55.4 (2013), 647–66.

Medici, Catherine. 'Using Network Analysis to Understand Early Modern Women', *Early Modern Women*, 13.1 (2018), 153–62.

CHAPTER 39

'ON THE PICTURE OF Y^E PRISONER'

Lucy Hutchinson and the Image of the Imprisoned King

HERO CHALMERS

Our understanding of the interface between early modern women's writing and various literary communities or networks most frequently leads us to locate the work of individual female authors within wider groupings—those with whom they share religious, political, or familial connections. Indeed, marriage and family ties lie at the heart of Lucy Hutchinson's manuscript elegies, catalysed by the imprisonment and death of her husband, the Parliamentarian colonel, John Hutchinson. The poems dwell on the final episode in a life which she unfolds in her manuscript memoir of Colonel Hutchinson. This details his role in the events of the Civil War, his part in signing the death warrant of Charles I, his imprisonment after the Restoration on charges of conspiring to rebel against Charles II, and his eventual death in prison in 1664.[1] This chapter contends that Hutchinson's engagements with marriage, family, and dynasty mobilise literary resources associated with royalist cultural networks which might, at first glance, appear inimical to her religious and political values. As Sarah C. E. Ross has shown, linking notions of dynasty with marriage and family proves more vexed for Hutchinson than for royalist women writers. While the royalist poets Jane Cavendish and Hester Pulter 'fuse the absent familial patriarch'—be he father or husband—with the king, as head of the Stuart dynasty, Hutchinson eschews the Filmerian patriarchalism which would allow her to draw an easy equivalence between her spouse and the monarch.[2] Instead, suggests Ross, Hutchinson 'establishes John as a political and a personally noble subject

[1] See Lucy Hutchinson, 'The Life of John Hutchinson', in James Sutherland (ed.), *Memoirs of the Life of Colonel Hutchinson* (London, 1973).

[2] Sarah C. E. Ross, *Women, Poetry, and Politics in Seventeenth-Century Britain* (Oxford, 2015), 180.

in a repeated reversal of royalist language'.[3] Similarly, David Norbrook observes that in the elegies, 'images of kingship are consistently directed away from the secular world into the saint's austere self-control'.[4] This chapter seeks to build on such observations by suggesting that in order fully to appreciate Hutchinson's engagements with royalist language, we need to understand more precisely how she is responding to the circulation of images associated with royalist representations of the imprisonment and death of Charles I. In particular, it draws attention to the way in which Hutchinson's elegies reconfigure the language and iconography of *Eikon Basilike*, the hugely successful royalist apologia for Charles I, written as if in the king's own voice and printed immediately after his execution in January 1649.

RESPONDING TO THE KING'S IMAGE

The overwhelming likelihood that Hutchinson had read *Eikon Basilike* (whose title means the 'portrait' or 'image' of the king) is confirmed by its enormous popularity in the months and years that followed its initial printing. As Andrew Lacey observes: 'with thirty-nine English editions in 1649 alone', it 'was the most successful book of the century'.[5] Two of the editions of 1649 were even printed by 'publishers normally associated with parliamentary literature'.[6] The degree to which the king's opponents recognised *Eikon Basilike* as 'a real political threat to the supporters of the newly established Commonwealth' is evident not only in Parliament's commissioning John Milton to write a counter-attack which appeared in October 1649 as *Eikonoklastes* ('the icon-breaker'), but in 'the large number of other writers who took up the arms of pen and pamphlet to counter... [its] persuasive influence'.[7] The early years of the Restoration (which immediately preceded the composition of Hutchinson's elegies) witnessed both the suppression of Milton's *Eikonoklastes* by royal proclamation and a lavish new edition of *Eikon Basilike*, reprinted as part of Charles I's works.[8] In reading Hutchinson as responding, along with fellow Puritans, to *Eikon Basilike*, it is important to acknowledge that the resonances

[3] Ross, *Women, Poetry, and Politics*, 179.

[4] David Norbrook, 'Lucy Hutchinson's "Elegies" and the Situation of the Republican Woman Writer (With Text)', *English Literary Renaissance*, 27 (1997), 468–521, 474. All references will be taken from this edition. See also Susan Wiseman, *Conspiracy and Virtue: Women, Writing, and Politics in Seventeenth-Century England* (Oxford, 2006), 223.

[5] Andrew Lacey, *The Cult of King Charles the Martyr* (Woodbridge, 2003), 81.

[6] Lois Potter, *Secret Rites and Secret Writing: Royalist Literature 1641–1660* (Cambridge, 1989), 7.

[7] David Ainsworth, *Milton and the Spiritual Reader* (New York, 2008), 35; John Milton, *Eikonoklastes*, in Merritt Y. Hughes (ed.), *The Complete Prose Works of John Milton, Volume III: 1648–1649* (New Haven, CT, 1962), 147.

[8] See *A Proclamation, for Calling in and Suppressing of Two Books Written by John Milton* (London, 1660); Robert Wilcher '*Eikon Basilike*: The Printing, Composition, Strategy, and Impact of "The King's Book"', in Laura Lunger Knoppers (ed.), *The Oxford Handbook of Literature and The English Revolution* (Oxford, 2012), 289–308, 291.

between her writings and the King's Book also depend on a number of shared biblical allusions, including the prominent portrayal of the king and John Hutchinson as Christ-like figures.[9] This chapter proposes that the sustained web of intertextual connections between her elegies and *Eikon Basilike* indicates that Hutchinson is responding directly to the latter as well as reworking common scriptural references.

Hutchinson's encounter with contemporary images of kingship in the elegies is far more fluid and allusive than that of printed polemics such as *Eikonoklastes*. Writing in manuscript, she would have been more able to control the circulation of her poems.[10] Indeed, we have no evidence that anyone else read them.[11] However, Hutchinson must have credited any imagined or intended readership with the mental flexibility to countenance an approach that, rather than obliterating the monarch's image, acknowledged its enduring capacity to evoke pathos. For, in setting up the narrative of John Hutchinson's imprisonment and death as a superior antitype to that of the king, Hutchinson also entertains the affective resonance of the discourses of royalist martyrology. As Lana Cable remarks, in discussing Milton's *Eikonoklastes*, 'to create a new icon is to lay claim to affective responses hitherto elicited by a different icon'.[12] This chapter will suggest that Hutchinson's elegies respond to the king's image both as shameful and as capable of eliciting pity and that they use it to frame representations not only of her dead husband but also of her own widowed grief. Such a reading is consistent with the substantial body of evidence that complicates too fixed or binary a sense of Lucy and John Hutchinson's political allegiances.[13] Norbrook asserts that in the 1650s, she became 'skillful in adopting a literary idiom that could appeal to royalists and republicans alike ... She had become well versed in the humanist skill of arguing *in utramque partem*, being able to present both sides of an argument with equal eloquence'.[14] Much as *Eikon Basilike* has been

[9] For discussions of the portrayal of Charles I and John Hutchinson as Christ-like, see, for example, Lana Cable, 'Milton's Iconoclastic Truth', in David Loewenstein and James Grantham Turner (eds), *Politics, Poetics and Hermeneutics in Milton's Prose* (Cambridge, 1990), 135–51,144; Pamela Hammons, *Gender, Sexuality, and Material Objects in English Renaissance Verse* (Farnham, 2010), 168; Erica Longfellow, *Women and Religious Writing in Early Modern England* (Cambridge, 2004), 196; Laura Blair McKnight, 'Crucifixion or Apocalypse: Reconfiguring the *Eikon Basilike*', in Donna B. Hamilton and Richard Strier (eds), *Religion, Literature and Politics in Post-Reformation England, 1540–1688* (Cambridge, 2009), 138–60, 138–9; Erin Murphy, *Familial Forms: Politics and Genealogy in Seventeenth-Century English Literature* (Newark, NJ, 2011), 166.

[10] Norbrook, 'Lucy Hutchinson's "Elegies"', 484.

[11] Norbrook, 'Lucy Hutchinson's "Elegies"', 483.

[12] Cable, 'Milton's Iconoclastic Truth', 136.

[13] For discussions of the complexity of the Hutchinsons' political loyalties, see Jerome De Groot, 'John Denham and Lucy Hutchinson's Commonplace Book', *SEL Studies in English Literature*, 48 (2008), 147–63; Norbrook, 'Lucy Hutchinson's "Elegies"', 469; David Norbrook, 'Lucy Hutchinson versus Edmund Waller: An Unpublished Reply to Waller's "A Panegyrick to my Lord Protector"', *The Seventeenth Century*, 11 (1996), 61–86; David Norbrook, 'Memoirs and Oblivion: Lucy Hutchinson and the Restoration', *Huntington Library Quarterly*, 75 (2012), 233–82; David Norbrook, '"Words More Than Civil": Republican Civility in Lucy Hutchinson's "The Life of John Hutchinson"', in Jennifer Richards (ed.), *Early Modern Civil Discourses* (Houndmills, 2003), 68–84, 71–4.

[14] Norbrook, 'Memoirs and Oblivion', 260.

read as crafted to appeal to a spectrum of political opinion, then, Lucy Hutchinson's appropriations of the king's image in responding to her husband's imprisonment and death may be read as available to readers whose political sympathies eschew straightforward binarism.[15]

A closer examination of her elegies indicates their appreciation of the power of visual representations of the suffering monarch, co-opting them as a means of evoking the political and spiritual superiority of John Hutchinson while borrowing their affective resonance to elicit pathos for his plight. A chief point of reference for the elegies is William Marshall's famous frontispiece to the *Eikon Basilike* (see Figure 39.1), with its accompanying poem, entitled 'The Explanation of the EMBLEME'.[16]

As Lacey intimates, 'this engraving, more than anything else, established the image of Charles as a Christian saint and martyr among a large section of the community'.[17] Hutchinson's repeated appeal to her readers' visual sense attests to her understanding of the cultural currency of the image of the imprisoned 'Prince' (as she refers to John) promoted in *Eikon Basilike* (4.2). With the repeated injunction to 'See him in Prison' (4.23, 6.3), Hutchinson's elegies invite readers to imagine her husband as if they are turning their gaze on an alternative spectacle of noble virtue incarcerated.

Where the subtitle of the *Eikon Basilike* offers readers *The Portraicture of His Sacred Majesty in His Solitudes and Sufferings*, Hutchinson's Elegies 4–6 foreground the iconographic dimension by presenting 'two pictures one a Gallant man drest vp in Armour The other y:^{e} Same Honorable P^{r}son looking Through a Prison Greate & leaneing on a Bible' (494). The description of the second picture here evokes comparison with Marshall's frontispiece in which Charles is also pictured with a Bible, looking towards a window. Hutchinson's representations of her own imprisoned prince tend to borrow significant components of the iconography of *Eikon Basilike* but place them in more emphatically prison-like settings, thereby enhancing the stoic, Puritan, moral authority of John Hutchinson. Whereas the frontispiece of the King's Book situates him kneeling at an altar in what appears to be a chapel, Hutchinson's 'On the Picture of ye Prisoner' depicts her husband 'Thurst [thrust] in a vile and mallancholy roome' (6.6). Yet, we are told, 'Close prisons meant his Innocence to Conceale / The glories of his Suffering grace reveale' (6.13–14). The very meanness of John Hutchinson's straitened environment acts as a foil to his spiritual virtue, figured elsewhere in the poem as a benevolent royal influence: 'But reigning Their Kings presence m:^{ks} ye Court' (6.7).

[15] For a discussion of the use of mixed genres in *Eikon Basilike* to appeal to a diversity of religious opinion, see Elizabeth P. Skerpan, 'Rhetorical Genres and the *Eikon Basilike*', *Explorations in Renaissance Culture*, 11 (1985), 99–111.

[16] For William Dugard's addition of the explanatory verses to the frontispiece, see Wilcher, '*Eikon Basilike*', 291.

[17] Lacey, *The Cult of King Charles*, 78. Kevin Sharpe, *Reading Authority and Representing Rule in Early Modern England* (London, 2013), 161, indicates that the Marshall's engraving was also widely disseminated in the form of 'woodcuts, badges and mementoes'.

FIGURE 39.1 *Eikon Basilike* (1649). Bodleian shelfmark, Vet. A3 e. 316. Frontispiece. This image is reproduced by kind permission of the Bodleian Library, The University of Oxford.

If Hutchinson's attention to the material details of her husband's imprisonment attempts to offer a more authentic image of faithful Christian suffering, her elegies also co-opt the regal imagery of *Eikon Basilike* to stress that he has exceeded Charles in rising above the lure of worldly kingdoms. In particular, she draws on the way in which the frontispiece emphasises the contrast between the eternal crown of glory (towards which

Charles raises his eyes), the earthly crown (which lies rejected at his feet), and the crown of thorns which he grasps in his hand, accepting his Christ-like destiny to suffer as a martyr.[18] Such symbolism in the engraving echoes the king's speech from the scaffold in which he announces, '*I go from a corruptible, to an incorruptible Crown*'.[19]

Hutchinson would have been familiar with the provenance of these words in 1 Corinthians 9.25. Indeed, the contrast between heavenly and earthly crowns recurs throughout the Bible, including the Book of Revelation in which its association with the notion of suffering in prison speaks eloquently to Hutchinson's framing of her husband's tribulations: 'behold, the devil shall cast *some* of you into prison, that ye may be tried ... be thou faithful unto death, and I will give thee a crown of life' (Revelation 2.10).[20] Yet, Hutchinson's elegies pointedly use the motif of crowns to pit her husband's spiritual 'Empire' against the earthly monarchy of Charles himself in a manner which seizes the iconography of crowns in the King's Book for its own purposes. The fourth elegy, 'Vpon two pictures', opens in a manner which makes such a contrast eminently clear:

The table you here See presents
A true-borne Princes Lyneaments
No Vulgar hands Sett on his Crowne
Nor could They cast his Empire downe
Whose Soule [Stoopt] not to servile Things
But triumpht ouer foyld Kings. (4.1–6)[21]

The next elegy links the rejection of an earthly crown to her husband's refusal of armed conflict after the king's execution. As the Latin motto, 'mundi calco' ('I tread on the world'), beneath Charles' right foot and next to the discarded earthly crown in the *Eikon Basilike* frontispiece marks the monarch's renunciation of worldly power, so John Hutchinson renounces military might and secular status: 'Brauely he Armd more brauely he lay armes downe / Thinking it more to win y^{n} to weare a Crowne' (5.59–60). These lines pick up on images of relinquishing the earthly crown, established in the first elegy of the sequence in which her husband's adherence to 'Love devine' (1.12) is said to have 'Maide Carnall reason freely to lay downe / At y:^{e} lords feete her Scepture & her Crowne' (21–2). Where the frontispiece figures the abasement of the symbol of secular power beneath the king's feet, Hutchinson here places it at the feet of the celestial ruler. Later in the same poem, her speaker champions the manner in which her husband's 'Constant loue' (1.50) 'put on honours Crowne upon disgrace' (62). Several of the

[18] For an analysis of the symbolism of the frontispiece, see Wilcher, '*Eikon Basilike*', 298.

[19] *King Charles His Trial at the High Court of Justice*, 2nd ed. (1650), quoted in Jim Daems and Holly Faith Nelson (eds), *Eikon Basilike with Selections from Eikonoklastes* (Peterborough, ON, 2006), 323. All references to *Eikon Basilike* will be taken from this edition.

[20] For other pertinent biblical references, see 2 Timothy 4.8 and 1 Peter 5.4.

[21] For a reading of this poem as contesting the imagery of Stuart Restoration, see Wiseman, *Conspiracy and Virtue*, 223.

putative epitaphs which follow the elegies return to ideas of John Hutchinson receiving a celestial crown after his death or crowning the allies who outlive him.[22]

Hutchinson's claim that her husband dies in 'Spite of his foes Crownd in his funerall' (6.56) not only extends her figuration of his demise as a spiritual coronation to outdo Charles' own, but leads her to identify him with the biblical figure of Samson with whom the king is linked in *Eikon Basilike*. John Hutchinson is figured as one who 'like great Sampson dying Threw downe more / Then he had vanquisht all his life before' (6.67–8), recalling how Samson's own death coincides with his triumphant demolition of the supposedly sacrilegious Philistine Temple of Dagon. The 'iconoclasm' against the realm of worldly images with which Norbrook connects Hutchinson's allusion to Samson here can also be seen to encompass an iconoclastic impulse towards the specific presentation of the king's image in the King's Book.[23] Although Murphy reads the reference to Samson as seeking to unite his identities as 'valiant soldier' and 'suffering prisoner', Hutchinson stresses his decisive final triumph whereas the allusions in *Eikon Basilike* evoke, at best, a spirit of patient endurance through suffering and, at worst, humiliation by one's enemies.[24] In the final chapter, entitled '*Meditations upon Death, after* ... HIS MAJESTY'S *closer Imprisonment in* Carisbrooke-Castle', Charles muses:

> The assaults of affliction may be terrible, like *Samson's* Lion, but they yield much sweetness to those, that dare to encounter and overcome them; who know how to overlive the witherings of their Gourds without discontent or peevishness. (196–7)

Here, unexpected bounty is conferred when Samson discovers honey in a beehive that occupies the carcass of a lion he slew, but the king's earlier comparison between himself and the biblical hero dwells more on the latter's abjection.[25] Charles considers the diminution of sovereignty represented by the Nineteen Propositions sent to him by Parliament in June 1642:

> as if *Sampson* should have consented, not only to bind his own hands, and cut off his hair, but to put out his own eyes, that the *Philistines* might with the more safety mock, and abuse him; which they chose rather to do, than quite to destroy him, when he was become so tame an object and fit occasion for their sport and scorn. (94–5)

Hutchinson may have been encouraged by Milton's *Eikonoklastes* to figure her husband as a triumphant Samson in contrast to Charles' defeated and resigned images of the biblical hero. As Elizabeth Scott-Baumann points out, Hutchinson shared Milton's puritan and republican convictions and appears to have been aware of his writings. Her own

22 See 15.20, 18.12, 18A.14, 21.12.

23 Norbrook, 'Lucy Hutchinson's "Elegies"', 475.

24 Erin Murphy, '"I remain, an airy phantasme": Lucy Hutchinson's Civil War Ghost Writing', *English Literary History*, 82 (2015), 87–113, 97–8.

25 The specific biblical allusion is to Judges 15.5–8.

Genesis paraphrase, *Order and Disorder*, is likely to have been written with *Paradise Lost* in mind. Although the latter was not printed until 1667, three years after the death of John Hutchinson occasioned Lucy Hutchinson's elegies, Milton and Hutchinson may have seen the manuscripts of each other's biblical epics before they were printed.[26] If Hutchinson read *Eikonoklastes*, she would have found Milton portraying the weakness of a monarch's pronouncements unsupported by the law, in terms of Samson's loss of his God-given strength as a Nazarite once his locks are shorn: '*The words of a King*, as they are *full of power*, in the autority and strength of Law, so like *Sampson*, without the strength of that *Nazarites* lock, they have no more power in them then the words of another Man' (545–6).

As Milton undermines the idea of sacred authority behind the monarch's words, so Hutchinson enhances her husband's spiritual authority by presenting him as interacting more profoundly with the scriptural word than the king does. Where the Charles of *Eikon Basilike* kneels in front of an altar or table bearing a Bible open at the words, 'In verbo tuo spes mea' ('My hope is in your word'), the elegies picture John Hutchinson not only as 'leaninge' on the Bible as his mainstay but as actively finding spiritual inspiration within it: 'Opening y:ᵗ booke when They had shut their Locks / Hee Their found liuing streames & diamond rocks' (6.19–20).[27] The contention that reading the Scriptures 'Brings to his viue old Prophetts martird sants' (6.26) sounds a warning against *Eikon Basilike*'s attempt to establish Charles as a thoroughly unscriptural martyr, whereas the speaker in Hutchinson's tenth elegy is granted a vision of 'The deare objet of my loue / Wearing yᵉ Martirs Crowne [enthroned] above' (10.23–4).[28] While Norbrook's transcription plausibly substitutes the more familiar verb '[enthroned]' for 'enthornd' from the original scribal manuscript of the elegies, his editorial emendation perhaps elides a further instance of Hutchinson's redeployment of images associated with the *Eikon Basilike*. It may be that the poem seeks to underline John Hutchinson's spiritual superiority over the king by imagining him triumphantly wearing the crown of thorns which Charles merely holds in his hand in the frontispiece of the King's Book.[29]

The manner in which Hutchinson depicts the inspiration received by her husband in studying the Scriptures makes reference to another notable facet of the iconography of the King's Book. John Hutchinson's reading the Bible, we are told, 'in his darkest sollitude shot rayes / That shamd yᵉ splendor of yᵉ brightest days' (6.21–2). While the foregrounding of 'sollitude' here recalls the subtitle of *Eikon Basilike*, the image of the

[26] Elizabeth Scott-Baumann, *Forms of Engagement: Women, Poetry, and Culture 1640–1680* (Oxford, 2013), 175. See also David Norbrook (ed.), *Order and Disorder* (Oxford, 2001), xvii.

[27] For Hutchinson's emphasis on her husband's Bible reading in prison, see also 'Life of John Hutchinson', 264, 270.

[28] For John Hutchinson as martyr, see also one of the proposed epitaphs, 16.20.

[29] For a discussion of the characteristics of the manuscript which contains Hutchinson's elegies and of Norbrook's principles in transcribing it, see 'Lucy Hutchinson's "Elegies"', 485.

shooting rays picks up on one of the most striking features of its frontispiece in which beams of light connect the king's head with the heavens as if the illumination emanates not only from the heavens but from Charles himself.[30] In contrast, Lucy Hutchinson's depiction of the shooting rays which attend Colonel Hutchinson in his final imprisonment indicate that they have their source in the Bible alone. However, the earlier elegy 'Vpon two pictures' also appears to reappropriate Charles' radiance in depicting prison as the place in which John Hutchinson's 'Courage Then most brightly shone', a riposte to the claim, in *Eikon Basilike*'s 'The Explanation of the EMBLEME', that Charles 'shine[s] more bright / In sad Affliction's Darksom night' (4.25). The depiction of Colonel Hutchinson in the ninth elegy draws more directly on the iconography of the frontispiece claiming that he:

> ... like days King brooke Through ye Clowd
> That did his rising glorie shrowd
> Quick rays shott from his Eies whose light
> Mad the whole spheare They moued in Bright. (9.45–8)

The figuration of the Puritan martyr as 'days King' stands as a response to earlier elegies in the sequence in which—as others have noted—hostile responses to the sun encode anti-royalist sentiments given the sun's status as an established symbol of monarchy.[31] Similarly, the contention that 'Quick rays shott from [John Hutchinson's] Eies' counters the earlier contemptuous portrayal, in Elegy 3, of a sun who, as 'gay courtier' (3.35) and 'Gawdy Masker' (11), 'This morning Through my window shot his rayes / Where with his hatefull & unwellcome beames / He guilt ye Surface of aflictions Streames' (2–4). The blending of courtly, royalist associations here with an allusion to the rays of illumination in Marshall's engraving of the embattled king also underpins the poem's embittered complaint to the sun that 'Thy staind beames into the Prison came' (3.31). However, the colonel's radiance once more outshines the king's as the 'staind beames' of the courtly sun 'los[e] their boasts outshind with vertues flame' (3.32). As Line Cottegnies comments, 'the prison to which many martyrs of the cause were condemned ... becomes the only place where true light can be found'.[32]

[30] See 1.37 for further emphasis on John Hutchinson's 'sollitude' in prison. See also Hutchinson, 'Life of John Hutchinson', 264.

[31] For readings which note the anti-monarchist sentiments implicit in the way Hutchinson's elegies respond to the sun, see Murphy, *Familial Forms*, 157; Norbrook, 'Lucy Hutchinson's "Elegies"', 475; Scott-Baumann, *Forms of Engagement*, 127–8, 133; Lauren Shohet, 'Women's Elegy: Early Modern', in Karen Weisman (ed.), *The Oxford Handbook of Elegy* [online edn] (2012), 5 [PDF pagination], *Oxford Handbooks Online*, DOI: 10.1093/oxfordhb/9780199228133.013.0025, accessed 30 June 2020.

[32] Line Cottegnies, 'The Garden and the Tower: Pastoral Retreat and Configurations of the Self in the Auto/Biographical Works of Margaret Cavendish and Lucy Hutchinson', in Frédéric Regard (ed.), *Mapping the Self: Space, Identity, Discourse in British Auto/Biography* (Saint-Étienne, 2003), 125–44, 137.

APPROPRIATING EMBLEMS AND METAPHORS

Lucy Hutchinson's reappropriation of imagery central to *Eikon Basilike* also encompasses what Wilcher calls the 'emblematic landscape' to the left of Charles in the frontispiece (see Figure 39.1), in the upper part of which 'a rock stands firm in a turbulent sea', bearing the legend 'IMMOTA TRIUMPHANS' ('unmoved, triumphant').[33] Hutchinson's elegies, like *Eikon Basilike*, are informed by recurrent biblical allusions to God as a rock, not least in the Psalms on which both draw.[34] However, the juxtapositions of the frontispiece make clear that the imagery of immoveable rock may be identified not only with God but with the king himself, just as Hutchinson identifies it both with divine constancy and the unshakeable spiritual fortitude of John Hutchinson: 'He like a rock of Vertuious Courage stood / And brooke ye force of ye Preualing flood' (5.51–2). The pivotal vision of 'Love's Rocke' in Hutchinson's tenth elegy, 'The Recovery', associates it with redemptive spiritual transformation implicitly cast in opposition to the idolatry of earthly monarchy. The rock acts as the location where the speaker sees their lost loved one achieve the 'Martirs Crowne' (10.24). The sense that Hutchinson's divine rock and her dead husband's celestial crown mount a challenge to the Caroline hagiography disseminated by the printing of *Eikon Basilike* is implied in the poem's claims that:

Created beauties w:c^h^ blind Soules adore
Here Sease to be [men's] Idolls any more
For here Their Seene but darke declining streams
Guilt as They pas w:^th^ lights reflected beames
The celebrated works of vane mens hands
Are paper frames erected on The Sands
Which loosened & disperst wth euery wind
No memory no empression leaue behind. (10.45–52)

[33] Wilcher, '*Eikon Basilike*', 298.

[34] Hutchinson, 'Life of John Hutchinson', 270, confides that he chose '48 selected psalms which he had applied to his present condition'. David Norbrook, '"But a Copie": Textual Authority and Gender in Editions of "The Life of John Hutchinson"', in W. Speed Hill (ed.), *New Ways of Looking at Old Texts, III: Papers of the Renaissance English Text Society, 1997–2001* (Tempe, AZ, 2004), 109–30, 113, notes that the manuscript containing the 'Life' is 'followed by a long section headed "Psalmes he had markd when he first began to be pers[ecuted]"'. For a list of these Psalms, see N. H. Keeble (ed.), *Memoirs of the Life of Colonel Hutchinson* (London, 1995), 275. Each section of *Eikon Basilike* concludes with prayers which draw heavily on the Psalms. Of the Psalms which Hutchinson lists as having been 'markd' by her husband and which are also alluded to in *Eikon Basilike*, numbers 18.2 and 71.3 figure God as a rock. See *Eikon Basilike*, 174, 203, for allusions to these two Psalms, albeit not to their specific image of God as a rock. Charles refers to 2 Samuel 23.3 in asserting, 'Though the Reeds of *Egypt* break under the hand of him that leans on them: yet the Rock of Israel will be an everlasting stay and defence', 166. Cottegnies, 'The Garden and the Tower', 140, notes that Psalm 18.2 also contains the image of the 'high tower' which she identifies as a key motif in Hutchinson's writings.

The 'paper frames' of the King's Book are scattered, the refulgent rays of the frontispiece become mere 'reflected beames' and the monarchical idol ceases to dominate the 'memory' of his subjects.

Beyond the specific imagery of the rock, Hutchinson's writings share with *Eikon Basilike* a related complex of metaphors around nautical peril. Charles establishes a connection between civil disobedience and 'the raging of the Sea' which he subsequently develops: 'With what unwillingness I withdrew from *Westminster*, let them judge, who, unprovided of tackling, and victual, are forced to Sea by a storm, yet better do so, than venture splitting or sinking on a Lee shore' (69).[35] The fact that the king's enemies could recognise the emotional persuasiveness of such metaphorical language is, as Cable suggests, apparent in the fact that Milton's *Eikonoklastes* specifically attacks Charles' use of this nautical 'Simily' as being too 'Poetical ... for a Statist' (406), yet resorts to the same kind of metaphor only two paragraphs later. Yet, *pace* Cable, Milton does not use it 'in much the same way'.[36] Whereas, for Charles, the image of the embattled mariner lends the gloss of heroic romance to his personal choice to withdraw from the fray, Milton repurposes the metaphor in a manner which reminds the reader that the king should be steering the ship of state for the benefit of his citizens. Yet, bemoans Milton, 'he left the City; and in a most tempestuous season forsook the Helme, and steerage of the Common-wealth' (408). Hutchinson's memoir of her husband follows suit in appropriating the nautical imagery used by *Eikon Basilike* to dramatise the fate of the royal martyr in a manner which promotes the puritan saint, John Hutchinson, as the true pilot of a godly commonwealth. The 'Life', like Hutchinson's autobiographical fragment, describes various historical vicissitudes as 'an approaching storme' (174) or 'horrid tempest', and intimates her husband's post-Restoration regret 'that ever he forsooke his owne blessed quiett to embarque in such a troubled sea, where he had made a shipwrack of all things but a good conscience' (228).[37] Her subsequent narrative of one of his dreams reinstates him as the trusted helmsman of the Good Old Cause. Colonel Hutchinson dreams that he is in a boat on the Thames which has run aground, beset by 'wind and tide' (242). Only by taking over from the crew, lying down in the boat, 'and applying his brest to the head of it' can he bring it safely to shore 'on Southworke side' which appears as a paradisal landscape in which his father bestows laurel leaves upon him (242). Puzzling over the meaning of the dream, his wife interprets 'the boate' as:

> representing the commonwealth, which several unquiet people sought to enfranchise by vaine endeavours ... his lying downe and shooving it with his breast might signifie the advancement of the Cause by the patient suffering of the Martyrs, among which his owne was to be eminent. (242)[38]

[35] *Eikon Basilike*, 69; see also 60, 63.

[36] Cable, 'Milton's Iconoclastic Truth', 140.

[37] Hutchinson, 'The Life of Mrs. Lucy Hutchinson', in Sutherland (ed.), *Memoirs of the Life of Colonel Hutchinson*, 279.

[38] Norbrook, 'Memoirs and Oblivion', 271, notes the use of 'nautical imagery' in a petition submitted to Parliament on John Hutchinson's behalf in August 1660.

We cannot determine for certain whether Hutchinson wrote this passage with *Eikon Basilike* directly in mind. However, the vision of the would-be martyr Colonel Hutchinson taking charge of the wind-swept bark undoubtedly presents a resonant counterpoint to the presentation of a saintly Charles as pilot of a storm-tossed ship.

The suggestion that such royalist figurations influenced Puritan writing in the period is borne out not only in the work of Hutchinson and Milton but also in Marvell's 'The Unfortunate Lover', composed around the time of Charles I's death.[39] Wilcher reads this poem's depiction of a lover shipwrecked on a rock as responding to the *Eikon Basilike* frontispiece while Peter Davidson also connects it to the circulation of 'royalist propaganda' images associating the fate of the Stuart princes after their father's execution with a perilous sea voyage.[40] Similarly, Nicholas McDowell argues that 'The Unfortunate Lover' responds to Thomas Stanley's versification of *Eikon Basilike*.[41] While Smith and McDowell warn against reading Marvell's characteristically elliptical poem as a crypto-royalist text, they acknowledge that it taps into a topical mood of royalist lament.[42] As Restoration texts, Hutchinson's elegies and her 'Life of John Hutchinson' coincide with a very different mood for royalists. Yet, her elegiac verse also suggests a recognition that tropes previously used to generate pathos in depicting the fate of Charles I (including that of the storm-tossed ship) could remain potent not only as a means of framing the counter-narrative of Puritan martyr John Hutchinson, but also in figuring her own bereavement.

REPRESENTING GRIEF

In order to understand these contrasting deployments of imagery associated with the defeated king, it is essential to recognise that the elegies combine the celebration of John Hutchinson with an emphasis on personal grief, a grief which, as others have noted, they manifestly struggle to tame within the bounds of Puritan spiritual consolation.[43] In presenting inconsolable feminine sorrow by means of images associated with the deposed monarch, Hutchinson both amplifies its tragic resonances and underscores its shameful, illicit transgression of puritan proprieties. Whereas the fourth elegy proudly claims of John Hutchinson that 'No Vulgar hand Sett on his Crowne / Nor could They

[39] For the date of composition, see Nigel Smith (ed.), *The Poems of Andrew Marvell* (Harlow, 2003), 86.

[40] Robert Wilcher, *The Writing of Royalism 1628–1660* (Cambridge, 2001), 306–7; Peter Davidson (ed.), *Poetry and Revolution: An Anthology of British and Irish Verse, 1625–1660* (Oxford, 1998), lxx–lxxi.

[41] Nicholas McDowell, *Poetry and Allegiance in the English Civil Wars: Marvell and the Cause of Wit* (Oxford, 2008), 218–19.

[42] Smith (ed.), *Poems of Andrew Marvell*, 88; McDowell, *Poetry and Allegiance*, 221, 222.

[43] See Kate Chedgzoy, *Women's Writing in the British Atlantic World: Memory, Place and History, 1550–1700* (Cambridge, 2007), 161–2; Scott-Baumann, *Forms of Engagement*, 140, 164–7; Susan Wiseman 'No "Publick Funerall"? Lucy Hutchinson's Elegy, Epitaph, Monument', *The Seventeenth Century*, 30 (2015), 207–28, 211.

cast his Empire downe' (4.3–4), the twelfth—which is presented as Lucy Hutchinson's 'Musings in my evening Walkes at O[wthorp]' (their country estate)—laments, 'What Tho Those glories were my [Crowne] / His death hath throne my empire downe' (12.49–50). As previously discussed, the first of these couplets contrasts John Hutchinson's confident possession of a spiritual 'Empire' with King Charles' loss of an earthly one, but the echoing couplet in the later elegy aligns Lucy Hutchinson (as the grieving wife) with the king's worldly depredations, a 'fallen Queene' (12.52), wailing the desertions of those 'flatterrers' (69) who 'once did me y^r princis Call' (72). Similarly, where the celestial virtues of the lamented male lover in the ninth elegy are figured in regal terms as 'Mixing his Majesty with grace' (9.28), the female voice which mourns him confesses, 'The shades of death hath hemd me round / My late Crowne lyes in ye cold ground' (53–4). It is noteworthy, then, that the fallen Eve's complaint from Hutchinson's *Order and Disorder* (5.401–42) which also appears amongst the elegies, presented as if it were her own lament for her husband's imprisonment, similarly figures shameful feminine mourning in terms of defeated monarchy.[44] 'Haue not our subjects their allegiance broke . . .?', asks Eve, going on to recall *Eikon Basilike*'s iconographic association of Charles with Christ's crown of thorns: 'Thorns prick my eyes when shame hath cast them down' (5.415, 424).

Hutchinson represents the state of widowed grief not only as the loss of an earthly crown but also in terms of the dangerous sea voyage which recurs as a metaphor for Charles I's toils in *Eikon Basilike*.[45] The connection between these two metaphorical strands is particularly marked at the start of Elegy 10, 'The Recovery':

> My loue life Crowne peace treasure Joys were lost
> And Seeking y:^m Long was my fraile Barke tost
> On Sorrowes raging flood where stormes p^r vaild
> And ye Poore Leaking Vessell euery way assaild
> The Cordage Crackt y:^e Shrowds & maine mast tore. (10.1–5)

In Hutchinson's hands, the nautical imagery used in *Eikon Basilike* to evoke a sense of royal heroism and resourcefulness in the face of an unavoidable 'storm' of popular opposition comes to represent the chaotic turbulence of overpowering, personal grief. Only the speaker's mysterious vision of a rock, associated with love, heaven, truth, and life, can provide respite.[46] Hutchinson's poem, like Marvell's 'The Unfortunate

44 See also Norbrook's discussion of Elegy 2A and its provenance in 'Lucy Hutchinson's "Elegies"', 480–2. The poem concludes with a note stating that, 'these verses were writ by Mrs Hutchinson on ye Coll: her Husbands being then a prisoner in ye Tower: 1664' (491). Danielle Clarke, 'Animating Eve: Gender, Authority, and Complaint', in Sarah C. E. Ross and Rosalind Smith (eds), *Early Modern Women's Complaint: Gender, Form, and Politics* (London, 2020), 157–81, 175, offers a salutary reminder of the need to consider Hutchinson's use of 'ethopoeia' in adopting Eve's first-person voice in *Order and Disorder* rather than allowing the duplication of this passage in the elegies to encourage us to assume that Hutchinson identifies herself wholly with Eve.

45 See also Hutchinson, 'Life of John Hutchinson', 1.

46 For other allusions to the rock in 'The Recovery', see lines 19, 63, 65.

Lover', appears to refract the nautical imagery of *Eikon Basilike*, albeit Marvell's possible allusions to the immoveable rock on the frontispiece present it in a largely antagonistic way as the site of the lover's shipwreck and, at best, a 'stubborn rock' (52) to which he clings. Although there is no firm evidence that Hutchinson read Marvell's poem in manuscript, both appear to offer responses to *Eikon Basilike* which explore the pathos of images associated with the defeated king while distancing themselves from him through realignment or distortion of those images.[47]

CONCLUSION

Whether or not Hutchinson read 'The Unfortunate Lover', placing her elegies alongside it serves as a reminder that she deserves a place in critical discussions of the circulation of royalist discourse and iconography in the middle decades of the seventeenth century. Reading her writings in tandem with *Eikon Basilike* highlights the fact that Puritan responses to the King's Book might take forms other than the systematic wrecking tactics of Milton's *Eikonoklastes*. In Hutchinson's case, the royalist hagiography of Charles I provides a template not only for the countervailing presentation of Puritan martyr and 'true-borne Prince' John Hutchinson, but also (more surprisingly) for the representation of her own unredeemed grief as his widow. Her elegies thus challenge us to recognise that, while they provide a corrective to representations of the monarch's imprisonment and death, they also borrow and repurpose the affective impact it undoubtedly possessed in the contemporary imagination.

FURTHER READING

Chedgzoy, Kate. *Women's Writing in the British Atlantic World: Memory, Place and History*. Cambridge, 2007.

Lacey, Andrew. *The Cult of King Charles the Martyr*. Woodbridge, 2003.

McDowell, Nicholas. *Poetry and Allegiance in the English Civil Wars: Marvell and the Cause of Wit*. Oxford, 2008.

Norbrook, David. 'Lucy Hutchinson's "Elegies" and the Situation of the Republican Woman Writer'. *English Literary Renaissance*, 27 (1997), 468–521.

Ross, Sarah C. E. *Women, Poetry, and Politics in Seventeenth-Century Britain*. Oxford, 2015.

47 In 1675, Hutchinson dedicated a new manuscript of her translation of Lucretius, *De Rerum Natura*, to her friend Arthur Annesley, Earl of Anglesey, who assisted Marvell in the publication of *The Rehearsal Tranpros'd* (1672, 1673); see Norbrook (ed.), *Order and Disorder*, xvii; Annabel Patterson and Martin Dzelzainis, 'Marvell and the Earl of Anglesey: A Chapter in the History of Reading', *The Historical Journal*, 44 (2001), 703–26.

Wilcher, Robert. '*Eikon Basilike*: The Printing, Composition, Strategy, and Impact of "The King's Book"'. In Laura Lunger Knoppers (ed.), *The Oxford Handbook of Literature and The English Revolution*. Oxford, 2012, 289–308.

Wiseman, Susan. 'No "Publick funerall"? Lucy Hutchinson's Elegy, Epitaph, Monument'. *The Seventeenth Century*, 30 (2015), 207–28.

CHAPTER 40

THE TOPOPOETICS OF RETIREMENT IN KATHERINE PHILIPS AND LUCY HUTCHINSON

JAMES LOXLEY

THE topos of retirement is a familiar presence in early modern poetry, appearing in genres as apparently distinct as satire, pastoral, elegy, and panegyric, and animating both secular and devotional work. In some ways, it underpins the distinctly early modern genre of estate poetry, taking its place in the formulation of a poetics of place, or a topopoetics, focused on ideas of a rural location distanced from a variously defined world of public business. Women writers participated as fully as their male counterparts in the development of this topopoetics, with Aemilia Lanyer's celebrated 'The Description of Cooke-ham' providing an instance of the mode as clearly foundational as Ben Jonson's 'To Penshurst'. But the fusion of a thematics of retirement with the poetic evocation of a particular place did not necessarily produce works of a uniform ethical or political orientation. That the retired life could be differently valorised was established by classical precedent as much as by early modern practice. This chapter explores how two key dimensions of this poetic practice could shape such valorisations: firstly, the acute shifts in fortune associated with the social and political upheavals of the mid-seventeenth century, and secondly, the gender both of the poet and the figure or persona of the retiree. How, in particular, might the topopoetics of retirement work differently for women than for men?

In the spring of 1653, Oliver Cromwell dissolved the Parliament which had been the heart of English government, *de facto* and then *de jure*, through wars and revolutions, for nearly thirteen years. Parliament's dissolution stripped many of its chief officers of their employment, and those for whom the more monarchical form of government now embodied in the Cromwellian protectorate held little appeal found themselves excluded from public business. Among them was Colonel John Hutchinson, Lucy Hutchinson's husband, and in her celebrated memoir of his life Hutchinson describes what the colonel did next. Abjuring any attempt to push back against Cromwell's coup, John Hutchinson retired to his estates in Nottinghamshire, where he busied himself 'with the surveying of his buildings and improving by enclosure the place he lived in', curating his newly acquired, ex-royal art collection, with hawking and with 'the practice of his viol'.[1] He also took charge of his children's education:

> He spared not any cost for the education of both his sons and daughters in languages, sciences, music, dancing, and all other qualities befitting their father's house. […] And as other things were his delight, this only he made his business, to attend the education of his children and the government of his own house and town which he performed so well that never was any man more feared and loved than he by all his domestics and tenants and hired workmen. (*Memoirs*, 255)

As the language of love and fear indicates, John Hutchinson is here being described as a sovereign—the authority over 'his own house and town'. Lucy Hutchinson's account casts him as the exemplary patriarch, the paradigmatic figure of social authority (see this volume, Chapter 39, Hero Chalmers, 'Lucy Hutchinson and the Image of the Imprisoned King').

Hutchinson's next paragraph, however, carefully stresses the nature and limits of the colonel's power:

> As for the public business of the country, he would not act in any office under the Protector's power, and therefore only confined himself to his own, which the whole country about him were very much grieved at, and would rather come to him for counsel as a private neighbour than to any of the men in power for greater help. And he now being reduced into an absolute private condition was very much courted and visited by all of all parties. (*Memoirs*, 255–6)

To speak of John Hutchinson as 'confined' or 'reduced' suggests that he is now less than he was, that the 'private condition' that Hutchinson here limits him to is more privation than privacy, an exclusion—voluntary or otherwise—from the 'public business' in which he would be—indeed, had been—fully himself. But as we have seen, her portrayal of his retirement contrastingly figures him as most powerfully himself in his patriarchal role at the apex of 'his own house and town', the woman writer here painting a portrait of the ideal father-ruler. The stress on what is John's 'own'—his family, his estate, his tenants—accentuates both his possessions and his self-possession. The 'absolute private condition' in which he subsists speaks not just of privation but, contrastingly, of the absoluteness of an authority which cannot be challenged or compromised.

[1] Lucy Hutchinson, in N. H. Keeble (ed.), *Memoirs of the Life of Colonel Hutchinson* (London, 1995), 255.

In this one vignette we can see many of the key dynamics of the writing of retirement and retreat in the central decades of the seventeenth century. Drawing on the precedent offered principally by the Roman poet Horace, poets evoking the retired life often worked through a topopoetic contrast between the country and the city, the former standardly valorised as innocent, peaceful, and the site of contentment when set against the restlessness and corruption of the latter. The genre of estate poetry initiated by Lanyer and Jonson but taken up by later generations also set a defined rural locale against a wider world of public business, while the enduring symbolism of the garden offered a potent resource for the figuration of a private retreat from the heat and bustle of a wider social world. Which is not to say that the poetry of retreat or retirement could only praise the retired life: a contrasting topopoetics of exile from the civilisation of court and town to rural rudeness or dullness was also exemplified in the classical and contemporary inheritance.

The upheavals and disruptions of the 1640s and 1650s, though, created a much more acutely fraught context for the writing of retirement or retreat. Government at both national and local levels was overwhelmed by a military conflict which generated huge emotional and intellectual turmoil among the populace, and was then subject to successive convulsive revolutions as stability eluded the victors. In such fraught circumstances, with many tender consciences the victims of rapid reversals of fortune, some found sanctuary in a withdrawal from public business; many others found themselves suddenly ejected from public roles in which they had previously thrived. The purges of the church, of universities, and of local and national administration cast many royalists and Episcopalians into a forced retirement over the course of the 1640s; the transition to a republic in 1649 and a Protectorate in 1653 saw moderate Parliamentarians, Presbyterians, and eventually republicans such as John Hutchinson join them. An Act of February 1650 implemented a form of internal exile for 'all Papists whatsoever, and all Officers and Soldiers of Fortune, and other persons who have borne Arms against the Parliament, or have adhered unto, or willingly assisted their Enemies in the late War', requiring them to 'depart out of the said Cities of London and Westminster, and late Lines of Communication, and all other places within Twenty miles of the said late Lines'.[2] Furthermore, all those subject to the Act's provisions were also required to:

> repair to the place of dwelling where they usually heretofore made their common abode; or not having any certain abode ... repair to the place where such person was born or where the Father or Mother of such person shal then be dwelling, and give such notice of their coming as is afterwards expressed; and shall not at any time

[2] 'February 1650: An Act for removing all Papists, and all Officers and Soldiers of Fortune, and divers other Delinquents removed from London and Westminster, and confining them within five miles of their dwellings, and for encouragement of such as discover Priests and Jesuits, their Receivers and Abettors.', in C. H. Firth and R. S. Rait (eds), *Acts and Ordinances of the Interregnum, 1642–1660* (London, 1911), 349–54.

> after pass or remove above five miles from thence, upon pain of Imprisonment, and Sequestration of all their Estates Real and Personal.[3]

This statute was widely understood, as the title of a poem by Katherine Philips' friend John Berkenhead puts it, as an 'Act for Banishment'.[4]

In such fraught conditions, retirement's ethical value and significance could vary wildly. For country gentlemen deprived of their expected place in the network of governance that made up a national commonwealth, retirement could represent an opportunity to build an alternative model of sociality, predicated on affectively potent bonds and domestic values such as friendship and hospitality. Thus we see the royalist gentleman Thomas Stanley practise the art of *amicitia* with those named in his 'Register of Friends'.[5] As Lucy Hutchinson says of her husband, retirement could also represent a chance for the excluded gentleman to reconstitute his status as 'the government of his own house and town'. But it could also speak not of bonds but of dissociation, and not of authority but of dissipation and disintegration. Berkenhead pointedly described himself and his fellow forcibly retired royalists as 'slaves to slaves in five mile chains'.[6]

In the strong assertion of autonomy and autarky that characterises the more affirmative vision of retirement can be seen a fear of its opposite—the subjection to limits from the outside, to heteronomy, that presages a loss of integration and self-sustenance. This sense of retirement's dangers is continuous with a classical *topos* opposing the life of public business—*negotium*—to that of *otium*, or retired and private leisure. This ethical perspective tended to assert the virtue of the *vita activa*, life lived in the exercise of the duties or offices of a citizen, and contrast this with the moral peril of idleness and pleasure.[7] While such a perspective was associated particularly with the traditions of thought that fed into seventeenth-century republicanism, it was widely shared and mobilised even by those who might be thought to place less emphasis on the need for a politically active citizenry. When both James VI and I and his successor issued proclamations requiring the landed gentry to leave London and return to their country estates, they were not seeking to send them on holiday—they were instead requesting that they cease their leisured indulgence in the pleasures of the town and resume their

[3] 'February 1650', n.p.

[4] See Philip Major, '"Twixt Hope and Fear": John Berkenhead, Henry Lawes and Banishment from London during the English Revolution', *Review of English Studies*, 59 (2008), 270–80.

[5] For Stanley, see Thomas Stanley, *The Poems and Translations of Thomas Stanley*, ed. Galbraith Crump (Oxford, 1962), xxiii–xxxiv, 354–66; Stella Revard, 'Thomas Stanley and "A Register of Friends"', in Claude J. Summers and Ted-Larry Pebworth (eds), *Literary Circles and Cultural Communities in Renaissance England* (London, 2000), 148–72, 148–9; on Philips' coterie see Catharine Gray, *Women Writers and Public Debate in Seventeenth-Century Britain* (London, 2007), 105–42.

[6] See Major, '"Twixt Hope and Fear"', 270–3.

[7] See Brian Vickers, 'Leisure and Idleness in the Renaissance: The Ambivalence of Otium', *Renaissance Studies*, 4 (1990), 1–37, 107–54; Markku Peltonen, *Classical Humanism and Republicanism in English Political Thought, 1570–1640* (Cambridge, 1995).

roles in the governance of their localities.[8] Lucy Hutchinson's portrait of her retired husband insists that his absence from what might be thought of as the political centre has not lessened his ability to embody virtue in a continued *vita activa*.

It is worthwhile, in this connection, contrasting her account of her husband's retreat from public business with what she says of two other notable Parliamentarians. In describing the events of 1650 she evokes the shock and betrayal felt by those at the top of the republican regime at Sir Thomas Fairfax's resignation of his commission as Lord General of the army, 'persuaded', Hutchinson is careful to note, 'by his wife and her Presbyterian chaplains'. Fairfax's retirement is anything but noble—indeed, as she says, 'this great man was then as immovable by his friends as he was pertinacious in obeying his wife; whereby he then died to all his former glory, and became the monument to his own name, which every day wore out' (*Memoirs*, 240–1). For Fairfax, there is no reconstitution of his status in retirement, but only a strange kind of living death. The retirement of the key Protectoral politician John Lambert in 1657 appears in differently dishonourable colours. Estranged from Cromwell's regime and deprived of his commissions, Major-General Lambert withdrew to his country house in Wimbledon, 'where he fell to dress his flowers in his garden and work at the needle with his wife and his maids', as Hutchinson tartly puts it (*Memoirs*, 257).

Hutchinson's varying characterisations of retirement in these three cases speak very clearly both to its ethical and spiritual risks—the potential loss of honour that comes with the loss or surrender of public status—and to the ways in which it is to be met. John Hutchinson avoids the dishonour she bestows on Fairfax and Lambert in his sustenance of an active life. And for those with literary inclinations, the writing of poetry could offer just such a means. It is noticeable, for example, that those exemplary Cavalier poets, Richard Lovelace and Robert Herrick, published collections of their poetry at the end of the 1640s, when the former had been effectively excluded from his family's traditionally prominent role in Kentish society, and the latter had been ejected from his church living in Devon.[9] As the profusion of printed verse written out of retirement in the 1640s and 1650s shows, they were far from alone. More than this, writing offered resources for the rhetorical as well as practical salvation of retirement from the shame of defeat and subjection, and the ethical peril of idleness. Rhetorical figures familiar from both classical rhetoric and devotional meditations enabled Lovelace, for example, to sing of his freedom even as he wrote 'To Althea, from Prison', and allowed Andrew Marvell to interanimate the formal gardens of Sir Thomas Fairfax's country estate at Nun Appleton metaphorically with the kingdom, the world, and paradise itself in a manner which seems both to acknowledge the ethical risks run by his patron in giving up his position while refuting, or at least confounding, the deathly imputations voiced by Hutchinson.[10]

[8] See, for a characteristic example, Charles I's Proclamation of 20 June 1632, in James Larkin (ed.), *Stuart Royal Proclamations, Vol 2: Royal Proclamations of King Charles I, 1625–46* (Oxford, 1983), 292–6.

[9] Robert Herrick, *Hesperides* (London, 1648); Richard Lovelace, *Lucasta* (London, 1649).

[10] On the occasion of Marvell's poem, see Derek Hirst and Steven Zwicker, *Andrew Marvell: Orphan of the Hurricane* (Oxford, 2012), 9–40.

Rather than instantiate the experience of retreat, the writing of retirement might seek, instead, to transform or transmute it. Thus, the apparently idle recreations of gentleman poets could be, in fact, at odds with this version of themselves. But what, then, of those poets who were not gentlemen? What of women writers? One of the most notable features of Lucy Hutchinson's characterisation of Fairfax and Lambert in retirement is the gendering of what is to her their shame: Fairfax's downfall is his uxoriousness, while Lambert with his flowers and sewing resembles nothing so much as Hercules brought low by Omphale.[11] Indeed, the language of *otium* is marked by its proximity to femininity, and the attendant risk—for men—of effeminacy.[12] As Bronwen Price has suggested, the topos of retirement can in some contexts furnish 'a topography which is implicitly feminised in that it is both an apparently private space fulfilling a maternal function of nurture and protection and one whose enclosed recesses are symbolically connected to the female body'.[13] So a key moralised way of thinking about retirement presumes a subject capable of being most themselves in a life lived in public duties and offices, and of recreating that form of life even in the more limited circumstances of the locality and household precisely in order to sustain or maintain their propriety and identity. But such a subject could not, therefore, standardly be coded feminine, since effeminacy was what it risked when it failed to be properly itself. Or, to look at it from the other side, Sarah Prescott has suggested that 'retirement had a gendered dimension in that women did not have anything to retire from in terms of public and professional life'.[14]

However, the picture is more complicated than this might suggest—particularly because retirement is precisely a topos for a number of prominent female poets of the mid-seventeenth century, including, in her 'Elegies', Lucy Hutchinson. Scholars of Caroline court culture have shown how Queen Henrietta Maria provided a feminocentric model for political agency during the 1630s, the power and influence of which was keenly understood by her contemporaries.[15] The inhabitation of the public realm evidenced in her queenship was followed by the evident political visibility and audibility of women from a range of social classes in the violent upheavals of the 1640s and after. Susan Wiseman, for example, has described how groups of urban women used the discursive genre of the petition to make addresses to king and parliament, modelled on the

[11] On the currency of this mythic image in the Renaissance, see Stephen Orgel, *Impersonations: The Performance of Gender in Shakespeare's England* (Cambridge, 1996), 82.

[12] James Loxley, 'Unfettered Organs: The Polemical Voices of Katherine Philips', in Danielle Clarke and Elizabeth Clarke (eds), *'This Double Voice': Gendered Writing in Early Modern England* (Basingstoke, 2000), 230–48, 238–42.

[13] Bronwen Price, 'Verse, Voice, and Body: The retirement mode and women's poetry 1680–1723', *Early Modern Literary Studies*, 12.3 (2007) 5.1–44 https://extra.shu.ac.uk/emls/12-3/priceve2.htm.

[14] Sarah Prescott, '"That private shade, wherein my Muse was bred": Katherine Philips and the Poetic Spaces of Welsh Retirement', *Philological Quarterly*, 88 (2009), 345–64, 354.

[15] On Henrietta Maria's court and her cultural influence, see especially Erica Veevers, *Images of Love and Religion: Queen Henrietta Maria and Court Entertainments* (Cambridge, 1989) and Karen Britland, *Drama at the Courts of Queen Henrietta Maria* (Cambridge, 2006).

biblical precedent of Esther, while the martial deeds of noblewomen such as Charlotte Stanley, the Countess of Derby, were widely noted and recounted.[16] When Henrietta Maria returned to England in 1643 with arms and money for the royalist cause she was hailed both as an 'epicene' military heroine and as possessed, courtesy of her beauty, of an ordering power comparable with Orpheus: 'Lawes will obtaine / Their Force, and be once Lawes againe' now that she has returned.[17] The context of war left any clear distinction between private and public realms harder to assert; by the same token, the place of women in relation to any such distinction became problematic enough for a queen to be labelled 'epicene' by her admirers. A simply gendered topopoetics of retirement becomes harder to assert in a context where poets are having to register like this the wartime disruption of the gendering of both roles and spaces.

KATHERINE PHILIPS: FRIENDSHIP AND RETIREMENT

We can see this clearly in relation to Katherine Philips' poetry of retired friendship, and the private 'Society' it seemingly instantiates. Such poetry is necessarily counterposed to a wider or more public world, but as Catharine Gray has documented most fully, the 'post-courtly coterie' within which it was written and circulated was itself more than private.[18] The publication of William Cartwright's *Comedies, Tragi-comedies, with Other Poems* in 1651 was perhaps this group's most public and political moment: Cartwright's works were prefaced by a lengthy series of commendatory poems including many by members of Philips' network, and headed up by a tribute by Philips herself. When she there describes Cartwright—whom she cannot have known personally—as her 'much valued friend', it is clear that the term is marking something more than its customary meaning. In this case, the community of friends is, in Benedict Anderson's sense, imagined—these bonds are at least as public as private. The same group contributed a number of poems to be set by Henry Lawes, presumably for performance during his semi-public recitals of the 1650s as well as for publication in his 1653 *Second Book of Ayres and Dialogues*.[19] Hero Chalmers has noted the extent to which Philips' feminocentric coterie recalled Henrietta Maria's court and its *précieux* culture, while the poet's somewhat ambiguous or conflicted approach to making her writing public is demonstrable

16 Susan Wiseman, *Conspiracy and Virtue: Women, Writing, and Politics in Seventeenth-Century England* (Cambridge, 2006), 46–8; Mihoko Suzuki, 'Daughters of Coke: Women's Legal Discourse in England, 1642–1689', in Sigrun Haude and Melinda Zook (eds), *Challenging Orthodoxies: The Social and Cultural Worlds of Early Modern Women* (Abingdon, 2016), 165–92, 176. See also this volume, Chapter 5, Michele Osherow, '"At My Petition": Embroidering Esther'.

17 *Musarum Oxoniensium Epibateria* (Oxford, 1643), sigs. A, [B1v].

18 Gray, *Women Writers*, 108–24.

19 Ian Spink, *Henry Lawes: Cavalier Songwriter* (Oxford, 2000), 94–113.

in the still not entirely resolved question of whether she assented to the 1664 edition of her works, as well as her involvement in preparations for the eventually posthumous edition of 1667.[20] As Elizabeth Scott-Baumann has argued, Philips' claim to have written 'only for own amusement, in a retir'd life', is belied by ample evidence of dialogue, interaction, and exchange with both other writers and admiring readers over the length of her career. As Scott-Baumann puts it: 'in the 1650s and 1660s, to be a poet *of* retreat was by no means to be a poet *in* retreat'.[21]

Something of the tension implicit in this way of living 'a retir'd life' is legible in Philips' understanding both of the nature of friendship and of the ills that might beset it. The commonplace link between retreat and the enjoyment of friendship is only intensified by Philips' explicit yoking of the two together in such poems as 'A Retir'd Friendship: to Ardelia'. Conventionally, this poem positions itself as an invitation, and in so doing establishes a dynamic relationship between the 'here' of the speaker and the less determinate elsewheres of what lies beyond it. The deictic 'here' is primarily defined negatively through this relationship:

> Here is no quarrelling for Crowns,
> Nor fear of changes in our fate;
> No trembling at the Great ones frowns,
> Nor any Slavery of State.
>
> Here's no disguise, nor treachery,
> Nor any deep conceal'd design;
> From blood and plots this place is free,
> And calme as are those looks of thine. (Philips, *Works*, 1. 97; 5–12)

'Not-here', in other words, is a non-specific milieu of threat where the danger is in general concealed—hence the affective predominance of fear and trembling, consonant with the epistemic uncertainty of treachery and plots. The 'here' to which it is opposed is a 'bowre', which has clear erotic connotations, while the friends themselves are imagined 'mingling souls'. In an echo of John Donne's 'A Valediction Forbidding Mourning', the poem's concluding stanza completes the picture:

> But we (of one another's mind
> Assur'd,) the boistrous world disdain;
> With quiet souls, and unconfin'd
> Enjoy what princes wish in vain. (33–6)

What is it that princes can only wish for? The simple answer would seem to be peace, but a peace predicated on security: friendship is a state of mutual openness, of presence to

[20] Hero Chalmers, *Royalist Women Writers, 1650–1689* (Oxford, 2004), 105–48.

[21] Elizabeth Scott-Baumann, *Forms of Engagement: Women, Poetry and Culture 1640–1680* (Oxford, 2013), 81, 90.

each other and shared interest, in which the friends live 'in one another's hearts' (16). This requires trust: what friendship both needs and provides is the *assurance* of 'one another's mind'. But that it should both provide it and require it poses a potential problem. Where there is trust there can also be treachery—indeed, treachery presupposes the bonds and commitments it breaks. Hence, perhaps, the insistence on assurance—but what assures the assurance? The poem's final line, which seeks to contrast the happy friends with troubled princes, actually shows how a friendship needing assurance is not in fact invulnerable to the kinds of ills that beset statesmen. The bonds instantiated in a retired life turn out to be not as absolutely different from those of the public realm after all.

Some of the same phrasing occurs in 'Invitation to the Countrey', addressed to Philips' friend Mary Aubrey. She again writes of the poet and addressee 'mingling souls' (1. 175; 47), but now paints a slightly more determinate picture of the rural 'here' to which she is inviting her. Only slightly, though, because 'here' is largely characterised negatively, as an 'empty, wild' place that offers 'nothing to satisfy or entertain' (4–5). Nonetheless, she goes on to note, 'a retirement from the noise of Towns' (11) is something that kings and conquerors have often sought, and gives voice to a strain of *contemptus mundi*:

> Thus all the glittering world is but a cheat,
> Obtruding on our sence things grosse for great. (31–2)

Once again, the public realm is figured as a place of treachery and disguise, but now Philips posits a somewhat different virtuous alternative, characterised not by the mutual assurance of friendship but by a rather more Stoic self-possession:

> Man, unconcern'd without, himself may be
> His own both prospect and security.
> Kings may be slaves by their own passions hurl'd,
> But who commands himself commands the World. (37–40)

The poem asserts that 'A country-life assists this study best, / When no distractions doth the soule arrest' (41–2)—retirement gives someone the space in which to learn self-mastery.

It is this sense of the retired life that predominates in Philips' 'Ode Upon Retirement', in which she praises Abraham Cowley for his retreat from worldly business. The second stanza of the ode gives a particularly resonant account of the poet's own enviable situation in its address to the scorned world:

> In my remote and humble seate
>   Now I'm again possest
> Of that late fugitive, my breast,
> From all thy tumult and from all thy heat
> I'le find a quiet and a cool retreate;
>   And on the fetters I have worne

Looke with experienced and revengefull scorne,
    In this my soveraigne privacie.
    'Tis true I cannot governe thee,
    But yet my selfe I can subdue;
And that's the nobler empire of the two. (1.193; 18–28)

The language of this stanza for the most part works against its assertion of peace and coolness. The poet's breast is a 'late fugitive' that has been recaptured, but taking possession of it equates to throwing off 'fetters'. She is striving to 'subdue' herself, animated by 'revengefull scorne'. The desired state here is 'soveraigne privacie', a powerful phrasing which couples the modern sense of privacy as one's own space, a kind of property right, with the charged idea of ultimate public authority.

Once again, then, we can see Philips' vision of the retired life inflected by the language and categories of the public world it is supposedly defined against. In this emphasis on self-possession and self-mastery her writing of retirement echoes the reconstitution of the *vita activa* that Hutchinson describes in her husband's response to his loss of a role in government. But the key point here is that Philips is not the patriarch, as John Hutchinson was, but (in Margaret J. M. Ezell's phrase) the patriarch's wife.[22] To say 'Who commands himself commands the World' in reference to herself, and to speak of her own 'soveraigne privacie', is to merge both gender and retirement in a single event of displacement. This is a displacement which, as Sarah Prescott has suggested, works figuratively on a standard topology of centre and margins.[23]

It is illuminating in this context to compare Philips' writing of retreat with that of her contemporaries. Hero Chalmers has discussed the extent to which Margaret Cavendish's closet drama features an 'espousal of pastoral retreat' as 'a pertinent rationalisation of disempowerment', a reaction to the displacement of Henrietta Maria's feminocentric court culture from its position near the centres of authority and its reconstitution in exile.[24] Her stepdaughters Jane Cavendish and Elizabeth Brackley give female seclusion a different colouring in their wartime writing, orientating such retreat more dolefully around the absent, authorising person of their father.[25] From the family house at Broadfield in Hertfordshire, Hester Pulter wrote a wartime poetry marked, as Sarah Ross has said, by 'royalism, tropes of geographical isolation and solitude … and a prevailing poetic aesthetic of sighs and tears', reproducing a 'paradigm of feminized retreat'.[26] But Pulter's poetry of retreat can be topopoetically unstable: 'The Invitation to the Country' addressed to her two daughters in 1647 'when His Sacred Majesty

22 Margaret J. M. Ezell, *The Patriarch's Wife: Literary Evidence and the History of the Family* (Chapel Hill, NC, 1987).

23 Sarah Prescott, '"That Private Shade"', and 'Archipelagic Coterie Space: Katherine Philips and Welsh Women's Writing', *Tulsa Studies in Women's Literature*, 33 (2014), 51–76.

24 Hero Chalmers, 'The Politics of Feminine Retreat in Margaret Cavendish's *The Female Academy* and *The Convent of Pleasure*', *Women's Writing*, 6 (1999), 81–94, 88.

25 Chalmers, 'Politics of Feminine Retreat', 89.

26 Sarah C. E. Ross, *Women, Poetry, and Politics in Seventeenth Century Britain* (Oxford, 2015), 137.

Was at Unhappy [Holmby]' (i.e., held in captivity by the New Model Army), begins by presenting Broadfield as a place of fullness and pastoral safety in contrast to the capital city deprived of the presence of its monarch. But after seventy lines the poem turns quite suddenly, and extends this apprehension of living on into absence to the rural landscape which had initially stood in contrast to it.[27] By the poem's end, its speaker's illocutionary stance has reversed itself from offering comfort to its addressees to seeking comfort from them, as the place of fullness becomes instead the site of grief.

LUCY HUTCHINSON: RETIREMENT IN VERSE

But perhaps the most illuminating complement to Philips' deft assertion of 'soveraigne privacie' is to be found in the verse treatments of retirement written by Lucy Hutchinson. A poem originally written in an autobiographical manuscript and published with the first printed edition of the *Memoirs* in 1806 offers smoothly eloquent praise of the retired life, and was presumed by its first editor to have been 'probably composed by her during her husband's retirement from public business to his seat at Owthorpe'.[28] It begins with three personifications of industry—the prince, the soldier, and the merchant—but asserts that theirs is merely instrumental labour, undertaken in the pursuit of 'the same end, contented quietness':

> Which none of them attain, for sweet repose
> But seldom to the splendid palace goes;
> A troop of restless passions wander there,
> And only private lives are free from care. (*Memoirs*, 339; 2, 9–12)

Here again we see the sharp counter-position of a public and a private life, the former now characterised not as a *vita activa* but as a kind of restless wandering. The perils of such restlessness are implicit in the collective term 'troop' for the passions, conjuring up the image of a palace coup. These passions, taking the specific forms of ambition, avarice, and voluptuousness, are restless precisely because they are incapable of satisfaction—they drive a pursuit that can never achieve its end. The only hope of peace, then, is to give up or overcome these desires, and this is a peace that Hutchinson both characterises as 'freedom' and locates 'in the country life' (31). Such freedom is princely, but the microcosmic commonwealth that such a prince governs is magically free of the social and political ills that beset its larger analogue—his sheep don't begrudge him their fleeces, and if one of them is killed for meat 'those who survive will raise no mutiny' (36). And 'if ambitiously he seeks for fame' beyond the walls of his own estate:

[27] For a full discussion of this poem, see Ross, *Women, Poetry, and Politics*, 140–6.

[28] Hutchinson, *Memoirs*, 339.

One village feast shall gain a greater name
Than his who wears the diadem,
Whom the rude multitude do still condemn. (54–6)

This is Hutchinson's estate poem, fashioning an epitome of the ideal society from the cycles of domestic production and consumption like Jonson's 'To Penshurst', but without Jonson's defining orientation to the validating presence of the monarch. The banishment from Owthorpe of 'pomp and majesty' excludes also a whole litany of sins and suffering, 'Fear, sorrow, envy, lust, revenge and care' (58, 60). The poem concludes with a flourish of rhetorical questions:

What court can then such liberty afford?
Or where is man so uncontroll'd a lord? (61–2)

Courts afford no liberty, clearly, but not just because they represent the public realm in general—the pomp and majesty against which the free landholder defines his own apparently unexploitative wealth is unsurprisingly monarchical.

Despite this political colouring, though, the poem is in some ways impersonal—unlike many others of its genre, narratorial focalisation is notably absent. There is, in other words, no deictic 'here' from which the poem and its readers can take their bearings. So while the poem might indeed date from the period of John Hutchinson's retirement, and it would certainly fit with the account of their life at Owthorpe after 1653 given in the *Memoirs*, it resists secure anchorage in a particular time and place. This is in startling contrast, however, to the sequence of 'Elegies' written by Hutchinson after her husband's death in 1664.[29] The 'Elegies' foreground their speaker, a lyric voice characterised by a bleak, raw timbre, functioning not as formal funeral verses but as the rhetorical articulation of the limits of experience—testimony to a grief which is only just properly nameable. They speak most powerfully of solitariness, though not as any kind of 'soveraigne privacie', and the lyric speaker does not express the secure self-possessed presence of Philips' most assertive poems. More than this, though, they function recursively, exploring the rhetorical composition of any such presence. 'To the Gardin att O[wthorpe]', for example, reworks the topopoetics of the garden as retreat, evoking not its sensory plenitude or its contrast with an urban elsewhere, but as a site of absence:

Poor desolate Gardin smile no more on me
To whome glad lookes rude entertainments be
While Thou and I for they deare Master mourne . . . (1–3)

[29] The 'Elegies' were first published from the surviving manuscript at Nottinghamshire Archives by David Norbrook, in 'Lucy Hutchinson's "Elegies" and the Situation of the Republican Woman Writer (with text)', *English Literary Renaissance*, 27 (1997), 468–521. I quote from Norbrook's text, but have silently expanded contractions and modernised u/v where necessary.

The garden's desolation is a function of the speaker's grief, and the poem goes on to insist that they are both bound together as creations of the now dead 'Master':

> He that empaled ye from the comon Ground
> Whoe all Thy walls with shining frutetrees Crownd
> Me alsoe above vulgar Girles did rayse
> And planted in me all that yelded prayse. (11–14)

The active life of the landholder is present here only in its products, both garden and wife, who are not themselves endowed with the same capacities. Flowers and daughters are paralleled, further strengthening the identity of garden and speaker, while the grief-stricken sense of the present's losses passes into a speculation on the entropic future.

But after thirty lines the poem turns to reflect on its own figurative work. The use of metaphor, which allows the garden to stand for the speaker and vice versa, is suddenly called into question:

> Too much alas This Parallil I find
> In the disordred passions of my mind [-]
> But Thy late lovelinesse is only hid
> Mine like the shadow with its substance fled[.]
> Annother Gardiner and another Spring
> May into ye new grace and new lustre bring
> While beauties seedes doe yet remain alive
> But ah my Glories never can revive. (31–8)

Just at the point where the poem explicitly names its figurative work in remarking the completeness of the parallel, figuration fails. The garden and the poet are not the same; something is 'too much'. Time is the problem here, or rather the possibility of time as potential—the garden might have a future with another gardener, incubating 'beauties seedes' even in its desolation, but such cyclical temporality is not the kind of time in which the poet lives. This, instead, is a linear temporality in which loss and death are absolute—glories once gone can never revive. The garden of the future might be, as the poem says, only a 'weak semblance' (44) of its predecessor, but it would still be its representation. To recover her 'vanisht glories', by contrast, the speaker would need to be able to 'call back hasty flying time' (47–8), which is not an option. Indeed, she raises the possibility only to insist that *even if* her own best qualities could be recovered from the past into which they have vanished, 'to me That resurrection would be vaine / And like ungathred flowers would die againe' (49–50). The explicit echo and nihilistic rewriting of the Christian promise of salvation makes the poem almost a triumph of death, clarifying the status of its speaker as a strict impossibility, like the elixir of the first nothing who speaks Donne's 'Nocturnal Upon St Lucy's Day'.

When she returns to the garden in a later poem in the sequence, it is in very similar terms. 'Musings in my evening Walkes at O[wthorpe]' begins not with the garden, this time, but with the poet herself:

> With unseene teares and unheard groanes
> Ore those cold ashes and dried bones
> I weepe my wretched life away
> No Joy comes with the Chearefull day
> No rest comes with the Silent Night
> What terrors my darke Soule affright
> What ever doth it Selfe present
> Brings foode unto my discontent. (1–8)

While the fact that the tears and groans are unseen and unheard marks the speaker as less than a full presence to others, she is fully present to herself and to her 'discontent'. The barren garden furnishes her with a scene in which to articulate the true extent of her desolation, an inability to take joy or comfort in her children (29–32) or her books (37–42). Any attempt at relief only deepens her suffering:

> While with his memory I converse
> His glories to my Selfe rehearse
> Hopeing They Should my greife abate
> I add to my owne Sorrowes weight[.]
> What Tho Those glories were my Crowne
> His death hath throne my empire downe[,]
> And better never to have bine
> Raysed high Then live a fallen Queene[.]
> Ah me where Shall I seeke releife
> If even my pleasurs feed my greife. (45–56)

In this articulation of her distress we can hear an inverted echo of the kind of figurative transformation of the shame of retirement into its opposite, and of defeat into victory, that we see in many such poems. Instead, Hutchinson turns the resources of paradox towards further and deeper negation rather than towards affirmation. Having reached this point, the poem concludes with bitter complaint at her abandonment by others—pointedly, she states that she has 'No frinds to Comfort me' (61), and that her 'flatterrers whoe did adore / My happier state knowe me no more' (69–70). This retired life is not one warmed by friendship, but is instead still marked by the kinds of enmity which the poetry of retreat customarily associates with the turmoil of the public realm. The last four lines of the poem are a starkly angry challenge to some of those who have abandoned her:

> Yee Servile Slaves where are you all
> Whoe once did me your princis Call[?]

Even then I loathed your flatteries
And your sicke soules dispise. (71–4)

This address, of course, goes unheard (initials in the margin of the manuscript next to the final lines perhaps indicate precisely who Hutchinson had in mind, but there is no evidence of the poem's circulation)[30].

The poem's 'musings' are to that extent akin to an inner monologue or a *cri decoeur*. Here, as elsewhere in the sequence, Hutchinson's grief at her widowhood merges with a wider sense of exclusion from the circuits both of sociality and—as her description of her former self as 'princis' shows—of power. To the displacements of political upheaval, in other words, have been added the displacements of widowhood, which furnishes Hutchinson at least with a sharply gendered loss of place and position. This is retirement as annihilation, grief, and anger at the unassuageable loss of a husband speaking also of a profound estrangement from the public life they enjoyed together. What remains, though, is the vocalisation of the desolate condition that is life's undoing. Even in the brutal loss of her pleasures and bonds, and even though her groans are unheard, the voice persists; even if retirement here is a condition in which the very possibility of a continuing life is called into question, the negation itself can still be articulated. Stripped of everything that made it a subject, this speaking is all the more starkly audible, and the extent of its loss all the more visible. As Susan Wiseman has said of the Hutchinson of the 'Elegies', 'a shade may not be there, but it makes its presence felt'.[31]

CONCLUSION

In reading Philips and Hutchinson together we can trace different but connected ways of writing retirement, which mark some (though not all) of the key elements of the genre in the singular circumstances of mid-seventeenth-century social and political turmoil. The poetry of retirement is a writing of displacement, of the removal from one place to another, which almost always involves a topopoetics of 'here' and 'there', and relationships of substantive negation or differentiation between those two poles. To speak out of retirement is to speak back to the world from which the poet has been displaced, or has displaced themselves; it involves, therefore, not just placemaking as a characterisation of the site of its utterance but placemaking as the transformation of that site into something more than a sheer outside to public visibility and audibility. In both Philips and Hutchinson we see that transformation taking place through and as a female poet's resort to an already gendered topopoetics of retirement—a resort which

[30] See Norbrook, 'Lucy Hutchinson's "Elegies"', 511; the poem appears on page xxxiii of the manuscript.

[31] Wiseman, *Conspiracy and Virtue*, 228.

transforms the terms of that articulation, whether it issues in an enduring claim to sovereign privacy or to unheard but insistently audible grief.

FURTHER READING

Chalmers, Hero. *Royalist Women Writers, 1650–1689*. Oxford, 2004.

Chedgzoy, Kate. *Women's Writing in the British Atlantic World: Memory, Place and History, 1550–1700*. Cambridge, 2009.

Gray, Catharine. *Women Writers and Public Debate in Seventeenth-Century Britain*. New York, 2007.

Ross, Sarah C. E. *Women, Poetry, and Politics in Seventeenth Century Britain*. Oxford, 2015.

Scott-Baumann, Elizabeth. *Forms of Engagement: Women, Poetry and Culture 1640–1680*. Oxford, 2013.

Wiseman, Susan. *Conspiracy and Virtue: Women, Writing, and Politics in Seventeenth-Century England*. Cambridge, 2006.

CHAPTER 41

EARLY MODERN WOMEN IN PRINT AND MARGARET CAVENDISH, WOMAN IN PRINT

LIZA BLAKE

In 1653, Margaret Cavendish, then Marchioness and eventually Duchess of Newcastle, published a volume of poetry entitled *Poems and Fancies*.[1] This book was the first of what would eventually be twenty-one print publications published during her lifetime, with two additional volumes published after her death.[2] The book begins with nine (and, in a few copies, ten) prefatory materials, each of which prepares different audiences (Cavendish's brother-in-law, her dedicatee; other women in general; her maidservant in particular; natural philosophers; sceptical or censuring readers) to read her collection.[3] One of these letters, addressed 'To All Noble and Worthy Ladies', begins by asking women to forgive her for her decision to put her work into print: 'Condemn

[1] For a modern critical edition collating the three editions of Cavendish's book, see Margaret Cavendish, in Liza Blake (ed.), *Margaret Cavendish's Poems and Fancies: A Digital Critical Edition* (2019), http://library2.utm.utoronto.ca/poemsandfancies/, accessed 8 November 2020. All quotations from Cavendish's *Poems and Fancies* are from this edition. I am grateful to my graduate research assistant Melanie Simoes Santos for her contributions to this chapter.

[2] The count of twenty-one does not include the putative 1663 edition of the *Orations*; every copy I have consulted is a 1662 edition with a small tail added by hand to the '2' in '1662' to turn it into a '3'. The two additional volumes were: a reprint of the biography of her husband, William Cavendish, first published in folio in 1667 and reprinted in 1675, two years after her death; and a collection of commendatory letters and poems addressed to Cavendish and her husband, published under the latter's direction in 1676. Some copies of this later text additionally appear with the date 1678, but a cursory textual collation across copies suggests to me that the 1678 edition in fact consists of copies from 1676 reissued with an updated title page.

[3] Most surviving copies of the 1653 edition of her poems have nine prefatory materials; five of the thirty-four I have consulted contain an additional poem by her husband lauding the poetic collection.

me not as if I should dishonor your sex in setting forth this work, for it is harmless and free from all dishonesty—I will not say from vanity, for that is so natural to our sex that it were unnatural not to be so'. With this opening salvo, Cavendish both seems to partake of the modesty *topos* (begging her women readers not to treat her book as a source of dishonour, admitting that vanity is a failing of her and their sex), and to distance herself from it: the potential dishonour that she tries to stave off comes not from a faulty book (the book is 'harmless and free from all dishonesty'), but from the crime of publishing while female, as if the mere act of print publication, of 'setting forth this work', might 'dishonor . . . your sex'.

The idea that a woman publishing in print might in itself be sufficient to dishonour not just herself but her entire sex may be one reason why relatively few women appeared in print until the mid-seventeenth century, compared to men—according to Patricia Crawford's calculations, women writers never made up more than 1.6 per cent of print output in the seventeenth century.[4] The 'stigma of print', as it has come to be known, may indeed have compelled many women to keep their writing circulating privately in manuscript rather than bringing it to the print house.[5] In the case of Cavendish, her decision to appear in print contrasts with the choices made by her stepdaughters Jane and Elizabeth to circulate their writing only in manuscript.[6] In addition, some women whose work went into print appeared to do so in an instance of what Margaret J. M. Ezell has called 'forced' publication, where texts circulating in manuscript were brought to the printer without the author's knowledge or permission—a position that then sometimes forced the authors to address these flawed versions and to issue later, corrected editions.[7] However, recent scholarship has also pushed back against the generalised assumption that print was an entirely inhospitable environment for women writers; as late as 2009, for instance, Marcy L. North was arguing that scholars' hyper-focus on exclusively *literary* writing had given the false impression of a lack of women writers.[8] Women made meaningful print contributions especially to didactic and religious literature throughout the sixteenth and seventeenth centuries, even if literary works by women are scarcer in print until the seventeenth century.[9]

[4] See Patricia Crawford, 'Women's Published Writings 1600–1700', in Mary Prior (ed.), *Women in English Society: 1500–1800* (London, 1985), 158–209, 196.

[5] See Wendy Wall, *The Imprint of Gender: Authorship and Publication in the English Renaissance* (Ithaca, NY, 1993); she also discusses the way that women writers who did go into print had to negotiate their self-presentation to overcome the stigma.

[6] See Katie Whitaker, *Mad Madge: The Extraordinary Life of Margaret Cavendish, Duchess of Newcastle, the First Woman to Live by Her Pen* (New York, 2002): 'Although Jane and Elizabeth [Margaret's stepdaughters] were keen writers (like Margaret herself), they conformed to their culture's ideal of feminine modesty, shunning publication and writing only for their inmost family circle' (233).

[7] Margaret J. M. Ezell, *Social Authorship and the Advent of Print* (Baltimore, MD, 1999), esp. ch. 2, 'Literary Pirates and Reluctant Authors: Some Peculiar Institutions of Authorship', 45–60.

[8] Marcy L. North, 'Women, the Material Book and Early Printing', in Laura Lunger Knoppers (ed.), *The Cambridge Companion to Early Modern Women's Writing* (Cambridge, 2009), 68–82.

[9] *Women Writers Online* shows thirty surviving printed books (or sections of books) authored or translated by women in the sixteenth century, and 174 from the seventeenth century; see *Women Writers Project* (1999–2016), Northeastern University, https://www-wwp-northeastern-edu, accessed 8

Cavendish certainly had the stigma of print in mind when writing the letter 'To All Noble and Worthy Ladies', where she writes, 'And very like[ly] they [men] will say to me, as to the lady that wrote the romance: "Work lady, work, let writing books alone, / For surely wiser women ne'er wrote one"'. The 'lady that wrote the romance' is Mary Wroth, whose prose romance *Urania* was printed in 1621; the couplet is a rough approximation of one written by Edward Denny at the end of a long poem attacking Wroth's act of publication.[10] Cavendish either alters or misremembers Denny to make his stricture more severe: while the four surviving manuscript copies of this poem tell Wroth to leave '*idle books* alone', Cavendish quotes the line as 'let *writing books* alone'.[11] Where Denny leaves potential space for women to write books that are not idle, Cavendish remembers him as having left no space at all for ladies to write books. Making the stricture more severe serves the larger rhetorical purpose of Cavendish's letter, which is to persuade women to take her side against any potentially critical men, and to defend the right of a woman to write, and to write books in particular. The letter's modest opening masks what will go on to become a call to female arms, reminding women that they are often told that their 'tongues are as sharp as two-edged swords' and inviting them to bring those swords to 'strengthen my side' in 'this battle'—where 'this battle' is somehow simultaneously both a battle over the reception of her book, and a battle over the rights of women (and the rights of writing women) more generally.[12] Dispensing entirely with the modesty of her opening, Cavendish sets the defence of her book up as the synecdoche for the defence of women's right to write more generally. She is the monument whose defence (by women) can in turn offer future defences on behalf of other women.

The extent to which Cavendish is actually able to speak to the experience of women writers more generally is, of course, debatable: as a woman writer who (apparently) self-funded all of her own publications, Cavendish's experience with her printer was very different than that of Isabella Whitney, for example, who several decades earlier had collaborated with her printer to maximise profits from her publications (see this volume, Chapter 20, Michelle O'Callaghan, 'London and the Book Trade').[13] In *The Textual Condition*, Jerome J. McGann famously argued for rethinking textual

November 2020. See also Crawford, 'Women's Published Writings 1600–1700', for a complete checklist of seventeenth-century works.

[10] Whitaker, *Mad Madge*, 152, suggests that Cavendish is likely paraphrasing Denny from memory. For a digital edition of the exchange between Denny and Wroth, see Paul Salzman (ed.), 'Hermaphrodite Poems', in *Mary Wroth's Poetry: An Electronic Edition* (2012), La Trobe University, http://wroth.latrobe.edu.au/hermaphrodite-poems.html, accessed 8 November 2020.

[11] Salzman, 'Modernisation Notes' to 'Hermaphrodite Poems' (italics mine).

[12] For an argument about (and demonstration of) the value of reading women's modesy *topoi* as literary performances rather than literally, see Patricia Pender, *Early Modern Women's Writing and the Rhetoric of Modesty* (New York, 2012).

[13] For an argument about how a focus on Cavendish can sometimes distort our understanding of women's literary history, see Lara Dodds, 'Affected and Disaffected Alike: Women, Print, and the Problem of Women's Literary History', Stephen B. Dobranski (ed.), *Political Turmoil: Early Modern British Literature in Transition, 1623–1660* (Cambridge, 2019), 205–20. I discuss Whitney in more detail below.

production not as the work of a singular author, but as the work of a collaborative network of agents, from authors to editors to typesetters.[14] Recent scholarship on women and book production by Helen Smith, Valerie Wayne, and others has shown the involvement of women in every node of this network, including not only women writers, translators, and editors but also female 'rag-pickers' who were vital to paper-making, women printers and publishers, and more—even as Gillian Wright has pointed out that a 'more diverse understanding of textual agency ... has challenging implications for the study of women's writing, for the obvious reason that not all of the agents in the textual process are likely to have been women'.[15] Groundbreaking work such as these studies and collections help us see Cavendish not just as the singular monumental author—'Margaret the First' as she calls herself in the *Blazing World*—but as a woman writer deeply entrenched in the communities and networks of book production in which she so actively participated.[16] In turn, this chapter will show how Cavendish's community—her networks—included not just other 'noble and worthy' women, but also what I call her print collaborators, from printers to binders to distributors. This chapter, then, is a study of what print meant to someone like Cavendish, and how her relationship to print may allow us to rethink some of the dichotomies that currently structure the way we talk about women writers, including the dichotomies of print versus manuscript and author versus publisher or printer.

ATTENDING TO THE MANUSCRIPT IN CAVENDISH'S PRINTED BOOKS

It may be that the writing of many women writers is lost to history because women had no opportunity to bring their works to the press, but many early modern women also deliberately chose not to print their works, and to publish them instead by other means. This was a common practice in the period for both male and female writers: 'scribal publication' or the circulation of manuscripts would allow a writer to share their works but maintain some control of their audience, whether that meant circulating one's writing to only a circle of family members (as seems to have been the case with a writer like Hester

[14] Jerome J. McGann, *The Textual Condition* (Princeton, NJ, 1991).

[15] Helen Smith, *Grossly Material Things: Women and Book Production in Early Modern England* (Oxford, 2012); and several of the essays in Valerie Wayne (ed.), *Women's Labour and the History of the Book in Early Modern England* (London, 2020). See also Anne Lawrence-Mathers and Philippa Hardman (eds), *Women and Writing, c.1340–c.1650: The Domestication of Print Culture* (York, 2010), and Julie Crawford, *Mediatrix: Women, Politics, and Literary Production in Early Modern England* (Oxford, 2014), who offers a study of the role of women patrons in the production of texts. Gillian Wright, *Producing Women's Poetry, 1600–1730: Text and Paratext, Manuscript and Print* (Cambridge, 2013), 18.

[16] Margaret Cavendish, *A Description of a New World Called the Blazing World* (London, 1666), sig. b*2r.

Pulter), or to a wider coterie of people that might still be limited to, for example, people with similar political leanings, or people of the same economic or social class as the author.[17] For those women writers who did go into print (including those whose works may have been printed without their permission), we are sometimes left with both print and manuscript texts, and the differences between manuscript and print versions of texts are often fascinating, and revealing of varying understandings of the differences between manuscript and print publication.[18] For Cavendish, however, manuscript copies of texts were only temporary backups for printed texts: she states explicitly that once a book had made it into print she would 'Commit the Originals to the Fire', because, like parents 'past Breeding, they are but Useless in this World'.[19] Other manuscripts, such as her self-described 'Baby Books' that contained her childhood writing, she promised she 'would never divulge'.[20]

Despite Cavendish's commitment to print as a medium—her explicit desire that her works survive in print rather than in manuscript—her books often blur the boundary between these two different modes of writing and textual distribution, in several ways. Although modern readers associate printed texts with uniformity, early modern printed books in general, and Cavendish's texts in particular, can display quite a lot of variance even across copies of the 'same' book.[21] Cavendish often includes multiple paratextual prefatory materials (letters to different imagined readers, explanatory prefaces, etc.) in her books, and those materials may be partially missing, or may be bound in different arrangements, in different surviving copies of her texts.[22] James Fitzmaurice has demonstrated that many (though not all) copies of a given Cavendish book have uniform or systematic handwritten corrections, made by a secretary seemingly at her direction,

[17] See Harold Love, *Scribal Publication in Seventeenth-Century England* (Oxford, 1993); Ezell, *Social Authorship*.

[18] See Sarah C. E. Ross and Elizabeth Scott-Baumann, '"Corrected by the Author"? Women, Poetry, and Seventeenth-Century Print Publication', *Huntington Library Quarterly* 84.2 (2021), 353–81; this article examines the relationship between manuscript and print in the writings of both Katherine Philips and Anne Bradstreet, as well as Cavendish's views on print. See also Wright, *Producing Women's Poetry*, and Paul Salzman's analysis of Wroth's poems appearing in manuscript and in print in his 'Textual Introduction', in Salzman (ed.), *Mary Wroth's Poetry*.

[19] Margaret Cavendish, *CCXI Sociable Letters* (London, 1664), 295–6; cited in Whitaker, *Mad Madge*, 173.

[20] Margaret Cavendish, *The Life of the Thrice Noble, High, and Puissant Prince William Cavendishe, Duke, Marquess, and Earl of Newcastle* (London, 1667), sig. (a)2r. Most of the manuscripts that survive in her hand are letters she wrote to William Cavendish while they were courting, now held in London, British Library, Additional MS 70499.

[21] For an excellent introduction to copy-specific variance in early print in general, see Adrian Johns, *The Nature of the Book: Print and Knowledge in the Making* (Chicago, IL, 1998).

[22] Some specific rearrangements are noted in Liza Blake, 'Close Reading (and) Textual Bibliography: How Many Parts Does Margaret Cavendish's *Blazing World* Have?', in Lisa Walters and Brandie Siegfried (eds), *'Margaret Cavendish: an Interdisciplinary Perspective'* (Cambridge, 2022), 233–47. See also Rebecca Bullard, 'Gatherings in Exile: Interpreting the Bibliographical Structure of *Natures Pictures Drawn by Fancies Pencil to the Life* (1656)', *English Studies*, 92 (2011), 786–805; and James Fitzmaurice, 'Front Matter and the Physical Make-up of Natures Pictures', *Women's Writing*, 4 (1997), 353–67.

and often matching exactly across multiple copies of a book.[23] However, there is also evidence that she sometimes ordered different sets of corrections for different imagined audiences, and there also survive several copies of what I call Cavendish's 'reading copies', or copies of her printed texts which contain *non-uniform* hand corrections, often in Cavendish's own hand, and which seem to indicate her looking back and making different notes on different copies of her texts.[24] The large amount of copy-specific variance that one encounters when reading her texts makes many of her printed texts unique, or close to unique, somewhere closer to the middle of the spectrum between individual manuscript and uniform printed text. And although the amount of attention Cavendish gives to her book is somewhat unusual, it is not unique; Vanessa Wilkie has shown how Lady Eleanor Douglas likewise continued to engage with her own writing post-print, and that she, like Cavendish, annotated her own texts differently for different readers.[25]

The post-print corrections Cavendish makes (or directs secretaries to make) to her books include, crucially, not only handwritten corrections, but also printed paper slips, pasted in after the fact. Her *Plays Never Before Printed* (1668) includes both kinds of post-print additions, and the printed paper slips (which get pasted in to mark out things written by her husband within her books) have been analysed by Jeffrey Masten.[26] As Masten points out, it was not entirely unusual for a printer to make slips to be inserted into a text, but the slips that appear in the 1668 *Plays* (five or six per corrected copy, all of which say 'Written by my Lord Duke' or 'VVritten by my Lord Duke') are unusual in that they do not replace erroneous text, but are inserted into white space.[27] Masten analyses, in particular, the strange way that these printed slips further blur the boundaries between manuscript and print, being both uniformly printed but also written in her voice ('*my* Lord Duke').[28] This strange dislocation of her voice from her hand happens elsewhere as well; while *Nature's Pictures* (1656) does not have any printed slips in it, different copies have manuscript notes that mark out passages written by her husband, always in her voice, but only sometimes in her own hand, in a way that can often confuse cataloguers. Of the two copies of the 1656 edition held at the British Library—both of which have first-person, handwritten notes on pages 20, 25, 64, and 271 attributing

[23] See James Fitzmaurice, 'Margaret Cavendish on Her Own Writing: Evidence from Revision and Handmade Correction', *Papers of the Bibliographical Society of America*, 85 (1991), 297–308; and Liza Blake, 'Pounced Corrections in Oxford copies of Cavendish's *Philosophical and Physical Opinions*; or, Margaret Cavendish's Glitter Pen', *New College Notes*, 10 (2018), no. 6, 1–11 [electronic journal], New College, Oxford, https://www.new.ox.ac.uk/sites/default/files/2018-12/10NCN6%20%282018%29%20Blake%20on%20Pouncing_0.pdf, accessed 8 November 2020.

[24] Liza Blake, "Margaret Cavendish's Reading Copies: Authorial Annotation and Reading Beyond Revision" (article in progress)

[25] Vanessa Wilkie, 'Reading and Writing Between the Lines: Lady Eleanor Douglas, a Midland Visionary and her Annotated Pamphlets', *Midland History*, 41 (2016), 168–83.

[26] Jeffrey Masten, 'Margaret Cavendish: Paper, Performance, "Sociable Virginity"', *Modern Language Quarterly*, 65 (2004), 49–68.

[27] Masten, 'Paper', 52–3.

[28] Masten, 'Paper', 58.

sections to her husband—both books are marked in the catalogue as containing her hand, though only one actually contains her handwriting.[29] Instances such as these complicate not only the dichotomies of (stable, uniform) print versus (unique) manuscript, but also the seemingly easy and fixed boundaries between the personal (typically associated with manuscript) and the impersonal.

Masten's essay explores how the printed slips in Cavendish's 1668 *Plays* help us imagine Cavendish not just as author but as co-author, an active collaborator with her husband.[30] I would build on that argument to suggest that the slips also suggest an ongoing collaboration with her printer Anne Maxwell, who, as the printer who printed all her texts (except for a Latin translation) after 1666, is most likely the one who provided her with the printed sheets that were then cut into slips and pasted into most of the books. Cavendish did not always have a close relationship with her printers, and changed printers frequently in her publishing career.[31] Early in her career, in particular, she seemed to think of her printers less as collaborators and more as (inadequate) employees:

> I think it is against Nature for a Woman to spell right, for my part I confess I cannot; and as for the Rimes and Numbers, although it is like I have erred in many, yet not so much as by the negligence of those that were to oversee it; for by the false printing, they have . . . done my Book wrong . . . so that my Book is lamed by an ill Midwife and Nurse, the Printer and Overseer . . .[32]

These complaints about sloppy printing, levelled in *World's Olio* (1655) against her first printer, Thomas Roycroft, appear again in *Nature's Pictures* (1656), where she notes that many of her books had been 'so cruelly disfigured by ill printing', including most recently her 1655 *Philosophical and Physical Opinions* (possibly printed by Thomas Warren, the husband of Alice Warren who would, as widow, go on to print Cavendish's 1662 *Plays*).[33] Though her practice of collecting and correcting her texts began as a reaction to the misprints of what she viewed as her sloppy printers, she (or her secretaries) continued

[29] Margaret Cavendish, *Natures Pictures, Drawn by Fancies Pencil to the Life* (London, 1656). Her hand is in the copy located at shelfmark 841.m.25, and the copy at shelfmark G.11599 has notes in her voice (e.g., on page 20, a marginal note reads 'These songes followinge: are my Lord Marquess' /'), but not in her hand.

[30] Masten, 'Paper', 56, does not present this collaboration as entirely uncomplicated; he highlights the belatedness of the slips, which were not included in the bulk of the text but added later, and observes that these 'either are an afterthought, or are performed as one'.

[31] For an overview of what we know about the printers and booksellers of Cavendish's work, see Cameron Kroetsch, 'List of Margaret Cavendish's Texts, Printers, and Booksellers (1653–1675)', *Digital Cavendish Project* (15 August 2013), http://digitalcavendish.org/original-research/texts-printers-booksellers/, accessed 8 November 2020.

[32] Cavendish, *The World's Olio* (London, 1655), 93–4.

[33] Cavendish, *Natures Pictures*, sig. 3E4r. On the possibility of Cavendish coming to the widowed printer Alice Warren first through her late husband, see Kroetsch, 'List', notes 2, 14; on women printers and evidence that they were working with their husbands in printshops well before their deaths, see essays by Valerie Wayne, Alan B. Farmer, Sarah Neville, Erika Mary Boeckeler, and Martine van Elk, in Wayne (ed.), *Women's Labour*.

the practice to the end of 1668, with uniform hand corrections appearing in four of the seven books printed by Anne Maxwell in that year, including the 1668 *Plays* that also had paper slips added.[34]

WOMEN IN PRINT APART FROM PROFIT

Though Cavendish seems to have had a more productive working relationship with Anne Maxwell than with any prior printer, the printers with whom she worked seem to have been, to her mind, sloppy at worst, and mere instruments at best. This puts Cavendish in stark contrast to an author like Isabella Whitney, who, as Kirk Melnikoff has persuasively demonstrated, worked in close collaboration with her printer and bookseller Richard Jones, not only reading and citing other books for sale in his bookshop, but also shaping her writing to suit his demands, deliberately '[taking] steps to fashion a volume that her "Printer" would consider a valuable commodity'.[35] Likewise, Erin McCarthy has shown that the multiplication of prefatory materials in Aemilia Lanyer's *Salve Deus Rex Judaeorum* (1611) may be attributed as much to her publisher's desire for a marketable book as to Lanyer's own authorial ambitions.[36] As Michelle O'Callaghan has noted, Whitney, who was writing towards the end of the sixteenth century, six decades before Cavendish, is most famous for being 'England's first professional woman writer'—where 'professional' means writing and publishing for profit.[37] Questions about the *commercial* possibilities available to women writers have long dominated conversations about women in print, partly because Virginia Woolf's landmark essay *A Room of One's Own* (1929) focuses not just on historical women's abilities and opportunities to write, but also on their ability to translate their writing into money, either to support their husbands or to establish financial independence—hence Woolf's privileging of Aphra Behn, who was able not just to write but also to turn her writing into a career that allowed her to support herself.[38] This valorisation of Behn (and her ability to translate her writing into a profitable enterprise), however, has obscured many

[34] Uniform corrections appear in multiple copies of *Plays Never Before Printed, Grounds of Natural Philosophy, Observations upon Experimental Philosophy*, and *Blazing World* (with these latter two texts usually circulating together, but sometimes separately).

[35] Kirk Melnikoff, 'Isabella Whitney Among the Stalls of Richard Jones', in Valerie Wayne (ed.), *Women's Labour*, 145–61, 156. See also this volume, Chapter 20, O'Callaghan.

[36] Erin A. McCarthy, 'Speculation and the Multiple Dedications in *Salve Deus Rex Judaeorum*', *SEL Studies in English Literature 1500–1900*, 55 (2015), 45–72.

[37] Michelle O'Callaghan, '"My Printer Must, Haue Somwhat to His Share": Isabella Whitney, Richard Jones, and Crafting Books', *Women's Writing*, 26 (2019), 15–34, 15. O'Callaghan argues that both women's writing and women's authorship were 'mediated through the work of booksellers, printers, and other agents in the print trade' (15).

[38] Virginia Woolf, *A Room of One's Own* (London, 1935), 95–9. Even Whitaker, Cavendish's most comprehensive biographer, attempts to put Cavendish in this camp with the subtitle of her biography, which names Cavendish as 'the First Woman to Live by her Pen'.

women writers whose printed works were not primarily designed for (their own) profit. Works printed for reasons other than financial profit include posthumous publications such as John Bale's and then John Foxe's publications of the *Examinations of Anne Askew* (first-person accounts of Askew's questionings and tortures as a Protestant martyr), works by royal women Katherine Parr (wife of Henry VIII) and Princess (and then Queen) Elizabeth I, and publications by noble women from Mary Sidney Herbert, Countess of Pembroke to Margaret Cavendish, Duchess of Newcastle.[39] These women, and others who chose to put their works into print for reasons other than financial gain, are, in fact, no different than their male counterparts, who also published for reasons other than profit, and Ezell's call for a way of understanding authorship 'that do[es] not consider the relationship between the writer and his or her reader as being governed only by commercial exchange or professional advancement' is just as timely today as it was when it was first published.[40]

Cavendish in particular offers a prime example of someone whose desire to go into print seems entirely divorced from questions of profit. Her *Poems and Fancies* has a poem called 'The Poetress' Hasty Resolution', in which her personified Reason attempts to convince her to delay publication, imploring her to 'the printer spare, / He'll lose by your ill poetry, I fear' (11–12). Though Cavendish's biographer Katie Whitaker argues that this poem offers evidence that 'it was the booksellers and not Margaret herself who paid for publishing the book', the preponderance of evidence that can be gleaned from her surviving texts suggests that her books were not primarily intended for financial profit, whether Cavendish's or the printers' and booksellers'.[41] With two exceptions (the 1653 *Philosophical Fancies* and the posthumous 1675 reissue of the *Life of the Duke*), all of her books were printed in folio, sometimes with large font and often (especially in the 1653 *Poems*) with large amounts of white space on each page—a sign that the printer was not economising on paper. While her first six publications list on their title pages the booksellers where her books can be purchased, from the *Orations* (1662) forward her title pages list printers (usually) but no booksellers.[42] This may just have been the result

[39] Anne Askew, *The First Examinacyon of Anne Askewe, Latelye Martyred in Smythfelde, by the Romysh Popes Upholders, with the Elucydacyon of Johan Bale* (Wesel, 1546); *The Lattre Examinacyon of Anne Askewe, Latelye Martyred in Smythfelde, by the Wycked Synagoge of Antichrist, with the Elucydacyon of Johan Bale* (Wesel, 1547); and *The Two Examinations*, in John Foxe (ed.), *Actes and Monuments of these Latter and Perillous Dayes Touching Matters of the Church* (London, 1563), sigs. 2O5r–2P3v; Katherine Parr, *Prayers Stirryng the Mynd unto Heavenlye Medytacions* (London, 1545), *The Lamentation of a Synner* (London, 1548); Elizabeth I, *The True Copie of a Letter from the Queenes Majestie, to the Lord Maior of London, and His Brethren* (London, 1586), and *Elizabetha Triumphans* [*The Tilbury Speech*] (London, 1588); Mary Sidney Herbert, Countess of Pembroke, 'The Doleful Lay of Clorinda', in Edmund Spenser, *Colin Clouts Come Home Againe* (London, 1595), sigs. G1r–G2v (she also had several translations appear in print).

[40] Ezell, *Social Authorship*, 12. See also Jane Stevenson, 'Women and the Cultural Politics of Printing', *The Seventeenth Century*, 24 (2009), 205–37, 209, for an analysis of the 'category of the wholly non-commercial printed book [as] relevant to the printing of women's writing'. Stevenson discusses Cavendish as a particular example of this type of publication, 210–13.

[41] Whitaker, *Mad Madge*, 375, n. 56.

[42] Kroetsch, 'List', 1.

of changing printers who had different preferences for what information should appear on the title page (beginning with the *Orations*, she moved to William Wilson and then to Anne Maxwell), or it might indicate that the majority of the newly printed books were sent not to a bookseller, but to Cavendish directly.

After her return to England in 1660 with the Restoration and the end of the English Civil Wars, Cavendish collected and controlled the distribution of a large number of her printed books, apparently receiving them directly from the printers to distribute as presentation copies, gifts to individuals and to private and institutional libraries. Cavendish donated copies of several of her books to every college (that existed as a college during her lifetime) of Oxford University and Cambridge University, as well as to the central libraries of each university: Oxford colleges received approximately six to eight books each, and Cambridge colleges received approximately ten to twelve.[43] That Cavendish was the source of these donations is evident from the large number of books held in Oxford and Cambridge, from the letters issued from Oxford and Cambridge thanking her for book donations, and from the many donor inscriptions in the front pages of copies still lodged in those college libraries.[44] As I show elsewhere, either Cavendish or her printer had the books batch-bound before they were distributed as gifts, though the evidence suggests that this batch-binding most likely happened after the books had left the printer's hands. Some books are bound identically across both Oxford and Cambridge, but two books, the *Orations* (1662) and *Philosophical and Physical Opinions* (1663), appear to have been bound locally in Oxford and Cambridge respectively. Of those books still in their original bindings, every Oxford copy is the same across colleges, as is every Cambridge copy, but the Oxford and Cambridge bindings are both different from one another and different from presentation copies given to people outside Oxford and Cambridge.[45] After 1664, the uniform bindings of donation copies often match across Oxford and Cambridge and in books given to people outside those two universities, suggesting that the batch-binding happened centrally, perhaps facilitated for Cavendish by the printer(s), or perhaps as part of a larger trade

[43] See Blake, 'Cavendish's University Years', which examines both her Oxford and Cambridge donations as well as the uniform bindings on donated books inside and outside of the universities. For an ungenerous account of Cavendish's donations to Oxford colleges, see William Poole, 'Margaret Cavendish's Books in New College, and around Oxford', *New College Notes*, 6 (2015), no. 5, 1–8 [electronic journal], New College, Oxford, https://www.new.ox.ac.uk/new-college-notes accessed 8 November 2020.

[44] The collection of copies in Oxford and Cambridge is detailed in Liza Blake, 'Locating Margaret Cavendish's Books: Database, Map, and Analysis', *Digital Cavendish Project* (14 November 2018, updated 6 December 2019), http://digitalcavendish.org/original-research/locating-margaret-cavendish/, accessed 8 November 2020. The letters, both Latin and English, are included in *A Collection of Letters and Poems Written by Several Persons of Honour and Learning Upon Divers Important Subjects to the Late Duke and Dutchess of Newcastle* (London, 1676), collected and printed after her lifetime.

[45] Blake, 'Cavendish's University Years', 51–67. David Pearson, who is studying local Cambridge binders, has confirmed that the binding present on Cambridge copies of the *Orations* (1662) and *Philosophical and Physical Opinions* (1663) seemed to match other books likely bound in Cambridge (private communication, 16 March 2019).

binding.[46] Still other donation copies were bound in upscale or 'extra' versions of these basic binding patterns, featuring the same rolls, fillets, and fleurons (decorative patterns pressed into the leather), but gilded (pressed with gold leaf), and on marbled or painted leather.[47] With these donations—given to domestic and continental universities, public and private libraries—Cavendish once again blurs print and manuscript cultures, taking the fairly standard practice in the early modern period of giving out individual 'presentation copies' of a text (crafting a copy as an upscale object and gifting it to a treasured recipient, such as a patron or prospective patron) and, with the help of print, massively scaling that practice up, giving out hundreds of her books over the course of her publishing lifetime.

CONCLUSION

Cavendish's prefatory letter 'To All Noble and Worthy Ladies' is a study in carefully balanced contradictions, starting as it does with an invocation of the modesty *topos* and ending with a call to arms to all women to support not just her writing but the right of all women to write. Does this letter hint at her motivations for going into print? Does she really see herself as a trailblazer, whose venture into publishing will make it easier for other women to write and publish? Determining Cavendish's views on printing is difficult from her prefatory materials, which often hold together contradictions not only within but also across letters in a single collection. In 'To All Noble and Worthy Ladies' she declares, 'I wish my book may set a-work every tongue', and it is not clear whether it is the printed book itself or the conversations of these tongues about her printed books that will construct the 'pyramid of fame' ('The Poetress' Hasty Resolution', 6) and 'pyramid of praise to my memory' ('To the Reader') that she wishes for in other *Poems and Fancies* prefatory materials. However, the idea that she potentially saw print as a lasting, public monument is also undercut in other letters, such as the 'Epistle to Mistress Toppe', where she demurs, 'I print this book to give an account to my friends how I spend the idle time of my life, and how I busy my thoughts when I think upon the objects of the world'. According to both her own writings and what we can learn about her agendas from surviving copies of her texts, Cavendish's printed books were both public and private, destined for bookshops and for carefully selected private libraries, sometimes uniform and sometimes capable of great copy-specific variance. This is why, as I have suggested, Cavendish's in many ways unique relationship to print as a

[46] On early modern trade bindings (bindings done to batches of books so that booksellers could sell not unbound sheets but pre-bound books), see Stuart Bennett, *Trade Bookbinding in the British Isles, 1660–1800* (New Castle, DE, 2004). That some of the bindings match even across books printed by different printers suggests to me that the bindings were not arranged by the printer, but by a separate binder.

[47] Blake, 'Cavendish's University Years', 74–81.

medium, and to her printed books, cuts through many of the assumptions about print, manuscript, and women writers that still motivate and structure much of the work in our field. In addition, the fact that so much of her interaction with her printed texts was mediated through different agents (printers, binders, secretaries making manuscript and print corrections, agents distributing her books) reminds us that although Cavendish presents herself to the world as a singular, monumental author, she exists at the centre of a network of what I have called her print collaborators, all of whom ensured the existence and survival of her hybrid books to the present day—and which books, in turn, still show traces of the print networks of which she was a part.

FURTHER READING

Crawford, Patricia. 'Women's Published Writings 1600–1700', in Mary Prior (ed.), *Women in English Society: 1500–1800*. London, 1985, 158–209.

Greetham, D. C. *Textual Scholarship: An Introduction*. New York, 1994.

Masten, Jeffrey. 'Margaret Cavendish: Paper, Performance, "Sociable Virginity"', *Modern Language Quarterly*, 65 (2004), 49–68.

McGann, Jerome J. *The Textual Condition*. Princeton, NJ, 1991.

Smith, Helen. *Grossly Material Things: Women and Book Production in Early Modern England*. Oxford, 2012.

Wayne, Valerie (ed.), *Women's Labour and the History of the Book in Early Modern England*. London, 2020.

Werner, Sarah. *Studying Early Printed Books 1450–1800: A Practical Guide*. Hoboken, NJ, 2019.

PART VI

TOOLS AND METHODOLOGIES

CHAPTER 42

EDITING EARLY MODERN WOMEN'S WRITING

Tradition and Innovation

PAUL SALZMAN

TAKEN at its most basic level, editing is the process whereby a text is transmitted to readers through one or more intermediaries. Recent work on transmission, and theories surrounding the material turn in early modern literary studies, have expanded our idea of what we mean by editing, for early modern writing in general, and for early modern women's writing in particular.[1] As the scope of the present volume indicates, early modern women wrote across an extremely heterogeneous range of forms, and the process of recovering that writing is ongoing, especially writing that exists in manuscript form. This chapter argues that the early transmission of women's writing was in itself a form of editing. By the twentieth century, when the editing of canonical authors was at its most authoritative, the transmission of early modern women's writing remained outside the dominant editorial tradition. The situation slowly changed at a time when some of the assumptions behind this form of editing began to be questioned, especially the idea that the editor's task was to construct a single, 'ideal' text from the textual material available. The challenge for editors of early modern women's writing across recent decades has been to respond to some of these theoretical issues, while at the same time continuing with the significant recovery process which has continued to make the range of that writing more visible.

[1] For a useful and provocative summary, see Peter Shillingsburg, *Textuality and Knowledge* (Philadelphia, PA, 2017); for a groundbreaking approach to women's writing, see Helen Smith, *'Grossly Material Things': Women and Book Production in Early Modern England* (Oxford, 2012).

ALWAYS EDITED

Anne Askew, Queen Katherine Parr, Elizabeth Tyrwhit, and Queen Elizabeth are four Tudor writers, the contemporaneous transmission of whose work can be seen as a form of editing. Anne Askew was tried as a heretic late in the reign of Henry VIII, and her testimonials were first published by John Bale in 1546 and 1547, and then later incorporated into Foxe's *Acts and Monuments* of 1563.[2] In her groundbreaking book on the rhetorical trope of women's modesty, Patricia Pender explains that 'Bale's editions of Askew represent some of the first early modern English versions of the "scholarly edition"'.[3] Pender goes on to note that all of Askew's texts are 'heavily mediated', and she offers a fruitful paradigm for reading these mediated texts that avoids any misplaced desire for an 'authentic' originary source. If we see mediation as an inevitable condition of writing and its transmission, we can approach that writing as, in a sense, always in a process of being edited. We have in recent years become used to thinking of that most canonical of all early modern writers, William Shakespeare, as always mediated, with any desire to recover or reconstruct an authentic authorial moment as misplaced,[4] but it is only relatively recently that we have taken this approach to writing by early modern women.

So Pender invites us to read Askew's writing as a kind of collaboration produced by Askew with Bale and Foxe. Both men frame Askew's narrative, and attempt to guide our interpretation of it; they engage in what we might call editing as retelling, though they offer us what they claim to be Askew's actual words. Bale's two accounts are in the form of an elaborate to and fro exchange: Askew's words are in dialogue with Bale's commentary, and indeed Bale's explication is often longer than Askew's comments. For example, Askew's seven-line account of her eighth examination includes the succinct response to the issue of private Masses: 'I sayd, it was great Idololatrye [sic] to beleve more in them, than in the deathe which Christ dyed for us'.[5] This evokes from Bale a two-and-a-half-page exposition on private Masses, and a 'correct' view of baptism and penance. Bale's two editions of Askew are like a dialogue, whereas Foxe produces a kind of précis edition, which cuts out Bale's lengthy explications.[6] This has been seen as a paradigm for the relationship between early modern women writers and their transmission by Jennifer Summit, whose concept of a more even balance between female writer and male editor is further developed by Pender.[7] These scholars, as well as those who have applied

[2] See Diane Watt, 'Askew [married name Kyme], Anne (*c.* 1521–1545)', *ODNB*.

[3] Patricia Pender, *Early Modern Women's Writing and the Rhetoric of Modesty* (Houndmills, 2012), 37.

[4] See, for example, Sonia Massai, *Shakespeare and the Rise of the Editor* (Cambridge, 2007).

[5] *The First Examination of Anne Askewe* (1546), sig. A6v.

[6] For a good comparison of the two, as well as Pender see Thomas S. Freeman and Sarah Wall, 'Racking the Body, Shaping the Text: The Account of Anne Askew in Foxe's "Book of Martyrs"', *Renaissance Quarterly*, 54 (2001), 1165–96.

[7] Jennifer Summit, *Lost Property: The Woman Writer and English Literary History, 1380–1589* (Chicago, IL, 2000), 10; and for a highly sophisticated account of how we might '"hear" Askew's physical

this paradigm to their overall interpretation of Tudor religious writing by women, have helped to undo a rigid, disempowering notion of the editing process.[8]

Katherine Parr, Henry VIII's final queen (survived), published an extremely popular religious work in 1545, commonly known as *Prayers or Meditations*.[9] This went through three editions in 1545 and thirteen altogether by the end of the sixteenth century. Parr's modern editor, Janel Mueller, notes how Parr would have had to negotiate the publication of this potentially controversial religious work with both the king and Archbishop Thomas Cranmer.[10] Parr's final published work, *The Lamentacion of a Synner* (1547) was introduced, and its interpretation guided, by an introduction from William Cecil. Cecil specifically instructs a female audience to appreciate the piety of this text: 'to all ladies of estate I wishe as ernest minde to folowe our queen in virtue, as in honour . . . so shall they . . . taste of this freedome of remission of this everlastyng blisse'.[11]

Elizabeth Tyrwhit was part of Katherine Parr's circle, and her published prayerbook has some of the same religious associations. Thanks to the meticulous work of Tyrwhit's modern editor, Susan Felch, it is now clear that the two early editions of Tyrwhit's *Morning and Evening Prayers* were misunderstood, and that the first, published in 1574, is a kind of abridgement of Tyrwhit's now lost manuscript, while the second, published in 1582 as part of Thomas Bentley's *Monument of Matrons*, is more complete, and can be presumed to be closer to Tyrwhit's original text.[12] The earliest printing, as Felch notes, is a silent editorial mediation, with Tyrwhit's text prefaced by a generic 'exhortation unto prayer', while Bentley's edition is part of a monumentalising (and anthologising) process, with Bentley himself functioning as 'a careful antiquarian and non-intrusive editor'.[13]

The most prominent of these four women was of course Queen Elizabeth, whose speeches and proclamations in particular were disseminated in a variety of forms. But the most interesting example of her work being edited comes from a poem included in George Puttenham's *The Arte of English Poesie* (1589). This poetry handbook cum critical assessment includes a number of poems as illustrations. For the final example of poetic ornament, *exargia*, defined as 'gorgeous' by Puttenham, who sees this as in essence a figure of amplification, he presents Elizabeth's now much anthologised 'The

voice', see Jennifer Richards, *Voices and Books in the English Renaissance: A New History of Reading* (Oxford, 2019), 190–201.

[8] For an excellent example of this process of interpretation see Kimberly Anne Coles, *Religion, Reform, and Women's Writing in Early Modern England* (Cambridge, 2008).

[9] See the fine edition of Parr's complete writing, in Janel Mueller (ed.), *Katherine Parr: Complete Works and Correspondence* (Chicago, IL, 2011).

[10] Mueller (ed.), *Katherine Parr*, 370–1.

[11] Katherine Parr, *The Lamentacion of a Synner* (1547), sig. ∏6v

[12] I am summarising Susan Felch's complex argument which is found in her essay 'The Backward Gaze: Editing Elizabeth Tyrwhit's Prayerbook', in Sarah C. E. Ross and Paul Salzman (eds), *Editing Early Modern Women* (Cambridge, 2016), Ch. 2; see also her edition *Elizabeth Tyrwhit's Morning and Evening Prayers* (Burlington, VA, 2008).

[13] Felch, 'The Backward Gaze', 32.

doubt of future foes'.[14] Puttenham offers a quite elaborate contextualisation and interpretation of Elizabeth's poem, beginning with an explanation that this figure is most appropriate for 'the arte of a ladies penne' because the queen herself is the epitome of beauty. But at the same time, Puttenham stresses the political implications of a figure (and poem) that is about penetrating deception in the realm and resisting the rebellious machinations deriving from Mary Queen of Scots, and opposing dangerous 'ambition and disloyaltie'.[15]

As noted above, Parr's, Tyrwhit's, and Elizabeth's writings were all published in what John N. King has described as 'the earliest printed collection of English women's writings'.[16] Thomas Bentley's *The Monument of Matrones* was published in 1582; it is a massive anthology of religious material relating to, and produced by, women. Bentley's edition is an exemplary compilation that both conveys the virtue of his numerous examples of female piety and offers instruction and spiritual sustenance to his 'Christian' (i.e., Protestant) readers. Bentley is happy to acknowledge his sources, and explains that his volume is indeed a compilation or edition, as when he notes Parr's work as 'first published in print by Sir William Cicill ... as by his verie godlie, learned, and eloquent Epistle thereunto prefixed, and here also in this edition now inserted'.[17] I have already noted Susan Felch's rehabilitation of Bentley as editor of Tyrwhit. To that we can add Louise Horton's uncovering of the complex process of transmission behind another noblewoman's writing: Frances, Lady Abergavenny, whose fifty prayers went through an extremely complex and multi-authored process of transmission that extended well beyond Bentley.[18] But Bentley is a significant starting point, because his anthologising and organising process can be seen as paradigmatic for the way that early modern women's writing was edited from his time all the way through to the twentieth century. Bentley's express purpose was to catalogue and reproduce texts by 'vertuous women of all ages'. In doing so, he acts as a didactic curator of works that will demonstrate learning and piety and build a 'monument' to female worth. He sets in train a method of selection and reproduction of women writers that tended to avoid the untidy, the unruly, and the uncategorisable.

[14] George Puttenham, *The Arte of English Poesie* (1589), 207–8.

[15] Puttenham, *Arte*, 207.

[16] John N. King, 'Thomas Bentley's Monument of Matrons', in Pamela Joseph Benson and Victoria Kirkham (eds), *Strong Voices, Weak History: Early Women Writers & Canons in England, France, and Italy* (Ann Arbor, MI, 2005), 216.

[17] Thomas Bentley, *The Monument of Matrones* (1582), sig. B1 (I have changed black-letter type to Roman).

[18] Louise Horton, '"Restore Me That Am Lost": Recovering the Forgotten History of Lady Abergavenny's Prayers', *Women's Writing*, 26 (2019), 3–14.

TRANSMISSION AND VISIBILITY

During the course of the seventeenth century, substantial collections of works by a single author also began to be published in monumental editions. The example usually cited here is Ben Jonson's 1616 folio *Works* (and the accompanying early modern joke 'Pray tell me Ben, where does the mystery lurk, / What others call a play, you call a work').[19] In the terms I have been outlining here, three women writers in particular had their work collected and edited in the seventeenth and through to the eighteenth century: Margaret Cavendish, Katherine Philips, and Aphra Behn. Cavendish constructed her own authorial presence with great care, publishing a series of impressive volumes of poetry, plays, philosophy, scientific studies, and stories. Cavendish was also a compulsive re-editor, especially of her own poetry, which appeared in substantially different versions in 1653, 1664, and 1668.[20] Cavendish's process both of revision and of the provision of numerous defensive prefaces enabled her to maintain control over her work even as she published it. She acted, in a sense, as her own gatekeeper. Philips' publishing history is somewhat controversial, but for my purposes it involves two significant editions of her *Poems*, the first possibly unauthorised, the second much more substantial. Philips' 1664 octavo *Poems* was followed in 1667 by a much more substantial folio which added her translations of Corneille's *Pompey* and *Horace*. At the same time, a number of manuscript 'editions' of Philips' poetry were compiled, notably the so-called Rosania manuscript, a presentation collection compiled by someone calling himself Polexander, and described by Marie-Louise Coolahan as 'a memorial volume'.[21] Both the folio *Poems* (1667) and the Rosania volume have all the hallmarks of an edition: where the manuscript is a personalised selection, the published volume is an embodiment of Philips' status as poet, complete with an engraved portrait of her.

Behn, as a professional writer, was constantly engaged in the process of the publication of individual plays, and she became a marketable commodity not only during her career, but posthumously, as is reflected in a series of collected editions of her works, which continued to be published through much of the eighteenth century.[22] Behn's plays and her fiction were published in multivolume editions, many of them accompanied by biographical introductions which tended to characterise her as somewhat disreputable

[19] John Mennes, *Recreation for Ingenious Head-Peeces* (London, 1654), sig. D7r.

[20] Margaret Cavendish, *Poems and Fancies* (1654), *Poems and Phansies* (1664), *Poems, or Several Fancies* (1668); on Cavendish's revising habits see Elizabeth Scott-Baumann, *Forms of Engagement: Women, Poetry and Culture 1640–1680* (Oxford, 2013), Ch. 2.

[21] Marie-Louise Coolahan, 'Single-Author Manuscripts, *Poems* (1664), and the Editing of Katherine Philips', in Ross and Salzman (eds), *Editing Early Modern Women*, 176–94, 177; and see the whole of Coolahan's essay which outlines some of the issues surrounding Philips' editions. Coolahan suggestively characterises compilers of some of these manuscripts as 'reader-editors' (184).

[22] See Jane Spencer, *Aphra Behn's Afterlife* (Oxford, 2000) and Paul Salzman, 'Aphra Behn's Fiction: Transmission, Editing, and Canonisation', in Brandie R Siegfried and Pamela S. Hammons (eds), *World-Making Women* (Cambridge, 2021), 37–53.

(this was when the comparison with the morally respectable Philips began to be established).[23] The editing of women's writing continued in this sporadic fashion during the eighteenth and nineteenth centuries. A lot of the collecting, anthologising, and transmission was virtually invisible, or perhaps more accurately largely forgotten, until it was outlined in Margaret Ezell's groundbreaking 1993 study, *Writing Women's Literary History*.[24] By the end of the seventeenth century, as Carol Barash has argued, there was a clear sense of women writers as a category, and this was reflected in editions; for example, in 1700 *The Nine Muses* was a commemorative volume for the death of Dryden, featuring poems by Mary Pix, Catherine Trotter, and other female poets.[25] More recently, Gillian Wright has examined how women writers such as Anne Southwell, Anne Bradstreet, Katherine Philips, and others constructed themselves as poets whose work deserved to be collected, as they self-consciously produced an oeuvre.[26] During the course of the eighteenth century, early modern women's poetry was given a constant presence through successive editions of George Coleman and Bonnell Thornton's *Poems By Eminent Ladies*, which was first published in 1755, and then in expanded editions in 1773 and 1780.

As editing of early modern literature became more expansive and adventurous in the nineteenth century, women writers remained visible, if far less prominent members of what was being established as the 'field' of Renaissance literature.[27] In 1825, Alexander Dyce edited a significant collection of women's poetry: *Specimens of British Poetesses*.[28] Dyce's anthology was scarcely bettered until the 1970s, and then mainly because he relied heavily on print and (understandably) did not access many manuscript sources for the earlier poetry. There were some other notable editing moments in the nineteenth century; for example, the eminent historian C. H. Firth edited Margaret Cavendish's *Life of William Cavendish* and a revised edition of Lucy Hutchinson's biography of her husband—a text that was already extremely popular, having gone through ten editions since first being edited by Julius Hutchinson in 1816.[29]

[23] For the shifting reputations and fortunes of Behn and Philips, see Paul Salzman, *Reading Early Modern Women's Writing* (Oxford, 2006).

[24] Margaret J. M. Ezell, *Writing Women's Literary History* (Baltimore, MD, 1993).

[25] See Carol Barash, *English Women's Poetry 1649–1714* (Oxford, 1996), 241; *The Nine Muses, or, Poems Written by Nine Several Ladies Upon the Death of the Late Famous John Dryden Esq* (London, 1700).

[26] Gillian Wright, *Producing Women's Poetry, 1600–1730: Text and Paratext, Manuscript and Print* (Cambridge, 2013).

[27] For an overview see Paul Salzman, *Editors Construct the Renaissance Canon 1825–1915* (Houndmills, 2018).

[28] See Paul Salzman, 'How Alexander Dyce Assembled *Specimens of British Poetesses*: A Key Moment in the Transmission of Early Modern Women's Writing', *Women's Writing*, 26 (2019), 88–105.

[29] C. H. Firth (ed.), *Memoirs of the Life of Colonel Hutchinson* (London, 1885); *The Life of William Cavendish* (London, 1886).

PROFESSIONAL EDITING, AUTHORITATIVE EDITIONS, AND THE RECOVERY OF EARLY MODERN WOMEN'S WRITING

The beginning of the twentieth century saw the foundations of a new and purportedly more scientific approach to scholarly editing.[30] Much of the theorising, and many of the practical editorial projects, were aimed at Shakespeare. In relation to women's writing, there was a moment when two pioneering editions that were published early in the twentieth century seemed to promise equal standing for women writers: R. B. McKerrow's edition of Thomas Nashe, published between 1904 and 1910, and Montague Summers' edition of Aphra Behn, published in 1915.[31] However, as the first half of the century unfolded, an increasing number of early modern male writers received the full 'authoritative edition' treatment, but no women writers, which reinforced the impression that there were either none (the missing output of Shakespeare's sister) or none of any importance. So, even in cases where some knowledge of a particular writer was present—such as, for example, Katherine Philips, who received careful attention from Louise Guiney, notably in her 1904 selection of Philips' poetry—there was no edition of the kind that established a canonical presence.[32]

This situation began to change with a variety of recovery projects spurred by second-wave feminism. Scholars began to be alerted to the rich diversity of women's writing, and a key moment for this, at least for printed writings, was Betty Travitsky's anthology *The Paradise of Women: Writings by Englishwomen of the Renaissance* (1981).[33] Not only did this include dozens of (brief) extracts from women's writing, but, even more importantly, it also contained an extensive bibliography of printed texts by women, spurring scholars to read and potentially edit them. Almost as if in response to this, a highly significant and profoundly influential project began at Brown University in 1986. The Brown *Women Writers Project* brought together the relatively new idea of an electronic archive with the enthusiasm being generated for the recovery of women's (printed) texts. It began with a corpus of 200 texts first published between 1526 and 1850, which were

[30] For a good if somewhat controversial summary, see Gabriel Egan, *The Struggle for Shakespeare's Text: Twentieth-Century Editorial Theory and Practice* (Cambridge, 2013).

[31] Thomas Nashe, in R. B. McKerrow (ed.), *The Works of Thomas Nashe*, 5 vols (London, 1904–1910); Aphra Behn, in Montague Summers (ed.), *The Works of Aphra Behn*, 6 vols (Stratford/London, 1915).

[32] See Andrea Sununu, '"I Long to Know Your Opinion of It": The Serendipity of a Malfunctioning Timing Belt or the Guiney-Tutin Connection in the Recovery of Katherine Philips', *Women's Writing*, 24 (2017), 258–79; and Kate Lilley, 'When Sapphos Meet: Louise Imogen Guiney and Katherine Philips' *Selected Poems* (1904)', *Women's Writing*, 26 (2019), 106–24.

[33] Betty Travitsky (ed.), *The Paradise of Women: Writings by English Women of the Renaissance* (Westport/London, 1981).

transcribed and encoded, and which at that point could be ordered as printouts. This was a notion of 'editing' as a minimalist production of cheap and easily accessible primary texts.

The project was transformative in a number of ways: it emphasised that the writings of early modern women were a resource that needed to be shared and taught; it harnessed the idea that there might be a productive partnership between the humanities and digital technology; and it changed, developed, and diversified in response to new opportunities.[34] The neglect of women's writing in manuscript was, at a slightly later date, rectified by the *Perdita* project, which began as a bibliographical database of manuscript sources, and was later the source for an online digital facsimile repository of 230 of those texts.[35] As Patricia Pender and Rosalind Smith note of the *Women Writers* and *Perdita* projects: 'both resources have opened up the field of early modern women's writing by providing access for scholars outside the elite library to not only a broad set of texts, some hitherto unknown, but also to genuinely new ways of looking at those texts'.[36] These two projects are best described as recovery and reproduction projects and are 'editions' only in the very broad sense discussed above. *Perdita* in particular signalled a somewhat delayed recognition of how much women's writing existed in manuscript, although the minimalist editorial practice of reproduction pointed to the limitations of this practice. The digital possibilities set out by these two projects will be examined in more detail in the final section of this chapter. Here, I want to consider two further editions which helped to transform the scholarship, but more particularly the pedagogical imperative, associated with the recovery of early modern women's writing.

Kissing the Rod, a weighty anthology of seventeenth-century women's poetry, was edited by Germaine Greer, Susan Hastings, Jeslyn Medoff, and Melinda Sansone, and was published in England by Virago in 1988 and by Farrar Strauss & Giroux in the United States in 1989.[37] It contains poems by dozens of writers, from the reasonably well known such as Philips, Bradstreet, and Wroth, through to a number who were obscure or even completely unknown. In 1989 Elspeth Graham, Hilary Hinds, Elaine Hobby, and Helen Wilcox published *Her Own Life*, a pioneering collection of autobiographical works by thirteen early modern women.[38] Where the editors of *Kissing the Rod* worked with relatively conventional notions of what constitutes the literary, given that poetry can be seen

[34] See 'Women Writers Project History', in *Women Writers Project*, Northwestern University, https://www.wwp.northeastern.edu/about/history/, accessed 17 April 2020. For important theoretical speculation about the implications of the project, see Julia Flanders, 'Gender and the Electronic Text', in Kathryn Sutherland (ed.), *Electronic Text: Investigations in Method and Theory* (Oxford, 1997), 127–43.

[35] The *Perdita* project was established in 1997 at Nottingham Trent University. It then transitioned to an online catalogue together with digital facsimiles of close to half the manuscripts. See the discussion by Rosalind Smith, 'Perdita Project', *Early Modern Women: An Interdisciplinary Journal*, 11 (2017), 145–51.

[36] Patricia Pender and Rosalind Smith, 'Editing Early Modern Women in the Digital Age', in Ross and Salzman (eds), *Editing Early Modern Women*, 262.

[37] Germaine Greer et al. (eds), *Kissing the Rod: An Anthology of Seventeenth-Century Women's Verse* (London, 1988).

[38] Elspeth Graham et al. (eds), *Her Own Life: Autobiographical Writings by Seventeenth-Century Englishwomen* (London, 1989).

as the most valued of all literary forms, *Her Own Life* exemplified the way in which a true understanding of what early modern women wrote challenges hierarchies of genres. *Her Own Life* is yet another example of the way the recovery stage of scholarship produced editions that were anthologies, and that were student-friendly. The equivalent volume for drama was the 1995 *Renaissance Drama by Women*, edited by S. P. Cerasano and Marion Wynne-Davies.[39] Given that there have been re-evaluations of this process that note some of the disadvantages of these supposedly less substantial types of edition, I want to recall here the immense excitement generated by the possibility of teaching the diverse writing by early modern women to students in affordable, accessible, but also truly scholarly editions.[40] The commitment to pedagogy has been a persistent force in the editing of early modern women's writing, from this period in the late 1980s through to the present day. The deep scholarly exploration of the diverse forms in which women wrote has also had an ongoing impact on editing. As Alice Eardley notes in her thoughtful account of the anthology in relation to early modern women's writing, the acknowledgement of the diverse forms of women's writing was extended even further when manuscripts were taken into account, a process which again accelerated during the 1990s and up to the present day.[41]

By the early 1990s, these anthologies were joined by a number of volumes that were more conventionally aligned to single-author editions or to more conventional ideas of genre. Katherine Philips presents a series of complex challenges for any editor because her poetry was transmitted across a number of manuscripts and printed texts. In 1990, the small Stump Cross Press, run by Germaine Greer, published Philips' poems edited by Patrick Thomas, making use of the full range of textual sources.[42] At the same time, the Brown *Women Writers Project* collaborated with Oxford University Press to produce a series of single-author editions (not always complete editions) in a generally affordable format. Fifteen volumes were published, though only half were early modern, with these again exemplifying a diverse range of genres: Anne Askew's examinations, Arbella Stuart's letters, Aemilia Lanyer's poetry, Rachel Speght's poetry and polemical work, Anne Weamys' *Arcadia* continuation, a selection of Eleanor Davies' prophecies, and Jane Sharp's *The Midwives Book*.[43] Unfortunately, the series was discontinued in 1999

[39] S. P. Cerasano and Marion Wynne-Davies (eds), *Renaissance Drama by Women: Texts and Documents* (London, 1995).

[40] For potential issues, see Jonathan Gibson and Gillian Wright, 'Editing Perdita: Texts, Theories, Readers', in Ann Holinshead Hurley and Chanita Goodblatt, (eds), *Women Editing/Editing Women: Early Modern Women Writers and the New Textualism* (Newcastle, 2009), 156–73.

[41] Alice Eardley, 'Recreating the Canon: Women Writers and Anthologies of Early Modern Verse', *Women's Writing*, 14 (2007), 270–89; see also Ramona Wray, 'Anthologising the Early Modern Female Voice', in Andrew Murphy (ed.), *The Renaissance Text: Theory, Editing, Textuality* (Manchester, 2000), 55–72.

[42] Katherine Philips, in Patrick Thomas (ed.), *The Collected Works of Katherine Philips: The Matchless Orinda*, 3 vols (Essex, 1990–1993); an authoritative edition of Philips is being edited for Oxford University Press by Elizabeth Hageman and Andrea Sununu.

[43] Anne Askew, in Elaine V. Beilin (ed.), *The Examinations of Anne Askew* (Oxford, 1997); Arbella Stuart, in Sara Jayne Steen (ed.), *The Letters of Lady Arbella Stuart* (Oxford, 1995); Aemilia Lanyer, in

after the publication of Elaine Hobby's intricately researched edition of *The Midwives Book*. The reins were indirectly picked up by The Other Voice series, which began in 1993 with translations of texts by European women writers and, after a move to Iter Press, added texts by women writing in English, including important editions of Hester Pulter's poetry, Margaret Fell's pamphlets, Margaret Cavendish's poetry, Mary Wroth's 'Pamphilia to Amphilanthus' sequence, drama by Wroth and the Cavendish sisters, and Anna Trapnel's *Report and Plea*.[44]

However, in the course of the 1990s, there were some important theoretical questions being asked about the relationship between the editing of early modern women's texts and editing in general.[45] Unsurprisingly, given the sophistication of her editorial work on Mary Wroth, Josephine Roberts summed up many of the issues for the editing of early modern women's writing raised by the questioning of editorial methods by scholars like Leah Marcus, whose provocative book on 'unediting' canonical Renaissance texts was published in 1996.[46] Roberts notes the growing recognition of the amount of women's writing in manuscript, rather than print, and also the need to understand the implications of a recovery project that fails to take into account issues surrounding the concept of authorship.[47] Roberts also responds to a now famous comment by W. Speed Hill: 'feminist scholars are actively engaged in recovering texts by and about women, scaling the very intentionalist mountain the other side of which their male confreres are descending'.[48] Roberts notes in response that already by 1996, 'the project of recovering women's writing involves more than simply the process of editing individual authors; it is ultimately an attempt to reconstruct a lost manuscript culture'.[49]

A few years later, though, Danielle Clarke produced a stringent critique that examined a number of issues that, she argued, still needed to be addressed by editors of early modern women's texts.[50] In essence, Clarke questioned the continuing desire

Susanne Woods (ed.), *The Poems of Aemilia Lanyer* (Oxford, 1995); Rachel Speght, in Barbara Kiefer Lewalski (ed.), *The Polemics of Rachel Speght* (Oxford, 1996); Anna Weamys, in Patrick Colborn Cullen (ed.), *A Continuation of Sir Philip Sidney's 'Arcadia'* (Oxford, 1995); Eleanor Davies, in Esther S. Cope (ed.), *Prophetic Writings of Lady Eleanor Davies* (Oxford, 1996); Jane Sharpe, in Elaine Hobby (ed.), *The Midwives Book* (Oxford, 1999).

44 Another press that has published a significant proportion of work by early modern women is Broadview, which has three volumes of works by Margaret Cavendish.

45 For a valuable collection of (mostly republished) essays exploring the implication of 'new textualism' and the editing of early modern women's writing, see Ann Hollinshead Hurley and Chanita Goodblatt (eds), *Women Editing/Editing Women: Early Modern Women Writers and the New Textualism* (Newcastle, 2009).

46 Leah S. Marcus, *Unediting the Renaissance: Shakespeare, Marlowe, Milton* (London, 1996).

47 Josephine A. Roberts, 'Editing the Women Writers of Early Modern England', *Shakespeare Studies*, 24 (1996), 63–70.

48 W. Speed Hill, 'Editing Nondramatic Texts of the English Renaissance: A Field Guide with Illustrations', in W. Speed Hill (ed.), *New Ways of Looking at Old Texts: Papers of the Renaissance English Text Society 1985–1991* (Binghamton, 1993), 1–24, 23.

49 Roberts, 'Editing the Women Writers', 70.

50 Danielle Clarke, 'Nostalgia, Anachronism, and the Editing of Early Modern Women's Texts', *Text*, 15 (2003), 187–209.

for women's texts to resemble the texts that were part of an established male canon. Clarke suggested that editors might put into practice some of the more truly radical possibilities opened up by a deep engagement with early modern women's writing. This vision of a more utopian future for editing requires taking into account the theoretical questions that fuelled the new textualism, as well as the historical context for early modern women's writing, and an editorial methodology that would facilitate a new approach without losing sight of the many women made visible by the recovery project.

In the two decades since, many of the issues raised by Clarke have been addressed. Indeed, one can argue that the process of discovery, recovery, and dissemination has meant that editors of early modern women's writing have been in a particularly advantageous position to address these issues, including the relationship between digital and 'conventional' editing, the material turn in early modern studies, and the idea of social editing. Editors have also, on the whole, been acutely aware of the need to consider an edition's audience. In some cases this has meant buying into the traditional single-author, complete works edition, notably in recent years with editions of Mary Sidney Herbert, Lucy Hutchinson, and Aphra Behn, but it has also meant an imaginative response to increasing possibilities for digital editions.

THE DIGITAL TURN

I have already noted the pioneering online presence of the Brown *Women Writers Project* and the *Perdita* project. We are now, in 2020, at a stage of increasing self-consciousness and, to a degree, of sophistication in relation to digital possibilities for editing. But before I examine some specific instances, I want to return to a very early online edition which underlines the fact that access remains of considerable importance in the editing process as it relates to early modern women's writing. In 1995, Sara Jayne Steen supervised a group of students who edited Isabella Whitney's *A Sweet Nosegay* (1573).[51] This is a lightly modernised and annotated text. While Whitney's book might not present many difficulties for the scholar, the fact that it was printed in black-letter type makes it a challenge for students and ordinary readers, so this readily accessible PDF, placed online, and importantly available for no charge, makes what we might term the simplest of all online editions extremely useful—and indeed it remains so, as we await the projected edition that will appear in The Other Voice series. In terms of printed texts, the greatest access was (and remains) through the *Early English Books* project, which began in 1938 as a microfilm series that aimed to photograph all printed books from 1475 to 1700.[52] In

[51] Isabella Whitney, in Nick Broyles et al. (eds), *A Sweet Nosegay* (1995), Montana State University, http://sjsteen.blogs.plymouth.edu/files/2008/04/a-sweet-nosegay.pdf, accessed 2 June 2020.

[52] For a succinct critical history, see https://folgerpedia.folger.edu/History_of_Early_English_Books_Online, accessed 2 June 2020.

the 1990s, this microfilm series was progressively digitised and became *Early English Books Online* (*EEBO*).

Initially, many innovative approaches to online editions relied upon the work that had gone into previous, conventional editions: work that, as I have been outlining, was seldom available in the case of early modern women's writing. Indeed, the amount of time required for that kind of edition meant that both publishers and scholars have been reluctant to commit to editions of less canonical authors, although many of the male authors now seem in retrospect no more significant than the women who have been overlooked. Many of the issues raised by scholars' confrontations with early modern women's writing speak directly to debates over how editing might function in a fragmented educational and scholarly environment. Editors of texts by early modern women have had to find imaginative answers to questions of how to contextualise myriad works outside conventional literary genres. Editors have had to pivot away from the obviously literary and its associated editorial conventions to take into account the heterogeneity of early modern women's writing, encompassing as it does letters, diaries, conduct books, so-called mother's advice, religious meditations, prophecy, treatises, receipt books, dialogues, and so on. This process has produced editions such as Elaine Hobby's of Jane Sharpe's *The Midwives Book* or Susan Felch's of Elizabeth Tyrwhit's prayers and meditations.

At the same time, these texts have also raised questions about the notion of a singular 'author' and, more recently, of a gendered author. The idea of editing that might have to come to terms with multiple exemplars of a text, with its history of transmission and reading, without being in thrall to a posited ideal version, has also been a productive paradigm for approaches to early modern women's writing. There has, in many respects, had to be a revolution in approaches to bibliography and book history, and in approaches to readership, transmission, and the material characteristics of texts, in order for scholars of early modern women's writing to achieve an understanding of the complexity required for new editions and theories of editing to flourish. A good example is the important work of Kate Ozment on what she terms feminist bibliography: a fundamental repositioning of ideas about texts and their nature that challenges the masculinist bias of traditional bibliography.[53] Together with the increasing attention to women's writing in manuscript since Margaret Ezell first asked for that lacuna to be addressed, this new awareness has generated a considerable amount of innovative editorial activity.

Experiments in digital editing in general have proliferated in recent years, along with some criticism of the utopianism that seemed to accompany early manifestations.[54] I want to end this chapter by looking at a few examples of digital editions that exemplify the imaginative response to ongoing questions about how best to represent the diversity,

[53] Kate Ozment, 'Rationale for Feminist Bibliography', *Textual Cultures*, 13 (2020), 149–78.

[54] See, for example, Margaret J. M. Ezell, 'Editing Early Modern Women's Manuscripts: Theory, Electronic Editions, and the Accidental Copy-Text', *Literature Compass*, 7 (2010), 102–9.

unique characteristics, and significance of early modern women's writing.[55] As I have already noted in relation to Steen's Whitney edition, given the ongoing recovery process, even quite simple digital editions of early modern women's writing can have a significant impact. However, there have been some especially imaginative editions that address the specific issues surrounding early modern women's writing outlined above, and that offer models for further work. I want to note five in particular that are quite distinctive, moving from the most to the least conventional.

'Traditional' printed editions have been adapted to reflect newer views on the circulation of manuscripts in particular, so that, for example, an edition like Harold Love's *The Works of John Wilmot, Earl of Rochester* moves away from single, reconstructed ideal texts to versions that reflect circulation and adaptation.[56] Online editions offer an even more flexible opportunity to explore multiple versions, or to allow for more 'reader control' over how a text is represented. And, somewhat paradoxically, a digital edition can better represent the physical characteristics of individual copies of books and manuscripts, compared to a conventional scholarly edition, given the potential for photographed copies to be magnified. For example, my own edition of Mary Wroth's poetry includes high-definition images of the whole of Wroth's manuscript 'Pamphilia to Amphilanthus' as part of a multi-column design that includes the printed version of the poetry, as well as modernised and unmodernised transcripts and annotations, which can be selected to allow for a custom-built edition for each individual reader.[57] This process is possible when there are only one or two textual sources, which allows for a particularly rich digital editorial environment. So, for example, Hester Pulter's single manuscript of poetry and a romance is able to be utilised for the online *Pulter Project* edition, with the texts treated in different ways and annotated and contextualised in considerable detail, in part because there is already a modernised print edition edited by Alice Eardley.[58] As noted above, labour is an under-discussed aspect of editing, and the more complex textual sources are, the more labour (and knowledge) is required to edit them, whether online or in a more conventional edition. This is, in part, why it has been difficult for scholars to commit to the time involved to produce an edition of a writer who publishers might consider to be too obscure. To some extent, online editions of complex texts have been able to bypass this potential reluctance of publishers. A good example is Liza Blake's elaborate, scholarly edition of Margaret Cavendish's *Poems and*

[55] For a useful review of nine websites/editions see *Early Modern Women: An Interdisciplinary Journal*, 11 (2017).

[56] Harold Love (ed.), *The Works of John Wilmot Earl of Rochester* (Oxford, 1999).

[57] Paul Salzman (ed.), *Mary Wroth's Poetry: An Electronic Edition* (2012), La Trobe University, http://Wroth.latrobe.edu.au, accessed 16 October 2020.

[58] Leah Knight and Wendy Wall (eds), *The Pulter Project: Poet in the Making* (2018), Northwestern University, http://pulterproject.northwestern.edu, accessed 16 October 2020 (only has the poetry); Alice Eardley (ed.), *Lady Hester Pulter: Poems, Emblems, and The Unfortunate Florinda* (Toronto, 2014).

Fancies, which exists in three distinct printed editions, but also with numerous stop press and hand-written corrections in individual copies.[59]

Online editing has also been able to expand the notion of what might constitute an 'edition', partly in reference to increasing interest in what might constitute an archive.[60] Two notable examples are the *Material Cultures of Early Modern Women's Writing Digital Archive*, an eclectic collection of texts treated in different ways to allow for a sense of what might be called differential circulation, and *Bess of Hardwick's Letters*, a comprehensive archive that houses images, transcripts in various modes, and tools for transcription exercises.[61] Instances like this stretch the idea of an edition to incorporate both a quantity of material, and ways to interact with it, that are unable to be achieved in a conventional print edition. And, as I have already noted, because editors of early modern women's writing have had to think through issues surrounding authorship and readership, their digital editing has had to be especially agile.

While digital editing has raised a number of theoretical issues, from the difficulty of ensuring that websites will remain active through to the limitations of the two-dimensional image of the three-dimensional book or manuscript, I have no doubt that digital editions will continue to have a positive effect on the dissemination and analysis of early modern women's writing. This is no more evident than under the circumstances current as I write this, with libraries closed and scholars restricted in movement owing to the Covid-19 pandemic. Digital access has been of major importance at this moment in time, and doubtless will be into the future. But for early modern women's writing in particular, the digital turn has meant an ever-greater engagement with what is required by the range of writing that extends beyond 'literary' boundaries. Expanded notions of the archive as interactive repository will surely continue to offer new ways of encompassing the heterogeneity of early modern women's writing. At the same time, the digital space also offers scope to incorporate previously under-recognised ways of analysing that writing in response to approaches such as critical race studies and queer theory.

[59] See Margaret Cavendish, in Liza Blake (ed.), *Margaret Cavendish's Poems and Fancies: A Digital Critical Edition* (2019), University of Toronto, http://library2.utm.utoronto.ca/poemsandfancies/, accessed 2 June 2020; Cavendish has a significant and sophisticated general online presence through the website *Digital Cavendish* (2015), The International Margaret Cavendish Society, http://digitalcavendish.org, accessed 2 June 2020; Liza Blake also has planned a much more adventurous 'edition' of Cavendish's poetry which will allow the user to plot different paths through the texts in a kind of choose-your-own-adventure format, see http://electric.press/books/cavendish.html.

[60] For important reflections on the idea of an archive in relation to early modern literature and the digital turn, see Alan Galey, *The Shakespearean Archive: Experiments in New Media from the Renaissance to Postmodernity* (Cambridge, 2014).

[61] *EMWRN: Material Cultures of Early Modern Women's Writing Digital Archive (2017–20)*, https://c21ch.newcastle.edu.au/emwrn/digitalarchive, accessed 2 June 2020; Alison Wiggins (leader), *Bess of Hardwick's Letters* (2013), University of Glasgow, https://www.bessofhardwick.org, accessed 2 June 2020.

FURTHER READING

Clarke, Danielle. 'Nostalgia, Anachronism, and the Editing of Early Modern Women's Texts'. *Text*, 15 (2003), 187–209.

Eardley, Alice. 'Recreating the Canon: Women Writers and Anthologies of Early Modern Verse'. *Women's Writing*, 14 (2007), 270–89.

Ezell, Margaret J. M. 'Editing Early Modern Women's Manuscripts: Theory, Electronic Editions, and the Accidental Copy-Text'. *Literature Compass*, 7 (2010), 102–9.

Flanders, Julia. 'Gender and the Electronic Text', in Kathryn Sutherland (ed.), *Electronic Text: Investigations in Method and Theory*. Oxford, 1997, 127–43.

Wright, Gillian. *Producing Women's Poetry, 1600–1730: Text and Paratext, Manuscript and Print*. Cambridge, 2013.

Ross, Sarah C. E. and Paul Salzman (eds). *Editing Early Modern Women*. Cambridge, 2016.

CHAPTER 43

RECEPTION, REPUTATION, AND AFTERLIVES

MARIE-LOUISE COOLAHAN

WHICH early modern female authors were read, and how? How did early modern women achieve reputations as writers in the early modern period? This chapter outlines theoretical and methodological developments at the intersection of reception studies and early modern women's writing, exploring the what and how of reception as a research practice and proposing future directions. Its focal example is the *RECIRC* project, which aimed to produce a large-scale quantitative analysis of the reception and circulation (the key terms of the acronym) of women's writing from 1550 to 1700, and offers an explicit nexus between reception studies and early modern women's writing.[1] These questions reflect a shift from the theorisation of the reader pursued by reader-response criticism to the historicisation of readers that has been the focus of the history of reading. Where reader-response criticism sought to pinpoint and categorise universal models for the reader (such as Wolfgang Iser's 'implied' versus 'actual' reader), early modernists working in the field have built upon Jardine and Grafton's seminal study of male scholarly reading, and developed a more materialist approach that uncovers how 'imagined actual readers' and 'less extraordinary readers' went about the act of reading in the period.[2] This approach has dovetailed with a renewed focus on the textuality and orality of reading, advocated by Jennifer Richards and Fred Schurink.[3] As book history

[1] 'Home', *RECIRC: The Reception and Circulation of Early Modern Women's Writing, 1550—1700*, National University of Ireland Galway, https://recirc.nuigalway.ie/, accessed 21 December 2020.

[2] Wolfgang Iser, *The Act of Reading: A Theory of Aesthetic Response* (Baltimore, MD, 1978); Lisa Jardine and Anthony Grafton, '"Studied for Action": How Gabriel Harvey Read His Livy', *Past and Present*, 129 (1990), 30–78; William H. Sherman, *Used Books: Marking Readers in Renaissance England* (Philadelphia, PA, 2008), 100; Heidi Brayman Hackel, *Reading Material in Early Modern England: Print, Gender, and Literacy* (Cambridge, 2005), 3, 8.

[3] Jennifer Richards and Fred Schurink, 'Introduction: The Textuality and Materiality of Reading in Early Modern England', *Huntington Library Quarterly*, 73 (2010), 345–61, 348. For a survey of the field, see Edith Snook, 'Recent Studies in Early Modern Reading', *English Literary Renaissance*, 43 (2013), 343–78.

has turned to the history of reading and feminist recovery research to questions of impact, scholars have combined the two to investigate the contemporary and posthumous effects of women who read and wrote in the sixteenth and seventeenth centuries. This productive intersection of disciplines and interests has tended to focus more on the history of women as readers than on how women writers were read. This was a necessary corrective to early modern histories of reading that had prioritised learned male readers; as Heidi Brayman Hackel and Catherine Kelly wrote in 2008, 'the field of women's reading is comparatively undeveloped for the periods before 1800'—a deficiency that has been considerably remedied since. In summary, scholarship on women's reading has pursued four main trajectories: prescriptions about female readers; direct addresses to women as patrons and readers; literary representations of women reading; and the archival, material history of women as readers.[4]

DEFINITIONS

The history of how women writers were read is distinct from the history of women as readers, although they are not mutually exclusive; we might, for example, be interested in the overlapping space where women are reading women. Indeed, reading—though central—is not the whole picture of the afterlives of female-authored texts. Reception captures all forms of impact, including and beyond reading. It involves a range of different agents. It is recorded in multiple sources, the genres of which shape the mode of reception. That reception studies has gained multidisciplinary currency is evidenced by Ika Willis' *Reception* (2018, 'The New Critical Idiom' series); two consecutive issues of *PMLA* on 'Cultures of Reading' (2018, 2019); and the flourishing of the *Classical Receptions Journal*, founded in 2009. Willis' identification of reception's agents and forms testifies to its breadth, insisting on its plurality by embracing a transhistorical perspective: 'Reception involves looking at texts from the point of view of the readers, viewers, listeners, spectators and audiences who read, watch or listen to cultural productions, interpret them, and respond to them in a myriad of different ways'.[5] This capacious reach is also found in historically focused projects such as the *Reading Experience Database* (*RED*), which defines a 'reading experience' as 'a recorded engagement with a written or

[4] Heidi Brayman Hackel and Catherine E. Kelly, 'Introduction', in *Reading Women: Literacy, Authorship, and Culture in the Atlantic World, 1500–1800* (Philadelphia, PA, 2008), 2, and *passim*. For this range of scholarship, see also: Edith Snook, *Women, Reading, and the Cultural Politics of Early Modern England* (Abingdon, 2005); Sasha Roberts, *Reading Shakespeare's Poems in Early Modern England* (Basingstoke, 2003), 20–61, 179–90; Brayman Hackel, *Reading Materials*, 196–255; Sherman, *Used Books*, 53–67; Leah Knight, Micheline White, and Elizabeth Sauer (eds), *Women's Bookscapes in Early Modern Britain: Reading, Ownership, Circulation* (Ann Arbor, MI, 2018).

[5] Ika Willis, *Reception* (Abingdon, 2018), 1.

printed text—beyond the mere fact of possession'.[6] The *RED*, founded in 2006, sought to capture as wide a range as possible of the evidence of reading in Britain between 1450 and 1945, encouraging the general public to contribute with the research team based at the Open University. Their exclusion of book ownership on its own frames reception as an evaluative engagement with an artistic work, and reflects their concern with reading, in particular. *RECIRC*, on the other hand, cast its net more widely to define reception as 'a record of engagement with a female author and/or her work'.[7] Here, the delimiting factors are the historical period and feminist focus, permitting wider scope in relation to the shape that engagement might take.

AGENTS OF RECEPTION

Willis' accommodation of literature, theatre, visual art, and digital forms extends the act of reception to hearing and seeing as well as reading. 'Receiver', then, is a useful catch-all designation for the agent of reception in its broadest sense; it reaches beyond reading to include all activities of reception and does not pre-empt the kinds of receiver or reception that may emerge. The agents of reception may be defined according to the kind of artistic work they encounter; the roles they play (critic, scholar, present audience member, later reader); situations (individually, in groups, at home, outdoors); or the media (screen, theatre, book, computer) through which they encounter it. The *RED*'s focus on reading experiences produced three categories of receiver: readers, listeners, and reading groups (with subcategories allowing for refinement according to gender, age, socio-economic group, occupation, religion, and country of origin). Categories of reading situation include time of day, century, country, and provenance.[8] However, the agency involved is quickly refined as researchers delve into sources and categories of reception.

SOURCES OF RECEPTION

Where is evidence of reception, particularly with regard to women writers, sought? With its aim to capture reading experiences from the fifteenth through to twentieth centuries, the *RED* urged contributors to:

[6] 'Frequently Asked Questions', *UK RED: Reading Experience Database*, Open University, https://www.open.ac.uk/Arts/reading/UK/faq.php, accessed 30 October 2020.

[7] 'About the Data', *RECIRC: The Reception and Circulation of Early Modern Women's Writing, 1550–1700*, National University of Ireland Galway, https://recirc.nuigalway.ie/about-data/data, accessed 15 November 2020.

[8] 'Search', *UK RED: Reading Experience Database*, Open University, https://www.open.ac.uk/Arts/reading/UK/search.php, accessed 11 November 2020.

> gather evidence of all sorts of reading, not only books but also newspapers, journals, posters, advertisements, magazines, letters, scripts, playbills, tickets, chapbooks and almanacs. We include the compilation of Books of Hours, commonplace books, etc. and the experience of reading aloud.[9]

For scholars of early modern reception, sources such as letters, chapbooks, almanacs, manuscripts, and commonplace books are equally important, as is any commentary or material trace of having been used. Such diverse sources are particularly important for the reception of early modern women, whose writings were more often circulated via manuscript culture and who wrote in genres far more varied than the literary trinity of poetry, drama, and fiction. Printed books bearing the marks of use—signatures, comments and annotations, manicules and underlinings, substitutions and emendments, doodles and drawings, for example—are treasure troves for reception researchers. The very prolixity of such sources means setting up boundaries and parameters, typically via author or work. For example, the studies of marginalia in print copies of Philip Sidney's *Arcadia* and George Herbert's *The Temple*; or Sherman's use of the Huntington Library's collection as the perimeter for his survey of 'used books'.[10] Taking manuscript evidence into account opens up the range of a single author's reception as, for example, in Sasha Roberts' study of the early readers of Shakespeare's poetry.[11] Scholars of early modern women have focused on individual receivers as building blocks towards understanding how women experienced and engaged with others' writing: the reader (e.g., Margaret Cavendish), annotator (e.g., Anne Clifford), book owner (e.g., Frances Wolfreston).[12]

The kinds of reception found are determined, to an important extent, by where researchers look. The *RECIRC* project, for example, which aimed to produce a quantitative picture of how women were received in the early modern period, sought large-scale sources in which, we hypothesised, we were most likely to find evidence of the transnational writings of women: in Catholic religious orders, in scientific correspondence networks, in manuscript culture, and in relation to book ownership. Thus, the project was divided into four work packages, corresponding to different categories of source: martyrologies and bibliographies; letters; manuscript miscellanies; and booklists and inventories. The first three of these were located in nominated collections where, again, we anticipated that large amounts of material would be found: convent archives, the Hartlib Papers archive, and four libraries with major early modern manuscript collections.[13] The evidence of reception we found, then, was the product of a targeted

[9] 'Frequently Asked Questions', n.p.

[10] Brayman Hackel, *Reading Materials*, 137–95; Joel Swann, '"In the hands and hearts of all true Christians": Herbert's *The Temple* (1633–1709) and Its Readers', *Journal of Medieval and Early Modern Studies*, 50 (2020), 115–37; Sherman, *Used Books*.

[11] Roberts, *Reading Shakespeare's Poems*.

[12] Julie Crawford, 'Margaret Cavendish's Books', in Knight, White, and Sauer (eds), *Women's Bookscapes*, 94–114; Stephen Orgel, *The Reader in the Book: A Study of Spaces and Traces* (Oxford, 2015), 138–57; Sarah Lindenbaum, 'Hiding in Plain Sight: How Electronic Records Can Lead Us to Early Modern Women Readers', in Knight, White, and Sauer (eds), *Women's Bookscapes*, 193–213.

[13] See 'About the Data', n.p.

set of decisions devised in relation to source material. Exclusions as well as inclusions shape our findings. For example, single-author manuscript collections, such as the 'Rosania' manuscript of poems and drama by Katherine Philips, are omitted from our calculations despite their rich evidence of the seriousness with which readers engaged with a woman's work because they are not miscellanies. Substantial collections held in other libraries and archives were not audited for pragmatic logistical reasons, meaning our results are not comprehensive but indicative. As Julia Flanders argues in Chapter 44 of this volume, transparency is therefore a crucial component of digital humanities and quantitative projects.

What researchers find is also determined by the laws of attrition and the privileges of literacy. It is likely that the most popular printed books were 'read to death', as Orgel notes; 'the higher the survival rate of any particular title, the less likely it is that the book got much use'.[14] Moreover, book ownership itself was a sign of economic comfort and education. As Brayman Hackel advises, 'Any examination of handwritten marginalia for clues about early modern reading, therefore, is inherently limited to a narrow group of readers, those with sufficient means to own substantial books and educated enough to be able to write in them'.[15] Women who enjoyed access to books may not have left marks in those they did not own. Jane Lumley is a case in point: the Lumley family library comprised 2,609 books by 1609 but the translator of Euripides into English wrote her name on only seven of the books in that collection.[16] Certainly, the evidence we find will never be wholly representative. Self-selection is always at play: we discover those who were moved to engage, not those who remained indifferent. But ultimately, the same goes for recovery research per se. What is lost to the historical record is tantalising to the recovery researcher, but in some cases, an account of its reception may be the best evidence for its having existed at all.[17] Moreover, reading literacy entailed a different skillset to writing literacy.[18] Accounts of reading communally—as for example, Hoby's accounts of household reading or convent readings of sacred texts—remind us that reading was not the preserve of an elite.[19] The documentary record may veer away from the lower social orders but it does not preclude their engagement.

[14] Orgel, *Reader in the Book*, 19.

[15] Brayman Hackel, *Reading Materials*, 141.

[16] Sears Jayne and Francis R. Johnson (eds), *The Lumley Library: The Catalogue of 1609* (London, 1956), 48, 60, 131, 149, 170, 198, 225. See also Marie-Louise Coolahan and Mark Empey, 'Women's Book Ownership and the Reception of Early Modern Women's Texts, 1545–1700', in Knight, White, and Sauer (eds), *Women's Bookscapes*, 231–52; Marie-Louise Coolahan, '"My lady's books": Devising a Toolkit for Quantitative Research; or, What Is a Book and How Do We Count it?', *Huntington Library Quarterly*, 84.1 (2021), 125–37; and Chapter 35 in this volume, Sebastiaan Verweij, 'Elizabeth Melville: Protestant Poetics, Publication, and Propaganda'.

[17] Marie-Louise Coolahan, 'Reception, Reputation, and Early Modern Women's Missing Texts', *Critical Quarterly*, 55 (2013), 3–14.

[18] Margaret W. Ferguson and Mihoko Suzuki, 'Women's Literacies and Social Hierarchy in Early Modern England', *Literature Compass*, 12 (2015), 575–90.

[19] See Andrew Cambers, 'Readers' Marks and Religious Practice: Margaret Hoby's Marginalia', in John N. King (ed.), *Tudor Books and Readers: Materiality and the Construction of Meaning* (Cambridge, 2010),

TYPES OF RECEPTION

What are these signs of engagement and how might we distinguish types of reception? Whether a single case study or a wide survey, the categories identified must be legible and meaningful within the field, even as they are refined through exposure to primary evidence. For this reason, I would like to share here the experience of the *RECIRC* project, which built a database to facilitate the cataloguing, sharing, and comparison of reception evidence. *RECIRC* devised a taxonomy based on models such as the *RED* and resources like Peter Beal's *Dictionary of Manuscript Terminology*. Initially intended for researchers based at different archives to pool their data, the first list imagined all possible types of reception we might find. This original version identified thirty-four types of reception (I omit here the shorter list of types of circulation): adaptation, annotation, answer, citation, dedication, diagram, drama, drawing, embroidery, equation, excerpt, extended commentary, funeral sermon, horoscope, imitation, marginalia, music-setting, obituary, paraphrase, performance, poem, portrait, print edition, reading, reading aloud alone, reading aloud in company, reading silently alone, reading silently in company, reference to named author, reference to specific work, reference to unspecified work(s), summary, transcription, and translation. Minimisation of subjective interpretation at the data-gathering phase was a primary rationale. For example, the basic category 'poem' was used to designate all kinds of verse about, or referring to, a woman writer. This liberated researchers from adjudicating poetic genres in the archive. However, all funded projects come to a definitive conclusion, and the public version of the database reflects the evidence we found, as opposed to what we had hoped or expected to find. The categories for which we found no evidence—diagram, embroidery, equation, horoscope, imitation, reading aloud alone, reading silently alone, reading silently in company—are supplied here as flags for future researchers.[20] On the same basis, I include three categories that I wish we had employed: prayer, legal document, and context reference (the deployment of a woman writer's name for a contextual purpose such as year-date, e.g., the specific year of Queen Elizabeth's reign). These emerged as major categories captured within 'extended commentary' and 'reference to named author', but only at a later stage. The discrepancy opens up in a very blunt way the distinction between theory and practice; we hypothesised that thirty-four types of reception would be found, a theory that was adjusted when tested (although our actual findings do not exhaust all possibilities). Contingency, of course, is a necessary precondition for classification. As Julia Flanders argues in this volume, this 'requires careful attention' to the 'natural heuristics of classification and differentiation'.[21]

212–18; Caroline Bowden, 'English Reading Communities in Exile: Introducing Cloistered Nuns to Their Books', in Knight, White, and Sauer (eds), *Women's Bookscapes*, 171–89.

[20] For definitions of these terms, see 'About the Data', n.p.

[21] See this volume, Chapter 44, Julia Flanders, '"A Telescope for the Mind": Digital Modelling and Analysis of Early Modern Women's Writing'; and see also Susan Brown, 'Categorically Provisional', *Publications of the Modern Language Association of America*, 135 (2020), 165–74.

If the recovery of reception evidence requires identification and classification of what it is we are trying to recover, the interpretation of that material generates further patterns. Brayman Hackel has proposed three categories in relation to book marginalia: marks of active reading, of ownership, and of record. She argues that these correspond to three distinct roles for the book: 'as intellectual process, as valued object, and as available paper'.[22] Orgel adverts to 'a whole other class of markings that are ubiquitous ... seemingly irrelevant markings'.[23] How might we group together the twenty-six types of reception located by the *RECIRC* team? Pursuing a broad remit to investigate what these traces can tell us about reception of an author and/or her work (rather than about the printed book), *RECIRC*'s categories embrace literary engagement (adaptation, answer, citation, extended commentary, paraphrase, reading, reading aloud in company, summary), material use (annotation, marginalia, print edition, transcription), creative reuse (adaptation, dedication, drama, excerpt, music-setting, performance, poem, portrait, translation), and reputational engagement (funeral sermon, obituary, reference to named author, reference to specific work, reference to unspecified work). These categories may overlap. For example, Katherine Philips' comments on having read 'Elégie sur une jalousie' by Henriette de Coligny, comtesse de La Suze, are tagged as 'extended commentary', 'reference to named author', and 'reference to specific work'.[24] Crucially, this grouping into four categories is the product of the present discussion; users may sort and analyse *RECIRC* categories as they see fit. Those interested in the reader as editor, for example, might drill down into the quality of marginalia or annotations (as well as consult the taxonomy of annotations devised by the *Archaeology of Reading* project).[25] Similarly, a researcher interested in poetic receptions of a woman writer or her work might gather all instances classed as poems in order to disentangle elegies from epithalamia. The student of literary influence might collate citation with dedication, performance, and the various forms of reference. Interpretative judgement is deferred to the user, both a pragmatic way to process quantities of material in the archive and (hopefully) a means of building in flexibility for other users and interpreters. A different approach again might stratify according to evaluative judgement, as exemplified by *Women Writers in Review*, a digitised collection of literary reviews, from 1770 to 1830, of women's writing. Here, reviews are classified on a spectrum from 'very positive' to 'very negative', a structure that supports the visualisation of

[22] Brayman Hackel, *Reading Materials*, 138.

[23] Orgel, *Reader in the Book*, 4. However, see the Voltaire Foundation parsing of the meanings of Voltaire's marginalia in Gillian Pink and Dan Barker, 'Digitising the Margins: A Classification of Voltaire's Squiggles', *Voltaire Foundation*, University of Oxford, 12 November 2020, https://voltairefoundation.wordpress.com/2020/11/12/digitising-the-margins-a-classification-of-voltaires-scribbles/, accessed 30 April 2022.

[24] 'Reception ID #4666', *RECIRC: The Reception and Circulation of Early Modern Women's Writing, 1550—1700*, National University of Ireland Galway, https://recirc.nuigalway.ie/receptions/reception/4666, accessed 16 November 2020.

[25] *The Archaeology of Reading* (2019), The Sheridan Libraries–Johns Hopkins University, Centre for Editing Lives and Letters–UCL, Princeton University Library, and The Andrew W. Mellon Foundation, https://archaeologyofreading.org/, accessed 16 November 2020.

reception in colour (green/positive; red/negative) across a timeline running from 1700 to 1840.[26] With a predetermined genre parameter (literary review), the user's interpretation is directed towards the quality of reception.

ROLES AND MODES OF ENGAGEMENT

The grouping of categories can illuminate the receiver's relationship with the author or work being received, as well as with the book or source in which the reception is recorded. But the distinction between the specific instance of reception and the source in which it occurs also disentangles the layers of responsibility involved. The receiver bifurcates into the person responsible for the specific act of reception and the person responsible for the source in which it is recorded. Both roles might coalesce in a heavily annotated book belonging to a single owner whose hand is responsible for all marginalia therein. But where multiple hands occur—as, for example, in Anne Clifford's copy of John Selden's *Titles of Honor*, which bears her own and her secretary's hand—the layers of responsibility multiply.[27] Where the source is a manuscript miscellany inscribed by various hands and owners, in which many individual items attest to the reception of women writers, levels of responsibility are further complicated. The difference between a large-scale source, such as a martyrology or manuscript miscellany, and the specific item of reception evidence that occurs within it, led *RECIRC* to distinguish the micro from the macro in terms of (receiver) responsibility. For example, William Browne's elegy on Mary Sidney, 'Underneath this sable hearse', is an instance of poetic reception authored by Browne, copied into the miscellany of Richard Boyle, Earl of Burlington. In order to distinguish the levels of responsibility, *RECIRC* separates roles according to scale: those responsible for the large-scale source are labelled 'owner/compiler/scribe' (Boyle, in this case), as opposed to those responsible for the individual items of reception evidence, labelled 'receiver' (Browne).[28] The type of reception further nuances the receiver, who could be an annotator, translator, performer, painter, or writer—categories that contain as well as refine the paradigmatic 'reader'. The roles of the agent of reception may overlap; they may be momentary rather than consistent practices over time. Hence, they are shifting rather than definitive of the receiver and they reflect her/his agency and agenda. These latter issues of motivation inflect the reception of any woman writer; why is she being read or engaged with?

[26] *Women Writers in Review, Northeastern University Women Writers Project*, Northeastern University, https://wwp.northeastern.edu/review/, accessed 12 November 2020.

[27] See Georgianna Ziegler, 'Lady Anne Clifford Reads John Selden', in Katherine Acheson (ed.), *Early Modern English Marginalia* (Abingdon, 2019), 134–54.

[28] 'Reception ID #1183', *RECIRC: The Reception and Circulation of Early Modern Women's Writing, 1550—1700*, National University of Ireland Galway, https://recirc.nuigalway.ie/receptions/reception/1183, accessed 16 November 2020.

The dominant model for understanding a reader's agenda—what the reader is reading for—has been the utilitarian, 'for action', prototype first established by Jardine and Grafton. Grounded in the humanist reading of Gabriel Harvey, this understanding of the reader's approach to the text is ensconced in humanist education and, therefore, leans towards learned men.[29] As scholars have excavated the world of women readers, this model has been extended—most notably, perhaps, in Julie Crawford's analysis of Margaret Hoby's reading as 'goal-directed', which argues that her diary is 'best understood as a record of a public career, and her reading as a form of political activism'.[30] This template reflects the reading practices of those who annotate and comment upon the textual content. But there are alternative models that better describe other reception practices. The transcription of a text is a function of the conservationist impulse, the urge to preserve it. Its compilation in a manuscript, juxtaposed with other cognate texts, might serve a memorialising purpose. The compiler of British Library Add MS 29921, for example, placed together three elegies on Queen Elizabeth's death.[31] Indeed, it might do both at the same time, as in Elizabeth Lucy's biography of her mother-in-law, Constance Lucy, followed by an account of Elizabeth written by her daughter (Constance's granddaughter), Martha Eyre.[32] Annotations can also be performative, as Micheline White has argued of Katherine Parr's practice. Self-fashioning and an awareness of the wider courtly audience inform her method, White argues: 'Parr's signature can be read as a visible marker that announces her commitment to humanist ideals and that identifies her as part of a community of cutting-edge, forward-thinking, reformist readers'.[33] A similar principle of monarchical self-construction is detected by Rosalind Smith, whose discussion of Mary Stuart's marginalia in her manuscript Book of Hours identifies its rippling impact: 'its circulation among her peers as a tool of alliance or remembrance and its use as the means of disseminating her secular poetry, means that it could never be an apolitical, private and domestic text'.[34] The strata of reception pile up: Parr and Stuart are

[29] For a critique of this model, see Richards and Schurink, 'Textuality and Materiality', 351–2.

[30] Julie Crawford, *Mediatrix: Women, Politics, and Literary Production in Early Modern England* (Oxford, 2014), 86–120.

[31] London, British Library, Add MS 29921, fol. 38r; 'Reception ID ##436–438', *RECIRC: The Reception and Circulation of Early Modern Women's Writing, 1550—1700*, National University of Ireland Galway, https://recirc.nuigalway.ie/receptions/reception/436-438, accessed 16 November 2020.

[32] Washington, DC, Folger Shakespeare Library, MS V.a.166; 'Reception ID #1390' and 'Reception ID #1392', *RECIRC: The Reception and Circulation of Early Modern Women's Writing, 1550—1700*, National University of Ireland Galway, https://recirc.nuigalway.ie/receptions/reception/1390 and https://recirc.nuigalway.ie/receptions/reception/1392, accessed 16 November 2020. See also Cambridge, MA, Houghton Library, Harvard University, MS Eng 729, and Alan Stewart, *The Oxford History of Life Writing: Volume 2: Early Modern* (Oxford, 2018), 188–98.

[33] Micheline White, 'Katherine Parr's Marginalia: Putting the Wisdom of Chrysostom and Solomon into Practice', in Knight, White, and Sauer (eds), *Women's Bookscapes*, 21–42, 26. See also Jason Scott-Warren, 'Reading Graffiti in the Early Modern Book', *Huntington Library Quarterly*, 73 (2010), 363–81, for the annotated page as a site for public performance.

[34] Rosalind Smith, '"Le pouvoir de faire dire": Marginalia in Mary Queen of Scots' Book of Hours', in Patricia Pender and Rosalind Smith (eds), *Material Cultures of Early Modern Women's Writing* (Basingstoke, 2014), 55–75, 60.

monarchs receiving devotional texts, but their marginalia (their reception of the texts) signal religio-political affiliations, acts of self-definition performed in full knowledge that their marginalia enjoyed an audience of courtier reader-receivers.

The level of agency and self-awareness inherent in the act of reception alerts us to its immersion in the generation of writing—reception as creative practice. Reading stimulates writing; reception becomes production. Both Roberts and Orgel highlight the reader's insertion of the self into the text, echoing each other: readers who 'copied, corrected, commonplaced, applied, annotated, emended, reformatted, reworked and responded to Shakespeare's poems made them their own'; 'you made yourself part of your book'.[35] This transmutation of the text into an artefact of the self derives from the reader's own sense of agency and picks up on the perception of marginalia as a form of life-writing.[36] But the receiver is not confined to self-articulation. If the receiver can be an annotator, translator, performer, painter, or writer, as outlined above, the act of reception is also an act of creating something new beyond the self. The cause-and-effect relationship between reception and creative practice was embedded in early modern education systems. Brayman Hackel identifies this as a key concern underpinning anxieties about women as readers, in particular relation to women's authorship of genres such as translation: 'For a period in which reading was so often figured as the first stage of writing, an understanding of the habits of reading illuminates the production as well as the reception of texts'.[37] The creative potential inherent in reception is also remarked by Acheson:

> Far from being derivative and dependent, then, marginalia ... are innovative and opportunistic, opening up the possibility of further transformation of the materials of writing and reading into acts of communication, works of literature, and interventions in the world of learning.[38]

The internationalist, multilingual frame informing these observations points us to the important role played by reception in building and consolidating transnational reputation. Translations of the autobiography of Teresa de Ávila serve as just one example; other trajectories are suggested by instances such as Anna Maria van Schurmann's epistolary reference to having heard about Dorothy Moore or the various accounts of Italian women poets in English bio-bibliographies.[39]

[35] Roberts, *Reading Shakespeare's Poems*, 8; Orgel, *Reader in the Book*, 56.

[36] For marginalia as life-writing, see Adam Smyth, *Autobiography in Early Modern England* (Cambridge, 2010), and Acheson, *English Marginalia*, 6–9.

[37] Brayman Hackel, *Reading Materials*, 55.

[38] Acheson, *English Marginalia*, 9.

[39] Danielle Clarke, 'Life Writing for the Counter-Reformation: The English Translation and Reception of Teresa de Ávila's Autobiography', *Journal of Medieval and Early Modern Studies*, 50 (2020), 75–94; Lynette Hunter (ed.), *The Letters of Dorothy Moore, 1612–64: The Friendships, Marriage and Intellectual Life of a Seventeenth-Century Woman* (Aldershot, 2004), 1; Bathsua Makin, *An Essay to Revive the Antient Education of Gentlewomen* (London, 1673), 20; or Charles Gildon, *The History of the Athenian Society* (London, 1692), 27, respectively. See also Julie D. Campbell and Anne R. Larsen (eds), *Early Modern Women and Transnational Communities of Letters* (Farnham, 2009).

CASE STUDY: KATHERINE PHILIPS

Katherine Philips, who was read in France and who read French women writers (see this volume, Chapter 29, Line Cottegnies, 'French Connections: English Women's Writing and *Préciosité*'), is illustrative of this range of approaches to assessing reception. As a writer careful to circulate her work in manuscript during her early career, Philips successfully built a reputation so that, by the time of reaching wider audiences, her forays into print publication were, if not uncontroversial, easily defended by her advocates and admirers. Philips' reputation has benefited enormously from the flourishing of manuscript studies in the early 1990s. Two landmark articles by Elizabeth Hageman and Andrea Sununu led the way for subsequent scholars, in the process showing how intertwined are reception and recovery research. Tracking down musical settings, manuscript compilations, and excerpts of her work, Hageman and Sununu's wide-reaching reappraisals of the archive simultaneously opened up new contexts for understanding how Philips was read and recycled by seventeenth-century readers.[40] Philips' own framing, courting, and assaying of her readership—most fully described by Gillian Wright—exhibits a canny manipulation of medium and audience to establish her own reputation, a poised anticipation of her readers that ensured her longevity as a model for later women writers.[41] The posthumous print edition, *Poems* (1667), was an immediate editorial intervention to frame her reception—an observation that supports Paul Salzman's treatment of early modern transmission as a form of editing, in Chapter 42 of this volume. *Poems* (1667) also facilitated the reabsorption of Philips' writing back into manuscript culture, as miscellany compilers selected passages from print, applying them to their own uses.[42] Scholars have tracked how Philips' poems were excerpted, appropriated, and reworked in manuscript, from Katherine Butler and Sarah Cowper's formally engaged appropriations of her poems in their commonplace books to Robert Overton's wholesale redeployment of her elegiac royalism to the service of Parliamentarian melancholy.[43] Hageman's study of over a hundred print editions of Philips encompasses ownership inscriptions and signatures, biographical information

[40] Elizabeth Hageman and Andrea Sununu, 'New Manuscript Texts of Katherine Philips, The "Matchless Orinda"', *English Manuscript Studies 1100–1700*, 4 (1993), 174–219; '"More Copies of it abroad than I could have imagin'd": Further Manuscript Texts of Katherine Philips, the Matchless Orinda', *English Manuscript Studies 1100–1700*, 5 (1995), 127–69.

[41] Gillian Wright, *Producing Women's Poetry, 1600–1730: Text and Paratext, Manuscript and Print* (Cambridge, 2013), 97–145.

[42] See Marie-Louise Coolahan, 'Single-Author Manuscripts, *Poems* (1664), and the Editing of Katherine Philips', in Sarah C. E. Ross and Paul Salzman (eds), *Editing Early Modern Women* (Cambridge, 2016), 176–94.

[43] Victoria E. Burke, 'The Couplet and the Poem: Late Seventeenth-Century Women Reading Katherine Philips', *Women's Writing*, 24 (2017), 280–97; David Norbrook, '"This Blushing Tribute of a Borrowed Muse": Robert Overton's Overturning of the Seventeenth-Century Poetic Canon', *English Manuscript Studies 1100–1700*, 4 (1993), 220–66.

and identification of pseudonyms, corrections, and symbols.[44] The ebbs and flows of an author's place in literary history are equally a matter of reception. Recent work on the recovery and representation of Philips for an early twentieth-century audience has placed her reception at that time as setting the tone for later scholarship and recuperated in turn the career of Louise Guiney.[45]

LITERARY HISTORY AS RECEPTION

To ask when women writers were read is to open up the *longue durée*, to think about afterlives and the conditions for longevity. Reception history is not only a matter for the woman writer's contemporaries, it extends to our critical work today as well as that of the centuries inbetween—and these latter dimensions are equally part of reception studies. Paul Salzman's insights on nineteenth-century editing as 'curated transmission', and editorial activity as 'curatorial, but also an intervention in the contemporary literary scene', are useful in this regard.[46] Salzman has argued that feminist critics have been too ready to dismiss the work of earlier generations; that, in reacting against immediately preceding critics, we overlook 'the life this writing had in the seventeenth, eighteenth, and nineteenth centuries'.[47] To look beyond the generation we are reacting against is to understand the vagaries and fashions of reception, and to historicise literary history as reception. Literary history is fundamentally about reception. It shapes and revises notions of literary value, presenting contexts for our understanding of literary texts. The literary historian shapes and determines the reception of an author and her works—or consigns them to history (for a time). Literary history is invested in framing reception for its audience, perennially open to revision and contestation.

Few early modern women writers have benefited from the *longue durée* perspective advocated by Salzman. The fullest picture we have is that for Aphra Behn, largely due to her status at the vanguard of professional women's writing, having earned her living

[44] Elizabeth H. Hageman, 'Afterword: The Most Deservedly Admired Mrs. Katherine Philips—Her Books', in David L. Orvis and Ryan Singh Paul (eds), *The Noble Flame of Katherine Philips: A Poetics of Culture, Politics, and Friendship* (Pittsburgh, PA, 2015), 311–24, 319–24.

[45] Andrea Sununu, '"I Long to Know Your Opinion of It": The Serendipity of a Malfunctioning Timing Belt or the Guiney-Tutin Collaboration in the Recovery of Katherine Philips', *Women's Writing*, 24 (2017), 258–79, repr. in Marie-Louise Coolahan and Gillian Wright (eds), *Katherine Philips: Form, Reception, and Literary Contexts* (New York, 2018), 129–50; Kate Lilley, 'When Sapphos Meet: Louise Imogen Guiney and Katherine Philips' *Selected Poems* (1904)', *Women's Writing*, 26 (2019), 106–24.

[46] Paul Salzman, *Editors Construct the Renaissance Canon, 1825–1915* (Basingstoke, 2018), 5; 'How Alexander Dyce Assembled *Specimens of British Poetesses*: A Key Moment in the Transmission of Early Modern Women's Writing', *Women's Writing*, 26 (2019), 88–105, 89. See also Margaret J. M. Ezell, *Writing Women's Literary History* (Baltimore, MD, 1993), and Melanie Bigold, '"Bookmaking Out of the Remains of the Dead": George Ballard's *Memoirs of Several Ladies* (1752)', *Eighteenth-Century Life*, 38 (2014), 28–46.

[47] Paul Salzman, *Reading Early Modern Women's Writing* (Oxford, 2006), 219.

by it. Jane Spencer's forensic account of her reception through the eighteenth century is equally a historical study of literary taste and genre. As the novel became increasingly associated with moral rectitude and Behn with the erotic, her fiction fell out of favour. The exception was *Oroonoko*, first adapted for the stage by Thomas Southerne in 1695 and regularly performed through the eighteenth century. Southerne's version pitched the narrative towards sentimentality and mixed-race romance, making the character of Imoinda racially white. In its various literary manifestations, the story came to play an influential part for the abolitionist movement. The earliest posthumous editions fleshed out Behn's biography, shifting her reputation 'from Behn the witty author to Behn the amorous adventuress', and the narrator's claims to autobiographical truth in *Oroonoko* grounded the place of biography within her critical reception.[48] As tastes in poetry shifted, Behn's verse fell out of favour; 'generally seen as un-feminine' by the 1840s. The pendulum swings, however, and Salzman pinpoints Montague Summers' 1915 edition as the moment of transition when 'Behn's reputation for moral laxity became, at least for some groups of people, a drawcard rather than a drawback'.[49]

By contrast, Katherine Jones, Viscountess Ranelagh, offers an example of a woman fêted as an intellectual in her own day, but whose reputation fell into abeyance until very recently. Acclaimed by Gilbert Burnet as 'the greatest Figure in all the Revolutions of these Kingdoms for above fifty Years, of any Woman of our Age … with a vast Reach both of Knowledg and Apprehensions', Ranelagh was a different kind of woman writer, a political activist and patron, centrally involved in Samuel Hartlib's correspondence network.[50] Author of letters and an alchemical treatise, collector of medical recipes, her surviving works are dispersed and operate outside the genres traditionally valued as literary. Thus, the trajectory of her reputation in history might be expected to diverge from that of Behn or Philips yet it illuminates the ease with which reputation declines without a champion. Divorced from any evidence of her writing, Ranelagh's reputation held on as she dropped from the view of literary historians. George Ballard lamented his inability to secure archival evidence of her achievements, including her in a list of women he had hoped to include in *Memoirs of Several Ladies of Great Britain* (1752):

> there are others, whom I well know to have been persons of distinguished parts and learning, but have been able to collect very little else relating to them. Such as, Lady Mary Nevil, Lady Anne Southwell … Lady Ranelagh … Mrs æmillia Lanyer, Mrs Makins (who corresponded in the learned languages with Mrs Anna Maria Van Schurman) … together with very many other learned and ingenious women.[51]

[48] Jane Spencer, *Aphra Behn's Afterlife* (Oxford, 2000), 34.

[49] Salzman, *Reading Early Modern Women*, 213, 214.

[50] Gilbert Burnet, *A Sermon Preached at the Funeral of the Honourable Robert Boyle* (London, 1692), 33.

[51] George Ballard, *Memoirs of Several Ladies of Great Britain* (London, 1752), vii.

Michelle DiMeo suggests that there are two dimensions to this. On the one hand, in order to build her impressive reputation in her own time, Ranelagh had to conform with socially prescribed models of womanhood: 'it was her ability to maintain a pious and charitable reputation alongside her bold activism that allowed her to be taken seriously as a female intellectual'. But that conformity entailed disinterest in one's legacy:

> A seventeenth-century woman could often be an active participant in the intellectual culture of her time, but the decision to plan actively for her memorialization through the collation of a personal archive was considered by her contemporaries to be inappropriate.[52]

Her subscription to contemporary ideals, so successful in establishing her reputation among contemporaries—that careful balance of public reputation, piety, and lack of interest in self-curation—means that Ranelagh's letters languished, scattered across the archives of the men with whom she debated. To rely on the vagaries of reception for one's afterlife is a passive and risky business for the early modern woman writer.

CONCLUSION

Reputations come and go. Fields of interest emerge from the pressures and exigencies of our own time, driving us back into the works of history to locate flashpoints, precursors that have undergone, mediated, or represented analogous moments. The first impulse of feminist recovery research—to locate and retrieve for critical discussion the writings of women in history—has allied with fields such as manuscript studies and book history to develop new methodologies for interpreting the works recovered, new modes of evaluating reputations; it is deeply concerned with matters of the afterlife. Moreover, criticism's immersion in and evolution out of its own moment—the search for contemporary resonance among historically produced texts—is reception: the publication of critical work on women's writing, the classroom discussion of women's writing, the production of artistic work inspired by or 'updating' women's writing, all constitute acts of reception in their own right.

To ask which female authors were read, and how, and when, is to wrestle with the literary history of the present as well as the past; to consider how reputations were made in the early modern period and since (and now), to include readers and cultural producers of all kinds as part of the investigation into impact and the conditions for relevance. Reception encompasses a host of critical and responsive activities. If it begins with the acts of reading, seeing, listening, these acts of reception diversify as the response is recorded and classified as annotation, translation, or compilation. The receiver's agency,

[52] Michelle DiMeo, *Lady Ranelagh: The Incomparable Life of Robert Boyle's Sister* (Chicago, IL, 2021), p. 2. I am grateful to Dr DiMeo for allowing me to consult her work while in press.

and agenda, inform how the work is reframed, reused, mediated, and understood. The reception of early modern women's writing contains multiple trajectories, stops and starts, audiences and agents. We are only beginning to track the patterns, models, and reiterative processes by which women writers of the sixteenth and seventeenth centuries were received.[53]

FURTHER READING

Brayman Hackel, Heidi. *Reading Material in Early Modern England: Print, Gender, and Literacy*. Cambridge, 2005.

Coolahan, Marie-Louise (ed.). 'Special Issue: The Cultural Dynamics of Reception'. *Journal of Medieval and Early Modern Studies*, 50.1 (2020).

Knight, Leah, Micheline White, and Elizabeth Sauer (eds). *Women's Bookscapes in Early Modern Britain: Reading, Ownership, Circulation*. Ann Arbor, MI, 2018.

Salzman, Paul (ed.). 'Special Issue: Early Modern Women's Writing and Transmission'. *Women's Writing*, 26.1 (2019).

Snook, Edith. *Women, Reading, and the Cultural Politics of Early Modern England*. Abingdon, 2005.

Willis, Ika. *Reception*. Abingdon, 2018.

[53] Research for this chapter was funded by the European Research Council under the European Union's Seventh Framework Programme (FP/2007-2013 / ERC Grant Agreement n. 615545.

CHAPTER 44

'A TELESCOPE FOR THE MIND'

Digital Modelling and Analysis of Early Modern Women's Writing

JULIA FLANDERS

INTRODUCTION: A CRITICAL APPROPRIATION

DIGITAL tools and methods in the humanities occupy contested ground, concerning the theoretical and practical significance of their entailments as products of the industrial, military, and scientific sectors. Certainly, there are ample examples that bear out early arguments for the recuperative potential of these technologies: some of their first applications in the humanities have been in efforts to recover and study the cultural legacy of marginalised groups, including women's writing. Indeed, some of the earliest digital humanities research projects focused on the recovery of women's writing: the *Women Writers Project*, *Project Orlando*, the *Victorian Women Writers Project*, and the *Perdita* project all date from the early 1990s or before.[1] The initial discourse surrounding digital approaches emphasised the emergent visibility of previously hidden phenomena and entities, offering a neo-Enlightenment epistemology anchored in the assistive powers of the digital tools. As Margaret Masterman described it in a 1962 article in the

[1] See *Women Writers Project*, Northeastern University, https://www.wwp.northeastern.edu, accessed 8 April 2021; Susan Brown, Patricia Clements, and Isobel Grundy (eds), *Orlando: Women's Writing in the British Isles from the Beginnings to the Present*, Cambridge, 2006–2021, http://orlando.cambridge.org, accessed 8 April 2021; *Victorian Women Writers Project*, Indiana University, http://webapp1.dlib.indiana.edu/vwwp/welcome.do, accessed 8 April 2021; and *Perdita*, University of Warwick, http://web.warwick.ac.uk/english/perdita/html/, accessed 8 April 2021.

Times Literary Supplement, the computer was 'a telescope for the mind', and this trope has been a staple of digital humanities imagery in describing the operation and benefits of digital scholarly tools.[2]

This early language of discovery and visibility served early modern women's writing well: it aligned with important research showing that the apparent lack of women's writing in early periods was in important ways an artefact of cataloguing practices, purchasing and retention habits, and self-serving ignorance. The digital archives of women's writing, like those of other marginalised groups, represent a step forward towards a fuller, more accurate, and more accessible record of culture. At the same time, the work of those very projects demonstrates the need to look more closely at the ways in which digital tools themselves can contribute to invisibility and marginalisation. As Safiya Noble has argued in *Algorithms of Oppression*, computational processes are trained on data that carries norms and assumptions that reflect deep-seated social inequities.[3] Similarly, digital standards that enact scholarly norms for describing cultural sources are necessarily reinscribing those norms upon the new digital cultural record. Digital humanities scholars have long understood digital technologies themselves as expressions of cultural knowledge systems. In the mystified interior of our digital infrastructure—metadata standards, tool design, selection practices, digitisation priorities—lies a fresh implementation of the hidden: that which is silenced and rendered structurally invisible through its incommensurability with our tools and descriptive practices.

Our awareness of this risk, and our scepticism of these tools, is crucial for their responsible use in humanities scholarship. The work being done by scholars of the early modern period on the early shaping and solidification of concepts of race, gender, sexuality, and nation also provides important tools for understanding how those concepts are reified in digital infrastructures, and where to look for their restrictive effects.[4] Despite their debt to scientific and progressivist forms of knowledge, digital technologies can also be critically appropriated for work that benefits from the scale and complexity of digital information but without falling prey to its mystifications. For the study of early modern women's writing, there are important technologies and methods, some of which have been established as foundational and others which are emergent, suggesting different analytical and interpretive tactics, and possibly new rhetorics and types of

[2] Margaret Masterman, 'The Intellect's New Eye', in *Freeing the Mind: Articles and Letters from The Times Literary Supplement during March-June, 1962* (London, 1962), 38–44. I am grateful to Willard McCarty for this reference.

[3] Safiya Umoja Noble, *Algorithms of Oppression: How Search Engines Reinforce Racism* (New York, 2018).

[4] For instance: Kim F. Hall, *Things of Darkness: Economies of Race and Gender in Early Modern England* (Ithaca, NY, 1995); Patricia Akhimie, *Shakespeare and the Cultivation of Difference: Race and Conduct in the Early Modern World* (New York, 2018); Jennifer L. Morgan, '"Some Could Suckle over Their Shoulder": Male Travelers, Female Bodies, and the Gendering of Racial Ideology, 1500–1770', *The William and Mary Quarterly*, 54.1, 167–92; and Jacqueline Wernimont, *Numbered Lives: Life and Death in Quantum Media*, Cambridge, MA, 2019.

argumentation. In exploring digital methodologies for early women's writing, therefore, we are both appropriating (somewhat against the grain) tools whose deepest ideological entailments are with global systems of power, and also working within a comparatively long tradition (in the field of digital humanities) of such appropriations, a history that has been directly shaped by the study of early women's writing and other 'peripheral' traditions.

DIGITAL MODELLING AND EDITING OF EARLY MODERN WOMEN'S WRITING

Digital catalogues, collections, and editions—the domain of the 'thematic research collection', as defined by Carole Palmer—constitute an early and still crucial move in establishing the very existence, as well as the legitimacy, of early modern women's writing.[5] Digital projects in the early 1990s, including *Perdita*, the *Women Writers Project*, and *Project Orlando*, established a conjoined research agenda on the digital collection and modelling of women's writing, and also made an authoritative set of contributions to these digital methodologies from the specific perspective of women's texts and their distinctive scholarly requirements.[6] These digital collections offer scholars the traditional practical advantages of discovery but with enhancements that twenty-first-century scholars now take more or less for granted: the ability to find not only a specific item or author, but groups of items and authors that meet certain search criteria, such as date ranges, genres, and document formats. Furthermore, while searches of early digital catalogues were often limited to bibliographic data, the expansion and interconnection of digital resources is now starting to make possible discovery processes that might involve, for instance, searching for items in a certain format, by authors possessing certain biographical traits (e.g., religion or marital status), on certain topics, containing certain combinations of words. The boundaries between the catalogue, the biographical dictionary, and the full-text collection are gradually becoming traversable.

[5] Carole L. Palmer, 'Thematic Research Collections', in Susan Schreibman, Ray Siemens, and John Unsworth (eds), *A Companion to Digital Humanities* (Oxford, 2004). http://digitalhumanities.org:3030/companion, accessed 8 April 2021.

[6] The genre continues into later periods in projects such as the *Victorian Women Writers Project*, Indiana University, http://webapp1.dlib.indiana.edu/vwwp/welcome.do, accessed 8 April 2021; the *British Women Romantic Poets Project*, University of Michigan, https://quod.lib.umich.edu/b/bwrp/, accessed 8 April 2021; *Women's Travel Writing 1830–1930* (originally at the University of Minnesota, now sadly unavailable); and the Digital Schomburg collection of *African American Women Writers of the 19th Century*, New York Public Library, http://digital.nypl.org/schomburg/writers_aa19/, accessed 8 April 2021.

Digital collections tend to offer a progressive narrative that responds to early problems of invisibility and inaccessibility of early women's writing by gathering and showing what is known. But they also risk thereby strengthening the epistemology of completeness and authority that already pervades our relationship with archives, as Jeannette Bastian and others have shown.[7] As Lauren Klein suggests, calling for digital projects and their users to '[reframe] the archive itself as a site of action rather than as a record of fixity or loss', it is as important for digital catalogues and collections to make visible their gaps, omissions, and scoping criteria, and the agencies by which they are produced, as it is to celebrate their plenitude.[8] A crucial element of the technologies that support digital collections is thus the use of explicit markup or text encoding, which serves a triple purpose: it supports the fine-grained description and analysis of research materials that is essential for digital scholarship; it does so in a way that allows different descriptive approaches to be mutually intelligible rather than isolated; and it supports the transparency and layered self-critique that are necessary for digital archives and collections to show their agency, motivations, and limitations.

Text markup or text encoding has its technical origins in digital typesetting systems, where it first emerged as a way of identifying the different textual components (headings, paragraphs, and so forth) that required different formatting, and ultimately grew to become a generalised approach to modelling textual data (and indeed, many other types of information) at a structural level. Its intellectual origins reach further back to traditions of scholarly editing and formal apparatus, with regular structures of lemma, textual variants, sigla, and so forth communicated by systematic typographical cues. Similarly, we can see in the early adoption of text markup in the digital humanities in the 1980s an emphasis on what we might call the 'old formalism': an emphasis on identifying and analysing textual components by their function and rhetorical role. But we can also read the operations of text markup in a New Formalist spirit that is more interested in systems of power and regulation that animate markup systems. The most common markup language used in the digital humanities is the Text Encoding Initiative (TEI) Guidelines, which establish a shared descriptive language for representing digital texts by identifying their signifying elements.[9] These include aspects of structure such as document sections and the identifiably different components of different textual genres such as verse lines, paragraphs, lists, and cast lists, but also aspects of intertextual reference (citations, quotations), contextual reference (named entities such as people and places), editorial intervention (annotation, emendation, conjecture), and many other aspects too numerous to name here.

[7] Jeannette Bastian, 'Reading Colonial Records Through an Archival Lens: The Provenance of Place, Space and Creation', *Archival Science*, 6 (2006), 267–84. DOI:10.1007/s10502-006-9019-1.

[8] Lauren Klein, 'The Image of Absence: Archival Silence, Data Visualization, and James Hemings', *American Literature*, 85.4 (2013), 661–88, 665.

[9] Text Encoding Initiative Consortium (eds), *TEI P5: Guidelines for Electronic Text Encoding and Interchange*, TEI Consortium, http://www.tei-c.org/Guidelines/P5, accessed 8 April 2021.

This language is defined and regulated, like all such markup languages, by a set of formal rules represented by a schema, and the process by which the schema produces and enforces systems of meaning within the digital text is itself a crucial site for critical scrutiny. Markup languages in industrial contexts are typically designed and maintained by a central authority, in a manner analogous to the forms of standardisation that produce standardised electrical outlets or building codes. However, the TEI Guidelines, as a humanities research technology, are designed so that its schema is more of a kit from which local schemas may be constructed, and to which local idioms and descriptive systems can be added, ideally in a manner that invites scrutiny, commentary, emulation, and experimentation. For scholars of the early modern period, this digital formalism thus entertains and risks the best and worst potential of new formalism as Marjorie Levinson characterises it. It enables 'scrupulous attention to the formal means that establish the conditions of possibility for experience—textual, aesthetic, and every other kind', but it risks projecting a kind of self-evidence and self-confidence that is unaware of its own complicities: 'sectarian, programmatic, and instrumental reading, geared toward the shaping or sustaining of the liberal bourgeois subject—the autonomous, self-transparent, complex but not conflicted subject'.[10]

The reimagination of traditional scholarly editing which these approaches propose has been an important issue in the theorisation and construction of digital resources for the study of early modern women's writing. Rosalind Smith, in a review of *Perdita*, argues that the scholarly edition is a technology whose legitimising force plays an important role in reframing the canon, while approaches with lesser claims to academic cultural capital (such as facsimile and documentary editions) tend to perpetuate the marginalisation of early women's writing.[11] At the same time, the genre of the individual edition has proven less viable than larger-scale approaches as a mode of digital publication, for reasons having less to do with its intellectual merits than with the realities of funding, institutional support, and audience. Important exceptions include Paul Salzman's digital editions of Lady Mary Wroth's work, Leah Knight and Wendy Wall's *The Pulter Project*, and Liza Blake's digital edition of Margaret Cavendish's *Poems and Fancies*, which are notable individually for the stature of their subjects and the distinctiveness of their approaches, rather than collectively as evidence of an easily reproducible praxis.[12] And although venues do exist for digital scholarly editions (notably

[10] Marjorie Levinson, 'What is New Formalism?', *Publications of the Modern Language Association*, 122.2 (2007), 558–69, 562.

[11] Rosalind Smith, 'Perdita Project', *Early Modern Women*, 11.2 (2017), 145–51. The term 'documentary editions' refers to the tradition of documentary editing (as promulgated by, for instance, the Association for Documentary Editing; see *The Association for Documentary Editing*, https://www.documentaryediting.org/wordpress/, accessed 8 April 2021) which emerges from the curation and editing of collections of personal papers as part of historical research. More broadly, documentary approaches to editing have become increasingly visible in digital editions of documents that exist only in a single instance (whether print or manuscript) and for which the chief goal is access and contextualisation rather than establishing a critically edited text.

[12] See Paul Salzman (ed.), *Mary Wroth's Poetry: An Electronic Edition* (2012), La Trobe University, http://wroth.latrobe.edu.au/ and https://c21ch.newcastle.edu.au/emwrn/marywroth, accessed 8 April

the *Scholarly Editing* journal, which publishes 'micro-editions' in TEI, and emerging initiatives such as the *Primary Source Cooperative* that seek to provide a sustainable platform for digital editions), they are scarce.[13] As a result, digital projects focused on gathering, representing, and publishing digital versions of early modern women's writing have tended to frame their missions in more broadly recuperative ways, focusing on editorial *processes* rather than *products*, while employing technical approaches that take advantage of the multilayered, semantically precise, expressive formalisms of systems like the TEI Guidelines and related standards. One very long-standing example is the *Women Writers Project*, whose digital collection of women's writing (published as *Women Writers Online*) is not strongly 'edited' in the conventional sense: the texts do not carry scholarly commentary and have not been corrected or reconstructed with reference to manuscript sources or multiple editions.[14] However, the text is strongly 'modelled' in ways that constitute a different kind of editing: the process of digital encoding produces an analytical representation of the text—expressed using the TEI language—that makes explicit the text's structures, genre-specific features, intertextual gestures, named entities, rhetorical texture, and typography. Scholars can also use such digital texts—lightly edited but strongly modelled—as the basis for more intensive editorial work and for specialised analysis using tools such as the Versioning Machine, which supports comparison between different textual versions.[15] This textual modelling has value in supporting the display and navigation of individual texts, but more importantly it puts the texts into conversation by organising them under a common descriptive rubric: it accomplishes for the collection as a whole what traditional scholarly editing does for the individual text, expressing the material through a single consistent and explicit scholarly rationale.

This collection-level digital modelling is also expressed through the metadata associated with each text, which represents bibliographic details but also information about editorial practices, languages used in the text, the text's producers, the topic and genre, and potentially much more. Many important digital resources for the study of early women's writing—including *Perdita, RECIRC, NEWW Women Writers, Bieses,* and *Early Modern Letters Online*—capture metadata but not full text, and can therefore

2021; Leah Knight and Wendy Wall (eds), *The Pulter Project: Poet in the Making* (2018), Northwestern University, http://pulterproject.northwestern.edu/, accessed 8 April 2021; Liza Blake (ed.), *Margaret Cavendish's Poems and Fancies* (2019), University of Toronto, http://library2.utm.utoronto.ca/poemsandfancies/, accessed 8 April 2021. I am grateful to Sarah Ross for drawing my attention to these examples.

[13] See *Scholarly Editing: The Annual of the Association for Documentary Editing*, Noelle Baker and Kathryn Tomasek (eds), https://scholarlyediting.org, accessed 8 April 2021; *Primary Source Cooperative*, Massachusetts Historical Society, http://primarysourcecoop.org, accessed 8 April 2021.

[14] See *Women Writers Project*, Northeastern University, https://www.wwp.northeastern.edu, accessed 8 April 2021; for editorial principles see 'Methodology for Transcription and Editing', *Women Writers Project*, Northeastern University, https://www.wwp.northeastern.edu/about/methods/editorial_principles.html, accessed 8 April 2021.

[15] See Susan Schreibman, *Versioning Machine 5.0*, http://v-machine.org, accessed 8 April 2021.

cover a much larger set of texts.[16] As with full-text modelling, this metadata supports the discovery of any individual text in the manner of a catalogue entry (still an important point for early women's writing) but also supports the exploration of the collection as a model of a specific cultural and textual space. This kind of modelling may also extend to include extra-textual information, as in *RECIRC*'s work to amass evidence of the impact of women's writing through studies of readership and reception. Each 'reception' is 'a record of engagement with a female author and/or her work': in other words, a parcel of data that connects an author, a reader, and possibly one or more texts.[17] *RECIRC*'s case study of the Hartlib Circle shows how these interconnections establish a social network in which women authors are situated in relation to authors and readers, both female and male.[18]

As with traditional scholarly editing and analysis, the value of these approaches depends on transparency and self-reflexivity. While text markup and digital modelling approaches have the capacity to express contingency, indeterminacy, and multivocality, doing so requires careful attention and critical resistance to their natural heuristics of classification and differentiation. Tools like the TEI, which are designed to encourage this critical approach, require greater effort to implement than those which offer to work 'out of the box'. Bringing the 'box' into critical visibility—being aware of it and critiquing it—is thus an important aspect of these digital methodologies as indeed of all digital methodologies. For the same reason, documentation of data and methods is urgently important and tends to be a focus of attention for projects working with early women's writing precisely because their positioning puts them from the start in a frictional position with fundamental assumptions and approaches.[19] This emphasis on transparency also has value in supporting the development of interconnections between data collections: for example, in the way that varied texts and data sets are being linked to *The Map of Early Modern London*.[20] In the further future, the use of linked open data methods (which make the individual items but also the concepts through which they

[16] See *Perdita*, University of Warwick, http://web.warwick.ac.uk/english/perdita/html/, accessed 8 April 2021; *RECIRC*, National University of Ireland, Galway, https://recirc.nuigalway.ie, accessed 8 April 2021; *NEWW Women Writers*, Huygens Institute, http://resources.huygens.knaw.nl/womenwriters/, accessed 8 April 2021; *Bieses: Bibliografía de Escritorias Españolas*, https://www.bieses.net, accessed 8 April 2021; and *Early Modern Letters Online*, University of Oxford, http://emlo.bodleian.ox.ac.uk, accessed 8 April 2021, respectively.

[17] 'Receptions', *RECIRC*, National University of Ireland, Galway, https://recirc.nuigalway.ie/explore, accessed 8 April 2021.

[18] 'The Hartlib Circle', *RECIRC*, National University of Ireland, Galway, https://recirc.nuigalway.ie/cases/hartlib-circle, accessed 8 April 2021.

[19] For some examples see, e.g., the *Women Writers Project*'s encoding documentation: 'Internal Encoding Documentation', *Women Writers Project*, Northeastern University, https://www.wwp.northeastern.edu/research/publications/documentation/internal/, accessed 8 April 2021; see also *RECIRC*'s documentation: 'About the Data', *RECIRC*, National University of Ireland, Galway, https://recirc.nuigalway.ie/about-data, accessed 8 April 2021. The *Scholarly Editing* journal is also exemplary in exposing the data underlying its editions and in treating encoding methods as integral to the scholarly publication.

[20] See *Map of Early Modern London*, University of Victoria, https://mapoflondon.uvic.ca/index.htm, accessed 8 April 2021.

are formalised publicly addressable) may further encourage this more social approach to knowledge production.

DATA ANALYSIS FOR EARLY WOMEN'S WRITING

Text markup and data modelling focus attention on the rhetorical, bibliographic, historical, and formal aspects of early women's texts, and propose an archival and editorial sensibility through which texts are anchored in documents and in the apparatus of authentication and curation. Complementing these approaches are digital methods of large-scale data analysis, which tend to focus on semantic and linguistic information and for which text is often represented as a large aggregate corpus rather than a collection of distinct documents: for example, the use of word embedding models in the *Women Writers Vector Toolkit*, or Mattie Burkert's comparison of male- and female-authored plays, both discussed below. (Indeed, for many such methods the boundaries between texts and even the original word order are entirely lost.) The simplest of such tools offer basic quantitative measures, such as word frequency within documents, distribution of word frequencies or metadata features across a collection of documents, or frequency of specific collocations of words. More complex approaches involve what is termed 'machine learning', in which a text corpus is analysed algorithmically to produce a statistical model of the corpus, which can then be queried and examined to yield insight about the texts or the language they contain. The term 'learning' marks the fact that the model is produced not by an a priori theory or set of categorisations established by the researcher, but rather inductively by the algorithm's own operations and observations over the text. In some cases, this learning is 'supervised' in the sense that the researcher provides a sample corpus in which some categorisations have already been performed by hand: for instance, to identify the genre of each text according to some scheme (e.g., verse, fiction, drama, letters, etc.). The algorithmic process then relies on this training data to identify correlations between those genres and the patterns it observes, and uses those patterns to propose genre identifications in a second, unmarked corpus. In 'unsupervised' machine learning, no training data is provided: the algorithmic process instead generates its model of the corpus based on its own iterative observations.[21] In practice, machine learning techniques in the humanities are used in combination with human interpretive work and modelling of the kind described in the previous section: what the *Visualizing English Print* project refers to as 'scalable scholarship', echoing Martin Mueller's 'scalable

[21] For a useful exploration of supervised and unsupervised text analysis methods for early modern scholarship, see Michael Witmore and Jonathan Hope, 'A Map of Early English Print', *Wine Dark Sea* (23 April 2019), http://winedarksea.org/?p=2703.

reading'.[22] These methods offer important opportunities to study women's writing from the perspective of language and discourse, as well as to study larger cultural patterns in publication. They give direct attention to early modern women's writing as a large-scale, pervasive, historical phenomenon—either on its own or in combination with male-authored texts—rather than an assemblage of individual, marginal, and isolated documents. They also open up the possibility that information drawn from large corpora of comparatively unknown texts might nuance our understanding of genres and periodisations based on better-known works.

A notable example of this 'scalable' intersection of human interpretive work and algorithmic text analysis at work as scholarly infrastructure is DocuScope, and its integration into research on early modern texts.[23] Based on a long-standing research initiative at Carnegie Mellon University and supported further by a Mellon-funded initiative at the University of Wisconsin, Madison, DocuScope provides an environment for annotating and analysing a text corpus using a dictionary of rhetorical effects or 'language action types' (LATs) that are mapped to specific verbal formulations. For example, words like 'premised' or 'predicated' might map to the LAT 'ReasonBackward'; words and phrases like 'doctrine', 'laws', 'the Public', and 'rules' might map to the LAT 'CommonAuthorities'.[24] At the University of Wisconsin, DocuScope has also been integrated into the Ubiqu+Ity text analysis environment by the *Visualizing English Print* project, which enables DocuScope to be used with the *VEP* corpus as well as with corpora uploaded by individual scholars.[25] A corpus annotated by DocuScope contains markup that associates specific words and phrases with specific LATs (which can thus be examined by the researcher to determine their appropriateness). More importantly, researchers can add their own custom LAT definitions or create their own dictionaries to enable DocuScope to annotate a corpus with, for instance, terms associated with gendered or racialised language, or archaisms, or regional idioms. Ubiqu+Ity also provides a text analysis platform in which the distribution of specific LATs within the corpus can be explored, and from which the results of the annotation can be downloaded for further analysis by the individual researcher.[26] DocuScope and Ubiqu+Ity thus establish a research environment within which some proposed generalisations (the dictionary of rhetorical features) are put into dialogue with specific insights and ideas from individual researchers (the custom dictionary) and applied algorithmically to either a standard

[22] See 'Methodology: Scalable Scholarship', *Visualizing English Print*, https://graphics.cs.wisc.edu/WP/vep/scalable-scholarship/, accessed 8 April 2021; Martin Mueller, 'Scalable Reading', https://sites.northwestern.edu/scalablereading/, accessed 8 April 2021.

[23] 'DocuScope Project', Carnegie Mellon University, https://www.cmu.edu/dietrich/english/research-and-publications/docuscope.html, accessed 8 April 2021.

[24] Witmore and Hope, 'Map'.

[25] See the *VEP* documentation: 'Documentation', *Visualizing English Print*, University of Wisconsin-Madison, https://graphics.cs.wisc.edu/WP/vep/tag/documentation/, accessed 8 April 2021.

[26] Heather Froelich, 'Making Your Own Rules for use with Ubiqu+Ity', *Visualizing English Print*, University of Wisconsin-Madison, 7 October 2016, https://graphics.cs.wisc.edu/WP/vep/tag/documentation/, accessed 8 April 2021.

corpus (for instance, any of the *Visualizing English Print* corpora, available for download from the *VEP* site) or researchers' own corpora (which can be uploaded for annotation using Ubiqu+Ity).

These forms of analysis have their roots (and strong current branches) in the social sciences, and early digital humanities research narratives involving such tools tended to be framed around hypothesis-testing and scientific modes of argumentation. More recently, scholars are finding ways to build more nuanced and exploratory literary arguments that draw on such quantitative tools, as two brief examples will help illustrate. The first is an article on the *Digital Cavendish* site in which Jacob Tootalian neatly demonstrates some of the possibilities of this tool set for a single-author corpus and how it can bring both genre and authorial maturation into view.[27] After creating a corpus of Margaret Cavendish's writings from the Text Creation Partnership's open-access corpora derived from *Early English Books Online*, and using DocuScope to annotate the texts, he performed further analysis of the results using principal component analysis (PCA), which seeks to identify the characteristics that most fully account for differences between groups of texts within a collection. In this case, the PCA was based upon the rhetorical gestures identified by DocuScope, and it separated the Cavendish texts into rough generic and to some extent chronological groupings (for instance, philosophical prose of the 1660s, plays, biographical prose). Tootalian's analysis shows how the specific rhetorical gestures contributed to the distribution of the texts: for instance, the 1660s philosophical prose tended to be characterised by LATs such as 'AbstractConcerns', 'Specifiers', and 'DenyDisclaim', while the plays tended to be characterised by LATs such as 'PersonProperty', 'BiographicalTime', and 'DirectAddress'. The article then goes on to look in detail at the language of the texts and its annotation by DocuScope, examining how specific rhetorical gestures (and the language through which they are enacted) perform within specific contexts of genre within Cavendish's oeuvre, arguing for an evolution in her philosophical writings over time in ways that move them away from her poetic language and into a more distinct generic category.

Using the same tool set, Mattie Burkert instead uses a multi-author corpus of dramatic texts to compare male-authored and female-authored plays and to examine a complex critical position: to 'understand why contemporaries experienced the revival of heroic tragedy in the 1690s as being different from the first wave in the 1670s, and also in order to determine whether gender had a role in that change'.[28] Like Tootalian, Burkert examines the gestures that seem to differentiate genres (in this case, dramatic genres such as comedy, farce, burlesque, pastoral), with particular attention to

[27] Jacob Tootalian, 'Cavendish and the Language of Genres', *Digital Cavendish Project* (28 August 2013), http://digitalcavendish.org/the-language-of-genres/, accessed 8 April 2021.

[28] Mattie Burkert, 'Plotting the "Female Wits" Controversy: Gender, Genre, and Printed Plays, 1670–1699', in Laura Estill, Diane K. Jakacki, and Michael Ullyot (eds), *Early Modern Studies after the Digital Turn* (Phoenix, AZ, 2016), 35–59, 42. https://digitalcommons.usu.edu/cgi/viewcontent.cgi?article=1794&context=english_facpub, accessed 8 April 2021.

characterising 'heroic' modes, and with the ultimate goal of distinguishing the heroic drama of the 1690s from that of the 1670s and questioning the possible contribution of women writers to that shift. Both of these articles are exemplary in documenting and explaining the details of their analytical process and its tools, and showing how the entire work process—from corpus construction to tool choices and parameters to interpretation of the results—contributes materially to the final argument. While both also offer useful models for using digital tools to study early modern texts, including women's writing, Burkert additionally demonstrates how comparative approaches enabled by an appropriately structured corpus can focus the analysis on gender and bring differences between male-authored and female-authored writing into clearer focus.

DocuScope's annotations focus on a very specific channel of information—the kinds of local rhetorical gestures that can be associated with specific patterns of words—and it does not (at least not yet) take into account the kinds of document structure represented by markup of the kind we examined in the previous section. Most large-scale text analysis tools operate on plain text and treat the text as either a simple series of words, or in some cases an unordered 'bag of words'. However, as humanities researchers work more intensively with these tools (and as corpora such as the Text Creation Partnership make TEI-encoded texts available in larger numbers) approaches are emerging that put information from text markup into play as part of large-scale analysis. The *Women Writers Project*, whose collection now includes over 450 texts and about eleven million words, has developed a toolkit through which researchers can use word embedding models to explore the *WWP* corpus as well as other corpora.[29] In word embedding models, the text analysis algorithm identifies words that occupy similar semantic spaces within the corpus (for instance, words related to royalty, or food, or domestic labour). While these models do not ordinarily take text structure into account, the *Women Writers Vector Toolkit* uses a corpus preparation process in which the original TEI-encoded texts are filtered, using the TEI markup, to extract or suppress specific features of interest: for instance, to retain original spellings, to exclude paratexts, or to include only poetic material. Most interestingly for the study of women's writing, the toolkit also presents multiple corpora (from the *WWP*, *EEBO-TCP*, and the *Victorian Women Writers Project*) some of which include only female-authored texts and some of which include mostly male-authored texts, making it possible to compare the language of female- and male-authored texts in very fine-grained ways. Even more powerful analyses are possible with deliberately constructed corpora and use of command-line tools which offer greater computational complexity.

Another important tool for the study of early modern women's writing is social network analysis, as we saw earlier in *RECIRC*'s work on the Hartlib Circle. In some cases, network analysis is used to learn about the connections between people so that we can

[29] *Women Writers Vector Toolkit, Women Writers Project*, Northeastern University, https://wwp.northeastern.edu/lab/wwvt/index.html, accessed 8 April 2021.

better understand their writing; sometimes, network analysis derives from specific textual forms like letters (what Ruth and Sebastian Ahnert in their study of Protestant letter networks call 'sociotexts', after Gary Schneider[30]) that themselves establish a network among a group of people. An example of the former type is *Six Degrees of Francis Bacon*, a research project which is building a very large data set representing the social network of early modern Britain.[31] This data was generated from documents—in this case, the *Oxford Dictionary of National Biography*—through a combination of techniques involving named entity recognition (to identify the people named in each biographical article) and then computational analysis which yielded information about the co-occurrence of people references within documents. Based on that information (and with certain parameters, limitations, validation, and hand curation), the project inferred a social network of people who actually had a relationship of relevance.[32] With the initial computationally generated data as a starting point, the project is expanding collaboratively through contributions of data to add both people and relationships, and the project's visualisations make clear which relationships are computationally inferred and which come from human contributors. As its creators make clear, the project's development illustrated some important lessons about the limitations of large-scale data sets, particularly where the study of marginalised groups is concerned.[33] For example, in order to achieve better precision and fewer false positives in the inferencing process (and to reduce computational overhead), the project decided to omit names that occurred in fewer than five documents. As they note, however, because women's names typically change at marriage, their visibility to the named entity recognition process within the source biographies is dispersed and they are less likely to reach the threshold of five references. Hand curation could address this problem (by instituting authority control and associating the different names with the single person) but would be costly. (For notable women such as Margaret Cavendish, *Six Degrees of Francis Bacon* offers interesting research possibilities, as explored for instance in Shawn Moore's posting on the *Digital Cavendish* site.[34]) Furthermore, within large-scale data sets characteristics like gender and race (which would be difficult to infer computationally even if they were simple to describe, which they are not) tend to be invisible: *Six Degrees of Francis*

[30] Ruth Ahnert and S. E. Ahnert, 'Protestant Letter Networks in the Reign of Mary I: A Quantitative Approach', *English Literary History*, 82.1 (2015), 1–33, 2.

[31] Christopher Warren, Daniel Shore, Jessica Otis, Scott Weingart, and John Ladd, *Six Degrees of Francis Bacon*, Carnegie Mellon University, http://www.sixdegreesoffrancisbacon.com, accessed 8 April 2021.

[32] Christopher N. Warren, Daniel Shore, Jessica Otis, Lawrence Wang, Mike Finegold, and Cosma Shalizi, 'Six Degrees of Francis Bacon: A Statistical Method for Reconstructing Large Historical Social Networks', *Digital Humanities Quarterly*, 10.3 (2016), http://digitalhumanities.org/dhq/vol/10/3/000244/000244.html, accessed 8 April 2021.

[33] Warren et al., 'Six Degrees'.

[34] Shawn Moore, 'Networks as Constructs: The Curious Case of Margaret Cavendish, Duchess of Newcastle (1623?—1673)', *Digital Cavendish Project* (22 June 2013), http://digitalcavendish.org/2013/06/22/networks-as-constructs/, accessed 8 April 2021.

Bacon includes many women, but the interface does not yet make it possible to select them as a group for special attention. Given the scale and difficulty of the task, these are understandable trade-offs, but they illustrate the challenges for researchers working on marginalised populations and also the importance of being transparent in describing the limitations of the data and tools, as this project does.

Although in this case the documents were taken from a modern reference source, a similar process could have been performed using other documentary sources, such as court records or accounts of public events, to generate a different kind of social network. The derivation of a network through the analysis of co-occurrence within documents is a powerful tool which can be extended beyond human social networks to include information about organisations (for instance, a network of authors, editors, illustrators, and publishing houses) or locations (for instance, a network of authors and locations they mention in their writing) or even abstractions (for instance, a network of authors and the topics that appear in their work, inferred from catalogue metadata or from topic analysis of the works themselves). In these cases, the network reveals connections between entities that may not involve human relationships but instead show intellectual alignments or correlated experiences. Furthermore, the network can be analysed in ways that go far beyond simply following connections between entities to discover relationships. Ruth and Sebastian Ahnert's work on social network analysis in the study of early modern England lays out the more complex mathematical elements of this analysis, through which researchers can discover which nodes in the network act as the 'hubs' that are most highly connected with other nodes, or which nodes are on the pathways that connect the greatest number of other nodes.[35] Applying this analysis to a collection of letters written by underground Protestant communities under Mary I, they derive a social network that reflects not only the actual exchange of letters but also forms of connection that are mentioned within the letters, such as acts of assistance on behalf of prisoners. Mathematical analysis of this network reveals not only the raw presence of women within the network, but also the distinctive and significant roles they play as 'infrastructural figures', revealed through measures like eigenvector centrality—roles which the authors note would be largely overlooked by other forms of analysis.[36] In an unpublished paper presented at *RECIRC*'s 2017 conference on 'Reception, Reputation and Circulation in the Early Modern World, 1500–1800', Ahnert and Ahnert presented a similar project focused on correspondence in the State Papers Archive, which revealed the distinctive characteristics of spies within a correspondence network: nodes that anomalously combine a high level of correspondence traffic with a small number of other nodes.[37]

[35] Ahnert and Ahnert, 'Protestant Letter Networks', 14.

[36] Ahnert and Ahnert, 'Protestant Letter Networks', 17.

[37] Ruth Ahnert and S. E. Ahnert, 'Reconstructing Correspondence Networks in the State Papers Archive' [audio recording], 'Reception, Reputation and Circulation in the Early Modern World, 1500–1800' plenary address, https://recirc.nuigalway.ie/conference2017, accessed 8 April 2021.

CONCLUSION: AND MUCH MORE

The full range of digital methods and tools that have been and can be applied to early modern women's writing is much wider than this brief survey can encompass, and I have focused here on the most complex approaches that seemed to benefit most from detailed explication and critical consideration. Among the most important omissions: platforms for collaborative editing, such as those explored by the editors of the Devonshire Manuscript, and digital exhibit-building tools and publication platforms (such as WordPress, Omeka, and Scalar) that enable researchers to create interactive publications, innovative forms of scholarly argumentation, and pedagogical resources.[38] But in many ways, the repertoire of digital methodologies for the study of early modern women's writing is the same as for other literary and historical research. The common strands are foundational: data whose representational structures are appropriate for the research being conducted; editorial and curatorial methods that are explicit, consistent, and critically theorised; tools whose interior workings and underlying assumptions are visible and ideally also configurable; researchers whose familiarity with these principles enables them to work knowledgeably and critically to build substantive interpretations and arguments. Scholars of early women's writing face practical challenges both in the comparative paucity of information on women within established data sets and in the extra effort needed to work around complexities such as naming, as well as subtler difficulties such as the tendency of classifying and terminological systems (such as lists of occupations or genres) to offer impoverished sets of descriptors in areas of female activity. But the potential value of both complex digital modelling and large-scale data analysis—to say nothing of the other digital tools not considered here—is very considerable, and it is likely that the field is still in its incunabular stage. At the same time, feminist theory (and related work in queer theory and critical race studies) offers a crucial programme of critical attention to the social and ideological foundations of information structures, which researchers in digital humanities now also use to scrutinise the many places within the tool set where harmful, outdated, and reductive information structures are invisibly naturalised. Scholars of early modern women's writing thus have an opportunity to use these digital methodologies with a far greater awareness of their limitations, and of the care needed to use them responsibly.

[38] Ray Siemens, Constance Crompton, Daniel Powell, Alyssa Arbuckle, Maggie Shirley, and the Devonshire Manuscript Editorial Group, 'Building *A Social Edition of the Devonshire Manuscript*'. Matthew James Driscoll and Elena Pierazzo (eds), *Digital Scholarly Editing* (Cambridge, 2016), 137–60.

FURTHER READING

Ahnert, Ruth and S. E. Ahnert. 'Protestant Letter Networks in the Reign of Mary I: A Quantitative Approach'. *English Literary History*, 82.1 (2015), 1–33.

Driscoll, Matthew James and Elena Pierazzo (eds). *Digital Scholarly Editing*. Cambridge, 2016.

Estill, Laura, Diane K. Jakacki, and Michael Ullyot (eds). *Early Modern Studies after the Digital Turn*. Phoenix, AZ, 2016.

Flanders, Julia, Sarah Connell, and Syd Bauman. 'Text Encoding', in Constance Crompton, Richard J. Lane, and Ray Siemens (eds), *Doing Digital Humanities*. New York, 2016, 104–22.

Wernimont, Jacqueline. *Numbered Lives: Life and Death in Quantum Media*. Cambridge, MA, 2019.

CHAPTER 45

MATERIAL TEXTS

Women's Paperwork in Early Modern England and Mary Wroth's Urania

ANNA REYNOLDS

I want to begin with an act of critical imagination. Picture three women: one of elite status, one middling, and one lower. They live in London, in the late sixteenth or early seventeenth century. We are imagining their everyday textual encounters, both professional and leisured, and extending beyond the reading and writing of books.

Our imaginations are barely needed for our elite woman. The historical record is replete with biographies of wealthy women who owned large libraries, who kept diaries, commonplace books and household accounts, who translated literary texts, and who wrote literary texts of their own.[1] Perhaps our woman is like Lady Anne Clifford, adorning her bedchamber with 'the flowers of a library', pinning paper texts to her walls and furniture.[2] Certainly she would have lived in a domestic environment rich in textual objects—mottos, emblems, proverbs, a coat of arms, all woven, sewn, tooled, painted, and carved in her textiles, furniture, tableware, bookbindings, portraits, and stonework, and even moulded into the foodstuffs of her banquets.[3] Most of these textual objects would have been commissioned or inherited rather than made with her own hands, but our woman might have produced fine embroideries, gifting them to other noble

[1] As well as female monarchs, we know much about the experience of elite women such as Elizabeth Talbot, Margaret Hoby, Frances Egerton, and Anne Clifford. See Heidi Brayman Hackel, *Reading Material in Early Modern England: Print, Gender, and Literacy* (Cambridge, 2005).

[2] Brayman Hackel, *Reading Material*, 232, and see this volume, Chapter 8, Leah Knight, 'Libraries Not Their Own' and this volume, Chapter 46, Patricia Phillippy, 'Memory and Matter: Lady Anne Clifford's "Life of Mee"'.

[3] See Susan Frye, *Pens and Needles: Women's Textualities in Early Modern England* (Philadelphia, 2010), 13–14; and Wendy Wall, *Recipes for Thought: Knowledge and Taste in the Early Modern Kitchen* (Philadelphia, PA, 2015), 18.

families.[4] Perhaps she scratched verses with a diamond onto windowpanes, or pasted and bound fragments of the Gospels into a reordered devotional text, like a Collet sister in the Ferrar community at Little Gidding.[5]

Again, the imaginative work is relatively easy for our middling status woman. We can model her on what we know of the gentry women who owned libraries, kept diaries, commonplace books, and household accounts, and who composed texts on a range of subjects. Her domestic environment is also rich in mottos, emblems, and proverbs, in the form of wall paintings and textiles, and on her tableware, though these objects would have been less numerous and their materials less opulent than her elite counterpart's. In addition to composing texts with both needle and pen, our middling woman might have authored a range of textual objects in her kitchen, crafting quills, following recipes for ink, and moulding marchpane fancies, perhaps serving them on trenchers bearing poesies.[6] In managing the economy of her household, she might have gathered unwanted paper for use as waste wrappers, linings, and kindling in her kitchen or as supports in her needlework.[7] She was, perhaps, an artisan, a widow printer, publisher, or stationer, or a bookbinder crafting—rather than commissioning—covers that might range from simple trade bindings to gorgeously tooled or embroidered cases.[8]

It is for our third woman, of the lowest socio-economic status, that we must exercise our imaginations most vigorously. Perhaps she owned no, or very few, books; perhaps she was illiterate, unable to write, or to read handwritten script.[9] Perhaps she could read the verses and proverbs scratched and traced in the city's churches and inns, in chalk, charcoal, paint, stone, or smoke, or the woodcuts, broadsheets, and title-pages pasted on its walls and posts.[10] She might have handled texts as she made her living: perhaps she was a hawker or pedlar of cheap print, or laboured in a print shop as one of the 'girles' who took 'sheets from the tinpin of the presse'.[11] Her relationship to the materials

[4] See Lisa M. Klein, 'Your Humble Handmaid: Elizabethan Gifts of Needlework', *Renaissance Quarterly*, 50.2 (1997), 459–93; and this volume, Chapter 5, Michele Osherow, '"At My Petition": Embroidering Esther'.

[5] See, for instance, Queen Elizabeth's 'Written on a Window Frame at Woodstock' and 'Written With a Diamond' in Leah S. Marcus, Janel Mueller, and Mary Beth Rose (eds), *Elizabeth I: Collected Works* (Chicago, IL, 2000), 45–6; and the verses from Tottel copied by Mary Queen of Scots' on a window at Fotheringhay, described in Ruth Hughey (ed.), *The Arundel Harington Manuscript of Tudor Poetry*, (Columbus, 1960) vol. 2, 19; and Whitney Trettien, *Cut/Copy/Paste: Fragments from the History of Bookwork* (Minneapolis, MN, 2021), 29–97.

[6] Wall, *Recipes*, 117; and see this volume, Chapter 22, Wendy Wall, 'The World of Recipes'.

[7] On the uses of waste paper see my forthcoming study *Privy Tokens: Waste Paper in Early Modern England.*

[8] See Helen Smith, *'Grossly Material Things': Women and Book Production in Early Modern England* (Oxford, 2012) and Valerie Wayne (ed.), *Women's Labour and the History of the Book* (London, 2020).

[9] For a discussion of the limitations of traditional definitions of literacy, see Hackel, *Reading Material*, 52–68. See also this volume, Chapter 38, Susan Wiseman, 'Non-elite Networks and Women'.

[10] See Juliet Fleming, *Graffiti and the Writing Arts of Early Modern England* (London, 2001), 29–72; Tessa Watt, *Cheap Print and Popular Piety, 1550–1640* (Cambridge, 1991), 6–7; and Tiffany Stern, *Documents of Performance in Early Modern England* (Cambridge, 2009), 50–3.

[11] Smith, *'Grossly Material Things'*, 96, and Sara Mendelson and Patricia Crawford, *Women in Early Modern England* (Oxford, 1998), 333.

of writing might have been extremely intimate, working as a ragpicker collecting the raw material for papermaking, or, later in paper's life cycle, hanging sheets to dry and examining them for damage in the paper mill.[12] Perhaps, even later still, she sorted, used, or sold waste paper in her own household or that of her mistress.[13]

This stratification into three sorts is of course overly simplistic, but it goes some way to demonstrating early modern women's varied engagements with the materials of reading and writing across the socio-economic spectrum. Furthermore, it suggests the authority and agency, as well as dexterity and skill, with which women handled textual stuff.[14] These are the themes that this chapter will explore. First, it will survey the critical field within which we have developed our understanding of the material variety of women's texts. This will be followed by a more detailed examination of women's practical knowledge of a specific writing material—paper—and a case study of one elite woman's figuring of this knowledge in a now-canonical example of early modern women's writing: Mary Wroth's *Urania*.

EARLY MODERN WOMEN AND THE MATERIAL TEXT

Any attempt to survey the place of material texts within scholarship on early modern women's writing is made difficult by the shifting definitions of the 'material' and the 'textual' in literary criticism since the 1980s. In using these freighted terms, we must also account for how they sit between early modern women's writing and numerous related fields of study: archival recovery and textual editing, book history and print and manuscript cultures, the history of reading, and the study of material culture. At stake in the term 'material text' is the history of the study of women's writing and its give and take with the 'isms'—almost invariably 'new'—of the last few decades: not just the successive waves of feminism, but also new textualism, cultural materialism, new historicism, new materialism, and new formalism.

Because of its roots in the recovery of texts that have been 'lost' or neglected in the archives, the study of early modern women's writing is grounded in an attention to texts as *objects*. In the 1980s and 1990s, influential scholarship attended to the circulation of manuscript poetry, the practice of commonplacing, and marginalia as evidence of early

[12] Heidi Craig, 'English Rag-Women and Early Modern Paper Production', in Valerie Wayne (ed.), *Women's Labour and the History of the Book* (London, 2020), 29–46.

[13] Reynolds, *Privy Tokens*.

[14] This reworks Catherine Richardson's assertion that women's 'relation to the material world' is 'analogous to that of servants—expert and dextrous but lacking in authority'. See Richardson, *Shakespeare and Material Culture* (Oxford, 2011), 15.

modern reading practices.[15] The wealth of material uncovered by scholars searching for literature written by women expanded the objects of study beyond texts produced and annotated by men, and, more gradually, beyond the comparative framework of print culture.[16] As Victoria E. Burke wrote in relation to four women's manuscript miscellanies in 1997, 'a new type of literary history needs to be written', one that gives 'a central position to the practice of compilation'.[17] Over the last two decades, the history of early modern literary culture has been rewritten along these lines. Forms of writing typically considered non-literary, such as letters, diaries, accounts, and recipes, have been reconceived as important intertexts to the poetry, drama, and prose they might sit alongside in early modern manuscripts.[18] Similarly, the evidence of women's book ownership and use, in the form of marginalia, ownership inscriptions, and inventories, has influenced broader studies of how early moderns engaged—materially and intellectually—with their books.[19]

It is no longer the case, then, that book history is a field primarily concerned with 'male writers seeking print', as Margaret J. M. Ezell characterised it in 2008.[20] It is also no longer a 'side-effect that women's participation ... has essentially been relegated to belonging in another category'.[21] Instead, the methodologies and primary concerns of scholarship on women's writing are now central to the broader field of book history—a field that has grown to encompass the unstable material history of both printed and manuscript texts, and the varied ways in which early modern men and women read, handled, and remade their textual objects. This is not to say, however, that early modern women's writing and reading practices are, themselves, now central to the history of the book. Though the findings of scholarship on women's writing have had a profound

[15] For instance, Peter Beal, *Index of Literary Manuscripts* (London, 1980–1993), Harold Love, *Scribal Publication in Seventeenth-Century England* (Oxford, 1993), and Lisa Jardine and Anthony Grafton, '"Studied for Action": How Gabriel Harvey Read his Livy', *Past and Present*, 129.1 (1990), 30–78.

[16] For instance, Margaret J. M. Ezell, *The Patriarch's Wife* (Chapel Hill, NC, 1987); Anne Southwell, in Jean Klene (ed.), *The Southwell-Sibthorpe Commonplace Book: Folger Ms. V.b. 198* (Tempe, 1997); and Elizabeth Clarke et al. (eds), *Perdita*, University of Warwick, http://web.warwick.ac.uk/english/perdita/html/, accessed 3 December 2020.

[17] Victoria E. Burke, 'Women and Early Seventeenth-Century Manuscript Culture: Four Miscellanies', *The Seventeenth Century*, 12.2 (1997), 135–50, 146 and see this volume, Chapter 15, Victoria Burke, 'Commonplacing, Making Miscellanies, and Interpreting Literature'.

[18] For an account of these developments see Margaret J. M. Ezell, 'The Laughing Tortoise: Speculations on Manuscript Sources and Women's Book History', *English Literary Renaissance*, 38.2 (2008), 331–55.

[19] See Leah Knight and Micheline White, 'The Bookscape', in Knight, White, and Elizabeth Sauer (eds), *Women's Bookscapes in Early Modern Britain* (Ann Arbor, MI, 2018), 1–18, 1–4; and Katherine Acheson's chapter, 'The Occupation of the Margins: Writing, Space, and Early Modern Women', in her edited collection, *Early Modern English Marginalia* (Abingdon, 2019), 70–90. For scholarship representative of this influence, see Jeffrey Todd Knight, *Bound to Read: Compilations, Collections, and the Making of Renaissance Literature* (Philadelphia, PA, 2013); and Adam Smyth, *Material Texts in Early Modern England* (Cambridge, 2018).

[20] Ezell, 'The Laughing Tortoise', 336.

[21] Ezell, 'The Laughing Tortoise', 336.

influence on the wider field of book history, women writers, printers, binders, compilers, and readers remain the exception, rather than the norm, in the majority of studies of early modern book production. Helen Smith's *'Grossly Material Things'* (2012) and Valerie Wayne's *Women's Labour and the History of the Book in Early Modern England* (2020) at once correct and bear out this perceived exceptionality.

A discussion of the place of the material text in scholarship on early modern women's writing also needs to account for the shifting use of the term 'material'. Although the physical nature of women's texts—particularly manuscripts—was central to the field from the 1980s onwards, scholars primarily attended to the broader sociological history of manuscripts, rather than the specificities of their material form. In the late 1990s, early modern scholarship experienced a 'material turn', also known as the advent of 'new materialism': attention to the relationship between texts and their material conditions narrowed to focus on the importance of things, objects, and matter in early modern literature.[22] A decade after Juliet Fleming's influential claim that 'the page is no longer an important boundary', scholars of early modern women's writing began to theorise material practices typically conceived as non-literary.[23] The work of Susan Frye and Wendy Wall in particular has redefined reading, writing, and textuality.[24] In light of their research, needlework and kitchenwork are conceived as both intellectual and manual practices akin to textual composition, allowing us to make the 'speculative leaps' that, as Rebecca Jarratt argues, are 'required to initiate feminist history—to imagine the world differently from the way it has been handed down to us'.[25] This research has borne out Fleming's tentative suggestion that, in expanding what we see as texts, we might begin 'to identify the poetic effects of other writing (including that by women) that has hitherto been discounted on the unexamined ground of its being "overly literal" '.[26] In attending to the histories of alternative forms of composition and consumption, it has become clear that early modern women were not limited to an understanding of the literary as it was inherited through male forms of authorship and canonicity. In addition to these existing traditions, they produced and consumed texts within distinct, often domestic, intellectual and material traditions.

What, then, is the current status of the material text in scholarship on early modern women's writing? As Patricia Phillippy observes in the introduction to the recent Cambridge *History of Early Modern Women's Writing*, many handbooks on the subject now have entire sections on material environments and practices.[27] But the rise in the status of the material has also brought about new concerns. Gillian Wright, writing on

[22] Margreta de Grazia, Maureen Quilligan, and Peter Stallybrass, *Subject and Object in Renaissance Culture* (Cambridge, 1996) is often cited as representative of this turn. For a critique of the material turn, see Douglas Bruster, *Shakespeare and the Question of Culture* (Basingstoke, 2003), 191–205.

[23] Fleming, *Graffiti*, 9.

[24] See Frye, *Pens and Needles* and Wall, *Recipes*.

[25] Susan C. Jarratt, 'Rhetoric and Feminism: Together Again', *College English*, 62.3 (2000), 390–3, 391.

[26] Fleming, *Graffiti and the Writing Arts*, 22.

[27] Patricia Phillippy, 'Introduction: Sparkling Multiplicity', in Patricia Phillippy (ed.), *A History of Early Modern Women's Writing* (Cambridge, 2018), 1–24, 5.

the production of seventeenth- and eighteenth-century women's poetry, suggests that there is a 'danger' in attending too narrowly 'to the material aspects of women's writing', because it 'may, under certain circumstances, serve to distract from, rather than illuminate, the writing itself'.[28] There is a long-standing and pervasive anxiety that a focus on the material is often, or even inevitably, at the expense of the formal and linguistic properties of the text.[29] This concern is certainly valid, but it can be overstated. Just as Wright's own study attends to both the material and the traditionally literary aspects of women's poetry, the formal turn now taking place in scholarship on early modern women's writing remains sensitive to the material.[30] The return to more traditional questions of form and genre is complicated and enriched by the long-standing commitment of the field to the investigation of the material history of texts and the material culture of women's literary production.

WOMEN'S PAPERWORK AND WROTH'S *URANIA*

In the rest of this chapter, I will seek to demonstrate the importance of a simultaneously central and easily overlooked material—paper—to the literary negotiations of Mary Wroth's *Urania*. Just as the work of Frye and Wall has demonstrated the importance of needlework and kitchenwork to our understanding of women's participation in early modern literary culture, we need to recognise the gendered knowledge that early modern women had of paper as both a material resource and a writing support. This paper knowledge was not homogenous, but was determined by the social status of the woman in question.[31] As a member of the Sidney family, Mary Wroth's knowledge of paper was shaped by her elite status. She would have been sensitive to the material qualities of the expensive white paper of her letters and manuscripts, as well as

[28] Gillian Wright, *Producing Women's Poetry, 1600–1730: Text and Paratext, Manuscript and Print* (Cambridge, 2013), 9.

[29] Margreta de Grazia, Maureen Quilligan, and Peter Stallybrass, *Subject and Object in Renaissance Culture* (Cambridge, 1996) is often cited as representative of this turn. For a critique of the material turn, see Douglas Bruster, *Shakespeare and the Question of Culture* (Basingstoke, 2003), 191–205.

[30] See, for instance, Elizabeth Scott-Baumann, *Forms of Engagement: Women, Poetry, and Culture, 1640–1680* (Oxford, 2013), and this volume , Chapter 13, Dianne Mitchell, 'Lyric Backwardness'.

[31] On the intimate knowledge that lower-status women might have had of paper, see Craig, 'English Rag-Women'. For the sorts of knowledge middling status women would have had of paper see Helen Smith, '"A Unique Instance of Art": The Proliferating Surfaces of Early Modern Paper', *Journal of the Northern Renaissance*, 8 (2017), http://www.northernrenaissance.org, accessed 12 July 2020; and Elaine Leong, 'Papering the Household: Paper, Recipes, and Everyday Technologies in Early Modern England', in Carla Bittel, Elaine Leong, and Christine von Oertzen (eds), *Working With Paper: Gendered Practices in the History of Knowledge* (Pittsburgh, PA, 2019), 32–45. Many elite women would also have used paper medicinally, though this context is less relevant to the paper knowledge figured in *Urania*.

the cheaper paper of her printed books.[32] She would also have been sensitive to the non-textual functions of paper in her household, particularly in relation to the use of sheets of paper as wrappers for textiles—laid between 'rich imbroyderies', as a character describes in *Urania*—and the use of smaller fragments of paper for needlework, as a surface in which to stick pins or around which to wind thread.[33] These loose sheets of wrapping paper and smaller slips and scraps are absent from the historical record because of their ephemerality and their apparent triviality. Wroth's *Urania*, however, is rich in these everyday materials and reveals an imaginative connection between household sheets and the pages that make up Wroth's romance. The ways in which paper—both textual and non-textual, literary and domestic—might be handled, preserved, and destroyed, proves to be vital in the way Wroth positions herself in relation to existing literary forms and traditions.

Attention to Wroth's figurative play with paper sheets sheds new light on the debates that have characterised Wroth scholarship since the 1990s. As Paul Salzman puts it:

> [c]ritical interpretation of Wroth's poetry has focused to a considerable degree on her rewriting of the male sonnet tradition, and a critical debate over whether to read her work as inherently about a private, female space, or as engaged in some version of a public debate.[34]

Much of this debate around interiority, privacy, and gendered subjectivity hinges on the way *Urania* stages the circulation of manuscripts within a coterie of predominantly female poets and readers.[35] This chapter builds on recent work, informed by the material turn, that attends not just to the manuscript culture that underpins the text, but the ways in which Wroth conceives of her text as an object and her literary composition as a material process.[36] The work of Jennifer Munroe and Susan Frye on needlework, textiles,

[32] On women's engagement with pen and paper, see Helen Smith, 'Women and the Materials of Writing', in Patricia Pender and Rosalind Smith (eds), *Material Cultures of Early Modern Women's Writing* (Basingstoke, 2014), 14–35. On the wider sensitivity to the varying grades of paper, see James Daybell, *The Material Letter in Early Modern England* (Basingstoke, 2012).

[33] Mary Wroth, *The Countesse of Mountgomeries Urania* (London, [1621]), 423. All subsequent references are from this edition and page numbers will be given in the text. On seventeenth-century 'papers of pins', see Mary Carolyn Beaudry, *Findings: The Material Culture of Needlework and Sewing* (New Haven, CT, 2006), 29. On the use of paper to wind thread, see Claire Canavan, '"Various Pleasant Fiction": Embroidering Textiles and Texts in Early Modern England' (PhD Diss., University of York, 2017), 254.

[34] Paul Salzman, *Reading Early Modern Women's Writing* (Oxford, 2006), 66.

[35] Jeffrey Masten sees Wroth's poems as an exception to the norms of manuscript circulation. See Masten, '"Shall I turne blabb?": Circulation, Gender, and Subjectivity in Mary Wroth's Sonnets', in Naomi J. Miller and Gary Waller (eds), *Reading Mary Wroth* (Knoxville, TN, 1991), 67–87. Edith Snook conceives of this coterie in more positive terms in *Women, Reading, and the Cultural Politics of Early Modern England* (Aldershot, 2005), 145–67.

[36] See Sarah Rodgers, 'Embedded Poetry and Coterie Readers in Mary Wroth's *Urania*', *Studies in Philology*, 111.3 (2014), 470–85; and Margaret Simon, 'Mary Wroth's Ephemeral Epitaph', *Studies in English Literature, 1500–1900*, 56.1 (2016), 45–69.

and gardening in *Urania* has revealed the 'alternative frameworks' available to women writers in the period, and how a poet might 'creat[e] a landscape of female textualities' in which to assert and explore her identity.[37] The terms of debate have expanded, therefore, beyond the privacy of a woman's closet and the strictures placed on female writers by patriarchal discourse and social structures. As a material that underpins both literary culture and domestic practice, paper is central to Wroth's exploration of both alternative and existing poetic frameworks. It also reveals the way in which Wroth conceived of the material make-up and life cycle of books, not as printed *or* manuscript, public *or* private, but as hybrid, mutable, and communal assemblies of paper sheets. In what follows, I focus on two moments in *Urania* when our attention is drawn to paper: the first is one of the many letter exchanges that takes place in the narrative, and the second, mentioned above, alludes to papers slipped between embroideries.

In a striking but far from unique moment in *Urania*, Melisinda receives a letter from her lover, Ollorandus: 'Shee kissed the letter, then opened it; but haveing read it, kissed it often' (226). 'O deare Paper', she apostrophises before burning the letter, reassuring it that 'the fire must consume you' but 'thy ashes yet shalbe preserv'd', as she places them 'in a daintie Cabinet' (227). Melisinda uses 'the same light' with which she sealed her reply 'to g[i]ve the death to the other', and proceeds to compose verses 'witnessing' the occasion. The scene is rich in the physical manipulation of a text's material form, and alludes extensively to the lyric tradition. This tradition is frequently parodied throughout the romance. The trope of the burning lover, for instance, is literalised in the ashes of burnt verses that litter *Urania*'s landscapes.[38] Elsewhere, the Petrarchan lover as a ship on a stormy sea is transformed into an actual boat carrying a forlorn woman and her faithful dog, which is in turn compared to 'the Boates boyes make of paper, and play withall' (421).

Wroth's investment in Petrarchism has been extensively explored, often underpinning interpretations of the inward or outward facing nature of her work.[39] The scholarship of Heather Dubrow and Danielle Clarke deals with Wroth's Petrarchism especially sensitively, demonstrating that Wroth's scepticism regarding the sonnet tradition's central conceits is not dissimilar to that of Renaissance sonnet sequences more broadly.[40] There is a tendency, however, to treat Wroth's Petrarchism, and *Urania* in general, too seriously. Clarke is one of the few scholars to point out the 'wit and comedy' that characterises the romance, and the often 'ludicrous' nature of Pamphilia's constancy.[41] Furthermore, this Petrarchan parody is in itself a convention of the romance tradition

[37] See Frye, *Pens and Needles*, 193; Jennifer Munroe, '"In This Strang Labourinth How Shall I Turne?": Needlework, Gardens, and Writing in Mary Wroth's 'Pamphilia to Amphilanthus', *Tulsa Studies in Women's Literature*, 24.1 (2005), 33–55, 36.

[38] *Urania*, 232–3, 266, 272.

[39] For instance, Masten, '"Shall I turne blabb?"'; and Nona Fienberg, 'Mary Wroth's Poetics of the Self', *Studies of English Literature, 1500–1900*, 42.1 (2002), 121–36.

[40] Clarke, *The Politics of Early Modern Women's Writing* (Harlow, 2001), 213–27; and Heather Dubrow, *Echoes of Desire: Petrarchism and its Counterdiscourses* (Ithaca, NY, 1995), 135–61.

[41] Clarke, *Politics*, 216.

that Wroth enters into in *Urania*. What is unique to *Urania*, though, is the pattern that emerges in its parody: when gesturing towards the Petrarchan tradition, Wroth often literalises its common conceits, and in doing so draws attention to the manipulation of the paper on which such poems are written. Paper ashes and children's paper boats suggest the fragility of textual objects, tapping into anxieties regarding textual vulnerability that were pervasive in early modern literature, often expressed alongside, or in contradiction to, rhetorical claims of literary endurance or immortality.[42] Through the frequent incineration of letters and verses, Wroth intervenes in contemporary discourse surrounding the capacity of especially good texts to survive independently of their material form. But rather than joining this tradition, Wroth parodies it, and does so most often in moments when women read texts written by men.

Edith Snook's interpretation of Melisinda's readerly act is one that overlooks Wroth's parodic intent: for Snook, transforming the text to ashes marks the letter as 'forever precious', guaranteeing its immaterial endurance in memory and averting the common waste paper fate of texts in early modern households.[43] It remains a 'treasure', rather than 'mundane or common' paper for 'wrapping fish, packaging spices, starting fires, or binding books'.[44] Snook is right that, when Melisinda incinerates her lover's letter, Wroth is gesturing towards the transcendental impulse present in much early modern poetry. But Melisinda's preservative act is undercut by the reduction of the text to raw, ashy matter, or 'relique'. Relics in post-Reformation England are loaded with significations too manifold to explore here, but elsewhere in *Urania* they suggest the inertness of objects placed within cabinets: one poem contains the lines, 'love which living lives as dead to me / As holy relics which in boxes be | Placed in a Chest, that overthrows my joy' (110).[45] Snook, otherwise sensitive to the way that manuscripts circulate in *Urania*, misunderstands Wroth's playful use of the tropes of textual treasure and endurance. Elsewhere in *Urania*, the 'mundane or common' circulation of paper in the household is far preferable to the illegibility and stagnancy of ashy relics.

Wroth proceeds to offer an alternative understanding of literary composition and transmission grounded in the very material use of paper in the household. In one of the many scenes where women rehearse and compose poetry in one another's company, we hear of Dorolina's concern for Pamphilia's state of mind. Dorolina is seeking to distract Pamphilia:

42 See Emily Butterworth, 'Apothecaries' Cornets: Books as Waste Paper in the Renaissance', *Modern Language Notes*, 133.4 (2018), 891–913; and Reynolds, *Privy Tokens*.

43 Snook, *Women, Reading*, 148. Clarke, in contrast, sees this as a moment in which a woman removes a man's text from circulation, and so 'makes Ollorandus her own, collapsing the distinction of self and other'. See Clarke, *Politics*, 226.

44 Snook, *Women, Reading*, 226.

45 See Lucy Razzall, '"A good Booke is the pretious life-blood of a master-spirit": Recollecting Relics in Post-Reformation English Writing', *Journal of the Northern Renaissance*, 2 (2010), http://northernrenaissance.org. Accessed 6 December 2020. See also Wroth, *Urania*, 490.

> to take her … from her continuall passions, which not utter'd did weare her spirits and waste them, as rich imbroyderies will spoyle one another, if laid without papers betweene them, fretting each other, as her thoughts and imaginations did her rich and incomprable minde. (423)

Although there are many Wroth figures and female poets in *Urania*, Pamphilia is the most central, granting this metaphor of authorship particular significance. It is very different from contemporary metaphors of textual production that, as Wendy Wall has demonstrated, typically refer to sexual procreation and childbirth, or an erotic 'pressing'.[46] Firmly situated in a domestic environment populated by female poets, readers, and listeners, Wroth's figurative account conforms more closely to the association of women's composition with weaving and needlework.[47] There are, though, important differences between the influential paradigm of Penelope weaving (and unweaving) a shroud, and the acts, objects, and agency in the description of Pamphilia's passions. In Wroth's peculiar simile, the female poet's passions and intellect are conceived as *already* being artworks, as 'rich imbroyderies' skilfully crafted and deserving admiration and careful storage. It is the combined weight of these two embroideries when they come into contact with a sheet of paper that imprint a text onto each side of the page—not, as contemporary tropes have it, the weight of the male body that stands in for the printing press, or the phallic point of the pen. The raised threads, if they don't press the paper, will simply 'fret' one another, wearing and wasting the surface and colour of each embroidery, and damaging the poet's passions and mind.

At first glance, this might seem a modesty topos framing female authorship as a necessary outlet for a dangerous excess of emotion. Composition figured as domestic work—or, more precisely, the storage of an embroidery—might provide further support for the widespread understanding of Wroth's poetics as one of privacy and withdrawal: the embroidery is *not* on display. Here, Wroth might be seen to figure her text as non-circulating, ostensibly staging what Jeffrey Masten perceives as an empty, interiorised space for the nascent female subject.[48] But the spatial poetics at work in this passage are, in fact, central to *Urania* as a whole, mirroring the kinetics of the moment, early in the romance, when we are first presented with Pamphilia's poetry. After reading her verses, we hear how Pamphilia took 'the new-writ lines, and as soone almost as shee

[46] Wendy Wall, *The Imprint of Gender: Authorship and Publication in the English Renaissance* (Ithaca, NY, 1993), 1–22.

[47] On the richness of Wroth's domestic imagery, see Frye, *Pens and Needles*, 221 and Helen Hackett, *Women and Romance Fiction* (Cambridge, 2000), 178. On the association of women's composition with weaving and needlework, see Sarah C. E. Ross, '"Like Penelope, Always Employed": Reading, Life-Writing, and the Early Modern Female Self in Katherine Austen's Book M', *Literature Compass*, 9.4 (2012), 306–16, 314. See also this volume, Chapter 5, Osherow, and Poem 90, 'A Gentlewoman yt married a yong Gent who after forsooke whereuppon she tooke hir needle in which she was excelent and worked upon hir Sampler thus', in Jane Stevenson and Peter Davidson (eds), *Early Modern Women Poets, 1520–1700: An Anthology* (Oxford, 2001). My thanks to Danielle Clarke for bringing these verses to my attention.

[48] Masten, '"Shall I turne blabb?"', 69.

had giuen them life, shee likewise gaue them buriall' (52). Crucially, though, this is not a permanent grave and Pamphilia's verses are resurrected repeatedly throughout the text, read by intruders into her cabinet or retrieved by the poet herself and read aloud.[49] As Vin Nardizzi and Miriam Jacobson hypothesise, Pamphilia's 'buriall' is perhaps simply the laying of 'the abandoned sonnet underneath a sheaf of paper at the bottom of her writing box'.[50]

There is a distinction, then, between the inert contents of ashy reliquaries, and the poetry that is buried—temporarily—in cabinets, like embroideries stored carefully, but intended to be retrieved, unfolded, displayed, and admired. Wroth's figure of frictional composition, like her parody of Petrarchism in kindling and paper boats, plays skilfully with the widespread poetic trope of textual immateriality. Embedded in Wroth's metaphor of authorship is an allusion to Horace's Ode 3.30, or perhaps more precisely, Shakespeare's reworking of this influential text, Sonnet 55.[51] The speaker of Shakespeare's sonnet claims that 'Not marble, nor the gilded monuments / Of princes, shall outlive this powerful rhyme' (1–2). In Shakespeare's poem, while 'sluttish time' and 'wasteful war' 'besmear' stone and statues, the sonnet itself ('this') will survive (4, 5, 14).[52] Wroth, in contrast, draws attention to the humdrum handling of paper, a material obscured in Shakespeare's poem: the friction, wasting, and wearing Wroth depicts take place in a domestic setting, not on the grand stage of monuments and martial history. This confirms Heather Dubrow's reading of the first song in *Pamphilia to Amphilanthus*: Wroth's poetry 'is figured not as an endless monument to herself or the immortalised beloved but rather as scribblings' with an uncertain fate.[53]

This should not, however, obscure what Wroth *does* claim for her work, in her embroidery analogy and throughout *Urania*. The text is not an 'endless monument' to her beloved because Amphilanthus is *not* her primary subject or the imagined reader of her text. Her subject is instead the composition of poetry by *Urania*'s coterie of predominantly elite women, and her imagined reader is, similarly, part of a community of typically sympathetic and highly literate women.[54] Shakespeare's sonnets are models for the sorts of poems that female readers burn and render inert in *Urania*. It is the sheets placed between embroideries—on which women's 'thoughts and imagination' are imprinted (423)—that emerge as, in Shakespeare's words, a 'living record'.[55]

[49] For instance, Wroth, *Urania*, 217, 266. Julie Crawford argues that this moment is 'an exemplum for the interpretive practices of the romance as a whole', demonstrating the 'possibility' for textual 'excavation' that persists throughout *Urania (Mediatrix: Women, Politics, and Literary Production in Early Modern England* (Oxford, 2014), 162).

[50] Vin Nardizzi and Miriam Jacobson, 'The Secrets of Grafting in Wroth's *Urania*', in Jennifer Munroe and Rebecca Laroche (eds), *Ecofeminist Approaches to Early Modernity* (Basingstoke, 2011), 183.

[51] Margaret Simon similarly finds Horatian and Shakespearean intertexts in the first song of *Pamphilia to Amphilanthus*. See Simon, 'Mary Wroth's Ephemeral Epitaph'.

[52] Shakespeare, Sonnet 55, in Gary Taylor, John Jowett, Terri Bourus, and Gabriel Egan (eds), *The New Oxford Shakespeare: Modern Critical Edition*, Vol. 1 (Oxford, 2017), 1470.

[53] Dubrow, *Echoes*, 159.

[54] See Crawford, *Mediatrix*, 167–70; and Hackett, *Women and Romance*, 161.

[55] Shakespeare, Sonnet 55, line 8.

Their 'posterity' is not proclaimed, but we see it in action within the narrative: poems written by both men and women in *Urania* are burnt and buried, whereas only women's verses—particularly Pamphilia's—circulate within a community of likeminded readers. Although the dangers of circulating intimate poems and revelatory letters is made very clear in *Urania*, a highly positive mode of transmission also emerges. Women in the romance regularly share their poetry with one another orally and textually:[56] one hears Pamphilia's verses and, 'desiring the Copy', has it 'promised ... and many more' (392). Elsewhere, Pamphilia hears a poetic dialogue between a shepherd and 'a dainty louing lass' and has it 'written out' (143). On another occasion, the absence of men's poetry from this network of transcription and circulation is made explicit: Pamphilia describes, as she often does, a male lover who commends variety in love and a woman who defends constancy. 'The coppie of his I have not', she tells her audience, but 'hers bee these' (315).

Urania has long been understood as a text about the gendered circulation of poetic manuscripts. I want to add to this a sense of the intricate physical detail with which Wroth imagines her literary work coming into being, and of how the multiple textual objects and embodied acts of writing in the romance add up to a complex whole. The landscape of *Urania* is analogous to a literary miscellany made up of countless loose sheets of paper that are repeatedly copied, lost, destroyed, imitated, and supplemented.[57] This miscellany is neither wholly manuscript nor print, but incorporates the diverse modes of textual production and consumption available in the early modern period. The papers laid between Pamphilia's 'rich imbroyderies', or creative intellect, form the imaginative centrepiece of this miscellany, similar to Pamphilia's grove which serves as a self-generative gathering of paper on which the poet, and those she inspires, 'engraue', 'insculpt', 'carue', 'write', and 'imbroider' texts.[58] Trees might seem wholly 'unlike paper', rooted to one place, permanently public, and enduring.[59] Trees, though, are organic, mutable beings, always transforming through growth and decay.[60] As a whole, the trees in Pamphilia's grove figure for the composite miscellany that makes up *Urania* and its imagined history as a published text: the acts of reading and writing Wroth imagines it inspiring extend beyond pen and paper to the engraving, sculpting, carving, and embroidering that took place in the early modern household.

The idea that Wroth's textual creation is the imprint of a 'rich imbroyder[y]' pressed against paper sheets might seem passive, downplaying the poet's agency, but the analogy

[56] See Barbara Kiefer Lewalski for precise figures regarding the gender ratio of poets in *Urania*; in *Writing Women in Jacobean England* (Harvard, MA, 1993), 279.

[57] On the 'polyvocality' of *Urania* and readers' manuscript additions to the incomplete, printed text, see Rodgers, 'Embedded Poetry'.

[58] Wroth, *Urania*, 75, 110, 161, 270, 273, 416. Tree-writing is a long-standing romantic trope. Pamphilia's grove differs from its predecessors in the number of readers that add to it, and in the variety of verbs used to describe the act of carving. See, for instance, Pamela and Musidorus in Philip Sidney's *Arcadia* and Orlando in Shakespeare's *As You Like It*.

[59] Nardizzi and Jacobson, 'Secrets of Grafting', 183.

[60] On the impermanence of trees as textual supports, see Leah Knight, *Reading Green in Early Modern England* (Farnham, 2014), 95–105.

is as much artful *sprezzatura* as modesty trope. The labour of writing is replaced by an effortless grazing against a paper sheet. We imagine ourselves within a domestic space, opening a chest that contains gorgeous embroideries and dwell, for a moment, on the demands of household work. As we do so, we admire the skilful way that Wroth embroiders her own highly sophisticated play with literary tradition, and the material rhythms of reading and household work. Neither this literary play nor the composite nature of Wroth's text are straightforwardly gendered: male poets of the period similarly query ideas of literary tradition and endurance, and, as book historians have argued with increasing frequency in the last decade, early modern textual culture more broadly was defined by its mutability. *Urania* is representative of this wider literary culture, and a small number of Pamphilia's readers and poetic imitators are men. It becomes clear, though, as we observe the process of composing, copying, circulating, and storing the miscellany that makes up *Urania*, that women are much better readers and poets than men, and that Pamphilia is the most skilful of them all.

The archival recovery of early modern women's writing is ongoing, and the texts produced and reading traces left behind by early modern women will continue to reshape the field of book history and our understanding of what constitutes texts and books. We should keep in mind the warnings of those wary of the material turn and be sure to attend to the 'writing itself'. Wroth's textual play with household paper in her *Urania* prompts us, however, to consider more carefully the interrelation of writing and its material forms. Understanding of what writing *is* has radically expanded in recent years, and our critical approaches must themselves expand to meet it, attending to the material knowledge figured in the works of early modern women in *conjunction* with, not instead of, their literary forms and textual peculiarities. After all, flimsy sheets of wrapping paper might prove to be, like the embroideries they encompass, figuratively rich, and so function imaginatively—as well as practically—in the early modern household.

FURTHER READING

Bittel, Carla, Elaine Leong, and Christine von Oertzen (eds). *Working With Paper: Gendered Practices in the History of Knowledge*. Pittsburgh, PA, 2019.

Brayman, Heidi. *Reading Material in Early Modern England*. Cambridge, 2005.

Fleming, Juliet. *Graffiti and the Writing Arts of Early Modern England*. London, 2001.

Frye, Susan. *Pens and Needles: Women's Textualities in Early Modern England*. Philadelphia, PA, 2010.

Wall, Wendy. *Recipes for Thought: Knowledge and Taste in the Early Modern Kitchen*. Philadelphia, PA, 2015.

Wayne, Valerie (ed.). *Women's Labour and the History of the Book*. London, 2020.

CHAPTER 46

MEMORY AND MATTER

Lady Anne Clifford's 'Life of Mee'

PATRICIA PHILLIPPY

A TRUE MEMORIALL

LADY Anne Clifford's manuscript writings are emporia of objects, artefacts, creations, and commodities; a vast network of goods that complicates conventional readings of Clifford's life and works as single-mindedly commemorating, and thereby promoting, her dynastic identity and claim. Clifford's textual storehouses include, among other things, wedding rings, buckskin gloves, Irish stitch work cushions, jewellery, portraits, 'doucets' of two deer, and a lock of a child's hair enclosed in a letter. Among the quantities of 'kitchen stuff' prepared or consumed by her households, Clifford numbers rosemary cakes, venison, quince marmalade, cherries, pancakes, beer, sack, white wine, and pulp of pomcitron, as well as medicinal 'cordials and concerves' and 'alchermy'. And, of course, there are books—Sidney's *Arcadia*, Montaigne's *Essays*, Spenser's *Faerie Queene*, Augustine's *City of God*—as well as manuscripts, maps, and chronicles which Clifford both read and wrote.[1]

This collection suggests the transient pleasures that Clifford's possessions must have afforded her, and highlights their commemorative afterlives in Clifford's writings. It serves as an apt starting point for this chapter, which situates Clifford's memorial project at the interfaces of materiality and memory in order, on the one hand, to escape

[1] This catalogue is based upon Anne Clifford, in Jessica L. Malay (ed.), *Anne Clifford's Autobiographical Writing, 1590–1676* (Manchester, 2018), hereafter cited as *AW*. The volume includes modernised texts of 'The Countess of Dorset's diary' (1616–1619), Clifford's 'Life of me' (written *c* 1649), her 'Yearly memoirs' from 1650 to 1675, and her 'Daybook', which covers January 1676 to Clifford's death on 22 March of the same year. 'Life of mee' and 'Yearly memoirs' are also published in original spelling in Anne Clifford, in Jessica L. Malay (ed.), *Anne Clifford's Great Books of Record* (Manchester, 2015), 795–905, hereafter cited as *GB*. Quotations are from *GB*, and to *AW* for sources not included in *GB*.

the confines of an exclusively dynastic reading of Clifford's archive and, on the other, to explore her productive engagement with the early modern art of memory. In fact, these two domains share similar features. 'Memory', as Garrett Sullivan asserts, is 'both a somatic activity and a social practice', and dynasty, likewise, inscribes the natural body within a symbolic order that bestows social meaning upon it. Moreover, both dynastic promotion and memory work are 'linked to, if not constitutive of... ideal conception[s] of masculinity'.[2] As such, both cast women as objects useful to the male subject, whether as ideas captured and retrieved by memory, or as female kin exchanged to consolidate dynastic power.[3]

Despite this masculine hegemony, Clifford's writings and commemorative works establish her as a remembering subject who employs the memory arts to create powerful social, personal, and dynastic interventions. Rather than simply displacing the male subject, or coexisting with the mnemonic objects she deploys, Clifford troubles the gendered division of subject and object, occupying a medial space where identities intertwine. She is a subject immersed in matter, whose memorial gestures and metaphors suggest an art of memory that is embodied, embedded, and transformative. When Clifford borrows a startlingly counter-dynastic image to recall her two marriages, she embodies this immersion, and employs strategies characteristic of her engagement with the 'mnemonic episteme' permeating the early modern world.[4] In 'A summary of the records and a true memoriall of the life of mee, the Ladie Anne Clifford', she recalls:

> So as in both their life tymes the marble pillers of Knolle in Kentt and Wilton in Wilteshire were to mee oftentimes but the gaie harbours of anguish, in somuch as a wise man that knew the inside of my fortunes would often saie thatt I lived in both these, my Lords' great families, as the river of Roane or Rhodamus runns through the lake of Geneva without mingling any part of its streams with that lake. (*GB*, 802)

Clifford's equation of 'great families' with their landed estates—the Sackvilles of Knole, the Herberts of Wilton—anticipates her recoveries and restorations of the Clifford castles: Skipton, Brougham, Brough, Appleby, and Pendragon.[5] The passage, further, embeds a memorial for Philip Herbert's uncle Philip Sidney that displays Clifford's art of memory in action; her retention and recollection of a passage from the *Old Arcadia*, whose 'marble bowers [were] many times the gay harbours of anguish', become the

[2] Garrett A. Sullivan, Jr., *Memory and Forgetting in English Renaissance Drama: Shakespeare, Marlowe, Webster* (Cambridge, 2005), 39.

[3] Peter of Ravenna's *Book of Memory*, published in English in 1545, advised the use of women as mnemonic objects: see Lina Perkins Wilder, 'Veiled Memory Traces in *Much Ado About Nothing*, *Pericles* and *The Winter's Tale*', in Andrew Hiscock and Lina Perkins Wilder (eds), *The Routledge Handbook of Shakespeare and Memory* (New York, 2018), 239–52, 240.

[4] William E. Engel, Rory Loughnane, and Grant Williams (eds), *The Memory Arts in Renaissance England: A Critical Anthology* (Cambridge, 2016), 11.

[5] See John A. A. Goodall, 'Lady Anne Clifford and the Architectural Pursuit of Nobility', in Karen Hearn and Lynne Hulse (eds), *Lady Anne Clifford: Culture, Patronage and Gender in 17th-century Britain*, Yorkshire Archaeological Society Occasional Papers No. 7 (2009), 73–86.

austere ports of call through which she has passed.[6] Moreover, the form of the work, as a 'summary of the records and a true memoriall', involves time shifts—like those observed in Clifford's *Great Picture*, discussed later—that rehearse a spatial precision amid blurring temporalities, arguing that the 'life of mee' has been submerged or suspended on a personal timeline between the loss of Clifford's inheritance in 1605 and its retrieval in 1643. This submersion and singularity are captured in the incongruous image of water within water, which defies the mixing of like elements to flow undiluted on an independent course.

Clifford's metaphor undoes the dynastic formula that unites noble families through the mingling of bloodlines. Clifford would have read in Fynes Moryson's *Itinerary* (1617) that the Rhodanus, 'falles into this Lake [Geneva], having so cleare a colour, as it seemes not at all to mingle with the standing water of the Lake', and she aligns herself with this amazing work of nature to extricate virginal corporeality from the cultural text of dynastic affiliation.[7] Forgetting the fact of physical intercourse, belied by the birth of two surviving daughters to Richard Sackville, Clifford slips between elements, intact and unsullied. Like Clifford herself, moreover, her daughters Margaret and Isabella Sackville are imagined as carrying exclusively the pure Clifford blood and legacy, marvellously emulating Idonea and Isabella de Veteripont, the thirteenth-century sisters who set the precedent for Clifford's claim to the masculine right of primogeniture.[8] Composed of countless physical, emotional, and intellectual droplets intermingling within a fluid form, Clifford remains, essentially, a Clifford. Memory, in this image and throughout Clifford's corpus, is a river that blends and dissolves oppositions; that adapts and retains its shape amid the shifting, shapeless flow of time and place; and that gives shape to the blended subject immersed within it. As Karen Barad writes: 'Memory—the pattern of sedimented enfoldings of iterative intra-activity—is written into the fabric of the world. The world "holds" the memory of all traces; or rather the world *is* its memory'.[9]

As memory studies have come to engage theories of embodiment, critics have usefully observed that the early modern art of memory is predicated, as Garrett Sullivan puts it, on 'a pre-Cartesian conception of mind and body as intertwined and imbricated in one

6 Philip Sidney, in Katherine Duncan Jones (ed.), *The Countess of Pembroke's Arcadia (The Old Arcadia)* (Oxford, 1985), 76. See Heidi Brayman Hackel, '"Turning to her 'Best Companion[s]": Lady Anne Clifford as Reader, Annotator and Book Collector', in Karen Hearn and Lynne Hulse (eds), *Lady Anne Clifford: Culture, Patronage and Gender in 17th-century Britain*, Yorkshire Archaeological Society Occasional Papers No. 7 (2009); and *AW*, 66.

7 Fynes Moryson, *An Itinerary* (London, 1617), 180. Jessica L. Malay, 'Reassessing Anne Clifford's Books: The Discovery of a New Manuscript Inventory', *Papers of the Bibliographical Society of America*, 115.1 (2021), 1–41, discusses a newly discovered manuscript inventory of Clifford's books (1684) which affirms that Clifford owned Moryson's *Itinerary*. James Halder et al., 'Mixing of Rhône River water in Lake Geneva (Switzerland–France) inferred from stable hydrogen and oxygen isotope profiles', *Journal of Hydrology*, 477 (2013), 152–64, concludes that the majority (63%) of the Rhône current remains distinct from the lake waters.

8 See *GB*, 113–56.

9 Karen Barad, 'Quantum Entanglements and Hauntological Relations of Inheritance: Dis/continuities, SpaceTime Enfoldings, and Justice-to-Come', *Derrida Today*, 3.2 (2010), 240–68, 261.

another'.[10] The mind and body in question are normatively masculine, propelled by a cognitive discipline that is mirrored in orthodox social behaviour. Women, meanwhile, are associated with an oblivion that undermines memorial discipline; their cold, moist bodies are prone to lethargy, etymologically and notionally wedded to the River Lethe. Clifford's incarnation as the tenacious Rhône rushing through the stagnant waters of Geneva seems pointedly to reverse memory's gendered figures. Clifford is one of many early modern women who employ mnemonic practices in quotidian activities, written works, and social performances. Yet, little attention has been given to women writers' engagements with the arts of memory.[11] This chapter begins to repair this critical lacuna by marrying memory studies to feminist new materialism, a methodology that maps the entanglements of gendered bodies with animated, 'vibrant' matter.[12] This reading of Lady Anne Clifford's memorial enterprises asserts that memory is embodied and, further, that the body is inseparable from and enmeshed in the agency of matter. Seeing Clifford as a creature intertwined with her world, and understanding her world *as* the memory of material entanglements enlivens the critical relationship between memory and matter and opens a space for women's identification as remembering subjects. Clifford's innovative, creative engagement with memorialisation breaks the restrictive confines of dynasty and of the period's mnemonic practices to pursue instead intra-actions—as Barad puts it, 'mutual constitutions of entangled agencies'—that dissolve oppositions and enfold past, present, and future.[13]

THE STOREHOUSE AND THE THREAD

The early modern art of memory, as Andrew Hiscock and Lina Perkins Wilder put it, 'was a practical and necessary skill, a discursive practice, a moral and religious imperative ... but also [a] gendered competency, an indication of a particular sensibility, [a]

[10] Sullivan, *Memory*, 39. See also Lina Perkins Wilder, *Shakespeare's Memory Theatre: Recollection, Properties, and Character* (Cambridge, 2010); Isabel Karremann, *The Drama of Memory in Shakespeare's History Plays* (Cambridge, 2015); and for discussion, see Kate Chedgzoy, Elspeth Graham, Katherine Hodgkin, and Ramona Wray, 'Researching Memory in Early Modern Studies', *Memory Studies*, 11.1 (2018), 5–20, 12–15. For an inclusive overview of recent work in memory studies, see Rebecca Helfer, "The State of the Art of Memory and Shakespeare Studies", in Andrew Hiscock and Lina Perkins Wilder (eds), *The Routledge Handbook to Shakespeare and Memory* (New York, 2018), 315–28.

[11] Notable exceptions to this trend are Danielle Clarke, 'Memory and Memorialization in the Psalms of Mary Sidney, Countess of Pembroke', *Memory Studies*, 11.1 (2018), 85–99; and Andrew Hiscock, *Reading Memory in Early Modern Literature* (Cambridge, 2011).

[12] Jane Bennett, *Vibrant Matter: The Political Ecology of Things* (Durham, NC, 2009). See also Karen Barad, *Meeting the Universe Halfway: Quantum Physics and the Entanglement of Meaning and Matter* (Durham, NC, 2007); Stacy Alaimo, *Bodily Natures: Science, Environment and the Material Self* (Bloomington, IN, 2010); and Rosi Braidotti, *The Posthuman* (Cambridge, 2013).

[13] Barad, *Meeting*, 33. She further explains, 'distinct agencies do not precede, but rather emerge through, their intra-action' (33).

human potential residing in the hindermost of the brain's three ventricles'.[14] Derived from classical sources (chiefly Aristotle, Galen, Cicero, and Augustine), early modern physiology located memory within the last of three compartments of the brain, preceded by imagination and reason.[15] Memory training pervaded nearly every aspect of life in the period, exploiting spatial metaphors of the palace, storehouse, or theatre, to improve natural memory with more infallible techniques. John Willis' *Mnemonica, or, The Art of Memory* (1618) teaches readers to construct a mental '*Repository*', 'an imaginary fabrick, fancied Artificially, built of hewen stone, in the form of a *Theater*'. This memory theatre is divided into 'places' where 'Ideas' ('visible representation[s] of things to be remember'd') are displayed.[16] His catalogue of Ideas makes of the memory theatre a cabinet of curiosities:

> Let the *Ideas* of things usually hanged against a Wall, be so disposed in the *Repository*, as Musical Instruments, Arms, Looking-Glasses, Pictures, Brushes, written tables... Title-pages of Books pasted against the Pillar, Proclamations, or printed pages nailed to the Wall [and] such things as lye, or are any ways situate on the ground [as] living Creatures, whether standing, sitting, or lying, *etc.*[17]

Willis' *Art of Memory*, 'drained out of the pure fountains of Art and Nature', acknowledges the coexistence of natural and artificial memories while promoting a *techne* to enhance nature with art.

If memory is 'a gendered competency', it was largely gendered masculine in the early modern period. Memory training consisted of 'rhetorical mnemotechnology', employed in schools to train boys destined for careers in the public sphere.[18] From a physiological standpoint, moreover, humoral theory informed mnemonic ability: women were considered phlegmatic, and, as Galen argued, 'phlegm causes lethargy with the loss of memory and intelligence'.[19] What was expected of women threatened men: the 'moyste and veraye colde humour wasshing the braine' produced an excess of phlegm which led to oblivion and effeminacy.[20] When Edward Rainbowe eulogises Clifford, praising her

[14] Andrew Hiscock and Lina Perkins Wilder, 'Introduction', in Andrew Hiscock and Lina Perkins Wilder (eds), *The Routledge Handbook to Shakespeare and Memory* (New York, 2018), 3.

[15] Foundational works include Frances Yates, *The Art of Memory* (London, 1966); Mary J. Carruthers, *The Book of Memory* (Cambridge, 1990); and Paolo Rossi, *Logic and the Art of Memory* (Chicago, IL, 1960). See also Lina Bolzoni, *The Gallery of Memory: Literary and Iconographic Models in the Age of the Printing Press* (Toronto, 2001); and William E. Engel, 'Mnemonic Criticism and Renaissance Literature: A Manifesto', *Connotations*, 1.1 (1991), 12–33. Hiscock, *Reading Memory*, 1–36, provides an astute summary of the early modern reception of classical and medieval memory arts.

[16] John Willis, *Mnemonica, or, The Art of Memory* (London, 1661), 52. Willis' treatise circulated in manuscript from 1618.

[17] Willis, *Mnemonica*, 62–3.

[18] Hiscock, *Reading Memory*, 17.

[19] Jacques Jouanna, in Philip van der Eijk (ed.) and Neil Allies (trans.), *Greek Medicine from Hippocrates to Galen: Selected Papers* (Leiden, 2012), 340 nn 22 and 23.

[20] Quoted in Sullivan, *Memory*, 31.

'great sharpness of Wit, a faithful Memory, and deep Judgment',[21] he credits Clifford with masculine attributes and habits that suggest her familiarity with the techniques of artificial memory:

> she would frequently bring out of the rich Store-house of her *Memory* ... Sentences, or Sayings of remark, which she had read or learned out of Authors, and with these her Walls, her Bed, her Hangings, and Furniture must be adorned; causing her Servants to write them in Papers, and her Maids to pin them up, that she, or they, in the time of their dressing, or as occasion served, might remember, and make their descants on them.[22]

This materialisation of Willis' imaginative memory theatre complements Clifford's recorded transformation of her closet at Knole into a cabinet of curiosities resembling Willis' repository, replete with books, portraits, rarities blending art and nature, and *naturalia* with occult powers (heliotrope, amber, and rock crystal). In her exercise of the discipline of memory, as in her activities as a collector, as Elizabeth Chew has noted, Clifford 'insert[ed] herself into what had traditionally been marked out as a predominantly male cultural space'.[23]

Although memorial *techne* was most often a masculine practice, Kate Chedgzoy has argued that the metaphors attending the arts of memory, specifically the wax tablet and the storehouse, resonated with women's experience. Figured as malleable and changeable, women were commonly associated with wax, available to receive impressions—whether offspring or moral instruction—from men. The storehouse, meanwhile, refers women's mnemonic skills to the domestic sphere, where *oeconomia* was 'a practical and ideologically valued form of memory work'.[24] Clifford certainly deployed her memorial skills in the domestic sphere: her 'Daybook' for 1676 records the quotidian workings of her household at Brougham Castle in exquisite detail. This textual storehouse was akin to her mother, Margaret Clifford's, manuscript 'Book of Physick & Alchemye', a volume memorialised in the central compartment of Clifford's *Great Picture*.[25]

Considering Clifford's household mnemonics, Chedgzoy nominates her as 'a Mistress of Memory' within a broader argument that the domestication of memory work constituted an internalisation of masculine discipline to which women were compelled and by which they were defined.[26] It should be noted, however, that this reading of

[21] Edward Rainbowe, *Sermon Preached at the Funeral of the Right Honorable ANNE, Countess of Pembroke, Dorset and Montgomery* (London, 1676), 38.

[22] Rainbowe, *Sermon*, 40. See also Clarke, 'Memory and Memorialization', 89–92.

[23] Elizabeth V. Chew, '"Your Honor's Desyres": Lady Anne Clifford and the World of Goods', in Karen Hearn and Lynne Hulse (eds), *Lady Anne Clifford: Culture, Patronage and Gender in 17th-century Britain*, Yorkshire Archaeological Society Occasional Papers No. 7 (2009), 25–42, 28.

[24] Kate Chedgzoy, *Women's Writing in the British Atlantic World: Memory, Place and History, 1550–1700* (Cambridge, 2007), 20.

[25] See Chedgzoy, *Women's Writing*, 20. The manuscript survives as Kendal, Cumbria Archive Service (CAS), cat. WDHOTH/1/5, 'Book of Physick & Alchemy (*c* 1550), with her annotations made 1598'.

[26] Chedgzoy, *Women's Writing*, 19, following Natasha Korda, *Shakespeare's Domestic Economies: Gender and Property in Early Modern England* (Philadelphia, PA, 2002), 49–51.

the imposition of mnemotechniques specifically on women underestimates the degree to which 'remembering', as Grant Williams puts it, 'could be said to overburden individuals' of either sex.[27] As a project intended to cultivate the subject—schoolboys, housewives, and citizens alike—this internalised discipline turns the individual towards approved, and distinctly external, objects and behaviours. Memory training is both an imposition on the subject and an artificial operation enacted on inert matter. If, as Wilder maintains, the disciplines of memory can only 'repeat and valorize patriarchal hierarchy', women are the passive material—the wax—on which patriarchy is imprinted.[28]

Clifford's intra-active memory work suggests a way beyond the passive gendering of the memory arts. When the housewife is christened a 'Mistress of Memory', a subtle slippage from the source for this figure reveals a mnemonic metaphor of a different order. In William Gouge's *Of Domesticall Duties*, this feminine figure is not the housewife but her (and Gouge's own) 'method':

> My method and manner of proceeding brought many things to my minde, which otherwise might have slipped by. For by method sundry and severall points appertaining to one matter are drawne forth, as in a chaine one linke draweth up another ... As method is an helpe to Invention, so also to retention. It is as the thread or wier whereon pearles are put, which keepeth them from scattering ... In which respects method is fitly stiled the Mother of the Minde, and Mistresse of Memorie.[29]

Gouge's method extemporises towards what Andrew Hiscock describes as 'imaginative memoryscapes' that replace rote learning with a mnemonic method based on 'carefully sequenced taxonomies'.[30] Accordingly, Gouge's method—like links in a chain, or a thread on which pearls are strung—displaces the static operations of subjects on objects with mingled 'cross-taxonomies', where 'objects are energetic mediators rather than passive tools'.[31]

Gouge's metaphor resonates in Clifford's memory work when she recalls, 'Upon the 22nd [of November, 1616], I did string the pearls and diamonds my mother left me into a necklace' (*AW*, 44). Six months after her mother's death, Clifford prolongs Margaret's life and memory by creating a personal token from the jewels that were her legacy. Like the potent gems in her cabinet of curiosities, Margaret Clifford's jewels also exert an aura and agency. Her mother's omnipresence throughout Clifford's life is associated with Margaret's 'profettick spiritt' (*GB*, 724), her 'discerning spiritt into the disposition of humane creatures and natural causes' (*GB*, 720), exercised in her alchemy and embodied

[27] Grant Williams, 'Monumental Memory and Little Reminders', in Andrew Hiscock and Lina Perkins Wilder (eds), *The Routledge Handbook to Shakespeare and Memory* (New York, 2018), 297–311, 307. See also Sullivan, *Memory*, 40; and Clarke, 'Memory and Memorialization', 87–9.

[28] Wilder, 'Veiled Memory Traces', 239.

[29] William Gouge, *Of Domesticall Duties* (London, 1622), sigs. f4v–A1r.

[30] Hiscock, *Reading Memory*, 17–18.

[31] Jeffrey Jerome Cohen, *Stone: An Ecology of the Inhuman* (Minneapolis, MN, 2015), 4–5.

in her possessions. Margaret Clifford's presence weaves through her daughter's life; the thread that joins past and future. Forging links in this chain, Clifford bequeaths the tokens most closely tied to her mother to her daughter Margaret in literal storehouses of memory: 'all those seaven or eight old truncks and all that is within them, being for the most part old things that were my deare and blessed mother's, which truncks commonly stand in my owne chamber'.[32] Clifford's bequests are 'a meshwork of connections' joining objects, subjects, forces, and agencies, past, present, and future.[33]

Gouge's vibrant thread suggests the vital entanglement of human and nonhuman partners in emergent memoryscapes and, as such, resonates in new materialist theory. Barad uses this figure to describe the intra-action of matter, space, and time:

> The past is not closed ... 'Past' and 'future' are iteratively reconfigured and enfolded through the world's ongoing intra-activity ... Phenomena are not located in space and time; rather, phenomena are material entanglements enfolded and threaded through the spacetimemattering of the universe.[34]

Clifford's memories are enmeshed in intertwined spaces, times, and matters. In 'The Life of mee' she situates her second marriage among the Russell tombs, amid her mother's networks of affiliation:

> And mee thinks it is remarkable thatt I should be this second time marryed in that church of Cheynis in the vault whereof be interred my great-grandfather and grandfather of Bedford and their wyves, auncestors to my blessed mother, and also her sonne the Lord Robert Clifford, and her eldest sister, Anne, Countess Dowager of Warwick, their neice the Lady Frances Bourchier ... and their nephew Edward Russell third Earl of Bedford. (*GB*, 809)

Immersed in matter and propelled by 'wonderful' providence (*GB*, 809), Clifford and her Russell ancestors—links in a chain joining her to her mother—are contemporarily present: the past is never closed. Enfolded in 'the fabric of the world', time is threaded through matter. Clifford's intra-action with the Russell monuments calls forth Margaret Clifford's 'profettick spiritt', an agential presence guiding her daughter's course.[35]

A similar intra-action is portrayed in Clifford's *Great Picture* (see Figure 46.1), where remembrance is embodied in the mingling of creatures across porous temporal borders. Clifford as subject materialises here in plural. She is doubly represented in the two interiors of the side panels, coexisting spatially in a pliable temporality. In the panel between them, as in the vault at Chenies, bodies congregate across the threshold between

[32] TNA, PROB 11/350/410, 'Will of Anne, Lady Clifford, Countess of Pembroke, Dorset and Montgomery', proved 3 April 1676. Chew suggests that Clifford transported her mother's trunks on travels between households ('"Your Honor's Desyres"', 41).

[33] Cohen, *Stone*, 2.

[34] Barad, 'Quantum Entanglements', 261.

[35] Chew, '"Your Honor's Desyres"', 30.

FIGURE 46.1 Jan van Belcamp, attrib. *The Great Picture* (1646). Lakeland Art Trust—Abbott Hall Gallery and Museum, Kendal. CC/PD.

life and death. All of the family members depicted in the central panel are dead, save Clifford herself: as the inscription tells us, she is present in her mother's pregnant body, already immersed in 'the flesh of the world'.[36] As Danielle Clarke notes, Margaret Clifford holds the Book of Psalms, 'the ultimate iterative text,' mobilising a chain of matrilineal inheritance, both spiritual and material, reaching backwards to include Clifford's predecessor, Mary Sidney Herbert, Countess of Pembroke, who finished her brother's incomplete translation of the Psalms.[37] The picture enlivens a meshwork of connections where memory and matter, past and present intertwine. In this memoryscape, matter is strung on an intra-active thread. For Clifford, her method is her memory.

LITTLE REMINDERS

The seams stitching past to present in *The Great Picture* have quotidian parallels in the porous edges of Clifford's noble households; places of continual circulation and exchange among her 'family', as she calls the collective body of kin, staff, and servants sharing these bustling spaces with creatures and commodities (*AW*, 231). Her daily

[36] Maurice Merleau-Ponty, in Claude Lefort (ed.) and Alphonso Lingis (trans.), *The Visible and Invisible* (Evanston, IL, 1968), 123. The family portraits were copied from portraits dating from 1589, when Anne would in fact have been *in utero*. Clifford's scribe Edmund Langley painted the inscriptions on the *Great Picture* and reproduced them in manuscript: see Malay, 'Reassessing', n.p.; and CAS cat. WDHOTH/1/16, 'Inscriptions on the Great Picture at Appleby Castle'.

[37] Clarke, 'Memory and Memorialization', 91–2.

remembrances in the 'Daybook' of 1676 are remarkable in their detailed record of corporeality, their author's immersion in matter, and their palimpsestic shifts between past and present. 'The 20th day [of January]', she writes, 'I remembered how this day it was fifty-nine years I went with my first Lord to Whitehall, where in the inner withdrawing room chamber King James desired and urged me to submit to the award which he would make concerning my Lands of Inheritance, but I absolutely denied to do so', and on the same day, 'I had a very ill fit of wind yet slept well in the night' (*AW*, 235). On 14 February, she reports, 'early in the morning, did my black spotted bitch called [Quinne] puppy in my bed and chamber four little puppies, but they were all dead' (*AW*, 247). In the chamber, as Clifford repeatedly notes, 'wherein my noble father was borne and my blessed mother dyed' (*GB*, 892), Quinne gives birth to death in what will be Clifford's own deathbed five weeks later.

Just as Clifford materialises Willis' memory theatre by posting scraps of text throughout her chamber, she refuses to symbolically craft the creaturely other: Quinne is a piece of matter that resists abstraction, whether memorial or textual. This insistently material creature reminds us of the imbrication of Clifford's 'true memoriall' with the material bodies, human and non, emerging together within an orderly succession of expressive sites, the 'carefully sequenced taxonomies' that comprise her method: the collusion of memory and materiality.[38]

The 'Daybook' documents the somatic conditions of the eighty-six-year-old Clifford, an exacting account including recurring episodes of 'loose stools downwards', incidents of 'wind', and details of her toilette that attend to the health of body and spirit. On the morning of 22 February, she recalls:

> did I pare off the tops of the nails of all my fingers and toes, and ... burnt them in the fire in the chimney in my Chamber at Brougham Castle. And a little after ... did George Goodgion clipp off all the hairs of my head, which I likewise burnt in the fire ... God grant that good may betide me and mine after it. Psalm 23.4–5. (*AW*, 251)

The burning of hair and nails speaks to the sympathetic connection between the body and those pieces severed from it, while the Psalm suggests that the cleansing of the physical body is a talismanic cleansing of the soul, beneficial to 'me and mine'; a material enactment of the psalmic anointing of the head.

The porous household described in the 'Daybook' is a sprawling web of sympathetic connections. Clifford recalls sixty-eight visits of guests to her chamber in the three months the manuscript covers, each time kissing the women and taking the men by the hand; gestures which root memory in the material nexus of somatic and social exchange. The 'Daybook' entangles and enmeshes bodies in a transactional theatre. This record of quotidian activities locates memory within the domestic sphere, not as an internalised discipline but as an insatiable appetite for chronicling the smallest event,

[38] Hiscock, *Reading Memory*, 17.

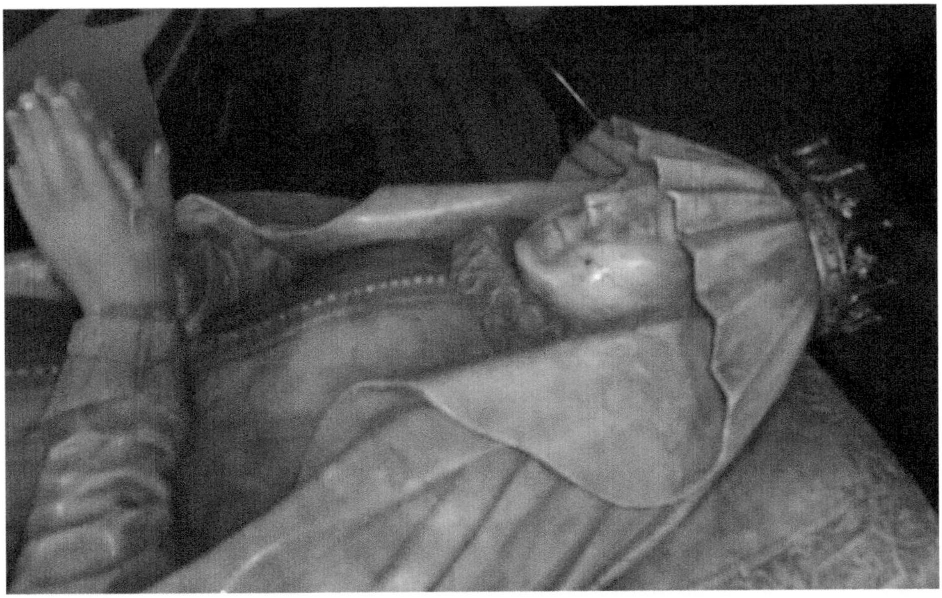

FIGURE 46.2 Maximillian Colt, Monument for Margaret Clifford, Countess of Cumberland (1617). St Lawrence's Church, Appleby, Westmorland. Photograph by Jessica L. Malay. Used with permission.

memorialising trivialities that seem unworthy of remembrance. As a work of memory, the 'Daybook' challenges assumptions of Clifford's dynastic motives. Certainly, Clifford made great use of the monumental, antiquarian, and heraldic structures available to elite men and women to celebrate noble ancestors, and her commemorative productions—from the *Great Books* to the rebuilding of the Clifford castles to her father's monument at Skipton—are well-known. The 'Daybook', however, points us towards what Grant Williams has called 'little reminders': personal, anti-monumental remembrances performed not for posterity, but enacted 'in real time … in natural memory'.[39] These contingent, temporary monuments bespeak 'a personal and private monumental practice … less material than mindful'.[40] In this context, we should note that of the eight funeral monuments Clifford erected in churches, only two—her father's and (perhaps) her own—can be said primarily to publish dynastic identity. Her monuments for poets Edmund Spenser and Samuel Daniel, for her girlhood companion and Russell relation, Frances Bourchier, and for Gabriel Vincent, Clifford's steward at Brough Castle, all attest to her 'great greife and sorrow' (*GB*, 869) at private losses. The remaining monument is her mother's (see Figure 46.2), erected in St Lawrence's Church in Appleby,

[39] Williams, 'Monumental Memories', 304 and 306.
[40] Williams, 'Monumental Memories', 308.

FIGURE 46.3 The Countess Pillar (1656). Brougham, Westmorland. Photograph by Ian Taylor. Creative Commons Attribution-Share Alike 2.0 Generic license.

Westmorland; the site appointed by her daughter and where Anne, too, 'caused [her] tomb to bee erected and sett upp for [her] selfe' in 1657 (*GB*, 835).[41]

Clifford's productive appropriation of mnemonic and monumental methods enables her to create a world of sympathetic connections; a network of intertwining spaces and times that are often reiterative and repetitious. This network weaves through Clifford's plural households, and expands beyond them as her memoryscape grows to coax from 'the landes of [her] inheritance' (*GB*, 809) their cooperation as Clifford lands. The Countess Pillar (see Figure 46.3) is an embodiment of and a monument to Clifford's matrilineal heritage; a needle whose thread weaves through her past, present, and future. The monument's intra-action with its setting enfolds the lingering presence of human love and loss: this agential place is a partner in creation. Erected near Brougham Castle,

[41] Clifford's non-dynastic monuments may have been influenced by her mother, who 'erected an obelisk in 1601 to her business confederate, Richard Cavendish with whom she had engaged in lead mining': see Adam White, 'Love, Loyalty and Friendship: Education, Dynasty and Service. Lady Anne Clifford's Church Monuments', in Karen Hearn and Lynne Hulse (eds), *Lady Anne Clifford: Culture, Patronage and Gender in 17th-century Britain*, Yorkshire Archaeological Society Occasional Papers No. 7 (2009), 43–71, 43.

at the site of Clifford's 'heavy and grievous parting' from her mother on 2 April 1616 (*AW*, 31), the Pillar commemorates the final encounter between mother and daughter, precisely marking the site in space, time, and matter. Rather than memorialising Margaret's *death*, Clifford acknowledges the *living* connection between the two women. The Pillar resurrects the pre-Reformation form of the roadside cross and its associations with powerful, remedial sites, but also redirects the contested memory of these Catholic monuments to sustain the bond joining Clifford women together across lifetimes and centuries. Clifford's memorial is both somatic and social, a blending realised in her bequest of an annual dole still given at the site on 2 April. The Pillar's meaning emerges from the cooperation between subject, structure, and site: the memory of a daughter's love and loss; the setting's suggestion of hallowed ground; and the charity that perpetually renews the connection between the Clifford women and their lands. The sundial surmounting the monument suggests at once the precision of its unique location in space and time, and its processual, transactional vitality.

Clifford's 'Yearly Memoirs' document her involvement—indeed, her love affair—with the North, and she clearly acts as co-author with the lands of her inheritance which unfold around her like palimpsests. 'I doe more and more fall in love with the contentments and innocent pleasures of a countrey life', she writes, 'for a wise body ought to make their owne homes the place of selfe-fruition' (*GB*, 818). This sense of self-fruition runs through Clifford's programmes of reparation and rebuilding, and through the stories of her progeny, which come vividly to life in the memoirs. Her accounts of the excursions of children and grandchildren 'to see the most remarkable thinges' (*GB*, 876) now include 'severall remarkable places' (*GB*, 888) near Clifford's castles: at Pendragon, Wildboar Fell, and Hugh Seat Morville; near Brougham, Whinfell Park and its landmarks, Harts Horne Tree, Three Brothers Tree, and Julian Bower. Clifford's continual chorographies between her castles passed these landmarks as well. Each of Clifford's progresses, its itinerary precisely, methodically recorded, is another thread in her web of relations and assemblages with others, objects, and sites; with past and present.[42]

One final landmark in this vibrant network expresses Clifford's co-creative engagements with the memorial agencies of the Clifford lands. Her progresses from Brougham to Pendragon Castles would lead her 'by the Pillar that I erected in memory of my last parting there with my blessed mother' (*GB*, 892) to a second pillar: on the border between Cumbria and North Yorkshire, on the summit of Hugh Seat Morville, Clifford placed a cairn (see Figure 46.4) consisting of stacked rocks, one of which is inscribed, 'A. P. 1664'.[43] 'Built of hewen stones', like Willis' memory theatre, the cairn materialises and externalises the 'imaginary fabrick' of memory. Although often interpreted as a memorial to Clifford's ancestor, Sir Hugh de Morville, his infamy as one of the assassins of Thomas à Becket complicates this reading. Rather, as Jessica L. Malay points out, the cairn is situated on the border joining Clifford's patrilineal Craven inheritance and

[42] Compare, for instance, *GB*, 892–3 and *GB*, 899.

[43] Anne, Countess of Pembroke. These initials also appear on Clifford's reconstructed buildings and churches.

FIGURE 46.4 'The Lady Pillar'. Hugh Seat Morville (1664). Photograph by Michael Graham, Creative Commons Attribution-Share Alike 2.0.

her Westmorland lands, which passed through the female co-heirs Idonea and Isabella de Veteripont, and which provided the dowers of Clifford women including Margaret Russell and Clifford herself.[44] Like Clifford, who claims in her 'Life of mee', 'never was there a childe more equally resembleinge both father and mother than my selfe' (*GB* 798), the cairn embeds and blends masculine and feminine. Clifford's memorial elides—or rather, forgets—her ancestor's murderous legacy in a hybrid memorialisation that both marks and dissolves borders.

Formally, the pillar is a subtle reminder of the trace of the human in this 'pure' landscape, but it also reveals the cultivation of matter free of human artistry. The cairn manifests, quite literally, the sedimented enfoldings of iterative intra-activity that, for Barad, define memory. Like the rarities in Clifford's cabinet of curiosities, the cairn merges human ingenuity and non-human agency. It speaks of 'human-lithic enmeshment', in Jeffrey Jerome Cohen's words, reminding us that, 'like stone, human flesh mingles dry earth with binding water: an unsettled union of wet and dry, cold and warm, fire and tears'; an unstable, supple material that describes Clifford's memorial method

[44] I am indebted to Malay, who shared this insight in conversation.

itself.[45] Situated at the source of the River Eden, the fluid border between counties, the cairn is a fountainhead of memory, mixing 'the pure fountains of Art and Nature' from which, according to Willis, memory drains. Etymologically, as William Camden notes, this Eden is unrelated to the biblical paradise with which it shares its name. Yet, as it rushes through the lands of Clifford's inheritance, the river recalls the Edenic narrative of 'self-fruition', the 'innocent pleasures' of human congruence with the non-human world. Rising below Clifford's cairn, the river 'seeketh a way Northwest, by Pendragon Castle, which hath nothing left unto it unconsumed by time, besides a bare name, and an heape of stones'; it makes its way to 'Apleby... in the upper part whereof standeth the castle aloft, environed wholly almost with the river'; until 'Eden holdeth on his course from hence... straight into the West by Whinfield, a large Parke shaded with trees, hard by... Brogham'.[46] If chorography, as Bart van Es argues, allows one 'to circumvent the established "staging- posts" of history', Clifford's fluid movements across the living map of her memoryscape—like those of the river joining her landmarks, holding a singular northward course—script an alternative, autonomous memory.[47] Blending past and present, Clifford engulfs, and is engulfed by, the fabric of the world.

A NEW MEMORYSCAPE

Women's agency as remembering subjects, Lina Perkins Wilder has argued, has the potential 'to challenge the whole structure of artificial memory' and, more fundamentally, the 'power relationships based on gender' that support it.[48] What is remarkable about this promising assessment is that it concludes a discussion of Shakespeare's female characters. Wilder typifies the tendency in the field of memory studies to attend to women, if at all, indirectly; mediated by female characters created by male authors.[49] This chapter, by contrast, has made use of feminist new materialism to alert us to the innovative means by which Lady Anne Clifford's writings and projects deploy the discipline of artificial memory while evading submission to masculine rule. Clifford's memorial work offers a case study showing how an early modern woman might destabilise the gendered dichotomies pervasive in memory work, not to tear down the structure but to redirect and appropriate it for her own use.

In the past four decades, a substantial body of criticism has brought to light a growing community of early modern women who wrote memorial works and commissioned

45 Cohen, *Stone*, 6 and 1.

46 William Camden, *Britain, or a Chorographical Description* (London, 1637), 761–2. Clifford repaired Pendragon Castle, 'the cheife and beloved habitation of Idonea, younger daughter and co-heire of Robert de Veteriponte', after 320 years of desolation (*GB*, 851).

47 Bart van Es, *Spenser's Forms of History* (Oxford, 2002), 50.

48 Wilder, 'Veiled Memory Traces', 251.

49 See, for instance, Sullivan, *Memory*, 88–108, for a discussion of Cleopatra's commemorative strategies that might usefully gloss those of early modern women.

or devised commemorative projects. Yet, this criticism has rarely addressed the arts of memory as pervasive features of culture, nor has it been in conversation with the critical field of memory studies. Focusing on women's 'natural memory', this criticism suggests that early modern women were not influenced by, or actively resisted, 'artificial memory' and the discipline it entailed. As a consequence, this work has run parallel to memory studies without intersecting that largely masculine field.[50] Clifford's project invites future research into early modern women writers' engagements with memory training and its role in the construction of subjectivity. Women's memory work can qualify the critical narrative that sees women only as the passive object of, or subordinate to, the masculine art of memory. Conversely, understanding the discipline imposed upon women as a pervasive condition in early modern culture can alert us to strategies employed by writers who, like Clifford, negotiate these limitations, clearing a space for autonomous legacies to emerge. Subtle shifts in perspective can bring into focus long-forgotten memorials in the fields of memory studies and women's writing. Such an act of collective remembrance can renew and transform our critical memoryscape.

FURTHER READING

Barad, Karen. *Meeting the Universe Halfway: Quantum Physics and the Entanglement of Meaning and Matter*. Durham, NC, 2007.

Clifford, Anne. In Jessica L. Malay (ed.), *Anne Clifford's Autobiographical Writings, 1590–1676*. Manchester, 2018.

Clifford, Anne. In Jessica L. Malay (ed.), *Anne Clifford's Great Books of Record*. Manchester, 2015.

Engel, William E., Rory Loughnane, and Grant Williams (eds). *The Memory Arts in Renaissance England: A Critical Anthology*. Cambridge, 2016.

Hiscock, Andrew and Lina Perkins Wilder (eds). *The Routledge Handbook of Shakespeare and Memory*. London, 2018.

Sullivan, Jr., Garrett A. *Memory and Forgetting in English Renaissance Drama: Shakespeare, Marlowe, Webster*. Cambridge, 2005.

Wilder, Lina Perkins. 'Veiled Memory Traces in *Much Ado About Nothing*, *Pericles* and *The Winter's Tale*', in Andrew Hiscock and Lina Perkins Wilder (eds), *The Routledge Handbook of Shakespeare and Memory*. London, 2018, 239–52.

[50] For discussion, see Chedgzoy et al., 'Researching Memory', 13.

CHAPTER 47

EARLY MODERN WOMEN, RACE, AND WRITING REVISITED

BERNADETTE ANDREA

TWENTY-FIVE years after the epochal publication of her co-edited collection, *Women, 'Race', and Writing in the Early Modern Period*, distinguished literary scholar and celebrated romance writer Margo Hendricks (Elysabeth Grace) opened her 2019 plenary address at the Folger Shakespeare Library, 'Coloring the Past, Rewriting Our Future: RaceB4Race', by evoking her 'ancestral privilege'.[1] This gesture signals her career-long commitment to a scholarly and political community that values 'the interconnectedness of gender, race, class, sexual orientation, age and other social categories which constitute cultural identity', as she wrote in her 1993 article 'Feminism, the Roaring Girls and Me'.[2] Her illustrious roll call of ancestors, interlocutors, and influences spans the 'four phases' in 'early modern race studies' documented in Kim F. Hall and Peter Erickson's 2016 *Shakespeare Quarterly* special issue.[3] It also encompasses the activists and

[1] Margo Hendricks and Patricia Parker (eds), *Women, 'Race', and Writing in the Early Modern Period* (New York, 1994); Hendricks, 'Coloring the Past, Rewriting Our Future: RaceB4Race', Folger Shakespeare Library, Washington, DC, 5 September 2019, https://www.folger.edu/institute/scholarly-programs/race-periodization/margo-hendricks, accessed 6 March 2021.

[2] Margo Hendricks, 'Feminism, the Roaring Girls and Me', in Gayle Green and Coppélia Kahn (eds), *Changing Subjects: The Making of Feminist Literary Criticism* (London, 1993), 147–53, 152.

[3] Peter Erickson and Kim F. Hall, '"A New Scholarly Song": Rereading Early Modern Race', *Shakespeare Quarterly*, 67 (2016), 1–13, 3. This special issue originated in the seminar on 'Early Modern Race/ Ethnic/ Diaspora Studies' at the 2015 meeting of the Shakespeare Association of America (3). As documented by the RaceB4Race Executive Board, 'in one flagship journal in our field [*Shakespeare Quarterly*], there have been no essays published on premodern critical race studies in the past five years aside from a special edition on the topic in 2016 (one and done?)'. See 'It's Time to End the Publishing Gatekeeping!: A Letter from RaceB4Race Executive Board', *The Sundial*, 11 June 2020, https://medium.com/the-sundial-acmrs/its-time-to-end-the-publishing-gatekeeping-75207525f587, accessed 6 March 2021.

intellectuals who shaped the 'historical materialist' standpoint of Hendricks' doctoral dissertation on early modern English and contemporary British and African American women's drama.[4] And it honours 'Zeola Culpepper Jones', her 'great-grandmother whose father was born enslaved. She was not'.[5] While ostensibly presented 'in no particular order', Hendricks' homage to her forebears and fellow travellers spotlights Black feminist scholars of early modern women's writing whose contributions were equally epochal: Hall, whose debut monograph, *Things of Darkness: Economies of Race and Gender in Early Modern England*, was published in 1995, and Joyce Green MacDonald, whose second book and first monograph, *Women and Race in Early Modern Texts*, was published in 2002.[6] In returning to these game-changing studies, I seek to elucidate 'an intellectual genealogy' that engages Hendricks', Hall's, and MacDonald's scholarship across their careers along with Hendricks' creative oeuvre.[7] This genealogy, to draw on Hendricks' key term from her 2019 plenary, confirms the indispensability of 'premodern critical race studies' (PCRS) for early modern women's studies *and* of early modern women's studies for PCRS.[8]

In his earlier assessment of the state of the field, 'The Moment of Race in Renaissance Studies' (1998), Erickson summarises:

> The principal body of second-phase work includes: Ania Loomba's *Gender, Race and Renaissance Drama* (1989); *Women, 'Race', and Writing in the Early Modern Period*, the 1994 collection edited by Margo Hendricks and Patricia Parker; Kim F. Hall's *Things of Darkness: Economies of Race and Gender in Early Modern England* (1995);

[4] Margo Hendricks [Margo Jennett Price-Hendricks], 'The Roaring Girls: A Study of Seventeenth-Century Century Feminism and the Development of Feminist Drama' (PhD Diss., University of California Riverside, 1987), 12, 35, 158, 216. Specifically, she applies '[a] materialist-feminist literary analysis' to the plays of Thomas Middleton, Aphra Behn, Caryl Churchill, and Alice Childress (10).

[5] Hendricks, 'Coloring the Past, Rewriting Our Future'.

[6] Hendricks, 'Coloring the Past, Rewriting Our Future'; Kim F. Hall, *Things of Darkness: Economies of Race and Gender in Early Modern England* (Ithaca, NY, 1995); Joyce Green MacDonald, *Women and Race in Early Modern Texts* (Cambridge, 2002).

[7] I draw the term 'intellectual genealogy' from Edward W. Said, *Orientalism* (New York, 1979), where it is never 'an exclusively academic matter' (24, 27).

[8] Hendricks, 'Coloring the Past, Rewriting Our Future'. Following Hall, *Things of Darkness*, I 'eschew the scare quotes' around race (6), as they can imply that an investigation of race and racism is anachronistic for the early modern period (Erickson and Hall, 'A New Scholarly Song', 4–5). That said, Hendricks and Parker, in their introduction to *Women, 'Race', and Writing*, place 'gender' and 'race' in scare quotes, thus signalling that both terms are 'complex, multiform and even contradictory' and require historical attention rather than erasure. See Hendricks and Parker, 'Introduction', in Margo Hendricks and Patricia Parker (eds), *Women, 'Race', and Writing in the Early Modern Period* (New York, 1994), 1–14, 7, 1. I also endorse Dympna Callaghan's dialogue with trans studies in her 'Preface to the Second Edition', in Dympna Callaghan (ed.), *A Feminist Companion to Shakespeare* (Malden, 2000, repr. 2016), xvii–xix, where she concludes: 'While "Woman" as a blanket designation with a capital letter may conflate a vast range of anatomical configurations and lived experiences, including but not limited to those related to religious identity, sexual orientation, class, race, and ethnicity, as a constitutive idea, "Woman" nonetheless remains a fully operative idea in our world, and those operations, past and present, demand critical analysis' (xix).

> *Race, Ethnicity, and Power in the Renaissance*, edited by Joyce Green MacDonald (1996); and the special issue of the *William and Mary Quarterly* 54, no. 1 (January 1997) entitled 'Constructing Race: Differentiating Peoples in the Early Modern World'.[9]

He concludes that 'the emergence of systematic, intensive investigation of race can be assigned to the period 1994–97'; at the same time, he queries 'the time lag of nearly fifteen years between addressing gender and turning to race'.[10] It is striking that the majority of these 'second-phase' works—particularly by Hendricks, Hall, and MacDonald—pursue an integrated and even intersectional analysis of race and gender; it is even more noteworthy that these three scholars do not limit themselves to Shakespeare's canon, but embrace the archive of early modern women's writing as essential for premodern critical race studies. Hall's evocation of Gloria T. Hull, Patricia Bell Scott, and Barbara Smith's groundbreaking anthology—*All the Women Are White, All the Blacks are Men, but Some of Us Are Brave: Black Women's Studies* (1982)—in her own essay for *Women, 'Race', and Writing* underscores the momentousness of this effort to rectify the neglect of women's writing in the first phase of early modern race studies from the 1970s through the 1980s and the effacement and even outright dismissal of race in the overlapping second wave of early modern women's studies.[11]

Nonetheless, as late as the 2010s, I received a reader's report recommending that I excise my extensive engagement with this scholarship on early modern women and race from a forthcoming chapter because it was 'dated', even though I cited other sources from the 1990s and before. I pushed back with a detailed rebuttal and my chapter—the only one in the collection to engage early modern women's writing—was published with its PCRS framework intact. As with the even more recent interrogation of the token inclusion of critical race scholarship in Shakespeare studies—'one and done?'—this report sought to enforce the erasures of colonialist 'premodern race studies (PRS)', which (as Hendricks elucidates) 'fails to acknowledge the scholarly ancestry (the genealogy) that

[9] Peter Erickson, 'The Moment of Race in Renaissance Studies', *Shakespeare Studies*, 26 (1998), 27–36, 33. He identifies 'the writings of Eldred Jones, Elliot Tokson, Jack D'Amico, and Anthony Barthelemy' as the first phase of early modern race studies (32–3).

[10] Erickson, 'The Moment of Race', 33–4. He refers to Carolyn Ruth Swift Lenz, Gayle Greene, and Carol Thomas Neely (eds), *The Woman's Part: Feminist Criticism of Shakespeare* (Urbana, IL, 1980).

[11] Kim F. Hall, '"I Rather Would Wish to Be a Black-Moor": Beauty, Race, and Rank in Lady Mary Wroth's *Urania*', in Margo Hendricks and Patricia Parker (eds), *Women, 'Race', and Writing in the Early Modern Period* (London, 1994), 178–94, 336 n7; and Hall, 'Reading What Isn't There: "Black" Studies in Early Modern England', *Stanford Humanities Review*, 3 (1993), 23–33, 30. She refers to Gloria T. Hull, Patricia Bell Scott, and Barbara Smith (eds), *All the Women Are White, All the Blacks are Men, but Some of Us Are Brave: Black Women's Studies* (New York, 1982). For a related intervention, see MacDonald, *Women and Race*, 147–51. For a more recent assessment, see MacDonald, 'How Race Might Help Us Find "Lost" Women's Writing', in Jaime Goodrich and Paula McQuade (eds), 'Special Issue: Beyond Canonicity: The Future(s) of Early Modern Women's Writing', *Criticism*, 63 (2021), 45–53.

continues to inhabit and nurture the critical process for the study of premodern race'.[12] Premodern critical race studies, by contrast:

> actively pursues not only the study of race in the premodern, not only the way in which periods helped to define, demarcate, tear apart, and bring together the study of race in the premodern era, but the way that outcome, the way those studies can effect a transformation of the academy and its relationship to our world.[13]

My aim in the present chapter, therefore, is to refute the sidelining of premodern critical race studies within early modern women's studies *and* to urge scholars of premodern critical race studies to integrate into their analyses (and not simply mention) historical women's cultural productions.[14] I accordingly begin with Hendricks' 'state of the field' essays, where she adjudicates 'the epistemology of race in the period' and engages with 'feminist historiography'.[15] I further adduce Hall's articulation of 'a semiotics of race' for assessing Renaissance art and literature and MacDonald's diachronic-dialogic approach to 'the intersection of race, gender, and performance' from the early modern era to the present.[16] Drawing on these theoretical and methodological interventions, I proceed to Hendricks', Hall's, and MacDonald's explications of early modern English women's writing across genres and their excavations of subaltern women's agency as English colonialism intensified over the course of the seventeenth century. I conclude with a case study that brings us to Elysabeth Grace's paranormal romance set in early modern England, the *Daughters of Saria* series, where she builds on these literary and historical investigations to imagine reparations on a cosmic scale.[17]

[12] 'It's Time to End the Publishing Gatekeeping!'; Hendricks, 'Coloring the Past, Rewriting Our Future'.

[13] Hendricks, 'Coloring the Past, Rewriting Our Future'.

[14] For some recent collections whose editors address this imperative in their introductions, see Kimberly Anne Coles and Eve Keller (eds), *The Routledge Companion to Women, Sex, and Gender in the Early British Colonial World* (London, 2018); Valerie Traub (ed.), *The Oxford Handbook of Shakespeare and Embodiment: Gender, Sexuality, and Race* (Oxford, 2016); and Ania Loomba and Melissa E. Sanchez (eds), *Rethinking Feminism in Early Modern Studies: Gender, Race, and Sexuality* (New York, 2016).

[15] Margo Hendricks, 'Surveying "Race" in Shakespeare', in Catherine M. S. Alexander and Stanley Wells (eds), *Shakespeare and Race* (Cambridge, 2000), 1–22; Hendricks, 'Feminist Historiography', in Anita Pacheco (ed.), *A Companion to Early Modern Women's Writing* (Oxford, 2002), 361–76.

[16] Hall, *Things of Darkness*, 5; MacDonald, *Women and Race*, 12.

[17] Hendricks [Elysabeth Grace], *Daughters of Saria*, https://www.elysabethgrace.com, last accessed 6 March 2021. While the setting for the entire series is global—and, indeed, cosmic—the first volume, *Fate's Match*, is mostly set in sixteenth-century England. The second volume, *Fate's Kiss*, is mostly set in seventeenth-century England. The third volume, *Fate's Consort*, is set in the contemporary San Francisco Bay Area. The fourth volume, *Fate's Promise*, appeared after the present chapter went into production, as did Hendricks, *Race and Romance: Coloring the Past* (Tempe, AZ, 2022).

THEORISING EARLY MODERN WOMEN AND RACE: EPISTEMOLOGIES, HISTORIOGRAPHIES, GENEALOGIES

In her 2019 plenary at the Folger Shakespeare Library, Hendricks recalled the 1994 publication of *Women, 'Race', and Writing in the Early Modern Period*, and shared:

> Of this book, I'm inordinately proud. It is a reflection of what I wanted to achieve as an early modern Shakespeare studies colonizer. The book was never intended solely for literary dialogue. Its purpose was to initiate conversations among and between academics working on race and gender in the early modern period.[18]

This co-edited collection's landmark essays deploy the theoretical and political perspectives of postcolonial and critical race studies to illuminate and interrogate the intersections of race, gender, and class in works by William Shakespeare, Ben Jonson, Michel de Montaigne, Thomas Heywood, Daniel Defoe, and Samuel Richardson, to name some of the canonical male writers covered in the collection. It also, and even more innovatively, engages English women's writing using the intersectional approach exemplified by, in Hendricks and Parker's words:

> Cherríe Moraga and Gloria Anzaldúa's *This Bridge Called My Back: Writings by Radical Women of Color*, Norma Alarcón's *Third Woman* journal, Amy Ling's *Between Worlds*, or Trinh T. Minh-ha's *Women, Native, Other: Writing, Postcoloniality, and Feminism*, as well as influential writing by Audre Lorde, Toni Morrison, Alice Walker, Maxine Hong Kingston, Paula Gunn Allen and others.[19]

With its stated commitment to interdisciplinarity, *Women, 'Race', and Writing* advanced literary critical treatments of then-neglected works by Elizabeth Cary, Viscountess Falkland, Lady Mary Wroth, and Aphra Behn along with contributions from historians assessing Inca and Iroquois women's agency. Hendricks' essay in this collection focuses on Aphra Behn; Hall's essay turns to Mary Wroth. Hall added Mary Sidney Herbert, Aemilia Lanyer, Elizabeth Cary, and Lady Anne Clifford in *Things of Darkness*. MacDonald covers Mary Sidney, Elizabeth Cary, Katherine Philips, and Aphra Behn in *Women and Race in Early Modern Texts*. As the field of premodern critical race studies has increasingly lodged itself within Shakespeare studies for a variety of reasons, Hendricks and Parker's aim 'to ask new questions about canonical and lesser-known

[18] Hendricks, 'Coloring the Past, Rewriting Our Future.'

[19] Hendricks and Parker, 'Introduction', 2.

texts, by both male and female authors, and to build bridges with contemporary work on "race", postcoloniality and difference' remains prescient and pressing.[20]

The precarity of the humanities and the pressures of the job market have certainly contributed to the concentration on canonical male writers, even in premodern critical race studies; still, as Ayanna Thompson explains in an interview: 'if you're really interested in the ideology of racism, then you have to start a lot earlier than people assumed. Once you move backwards in time, and you land in ... the 16th century, you have to deal with Shakespeare'.[21] Hendricks herself, even as she is recalling *Women, 'Race', and Writing* in her 2019 plenary, identifies as 'an early modern Shakespeare studies colonizer'.[22] From that standpoint, in her introduction to an anthology of previously published articles from *Shakespeare Survey*, 'Surveying "Race" in Shakespeare' (2000), she acknowledges that '[t]he one area which interests me and which I believe remains under-scrutinized is the epistemological and philosophical conceptualization of race in the early modern period'.[23] In setting this theoretical task for premodern critical race studies, she proceeds to model 'how a philological inquiry can shed light on the multivalent nature of the idea of race in Shakespeare's England'.[24]

Her close reading of two Spanish-English dictionaries published around the turn of the seventeenth century highlights 'the curious absence of the Spanish word *raza*—"race"—as a main entry in the dictionary' from 1591 and the inclusion of 'not only an entry for "raza" but one term that will have major ideological consequences in the long run, "mestizo"', which overlaps with the meaning of 'mulatto' in the dictionary from 1611.[25] As she ascertains, 'these dictionaries represent a major attempt to localize the semantic possibilities of the word "race" in the face of increasing perturbations within

[20] Hendricks and Parker, 'Introduction', 4.

[21] For the audio and transcript of Ayanna Thompson's conversation with Gene Demby and Shereen Marisol Meraji, see 'All That Glisters Is Not Gold', *Code Switch*, National Public Radio, 21 August 2019, https://www.npr.org/transcripts/752850055, accessed 6 March 2021.

[22] Hendricks, 'Coloring the Past, Rewriting Our Future'. Her essays on Marlowe and Shakespeare include: Hendricks, 'Managing the Barbarian: *The Tragedy of Dido, Queen of Carthage*', *Renaissance Drama*, 23 (1992), 165–88; Hendricks, '"Obscured by dreams": Race, Empire, and Shakespeare's *A Midsummer Night's Dream*', *Shakespeare Quarterly*, 47 (1996), 37–60; Hendricks, '"The Moor of Venice", or the Italian on the English Renaissance Stage', in Shirley Nelson Garner and Madelon Sprengnether (eds), *Shakespearean Tragedy and Gender* (Bloomington, IN, 1996), 193–209; and Hendricks, '"A word, sweet Lucrece": Confession, Feminism, and *The Rape of Lucrece*', in Dympna Callaghan (ed.), *A Feminist Companion to Shakespeare* (Malden, 2000, repr. 2016), 121–36.

[23] Catherine M. S. Alexander and Stanley Wells, 'Editorial Note', in *Shakespeare and Race*, ix; Hendricks, 'Surveying "Race"', 15. For related studies, see Margo Hendricks, 'Race and Nation', in Bruce R. Smith and Katherine Rowe (eds), *The Cambridge Guide to the Worlds of Shakespeare* (Cambridge, 2016), 663–8; and Hendricks, 'Race: A Renaissance Category', in Michael Hattaway (ed.), *A New Companion to English Renaissance Literature and Culture*, 2 vols (Malden, 2010), *i*, 535–44.

[24] Hendricks, 'Surveying "Race"', 15.

[25] Hendricks, 'Surveying "Race"', 15–17. For related genealogies, see B. V. Olguín, 'Raza', in Deborah R. Vargas, Nancy Raquel Mirabal, and Lawrence La Fountain-Stokes (eds), *Keywords for Latina/o Studies* (New York, 2017), 188–92; and Tessie P. Liu, 'Race', in Richard Wrightman Fox and James T. Kloppenberg (eds), *A Companion to American Thought* (Malden, 1998), 564–7. For a fuller analysis, see Ana M. Gómez-Bravo, 'The Origin of *Raza*: Racializing Difference in Early Spanish', *Interfaces*, 7 (2020), 64–114.

existing social relations'.[26] Furthermore, this construction of knowledge about 'race' and the concomitant constitution of racialised knowledge connects not only to 'the colonial practices under way in the Americas but also to the changing class and social dynamics in England itself' as they were mediated through the patriarchal family.[27] Hence, race, whether as residual feudal 'notions of lineage or genealogy' or emergent capitalist/mercantile 'paradigms of physical and phenotypical differences that would become the basis of later discourses of racism and racial difference', is inextricably linked to gender.[28]

In her assessment of 'Feminist Historiography' (2002) as it pertains to early modern women's writing, Hendricks similarly seeks to shed light on the blind spots in traditional Renaissance studies, which excluded women from its celebration of 'the universal man' (*l'uomo universale*), and in early feminist correctives, which excluded considerations of race from its celebration of universal 'sisterhood'.[29] Given that from the inception of the transatlantic slave trade whiteness was racialised as universal and invisible, and thus the measure of humanness, Hendricks interjects: 'in all that is "new" it is intriguing that feminist historiography continues to reflect an unconscious complicity in positing a portrait of early modern English culture that is singularly homogenous and white'.[30] As she stresses, 'it is both ironic and troubling that, despite the current critical engagement with ethnicity and race in early modern English studies, the histories of non-European (and even some European) women residing in England (especially in the larger towns and cities) remain untold or under-told'.[31] In dialogue with postcolonial feminist scholarship, she locates *Women, 'Race', and Writing* as 'an epistemological attempt' to address and redress, in the words of Chandra Talpade Mohanty, '(usually white) Western feminists' and their presumption of 'ethnocentric universalism'.[32] Hendricks asserts, quite rightly, that '*Women, 'Race', and Writing* marked a sea-change

[26] Hendricks, 'Surveying "Race"', 17.

[27] Hendricks, 'Surveying "Race"', 17–18.

[28] Hendricks and Parker, Introduction to *Women, 'Race', and Writing*, 2.

[29] Ania Loomba articulates a trenchant critique of this imperialist form of 'sisterhood' (19–21). See Loomba, 'The Color of Patriarchy: Critical Difference, Cultural Difference, and Renaissance Drama', in Margo Hendricks and Patricia Parker (eds), *Women, 'Race', and Writing in the Early Modern Period* (New York, 1994), 17–34. For the construction of 'the human' in the context of racial slavery and global imperialism, see Sylvia Wynter, 'Unsettling the Coloniality of Being/Power/Truth/Freedom: Towards the Human, After Man, Its Overrepresentation—An Argument', *CR: The New Centennial Review*, 3 (2003), 283–311.

[30] Hendricks, 'Feminist Historiography', 364. On the operations of whiteness in early modern English racial formation, with particular attention to gender, see Hall, *Things of Darkness*, 62–122; Hall, 'Beauty and the Beast of Whiteness: Teaching Race and Gender', *Shakespeare Quarterly*, 47 (1996), 461–75; Hall, '"These Bastard Signs of Fair": Literary Whiteness in Shakespeare's Sonnets', in Ania Loomba and Martin Orkin (eds), *Post-Colonial Shakespeares* (London, 1998), 64–83; and MacDonald, *Women and Race*, 21–44.

[31] Hendricks, 'Feminist Historiography', 365.

[32] Chandra Talpade Mohanty, 'Under Western Eyes: Feminist Scholarship and Colonial Discourses', in Chandra Talpade Mohanty, Ann Russo, and Lourdes Torres (eds), *Third World Women and the Politics of Feminism* (Bloomington, 1991), 51–80, 53, 55; Hendricks, 'Feminist Historiography', 365. Mohanty's essay first appeared in a special issue on 'The Discourse of Humanism', *boundary 2*, 12 (1984), 333–58.

for feminist historiography; Woman suddenly became women, and Women became women individuated by ethnicity'.[33]

As Hendricks recognises, Hall's *Things of Darkness* concurrently illustrated how 'within the epistemology and historiography of Renaissance Studies (whether literary, historical or visual), non-European women play an important role in the definition(s) of the category of Woman'.[34] MacDonald's *Women and Race in Early Modern Texts*, which appeared the same year as Hendricks' essay on feminist historiography, likewise seeks to revivify these traces and erasures, starting with her opening explication of the 1507/8 'tournament of the wild knight and the black lady'.[35] The former was impersonated by King James IV of Scotland. The latter may have been among the several women of African descent at the early sixteenth-century Scottish court or she may have been a white woman masquerading as 'the black lady', as Queen Anna, wife of King James VI of Scotland and I of England, did in the *Masque of Blackness* at the English court almost one hundred years later.[36] In concert with Hall and MacDonald, Hendricks counsels that 'we must read archival materials with the expectation that they will conceal as much as they reveal, and our task is to account for both'.[37] She does this through her case study of 'the Negress Maria', a woman (or perhaps girl) captured by Francis Drake on his famous circumnavigation the globe.[38] More infamously, he took her from a Spanish ship close to the coast of Panama, impregnated her, and abandoned her on a desolate island in the Indonesian archipelago. Her subaltern life, glimpsed in the depositions of Spanish and English men on these ships, is one Hendricks revisits throughout her oeuvre, culminating in her paranormal romance.[39] It is to this genealogy—historical, literary, and speculative—that I now turn.

33 Hendricks, 'Feminist Historiography', 365.

34 Hendricks, 'Feminist Historiography', 365–6.

35 MacDonald, *Women and Race*, 1.

36 MacDonald, *Women and Race*, 1–3. In her discussion in this book of the *Masque of Blackness* (performed at court on January 6, 1604 O. S./ 1605 N. S.), MacDonald generously acknowledges my article 'Black Skin, the Queen's Masques: Africanist Ambivalence and Feminine Author(ity) in the Masques of *Blackness* and *Beauty*', *English Literature Renaissance*, 29 (1999), 246–81, noting that its 'view of the complication of female authorship by race is similar to' hers (7 n14). MacDonald continues her commitment to accessing subaltern lives in the documentary archives and in the interstices of literary texts in 'The Legend of Lucy Negro', in Janell Hobson (ed.), *The Routledge Companion to Black Women's Cultural Histories* (New York, 2021), 66–74. See also MacDonald, 'Dark Ladies, Black Bodies: Animating Lucy Negro in Caroline Randall Williams' *Lucy Negro Redux*', Annual Shakespeare Lecture, George Washington University, 18 September 2020, https://www.youtube.com/watch?v=p41IFoBWK_A, accessed 6 March 2021.

37 Hendricks, 'Feminist Historiography', 367.

38 Hendricks, 'Feminist Historiography', 367–9. For more on Maria (likely an imposed name), see Jennifer L. Morgan, '*Partus sequitur ventrem*: Law, Race, and Reproduction in Colonial Slavery', *Small Axe*, 55 (2018), 1–17, 6–8.

39 Hendricks' attention to Maria's life was my touchstone as I investigated the historical agency and cultural resonance of gendered subalterns in *The Lives of Girls and Women from the Islamic World in Early Modern British Literature and Culture* (Toronto, 2017), 13, 39, 161 n111. My case studies address the racialisation of Central and West Asian girls and women, who were assimilated as 'white but not quite', and of the West African women who were increasingly denigrated as 'blackamoors'. Related studies

(RE)WRITING EARLY MODERN WOMEN AND RACE: FROM APHRA BEHN TO THE *DAUGHTERS OF SARIA*

In an essay that resonates with Hendricks' focus on epistemologies of race and feminist historiography in relation to early modern studies, Hall in 'Reading What Isn't There: "Black" Studies in Early Modern England' (1993) foregrounds 'the absence of black women' in the scholarly books on 'the black presence' that typified the first phase of early modern race studies.[40] In response to this symptomatic gap, she proposes to 'use the figure of the black woman as an example for the problematics of the historical study of race and gender'.[41] She starts by attending to '[t]he unnoticed black women' in Shakespeare's plays, even if they have no lines and may not appear on stage. Yet she goes beyond Shakespeare and other early modern male dramatists in attending to the 'narrative fragments' attesting to the lives of African-descended women in the British Isles as early as the turn of the sixteenth century, such as the 'black laundrymaid' (Grace Robinson) mentioned in Lady Anne Clifford's well-known diary. Hall explains that '[s]uch narrative fragments hint at the possibilities for the study of race in early modern England; however, they should also represent a cautionary tale about the ways in which the terms of representation dictate the terms of critical analysis'.[42] In other words, race as a category of analysis is indispensable not merely for investigating early modern English women's writing, which more often than not effaces its white privilege, but simultaneously for excavating subaltern women's historical agency and cultural inscriptions.[43]

As Hall expands in her essay on 'Women and Race' (1999) for the Women Writers Project, '[r]ather than isolating race as a focus, the best research sees race in relation to concerns of gender, class, religion and sexuality'.[44] Canvassing published writers such

include Bindu Malieckal, 'Mariam Khan and the Legacy of Mughal Women in Early Modern Literature of India', in Bernadette Andrea and Linda McJannet (eds), *Early Modern England and Islamic Worlds* (New York, 2011), 97–121; Amrita Sen, 'Traveling Companions: Women, Trade, and the Early East India Company', *Genre*, 48 (2015), 193–214; as well as Sen, 'Sailing to India: Women, Travel, and Crisis in the Seventeenth-Century', and Elisa Oh, 'Advance and Retreat: Reading English Colonial Choreographies of Pocahontas', in Patricia Akhimie and Bernadette Andrea (eds), *Travel and Travail: Early Modern Women, English Drama, and the Wider World* (Lincoln, NE, 2019), 64–80 and 139–57 respectively.

40 Hall, 'Reading What Isn't There', 23, 25.

41 Hall, 'Reading What Isn't There', 23.

42 Hall, 'Reading What Isn't There', 30–1.

43 For a salient intervention into current debates about subaltern agency, see Marisa J. Fuentes, *Dispossessed Lives: Enslaved Women, Violence, and the Archive* (Philadelphia, PA, 2016), which focuses on eighteenth-century Barbados. Fuentes acknowledges Saidiya Hartman's foundational work in this field, including 'Venus in Two Acts', *Small Axe*, 12 (2008), 1–14; *Lose Your Mother: A Journey Along the Atlantic Slave Route* (New York, 2008); and *Scenes of Subjection: Terror, Slavery, and Self-Making in Nineteenth-Century America* (Oxford, 1997).

44 Kim F. Hall, 'Women and Race', in *Women Writers in Context*, Women Writers Project, September 1999, repr. January 2013, https://www.wwp.northeastern.edu/context/index.html#rEss.race.xml,

as Margaret Cavendish, Duchess of Newcastle, Elizabeth Cary, Aemilia Lanyer, Mary Sidney, Mary Wroth, Aphra Behn, Jane Sharp, and Anne Clifford, she also dwells on the marginalised women inscribed in their works. As she concludes:

> [w]hile texts like *The Diary of Lady Anne Clifford* (which lists John Morocco and Grace Robinson as 'blackmoor' family servants) give evidence that women of African, [Native] American and East Indian descent lived in Renaissance England, scholars have not yet uncovered their voices.[45]

As such, '[t]hey are spoken about rather than talked with in the emerging voices of European women writers'.[46] The task, therefore, is to develop the critical and political tools to 'speak with the dead' through a premodern critical race studies and intersectional feminist engagement rather than from a '"premodern race studies" (PRS)' appropriation that 'fails to acknowledge the scholarly ancestry (the genealogy) that continues to inhabit and nurture the critical process for the study of premodern race'.[47]

In seeking to redress the muting of these subaltern voices, Hall in *Things of Darkness* drew attention to 'the Negress Maria' in the course of her discussion of the pendant Queen Elizabeth gifted to Francis Drake in the 1580s only a few years after she knighted him upon his return from his circumnavigation of the globe.[48] Dubbed 'the Drake jewel', it showcases 'a black male head superimposed on a white female head'.[49] As Hall glosses, this royal gift becomes 'a highly ironic gesture' when set against Drake's abduction, abuse, and abandonment of Maria during his celebrated (at least in England) voyage, as detailed earlier.[50] Hall delves into this visual archive in 'Object into Object?: Some Thoughts on the Presence of Black Women in Early Modern Culture' (2000), where she challenges the 'call to "transcend" black presence studies' and replace it with a deracinated model of fluidity.[51] In this essay, she counters the simplistic assumption

accessed 6 March 2021. Joyce Green MacDonald has a related essay on this site: 'Reading Race in *Women Writers Online*: Thirty Years On', in *Women Writers in Context*, Women Writers Project, September 2018, https://wwp.northeastern.edu/context/#macdonald.30race.xml, accessed 6 March 2021.

45 Hall, 'Women and Race'.

46 Hall, 'Women and Race'.

47 Stephen Greenblatt opens his influential book *Shakespearean Negotiations: The Circulation of Social Energy in Renaissance England* (Berkeley, CA, 1988) with the sentence: 'I began with the desire to speak with the dead' (1). Hendricks identifies Greenblatt as an arch-premodern race scholar (PRS) whose online course on Shakespeare's *Othello* 'typifies ... a classic, "white settler colonialist" move'. See Hendricks, 'Coloring the Past, Rewriting Our Future'.

48 Hall, *Things of Darkness*, 222. Drake returned to Plymouth Harbour, England, in September 1580; Queen Elizabeth knighted him in April 1581. Hall specifies that Drake received this gift sometime in 'the winter of 1586–87' (222), although the exact date varies in other sources.

49 Hall, *Things of Darkness*, 223, figure 12.

50 Hall, *Things of Darkness*, 222 n10.

51 Kim F. Hall, 'Object into Object?: Some Thoughts on the Presence of Black Women in Early Modern Culture', in Peter Erickson and Clark Hulse (eds), *Early Modern Visual Culture: Representation, Race, and Empire in Renaissance England* (Philadelphia, PA, 2000), 346–79, 349; here Hall takes issue with Loomba's 'The Color of Patriarchy'. Erickson and Hall return to this point in 'A New Scholarly Song', 10–11.

that representations of Black women in premodern European art and sculpture offer an unmediated window into these women's lives. Yet she also grants that some of their subjectivity and even agency can be limned in the visual archive, just as they can in the documentary and literary ones, with the qualification that the 'field of action requires a greater act of imagination when looking at black women in Europe'.[52]

This scholarly 'act of imagination' also informs MacDonald's *Women and Race in Early Modern Texts*, as when she adduces the aforementioned 'black lady's sudden disappearance' during the early sixteenth-century tournaments at the Scottish court as an instance of 'racial cross-dressing' in service of the king-cum-wild knight's imperial programme.[53] Whether or not 'the black lady' was one of the 'More lassis [Moor lasses or girls]' documented in the Lord High Treasurer's accounts is a moot point.[54] Rather, her absent presence viewed from a premodern critical race studies perspective illuminates the 'gendered tactics of communicating empire' that MacDonald assesses in the balance of her study: namely, 'the removal of dark-skinned women from representation, and the submersion of English women's racial identity into gender'.[55] While MacDonald does not address early modern women as such in her most recent book, *Shakespearean Adaptation, Race and Memory in the New World* (2020), she continues to explore 'the ways in which black women appear and disappear' in adaptations by contemporary novelists and playwrights of the African diaspora who 'do not so much "write back" to Shakespeare, seeking to erase his formulations of hierarchy, identity, and relationship, as they seek to imagine a world in which they can engage in *recreative dialogue* with him' (my emphasis).[56] This creative act of imagination starts with filling gaps and silences in the early modern canon and archive, but goes further in creating 'local worlds' no longer determined by the material practices of colonialism, empire, and slavery that shaped both.[57] And it necessarily 'engage[s] in critical analysis of the lingering potency of those after-effects as they seek to free themselves from them'.[58] Hendricks, in her paranormal romance *Daughters of Saria*, pursues a similar 'recreative dialogue' by fleshing out those subaltern lives that persist as traces in early modern sources and reimagining their futures.

As previously noted, Hendricks' essay in *Women, 'Race', and Writing* focuses on Aphra Behn, particularly her final play, *The Widow Ranter, or The History of Bacon in Virginia*, staged posthumously in 1689.[59] Here Hendricks explicates 'a racialized

52 Hall, 'Object into Object?', 374.

53 MacDonald, *Women and Race*, 2–3. Interestingly, the planned title for MacDonald's first monograph was 'Disappearing Acts: African Women in Early Modern Texts', as indicated in her review essay, 'Race Matters in American Culture', *College Literature*, 26 (1999), 193–9.

54 Andrea, *Lives*, 12, 22–6.

55 MacDonald, *Women and Race*, 10.

56 MacDonald, *Shakespearean Adaptation, Race and Memory in the New World* (New York, 2020), 1, 6.

57 MacDonald, *Shakespearean Adaptation*, 6.

58 MacDonald, *Shakespearean Adaptation*, 6.

59 David McInnis argues that *The Widow Ranter* is 'the first play purporting to represent New World life in and of itself, rather than arbitrarily selecting the New World as a spatial-temporal displacement of English concerns'. See McInnis, 'Virginian Culture and Experimental Genre in Aphra Behn's *The Widow*

discourse of civility' that 'allowed Behn to invent an "American Indian" who is both assimilable and unequivocally alien'.[60] Adducing the Powhatan woman Pocahontas ('Matoaka alias Rebecca')—who, as Hall speculates, may have crossed paths with Mary Wroth during her stay in England—Hendricks shows how, 'from the standpoint of the civilizing mission propounded by the English, miscegenation is both desirable *and* dangerous'.[61] In 'Alliance and Exile: Aphra Behn's Racial Identity' (1999), Hendricks situates Behn as a pioneer in all senses of the word who not only crossed genres, but also crossed continents to enable England's overseas colonial enterprise. She then poses a series of provocative questions that extend to Behn's subjectivity: 'Was Aphra Behn passing?'; 'If Behn was a "passer," from which parent did she inherit her black African ancestry?'; and '... what sort of "evidence," did she leave behind for an inquisitive reader, and can her writings be used to decipher the enigma?'.[62] As Hendricks reminds us, 'in the early modern English colonial spaces, not all relations of miscegenation necessarily ended as in *Othello* or *Titus Andronicus*', two Shakespearean tragedies that appear to foreclose the possibility of the 'mixed' child.[63] Rather, 'within four generations of miscegenation [the time between Shakespeare's and Behn's births], the "White Ethiop" was a very real possibility, and with it the passing subject'.[64] Hendricks thus interrogates 'Behn's texts and her position as an authorial subject in early modern England in a manner that permits an epistemological realignment of the early modern concept of race' and that enables the 'plausible history' she will develop in her subsequent scholarly and imaginative writings.[65]

In the epilogue to her 2019 plenary, Hendricks shifts more explicitly to the speculative as she weaves the archival threads she had recovered in her scholarship on 'colonialism/ imperialism, capitalism, and white sovereignty' into a lineage stretching from

Ranter', in Jo Wallwork and Paul Salzman (eds), *Early Modern Englishwomen Testing Ideas* (Farnham, 2011), 89–104, 89. In chapters four, five, and seven of *Women and Race*, MacDonald examines Behn's writing across multiple genres, along with the 'constellation of texts' and performances that preceded and proceeded from them (90). However, she mentions *The Widow Ranter* only once (148).

[60] Hendricks, 'Civility, Barbarism, and Aphra Behn's *The Widow Ranter*', in Margo Hendricks and Patricia Parker (eds), *Women, 'Race', and Writing in the Early Modern Period* (New York, 1994), 225–39, 227, 238.

[61] Hendricks, 'Civility, Barbarism', 236–7; Hall, 'I Rather Would Wish to Be a Black-Moor', 193. For Simon van de Passe's engraving of Pocahantas with her aliases (153), see Camilla Townsend, *Pocahontas and the Powhatan Dilemma* (New York, 2004), 135–58. For more on her names, see Paula Gunn Allen, *Pocahontas: Medicine Woman, Spy, Entrepreneur, Diplomat* (New York, 2003), 17–19.

[62] Hendricks, 'Alliance and Exile: Aphra Behn's Racial Identity', in Susan Frye and Karen Robertson (eds), *Maids and Mistresses, Cousins and Queens: Women's Alliances in Early Modern England* (New York, 1999), 259–73, 266–7; for more questions, see 270–2.

[63] Hendricks, 'Alliance and Exile', 271.

[64] Hendricks, 'Alliance and Exile', 271. Hendricks subsequently recognises that of 'the two mixed-race infants' with African fathers (Aaron and Muliteus) in Shakespeare's *Titus Andronicus*, one presents as black and one presents as white. See Hendricks, 'Visions of Color: Spectacle, Spectators, and the Performance of Race', in Barbara Hodgdon and W. B. Worthen (eds), *A Companion to Shakespeare and Performance* (Malden, 2005), 511–26, 517–18.

[65] Hendricks, 'Alliance and Exile', 272.

'the Negress Maria' to 'Francisco', her supposed child with Francis Drake.[66] Francisco, in turn, is figured as the great-grandfather of a girl whose given name was meant '[t]o remind her that, despite her whiteness, she was of the land, of Africa, was forever *mestizaje*, forever *desterrado*', mixed and exiled.[67] This girl became the first professional English woman writer, Aphra Behn. With this shift, Hendricks opens up a space for what Ramón Saldívar terms 'historical fantasy' and 'postrace aesthetics' in relation to early modern women's narratives of trauma and agency. Saldívar specifies that his use of:

> [t]he *post* of postrace is not like the *post* of post-structuralism; it is more like the *post* of postcolonial, that is, a term designating not a chronological but a conceptual frame, one that refers to the logic of something having been 'shaped as a consequence of' imperialism and racism.[68]

As he clarifies:

> historical fantasy is a way of describing the 'something more' that the literary works I refer to as postrace fictions do in linking fantasy, history, and the imaginary in the mode of speculative realism in order to remain true to ethnic literature's utopian allegiance to social justice.[69]

Hendricks invents just such an imaginary in her *Daughters of Saria* series when she dedicates the first volume, *Fate's Match*, to 'the Negress Maria', for '[w]ithout "Maria," Amina would not have been born'.[70] Amina is a Tamahaq—of the 'women who are direct human descendants of the archangel Lilith'—whose mother 'was given to Mali's king as a peace offering'.[71] Her story begins in 1587 as a captive on a Spanish galleon whose seizure by an English privateer propels her fate, which is to marry Captain Drake (not Francis, but his ostensible nephew Michael, who also turns out to have Tamahaq ancestry) and to bear their son (Raphael Francis Drake) in England.[72] As Hendricks elaborates in her 'Author's Notes':

66 Hendricks, 'Coloring the Past, Rewriting Our Future'.

67 Hendricks, 'Coloring the Past, Rewriting Our Future'.

68 Ramón Saldívar, 'Historical Fantasy, Speculative Realism, and Postrace Aesthetics in Contemporary American Fiction', *American Literary History*, 23 (2011), 574–99, 575.

69 Saldívar, 'Historical Fantasy', 585.

70 Hendricks [Elysabeth Grace], *Fate's Match*, 292, in *The Daughters of Saria* series.

71 Hendricks, *Fate's Match*, 11, 152.

72 Hendricks, *Fate's Match*, 250. Michael believes he is Francis Drake's nephew; however, the archangel Raphael reveals to Amina that he is Francis Drake's son with 'a Moorish Tamahaq. Enslaved by the Portuguese, Mariam was being transported to the Spanish-held island of Jamaica when Francis Drake attacked the galleon' (96). In a variation on Maria's story, Francis Drake captured, impregnated, and deposited Mariam in England to bear their child, Michael. When the child turned five, '[Francis] Drake gave his son to his childless brother with the promise of an inheritance' (96). Mariam 'died in the year 1578, not knowing where her son resided or even if he lived' (96).

> The story of Amina and Michael has its roots in an historical and troubling narrative about a Black African woman ('the negress Maria') and the Englishman Francis Drake ... After years of writing academically, I returned to my first love, writing romance, and began to ask 'what ifs' in relation to Maria's story. I realized very quickly it was impossible to recast her actual history as romance fiction and to give her the possibility of a HEA ['Happily Ever After'] even under the guise of a paranormal world. So, while *Fate's Match* is inspired by my familiarity with 'the negress Maria' account, it is not her story. In the end, *Fate's Match*, and the *Daughters of Saria* paranormal series, is my fictional homage to all women of African descent who enjoyed an HEA.[73]

Blending Amina and her female descendants' lives with angels, demons, shape shifters, and other 'supernaturals' in a narrative that spans Africa, Europe, and the Americas and conjoins lovers across ethnic and racial lines, Hendricks envisions a 'Raza Cósmica', which, as B. V. Olguín explains in *Keywords for Latina/o Studies*, 'presumably consists of the best of all peoples in a new amalgamated race' even as it can perpetuate its own exclusions.[74] Hendricks' desire to imagine a heroic life and happy ending for Maria-cum-Amina, without erasing the traumas of the history that weds her fate to Drake's, thus raises even more questions about women, 'race', and writing in the early modern period, to harken back to this generative collection and its provisional scare quotes, even as it urges the centring of gendered *and* racialised subalterns as agents of history and of its interrogation in the present.

FURTHER READING

Hall, Kim F. *Things of Darkness: Economies of Race and Gender in Early Modern England.* Ithaca, NY, 1995.

Hendricks, Margo. *Race and Romance: Coloring the Past.* Tempe, AZ, 2022.

Hendricks, Margo and Patricia Parker (eds). *Women, 'Race', and Writing in the Early Modern Period.* New York, 1994.

Loomba, Ania and Melissa E. Sanchez (eds). *Rethinking Feminism in Early Modern Studies: Gender, Race, and Sexuality.* New York, 2016.

MacDonald, Joyce Green. *Women and Race in Early Modern Texts.* Cambridge, 2002.

Traub, Valerie (ed.). *The Oxford Handbook of Shakespeare and Embodiment: Gender, Sexuality, and Race.* Oxford, 2016.

[73] Hendricks, *Fate's Match*, 289–90.

[74] Hendricks, *Fate's Match*, 11; Olguín, 'Raza', 189.

CHAPTER 48

TOUCHES ACROSS TIME

Queer Feminism, Early Modern Studies, and Aemilia Lanyer's 'Rich Chains'

ERIN MURPHY

As queer studies became institutionalised in the academy in the 1990s, two of its most influential figures argued for its need to distinguish itself from feminist inquiry. In 'Thinking Sex', Gayle Rubin argued 'it is essential to separate gender and sexuality analytically to more accurately reflect their separate social existence'.[1] In her pivotal *Epistemology of the Closet*, Eve Kosofsky Sedgwick proclaimed that 'the study of sexuality is not coextensive with the study of gender; correspondingly, antihomophobic inquiry is not coextensive with feminist inquiry. But we can't know in advance how they will be different'.[2] Sedgwick's statement marked its own provisionality, and not all schools of queer studies argued for such a distinction from feminist scholarship, but the reach of Rubin's and Sedgwick's declarations of a break were particularly formative, and too often led to a sense that either feminism and queer studies had little to say to each other, or that feminism was over, and queer studies was its successor. This chapter charts some of the results of this vexed relationship, in order to explore how more recent scholars have embraced a 'queer feminism' that eschews 'narratives that privilege antagonism and dissensus as the political and analytic relation between queer critique and feminist criticism'.[3] Challenging the 'theoretical universalism' of some strains of queer studies, feminist, queer of colour, and transgender theorists have refused the distinction between sexuality and gender posited by Rubin and deployed by Sedgwick. In early modern studies, a queer feminism has emerged, including work by Carla Freccero, Valerie Traub, Melissa Sanchez, Penelope Anderson, and others that explicitly builds

[1] Gayle Rubin, 'Thinking Sex: Notes for a Radical Theory of the Politics of Sexuality', in Carole S. Vance (ed.), *Pleasure and Danger: Exploring Female Sexuality* (Boston, MA, 1984), 267–319, 308.

[2] Eve Kosofsky Sedgwick, *Epistemology of the Closet* (Berkeley, CA, 1990), 27.

[3] Robyn Wiegman, 'The Times We're In: Queer Feminist Criticism and the Reparative "Turn"', *Feminist Theory*, 15.1 (2014), 4–25, 19–20.

on and intervenes in these theoretical conversations to illuminate the value of queer theorisations to understanding the past, to show how the past must be part of queer analysis, and to analyse the conceptualisation of the past itself. Through an analysis of the work of Aemilia Lanyer, this chapter illuminates how women's writing helps us reconsider the possibilities of queer feminism for early modern studies, especially a queer feminism that does not unintentionally perpetuate its own exclusions and hierarchies of race and gender. I will end with a brief meditation on Morgan Lloyd Malcolm's 2018 play *Emilia*, originally performed at the Globe Theatre and then in London's West End, to consider this popular mode of what Carolyn Dinshaw has called 'a touch across time'.[4] The complex dynamics of identification, erotics, and appropriation that mark Lanyer's use of biblical typology, as well as the way she has been taken up recently in the popular imagination, will show how early modern studies can contribute to the development of queer feminist analyses that attend to the mutually constitutive forces of gender, race, sexuality, religion, and status.

Early modern studies has largely moved past an oppositional moment in which queer scholars accused feminists of homophobia and heteronormativity and feminists accused 'queer scholars of misogyny and blindness to male privilege', but the earlier split still lingers.[5] Though debates about history and temporality have been central to the last two decades of queer studies, 'gender has been largely left out of these discussions', leading Loomba and Sanchez to hypothesise that the queer turn from historicism and feminism 'is an attempt to move out of the material and specific that both have (wrongly) come to represent'.[6] This double departure can lead to a kind of false universalising, which in some queer studies work ends up looking quite specific in its whiteness and masculinity.[7] A different way to narrate this scholarly moment, of course, would be to say that feminist literary criticism turned towards historicism at the same time it turned away from queer studies, which entailed risks of its own. Jonathan Goldberg and Madhavi Menon have argued that historicism's turn against universalism 'has replicated universalist assumptions; refusing, in the name of presentism, for example, the difficult task of thinking the relations between a past and present, neither of which is self-identical or identical to the other'.[8] Here, I argue that the way in which the two fields have taken up questions of history and temporality is symptomatic of the separation of these two fields more generally, with the consequence that investigations of the past, including

[4] Carolyn Dinshaw, *Getting Medieval: Sexualities and Communities, Pre- and Postmodern* (Durham, NC, 1999), 21.

[5] Ania Loomba and Melissa Sanchez, 'Feminism and the Burdens of History', in Ania Loomba and Melissa Sanchez (eds), *Rethinking Feminism in Early Modern Studies: Gender, Race and Sexuality* (New York, 2016), 15–41, 21–2.

[6] Loomba and Sanchez, 'Feminism', 22.

[7] See David Eng, Jack Halberstam, and José Esteban Muñoz, 'What's Queer About Queer Studies?', *Social Text*, 84–5 (2005), 1–18.

[8] Jonathan Goldberg and Madhavi Menon, 'Queering History', *PMLA*, 120.5 (2005), 1608–17, 1610. For an excellent summary of the heated debates on the 'queer unhistoricism', see Ari Friedlander, 'Desiring History and Historicizing Desire', *Journal for Early Modern Cultural Studies*, 16.2 (2016), 1–20.

explorations of early modern women writers, will be critical to efforts to rethink conceptualisations of gender and sexuality.

TOUCHING THE PAST

Given how fully early modern gender studies has embraced historicism, it is sometimes hard to remember that the 1980s were marked by debates between feminist scholars and New Historicists over the 'return to history'. Wai Chee Dimock offered a subtle way forwards, arguing for the importance of gender as a 'principle of unevenness' that would be critical to conceptualisations of history as it 'breaks up the seeming unity of time into its multiple sediments and infinite relays' and for historical analysis as a way to denaturalise gender.[9] Such analysis shaped the consensus that has informed scholarship on early modern studies for much of the last three decades that feminist criticism should 'be more fully historical, and a fuller historicism depended on the insights of feminism'.[10] The anti-essentialising energies underlying this consensus, however, have become muted over time, causing some of these earlier insights to lose their force, and leading to the kinds of critique offered by Goldberg and Menon in 2005. Reinvigorating these interventions will be particularly important as transgender studies provides new opportunities to rethink how gender is conceptualised across time. Queer studies' questioning of the centrality of difference to understandings of history can illuminate how claims of difference can be as damaging and narcissistic as claims of similarity as they function to consolidate a falsely unified sense of the present. In turn, feminist historicist work will be a crucial part of efforts to prevent queer studies from inadvertently reinstituting yet another disembodied universal subject.

Over the last two decades, a vast array of queer scholars have explored and vigorously debated questions of historical method and queer temporality, defined by Annamarie Jagose as 'a mode of inhabiting time that is attentive to the recursive eddies and back-to-the-future loops that often pass undetected or uncherished beneath the official narrations of the linear sequence that is taken to structure normative life'.[11] In order to bring this work more fully into conversation with scholarship on early modern women, I want to bring to the fore three threads: anachronism, desire, and reproductive temporality. As scholars deployed history to debunk essentialised understandings of sexuality, some produced a history of types, or 'taxonomy of categories or figures' that emphasised historical breaks and criticised anachronism.[12] Most influentially, a reading of Michel

[9] Wai Chee Dimock, 'Feminism, New Historicism, and the Reader', *American Literature*, 64 (1991), 601–22, 622.

[10] Jennifer L. Fleissner, 'Is Feminism a Historicism?', *Tulsa Studies in Women's Literature*, 21.1 (2002), 45–66, 46.

[11] Annamarie Jagose, 'Feminism's Queer Theory', *Feminism & Psychology*, 19.2 (2009), 157–74, 158.

[12] Valerie Traub, *Thinking Sex With the Early Moderns* (Philadelphia, PA, 2015), 87.

Foucault's *History of Sexuality* produced a narrative of the 'birth of the homosexual'.[13] Sedgwick critiqued such understandings of a 'grand paradigm shift' as producing a false sense of synchrony. In other words, narratives of historical particularity could obscure the multiple and unstable understandings of sexuality in both the past and the present, producing rather than merely describing coherent sexual categories. Thus, attempts to dislodge universalised discourses of transhistorical sexuality by emphasising historical difference had the unintended effect of erasing difference in supposedly discrete historical moments.

Critics such as Traub tried to move past the impasse over continuity and alterity by deploying what she called 'strategic historicism', 'a mode of historical inquiry attuned simultaneously to continuity and rupture, similarity and difference'.[14] Arguing that such positions did not go far enough, Goldberg and Menon advocated 'homohistory', a history 'invested in suspending determinate sexual and chronological differences while expanding the possibilities of the nonhetero, with all its connotations of sameness, similarity, proximity, and anachronism'.[15] The centrality of questions of difference and similarity to queer studies' ongoing debates about historical method show its relevance to early modern studies' efforts to remain critically reflective about its own historical practices, as well as demonstrating how writing by early modern women will provide an invaluable archive for queer studies.

Intertwined in debates over anachronism is the second thread: the role of desire in history. In the work that inspires the title of this chapter, Dinshaw argued for the importance of desire in the making of 'queer histories—affective relations across time' that recognise 'the historical past as a vibrant and heterogenous source of self-fashioning as well as community building'.[16] Arguing that the motivating force of queer time is desire, Carla Freccero offers the deliberate anachronism of the 'lesbian premodern' not as a point of origin or a lineal connection, but rather as 'a fantasmatic creature conjured for the sake of present and future survival'.[17] By emphasising the affect and desire present in all history, Dinshaw and Freccero make space for queer connections across time that do not adhere to the linearity of generations or logics of inheritance.

This brings me to the third and final thread: reproductive temporality. Freccero argues for queer time as an alternative to 'the heteronormative reproductivity of time, conceived as generations following upon generations culminating in the present and on its way to a future that will be time's fruition'.[18] Anderson has contended that queer arguments about reproductive temporality, most influentially articulated in Lee Edelman's concept of 'reprofuturism', often lend themselves to narratives of theoretical

[13] For a key intervention regarding this reading of Foucault, see Lynne Huffer, *Mad for Foucault: Rethinking the Foundations of Queer Theory* (New York, 2009).

[14] Traub, *The Renaissance of Lesbianism in Early Modern England* (Cambridge, 2002), 28.

[15] Goldberg and Menon, 'Queering History', 1609.

[16] Dinshaw, *Getting Medieval*, 142.

[17] Dinshaw, *Getting Medieval*, 70.

[18] Carla Freccero, 'The Queer Time of the Lesbian Premodern', in Noreen Giffney, Maureen M. Sauer, and Diane Watt (eds), *The Lesbian Premodern* (New York, 2011), 61–73, 64.

supersession, in which queer studies replaces a retrograde feminism: 'Following Edelman, critics often characterise the facts and metaphors of biological reproduction as problematically teleological, dismissing the feminist emphasis on those bodies most associated with pregnancy and childbirth: the bodies of women.'[19] Attending to the complex ways in which early modern women writers have represented the multiple lived and ideological temporalities of maternity as unteleological, a queer feminist analysis can prevent queer studies from inadvertently reinforcing the heteronormative narrative of reproduction it aims to contest.

Much like early modern women's representation of maternity, the particularity of seventeenth-century politics can disrupt heteronormative understandings of the reproductive temporality of politics. Shaped by a series of succession crises and civil war, seventeenth-century England was obsessed with the ability, or perhaps more importantly the inability, of reproduction to structure a stable sense of political time. Far from a guiding principle, reprofuturism in this time and place was an open debate, though in different terms.[20] Despite queer studies' many debates about how to do history, it has not been particularly interested in the ways in which history was being thought in these earlier moments. My analysis of Lanyer in this chapter focuses on her use of typology to show how histories of historical thinking can help us think beyond splits between feminism and queer theory, or historicism and queer studies.

Typology can function as a support for heteronormative thinking, whether through a divine reinforcement of lineage, or by recirculating religious desires through Edenic images of marriage that help to create a secular temporality infused with heterosexual desire. But, as we will see in the work of Lanyer, it also holds the potential to create queer connections across time.

THE INSISTENCE OF THE PAST: ELEGY, TYPOLOGY, AND QUEER HISTORY

Like many seventeenth-century English writers, Lanyer uses typology not only to connect Old and New Testament figures, but also to link the seventeenth century, particularly seventeenth-century women, to biblical figures.[21] In doing so, her poem

[19] Lee Edelman, *No Future: Queer Theory and the Death Drive* (Durham, NC, 2004); Penelope Anderson, 'Lucy Hutchinson's Sodom and the Backward Glance of Feminist Queer Temporality', *Seventeenth Century*, 30.2 (2015), 249–64, 249. For more historical accounts of reproduction, sexuality, and political temporality, see Michael Warner, 'Irving's Posterity', *English Literary History*, 67.3 (2000), 773–9; and Elizabeth Povinelli, 'Notes on Gridlock: Genealogy, Intimacy, Sexuality', *Public Culture*, 14.1 (2002), 215–38.

[20] See Erin Murphy, *Familial Forms: Politics and Genealogy in Seventeenth-Century English Literature* (Newark, DE, 2011).

[21] Donald R. Dickson, 'The Complexities of Biblical Typology in the Seventeenth Century', *Renaissance and Reformation*, 11.3 (1987), 253–72, 254.

also draws on another key characteristic of the Reformed understanding of typology: its grounding in the materiality of history.[22] Rather than merely displacing the past with the future, the move to acknowledge the lived particulars of seventeenth-century England as part of Christian history also expanded what counted as part of that history. The insistent presence of the past creates a kind of historical accretion that competes with the forward thrust of typology's structure of promise, fulfilment, and supersedure.

The refusal to leave the past behind has particular significance in Lanyer's *Salve Deus*, which is famously written by a poet whose patrons have left her behind, but also in terms of the poem's queer temporality. In *The Renaissance of Lesbianism*, Traub describes seventeenth-century literary representations of femme-femme erotics as operating in the elegiac mode, which 'renders "feminine" homoeroticism as insignificant by situating it safely in a spatially and temporally distant golden age'.[23] Lanyer, however, offers something different. Though the speaker describes the idyllic female relations of Cookeham as 'those pleasures past, which will not turne again', she refuses to leave the past in the past.[24] As Michael Morgan Holmes explains, the pleasures of the past 'are not simply lost but remade through memory as a force of "creative manipulation", intimacy, and eroticism'.[25] Through its mournful account of her relationship to Lady Margaret Clifford, Countess of Cumberland, Lanyer's poem both registers and, ultimately, resists the heteronormative closure found in Traub's examples.

But registering the productive refusal to leave the past behind as resistant elegy alone can miss the way in which the poems evince a queer temporality that extends beyond the speaker's individual loss. Lanyer's deployment of typology, particularly seventeenth-century Reformed typology, also functions as a hermeneutic through which the past asserts itself. Moving from 'a singular psychic experience of melancholic hauntedness' to 'the hauntedness that comes to us as a form of historicity', typology offers Lanyer what Freccero has referred to as 'queer historiography'.[26]

Since typology does not erase the past but instead insists upon its distinct historicity, it holds within it a resistant shard that can jam the works of supersedure.[27] Enacting

[22] Dickson, 'The Complexities of Biblical Typology', 259. Erich Auerbach also contends that typology 'differs from most of the allegorical forms known to us by the historicity both of the sign and what it signifies'. See Auerbach, 'Figura', in Ralph Manheim (trans.), *Scenes from the Drama of European Literature* (New York, 1959): 11–76, 54.

[23] Traub, *Renaissance*, 175; James Holstun, 'Will You Rent Our Ancient Love Asunder?: Lesbian Elegy in Donne, Marvell, and Milton', *English Literary History*, 54.4 (1987), 835–67.

[24] Aemilia Lanyer, 'The Description of Cooke-ham', in Susanne Woods (ed.), *The Poems of Aemilia Lanyer: Salve Deus Rex Judaeorum* (Oxford, 1993), line 18. Subsequent references are to this edition, and are cited parenthetically by poem and line number.

[25] Michael Morgan Holmes, 'The Love of Other Women: Rich Chains and Sweet Kisses', in Marshall Grossman (ed.), *Aemilia Lanyer: Gender, Genre, and the Canon* (Lexington, KY, 1998), 167–90, 181.

[26] Freccero, 'Premodern Lesbian', 65.

[27] Freccero, 'Premodern Lesbian', 64; Elizabeth Freeman, 'Time Binds, or Erotohistoriography', *Social Text*, 23.3–4 (2005), 57–68, 63.

a process of incorporation rather than introjection, typology preserves the past as an embedded object that carries the potential 'to be released as pleasure', which Elizabeth Freeman refers to as 'historicist jouissance'.[28] Of course, one could argue that a typological vision of Christian eternity that synchronises the Old and New Testament has no need for such processes, which are bound by secular understandings of time, but that would ignore what Richard Rambuss has described as the 'heterodoxies of gender and eroticism that can be embraced and inhabited through mechanisms of devotion'.[29] Rather than disinheriting the past, Lanyer's poem sustains the past in the present, and projects the past and present into the future. In the final image of the final poem in the book, 'The Description of Cooke-ham', the 'rich chains' (218) not only bind Lanyer to her mistress, but also bind her mistress to her past.

This Reformed version of typology was an inherently ambivalent hermeneutic, as can be seen in its often anti-Judaic appropriations of the past. As Achsah Guibbory explains: 'For Christians to use the Hebrew Bible in claiming to be the true Israel was an act of appropriation disinheriting the Jews, but simply to call it that does not tell the whole story'.[30] Guibbory shows how seventeenth-century English Protestants used typology to connect to 'Jews' from the biblical past while still reviling 'Jews' in the present, demonstrating the paradoxical dynamics of empathetic affiliation and violent appropriation that lie at the heart of this biblical hermeneutic. Lanyer's deployment of typology has sometimes been read in relation to hypotheses about her Jewish lineage, but the evidence of that lineage remains speculative.[31] She did, however, spend time as a child in the Calvinist household of Susan Bertie, Countess of Kent, and Guibbory has shown that Calvin's *Institutes* offered 'an alternative to Luther's Judaeo-phobia' that 'led some English people to feel a sense of connection with the Jews'.[32] Lanyer's particular emphasis on the past, in both personal and biblical terms, and the way that she brings the past, the present, and the future into coexistence resonates with a more resistant vision of typology, in which the past refuses to be disinherited by the future. Attending to Lanyer's mobilisation of typology allows us to reconsider this resistant and reparative strain of her poetry without imposing a false sense of erotic pastoralism or female community, nor ignoring its dangerously anti-Judaic valences.[33]

[28] Freeman, 'Time Binds', 64.

[29] Richard Rambuss, *Closet Devotions* (Durham, NC, 1998), 5.

[30] Achsah Guibbory, *Christian Identity, Jews and Israel in Seventeenth-Century England* (Oxford, 2010), 13.

[31] Susanne Woods, *Lanyer: A Renaissance Woman Poet* (Oxford, 1999), 5–6, 9–14.

[32] Woods, *Lanyer*, 17.

[33] Contra Butler's emphasis on loss and pain, Freeman offers the reparative mode of 'erotohistoriography: a politics of unpredictable, deeply embodied pleasures that counters the logic of development'. See Freeman, 'Time Binds', 59.

REFUSING REPRODUCTION: THE LINEAL AMBIVALENCE OF LANYER'S TYPOLOGY

Lanyer's *Salve Deus Rex Judaeoreum* appeared in print in 1611, the same year that King James I commissioned John Speed to add a genealogy tracing his Tudor lineage back to Adam and Eve to the official English translation of the Bible. As the king attempted to bolster his hereditary right by aligning it with the hereditary right of Christ, Lanyer uses a similar strategy to support her aristocratic patrons, as *Salve Deus*' 'typological structure of promise, fulfillment, and supersedure employs a pattern of spiritual inheritance and lineage, which simultaneously resounds to a similar pattern of material inheritance and lineage through which so many of Lanyer's dedicatees define themselves'.[34] As Marie Loughlin and others have shown, the poem lauds the connections between some of its hoped-for patrons and their daughters, particularly the bond between Lady Margaret Clifford and her daughter Anne, who spent much of her life arguing for her right to inherit her father's land. In Loughlin's reading of the poem, Lanyer's typology creates an alternative feminist genealogy in support of her patrons' struggles against the injustice of patrilineage. Thus, biblical typology supports female inheritance just as it supported Stuart monarchy. Perhaps for this reason, a carefully curated version of the book was presented to James I's heir, Prince Henry, the same prince to whom the king wrote his famous patriarchal text *Basilicon Doron*.[35]

Typology, however, also has the potential to compete with the lineal systems that claim it as reinforcement, and the models of kinship that Lanyer draws from the Bible reflect this paradox. Though Speed's biblical genealogy linked the Stuarts to Adam and Eve, Lanyer's turn to Genesis implicitly calls such claims of lineal authority into question:

> What difference was there when the world began,
> Was it not Virtue that distinguisht all?
> All sprang but from one woman and one man,
> Then how doth Gentry come to rise and fall?
>
> ('To the Ladie Anne', 33–7)

[34] Marie Loughlin, '"Fast Ti'd Unto Them In a Golden Chaine": Typology, Apocalypse, and Woman's Genealogy in Aemilia Lanyer's *Salve Deus Rex Judaeorum*', *Renaissance Quarterly*, 53.1 (2000), 133–79, 139.

[35] The version presented to James's heir, Henry, significantly edited the front matter to de-emphasise its challenges to lineage, suggesting that readers at the time understood its subversive potential. See Murphy, *Familial Forms*, 61–70.

Here, the poem does something more radical than substituting matrilineal for patrilineal right. By distinguishing between virtue and inheritance, the verse questions the significance of all lineal authority, contesting a system grounded in biological inheritance despite the status of Lanyer's potential patrons.

Even the depictions of female kinship suggest something queerer than matrilineage. 'To the Ladie Susan, Countesse Dowager of Kent, and Daughter to the Duchesse of Suffolke', describes the mother and daughter as lovers of Christ, representing them more as spiritual in-laws than as parent and child. Their shared love of Christ could be considered an aristocracy of faith reinforcing the aristocracy of blood, but it also offers a non-lineal connection as an alternative to material inheritance more consistent with Lanyer's query 'What difference was there when the world began'.

The community of spiritual in-laws extends beyond Lady Susan and her daughter to the many brides of Christ. Focusing on marital connections rather than lineal ones, Lanyer elevates her dedicatees as brides of Christ rather than daughters of the gentry:

> Our Lampes with oyle, ready when he doth call
> To enter with the Bridegroome to the feast,
> Where he that is the greatest may be least.
>
> ('To the Ladie Anne', 14–16)

The poet creates a shared relation to Christ, 'Our' Savior. The primary marital relation here is not the union of Adam and Eve, but rather the many unions of contemporary women and Christ. The lateral replaces the lineal and couples replace *the* couple. The hierarchical kinship of aristocracy and monarchy fades in this vision of 'the feast, / Where he that is the greatest may be least'.

EMBRACING MARRIAGE, REFUSING THE COUPLE

Of course, although challenging aristocratic and monarchic lineage could produce a queer sense of time by undermining the centrality of reproduction, using marriage as a new way to create community and continuity could defy such queer effects. For instance, John Milton's work continuously argues against hereditary government and pushes against the primacy of reproduction, but uses typology to help make normative a direct temporal connection between the marital relations of Adam and Eve and contemporary, seventeenth-century married couples.[36] Thus, by recirculating the religious desires for eternity and connection through Edenic images of marriage, Milton's work infuses secular temporality with heterosexual desire despite his distrust of reproduction.

36 Murphy, *Familial Forms*, 73–141.

But rather than privileging Adam and Eve as figures of a paradise lost (and the full complexities of Milton's couple warrant more analysis than I can provide here), Lanyer's typology of couples takes a different turn. In addition to the multiplicity of brides, the much-noted multiplicity or fluidity of Christ's gender also offers a very different idea of marriage than one bound by the conception of 'one woman and one man'.[37] Though the poem describes Christ as 'the Bridegroome' ('To All the Vertuous Ladies', 9), it also often endows him with feminine characteristics, and uses the form of the blazon to praise him:

> This is that Bridegroome that appeares so faire,
> So sweet, so lovely in his Spouses sight...
> Blacke as a Raven in her blackest hew;
> His lips like skarlet threeds, yet much more sweet
> Than is the sweetest hony dropping dew,
> Or hony combes, where all the Bees do meet;
> Yea, he is constant, and his words are true,
> His cheekes are beds of spices, flowers sweet;
> His lips, like Lillies, dropping downe pure mirrhe,
> Whose love, before all worlds we doe preferre.
>
> (*Salve Deus*, 1305–20)

As the poem proceeds, the gendered pronouns shift, as Christ is both 'him' (1342) and has 'her brests' (1343). Describing the femininity of Lanyer's Jesus as 'not gender-bound', Goldberg argues that the poem represents 'heterosexual relations and religious passion that coincide with female-female eroticism'.[38] The queerness of these relations defies an understanding of marriage as a heterosexual union.

The relation to Christ is also more than just a model of femme-femme erotics since, as Holmes argues, the poem offers 'him as the locus of triangulated eroticism between women themselves'.[39] The eroticised image of Christ's 'bleeding body', which the Countess of Cumberland can 'embrace, / And kisse' (1332–3) is 'Deepely engraved' (1327) in her heart by the female poet, leading critics to argue that the poem configures 'Christ's body as a kind of supplementary instrument' that 'vehiculates' her desire.[40] Thus, the

[37] Lynette McGrath, '"Let Us Have Our Libertie Againe": Amelia Lanier's 17th-Century Feminist Voice', *Women's Studies*, 20 (1992), 331–48, 343. On Lanyer's Christ's femininity, see also Wendy Wall, *The Imprint of Gender: Authorship and Publication in the English Renaissance* (Ithaca, NY, 1993); Michael Schoenfeldt, 'The Gender of Religious Devotion: Aemilia Lanyer and John Donne', in Claire McEachern and Deborah Shuger (eds), *Religion and Culture in Renaissance England* (Cambridge, 1997), 209–33; Janel Mueller, 'The Feminist Poetics of *Salve Deus Rex Judaeorum*', in Marshall Grossman (ed.), *Aemilia Lanyer: Gender, Genre, and the Canon* (Lexington, 1998), 99–127; Holmes, 'Love of Other Women'; and John Rogers, 'The Passion of a Female Literary Tradition: Aemilia Lanyer's *Salve Deus Rex Judaeorum*', in Anne K. Mellor, Felicity Nussbaum, and Jonathan F. S. Post (eds), *Forging Connections: Women's Poetry from the Renaissance to Romanticism* (San Marino, CA, 2002), 7–18.

[38] Jonathan Goldberg, *Desiring Women: English Renaissance Examples* (Stanford, CA, 1997), 34.

[39] Holmes, 'Love of Other Women', 180.

[40] Goldberg, *Desiring Women Writing*, 31.

seemingly heterosexual framing of bride and bridegroom quickly opens up into a plethora of erotic and affective relations. Far from converting a moment of homoerotic paradise lost into one of heterosexual coupledom found, Lanyer's poem reimagines this spiritual marriage in a way that enables queer erotics extending beyond the form of the couple.

LANYER'S PROMISCUOUS TYPOLOGY—REACHING ACROSS TIME

Critics have shown how Lanyer's blazon of Christ defies the gendered expectations of the form by placing the female speaker in the position of desiring subject, and also by calling into question the dynamics of subject and object in ways that challenge gender binaries. Holmes argues that by representing female desire for a feminine Christ, the poem imagines an erotics in which identification and desire, sameness and difference can coexist. Here, I want to explore how Lanyer's typology deploys temporality to a similar end, as she refuses the distinction of past, present, and future in ways that open up onto non-binary conceptions of gender identification.

'The Description of Cooke-ham', the collection's final poem, deploys some of the most typological language in the book. The Countess walks with Christ and his Apostles in the woods of the estate, but this is not an image of a time beyond time; rather, it is one of multiple times. The Countess coexists not only with Christ, but also with several Old Testament men:

> With *Moyses* you did mount his holy Hill,
> To know his pleasure, and performe his Will.
> With lovely *David* you did often sing,
> His holy Hymnes to Heavens Eternall King...
> With blessed *Joseph* you did often feed
> Your pined brethren, when they stood in need.
>
> ('Cooke-ham', 85–92)

Loughlin describes these lines as depicting the Countess as 'the last in a long line of Christ's biblical types', which includes Moses, Joseph, and David.[41] Earlier in the book types were divided by gender, as the Countess was placed in relation to Esther, Susanna, and Sheba. Here, however, she acts 'with' Christ to Moses, David, and Daniel, joining these male types of Christ. This defies both a binary sense of gender, and a sense of distinct historical moments. Here, we might say that by representing the Countess sharing devotional activities 'with' male types, the poem's typology masculinises the Countess,

[41] Loughlin, '"Fast Ti'd"', 171.

following the ways that the blazon feminises Christ. But just as the blazon represents Chris as 'not gender bound', typology creates a queer imagining of gender and temporality that exceeds such binary descriptions. Though the shared devotional activities are now the 'pleasure that have passed', they have already fused the past and present, male and female type in their contemporaneous performances of devotion.

REFUSING REPLACEMENT

In 'The Description of Cooke-ham', the poet pleads 'sweet Memorie doe thou retaine / Those pleasures past, which will not turne againe' (117–18), but she is not the only one looking back. The Countess also 'did repeat the pleasures which had past' (163), but she grieves and takes her leave. Her process of mourning contrasts with the speaker's melancholia. Left behind with the weeping garden, the speaker famously steals the kiss the Countess has given her favourite tree. Refusing to move on, she imaginatively keeps the past close. Holmes argues that the poet's active memory of this erotic scene avoids the heteronormative closure of lesbian elegy that Traub shows so often represented femme-femme eroticism as only a temporary state in the early modern period. It is not just the activity of individual memory, however, but also the typological structure of the poem that provides a conception of temporality that enables this erotic connection across time.

Starting with Ann Coiro's foundational reading, scholars have cautioned against a naïve reading of female community in Lanyer's work.[42] Coiro illuminated the speaker's moments of status antagonism, as the poet both reaches out to her patrons but also decries the neglect those of her rank are shown by the superiors they love: 'Neerer in show, yet farther off in love, / In which, the lowest alwayes are above' ('Cooke-ham', 109–10).[43] Lanyer's poem uses typology in a similarly ambivalent way, reading history both diachronically and synchronically, reflecting desires for sameness and difference, proximity and distance, community and competition. By arguing for typology's erotic affordances, I am not claiming that they offer a pastoral redemption of sexuality or of female-female relations more generally. Quite to the contrary, part of what allows typology to function as a productive erotic structure is its accommodation of ambivalence.

Lanyer's representation of the Queen of Sheba and King Solomon provides a key site for understanding the way that both connection and aggression mark typology in her poem. The poem explicitly uses typological language to describe this royal relationship as a 'figure' for the relationship of identification and desire of the Countess of

[42] Ann Baynes Coiro, 'Writing in Service: Sexual Politics and Class Position in the Poetry of Aemilia Lanyer and Ben Jonson', *Criticism*, 35.3 (1993), 357–76.

[43] Rogers reads Lanyer's typology as a structure of aggressive replacement through which Lanyer elevates her own status by degrading the work of Mary Sidney as a literary predecessor.

Cumberland and Jesus: 'Yet this faire map of majestie and might, / Was but a figure of thy deerest Love' (*Salve Deus*, 1609–10). The mirroring of David and Sheba in these lines has been read as representing heterosexual mutuality:[44]

> Here Majestie with Majestie did meete,
> Wisdome to Wisdome yeelded true content,
> One Beauty did another Beauty greet,
> Bounty to Bountie never could repent...
> Spirits affect where they doe sympathize,
> Wisdom desires Wisdome to embrace...
> Both good and bad in this point doe agree,
> That each desireth with his like to be.
>
> (*Salve Deus*, 1585–1600)

The emphasis on the desire for similarity, however, has led other critics to note the homoeroticism in these lines. Michael Schoenfeldt has connected this homoeroticism to the relations of the 'feminized Christ and his female devotees', though he follows the logic of the lesbian elegy by arguing that the homoerotic desire in these lines serves as a model for heterosexual marriage.[45] By contrast, Holmes and Goldberg read the relation between David and Sheba as a model for homoeroticism in the poem, as their likeness is 'only a simile for the relationship of identity between the Countess of Cumberland and Jesus, a likeness that overcomes gendered difference'.[46] The poem represents this simultaneity of similarity and difference, however, not through a simile, but through typology.

Just as Sheba sees her own majesty and beauty in Solomon but with a difference, the Countess of Cumberland recognises Solomon as a type or 'shadow' (1682) of Christ:

> Yet this rare Phoenix of that worne-out age,
> This great majesticke Queene comes short of thee,
> Who to an earthly Prince did then ingage
> Her hearts desires, her love, her libertie...
>   Giving all honour to a Creature, due
>   To her Creator, whom shee never knew.
>
> (*Salve Deus*, 1689–96)

44 Theresa Di Pasquale, 'Woman's Desire for Man in Lanyer's *Salve Deus Rex Judaeoreum*', *The Journal of English and Germanic Philology*, 99.3 (2000), 356–78, 358. In contrast, Guibbory argues Lanyer's reading rejects earthly marriage unlike interpretations in the Middle Ages, which saw Solomon and Sheba's marriage as both 'describing the relation between Christ and the Church' and 'as validating or sacramentalizing human marriage'. See Guibbory, 'The Gospel According to Aemilia: Women and the Sacred', in Marshall Grossman (ed.), *Aemilia Lanyer* (Lexington, KY, 1998), 191–211, 203.

45 Schoenfeldt, 'The Gender of Religious Devotion', 220–1.

46 Goldberg, *Desiring Women*, 27; Holmes, 'Love of Other Women', 174.

Though here Christ 'her Creator' is the anti-type of Solomon ('a Creature'), making the countess the anti-type of the Queen of Sheba, this typological moment calls into question the logic of supersedure, since the queen is not replaced by the countess but joins with her at the Day of Judgement: 'By honouring but the shadow of his Love / That great Judiciall day to have a place' (1682–3).[47] As a type, rather than a 'simile', Sheba here is a historical entity who carries her homoerotic desire to the judgement day. Infusing relations of male/female, female/divine, and type/anti-type with the desire for the same, the poem creates a homoerotics that does not fade away but remains embedded in these relations of difference.

As the poem positions the queen as the type of the Countess, it also deploys a hierarchy as the latter 'comes short of' (*Salve Deus*, 1690) the former. Just as Christ is 'greater' (*Salve Deus*, 1697) than Solomon, the Countess is greater than Sheba. Analysing the connection between typology and the poem's racial and religious hierarchies, Sanchez argues that 'insofar as typology sees the material as a temporal, imperfect figure for the eternal truth that eludes sense, and insofar as Lanyer situates Hebrew, Eastern, and African women as types of the Countess of Cumberland, she similarly aligns racial with epistemological hierarchies and teleologies'.[48] Sanchez offers Sheba as a key example of this vicious displacement, which recalls the double vision that Guibbory notes in the way that even as typology represented affinity with 'Jews' in the past, it served to disinherit seventeenth-century Jews in the present.

And this is where an intersectional analysis is so critical to analysing the case of Sheba. Shortly after the lines in which the typological identifications of Solomon/Christ and queen/countess are structured hierarchically as relations of lesser and 'greater', the greatness of Christ is reframed yet again (1706–20). The poet particularly praises the countess for seeking 'thy love in lowly shepheards weed' (1714), emphasising that Jesus was 'extreame poore' (1720). The description of Jesus as a lowly shepherd could not be more ordinary, but the countess's ability to love the lowly here stands in contrast to her failure to love the poet, cast in 'so lowe a frame' ('Cooke-ham', 104). As the feminised Christ provides a model of femme-femme erotics, the 'extreame poore' Christ provides a model for love across status. Both offer a model for love between the countess and the poet. The poem moves from the love of Sheba for Solomon, to the love of the countess for Christ, to the love of the countess for the poet. Not only does the countess appear as both an anti-type of Sheba and a type of Christ, 'with' Moses, Noah, and David, but the emphasis on Christ's lowness yet again reveals the poem's resistant deployment of biblical hermeneutics. This in no way negates the racialised hierarchy that Sanchez traces, but it does show how that hierarchy intersects with the flexibility of identification that negotiates hierarchies of sexuality and status. The poem's use of typology to accommodate certain kinds of desire underscores its exclusions, and serves as a reminder that desire is not immune to violence and coercion.

47 See Di Pasquale, 'Woman's Desire for Man', 371; and Loughlin, '"Fast Ti'd"', 144.

48 Melissa Sanchez, 'Ain't I a Ladie?: Race, Sexuality, and Early Modern Women Writers', in Kimberly Anne Coles and Eve Keller (eds), *Women, Sex, and Gender in the Early Modern World* (New York, 2018), 15–32; 20.

What are we reaching for when we 'touch across time'? And who is the 'we' that is reaching? When Lanyer creates her elegiac, typological text, she creates a poem spoken by the one left behind. She imagines the Queen of Sheba joining the Countess of Clifford at the end of time. Do these elements undermine the hierarchies of race and religion that are expressed through a typological structure of supersedure, or perhaps even challenge the teleology of that structure? Or, as Sanchez argues, does Lanyer merely appropriate the past in order to write herself and her patrons into a white, Christian future? And if that is the case, does the queer potential of typology I have been charting only exist if queerness denotes a disembodied and universal subject, and overlooks hierarchies of race and religion? If so, interpreting Lanyer's text as queer would exemplify one of the reasons that some feminists and scholars of race have been critical of queer studies. As Freccero writes, there is 'latent violence in even the friendliest of approaches'.[49] Lanyer's own complex, resistant identification with her aristocratic patrons in the poem thematises such dangers, refusing any comfortable resolution with the closing image of the bondage of the 'rich chains' that connect the poet and the patron.

CODA: 'A MEMORY, A DREAM, A FEELING OF HER'—*EMILIA* ON STAGE

In 2018, at perhaps the most explosive moment of the #MeToo movement, Morgan Lloyd Malcolm collaborated with the director Nicole Charles and a much-cited 'all female' cast to create *Emilia*, first performed at the Globe Theatre in 2018 and then at the Vaudeville Theatre in the West End in 2019. Malcolm describes the complex temporality of this bio-play's representation of Lanyer's life:

> This Play was also written to challenge the notion that a play about a person needs to be a vehicle for one actress. This is very much an ensemble piece hence the three Emilias. It takes place in several time zones at one time. It isn't an accurate representation of Renaissance England, it isn't a historical representation. It is a memory, a dream, a feeling of her.[50]

Despite the many intriguing elements of this play, its representations of erotics are hardly queer. The only female-female sexuality in the play comes in the predatory advances of Mary Sidney, in a moment far more homophobic than homoerotic, while Lanyer's husband is rather flatly depicted as having a homoerotic life beyond their marriage. The play exalts Lanyer as a writer, but is at least as interested in the hypothesis that Lanyer wrote part of Shakespeare's *Othello* as it is in her own writing, and it describes her religious

[49] Freccero, 'Tangents of Desire', *Journal for Early Modern Cultural Studies*, 16.2 (2016), 91–105, 92.
[50] Morgan Lloyd Malcolm, *Emilia* (London, 2018), vii.

writing as only a ruse to avoid censorship. It does, however, follow Lanyer's own deployment of typology as it solidifies a 'we' around 'Eve', with Emilia ending the play with a blistering monologue: 'I am seventy-six years old and I hold in me a muscle memory of every woman who came before me and I will send more for those that will come after. For Eve. For every Eve. I don't know if you can feel it. Do you? Do you feel it?'[51] This re-envisioning of Lanyer's life deserves its own essay, but I want to close with it to signal some of the ways that the issues raised here have implications beyond the scholarly.

Far from registering the typological displacement of women of colour, the play riffs on the debunked myth of Lanyer as Shakespeare's 'dark lady' to open up an identification across time that defies such racial hierarchies and encourages affiliations of gender. The character of Shakespeare describes his own limited knowledge of his lover, Emilia, as 'Italian. Maybe even North African. Jewish probably but you hid it'.[52] The casting note reads: 'This play was written to be performed by an all-female cast of diverse women. It would not be the same play if this is ignored. If being performed in a school where it is impossible to adhere to this then please cast against the "usual type". Be bold'.[53] The meaning of 'diverse' goes undefined, but in performances at the Globe and in the West End, the three Emilias, who represent her at different ages while also blurring such temporal distinctions, were played by black actors. The director Nicole Charles implicitly denies that the production has made Lanyer 'into a black British woman', explaining the casting by saying 'Emilia might have been of color, might have had a mixed heritage'.[54] Charles focuses on Lanyer's biography, but it is the play's experimentation with touches across time that I propose shares some of the complex historical impulses of *Salve Deus Rex Judaeorum*, despite that poem's anti-Semitic and racist elements.

What does it mean that a poem that deploys what Sanchez calls a 'typology of whiteness' provokes a play that refuses such a racialised teleology? Is this part of *Emilia*'s own flattening of a female 'we', or its lack of interest in Lanyer's actual writing, or is this play participating in a tradition of subversive appropriation in which Lanyer's poem also engaged? Answering this question would require a fuller engagement with *Emilia*, but I pose it here to illuminate the ongoing relevance of scholarship exploring such touches across time. Particularly as humanities fields are rethinking (both voluntarily and under the pressures of the neo-liberal university) how to be more 'public-facing', and recent novels on Mary Sidney and Margaret Cavendish join *Emilia* in reviving women authors for audiences beyond academia, a self-reflective queer feminism can help us to keep thinking about the affordances and dangers of touches across time.[55]

[51] Malcolm, *Emilia,*100.

[52] Malcolm, *Emilia,* 99.

[53] Malcolm, *Emilia,* vii.

[54] Bonnie Greer, 'Who Was Shakespeare's Muse? A Black Woman, This Play Imagines', *New York Times* (August 22, 2018), https://www.nytimes.com/2018/08/22/arts/shakespeare-globe-emilia.html, accessed July 1, 2020.

[55] See the bio-fictional works on Cavendish: Danielle Dutton, *Margaret the First: A Novel* (New York, 2016) and Siri Hustvedt, *The Blazing World* (New York, 2014); and on Mary Sidney, Naomi Miller,

FURTHER READING

Dinshaw, Carolyn. *Getting Medieval: Sexualities and Communities, Pre- and Postmodern*. Durham, NC, 1999.

Freccero, Carla. 'The Queer Time of the Lesbian Premodern', in Noreen Giffney, Maureen M. Sauer, and Diane Watt (eds), *The Lesbian Premodern*. New York, 2011, 61–73.

Jagose, Annamarie. 'Feminism's Queer Theory'. *Feminism & Psychology*, 19.2 (2009), 157–74.

Loomba, Ania and Melissa Sanchez (eds). *Rethinking Feminism in Early Modern Studies: Gender, Race and Sexuality*. New York, 2016.

Sanchez, Melissa. 'Ain't I a Ladie?: Race, Sexuality, and Early Modern Women Writers', in Kimberly Anne Coles and Eve Keller (eds), *Women, Sex, and Gender in the Early Modern World*. New York, 2018, 15–32.

Sedgwick, Eve Kosofsky. *Epistemology of the Closet*. Berkeley, CA, 1990.

Traub, Valerie. *The Renaissance of Lesbianism in Early Modern England*. Cambridge, 2002.

Traub, Valerie. *Thinking Sex With the Early Moderns*. Philadelphia, PA, 2015.

Imperfect Alchemist: A Novel of Mary Sidney Herbert, Renaissance Pioneer (London, 2020). Miller's novel is the first in her series of planned novels called 'Shakespeare's Sisters'.

CHAPTER 49

UNTIMELY DEVELOPMENTS

Periodisation, Early Modern Women's Writing, and Literary History

MICHELLE M. DOWD

In the opening sentences of her classic essay, 'Did Women Have a Renaissance?', Joan Kelly brought novel and urgent attention to the significance of periodisation to the study of premodern women. As she wrote:

> one of the tasks of women's history is to call into question accepted schemes of periodisation. To take the emancipation of women as a vantage point is to discover that events that further the historical development of men, liberating them from natural, social, or ideological constraints, have quite different, even opposite, effects upon women.[1]

Kelly would go on, famously, to conclude that the Renaissance was an excellent example of this phenomenon, arguing that 'there was no renaissance for women—at least, not during the Renaissance'.[2] Since its publication in 1977, many scholars have challenged and reworked Kelly's answer to her titular question. But although the conclusions may have changed, the concerns that Kelly raised about the problems for women's history that ensue when standards of periodisation are derived from male experiences and histories remain vital. This is especially true for the study of early modern women writers, as historical and literary periodisation markers jointly conspire to limit our understanding of women's textual production.

Some questions to consider: do the categories and temporal divisions that scholars have traditionally used to describe this period—such as 'Renaissance' or 'Restoration'

[1] Joan Kelly, 'Did Women Have a Renaissance?' in *Women, History, and Theory: The Essays of Joan Kelly* (Chicago, IL, 1984), 19.

[2] Kelly, 'Did Women Have a Renaissance?', 19.

or 'seventeenth century'—offer useful rubrics for understanding women's writing across these periods, or do they reflect an exclusively male-oriented model of literary history? How do such literary periodisations inform our scholarship and pedagogy on early modern women? What interpretive work do period-based frameworks do, and what limitations or critical weak spots do they produce? This chapter will explore these and other related questions in order to consider what periodisation means for the study of early modern women, and for early modern studies more generally. In particular, this chapter will demonstrate the ways in which early modern women's writing as a field challenges or helps to reconfigure conventional literary periodisations. How might traditional period markers impede our understanding of women's textual production by obscuring important developments or continuities? What happens if, rather than attempting to fit women's writing into pre-existing literary narratives, we use women's writing as our critical jumping-off point? Spotlighting women's writing as central to broader accounts of literary development, this chapter argues, can help sidestep the logic of exceptionalism that still governs how women's writing is often framed within early modern studies as a whole. This chapter considers several authors and texts that have been labelled as either 'exceptional' or 'belated' or otherwise out of sync with the dominant (primarily male-driven) modes and movements that have formed the basis for an orderly, sequential narrative of literary history (such as the popularity of the sonnet sequence in the 1590s or the stylistic development of professional drama in the early seventeenth century). It explores how centring women's writing within our literary analysis necessarily alters the critical narratives we tell. I suggest that attending to women writers' use of genre can be especially productive in this regard, enabling us to challenge temporal divisions and rethink traditional accounts of literary development. By considering women writers not as exceptions to some arbitrary 'rule', but as active participants within a literary culture whose writing encourages us to change the rules that we have learned, we can transform our understanding of literary influence, generic development, and periodisation in the process.

WHERE TO PUT EARLY MODERN WOMEN? TRADITIONAL NARRATIVES AND CRITICAL CHALLENGES

For scholars and students of early modern English literature, the year 1660 has long marked a traditional division between texts of the 'Renaissance' through to the Civil War and Interregnum on the one hand and literature of the Restoration on the other.[3]

[3] Mihoko Suzuki notes that literary scholars tend to treat 'the years up to 1642, 1642–1660, and after 1600 as three separate periods'; *Subordinate Subjects: Gender, the Political Nation, and Literary Form in England, 1588–1688* (Aldershot, 2003), 4.

This break is perhaps nowhere more firmly ensconced than in the practical mechanisms and artefacts of academic institutions, all of which tend to change much more slowly than does (say) scholarship on the question of periodisation.[4] But a quick glance at university course catalogues, textbooks, and publicly displayed areas of research speciality, as reflected on departmental websites, faculty job descriptions, and doctoral exam fields, reveals that 1660 remains an important marker of literary periodisation. The tenth edition of *The Norton Anthology of English Literature*, for instance, continues a long-standing practice of dividing its volumes between *The Sixteenth Century/The Early Seventeenth Century* (Volume B) and *The Restoration and the Eighteenth Century* (Volume C).[5] Enshrined in one of the most widely used college and university teaching editions in the United States, this division reflects and helps to codify standard practices throughout the academy, enforcing an asymmetrical splitting of the seventeenth century into distinct fields of study.

Historians and literary scholars have challenged this period division, arguing for greater continuity across the sixteenth and seventeenth centuries rather than a definitive break coinciding with the Stuart Restoration. Jonathan Scott, for instance, has argued that one of the results of the 'historiographical division at 1660' is a 'restoration period artificially wedded to its future, and severed from its past'.[6] Similarly, Keith Wrightson has urged historians to reject 'conventional terminal dates in order to pursue particular problems over spans of time'.[7] This attention to continuities rather than stark rifts also characterises the critiques of periodisation offered by literary critics. Literary periods across the board, as Eric Hayot has argued, 'instantiate more or less untheorised and inherited notions of totality' that resist more nuanced approaches to textual production.[8] Furthermore, where the specific case of England in the seventeenth century is concerned, fixing the dividing line at 1660 suggests that literary works largely pattern themselves on historical and political events. Periodisation in this instance thus grants primacy to historical events by assuming that literature mirrors the ebbs and flows of history.

But literary texts do not always play by history's rules, a point to which I will return. Furthermore, the assignment of a literary 'period' to a text can often seem arbitrary, especially when seemingly straightforward markers such as publication dates are taken into account. In the *Norton Anthology of English Literature*, for instance, both Katherine Philips and Margaret Cavendish are included along with John Milton under 'The Early Seventeenth Century' in Volume B. And although Cavendish's *Poems and Fancies* (of which the Norton includes some excerpts) was published in 1653, *The Blazing World*

[4] On the institutional effects of a continued adherence to literary periodisation, see Eric Hayot, 'Against Periodization; or, On Institutional Time', *New Literary History*, 42 (2011), 739–56.

[5] Stephen Greenblatt (ed.), *The Norton Anthology of English Literature*, 10th edn (New York, 2018).

[6] Jonathan Scott, *England's Troubles: Seventeenth-Century English Political Instability in European Context* (Cambridge, 2000), 25.

[7] Keith Wrightson, 'The Enclosure of English Social History', in Adrian Wilson (ed.), *Rethinking Social History: English Society 1520–1970 and Its Interpretation* (Manchester, 1993), 59–77, 70.

[8] Hayot, 'Against Periodization', 744.

(excerpts of which are also included) was not published until 1666, a year before the first publication of *Paradise Lost* and of Philips' *Poems*. As it happens, it is also just a year before the 1667 publication of John Dryden's *Annus Mirabilis*. But to find Dryden's poem in the Norton, we must look to the next volume, under the 'Restoration' in Volume C. These distinctions have become normalised over time, but it is valuable, I think, to revisit and highlight their tenuousness as we consider the place of women's writing in this larger narrative.

As Kelly and numerous feminist scholars have argued, periodisation is largely a patriarchal construct. As a result, traditional period divisions, such as the divide between the medieval and the early modern eras and the split at 1660 between 'Renaissance' and 'Restoration' literature, do not always line up neatly with women's textual production, and they can easily obscure significant continuities in discursive practice. In the decades following Kelly's crucial intervention, literary scholars have continued to contest and reframe markers of periodisation by noting that women's writing frequently resists standard period divides. Considering literary production in England that spans across the 1660 boundary, for instance, Paul Salzman argued in 2006 that 'the artificial dividing line that is drawn at 1660' has often had a 'disorienting effect on the approach to many women writers who flourished during the intensely productive period of the Civil War and its aftermath', leading to the 'considerable fragmentation in the presentation and representation of early modern women's writing'.[9] Writers such as the mid-century prophets Anna Trapnel and Elizabeth Poole, for instance, often fall through the cracks of these traditional divisions and, as a result, they are frequently excluded from both 'Renaissance' and 'Restoration' paradigms.

Scholars of women's writing have increasingly sought to resist such fragmentation by pursuing alternative temporal frameworks for analysis. Mihoko Suzuki, for example, makes the compelling case that a focus on 'the long seventeenth century' is more suitable for tracing continuities in literary forms across the century and for considering the 'extended afterlife' of many popular texts long after their date of first publication. Furthermore, she notes that attending to the 'long seventeenth century' helps us to assess more accurately the influence of women writers, since, for instance, 'following the publication of women's petitions during the Revolution, the Restoration saw a continued expansion of the public addressed by women's writing'.[10] Similarly, Sarah C. E. Ross and Gillian Wright have each explored how the work of female poets develops in significant ways *across* the artificial boundary of 1660. Ross, for instance, astutely discusses

[9] Paul Salzman, *Reading Early Modern Women's Writing* (Oxford, 2006), 2–3. Sharon Achinstein also noted that the strict break at 1660 often led scholars interested in gender to neglect the 'resources of the Civil War years'. Instead, she proposed viewing the Civil Wars not as a 'punctual mid-century event, but rather a shift in cultural definitions'; 'Introduction: Gender, Literature, and the English Revolution', *Women's Studies*, 24 (1994), 1–13, 2–3. The publication of recent anthologies such as Sarah C. E. Ross and Elizabeth Scott-Baumann (eds), *Women Poets of the English Civil War* (Manchester, 2018), demonstrates how scholars are continuing to resist the 1660 divide, bringing needed attention (and, crucially, increased access) to women's literary outputs at mid-century.

[10] Suzuki, *Subordinate Subjects*, 4–5.

the 'ways in which women's "poetry of state" in the years of the revolution and beyond extends and develops earlier female modes of expression', whereas Wright, focusing on the 'long seventeenth century' as Suzuki does, advocates cogently for the benefits of adopting an expanded time frame, one that allows us to see 'the seventeenth and early eighteenth centuries as a time of expanding possibilities for English women poets'.[11]

One of the continuities to which Ross draws particular attention is that of religion. As she notes, despite women's heightened attention to political discourse at mid-century, 'women continued to write prevalently in religious modes' across the seventeenth century.[12] Women such as Jane Cavendish and Hester Pulter, for instance, continued to engage political issues through religious verse in the second half of the century, a practice they shared with earlier writers such as Elizabeth Melville and Anne Southwell. Such a focus on women's religious writing marks one important way in which scholars have allowed women's texts to guide and reframe narratives about periodisation. In some instances (as Ross' work demonstrates) the result is a rejection of standard period divisions, such as the break at 1660. But attention to female religiosity also allows for a reclamation and reevaluation of another traditional period marker, namely the Reformation. Following Kelly, who assessed and ultimately challenged the applicability of the label 'Renaissance' to women's history, Margaret Ferguson has considered the historiographic significance of the profound engagement with religion displayed by many early modern women writers. As she notably concluded, 'if women did not have a Renaissance, they did at least have a Reformation'.[13] Centring women in our critical discussions, in other words, does not always mean throwing out received categories; rather, it means thinking seriously about *which* divisions and temporal shifts are important for understanding women's texts and histories, and which are not.

So, while drawing a rigid divide at 1660 (for instance) tends to hinder rather than support analysis of women's literary production across the seventeenth century, other periodisation markers can still prove very fruitful for analysing women's writing, as long as gender is maintained as a central category of analysis. Furthermore, periodisation itself as a historiographical practice can help to draw attention to important shifts and developments to which women contributed significantly. As Merry Wiesner-Hanks and others have argued, it is thus important both to question 'the applicability of chronological categories derived from male experience' and also ask how discussions of periodisation might be transformed by deeper attention to women's lives and literary engagements.[14] Rather than embracing a 'wholesale rejection' of

[11] Sarah C. E. Ross, *Women, Poetry, and Politics in Seventeenth-Century Britain* (Oxford, 2015), 11; Gillian Wright, *Producing Women's Poetry, 1600–1730: Text and Paratext, Manuscript and Print* (Cambridge, 2013), 239, 242.

[12] Ross, *Women, Poetry, and Politics*, 16.

[13] Margaret W. Ferguson, 'Moderation and Its Discontents: Recent Work on Renaissance Women', *Feminist Studies*, 20 (1994), 349–66, 352. Merry Wiesner-Hanks has likewise argued that the Reformation remains a useful category for analysing women's history in 'Do Women Need the Renaissance?', *Gender and History*, 20 (2008), 539–57, 545.

[14] Wiesner-Hanks, 'Do Women Need the Renaissance?', 539.

period categories, such as the 'early modern', then, we can consider instead how the early modern period 'needs women'.[15] Indeed, scholars have demonstrated that, like the Reformation, the 'early modern' remains a highly useful category for thinking about gender history and, specifically, women's contributions to important social, political, and economic developments. As Wiesner-Hanks has argued, one of the key developments that distinguishes the early modern period from those preceding it was the exponential growth of global interactions: 'new contacts between peoples brought about primarily—though not only—by European voyages'. And 'every one of these global interactions', she notes, 'was gendered'.[16] By widening the scope of our investigations to examine how women helped to shape the early modern world and its literatures as a distinctly global phenomenon, we can in turn productively redefine the category of the 'early modern' itself. Indeed, scholars such as Bernadette Andrea and Patricia Akhimie have recently investigated English women writers within a specifically global context and, in doing so, they have put pressure on traditional accounts of literary development.[17] This is but one way in which our attention to conventional markers of periodisation can be 'constructively enriched and challenged by gender history and the analysis of women's agency in the past'.[18]

If we begin our story with women, in other words, we get a different story—one that may or may not match up with conventional accounts of periodisation. Such a rethinking is necessary in order to continue to put pressure on mainstream literary histories of the early modern period, which remain predominantly shaped by male models. As Lara Dodds and I have argued elsewhere, 'early modern studies remains lopsidedly male in focus' in part because '"women's writing" is still often considered to be about women first and writing second'.[19] This is particularly true when we consider accounts of literary development, including (for example) the presumed dominance of specific genres or modes at a given historical time. As Margaret J. M. Ezell has argued, women's writing included in many mainstream anthologies tends to accord with standard definitions of literary modes and movements. 'The implication', she concludes 'is that women's literary history thus fits within the existing literary framework'—an existing framework determined solely by the output of male authors.[20] At other times, women's writing that does not fit into conventional narratives is included, but only to be

[15] Wiesner-Hanks, 'Do Women Need the Renaissance', 544, 551. See also Alexandra Shepard and Garthine Walker, 'Gender, Change and Periodisation', *Gender and History*, 20 (2008), 453–62, 454.

[16] Wiesner-Hanks, 'Do Women Need the Renaissance?', 549.

[17] See Bernadette Andrea, *Women and Islam in Early Modern English Literature* (Cambridge, 2008) and the essays collected in Patricia Akhimie and Bernadette Andrea (eds), *Travel and Travail: Early Modern Women, English Drama, and the Wider World* (Nebraska, 2019). See also the chapters in Part IV of the current volume ('Translingual and Transnational') as well as Chapter 47, Andrea, 'Early Modern Women, Race, and Writing Revisited'.

[18] Shepard and Walker, 'Gender, Change and Periodisation', 462.

[19] Lara Dodds and Michelle M. Dowd, 'Happy Accidents: Critical Belatedness, Feminist Formalism, and Early Modern Women's Writing', *Criticism*, 62 (2020), 169–93.

[20] Margaret J. M. Ezell, *Writing Women's Literary History* (Baltimore, MD, 1993), 62.

marked as exceptional, the 'road not taken'.[21] But might we produce a different roadmap entirely if we start by considering women writers' literary choices as primary rather than secondary to our broader scholarly conversations about the early modern period? What happens to our narratives of literary development vis-à-vis periodisation if we let women's writing guide them?

One way to reframe our literary narratives, I argue, is to attend to women writers use of genre across the early modern period (and across the divides that typically separate 'medieval' from 'Renaissance' and from 'Restoration'). Reading for genre can be a productive way to incorporate women's writing fully into our critical narratives while avoiding overly simplistic or misleading period divisions that tend to privilege male writings and narratives. Tracing women's deployment of literary modes and genres can, for one thing, help us to trace longer lines of connection than traditional period divides allow. Genres such as religious lyric, elegy, closet drama, the sonnet, romance, and life-writing all had long lifespans throughout the early modern period (and often beyond) as women writers built upon and transformed earlier models.[22]

But the *longue durée* of these forms is not typically accounted for in conventional literary histories. As Laura Lunger Knoppers writes:

> traditional literary historical periods only in part attend to women's writing in such genres as narrative and lyric poetry, drama, fictional and non-fictional prose. And attending to non-literary genres moves women's writing even further outside of the traditional literary historical rubrics.[23]

Rather than assuming that women's texts align with the literary histories demarcated by male textual production (or, indeed, with the dominant patterns of political or social history as conventionally understood), we can instead shift our focus by following the formal paths mapped out by early modern women. To explore how we might do that, I turn now to a few examples of texts by early modern women that do not neatly fit into standard accounts of literary genre, as defined in and through male-authored works. But by centring these texts—rather than labelling them as exceptional or out of place—we can begin to trace alternative narratives of literary history that are neither fragmented nor exclusively male.

[21] David Bevington uses this phrase to describe Elizabeth Cary's *The Tragedy of Mariam* in his introduction to the play in David Bevington et al. (eds), *English Renaissance Drama: A Norton Anthology* (New York, 2002), 620.

[22] For genre as a 'chronology-exploding' framework that privileges a 'continuist narrative' over one of rupture, see David Matthews, 'The Medieval Invasion of Early Modern England', *New Medieval Literatures*, 10 (2008), 223–44, 236. Hayot also lists genre as one of the few 'institutionally viable nonperiodizing concepts', as evidenced in part by the MLA job list; 'Against Periodization', 743.

[23] Laura Lunger Knoppers, 'Introduction: Critical Framework and Issues', in Knoppers (ed.), *The Cambridge Companion to Early Modern Women's Writing* (Cambridge, 2009), 8.

TAKING THE THREAD: THE *LONGUE DURÉE* OF WOMEN'S LYRIC

As scholars such as Ross and Wright have demonstrated, women's innovations in the lyric span across the early modern period, and they are often best understood when situated within a broader and more flexible time frame than traditional periodisation allows. Reading women's lyric in terms of a *longue durée* (or, at least, in terms of a more elastic chronology than those marked by strict divides between 'medieval' and 'Renaissance' and 'Reformation') often enables the seemingly odd or anomalous to take on new resonance, while also acknowledging the crucial role of women's verse in the history of English lyric.

Aemilia Lanyer's *Salve Deus Rex Judaeorum* (1611) is an excellent example of this. Lanyer's passion poem has frequently been discussed in terms of its exceptionalism, and Lanyer has been hailed as a pathbreaking proto-feminist poet whose defence of women was unusual for a printed, female-authored text of this period. But as Erica Longfellow and other critics have remarked, one of the problems of focusing on Lanyer's status as exceptional is that it tends to isolate her from history and from her literary contemporaries, both male and female.[24] If we instead read Lanyer as part of a longer tradition of devotional writing extending back well into the medieval period, *Salve Deus* looks less unique yet arguably more complex. Theresa Coletti and Nancy Bradley Warren, for instance, note the generic hybridity of the *Salve* (which encompasses devotional meditation on the Passion, dream vision, panegyric, and tropes from the mystical marriage tradition) as well as its confessional complexity. These elements of Lanyer's texts, as Coletti argues, are best illuminated by situating the *Salve* 'within the frame of reference provided by recent revisions of medieval and early modern periodisation'. Her reimagining of the scriptural account is 'rhetorically and exegetically reminiscent of medieval efforts to tell and retell that story', and she deftly repurposes 'strategies of late medieval devotional texts in various genres'.[25] Not only did Lanyer inherit and reshape medieval devotional traditions, but she also contributed to the development of other genres and motifs that would extend through the early modern period and into the eighteenth century. Her creative reimagining of the biblical story of Eve, for instance, as well as her country house poem, 'The Description of Cooke-ham', connect her to a

[24] See Erica Longfellow, *Women and Religious Writing in Early Modern England* (Cambridge, 2004), 60. For other examples of scholarship that has resituated Lanyer within the context of broader literary, print, and religious traditions, see Kimberly Anne Coles, *Religion, Reform, and Women's Writing in Early Modern England* (Cambridge, 2008), and Erin A. McCarthy, 'Speculation and Multiple Dedications in *Salve Deus Rex Judaeorum*', *SEL Studies in English Literature 1500–1900*, 55 (2015), 45–72.

[25] Theresa Coletti, '"Did Women Have a Renaissance?" A Medievalist Reads Joan Kelly and Aemilia Lanyer', *Early Modern Women: An Interdisciplinary Journal*, 8 (2013), 249–59, 254–5. See also Nancy Bradley Warren, *The Embodied Word: Female Spiritualities, Contested Orthodoxies, and English Religious Cultures, 1350–1700* (Notre Dame, IN, 2010).

long line of both earlier and later authors who experimented with these literary modes, including Geoffrey Chaucer, Ben Jonson, Mary Astell, Lucy Hutchinson, and Anne Finch. Understood in these more expansive literary contexts, Lanyer's work becomes less 'exceptional' and more central to the development of the religious lyric in English.

Put another way, our analysis of Lanyer's literary production is necessarily limited if we read her exclusively in the context of the 'Early Seventeenth Century'—the heading under which excerpts of the *Salve* can be found in Volume B of the tenth edition of *The Norton Anthology of English Literature*. The same can be said for the poetry of Mary Wroth, which is also included along with Lanyer in this section of the *Norton Anthology*. As Dianne Mitchell notes in Chapter 13 of this volume, Wroth's sonnet sequence *Pamphilia to Amphilanthus* (published in 1621, although likely circulating in manuscript earlier) is often described by critics as 'backward' or belated, returning to a lyric form (the Petrarchan sonnet) that had come to prominence in England in the 1590s and was widely considered *passé* by the 1610s. But as with Lanyer's verse, why assume that Wroth's sequence is necessarily the exception? If we start with *Pamphilia to Amphilanthus* when analysing Petrarchan sonnets, we potentially get a very different literary narrative than if we start with Sidney or Shakespeare and try to fit Wroth into their frame. Wroth's sequence has frequently been characterised as abstract, private, and inward-looking, features that, like its belated publication date, tend to mark the poems as tonally distinct from other sonnets of the period. But the distinctiveness of *Pamphilia to Amphilanthus* looks different when we regard it not as a failed derivative but as a model sequence in its own right. For instance, as Leila Watkins has compelling argued, 'Wroth's model of literary exchange' in which the reader acts 'as a crucial agent of artistic production' might seem initially to stand 'in striking contrast to other early modern sonnet sequences' disproportionate focus on the author'. However, 'by imagining a situation in which literary posterity is uncertain, Wroth shows the limitations of this genre's ability to sublimate frustrated desire into a lasting work of art'.[26] Wroth, in other words, is not an island unto herself: she is directly in dialogue with other English sonneteers. At the same time, our basic understanding of what constitutes an early modern sonnet sequence looks quite different if we centre Wroth's vision of readerly community rather than a predominantly male model of self-memorialisation through verse.

Taking this argument one step further, we can follow Mitchell in linking Wroth's sonnets to later poets, rather than limiting our discussion to the narrow period of the Elizabethan sonnet, by which standard Wroth appears belated. Mitchell reads Wroth together with the poems of Anne Southwell and Hester Pulter (see this volume, Mitchell, Chapter 13), but we can also look further afield in order to consider the specific literary afterlives of Wroth's 'A Crown of Sonnets Dedicated to Love'. Jennifer Higginbotham has written about Patience Agbabi's sonnet crown, 'Vicious Cycle', which appeared in her 2014 collection *Bloodshot Monochrome*. Agbabi specifically cites Wroth as an

[26] Leila Watkins, 'The Poetics of Consolation and Community in Mary Wroth's *Pamphilia to Amphilanthus*', *Studies in Philology*, 112 (2015), 139–61, 146–7.

influence and includes an imagined dialogue with her in 'Problem Pages', from the same collection.[27] Even more recently, Kwoya Fagin Maples includes a sonnet corona ('What Yields') at the conclusion of her 2018 volume *Mend*, a collection of poetry that examines the role that enslaved black women played in the development of modern gynaecology.[28] Rather than positioning the Elizabethan sonnet as the precursor to Wroth's 'belated' sequence, then, what if we instead considered more deeply the afterlife of the sonnet corona, a form that has been notably taken up by a wide range of women writers? By easing up on the strict boundaries of periodisation, we can start to create new narratives of the lyric in English that 'take the thread' of Wroth's sequence as a starting point, not an afterthought.[29]

RETHINKING PERIODISATION AND EARLY MODERN DRAMA

A similar logic can be applied to the writings of early modern women in other genres. Drama, for instance, is a particularly illustrative mode for examining critical narratives about women's writing vis-à-vis traditional accounts of periodisation. As Ramona Wray notes in Chapter 11 of this volume ('Receiving Early Modern Women's Drama'), the canon of early modern drama remains overwhelmingly male. Mainstream criticism of early modern drama rarely considers plays by women; even with the push over the past few decades to expand the dramatic canon beyond canonical figures such as Shakespeare, Marlowe, and Jonson, women writers still rarely make the cut.[30] When women's drama *is* included, it tends to be deliberately marked as an exception to the norm—a norm defined by the male-dominated professional theatre. Because most women from the period wrote not for the professional stage but for more informal venues (including household readings), their 'closet dramas' are frequently dismissed as tangential to the dominant literary phenomenon of the day: the commercial theatre.

[27] Jennifer Higginbotham, 'Taking the Thread of Mary Wroth's "A Crown of Sonnets Dedicated to Love"', in Lara Dodds and Michelle M. Dowd (eds), *Feminist Formalism and Early Modern Women's Writing: Readings, Conversations, Pedagogies* (Lincoln, NE, 2022), 23–37. See also Patience Agbabi, *Bloodshot Monochrome* (Edinburgh, 2014).

[28] See Kwoya Fagin Maples, *Mend* (Lexington, KY, 2018).

[29] The final line of the opening sonnet in Wroth's crown reads: 'Is to leave all, and take the thread of love'. See *Pamphilia to Amphilanthus*, in Josephine A. Roberts (ed.), *The Poems of Lady Mary Wroth* (Baton Rouge, LA, 1983), 128.

[30] Examples include Jeremy Lopez, *Constructing the Canon of Early Modern Drama* (Cambridge, 2014), and Tiffany Stern, 'Renaissance Drama: Future Directions', *Renaissance Drama*, 40 (2012), 151–60. Despite their scope, neither of these studies makes mention of any female-authored plays. And although the *Routledge Anthology of Renaissance Drama*, first published in 2003, included Elizabeth Cary's *The Tragedy of Mariam* as one of its eleven plays, the 2020 *Routledge Anthology of Early Modern Drama* does not include a single play by a woman, even though it has expanded to include seventeen plays.

As Wray demonstrates in her chapter in this volume, women's drama was actually very closely aligned with more mainstream forms of cultural production (see also this volume, Chapter 23, Julie Sanders, 'Daughters of the House: Women, Theatre, and Place in the Seventeenth Century'). And Marta Straznicky has argued that the public theatre should not be held up as the unquestioned ideal, the 'standard against which closet drama need be examined' because the 'closet and stage were distinct but continuous traditions'.[31] But women's drama still remains marginalised in the field, and periodisation, I would argue, is part of the problem. Indeed, 'early modern drama' as a field of study is a perfect example of a literary period whose temporal boundaries are defined exclusively through male authors and primarily through the literary output of a single author: William Shakespeare. Generally speaking, the study of early modern drama encompasses the period between the late 1580s and 1642, when the beginning of the Civil Wars forced the closing of England's professional theatres. But in practice, most criticism of early modern drama focuses even more narrowly on the period from about 1590 to 1620, dates that more closely correspond with the years of Shakespeare's active career as a playwright.[32] In many cases, then, studies of 'early modern drama' cover only a few decades of work; unlike the study of early modern poetry, it is a field that seems particularly resistant to the 'long-seventeenth century' model of literary history. But defining the field in these narrow terms, dictated by the temporal and practical constraints of commercial dramatic production, necessarily skews our understanding of 'drama' by leaving many later seventeenth-century women dramatists (such as Aphra Behn or Margaret Cavendish) out of consideration and excluding others (such as Mary Wroth or Elizabeth Cary) based on the privileging of the stage over the 'closet'. There is an odd circular logic (and intellectual slippage) at work here: what 'counts' as early modern drama has been delimited by the career lifespan of Shakespeare and (to a lesser extent) his contemporary male dramatists. That critical presumption has not only relegated 'early modern drama' to a curiously narrow period in time but it also, as a result, has led to distinct conclusions about early modern drama *as a genre* that have come to define the field (e.g., that it was primarily commercial, public-facing, and often collaborative). Even when critics extend the timeline, they still tend to start with Shakespeare and work outwards—meaning that he remains very much the default.[33]

Like lyric poetry, drama is another example of how attending to genre can help us push back against traditional periodisation markers in productive ways. We can begin

[31] Marta Straznicky, *Privacy, Playreading, and Women's Closet Drama, 1550–1700* (Cambridge, 2004), 112, and Straznicky, 'Closet Drama', in Arthur Kinney (ed.), *A Companion to Renaissance Drama* (Malden, MA: 2002), 416–30, 428.

[32] As Adam Zucker and Alan B. Farmer note, Caroline drama (which dates from roughly 1625 to 1642) has received relatively little attention until quite recently, as it has usually been 'better known for its abrupt conclusion than for its constituent parts'. See 'Introduction', in Adam Zucker and Alan B. Farmer (eds), *Localizing Caroline Drama: Politics and Economics of the Early Modern Stage, 1625–1642* (Houndmills, 2008), 1.

[33] See, for example, the important work being done by Andy Kesson, Lucy Munro, and Callen Davies for the *Before Shakespeare* project: https://beforeshakespeare.com

by opening up the field of 'early modern drama' to the full range of dramatic production across the period so that the closing of the theatres does not dictate the endings and beginnings of our critical narratives. But we can also strive to decentre the work of male dramatists (and the commercial stage) within those narratives by recognising the broader continuum of dramatic production even during Shakespeare's lifetime. Elizabeth Cary's *The Tragedy of Mariam* (1613) is an excellent example for this purpose: although it is one of the few female-authored plays that has been regularly included in anthologies, courses, and critical discussions of early modern drama, it is often brought into these conversations as an exception, a curiosity that does not fit the dramatic tradition of the period. But if we shift focus and start our analysis with plays such as *Mariam*, might we in fact broaden our understanding of dramatic production and potentially reach different conclusions about the contours of early modern drama as a genre? More detailed and sustained attention to *Mariam* as a Senecan tragedy, for instance, could yield new insights into the dramaturgical construction of tragic *pathos* and how that construct is defined in and through gendered terms. The neoclassical elements of Cary's play—which can look like oddities if our primary frame of reference is the plays of Shakespeare, Dekker, or Middleton—are in fact part of a long and robust English dramatic tradition that continued throughout the seventeenth century.[34] By ensuring that women's dramatic innovations across the period are regularly included in our critical conversations, we can produce vibrant new narratives about the English dramatic tradition that can complicate, enrich, and potentially revise the field of 'early modern drama' as we currently know it.

CONCLUSION: UNTIMELY POSSIBILITIES

Reading women's writing for its engagements and innovations with genre, I have argued, can help us trace literary continuities that transcend strict (and often male-oriented) period divisions. Such a strategy can help us re-evaluate the works of well-known writers such as Lanyer, Wroth, and Cary, but it can also enable fruitful analysis of the works of lesser-known or more recently 'discovered' writers, such as Hester Pulter or Dorothy Calthorpe. Reading for generic intersections, indebtedness, and transformations can help us avoid pigeonholing individual authors as exclusively 'of' their specific historical moment, encouraging us instead to think more expansively about how these authors are

[34] For a fuller discussion of *pathos* in *Mariam*, see Lara Dodds and Michelle M. Dowd, 'The Case for a Feminist Return to Form', *Early Modern Women: An Interdisciplinary Journal*, 13 (2018), 82–91. In *What Was Tragedy?: Theory and the Early Modern Canon* (Oxford, 2015), Blair Hoxby expands the discussion of early modern drama to include neoclassical plays, but strikingly he does not discuss *Mariam* or any female-authored plays.

part of literary conversations that extend well before and beyond their immediate temporal milieu. For those of us trained in historicist methods (myself included), it can at times feel counter-intuitive to loosen up a bit on the exactitude of historical specificity when it comes to contextualising a literary work. But being willing to let go of narrowly defined periodisation frameworks need not equate to a complete dismissal of historical sensitivity: we can still attend to nuance and change over time while refusing to cut off the story abruptly at 1642 or 1660 or 1700. By extending the temporal scope of our analysis, we will get a better understanding of the range of women's literary innovations over time, and we can use that analysis in turn to reshape the received narratives about literary history that we have inherited from a long-standing tradition of criticism biased by patriarchal constraints.

Furthermore, if we loosen the grip of periodisation, we can more fully explore the untimely resonances of early modern women's writing. In theorising what he refers to as 'untimely matter' in early modern England—a concept that acknowledges the 'simultaneous agency of past matter and present subject'—Jonathan Gil Harris emphasises that temporality is not simply the property of an individual text or object, but it 'is also generated by the work we do with that object'.[35] Similarly, Kathleen Davis argues that 'periodisation is never simply a line drawn through time: it is a discursive intervention in the present that, in part, sorts out and defines which elements of the past are relevant for thinking about the relationship between past and future'.[36] In our research and teaching of women's writing, we would do well to consider not only how this writing challenges traditional periodisation, but also how taking a longer view of women's literary production can enable us to connect those works meaningfully to our present moment. In arguing for such an approach, I am guided by the intersectional feminist scholarship of Kim F. Hall, who has advocated for what she calls strategic anachronism: a critical practice that holds a literary text in productive tension with its historical moment or period.[37] Such a critical methodology can help us reimagine what we might *do* with women's writing, what untimely new narratives it might allow us to tell.

FURTHER READING

Ezell, Margaret J. M. *Writing Women's Literary History*. Baltimore, 1993.

Ferguson, Margaret W. 'Moderation and Its Discontents: Recent Work on Renaissance Women'. *Feminist Studies*, 20 (1994), 349–66.

Hayot, Eric. 'Against Periodization; or, On Institutional Time'. *New Literary History*, 42 (2011), 739–56.

[35] Jonathan Gil Harris, *Untimely Matter in the Time of Shakespeare* (Philadelphia, 2009), 13, 16.

[36] Kathleen Davis, 'Periodization and the Matter of Precedent', *postmedieval: a journal of medieval cultural studies*, 1 (2010), 354–60, 357.

[37] See Kim F. Hall, *Things of Darkness: Economies of Race and Gender in Early Modern England* (Ithaca, 1995), 261.

Kelly, Joan. 'Did Women Have a Renaissance?' in *Women, History, and Theory: The Essays of Joan Kelly*, 19–50. Chicago, 1984.

Shepard, Alexandra, and Garthine Walker. 'Gender, Change and Periodisation'. *Gender and History*, 20 (2008), 453–62.

Suzuki, Mihoko. *Subordinate Subjects: Gender, the Political Nation, and Literary Form in England, 1588–1688*. Aldershot, 2003.

Wiesner-Hanks, Merry. 'Do Women Need the Renaissance?' *Gender and History*, 20 (2008), 539–57.

Bibliography

Manuscripts

Ampleforth Abbey, Ampleforth

MS SS84
MS SS85c
MS SS118

Archdiocesan Archives of Mechelen-Brussels

Engelse Benedictinessen/12.2

Archives départementales du Nord Lille, Lille

MS 20 H 18, 1

Bayerische Statsbibliothek, München

MS Latin 10369

Beinecke Rare Books Library, Yale University, New Haven

The James Marshall and Marie-Louise Osborn Collection, Document 38, 1A–B

Berkeley Castle, Gloucester

Berkeley Manuscripts General Series, Miscellaneous Papers 31/15

Bodleian Library, University of Oxford

MS Rawl. poet. 16
MS Tanner 169

British Library, London

Add MS 10,037
Add MS 12,507
Add MS 15,117
Add MS 15,950
Add MS 17,012
Add MS 23,212
Add MS 23,229
Add MS 27,351
Add MS 29,921
Add MS 45,196
Add MS 45,720
Add MS 53,723
Add MS 70,499
MS Harley 1860
MS Harley 2342
MS Harley 7001
MS Harley 7392
MS Royal 7 D X
MS Royal 12 A i
MS Royal 12 A ii
MS Royal 12 A iii
MS Royal 12 A iv
MS Royal 15 A i
MS Royal 15 A ix
MS Royal 17 B xviii
MS Sloane 1367

Cambridge University Library, Cambridge

MS Dd.i.18
MS Dd.i.19
MS Ii.5.37
MS Mm.3.32

Chatsworth House Library, Derbyshire

Cork MSS. Miscellaneous Box 5

Christ Church College Library, Oxford

MS Mus. 87

Colwich Abbey, Colwich

MS 629

Cumbria Archive Service, Kendal

WDHOTH/1/5
WDHOTH/1/16

Derbyshire Record Office, Matlock

D331/10/15
D331/19/23
D331/19/1718

Douai Abbey, Berkshire

Box O IV 1, MS G 13

Downside Abbey, Stratton-on-the-Fosse, Somerset

MS 66812

Folger Shakespeare Library, Washington, DC

MS V.a.20
MS V.a.91
MS V.a.104
MS V.a.166
MS V.a.425
MS V.a.430

MS V.a.450
MS V.b.198
MS V.b.301

Hertfordshire Archives and Local Studies, Hertford

MS D/EP F36
Penshanger MS D/EP F37

Houghton Library, Harvard University, Cambridge MA

MS Eng 729

Kislak Center for Special Collections, Philadelphia

Rare Book Collection. Fol. PR2399.W7 C68 1621

Lambeth Palace Library, London

MS 683

The National Archives, London

PROB 11/350/410
SP 12/175
SP 12/256
SP 16/506
SP 29/167
SP 106

National Library of Scotland, Edinburgh

Acc. 9270, Pt. 6
Crawford Collections, Acc. 9769, Personal Papers 84/1/1
GD 26/6/124
GD 26/6/136
MS 15937
MS Dep. 314/24
MS W10231
MS Wod. Qu XXIX

National Library of Wales, Aberystwyth

MS4340A

New College Library, University of Edinburgh

MS Bru. 2

New York Public Library, New York

MssCol 3318

Royal College of Physicians, London

MS 65
MS 654

Trinity College Dublin

MS 1995–2008/752

University of Leeds Library, Leeds

Brotherton Collection, MS Lt q 32

The University Library, Sheffield

Hartlib Papers, MS 61, 66/8, 1A

University of Pennsylvania Library, Philadelphia

Esther Aresty Collection. MS Codex 626

Wellcome Library, London

MS 363
MS 1127

MS 3712
MS 4683
MS 7113

William Andrews Clarke Memorial Library, Los Angeles

MS 2009.015
MS L6815 M3 C734

Printed Primary Sources

1641 Depositions. http://1641.tcd.ie. Accessed 30 June 2021.

A Blow at the Serpent; or a Gentle Answer from Madiston Prison. London, 1655.

A Collection of Letters and Poems Written by Several Persons of Honour and Learning upon Divers Important Subjects to the Late Duke and Dutchess of Newcastle. London, 1676.

A Proclamation, for Calling in and Suppressing of Two Books Written by John Milton. London, 1660.

A Relation of the Death of the Most Illustrious Lord, Sigr. Troilo Savelli. Trans. Toby Matthew. St Omer, 1620.

A Transcript of the Registers of the Worshipful Company of Stationers; from 1640–1708 A.D., 3 vols. London, 1913.

A True Copy of the Petition of The Gentlewomen, and Tradesmens-Wives in and about the City of London. London, 1642.

Adams, Thomas. *A Commentary or, Exposition upon the Divine Second Epistle Generall*. London, 1633.

Adcock, Rachel, Sara Read, and Anna Ziomek (eds). *Flesh and Spirit: An Anthology of Seventeenth-Century Women's Writing*. Manchester, 2014.

Agrippa, Heinrich Cornelius. In David Clapham (trans.), *A Treatise of the Nobilitie and Excellencye of Woman Kinde*. London, 1542.

Ainsworth, Henry. *Annotations upon the Five Bookes of Moses*. London, 1627.

Ainsworth, William. *Medulla Bibliorum, the Marrow of the Bible*. London, 1652.

Ambrose, Isaac. *Prima, Media, & Ultima, the First, Middle, and Last Things in Three Treatises*. London, 1659.

An Answer to a Printed Book, Falsely Intituled, A Blow at the Serpent. London, 1656.

Arnold, Elizabeth. 'The Invective of Doctor Andreas de Laguna, a Spaniard and Physition to Pope Julius the Third, against the Painting of Women, in His Annotations upon Dioscorides, li.5.cap.62', in Thomas Tuke, *A Discourse against Paintng and Tincturing of Men and Women*. London, 1616, sigs B3r–B4v.

Ascham, Roger. *The Scholemaster*. London, 1570.

Ashton, Robert (ed.). *James I by His Contemporaries*. London, 1969.

Askew, Anne. In Elaine V. Beilin (ed.). *The Examinations of Anne Askew*. Oxford, 1997.

Askew, Anne. *The First Examinacyon of Anne Askewe, Latelye Martyred in Smythfelde by the Romysh Popes Upholders, with the Elucydacyon of Johan Bale*. Wesel, 1546.

Askew, Anne. *The Lattre Examinacyon of Anne Askewe, Latelye Martyred in Smythfelde, by the Wycked Synagoge of Antichrist, with the Elucydacyon of Johan Bale*. Wesel, 1547.

Askew, Anne. *The Two Examinations*, in John Foxe (ed.), *Actes and Monuments*. London, 1563.
Astell, Mary. *A Serious Proposal to the Ladies for the Advancement of Their True and Greatest Interest*. London, 1694.
Aubrey, John. In Kate Bennett (ed.), *Brief Lives with an Apparatus for the Lives of Our English Mathematical Writers*. Oxford, 2015.
Augustine, St. In Toby Matthew (trans.), *The Confessions of the Incomparable Doctour S. Augustine*. St Omer, 1620.
Austen, Katherine. In Sarah C. E. Ross (ed.), *Katherine Austen's Book M: British Library, Additional Manuscript 4454*. Tempe, AZ, 2011.
Aylmer, John. *An Harborowe for Faithful and Trewe Subjectes agaynst the Late Blowne Blaste, Concerninge the Government of Wemen*. London, 1559.
Bacon, Lady Anne (née Cooke). *An Apologie or Answere in Defence of the Churche of Englande, with a Briefe and Plaine Declaration of the True Religion Professed and Used in the Same*. London, 1564.
Ballard, George. *Memoirs of Several Ladies of Great Britain*. London, 1752.
Basset, Mary. *Of the Sorowe, Weriness, Feare, and Prayer of Christ Before Hys Taking*, in *The Workes of Sir Thomas More Knyght, Sometime Lorde Chauncellour of England, Wrytten by Him in the Englysh Tonge*. London, 1557.
Beale, Robert. 'A Treatise of the Office of a Councellor and Principall Secretarie to Her Ma[jes]tie', in Conyers Read, *Mr. Secretary Walsingham and the Policy of Queen Elizabeth*, [x] vols. Oxford, 1925. I, 423–43.
Beaufort, Margaret. *A Full Devout and Gostely Treatyse of the Imytacion and Folowynge the Blessed Lyfe of Oure Moste Mercyfull Sauyoure Criste*. London, 1504.
Beaufort, Lady Margaret. *Here Begineth the Forthe Boke of the Folowynge Jesu Cryst out of the Contemninge of the Worlde. Imprynted at the Commaundement of Margarete aud by the Same Prynces Translated out of Frenche*, in *A Ful Devout Savyour Cryste*. London, 1504.
[Beaufort, Margaret]. *The Mirror of God to the Sinful Soul*. London, 1507.
Beaufort, Lady Margaret. *The Mirroure of Golde for the Synfull Soule. Translated out of Laten in to Frensshe, and Nowe of Late in to Englisshe by Margaret Countess of Richmond & Derby*. London, [1506?].
Beaumont, Agnes. 'The Narrative of the Persecution of Agnes Beaumont', in John Stachniewski with Anita Pacheco (eds.) *Grace Abounding with Other Spiritual Autobiographies*. Oxford, 1998.
Bede. In Thomas Stapleton (trans.), *The History of the Church of Englande. Compiled by Venerable Bede, Englishman*. Antwerp, 1565.
Beecher, Donald (ed.). *Characters*. Ottawa, 2003.
Behn, Aphra. *Miscellany*. London, 1685.
Behn, Aphra. In Joanna Lipking (ed.), *Oroonoko*. New York, 1997.
Behn, Aphra. *A Pindaric Poem to the Reverend Doctor Burnet, on the Honour He Did Me of Enquiring after Me and My Muse*. London, 1689.
Behn, Aphra. *Poems on Several Occasions*. London, 1684.
Behn, Aphra. In Montague Summers (ed.), *The Works of Aphra Behn*, 6 vols. Stratford, 1915.
Belcamp, Jan van. *The Great Picture* (1646). Google Arts and Culture. artsandculture.google.com/asset/the-great-picture/ugHL4_ozVj1f3g. Accessed 2 February 2021.
Bellany, Alastair and Andrew McRae (eds). *Early Stuart Libels: An Edition of Poetry from Manuscript Sources*. Early Modern Literary Studies Text Series I (2005). http://www.earlystuartlibels.net/. Accessed 28 November 2020.

Bentley, Thomas. *The Monument of Matrons, The Seventh Lampe of Virginitie*. London, 1582.

The Bible and Holy Scriptures Conteyned in the Olde and Newe Testament [The Geneva Bible]. Geneva, 1560.

Boate, Arnold. *The Character of a Trulie Vertuous and Pious Woman*. Paris, 1651.

Bodin, Jean. In Richard Knolles (trans.) and Kenneth Douglas McRae (ed.), *The Six Bookes of a Common-weale*. Cambridge, MA, 1962.

Bonnecorse, Balthazar de. In Aphra Behn (trans.), *La Montre, or The Lover's Watch*. London, 1686.

The Booke of Common Praier, and Administration of the Sacramentes, and Other Rites and Ceremonies in the Churche of Englande. London, 1559.

Bosc, Jacques du. In Walter Montagu (trans.), *The Accomplish't Woman*. London, 1639.

Boyle, Robert. In Michael Hunter, et al. (eds.) *The Correspondence of Robert Boyle*, vol 4. London, 2001.

Bernard, St. In Jean Leclercq and Henri Rochais (eds), *Sancti Bernardi Opera, vol. 4: Sermones I*. Rome, 1966.

Bethune, George (ed.). *The British Female Poets*. London, 1848.

Bradstreet, Anne. In Margaret Olofson Thickstun (ed.), *Poems and Meditations*. Toronto, 2019.

Bradstreet, Anne. *Several Poems*. Boston, MA, 1678.

Bradstreet, Anne. *The Tenth Muse Lately Sprung up in America*. London, 1650.

Bradstreet, Simon. *An Advertisement*. Boston, MA, 1678.

Brathwait, Richard. *The English Gentlewoman*. London, 1631.

Brewer, Thomas. *Mistres Turners Repentance*. London, 1615.

[Brilhac, Jean-Baptiste de]. In Aphra Behn (trans.), *Agnes de Castro*. London, 1688.

Broad, Jacqueline (ed.). *Women Philosophers of Seventeenth-Century England: Selected Correspondence*. Oxford, 2019.

Bunyan, John. In John Stachniewski with Anita Pacheco (eds.) *Grace Abounding with Other Spiritual Autobiographies*. Oxford, 1998.

Burgess, Anthony. *Spiritual Refining*. London, 1652.

Burnet, Gilbert. *A Sermon Preached at the Funeral of the Honourable Robert Boyle*. London, 1692.

Byfield, Nicholas. *Directions for the Private Reading of the Scriptures*. London, 1618.

Caccini, Giulio. In H. Wiley Hitchcock (ed.), *Le nuove musiche*. Madison, WI, 1970.

Calthorpe, Dorothy. In Julie A. Eckerle (ed.), *News from the Midell Regions and Calthorpe's Chapel*. Toronto, forthcoming.

Camden, William. In Philemon Holland (trans.), *Britain, or a Chorographical Description of the Most Flourishing Kingdomes, England, Scotland and Ireland*. London, 1637.

Camden, William. *Remaines of a Greater Worke, Concerning Britaine*. London, 1605.

Carew, Richard. *The Survey of Cornwall*. London, 1602.

Cartwright, William. *Comedies, Tragi-Comedies, with Other Poems*. London, 1651.

Cary, Elizabeth. In Heather Wolfe (ed.). *Elizabeth Cary, Lady Falkland: Life and Letters*. Cambridge, 2001.

Cary, Elizabeth. *The History of the Life, Reign, and Death of Edward II*. London, 1680.

Cary, Elizabeth. 'The Mirror of the Worlde Translated out of French into Englishe by E.T.' Oxford, Bodleian Library. Dep.d.817, in Lesley Peterson (ed.), *The Mirroure of the Worlde: A Translation by Elizabeth Tanfield Cary*. Montreal, 2012.

Cary, Elizabeth. *The Reply of the Most Illustrious Cardinall of Perron, to the Answeare of the King of Great Britaine. The First Tome Translated into English*. Douay, 1630.

Cary, Elizabeth. In A. C. Dunstan and W. W. Greg (eds), *The Tragedy of Mariam*. Oxford, 1914.

Cary, Elizabeth. In Ramona Wray (ed.), *The Tragedy of Mariam*. London, 2012.
Cary, Lucy. 'The Lady Falkland: Her Life', in Barry Weller and Margaret W. Ferguson (eds), *The Tragedy of Mariam the Fair Queen of Jewry, with The Lady Falkland by One of Her Daughters*. Berkeley, CA, 1994, 183–275.
Catalogue of the Pamphlets, Books, Newspapers, and Manuscripts ... Collected by George Thomason, 1640–1661, vol. i. London, 1908.
Cavendish, Margaret. In Kate Lilley (ed.), *The Blazing World & Other Writings*. London, 1994.
Cavendish, Margaret. *CCXI Sociable Letters Written by the Thrice Noble, Illustrious, and Excellent Princess, the Lady Marchioness of Newcastle*. London, 1664.
Cavendish, Jane. In Alexandra G. Bennett (ed.), *The Collected Works of Jane Cavendish*. London, 2018.
Cavendish, Margaret. *A Description of a New World Called the Blazing World*. London, 1666.
Cavendish, Margaret. In Shawn Moore, Jacob Tootalian and Liza Blake (eds), *Digital Cavendish: A Scholarly Collaborative* (2015). http://digitalcavendish.org/complete-works. Accessed 20 July 2021.
Cavendish, Margaret. *The Life of the Thrice Noble, High, and Puissant Prince William Cavendishe, Duke, Marquess, and Earl of Newcastle*. London, 1667.
Cavendish, Margaret. In C. H. Firth (ed.), *The Life of William Cavendish Duke of Newcastle*. London, 1886.
Cavendish, Margaret. In Liza Blake (ed.), *Margaret Cavendish's Poems and Fancies: A Digital Critical Edition* (2019). University of Toronto. http://library2.utm.utoronto.ca/poemsandfancies/. Accessed 8 November 2020.
Cavendish, Margaret. *Natures Pictures, Drawn by Fancies Pencil to the Life*. London, 1656.
Cavendish, Margaret. *Observations upon Experimental Philosophy*. London, 1666.
Cavendish, Margaret. In Eileen O'Neill (ed.), *Observations upon Experimental Philosophy*. Cambridge, 2001.
Cavendish, Margaret. *Orations of Divers Sorts Accommodated to Divers Places*. London, 1662.
Cavendish, Margaret. In Sylvia Bowerbank and Sara Mendelson (eds), *Paper Bodies: A Margaret Cavendish Reader*. Peterborough, ON, 2000.
Cavendish, Margaret. *Philosophical Letters, or, Modest Reflections upon Some Opinions in Natural Philosophy*. London, 1664.
Cavendish, Margaret. *Playes*. London, 1662.
Cavendish, Margaret. *Plays, Never Before Printed*. London, 1668.
Cavendish, Margaret. *Poems and Fancies*. London, 1654.
Cavendish, Margaret. In Brandie Siegfried (ed.), *Poems and Fancies with the Animal Parliament*. Toronto, 2018.
Cavendish, Margaret. *Poems and Phansies*. London, 1664.
Cavendish, Margaret. *Poems, or Several Fancies*. London, 1668.
Cavendish, Margaret. In James Fitzmaurice (ed.), *Sociable Letters*. New York, 2004.
Cavendish, Margaret. *The Worlds Olio*. London, 1655.
Cervantes Saavedra, Miguel de. In J. M. Cohen (trans.), *The Adventures of Don Quixote*. London, 1950.
Chapman, George. In Akihiro Yamada (ed.), *The Widow's Tears*. London, 1975.
Clarke, Samuel. *The Lives of Sundry Eminent Persons in this Later Age*, Part 2. London, 1683.
Clifford, Anne. In Jessica L. Malay (ed.), *Anne Clifford's Autobiographical Writings, 1590–1676*. Manchester, 2018.
Clifford, Anne. In Jessica L. Malay (ed.), *Anne Clifford's Great Books of Record*. Manchester, 2015.

Clifford, Anne. 'The Diary of Lady Anne Clifford', in Randall Martin (ed.), *Women Writers in Renaissance England*. New York, 2010, 245–75.

Collective. *Recueil de pièces galantes en prose et en vers de Madame la Comtesse de la Suze, et de Monsieur Pelisson*. Paris, 1663, repr. 1684.

Collins, An. In Sidney Gottlieb (ed.), *An Collins: Divine Songs and Meditacions*. Tempe, AZ, 1996.

Conway, Anne. In Marjorie Hope Nicolson and Sarah Hutton (eds), *The Conway Letters: The Correspondence of Anne, Viscountess Conway, Henry More, and their Friends, 1642–1684*. Oxford, 1992.

Conway, Anne. *The Principles of the Most Ancient and Modern Philosophy*. London, 1692.

The Conway Papers (1576–1606), in Charles Angell Bradford, unpublished typescript, Washington, DC, Folger Shakespeare Library call number DA378.C6 B6.

Cooke, Anne. *Fouretene Sermons of Barnardine Ochyne, Concernyng the Predestinacion and Eleccion of God: Very Expediente to the Setynge Forth of Hys Glorye among Hys Creatures. Translated out of Italian in to Oure Natyve Tounge by A. C.* London, [1551?].

Cooke, Anne. *Sermons of Barnardine Ochine of Sena, Godeley, Frutfull, and Very Necessary for All True Christians Translated out of Italien into Englisshe*. London, 1548.

Cooke, John. 'An Apparatour', in Donald Beecher (ed.), *Characters*. Ottawa, 2003.

Coverdale, Miles (trans.). *The Psalter or Boke of Psalmes Both in Latyn and Englyshe*. London, 1540.

Cummings, Brian (ed.). *The Book of Common Prayer: The Texts of 1549, 1559, and 1662*. Oxford, 2011.

Dalrymple, David (ed.). *Secret Correspondence of Sir Robert Cecil with James VI, King of Scotland*. Edinburgh, 1766.

Daniel, Samuel. 'Samuel Daniel to Mary Sidney', in S. P. Cerasano and Marion Wynne-Davies (eds), *Readings in Renaissance Women's Drama*. London, 1998, 10–12.

Davidson, Peter (ed.). *Poetry and Revolution: An Anthology of British and Irish Verse, 1625–1660*. Oxford, 1998.

Davies, John. *The Muses Sacrifice*. London, 1612.

Davies, Lady Eleanor. In Esther S. Cope (ed.). *Prophetic Writings of Lady Eleanor Davies*. Oxford, 1996.

Deacon, Pudentiana. *Delicious Entertainments of the Soule. Written by the Holy and Most Reverend Lord Francis de Sales, Bishop and Prince of Geneva. Translated by a Dame of Our Ladies of Comfort of the Order of S. Bennet in Cambray*. Douai, 1632.

Dod, John and Robert Cleaver. *A Godlie Forme of Householde Government: For the Ordering of Private Families, According to the Direction of Gods Word*. London, 1598.

Drayton, Michael. *Englands Herociall Epistles*. London, 1597.

Drummond, William. *Poems by That Most Famous Wit, William Drummond of Hawthornden*. London, 1656.

Du Verger, Susan. *Admirable Events: Selected out of Four Bookes, Written in French by the Right Reverend, John Peter Camus, Bishop of Belley. Together with Morall Relations, Written by the Same Author. And Translated into English by S. Du Verger*. London, 1639.

Du Verger, Susan. *Diotrephe, or, An Historie of Valentines. Written in French by the Right Reverend John Peter Camus, Bishop and Lord of Belley, a Prince of the Holy Empire, and Privie Councellour to the Most Christian King Lewis the 14. Now Reigning*. London, 1641.

Dugdale, William. *The Antiquities of Warwickshire Illustrated: From Records, Ledger Books, Manuscripts, Charters, Evidences, Tombs, and Armes: Beautified with Maps, Prospects, and Portraitures*. London, 1656.

Dyce, Alexander (ed.). *Specimens of British Poetesses*. London, 1825.

E., T. [Thomas Edgar?]. *The Lawes Resolution of Womens Rights*. London, 1632.

Early Modern Recipes Online Collective. Hypotheses (2012). https://emroc.hypotheses.org/. Accessed 5 December 2020.

Eikon Basilike. In Jim Daems and Holly Faith Nelson (eds), *Eikon Basilike with Selections from Eikonoklastes*. Peterborough, ON, 2006.

Elisabeth of Bohemia and René Descartes. In Lisa Shapiro (ed. and trans.), *The Correspondence between Princess Elisabeth of Bohemia and René Descartes*. Chicago, IL, 2007.

[Eliza]. *Eliza's Babes*. London, 1652.

[Eliza]. In L. E. Semler (ed.), *Eliza's Babes: or The Virgin's Offering (1652): A Critical Edition*. Madison, NJ, 2001.

Elizabeth I, Queen of England and Ireland. In Leah S. Marcus, Janel Mueller, and Mary Beth Rose (eds), *Elizabeth I: Collected Works*. Chicago, IL, 2002.

Elizabeth I, Queen of England and Ireland. In Janel Mueller and Joshua Scodel (eds), *Elizabeth I: Translations*, 2 vols. Chicago, IL, 2009.

Elizabeth I, Queen of England and Ireland. *Elizabetha Triumphans* [*The Tilbury Speech*]. London, 1588.

Elizabeth I, Queen of England and Ireland. 'A Godlie Meditation of the Inwarde Love of the Christian Soule towards Christ our Lord', in Thomas Bentley (ed.), *The Monument of Matrones Conteining Seuen Severall Lamps of Virginitie, or Distinct Treatises*, Parts 1–4. London, 1582; Lamp 2, 1–34.

Elizabeth I, Queen of England and Ireland. *A Godly Meditation of the Inwarde Love of the Soule. First Printed in the Yeare 1548*. London, 1567–1568.

Elizabeth I, Queen of England and Ireland. *A Godly Medytacyon of the Christen Sowle Concerninge a Love towards God and Hys Christ, Compiled in Frenche by the Lady Margarete Quene of Naver, and Aptely Translated into Englysh by the Right Vertuouse Lady Elizabeth Doughter to our Late Soverayne Kynge Heneri the viii*. Wesel [Marburg], 1548.

Elizabeth I, Queen of England and Ireland. *The True Copie of a Letter from the Queenes Majestie, to the Lord Maior of London, and His Brethren*. London, 1586.

Elizabeth Stuart, Queen of Bohemia. In Nadine Akkerman (ed.), *The Correspondence of Elizabeth Stuart, Queen of Bohemia*, 3 vols. Oxford, 2015.

Elyot, Thomas. *The Defence of Good Women*. London, 1540.

Erasmus, Desidarius. *De conscribendis epistolis*, in J. K. Sowards (ed.) and Charles Fantazzi (trans.), *Collected Works of Erasmus: Literary and Educational Writings*. Toronto, 1985.

Erasmus, Desiderius. *The First Tome or Volume of the Paraphrase of Erasmus*. London, 1548.

Erundell, Peter. *The French Garden: For English Ladyes and Gentlewomen to Walke In. Or, A Sommer Dayes Labour*. London, 1605.

Evelinge, Elizabeth. *The Admirable Life of the Holy Virgin S. Catherine of Bologna, Abbess of the Monastery of the Sacred Virgins of the Order of S. Clare in the Citty of Bologna*. St. Omer, 1621.

Evelinge, Elizabeth. *The Declarations and Ordinances Made upon the Rule of Our Holy Mother S. Clare*. St. Omer, 1622.

Evelinge, Elizabeth. *The History of the Angellical Virgin Glorious S. Clare, Dedicated to the Queens Most Excellent Majesty. Extracted out of the R.F. LUKE Wadding His Annals of the*

Freer Minors Chiefely by Francis Hendricque and Now Donne into English, by Sister Magdalen Augustine, of the Holy Order of the Poore Clares in Aire. Douay, 1635.

Fehrenbach, R. J. (ed.), '*A Letter Sent by the Maydens of London* (1567)'. *English Literary Renaissance*, 14 (1984), 285–304.

Fell, Margaret. *Womens Speaking Justified, Proved and Allowed of by the Scriptures*. London, 1667.

Fell, Sarah. In Norman Penney (ed.), *The Household Account Book of Sarah Fell of Swarthmoor Hall*. Cambridge, 1920.

[Feltham, Owen]. *Batavia, of den ontployden Hollander*. Amsterdam, 1684.

[Feltham, Owen]. *Batavia, or the Hollander Displayed*. Amsterdam, 1675.

Finch, Anne. In Myra Reynolds (ed.), *The Poems of Anne Countess of Winchilsea*. Chicago, IL, 1903.

Finch, Anne et al. In Marjorie Hope Nicolson and Sarah Hutton (eds), *The Conway Letters: The Correspondence of Anne, Viscountess Conway, Henry More, and Their Friends 1642–1684*. Oxford, 1992.

Firth, C. H. and R. S. Rait (eds). *Acts and Ordinances of the Interregnum, 1642–1660*. London, 1911.

Florio, Michelangelo. *Historia de la vita e de la morte de l'illustriss, Signora Giovanna Graia*. Middelburgh, 1607.

Fontenelle, Bernard Le Bovier de. In Aphra Behn (trans.), *A Discovery of New Worlds*. London, 1688.

Foxe, John. *Actes and Monuments of These Latter and Perillous Dayes Touching Matters of the Church*. London, 1563.

Foxe, John. *Actes and Monuments of These Latter and Perillous Dayes Touching Matters of the Church*. London, 1570.

Fraunce, Abraham. *The Arcadian Rhetorike*. London, 1588.

G[ainsford], T[homas]. *The Rich Cabinet; Furnished with Varietie of Excellent Discriptions, Exquisite Charracters, Witty Discourses, and Delightfull Histories*. London, 1616.

Garland, Edward. *An Answer to a Printed Book, Falsely Entitled, A Blow at the Serpent*. London, 1657.

The Geneva Bible: A Facsimile of the 1560 Edition. Madison, WI, 1969.

Gertrude the Great. *Les insinuations de la divine piété*. Paris, 1634.

Gildon, Charles. *The History of the Athenian Society*. London, 1692.

Gouge, William. *Of Domesticall Duties: Eight Treatises*. London, 1622.

Goureau, Angeline (ed.). *The Whole Duty of a Woman: Female Writers in Seventeenth-Century England*. New York, 1985.

Graham, Elspeth et al. (eds). *Her Own Life: Autobiographical Writings by Seventeenth-Century Englishwomen*. London, 1989.

Gray, Thomas. In Duncan C. Tovey (ed.), *The Letters of Thomas Gray*, 3 vols. London, 1900–1912.

Green, Mary Anne Everett (ed. and trans.). *Letters of Queen Henrietta Maria, Including Her Private Correspondence with Charles I*. London, 1857.

Greenblatt, Stephen (ed.). *The Norton Anthology of English Literature*, 10th edn. New York, 2018.

Greenbury, Catherine. *A Short Relation, of the Life, Virtues, and Miracles, of S. Elizabeth, Called the Peacemaker. Queen of Portugall. Of the Third Rule of S. Francis. Translated out of Dutch by Sister Catherine Francis, Abbess of the English Monasteries of S. Francis Third Rule in Bruxelles*. Brussels, 1628.

Greer, Germaine et al. (eds). *Kissing the Rod: An Anthology of Seventeenth-Century Women's Verse*. London, 1988.

Grey, Elizabeth (Countess of Kent). *A Choice Manuall, or Rare and Select Secrets in Physick and Chirurgery*. London, 1653.

Grey, Lady Jane. *An Epistle of the Ladye Jane a Righte Vertuous Woman, to a Learned Man of Late Falne from the Truth of Gods Most Holy Word, for Fear of the Worlde*. [London?], [1554?].

Grey, Lady Jane. *Here in This Booke Ye Have a Godly Epistle Made by a Faithful Christian. A Comunication betwene Fecknam and the Lady Jane Dudley. A Letter That She Wrote to Her Syster Lady Katherin. The Ende of the Ladye Jane upon the Scaffolde. Ye Shal Have Also Herein a Godly Prayer Made by Maister John Knokes*. London, [1554?].

Grey, Lady Jane. In Nicolas, Nicholas Harris [(ed.)?], *The Literary Remains of Lady Jane Grey: With a Memoir of Her Life*. London, 1825.

Grotius, Hugo. In P.C. Molhuysen, B. L. Meulenbreuk, P. P. Witkam et al. (eds), *Briefwisseling*, 17 vols. *The Correspondence of Hugo Grotius*. http://www.grotius.huygens.knaw.nl. Accessed 2 June 2021.

Grymeston, Elizabeth. *Miscellanea, Meditations, Memoratives*. London, 1604.

[Guillerargues, Gabriel de]. *Lettres portugaises*. Paris, 1669.

Halkett, Anne. In Suzanne Trill (ed.), *Lady Anne Halkett: Selected Self-Writings*. Aldershot, 2007.

Hall, Joseph. *Contemplations upon the Principall Passages of the Holy Storie*. London, 1626.

Hamilton, Adam (ed.). *The Chronicle of the English Augustine Canonesses Regular of the Lateran at St Monica's in Louvain, 1625–1644*, 2 vols. Edinburgh, 1906.

Hamilton, William. *The Exemplary Life and Character of James Bonnell*. London, 1704.

Hasted, Edward. *The History and Topographical Survey of the County of Kent*, vol. 1. Canterbury, 1797.

Hasted, Edward. *The History and Topographical Survey of the County of Kent*, vol. 3. Canterbury, 1797. *British History Online*. https://www.british-history.ac.uk/survey-kent/vol3. Accessed 19 August 2020.

Heliodorus. In William L'Isle (trans.), *The Faire Æthiopian*. London, 1631.

Heliodorus. In Thomas Underdown (trans.), *An Æthiopian Historie*. London, 1659.

Herbert, George. In Helen Wilcox (ed.), *The English Poems of George Herbert*. Cambridge, 2007.

Herrick, Robert. *Hesperides*. London, 1648.

Heyrick, Richard. *Queen Esthers Resolves: or, A Princely Pattern of Heaven-Born Resolution, for All The Lovers of God and Their Country*. London, 1646.

Heywood, John. In John S. Farmer (ed.), *The Proverbs, Epigrams, and Miscellanies*. London, 1906.

Heywood, Thomas. *The Exemplary Lifes and Remarkable Acts of Nine the Most Worthy Women of the World: Three Jewes, Three Gentiles, Three Christians*. London, 1640.

Heywood, Thomas. *The Generall Historie of Women*. London, 1657.

Heywood, Thomas. *Gynaikeion: or Nine Bookes of Various History Concerning Women*. London, 1624.

Hoby, Margaret. In Joanna Moody (ed.), *The Private Life of an Elizabethan Lady: The Diary of Lady Margaret Hoby, 1599–1605*. Stroud, 1998.

The Holy Bible, King James Version (1611) 400th Anniversary Edition. Peabody, MA, 2010.

Homer. In Wilson, Emily (trans.), *The Odyssey*. New York, 2018.

Hume, Anna. *The Triumphs of Love: Chastity; Death; Translated out of Petrarch by Mrs. Anna Hume*. Edinburgh, 1644.

Hutchinson, Lucy. 'The Life of John Hutchinson', in James Sutherland (ed.), *Memoirs of the Life of Colonel Hutchinson*. London, 1973.

Hutchinson, Lucy. 'The Life of Mrs Lucy Hutchinson, Written by Herself', in Julius Hutchinson (ed.), *Memoirs of the Life of Colonel Hutchinson, Governor of Nottingham Castle and Town*. London, 1806, 1–18.

Hutchinson, Lucy. In C. H. Firth (ed.), *Memoirs of the Life of Colonel Hutchinson*. London, 1885.

Hutchinson, Lucy. In N. H. Keeble (ed.), *Memoirs of the Life of Colonel Hutchinson with a Fragment of Autobiography*. London, 1995.

Hutchinson, Lucy. In David Norbrook (ed.), *Order and Disorder*. Oxford, 2001.

Hutchinson, Lucy. In Reid Barbour and David Norbrook (eds), *Translation of Lucretius*. Oxford, 2012.

Hutchinson, Lucy. *Of Theologie*, in David Norbrook, Elizabeth Clarke, and Jane Stevenson (eds), *The Works of Lucy Hutchinson, vol. II: Theological Writings and Translations*. Oxford, 2018.

Jackson, Arthur. *Annotations upon the Remaining Historicall Part of the Old Testament*. Cambridge, 1646.

James VI and I, King of England, Ireland, and Scotland. In Charles H. McIlwain (ed.), *Political Works of James I*. New York, 1965.

Jehlen, Myra and Michael Warner (eds). *The English Literatures of America, 1500–1800*. London, 1997.

Jenkinson, Anne. *Meditations upon the Lamentations of Jeremy, Translated out of French by A. I. Every Verse Beginning with the Hebrew Alphabet*. London, 1609.

Jessey, Henry. *The Exceeding Riches of Grace*. London, 1647.

Jevon, Rachel. *Carmen Piambeyikon Regiae Majestati Caroli II. Principum et Christianorum Optimi in Exoptatissimum Eius Restaurationem*. London, 1660.

Jevon, Rachel. *Exultationis Carmen. To the Kings Most Excellent Majesty upon His Most Desired Return*. London, 1660.

Jones, Robert. *The Muses Gardin for Delights*. London, 1610.

Jinner, Sarah. *An Almanack and Prognostication for the Year of Our Lord 1659*. London, 1659.

Jonson, Ben. 'Jonson and Wroth', in S. P. Cerasano and Marion Wynne-Davies (eds), *Readings in Renaissance Women's Drama*. London, 1998.

Jonson, Ben. *Timber: Or, Discoveries; Made upon Men and Matter: As They Have Flow'd out of His Daily Readings; or Had Their Refluxe to His Peculiar Notion of the Times*, in *Works*. London, 1641.

Kennedy, George A. (trans. and ed.). *Progymnasmata: Greek Textbooks of Prose Composition and Rhetoric*. Atlanta, 2003.

Kowalchuk, Kristine (ed.). *Preserving on Paper: Seventeenth-Century Englishwomen's Receipt Books*. Toronto, 2017.

La Calprenède, Gautier de Costes de. *Cassandra*, in Charles Cotterell (trans.), London, 1652.

La Calprenède, Gautier de Costes de. In John Davies (trans.), *Hymen's Praeludia, or, Loves Master-Piece Being the Ninth, and Tenth Part*. London, 1659.

Lambarde, William. *A Perambulation of Kent: Conteining the Description, Hystorie, and Customes of That Shire*. London, 1570.

Lanyer, Aemilia. In Susanne Woods (ed.), *The Poems of Aemilia Lanyer*. Oxford, 1993.

Larkin, James (ed.). *Stuart Royal Proclamations, vol. 2: Royal Proclamations of King Charles I, 1625–46*. Oxford, 1983.

Lawes, Henry. *Ayres and Dialogues*. London, 1653.

Lawes, Henry. *The Second Book of Ayres, and Dialogues*. London, 1655.
Le Moyne, Pierre. *The Gallery of Heroick Women*. Trans. John Paulet, Marquess of Winchester. London, 1652.
Lee, Nathaniel. *The Princess of Cleves*. London, 1689.
Lescailje, Kataryne. *Rouwklagt over de dood van de koninginne van Grootbrittanje*. Amsterdam, 1695.
Lescailje, Katharina. *Tooneel- en mengelpoëzy*, 3 vols. Amsterdam, 1731.
Letters and Poems in Honour of the Incomparable Princess, Margaret, Dutchess of Newcastle. London, 1676.
Lipsius, Justus. In William Jones (trans.), *Six Bookes of Politickes or Civill Doctrine*. London, 1594.
Locke, Anne. In Susan Felch (ed.), *The Collected Works of Anne Vaughan Lock*. Tempe, AZ, 1999.
Locke, Anne. '*A Meditation of a Penitent Sinner: Written in Maner of a Paraphrase upon the 51. Psalme of David*', in *Sermons of John Calvin, upon the Songe That Ezechias Made after He Had Bene Sicke, and Afflicted by the Hand of God, Conteyned in the 38. Chapiter of Esay. Translated out of Frenche into Englishe*. London, 1560.
Locke, Anne (Prowse). *Of the Markes of the Children of God, and of Their Comforts in Afflications. To the Faithfull of the Low Countrie. Overseene againe and Augmented by the Author, and Translated out of French by A. Prowse*. London, 1590.
Lorich, Reinhard. *Aphthonii Progymnasmata*. Cambridge, 1631.
Lovelace, Richard. *Lucasta*. London, 1649.
Lumley, Lady Jane. *Iphigenia at Aulis*. The Malone Society Reprints. London, 1909.
Lumley, Lady Jane. In Diane Purkiss (ed.), *Three Tragedies by Renaissance Women*. London, 1998.
Lydgate, John. 'London Lickpenny'. In Lawrence Manley (ed.), *London in the Age of Shakespeare: An Anthology*. University Park, PA, 1986.
Lyly, John. *Euphues and His England*. London, 1580.
Lyly, John. *Sixe Court Comedies*. London, 1632.
Machiavelli, Niccolò. In Bernard Crick (ed.), *The Discourses*. Harmondsworth, 1970.
Machiavelli, Niccolò. In George Bull (trans.), *The Prince*. Harmondsworth, 1999.
Major, Elizabeth. *Honey on the Rod*. London, 1656.
Makin, Bathsua. *An Essay to Revive the Antient Education of Gentlewomen*. London, 1673.
Man, Judith. *An Epitome of the History of Faire Argenis and Polyarchus, Extracted out of the Latin, and Put in French, by That Great and Famous Writer, M. N. Coeffeteau, Bishop of Marseilles. And Translated out of the French into English by a Young Gentlewoman. Dedicated to the Lady Anne Wentworth*. London, 1640.
Markham, Gervase. *The English Housewife*. London, 1623.
Markham, Gervase. In Michael R. Best (ed.), *The English Housewife*. Montréal, 1986.
Marprelate, Martin (pseud.). *Oh Read over D. John Bridges, for It Is Worthy Worke: Or an Epitome of the Fyrste Booke, of that Right Worshipfull Volume, Written against the Puritans, in the Defence of the Noble Cleargie, by as Worshipfull a Prieste, John Bridges, Presbyter, Priest or Elder, Doctor of Divillitie, and Deane of Sarum* [The Epistle]. East Molesey, 1588.
Marston, John. *The Workes*. London, 1633.
Martin, Dorcas. *An Instruction for Christians, Conteining a Fruitfull and Godlie Exercise, as Well in Wholesome and Fruitfull Praiers, as in Reverend Discerning of Gods Holie Commandemts and Sacraments: Translated out of French into English by a Right Vertuous and Godlie Matrone*

and Gentlewoman Named Mistress Dorcas Martin, in Thomas Bentley (ed.), *The Monument of Matrones: Conteining Seven Severall Lampes of Virginitie, or Distinct Treatises; Whereof the First Five Concerne Praier and Meditation: the Other Two, Last Precepts and Examples*, Parts 14. London, 1582; Lampe 2, 220–46.

Marvell, Andrew. In Nigel Smith (ed.), *The Poems of Andrew Marvell*. Harlow, 2003.

Mary I, Queen of England and Ireland. *Paraphrase of the Gospel of St. John. The First Tome or Volume of the Paraphrase of Erasmus upon the Newe Testament*. London, 1548.

Matthew, Toby. In David Knowles (ed.), *The Life of Lady Lucy Knatchbull*. London, 1931.

Matthew, Toby. 'The Life of Lady Lucy Knatchbull'. In Caroline Bowden (ed.), *English Convents in Exile, 1600–1800*, vol. 3. Nicky Hallett (ed.), *Life Writing I*. London, 2012.

May, Robert. *The Accomplisht Cook, or, The Art and Mystery of Cookery*. London, 1660.

Mayer, John. *Many Commentaries in One: Upon Joshuah, Judges, Ruth, 1 and 2 of Samuel, 1 and 2 of Kings, 1 and 2 of Chronicles, Ezra, Nehemiah, Esther*. London, 1647.

Melville, Elizabeth. *Ane Godlie Dreame, Compylit in Scottish Meter be M. M. Gentelwoman in Culross, at the Requeist of Her Freindes*. Edinburgh, 1603.

Melville, Elizabeth. In Jamie Reid Baxter (ed.), *Poems of Elizabeth Melville, Lady Culross*. Edinburgh, 2010.

Mennes, John. *Recreation for Ingenious Head-Peeces*. London, 1654.

Milton, John. *Eikonoklastes*. In Merritt Y. Hughes (ed.), *The Complete Prose Works of John Milton, vol III: 1648–1649*. New Haven, CT, 1962.

Milton, John. In Merritt Y. Hughes (ed.), *John Milton: Complete Poems and Major Prose*. New York, 1957.

Miola, Robert S. (ed.). *Early Modern Catholicism: An Anthology of Primary Sources*. Oxford, 2007.

Mollineux, Mary. *Fruits of Retirement: or Miscellaneous Poems, Moral and Divine*. London, 1702.

Mollineux, Mary, *Fruits of Retirement: or, Miscellaneous Poems, Moral and Divine: Being Some Contemplations, Letters, &c. Written on Variety of Subjects and Occasions*, 5th edn. London, 1761.

Montagu, Lady Mary Wortley. In Dallaway, James (ed.), *The Works of ... Lady Mary Wortley Montagu, Including Her Correspondance, Poems and Essays*, 5 vols. London, 1803.

Montagu, Walter. *The Shepheard's Paradise*. London, 1659.

Montaigne, Michel de. In John Florio (trans.). *The Essayes or Morall, Politike and Millitarie Discourses of Lord Michaell de Montaigne*. London, 1603.

Montgomerie, Alexander. In Parkinson, David J. (ed.), *Alexander Montgomerie: Poems*. Edinburgh, 2000.

Montgomerie, Alexander. In James Cranstoun (ed.), *The Poems of Alexander Montgomerie*. Edinburgh, 1887.

Morata, Olimpia. In Holt N. Parker (ed.), *Olimpia Morata: The Complete Writings of an Italian Heretic*. Chicago, IL, 2003.

More, Gertrude. In Augustine Baker (ed.), *The Spiritual Exercises of the Most Vertuous and Religious D. Gertrude More*. Paris, 1658.

Moryson, Fynes. *An Itinerary Written by Fynes Moryson, Gent*. London, 1617.

Munda, Constantia. *The Worming of a Mad Dogge: or, A Soppe for Cerberus the Jaylor of Hell*. London, 1617.

Murrell, John. *Daily Exercise for Ladies and Gentlewomen*. London, 1617.

Nashe, Thomas. In R. B. McKerrow (ed.), *The Works of Thomas Nashe*, 5 vols. London, 1904–1910.

Niccols, Richard. *Sir Thomas Overburies Vision*. London, 1616.

Norden, John. *Speculi Britan[n]icæ Pars the Description of Hartfordshire*. London, 1598.
'Obituary Notices of the Nuns of the English Benedictine Abbey of Ghent in Flanders 1627–1811'. *Miscellanea XI*. London, 1917, 1–92.
Oldenburg, Henry. In A. Rupert Hall and Marie Boas Hall (eds), *The Correspondence of Henry Oldenburg*, 9 vols. Madison, 1965–1973.
Ortúñez de Calahorra, Diego. In Daniel Eisenberg (ed.), *Espejo de príncipes y cavalleros*, 6 vols. Madrid, 1975.
Osborne, Dorothy. In G. C. Moore Smith (ed.), *The Letters of Dorothy Osborne to William Temple*. Oxford, 1928.
Overbury, Thomas. *New and Choise Characters*. London, 1615.
Overbury, Thomas. *His Wife with Additions of New Characters*. 1614. Reprinted in Edward F. Rimbaul (ed.), *The Miscellaneous Works in Prose and Verse of Sir Thomas Overbury*. London, 1890.
Owen, Jane. *An Antidote against Purgatory*. [St. Omer], 1634.
Palmer, Julia. In Victoria Burke and Elizabeth Clarke (eds), *The 'Centuries' of Julia Palmer*. Nottingham, 2001.
Parr, Katherine. In Janel Mueller (ed.), *Katherine Parr: Complete Works and Correspondence*. Chicago, IL, 2011.
Parr, Katherine. *The Lamentation of a Synner*. London, 1547.
Parr, Katherine. *Prayers or Meditacions, Wherin the Mynde is Styrred Paciently to Suffre All Afflictions Here*. London, 1545.
Parr, Katherine. *Prayers Stirryng the Mynd unto Heavenlye Medytacions*. London, 1545.
Partridge, John. *The Treasurie of Commodious Conceits, & Hidden Secrets and May Be Called, the Huswives Closet, of Healthfull Prouision*. London, 1573.
Percy, Mary. *An Abridgement of Christian Perfection. Wherein Are Conteyned Many Excellent Documents, Precepts, & Advertisements, Touching the Holy, & Sacred Mysticall Divinity. Translated out of the French Corrected Copie, into English*. [St Omer], 1612.
Percy, Thomas (ed.). *Reliques of English Poetry of the Latter Part of the Sixteenth Century*. London, 1765.
Philipot, John. *Villare Cantianum, or, Kent Surveyed and Illustrated*. London, 1659.
Philips, Katherine. In Patrick Thomas (ed.). *The Collected Works of Katherine Philips: The Matchless Orinda*, 3 vols. Essex, 1990–1993.
Philips, Katherine. *Letters from Orinda to Poliarchus*. London, 1705.
Philips, Katherine. *Poems. By the Most Deservedly Admired Mrs. Katherine Philips the Matchless Orinda*. London, 1667.
Phillips, Edward. *Theatrum Poetarum, or A Compleat Collection of the Poets*. London, 1675.
Pizan, Christine de. In Kate Langdon Forhan (trans. and ed.), *The Book of the Body Politic*. Cambridge, 1994.
Pizan, Christine de. In William Caxton (trans.) and A. T. P. Byles (ed.), *Book of Fayttes of Armes and of Chyvalrie*. London, 1932.
Pizan, Christine de. In Bryan Anslay (trans.), *Here Begynneth the Boke of the Cyte of Ladyes*. London, 1521.
Plat, Hugh. *Delightes for Ladies*. London, 1602.
Plat, Hugh. *Divers Chimicall Conclusions* (separate dated title page, pagination and register), in Hugh Plat, *The Jewell House of Art and Nature*. London, 1594.
Plomer, Henry (ed.). *The Churchwardens' Accounts of St. Nicholas, Strood*. Kent, 1927.
Pontaymeri, Alexandre de. *A Womans Woorth, Defended against All the Men in the World*, Attrib. Anthony Gibson. London, 1599.

Powell, Vavasor. *The Scriptures Concord or a Catechisme*. London, 1646.

Pulter, Hester. In Alice Eardley (ed.), *Lady Hester Pulter: Poems, Emblems, and The Unfortunate Florinda*. Toronto, 2014.

Pulter, Hester. In Leah Knight and Wendy Wall (eds), *The Pulter Project: Poet in the Making* (2018). Northwestern University. http://pulterproject.northwestern.edu.

Puttenham, George. *The Arte of English Poesie*. London, 1589.

Quarles, Francis. *Hadassa or The History of Queene Ester with Meditations Thereupon, Diuine and Morall*. London, 1621.

Rainbowe, Edward. *A Sermon Preached at the Funeral of the Right Honorable Anne, Countess of Pembroke, Dorset, and Montgomery*. London, 1677.

Rainolde, Richard. *A Booke Called the Foundacion of Rhetorike*. London, 1563.

Ralegh, Walter. In Michael Rudick (ed.), *The Poems of Sir Walter Ralegh: A Historical Edition*. Tempe, AZ, 2000.

Ravenscroft, Thomas. *The Whole Booke of Psalmes*. London, 1621.

Rich, Barnaby. *The Excellency of Good Women*. London, 1613.

Rich, Mary. *Memoir of Lady Warwick: Also Her Diary*. London, 1847.

Rich, Mary. *Some Specialities in the Life of M. Warwicke*. In T. C. Croker (ed.), *The Autobiography of Mary Countess of Warwick*. London, 1848, 1–38.

Ridley, Thomas. *A View of the Civile and Ecclesiasticall Law*. London, 1607.

Robinson, Clement (ed.). *A Handefull of Pleasant Delites*. London, 1584.

Romieu, Marie de. *Les Premiers Oeuvres Poetiques de M. Damoiselle Marie de Romieu, Vivaroise*. Paris, 1581.

Roper, Margaret. *A Devoute Treatise upon the Pater Noster, Made Fyrst in Latyn by the Moost Famous Doctour Mayster Erasmus Roterdamus, and Torned into Englisshe by a Yong Vertuous and Well Lerned Gentylwoman of .xix. Yere of Age*. London, [1531?].

Rosewell, Walter. *The Serpents Subtilty Discovered, or a True Relation of What Passed in the Cathedrall Church of Rochester*. London, 1656.

Rowlandson, Mary. In Neal Salisbury (eds). *Soveraignty and Goodness of God (1682)*. Boston, MA, 1997.

The Rule of the Most Blissed Father Saint Benedict. Ghent, 1632.

Russell, Elizabeth. *A Way of Reconciliation of a Good and Learned Man, Touching the Nature and Substance of the Body and Blood in the Sacrament*. London, 1605.

Schurman, Anna Maria van. In Clement Barksdale (trans.), *The Learned Maid; or, Whether a Maid May Be a Scholar?* London, 1659.

Schurman, Anna Maria van. *Opuscula Hebræa, Græca, Latina, Gallica, Prosaica et Metrica*. Leiden, 1648.

Scudéry, George and Madeleine de. *Artamenes. Or The Grand Cyrus*. Trans Francis Gifford, 5 vols. London, 1653.

Scudéry, George and Madeleine de. *Ibrahim. Or The Illustrious Bassa*. Trans. Henry Cogan. London, 1652–1655.

Scudéry, Madeleine de. *Clelia*. Trans. John Davies. 1655–1661, 1678.

Scudéry, Madeleine de. *Conversations upon Several Subjects*. London, 1683.

Selden, John. *Titles of Honor*. London, 1631.

Shakespeare, William. *Hamlet*. In Stephen Greenblatt et al. (eds), *The Norton Shakespeare Based on the Oxford Edition: Tragedies*. New York, 1997, 296–384.

Shakespeare, William. *Measure for Measure*. In Jonathan Bate and Eric Rasmussen (eds), *William Shakespeare: Complete Works*. Basingstoke, 2007, 159–214.

Shakespeare, William. *The Tragedy of Antony and Cleopatra*. In Stanley Wells, Gary Taylor, John Jowett, and William Montgomery (eds), *The Oxford Shakespeare: The Complete Works*, 2nd edn. Oxford, 2005.

Shapiro, Lisa (ed. and trans.). *The Correspondence between Princess Elisabeth of Bohemia and René Descartes*. Chicago, IL, 2007.

Sharp, Jane. *The Midwives Book. Or the Whole Art of Midwifery Discovered*. London, 1671.

Sharpe, Jane. In Elaine Hobby (ed.), *The Midwives Book*. Oxford, 1999.

Sidney, Mary. In Hannibal Hamlin, Michael G. Brennan, Margaret P. Hannay, and Noel J. Kinnamon (eds), *The Sidney Psalter: The Psalms of Sir Philip and Mary Sidney*. Oxford, 2009.

Sidney Herbert, Mary. In Margaret P. Hannay, Noel J. Kinnamon, and Michael G. Brennan (eds), *The Collected Works of Mary Sidney Herbert, Countess of Pembroke*, 2 vols. Oxford, 1998.

Sidney Herbert, Mary. *A Discourse of Life and Death. Written in French by Ph. Mornay. Antonius, A Tragoedie Written Also in French by Ro. Garnier. Both Done in English by the Countesse of Pembroke*. London, 1592.

Sidney Herbert, Mary. 'The Doleful Lay of Clorinda'. In Edmund Spenser, *Colin Clouts Come Home Againe*. London, 1595.

Sidney, Philip. In Katherine Duncan Jones (ed.), *The Countess of Pembroke's Arcadia (The Old Arcadia)*. Oxford, 1985.

Sidney, Philip. *The Countesse of Pembrokes Arcadia*. London, 1593.

Somner, William. *The Antiquities of Canterbury*. London, 1640.

Sophia of Hanover. In Sean Ward (ed. and trans.), *Memoirs (1630–1680)*. Toronto, 2013.

Southwell, Anne. In Jean Klene (ed.), *The Southwell-Sibthorpe Commonplace Book*. Tempe, AZ, 1997.

Sowernam, Ester. *Ester Hath Hang'd Haman*. London, 1617.

Speght, Rachel. In Barbara Kiefer Lewalski (ed.), *The Polemics and Poems of Rachel Speght*. Oxford, 1996.

Spenser, Edmund. In William A. Oram et al. (eds), *The Yale Edition of the Shorter Poems of Edmund Spenser*. New Haven, CT, 1989.

Stanford, Ann (ed.). *The Women Poets in English: An Anthology*. New York, 1972.

Stanley, Thomas. In Galbraith Crump (ed.). *The Poems and Translations of Thomas Stanley*. Oxford: Clarendon Press, 1962.

Stapleton, Thomas. In E. E. Reynolds (trans.). *The Life and Illustrious Martyrdom of Sir Thomas More*. London, 1967.

Stephens, John. *Satyrical Essayes, Characters and Others*. London, 1615.

Stevenson, Jane and Peter Davidson (eds). *Early Modern Women Poets, 1520–1700: An Anthology*. Oxford, 2001.

Stow, John. *A Survay of London Contayning the Originall, Antiquity, Increase, Moderne Estate, and Description of That Citie*. London, 1598.

Strype, John. *David and Saul a Sermon Preached on the Day of National Thanksgiving*. London, 1696.

Stuart, Arbella. In Sara Jayne Steen (ed.), *The Letters of Lady Arbella Stuart*. Oxford, 1995.

Swetnam, Joseph. *The Araignment of Lewd, Idle, Froward and Unconstant Women*. London, 1615.

Talbot, Alethia. *Natura Exenterata: Or Nature Unbowelled*. London, 1655.

Tallemant, Paul. In Aphra Behn (trans.), *Lycidus*. London, 1688.

Taylor, Jeremy. *Discourse of the Nature, Offices and Measures of Friendship, with the Rules of Conducting It*. London, 1657.
Taylor, John. *The Needles Excellency: A New Booke Wherin Are Divers Admirable Workes Wrought with the Needle*. London, 1631.
Temple, William. *Aenmerckingen over de Vereenigde Nederlandtsche Provintien*. Amsterdam, 1673.
Temple, William. *Observations upon the United Provinces of the Netherlands*. London, 1673.
The Account Audited, or the Date of the Resurrection of the Witnesses, Pretended to Be Demonstrated by M. Cary a Minister. Examined by a Friend to the Truth and Ministry. London, 1648.
The Just Downefall of Ambition Adultery and Murder. London, 1615.
The Nine Muses, or, Poems Written by Nine Several Ladies upon the Death of the Late Famous John Dryden Esq. London, 1700.
Thomas, William. *An Argument Wherin the Apparaile of Women is Both Reproved and Defended*. London, 1551.
Thomas, William. *The Vanitie of this Worlde*. London, 1549.
Thoms, William J. (ed.). *Anecdotes and Traditions illustrative of Early English History and Literature*. London, 1839.
Thoroton, Robert. *The Antiquities of Nottinghamshire*. London, 1677.
Tillotson, Johan. *Predicatie Gedaan in de Kapel van Lincolns-Inn, tot London, op den 10. February. 1689*. Amsterdam, 1689.
Trapnel, Anna. In Hilary Hinds (ed.), *Anna Trapnel's Report and Plea; or, a Narrative of Her Journey from London into Cornwall*. Tempe, AZ, 2016.
Trapp, John. *A Commentary or Exposition upon the Books of Ezra, Nehemiah, Ester, Job and Psalms*. London, 1657.
Travitsky, Betty (ed.). *The Paradise of Women: Writings by English Women of the Renaissance*. New York, 1982, repr. 1989.
Tuvil, Daniel. *Asylum Veneris, or a Sanctuary for Ladies*. London, 1616.
Tuvil, Daniel. 'On Sir Thomas Overburies Poem The Wife'. In Donald Beecher (ed.), *Characters*. Ottawa, 2003.
Tweedie, W. K. (ed.). *Select Biographies*. Edinburgh, 1845.
Tyler, Margaret. In Joyce Boro (ed.), *Mirror of Princely Deeds and Knighthood*. London, 2014.
Tyler, Margaret. *The Mirrour of Princely Deedes and Knighthood*. London, [1578].
Tyrwhit, Elizabeth. In Susan Felch (ed.), *Elizabeth Tyrwhit's Morning and Evening Prayers*. Burlington, VA, 2008.
University of Oxford. *Musarum Oxoniensium Epibateria*. Oxford, 1643.
Unto Every Individual Member of Parliament the Humble Representation of Divers Afflicted Women-Petitioners to the Parliament, on the Behalf of Mr. John Lilburn. London, 1653.
Urfé, Honoré d'. *L'Astrée*. Paris, 1607.
Urfé, Honoré d'. In John Pyper (trans.), *The History of Astrea*. London, 1620.
Villiers, George, second duke of Buckingham. In Robert D. Hume and Harold Love (eds), *Plays, Poems, and Miscellaneous Writings Associated with George Villiers, Second Duke of Buckingham*, vol. 2. Oxford, 2007.
Vives, Juan Luis. In Richard Hyrde (ed.), *A Very Frutful and Pleasant Boke Called the Instruction of a Christen Woman*. London, 1547.

Vives, Juan Luis. In Foster Watson (ed.), *Vives and the Renascence Education of Women*. London, 1912.

Walker, Anthony. *Eureka, or, the Virtuous Woman Found*. London, 1678.

Walpole, Horace (ed.). *A Journey into England by Paul Hentzner, in the Year 1598*. London, 1758.

Weamys, Anna. In Patrick Colborn Cullen (ed.), *A Continuation of Sir Philip Sidney's Arcadia*. Oxford, 1995.

Weber, Alan S. (ed.). *Almanacs: Printed Writings, 1641–1700: Series II, Part One, vol. 6: The Early Modern Englishwoman: A Facsimile Library of Essential Works & Printed Writings*. London, 2002.

Weldon, Anthony. *The Court and Character of King James, and the Court of King Charles*. London, 1651.

Whitney, Isabella. *The Copy of a Letter*. London, [*c.* 1567].

Whitney, Isabella. In Danielle Clarke (ed.), *Isabella Whitney, Mary Sidney and Aemilia Lanyer: Renaissance Women Poets*. London, 2000.

Whitney, Isabella. *A Sweet Nosgay*. London, 1573.

Whitney, Isabella. In Nick Broyles et al. (eds), *A Sweet Nosegay* (1995). Montana State University. http://sjsteen.blogs.plymouth.edu/files/2008/04/a-sweet-nosegay.pdf. Accessed 2 June 2020.

Williamson, George Charles. *Lady Anne Clifford*. Kendal, 1922.

Willis, John. *Mnemonica, or The Art of Memory*. London, 1661.

Wilmot, John, Earl of Rochester. In Harold Love (ed.), *The Works of John Wilmot Earl of Rochester*. Oxford, 1999.

Winthrop, John and Margaret Tyndal. In Joseph Hopkins Twichell (ed.), *Some Old Puritan Love-Letters: John and Margaret Winthrop, 1618–1638*. New York, 1894.

Woodcoke, Richard. *Godly and Learned Answer to a Lewd and Unlearned Pamphlet*. London, 1608.

Woolley, Hannah. *The Gentlewomans Companion; or, A Guide to the Female Sex*. London, 1673.

Woolley, Hannah. *Supplement to the Queen-Like Closet*. London, 1674.

Wroth, Lady Mary. *The Countess of Montgomery's Urania*. London, 1621.

Wroth, Lady Mary. In Josephine A. Roberts (ed.), *The First Part of the Countess of Montgomery's Urania*. Binghamton, NY, 1995.

Wroth, Mary. In Paul Salzman (ed.), 'Lady Mary Wroth: *Love's Victory*'. Early Modern Women Research Network (2017–2020). https://c21ch.newcastle.edu.au/emwrn/. Accessed 20 December 2020.

Wroth, Lady Mary. In Michael G. Brennan (ed.), *Lady Mary Wroth's Love's Victory: The Penshurst Manuscript*. London, 1988.

Wroth, Lady Mary. *Love's Victory*. In S. P. Cerasano and Marian Wynne Davies (eds), *Renaissance Drama by Women: Texts and Documents*. London, 1996, 91–126.

Wroth, Lady Mary. In Paul Salzman (ed.), *Mary Wroth's Poetry: An Electronic Edition*. http://wroth.latrobe.edu.au/index.html. Accessed 30 December 2020.

Wroth, Lady Mary. *Pamphilia to Amphilanthus*. In Josephine A. Roberts (ed.), *The Poems of Lady Mary Wroth*. Baton Rouge, MO, 1983.

Wroth, Lady Mary. In Ilona Bell and Steven May (eds), *Pamphilia to Amphilanthus in Manuscript and Print*. Toronto, 2017.

Wroth, Lady Mary. In Josephine A. Roberts (ed.), *The Second Part of The Countess of Montgomery's Urania*. Completed by Suzanne Gossett and Janel Mueller. Binghamton, NY, 1999.

Wycherley, William. *The Plain Dealer*. In Peter Dixon (ed.), *The Country Wife and Other Plays*. Oxford, 1996, 283–399.

Secondary Sources

Abbate, Carolyn. 'Music—Drastic or Gnostic?'. *Critical Inquiry*, 30 (2004), 505–36.

Acheson, Katherine (ed.). *Early Modern English Marginalia*. Abingdon, 2019.

Acheson, Katherine. 'The Occupation of the Margins: Writing, Space, and Early Modern Women'. In K. Acheson (ed.), *Early Modern English Marginalia*. Abingdon, 2019, 70–90.

Acheson, Katherine. '"Outrage your face": Anti-Theatricality and Gender in Early Modern Closet Drama by Women'. *Early Modern Literary Studies*, 6.7 (2001), 1–16.

Achinstein, Sharon. 'Introduction: Gender, Literature, and the English Revolution'. *Women's Studies*, 24 (1994), 1–13.

Aebischer, Pascale and Kathryn Prince. 'Introduction'. In Pascale Aebischer and Kathryn Prince (eds), *Performing Early Modern Drama Today*. Cambridge, 2012, 1–16.

African American Women Writers of the 19th Century. New York Public Library. http://digital.nypl.org/schomburg/writers_aa19/. Accessed 8 April 2021.

Agbabi, Patience. *Bloodshot Monochrome*. Edinburgh, 2014.

Agnew, John. *Place and Politics: The Geographical Mediation of State and Society*. Winchester, MA, 1987.

Ahnert, Ruth. *The Rise of Prison Writing in the Sixteenth Century*. Cambridge, 2013.

Ahnert, Ruth. 'Writing in the Tower of London during the Reformation, ca. 1530–1558'. *Huntington Library Quarterly*, 72 (2009), 168–92.

Ahnert, Ruth and Sebastian E. Ahnert. 'Metadata, Surveillance and the Tudor State'. *History Workshop Journal*, 87 (2019), 27–51.

Ahnert, Ruth and Sebastian E. Ahnert. 'Protestant Letter Networks in the Reign of Mary I: A Quantitative Approach'. *English Literary History*, 82.1 (2015), 1–33.

Ahnert, Ruth and Sebastian E. Ahnert. 'Reconstructing Correspondence Networks in the State Papers Archive'. Audio recording. 'Reception, Reputation and Circulation in the Early Modern World, 1500–1800'. Plenary address, 22–25 March 2017. https://recirc.nuigalway.ie/conference2017. Accessed 8 April 2021.

Ainsworth, David. *Milton and the Spiritual Reader*. New York, 2008.

Akhimie, Patricia. *Shakespeare and the Cultivation of Difference: Race and Conduct in the Early Modern World*. New York, 2018.

Akhimie, Patricia and Bernadette Andrea (eds). *Travel and Travail: Early Modern Women, English Drama, and the Wider World*. Nebraska, 2019.

Akkerman, Nadine. *Courtly Rivals in The Hague: Elizabeth Stuart (1596–1662) & Amalia von Solms (1602–1675)*. The Hague, 2014.

Akkerman, Nadine. 'Enigmatic Cultures of Cryptology'. In Daybell and Gordon (eds), *Cultures of Correspondence*, 69–84.

Akkerman, Nadine. *Invisible Agents: Women and Espionage in Seventeenth-Century Britain*. Oxford, 2018.

Alaimo, Stacy. *Bodily Natures: Science, Environment and the Material Self*. Bloomington, IN, 2010.

Albala, Ken. *The Banquet: Dining in the Great Courts of Late Renaissance Europe*. Champaign, IL, 2007.

Alexander, Gavin. 'The Musical Sidneys'. *John Donne Journal*, 25 (2006), 65–105.

Alexander, Gavin. 'Prosopopoeia: The Speaking Figure'. In Sylvia Adamson, Gavin Alexander, and Katrin Ettenhuber (eds), *Renaissance Figures of Speech*. Cambridge, 2007, 97–112.

Alfar, Cristina Léon. *Women and Shakespeare's Cuckoldry Plays: Shifting Narratives of Marital Betrayal*. New York, 2017.

Alfar, Cristina Léon and Emily G. Sherwood (eds). *Reading Mistress Elizabeth Bourne: Marriage, Separation, and Legal Controversies*. New York, 2021.

Allen, Gemma. '"A Briefe and Plaine Declaration": Lady Anne Bacon's 1564 Translation of the *Apologia Ecclesiasticae Anglicanae*'. In Anne Lawrence-Mathers and Phillipa Hardman (eds), *Women and Writing, c.1340–c.1650: The Domestication of Print Culture*. York, 2010, 62–76.

Allen, Gemma. *The Cooke Sisters: Education, Piety and Politics in Early Modern England*. Manchester, 2013.

Allen, Paula Gunn. *Pocahontas: Medicine Woman, Spy, Entrepreneur, Diplomat*. New York, 2003.

Allut, Paul. *Aloysia Sygea et Nicolas Chorier*. Lyon, 1862.

Anderson, Linda. *Autobiography*. London, 2001.

Anderson, Penelope. *Friendship's Shadows: Women's Friendship and the Politics of Betrayal in England, 1640–1705*. Edinburgh, 2012.

Anderson, Penelope. 'Lucy Hutchinson's Sodom and the Backward Glance of Feminist Queer Temporality'. *Seventeenth Century*, 30.2 (2015), 249–64.

Anderson, Penelope and Whitney Sperrazza. 'Feminist Queer Temporalities in Aemilia Lanyer and Lucy Hutchinson'. In Merry E. Wiesner–Hanks (ed.), *Gendered Temporalities in the Early Modern World*. Amsterdam, 2018, 159–84.

Andrea, Bernadette. 'Black Skin, the Queen's Masques: Africanist Ambivalence and Feminine Author(ity) in the Masques of *Blackness* and *Beauty*'. *English Literary Renaissance*, 29 (1999), 246–81.

Andrea, Bernadette. *The Lives of Girls and Women from the Islamic World in Early Modern British Literature and Culture*. Toronto, 2017.

Andrea, Bernadette. *Women and Islam in Early Modern English Literature*. Cambridge, 2008.

Andreadis, Harriette. 'Re-Configuring Early Modern Friendship: Katherine Philips and Homoerotic Desire'. *SEL: Studies in English Literature 1500–1900*, 46.3 (2006), 523–42.

Anselment, Raymond A. 'Introduction'. In Raymond A. Anselment (ed.), *The Occasional Meditations of Mary Rich, Countess of Warwick*. Tempe, AZ, 2009, 1–39.

Anselment, Raymond A. 'Introduction'. In Raymond A. Anselment (ed.), *The Remembrances of Elizabeth Freke, 1671–1714*. Cambridge, 2001, 1–36.

Anselment, Raymond A. 'Katherine Austen and the Widow's Might'. *Journal for Early Modern Cultural Studies*, 5 (2005), 5–25.

Anselment, Raymond A. '"My First Booke of my Life": The Apology of a Seventeenth-Century Gentry Woman'. *Prose Studies*, 24 (2001), 1–14.

Anselment, Raymond A. 'Seventeenth-Century Manuscript Sources of Alice Thornton's Life'. *SEL: Studies in English Literature 1500–1900*, 45.1 (2005), 135–55.

Antonio, Nicolás. *Biblioteca Hispana*, 4 vols. Madrid, 1783–1788, vol. 2.

Appelbaum, Robert. *Aguecheek's Beef, Belch's Hiccup, and Other Gastronomic Interjections*. Chicago, IL, 2006.

Applegate, Joan. 'Katherine Philips's "Orinda upon Little Hector": An Unrecorded Musical Setting by Henry Lawes'. *English Manuscript Studies, 1100–1700*, 4 (1993), 272–80.

The Archaeology of Reading. c. 2019. The Sheridan Libraries—Johns Hopkins University, Centre for Editing Lives and Letters—UCL, Princeton University Library, and The Andrew W. Mellon Foundation. https://archaeologyofreading.org/. Accessed 16 November 2020.

Archer, Jayne Elisabeth. 'The Queens' Arcanum: Authority and Authorship in *The Queens Closet Opened* (1655)'. *Renaissance Journal*, 1 (2002), 14–25.

Archer, Jayne Elisabeth. 'Women and Chymistry in Early Modern England: The Manuscript Receipt Book (*c.* 1616) of Sarah Wigges'. In Kathleen P. Long (ed.), *Gender and Scientific Discourse in Early Modern Culture*. London, 2010,191–216.

Armstrong, Guyda. 'Coding Continental: Information Design in Sixteenth-Century English Vernacular Language Manuals and Translations'. *Renaissance Studies*, 29 (2015), 78–102.

Armstrong, Guyda. *The English Boccaccio: A History in Books*. Toronto, 2013.

Arthur, Jake. 'Anne Lock or Thomas Norton? A Response to the Re-attribution of the Rirst Sonnet Sequence in English'. *Early Modern Women: An Interdisciplinary Journal*, 16.2 (2022), 214–36.

Arthur, Jake and Rosalind Smith. 'Women's Complaint, 1530–1680: Taxonomy, Voice, and the Index in the Digital Age'. In Ross and Smith (eds), *Early Modern Women's Complaint*, 291–312.

Arthur, Liz. *Embroidery 1600–1700 at the Burrell Collection*. Glasgow, 1995.

Arthurson, Ian. 'Espionage and Intelligence from the Wars of the Roses to the Reformation'. *Nottingham Medieval Studies*, 35 (1991), 134–54.

Association for Documentary Editing (n.d.) https://www.documentaryediting.org/wordpress/. Accessed 8 April 2021.

Auerbach, Erich. In Ralph Manheim (trans.), *Scenes from the Drama of European Literature*. New York, 1959.

Auger, Peter. *Du Bartas' Legacy in England and Scotland*. Oxford, 2019.

Aughterson, Kate (ed.). *Renaissance Women: A Sourcebook*. London, 1995.

Austern, Linda Phyllis. *Both from the Ears and Mind: Thinking About Music in Early Modern England*. Chicago, IL, 2020.

Austern, Linda Phyllis. '"For Musicke Is the Handmaid of the Lord": Women, Psalms, and Domestic Music-Making in Early Modern England'. In Linda Phyllis Austern, Kari Boyd McBride, and David L. Orvis (eds), *Psalms in the Early Modern World*. Farnham, 2011, 77–114.

Austern, Linda Phyllis. 'Portrait of the Artist as (Female) Musician'. In Thomasin LaMay (ed.), *Musical Voices of Early Modern Women: Many-Headed Melodies*. Aldershot, 2005, 15–59.

Bachelard, Gaston. *The Poetics of Space*. New York, 2014.

Barabási, Albert-László. *Network Science*. Cambridge, 2016.

Barad, Karen. *Meeting the Universe Halfway: Quantum Physics and the Entanglement of Meaning and Matter*. Durham, NC, 2007.

Barad, Karen. 'Quantum Entanglements and Hauntological Relations of Inheritance: Dis/continuities, SpaceTime Enfoldings, and Justice-to-Come'. *Derrida Today*, 3.2 (2010), 240–68.

Barash, Carol. *English Women's Poetry 1649–1714: Politics, Community, and Linguistic Authority*. Oxford, 1996.

Barish, Jonas. 'Language for the Study; Language for the Stage'. In A. L. Magnusson and C. E. McGee (eds), *The Elizabethan Theatre XII*. Toronto, 1993, 19–43.

Barker, Simon and Hilary Hinds. 'Elizabeth Cary, *The Tragedy of Mariam*'. In Simon Barker and Hilary Hinds (eds), *The Routledge Anthology of Renaissance Drama*. Abingdon, 2003, 191–3.

Barnes, Diana G. *Epistolary Community in Print, 1580–1664*. Abingdon, 2013.

Barroll, Leeds. *Anna of Denmark, Queen of England: A Cultural Biography*. Philadelphia, PA, 2001.

Bassnett, Madeline. 'A Language Not One's Own: Translational Exchange in Seventeenth-Century Englishwomen's Iberian Recipes'. *Journal for Early Modern Cultural Studies*, 19 (2019), 1–27.

Bassnett, Susan. 'The Translation Turn in Cultural Studies'. In Susan Bassnett and André Lefevere (eds), *Constructing Cultures: Essays on Literary Translation*. Clevedon, OH, 1998, 123–140.

Bastian, Jeannette. 'Reading Colonial Records through an Archival Lens: The Provenance of Place, Space and Creation'. *Archival Science*, 6 (2006), 267–84.

Bates, Catherine (ed.). *A Companion to Renaissance Poetry*. Oxford, 2018.

Bates, Catherine. 'Recent Studies in the Renaissance'. *SEL: Studies in English Literature, 1500–1900*, 59.1 (2019), 203–41.

Battigelli, Anna. *Margaret Cavendish and the Exiles of the Mind*. Lexington, KY, 1998.

Beadle, Richard and Colin Burrow (eds). *Manuscript Miscellanies c.1450–1700*. Special Issue of *English Manuscript Studies, 1100–1700*, 16 (2011).

Beal, Peter. *A Dictionary of Manuscript Terminology, 1450–2000*. Oxford, 2009.

Beal, Peter. *Index of Literary Manuscripts*. London, 1980–1993.

Beal, Peter. 'Notions in Garrison: The Seventeenth-Century Commonplace Book'. In Hill (ed.), *New Ways of Looking at Old Texts*, 131–47.

Beal, Peter. *In Praise of Scribes: Manuscripts and Their Makers in Seventeenth-Century England*. Oxford, 1998.

Beasley, Faith H. *Salons, History, and the Creation of 17th-Century France*. London, 2006.

Beaudry, Mary Carolyn. *Findings: The Material Culture of Needlework and Sewing*. New Haven, CT, 2006.

Beek, Pieta van. In Anna-Mart Bonthuys and Dineke Ehlers (trans.), *The First Female University Student: Anna Maria van Schurman (1636)*. Utrecht, 2010.

Beek, Pieta van. *Klein werk: de Opuscula Hebraea Graeca Latina et Gallica, prosaica et metrica van Anna Maria van Schurman (1607–1678)*. PhD Diss., University of Stellenbosch, 1997.

Beemer, Suzy. 'Masks of Blackness, Masks of Whiteness: Coloring the (Sexual) Subject in Jonson, Cary, and Fletcher'. *Thamyris*, 4 (1997), 223–4.

Bell, Ilona. 'The Circulation of Writings by Lady Mary Wroth'. In Hannay, Lamb, and Brennan (eds), *The Ashgate Research Companion to the Sidneys*, 77–87.

Bell, Ilona. '"Joy's Sports": The Unexpurgated Text of Mary Wroth's *Pamphilia to Amphilanthus*'. *Modern Philology*, 111 (2013), 231–52.

Bell, Susan Groag. *The Lost Tapestries of the City of Ladies: Christine de Pizan's Renaissance Legacy*. Berkeley, CA, 2004.

Bellany, Alastair. *The Politics of Court Scandal: News Culture and the Overbury Affair, 1603–1666*. Cambridge, 2002.

Belle, Marie-Alice. 'Locating Early Modern Women's Translations: Critical and Historiographical Issues'. *Renaissance and Reformation / Renaissance et Réforme*, 35 (2012), 5–23.

Belle, Marie-Alice and Line Cottegnies (eds). *Robert Garnier in Elizabethan England, Mary Sidney Herbert's Antonius, and Thomas Kyd's Cornelia*. Cambridge, 2017.

Belle, Marie-Alice and Brenda M. Hosington (eds). *Thresholds of Translation: Paratexts, Print and Cultural Exchange in Early Modern Britain (1473–1660)*. Cham, 2018.

Bennett, Jane. *Vibrant Matter: The Political Ecology of Things*. Durham, NC, 2009.

Bennett, Stuart. *Trade Bookbinding in the British Isles, 1660–1800*. New Castle, DE, 2004.

Bennett, Susan and Mary Polito. 'Thinking Site: An Introduction'. In Susan Bennett and Mary Polito (eds), *Performing Environments: Site-Specificity in Medieval and Early Modern English Drama*. London, 2014, 1–13.

Bennett, Susan and Julie Sanders. 'Rehearsing across Space and Place: Rethinking *A Masque Presented at Ludlow Castle*'. In Anna Birch and Joanne Tompkins (eds), *Performing Site-Specific Theatre: Politics, Place, Practice*. London, 2012, 37–53.

Benstock, Shari (ed.). *The Private Self: Theory and Practice of Women's Autobiographical Writings*. Chapel Hill, NC, 1988.

Berg, Christine and Philippa Berry. '"Spiritual Whoredom": An Essay on Female Prophets in the Seventeenth Century'. In Francis Barker et al. (eds), *1642: Literature and Power in the Seventeenth Century*. Colchester, 1981, 37–54.

Bergenroth, G. A. (ed.). *Calendar of State Papers, Spain*. London, 1862.

Bergeron, David M. 'Women as Patrons of English Renaissance Drama'. In Cerasano and Wynne-Davies (eds), *Readings in Renaissance Women's Drama*, 69–80.

Berlin, Adele. *The JPS Bible Commentary: Esther*. Philadelphia, PA, 2001.

Bevington. David. 'Introduction to *The Tragedy of Mariam* by Elizabeth Cary'. In David Bevington, Katharine Eisaman Maus, Lars Engle, and Eric Rasmussen (eds), *English Renaissance Drama: A Norton Anthology*. New York, 2002, 615–20.

Bevington, David and Peter Holbrook (eds). *The Politics of the Stuart Court Masque*. Cambridge, 1998.

Bieses: Bibliografía de Escritorias Españolas. https://www.bieses.net. Accessed 8 April 2021.

Bigold, Melanie. '"Bookmaking out of the Remains of the Dead": George Ballard's *Memoirs of Several Ladies* (1752)'. *Eighteenth-Century Life*, 38 (2014), 28–46.

Bilinkoff, Jodi. *Related Lives: Confessors and Their Female Penitents, 1450–1750*. Ithaca, NY, 2005.

Bistué, Belén. *Collaborative Translation and Multi-Version Texts*. Farnham, 2013.

Black, Joseph. 'Manuscript and Women's Booklists'. In Pender and Smith (eds), *Palgrave Encyclopedia*.

Black, Joseph. 'Women's Libraries in the *Private Libraries in Renaissance England Project*'. In Knight, White, and Sauer (eds), *Women's Bookscapes*, 214–31.

Blaisdell, C. J. 'Marguerite de Navarre and Her Circle (1492–1549)'. In Jean R. Brink (ed.), *Female Scholars: A Tradition of Learned Women before 1800*. Montréal, 1980, 36–53.

Blake, Liza. 'After Life in Margaret Cavendish's Vitalist Posthumanism'. *Criticism*, 62.3 (2020), 433–56.

Blake, Liza. 'Close Reading (and) Textual Bibliography: How Many Parts Does Margaret Cavendish's *Blazing World* Have?'. In Lisa Walters and Brandie Siegfried (eds), *Margaret Cavendish: An Interdisciplinary Perspective*. Cambridge, 2022. 233–47..

Blake, Liza. 'Locating Margaret Cavendish's Books: Database, Map, and Analysis'. *The Digital Cavendish Project*, 14 November 2018, updated 6 December 2019. http://digitalcavendish.org/original-research/locating-margaret-cavendish/. Accessed 8 November 2020.

Blake, Liza. 'Pounced Corrections in Oxford Copies of Cavendish's *Philosophical and Physical Opinions*; or, Margaret Cavendish's Glitter Pen'. *New College Notes*, 10 (2018), 1–11. https://www.new.ox.ac.uk/sites/default/files/2018-12/10NCN6%20%282018%29%20Blake%20on%20Pouncing_0.pdf. Accessed 8 November 2020.

Blake, Liza. 'Reading Poems (and Fancies): An Introduction to Margaret Cavendish's *Poems and Fancies*'. In Liza Blake (ed.), *Margaret Cavendish's Poems and Fancies: A Digital Critical*

Edition (2019). University of Toronto. http://library2.utm.utoronto.ca/poemsandfancies/introduction-to-cavendishs-poems-and-fancies/. Accessed 16 November 2020.

Blake, Liza. 'Margaret Cavendish's University Years: Batch Bindings and Trade Bindings in Cambridge and Oxford'. *Papers of the Bibliographical Society of America*, 116.1 (2022), 21–91.

Bloom, Gina. *Voice in Motion: Staging Gender, Shaping Sound*. Philadelphia, PA, 2007.

Boleyn, Deirdre. 'Because Women Are Not Women, Rather Might Be a Fit Subject of an Ingenious Strategist'. *Prose Studies*, 32 (2010), 38–55.

Bolzoni, Lina. *The Gallery of Memory: Literary and Iconographic Models in the Age of the Printing Press*. Toronto, 2000.

Bond, Gerald A. *The Loving Subject: Desire, Eloquence and Power in Romanesque France*. Philadelphia, PA, 1995.

Booy, David. 'General Introduction'. In David Booy (ed.), *Personal Disclosures: An Anthology of Self-Writings from the Seventeenth Century*. Aldershot, 2002, 1–19.

Bourdieu, Pierre and Jean-Claude Passeron. In Richard Nice (trans.), *Reproduction in Education, Society and Culture*. London, 1990.

Bourke, Evan. 'Female Involvement, Membership, and Centrality: A Social Network Analysis of the Hartlib Circle'. *Literature Compass*, 14.4 (2017), 1–17.

Boutcher, Warren. 'Marginal Commentaries: The Cultural Transmission of Montaigne's *Essais* in Shakespeare's England'. *Actes des congrès de la Société française Shakespeare*, 21 (2004), 13–28.

Bowden, Caroline. 'The Abbess and Mrs. Brown: Lady Mary Knatchbull and Royalist Politics in Flanders in the Late 1650s'. *Recusant History*, 24 (1999), 288–308.

Bowden, Caroline. 'Books and Reading at Syon Abbey, Lisbon in the Seventeenth Century'. In E. A. Jones and Alexandra Walsham (eds), *Syon Abbey and Its Books: Religious Communities and Communication in Late Medieval and Early Modern England*. Woodbridge, 2010, 177–202.

Bowden, Caroline. 'Building Libraries in Exile: The English Convents and Their Book Collections in the Seventeenth Century'. *British Catholic History*, 32.3 (2015), 343–382.

Bowden, Caroline. '"A Distribution of Tyme": Reading and Writing Practices in the English Convents in Exile'. *Tulsa Studies in Women's Literature*, 31 (2012), 99–116.

Bowden, Caroline. 'English Reading Communities in Exile: Introducing Cloistered Nuns to Their Books'. In Knight, White, and Sauer (eds), *Women's Bookscapes*, 171–92.

Bowden, Caroline. 'The Library of Mildred Cooke Cecil, Lady Burghley'. *The Library*, 6.1 (2005), 3–29.

Bowden, Caroline and Catherine E. Kelly (eds). *Reading Women: Literacy, Authorship, and Culture in the Atlantic World, 1500–1800*. Philadelphia, PA, 2008.

Bowie, Karin. 'Cultural, British and Global Turns in the History of Early Modern Scotland'. *The Scottish Historical Review*, 92.234 (2013), 38–48.

Boyer, Abel. *Dictionnaire royal françois et anglois*. The Hague, 1702.

Braganza, V. M. '"Many Ciphers, although But One for Meaning": Lady Mary Wroth's Many-Sided Monogram'. *English Literary Renaissance* 52.1 (2022), 124–52.

Braidotti, Rosi. *The Posthuman*. Cambridge, 2013.

Brayman Hackel, Heidi. 'The Countess of Bridgewater's London Library'. In Jennifer Andersen and Elizabeth Sauer (eds), *Books and Readers in Early Modern England: Material Studies*. Philadelphia, PA, 2002, 138–59.

Brayman Hackel, Heidi. *Reading Material in Early Modern England: Print, Gender, and Literacy*. Cambridge, 2005.

Brayman Hackel, Heidi. '"Turning to Her 'Best Companion[s]'": Lady Anne Clifford as Reader, Annotator and Book Collector'. In Hearn and Hulse (eds), *Lady Anne Clifford*, 99–108.

Brayman Hackel, Heidi and Catherine E. Kelly (eds). *Reading Women: Literacy, Authorship, and Culture in the Atlantic World, 1500–1800*. Philadelphia, PA, 2008.

Brennan, Michael G. 'The Queen's Proposed Visit to Wilton House in 1599 and the "Sidney Psalms"'. In Margaret P. Hannay (ed.), *Mary Sidney, Countess of Pembroke*. Surrey, 2009, 175–201.

Brenner, Athalya. 'Looking at Esther through the Looking Glass'. In Athalya Brenner (ed.), *A Feminist Companion to the Bible: Esther, Judith and Susanna*. Sheffield, 1995, 71–80.

Brenner, Robert. *Merchants and Revolution: Commercial Change, Political Conflict, and London's Overseas Traders, 1550–1653*. London, 2003.

Brewster, Scott. *Lyric*. London, 2009.

British Women Romantic Poets Project. University of Michigan. https://quod.lib.umich.edu/b/bwrp/. Accessed 8 April 2021.

Britland, Karen. 'Conspiring with "Friends": Hester Pulter's Poetry and the Stanley Family at Cumberlow Green'. *Review of English Studies*, 69 (2018), 832–54.

Britland, Karen. *Drama at the Courts of Queen Henrietta Maria*. Cambridge, 2006.

Britland, Karen. 'Women in the Royal Courts'. In Knoppers (ed.), *Cambridge Companion to Early Modern Women's Writing*, 124–39.

Brodsky, Vivien. 'Widows in Late Elizabethan London: Remarriage, Economic Opportunity and Family Orientations'. In Lloyd Bonfield, Richard M. Smith, and Keith Wrightson (eds), *The World We Have Gained: Histories of Population and Social Structure*. Oxford, 1986, 122–54.

Brooks, Christopher W. *Lawyers, Litigation and English Society since 1450*. London, 1998.

Brooks, Christopher W. *Pettyfoggers and the Vipers of the Commonwealth*. Cambridge, 1986.

Bross, Kristina. *Future History: Global Fantasies in Seventeenth-Century American and British Writings*. New York, 2017.

Brown, Cedric. 'William Smith, Vere Southerne, Jesuit Missioner, and Three Linked Manuscript Miscellanies'. In Eckhardt and Starza Smith (eds), *Manuscript Miscellanies in Early Modern England*, 113–32.

Brown, Laura. *Ends of Empire: Women and Ideology in Early Eighteenth-Century English Literature*. Ithaca, NY, 1993.

Brown, Pamela Allen and Peter Parolin (eds). *Women Players in England, 1500–1660: Beyond the All-Male Stage*. Aldershot, 2005.

Brown, Susan. 'Categorically Provisional'. *PMLA*, 135 (2020), 165–74.

Brownlee, Victoria. *Biblical Readings and Literary Writings in Early Modern England, 1558–1625*. Oxford, 2018.

Bruster, Douglas. *Shakespeare and the Question of Culture: Early Modern Literature and the Cultural Turn*. Basingstoke, 2003.

Bullard, Rebecca. '"A Bright Coelestiall Mind": A New Set of Writings by Lady Dorothy Browne (1621–1685)'. *Huntington Library Quarterly*, 73.1 (2010), 99–122.

Bullard, Rebecca. 'Gatherings in Exile: Interpreting the Bibliographical Structure of *Natures Pictures Drawn by Fancies Pencil to the Life* (1656)'. *English Studies*, 92 (2011), 786–805.

Burgess, Glenn. 'Bodin in the English Revolution'. In Howell A. Lloyd (ed.), *The Reception of Bodin*. Leiden, 2013, 387–407.

Burke, Peter. 'Cultures of Translation in Early Modern Europe'. In Peter Burke and R. Po-Chia Hsia (eds), *Cultural Translation in Early Modern Europe*. Cambridge, 2007, 7–38.

Burke, Victoria E., 'Ann Bowyer's Commonplace Book (Bodleian Library Ashmole MS 51): Reading and Writing among the "Middling Sort"'. *Early Modern Literary Studies*, 6 (2001),

1–28 paragraphs. Sheffield Hallam University. https://extra.shu.ac.uk/emls/06-3/burkbowy.htm. Accessed 23 November 2020.

Burke, Victoria. 'Contexts for Women's Manuscript Miscellanies: The Case of Elizabeth Lyttelton and Sir Thomas Browne'. *The Yearbook of English Studies*, 33 (2003), 316–28.

Burke, Victoria E. 'The Couplet and the Poem: Late Seventeenth-Century Women Reading Katherine Philips'. *Women's Writing*, 24 (2017), 280–97.

Burke, Victoria E. 'Recent Studies in Commonplace Books'. *English Literary Renaissance*, 43 (2013), 153–77.

Burke, Victoria E. 'Women and Early Seventeenth-Century Manuscript Culture: Four Miscellanies'. *The Seventeenth Century*, 12.2 (1997), 135–50.

Burke, Victoria E. 'Women's Verse Miscellany Manuscripts in the Perdita Project: Examples and Generalizations'. In Denbo (ed.), *New Ways of Looking at Old Texts, IV*, 141–54.

Burkert, Mattie. 'Plotting the "Female Wits" Controversy: Gender, Genre, and Printed Plays, 1670–1699'. In Laura Estill, Diane K. Jakacki, and Michael Ullyot (eds), *Early Modern Studies after the Digital Turn*. Phoenix, AZ, 2016, 35–59.

Burlinson, Christopher and Ruth Connolly (eds). 'Editing Stuart Poetry'. *Studies in English Literature*, 52 (2012), 1–12.

Burton, Ben and Elizabeth Scott-Baumann (eds). *The Work of Form: Poetics and Materiality in Early Modern Culture*. Oxford, 2014.

Buss, Helen M. *Repossessing the World: Reading Memoirs by Contemporary Women*. Waterloo, ON, 2002.

Butler, Martin. 'Private and Occasional Drama'. In A. R. Braunmuller and Michael Hattaway (eds), *The Cambridge Companion to English Renaissance Drama*. Cambridge, 1990, 131–63.

Butterworth, Emily. 'Apothecaries' Cornets: Books as Waste Paper in the Renaissance'. *Modern Language Notes*, 133 (2018), 891–913.

Butzner, Alexis. '"Taken Weak in My Outward Man": The Paradox of the Pathologized Female Prophet'. *Early Modern Women*, 13 (2018), 30–57.

Cable, Lana. 'Milton's Iconoclastic Truth'. In David Loewenstein and James Grantham Turner (eds), *Politics, Poetics and Hermeneutics in Milton's Prose*. Cambridge, 1990, 135–51.

Caldwell, Tanya. 'The Rise and Fall of Absolutism: Margaret Cavendish's Manipulation of Masque Conventions in "The Claspe: *Fantasmes* Masque" and *The Blazing World*'. *In-Between: Essays & Studies in Literary Criticism*, 9 (2000), 287–99.

Callaghan, Dympna (ed.). *A Feminist Companion to Shakespeare*. Malden, 2000, repr. 2016.

Callaghan, Dympna. 'Re-reading Elizabeth Cary's *The Tragedy of Mariam, Faire Queene of Jewry*'. In Hendricks and Parker (eds), *Women, 'Race', and Writing*, 163–77.

Cambers, Andrew. 'Readers' Marks and Religious Practice: Margaret Hoby's Marginalia'. In John N. King (ed.), *Tudor Books and Readers: Materiality and the Construction of Meaning*. Cambridge, 2010, 211–31.

Cameron, W. J. *New Light on Aphra Behn*, Auckland, 1961.

Campbell, Julie D. 'Masque Scenery and the Tradition of Immobilization in *The First Part of the Countess of Montgomery's Urania*'. *Renaissance Studies*, 22 (2008), 221–39.

Campbell, Julie D. and Anne R. Larsen (eds). *Early Modern Women and Transnational Communities of Letters*. Farnham, 2009.

Canavan, Claire. '"Various Pleasant Fiction": Embroidering Textiles and Texts in Early Modern England'. PhD Diss., University of York, 2017.

Capello, Sergio. 'Jean Du Nesme'. In Michel Simonin (ed.), *Dictionnaire des lettres françaises. Le XVIe siècle*. Paris, 2001, 434.

Capp, Bernard. *Astrology and the Popular Press: English Almanacs, 1500–1800*. London, 1979, repr. 2008.

Carrell, Jennifer Lee. 'A Pack of Lies in a Looking Glass: Lady Mary Wroth's *Urania* and the Magic Mirror of Romance'. *SEL: Studies in English Literature 1500–1900*, 34 (1994), 79–107.

Carruthers, Mary J. *The Book of Memory: A Study of Memory in Medieval Culture*. Cambridge, 1990.

Cavanagh, Jean C. 'Lady Southwell's Defense of Poetry'. *English Literary Renaissance*, 14.3 (1984).

Cerasano, S. P. and Marion Wynne-Davies (eds). *Readings in Renaissance Women's Drama*. London, 1998.

Cerasano, S. P. and Marion Wynne-Davies (eds). *Renaissance Drama by Women: Texts and Documents*. London, 1995.

Certeau, Michel de. In Steven Rendall (trans.), *The Practice of Everyday Life*. Berkeley, CA, 1984.

Chalmers, Hero. 'The Politics of Feminine Retreat in Margaret Cavendish's *The Female Academy* and *The Convent of Pleasure*'. *Women's Writing*, 6 (1999), 81–94.

Chalmers, Hero. *Royalist Women Writers 1650–1689*. Oxford, 2004.

Charnell-White, Cathryn A. *Beirdd Ceridwen: Blodeugerdd Barddas o Ganu Menywod hyd tua 1800*. Swansea, 2005.

Charnell-White, Cathryn A. 'Problems of Authorship and Attribution: The Welsh-Language Women's Canon before 1800'. *Women's Writing*, 24.4 (2017), 398–417.

Chedgzoy, Kate. 'The Cultural Geographies of Early Modern Women's Writing: Journeys across Spaces and Times'. *Literature Compass*, 3.4 (2006), 884–95.

Chedgzoy, Kate. 'Female Prophecy in the Seventeenth Century: The Case of Anna Trapnel'. In William Zunder and Suzanne Trill (eds), *Writing and the English Renaissance*. London, 1996, 238–54.

Chedgzoy, Kate. *Women's Writing in the British Atlantic World: Memory, Place and History, 1550–1700*. Cambridge, 2007.

Chedgzoy, Kate, Elspeth Graham, Katherine Hodgkin, and Ramona Wray. 'Researching Memory in Early Modern Studies'. *Memory Studies*, 11.1 (2018), 5–20.

Chew, Elizabeth V. '"Your Honor's Desyres": Lady Anne Clifford and the World of Goods'. In Hearn and Hulse (eds), *Lady Anne Clifford*, 25–42.

Chowdhury, Sajed. 'The Poetics of "Making" in the Manuscript Writings of Constance Aston Fowler'. *The Seventeenth Century*, 35 (2020), 337–61.

Clark, Ira. 'The Widow Hunt on the Tudor–Stuart Stage'. *SEL: Studies in English Literature 1500–1900*, 41 (2001), 399–416.

Clark, Sandra. 'The Broadside Ballad and the Woman's Voice'. In Malcolmson and Suzuki (eds), *Debating Gender*, 103–20.

Clarke, Danielle. 'Animating Eve: Gender, Authority, and Complaint'. In Ross and Smith (eds), *Early Modern Women's Complaint*, 157–81.

Clarke, Danielle. '"In sort as she it sung": Spenser's "Doleful Lay" and the Construction of Female Authorship'. *Criticism*, 42.4 (2000), 451–68.

Clarke, Danielle. 'Life Writing for the Counter-Reformation: The English Translation and Reception of Teresa de Ávila's Autobiography'. *Journal of Medieval and Early Modern Studies*, 50 (2020), 75–94.

Clarke, Danielle. 'Memory and Memorialization in the Psalms of Mary Sidney, Countess of Pembroke'. *Memory Studies*, 11.1 (2018), 85–99.

Clarke, Danielle. 'Nostalgia, Anachronism, and the Editing of Early Modern Women's Texts'. *Text*, 15 (2003), 187–209.

Clarke, Danielle. *The Politics of Early Modern Women's Writing*. Harlow, 2001.
Clarke, Danielle. 'Speaking Women: Rhetoric and the Construction of Female Talk'. In Richards and Thorne (eds), *Rhetoric, Women and Politics in Early Modern England*, 70–88.
Clarke, Danielle. 'Translation'. In Knoppers (ed.), *The Cambridge Companion to Early Modern Women's Writing*, 167–80.
Clarke, Danielle and Elizabeth Clarke (eds). *'This Double Voice': Gendered Writing in Early Modern England*. Basingstoke, 2000.
Clarke, Danielle and Sarah McKibben. 'Seventeenth-Century Women's Poetry in Ireland'. In Ailbhe Darcy and David Wheatley (eds), *A History of Irish Women's Poetry*. Cambridge, 2021, 57–73.
Clarke, Elizabeth. 'Anne, Lady Southwell: Coteries and Culture'. In Harris and Scott-Baumann (eds), *Intellectual Culture of Puritan Women*, 57–70.
Clarke, Elizabeth. 'Anne Southwell and the Pamphlet Debate: The Politics of Gender, Class and Manuscript'. In Malcolmson and Suzuki (eds), *Debating Gender*, 37–53.
Clarke, Elizabeth. *Politics, Religion and the Song of Songs in the Seventeenth Century*. Basingstoke, 2011.
Cohen, Jeffrey Jerome. *Stone: An Ecology of the Inhuman*. Minneapolis, MN, 2015.
Cohen, Matt. *The Networked Wilderness: Communicating in Early New England*. Minneapolis, MN, 2010.
Coiro, Ann Baynes. 'Writing in Service: Sexual Politics and Class Position in the Poetry of Aemilia Lanyer and Ben Jonson'. *Criticism*, 35.3 (1993), 357–76.
Colclough, David. *Freedom of Speech in Early Stuart England*. Cambridge, 2005.
Colclough, Stephen. *Consuming Texts: Readers and Reading Communities, 1695–1870*. Houndmills, 2007.
Coldiron, A. E. B. *English Printing, Verse Translation, and the Battle of the Sexes: 1476–1557*. Burlington, VT, 2009.
Coldiron, A. E. B. *Printers without Borders: Translation and Textuality in the Renaissance*. Cambridge, 2015.
Coldiron, A. E. B. 'Visibility Now: Historicizing Foreign Presences in Translation'. *Translation Studies*, 5 (2012), 189–200.
Coles, Kimberly Anne. *Religion, Reform, and Women's Writing in Early Modern England*. Cambridge, 2008.
Coles, Kimberly Anne. '"Undisciplined": Early Modern Women's Writing and the Urgency of Scholarly Activism'. In Goodrich and McQuade (eds), *'Special Issue'*, 55–62.
Coles, Kimberly Anne and Eve Keller (eds). *The Routledge Companion to Women, Sex, and Gender in the Early British Colonial World*. London, 2018.
Coletti, Theresa. '"Did Women Have a Renaissance?" A Medievalist Reads Joan Kelly and Aemilia Lanyer'. *Early Modern Women: An Interdisciplinary Journal*, 8 (2013), 249–59.
Colie, Rosalie. *The Resources of Kind: Genre Theory in the Renaissance*. Los Angeles, CA, 1973.
Collar, Anna, Fiona Coward, and Barbara J. Mills. 'Networks in Archaeology: Phenomena, Abstraction, Representation'. *Journal of Archaeological Method and Theory*, 22.1 (2015), 1–32.
Collinson, Patrick. 'The Role of Women in the English Reformation Illustrated by the Life and Friendships of Anne Locke'. *Studies in Church History*, 2 (1965), 258–72.
Cooke, George Alexander. *Topographical and Statistical Description of the County of Hereford*. London, 1805.
Coolahan, Marie-Louise. 'Caitlín Dubh's Keens: Literary Negotiations in Early Modern Ireland'. In Burke and Gibson (eds), *Early Modern Women's Manuscript Writing*, 99–102.

Coolahan, Marie-Louise. 'Loss and Longevity: Rhetorics and Tactics of Early Modern Women's Writing'. In Goodrich and McQuade (eds), '*Special Issue*', 23–32.

Coolahan, Marie-Louise. '"My lady's books": Devising a Toolkit for Quantitative Research; or, What Is a Book and How Do We Count It?'. *Huntington Library Quarterly*, 84.1 (2021), 125–37.

Coolahan, Marie-Louise. 'Nuns' Writing: Translation, Textual Mobility, and Transnational Networks'. In Phillippy (ed.), *A History of Early Modern Women's Writing*, 257–75.

Coolahan, Marie-Louise. 'Reception, Reputation, and Early Modern Women's Missing Texts'. *Critical Quarterly*, 55.4 (2013), 3–14.

Coolahan, Marie-Louise. 'Single-Author Manuscripts, *Poems* (1664), and the Editing of Katherine Philips'. In Ross and Salzman (eds), *Editing Early Modern Women*, 176–94.

Coolahan, Marie-Louise (ed.). 'Special Issue: The Cultural Dynamics of Reception'. *Journal of Medieval and Early Modern Studies*, 50.1 (2020).

Coolahan, Marie-Louise. 'Whither the Archipelago? Stops, Starts, and Hurdles on the Four Nations Front'. *Literature Compass*, 15.11 (2018), 1–12.

Coolahan, Marie-Louise. *Women, Writing, and Language in Early Modern Ireland*. Oxford, 2010.

Coolahan, Marie-Louise. 'Writing before 1700'. In Heather Ingman and Clíona Ó Gallchóir (eds), *A History of Modern Irish Women's Literature*. Cambridge, 2018, 18–36.

Coolahan, Marie-Louis and Mark Empey. 'Women's Book Ownership and the Reception of Early Modern Women's Texts, 1545–1700'. In Knight, White, and Sauer (eds), *Women's Bookscapes*, 231–52.

Coolahan, Marie-Louise and Erin A. McCarthy. 'From Manuscript to Metadata: Understanding and Structuring Female-Attributed Complaints'. In Ross and Smith (eds), *Early Modern Women's Complaint*, 269–90.

Cooper, Helen. *The English Romance in Time: Transforming Motifs from Geoffrey of Monmouth to the Death of Shakespeare*. Oxford, 2004.

Cope, Sophie. 'Marking the New Year: Dated Objects and the Materiality of Time in Early Modern England'. *Journal of Early Modern Studies*, 6 (2017), 89–111.

Corens, Liesbeth, Kate Peters, and Alexandra Walsham. 'Introduction'. In Liesbeth Corens, Kate Peters, and Alexandra Walsham (eds), *Archives and Information in the Early Modern World*. London, 2018.

Costello, William T. *The Scholastic Curriculum at Early Seventeenth-Century Cambridge*. Cambridge, MA, 1958.

Cottegnies, Line. 'Aphra Behn's French Translations'. In Janet Todd and Derek Hughes (eds), *The Cambridge Companion to Aphra Behn*. Cambridge, 2004, 221–34.

Cottegnies, Line. 'The Garden and the Tower: Pastoral Retreat and Configurations of the Self in the Auto/Biographical Works of Margaret Cavendish and Lucy Hutchinson'. In Frédéric Regard (ed.), *Mapping the Self: Space, Identity, Discourse in British Auto/Biography*. Saint-Étienne, 2003, 125–44.

Cottegnies, Line. 'Katherine Philips's French Translations: Between Mediation and Appropriation'. *Women's Writing*, 23.4 (2016), 445–64.

Cottegnies, Line. 'Leaves of Fame: Katherine Philips and Robert Herrick's Shared Community'. In Tom Cain and Ruth Connolly (eds), *Lords of Wine and Oile: Community and Conviviality in Robert Herrick*. Oxford, 2011, 127–54.

Craig, Heidi. 'English Rag-Women and Early Modern Paper Production'. In Wayne (ed.), *Women's Labour and the History of the Book*, 29–46.

Craig, Hugh. 'Style, Statistics, and New Models of Authorship'. *Early Modern Literary Studies*, 15.1 (2009), 41 paras.

Craig, Hugh and Brett Greatley-Hirsch. *Style, Computers, and Early Modern Drama: Beyond Authorship*. Cambridge, 2017.
Crane, Mary Thomas. *Framing Authority: Sayings, Self, and Society in Sixteenth-Century England*. Princeton, NJ, 1993.
Crawford, Julie. 'Margaret Cavendish's Books'. In Knight, White, and Sauer (eds), *Women's Bookscapes*, 94–116.
Crawford, Julie. *Mediatrix: Women, Politics and Literary Production in Early Modern England*. Oxford, 2014.
Crawford, Julie. 'Transubstantial Bodies in *Paradise Lost* and *Order and Disorder*'. *Journal for Early Modern Cultural Studies*, 19.4 (2019), 75–93.
Crawford, Patricia. *Women and Religion in England 1500–1720*. New York, 1993.
Crawford, Patricia. 'Women's Published Writings 1600–1700'. In Prior (ed.), *Women in English Society*, 158–209.
Crawforth, Hannah J. 'Court Hieroglyphics: The Idea of the Cipher in Ben Jonson's Masque'. In Robyn Adams and Rosanna Cox (eds), *Diplomacy and Early Modern Culture*. Basingstoke, 2011, 138–54.
Cresswell, Tim. 'Place; Part I'. In John A. Agnew and James S. Duncan (eds), *The Wiley-Blackwell Companion to Human Geography*. Oxford, 2011, 235–44.
Cresswell, Tim. *Place: A Short Introduction*. Oxford, 2004.
Cressy, David. *Coming Over: Migration and Communication between England and New England in the Seventeenth Century*. Cambridge, 1987.
Cressy, David. *Literacy and the Social Order: Reading and Writing in Tudor and Stuart England*. Cambridge, 1980, repr. 2009.
Cripps, Doreen. *Elizabeth of the Sealed Knot: A Biography of Elizabeth Murray, Countess of Dysart*. Kineton, 1975.
Crowley, Joseph. 'Rachel Jevon, *Exultationis Carmen*, 1660'. In Helen Ostovich and Elizabeth Sauer (eds), *Reading Early Modern Women: An Anthology of Texts in Manuscript and Print 1550–1700*. New York, 2004, 393–4.
Crowley, Lara M. *Manuscript Matters: Reading John Donne's Poetry and Prose in Early Modern England*. Oxford, 2018.
Culler, Jonathan. *Theory of the Lyric*. Cambridge, 2015.
Cummings, Brian. *The Literary Culture of the Reformation: Grammar and Grace*. Oxford, 2002.
Cunnar, Eugene R. and Jeffrey Johnson (eds). *Discovering and (Re)Covering the Seventeenth Century Religious Lyric*. Pittsburgh, PA, 2001.
D'Addario, Christopher. *Exile and Journey in Seventeenth-Century Literature*. Cambridge, 2007.
Dambrogio, Jana and Daniel Starza Smith (eds). *Letterlocking: A Global Technology of Communication Security*. Massachusetts Institute of Technology. www.letterlocking.org. Accessed 20 July 2021.
Das, Nandini. *Renaissance Romance: The Transformation of English Prose Fiction, 1570–1620*. New York, 2011.
Davis, Alex. *Chivalry and Romance in the English Renaissance*. Cambridge, 2003.
Davis, Kathleen. 'Periodization and the Matter of Precedent'. *postmedieval: a journal of medieval cultural studies*, 1 (2010), 354–60.
Davis, Natalie Zemon. *The Gift in Sixteenth-Century France*. Oxford, 2000.
Davison, Kate. 'Early Modern Social Networks: Antecedents, Opportunities, and Challenges'. *American Historical Review*, 124.2 (2019), 456–82.

Day, Alexandra. 'Literary Gifts: Performance and Collaboration in the Arundel/Lumley Family Manuscripts'. In Pender (ed.), *Gender, Authorship, and Early Modern Women's Collaboration*, 125–48.

Daybell, James (ed.). *Early Modern Women's Letter Writing, 1450–1700*. New York, 2001.

Daybell, James. 'Elizabeth Bourne (fl. 1570s–1580s): A New Elizabethan Woman Poet'. "*Notes & Queries*", 52 (2005), 176–8.

Daybell, James. 'Interpreting Letters and Reading Script: Evidence for Female Education and Literacy in Tudor England'. *History of Education*, 34 (2005), 695–715.

Daybell, James. *The Material Letter in Early Modern England*. Basingstoke, 2012.

Daybell, James. 'Recent Studies in Sixteenth-Century Letters'. *English Literary Renaissance*, 35.2 (2005), 331–62.

Daybell, James. 'Recent Studies in Seventeenth-Century Letters'. *English Literary Renaissance*, 36 (2006), 135–70.

Daybell, James. 'Secret Letters in Elizabethan England'. In James Daybell and Peter Hinds (eds), *Material Readings of Early Modern Culture: Texts and Social Practices, 1580–1730*. Basingstoke, 2010, 47–64.

Daybell, James. *Women Letter-Writers in Tudor England*. Oxford, 2006.

Daybell, James and Andrew Gordon (eds). *Cultures of Correspondence in Early Modern Britain*. Philadelphia, PA, 2016.

de Grazia, Margreta, Maureen Quilligan, and Peter Stallybrass (eds). *Subject and Object in Renaissance Culture*. Cambridge, 1996.

de Groot, Jerome. 'John Denham and Lucy Hutchinson's Commonplace Book'. *SEL: Studies in English Literature*, 48 (2008), 147–63.

DeJean, Joan. *Tender Geographies: Women and the Origins of the Novel in France*. New York, 1991.

Demers, Patricia. '"God May Open More Than Man Maye Vnderstande": Lady Margaret Beaufort's Translation of the De "Imitatione Christi"'. *Renaissance and Reformation/Renaissance et Réforme*, 35.4 (2012), 45–61.

Demers, Patricia. 'The Presence of the Now'. In Goodrich and McQuade (eds), 'Special Issue', 161–8.

Demers, Patricia. '"Warpe and Web" in the Sidney Psalms: The "Coupled Worke" of the Countess of Pembroke and Sir Philip Sidney'. In Marjorie Stone and Judith Thompson (eds), *Literary Couplings: Writing Couples, Collaborators, and the Construction of Authorship*. Madison, WI, 2006, 41–59.

Denbo, Michael (ed.). *New Ways of Looking at Old Texts, IV: Papers of the Renaissance English Text Society, 2002–2006*. Tempe, AZ, 2008.

Denis, Delphine. *Le Parnasse galant: Institution d'une catégorie littéraire au XVIIe siècle*. Paris, 2001.

Denis, Delphine. 'Sçavoir la carte': Voyage au Royaume de Galanterie'. *Espaces classiques*, 34 (2002), 179–89.

Dickson, Donald R. 'The Complexities of Biblical Typology in the Seventeenth Century'. *Renaissance and Reformation/Renaissance et Reforme*, 11.3 (1987), 253–72.

DiMeo, Michelle. 'Authorship and Medical Networks: Reading Attributions in Early Modern Manuscript Recipes'. In DiMeo and Pennell (eds), *Reading and Writing Recipe Books*, 25–46.

DiMeo, Michelle. *Lady Ranelagh: The Incomparable Life of Robert Boyle's Sister*. Chicago, IL, 2021.

DiMeo, Michelle and Rebecca Laroche. 'On Elizabeth Isham's "Oil of Swallows": Animal Slaughter and Early Modern Women's Medical Recipes'. In Jennifer Munroe and Rebecca Laroche (eds), *Ecofeminist Approaches to Early Modernity*. London, 2011, 87–104.

DiMeo, Michelle and Sara Pennell (eds). *Reading and Writing Recipe Books 1550–1800*. Manchester, 2013.

Dimock, Wai Chee. 'Feminism, New Historicism, and the Reader'. *American Literature*, 64 (1991), 601–22.

Dinshaw, Carolyn. *Getting Medieval: Sexualities and Communities, Pre- and Postmodern*. Durham, NC, 1999.

Dinshaw, Carolyn. *How Soon Is Now? Medieval Texts, Amateur Readers, and the Queerness of Time*. Durham, NC, 2012.

DiPasquale, Theresa. 'Woman's Desire for Man in Lanyer's *Salve Deus Rex Judaeoreum*'. *The Journal of English and Germanic Philology*, 99.3 (2000), 356–78.

'DocuScope Project'. Carnegie Mellon University. https://www.cmu.edu/dietrich/english/research-and-publications/docuscope.html. Accessed 8 April 2021.

Dodds, Lara. 'Affected and Disaffected Alike: Women, Print, and the Problem of Women's Literary History'. In Stephen B. Dobranski (ed.), *Political Turmoil: Early Modern British Literature in Transition, 1623–1660*. Cambridge, 2019, 205–20.

Dodds, Lara. 'Form, Formalism, and Literary Studies: The Case of Margaret Cavendish'. In Siegfried and Hammons (eds), *World-Making Renaissance Women*, 136–50.

Dodds, Lara. *The Literary Invention of Margaret Cavendish*. Pittsburgh, PA, 2013.

Dodds, Lara. 'Reading and Writing in Sociable Letters; Or, How Margaret Cavendish Read Her Plutarch'. *English Literary Renaissance*, 41 (2011), 189–218.

Dodds, Lara and Michelle M. Dowd. 'The Case for a Feminist Return to Form'. *Early Modern Women: An Interdisciplinary Journal*, 13 (2018), 82–91.

Dodds, Lara and Michelle M. Dowd. 'Happy Accidents: Critical Belatedness, Feminist Formalism, and Early Modern Women's Writing'. *Criticism*, 62.2 (2020), 169–93.

Dodds, Lara and Michelle M. Dowd (eds), *Feminist Formalism and Early Modern Women's Writing: Readings, Conversations, Pedagogies*. Lincoln, NE, 2022.

Doody, Margaret. *The True Story of the Novel*. Newark, NJ, 1997.

Douglas, Mary. 'Foreword'. In Marcel Mauss, *The Gift: The Form and Reason for Exchange in Archaic Societies*, trans. W. D. Halls. Abingdon, 2008, ix–xxiii.

Dow, Gillian. 'Criss-Crossing the Channel'. In J. A. Downie (ed.), *The Oxford Handbook of the Eighteenth-Century Novel*. Oxford, 2016, 88–104.

Dowd, Michelle M. 'Dramaturgy and the Politics of Space in *The Tragedy of Mariam*'. *Renaissance Drama*, 44.1 (2016), 101–22.

Dowd, Michelle M. 'Structures of Piety in Elizabeth Richardson's *Legacie*'. In Dowd and Eckerle (eds), *Genre and Women's Life Writing*, 115–30.

Dowd, Michelle M. and Julie A. Eckerle (eds). *Genre and Women's Life Writing in Early Modern England*. Aldershot, 2007.

Dowling, Maria. *Humanism in the Age of Henry VIII*. London, 1986.

Downes, Stephanie. 'Fashioning Christine de Pizan in Tudor Defenses of Women'. *Parergon*, 23 (2006), 71–92.

Dubrow, Heather. '"And Thus Leave off": Reevaluating Mary Wroth's Folger Manuscript, V.a.104'. *Tulsa Studies in Women's Literature*, 22 (2003), 273–91.

Dubrow, Heather. *Echoes of Desire: Petrarchism and its Counterdiscourses*. Ithaca, NY, 1995.

Duffy, Eamon. *The Voices of Morebath: Reformation and Rebellion in an English Village*. New Haven, CT, 2001.

Duncan-Jones, Katherine. 'Bess Carey's Petrarch: Newly Discovered Elizabethan Sonnets'. *The Review of English Studies*, 50 (1999), 304–20.

Dunn, Leslie C. and Katherine R. Larson (eds). *Gender and Song in Early Modern England*. Farnham, 2014.

Dunnigan, Sarah M. 'Daughterly Desires: Representing and Reimagining the Feminine in Anna Hume's *Triumphs*'. In Dunnigan, Harker, and Newlyn (eds), *Woman and the Feminine*, 120–35.

Dunnigan, Sarah M. 'Sacred Afterlives: Mary, Queen of Scots, Elizabeth Melville, and the Politics of Sanctity'. *Women's Writing*, 10.3 (2003), 401–24.

Dunnigan, Sarah M. 'Scottish Women Writers *c*. 1560–*c*. 1650'. In Douglas Gifford and Dorothy McMillan (eds), *A History of Scottish Women's Writing*. Edinburgh, 1997, 15–43.

Dunnigan, Sarah M., C. Marie Harker, and Evelyn S. Newlyn (eds). *Woman and the Feminine in Medieval and Early Modern Scottish Writing*. Basingstoke, 2004.

Durrant, C. S. *A Link between Flemish Mystics and English Martyrs*. London, 1925.

Durston, Christopher and Judith D. Maltby. *Religion in Revolutionary England*. Manchester, 2006.

Dutton, Danielle. *Margaret the First: A Novel*. New York, 2016.

Eamon, William. *Science and the Secrets of Nature: Book of Secrets in Medieval and Early Modern Culture*. Princeton, NJ, 1994.

Eardley, Alice. 'Marketing Aspiration: Fact, Fiction, and the Publication of French Romance in Mid-Seventeenth-Century England'. In Jacqueline Glomski and Isabelle Moreau (eds), *Seventeenth-Century Fiction: Text and Transmission*. Oxford, 2016, 130–42.

Eardley, Alice. 'Recreating the Canon: Women Writers and Anthologies of Early Modern Verse'. *Women's Writing*, 14 (2007), 270–89.

Eardley, Alice. '"Saturn (whose aspects soe sads my soule)": Lady Hester Pulter's Feminine Melancholic Genius'. In Denbo (ed.), *New Ways of Looking at Old Texts, IV*, 239–54.

Early Modern Letters Online. University of Oxford. http://emlo.bodleian.ox.ac.uk. Accessed 8 April 2021.

Eckerle, Julie A. 'Prefacing Texts, Authorizing Authors, and Constructing Selves: The Preface as Autobiographical Space'. In Dowd and Eckerle (eds), *Genre and Women's Life Writing*, 97–113.

Eckerle, Julie A. *Romancing the Self in Early Modern Englishwomen's Life Writing*. Farnham, 2013.

Eckerle, Julie A. and Naomi McAreavey (eds). *Women's Life Writing and Early Modern Ireland*. Lincoln, 2019.

Eckhardt, Joshua and Daniel Starza Smith (eds). *Manuscript Miscellanies in Early Modern England*. Farnham, 2014.

Edelman, Lee. *No Future: Queer Theory and the Death Drive*. Durham, NC, 2004.

Edwards, Michael. 'The Lost Library of Anne Conway'. *The Seventeenth Century* (2019), 1–29.

Egan, Gabriel. *The Struggle for Shakespeare's Text: Twentieth-Century Editorial Theory and Practice*. Cambridge, 2013.

Ellinghausen, Laurie. *Labor and Writing in Early Modern England, 1567–1667*. Aldershot, 2008.

Ellis, Roger. 'The Juvenile Translations of Elizabeth Tudor'. *Translation and Literature*, 18.2 (Autumn 2009), 157–80.

Eng, David, Jack Halberstam, and José Esteban Muñoz. 'What's Queer about Queer Studies?'. *Social Text*, 84–5 (2005), 1–18.

Engel, William E. 'Mnemonic Criticism and Renaissance Literature: A Manifesto'. *Connotations*, 1.1 (1991), 12–33.

Engel, William E., Rory Loughnane, and Grant Williams (eds). *The Memory Arts in Renaissance England: A Critical Anthology*. Cambridge, 2016.

Engen, Abram Van. *Sympathetic Puritans: Calvinist Fellow Feeling in Early New England*. New York, 2015.

Enterline, Lynn. '"Past the Help of Law": Epyllia and the Female Complaint'. In Ross and Smith (eds), *Early Modern Women's Complaint*, 315–27.

Enterline, Lynn. *Shakespeare's Schoolroom: Rhetoric, Discipline, Emotion*. Philadelphia, PA, 2012.

Ephraim, Michelle. *Reading the Jewish Woman on the Elizabethan Stage*. Burlington, VT, 2008.

Erickson, Amy Louise. *Women and Property in Early Modern England*. London, 1993.

Erickson, Peter. 'The Moment of Race in Renaissance Studies'. *Shakespeare Studies*, 26 (1998), 27–36.

Erickson, Peter and Kim F. Hall. '"A New Scholarly Song": Rereading Early Modern Race'. *Shakespeare Quarterly*, 67 (2016), 1–13.

Es, Bart van. *Spenser's Forms of History*. Oxford, 2002.

Estill, Laura. '"All the Adulteries of Art": The Dramatic Excerpts of Margaret Bellasys's BL MS. Add. 10309'. In Michael Denbo (ed.), *New Ways of Looking at Old Texts, V: Papers of the Renaissance English Text Society, 2007–2010*. Tempe, AZ, 2014, 235–45.

Evans, Deanna Delmar. 'Holy Terror and Love Divine: The Passionate Voice in Elizabeth Melville's *Ane Godlie* Dreame'. In Dunnigan, Harker, and Newlyn (eds), *Woman and the Feminine*, 153–61.

Ezell, Margaret J. M. 'Cooking the Books; or, The Three Faces of Hannah Woolley'. In DiMeo and Pennell (eds), *Reading and Writing Recipe Books*, 159–78.

Ezell, Margaret J. M. 'Domestic Papers: Manuscript Culture and Early Modern Women's Life Writing'. In Dowd and Eckerle (eds), *Genre and Women's Life Writing*, 33–48.

Ezell, Margaret J. M. 'Editing Early Modern Women's Manuscripts: Theory, Electronic Editions, and the Accidental Copy-Text'. *Literature Compass*, 7 (2010), 102–9.

Ezell, Margaret J. M. 'Invisibility Optics: Aphra Behn, Esther Inglis and the Fortunes of Women's Works'. In Phillippy (ed.), *A History of Early Modern Women's Writing*, 27–45.

Ezell, Margaret J. M. 'The Laughing Tortoise: Speculations on Manuscript Sources and Women's Book History'. *English Literary Renaissance*, 38.2 (2008), 331–55.

Ezell, Margaret J. M. *The Patriarch's Wife: Literary Evidence and the History of the Family*. Chapel Hill, NC, 1987.

Ezell, Margaret J. M. *Social Authorship and the Advent of Print*. Baltimore, MD, 1999.

Ezell, Margaret J. M. 'To Be Your Daughter in Your Pen: The Social Functions of Literature in the Writings of Lady Elizabeth Brackley and Lady Jane Cavendish'. *Huntington Library Quarterly*, 51 (1988), 281–96.

Ezell, Margaret J. M. *Writing Women's Literary History*. Baltimore, MD, 1993.

Fall, Rebecca L. 'Pamphilia Unbound: Digital Re-Visions of Mary Wroth's Folger Manuscript, V.a.104'. In Larson and Miller (eds), *Re-Reading Mary Wroth*, 193–207.

Fehrenbach, R. J. and Joseph L. Black. 'General Introduction'. In Fehrenbach and Black (eds), *Private Libraries in Renaissance England*, xxiii–xxx.

Fehrenbach, R. J. and Joseph L. Black (eds), *Private Libraries in Renaissance England: A Collection and Catalogue of Tudor and Early Stuart Book-Lists*, X. Tempe, AZ, 2020.

Felch, Susan M. 'The Backward Gaze: Editing Elizabeth Tyrwhit's Prayerbook'. In Ross and Salzman (eds), *Editing Early Modern Women*, 21–39.

Felch, Susan M. "The Public Life of Anne Vaughan Lock: Her Reception in England and Scotland'. In Julie D. Campbell and Anne R. Larsen (eds), *Early Modern Women and Transnational Communities of Letters*. Farnham, 2009, repr. 2016, 137–58.

Felski, Rita. 'Latour and literary studies'. *PMLA*, 130.3 (2015), 727–42.

Ferguson, George. *Signs and Symbols in Christian Art*. London, 1961.

Ferguson, Margaret W. 'The Authorial Ciphers of Aphra Behn'. In Steven N. Zwicker (ed.), *The Cambridge Companion to English Literature, 1650–1740*. Cambridge, 1998, 225–49.

Ferguson, Margaret W. 'Moderation and Its Discontents: Recent Work on Renaissance Women'. *Feminist Studies*, 20 (1994), 349–66.

Ferguson, Margaret W. and Mihoko Suzuki. 'Women's Literacies and Social Hierarchy in Early Modern England'. *Literature Compass*, 12 (2015), 575–90.

Feroli, Teresa. *Political Speaking Justified: Women Prophets and the English Revolution*. Newark, 2006.

Ferszt, Elizabeth and Ivy Schweitzer. 'A Different, More Complicated Bradstreet: Interview with Charlotte Gordon'. *Women's Studies*, 43 (2014), 372–8.

Field, Catherine. '"Many Hands Hands": Writing the Self in Early Modern Recipe Books'. In Dowd and Eckerle (eds), *Genre and Women's Life Writing*, 49–64.

Fienberg, Nona. 'Mary Wroth and the Invention of Female Poetic Subjectivity'. In Miller and Waller (eds), *Reading Mary Wroth*, 175–90.

Fienberg, Nona. 'Mary Wroth's Poetics of the Self'. *SEL Studies in English Literature, 1500–1900*, 42.1 (2002), 121–36.

Findlay, Alison. '*Love's Victory* in Production at Penshurst'. *Sidney Journal*, 34 (2016), 107–22.

Findlay, Alison. 'The Manuscripts of *Love's Victory*'. Shakespeare and His Sisters. wp.lancs.ac.uk/shakespeare-and-his-sisters. Accessed 20 December 2020.

Findlay, Alison. *Playing Spaces in Early Modern Women's Drama*. Cambridge, 2006.

Findlay, Alison. 'Reproducing *Iphigenia at Aulis*'. *Early Theatre*, 17 (2014), 133–48.

Findlay, Alison, Stephanie Hodgson-Wright, and Gweno Williams. *Women and Dramatic Production 1500–1700*. Harlow, 2000.

Fischlin, Daniel (ed.). *OuterSpeares: Shakespeare, Intermedia, and the Limits of Adaptation*. Toronto, 2014.

Fisken, Beth Wynne. '"The Art of Sacred Parody" in Mary Sidney's Psalmes'. *Tulsa Studies in Women's Literature*, 8.2 (1989), 223–39.

Fissell, Mary E. 'Women in Healing Spaces'. In Knoppers (ed.), *The Cambridge Companion to Early Modern Women's Writing*, 153–64.

Fitzmaurice, James. 'Front Matter and the Physical Make-up of Natures Pictures'. *Women's Writing*, 4 (1997), 353–67.

Fitzmaurice, James. 'Margaret Cavendish on Her Own Writing: Evidence from Revision and Handmade Correction'. *Papers of the Bibliographical Society of America*, 85 (1991), 297–308.

Fitzmaurice, James. "When an Old Ballad is Plainly Sung': Musical Lyrics in the Plays of Margaret and William Cavendish'. In Lamb and Bamford (eds), *Oral Traditions and Gender*, 153–68.

Flanders, Julia. 'Gender and the Electronic Text'. In Kathryn Sutherland (ed.), *Electronic Text: Investigations in Method and Theory*. Oxford, 1997, 127–43.

Flather, Amanda. *Gender and Space in Early Modern England.* Woodbridge, 2007.

Fleissner, Jennifer L. 'Is Feminism a Historicism?'. *Tulsa Studies in Women's Literature,* 21.1 (2002), 45–66.

Fleming, Juliet. *Graffiti and the Writing Arts of Early Modern England.* London, 2001.

Foucault, Michel. In Frédéric Gros (ed.) and Graham Burchell (trans.), *The Government of the Self and Others: Lectures at the Collège de France 1982–1983.* New York, 2010.

Foyster, Elisabeth. 'Marrying the Experienced Widow in Early Modern England: The Male Perspective'. In Sandra Cavallo and Lyndan Warner (eds), *Widowhood in Medieval and Early Modern Europe.* Harlow, 1999, 108–24.

Fraser, Nancy. 'Rethinking the Public Sphere: A Contribution to the Critique of Actually Existing Democracy'. *Social Text,* 25/26 (1990), 56–80.

Freccero, Carla. 'The Queer Time of the Lesbian Premodern'. In Noreen Giffney, Maureen M. Sauer, and Diane Watt (eds), *The Lesbian Premodern.* New York, 2011, 61–73.

Freccero, Carla. 'Queer Times'. *South Atlantic Quarterly,* 106 (2007), 485–94.

Freccero, Carla. 'Tangents of Desire'. *Journal for Early Modern Cultural Studies,* 16.2 (2016), 91–105.

Freeman, Elizabeth. 'Time Binds, or Erotohistoriography'. *Social Text,* 23.3–4 (2005), 57–68.

Freeman, Thomas S. and Sarah Wall. 'Racking the Body, Shaping the Text: The Account of Anne Askew in Foxe's "Book of Martyrs"'. *Renaissance Quarterly,* 54 (2001), 1165–96.

Friedlander, Ari. 'Desiring History and Historicizing Desire'. *Journal for Early Modern Cultural Studies,* 16.2 (2016), 1–20.

Froelich, Heather. 'Making Your Own Rules for use with Ubiqu+Ity'. *Visualizing English Print.* University of Wisconsin-Madison, 7 October 2016. https://graphics.cs.wisc.edu/WP/vep/2016/10/07/making-your-own-rules-for-use-with-ubiquity/. Accessed 8 April 2021.

Froide, Amy M. 'Marital Status as a Category of Difference: Singlewomen and Widows in Early Modern England'. In Judith M. Bennett and Amy M. Froide (eds), *Singlewomen in the European Past, 1250–1800.* Philadelphia, PA, 1998, 236–69.

Froide, Amy M. *Never Married: Singlewomen in Early Modern England.* Oxford, 2005.

Frye, Susan. 'Materializing Authorship in Esther Inglis's Books'. *Journal of Medieval and Early Modern Studies,* 32 (2002), 469–91.

Frye, Susan. *Pens and Needles: Women's Textualities in Early Modern England.* Philadelphia, PA, 2010.

Frye, Susan. 'Sewing Connections: Elizabeth Tudor, Mary Stuart, Elizabeth Talbot, and Seventeenth-Century Anonymous Needleworkers'. In Frye and Robertson (eds), *Maids and Mistresses,* 165–82.

Frye, Susan and Karen Robertson (eds). *Maids and Mistresses, Cousins and Queens: Women's Alliances in Early Modern England.* Oxford, 1999.

Fuchs, Barbara. *The Poetics of Piracy: Emulating Spain in English Literature.* Philadelphia, PA, 2013.

Fuchs, Barbara. *Romance.* New York, 2004.

Fudge, Erica. 'Renaissance Animal Things'. *New Formations,* 76 (2012), 86–100.

Fuentes, Marisa J. *Dispossessed Lives: Enslaved Women, Violence, and the Archive.* Philadelphia, PA, 2016.

Fulton, Thomas. *Historical Milton: Manuscript, Print, and Political Culture in Revolutionary England.* Amherst, MA, 2010.

Fumerton, Patricia. *The Broadside Ballad: Moving Media, Tactical Publics.* Philadelphia, PA, 2020.

Fumerton, Patricia (ed.). *English Broadside Ballad Archive.* https://ebba.english.ucsb.edu. Accessed 12 March 2021.

Fumerton, Patricia. *Unsettled: The Culture of Mobility and the Working Poor in Early Modern England*. Chicago, IL, 2006.

Fumerton, Patricia and Anita Guerrini (eds), with the assistance of Kris McAbee. *Ballads and Broadsides in Britain, 1500–1800*. Farnham, 2010.

Furey, Constance M. *Poetic Relations: Intimacy and Faith in the English Reformation*. Chicago, IL, 2017.

Gabbard, D. Christopher. 'Gender Stereotyping in Early Modern Travel Writing on Holland'. *SEL: Studies in English Literature, 1500–1900*, 43 (2003), 83–100.

Gajowski, Evelyn. 'Intersecting Discourses of Race and Gender in Elizabeth Cary's *The Tragedy of Mariam*'. *Early Modern Literary Studies*, 27 (2017), 297–314.

Galey, Alan. *The Shakespearean Archive: Experiments in New Media from the Renaissance to Postmodernity*. Cambridge, 2014.

Gallagher, Catherine. 'The Rise of Fictionality'. In Franco Moretti (ed.), *The Novel*. Princeton, NJ, 2006, 336–63.

Gaudio, Michael. *The Bible and the Printed Image in Early Modern England: Little Gidding and the Pursuit of Scriptural Harmony*. London, 2017.

Geerdink, Nina. 'Cultural Marketing of William III: A Religious Turn in Katharina Lescailje's Political Poetry'. *Dutch Crossing*, 34 (2010), 25–41.

Geerdink, Nina. 'Rouw om een "cieraad grooter vrouwen": Lijkdichten bij de dood van Maria Stuart (1695) door mannen en vrouwen'. *Historica*, 32 (2009), 3–5.

Genette, Gérard. In Jane E. Lewin (trans.), *Paratexts: Thresholds of Interpretation*. Cambridge, 1997.

Gentzler, Edwin. 'Interdisciplinary Connections'. *Perspectives: Studies in Translatology*, 11 (2003), 11–24.

Geuter, Ruth. 'Embroidered Biblical Narratives and Their Social Context'. In Andrew Morrall and Melinda Watt (eds), *English Embroidery from the Metropolitan Museum of Art, 1580–1700*. New Haven, CT, 2009, 57–77.

Geuter, Ruth. 'Reconstructing the Context of Seventeenth-Century English Figurative Embroideries'. In Moira Donald and Linda Hurcombe (eds), *Gender and Material Culture in Historical Perspective*. London, 2001, 97–111.

Gheeraert-Graffeuille, Claire. 'Margaret Cavendish's *Femmes Fortes*: The Paradoxes of Female Heroism in *Bell in Campo* (1662)'. *Revue de la Société d'études anglo-américaines des XVIIe et XVIIIe siècles*, 73 (2016), 243–65.

Gibbon, C. R. A. 'The Literary Cultures of the Scottish Reformation'. *The Review of English Studies*, 57.288 (2006), 64–82.

Gibson, Jonathan. 'Synchrony and Process: Editing Manuscript Miscellanies'. *SEL: Studies in English Literature*, 52 (2012), 85–100.

Gibson, Jonathan and Victoria E. Burke. *Early Modern Women's Manuscript Writing: Selected Papers from the Trinity/Trent Colloquium*. Aldershot, 2004.

Gill, Catie. '"All the Monarchies of This World Are Going down the Hill": The Anti-Monarchism of Anna Trapnel's *The Cry of a Stone* (1654)'. *Prose Studies*, 29 (2007), 19–35.

Gillespie, Katharine. *Domesticity and Dissent in the Seventeenth Century: English Women Writers and the Public Sphere*. Cambridge, 2004.

Gillespie, Katharine. *Women Writing the English Republic, 1625–1681*. Cambridge, 2017.

Glaisyer, Natasha. 'Popular Didactic Literature'. In Joad Raymond (ed.), *The Oxford History of Popular Print Culture, vol. I: Cheap Print in Britain and Ireland to 1660*. Oxford, 2011, 510–19.

Glomski, Jacqueline and Isabelle Moreau (eds). *Seventeenth-Century Fiction: Text and Transmission*. Oxford, 2016.

Goggin, Maureen Daly. 'Introduction: Threading Women'. In Goggin and Tobin (eds), *Women and the Material Culture of Needlework*, 1–12.
Goggin, Maureen Daly. 'Stitching a Life in "Pen of Steele and Silken Inke": Elizabeth Parker's *circa* 1830 Sampler'. In Goggin and Tobin (eds), *Women and the Material Culture of Needlework*, 31–50.
Goggin, Maureen Daly and Beth Fowkes Tobin (eds). *Women and the Material Culture of Needlework and Textiles, 1750–1950*. Burlington, VT, 2009.
Goh, Madeleine and Chad Schroeder (eds). *The Brill Dictionary of Ancient Greek*. London, 2015.
Goldberg, Jonathan. *Desiring Women: English Renaissance Examples*. Stanford, CA, 1997.
Goldberg, Jonathan and Madhavi Menon. 'Queering History'. *PMLA*, 120.5 (2005), 1608–17.
Goldstein, David. *Eating and Ethics in Shakespeare's England*. Cambridge, 2013.
Goldstein, David. 'Woolley's Mouse: Early Modern Recipe Books and the Uses of Nature'. In Jennifer Munroe and Rebecca Laroche (eds), *Ecofeminist Approaches to Early Modernity*. London, 2011, 105–27.
Gómez-Bravo, Ana M. 'The Origin of *Raza*: Racializing Difference in Early Spanish'. *Interfaces*, 7 (2020), 64–114.
Goodall, John. 'Lady Anne Clifford and the Architectural Pursuit of Nobility'. In Hearn and Hulse (eds), *Lady Anne Clifford*, 73–86.
Goodrich, Jaime. 'Authority, Gender, and Monastic Piety: Controversies at the English Benedictine Convent in Brussels, 1620–1623'. *British Catholic History*, 33 (2016), 91–114.
Goodrich, Jaime. 'Common Libraries: Book Circulation in English Benedictine Convents, 1600–1700'. In Knight, White, and Sauer (eds), *Women's Bookscapes*, 153–70.
Goodrich, Jaime. '"Enseigne-Bearers of Saint Clare": Elizabeth Evelinge's Early Translations and the Restoration of English Franciscanism'. In White (ed.), *English Women, Religion, and Textual Production*, 83–100.
Goodrich, Jaime. *Faithful Translators: Authorship, Gender, and Religion in Early Modern England*. Evanston, IL, 2013.
Goodrich, Jaime. '"Low and plain stile": Poetry and Piety in English Benedictine Convents, 1600–1800'. *British Catholic History*, 33 (2019), 599–618.
Goodrich, Jaime. 'Reconsidering the Woman Writer: The Identity Politics of Anne Cooke Bacon'. In Phillippy (ed), *A History of Early Modern Women's Writing*, 46–65.
Goodrich, Jaime. 'Thomas More and Margaret Roper: A Case for Rethinking Women's Participation in the Early Modern Public Sphere'. *Sixteenth Century Journal*, 39 (2008), 1021–40.
Goodrich, Jaime. 'Translating Lady Mary Percy: Authorship and Authority among the Brussels Benedictines'. In Caroline Bowden and James E. Kelly (eds), *The English Convents in Exile, 1600–1800: Communities, Culture and Identity*. Farnham, 2013, 109–22.
Goodrich, Jaime and Paula McQuade (eds). 'Special Issue: The Future(s) of Early Modern Women Writers'. *Criticism* 63.1–2 (2021).
Gordon, Andrew. *Writing Early Modern London: Memory, Text and Community*. Basingstoke, 2013.
Goreau, Angeline. *The Whole Duty of a Woman: Female Writers in Seventeenth-Century England*. New York, 1985.
Gorman, Cassandra. 'Allegorical Analogies: Henry More's Poetical Cosmology'. *Studies in Philology*, 114.1 (2017), 148–70.
Gorman, Cassandra. 'The Imperfect Circle: Hester Pulter's Alchemical Forms'. In Subha Mukherji and Elizabeth Swann (eds), *The Poetics of Scientia in Early Modern England*. London, forthcoming.
Gorst-Williams, Jessica. *Elizabeth, The Winter Queen*. London, 1977.

Gough, Richard. *The History of Myddle*. New York, 1986.

Gouk, Penelope. 'Raising Spirits and Restoring Souls: Early Modern Medical Explanations for Music's Effects'. In Veit Erlmann (ed.), *Hearing Cultures: Essays on Sound, Listening, and Modernity*. Oxford, 2004, 87–105.

Gouk, Penelope. 'Some English Theories of Hearing in the Seventeenth Century: Before and After Descartes'. In Charles Burnett, Michael Fend, and Penelope Gouk (eds), *The Second Sense: Studies in Hearing and Musical Judgment from Antiquity to the Seventeenth Century*. London, 1991, 95–113.

Gowing, Laura. *Domestic Dangers: Women, Words, and Sex in Early Modern London*. Oxford, 1996.

Graham, Elspeth. 'Women's Writing and the Self'. In Helen Wilcox (ed.), *Women and Literature in Britain, 1500–1700*. Cambridge, 1996, 209–33.

Gray, Catharine. *Women Writers and Public Debate in Seventeenth-Century Britain*. New York, 2007.

Gray, Kathryn N. *John Eliot and the Praying Indians of Massachusetts Bay*. Plymouth, MA, 2013.

Gray, Todd (ed.). *Devon Household Accounts, Part II: Henry 5th Earl of Bath and Rachel, Countess of Bath, Tavistock and London 1637–1655*. Exeter, 1996.

Green, Ian. *The Christian's ABC: Catechisms and Catechizing in England, 1550–1700*. Oxford, 1996.

Green, Ian. *Print and Protestantism in Early Modern England*. Oxford, 2000.

Green, Mary Anne Everett. *Elizabeth, Electress Palatine and Queen of Bohemia*. London, 1855, repr. 1909.

Green, Monica H. *Making Women's Medicine Masculine: The Rise of Male Authority in Pre-Modern Gynaecology*. Oxford, 2008.

Greenblatt, Stephen. *Shakespearean Negotiations: The Circulation of Social Energy in Renaissance England*. Berkeley, CA, 1988.

Greer, Bonnie. 'Who Was Shakespeare's Muse? A Black Woman, This Play Imagines'. *New York Times*, 22 August 2018. https://www.nytimes.com/2018/08/22/arts/shakespeare-globe-emilia.html. Accessed 2 June 2021.

Greer, David. 'Five Variations on "Farewell Dear Loue"'. In John Caldwell, Edward Olleson, and Susan Wollenberg (eds), *The Well Enchanting Skill: Music, Poetry, and Drama in the Culture of the Renaissance*. Oxford, 1990, 213–29.

Greer, Germaine, Susan Hastings, Jeslyn Medoff, and Melinda Sansone (eds). *Kissing the Rod: An Anthology of Seventeenth-Century Women's Verse*. New York, 1988.

Griffey, Erin. *Henrietta Maria: Piety, Politics and Patronage*. Aldershot, 2008.

Griffin, Carrie. *Instructional Writing in English, 1350–1650: Materiality and Meaning*. London, 2019.

Griffiths, Huw. 'Letter-Writing Lucrece: Shakespeare in the 1590s'. In Richards and Thorne (eds), *Rhetoric, Women and Politics in Early Modern England*, 89–110.

Grossman, Marshall (ed.) *Aemilia Lanyer: Gender, Genre, and the Canon*. Lexington, MD, 1998.

Gruber, Elizabeth. 'Insurgent Flesh: Epistemology and Violence in *Othello* and *Mariam*'. In Karen Raber (ed.), *Ashgate Critical Essays on Women Writers in England, 1550–1700: Elizabeth Cary*. Farnham, 2009, 477–94.

Guerrini, Anita. 'The Ghastly Kitchen'. *History of Science*, 51 (2016), 71–97.

Guibbory, Achsah. *Christian Identity, Jews and Israel in Seventeenth-Century England*. Oxford, 2010.

Guibbory, Achsah. 'The Gospel According to Aemilia: Women and the Sacred'. In Grossman (ed.), *Aemilia Lanyer: Gender, Genre, and the Canon*, 191–211.

Guy, John. *My Heart Is My Own: The Life of Mary Queen of Scots*. London, 2004.

Habermas, Jürgen. In Thomas Burger (trans.), *The Structural Transformation of the Public Sphere: An Inquiry into a Category of Bourgeois Society*. Cambridge, MA, 1991.
Hackett, Helen. 'Lady Mary Sidney Wroth: *The Countess of Montgomery's Urania*'. In Hannay, Lamb, and Brennan (eds), *The Ashgate Research Companion to the Sidneys*, 127–49.
Hackett, Helen. 'Unlocking the Mysteries of Constance Aston Fowler's Verse Miscellany (Huntington Library MS HM 904): The Hand B Scribe Identified'. In Eckhardt and Starza Smith (eds), *Manuscript Miscellanies in Early Modern England*, 91–112.
Hackett, Helen. 'Women and Catholic Manuscript Networks in Seventeenth-Century England: New Research on Constance Aston Fowler's Miscellany of Sacred and Secular Verse'. *Renaissance Quarterly*, 65.4 (2012), 1094–124.
Hageman, Elizabeth. 'Afterword: The Most Deservedly Admired Mrs. Katherine Philips—Her Books'. In David L. Orvis and Ryan Singh Paul (eds), *The Noble Flame of Katherine Philips: A Poetics of Culture, Politics, and Friendship*. Pittsburgh, PA, 2015, 311–24.
Hageman, Elizabeth. '"More Copies of it abroad than I could have imagin'd": Further Manuscript Texts of Katherine Philips, the Matchless Orinda'. *English Manuscript Studies 1100–1700*, 5 (1995), 127–69.
Hageman, Elizabeth and Andrea Sununu. 'New Manuscript Texts and Katherine Philips, the "Matchless Orinda"'. *English Manuscript Studies, 1100–1700*, 4 (1993), 174–219.
Halberstam, Jack. *The Queer Art of Failure*. Durham, NC, 2011.
Halder, Janine, Laurent Decrouy, and Torsten W. Vennemann. 'Mixing of Rhône River Water in Lake Geneva (Switzerland–France) Inferred from Stable Hydrogen and Oxygen Isotope Profiles'. *Journal of Hydrology*, 477 (2013), 152–64.
Hall, Kim F. 'Beauty and the Beast of Whiteness: Teaching Race and Gender'. *Shakespeare Quarterly*, 47 (1996), 461–75.
Hall, Kim F. 'Culinary Spaces, Colonial Spaces: The Gendering of Sugar in the Seventeenth Century'. In Valerie Traub, M. Lindsay Kaplan, and Dympna Callaghan (eds), *Feminist Readings of Early Modern Culture: Emerging Subjects*. Cambridge, 1996, 168–90.
Hall, Kim F. '"I Rather Would Wish to Be a Black-Moor": Beauty, Race, and Rank in Lady Mary Wroth's *Urania*'. In Hendricks and Parker (eds), *Women, 'Race', and Writing*, 178–94.
Hall, Kim F. 'Object into Object? Some Thoughts on the Presence of Black Women in Early Modern Culture'. In Peter Erickson and Clark Hulse (eds), *Early Modern Visual Culture: Representation, Race, and Empire in Renaissance England*. Philadelphia, PA, 2000, 346–79.
Hall, Kim F. 'Reading What Isn't There: "Black" Studies in Early Modern England'. *Stanford Humanities Review*, 3 (1993), 23–33.
Hall, Kim F. '"These Bastard Signs of Fair": Literary Whiteness in Shakespeare's Sonnets'. In Ania Loomba and Martin Orkin (eds), *Post-Colonial Shakespeares*. New York, 1998, 64–83.
Hall, Kim F. *Things of Darkness: Economies of Race and Gender in Early Modern England*. Ithaca, NY, 1995.
Hall, Kim F. 'Women and Race'. *Women Writers in Context. Women's Writers Project*. September 1999, repr. January 2013. https://www.wwp.northeastern.edu/context/index.html#rEss.race.xml. Accessed 2 June 2021.
Hallett, Nicky. 'Philip Sidney in the Cloister: The Reading Habits of English Nuns in Seventeenth-Century Antwerp'. *Journal for Early Modern Cultural Studies*, 12.3 (2012), 87–115.
Halsband, Robert. *The Life of Lady Mary Wortley Montagu*. Oxford, 1956.
Hamlin, Hannibal. *Psalm Culture and Early Modern English Literature*. Cambridge, 2004.
Hammons, Pamela. *Gender, Sexuality, and Material Objects in English Renaissance Verse*. Farnham, 2010.

Hammons, Pamela S. 'Introduction'. In Pamela S. Hammons (ed.), *Book M: A London Widow's Life Writings*. Toronto, 2013.

Hammons, Pamela. 'Widow, Prophet, and Poet: Lyrical Self-Figurations in Katherine Austen's "Book M" (1664)'. In Barbara Smith and Ursula Appelt (eds), *Write or Be Written: Early Modern Women Poets and Cultural Constraints*. Aldershot, 2001, 3–27.

Hannay, Margaret P. '"Doo What Men May Sing": Mary Sidney and the Tradition of Admonitory Dedication'. In Hannay (ed.), *Silent but for the Word*, 149–281.

Hannay, Margaret P. '"How I These Studies Prize": The Countess of Pembroke and Elizabethan Science'. In Hunter and Hutton (eds), *Women, Science and Medicine*, 10–21.

Hannay, Margaret P. *Mary Sidney, Lady Wroth*. Farnham, 2010.

Hannay, Margaret P. *Philip's Phoenix: Mary Sidney, Countess of Pembroke*. Oxford, 1990.

Hannay, Margaret P. '"Princes You as Men Must Dy": Genevan Advice to Monarchs in the Psalmes of Mary Sidney'. *English Literary Renaissance*, 19 (1989), 22–41.

Hannay, Margaret P. (ed.). *Silent But for the Word*. Kent, OH, 1985.

Hannay, Margaret P. 'Sleuthing in the Archives'. In Larson and Miller (eds), *Re-reading Mary Wroth*, 19–36.

Hannay, Margaret P. '"Unlock My Lipps": The Miserere mei Deus of Anne Vaughan Lock and Mary Sidney Herbert'. In Jean M. Brink (ed.), *Privileging Gender in Early Modern England*. Kirkesville, MO, 1993, 19–36.

Hannay, Margaret P., Mary Ellen Lamb, and Michael G. Brennan (eds). *The Ashgate Research Companion to the Sidneys, 1500–1700, vol. 2: Literature*. Burlington, VT, 2015.

Hanson, Elizabeth. 'Boredom and Whoredom: Reading Renaissance Women's Sonnet Sequences'. *The Yale Journal of Criticism*, 10 (1997), 165–91.

Harkness, Deborah. *The Jewel House: Elizabethan London and the Scientific Revolution*. New Haven, CT, 2007.

Harris, Barbara. 'Women and Politics in Early Tudor England'. *The Historical Journal*, 33.2 (1990), 259–81.

Harris, Frances. 'Living in the Neighbourhood of Science: Mary Evelyn, Margaret Cavendish and the Greshamites'. In Hunter and Hutton (eds), *Women, Science and Medicine*, 198–217.

Harris, Frances. *Transformations of Love: The Friendship of John Evelyn and Margaret Godolphin*. Oxford, 2002.

Harris, Johanna and Elizabeth Scott-Baumann (eds). *The Intellectual Culture of Puritan Women, 1558–1689*. Basingstoke, 2010.

Harris, Wendell V. 'Canonicity'. *PMLA* 106.1 (1991), 110–21.

Harris Sacks, David. 'The Promise and the Contract in Early Modern England: Slade's Case in Perspective'. In Kahn and Hutson (eds), *Rhetoric and Law in Early Modern Europe*, 28–53.

Hartman, Saidiya. *Lose Your Mother: A Journey along the Atlantic Slave Route*. New York, 2008.

Hartman, Saidiya. *Scenes of Subjection: Terror, Slavery, and Self-Making in Nineteenth-Century America*. Oxford, 1997.

Hartman, Saidiya. 'Venus in Two Acts'. *Small Axe*, 12 (2008), 1–14.

Hawes, Clement. *Mania and Literary Style: The Rhetoric of Enthusiasm from the Ranters to Christopher Smart*. Cambridge, 1996.

Hayot, Eric. 'Against Periodization; or, On Institutional Time'. *New Literary History*, 42 (2011), 739–56.

Hayward, Maria. 'Gift Giving at the Court of Henry VIII: The 1539 New Year's Gift Roll in Context'. *The Antiquaries Journal*, 85.1 (2005), 126–75.

Heal, Felicity. *The Power of Gifts: Gift Exchange in Early Modern England*. Oxford, 2014.

Heale, Elizabeth. '"Desiring Women Writing": Female Voices and Courtly "Balets" in Some Early Tudor Manuscript Albums'. In Burke and Gibson (eds), *Early Modern Women's Manuscript Writing*, 9–31.

Hearn, Karen and Lynne Hulse (eds). *Lady Anne Clifford: Culture, Patronage and Gender in 17th-century Britain*. Yorkshire Archaeological Society Occasional Papers No. 7. Leeds, 2009.

Helfer, Rebecca. 'The State of the Art of Memory and Shakespeare Studies'. In Andrew Hiscock and Lina Perkins Wilder (eds), *The Routledge Handbook of Shakespeare and Memory*. London, 2018, 315–28.

Heller, Jennifer L. 'Space, Violence, and Bodies in Middleton and Cary'. *SEL: Studies in English Literature 1500–1900*, 45.2 (2005), 425–41.

Hellwarth, Jennifer Wynne. *The Reproductive Unconscious in Medieval and Early Modern England*. London, 2002.

Helmers, Helmer J. 'Popular Participation and Public Debate'. In Helmer J. Helmers and Geert H. Janssen (eds), *The Cambridge Companion to the Dutch Golden Age*. Cambridge, 2018, 124–46.

Helmers, Helmer J. *The Royalist Republic: Literature, Politics, and Religion in the Anglo-Dutch Public Sphere, 1639–1660*. Cambridge, 2015.

Henderson, Katherine Usher and Barbara F. McManus (eds). *Half Humankind: Contexts and Texts of the Controversy about Women in England, 1540–1640*. Urbana, IL, 1985.

Hendricks, Margo. 'Alliance and Exile: Aphra Behn's Racial Identity'. In Frye and Robertson (eds), *Maids and Mistresses*, 259–73.

Hendricks, Margo. 'Civility, Barbarism, and Aphra Behn's *The Widow Ranter*'. In Hendricks and Parker (eds), *Women, 'Race', and Writing*, 225–39.

Hendricks, Margo. 'Coloring the Past, Rewriting Our Future: RaceB4Race'. Folger Shakespeare Library, Washington, DC, 5 September 2019. https://www.folger.edu/institute/scholarly-programs/race-periodization/margo-hendricks. Accessed 6 March 2021.

Hendricks, Margo. [Elysabeth Grace]. *Daughters of Saria, vol. 1: Fate's Match* (2019); *vol. 2: Fate's Kiss* (2020); *vol. 3: Fate's Consort* (2020). https://www.elysabethgrace.com/daughtersofsariaseries. Accessed 6 March 2021.

Hendricks, Margo. 'Feminism, the Roaring Girls and Me'. In Gayle Green and Coppélia Kahn (eds), *Changing Subjects: The Making of Feminist Literary Criticism*. London, 1993, 147–53.

Hendricks, Margo. 'Feminist Historiography'. In Anita Pacheco (ed.), *A Companion to Early Modern Women's Writing*. Oxford, 2002, 361–76.

Hendricks, Margo. 'Managing the Barbarian: *The Tragedy of Dido, Queen of Carthage*'. *Renaissance Drama*, 23 (1992), 165–88.

Hendricks, Margo. '"The Moor of Venice", or the Italian on the English Renaissance Stage'. In Shirley Nelson Garner and Madelon Sprengnether (eds), *Shakespearean Tragedy and Gender*. Bloomington, IN, 1996, 193–209.

Hendricks, Margo. '"Obscured by Dreams": Race, Empire, and Shakespeare's *A Midsummer Night's Dream*'. *Shakespeare Quarterly*, 47.1 (1996), 37–60.

Hendricks, Margo. 'Race: A Renaissance Category'. In Michael Hattaway (ed.), *A New Companion to English Renaissance Literature and Culture*, 2 vols. Malden, MA, 2010, I.535–44.

Hendricks, Margo. 'Race and Nation'. In Bruce R. Smith and Katherine Rowe (eds), *The Cambridge Guide to the Worlds of Shakespeare*. Cambridge, 2016, 663–8.

Hendricks, Margo [Margo Jennett Price-Hendricks]. 'The Roaring Girls: A Study of Seventeenth-Century Century Feminism and the Development of Feminist Drama'. PhD Diss., University of California Riverside, 1987.

Hendricks, Margo. 'Surveying "Race" in Shakespeare'. In Catherine M. S. Alexander and Stanley Wells (eds), *Shakespeare and Race*. Cambridge, 2000, 1–22.

Hendricks, Margo. 'Visions of Color: Spectacle, Spectators, and the Performance of Race'. In Barbara Hodgdon and W.B. Worthen (eds), *A Companion to Shakespeare and Performance*. Malden, MA, 2005, 511–26.

Hendricks, Margo. '"A word, sweet Lucrece": Confession, Feminism, and *The Rape of Lucrece*'. In Callaghan (ed.), *A Feminist Companion to Shakespeare*, 121–36.

Hendricks, Margo and Patricia Parker (eds). *Women, 'Race', and Writing in the Early Modern Period*. New York, 1994.

Henke, Robert and Eric Nicholson. 'Introduction'. In Robert Henke and Eric Nicholson (eds), *Transnational Exchange in Early Modern Theatre*. Aldershot, 2008, 1–22.

Herissone, Rebecca. *Musical Creativity in Restoration England*. Cambridge, 2013.

Herman, Peter C. 'Lady Hester Pulter's *The Unfortunate Florinda*: Race, Religion, and the Politics of Rape'. *Renaissance Quarterly*, 63.4 (2010), 1206–46.

Hey, David (ed.). *The Oxford Companion to Family and Local History*. Oxford, 2010.

Hickerson, Megan L. *Making Women Martyrs in Tudor England*. Basingstoke, 2005.

Higginbotham, Jennifer. 'Taking the Thread of Mary Wroth's "A Crown of Sonnets Dedicated to Love"'. In Lara Dodds and Michelle M. Dowd (eds), *Feminist Formalism and Early Modern Women's Writing: Readings, Conversations, Pedagogies*. Lincoln, NE, 2022, 23–37.

Hill, W. Speed. 'Editing Nondramatic Texts of the English Renaissance: A Field Guide with Illustrations'. In Hill (ed.), *New Ways of Looking at Old Texts*, 1–24.

Hill, W. Speed (ed.). *New Ways of Looking at Old Texts: Papers of the Renaissance English Text Society, 1985–1991*. Binghamton, NY, 1993.

Hinds, Hilary. *God's Englishwomen: Seventeenth-Century Radical Sectarian Writing and Feminist Criticism*. Manchester, 1996.

Hiscock, Andrew. '"A Dialogue between Old England and New": Anne Bradstreet and her Negotiations with the Old World'. In Andrew Hiscock (ed.), *Mighty Europe 1400–1700: Writing an Early Modern Continent*. Bern, 2007, 185–220.

Hiscock, Andrew. *Reading Memory in Early Modern Literature*. Cambridge, 2011.

Hiscock, Andrew and Helen Wilcox (eds). *The Oxford Handbook of Early Modern English Literature and Religion*. Oxford, 2017.

Hobbs, Mary. *Early Seventeenth-Century Verse Miscellany Manuscripts*. Aldershot, 1992.

Hobby, Elaine. '"Dreams and plain dotage": The Value of *The Birth of Mankind*'. *Essays and Studies*, 61 (2008), 35–52.

Hobby, Elaine. 'Katherine Philips: Seventeenth-Century Lesbian Poet'. In Elaine Hobby and Chris White (eds), *What Lesbians Do in Books*. London, 1991, 183–204.

Hobby, Elaine. *The Virtue of Necessity: English Women's Writing 1649–88*. Ann Arbor, MI, 1988.

Hoffman, C. F. 'Catherine Parr as a Woman of Letters'. *The Huntington Library Quarterly*, 23.4 (1960), 349–67.

Hoftijzer, P. G. *Engelse boekverkopers bij de Beurs: De geschiedenis van de Amsterdamse boekhandels Bruyning en Swart, 1637–1724*. Amsterdam, 1987.

Holberton, Edward. 'Prophecy and Geography in Anne Bradstreet's "Contemplations": A Transatlantic Reading'. In Robin Peel and Daniel Maudlin (eds), *Transatlantic Traffic and (Mis)Translations*. Durham, NH, 2013, 157–75.

Holdsworth, R. V. 'Middleton and *Mariam*'. *Notes and Queries*, 33 (1986), 379–80.

Holmes, Michael Morgan. 'The Love of Other Women: Rich Chains and Sweet Kisses'. In Grossman (ed.), *Aemilia Lanyer: Gender, Genre, and the Canon*, 167–90.

Holstun, James. *Ehud's Dagger: Class Struggle in the English Revolution.* London, 2000.
Holstun, James. 'Will You Rent Our Ancient Love Asunder? Lesbian Elegy in Donne, Marvell, and Milton'. *English Literary History*, 54.4 (1987), 835–67.
Horton, Louise. 'The Clerics and the Learned Lady: Intertextuality in the Religious Writings of Lady Jane Grey'. In Pender (ed.), *Gender, Authorship, and Early Modern Women's Collaboration*, 149–74.
Horton, Louise. '"Restore Me That Am Lost": Recovering the Forgotten History of Lady Abergavenny's Prayers'. *Women's Writing*, 26 (2019), 3–14.
Hosington, Brenda M. 'Collaboration, Authorship, and Gender in the Paratexts Accompanying Translations by Susan Du Verger and Judith Man'. In Pender (ed.), *Gender, Authorship, and Early Modern Women's Collaboration*, 95–121.
Hosington, Brenda M. 'Commerce, Printing, and Patronage'. In Gordon Braden, Robert Cummings, and Stuart Gillespie (eds), *The Oxford History of Literary Translation in English, vol. II: 1550–1660*. Oxford, 2010, 47–57.
Hosington, Brenda M. 'Fact and Fiction in Susan Du Verger's Translations of Jean-Pierre Camus's *Les Euenemens singuliers, Les Relations morales*, and *Diotrephe. Histoire Valentine*'. In Jacqueline Glomski and Isabelle Moreau (eds), *Seventeenth-Century Fiction: Text and Transmission*. Oxford, 2016, 115–29.
Hosington, Brenda M. '"How we ought to knowe God": Princess Elizabeth's Presentation of her Calvin Translation to Katherine Parr'. In Catherine Batt and René Tixier (eds), *Booldly Bot Meekly: Essays on the Theory and Practice of Translation in the Middle Ages in Honour of Roger Ellis*. Turnhout, 2018, 499–513.
Hosington, Brenda M. 'Women Translators and the Early Printed Book'. In Vincent Gillespie and Susan Powell (eds), *A Companion to the Early Printed Book in Britain 1476–1558*. Woodbridge, 2014, 248–71.
Hosington, Brenda and Marie-Alice Belle. *Renaissance Cultural Crossroads* (2010). The University of Warwick. www.dhi.ac.uk/rcc. Accessed 20 December 2020.
Hoskins, W. G. *Local History in England*. London, 1984.
Howard, Jean. 'Textualizing an Urban Life: The Case of Isabella Whitney'. In Ronald Bedford, Lloyd Davis, and Philippa Kelly (eds), *Early Modern Autobiography: Theories, Genres, Practices*. Ann Arbor, MI, 2006, 217–33.
Hoxby, Blair. *What Was Tragedy? Theory and the Early Modern Canon*. Oxford, 2015.
Hubbard, Eleanor. *City Women: Money, Sex, and the Social Order in Early Modern London*. Oxford, 2012.
Hubbard, Eleanor. 'Reading, Writing, and Initialing: Female Literacy in Early Modern London'. *Journal of British Studies*, 54.3 (2015), 553–77.
Huffer, Lynne. *Mad for Foucault: Rethinking the Foundations of Queer Theory*. New York, 2009.
Hull, Gloria T., Patricia Bell Scott, and Barbara Smith (eds). *All the Women Are White, All the Blacks Are Men, but Some of Us Are Brave: Black Women's Studies*. New York, 1982.
Humfrey, Paula. *The Experience of Domestic Service for Women in Early Modern London*. Abingdon, 2011.
Humphrey, Carol. *Sampled Lives: Samplers from the Fitzwilliam Museum*. Cambridge, 2017.
Hunt, Arnold. 'The Books, Library, and Literary Patronage of Mrs. Anne Sadleir (1585–1670)'. In Burke and Gibson (eds), *Early Modern Women's Manuscript Writing*, 205–36.
Hunter, Lynette. 'Books for Daily Life: Household, Husbandry, Behaviour'. In J. Barnard and D. F. McKenzie (eds), *The Cambridge History of the Book in Britain, vol. IV: 1557–1695*. Cambridge, 2002, 514–32.

Hunter, Lynette (ed.). *The Letters of Dorothy Moore, 1612–64: The Friendships, Marriage and Intellectual Life of a Seventeenth-Century Woman*. Aldershot, 2004.

Hunter, Lynette and Sarah Hutton (eds), *Women, Science and Medicine, 1500–1700: Mothers of the Royal Society*. Stroud, 1997.

Hurley, Ann Hollinshead and Chanita Goodblatt (eds). *Women Editing/Editing Women: Early Modern Women Writers and the New Textualism*. Newcastle, 2009.

Hustvedt, Siri. *The Blazing World*. New York, 2014.

Hutson, Lorna. *The Usurer's Daughter: Male Friendship and Fictions of Women in Sixteenth-Century England*. London, 1994.

Hutton, Sarah. 'Ancient Wisdom and Modern Philosophy: Anne Conway, F. M. van Helmont, and the Seventeenth-Century Dutch Interchange of Ideas'. *Quaestiones Infinitae*, 4 (1994), 1–16.

Hutton, Sarah. 'Lady Damaris Masham'. https://plato.stanford.edu/entries/lady-masham/. Accessed 22 May 2021.

Hyning, Victoria van. *Convent Autobiography: Early Modern English Nuns in Exile*. Oxford, 2019.

Ibbetson, David. 'Sixteenth Century Contract Law: Slade's Case in Context'. *Oxford Journal of Legal Studies*, 4/3 (1984), 295–317.

Ingram, Jill. *Idioms of Self-Interest: Credit, Identity and Property in English Renaissance Literature*. New York, 2006.

Ingram, Martin. *Church Courts, Sex and Marriage in England, 1570–1640*. Cambridge, 1990.

Iser, Wolfgang. *The Act of Reading: A Theory of Aesthetic Response*. Baltimore, MD, 1978.

Ives, Eric. *Lady Jane Grey: A Tudor Mystery*. Chichester, 2011.

Ivic, Christopher. '"Our British Land": Anne Bradstreet's Atlantic Perspective'. In Philip Schwyzer and Simon Mealor (eds), *Archipelagic Identities: Literature and Identity in the Atlantic Archipelago, 1550–1800*. Aldershot, 2004, 195–204.

Iyengar, Sujata. 'Royalist, Romancist, Racialist: Rank, Gender and Race in the Science and Fiction of Margaret Cavendish'. *English Literary History*, 69 (2002), 649–72.

Jagose, Annamarie. 'Feminism's Queer Theory'. *Feminism & Psychology*, 19.2 (2009), 157–74.

Jameson, Frederic. 'Magical Narratives: Romance as Genre'. *New Literary History*, 7.1 (1975), 135–63.

Jardine, Boris. 'The Book as Instrument: Craft and Technique in Early Modern Practical Mathematics'. *Learning by the Book: Manuals and Handbooks in the History of Science*, 5 (2020), 111–29.

Jardine, Lisa. *Going Dutch: How England Plundered Holland's Glory*. New York, 2008.

Jardine, Lisa and Anthony Grafton. '"Studied for Action": How Gabriel Harvey Read His Livy'. *Past and Present*, 129 (1990), 30–78.

Jarratt, Susan. 'Rhetoric and Feminism: Together Again'. *College English*, 62.3 (2000), 390–3.

Jarrett-Macaulay, Delia. 'Introduction'. In Delia Jarrett-Macaulay (ed.), *Shakespeare, Race and Performance: The Diverse Bard*. New York, 2017, 1–19.

Jayne, Sears and Francis R. Johnson (eds). *The Lumley Library: The Catalogue of 1609*. London, 1956.

Johns, Adrian. *The Nature of the Book: Print and Knowledge in the Making*. Chicago, IL, 1998.

Johnston, Hope. 'How *Le livre de la Cite des Dames* First Came to be Printed in England'. In Liliane Dulac, Anne Paupert, Anne, Christine Reno, and Bernard Ribémont (eds), *Desireuse de plus avant enquerre*. Paris, 2008, 385–96.

Jones, Ann Rosalind and Peter Stallybrass. *Renaissance Clothing and the Materials of Memory*. Cambridge, 2002.

Jones, Emily Griffiths. *Right Romance: Heroic Subjectivity and Elect Community in Seventeenth-Century England*. University Park, PA, 2020.
Jordan, Constance. 'Feminism and the Humanists: The Case of Sir Thomas Elyot's *Defence of Good Women*'. *Renaissance Quarterly*, 36 (1983), 242–58.
Jordan, Constance. *Renaissance Feminism: Literary Texts and Political Models*. Ithaca, NY, 1990.
Jouanna, Jacques. In Philip van der Eijk (ed.) and Neil Allies (trans.), *Greek Medicine from Hippocrates to Galen: Selected Papers*. Leiden, 2012.
Judson, J. Richard and Rudolf Ekkart. *Gerrit van Honthorst, 1592–1656*. Doornspijk, 1999.
Juneja, Renu. 'The Widow as Paradox and Paradigm in Middleton's Plays'. *The Journal of General Education*, 34 (1982), 3–19.
Juneja, Renu. 'Widowhood and Sexuality in Chapman's "The Widow's Tears"'. *Philological Quarterly*, 67 (1988), 157–75.
Justice, George L. and Nathan Tinker (eds). *Women's Writing and the Circulation of Ideas: Manuscript Publication in England, 1550–1800*. Cambridge, 2002.
Kahn, David. *The Codebreakers: The Story of Secret Writing*. New York, 1967, repr. 1996.
Kahn, Victoria and Lorna Hutson (eds). *Rhetoric and Law in Early Modern Europe*. New Haven, CT, 2001.
Kaplan, M. Lindsay. 'The Jewish Body in Black and White in Medieval and Early Modern England'. *PQ*, 92 (2013), 41–65.
Karremann, Isobel. *The Drama of Memory in Shakespeare's History Plays*. Cambridge, 2015.
Kearns, Judith. 'Fashioning Innocence: Rhetorical Construction of Character in the Memoirs of Anne, Lady Halkett'. *Texas Studies in Literature and Language*, 46 (2004), 340–62.
Keens-Soper, Maurice. 'Wicquefort'. In G. R. Berridge, Maurice Keens-Soper, and T. G. Otto (eds), *Diplomatic Theory from Machiavelli to Kissinger*. New York, 2001, 88–105.
Kelly, James E. *English Convents in Catholic Europe, c 1600–1800*. Cambridge, 2020.
Kelly, Joan. 'Did Women Have a Renaissance?'. In *Women, History, and Theory: The Essays of Joan Kelly*. Chicago, IL, 1984, 19–50.
Kennedy, Gwynne. *Just Anger: Representing Women's Anger in Early Modern England*. Carbondale, IL, 2000.
Kenny, Neil. *Born to Write: Literary Families and Social Hierarchy in Early Modern France*. Oxford, 2020.
Kerrigan, John. *Archipelagic English: Literature, History, and Politics, 1603–1707*. Cambridge, 2006.
Kibbee, Douglas A. *For to Speke Frenche Trewely: The French Language in England, 1000–1600*. Amsterdam, 1991.
Kidnie, M. J. 'Near Neighbours: Another Early Seventeenth-Century Manuscript of *The Humorous Magistrate*'. *Renaissance Quarterly*, 52 (1999), 402–39.
Killeen, Kevin. 'Coles from Thine Altar Tipp'd Theyr Tongues With Cunning': The Decalogue Poetry of Anne Southwell'. In Sophie Read (ed.), *Literature and the Bible*. London, forthcoming.
Killeen, Kevin, Helen Smith, and Rachel Willie (eds). *The Oxford Handbook of the Bible in Early Modern England*. Oxford, 2015.
King, John N. *English Reformation Literature: The Tudor Origins of the Protestant Tradition*. Princeton, NJ, 1982.
King, John N. *Foxe's Book of Martyrs and Early Print Culture*. Cambridge, 2006.
King, John N. 'How Anne Askew Read the Bible'. *Reformation*, 25 (2020), 47–68.
King, John N. 'Thomas Bentley's Monument of Matrons'. In Pamela Joseph Benson and Victoria Kirkham (eds), *Strong Voices, Weak History: Early Women Writers and Canons in England, France, and Italy*. Ann Arbor, MI, 2005, 2016–38.

King, Margaret L. and Alfred Rabil (trans.). *Her Immaculate Hand: Selected Works by and about the Women Humanists of Quattrocento Italy*. Asheville, NC, 1997.

Kinney, Clare R. 'Turn and Counterturn: Reappraising Mary Wroth's Poetic Labyrinths'. In Larson and Miller (eds), *Re-Reading Mary Wroth*, 85–102.

Klein, Lauren. 'The Image of Absence: Archival Silence, Data Visualization, and James Hemings'. *American Literature*, 85.4 (2013), 661–88.

Klein, Lisa M. 'Your Humble Handmaid: Elizabethan Gifts of Needlework'. *Renaissance Quarterly*, 50.2 (1997), 459–93.

Knight, Jeffrey Todd. *Bound to Read: Compilations, Collections, and the Making of Renaissance Literature*. Philadelphia, 2013.

Knight, Leah. 'Anne Clifford'. In Fehrenbach and Black (eds), *Private Libraries in Renaissance England*, 347–63.

Knight, Leah. 'Margaret Clifford'. In Fehrenbach and Black (eds), *Private Libraries in Renaissance England*, 157–61.

Knight, Leah. 'Reading across Borders: The Case of Anne Clifford's "Popish" Books'. *Journal of the Canadian Historical Association*, n.s. 25.2 (2014), 27–57.

Knight, Leah. *Reading Green in Early Modern England*. Farnham, 2014.

Knight, Leah. 'Reading Proof: Or, Problems and Possibilities in the Text Life of Anne Clifford'. In Knight, White, and Sauer (eds), *Women's Bookscapes*, 253–73.

Knight, Leah and Wendy Wall (eds). 'Special Issue: The Poetry of Hester Pulter: Revolution and Remediation'. *Journal for Early Modern Cultural Studies*, 20.2 (2020).

Knight, Leah, Micheline White, and Elizabeth Sauer (eds). *Women's Bookscapes in Early Modern Britain: Reading, Ownership, Circulation*. Ann Arbor, MI, 2018.

Knoppers, Laura Lunger (ed.). *The Cambridge Companion to Early Modern Women's Writing*. Cambridge, 2009.

Knoppers, Laura Lunger. 'Introduction: Critical Framework and Issues'. In Knoppers (ed.), *The Cambridge Companion to Early Modern Women's Writing*, 1–17.

Knoppers, Laura. *Politicizing Domesticity from Henrietta Maria to Milton's Eve*. Cambridge, 2011.

Kolkovich, Elizabeth Zeman. 'In Defense of Indulgence: Hester Pulter's Maternal Elegies'. *Journal for Early Modern Cultural Studies*, 20.2 (2021), 43–70.

Kolkovich, Elizabeth Zeman. 'Reader, Maker, Mentor: The Countess of Huntingdon and Her Networks'. In Wayne (ed.), *Women's Labour and the History of the Book*, 225–42.

Korda, Natasha. 'Gender at Work in the Cries of London'. In Lamb and Bamford (eds), *Oral Traditions and Gender*, 117–35.

Korda, Natasha. 'Insubstantial Pageants: Women's Work and the (Im)material Culture of the Early Modern Stage'. *Shakespeare*, 7 (2011), 413–31.

Korda, Natasha. *Labors Lost: Women's Work and the Early Modern English Stage*. Philadelphia, PA, 2011.

Korda, Natasha. *Shakespeare's Domestic Economies: Gender and Property in Early Modern England*. Philadelphia, PA, 2002.

Korda, Natasha. 'Shakespeare's Laundry'. In Loomba and Sanchez (eds), *Rethinking Feminism in Early Modern Studies*, 93–111.

Kroetsch, Cameron. 'List of Margaret Cavendish's Texts, Printers, and Booksellers (1653–1675)'. *Digital Cavendish Project*, 15 August 2013. http://digitalcavendish.org/original-research/texts-printers-booksellers/. Accessed 8 November 2020.

Krontiris, Tina. 'Breaking Barriers of Genre and Gender: Margaret Tyler's Translation of 'The Mirrour of Knighthood'. *English Literary Renaissance*, 18 (1988), 19–39.

Krontiris, Tina. *Oppositional Voices: Women and Writers and Translators of Literature in the English Renaissance*. London, 1992.

Kyle, Chris R. *Theater of State: Parliament and Political Culture in Early Stuart England*. Stanford, CA, 2012.

La Bouff, Nicole. 'An Unlikely Christian Humanist: How Bess of Hardwick (ca. 1527–1608) Answered "the Woman Question"'. *Sixteenth Century Journal*, 4.7 (2016), 847–82.

Lacey, Andrew. *The Cult of King Charles the Martyr*. Woodbridge, 2003.

Laclau, Ernesto and Chantal Mouffe. *Hegemony and Socialist Strategy: Toward a Radical Democratic Politics*. London, 1985.

Lamb, Mary Ellen. 'The Cooke Sisters: Attitudes toward Learned Women in the Renaissance'. In Hannay (ed.), *Silent But for the Word*, 107–25.

Lamb, Mary Ellen. 'Isabella Whitney and Reading Humanism'. In Knight,White, and Sauer (eds), *Women's Bookscapes*, 43–58.

Lamb, Mary Ellen. 'Topicality in Mary Wroth's *Countess of Montgomery's Urania*: Prose Romance, Masque, and Lyric'. In Andrew Hadfield (ed.), *The Oxford Handbook of English Prose, 1500–1640*. Oxford, 2013, 235–50.

Lamb, Mary Ellen and Karen Bamford (eds). *Oral Traditions and Gender in Early Modern Literary Texts*. Aldershot, 2008.

Lambley, Kathleen. *The Teaching and Cultivation of the French Language in England during Tudor and Stuart Times*. Manchester, 1920.

Laroche, Rebecca. *Medical Authority and Englishwomen's Herbal Texts, 1550–1650*. Farnham, 2009.

Larsen, Anne R. *Anna Maria van Schurman, 'The Star of Utrecht': The Educational Vision and Reception of a Savante*. London, 2016.

Larson, Katherine R. *The Matter of Song in Early Modern England: Texts in and of the Air*. Oxford, 2019.

Larson, Katherine R. and Naomi J. Miller (eds). *Re-Reading Mary Wroth*. New York, 2015.

Larson, Katherine R., Scott Trudell, and Sarah Williams (eds). *Early Modern Songscapes*. http:// songscapes.org. Accessed 12 March 2021.

Larson, Katherine. OUP Companion Website: The Matter of Song in Early Modern England'. https:// glo bal.oup.com/ booksites/content/9780198843788/. Accessed 12 March 2021.

Latour, Bruno. *Reassembling the Social*. Oxford, 2007.

Lawrence, Dana E. 'Isabella Whitney's "Slips": Poetry, Collaboration, and Coterie'. In Phillippy (ed.), *A History of Early Modern Women's Writing*, 119–36.

Lawrence-Mathers, Anne and Philippa Hardman (eds). *Women and Writing, c.1340–c.1650: The Domestication of Print Culture*. York, 2010.

Lay, Jenna. *Beyond the Cloister: Catholic Englishwomen and Early Modern Literary Culture*. Philadelphia, PA, 2016.

Leach, Edmund. *Culture and Nature, or La Femme Sauvage [The Stevenson Lecture]*. London, 1968.

Lee, Christine S. 'The Meanings of Romance: Rethinking Early Modern Fiction'. *Modern Philology*, 112.2 (2014), 287–311.

Lefevere, André. 'Mother Courage's Cucumbers: Text, System and Refraction in a Theory of Literature'. *Modern Language Studies*, 12 (1982), 3–20.

Lefevere, André. *Translation, Rewriting and the Manipulation of Literary Fame*. New York, 1992.

Lenz, Carolyn Ruth Swift, Gayle Greene, and Carol Thomas Neely (eds). *The Woman's Part: Feminist Criticism of Shakespeare*. Urbana, IL, 1980.

Leonard, Irving A. *Books of the Brave*. Berkeley, CA, 1992.

Leonardi, Susan. 'Recipes for Reading: Pasta Salad, Lobster a la Riseholme, Key Lime Pie'. *PMLA*, 104.3 (1989), 340–7.

Leong, Elaine. 'Collecting Knowledge for the Family: Recipes, Gender and Practical Knowledge in the Early Modern English Household'. *Centarus*, 55 (2013), 81–103.

Leong, Elaine. '"Herbals she peruseth": Reading Medicine in Early Modern England'. *Renaissance Studies*, 28.4 (2014), 556–78.

Leong, Elaine. 'Making Medicines in the Early Modern Household'. In *Bulletin of the History of Medicine*, 82 (2008), 145–68.

Leong, Elaine. 'Papering the Household: Paper, Recipes, and Everyday Technologies in Early Modern England'. In Carla Bittel, Elaine Leong, and Christine von Oertzen (eds), *Working with Paper: Gendered Practices in the History of Knowledge*. Pittsburgh, 2019, 32–45.

Leong, Elaine, Amanda E. Herbert, R. A. Kashanipour, Sarah Peters Kernan, Joshua Schlachet, Laurence Totelin, and Jess Clark (eds). *The Recipes Project*. Hypotheses. https://recipes.hypotheses.org/. Accessed 5 December 2020.

Leppert, Richard. *The Sight of Sound: Music, Representation, and the History of the Body*. Berkeley, CA, 1993.

Levenson, Jon D. *The Old Testament Library: Esther, A Commentary*. Louisville, KY, 1997.

Levine, Caroline. 'From Nation to Network'. *Victorian Studies*, 55.4 (2013), 647–66.

Levine, Caroline. *Forms: Whole, Rhythm, Hierarchy, Network*. Princeton, NJ, 2015.

Levinson, Marjorie. 'What Is New Formalism?' *PMLA*, 122.2 (2017), 558–69.

Lewalski, Barbara Kiefer. *Protestant Poetics and the Seventeenth-Century Lyric*. Princeton, NJ, 1979.

Lewalski, Barbara Kiefer. 'Re-Writing Patriarchy and Patronage: Margaret Clifford, Anne Clifford, and Aemilia Lanyer'. *The Yearbook of English Studies*, 21 (1991), 87–106.

Lewalski, Barbara Kiefer. *Writing Women in Jacobean England*. Cambridge, MA, 1993.

Lilley, Kate. '"Dear Object": Katherine Philips's Love Elegies and Their Readers'. In Wallwork and Salzman (eds), *Women Writing*, 163–78.

Lilley, Kate. 'Fruits of Sodom: The Critical Erotics of Early Modern Women's Writing'. *Parergon*, 29 (2012), 175–92.

Lilley, Kate. 'Katherine Philips, "Philo-Philippa" and the Poetics of Association'. In Pender and Smith (eds) *Material Cultures of Early Modern Women's Writing*, 118–39.

Lilley, Kate. 'When Sapphos Meet: Louise Imogen Guiney and Katherine Philips' Selected Poems (1904)'. *Women's Writing*, 26 (2019), 106–24.

Lindenbaum, Sarah. 'Hiding in Plain Sight: How Electronic Records Can Lead Us to Early Modern Women Readers'. In Knight, White, and Sauer (eds), *Women's Bookscapes*, 193–213.

Lindenbaum, Sarah. 'Written in the Margent: Frances Wolfreston Revealed'. *The Collation: Research and Exploration at the Folger*, 21 June 2018. https://collation.folger.edu/2018/06/frances-wolfreston-revealed/. Accessed 2 February 2021.

Lindley, David. *Lyric*. London, 1985.

Lindley, David. *The Trials of Frances Howard: Fact and Fiction at the Court of King James*. London, 1993.

Liu, Tessie P. 'Race'. In Richard Wrightman Fox and James T. Kloppenberg (eds), *A Companion to American Thought*. Malden, MA, 1998, 564–7.

Livingston, Carole Rose. *British Broadside Ballads of the Sixteenth Century: A Catalogue of the Extant Sheets and an Essay*. New York, 1991.

Llewellyn, Mark. 'Katherine Philips: Friendship, Poetry and Neo-Platonic Thought in Seventeenth Century England'. *Philological Quarterly*, 81 (2002), 441–68.

Loades, David. *Mary Tudor*. Oxford, 1997.

Loar, Christopher F. 'Exclusion and Desecration: Aphra Behn, Liberalism, and the Politics of the Pindaric Ode'. *Restoration*, 39 (2015), 125–36.

Loewenstein, David. *Representing Revolution in Milton and His Contemporaries: Religion, Politics, and Polemics in Radical Puritanism*. Cambridge, 2001.

Loewenstein, David. 'Scriptural Exegesis, Female Prophecy, and Radical Politics in Mary Cary'. *SEL: Studies in English Literature 1500–1900*, 46 (2001), 133–53.

Longfellow, Erica. *Women and Religious Writing in Early Modern England*. Cambridge, 2004.

Loomba, Ania. 'The Color of Patriarchy: Critical Difference, Cultural Difference, and Renaissance Drama'. In Hendricks and Parker (eds), *Women, 'Race', and Writing*, 17–34.

Loomba, Ania and Melissa Sanchez. 'Feminism and the Burdens of History'. In Loomba and Sanchez (eds), *Rethinking Feminism in Early Modern Studies*, 15–41.

Loomba, Ania and Melissa E. Sanchez (eds). *Rethinking Feminism in Early Modern Studies: Gender, Race, Sexuality*. London, 2016.

Lopez, Jeremy. *Constructing the Canon of Early Modern Drama*. Cambridge, 2014.

Lopez, Jeremy. 'General Introduction'. In Jeremy Lopez (ed.), *The Routledge Anthology of Early Modern Drama*. Abingdon, 2020, 1–3.

Loscocco, Paula. '"Manly Sweetness": Katherine Philips among the Neoclassicals'. *The Huntington Library Quarterly*, 56.3 (1993), 259–79.

Loughlin, Marie. '"Fast Ti'd unto Them in a Golden Chaine": Typology, Apocalypse, and Woman's Genealogy in Aemilia Lanyer's *Salve Deus Rex Judaeorum*'. *Renaissance Quarterly*, 53.1 (2000), 133–79.

Love, Harold. 'How Personal is a Personal Miscellany? Sarah Cowper, Martin Clifford, and the "Buckingham Commonplace Book"'. In R. C. Alston (ed.), *Order and Connexion: Studies in Bibliography and Book History*. Cambridge, 1997, 111–26.

Love, Harold. *Scribal Publication in Seventeenth-Century England*. Oxford, 1993.

Love, Heather. *Feeling Backward: Loss and the Politics of Queer History*. Cambridge, MA, 2007.

Low, Jennifer. 'Surface and Interiority: Self-Creation in Margaret Cavendish's *The Claspe*'. *Philological Quarterly*, 77 (1998), 149–69.

Loxley, James. 'Unfettered Organs: The Polemical Voices of Katherine Philips'. In Clarke and Clarke (eds), *'This Double Voice'*, 230–48.

Luckyj, Christina. *Liberty and the Politics of the Female Voice in Early Stuart England*. Cambridge, 2022.

Luckyj, Christina. '*A Mouzell for Melastomus* in Context: Rereading the Swetnam-Speght Debate'. *English Literary Renaissance*, 40 (2010), 113–31.

Luckyj, Christina. *'A Moving Rhetoricke': Gender and Silence in Early Modern England*. Manchester, 2002.

Luckyj, Christina. 'Reading Overbury's *Wife*: Politics and Marriage in 1616'. In Hannah Crawforth and Sarah Lewis (eds), *Family Politics in Early Modern Literature*. London, 2017, 39–56.

Lux-Sterritt, Laurence. *English Benedictine Nuns in Exile in the Seventeenth Century: Living Spirituality*. Manchester, 2017.

Lyons, Tara L. 'Lady Elizabeth Grey'. In Fehrenbach and Black (eds), *Private Libraries in Renaissance England*, 324–61.

MacDonald, Joyce Green. 'Dark Ladies, Black Bodies: Animating Lucy Negro in Caroline Randall Williams' *Lucy Negro Redux*'. Annual Shakespeare Lecture, George Washington University, 18 September 2020. https://www.youtube.com/watch?v=p41IFoBWK_A. Accessed 6 March 2021.

MacDonald, Joyce Green. 'The Legend of Lucy Negro'. In Janell Hobson (ed.), *The Routledge Companion to Black Women's Cultural Histories*. New York, 2021.

MacDonald, Joyce. 'How Race Might Help Us Find "Lost" Women's Writing'. In Goodrich and McQuade (eds), 'Special Issue', 45–54.

MacDonald, Joyce Green. 'Reading Race in *Women Writers Online*: Thirty Years On'. *Women Writers in Context. Women's Writers Project*. September 2018. https://wwp.northeastern.edu/context/#macdonald.30race.xml. Accessed 6 March 2021.

MacDonald, Joyce Green. *Shakespearean Adaptation, Race and Memory in the New World*. London, 2020.

MacDonald, Joyce Green. *Women and Race in Early Modern Texts*. Oxford, 2002.

Macherey, Pierre. In Geoffrey Wall (trans.), *A Theory of Literary Production*. London, 1978.

Mack, Peter. *Elizabethan Rhetoric: Theory and Practice*. Cambridge, 2002.

Mack, Phyllis. *Visionary Women: Ecstatic Prophecy in Seventeenth-Century England*. Berkeley, CA, 1994.

Maclean, G. M. 'An Edition of Poems on the Restoration'. *Restoration: Studies in English Literary Culture, 1660–1700*, 11 (1987), 117–21.

Maître, Myriam. *Les Précieuses. Naissance des femmes de lettres en France au XVIIe siècle*. Paris, 1999.

Major, Philip. '"Twixt Hope and Fear": John Berkenhead, Henry Lawes and Banishment from London during the English Revolution'. *Review of English Studies*, 59 (2008), 270–80.

Malay, Jessica L. 'Jane Seager's Sibylline Poems: Maidenly Negotiations Through Elizabethan Gift Exchange'. *English Literary Renaissance*, 36 (2006), 173–93.

Malay, Jessica L. 'Positioning Patronage: Lanyer's *Salve Deus Rex Judaeorum* and the Countess of Cumberland in Time and Place'. *The Seventeenth Century*, 28 (2013), 251–74.

Malay, Jessica L. 'Reassessing Anne Clifford's Books: The Discovery of a New Manuscript Inventory'. *Papers of the Bibliographical Society of America*, 115.1 (2021), 1–41.

Malay, Jessica L. 'To Be a Sibyl: Jane Seager's Sibylline Poems'. In Jessica L. Malay (ed.), *Prophecy and Sibylline Imagery in the Renaissance*. New York, 2010, 121–36.

Malcolm, Morgan Lloyd. *Emilia*. London, 2018.

Malcolmson, Cristina. 'Christine de Pizan's *City of Ladies* in Early Modern England'. In Malcolmson and Suzuki (eds), *Debating Gender*, 15–35.

Malcolmson, Cristina and Mihoko Suzuki (eds). *Debating Gender in Early Modern England 1500–1700*. New York, 2002.

Malieckal, Bindu. 'Mariam Khan and the Legacy of Mughal Women in Early Modern Literature of India'. In Bernadette Andrea and Linda McJannet (eds), *Early Modern England and Islamic Worlds*. New York, 2011, 97–121.

Mallinson, Jonathan. '*L'Astrée* en Angleterre au XVIIe siècle'. *Cahiers de l'Association internationale des études françaises*, 60 (2008), 207–24.

Manley, Lawrence. *Literature and Culture in Early Modern London*. Cambridge, 1995.

Manning, David. 'What Was Devotional Writing? Revisiting the Community at Little Gidding, 1626–33'. In Elizabeth Clarke and Robert W. Daniel (eds), *People and Piety: Protestant Devotional Identities in Early Modern England*. Manchester, 2012, 25–42.

Map of Early Modern London. University of Victoria. https://mapoflondon.uvic.ca/index.htm. Accessed 8 April 2021.

Maples, Kwoya Fagin. *Mend*. Lexington, KY, 2018.

Marcus, Leah S. 'Editing Queen Elizabeth I'. In Ross and Salzman (eds), *Editing Early Modern Women's Writing*, 139–55.

Marcus, Leah S. *Unediting the Renaissance: Shakespeare, Marlowe, Milton*. London, 1996.

Marotti, Arthur F. *Manuscript, Print, and the English Renaissance Lyric*. Ithaca, NY, 1995.

Marsh, Christopher. *Music and Society in Early Modern England*. Cambridge, 2010.

Marsh, Christopher. 'The Sound of Print in Early Modern England: The Broadside Ballad as Song'. In Julia Crick and Alexandra Walsham (eds), *The Uses of Script and Print, 1300–1700*. Cambridge, 2004, 171–90.

Marshall, Alan. *Intelligence and Espionage in the Reign of Charles II, 1660–1685*. Cambridge, 1994.

Marshall, Rosalind K. *The Winter Queen: The Life of Elizabeth of Bohemia 1596–1662*. Edinburgh, 1998.

Martin, Jessica and Alec Ryrie (eds). *Private and Domestic Devotion in Early Modern Britain*. Abingdon, 2012.

Martin, Randall. 'Isabella Whitney's "Lamentation upon the Death of William Gruffith"'. *Early Modern Literary Studies*, 3 (1997), 2.1–15.

Maruca, Lisa. *The Work of Print: Authorship and the English Text Trades, 1660–1760*. Seattle, 2007.

Mascuch, Michael. *Origins of the Individualist Self: Autobiography and Self-Identity in England, 1592–1791*. Stanford, CA, 1996.

Mason, Rebecca. 'Women, Marital Status, and Law: The Marital Spectrum in Seventeenth-Century Glasgow'. *Journal of British Studies*, 58 (2019), 787–804.

Massai, Sonia. *Shakespeare and the Rise of the Editor*. Cambridge, 2007.

Massardier-Kenney, Françoise. 'Towards a Redefinition of Feminist Translation Practice'. *The Translator*, 3 (1997), 55–69.

Masten, Jeffrey. 'Margaret Cavendish: Paper, Performance, "Sociable Virginity"'. *Modern Language Quarterly*, 65 (2004), 49–68.

Masten, Jeffrey. '"Shall I Turn Blabb?": Circulation, Gender, and Subjectivity in Mary Wroth's Sonnets'. In Miller and Waller (eds), *Reading Mary Wroth*, 67–87.

Masterman, Margaret. 'The Intellect's New Eye'. In *Freeing the Mind: Articles and Letters from The Times Literary Supplement during March–June, 1962*. London, 1962, 38–44.

Matchinske, Megan. 'Serial Identity: History, Gender, and Form in the Diary Writing of Lady Anne Clifford'. In Dowd and Eckerle (eds), *Genre and Women's Life Writing*, 65–80.

Matthews, David. 'The Medieval Invasion of Early Modern England'. *New Medieval Literatures*, 10 (2008), 223–44.

Matthiessen, F. O. *Translation: An Elizabethan Art*. New York, 1965.

Mauss, Marcel. In W. D. Halls (trans.), *The Gift: The Form and Reason for Exchange in Archaic Societies*. Abingdon, 2008.

May, Steven W. 'Anne Lock and Thomas Norton's Meditation of a Penitent Sinner'. *Modern Philology*, 114.4 (2017), 793–819.

May, Steven W. 'The Renaissance Women's Canon, Past, Present, and Future'. In Goodrich and McQuade (eds), 'Special Issue', 131–40.

May, Steven W. and Arthur F. Marotti. 'Manuscript Culture: Circulation and Transmission'. In Bates (ed.), *A Companion to Renaissance Poetry*, 78–102.

Mazzola, Elizabeth. 'The Renaissance Englishwoman in Code: "Blabbs" and Cryptographers at Elizabeth I's Court'. *Critical Survey*, 22.3 (2010), 1–20.

Mazzola, Elizabeth. 'Schooling Shrews and Grooming Queens in the Tudor Classroom'. *Critical Survey*, 22 (2010), 1–25.

McAreavey, Naomi. 'An Epistolary Account of the Irish Rising of 1641 by the Wife of the Mayor of Waterford [with Text]'. *English Literary Renaissance*, 42.1 (2012), 90–118.

McAreavey, Naomi. '"This is that I may remember what passings that happened in Waterford": Inscribing the 1641 Rising in the Letters of the Wife of the Mayor of Waterford'. *Early Modern Women: An Interdisciplinary Journal*, 5 (2010), 77–109.

McAuley, Gay. 'Place in the Performance Experience'. *Modern Drama*, 46 (2003), 598–613.

McCarthy, Erin A. 'Is There Room for Judith Shakepeare and Her Brother, Too?'. In Goodrich and McQuade (eds), 'Special Issue', 33–44.

McCarthy, Erin A. 'Reading Women Reading Donne in Manuscript and Printed Miscellanies: A Quantitative Approach'. *The Review of English Studies*, 69.291 (2018), 661–85.

McCarthy, Erin A. 'Speculation and Multiple Dedications in *Salve Deus Rex Judaeorum*'. *SEL: Studies in English Literature 1500–1900*, 55 (2015), 45–72.

McCarthy, Penny. 'Autumn 1604: Documentation and Literary Coincidence'. In Paul Salzman and Marion Wynne-Davies (eds), *Mary Wroth and Shakespeare*. London, 2014, 37–46.

McClain, Lisa. *Divided Loyalties? Pushing the Boundaries of Gender and Lay Roles in the Catholic Church, 1534–1829*. London, 2018.

McConica, James. *English Humanists and Reformation Politics under Henry VIII and Edward VI*. Oxford, 1968.

McCray, Lucinda. *Sufferers and Healers: The Experience of Illness in Seventeenth-Century England*. London, 1987.

McCutcheon, Rebecca. 'A Performance Studies Approach to *The Tragedy of Mariam*'. *Early Theatre*, 17 (2014), 187–201.

McDowell, Nicholas. *Poetry and Allegiance in the English Civil Wars: Marvell and the Cause of Wit*. Oxford, 2008.

McDowell, Paula. *The Women of Grub Street: Press, Politics, and Gender in the London Literary Marketplace 1678–1730*. Oxford, 1998.

McGann, Jerome J. *The Textual Condition*. Princeton, NJ, 1991.

McGrath, Lynette. '"Let Us Have Our Libertie Againe": Amelia Lanier's 17th-Century Feminist Voice'. *Women's Studies*, 20 (1992), 331–48.

McGrath, Lynette. *Subjectivity and Women's Poetry in Early Modern England: Why on the Ridge Should She Desire to Go?* New York, 2017.

McIlvenna, Una. 'When the News Was Sung: Ballads as News Media in Early Modern Europe'. *Media History*, 22 (2016), 1–17.

McInnis, David. 'Virginian Culture and Experimental Genre in Aphra Behn's *The Widow Ranter*'. In Jo Wallwork and Paul Salzman (eds), *Early Modern Englishwomen Testing Ideas*. Farnham, 2011, 89–104.

McKeon, Michael. *The Secret History of Domesticity: Public, Private, and the Division of Knowledge*. Baltimore, MD, 2005.

McKitterick, David. 'Women and Their Books in Seventeenth-Century England: The Case of Elizabeth Puckering'. *The Library*, 1.4 (2000), 359–80.

McKnight, Laura Blair. 'Crucifixion or Apocalypse: Reconfiguring the *Eikon Basilike*'. In Donna B. Hamilton and Richard Strier (eds), *Religion, Literature and Politics in Post-Reformation England, 1540–1688*. Cambridge, 2009, 138–60.

McManus, Clare. '"Sing It Like Poor Barbary": *Othello* and Early Modern Women's Performance'. In Clare McManus and Lucy Munro (eds), 'Special Issue: Renaissance Women's Performance and the Dramatic Canon'. *Shakespeare Bulletin*, 33 (2015), 99–120.

McManus, Clare (ed.). *Women and Culture at the Courts of the Stuart Queens*. New York, 2003.

McManus, Clare. *Women on the Renaissance Stage: Anna of Denmark and Female Masquing in the Stuart Court, 1590–1619*. Manchester, 2002.

McManus, Clare and Lucy Munro. 'Renaissance Women's Performance and the Dramatic Canon'. *Shakespeare Bulletin*, 33 (2015), 1–7.

McMullan, Gordon. '"Our Whole Life Is Like a Play": Collaboration and the Problem of Editing'. *Textus*, 9 (1996), 437–60.

McMullen, Norma. 'The Education of English Gentlewomen 1540–1640'. *History of Education*, 6 (1977), 87–101.

McMurran, Mary Helen. *The Spread of Novels. Translation and Prose Fiction in the Eighteenth Century*. Princeton, NJ, 2010.

McQuade, Paula. '"A Knowing People": Early Modern Motherhood, Female Authorship, and Working-Class Community in Dorothy Burch's *A Catechism of the Several Heads of the Christian Religion* (1646)'. *Prose Studies*, 32 (2010), 167–86.

McQuade, Paula. *Catechisms and Women's Writing in Seventeenth-Century England*. Cambridge, 2017.

McQuade, Paula. *Catechisms Written for Mothers, Schoolmistresses, and Children, 1575–1750*. Aldershot, 2008.

McShane, Angela. '*The Gazet in Metre; or the Rhiming Newsmonger*: The English Broadside Ballad as Intelligencer'. In Joop W. Koopmans (ed.), *News and Politics in Early Modern Europe (1500–1800)*. Leuven, 2005, 131–52.

McShane, Angela. 'Political Street Songs and Singers in Seventeenth-Century England'. In Luca Degl'Innocenti and Massimo Rospocher (eds), 'Special Issue: Street Singers in Renaissance Europe'. *Renaissance Studies*, 33 (2018), 94–118.

McShane, Bronagh Ann. 'Visualising the Reception and Circulation of Early Modern Nuns' Letters'. *Journal of Historical Network Research*, 2 (2018), 1–25.

Medici, Catherine. 'Using Network Analysis to Understand Early Modern Women'. *Early Modern Women*, 13.1 (2018), 153–62.

Mejia-LaPerle, Carol. 'Access and Agency in Elizabeth Cary's *The Tragedy of Mariam*: Early Modern Closet Drama and the Spatialization of Power'. *Literature Compass*, 3.2 (2006), 80–94.

Melnikoff, Kirk. 'Isabella Whitney among the Stalls of Richard Jones'. In Wayne (ed.), *Women's Labour and the History of the Book*, 145–61.

Melnikoff, Kirk. 'Thomas Hacket and the Ventures of an Elizabethan Publisher'. *The Library*, 10 (2009), 257–71.

Mendelson, Sara and Patricia Crawford. *Women in Early Modern England*. Oxford, 1998.

Merleau-Ponty, Maurice. In Claude Lefort (ed.) and Alphonso Lingis (trans.), *The Visible and Invisible*. Evanston, IL, 1968.

Miller, Naomi. *Imperfect Alchemist: A Novel of Mary Sidney Herbert, Renaissance Pioneer*. London, 2020.

Miller, Naomi J. '"Not Much to Be Marked": Narrative of the Woman's Part in Lady Mary Wroth's Urania'. *SEL: Studies in English Literature 1500–1900*, 29 (1989), 121–37.

Miller, Naomi J. 'Playing with Margaret Cavendish and Mary Wroth'. *Early Modern Women: An Interdisciplinary Journal*, 10 (2016), 95–110.

Miller, Naomi J. and Gary Waller (eds). *Reading Mary Wroth: Representing Alternatives in Early Modern England.* Knoxville, TN, 1996.

Millman, Jill Seal and Gillian Wright (eds). *Early Modern Women's Manuscript Poetry.* Manchester, 2005.

Milsom, John. 'The Nonsuch Music Library'. In Chris Banks, Arthur Searle, and Malcolm Turner (eds), *Sundry Sorts of Music Books: Essays on the British Library Collections.* London, 1993, 146–82.

Mistress Elizabeth Davenant, Her Songes. Performed by Rebecca Ockenden and Sofie Vanden Eynde. Ramée Records, 2011.

Mohanty, Chandra Talpade. 'Under Western Eyes: Feminist Scholarship and Colonial Discourses'. *boundary 2*, 12.3 (1984), 333–58.

Mohanty, Chandra Talpade. 'Under Western Eyes: Feminist Scholarship and Colonial Discourses'. In Chandra Talpade Mohanty, Ann Russo, and Lourdes Torres (eds), *Third World Women and the Politics of Feminism.* Bloomington, IN, 1991, 51–80.

Molekamp, Femke. *Women and the Bible in Early Modern England: Religious Reading and Writing.* Oxford, 2013.

Moncrief, Kathryn M. and Kathryn R. McPherson. '"Shall I Teach You to Know?": Intersections of Pedagogy, Performance, and Gender'. In Moncrief and McPherson (eds), *Performing Pedagogy in Early Modern England: Gender, Instruction, and Performance.* Farnham, 2011, 1–20.

Moody, Ellen. 'List and Bibliography: All Sources for Finch's Fables, Plays, Lyrics, Satires and Devotional Poetry'. http://www.jimandellen.org/masterlist.fables.html. Accessed 30 September 2020.

Moore, Shawn. 'Networks as Constructs: The Curious Case of Margaret Cavendish, Duchess of Newcastle (1623?–1673)'. *The Digital Cavendish Project*, 22 June 2013. http://digitalcavendish.org/2013/06/22/networks-as-constructs/. Accessed 8 April 2021.

Morgan, Jennifer L. '*Partus sequitur ventrem*: Law, Race, and Reproduction in Colonial Slavery'. *Small Axe*, 55 (2018), 1–17.

Morgan, Jennifer L. '"Some Could Suckle over Their Shoulder": Male Travelers, Female Bodies, and the Gendering of Racial Ideology, 1500–1770'. *The William and Mary Quarterly*, 54.1, 167–92.

Moro, António and Sánchez Coello. 'A princesa esquecida: D. Maria de Portugal (1521–1578)'. In Annemarie Jordan (ed.), *Retrato de corte em Portugal: O Legado de António Moro (1552–1572).* Lisbon, 1994, 63–72.

Morris, Christopher (ed.). *The Illustrated Journeys of Celia Fiennes, 1685–1712.* London, 1982.

Morris, John and Philip Oldfield. *British Armorial Bindings.* University of Toronto. armorial.library.utoronto.ca/stamp-owners-by-centuries?field_gender_value=F&items_per_page=100. Accessed 2 February 2021.

Morrissey, Lee. '"Behold This Creature's form and State": Katherine Philips and the Early Ascendancy'. *Women's Writing*, 24.3 (2017), 298–312.

Moss, Ann. *Printed Common-Place Books and the Structuring of Renaissance Thought.* Oxford, 1996.

Mueller, Janel. 'Complications of Intertextuality: John Fisher, Katherine Parr and "The Book of the Crucifix"'. In Cedric C. Brown and Arthur F. Marotti (eds), *Texts and Cultural Change in Early Modern England.* Basingstoke, 1997, 15–36.

Mueller, Janel. 'Devotion as Difference: Intertextuality in Queen Katherine Parr's "Prayers or Meditations" (1545)'. *The Huntington Library Quarterly*, 53.3 (1990), 171–97.

Mueller, Janel. 'The Feminist Poetics of *Salve Deus Rex Judaeoreum*'. In Grossman (ed.), *Aemilia Lanyer: Gender, Genre, and the Canon*, 99–127.

Mueller, Janel. 'Prospecting for Common Ground in Devotion: Queen Katherine Parr's Personal Prayer Book'. In White (ed.), *English Women, Religion, and Textual Production*, 127–46.

Mukherji, Subha. *Law and Representation in Early Modern Drama*. Cambridge, 2006.

Muldrew, Craig. *The Economy of Obligation: The Culture of Credit*. London, 1998.

Mullan, David George (ed.). *Women's Life Writing in Early Modern Scotland: Writing the Evangelical Self, c. 1670–1730*. Aldershot, 2003.

Munroe, Jennifer. '"In this Strang Labourinth, How Shall I Turne": Needlework, Gardens and Writing in Mary Wroth's Pamphilia to Amphilanthus'. *Tulsa Studies in Women's Literature*, 24 (2005), 33–55.

Murphy, Emilie K. M. 'Exile and Linguistic Encounter: Early Modern English Convents in the Low Countries and France'. *Renaissance Quarterly*, 73 (2020), 132–64.

Murphy, Emilie K. M. 'Language and Power in an English Convent in Exile, *c* 1621–1631'. *The Historical Journal*, 62 (2019), 101–25.

Murphy, Erin. '"I remain, an airy phantasme": Lucy Hutchinson's Civil War Ghost Writing'. *English Literary History*, 82 (2015), 87–113.

Nardizzi, Vin and Miriam Jacobson. 'The Secrets of Grafting in Wroth's *Urania*'. In Jennifer Munroe and Rebecca Laroche (eds), *Ecofeminist Approaches to Early Modernity*. Basingstoke, 2011, 175–94.

Narveson, Kate. 'Authority, Scripture, and Typography in Lady Grace Mildmay's Manuscript Meditations'. In White (ed.), *English Women, Religion, and Textual Production*, 167–84.

Narveson, Kate. *Bible Readers and Lay Writers in Early Modern England: Gender and Self-Definition in an Emergent Writing Culture*. Farnham, 2012.

Nelson, Holly Faith and Sharon Alker. 'Memory, Monuments, and Melancholic Genius in Margaret Cavendish's *Bell in Campo*'. *Eighteenth Century Fiction*, 21 (2008), 13–35.

Nelson, Katie. 'Love in the Music Room: Thomas Whythorne and the Private Affairs of Tudor Music Tutors'. *Early Music*, 40 (2012), 15–26.

Nesler, Miranda. 'Closeted Authority in *The Tragedy of Mariam*'. *SEL: Studies in English Literature 1500–1900*, 52.2 (2012), 363–85.

Nevitt, Marcus. '"Blessed, Self-Denying, Lambe-Like"? The Fifth Monarchist Women'. *Critical Survey*, 11 (1999), 83–97.

Newcomb, Lori Humphrey. 'Frances Wolfreston's Annotations as Labours of Love'. In Wayne (ed.), *Women's Labour and the History of the Book*, 243–66.

Newcomb, Lori Humphrey. 'Gendering Prose Romance in Renaissance England'. In Corinne Saunders (ed.), *A Companion to Romance: From Classical to Contemporary*. Malden, MA, 2004.

Newdigate, Bernard. *Michael Drayton and His Circle*. Oxford, 1941.

Newell, Aimee E. 'Tattered to Pieces: Amy Fiske's Sampler and the Changing Roles of Women in Antebellum New England'. In Goggin and Fowkes Tobin (eds), *Women and the Material Culture of Needlework*, 51–68.

Newlyn, Evelyn S. 'A Methodology for Reading against the Culture: Anonymous, Women Poets, and the Maitland Quarto Manuscript (c. 1586)'. In Dunnigan, Harker, and Newlyn (eds), *Woman and the Feminine*, 89–103.

NEWW Women Writers. Huygens Institute. http://resources.huygens.knaw.nl/womenwriters/ . Accessed 8 April 2021.

Nicolas, Nicholas Harris. *The Literary Remains of Lady Jane Grey: With a Memoir of Her Life*. London, 1825.

Noble, Safiya Umoja. *Algorithms of Oppression: How Search Engines Reinforce Racism*. New York, 2018.

Norbrook, David. 'Autonomy and the Republic of Letters: Michèle le Dœuff, Anna Maria van Schurman, and the History of Women Intellectuals'. *Australian Journal of French Studies*, 40 (2003), 275–87.

Norbrook, David. '"But a Copie": Textual Authority and Gender in Editions of "The Life of John Hutchinson"'. In W. Speed Hill (ed.), *New Ways of Looking at Old Texts, III: Papers of the Renaissance English Text Society, 1997–2001*. Tempe, AZ, 2004, 109–30.

Norbrook, David. 'Memoirs and Oblivion: Lucy Hutchinson and the Restoration'. *Huntington Library Quarterly*, 75 (2012), 233–82.

Norbrook, David. 'Women, the Republic of Letters, and the Public Sphere in the Mid-Seventeenth Century'. *Criticism*, 46 (2004), 223–40.

Norbrook, David. '"Words More Than Civil": Republican Civility in Lucy Hutchinson's "The Life of John Hutchinson"'. In Jennifer Richards (ed.), *Early Modern Civil Discourses*. Houndmills, 2003, 68–84.

Nord, Christiane. *Translation as a Purposeful Activity: Functionalist Approaches Explained*. Manchester, 1997.

North, Marcy L. 'Ambiguities of Female Authorship and the Accessible Archive'. In Coles and Keller (eds), *The Routledge Companion to Women, Sex and Gender in the British Colonial World*, 73–87.

North, Marcy L. *The Anonymous Renaissance: Cultures of Discretion in Tudor-Stuart England*. Chicago, IL, 2003.

North, Marcy L. 'Women, the Material Book and Early Printing'. In Knoppers (ed.), *The Cambridge Companion to Early Modern Women's Writing*, 68–82.

Nussbaum, Felicity A. *The Autobiographical Subject: Gender and Ideology in Eighteenth-Century England*. Baltimore, MD, 1989.

Ó Baoill, Colm. '"Neither out Nor in": Scottish Gaelic Women Poets, 1650–1750'. In Dunnigan, Harker, and Newlyn (eds), *Woman and the Feminine*, 136–52.

O'Callaghan, Michelle. *Crafting Poetry Anthologies in Renaissance England: Early Modern Cultures of Recreation*. Cambridge, 2020.

O'Callaghan, Michelle. '"Good Ladies Be Working": Singing at Work in Tudor Woman's Song'. In Jennifer Richards and Richard Wistreich (eds), 'Special Issue: Voicing Text 1500–1700'. *Huntington Library Quarterly*, 82 (2019), 107–26.

O'Callaghan, Michelle. '"My Printer Must, Haue Somwhat to his Share": Isabella Whitney, Richard Jones, and Crafting Books'. *Women's Writing*, 26 (2019), 15–34.

O'Callaghan, Michelle. *'The Shepheards Nation': Jacobean Spenserians and Early Stuart Political Culture, 1612–1625*. Oxford, 2000.

O'Connor, Marion. 'Rachel Fane's May Masque at Apethorpe, 1627'. *English Literary Renaissance*, 36 (2006), 90–213.

Oh, Elisa. 'Advance and Retreat: Reading English Colonial Choreographies of Pocahontas'. In Akhimie and Andrea (eds), *Travel and Travail*, 139–57.

Olguín, B. V. 'Raza'. In Deborah R. Vargas, Nancy Raquel Mirabal, and Lawrence La Fountain-Stokes (eds), *Keywords for Latina/o Studies*. New York, 2017, 188–92.

Oman, Carola. *Mary of Modena*. London, 1962.

Orgel, Stephen. *The Illusion of Power: Political Theatre in the English Renaissance*. Berkeley, CA, 1975.

Orgel, Stephen. *Impersonations: The Performance of Gender in Shakespeare's England*. Cambridge, 1996.

Orgel, Stephen. *The Reader in the Book: A Study of Spaces and Traces*. Oxford, 2015.

Orgel, Stephen and Roy Strong. *Inigo Jones: The Theatre of the Stuart Court*, 2 vols. Berkeley, CA, 1973.

Orlemanski, Julie. 'Who Has Fiction? Modernity, Fictionality, and the Middle Ages'. *New Literary History*, 50 (2019), 145–70.

Orlin, Lena Cowen. *Elizabethan Households: An Anthology*. Washington, DC, 1995.

Orlin, Lena Cowen. *Locating Privacy in Early Modern London*. Oxford, 2007.

Orr, Leah. *Novel Ventures: Fiction and Print Culture in England, 1690–1730*. Charlottesville, VA, 2017.

Ostovich, Helen. 'Hell for Lovers: Shades of Adultery in *The Devil Is an Ass*'. In Julie Sanders with Kate Chedgzoy and Susan Wiseman (eds), *Refashioning Ben Jonson: Gender, Politics and the Jonsonian Canon*. London, 1998, 155–82.

Ottway, Sheila. 'They Only Lived Twice: Public and Private Selfhood in the Autobiographies of Anne, Lady Halkett and Colonel Joseph Bampfield'. In Henk Dragstra, Sheila Ottway, and Helen Wilcox (eds), *Betraying Our Selves: Forms of Self-Representation in Early Modern English Texts*. Basingstoke, 2000, 136–47.

Ozment, Kate. 'Rationale for Feminist Bibliography'. *Textual Cultures*, 13 (2020), 149–78.

Pal, Carol. *Republic of Women: Rethinking the Republic of Letters in the Seventeenth Century*. Cambridge, 2012.

Palmer, Carole L. 'Thematic Research Collections'. In Susan Schreibman, Ray Siemens, and John Unsworth (eds), *A Companion to Digital Humanities*. Oxford, 2004. http://digitalhumanities.org:3030/companion. Accessed 8 April 2021.

Parker, Patricia. *Inescapable Romance: Studies in the Poetics of a Mode*. Princeton, NJ, 1979.

Parker, Patricia. *Shakespeare from the Margins: Language, Culture, Context*. Chicago, IL, 1996.

Parker, Rozsika. *The Subversive Stitch: Embroidery and the Making of the Feminine*. London, 1984, repr. 1989.

Parry, Glynn and Cathryn Enis. *Shakespeare before Shakespeare: Stratford upon Avon, Warwickshire and the Elizabethan State*. Oxford, 2020.

Passanante, Gerard. *The Lucretian Renaissance: Philology and the Afterlife of Tradition*. Chicago, IL, 2011.

Patterson, Annabel and Martin Dzelzainis. 'Marvell and the Earl of Anglesey: A Chapter in the History of Reading'. *The Historical Journal*, 44 (2001), 703–26.

Patton, Elizabeth. 'Women, Books, and the Lay Apostolate: A Catholic Literary Network in Late Sixteenth-Century England'. In Knight, White, and Sauer (eds), *Women's Bookscapes*, 117–34.

Pearson, David. *Book Owners Online*. University College London Centre for Editing Lives and Letters. https://bookowners.online/Main_Page. Accessed 2 February 2021.

Pearson, David. *English Book Owners in the Seventeenth Century: A Work in Progress Listing*. https://bibsocamer.org/BibSite/Pearson/Pearson.pdf. Accessed 2 February 2021.

Pelling, Margaret. *Medical Conflicts in Early Modern London: Patronage, Physicians, and Irregular Practitioners, 1550–1640*. Oxford, 2003.

Peltonen, Markku. *Classical Humanism and Republicanism in English Political Thought, 1570–1640*. Cambridge, 1995.

Pender, Patricia. 'Disciplining the Imperial Mother: Anne Bradstreet's *A Dialogue between Old England and New*'. In Wallwork and Salzman (eds), *Women Writing*, 115–31.

Pender, Patricia. 'Dispensing Quails, Mincemeat, Leaven: Katherine Parr's Patronage of the *Paraphrases* of Erasmus'. In Pender and Smith (eds), *Material Cultures*, 36–54.

Pender, Patricia. *Early Modern Women's Writing and the Rhetoric of Modesty*. New York, 2012.

Pender, Patricia (ed.). *Gender, Authorship, and Early Modern Women's Collaboration*. Basingstoke, 2017.

Pender, Patricia. 'The Ghost in the Machine in the Sidney Family Corpus'. *SEL: Studies in English Literature 1500–1900*, 51 (2011), 65–85.

Pender, Patricia. '"A worme most abjecte": *Sermo Humilis* as Reformation Strategy in Katherine Parr's *Prayers or Medytacions*'. In Pender (ed.), *Early Modern Women's Writing and the Rhetoric of Modesty*. New York, 2012, 64–91.

Pender, Patricia and Alexandra Day. 'Introduction: Gender, Authorship, and Early Modern Women's Collaboration'. In Pender (ed.), *Gender, Authorship and Early Modern Women's Collaboration*, 1–19.

Pender, Patricia and Rosalind Smith. 'Editing Early Modern Women in the Digital Age'. In Ross and Salzman (eds), *Editing Early Modern Women*, 255–69.

Pender, Patricia and Rosalind Smith (eds). *Material Cultures of Early Modern Women's Writing*. Basingstoke, 2014.

Pender, Patricia and Rosalind Smith (eds). *The Palgrave Encyclopedia of Early Modern Women's Writing in English*. London, 2021–.

Pennell, Sara. 'Perfecting Practice? Women, Manuscript Recipes and Knowledge in Early Modern England'. In Burke and Gibson (eds), *Early Modern Women's Manuscript Writing*, 237–58.

Perdita. University of Warwick. http://web.warwick.ac.uk/english/perdita/html/. Accessed 8 April 2021.

Perdita Manuscripts, 1500–1700. Adam Matthew Digital. https://www.amdigital.co.uk/primary%E2%80%93sources/index.php?option=com_content&view=featured&Itemid=101. Accessed 12 June 2021.

Performing the Queen's Men: Exploring Theatre History through Performance. http://thequeensmen.mcmaster.ca. Accessed 12 March 2021.

Performance as Research in Early English Theatre Studies: The Three Ladies of London in Context. http://threeladiesoflondon.mcmaster.ca. Accessed 12 March 2021.

Pestana, Carla Gardina. *The English Atlantic in an Age of Revolution, 1640–1661*. Cambridge, MA, 2004.

Phillippy, Patricia. 'Anne Bradstreet's Family Plots: Puritanism, Humanism, Posthumanism'. *Criticism*, 62.1 (2020), 29–68.

Phillippy, Patricia (ed.). *A History of Early Modern Women's Writing*. Cambridge, 2018.

Pink, Gillian and Dan Barker. 'Digitising the Margins: A Classification of Voltaire's Squiggles'. Voltaire Foundation, University of Oxford, 12 November 2020. https://voltairefoundation.wordpress.com/2020/11/12/digitising-the-margins-a-classification-of-voltaires-scribbles/. Accessed 30 April 2022.

Pizzagalli, Daniela. *Tra due dinastie. Bianca Maria Visconti e il ducato di Milano*. Milan, 1988.

Plane, Ann Marie and Leslie Tuttle. 'Review Essay: Dreams and Dreaming in the Early Modern World'. *Renaissance Quarterly*, 67.3 (2014), 917–31.

Poitevin, Kimberly. '"Counterfeit Colour": Making up Race in Elizabeth Cary's *The Tragedy of Mariam*'. *Tulsa Studies in Women's Literature*, 24.1 (2005), 13–34.

Pollmann, Judith. 'Archiving the Present and Chronicling the Future in Early Modern Europe'. *Past and Present* Supplement 11 (2016), 232–52.

Pollnitz, Aysha. *Princely Education in Early Modern Britain*. Cambridge, 2015.

Pollock, Linda. *With Faith and Physic: The Life of a Tudor Gentlewoman, Lady Grace Mildmay 1552–1620*. London, 1993.

Poole, William. 'Margaret Cavendish's Books in New College, and around Oxford'. *New College Notes*, 6 (2015), 1–8. New College, University of Oxford. https://www.new.ox.ac.uk/new-college-notes. Accessed 8 November 2020.

Potter, Lois. *Secret Rites and Secret Writing: Royalist Literature 1641–1660*. Cambridge, 1989.

Povinelli, Elizabeth. 'Notes on Gridlock: Genealogy, Intimacy, Sexuality'. *Public Culture*, 14.1 (2002), 215–38.

Prendergast, Maria. *Railing, Reviling and Invective in English Literary Culture 1588–1617: The Anti-Poetics of Theater and Print*. London, 2016.

Prescott, Anne Lake. 'A Year in the Life of King Saul: 1643'. In Kevin Killeen, Helen Smith, and Rachel Willie (eds), *Oxford Handbook of the Bible in Early Modern England, c. 1530–1700*. Oxford, 2015, 412–26.

Prescott, Sarah. 'Archipelagic Coterie Space: Katherine Philips and Welsh Women's Writing'. *Tulsa Studies in Women's Literature*, 33 (2014), 51–76.

Prescott, Sarah. '"That private shade, wherein my Muse was bred": Katherine Philips and the Poetic Spaces of Welsh Retirement'. *Philological Quarterly*, 88 (2009), 345–64.

Preston, Claire. *The Poetics of Scientific Investigation in Seventeenth-Century England*. Oxford, 2015.

Preston, Claire. 'Utopian Intelligences: Scientific Correspondence and Christian Virtuousos'. In Anne Dunan-Page and Clotilde Prunier (eds), *Debating the Faith: Religion and Letter Writing in Great Britain, 1550–1800*. Dordrecht, 2012, 139–58.

Price, Bronwen. 'Verse, Voice, and Body: The Retirement Mode and Women's Poetry 1680–1723'. *Early Modern Literary Studies*, 12.3 (2007), 5.1–5.44, http://purl.oclc.org/emls/12-3/priceve2.htm. Accessed 2 June 2021.

Primary Source Cooperative. Massachusetts Historical Society. http://primarysourcecoop.org. Accessed 8 April 2021.

Prior, Mary (ed.). *Women in English Society 1500–1800*. London, 1985.

Pristash, Heather, Inez Schaechterle, and Sue Carter Wood. 'The Needle as Pen: Intentionality, Needlework and the Production of Alternate Discourses of Power'. In Goggin and Tobin (eds), *Women and the Material Culture of Needlework*, 15–27.

Purdie, Rhiannon. 'Medieval Romance in Scotland'. In Priscilla Bawcutt and Janet Hadley Williams (eds), *A Companion to Medieval Scottish Poetry*. Cambridge, 2006, 165–77.

Purkiss, Diane. 'Anna Trapnel's Literary Geography'. In Harris and Scott-Baumann (eds), *The Intellectual Culture of Puritan Women*, 162–75.

Purkiss, Diane. 'Material Girls: The Seventeenth-Century Woman Debate'. In Clare Brant and Diane Purkiss (eds), *Women Texts and Histories 1575–1760*. London, 1992, 69–101.

Purkiss, Diane. 'Producing the Voice, Consuming the Body: Women Prophets of the Seventeenth Century'. In Isobel Grundy and Susan Wiseman (eds), *Women, Writing, History 1640–1740*. London, 1992.

Purkiss, Diane. 'Rooms of All Our Own: A History of Ignoring Early Women Writers'. *Times Literary Supplement* (15 February 2019), 10–11.

Quilligan, Maureen. 'Elizabeth's Embroidery'. *Shakespeare Studies*, 28 (2000), 208–14.

Quilligan, Maureen. *Incest and Agency in Elizabeth's England*. Philadelphia, PA, 2005.

Quilligan, Maureen. 'Staging Gender: William Shakespeare and Elizabeth Cary'. In Karen Raber (ed.), *Ashgate Critical Essays on Women Writers in England, 1550–1700: Elizabeth Cary*. Farnham, 2009, 527–51.

Raab, Felix. *The English Face of Machiavelli: A Changing Interpretation 1500–1700*. London, 1964.

Raber, Karen. *Dramatic Difference: Gender, Class, and Genre in the Early Modern Closet Drama*. Newark, 2001.

RaceB4Race Executive Board. 'It's Time to End the Publishing Gatekeeping! A Letter from RaceB4Race Executive Board'. *The Sundial*, 11 June 2020, https://medium.com/the-sundial-acmrs/its-time-to-end-the-publishing-gatekeeping-75207525f587. Accessed 6 March 2021.

Rambuss, Richard. *Closet Devotions*. Durham, NC, 1998.

Ravelhofer, Barbara. *The Early Stuart Masque: Dance, Costume, and Music*. Oxford, 2006.

Raymond, Joad. *Pamphlets and Pamphleteering in Early Modern Britain*. Cambridge, 2003.

Razzall, Lucy. '"A good Booke is the pretious life-blood of a master-spirit": Recollecting Relics in Post-Reformation English Writing'. *Journal of the Northern Renaissance*, 2 (2010), http://northernrenaissance.org. Accessed 6 December 2020.

RECIRC: The Reception and Circulation of Early Modern Women's Writing, 1550–1700. Directed by Marie-Louise Coolahan. https://recirc.nuigalway.ie/. Accessed 23 November 2020.

Reid, Lindsay Ann. 'The Brief Ovidian Career of Isabella Whitney: From Heroidean to Tristian Complaint'. In Ross and Smith (eds), *Early Modern Women's Complaint*, 89–113.

Reid, W. Stanford. *Trumpeter of God: A Biography of John Knox*. New York, 1974.

retroReveal. retroreveal.org. Accessed 2 February 2021.

Reid Baxter, Jamie. 'Elizabeth Melville, Calvinism and the Lyric Voice'. In David J. Parkinson (ed.), *James VI and I, Literature and Scotland: Tides of Change, 1567–1625*. Leuven, 2013, 151–72.

Reid Baxter, Jamie. 'Elizabeth Melville, Lady Culross: 3500 New Lines of Verse'. In Dunnigan, Harker, and Newlyn (eds), *Woman and the Feminine*, 195–200.

Reid Baxter, Jamie. 'Elizabeth Melville, Lady Culross: New Light from Fife'. *Innes Review*, 68.1 (2017), 38–77.

Reid Baxter, Jamie. 'Presbytery, Politics and Poetry: Maister Robert Bruce, John Burel and Elizabeth Melville, Lady Culross'. *Records of the Scottish Church History Society*, 33 (2003), 6–27.

Reid Baxter, Jamie. 'The Songs of Lady Culross'. In Gordon Munro, Stuart Campbell, Greta-Mary Hair, Margaret Mackay, Elaine Moohan, and Graham Hair (eds), *Notis Musycall: Essays on Music and Scottish Culture in Honour of Kenneth Elliott*. Glasgow, 2005, 143–63.

Revard, Stella. 'Thomas Stanley and "A Register of Friends"'. In Claude J. Summers and Ted-Larry Pebworth (eds), *Literary Circles and Cultural Communities in Renaissance England*. London, 2000, 148–72.

Rhodes, Neil. *Common: The Development of Literary Culture in Sixteenth-Century England*. Oxford, 2018.

Richards, Jennifer. *Voices and Books in the English Renaissance: A New History of Reading*. Oxford, 2019.

Richards, Jennifer and Fred Schurink. 'Introduction: The Textuality and Materiality of Reading in Early Modern England'. *Huntington Library Quarterly*, 73 (2010), 345–61.

Richards, Jennifer and Alison Thorne (eds). *Rhetoric, Women and Politics in Early Modern England*. London, 2007.

Richardson, Catherine. 'Early Modern Plays and Domestic Space'. *Home Cultures*, 2.3 (2005), 269–83.

Richardson, Catherine. 'Household Writing'. In Caroline Bicks and Jennifer Summit (eds), *The History of British Women's Writing, 1500–1610*, vol. 2. London, 2010, 89–107.

Richardson, Catherine. *Shakespeare and Material Culture*. Oxford, 2011.

Riley, Denise. *'Am I That Name?' Feminism and the Category of 'Woman' in History*. Minneapolis, MN, 1988.

Roberts, Josephine A. 'Editing the Women Writers of Early Modern England'. *Shakespeare Studies*, 24 (1996), 63–70.
Roberts, Josephine A. 'The Phallacies of Authorship'. In Susan Dwyer Amussen and Adele F. Seeff (eds), *Attending to Early Modern Women*. Newark, 1998, 38–57.
Roberts, J. R. (ed.). *New Perspectives on the Seventeenth-Century Religious Lyric*. Columbia, MO, 1994.
Roberts, Sasha. 'Engendering the Female Reader: Women's Recreational Reading of Shakespeare in Early Modern England'. In Brayman Hackel and Kelly (eds), *Reading Women*, 36–54.
Roberts, Sasha. *Reading Shakespeare's Poems in Early Modern England*. Houndmills, 2003.
Rodgers, Sarah. 'Embedded Poetry and Coterie Readers in Mary Wroth's *Urania*'. *Studies in Philology*, 111.3 (2014), 470–85.
Rogers, John. 'The Passion of a Female Literary Tradition: Aemilia Lanyer's *Salve Deus Rex Judaeoreum*'. In Anne K. Mellor, Felicity Nussbaum, and Jonathan F. S. Post (eds), *Forging Connections: Women's Poetry from the Renaissance to Romanticism*. San Marino, CA, 2002, 7–18.
Roper, Lyndal. *Oedipus & the Devil: Witchcraft, Sexuality and Religion in Early Modern Europe*. London, 1994.
Ross, Sarah C. E. 'Coteries, Circles, Networks: The Cavendish Circle and Civil War Women's Writing'. In Phillippy (ed.), *A History of Early Modern Women's Writing*, 332–47.
Ross, Sarah C. E. 'Early Modern Women and the Apparatus of Authorship'. *Parergon*, 29 (2012), 1–8.
Ross, Sarah C. E. 'Elizabeth Melville: Textual History'. *Early Modern Women Research Network*, 2017. https://c21ch.newcastle.edu.au/emwrn/elizabethmelville. Accessed 2 June 2021.
Ross, Sarah C. E. 'Elizabeth Melville and the Religious Sonnet Sequence in Scotland and England'. In Susan Wiseman (ed.), *Early Modern Women and the Poem*. Manchester, 2013, 42–59.
Ross, Sarah C. E. '"Like Penelope, Always Employed": Reading, Life-Writing, and the Early Modern Female Self in Katherine Austen's *Book M*'. *Literature Compass*, 9 (2012), 306–16.
Ross, Sarah C. E. 'Peripatetic Poems: Sites of Production and Routes of Exchange in Elizabeth Melville's Scotland'. *Women's Writing*, 26.1 (2019), 53–70.
Ross, Sarah C. E. *Women, Poetry, and Politics in Seventeenth-Century Britain*. Oxford, 2015.
Ross, Sarah C. E. and Paul Salzman (eds). *Editing Early Modern Women*. Cambridge, 2016.
Ross, Sarah C. E. and Elizabeth Scott-Baumann. '"Corrected by the Author": Women, Poetry, and Seventeenth-Century Print Publication'. *Huntington Library Quarterly*, 84.2 (2021), 353–81.
Ross, Sarah C. E. and Elizabeth Scott-Baumann (eds). *Women Poets of the English Civil War*. Manchester, 2018.
Ross, Sarah C. E. and Rosalind Smith. 'Beyond Ovid: Early Modern Women's Complaint'. In Ross and Smith (eds), *Early Modern Women's Complaint*, 1–26.
Ross, Sarah C. E. and Rosalind Smith (eds). *Early Modern Women's Complaint: Gender, Form, and Politics*. London, 2020.
Rossi, Carla. *Italus ore, Anglus pectore: studi su John Florio*, vol. 1. London, 2018.
Rossi, Paolo. *Logic and the Art of Memory*. Chicago, IL, 1960.
Round, Phillip H. *By Nature and by Custom Cursed: Transatlantic Civil Discourse and New England Cultural Production, 1620–1660*. Hanover, NH, 1999.
Rubin, Gayle. 'Thinking Sex: Notes for a Radical Theory of the Politics of Sexuality'. In Carole S. Vance (ed.), *Pleasure and Danger: Exploring Female Sexuality*. Boston, MA, 1984, 267–319.
Rubright, Marjorie. *Doppelgänger Dilemmas: Anglo-Dutch Relations in Early Modern English Literature and Culture*. Philadelphia, PA, 2014.

Russ, Joanna. *How to Suppress Women's Writing*. Austin, TX, 2018.

Ryrie, Alec. *Being Protestant in Reformation Britain*. Oxford, 2013.

Sae, Kitamura. 'A Shakespeare of One's Own: Female Users of Playbooks from the Seventeenth to the Mid-Eighteenth Century'. *Palgrave Communications*, 3 (2017). doi: 10.1057/palcomms.2017.21.

Said, Edward W. *Orientalism*. New York, 1979.

Saldívar, Ramón. 'Historical Fantasy, Speculative Realism, and Postrace Aesthetics in Contemporary American Fiction'. *American Literary History*, 23 (2011), 574–99.

Salmon, J. H. M. 'The Legacy of Jean Bodin: Absolutism, Populism, or Constitutionalism?' *History of Political Thought*, 17 (1996), 500–22.

Salzburg, Rosa. *Ephemeral City: Cheap Print and Urban Culture in Renaissance Venice*. Manchester, 2014.

Salzman, Paul. 'Aphra Behn's Fiction: Transmission, Editing, and Canonisation'. In Siegfried and Hammons (eds), *World-Making Renaissance Women*, 37–53.

Salzman, Paul. *Editors Construct the Renaissance Canon 1825–1915*. Cham, 2018.

Salzman, Paul. *English Prose Fiction: 1588–1700*. Oxford, 1985.

Salzman, Paul. 'Hidden in Plain Sight: Editing and (Not) Canonizing Early Modern Women's Writing'. In Goodrich and McQuade (eds), 'Special Issue', 121–30.

Salzman, Paul. 'How Alexander Dyce Assembled *Specimens of British Poetesses*: A Key Moment in the Transmission of Early Modern Women's Writing'. *Women's Writing*, 26 (2019), 88–105.

Salzman, Paul (ed.). *Mary Wroth's Poetry: An Electronic Edition* (2012). La Trobe University. http://wroth.latrobe.edu.au/index.html. Accessed 8 November 2020.

Salzman, Paul. 'Not Understanding Mary Wroth's Poetry'. *Parergon*, 29 (2012), 133–48.

Salzman, Paul. *Reading Early Modern Women's Writing*. Oxford, 2006.

Salzman, Paul. 'Theories of Prose Fiction in England: 1558–1700'. In Glyn P. Norton (ed.), *The Cambridge History of Literary Criticism*. Cambridge, 1989, 295–304.

Salzman, Paul and Marion Wynne-Davies (eds). *Mary Wroth and Shakespeare*. London, 2014.

Sanchez, Melissa E. 'Ain't I a Ladie?: Race, Sexuality, and Early Modern Women Writers'. In Coles and Keller (eds), *The Routledge Companion to Women, Sex, and Gender in the Early Modern World*, 15–32.

Sanchez, Melissa E. '"In My Selfe the Smart I Try": Female Promiscuity in *Astrophil and Stella*. *English Literary History*, 80 (2013), 1–27.

Sanchez, Melissa E. 'What Were Women Writers?'. In Goodrich and McQuade (eds), 'Special Issue', 63–74.

Sanders, Julie. *The Cultural Geography of Early Modern Drama, 1620–1650*. Cambridge, 2011.

Sanders, Julie. 'Geographies of Performance in the Early Modern Midlands'. In Susan Bennett and Mary Polito (eds), *Performing Environments: Site-Specificity in Medieval and Early Modern English Drama*. London, 2014, 119–37.

Sanders, Julie. 'Making the Land Known: *Henry IV, Parts 1 and 2* and the Literature of Perambulation'. In Claire Jowitt and David McInnis (eds), *Travel and Drama in Early Modern England*. Cambridge, 2018, 72–91.

Sarasohn, Lisa T. 'Margaret Cavendish, William Newcastle, and Political Marginalization'. *English Studies*, 92 (2011), 806–17.

Sarasohn, Lisa T. *The Natural Philosophy of Margaret Cavendish: Reason and Fancy During the Scientific Revolution*. Baltimore, MD, 2010.

Sauer, Elizabeth. 'Anthologizing Practices, Women's Literary History, and the Case of Isabella Whitney'. In Arthur F. Marotti (ed.), *New Ways of Looking at Old Texts, VI: Papers of the Renaissance English Text Society, 2011–2016*. Tempe, AZ, 2019, 103–16.

Sauer, Elizabeth. '"Book Passages and the Reconstruction of the Bradstreets": New England Library'. In Knight, White, and Sauer (eds), *Women's Bookscapes*, 59–77.

Schafer, Elizabeth. 'An Early Modern Feminist'. *Times Higher Education* (6 June 2013). https://www.timeshighereducation.com/features/an-early-modern-feminist/2004327.article?nopaging=1. Accessed 20 December 2020.

Schafer, Elizabeth. 'Introduction'. *Early Theatre*, 17 (2014), 125–32.

Schleiner, Louise. 'Margaret Tyler, Translator and Waiting Woman'. *English Language Notes*, 29 (1992), 1–8.

Schneider, Gary. *The Culture of Epistolarity: Vernacular Letters and Letter Writing in Early Modern England, 1500–1700*. Newark, DE, 2005.

Schoenfeldt, Michael. 'The Gender of Religious Devotion: Aemilia Lanyer and John Donne'. In Claire McEachern and Deborah Shuger (eds), *Religion and Culture in Renaissance England*. Cambridge, 1997, 209–33.

Scholarly Editing: The Annual of the Association for Documentary Editing. Noelle Baker and Kathryn Tomasek (eds). https://scholarlyediting.org. Accessed 8 April 2021.

Schoneveld, Cornelis W. *Intertraffic of the Mind: Studies in Seventeenth-Century Anglo-Dutch Translation with a Checklist of Books Translated from English into Dutch, 1600–1700*. Leiden, 1983.

Schreibman, Susan. *Versioning Machine 5.0*. http://v-machine.org. Accessed 8 April 2021.

Schwarz, Kathryn. 'Chastity, Militant and Married: Cavendish's Romance, Milton's Masque'. *PMLA*, 118 (2003), 270–85.

Scott, Jonathan. *England's Troubles: Seventeenth-Century English Political Instability in European Context*. Cambridge, 2000.

Scott-Baumann, Elizabeth. *Forms of Engagement: Women, Poetry, and Culture 1640–1680*. Oxford, 2013.

Scott-Baumann, Elizabeth. 'Hester Pulter's Well-Wrought Urns: Early Modern Women, Sonnets, and the New Criticism'. *Journal for Early Modern Cultural Studies*, 20.2 (2020), 120–43.

Scott-Warren, Jason. 'News, Sociability, and Bookbuying in Early Modern England: The Letters of Sir Thomas Cornwallis'. *The Library*, 1.4 (2000), 381–402.

Scott-Warren, Jason. 'Reading Graffiti in the Early Modern Book'. *Huntington Library Quarterly*, 73 (2010), 363–81.

Scott-Warren, Jason. *Sir John Harington and the Book as Gift*. Oxford, 2001.

Sedgwick, Eve Kosofsky. *Epistemology of the Closet*. Berkeley, CA, 1990.

Sedgwick, Eve Kosofsky. *Touching Feeling: Affect, Pedagogy, Performativity*. Durham, NC, 2003.

Sellier, Philippe. '"Se tirer du commun des femmes": La constellation précieuse'. In Sellier (ed.), *Essais sur l'imaginaire classique*. Paris, 2005, 197–213.

Siegfried, Brandie R. and Pamela S. Hammons (eds). *World-Making Renaissance Women: Rethinking Early Modern Women's Place in Literature and Culture*. Cambridge, 2021.

Sen, Amrita. 'Sailing to India: Women, Travel, and Crisis in the Seventeenth-Century'. In Akhimie and Andrea (eds), *Travel and Travail*, 64–80.

Sen, Amrita. 'Traveling Companions: Women, Trade, and the Early East India Company'. *Genre*, 48 (2015), 193–214.

Shahani, Gitanjali. *Tasting Difference: Food, Race, and Cultural Encounters in Early Modern Literature*. Ithaca, NY, 2020.

Shami, Jeanne and Anne James. *Gateway to Early Modern Manuscript Sermons*. https://gemms.itercommunity.org. Accessed 18 July 2021.

Shapiro, Lisa. 'Elizabeth, Princess of Bohemia'. In *The Stanford Encyclopedia of Philosophy* https://plato.stanford.edu/entries/elisabeth-bohemia/. Accessed 22 May 2021.

Shapiro, Lisa. 'Princess Elizabeth [*sic*] and Descartes: The Union of Mind and Body and the Practice of Philosophy'. *British Journal for the History of Philosophy*, 7.3 (1999), 503–20.

Sharpe, James. *Instruments of Darkness: Witchcraft in Early Modern England*. Philadelphia, PA, 1996.

Sharpe, Kevin. *Politics and Ideas in Early Stuart England*. London, 1989.

Sharpe, Kevin. *Reading Authority and Representing Rule in Early Modern England*. London, 2013.

Shepard, Alexandra and Garthine Walker. 'Gender, Change and Periodisation'. *Gender and History*, 20 (2008), 453–62.

Shepherd, Amanda. *Gender and Authority in Sixteenth-Century England*. Keele, 1994.

Sherman, Sandra. *Invention of the Modern Cookbook*. Santa Barbara, CA, 2010.

Sherman, William H. *Used Books: Marking Readers in Renaissance England*. Philadelphia, PA, 2008.

Shinn, Abigail and Angus Vine. 'Introduction: Theorizing Copiousness'. *Renaissance Studies*, 28 (2014), 167–82.

Shohet, Lauren. 'Women's Elegy: Early Modern'. In Karen Weisman (ed.), *The Oxford Handbook of Elegy* (2012). DOI: 10.1093/oxfordhb/9780199228133.013.0025. Accessed 30 June 2020.

Siemens, Ray, Constance Crompton, Daniel Powell, Alyssa Arbuckle, Maggie Shirley, and the Devonshire Manuscript Editorial Group. 'Building *A Social Edition of the Devonshire Manuscript*'. In Matthew James Driscoll and Elena Pierazzo (eds), Digital Scholarly Editing (Cambridge, 2016), 137– 60.

Simon, Margaret. 'Mary Wroth's Ephemeral Epitaph'. *SEL: Studies in English Literature, 1500–1900*, 56.1 (2016), 45–69.

Simpson, D. P. (ed.). *Cassell's Latin Dictionary*. New York, 1977.

Singh, Jyotsna G. '"Th'expense of spirit in a waste of shame": Mapping the "Emotional Regime" of Shakespeare's Sonnets'. In Michael Schoenfeldt (ed.), *A Companion to Shakespeare's Sonnets*. Oxford, 2007, 277–89.

Skerpan, Elizabeth P. 'Rhetorical Genres and the *Eikon Basilike*'. *Explorations in Renaissance Culture*, 11 (1985), 99–111.

Slater, Miriam. *Family Life in the Seventeenth Century: The Verneys of Claydon House*. London, 1984.

Smetham, Henry. *History of Strood*. Rochester, 1899.

Smith, Barbara and Ursula Appelts (eds). *Write or Be Written: Early Modern Women Poets and Cultural Constraints*. Aldershot, 2001.

Smith, Bruce R. *The Acoustic World of Early Modern England: Attending to the O-Factor*. Chicago, IL, 1999.

Smith, Bruce R. 'Female Impersonation in Early Modern Ballads'. In Pamela Allen Brown and Peter Parolin (eds), *Women Players in England: Beyond the All-Male Stage*. Aldershot, 2005, 281–304.

Smith, Daniel Starza. *John Donne and the Conway Papers: Patronage and Manuscript Circulation in the Early Seventeenth Century*. Oxford, 2014.

Smith, Emma. 'Marital Marginalia: The Seventeenth-Century Library of Thomas and Isabella Hervey'. In Acheson (ed.), *Early Modern English Marginalia*, 155–72.

Smith, Hallett. 'English Metrical Psalms in the Sixteenth Century and Their Literary Significance'. *Huntington Library Quarterly*, 9 (1946), 249–71.

Smith, Helen. *'Grossly Material Things': Women and Book Production in Early Modern England*. Oxford, 2012.

Smith, Helen. 'Women and the Materials of Writing'. In Pender and Smith (eds), *Material Cultures*, 14–35.
Smith, Helen and Louise Wilson (eds). *Renaissance Paratexts*. Cambridge, 2011.
Smith, Nigel. *Perfection Proclaimed: Language and Literature in English Radical Religion, 1640–60*. Oxford, 1989.
Smith, Pamela. *The Body of the Artisan: Art and Experience in the Scientific Revolution*. Chicago, IL, 2004.
Smith, Rochelle. 'Admirable Musicians: Women's Songs in *Othello* and *The Maid's Tragedy*'. *Comparative Drama*, 28 (1994), 311–23.
Smith, Rosalind. '"Le pouvoir de faire dire": Marginalia in Mary Queen of Scots' Book of Hours'. In Pender and Smith (eds), *Material Cultures*, 55–75.
Smith, Rosalind. 'Perdita Project'. *Early Modern Women: An Interdisciplinary Journal*, 11.2 (2017), 145–51.
Smith, Rosalind. 'Reading Mary Stuart's Casket Sonnets: Reception, Authorship, and Early Modern Women's Writing'. *Parergon*, 29.2 (2012), 149–76.
Smith, Rosalind. *Sonnets and the English Woman Writer, 1560–1621: The Politics of Absence*. Basingstoke, 2005.
Smyth, Adam. *Autobiography in Early Modern England*. Cambridge, 2010.
Smyth, Adam. 'Commonplace Book Culture: A List of Sixteen Traits'. In Anne Lawrence-Mathers and Phillipa Hardman (eds), *Women and Writing, c.1340–c.1650: The Domestication of Print Culture*. Woodbridge, 2010, 90–110.
Smyth, Adam. 'Introduction'. In Adam Smyth (ed.), *A History of English Autobiography*. Cambridge, 2016, 1–10.
Smyth, Adam. *Material Texts in Early Modern England*. Cambridge, 2018.
Snively, Samantha. '"The Quintessence of Wit": Domestic Labor, Science, and Margaret Cavendish's Kitchen Fancies'. *Newberry Essays in Medieval and Early Modern Studies*, 9 (2015), 21–8.
Snook, Edith. 'Elizabeth Isham's "Own Bookes": Property, Propriety, and the Self as Library'. In Knight, White, and Sauer (eds), *Women's Bookscapes*, 77–93.
Snook, Edith. 'English Women's Writing and Indigenous Medical Knowledge in the Early Modern Atlantic World'. In Phillippy (ed.), *A History of Early Modern Women's Writing*, 382–97.
Snook, Edith. 'Jane Grey, "Manful" Combat, and the Female Reader in Early Modern England'. *Renaissance and Reformation / Renaissance et Réforme*, 32 (2009), 47–81.
Snook, Edith. 'Recent Studies in Early Modern Reading'. *English Literary Renaissance*, 43.2 (2013), 343–78.
Snook, Edith. *Women, Reading, and the Cultural Politics of Early Modern England*. Abingdon, 2005.
Spence, Richard T. *Lady Anne Clifford, Countess of Pembroke, Dorset and Montgomery (1590–1676)*. Sutton, 1997.
Spencer, Gilbert. In Germaine Warkentin, Joseph L. Black, and William R. Bowen (eds), *The Library of the Sidneys of Penshurst Place Circa 1665*. Toronto, 2013.
Spencer, Jane. *Aphra Behn's Afterlife*. Oxford, 2000.
Sperrazza, Whitney. 'Knowing Mary Wroth's Pamphilia'. *Journal for Early Modern Cultural Studies*, 19 (2019), 1–35.
Spiller, Elizabeth A. *Reading and the History of Race in the Renaissance*. Cambridge, 2011.
Spiller, Elizabeth A. *Science, Reading, and Renaissance Literature: The Art of Making Knowledge, 1580–1670*. Cambridge, 2004, 137–77.

Spiller, Elizabeth A. (ed.). *Seventeenth-Century English Recipe Books: Cooking, Physic and Chirurgery in the Works of Elizabeth Grey and Aletheia Talbot*. Burlington, VT, 2008.
Spiller, Michael R. G. *The Development of the Sonnet*. New York, 1992.
Spink, Ian. *English Song: Dowland to Purcell*. London, 1974.
Spink, Ian. *Henry Lawes: Cavalier Songwriter*. Oxford, 2000.
Stallybrass, Peter. 'Against Thinking'. *PMLA*, 122 (2007), 1580–7.
Stanivukovic, Goran. *Timely Voices: Romance Writing in English Literature*. Montreal, 2017.
Stanton, Domna C. 'The Fiction of *Préciosité* and the Fear of Women'. *Yale French Studies*, 62 (1981), 107–34.
Stedman, Gera. *Cultural Exchanges in Seventeenth-Century France and England*. Farnham, 2013.
Stern, Tiffany. *Documents of Performance in Early Modern England*. Cambridge, 2009.
Stern, Tiffany. 'Renaissance Drama: Future Directions'. *Renaissance Drama*, 40 (2012), 151–60.
Sternfeld, Frederick W. and Mary Joiner Chan. 'Come Live with Me and Be My Love'. *Comparative Literature*, 22.2 (1970), 173–87.
Stevenson, Jane. 'Reading, Writing and Gender in Early Modern Scotland'. *The Seventeenth Century*, 27.3 (2012), 335–74.
Stevenson, Jane. 'Women and the Cultural Politics of Printing'. *The Seventeenth Century*, 24 (2009), 205–37.
Stevenson, Jane. 'Women's Education'. In Philip Ford, Jan Bloemendal, and Charles Fantazzi (eds), *Brill's Encyclopaedia of the Neo-Latin World*. Leiden, 2014, 87–99.
Stevenson, Jay. 'The Mechanist-Vitalist Soul of Margaret Cavendish'. SEL: *Studies in English Literature, 1500–1900*, 36.3 (1996), 527–43.
Stewart, Alan. *The Oxford History of Life Writing, vol. 2: Early Modern*. Oxford, 2018.
Stewart, Alan. *Shakespeare's Letters*. Oxford, 2008.
Stiebel, Arlene. 'Subversive Sexuality: Masking the Erotic in Poems by Katherine Philips and Aphra Behn'. In Claude J. Summers and Ted-Larry Pebworth (eds), *Renaissance Discourses of Desire*. Columbia, MO, 1993, 223–36.
Stighelen, Katlijne van der. *Anna Maria van Schurman of 'Hoe hooge dat een maeght kan in de konsten stijgen'*. Leuven, 1987.
Stokes, James. 'The Ongoing Exploration of Women and Performance in Early Modern England'. *Shakespeare Bulletin*, 33 (2015), 9–31.
Straznicky, Marta. 'Closet Drama'. In Arthur F. Kinney (ed.), *A Companion to Renaissance Drama*. Oxford, 2002, 416–30.
Straznicky, Marta. 'Lady Mary Wroth's Patchwork Play: The Huntington Manuscript of *Love's Victory*'. *Sidney Journal*, 34 (2016), 81–91.
Straznicky, Marta. *Privacy, Playreading, and Women's Closet Drama, 1550–1700*. Cambridge, 2004.
Straznicky, Marta. 'Private Drama'. In Knoppers (ed.), *The Cambridge Companion to Early Modern Women's Writing*, 247–59.
Straznicky, Marta. 'Reading through the Body'. In Marta Straznicky (ed.), *The Book of the Play: Playwrights, Stationers, and Readers in Early Modern England*. Amherst, MA, 2006, 59–79.
Straznicky, Marta and Sara Mueller (eds). *Women's Household Drama: 'Loves Victorie', 'A Pastorall', and 'The Concealed Fansyes'*. Tempe, AZ, 2018.
Stretton, Tim. 'The Legal Identity of Married Women'. In Andreas Bauer and Karl H. L. Welker (eds), *Europa und Seine Regionen: 2000 Jahre Rechtsgeschichte*. Cologne, 2007, 309–21.
Stretton, Tim. 'Widows at Law in Tudor and Stuart England'. In Sandra Cavallo and Lyndan Warner (eds), *Widowhood in Medieval and Early Modern Europe*. Abingdon, 2014, 193–208.
Stretton, Tim. *Women Waging Law in Elizabeth England*. Cambridge, 2005.

Strong, John A. 'Algonquian Women as Sunksquaws and Caretakers of the Soil: The Documentary Evidence of the Seventeenth-Century Records'. In Susan Castillo and Victor M. P. Da Rossa (eds), *Native American Women in Literature and Culture*. Porto, 1997.

Sullivan, Garrett A., Jr. *Memory and Forgetting in English Renaissance Drama: Shakespeare, Marlowe, Webster*. Cambridge, 2005.

Summit, Jennifer. *Lost Property: The Woman Writer and English Literary History, 1380–1589*. Chicago, IL, 2000.

Sununu, Andrea. '"I Long to Know Your Opinion of It": The Serendipity of a Malfunctioning Timing Belt or the Guiney-Tutin Connection in the Recovery of Katherine Philips'. *Women's Writing*, 24 (2017), 258–79.

Suzuki, Mihoko. *Antigone's Example: Early Modern Women's Political Writing in Times of Civil War from Christine de Pizan to Helen Maria Williams*. New York, 2022.

Suzuki, Mihoko. 'Daughters of Coke: Women's Legal Discourse in England, 1642–1689'. In Sigrun Haude and Melinda Zook (eds), *Challenging Orthodoxies: The Social and Cultural Worlds of Early Modern Women*. Abingdon, 2016, 165–92.

Suzuki, Mihoko. 'Elizabeth, Gender and the Political Imaginary of Seventeenth-Century England'. In Malcolmson and Suzuki (eds), *Debating Gender*, 231–54.

Suzuki, Mihoko. 'Political Writing across Borders'. In Phillippy (ed.), *A History of Early Modern Women's Writing*, 364–81.

Suzuki, Mihoko. *Subordinate Subjects: Gender, the Political Nation, and Literary Form in England, 1588–1688*. Aldershot, 2003.

Suzuki, Mihoko. 'What's Political in Seventeenth-Century Women's Political Writing?'. *Literature Compass*, 6 (2009), 927–41.

Swaim, Kathleen. 'Matching the "Matchless Orinda" to Her Times'. In Kevin L. Cope (ed.), *1650–1850: Ideas, Aesthetics, and Inquiries in the Early Modern Era*, vol. 3. New York, 1997, 77–108.

Swain, Margaret H. 'A New Year's Gift from the Princess Elizabeth'. *Connoisseur*, 183 (1973), 258–66.

Swain, Margaret H. *Figures on Fabric: Embroidery Design Sources and Their Application*. London, 1980.

Swann, Joel. '"In the hands and hearts of all true Christians": Herbert's *The Temple* (1633–1709) and Its Readers'. *Journal of Medieval and Early Modern Studies*, 50 (2020), 115–37.

Szmuk-Tanenbaum, Szilvia and Stephen Schmidt (eds). *Manuscript Cookbook Survey*. https://www.manuscriptcookbookssurvey.org/. Accessed 30 June 2020.

Taavitsainen, Irma and Päivi Pahta. 'Authority and Instruction in Two Sixteenth-Century Medical Dialogues'. In Matti Peikola, Janne Skaffari, and Sanna-Kaisa Tanskanen (eds), *Instructional Writing in English: Studies in Honour of Risto Hiltunen*. Amsterdam, 2009, 105–24.

Tancke, Ulrike. *'Bethinke Thy Selfe' in Early Modern England: Writing Women's Identities*. Leiden, 2010.

Teague, Frances. *Bathsua Makin, Woman of Learning*. Lewisburg, PA, 1998.

Teague, Frances. 'The Identity of Bathsua Makin'. *Biography*, 16 (1993), 1–17.

Text Encoding Initiative Consortium (ed.). *TEI P5: Guidelines for Electronic Text Encoding and Interchange*. TEI Consortium. http://www.tei-c.org/Guidelines/P5. Accessed 8 April 2021.

Thain, Marion (ed.). *The Lyric Poem: Formations and Transformations*. Cambridge, 2013.

Theophano, Janet. *Eat My Words: Reading Women's Lives through the Cookbooks They Wrote*. New York, 2002.

Thickstun, Margaret Olofson. 'Contextualizing Anne Bradstreet's Literary Remains: Why We Need a New Edition of the Poems'. *Early American Literature*, 52 (2017), 389–422.

Thomas, Emily (ed.). *Early Modern Women on Metaphysics*. Cambridge, 2018.
Thompson, Ayanna, Gene Demby, and Shereen Marisol Meraji. 'All That Glisters Is Not Gold'. *Code Switch*, National Public Radio, 21 August 2019, https://www.npr.org/transcripts/752850055. Accessed 6 March 2021.
Thorne, Alison. '"Large Complaints in Little Papers": Negotiating Ovidian Genealogies of Complaint in Drayton's *Englands Heroicall Epistles*'. *Renaissance Studies*, 22 (2008), 368–84.
Thorne, Alison. 'The Politics of Female Supplication in the Book of Esther'. In Victoria Brownlee and Laura Gallagher (eds), *Biblical Women in Early Modern Literary Culture 1550–1700*. Manchester, 2016, 95–110.
Tigner, Amy. 'Preserving Nature in Hannah Woolley's *The Queen-Like Closet; or Rich Cabinet*'. In Jennifer Munroe and Rebecca Laroche (eds), *Ecofeminist Approaches to Early Modernity*. London, 2011, 129–49.
Tigner, Amy. 'Trans-Border Kitchens: Iberian Recipes in Seventeenth-Century English Manuscripts'. In Vicki Howard and Jon Stobart (eds), *History of Retailing and Consumption*, 5 (2019), 51–70.
Todd, Barbara J. 'The Remarrying Widow: A Stereotype Reconsidered'. In Prior (ed.), *Women in English Society*, 54–92.
Tootalian, Jacob. 'Cavendish and the Language of Genres'. *The Digital Cavendish Project*, 28 August 2013. http://digitalcavendish.org/the-language-of-genres/. Accessed 8 April 2021.
Townsend, Camilla. *Pocahontas and the Powhatan Dilemma*. New York, 2004.
Traub, Valerie (ed.). *The Oxford Handbook of Shakespeare and Embodiment: Gender, Sexuality, and Race*. Oxford, 2016.
Traub, Valerie. *The Renaissance of Lesbianism in Early Modern England*. Cambridge, 2002.
Traub, Valerie. *Thinking Sex with the Early Moderns*. Philadelphia, PA, 2015.
Trettien, Whitney. *Cut/Copy/Paste: Fragments from the History of Bookwork*. Minneapolis, MN, 2021.
Trettien, Whitney. 'Isabella Whitney's Slips: Textile Labour, Gendered Authorship, and the Early Modern Miscellany'. Special Issue of *Journal of Medieval and Early Modern Studies*, 45 (2015), 505–21.
Trill, Suzanne. 'Beyond Romance? Re-Reading the "Lives" of Anne, Lady Halkett (1621/2?–1699)'. *Literature Compass*, 6 (2009), 446–59.
Trill, Suzanne. 'Early Modern Women's Writing in the Edinburgh Archives, c. 1550–1740: A Preliminary Checklist'. In Dunnigan, Harker, and Newlyn (eds), *Woman and the Feminine*, 196–201.
Trill, Suzanne. 'A Feminist Critic in the Archives: Reading Anna Walker's A Sweete Savor for Woman (c. 1606)'. *Women's Writing*, 9.2 (2002), 199–214.
Trill, Suzanne, Kate Chedgzoy, and Melanie Osborne (eds). *'Lay by Your Needles, Ladies, Take the Pen': Writing Women in England, 1500–1700*. London, 1997.
Trudell, Scott A. 'Performing Women in English Books of Ayres'. In Dunn and Larson (eds), *Gender and Song in Early Modern England*, 15–30.
Trudell, Scott A. *Unwritten Poetry: Song, Performance, and Media in Early Modern England*. Oxford, 2019.
Turner, Denys. *The Darkness of God: Negativity in Christian Mysticism*. Cambridge, 1995.
Turner, James Grantham. '"Romance" and the Novel in Restoration England'. *The Review of English Studies*, 63 (2011), 58–85.
UK Reading Experience Database. The Open University. open.ac.uk/Arts/reading/UK/. Accessed 2 February 2021.

Uman, Deborah. *Women as Translators in Early Modern England*. Newark, 2012.
Uman, Deborah and Belén Bistué. 'Translation as Collaborative Authorship: Margaret Tyler's *The Mirrour of Princely Deedes and Knighthood*'. *Comparative Literature Studies*, 44/3 (2007), 298–323.
Underdown, David. *A Freeborn People: Politics and the Nation in Seventeenth-Century England*. Oxford, 1996.
Upham, Alfred Horatio. *The French Influence in English Literature from the Accession of Elizabeth to the Restoration*. New York, 1908.
Veevers, Erica. *Images of Love and Religion: Queen Henrietta Maria and Court Entertainments*. Cambridge, 1989.
Venuti, Lawrence. *The Translator's Invisibility. A History of Translation*, 2nd edn. Abingdon, 2008.
Veracini, Lorenzo. *Settler Colonialism: A Theoretical Overview*. Basingstoke, 2010.
Veronese, Leah and Daniel Starza Smith. 'Elizabeth Bourne'. In Pender and Smith (eds), *Palgrave Encyclopedia*.
Verweij, Sebastiaan. *The Literary Culture of Early Modern Scotland: Manuscript Production and Circulation, 1560–1625*. Oxford, 2016.
Vickers, Brian. 'Leisure and Idleness in the Renaissance: The Ambivalence of Otium'. *Renaissance Studies*, 4 (1990), 1–37, 107–54.
Victorian Women Writers Project. Indiana University. http://webapp1.dlib.indiana.edu/vwwp/welcome.do. Accessed 8 April 2021.
Viennot, Eliane and T. Clavier (eds). *Anne de France: Enseignements à sa fille, suivis de l'Histoire du siège de Brest*. Saint-Etienne, 2007.
Vine, Angus. *Miscellaneous Order: Manuscript Culture and the Early Modern Organization of Knowledge*. Oxford, 2019.
Viroli, Maurizio. *Machiavelli*. Oxford, 1998.
Visualizing English Print. University of Wisconsin-Madison. https://graphics.cs.wisc.edu/WP/vep/. Accessed 8 April 2021.
Walker, Claire. 'Crumbs of News: Early Modern English Nuns and Royalist Intelligence Networks'. *Journal of Medieval and Early Modern Studies*, 42 (2012), 635–55.
Walker, Claire. '"Doe Not Supose Me a Well Mortifyed Nun Dead to the World": Letter-Writing in Early Modern English Convents'. In Daybell (ed.), *Early Modern Women's Letter Writing*, 159–76.
Walker, Claire. *Gender and Politics in Early Modern Europe: English Convents in France and the Low Countries*. New York, 2003.
Walker, Claire. 'Loyal and Dutiful Subjects: English Nuns and Stuart Politics'. In James Daybell (ed.), *Women and Politics in Early Modern England, 1450–1700*. Farnham, 2004, 228–42.
Walker, Claire. 'Prayer, Patronage, and Political Conspiracy: English Nuns and the Restoration'. *The Historical Journal*, 43 (2000), 1–23.
Walker, Claire. '"When God Shall Restore Them to Their Kingdoms": Nuns, Exiled Stuarts and English Catholic Identity, 1688–1745'. In Sarah Apetrei and Hannah Smith (eds), *Religion and Women in Britain, c 1600–1760*. Farnham, 2014, 79–97.
Wall, Wendy. 'Female Authorship'. In Bates (ed.), *A Companion to Renaissance Poetry*, 128–40.
Wall, Wendy. 'Household "Writing": or the Joys of Carving'. In Rebecca Ann Bach and Gwynne Kennedy (eds), *Feminisms and Early Modern Texts: Essays for Phyllis Rackin*. Cranbury, NJ, 2010, 25–42.

Wall, Wendy. *The Imprint of Gender: Authorship and Publication in the English Renaissance*. Ithaca, NY, 1993.

Wall, Wendy. 'Reading the Home: The Case of *The English Housewife*'. In Smith and Wilson (eds), *Renaissance Paratexts*, 165–84.

Wall, Wendy. *Recipes for Thought: Knowledge and Taste in the Early Modern English Kitchen*. Philadelphia, PA, 2015.

Wall, Wendy. *Staging Domesticity: Household Work and English Identity in Early Modern Drama*. Cambridge, 2002.

Wall, Wendy and Leah Knight (eds). *The Pulter Project: Poet in the Making*. http://pulterproject.northwestern.edu. Accessed 12 March 2021.

Wall-Randell, Sarah. '"All by Her Directing": The Countess of Pembroke and Her *Arcadia*'. In Wayne (ed.), *Women's Labour and the History of the Book*, 163–85.

Wallace, Bronwyn. 'Intimate Exegesis: Reading and Feeling in Early Modern Devotional Literature'. PhD Diss., University of Pennsylvania, 2015.

Wallwork, Jo and Paul Salzman (eds). *Women Writing 1550–1750*. Bundoora, 2001.

Walsh, Ann-Maria. 'The Boyle Women and Familial Life Writing'. In Julie A. Eckerle and Naomi McAreavey (eds), *Women's Life Writing and Early Modern Ireland*. Lincoln, 2019, 79–98.

Walsh, Ann-Maria. *The Daughters of the First Earl of Cork: Writing Family, Faith, Politics and Place*. Dublin, 2020.

Waquet, Françoise. In John Howe (trans.), *Latin, or the Empire of a Sign from the Sixteenth to Twentieth Centuries*. London, 2001.

Warley, Christopher. 'Un-canonizing Lady Mary Wroth?'. In *Arcade: Literature, the Humanities, & the World* (2010). Stanford University. https://arcade.stanford.edu/blogs/un-canonizing-lady-mary-wroth. Accessed 16 November 2020.

Warner, Michael. 'Irving's Posterity'. *English Literary History*, 67.3 (2000), 773–9.

Warnicke, Retha M. *Women of the English Renaissance and Reformation*. Westport, CT, 1987.

Warren, Charles W. 'Music at Nonesuch'. *The Musical Quarterly*, 54 (1968), 47–57.

Warren, Christopher N., Daniel Shore, Jessica Otis, Scott Weingart, and John Ladd. *Six Degrees of Francis Bacon*. Carnegie Mellon University. http://www.sixdegreesoffrancisbacon.com. Accessed 8 April 2021.

Warren, Christopher N., Daniel Shore, Jessica Otis, Lawrence Wang, Mike Finegold, and Cosma Shalizi. 'Six Degrees of Francis Bacon: A Statistical Method for Reconstructing Large Historical Social Networks'. *Digital Humanities Quarterly*, 10.3 (2016). http://digitalhumanities.org/dhq/vol/10/3/000244/000244.html. Accessed 8 April 2021.

Warren, Nancy Bradley. *The Embodied Word: Female Spiritualities, Contested Orthodoxies, and English Religious Cultures, 1350–1700*. Notre Dame, IN, 2010.

Watkins, Leila. 'The Poetics of Consolation and Community in Mary Wroth's *Pamphilia to Amphilanthus*'. *Studies in Philology*, 112 (2015), 139–61.

Watt, Tessa. *Cheap Print and Popular Piety, 1550–1640*. Cambridge, 1991.

Wayne, Valerie (ed.). *Women's Labour and the History of the Book in Early Modern England*. London, 2020.

Weiner, Annette. *Inalienable Possessions: The Paradox of Keeping-While-Giving*. Berkeley, CA, 1992.

'Wellcome Library: Recipe Books'. The Wellcome Library. https://wellcomelibrary.org/collections/digital-collections/recipe-books/. Accessed 30 June 2020.

Werness, Hope B. *The Encyclopedia of Animal Symbolism in World Art*. New York, 2006.

Wernimont, Jacqueline. *Numbered Lives: Life and Death in Quantum Media*. Cambridge, MA, 2019.

Westerkamp, Marilyn J. *Women and Religion in Early America 1600–1850: The Puritan and Evangelical Traditions*. New York, 1999.

Whitaker, Katie. *Mad Madge: The Extraordinary Life of Margaret Cavendish, Duchess of Newcastle, the First Woman to Live by Her Pen*. New York, 2002.

White, Adam. 'Love, Loyalty and Friendship: Education, Dynasty and Service. Lady Anne Clifford's Church Monuments'. In Hearn and Hulse (eds), *Lady Anne Clifford*, 43–71.

White, Elizabeth Wade. *Anne Bradstreet: The Tenth Muse*. New York, 1971.

White, Micheline. 'Dismantling Catholic Primers and Reforming Private Prayer: Anne Lock, Hezekiah's Song, and Psalm 51'. In Alec Ryrie and Jessica Martin (eds), *Private and Domestic Devotion in Early Modern Britain*. Farnham, 2012, 93–114.

White, Micheline (ed.). *English Women, Religion, and Textual Production 1500–1625*. Farnham, 2011.

White, Micheline. 'Katherine Parr, Henry VIII, and Royal Literary Collaboration'. In Pender (ed.), *Gender, Authorship, and Early Modern Women's Collaboration*, 23–46.

White, Micheline. 'Katherine Parr and Royal Religious Complaint: Complaining For and About Henry VIII'. In Ross and Smith (eds), *Early Modern Women's Complaint*, 47–65.

White, Micheline. 'Katherine Parr, Translation, and the Dissemination of Erasmus's Views on War and Peace'. *Renaissance and Reformation/Renaissance et Réforme*, 43 (2020), 67–91.

White, Micheline. 'Katherine Parr's Marginalia: Putting the Wisdom of Chrysostom and Solomon into Practice'. In Knight, White, and Sauer (eds), *Women's Bookscapes*, 21–42.

White, Micheline. 'The Perils and Possibilities of the Book Education: Anne Lock, John Knox, John Calvin, Queen Elizabeth, and the Duchess of Suffolk'. *Parergon*, 29.2 (2012), 9–27.

White, Micheline. 'Protestant Women's Writing and Congregational Psalm Singing: From the Song of the Exiled 'Handmaid' (1555) to the Countess of Pembroke's *Psalmes* (1599)'. *Sidney Journal*, 23 (2005), 61–82.

White, Micheline. 'The Psalms, War, and Royal Iconography: Katherine Parr's *Psalms or Prayers* (1544) and Henry VIII as David'. *Renaissance Studies*, 29 (2015), 554–75.

White, Micheline. 'Renaissance Englishwomen and Religious Translations: The Case of Anne Lock's *Of the Markes of the Children of God* (1590)'. *English Literary Renaissance*, 29 (1999), 375–400.

White, Micheline. 'Women Writers and Literary-Religious Circles in the Elizabethan West Country: Anne Dowriche, Anne Lock Prowse, Anne Lock Moyle, Ursula Fulford, and Elizabeth Rous'. *Modern Philology*, 103 (2005), 187–214.

White, Robert. *Cupid's Banishment*. In Cerasano and Wynne-Davies (eds), *Renaissance Drama by Women*, 76–126.

Whyman, Susan. *The Pen and the People*. New Haven, CT, 2009.

Wiegman, Robyn. 'The Times We're In: Queer Feminist Criticism and the Reparative "Turn"'. *Feminist Theory*, 15.1 (2014), 4–25.

Wiesner-Hanks, Merry E. 'Do Women Need the Renaissance?' *Gender and History*, 20 (2008), 539–57.

Wiggins, Alison. *Bess of Hardwick's Letters: Language, Materiality, and Early Modern Epistolary Culture*. Abingdon, 2016.

Wilcher, Robert. '*Eikon Basilike*: The Printing, Composition, Strategy, and Impact of "The King's Book"'. In Laura Lunger Knoppers (ed.), *The Oxford Handbook of Literature and The English Revolution*. Oxford, 2012, 289–308.

Wilcher, Robert. *The Writing of Royalism 1628–1660*. Cambridge, 2001.

Wilcox, Helen (ed.). *Women and Literature in Britain, 1500–1700*. Cambridge, 1996.

Wilcox, Kirstin. 'American Women's Writing in the Colonial Period'. In Dale M. Bauer (ed.), *The Cambridge History of American Women's Literature*. Cambridge, 2012, 55–73.

Wilder, Lina Perkins. *Shakespeare's Memory Theatre: Recollection, Properties, and Character*. Cambridge, 2010.

Wilder, Lina Perkins. 'Veiled Memory Traces in *Much Ado about Nothing*, *Pericles* and *The Winter's Tale*'. In Andrew Hiscock and Lina Perkins Wilder (eds), *The Routledge Handbook of Shakespeare and Memory*. London, 2018, 239–52.

Wilkie, Vanessa. 'Reading and Writing between the Lines: Lady Eleanor Douglas, a Midland Visionary and Her Annotated Pamphlets'. *Midland History*, 41 (2016), 168–83.

Wilkins, Emma. 'Margaret Cavendish and the Royal Society'. *Notes and Records of the Royal Society of London*, 68.3 (2014), 245–60.

Williams, Grant. 'Monumental Memory and Little Reminders'. In Andrew Hiscock and Lina Perkins Wilder (eds), *The Routledge Handbook of Shakespeare and Memory*. London, 2018, 297–311.

Williams, Sarah F. *Damnable Practises: Witches, Dangerous Women, and Music in Seventeenth-Century English Broadside Ballads*. Farnham, 2015.

Williams, Sarah F. 'Witches, Lamenting Women, and Cautionary Tales: Tracing "The Ladies Fall" in Early Modern English Broadside Balladry and Popular Song'. In Dunn and Larson (eds), *Gender and Song in Early Modern England*, 31–46.

Willis, Ika. *Reception*. Abingdon, 2018.

Wilson, Luke. 'Ben Jonson and the Law of Contract'. In Kahn and Hutson (eds), *Rhetoric and Law in Early Modern Europe*, 143–65.

Wilson, Luke. 'Contract'. In Lorna Hutson (ed.), *The Oxford Handbook of English Law and Literature, 1500–1700*. Oxford, 2017, 393–409.

Winkler, Amanda Eubanks. *Music, Dance, and Drama in Early Modern English Schools*. Cambridge, 2020.

Winkler, Amanda Eubanks and Richard Schoch (eds). *Performing Restoration Shakespeare*. Shakespeare/ResearchProject/. Accessed 12 March 2021.

Winner, Lauren F. 'The Foote Sisters' Compleat Housewife: Cookery Texts as a Source in Lived Religion'. In DiMeo and Pennell (eds), *Reading and Writing Recipe Books*, 135–55.

Wiseman, Susan. *Conspiracy and Virtue: Women, Writing, and Politics in Seventeenth-Century England*. Oxford, 2006.

Wiseman, Susan. '"The Most Considerable of My Troubles": Anne Halkett and the Writing of Civil War Conspiracy'. In Wallwork and Salzman (eds), *Women Writing*, 25–45.

Wiseman, Susan. 'No "Publick Funerall"? Lucy Hutchinson's Elegy, Epitaph, Monument'. *The Seventeenth Century*, 30 (2015), 207–28.

Wiseman, Susan. 'Unsilent Instruments and the Devil's Cushions: Authority in Seventeenth–Century Women's Prophetic Discourse'. In Isobel Armstrong (ed.), *New Feminist Discourses*. London, 1992, 176–96.

Wistreich, Richard. 'Vocal Performance in the Seventeenth Century'. In Colin Lawson and Robin Stowell (eds), *The Cambridge History of Musical Performance*. Cambridge, 2012, 398–420.

Witmore, Michael and Jonathan Hope. 'A Map of English Print'. *Wine Dark Sea*, 23 April 2019. http://winedarksea.org/?p=2703. Accessed 8 April 2021.

Wogan-Browne, Jocelyn, Nicholas Watson, Andrew Taylor, and Ruth Evans (eds). *The Idea of the Vernacular: An Anthology of Middle English Literary Theory, 1280–1520.* Exeter, 1999.

Wolfe, Heather. 'Dame Barbara Constable: Catholic Antiquarian, Advisor, and Closet Missionary'. In Ronald Corthell, Frances E. Dolan, Christopher Highley, and Arthur F. Marotti (eds), *Catholic Culture in Early Modern England.* Notre Dame, IN, 2007, 158–88.

Wolfe, Heather. 'Manuscripts in Early Modern England.' In Donna B. Hamilton (ed.), *A Concise Companion to English Renaissance Literature.* Malden, MA, 2006, 114–35.

Wolfe, Heather. 'Uncancelling the Cancelled: Recovering Obliterated Owners of Old Books'. *The Collation: Research and Exploration at the Folger*, 3 April 2019. collation.folger.edu/2019/04/uncancelling-the-cancelled. Accessed 2 June 2021.

Wolsk, Rebecca S. 'Muddy Allegiance and Shiny Booty: Aphra Behn's Anglo-Dutch Politics'. *Eighteenth-Century Fiction*, 17 (2004), 1–33.

Women Writers Project (1999–2016). Northeastern University. https://www.wwp.northeastern.edu/. Accessed 8 November 2020.

Wood, Diane S. 'In Praise of Women's Superiority: Heinrich Cornelius Agrippa's *De nobilitate*'. In Barbara K. Gold, Paul Allen Miller, and Charles Platter (eds), *Sex and Gender in Medieval and Renaissance Texts: The Latin Tradition.* Albany, NY, 1997.

Woodbridge, Linda. 'Resistance Theory Meets Drama: Tudor Seneca'. *Renaissance Drama*, 38 (2010), 115–39.

Woodbridge, Linda. *Women and the English Renaissance: Literature and the Nature of Womankind, 1540–1620.* Urbana, IL, 1984.

Woods, Susanne. *Lanyer: A Renaissance Woman Poet.* Oxford, 1999.

Woolf, Virginia. *A Room of One's Own.* London, 1935.

Woolf, Virginia. *A Room of One's Own.* New York, 1989.

Woolf, Viriginia. *A Room of One's Own.* London, 2004.

Woudhuysen, H. R. *Sir Philip Sidney and the Circulation of Manuscripts, 1558–1640.* Oxford, 1996.

Wray, Ramona. 'Anthologising the Early Modern Female Voice'. In Andrew Murphy (ed.), *The Renaissance Text: Theory, Editing, Textuality.* Manchester, 2000, 55–72.

Wray, Ramona. 'Autobiography'. In Knoppers (ed.), *The Cambridge Companion to Early Modern Women's Writing*, 194–207.

Wray, Ramona. 'Performing *The Tragedy of Mariam* and Constructing Stage History'. *Early Theatre*, 17 (2014), 149–66.

Wray, Ramona. '[Re]Constructing the Past: The Diametric Lives of Mary Rich'. In Henk Dragstra, Sheila Ottway, and Helen Wilcox (eds), *Betraying our Selves: Forms of Self-Representation in Early Modern English Texts.* London, 2000, 148–65.

Wray, Ramona. 'What Say You to [This] Book? . . . Is It Yours?': Oral and Collaborative Narrative Trajectories in the Mediated Writings of Anna Trapnel'. *Women's Writing*, 16 (2009), 408–24.

Wright, Gillian. 'Delight of Good Books: Family, Devotional Practice and Textual Circulation in Sarah Savages's Diaries'. *Book History*, 8, 45–74.

Wright, Gillian. *Producing Women's Poetry, 1600–1730: Text and Paratext, Manuscript and Print.* Cambridge, 2013.

Wright, Louis B. *Middle-Class Culture in Elizabethan England.* Chapel Hill, NC, 1935.

Wright, Louis B. 'The Reading of Renaissance English Women'. *Studies in Philology*, 28 (1931), 671–89.

Wrightson, Keith. 'The Enclosure of English Social History'. In Adrian Wilson (ed.), *Rethinking Social History: English Society 1520–1970 and Its Interpretation*. Manchester, 1993, 59–77.

Wrightson, Keith. *Ralph Tailor's Summer: A Scrivener, His City, and the Plague*. Princeton, NJ, 2011.

Wroth, Lady Mary. *Love's Victory*. Directed by Martin Hodgson. Performed by Shakespeare's Globe. Penshurst Place, Kent, 8 June 2014.

Wroth, Lady Mary. *Love's Victory*. Directed by Martin Hodgson. Penshurst Place, Kent, 16 September 2018.

Wynne-Davies, Marion. 'Editing Early Modern Women's Dramatic Writing'. In Ross and Salzman (eds), *Editing Early Modern Women*, 156–75.

Wynne-Davies, Marion. 'The Good Lady Lumley's Desire: *Iphigeneia* and the Nonsuch Banqueting House'. In Rina Walthaus and Marguérite Corporaal (eds), *Heroines of the Golden Stage: Women and Drama in Spain and England 1500–1700*. Kassel, 2008, 111–28.

Wynne-Davies, Marion. '"My Seeled Chamber and Dark Parlour Room": The English Country House and Renaissance Women Dramatists'. In Cerasano and Wynne-Davies (eds), *Readings in Renaissance Women's Drama*, 60–8.

Wynne-Davies, Marion. 'The Queen's Masque: Renaissance Women and the Seventeenth-Century Court Masque'. In S. P. Cerasano and Marion Wynne-Davies (eds), *Gloriana's Face: Women, Public and Private, in the English Renaissance*. Detroit, MI, 1992, 79–104.

Wynter, Sylvia. 'Unsettling the Coloniality of Being/Power/Truth/Freedom: Towards the Human, after Man, Its Overrepresentation—an Argument'. *CR: The New Centennial Review*, 3 (2003), 257–337.

Wyss, Hilary E. *Writing Indians: Literacy, Christianity and Native Community in Early America*. Amherst, MA, 2000.

Yakimyshyn, Lindsay J. 'Security and Instability: Mary Wroth, the Cavendish Sisters and Early Stuart Household Plays'. PhD Diss., University of Alberta, 2014.

Yates, Frances. *The Art of Memory*. London, 1966.

Yates, Frances. *The French Academies of the Sixteenth Century*. London, 1947.

Ziegler, Georgianna. 'Esther Inglis (c1570–1624): Calligrapher, Artist, Embroiderer, Writer'. https://estheringliscreativewoman.wordpress.com/.

Ziegler, Georgianna. 'Lady Anne Clifford Reads John Selden'. In Acheson (ed.), *Early Modern English Marginalia*, 134–54.

Ziegler, Georgianna. '"More Than Feminine Boldness": The Gift Books of Esther Inglis'. In Mary E. Burke, Jane Donawerth, Linda L. Dove, and Karen Nelson (eds), *Women, Writing and the Reproduction of Culture in Tudor and Stuart Britain*. Syracuse, NY, 2000, 19–37.

Ziegler, Georgianna. 'Patterns in Women's Book Ownership, 1500–1700'. In Wayne (ed.), *Women's Labour and the History of the Book*, 207–24.

Zucker, Adam and Alan B. Farmer (eds). *Localizing Caroline Drama: Politics and Economics of the Early Modern Stage, 1625–1642*. Houndmills, 2008, 1–16.

Zwicker, Steven and Derek Hirst. *Andrew Marvell: Orphan of the Hurricane*. Oxford, 2012.

Index

For the benefit of digital users, indexed terms that span two pages (e.g., 52–53) may, on occasion, appear on only one of those pages.

C

E

F

I

S

T

U

V